Mastering
Maya® 2009

Mastering
Maya® 2009

Eric Keller

WILEY

Wiley Publishing, Inc.

Acquisitions Editor: Mariann Barsolo
Development Editor: Lisa Bishop
Technical Editor: Gael McGill
Production Editor: Dassi Zeidel
Copy Editor: Linda Recktenwald
Production Manager: Tim Tate
Vice President and Executive Group Publisher: Richard Swadley
Vice President and Publisher: Neil Edde
Media Development Assistant Project Manager: Jenny Swisher
Media Development Associate Producer: Angie Denny
Media Development Quality Assurance: Josh Frank
Book Designers: Maureen Forys, Happenstance Type-O-Rama; Judy Fung
Compositors: Chris Gillespie and Jeffrey Lytle, Happenstance Type-O-Rama
Proofreaders: Jen Larsen, Amy Morales, Nate Pritts, and Scott Klemp, Word One New York
Indexer: Robert Swanson
Cover Designer: Ryan Sneed
Cover Image: Eric Keller

Dear Reader,

Thank you for choosing *Mastering Maya 2009*. This book is part of a family of premium-quality Sybex books, all written by outstanding authors who combine practical experience with a gift for teaching.

Sybex was founded in 1976. More than 30 years later, we're still committed to producing consistently exceptional books. With each of our titles we're working hard to set a new standard for the industry. From the authors we work with to the paper we print on, our goal is to bring you the best books available.

I hope you see all that reflected in these pages. I'd be very interested to hear your comments and get your feedback on how we're doing. Feel free to let me know what you think about this or any other Sybex book by sending me an email at nedde@wiley.com, or if you think you've found a technical error in this book, please visit http://sybex.custhelp.com. Customer feedback is critical to our efforts at Sybex.

Best regards,

Neil Edde
Vice President and Publisher
Sybex, an Imprint of Wiley

To Zoe

Acknowledgments

I'd like to thank all the people who worked so hard on this project, most especially the editors Lisa Bishop, Gael McGill, Linda Recktenwald, and Dassi Zeidel. I'd also like to thank Mariann Barsolo and Pete Gaughan. I thank all the folks at Autodesk who provided excellent support throughout the writing of this book.

I'd like to thank Eric Allen for his help in writing the rigging chapter and Michael Comet for agreeing to be interviewed. Several of my good friends contributed artwork that is used in the book. Anthony Honn built the car model used in many of the example scenes, and Chris Sanchez provided the fantastic design used in the modeling chapters. I've worked with these artists at several studios; they are both examples of the best of the talent working in the design and entertainment industry today.

Special thanks go to Ara Kermankian, Mike Wahlberg, and Gael McGill, who provided some of the artwork in the color insert.

I'd like to thank the following artists, teachers, and authors for their inspiration over the years: Drew Berry, Boaz Livny, Lee Lanier, Dariush Derakhshani, Kevin Llewellyn, John Brown, Scott Spencer, Alex Alvarez, Duncan Brinsmead, Danny Yount, Nate Homan, Chris Vincola, Kamal Hatami, Adam Newman, Roy Cullen, Geordie Martinez, Hiroshi Endo, Bill Pietsch, Davey Thomas, Chris Vargas, Dennis Liu, Satoshi Amagai, Sean Wehrli, and all the great people at Imaginary Forces, Prologue, and Yu and Company.

Naturally, all the programmers and designers who work so hard to develop this software deserve special recognition for their hard work. They are the true artists who allow the rest of us to create such fantastic things.

Extra special thanks go to Daisy, Joe, and Blue, who all forced me to get away from the computer for some much-needed exercise.

About the Authors

Eric Keller is a freelance visual effects artist working in Hollywood. He divides his time between the entertainment industry and scientific visualization. He teaches an introductory ZBrush class at the Gnomon School of Visual Effects and has authored numerous animation  and visualization tutorials for the Harvard Medical School course Maya for Molecular Biologists, taught by Gael McGill. Eric started out as an animator at the Howard Hughes Medical Institute, where he created animations for science education for seven years. In 2005, he and his wife moved to Los Angeles, where he could study and learn from the masters of visual effects. His goal is to bring the artistry and technology of Hollywood computer graphics to the field of scientific research in the hope that it can inspire and inform the scientific community and the general public.

Eric has worked at some of the best design studios in Los Angeles, including Prologue Films, Imaginary Forces, Yu and Company, BLT and Associates, and The Syndicate. Projects include feature film title animations for *The Invasion, Enchanted, Sympathy for Lady Vengeance,* and *Dragon Wars*. He has also contributed to numerous commercials, television shows, and design projects.

Other books by Eric Keller include *Maya Visual Effects: The Innovator's Guide* (Sybex, 2007) and *Introducing ZBrush* (Sybex, 2008). He was a contributing author to *Mastering Maya 7* (Sybex, 2006). He has authored the video series *Essential ZBrush 3.1* for Lynda.com as well as numerous tutorials and articles for industry magazines. Many of his tutorials are available online at www.highend3d.com and www.molecularmovies.org.

Eric Allen wrote Chapter 7, "Rigging and Muscle Systems." He has worked in the 3D industry for a decade. He was a modeling lead and expression artist on several widely used 3D figures, some of which have been downloaded over 200,000 times. He also worked for Tandem Motion Picture Studios as a modeler and character setup artist. He wrote *Body Language: Advanced 3D Character Rigging* (Sybex, 2008) and has written for *HDRI3D* magazine. Eric was a guest presenter at 3December. He graduated from BYU, where he worked on a short film titled *Lemmings*, which received multiple awards including a Student Emmy and a Bronze Student Academy Award. *Lemmings* was screened at the Cannes Film Festival. He is currently employed as a medical animator/visualizer at Interact Medical.

Anthony Honn created the vehicle model used in the example scenes throughout this book. Anthony originally trained in industrial design and architecture. After having graduated from the Art Center College of Design, a series of fateful events resulted in a career within the film and design industries. His clients have included multiple recording artists such as Janet Jackson as well as lifestyle brands such as Nike. Arguably, the industrial designer still lurks beneath, with his continued passion for robotics, automobiles, and furniture. For more of Anthony's work visit www.anthonyhonn.com.

Contents at a Glance

Contents

Introduction

Maya is big. It is really, really huge. The book you hold in your hands and all the exercises within represent a mere sliver of what can be created in Maya. Mastering Maya takes years of study and practice. I have been using Maya almost every day for ten years, and I'm still constantly faced with new challenges and making new discoveries.

Learning Maya is similar to learning a musical instrument. Both Maya and music require practice, study, patience, and determination. Just as the best musicians make playing their instruments seem effortless, the best Maya artists make visualizing the impossible seem easy. This is because the musician who masters music and the artist who masters Maya have spent years and years studying, practicing, and perfecting their skills and understanding.

This book is meant to be a guide to help you not only understand Maya but understand how to learn about Maya. The title *Mastering Maya* implies an active engagement with the software. This book is packed with as many hands-on tutorials as I could provide to keep you actively engaged. If you're looking for a quick reference guide that simply describes each and every button, control, and tool in the Maya interface, use the Maya documentation that comes with the software instead. This book is not a description of Maya; it is an explanation illustrated with practical examples.

The skills you acquire through the examples in this book should prepare you for using Maya in a professional environment. To that end, some features, such as lighting and rendering with mental ray, nDynamics, and Maya Muscle, have received more emphasis and attention. Features that have not changed significantly over the past few versions of the software, such as Maya Software rendering, standard Maya shaders, and older rigging techniques, receive less attention since they have been thoroughly covered elsewhere.

Maya 2009 is significantly different from Maya 2008. It is clear, from the changes made in this version, that Autodesk is fully committed to the continued evolution of Maya as a visual effects tool. Features such as the Nucleus dynamics solver are now firmly established and will continue to incorporate other aspects of Maya in future versions.

When you read this book and work through the exercises, do not hesitate to use the Maya help files. The authors of this book will not be insulted! The Maya documentation has a very useful search function that allows you to find complete descriptions of each control in the software. To use the help files, click the Help menu in the Maya menu interface. The documentation consists of a large library of Maya resources, which will appear in your default web browser when you access Help. Experienced Maya artists never hesitate to use the help files to find out more information about the software; there is no shame in asking questions!

Who Should Buy This Book

This book is written for intermediate Maya users and users who are advanced in some aspects of Maya and wish to learn more about other aspects. The book is intended to be used by artists who are familiar with Maya and the Maya interface or who have significant experience using similar 3D packages. If you have used older versions of Maya, this book will help you catch up on the newer features in Maya 2009.

If you have never used Maya or any other 3D software on a computer before, this book will be too challenging and you will quickly become frustrated. You are encouraged to read *Introducing Maya 2009* (Derakshani, Sybex 2009) or to read through the tutorials in the Maya documentation before attempting this book.

Here are some principles you should be familiar with before reading this book:

◆ The Maya interface

◆ Computer image basics such as color channels, masking, resolution, and image compression

◆ Computer animation basics such as keyframes, squash and stretch, and 3D coordinate systems

◆ Standard Maya shaders, such as the Blinn, Phong, Lambert, Layered, and Anisotropic materials, as well as standard textures, such as Fractal, Ramp, Noise, and Checker

◆ Lighting and rendering with standard Maya lights and the Maya Software rendering engine

◆ The basics of working with NURBS curves, polygon surfaces, and NURBS surfaces

◆ Your operating system. You need to be familiar with opening and saving files and the like. Basic computer networking skills are helpful as well.

What's Inside

Here is a description of the chapters in this book. The lessons in each chapter are accompanied by example scenes from the DVD included with the book.

Chapter 1: Working in Maya discusses how to work with the various nodes and the node structure that make up a scene. Using the Hypergraph, Outliner, Hypershade, Attribute Editor, and Connection Editor to build relationships between nodes is demonstrated through a series of exercises. References, the Asset Editor, and containers are also introduced. These features have been created to aid with large Maya projects that are divided between teams of artists.

Chapter 2: Maya Cameras provides an in-depth discussion of the Maya virtual camera and its attributes. A number of exercises provide examples of standard and custom camera rigs. Stereo 3D cameras are also introduced as a new feature.

Chapter 3: NURBS Modeling in Maya walks you through numerous approaches for modeling parts of a helmet for a space suit based on a concept drawing created by a professional artist.

Chapter 4: Polygon and Subdivision Surface Modeling continues to build on the model started in Chapter 3 using polygon and subdivision surface techniques. Smooth mesh polygons, creasing, and soft selection are demonstrated on various parts of the model.

Chapter 5: Animation demonstrates basic rigging with Inverse Kinematics as well as animating with keyframes, expressions, and constraints. Animation layers, which are new in Maya 2009, are explained.

Chapter 6: Animating with Deformers takes you through the numerous deformation tools available in Maya. Creating a facial animation rig using blend shapes is demonstrated, along with using lattices, non-linear deformers, and the geometry cache.

Chapter 7: Rigging and Muscle Systems explains joints, Inverse Kinematics, smooth binding, and proper rigging techniques. Maya Muscle is introduced and demonstrated on a character's arm. This chapter was cowritten by Eric Allen, author of *Body Language: Advanced 3D Character Rigging.*

Chapter 8: Paint Effects and Toon Shading provides a step-by-step demonstration of how to create a custom Paint Effects brush as well as how to animate and render with Paint Effects. Toon shading is also explained.

Chapter 9: mental ray Lights demonstrates a variety of lighting tools and techniques that can be used when rendering scenes with mental ray. Indirect lighting using Global Illumination, Final Gathering, and the Physical Sun and Sky Shader are all demonstrated.

Chapter 10: mental ray Shaders describes the more commonly used mental ray Shaders and how they can be used to add material qualities to the space helmet created in Chapter 3. Tips on how to use the shaders together as well as how to light and render them using mental ray are discussed.

Chapter 11: Texture Mapping demonstrates how to create UV texture coordinates for a character's head. Applying textures painted in other software packages, such as Adobe Photoshop and Pixologic's ZBrush, is discussed as well as displacement and normal maps and sub-surface scattering Shaders.

Chapter 12: Rendering for Compositing introduces render layers and render passes, which can be used to split the various elements of a render into separate files that are then recombined in compositing software.

Chapter 13: Introducing nParticles provides numerous examples of how to use Maya 2009's most powerful new feature: nParticles. In this chapter, you'll use fluid behavior, particle meshes, internal force fields, and other techniques to create amazing effects.

Chapter 14: Advanced nDynamic Effects demonstrates a variety of techniques that can be used with nCloth to create effects. Traditional rigid body dynamics are compared with nCloth, and combining nCloth and nParticles is illustrated.

Chapter 15: Fur, Hair, and Clothing discusses how to augment your Maya creatures and characters using Maya Fur, Maya Hair, and nCloth. Using dynamic curves to create a rig for a dragon's tail is also demonstrated.

Chapter 16: Maya Fluids explains how 2D and 3D fluids can be used to create smoke, cloud, and flame effects. The fluid pond effect is used to create milk for a hypothetical cereal commercial, and a demonstration of how to render using the Ocean shader is given.

Chapter 17: MEL and Python walks you through the process of creating a time- and labor-saving MEL script, illustrating how MEL is a very useful tool for all Maya artists. The Python interface is also explained.

> The companion DVD is home to all the demo files, samples, and bonus resources mentioned in the book. See Appendix B for more details on the contents and how to access them.

How to Contact the Author

I enjoy hearing from the readers of my books. Feedback helps me to continually improve my skills as an author. You can contact me through my website www.bloopatone.com as well as see examples of my own artwork there.

Sybex strives to keep you supplied with the latest tools and information you need for your work. Please check the book's website at www.sybex.com/go/masteringmaya2009, where we'll post additional content and updates that supplement this book should the need arise.

Chapter 1

Working in Maya

Maya's working environment has evolved to accommodate both the individual artist as well as a team of artists working in a production pipeline. The interface in Maya 2009 has changed significantly from previous versions of the program to reflect this evolution. This chapter is a brief overview of what professionals need to understand when working in Maya, the interface changes, and the new tools. If you've never used Maya before, you are strongly encouraged to read the Maya documentation as well as *Introducing Maya 2009* by Dariush Derakhshani (Sybex, 2009).

In this chapter, you will learn to:

◆ Understand transform and shape nodes

◆ Create a project

◆ Use assets

◆ Create file references

Maya Nodes

A Maya scene is a system of interconnected nodes. The nodes are the building blocks you, as the artist, put together to create the 3D scene and animation that will finally be rendered for the world to see. So if you can think of the objects in your scene, their motion, and appearance as nodes, think of the Maya interface as the tools and controls you use to connect those nodes.

Any given workflow in Maya is much like a route on a city map. There are usually many ways to get to your destination, and some of these make more sense than others depending on where you're going. In Maya, the best workflow depends on what you're trying to achieve, and there is usually more than one possible ideal workflow.

This section briefly explains how nodes work in Maya and then looks at the many ways these nodes and their connections are depicted in the interface. A thorough tour of all of the interface panels, controls, buttons, and tools can be found in the Maya documentation as well as in the book *Introducing Maya 2009* by Dariush Derakhshani (Sybex, 2009).

There are many types of nodes in Maya that serve any number of different functions. Most of the objects that you actually place on the grid in the viewport consist of two types of connected nodes: transform and shape. This two-node network is known as a Directed Acyclic Graph, or DAG. The arrangement of DAG nodes consists of a hierarchy in which the shape node is a child of the transform node.

The easiest way to understand the difference between the transform and shape node types is to think of a transform node as describing where an object is *located* and a shape node as describing what an object *is*.

The simple polygon cube in Figure 1.1 consists of six flat squares attached at the edges to form a box. Each side of the cube is subdivided twice, creating four polygons per side. That basically describes what the object is, and the description of the object would be contained in the shape node. This simple polygon cube may be 4 centimeters above the grid, rotated 35 degrees on the X axis, and scaled four times its original size based on the cube's local X and Y axes and six times its original size in the cube's local Z axis That description would be in the transform node (see Figure 1.1).

FIGURE 1.1

A shape node describes the shape of an object and how it has been constructed; a transform node describes where the object is located in the scene.

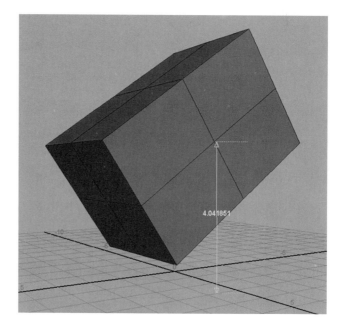

Maya has a number of workspaces that enable you to visualize and work with the nodes and their connections. The following sections describe how these workspaces work together when building a node network in a Maya scene.

Using the Hypergraph

The Hypergraph is literally a picture of the nodes and their connections in Maya. A complex scene can look like a very intricate web of these connections. When you really need to know how a network of nodes is connected, the Hypergraph gives you the most detailed view. There are two ways to view the Hypergraph: the hierarchy view and the connections view. The hierarchy view shows the relationships between nodes as a tree structure; the connections view shows how the nodes are connected as a web. You can have more than one Hypergraph window open at the same time, but you are still looking at the same scene with the same nodes and connections.

This short exercise gives you a sense of how you would typically use the Hypergraph:

1. Create a new Maya scene. Create a polygon cube by choosing Create ➢ Polygon Primitives ➢ Cube.

2. You will be prompted to draw a polygon on the grid by dragging on the surface. Drag a square on the grid, release the cursor, and then drag upward on the square to turn it into a three-dimensional cube (see Figure 1.2). Release the mouse button to complete the cube. At this point feel free to make your own decisions about the size and position of the cube on the grid.

FIGURE 1.2
When Interactive Creation is on, Maya prompts you to draw the object on the grid in the scene.

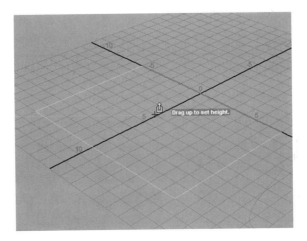

Drag up to set height.

INTERACTIVE CREATION

By default Maya creates objects using the interactive creation method, which allows you to draw on the canvas as you create your geometry. To turn this feature off, open the Create ➤ Polygon Primitives menu and deselect the Interactive Creation option at the bottom of the menu. While the interactive creation mode is on, you can uncheck the Exit On Completion method; this means that each time you draw on the grid, you will continue to create cubes until you switch to another tool.

---

3. Select the cube in the viewport, and choose Window ➤ Hypergraph ➤ Hierarchy to open the Hypergraph in Hierarchy mode. You'll see a yellow rectangle on a black field labeled pCube1. The rectangle turns gray when deselected.

4. Hold the right mouse button down and hover the cursor over the pCube rectangle. Choose Rename from the pop-up window. Rename the cube **myCube**.

5. Select myCube and choose, from the Hypergraph menu, Graph ➤ Input And Output connections. This switches the view to the connections view just as if you had originally opened the Hypergraph by choosing Windows ➤ Hypergraph:Connections. It's the same Hypergraph, but the view mode has changed, allowing you to see more of the scene.

NAVIGATING THE HYPERGRAPH

You can navigate the Hypergraph by using the same hot-key combination you use in the viewport: Alt+MMB (Middle-Mouse Button)-drag pans through the Hypergraph workspace, Alt+right-click-drag zooms in and out. Selecting a node and pressing the f hot key focuses the view on the currently selected node.

When you graph the input and output connections, you see the connected nodes that make up an object and how the object appears in the scene. In the current view, you should see the myCube node next to a stack of connected nodes labeled polyCube1, myCubeShape, and initial-ShadingGroup, as shown in Figure 1.3 (the nodes may also be arranged in a line; the actual position of the nodes in the Hypergraph does not affect the nodes themselves).

FIGURE 1.3

The node network appears in the Hypergraph. This shape node (myCubeShape) is connected to two other nodes, while the transform node (myCube) appears off to the side.

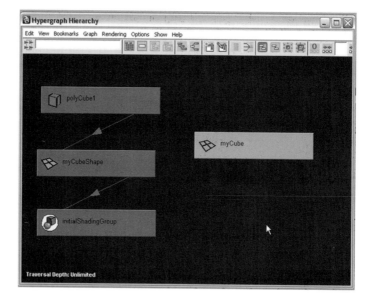

The myCube node is the transform node. The myCubeShape node is the shape node. In the Hypergraph the shape and transform nodes are depicted as unconnected; however, there is an implied connection, as you'll see later. This is demonstrated when you rename the myCube node; the shape node is renamed as well.

The polyCube1 node is the construction history node for the myCubeShape node. In Maya the construction history feature stores a record of the changes used to create a particular node. When you first create a piece of geometry, you can set options to the number of subdivisions, spans, width, height, depth, and many other features that are stored as a record in this history node. Additional history nodes are added as you make changes to the node. You can go back and change these settings as long as the history node still exists. Deleting a history node makes all previous changes to the node permanent (however, deleting history is undoable).

6. Keep the Hypergraph open, but select the cube in the viewport. Set the current menu to Polygons (you can change the menu set by choosing Polygons from the menu in the upper left of the Maya interface).

7. Choose Mesh ➤ Smooth. The cube will be subdivided and smoothed in the viewport. In the Hypergraph you'll see a new polySmoothFace1 node between the polyCube1 node and the myCubeShape node (see Figure 1.4). This new node is part of the history of the cube. Select the polySmoothFace1 node, and delete it by pressing the Backspace key on the keyboard. The cube will return to its unsmoothed state.

FIGURE 1.4
Performing a smooth operation on the cube when construction history is activated causes a new polySmoothFace node to be inserted into the node network.

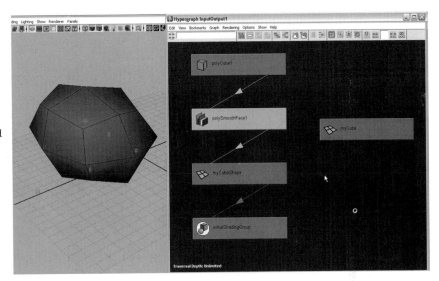

WORKING WITH HISTORY

Over the course of a modeling session, the history for any given object can become quite long and complex. This can slow down performance. It's a good idea to periodically delete history on an object by selecting the object and choosing Edit ➤ Delete By Type ➤ History. You can also choose to delete all the history in the scene by choosing Edit ➤ Delete All By Type ➤ History. History can also be turned off globally by clicking the history toggle switch on the status line.

8. Select the transform node (myCube), and press the s hot key. This creates a keyframe on all of the channels of the transform node. You'll see a new node icon appear for each keyframed channel with a connection to the transform node. The transform node itself becomes a slanted rectangle, indicating that it is animated using an input connection (see Figure 1.5).

9. Hold the cursor over any line that connects one node to another. A label appears describing the output and input attributes indicated by the connection line.

FIGURE 1.5
The attributes of myCube's transform node have been keyframed. The keyframe nodes appear in the Hypergraph, and the icon for myCube becomes a slanted rectangle, indicating it is animated.

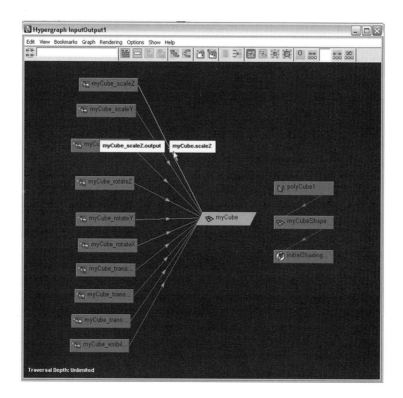

The Connection Editor

Connections between nodes can be added, deleted, or changed using the Hypergraph and the Connection Editor.

1. Start a new Maya Scene.

2. Create a locator in the scene by choosing Create ➤ Locator. A simple cross appears at the center of the grid in the viewport. This locator is a simple nonrendering null that indicates a point in space. Locators are handy tools that can be used for a wide variety of things in Maya.

3. Press the **w** hot key to switch to the Move tool, select the locator at the center of the grid, and move it out of the way.

4. Press the **g** hot key to create another locator. The g hot key repeats the last action you performed, in this case the creation of the locator.

5. Create a NURBS (Non-Uniform Rational B-Splines) sphere in the viewport by choosing Create ➤ NURBS Primitives ➤ Sphere. If you have Interactive Creation selected, you'll be prompted to drag on the grid in the viewport to create the sphere; otherwise, the sphere will be created at the center of the grid based on its default settings.

6. Move the sphere away from the center of the grid so you can clearly see both locators and the sphere. Use the Select tool (hot key = q) to drag a selection marquee around all three objects.

7. Open the Hypergraph in connections mode by choosing Window ➤ Hypergraph:Connections. You should see eight nodes in the Hypergraph (see Figure 1.6).

FIGURE 1.6
The input and output connections of the two locators and the sphere are graphed in the Hypergraph.

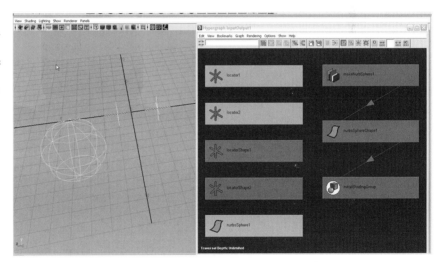

Locator1 and locator2 are the two transform nodes for the locators. LocatorShape1 and locatorShape2 are the two shape nodes for the locators. NurbsSphere1 is the transform node for the NURBS sphere. And nurbsSphereShape1 is the shape node for the sphere; it's connected to MakeNurbsSphere1, which is the history node, and to initialShadingGroup. The initialShadingGroup node is the default shading group that is applied to all geometry; without this node the geometry can't be shaded or rendered. When you apply a new shader to an object, the connection to initialShadingGroup is replaced with a connection to the new shader.

8. Use Alt+RMB (Right Mouse Button) to zoom out a little in the Hypergraph. Select the locator1, locator2, and nurbsSphere1 nodes, and use the Move tool to move them away from the other nodes so you can work on them in their own space.

9. In the viewport, switch to wireframe mode. You can do this by pressing 4 on the keyboard or clicking the wireframe icon on the icon bar at the top of the viewport window; the wireframe icon is the wireframe cube.

10. In the Hypergraph, MMB-drag the locator1 node over the nurbsSphere1 node. From the pop-up menu, choose Other at the bottom (Figure 1.7). A new dialog box will open; this is the Connection Editor.

FIGURE 1.7
You can connect two nodes in the Hypergraph by MMB-dragging one on top of the other and choosing from the options in the pop-up menu.

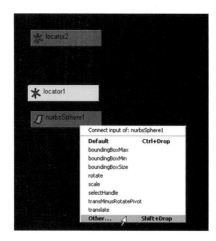

The Connection Editor is where you create and edit connections between nodes. The left side of the panel represents the output of a selected node, in this case the locator1 node. The output is the controlling node; the right side is the input, and in this case nurbsSphere1, which will be controlled based on whatever connections you make in the list below.

The list represents the attributes of each node. Any of the attributes that have a plus sign next to them can be expanded to reveal nested attributes. For instance, find the Translate attribute in the left side of the column and expand it by clicking the plus sign. You'll see that Translate has Translate X, Translate Y, and Translate Z. This means you can choose either to select the Translate attribute, which will automatically use all three nested attributes as the output connection, or to expand Translate and choose one or more of the nested Translate X, Y, or Z attributes as the output connection. In some situations, a connection becomes grayed out, indicating that the connection between the two attributes cannot be made, usually because the connection is not appropriate for the selected attributes.

11. Select the Translate attribute on the left. You'll notice that many of the selections in the right side become grayed out, meaning that they cannot be connected to Translate. This is because Translate is a vector—it is an output consisting of three connections (Translate X, Translate Y, Translate Z). The vector can be connected only to other vectors on the right side of the list.

12. On the right side, scroll down and select Translate. Both connections in the list are italicized, indicating that there is a connection to this attribute. If one of the other attributes

on the right were italicized, it would indicate that another node is already connected to that attribute (see Figure 1.8).

FIGURE 1.8
The Connection Editor specifies which attributes are connected between nodes.

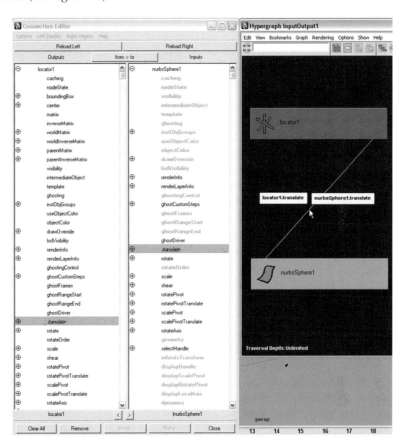

13. In the viewport, you'll notice that the sphere has snapped to the same position as the locator. Select the sphere, and try to move it using the Move tool (hot key = w). The sphere is locked to the locator. Select the locator and try to move it; the sphere moves with the locator. The output of the locator's Translate attributes are the input for the sphere's Translate.

INCOMING CONNECTIONS

In wireframe view, an object will be highlighted in purple if it has an incoming connection from the selected object.

---

14. Select the nurbsSphere1 node in the Hypergraph, and MMB-drag it on top of locator2. From the pop-up list, choose Rotate (see Figure 1.09). The Connection Editor opens again.

FIGURE 1.09

The nurbsSphere1 node is MMB-dragged on top of the locator2 node, making the sphere the input connection for locator2.

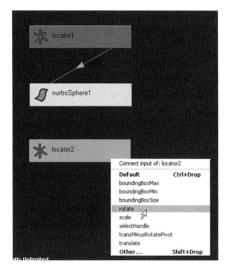

SPECIFYING CONNECTIONS

In some cases when you choose to make a connection from the pop-up window, Maya will automatically make it for you without opening the Connection Editor; however, in other cases, even when you choose what seems like an obvious connection from the list, Maya will still open the Connection Editor so you can make exactly the connection you want.

15. Now the nurbsSphere1 node is listed on the left, and the locator is on the right. Find the Rotate attributes and expand the list; choose Rotate X from the list. On the right side, find the Rotate attributes, expand them, and choose Rotate Y. This causes the Rotate X of the nurbsSphere1 node to control the Rotate Y of the locator.

16. In the viewport, select the sphere, and switch to the Rotate tool (hot key = e). Drag up and down on the red circle of the tool to rotate the sphere in X only. The locator rotates around its Y axis.

USE THE CONNECTION EDITOR TO MAKE SIMPLE CONNECTIONS

The Connection Editor is best used when you want to make a one-to-one relationship between attributes on two nodes. In other words, the value of the output connection needs to equal exactly the value of the input connection. More complex connections can be made using expressions, special nodes, or Set Driven Key. All of these options will be discussed throughout the book.

17. You can break a connection by reselecting the connected node on either side of the Connection Editor so that the attribute is no longer highlighted. You can also select the connecting line in the Hypergraph and press the Delete key to break the connection.

Using the Outliner

The Outliner is an alternative way to view the transform and shape nodes in a scene. The Outliner shows a hierarchical list of the nodes in the scene in a form similar to the outline of a book. The Outliner does not show the connections between nodes; rather it shows the hierarchy of the nodes in the scene. To see how this works try the following exercise:

1. Open the `miniGun_v01.ma` file from the `Chapter1/scenes` directory on the DVD. The scene consists of a minigun model in three parts.

2. Open the Outliner by Choosing Window ➤ Outliner.

OUTLINER LAYOUT PRESETS

The Outliner can be opened as a separate panel or, like many of the panels in Maya, it can be opened in a viewport. A popular window arrangement is to split the viewports into two views, with the left view set to the Outliner and the right view set to the perspective view. You can open this arrangement by going to the menu bar in a viewport window and choosing Panels ➤ Saved Layouts ➤ Persp/Outliner. You can also click the third layout button on the left side of the interface just below the toolbox.

---

3. At the top of the Outliner is a menu bar. In the Display menu, make sure DAG Objects only is checked and Shapes is unchecked (see Figure 1.10).

You'll see three nodes: gunBarrels, housing, and mount. These are the three transform nodes for the pieces of the minigun. Select each node, and you'll see the corresponding part highlighted in the perspective view. At the moment each piece is completely separate and unconnected.

FIGURE 1.10
The Display menu at the top of the Outliner

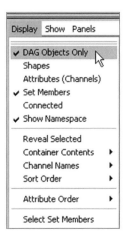

4. Select the housing node and switch to the Rotate tool (hot key = e). Rotate the objects; nothing else is affected. Try moving housing (hot key = w); again, nothing else is affected.

5. Hit Undo a few times until the housing node returns to its original location and orientation.

6. In either the perspective view or the Outliner, select the gunBarrels object, and then Shift+click the housing object and choose Edit ➢ Parent.

Parenting one object to another means you have made one transform node the child of the second. When an object is a child node, it inherits its position, rotation, scale, and visibility from the parent node. In the Outliner, you'll notice that the housing node has a plus sign beside it and the gunBarrels node is not visible. The plus sign indicates that the node has a child node.

7. Click the plus sign next to the housing node to expand this two-node hierarchy. The gunBarrels node is now visible as the child of the housing node. Select the housing node, and try rotating and translating it. The gunBarrels node follows the rotation of the housing node (see Figure 1.11).

FIGURE 1.11

When the gun-Barrels node is made a child of the housing object, it inherits changes made to the housing object's transform node.

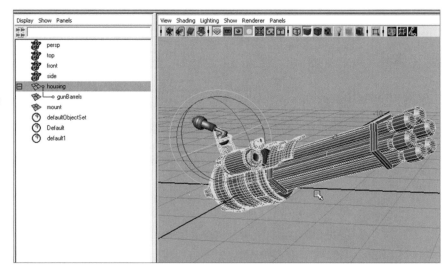

Unlike the situation presented in the Connection Editor section of the chapter, the rotation and translation of the gunBarrels object are not controlled by the rotation and translation of the housing node; rather, as a child, its rotation, translation, scale, and visibility are all relative to that of its parent.

8. Select the gunBarrels node, and try rotating and translating the object; then rotate and translate the housing node. You'll see the gun barrels maintain their position relative to the housing node. You could create an animation in which the gun barrels rotate on their own Z axis to spin around while firing, while the housing node is animated, rotating on all three axes in order to aim.

9. Hit Undo a few times (hot key = Ctrl+z) until both the housing and gunBarrel objects are back to their original position. In the Outliner, select the housing node, and MMB-drag it on top of the mount node. This is a way to quickly parent objects in the Outliner.

10. Click the plus signs next to the mount and housing nodes in the Outliner to expand the hierarchy. The lines indicate the organization of the hierarchy; the gun barrels are parented to the housing node, which is parented to the mount node.

SHIFT+CLICK TO EXPAND THE HIERARCHY

You can expand an entire hierarchy with one click in the Outliner. Just Shift+click the arrow for the hierarchy you want to expand.

---

11. In the Outliner, MMB-drag the gunBarrels node on top of the mount node. This rearranges the hierarchy so that now both the housing and gunBarrels nodes are children of the mount node. They are sibling nodes. Note the arrangement of the lines in the Outliner, indicating that the two nodes share the same parent.

12. Press Ctrl+z to undo the last action and return the gunBarrels node to its former place as a child of the housing node.

13. Select the mount node, and choose Edit ➤ Duplicate (hot key = Ctrl+d). This makes a copy of the entire hierarchy named mount1. Select the mount1 node, and switch to the Move tool (hot key = w). Pull on the red arrow of the tool to move the duplicate along the X axis about two units.

14. Select the mount node, and then Ctrl+click the mount1 node in the Outliner. Choose Edit ➤ Group (hot key = Ctrl+g) to group these two nodes under a single parent node.

A group node is a transform node that has no shape node. It's just a location in space used to organize a hierarchy. Like a parent node, its children inherit its rotation, translation, scale, and visibility.

15. Select the group1 node and Shift+click the plus sign next to it in the Outliner to expand the group and all its children. Double-click the label for the group1 node in the Outliner to rename it; rename the group **Guns**.

RENAMING NODES

You'll notice that the duplicate mount node has been renamed mount1 automatically. Nodes on the same level of the hierarchy can't have the same name. The child nodes do have the same name, and this is usually a bad idea. It can confuse Maya when more complex connections are made between nodes. Whenever you encounter this situation, you should take the time to rename the child nodes so that everything in the scene has a unique name.

16. Select the mount1 node in the Guns hierarchy, and choose Modify ➢ Prefix Hierarchy Names. In the pop-up window, type **right_**. This renames the top node and all its children so that "right_" precedes the name. Do the same with the other gun, but change the prefix to **left_**.

17. Select the Guns group and choose Modify ➢ Center Pivot. This places the pivot at the center of the group. Try rotating the Guns group, and you'll see both guns rotate together (see Figure 1.12).

FIGURE 1.12
The Guns group is rotated as a single unit.

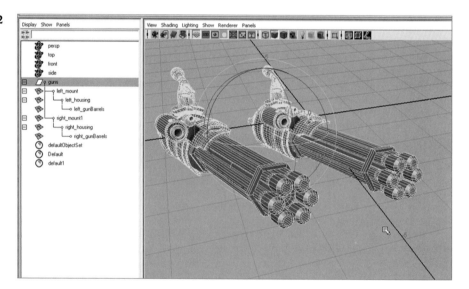

Each member of the hierarchy can have its own animation, so both gun barrels can rotate around their Z axes as they fire, the two housing nodes could be animated to aim in different directions, and the two guns could rotate as one unit, all at the same time. The entire group can be parented to another node that is part of a vehicle.

Real World Scenario

CREATE A CLASSIC SOLAR SYSTEM USING HIERARCHIES

A classic example of how parent-child relationships work in Maya is the solar system model. You can easily visualize how parenting works by creating simple sun, moon, and planet models and then parenting the models in such a way that the planets revolve around the sun and the moons revolve around the planets.

1. Create a simple NURBS sphere at the center of the grid.

2. Turn on Grid Snapping, and create a smaller sphere 10 units away from the center of the grid. This is your first planet.

3. Select the planet sphere, and choose the Move tool from the toolbox (hot key = w). Hold the **d** hot key to switch to the Pivot tool. The center of the icon for the Move tool changes to a circle when the Pivot tool is active.

4. While holding the **d** key, move the pivot point to the center of the sun; the planet should not move, just its pivot point. With Grid Snapping on, you should be able to snap the planet's pivot to the center of the grid.

5. Try rotating the planet on its Y axis. You'll see that it now rotates around the sun.

6. Undo changes to the planet's rotation, and create a third sphere. Make it smaller than the planet; this will be the planet's moon.

7. Place the moon sphere two units away from the planet. Using the d hot key, place the moon's pivot point at the center of the planet. Grid Snapping should help you achieve this as long as the planet is snapped to the grid.

8. Parent the moon to the planet and the planet to the sun.

9. Create keyframes on the moon's Y rotation and the planet's Y rotation so that the planet revolves around the sun and the moon revolves around the planet.

You can expand an entire hierarchy with one click in the Outliner. Just Shift+click the arrow for the hierarchy you want to expand.

Display Options in the Outliner

There are several options in the Outliner for displaying nodes and their hierarchical arrangements. You can see that the default perspective, top, side, and front cameras are visible as nodes at the top of the Outliner. Also there are a number of sets such as the defaultLightSet that appear at the bottom of the Outliner. These sets are mainly used for organization of data by Maya and are usually not directly edited or altered.

1. In the Display menu of the Outliner, check the Shapes option to display the shape nodes of the objects. The shape nodes appear parented to their respective transform node. You can select either the transform or the shape node in the Outliner to select the object.

ACCESSING OUTLINER OPTIONS

You can right-click in the Outliner to quickly access the Outliner's display options rather than use the menu at the top of the Outliner.

---

2. In the Display menu, activate the visibility of attributes by selecting the Attributes (Channels) option. Each node now has an expandable list of attributes. Most of the time you may want this option off because it clutters the Outliner and there are other ways to get to these attributes. Ultimately, how you use these options is up to you.

3. Turn off the Attributes display, and turn off the DAG Objects Only option.

4. To see a finished version of the scene, open miniGun_v02.ma from the chapter1\scenes directory on the DVD.

DAG stands for "Directed Acyclic Graph," and DAG objects are those objects that have both a shape and transform node. It's not really crucial to understand exactly what Directed Acyclic Graph means as long as you understand that it is an arrangement in which a shape node is parented to a transform node. When you turn off DAG Objects Only in the Outliner, you'll see all of the nodes in the Maya scene appear. Many of these are default utility nodes required to make Maya function, such as the renderLayerManager node or the dynController1 node. Many other nodes appear when you create a new node or connection. An example of this would be a keyframe or an expression node.

When you turn off DAG Objects Only, the list can get quite long. To find a node quickly, you can type the node's name in the field at the very top of the Outliner. This hides all nodes except the named node. Clearing the field restores the visibility of all nodes in the Outliner (see Figure 1.13).

Additional viewing options are available in the Show menu, which contains options for displaying only nodes of a certain type. Throughout this book the Outliner will be used extensively, so you'll have lots of practice working with this panel.

The Channel Box

The term *channel* is, for the most part, interchangeable with *attribute*. You can think of a channel as a container that holds the attribute's value. The Channel Box is an editor that lists a node's attributes for quick access. The Channel Box displays the node's attributes, which are most frequently keyframed for animation.

The Channel Box is located on the right side of the screen when the view mode button in the upper right of the status line is set to Show The Channel Box/Layer Editor. This short exercise gives a quick tour of how to work in the Channel Box.

1. Create a new scene in Maya, and create a NURBS Sphere on the grid (Create ➢ NURBS Primitives ➢ Sphere). You'll be prompted to draw the sphere on the grid if Interactive Creation mode is on; if not, the sphere will appear at the center of the grid. Either option is fine.

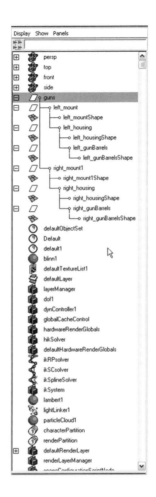

2. Make sure the Channel Box is visible on the right side of the screen. To do this, click the icon at the farthest right of the status bar (shown in Figure 1.14). This is a toggle to display the Channel Box. Click it until the Channel Box appears, as in Figure 1.15.

3. The Channel Box will list the currently selected object. Select the sphere, and you'll see nurbsSphere1 appear. The list below it is the attributes for the nurbsSphere1's transform node.

FIGURE 1.15
The Channel Box appears on the right side of the Maya interface.

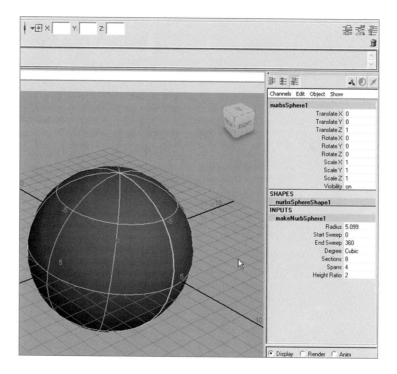

The lower half of the Channel Box lists the connections to this node. You'll see the name of the associated shape node under SHAPES and below this a section for the inputs. In this case the input is the history node, named makeNurbSphere1, which contains the original settings used to create the sphere. If you delete history on the sphere, these attributes will no longer be accessible.

4. In the upper section of the Channel Box, under nurbsSphere1, try selecting the fields and inputting different values for Translate, Scale, and Rotate. The sphere updates its position, orientation, and size.

5. In the Visibility channel, select the word *On* in the field and type **0**. The sphere disappears. Input the value **1** and it reappears. Visibility is a Boolean, meaning it is either on or off, 1 or 0.

6. Select the Translate X field so it is highlighted. Shift+click the Rotate Z value, and all the values in between are also selected. Type **0** in the Translate X field while they are selected, and all the Translate and Rotate values are set to the same value, which places the sphere at the center of the grid and returns it to its original orientation (see Figure 1.16).

FIGURE 1.16
You can quickly
"zero out" the
Translate and
Rotate channels
by Shift+clicking
their fields and
entering **0**.

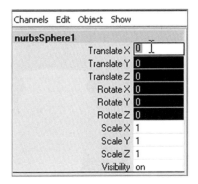

7. In the makeNurbsSphere section, highlight the Start Sweep channel. Enter a value of **90**, and the sphere opens up. You're altering the construction history of the sphere so it is no longer a closed surface.

8. Select the word *Sections* so it is highlighted in black. MMB-drag in the viewport view back and forth. Doing this creates a virtual slider so you can change the value of the field interactively instead of numerically. This should work for all of the channels (most of the time).

9. Set the timeline to frame 1 and press the **s** hot key. You'll see all of the channels turn orange, indicating that they have been keyframed. The s hot key keyframes all of the available channels.

10. Move the timeline to frame 24, and change some settings on both the transform node (the upper half of the Channel Box) and under makeNurbsSphere1. Press the **s** hot key again to set another key. Play the animation, and you'll see the sphere update based on the keyframed changes.

The s hot key keyframes everything, even those channels you may not need to keyframe. You can use the Channel Box to keyframe specific channels.

11. Rewind the timeline, and choose Edit ➤ Keys ➤ Delete Keys to remove all of the keyframes on the sphere.

12. Highlight Translate X and Shift+click Translate Z so that the translation channels are all selected. Right-click these values, and choose Key Selected (see Figure 1.17).

13. Move to frame 24, and enter different values in the Translate fields. Right-click and choose Key Selected. This places a keyframe on just the selected channels, which is often a cleaner and more efficient way to work.

BE THRIFTY WITH KEYFRAMES

Creating extra, unnecessary keys leads to a lot of problems, especially when you start to refine the animation on the Graph Editor. Keyframes also can increase the scene size (the amount of storage space the scene uses on disk). Be cheap with your keyframes, and use the Key Selected feature to keyframe only the channels you need. Avoid using the s hot key to create keys on everything.

---

14. To remove keys you can highlight the channels, right-click, and choose Break Connections. This removes any inputs to those channels. The values for the current keyframe will remain in the channels.

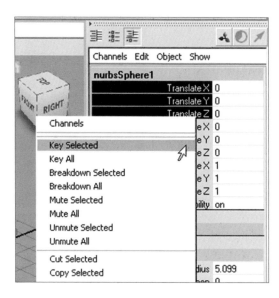

The channels are color coded to show what kind of input drives the channel. Orange indi-cates a keyframe, purple indicates an expression, yellow indicates a connection (as in a connec-tion from another node or channel made in the Connection Editor), brown indicates a muted channel, gray means the channel is locked, and green indicates a breakdown, which is a special type of keyframe (breakdowns are discussed in Chapter 5).

The Channel Box will be explored throughout the book and used frequently, particularly in the chapters concerning animation.

The Attribute Editor

The Attribute Editor is a tabbed panel that gives detailed information and access to a node's attributes. The tabs at the top of the editor allow you to move between the attributes of all the upstream (input) and downstream (output) connected nodes. This exercise gives a brief tour on how to use the Attribute Editor.

1. Create a new scene in Maya. Create a polygon cube on the grid (Create ➤ Polygon Primitives ➤ Cube).

2. Select the cube and open its Attribute Editor. There are several ways to do this:

Right-click on the cube and choose pCube1.

Select the cube and choose Windows ➤ Attribute Editor.

Click the Show/Hide Attribute Editor icon in the upper right of the Maya interface (Figure 1.18).

3. With the Attribute Editor open, choose the pCube1 tab at the top (Figure 1.19). The panel that opens contains the attributes for the cube's transform node, much like the upper section of the Channel Box described in the previous section. It also contains options for setting limits on the transform attributes.

FIGURE 1.18
The Show/Hide Attribute Editor icon resides in the upper-right corner of the Maya interface.

FIGURE 1.19
The Attribute Editor contains tabs that allow you to move through the connected nodes of a network.

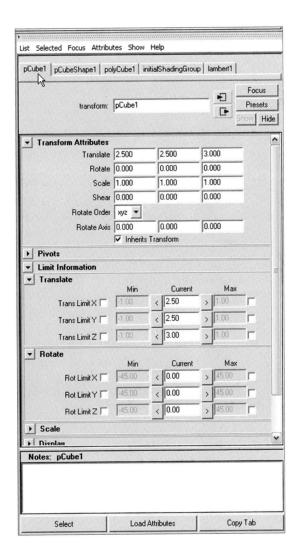

Many of the settings can be accessed through the Attribute Editor's rollout panels. These are collapsible sections of grouped settings.

4. In the Attribute Editor, under the pCube1 tab, click the triangle next to mental ray. This reveals mental ray–specific settings related to the cube. Note that there are subsections under mental ray that are also collapsible.

5. Choose the pCubeShape1 tab at the top of the Attribute Editor. This tab contains settings related to the shape node. For example, expand the Render Stats section, and you'll see a list of settings that control how the shape will appear in a render.

6. Choose the polyCube1 tab, and you'll see the construction history settings. If you delete history on the cube, this tab will no longer appear.

7. Expand the Poly Cube History rollout. If you right-click any of the fields, you get a pop-up menu that offers options, such as expressions, key setting, or locking, much like the fields in the Channel Box (Figure 1.20).

FIGURE 1.20

Right-clicking over an Attribute Field reveals a menu with options for animating the attribute value.

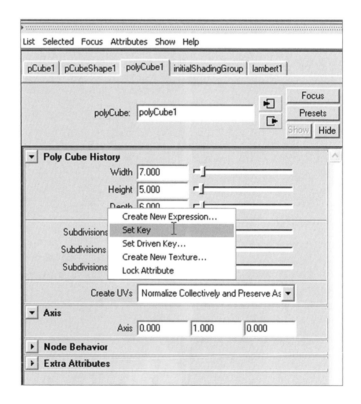

8. In the Subdivisions Width field type =. The field expands so you can add an expression. Type **=9*2;** and press the **Enter** key on your keyboard's numeric keypad (see Figure 1.21). This adds an expression to this attribute that makes the Subdivisions Width value equal to 18. Note that the field turns purple, and the slider can no longer be moved.

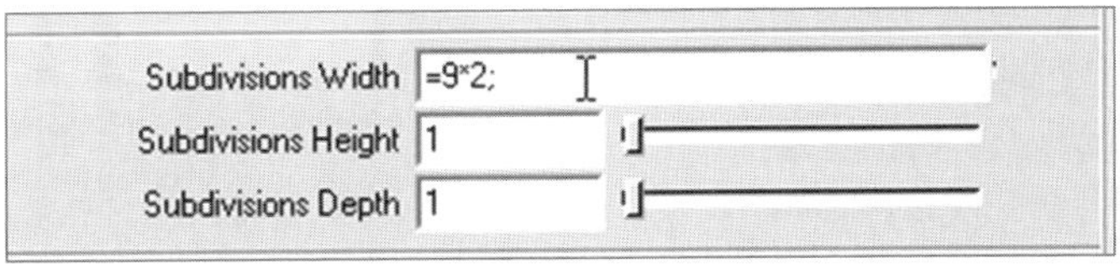

FIGURE 1.21
You can enter simple mathematical expressions directly into a field in the Attribute Editor.

Subdivisions Width	=9*2;
Subdivisions Height	1
Subdivisions Depth	1

9. Note that a new tab called Expression1 is added to the top of the Attribute Editor; this is a new expression node that is now part of the cube's node network.

If the number of connected nodes is too large to fit within the tab listing at the top, you can use the two arrow buttons to the right of the tabs (on a Mac, a single down-arrow button is displayed) to move back and forth between the tab listings. Likewise, if not all connections are visible, you can use the Go To Input and Go To Output connections buttons to the right of the field indicating the node name.

The Notes field at the bottom is useful for typing your own notes if you need to keep track of particular settings or leave a message for yourself or other users.

LOAD ATTRIBUTES

The Load Attributes button can be used if the attribute display needs to be refreshed. Maya automatically updates the editor when new attributes are added, but occasionally it misses an update and needs to be refreshed.

The Attribute Editor is the workhorse panel of Maya. Throughout this book we will use it constantly. Make sure you are comfortable with the core concepts of how to switch between node settings using the tabs as well as how to change the available values.

The Hypershade

The Hypershade, as the name suggests, is similar in function to the Hypergraph. It gives a visual display of how nodes in a Maya scene are connected. The Hypershade is mostly concerned with shaders—nodes used to define the color and material properties of renderable objects in a scene. These include materials (also known as shaders), textures, lights, cameras, and shading utilities. However, it is not unusual to use the Hypershade Work Area to make connections between other types of nodes as well. In this exercise you'll use the Hypershade to connect several types of nodes.

1. Create a new scene in Maya. Create a NURBS cone on the grid. You'll be prompted to draw the cone on the grid if Interactive Creation mode is on; if it is not, the sphere will appear at the center of the grid. Either option is fine.

2. Switch to smooth shaded mode by pressing **6** on the keyboard, or click on the smooth shade all and textured icons on the viewport's menu bar (Figure 1.22). Press **3** on the keyboard to switch to a high quality display of the geometry.

3. Open the Hypershade by choosing Window ➤ Rendering Editors ➤ Hypershade.

The Hypershade comprises several frames. On the left side is a visual menu of the nodes you can create in the Hypershade. You can choose between displaying the Maya nodes (Create Maya Nodes), mental ray nodes (Create mental ray Nodes), or all nodes (Create All Nodes). Since the list of both nodes can get very long, it is best to choose either Maya nodes or mental ray nodes depending on what you need.

The right side of the Hypershade contains a visual display of the nodes in the scene at the top and the Work Area at the bottom (Figure 1.23). The upper section is organized by tabs named Materials, Textures, Utilities, Lights, Cameras, Shading Groups, Bake Sets, Projects, and Container Nodes. If you want to access all the file textures used in the scene, you can choose the Textures tab to see them listed with preview icons.

4. On the left side of the Hypershade, make sure the menu mode is set to Create Maya Nodes. Click the Blinn button to create a new Blinn material.

FIGURE 1.23

The Hypershade organizes render nodes and offers a workspace for constructing render node networks.

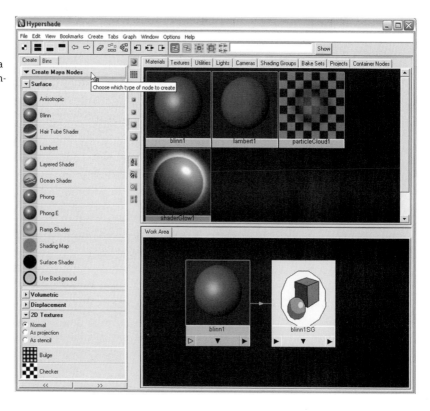

DEFAULT SCENE MATERIALS

All Maya scenes start with three materials already created: lambert1, particleCloud, and shaderGlow. The lambert1 material is the default material applied to all newly created geometry, the particleCloud material is a special material reserved for particle cloud objects, and the shaderGlow node sets the glow options for all shaders in the scene.

5. You can see the new blinn1 material listed under the Materials tab; it also appears in the Work Area.

6. Select the blinn1 material in the Work Area, and from the menu at the top of the Hypershade choose Graph ➤ Input And Output Connections. This displays all of the upstream and downstream nodes connected to blinn1.

The blinn1SG node is a downstream node known as a shader group, connected to blinn1. All materials have a shader group node connected to them. This node is a required part of the network that defines how the shader is applied to a surface and is often used when creating complex mental ray shader networks and overrides (see Figure 1.24).

FIGURE 1.24
Shaders all have shading group nodes attached, which define how the shader is applied to the geometry.

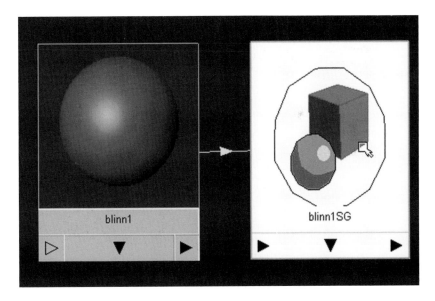

7. Select the blinn1 node, right-click it, and choose blinn1. This opens the Attribute Editor for the Blinn shader, if it's not open already. This is where you adjust the settings that define the look of the material.

8. In the viewport, select the cone. There are several ways you can apply the blinn1 material to the cone:

MMB-drag the material icon from the Hypershade on top of the cone in the viewport window.

Select the cone, right-click the blinn1 node in the Hypershade, and choose Assign Material To Selection (Figure 1.25).

Select the cone, and then click one of the shader icons under the Rendering tab of the shelf. The new material is created automatically when chosen from the shelf.

Right-click on the surface in the viewport, and choose Assign New Shader to create a new shader or Assign Existing Material to assign a shader you've already created.

FIGURE 1.25
Right-click on a shader and drag upward on the marking menu to choose Assign Material To Selection.

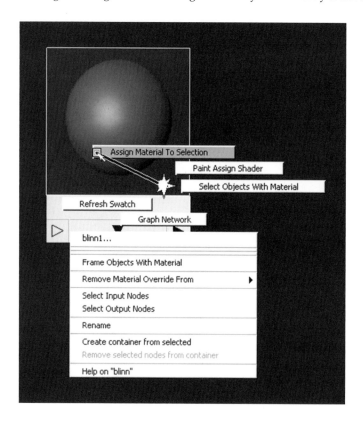

9. In the Attribute Editor for the blinn1 node, rename the material **coneShader**. Click the checkered box to the right of the Color slider. This opens the Create Render Node window (Figure 1.26).

FIGURE 1.26
Click the checkered
box next to the
Color slider to open
the Create Render
Node window.

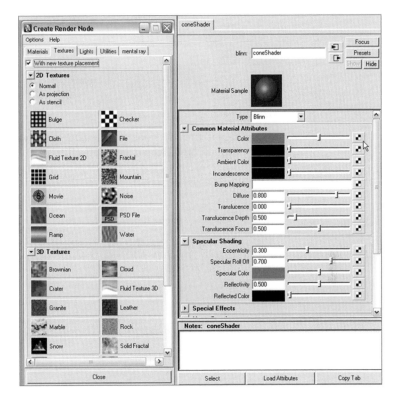

10. Click on the Grid button in the Create Render Node window to create a grid texture; this is applied to the color channel of the cone and is visible on the cone in the viewport when textured and smooth shaded mode is on (hot key = 6).

11. Select coneShader in the Work Area, and right-click its icon. Choose Graph Network. You'll see that the coneShader node now has the grid1 texture node as well as the place2dTexture1 node attached (Figure 1.27).

12. Click the place2dTexture1 node in the Work Area, and its attributes will be displayed in the Attribute Editor. Type **0.5** in the first field next to Coverage. This reduces the coverage of the grid texture in U space by one half.

NURBS UV TEXTURE COORDINATES

NURBS surfaces have their U and V texture coordinates based on the parameterization of the surface, unlike polygon meshes, which require defined UV coordinates. You can use the attributes in the place2dTexture node to position textures on NURBS surfaces. NURBS surfaces are discussed in Chapter 3, and texturing NIRBS surfaces is discussed in Chapter 11.

FIGURE 1.27
Applying the grid texture to the color channel of the coneShader adds two new nodes to the shader network.

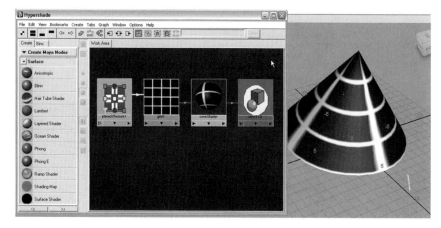

13. Select the grid1 node in the Work Area of the Hypershade to open its settings in the Attribute Editor. Under Color Balance, click on the color swatch next to Default Color. This opens the Color Chooser. Set the color to red.

DEFAULT COLOR

The Default Color of the texture is the color "behind" the grid texture. Any part of the surface that is not covered by the grid (based on the settings in the place2dTexture node) will use the default color.

---

14. In the left panel of the Hypershade, under Create Maya Nodes, scroll down to the 2D Textures and click Ramp to create a ramp node. At the moment it is not connected to any part of the coneShader network. This is another way to create render nodes in the Hypershade.

NAVIGATING THE HYPERSHADE WORK AREA

You can zoom out in the work area of the Hypershade by holding the Alt button while dragging with the right mouse button; likewise, you can pan by holding the Alt button while MMB-dragging.

---

15. Select the grid texture to open its settings in the Attribute Editor. In the Work Area of the Hypershade, MMB-drag the ramp texture from the Work Area all the way to the color swatch next to the Filler color in the grid's Attribute Editor. If you do not use the middle mouse button while dragging, you'll switch to the ramp texture in the Attribute Editor (see Figure 1.28).

16. Select the coneShader node in the Work Area of the Hypershade. Click the graph input and output connections icon on the top menu of the Hypershade. This graphs the network. You can see that the ramp texture is connected to the grid texture. The grid texture is connected to the coneShader, and the shader is connected to the blinn1SG node (see Figure 1.29).

FIGURE 1.28
A texture node can be MMB-dragged from the Hypershade into an attribute slot in the Attribute Editor.

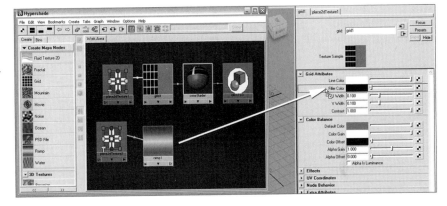

FIGURE 1.29
The coneShader network has grown with the addition of new nodes.

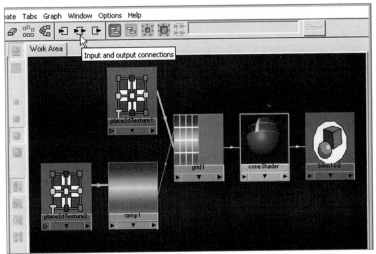

17. Select the blinn1SG node, and graph its input and output connections. The cone's shape node appears (if the bottom caps option was on in the creation options for the NURBS cone you'll see a second shape node for the cone's bottom cap surface). The blinn1SG node is also connected to the render partition and the light linker, which defines which lights are used to light the cone (see Figure 1.30).

NAVIGATING THE HYPERSHADE WORK AREA

You can MMB-drag nodes in and out of the work area of the Hypershade. Try MMB-dragging the nurbsCone1 transform node from the Outliner into the work area of the Hypershade.

The Hypershade is a very powerful and easy-to-use editor. You can build complex networks of nodes quickly just like rearranging building blocks. You can see how nodes are connected by holding the mouse over the lines that connect the nodes.

This section revealed the many ways Maya nodes can be displayed and connected in a Maya scene. You should make sure that you are comfortable with the basics of working with the editors described in this section. You will rely on them heavily throughout the book, and through the various exercises you will gain proficiency in using them.

FIGURE 1.30
The shape nodes for the cone are included in the graph when the input and output connections of the blinn1SG node are graphed.

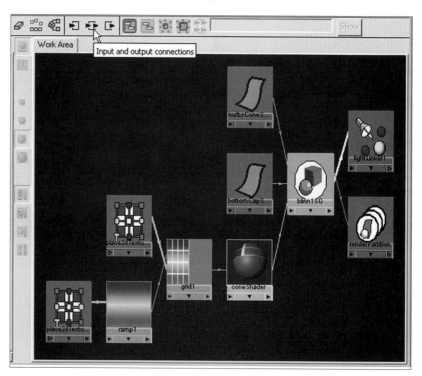

Maya Projects

Organization is the key to creating a successful animation. Whether you are working by yourself or with others in a production pipeline, you'll want to know where to find every file related to a particular project, whether it's a scene file, a texture map, an image sequence, or a particle disk cache. To help you organize all the files you use to create an animation, Maya offers you the option of easily creating a Maya project, which is simply a directory with subfolders where each file type related to your scenes can be stored.

Create a New Project

Creating a new project is very simple. Projects can be created on your local C drive, a secondary drive, or a network. The scene files used for each chapter in this book are stored in their own project directories on the DVD that comes with the book. Maya uses a default project directory when one has not been specified. This is located in your My Documents\maya\projects folder in Windows or Documents\maya\projects on a Mac. As an example you'll create a Project directory structure for the examples used in this chapter.

1. Start a new Maya 2009 session. You'll note that an empty scene is created when you run Maya.

2. Choose File ➢ Project➢ New.

3. The New Project dialog box opens. In the Name field, type **Mastering_Maya_Chapter01**.

4. In the Location field, use the Browse button to find where on your computer or network you want the project to be stored, or simply type the path to the directory. The project folder can be a subfolder of another folder if you like (see Figure 1.31).

FIGURE 1.31
The New Project dialog box lets you set the location of a new project directory structure on your hard drive.

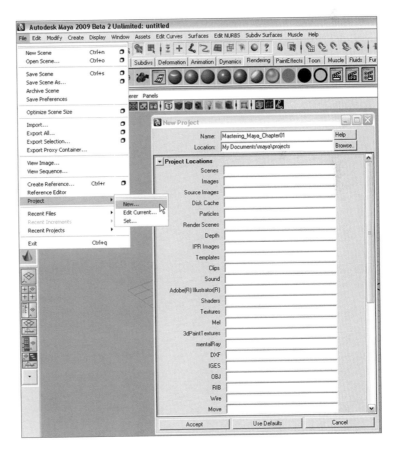

In the Project Locations section, you'll see a large number of labeled fields. The labels indicate the different types of files a Maya scene may or may not use. The fields indicate the path to the subdirectory where these types of files will be located.

5. At the bottom of the New Project Dialog, click the Use Defaults button. This automatically fills in all the fields (see the left side of Figure 1.32).

The fields contain the name of the subdirectory relative to the project file. So when you choose to use the default settings, all Maya scene files (files with the `.mb` or `.ma` file extension) will be stored in a folder labeled `Scenes`. The path to that folder will be, in this example, `Mastering_Maya_Chapter01\Scenes`.

EDITING DEFAULT FILE LOCATIONS

If you decide you want to store the scene files in a different directory, you can type the path to that directory in the field or type a name of a directory you'd like Maya to create when it makes the project.

---

6. Click Accept. Maya will take a few moments to create the Project directory and all subfolders on the specified disk drive.

7. Use your computer's file browser to locate the new project; then expand the folder and you'll see all the subfolders (see the right side of Figure 1.32).

FIGURE 1.32
Clicking the Use Defaults button fills in all of the fields with Maya's preferred default file structure (left side of the image). The directory structure is created on the specified drive (right side of the image).

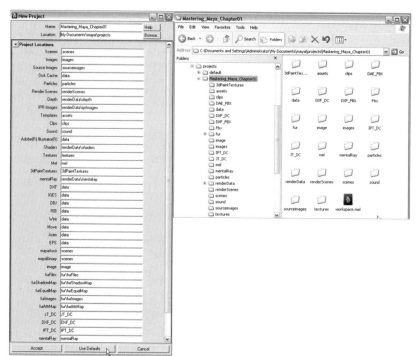

Edit and Change Projects

You may not need to use every folder Maya creates for you, or you may decide to change where Maya looks for elements, such as file textures. If you're working on a number of different projects, you may need to switch the current project. All of these options are available in the Maya File menu.

1. To edit the current Project, choose File ➤ Project ➤ Edit Current. The Edit Project window opens with all of the paths to the project subdirectories. You can type a new directory path into any one of these fields.

RELINKING FILES AFTER CHANGING PROJECT SETTINGS

If you edit the project, Maya will look in the newly specified folders from this point on, but files used prior to editing the project will not be copied or moved. You'll need to move these files using the computer's file browser if you want Maya to easily find them after editing the project.

---

2. If you don't want a particular directory to be created when you set up a project, leave the field blank.

3. To switch Projects, you can choose File ➤ Project Set, or choose a project listed in the Recent Projects menu.

RECENT PROJECT HISTORY

To change the number of projects listed in the Recent Projects menu, choose Window ➤ Settings/ Preferences ➤ Preferences. In the Preferences dialog box, choose the Files/Projects listing from the Categories column, and increase or decrease the value in the Recent History Size For Projects field.

When working on a project with a number of other animators, you can choose to share the same project, which is a little risky, or each animator can create their own project directory structure within a shared folder. The latter example is a little safer as it prevents two people from having the same project open or overwriting each other's work. Later on in the chapter you'll learn how multiple animators can share parts of the scene using file references.

OVERRIDING PROJECT SETTINGS

You can choose to override a project setting for an individual scene element. For instance, by default, Maya looks to the source images directory for file textures. However, when you create a file texture node, you can use the Browse button to reference a file anywhere on your machine or the network. This is usually not a great idea; it defeats the purpose of organizing the files in the first place and can easily lead to broken links between the scene and the texture file. It's a better idea to move all file textures used in the scene to the sourceimages directory or whatever directory is specified in your project settings.

Assets

A production pipeline consists of a number of artists with specialized tasks. Modelers, riggers, animators, lighting technical directors (TDs), and many others work together to create an animation from a director's vision. Organizing a complex animation sequence from all the nodes in a scene can be a daunting task. Maya 2009 introduces Assets, a workflow management tool designed to help a director separate the nodes in a scene and their many attributes into discrete interfaces so each team of specialized artists can concern itself only with its own part of the project.

Containers

Assets are created from containers. A container is a collection of nodes you choose to group together for the purpose of organization. A container is not the same as a group node; containers do not have an associated transform node and do not appear in the viewport of a scene. For example, a model, its animation controls, and its shaders can all be placed in a single container. This example demonstrates some of the ways you can create and work with containers.

CONTAINERS VERSUS FLUID CONTAINERS

Containers in this sense are not the same as Maya Fluid containers, which are a node related to fluid dynamics.

In this example you'll create a container for the front wheels of a vehicle.

1. Open the vehicle_v01.ma file from the Chapter1\scenes directory on the DVD. You'll see a three-wheeled vehicle. In the Outliner the vehicle is grouped.

2. Expand the vehicle group in the Outliner. The group consists of subgroups for the two front wheels, the rear wheel, the chassis, the suspension, and a NURBS curve named steering.

3. Select the steering node in the Outliner. This is the animation control for the steering. Switch to the Rotate tool (hot key = e), and drag the green circular handle of the Rotate tool to rotate the steering node on the Y axis. The front wheels match the arrow's orientation (see Figure 1.33).

FIGURE 1.33
The Y rotation of each front wheel is connected to the Y rotation of the steering control.

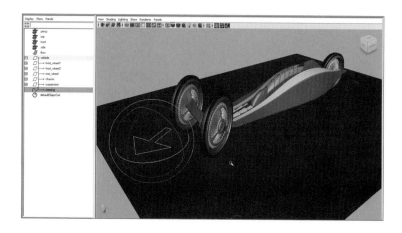

If you select one of the front_wheel groups in the Outliner, you'll see that its Rotate Y channel is colored yellow, indicating it has an incoming connection. The steering curve's Y rotation is connected to both front_wheel groups' Y connection.

4. Select steering again, and switch to the Move tool (hot key = w). Move steering up and down along the Y axis by dragging the green arrow of the Move tool. The front wheels rotate on the X axis based on the height of the steering object (see Figure 1.34).

FIGURE 1.34
The X rotation of each front wheel is connected to the Y translate of the steering control, giving the animator the ability to tilt the wheels if needed.

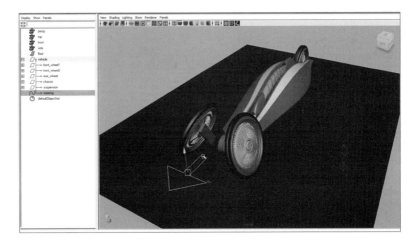

If you look in the Channel Box for either of the front_wheel groups, you'll see that the Rotate X channel is colored orange, indicating that it has been keyframed. In fact, the Rotate channels of the group use what's known as a driven key to determine their values. The keyframe's driver is the Y translation of the arrow group. You'll learn more about this technique in Chapter 5.

5. Select the vehicle group node and switch to the Move tool. Drag the red arrow of the Move tool to translate the vehicle back and forth along the X axis. All three wheels rotate as the car moves.

If you expand the front_wheel1 group in the Outliner and select the wheel1Rotate child group node, you'll see that the Rotate Z channel is colored purple in the Channel Box, indicating an expression is controlling its Z-axis rotation. You can open the Attribute Editor for the front_wheel1 group and switch to the Expression4 tab to see the expression; see Figure 1.35 (the field isn't large enough to display the entire expression; you can click on the field and hold down the right-arrow button on the keyboard to read the whole expression). Creating expressions will be covered in Chapter 5.

This model uses a very simple rig, but already there are a lot of nodes connected to the vehicle geometry to help the job of the animator. To simplify, you can create a container for just the wheels and their connected nodes so the animator can focus on just this part of the model to do his job.

6. In the Outliner, expand the vehicle group and the two front_wheel groups. Select the front_wheel1 group, Ctrl+click (on the Mac hold the Command button) wheel1Rotate, front_wheel2, wheel2Rotate, and the steering curve node. Open the Hypergraph in connections mode (Window ➢ Hypergraph:Connections).

7. In the Hypergraph menu choose Graph ➤ Input And Output Connections (see Figure 1.36).

8. Select the node named time1 and the vehicle node, and drag them below the other nodes, out of the way of the other nodes.

9. Drag a selection over all of the nodes at the top (excluding time1 and vehicle). These nodes include the group nodes, keyframe nodes, and expression nodes all related to controlling the rotation of the front wheel groups. In the Hypergraph menu, choose Edit ➤ Create Container ➤ Options.

FIGURE 1.35

The Z rotation of the wheels is controlled by an expression node. The expression node is a separate tab in the Attribute Editor.

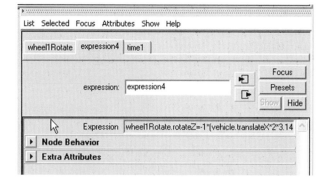

FIGURE 1.36

The vehicle group is expanded, and several of the nodes related to the front wheels are selected and graphed on the Hypergraph.

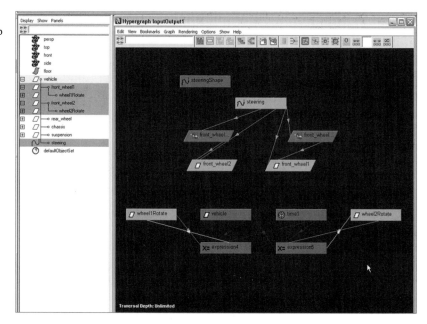

THE OPTIONS BOX

The small square to the right of a listing in the menu indicates the options. When you select just the listing in the menu, the action will be performed using the default settings. When you click the Options box to the right of the menu listing, a dialog box will open allowing you to change the options for the action. In this book, when you're asked to choose options, it means you need to click the Options box to the right of the menu listing.

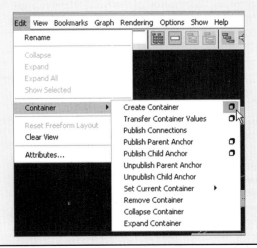

10. In the Create Container Options dialog box, set the Name of the container to **front_ wheels**. Turn off all of the settings under Include Options and Publish Options. All of the keyframes and expressions are applied to rotation of the wheel groups, not the geometry nodes contained in the groups, so you needn't worry about including the contents of the groups in the container (see Figure 1.37).

FIGURE 1.37
The options are set for the container that will hold all of the selected nodes in the Hypergraph.

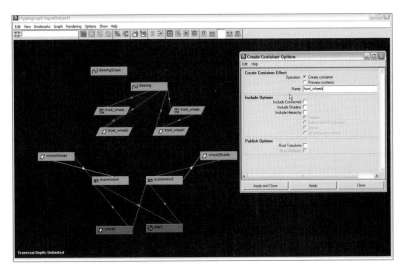

11. Click Apply and Close to create the container. In the Hypergraph, you'll see a gray box labeled front_wheels; this box is also visible in the Outliner. The time1 and vehicle nodes are still visible in the Hypergraph. It may appear as though they have been disconnected, but that's not actually the case.

12. Select the front_wheels container in the Hypergraph, and graph its input and output connections (Graph ➢ Input And Output Connections). The connections to the time1 and vehicle nodes are visible again.

13. Select the front_wheels container in the Hypergraph, and choose Options ➢ Merge Connections. Both the time1 and vehicle nodes have several lines connecting them to the front_wheels container. Choosing Merge Connections toggles a display mode in which multiple connections are displayed as a single bold line. This does not affect the connections themselves; it is just a display option that can be turned on and off as needed (see Figure 1.38).

FIGURE 1.38
Turning on Merge Connections groups multiple connection lines between nodes into a single bold line. This helps keep the Hypergraph neat but does not affect how the nodes function.

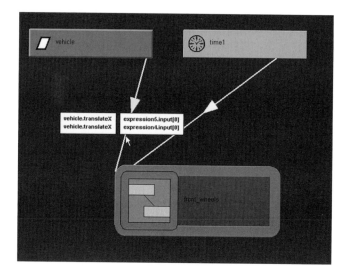

14. Select the front_wheels container in the Hypergraph, and click the Expand Selected Container(s) icon on the Hypergraph menu bar (or double-click on the container). You will see the nodes within the container. The merge connections view is disabled when you expand a container (see Figure 1.39).

You can select a node inside the container and remove it from the container by right-clicking the node and choosing Remove From Container.

15. Save the scene as **vehicle_v02.ma**.

FIGURE 1.39
Expanding the view of a container in the Hypergraph makes the connections between nodes within the container visible.

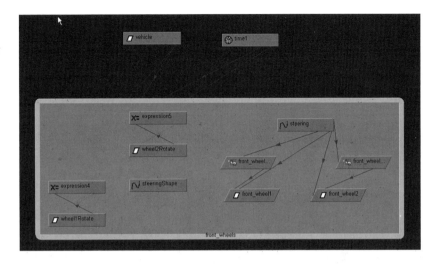

TIPS ON WORKING WITH CONTAINERS

◆ To delete a container, select it and choose (from the Hypergraph menu) Edit ➢ Container ➢ Remove Container. Don't select the container and delete it; deleting the container will delete the contents from the scene as well.

◆ You can remove all the containers in a scene, without deleting their contents, by choosing Edit ➢ Delete By Type ➢ Containers.

◆ In the Outliner, the container node can be expanded to reveal the contents. Note that the wheel groups are no longer shown as children of the vehicle group but are now inside the container group. The nodes themselves still behave as children of the vehicle group. If you change the position of the vehicle, the wheels will still rotate and move with the vehicle.

◆ Containers can be created in the Hypershade as well and can contain any type of node including shaders and textures.

◆ You can create containers without going into the Hypershade. Just select the nodes in the scene and choose Assets ➢ Create Container.

◆ If you choose Set Current Container from the Assets menu, all new nodes created in the scene will automatically become part of the specified container.

Creating Assets from Containers

You create an asset by publishing selected attributes of the container's nodes to the top level of the container. This means that the animator can select the container node and have all the custom controls available in the Channel Box without having to hunt around the various nodes in the network. You can also template your container for use with similar animation rigs.

In this exercise you'll create an asset based on the container created in the previous section.

1. Continue with the file from the previous section or open vehicle_v02.ma from the chapter1\scenes folder on the DVD.

2. In the Outliner, select the front_wheels container and expand the node by clicking the plus sign to the left of the node. Select the steering node from within the container.

3. In the Channel Box, select the Translate Y channel, and from the Edit menu in the Channel Box, choose Publish To Container ➢ Options. In the Publish Attribute Options box, choose both Selected Channel Box Attributes and Custom Name. Type **wheelTilt** in the Custom String field. Click Apply and Close (see Figure 1.40).

4. Select the front_wheels container in the Outliner; you'll see the wheelTilt channel has been added in the Channel Box. If you change this value between -1 and 1, the arrow controller moves up and down and the front wheels tilt.

FIGURE 1.40
The Translate Y attribute of the steering node is published to the container under the name wheelTilt.

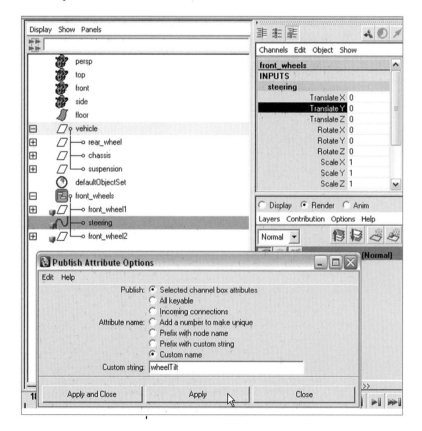

PUBLISH ATTRIBUTES FROM THE ATTRIBUTE EDITOR

If you need to publish a specific attribute that does not appear in the Channel Box, you can open the Attribute Editor for the appropriate node, right-click the attribute name, and choose the Publish options from the pop-up menu.

Using the Asset Editor

The Asset Editor can help you further customize and manage your scene's assets.

1. Open the scene vehicle_v03.ma from the chapter1\scenes folder on the DVD.

2. In the Outliner you'll see two containers: one for the wheels and another named carPaint, which holds the blue paint shader applied to the car.

3. To open the Asset Editor, choose Assets ➤ Asset Editor. The editor is in two panels; on the left side you'll see all the assets in the scene.

The Asset Editor opens in view mode. You can click the plus sign in the square to see the nodes contained within each container. You can see the attributes of each node listed by clicking the plus sign in the circle next to each node.

4. Select the front_wheels container, and click the push pin icon above and to the right of the asset list to switch to edit mode. On the right-hand side of the editor, you'll see the wheelTilt attribute we created in the previous section.

5. Select the arrow next to wheelTilt on the right-hand panel, and the wheels container expands to reveal the Translate channel of the steering node. This is the attribute originally published to the container as wheelTilt.

6. Expand the Rotate attributes of the steering node immediately below the Translate attributes. Select Rotate Y, and click the second icon from the top in the middle bar of the Asset Editor. This publishes the selected attribute to the container with a custom name (see Figure 1.41).

7. A dialog box will open, prompting you to name the selected attribute. Name it **steer**.

Note that steps 6 and 7 are just another way to publish an attribute; the end result is the same as when you published the wheelTilt attribute in the previous section.

8. Steer now appears in the right-hand side of the screen. The view on the right side of the Asset Editor shows the attributes grouped by node. If you want to see just the attributes themselves, choose View ➤ Mode ➤ Flat from the Asset Editor's menu bar.

9. Select the front_wheels container in the Outliner, and open its Attribute Editor. Expand the Container Attributes rollout and turn on Black Box (see Figure 1.42). When you do this, the only attributes that appear in the Channel Box are the ones that have been published to the container (wheelTilt and steer). Likewise, in the Outliner, you can no longer expand the container node.

FIGURE 1.41
Attributes can be published to the container from within the Asset Editor.

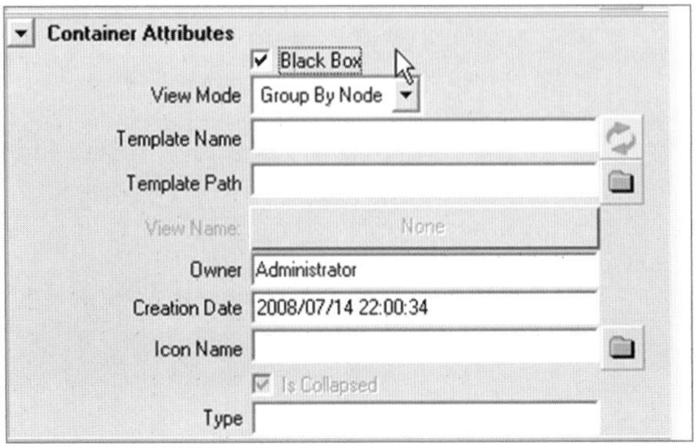

FIGURE 1.42
Turning on Black Box restricts access to the container's contents and their attributes.

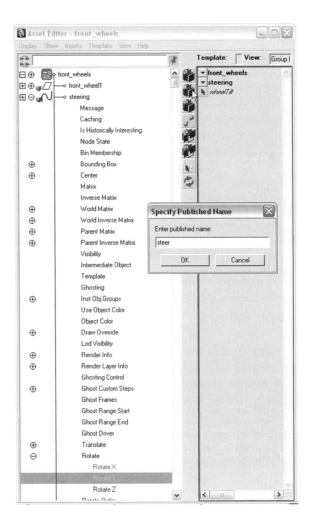

Template Containers

If you have a number of animation rigs that use a similar setup, you can template a container and its custom attributes and apply this container to similar node networks.

1. In the Asset Editor, click the push pin icon so you're still in edit mode. Select the front_wheels container and choose Template ➤ Save as. Container templates are saved to the assets folder of the current project. Name the container **wheelControl** and save it.

2. Save your current version of the scene. Open the file vehicle_v04.ma from the chapter1\ scenes folder on the DVD. This scene contains an identical version of the vehicle painted orange instead of blue.

3. In the Outliner, note that a container named front_wheels has been created; however, no attributes of the contained nodes have been published to the container.

4. Select the front_wheels container and open the Asset Editor (Assets ➤ Asset Editor). In the Asset Editor, select the front_wheels container, and click the push pin icon to switch to edit mode.

5. Choose Template ➤ Assign ➤ Assign New Template. From the File Browser dialog box choose the wheelControl.template file from the assets folder of the current project (this folder should open by default). A copy of the wheelControl.template file can be found in the chapter1\assets directory on the DVD.

6. In the Asset Editor you'll see the wheelTilt and steer attributes you created in the previous section; however, they are not bound to the wheels template, meaning they are not connected.

7. Click the plus sign in the square next to the front_wheels container on the left side of the Asset Editor; this will expand the front_wheels container. Click the plus sign in the circle next to the steering subgroup to expand its list of attributes.

8. Scroll down the list and find the Translate attribute; expand this attribute and select Translate Y. Click the connection icon to the right of wheelTilt in the right side of the Asset Editor. This will bind this attribute to the Translate attributes of the steering group (see Figure 1.43).

FIGURE 1.43

Attributes from the template on the right side of the panel can be bound to attributes of the containers on the left side of the panel.

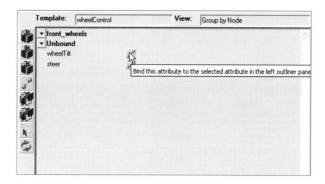

9. Expand the Rotate attributes below the Translate attributes, select the Rotate Y attribute on the left side of the editor, and click the connection icon to the right of steer to bind the attribute.

10. Close the Asset Editor, and select the front_wheels container in the Outliner. In the Channel Box the Wheel Tilt and Steer channels are now available. Change their values, and you'll see the wheels on the car update.

This example is very simple; the usefulness of this workflow is much more obvious when working with complex node networks that have equally complex interfaces. You can create container interfaces at an early stage of the project as a way to keep artists organized.

File References

File referencing is another workflow tool that can be used when a team of artists is working on the same scene. For example, by using file references an animator can begin animating a scene while the modeler is still perfecting the model. This is also true for any of the other team members. A texture artist can work on textures for the same model at the same time. The animator and texture artist can import a reference of the model into their Maya scene, and each time the modeler saves a change, the model reference in the other scenes will update (when the animator and texture artist reload either the scene or the reference).

FILE REFERENCING VERSUS IMPORTING

File referencing is not the same as importing a Maya scene into another Maya scene. When you import a Maya scene, all of the imported nodes become fully integrated into the new scene and have no links to any external files. On the other hand, file references maintain a link to external files regardless of whether the referenced files are open or closed. You can alter a referenced file in a scene, but it's not a great idea; it can break the link to the referenced file and defeats the purpose of file referencing in the first place.

Referencing a File

In this example you'll reference a model into a scene, animate it, and then make changes to the original reference to get a basic idea of the file referencing workflow.

1. Find the vehicleReference_v01.ma scene and the street_v01.ma scene in the chapter1\ scenes directory of the DVD. Copy both of these files to your local hard drive. Put them in the scenes directory of your current project.

2. Open the scene street_v01.ma from the scenes directory of the current project (or wherever you placed the file on your local drive). The scene contains a simple street model. A locator named carAnimation is attached to a curve in the center of the street. If you play the animation, you'll see the locator zip along the curve.

3. To bring in a file reference, choose File ➢ Create Reference. The File Browser will open; find the vehicleReferenc_v01.ma scene that you copied to your local drive. Select it and choose Reference from the File dialog box. After a few moments the car will appear in the scene (see Figure 1.44).

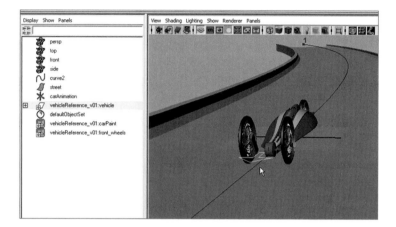

4. In the Outliner, you'll see the vehicleReference_v01:vehicle node as well as the vehicleReference_v01:front_wheels and carPaint container nodes. The container node is an asset with both the wheelTilt and steer attributes created in the previous section.

REFERENCING MAYA SCENES

You don't need to do anything special to the scene you want to reference; it can be a standard Maya scene. When you reference a file in a scene, all of its associated nodes appear using the referenced file's scene name as a prefix. You can change this to a custom string using the options in the Create Reference command.

---

5. In the Outliner, select the carAnimation locator, then Ctrl+click the vehicleReference_v01:vehicle node. Switch to the Animation menu set and choose Constrain ➢ Parent ➢ Options. In the options for the Parent constraint, turn off Maintain Offset, make sure both Translate All and Rotate All are selected, and set the weight to **1**. Click Add to make the constraint. The car is now constrained to the locator and will zip along the curve in the center of the street.

6. Try setting keyframes on the wheelTilt and steer attributes of the vehicleReference_v01:front_wheels node.

7. Save the scene to your local scenes directory as **street_v02.ma**.

8. Open the vehicleReference_v01.ma scene from the directory where you copied this file on your local drive.

9. Expand the Vehicle group and the Chassis subgroup. Select the Body subgroup. Set its Scale Y attribute to **0.73** and its Scale Z attribute to **1.5**.

10. Open the Hypershade (Window ➢ Rendering Editors ➢ Hypershade). Select the blue-Paint material. Click on the blue color swatch next to the Color channel, and use the Color Chooser to change the color to red.

11. Save the scene using the same name (vehicleReference_v01.ma). Open the street_v02.ma scene. The car model has all of the changes you created in the vehicleReference_v01.ma scene. It is red and the body is much wider (see Figure 1.45).

FIGURE 1.45

The changes made to the body shape and color in the vehicleRefer-ence_v01.ma file are reflected in the referenced model in the street scene.

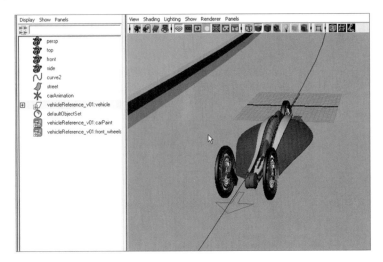

This is the basic file referencing workflow; however, a file referencing structure can be made much more complex to accommodate the needs of multiple teams. In addition, a referenced file can also use other references, so that a file referencing tree can be constructed layering several levels of file references. This kind of structure is best planned out and agreed upon in the beginning in order to minimize confusion and keep a consistent workflow.

Using Reference Proxies

You can use proxy objects for your file references to temporarily substitute higher-resolution objects with lower-resolution objects. This can make animating the scene a little easier because the lower-resolution objects will improve performance and update faster in Maya as you play the animation on the timeline.

Multiple versions of the model can be created and used as proxies to facilitate different needs in the scene. A proxy should be the same size and roughly the same shape as the referenced file.

1. Open the street_v03.ma scene from the chapter1\scenes directory on the DVD. This scene has the same street as before with the same animated locator.

2. First bring in the file reference by choosing File ➢ Create Reference ➢ Options. Under General Options in the Reference Options dialog box, turn on Group and Locator (see Figure 1.46). This will create a locator in the scene and a parent reference to the locator.

FIGURE 1.46

In the file reference options, make sure Group is on if you want to animate the reference and proxies.

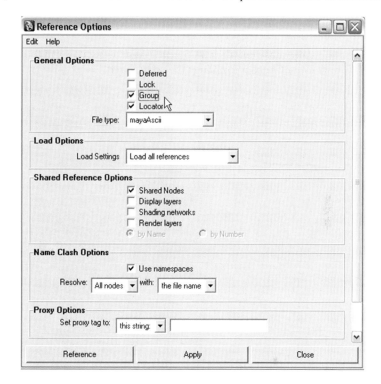

REFERENCE GROUPING

In order for the reference and proxy to share the same translation, rotation, and scale animation, the reference must have grouping enabled when it is brought into the scene. Otherwise, when you animate the proxy and then switch to the reference, animation placed on the transform node of the proxy will not be transferred to the reference.

3. Click the Reference button, and choose the vehicleReference_v01.ma file from the chapter1\scenes directory on the DVD.

4. When the reference loads, you'll see that it is parented to a locator named vehicleReference_v01RNlocator in the Outliner. In the Outliner, MMB-drag the vehicleReference_v01RNlocator on top of the carAnimation locator. Then select the vehicleReference_v01RN locator, open the Channel Box, and set all of its Translate and Rotate channels to **0**. This places the parent locator for the reference at the same position as the car animation

locator; when you play the animation, you'll see the car zip down the track. This is an alternate workflow to creating a parent constraint between the reference locator and the animated locator (see Figure 1.47).

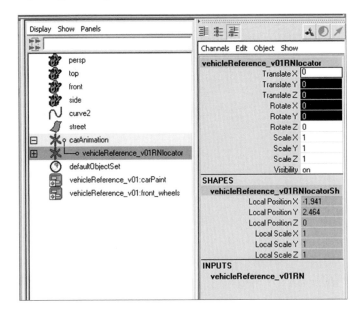

5. Choose File ➤ Reference Editor to open the Reference Editor window. In the bottom half of the Reference Editor window, select the vehicleReference_v01RN node. Choose Proxy ➤ Add Proxy ➤ Options.

6. In the Proxy Options, type **loRes** into the Set Proxy Tag To field. Click the Apply button, and use the File Browser dialog box to choose the loResCar_v01.ma scene from the chapter1\scenes directory on the DVD.

7. The Proxy Options dialog box should remain open after you add the loRes proxy. Change the field so that it reads **mediumRes**, click the Proxy button, and use the File Browser to select the medResCar_v01.ma scene from the chapter1\scenes folder on the DVD.

8. The Reference Editor won't look much different except that the icon next to the vehicle-Reference listing in the lower half has changed to the double-diamond icon, indicating that the reference has proxies available.

9. To switch to the proxy, make sure vehicleReference_v01PM is selected in the Reference Editor. From the menu bar in the Reference Editor, choose Proxy ➤ Reload Proxy As ➤ loRes. After a moment the original vehicle is replaced with the lower-resolution version.

10. Try using this menu to switch to the mediumRes version of the vehicle. The vehicle should be replaced with a slightly higher-resolution version. If you play the animation, the vehicle still moves along the animation curve (Figure 1.48).

11. To bring back the reference, select the original from the list in the Reload Proxy As menu.

The Reference Editor can be used to change proxies, remove proxies, and load, duplicate, unload, and reload references. When a reference is unloaded, it is removed from the scene.

FIGURE 1.48
The Reference Editor is used to switch between different versions of the proxy and the original referenced model.

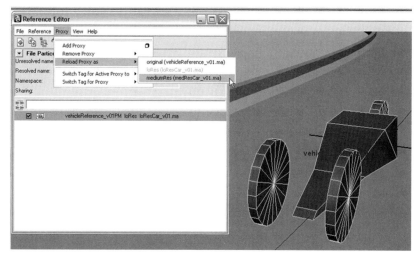

The Bottom Line

Understand transform and shape nodes.   DAG nodes have both a transform and a shape node. The transform node tells where an object is located; the shape node describes how it is made. Nodes can be parented to each other to form a hierarchy.

Master it   Arrange the nodes in the miniGun_v03.ma file in a hierarchical structure so the barrels of the guns can rotate on their Z axis, the guns can be aimed independently, and the guns rotate with the turret.

Create a project.   Creating a project directory structure keeps Maya scene files and connected external files organized to ensure the animation project is efficient.

Master it   Create a new project named Test, but make sure the project has only the scene, source images, and data subfolders.

Use assets.   An asset is a container in which the contained nodes have specific attributes published to the top level of the container. This means that members of each team in a pipeline have easy access to the attributes they need, thus streamlining production.

Master it   Create an asset from the nodes in the miniGun_v04.ma scene in the chapter1\ scenes folder. Make sure that only the Y rotation of the turret, the X rotation of the guns, and the Z rotation of the gun barrels are available to the animator.

Create file references.   File references can be used so that as part of the team works on a model, the other members of the team can use it in the scene. As changes to the original file are made, the referenced file in other scenes will update automatically.

Master it   Create a file reference for the miniGun_v04.ma scene; create a proxy from the miniGun_loRes.ma scene.

Chapter 2

Maya Cameras

Maya is a visual effects studio designed with the art of filmmaking in mind. Maya's virtual camera replicates real-world cameras as much as possible, while at the same time offering enough flexibility in the settings to allow for a wide variety of creative uses. This chapter introduces the core concepts of how to work with Maya's virtual cameras.

In this chapter, you'll learn to:

- ◆ Determine image size and resolution
- ◆ Work with camera settings
- ◆ Create custom camera rigs
- ◆ Use Depth of Field and Motion Blur
- ◆ Create orthographic and stereoscopic cameras

Image Size and Resolution

When starting a new project in Maya, you should first determine the final size of the rendered image or image sequence. These settings will affect every aspect of the project, including texture size, model tessellation, render time, how the shots are framed, and so on. You should raise this concern as soon as possible and make sure every member of the team, from the producer to the art director to the compositor to the editor, is aware of the final output of the animation. This means the image size, the resolution, the frames per second, and any image cropping that may occur after rendering. Nothing is worse than having to redo a render or even an animation because of a miscommunication concerning details, such as resolution settings or frames per second.

TAKING OVER A PROJECT

If you inherit a shot or a project from another animator, double-check that the resolution and camera settings are correct before proceeding. Never assume that the animation is set up properly. It's always possible that something has changed between the time the project started and the moment you took over someone else's scene files.

Set Image Size

The settings for the image size and resolution are located in the Render Settings window under the Common tab (shown in Figure 2.1). When you start a new scene, visit this panel first and make sure these settings are what you need.

NEW MENTAL RAY TABS

In Maya 2009 the mental ray settings are organized into five tabs. The tabs are labeled Common, Passes, Features, Quality, Indirect Lighting, and Options. This division of the Render Settings window adds a few new features, such as Render Passes, and also helps to better organize other aspects of rendering with mental ray. These tabs will be discussed in Chapter 12, "Rendering for Compositing."

FIGURE 2.1

The Common tab in the Render Settings window is where the image size and image resolution are established. Visit this panel when you start a new project.

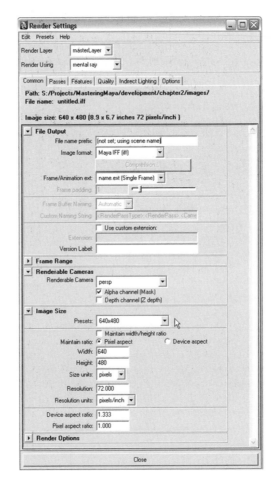

Image size refers to the number of pixels on the horizontal axis by the number of pixels on the vertical axis. So a setting of 640×480 means 640 pixels wide by 480 pixels tall.

Resolution refers to how many pixels fit within an inch (or centimeter, depending on the setting). Generally you'll use a resolution of 72 pixels per ich when rendering for animations displayed on computer screens, television screens, and film. Print resolution is much higher, usually 300 pixels per inch.

You can create any settings you'd like for the image size and resolution, or you can use one of the Maya Image Size presets. The list of presets is divided so that common film and video presets are at the top of the list and common print settings are at the bottom of the list. Size and resolution units can be changed in the Common tab of the Render Settings window as well.

ADJUSTING SIZE FOR RENDER TEST PREVIEWS

If you need to create test renders at a smaller size, you can change the size of just the images you see in the Render Preview window by choosing a setting from the Render ➤ Test Resolution menu in the Rendering menu set. This option only affects images displayed in the Render Preview window, it does not change the final output settings. When you render your final animation using a batch render, your images will use the size settings specified in the Common tab of the Render Settings window.

Resolution is expressed in a number of ways in Maya:

Image aspect ratio   The ratio of width over height. An image that is 720 by 540 has a ratio of 1.333.

Pixel aspect ratio   The ratio of the actual pixel size. Computer monitors use square pixels: the height of the pixel is 1 and the width of the pixel is 1; thus the pixel aspect ratio is 1. Standard video images use nonsquare pixels that are 1 in. height by 1.1 in. width, giving them a pixel aspect ratio of 0.9.

Device aspect ratio   The image aspect ratio multiplied by the pixel aspect ratio. For a video image that is 720×486 (1.48) using nonsquare pixels (0.9), this would be 1.48 × 0.9 = 1.333.

Film aspect ratio   The camera aperture attribute (found in the Attribute Editor for a camera) represented as a ratio. For a typical 35mm video image, this would be 0.816/0.612 = 1.333.

VIEWING NONSQUARE PIXELS ON A COMPUTER MONITOR

Viewing nonsquare pixels on a computer monitor makes the image look squished. Typically you would test render your animation using a pixel aspect ratio of 1.0 with an image size of 720×540. When you are ready for final output, you can switch your resolution to a standard video resolution using a pixel aspect ratio of 0.9 and an image size of 720×486.

Set Film Speed

The film speed (also known as transport speed) is specified in frames per second. This setting is found in the Maya Preferences window (Window ➤ Settings/Preferences ➤ Preferences). Under the Categories column on the left side of the window, choose Settings. In the Working Units area, use the Time drop-down list to specify the frames per second of the scene. You can change this setting after you've started animating, but it's a good idea to set this at the start of a project to avoid confusion or mistakes. When changing this setting on a scene that already has keyframed animation, you can choose to keep the keyframes at their current frame numbers or have Maya adjust the keyframe position automatically based on the new time setting (see Figure 2.2).

FIGURE 2.2

The animation speed (frames per second) is set in the Preferences window.

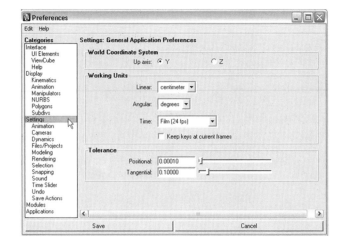

Camera Settings

The settings found in a camera's Attribute Editor greatly impact the look of a rendered animation. In this section, you'll practice using these settings on an animatic of a sci-fi car chase.

ANIMATICS

An *animatic* is a film industry term referring to a rough animation designed to help plan out a shot, like a moving storyboard. Typically models in an animatic are very low resolution and untextured with simple lighting. Animatics are used to plan out both computer-generated (CG) and live-action shots. Camera work, timing, and the composition of elements within the frame are the most important aspects of an animatic.

Creating a Camera

Every new Maya scene has four preset cameras by default. These are the front, side, top, and perspective (persp) cameras. You can render using any of these cameras; however, their main purpose is to navigate and view the 3D environment shown in the viewport. It's always a good idea to create new cameras in the scene for the purpose of rendering the animation.

1. Open the chase_v01.ma scene from the chapter2/scenes folder on the DVD. You'll find that a simple animatic of a car racing down a track has been created.

2. Create a new camera (Create ➤ Cameras ➤ Camera). Open the Outliner and select the new camera1 node. Double-click its transform node in the Outliner and rename it **shotCam1** (see Figure 2.3).

FIGURE 2.3

A new camera is created and renamed in the Outliner.

3. In the Display Layer Editor, turn off the visibility of all the layers except street to hide the unnecessary geometry in the scene.

DISPLAY LAYERS

Display layers are found below the Channel Box on the right side of the screen. Clicking the V button toggles the visibility of the layer.

---

4. Select shotCam1 in the Outliner, and press the **f** hot key to focus on this camera in the viewport.

The icon for the camera looks like a movie camera. It has a transform node and a shape node. The camera attributes are located on the shape node.

5. Select shotCam1, and switch to the Move tool (hot key = w). Move the camera up from the center of the grid to the level of the street. Set the Translate X, Y, and Z channels to **1.382**, **4.138**, and **-3.45**.

6. In the toolbox, click the Show Manipulator tool (the bottom icon in the toolbox). If you zoom out in the viewport, you'll see the camera has a second positional icon; this is the center of interest (see Figure 2.4). The value shown in the camera's Channel Box for the center of interest is the distance (in the scene's working units—meters for this scene) between the camera and the center of interest. Grab this part of the manipulator and position it on the street so the camera is looking up the road (toward the beginning of the track where the car starts). This is one technique for aiming the camera.

7. In the Viewport panel menu, choose Panels ➢ Perspective ➢ shotCam1. This will switch the view to shotcam1.

FIGURE 2.4
The Show Manipulator tool allows you to aim the camera using a second transform manipulator.

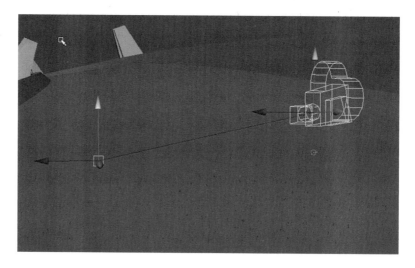

Maya 2009 has added icons to the Viewport panel so that you can quickly access common viewport settings (see Figure 2.5). The first group of icons on the left side is directly related to camera display options. Starting from the left, here is a list of the actions associated with each icon:

♦ **Select Camera**—Selects the transform node of the current viewing camera.

♦ **Camera Attributes**—Opens the Attribute Editor for the current viewing camera.

♦ **Bookmark**—Stores a bookmark for the current camera position. To move the camera to a bookmarked position, choose View ➢ Bookmarks and choose the bookmark from the list.

FIGURE 2.5
The new panel icon bar provides easy access to common viewport commands. The first two groups of icons on the left side are camera-related options.

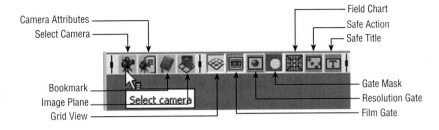

CAMERA BOOKMARKS

You can name your stored bookmarks and create a shelf button for each using the Bookmark Editor (View ➤ Bookmarks ➤ Edit Bookmarks).

◆ **Image Plane**—Creates an image plane for the current camera. Image planes are discussed in Chapter 3.

◆ **Grid View**—Turns the Grid display on or off.

◆ **Film Gate**—Turns the Film Gate display on or off.

◆ **Resolution Gate**—Turns the Resolution Gate display on or off.

◆ **Gate Mask**—Turns the shaded Gate Mask on or off when either the Resolution Gate or Film Gate display is activated.

◆ **Field Chart**—Turns the Field Chart display on or off.

◆ **Safe Action**—Turns the Safe Action display on or off.

◆ **Safe Title**—Turns the Safe Title display on or off.

DISPLAY SETTINGS

These same settings can be found in the Attribute Editor for the camera's shape node under the Display Options roll-out. You can use these settings to change the opacity or the color of the gate mask: Turn on both the Resolution and Film Gate displays at the same time, and change the Overscan setting, which changes the amount of space between the gate and the edge of the viewport.

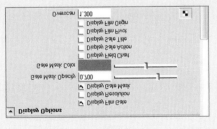

8. In the Display Layer Editor, turn on the buildings layer so the buildings are visible. Tumble around in the viewport (LMB-drag while holding down the Alt key) so you can see part of the large building to the left of the street.

9. In the panel view, turn on the Resolution Gate. Click the Camera Attributes icon to open the Attribute Editor for shotCam1.

The image size of this scene is set to 1280×720, which is the HD 720 preset. You can see the image resolution at the top of the screen when the Resolution Gate is activated. Working with the Resolution Gate on is extremely helpful when you're establishing the composition of your shots (Figure 2.6).

FIGURE 2.6
The Resolution Gate is a helpful tool when framing a shot.

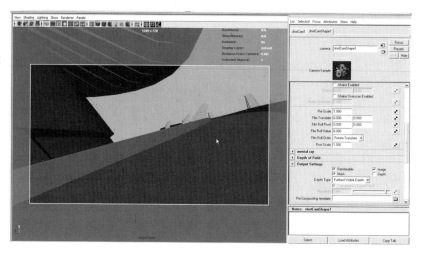

When you create a new camera to render the scene, you need to add it to the list of renderable cameras in the Render settings. You can render the scene using more than one camera.

10. Scroll down in the Attribute Editor for shotCam1 and expand the Output Settings area. Make sure the Renderable option is selected.

11. Open the Render Settings window. In the Renderable Cameras area, you'll see both the shotCam1 and persp cameras listed (see Figure 2.7). To remove the perspective camera, click the trashcan to the right of the listing.

FIGURE 2.7
Cameras can be added to the list of renderable cameras in the Render Settings window.

To change the renderable camera, choose a different camera from the list. To add another camera, choose Add Renderable Camera at the bottom of the list. The list shows all available cameras in the scene.

When batch rendering a scene with more than one renderable camera, Maya creates a subdirectory named after each renderable camera in the image directory of the project. You can add the camera name to the name of the image sequence by adding **%c** to the name listed in the File Name Prefix field in the Render Settings window. For example, setting the File Name Prefix to **myAnimation_%c** in a scene with two renderable cameras creates two image sequences named `myAnimation_camera1.#.tif` and `myAnimation_camera2.#.tif`. See Figure 2.8.

FIGURE 2.8
The camera name can be appended to the image name in the rendered sequence by adding **%c**.

Camera Attributes

At the top of the Attribute Editor for the camera's shape node, you'll find the basic settings for the camera available in the Camera Attributes rollout.

1. Select shotCam1 and open its Attribute Editor to the shotCam1Shape tab. In the Controls drop-down list, you have the option of switching to a camera with an aim node or to a camera with an aim and an up control. Set the camera to Camera And Aim (Figure 2.9).

A single-node camera is just a plain camera like the perspective camera. You can change its rotation and translation by setting these channels in the Channel Box, using the Move and Rotate tools, or tumbling and tracking while looking through the camera.

FIGURE 2.9
You can add additional camera controls using the Controls menu in the Attribute Editor. The camera is then grouped in the Outliner with a separate aim control.

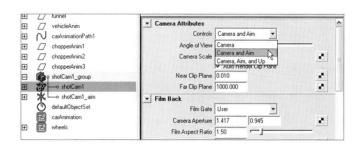

MOVING THE CAMERA

A camera can be translated and rotated using the standard transform tools. This is done when you are viewing the camera from another camera. When you are looking through a camera, you can use the same hot keys you use while moving around the perspective camera:

Alt+LMB = Tumble, also known as rotating the camera.

Alt+MMB = Track; this is the same as moving the camera on the X and Y axes.

Alt+RMB = Dolly; this is the same as moving the camera on the Z axis, also known as pushing the camera.

Additional camera movement controls are found in the panel's View menu; just choose View ➤ Camera Tools and choose one of the tools from the list.

By default, each change in position that results from tumbling, tracking, or dollying a camera view is not undoable. You can change this default by activating the Undoable Movements option in the camera's Attribute Editor; however, this may add a lot to the Undo cue. Alternatively, you can use the bracket hot keys, [and], to move between previous views. Bookmarks are also a good way to store camera views. It's also common to set a keyframe on a camera's Translation and Rotation settings as a way of storing the position. The keyframe can be used as part of an animation or deleted if it's not needed in the final animation.

A two-node camera is a camera with a separate aim control grouped together. When you switch to this type of camera (or create this type of camera from the Create ➤ Cameras menu), the rotation of the camera is controlled by the position of the aim node, which is simply a locator. It works much like the Show Manipulators tool except that the locator itself has a transform node. This makes it easy to visualize where the camera is looking in the scene and makes animation easier. You can keyframe the position of the aim locator and the position of the camera separately and easily edit their animation curves on the Graph Editor.

A three-node camera is created when you choose Camera, Aim, And Up from the Controls menu. This adds a third locator, which is used to control the camera's rotation around the Z axis. These controls and alternative arrangements will be explored later in the section on camera rigs.

When working with two- or three-node cameras, resist the temptation to move or keyframe the position of the group node that contains both the camera and the aim locator. Instead, expand the group in the Outliner and keyframe the camera and aim nodes separately. This will keep the animation simple and help to avoid confusion when editing the animation. If you need to move the whole rig over a large distance, Shift+click both the camera and the aim locator, and move them together. Moving the group node separately is asking for trouble.

CAMERA TWIST

The Camera And Aim type of rig has a twist attribute on the group node above the camera and aim nodes. Twist controls the Z rotation of the camera much like the up control on the three-node camera. This is the only control on the group node that you may want to adjust or keyframe.

---

2. Expand the shotCam1_group node that now appears in the Outliner, and select the shotCam_aim node. In the Channel Box, set its Translate X, Y, and Z settings to **-0.155**, **4.206**, **-2.884**. (The camera's node should still have its X, Y, and Z translation settings at 1.382, 4.138, and -3.45.)

3. In the Display Layer menu, turn on the car layer. Set the current frame to **60** so that the car is in view of the camera.

4. In the Attribute Editor for shotCam1, adjust the Angle Of View slider. Decreasing this setting flattens the perspective in the image and zooms in on the scene; increasing this setting exaggerates the perspective and zooms out.

5. With the camera still selected, switch to the Channel Box and find the Focal Length setting under the shotCamShape1 node. Highlight the Focal Length channel label, and MMB-drag back and forth in the viewport window. Set the Focal Length to **20** (see Figure 2.10).

FIGURE 2.10
The Angle Of View slider in the Attribute Editor and the focal length attribute in the Channel Box both adjust the zoom of the camera.

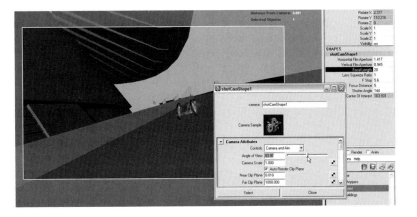

Adjusting the focal length of the camera has a similar effect on the camera as changing the angle of view; however, it is inversely related to the angle of view. Increasing the focal length zooms in on the scene, and decreasing it zooms out. The two settings are connected; they can't be set independently of each other.

In a real camera as you adjust the focal length, you are essentially repositioning the lens in the camera so that the distance between the lens and the film gate (where the film is exposed to light) is increased or decreased. As you increase the focal length, objects appear larger in frame. The camera zooms in on the subject. The viewable area also decreases—this is the angle of view. As you decrease the focal length, you move the lens back toward the film gate, increasing the viewable area in the scene and making objects in the frame appear smaller. You're essentially zooming out (see Figure 2.11).

By default, Maya cameras have a focal length of 35. Roughly speaking, the human eye has a focal length of about 50. A setting of 20 is a good way to increase drama in an action scene by exaggerating the perspective.

FIGURE 2.11
Two Maya cameras seen from above. A longer focal length produces a smaller angle of view (left camera); a shorter focal length produces a larger angle of view (right camera)

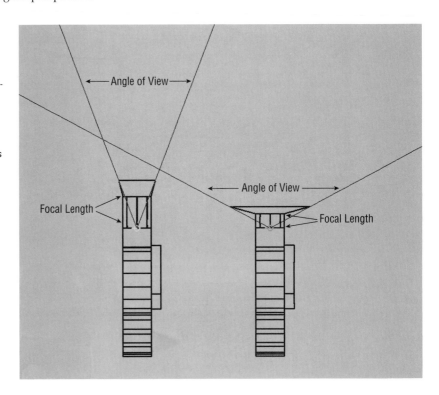

Real World Scenario

RENDERING A PORTRAIT

When you want to render a close-up of a character, a short focal length can distort the features of your character's face. To achieve the best results, you want to push the camera back in the scene and then zoom in. This flattens the depth of the scene and creates a more accurate portrayal of the character. Try these steps:

1. In the Render settings, create an image size suitable for a portrait—try something like **990×1220**.

2. Create a new camera and turn on the Resolution Gate so that you can properly frame the face.

3. Set the camera to focal length of **50**, and dolly the camera back (Alt+RMB) and frame the face.

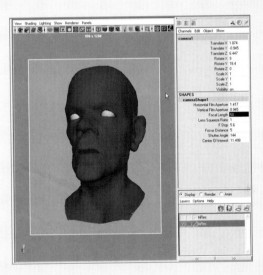

A good portrait should be slightly off center. Divide the frame horizontally into thirds, and position the eyes at about the place where the top and middle thirds meet. You can always experiment with different camera positions relative to the subject to see how it affects the emotional impact of the image. Unless you want to create a very confrontational image, try not to put the subject dead center in the frame.

Clipping Planes

Clipping planes are used to determine the range of renderable objects in a scene. Objects that lie outside of the clipping planes are not visible or renderable in the current camera. Clipping planes can affect the quality of the rendered image; if the ratio between the near clipping plane and the far clipping plane is too large, image quality can suffer (if the near clipping plane is 0.1, the far clipping plane should be no more than 20,000). Keep the far image plane just slightly beyond the farthest object that needs to be rendered in the scene, and keep the detail of distant objects fairly low.

The Auto Render Clip Plane option automatically determines the position of the clipping planes when rendering with Maya software (this setting does not affect animations rendered with mental ray, Maya hardware, or Vector renders). It's always a good idea to turn off this option and set the clipping plane values manually.

1. From the Panel menu choose Panels ➤ Layouts ➤ Two Panes Side By Side. Set the left pane to the Perspective view and the right pane to shotCam1.

2. Select shotCam1 and choose the Show Manipulators tool from the toolbox. Zoom in on the shot cam, and click the blue manipulator switch (located just below the camera when the Show Manipulators tool is active; see Figure 2.12) twice to switch to the clipping plane display.

FIGURE 2.12
Clicking the blue switch below the Show Manipulators tool cycles through the various actions of the tool. Clicking twice activates the manipulators for the clipping planes.

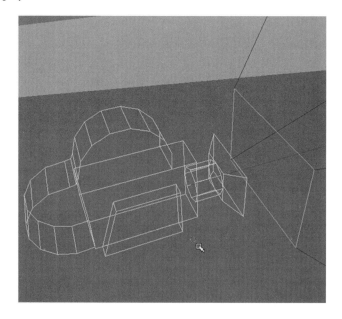

The clipping plane manipulator consists of two blue rectangles connected by lines. The near clipping plane is a small rectangle very close to the camera; the far clipping plane is very large and far from the camera

3. Zoom in close to the shot cam and MMB-drag the near clipping plane manipulator. You can set the position of this clipping plane interactively. Note that as you move the plane away from the camera, the geometry in the shotCam1 view is cut off. Any object between the camera and the near clipping plane will not render or will only partially render.

4. Zoom out until you can see the far clipping plane manipulator. MMB-drag on this and bring it in closer to the camera. Objects beyond this clipping plane will not be rendered by the camera or will appear cut off.

5. In the Attribute Editor for the shotCam1Shape node, set Near Clip Plane to **.05** and Far Clip Plane to **85** (the units for this scene are set to meters). This is a good starting place; if the positions of the planes need to change later on, they can be adjusted (see Figure 2.13).

6. Save the scene as **chase_v02.ma**. To see a version of the scene to this point, open chase_v02.ma from the chapter2/scenes directory on the DVD.

FIGURE 2.13
The positions of the clipping planes are set for the shotCam.

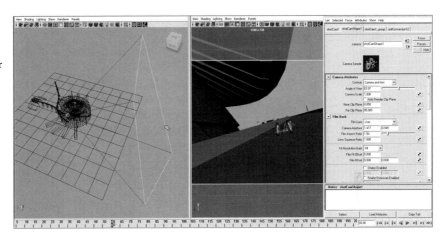

CLIPPING PLANE PROBLEMS

Sometimes you may find that everything disappears in a scene when you change the working units in the preferences or when you open a scene. This usually happens when the clipping planes have been set incorrectly or have changed. Try opening the Attribute Editor for the current camera and adjusting the values. This is true for the front, side, and top cameras as well as the perspective camera.

Film Back

In an actual camera the *film back* refers to the plate where the negative is placed when it is exposed to light. The size of the film determines the film back setting, so 35mm film uses a 35mm film back. The *film gate* is the gate that holds the film to the film back. Unless you are trying to match actual footage in Maya, you shouldn't need to edit these settings. Ideally you want the film gate and the resolution gate to be the same size. If you turn on the display of both the Film Gate and the Resolution Gate in the camera's Display Options rollout (toward the bottom of the Attribute Editor—you can't turn on both the Film Gate and Resolution Gate using the icons in the panel menu bar), you may see that the Film Gate is larger than the Resolution Gate. You can fix this by adjusting the Film Aspect Ratio. Simply divide the resolution width by the resolution height (1280 ÷ 720 = 1.777777), and put this value in the Film Aspect Ratio (see Figure 2.14).

FIGURE 2.14
In the top image, the Film Gate and Resolution Gate settings do not match. In the bottom image, the Film Aspect Ratio has been changed so that Film Gate and Resolution Gate match.

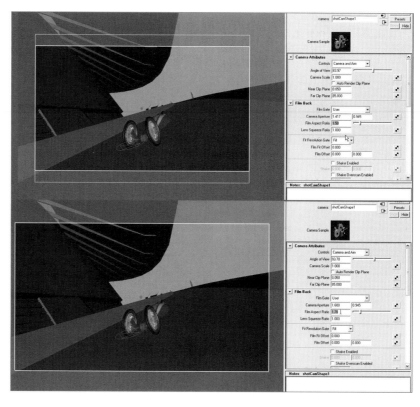

The Film Gate drop-down list has presets available that you can use to match footage if necessary. The presets will adjust the aperture, film aspect ratio, and lens squeeze ratio as needed. If you're not trying to match film, you can safely leave these settings at their default and concern yourself only with the Image Size and Resolution attributes in the Render Settings window.

The Film Fit Offset and Film Offset controls can be very useful in special circumstances where you need to change the center of the rendered area without altering the position of the camera. The parallax caused by the perspective of the 3D scene in the frame does not change even though the camera view has. Creating an offset in an animated camera can create a strange but very stylistic look.

The Film Fit Offset value has no effect if Fit Resolution Gate is set to Fill or Overscan. If you set the Fit Resolution Gate to Horizontal or Vertical and then adjust the Film Fit Offset, the offset will be either horizontal or vertical based on the Fit Resolution Gate setting. The Film Offset values accomplish the same thing; however, they don't depend on the setting of Fit Resolution Gate.

1. Continue with the scene from the previous section or open the chase_v02.ma scene from the chapter2/scenes directory on the DVD. Set the current camera in the viewport to shotCam1 and the timeline to frame 61.

2. In the Display layers, turn on the choppers layer so that the helicopter is visible in the shot.

3. Open the Attribute Editor for shotCam1, and switch to the shape node (shotCam1Shape) tab. In the Film Back rollout, set the Film Offset to **0.2** and **-.05**. Notice how this change alters the composition of the frame. Even a small change can affect the emotional impact of a shot (see Figure 2.15).

FIGURE 2.15
Adjusting the Film Offset changes the framing of the shot without actually moving the camera or the perspective of the image.

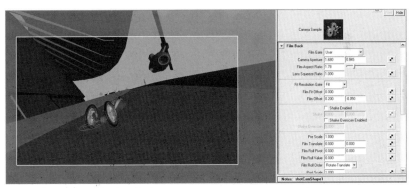

Camera Shake

Maya 2009 introduces the new Shake attribute, which is an easy way to add a shaky vibrating motion to a camera. The first field is the Horizontal shake, and the second field is the Vertical shake. The values you enter in the shake fields modify the current settings for the Film Offset. When you are applying a shake, you're essentially shaking the film back, which is useful because this does not change how the camera itself is animated. You can apply expressions, keyframes, or animated textures to one or both of these fields. The Shake Enabled option allows you to turn the shaking on or off while working in Maya; it can't be keyframed. However, you can easily animate the amount of shaking over time.

In this example, you'll use an animated fractal texture to create the camera shaking effect. You can use an animated fractal texture anytime you need to generate random noise values for an attribute. One advantage fractal textures have over mathematical expressions is that they are easier to animate over time.

1. Turn on the Shake Enabled option. Right-click the first field in the Shake option, and choose Create New Texture from the pop-up window (see Figure 2.16).

2. Switch to the Textures tab in the Create Render Node window, choose Fractal from the 2D Textures section, and make sure Normal is selected. The camera view will move when you add the texture, and that's okay.

FIGURE 2.16
Right-click the attribute field and choose Create New Texture. The Create Render Node window will open.

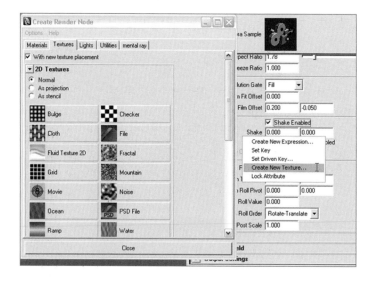

3. The attributes for the fractal texture will appear in the Attribute Editor. Set the Amplitude to **0.1**.

4. Check the Animated check box to enable the animation of the texture. Rewind the animation. Right-click the Time attribute, and choose Set Key (see Figure 2.17).

FIGURE 2.17
To animate a fractal texture, turn on the Animated option and set keyframes on the time slider.

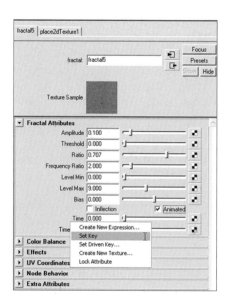

5. Set the Timeline to frame 200. Set the Time attribute to **100**, and set another key. Rewind and play the animation; you'll see the camera move back and forth.

6. Repeat steps 1 though 5 for the Vertical setting in Shake to add another animated fractal texture to this attribute. You want to have a different texture for each setting so that horizontal and vertical shaking of the camera are not the same value; otherwise the camera will appear to shake diagonally.

7. Select the second fractal texture, expand its UV Coordinates rollout, and click the arrow to the right of it to go to the fractal texture's place2dTexture node. Set the Rotate UV value to **45**. This rotates the texture so that the output of this animated texture is different from the other, ensuring a more random motion.

You may notice that the shaking is nice and strong but that you've lost the original composition of the frame. To bring it back to where it was, adjust the range of values created by each texture. The Fractal Amplitude of both textures is set to 0.1, which means each texture is adding a random value between 0 and 0.1 to the film offset. You need to equalize these values by adjusting the Alpha Offset and Alpha Gain of the textures.

8. Open the Hypershade by choosing Window ➤ Rendering Editors ➤ Hypershade. Click the Textures tab, and Shift+click the two fractal textures. From the Hypershade menu choose Graph ➤ Input And Output Connections. In the Work Area, you'll see the two textures connected to the camera.

9. Hold the mouse over the line connecting one of the textures to the shotCamShape1 node. The pop-up label shows that the `outAlpha` attribute of the texture is connected to the vertical or `horizontal shake` of the camera. This means that the `outAlpha` value must be adjusted to compensate for the change made to the camera's offset (see Figure 2.18).

If you look at what's going on with the fractal texture, you'll see that when the Amplitude of the texture is set to 0, the outAlpha value is 0.5 (you can see this by switching to the shotCamShape1 tab and looking at the Horizontal Shake field). The fractal texture itself is a flat gray color (value = 0.5). As you increase the Amplitude, the variation in the texture is amplified. At an Amplitude of 1, the outAlpha ranges from 0 to 1. You can see this in the values generated for the Shake attribute in the camera node. This is a very large offset and causes the shaking of the camera to be very extreme. You can set the amplitude to a very low value, but this means that the outAlpha value generated will remain close to 0.5, so as the shake values are added to the film offset, the composition of the frame is changed—the view shifts up to the right.

To fix this, you can adjust the Alpha Gain and Alpha Offset attributes found in the Color Balance section of each fractal texture. Alpha Gain is a scaling factor. When Alpha Gain is set to 0.5, the outAlpha values are cut in half; when Alpha Gain is set to 0, the outAlpha is also 0, and thus the Shake values are set to 0 and the camera returns to its original position. So if you want to shake the camera but keep it near its original position, it seems as though the best method is to adjust the Alpha Gain of the fractal texture.

FIGURE 2.18
The outAlpha value generated by the animated fractal texture is connected to the camera's horizontal shake.

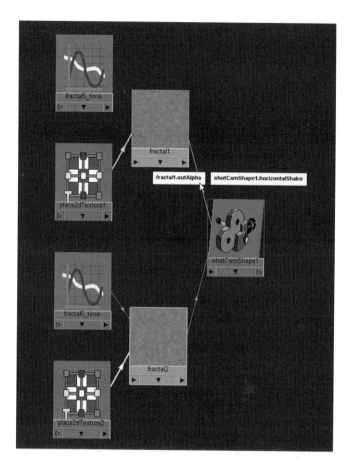

However, there is still one problem with this method. You want the outAlpha of the fractal to produce both negative and positive values so that the camera shakes around its original position in all directions. If you set the Alpha Gain to a positive or negative number, the values produced will be either positive or negative, which makes the view appear to shift in one direction or the other. To properly adjust the output of these values, you can use the Alpha Offset attribute to create a shift.

Set the Alpha Offset to negative one-half the Alpha Gain to get a range of values that are both positive and negative; 0 will be in the middle of this range. Figure 2.19 shows how adjusting the Amplitude, Alpha Gain, and Alpha Offset attributes affect the range of values produced by the animated fractal texture.

FIGURE 2.19
The range of values
produced by the
animated fractal
texture can be
adjusted using the
Amplitude, Alpha
Offset, and Alpha
Gain attributes.

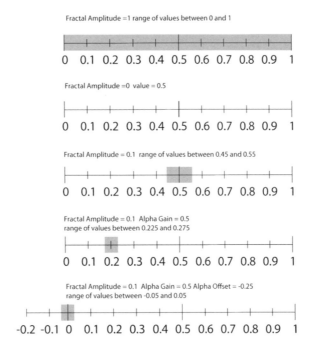

Fractal Amplitude =1 range of values between 0 and 1

0   0.1   0.2   0.3   0.4   0.5   0.6   0.7   0.8   0.9   1

Fractal Amplitude =0 value = 0.5

0   0.1   0.2   0.3   0.4   0.5   0.6   0.7   0.8   0.9   1

Fractal Amplitude = 0.1 range of values between 0.45 and 0.55

0   0.1   0.2   0.3   0.4   0.5   0.6   0.7   0.8   0.9   1

Fractal Amplitude = 0.1 Alpha Gain = 0.5
range of values between 0.225 and 0.275

0   0.1   0.2   0.3   0.4   0.5   0.6   0.7   0.8   0.9   1

Fractal Amplitude = 0.1 Alpha Gain = 0.5 Alpha Offset = -0.25
range of values between -0.05 and 0.05

-0.2 -0.1   0   0.1   0.2   0.3   0.4   0.5   0.6   0.7   0.8   0.9   1

The best way to set this up is to create a simple expression where the Alpha Offset is multiplied by negative one-half of the Alpha Gain. This technique can be used any time you need to shift the range of the fractal texture's outAlpha to give both positive and negative values.

10. Select the fractal1 node and open its attributes in the Attribute Editor. Expand the Color Balance rollout and set the Alpha Gain of fractal1 to **0.25**.

11. In the field for Alpha Offset, type **=-0.5*fractal1.alphaGain;**. Then hit the **Enter** key on the numeric keypad to enter the expression (Figure 2.20).

12. You can create the same setup for the fractal2 node. However, it might be a better idea to create a direct connection between the attributes of fractal1 and fractal2, so you need only adjust the Alpha Gain of fractal1, and all other values will update accordingly.

FIGURE 2.20
An expression is
created to auto-
matically set the
Alpha Offset of
fractal1 to nega-
tive one-half of the
Alpha Gain.

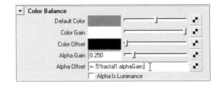

13. In the Hypershade, MMB-drag fractal1 on top of fractal2, and choose Other from the pop-up menu to open the Connection Editor. On the left side of the Connection Editor, select alphaGain; on the right side, select alphaGain to connect these two attributes. Select alphaOffset on the left side, and then select alphaOffset on the right side to connect these two attributes. Select Amplitude on the left, and then select Amplitude on the right to connect these two attributes as well (see Figure 2.21).

14. Play the animation, and you'll see the camera shake. To tone down the movement, reduce the Alpha Gain of fractal1.

15. Set the timeline to frame 60, and set the Alpha Gain of fractal1 to **0**. Right-click over the Alpha Gain field and choose Set key.

16. Set the timeline to frame 65. Set the Alpha Gain of fractal1 to **0.5**, and set another key.

17. Set the timeline to frame 90. Set the Alpha Gain of fractal1 to **0**, and set a third key. Play back the animation, and you'll see the camera shake as the car and helicopter fly by.

18. Save the scene as **chase_v03.ma**. To see a version of the scene to this point, open the chase_v03.ma file from the chapter2\scenes directory.

The Shake Overscan attribute moves the film back and forth on the Z axis of the camera as opposed to the Shake settings, which move the film back and forth horizontally and vertically. This can be used to create some great horror-movie effects.

FIGURE 2.21

The Connection Editor is used to connect the Alpha Gain, Alpha Offset, and Amplitude of fractal2 to fractal1.

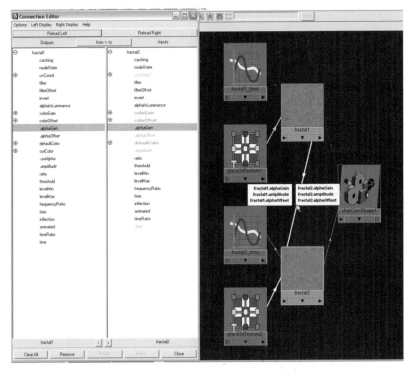

SHAKING CAMERA ASSET

This camera arrangement is a good candidate for an asset. You can create an asset from nodes that have already been connected and animated. Select the camera's shape node, expression, and fractal textures, and create a container. You can then use the Asset Editor to publish the Amplitude and Alpha Gain attributes of fractal1 to the container as custom attributes (give the attributes descriptive names, such as **shakeAmplitude** and **shakeScale**). When you need to make changes to the animation of the shake, you can simply set keyframes on the published shakeScale attribute. For more information on assets, consult Chapter 1.

Custom Camera Rigs

Maya's three camera types (camera, camera and aim, camera aim and up) work well for many common animation situations. However, you'll find that sometimes a custom camera rig gives you more creative control over a shot. This section shows how to create a custom camera rig for the car chase scene. Use this example as a springboard for ideas to design your own custom camera rigs and controls.

Swivel Camera Rig

This rig involves attaching a camera to a NURBS circle so that it can easily swivel around a subject in a perfect arc.

1. Open the chase_v03.ma scene from the chapter2\scenes directory on the DVD, or continue with the scene from the previous section. In the Display layers, turn off both the choppers and buildings layers.

2. Switch to the Persp camera in the viewport. Create a NURBS circle by choosing Create ➢ NURBS Primitives ➢ Circle. Name the circle **swivelCamRig**.

3. Create a new camera (Create ➢ Cameras ➢ Camera) and name it **swivelCam**.

4. Open the Attribute Editor for swivelCam to the swivelCamShape tab. Set the Controls to Camera and Aim.

5. Expand the new swivelCam_group node in the Outliner. Select the swivelCam and press the **f** hot key to focus on the camera in the viewport.

6. In the Outliner, select swivelCam and Ctrl+click the swivelCamRig circle. Switch to the Animation menu set, and choose Animate ➢ Motion Paths ➢ Attach To Motion Paths ➢ Options. In the options, set the Time Range to Start and turn off Follow. Click Attach to attach the camera to the circle (see Figure 2.22).

TURN OFF THE FOLLOW OPTION

The camera's rotation channels are already controlled by the Aim locator. If you leave the Follow option selected in the Attach To Motion Path options, you'll get an error message in the Script Editor bar.

FIGURE 2.22
The swivelCam
is attached to the
NURBS circle using
the Attach
To Motion Path
command.

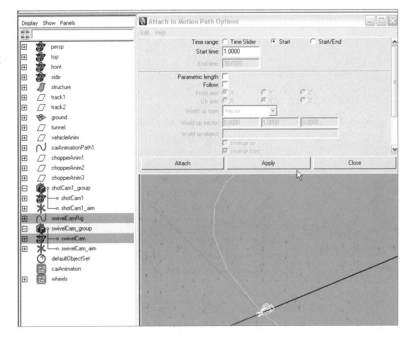

The camera is now attached to the circle via the motion path; the camera will stay in a fixed position on the circle curve. This is a fast and easy way to attach any object or other type of transform node (such as a group) to a curve.

7. Turn on the street and car display layers, and rewind the animation.

8. Zoom out in the viewport. In the Outliner, select the swivelCamRig and MMB-drag it up in the Outliner into the vehicleAnim group. Expand the vehicleAnim group, and select the swivelCamRig. Open the Channel Box, and set the Translate and Rotate channels to **0**. The circle will be repositioned around the car.

9. Select the swivelCam_aim locator from within the swivelCam_group. In the Outliner, MMB-drag this up into the vehicleAnim group as well. Set its Translate and Rotate channels to **0**. This will move to the pivot point of the vehicleAnim group.

10. Select the swivelCamRig, and in the Channel Box set Translate Y to **0.4**. Set the Scale attributes to **0.5** (see Figure 2.23).

11. Set the viewport to the swivelCam, and turn on the Resolution Gate. Select the swivelCam node, and set its focal length to **20**. Play the animation.

Swivel Camera Rig Asset

The camera follows the car, but things don't get interesting until you start to animate the attributes of the rig. To cut down on the number of node attributes that you need to hunt through to animate the rig, you'll create a container for the camera and rig and publish attributes to the container, thus turning the rig into an asset. For more information on assets, consult Chapter 1.

1. In the Outliner, Ctrl+click the swivelCam node, swivelCamShape, the swivelCam_aim locator, and the swivelCamRig node. Choose Assets ➤ Create Container ➤ Options. Set the operation to Create Container and the name to **swivelCamera**. Click Apply And Close to create the container (Figure 2.24).

2. Choose Assets ➤ Asset Editor. On the left side of the Asset Editor, select the swivelCamera container, and click the push pin icon to edit the container.

FIGURE 2.23
The NURBS circle (swivelCamRig) and the swivel-Cam_aim have been parented to the vehicleAnim group.

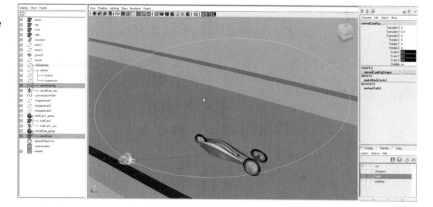

FIGURE 2.24
A container is created from nodes selected in the Outliner.

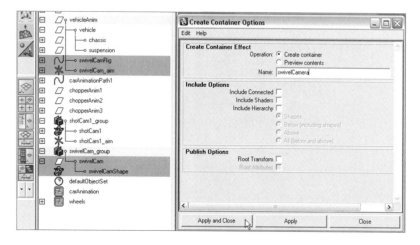

3. Click the plus sign in the square to expand the swivelCamera container, and then expand the swivelCam rig node (click the plus sign in the circle next to swivelCamRig). From the list of Attributes, select the Translate Y attribute. Click the second icon from the top at the center of the Asset Editor. Set the published name to **rise**.

4. Select the Rotate Y attribute, and publish it using the name **swivel**. Select Scale Z, and publish it using the name **push**.

5. Expand the swivelCam_aim node, and select its Translate attribute. Publish it using the name **aim** (see Figure 2.25). The three attributes Aim X, Aim Y, and Aim Z will be created at once.

6. Expand the swivelCam (click the plus sign in the square) and the swivelCamShape nodes (click the plus sign in the circle). Select the Focal Length attribute, and publish it using the name **zoom**.

7. Close the Asset Editor, and select the swivelCamera container node in the Outliner. Try changing the values of the published attributes and play the animation.

LOCK UNUSED ROTATION CHANNELS

To cut down on rotation problems, you'll want to lock the Rotate X and Rotate Z values of the swivel-CamRig. Select the node in the INPUTS section of the Channel Box, set the values to **0**, right-click these attributes, and choose Lock Selected. This keeps the rotation nice and simple.

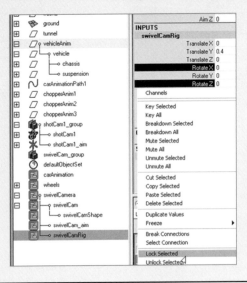

FIGURE 2.25
Various attri-
butes are chosen
from the nodes
in the swivelCam
container and
published to the
container using
the Asset Editor.

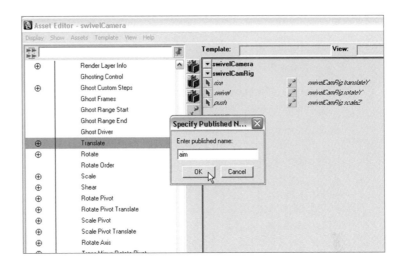

8. Open the Preferences panel (Window ➤ Settings/Preferences ➤ Preferences), and select
   Animation from the left-hand column. Make sure the Default In Tangent and Default
   Out Tangent are set to Clamped. Try setting the following keyframes to create a dramatic
   camera move using the rig (see Figure 2.26):

◆ Frame 1

   ◆ Rise: 3.227

   ◆ Swivel: 48.411

   ◆ Push: 6

   ◆ Aim X: 0

   ◆ Aim Y: 0

   ◆ Aim Z: 0

◆ Frame 41

   ◆ Rise: 0.06

   ◆ Swivel: 134.265

   ◆ Push: 0.3

   ◆ Aim X: 0

   ◆ Aim Y: 0

   ◆ Aim Z: 0

- Frame 92
  - Rise: 0.06
  - Swivel: 246.507
  - Push: 0.3
  - Aim X: 0
  - Aim Y:0 .091
  - Aim Z: 0.046
- Frame 145
  - Rise: 0.13
  - Swivel: 290.819
  - Push: 0.8
  - Aim X: 0
  - Aim Y: 0.167
  - Aim Z: -0.087
- Frame 160
  - Rise: 0
  - Swivel: 458.551
  - Push: 0.4
  - Aim X: 0
  - Aim Y: 0.132
  - Aim Z: -0.15
- Frame 200
  - Rise:0 .093
  - Swivel: 495.166
  - Push: 0.4
  - Aim X: 0
  - Aim Y: 0.132
  - Aim Z: -0.015

9. Set the view in the perspective window to swivelCam (Panels➤ Perspective➤ swivelCam) Turn on all the display layers and play the animation (Figure 2.27). Save the scene as **chase_v04.ma**. To see a finished version of the animation, open the chase_v04.ma scene from the chapter2\scenes directory on the DVD.

FIGURE 2.26
The attributes of the container are selected and key-framed.

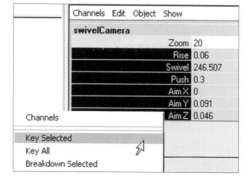

FIGURE 2.27
A custom camera rig can make exciting camera animation easy to create and edit.

Depth of Field and Motion Blur

Depth of field and motion blur are two effects meant to replicate real-world camera phenomena. Both of these effects can be used to increase the realism of a scene as well as the drama. However, they can both increase render times significantly, so it's important to learn how to efficiently apply them when rendering a scene. In this section, you'll learn how to activate these effects and the basics of how to work with them. Using both effects effectively is closely tied to render-quality issues. Render-quality issues are discussed more thoroughly in Chapter 12.

Depth of Field Settings

The Depth of Field (DOF) settings in Maya simulate the photographic phenomena where some areas of an image are in focus and other areas are out of focus. Artistically this can greatly increase the drama of the scene, as it forces the viewers to focus their attention on a specific element in the composition of a frame.

Depth of field is a ray-traced effect and can be created using both Maya software and mental ray; however, the mental ray Depth of Field feature is far superior to that of Maya software. This section describes how to render depth of field using mental ray.

DEPTH OF FIELD AND RENDER TIME

Depth of Field adds a lot to render time, as you'll see from the examples in this section. When working on a project that is under time constraints, you will need to factor DOF rendering into your schedule. If a scene requires an animated depth of field, you'll most likely find yourself re-rendering the sequence a lot. As an alternative, you may want to create the DOF using compositing software after the sequence has been rendered. It may not be as physically accurate as mental ray's DOF, but it will render much faster, and you can easily animate the effect and make changes in the compositing stage. To do this you can use the Camera Depth Render Pass preset (discussed in Chapter 12) to create a separate depth pass of the scene and then use the Luminance values of the depth pass layer to create DOF in your compositing software.

There are two ways to apply the mental ray Depth of Field effect to a camera in a Maya scene. You can activate the Depth Of Field option in the camera's Attribute Editor, or you can add a mental ray physical_lens_dof lens shader to the camera (mental ray has special shaders for lights and cameras, as well as surface materials). Both methods produce the same effect. In fact, when you turn on the DOF option in the Camera Attributes settings, you're essentially applying the mental ray DOF lens shader to the camera. The controls in the camera's Attribute Editor are easier to use than the controls in the physical DOF shader, so this example will describe only this method of applying DOF.

LENS SHADERS

There are a number of mental ray lens shaders you can apply to your camera to simulate real photographic phenomena. These shaders are discussed in Chapter 10.

---

1. Open the chase_v05.ma scene from the chapter2/scenes directory on the DVD. In the viewport, switch to the DOF_cam camera. If you play the animation (which starts at frame 100 in this scene), you'll see the camera move from street level upward as two helicopters come into view.

2. In the Panel menu bar, click the second icon from the left to open the DOF_cam's Attribute Editor. Expand the Environment settings, and click on the color swatch. Use the Color Chooser to create a pale blue color for the background (Figure 2.28).

FIGURE 2.28
A new background
color is chosen for
the DOF_cam.

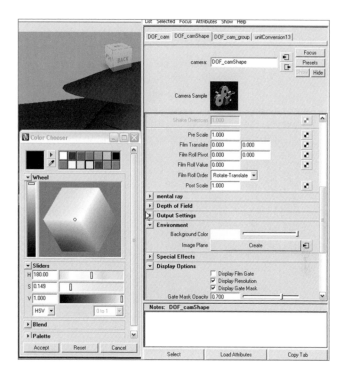

FIGURE 2.28
A new background
color is chosen for
the DOF_cam.

3. Open the Render settings and make sure the Render Using menu is set to mental ray. If mental ray does not appear in the list, you'll need to load the `Mayatomr.mll` plug-in found in the Window ➢ Settings/Preferences ➢ Plug-in Manager window.

4. Select the Quality tab in the Render settings, and set the Quality preset to Preview:Final Gather.

5. Switch to the Rendering menu set. Choose Render ➢ Test Resolution ➢ 50% Settings. This way any test renders you create will be at half resolution, which will save a lot of time but will not affect the size of the batch-rendered images.

6. Set the timeline to frame 136, and Choose Render ➢ Render Current Frame to create a test render (see Figure 2.29).

The Render View window will open and render a frame. Even though there are no lights in the scene, even lighting is created when Final Gather is activated in the Render settings (it's activated automatically when you choose the Preview:Final Gather Quality preset). The pale blue background color in the current camera is used in the Final Gather calculations. More sophisticated environmental lighting is discussed in Chapter 10. This particular lighting arrangement is simple to set up and works fine for an animatic.

As you can see from the test render, the composition of this frame is confusing to the eye and does not read very well. There are many conflicting shapes in the background and foreground. Using Depth of Field can help the eye to separate background elements from foreground elements and sort out the overall composition.

FIGURE 2.29
A test render is created for frame 136.

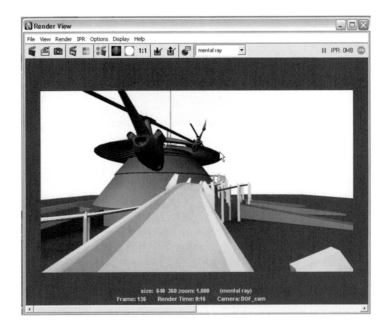

7. In the Attribute Editor for the DOF_Cam expand the Depth Of Field rollout and activate Depth Of Field. Store the current image in the Render Preview window (from the Render Preview window menu choose File ➤ Keep Image In Render View), and create another test render using the default DOF settings.

8. Use the scroll bar at the bottom of the Render View window to compare the images. There's almost no discernable difference. This is because the Depth of Field settings need to be adjusted. There are only three settings:

   ◆ **Focus Distance**: This determines the area of the image that is in focus. Areas in front or behind this area will be out of focus.

   ◆ **F Stop**: This describes the relationship between the diameter of the aperture and the focal length of the lens. Essentially it is the amount of blurriness seen in the rendered image. F Stop values used in Maya are based on real-world f-stop values. The lower the value, the blurrier the areas beyond the focus distance will be. Changing the focal length of the lens will affect the amount of blur as well. If you are happy with a camera's Depth of Field settings but then change the focal length or angle of view, you'll probably need to reset the F Stop setting. Typically values range from 2.8 to around 12.

   ◆ **Focus Region Scale**: This is a scalar value that you can use to adjust the area in the scene you want to stay in focus. Lowering this value will also increase the blurriness. Use this to fine-tune the DOF effect once you have the Focus Distance and F Stop settings.

9. Set the Focus Distance to **15**, the F Stop to **2.8**, and the Focus Region Scale to **0.1**, and create another test render.

The blurriness in the scene is much more obvious and the composition is a little easier to understand. The blurring is very grainy. You can improve this by adjusting the Quality settings in the Render Settings window. Increasing the Max Sample level and decreasing the Anti-Aliasing Contrast will smooth the render, but it will take much more time to render the image. For now you can leave the settings where they are as you adjust the DOF. Render-quality issues are discussed in Chapter 12 (see Figure 2.30).

10. Save the scene as **chase_v06.ma**. To see a version of the scene so far, open chase_v06.ma from the chapter2\scenes directory on the DVD.

FIGURE 2.30
Adding depth of field can help sort out the elements of a composition by increasing the sense of depth.

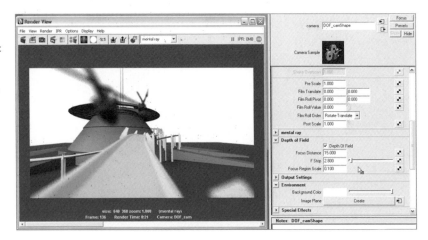

Creating a Rack Focus Rig

A *rack focus* refers to a depth of field that changes over time. It's a common technique used in cinematography as a storytelling aid. By changing the focus of the scene from elements in the background to the foreground (or vice versa), you control what the viewer looks at in the frame. In this section, you'll set up a camera rig that you can use to interactively change the focus distance of the camera.

1. Continue with the scene from the previous section or open the chase_v06.ma file from the Chapter2\scenes directory of the DVD.

2. Switch to the perspective view. Choose Create ➤ Measure Tools ➤ Distance Tool, and click on two different areas on the grid to create the tool. Two locators will appear with an annotation that displays the distance between the two locators in scene units (meters for this scene).

3. In the Outliner, rename locator1 **camPosition** and rename locator2 **distToCam** (see Figure 2.31).

4. In the Outliner, expand the DOF_cam_group. MMB-drag camPosition on top of the DOF_cam node to parent the locator to the camera. Open the Channel Box for the camPosition locator, and set all of its Translate and Rotate channels to **0**; this will snap camPosition to the center of the camera.

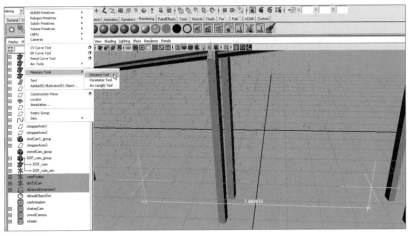

5. Shift-select the camPosition's Translate and Rotate channels in the Channel Box, right-click the fields, and choose Lock Selected so that the locator can no longer be moved.

6. In the Outliner, MMB-drag distToCam on top of the camPosition locator to parent distToCam to camPosition. Select distToCam, and in the Channel Box set its Translate X and Y channels to **0** and lock these two channels (see Figure 2.32). You should be able to move distToCam only along the Z axis.

FIGURE 2.32
The Translate X and
Y channels of the
distToCam node
are locked so that
it can move only
along the Z axis.

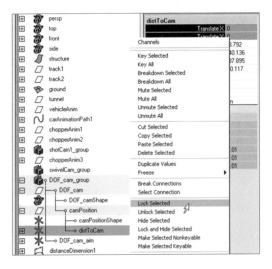

7. Open the Connection Editor by choosing Window ⟩ General Editors ⟩ Connection Editor. In the Outliner, select the distanceDimension1 node, and expand it so you can select the distanceDimensionShape1 node (make sure the Display menu in the Outliner

is set so that shape nodes are visible). Click the Reload Left button at the top of the Connection Editor to load this node.

8. Expand the DOF_Cam node in the Outliner, and select DOF_camShape. Click Reload Right in the Connection Editor.

9. From the bottom of the list on the left, select Distance. On the right side, select FocusDistance (see Figure 2.33).

FIGURE 2.33

The Distance attribute of the distanceDimensionShape1 node is linked to the focusDistance attribute of the DOF_camShape node using the Connection Editor.

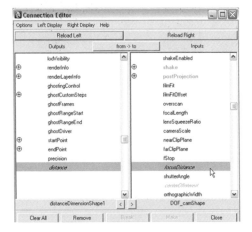

10. Look in the perspective view at the distance measured in the scene, select the distToCam locator, and move it so that the annotation reads about 5.5 units.

11. Select the DOF_camShape node and look at its focusDistance attribute. If it says something like 550 units, than there is a conversion problem. Select the distanceDimensionShape node in the Outliner, and open the Attribute Editor. From the menu in the Attribute Editor, click Focus, and select the node that reads unitConversion14. If you are having trouble finding this node, turn off DAG Objects Only in the Outliner's Display menu, and turn on Show Auxiliary Nodes in the Outliner's Show menu. You should see the unitConversion nodes at the bottom of the Outliner. Select unitConversion14 from the list to switch to the unitConversion node, and set the Conversion Factor to **1**.

Occasionally when you create this rig and the scene size is set to something other than centimeters, Maya converts the units automatically, and you end up with an incorrect number for the Focus Distance attribute of the camera. This node may not always be necessary when setting up this rig. If the value of the Focus Distance attribute of the camera matches the distance shown by the distanceDimension node, then you don't need to adjust the unitConversion's Conversion Factor.

12. Set the timeline to frame 138. In the Perspective window, select the distToCam locator and move it along the Z axis until its position is near the position of the car (about -10.671). In the Channel Box, right-click the Translate Z channel, and choose Key Selected (see Figure 2.34).

FIGURE 2.34
The distToCam locator is moved to the position of the car on frame 138 and keyframed.

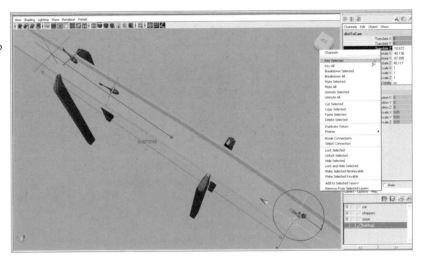

13. Switch to the DOF_cam in the viewport, and create a test render. The helicopters should be out of focus, and the area near the car should be in focus.

14. Set the timeline to frame 160. Move the distToCam node so it is at about the same position as the closest helicopter (around -1.026). Set another keyframe on its Z translation. Render another test frame. The area around the helicopter is now in focus (see Figure 2.35).

If you render a sequence of this animation for the frame range between 120 and 180, you'll see the focus change over time. To see a finished version of the camera rig, open chase_v07.ma from the chapter2\scenes directory on the DVD.

FIGURE 2.35
The focus distance of the camera has been animated using the rig so that at frame 160 the helicopter is in focus and the background is blurry.

Motion Blur

If an object changes position while the shutter on a camera is open, this movement shows up as a blur. Maya cameras can simulate this effect using the Motion Blur settings found in the Render settings as well as in the camera's Attribute Editor. Not only can Motion Blur help make an animation look more realistic, it can also help smooth the motion in the animation.

Like Depth of Field, Motion Blur is very expensive to render, meaning it can take a long time. Also much like Depth of Field, there are techniques for adding Motion Blur in the compositing stage after the scene has been rendered. You can render a Motion Vector pass using mental ray's passes (Render passes are discussed in Chapter 12) and then adding the motion blur using the Motion Vector pass in your compositing software. For jobs that are on a short timeline and a strict budget, this is often the way to go. In this section, however, you'll learn how to create Motion Blur in Maya using mental ray.

There are many quality issues closely tied to rendering with Motion Blur. In this chapter, you'll learn the basics of how to apply the different types of Motion Blur. Chapter 12 will discuss issues related to improving the quality of the render.

MENTAL RAY MOTION BLUR

mental ray Motion Blur supports all rendering features such as textures, shadows (ray trace and depth map), reflections, refractions, and caustics.

Motion Blur is enabled in the Render Settings window, so unlike Depth of Field, which is activated per-camera, all cameras in the scene will render with Motion Blur once it has been turned on. Likewise all objects in the scene have Motion Blur applied to them by default. You can, and should, turn off Motion Blur for those objects that appear in the distance or do not otherwise need motion blur. If your scene involves a close up of an asteroid whizzing by the camera while a planet looms in the distance surrounded by other slower-moving asteroids, you should disable Motion Blur for those distant and slower-moving objects. Doing so will greatly reduce render time.

To disable Motion Blur for a particular object, select the object, open its Attribute Editor to the shape node tab, expand the Render Stats rollout, and deselect the Motion Blur option. To disable Motion Blur for a large number of objects at the same time, select the objects and open the Attribute Spread Sheet (Window ➤ General Editors ➤ Attribute Spread Sheet). Switch to the Render tab, and select the Motion Blur header at the top of the column to select all of the values in the column. Enter **0** to turn off Motion Blur for all of the selected objects (see Figure 2.36).

MOTION BLUR AND RENDER LAYERS

Motion Blur can be active for an object on one render layer and disabled for the same object on another render layer using render layer overrides. For more information on using render layers, consult Chapter 12.

FIGURE 2.36

Motion Blur can be disabled for a single object in the Render Stats section of its Attribute Editor or for a large number of selected objects using the Attribute Spread Sheet.

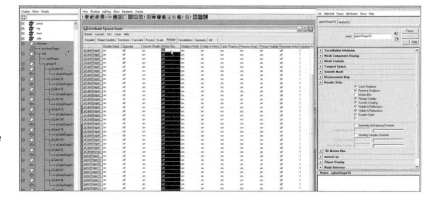

There are two types of Motion Blurs in mental ray for Maya: No Deformation and Full. No Deformation calculates only the blur created by an object's transformation—meaning its translation, rotation, and scale. A car moving past a camera or a helicopter blade should be rendered using No Deformation.

The Full setting calculates motion vectors for all of an object's vertices as they move over time. Full Motion Blur should be used when an object is being deformed, such as when a character's arm geometry is skinned to joints and animated moving past the camera. Using Full Motion Blur will give more accurate results for both deforming and nondeforming objects, but it will take a longer time to render than using No Deformation.

MOTION BLUR FOR MOVING CAMERAS

If a camera is moving past a stationary object, the object will be blurred just as if the object were moving passed a stationary camera.

The following exercise shows how to render with Motion Blur.

1. Open the scene chase_v08.ma from the chapter2\scenes directory of the DVD.

2. In the Display Layer panel, right-click on the buildings display layer and choose Select Objects. This will select all of the objects in the layer. Open the Attribute Spread Sheet (Window ➤ General Editors ➤ Attribute Spread Sheet), and switch to the Render tab. Select the Motion Blur header to select all of the values in the Motion Blur column, and turn the settings to Off (shown in Figure 2.36). Do the same for the objects in the street layer.

3. Switch to the Rendering menu set. Choose Render ➤ Test Resolution ➤ Render Settings. This will set the test render in the Render View window to 1280×720, the same as in the Render Settings window.

4. Switch to the shotCam1 camera in the viewport. Set the timeline to frame 59, and open the Render View window (Window ➤ Rendering Editors ➤ Render View).

5. Create a test render of the current view. From the Render View panel, choose Render ➢ Render ➢ ShotCam1. The scene will render. At the moment, the Render Quality is set to Preview:Final Gather, so the scene will render with very basic Final Gather lighting.

6. In the Render View panel, drag a red rectangle over the blue helicopter. To save time while working with Motion Blur, you'll render just this small area.

7. Open the Render Settings window. Switch to the Quality tab. Expand the Motion Blur rollout, and set Motion Blur to No Deformation. Leave the settings at their default, and in the Render View panel, click the render region icon (second icon from the left) to render the selected region in the scene. It will take a couple minutes. When it's finished, store the image in the render view. You can use the scroll bar at the bottom of the render view to compare stored images (see Figure 2.37).

FIGURE 2.37

The region around the helicopter is selected and rendered using Motion Blur. Just this small area took two minutes!

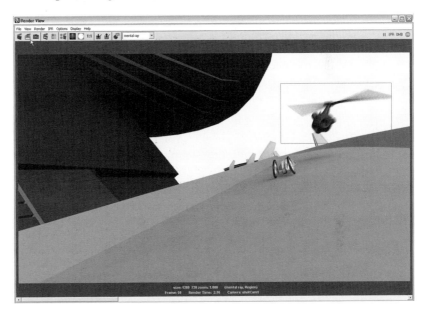

Immediately it should become apparent that Motion Blur adds a lot to render time, considering that this scene has no textures and simple geometry. It's true that Final Gather will add time to the render, but if you compare the time it took to render the full frame using the Final Gather Preview Render preset and the time it takes to render just a small portion of the frame with default settings, the difference is very significant. Clearly, optimizing Motion Blur is extremely important, and you should always consider balancing the quality of the final render with the amount of time it takes to render the sequence. Remember that if an object is moving quickly in the frame, some amount of graininess may actually be unnoticeable to the viewer.

8. In the Render Settings window, switch to the Features tab and set the Primary Renderer to Rasterizer (Rapid Motion) (see Figure 2.38). Click the Render Region button again to re-render the helicopter. This time it renders much faster. Store the image in the render view and compare it to the previous render.

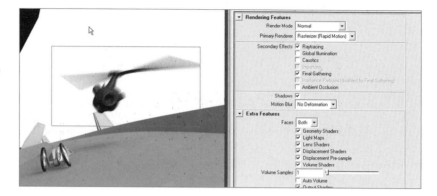

FIGURE 2.38
Changing the Primary Renderer to Rasterizer (Rapid Motion) reduces the render time for the helicopter region to 12 seconds.

The Rapid Motion setting uses a different algorithm to render motion blur, which is not quite as accurate but much faster. However, it does change the way mental ray renders the entire scene.

If you render the buildings, you'll notice that the shading when you use Rasterizer (Rapid Motion) is different from when you use Scanline. The Rasterizer does not calculate motion blurring for ray-traced elements (such as reflections and shadows). You can solve some of the problem by using detailed shadow maps instead of ray-traced shadows (discussed in Chapter 9), but this won't solve the problem that reflections lack motion blur.

9. Switch back to the Quality tab and take a look at the settings under Motion Blur:

   Motion Blur-By   This setting is a multiplier for the motion blur effect. A setting of 1 produces a realistic motion blur. Higher settings create a more stylistic or exaggerated effect.

   Shutter Open and Shutter Closed   These two settings establish the range within a frame where the shutter is actually opened or closed. By increasing the Shutter Open setting, you're actually creating a delay for the start of the blur; by decreasing the Shutter Close setting, you're moving the end time of the blur closer to the start of the frame.

10. Render the region around the helicopter. Store the frame, and then set Shutter Open to **0.25** and render the region again. Store the frame and compare the two images. Try a Shutter Close setting of **0.75**. Figure 2.39 shows the results of different settings for Shutter Open and Shutter Close.

Setting Shutter Open and Shutter Close to the same value effectively disables Motion Blur. You're basically saying that the shutter opens and closes instantaneously, and therefore there's no time to calculate a blur.

USING THE SHUTTER ANGLE ATTRIBUTE

You can achieve results similar to the Shutter Open and Shutter Close settings by changing the Shutter Angle attribute on the camera's shape node. The default setting for Maya cameras is 144. If you set this value to 72 and render, the resulting blur would be similar to setting Shutter Angle to 144, Shutter Open to 0.25, and Shutter Close to 0.75 (effectively halving the total time the shutter is open). The Shutter Angle setting on the camera is meant to be used with Maya software to provide the same functionality as mental ray's Shutter Open and Shutter Close settings. It's a good idea to stick to one method or the other—try not to mix the two techniques or the math will start to get a little fuzzy.

---

11. Return the Shutter settings to **0** for Shutter Open and **1** for Shutter Closed. In the Quality section below the Motion Blur settings, increase the Motion Steps to **6** and render the helicopter region again. Store the image and compare it to the previous renders. Notice that the blur on the helicopter blade is more of an arc, whereas in previous renders, the blur at the end of the blade is a straight line (Figure 2.40).

The Motion Steps attribute increases the number of times between the opening and closing of the shutter that mental ray samples the motion of the moving objects. If Motion Steps is set to 1, the motion of the object when the shutter opens is compared to the motion when the shutter is closed. The blur is calculated as a linear line between the two points. When you increase the number of Motion Steps, mental ray increases the number of times it looks at the motion of an object over the course of time in which the shutter is open and creates a blur between these samples. This produces a more accurate blur in rotating objects, such as wheels or helicopter blades.

FIGURE 2.39
Different settings for Shutter Open and Shutter Close affect how Motion Blur is calculated. From left to right, the Shutter Open and Shutter Close settings for the three images are (0, 1), (0.25, 1), and (0.25, 0.75). The length of time the shutter is open for the last image is half of the length of time for the first image.

FIGURE 2.40
Increasing Motion Steps increases the number of times the motion of the objects is sampled, producing more of an accurate blur in rotating objects.

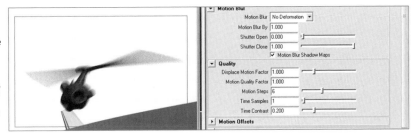

The other settings in the Quality section include:

Displace Motion Factor   This is new to Maya 2009. The setting adjusts the quality of motion-blurred objects using a displacement map. It effectively reduces geometry detail on those parts of the model that are moving past the camera based on the amount of detail and the amount of motion as compared to a nonmoving version of the same object. Slower-moving objects should use higher values.

Motion Quality Factor   This is used when the Primary Renderer is set to Rasterizer (Rapid Motion). Increasing this setting lowers the sampling of fast-moving objects and can help reduce render times. For most cases a setting of 1 should work fine.

Time Samples   This controls the quality of the motion blur. Raising this setting adds to render time but increases quality. As mental ray renders a two-dimensional image from a three-dimensional scene, it takes a number of spatial samples at any given point on the two-dimensional image. The number of samples taken is determined by the anti-alias settings (discussed further in Chapter 12). For each spatial sample a number of time samples can also be taken to determine the quality of the motion blur effect; this is determined by the Time Samples setting.

Time Contrast   Like Anti-Aliasing contrast (discussed in Chapter 12), lower Time Contrast values improve the quality of the motion blur but also increase render time. Note that the Time Samples and Time Contrast settings are linked. Moving one automatically adjusts the other in an inverse relationship.

Motion Offsets   These controls enable you to set specific time steps where you want motion blur to be calculated.

Orthographic and Stereo Cameras

Orthographic cameras are generally used for navigating a Maya scene and for modeling from specific views. A stereoscopic or stereo camera is actually a special rig that can be used for rendering stereoscopic 3D movies.

Orthographic Cameras

The front, top, and side cameras that are included in all Maya scenes are orthographic cameras. An orthographic view is one that lacks perspective. Think of a blueprint drawing, and you get the basic idea. There is no vanishing point in an orthographic view.

Any Maya camera can be turned into an orthographic camera. To do this, open the Attribute Editor for the camera, and in the Orthographic Views rollout, turn on the Orthographic option. Once a camera is in orthographic mode, it appears in the Orthographic section of the viewport's Panels menu. You can render animations using orthographic cameras; just add the camera to the list of renderable cameras in the Render Settings window. The Orthographic Width is changed when you dolly an orthographic camera in or out (see Figure 2.41).

FIGURE 2.41
The Orthographic option for the perspective camera is activated, flattening the image seen in the perspective view.

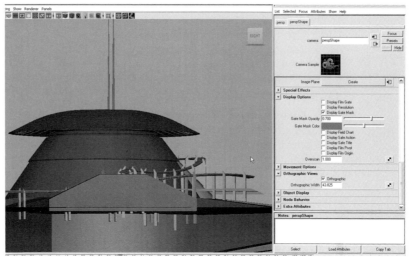

Stereo Cameras

Stereo cameras are new to Maya 2009. These can be used when rendering a movie that is meant to be seen using special 3D glasses. Follow the steps in this example to learn how to work with stereo cameras.

1. Create a new scene in Maya. From the Create menu choose Cameras ➢ Stereo Camera. You'll see three cameras appear on the grid.

2. Switch the panel layout to Panels ➢ Saved Layouts ➢ Four View. Set the upper-left panel to the perspective view and the upper right to Panels ➢ Stereo ➢ Stereo Camera. Set the lower left to StereoRigLeft and the lower right to StereoRigRight.

3. Create a NURBS sphere (Create ➢ NURBS Primitives ➢ Sphere). Position it in front of the center camera of the rig, and push it back in the Z axis about -10 units.

4. In the perspective view, select the center camera, and open the Attribute Editor to stereoRigCenterCamShape.

In the Stereo settings you can choose which type of stereo setup you want; this is dictated by how you plan to use the images in the compositing stage. The interaxial separation adjusts the distance between the left and right cameras, and the zero parallax defines the point on the Z axis (relative to the camera) at which an object directly in front of the camera appears in the same position in the left and right cameras.

5. In the Attribute Editor, under the Stereo Display Controls rollout, set Display Frustum to All. In the perspective view you can see the overlapping angle of view for all three cameras.

6. Turn on Display Zero Parallax Plane. A semitransparent plane appears at the point defined by the Zero Parallax setting.

7. Set the Stereo setting in the Stereo rollout to Converged.

As you change the Zero Parallax value, the left and right cameras will rotate on their Y axis to adjust, and the Zero Parallax Plane will move back and forth depending on the setting.

8. Set the Zero Parallax attribute to **10** (see Figure 2.42). In the perspective view, switch to a top view and make sure the NURBS sphere is directly in front of the center camera and at the same position as the zero parallax plane (Translate Z = -10).

FIGURE 2.42

A stereo camera uses three cameras to render out an image for 3D movies. The zero parallax plane is positioned at the point where objects in front of the center camera appear in the same position in the left and right cameras.

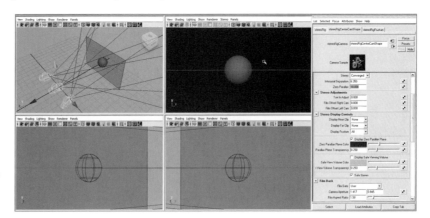

9. In the top view, move the sphere back and forth toward and away from the camera rig. Notice how the sphere appears in the same position in the frame in the left and right camera view when it is at the zero parallax plane. However, when it is in front of or behind the plane, it appears in different positions in the left and right views.

If you hold a finger up in front of your eyes and focus on the finger, the position of the finger is at the zero parallax point. Keep your eyes focused on that point, but move your finger toward and away from your face. You see two fingers when it's before or behind the zero parallax point (more obvious when it's closer to your face). When a stereo camera rig is rendered and composited, the same effect is achieved and, with the help of 3D glasses, the image on the two-dimensional screen appears in three dimensions.

10. Turn on the Safe Viewing Volume option in the Attribute Editor. This displays the area in 3D space where the views in all three cameras overlap. Objects should remain within this volume in the animation so that they render correctly as a stereo image.

11. Open the Render settings to the Common tab. Under Renderable cameras you can choose to render each camera of the stereo rig separately, or you can select the stereo pair option to add both the right and left camera at the same time. Selecting the stereoCamera option renders the scene using the center camera in the stereo camera rig. This can be useful if you want to render a nonstereoscopic version of the animation.

The cameras will render as separate sequences, which can then be composited together in compositing software to create the final output for the stereo 3D movie.

COMPOSITING STEREO RENDERS IN ADOBE AFTER EFFECTS

Adobe After Effects has a standard plug-in called 3D Glasses (Effects ➤ Perspective ➤ 3D Glasses) that can be used to composite renders created using Maya's stereo rig. From Maya you can render the left and right camera images as separate sequences and import them into After Effects and apply the 3D Glasses effect.

You can preview the 3D effect in the Render View window by choosing Render ➤ Stereo Camera. The Render View will render the scene and combine the two images. You can then choose one of the options in the Display ➤ Stereo Display menu to preview the image. If you have a pair of 3D glasses handy, choose the Anaglyph option, put on the glasses, and you'll be able to see how the image will look in 3D.

The Bottom Line

Determine image size and resolution.   The final image size of your render should be determined at the earliest possible stage in a project. It will affect everything from texture resolution to render time. Maya has a number of presets that can be used to set the image resolution.

> **Master it**   Set up an animation that will be rendered to be displayed on a high-definition progressive-scan television.

Work with camera settings.   The settings found in the Attribute Editor for a camera enable you to replicate real-world cameras as well as add effects such as camera shaking.

> **Master it**   Create a camera setting where the film back shakes back and forth in the camera. Set up a system where the amount of shaking can be animated over time.

Create custom camera rigs.   Dramatic camera moves are easier to create and animate when you build a custom camera rig.

> **Master it**   Create a camera in the car chase scene that films from the point of view of chopperAnim3 but tracks the car as it moves along the road.

Use Depth of Field and Motion Blur.   Depth of Field and Motion Blur replicate real-world camera effects and can add a lot of drama to a scene. Both are very expensive to render and should be applied with care.

> **Master it**   Create a camera asset with a built-in focus distance control.

Create orthographic and stereoscopic cameras.   Orthographic cameras are used primarily for modeling because they lack a sense of depth or a vanishing point. A stereoscopic rig uses three cameras and special parallax controls that enable you to render 3D movies from Maya.

> **Master it**   Create a 3D movie from the point of view of the driver in the chase scene.

Chapter 3

NURBS Modeling in Maya

Creating 3D models in computer graphics is an art form and a discipline unto itself. It takes years to master and requires an understanding of form, composition, anatomy, mechanics, gesture, and so on. It's an addictive art that never stops evolving. This chapter and Chapter 4 will introduce you to the different ways the tools in Maya can be applied to various modeling tasks. With a firm understanding of how the tools work, you can master the art of creating 3D models.

Together, Chapters 3 and 4 demonstrate various techniques for modeling with NURBS, polygons, and subdivision surfaces to create a single model of a woman in a space suit. Chapter 3 begins with using NURBS surfaces to create a detailed helmet for the space suit.

In this chapter you will learn to:

◆ Use image planes

◆ Apply NURBS curves and surfaces

◆ Model with NURBS surfaces

◆ Create realistic surfaces

◆ Adjust NURBS render tessellation

Image Planes

The example used in this chapter is based on a design created by Chris Sanchez. Chris is a professional concept artist and designer working in film production at Prologue Films in Venice, California. For this book I asked Chris to design a character in an environment suit that is heavily detailed and stylish in the hope that as many modeling techniques as possible could be demonstrated using a single project. Figure 3.1 shows Chris's drawing.

CHRIS SANCHEZ

Chris Sanchez is Los Angeles–based concept artist/illustrator/storyboard artist. He attained his BFA in Illustration from the Ringling College of Art and Design. He has foundations in traditional and digital techniques of drawing and painting. Chris has contributed to numerous film projects including *Spider-Man 3*, *Iron Man*, *The Hulk*, *Bridge to Terabithia*, *RocknRolla*, and *Tropic Thunder*. For more of Chris's work visit www.chrissanchezart.com.

FIGURE 3.1
The concept
drawing for the
project, drawn by
Chris Sanchez

It's not unusual in the fast-paced world of production to be faced with building a model based on a single view of the subject. You're also just as likely to be instructed to blend together several different designs. You can safely assume that the concept drawing you are given has been approved by the director. It's your responsibility to follow the spirit of that design as closely as possible, with an understanding that, at the same time, the technical aspects of animating and rendering the model may force you to make some adjustments. Some design aspects that work well in a two-dimensional drawing don't always work as well when translated into a three-dimensional model.

The best way to start is to create some orthographic drawings based on the sketch. You can use these as a guide in Maya to ensure that the placement of the model's parts and the proportions are consistent. Sometimes the concept artist creates these drawings for you; sometimes you need to create them yourself (sometimes you may be both the modeler and the concept artist). When creating the drawings, it's usually a good idea to focus on the major forms, creating bold lines and leaving out most of the details. A heavily detailed drawing can get confusing when working in Maya. You can always refer to the original concept drawing as a guide for the details. Since there is only one view of the design, some parts of the model need to be invented for the three-dimensional model. The orthographic drawings for this project are shown in Figure 3.2.

FIGURE 3.2
Simplified drawings have been created for the side and front views of the concept.

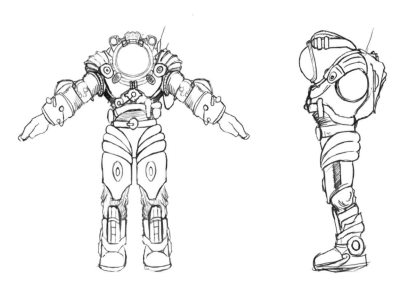

After you create the orthographic drawings, your first task is to bring them into Maya and apply them to image planes.

Creating Image Planes

Image planes are often used as a modeling guide. They are attached to the cameras in Maya and have a number of settings that you can adjust to fit your own preferred style.

1. Create a new scene in Maya.

2. Switch to the side view. From the View menu in the viewport panel, choose Image Plane ➢ Import Image (see Figure 3.3). A dialog box will open; browse the file directory on your computer and choose the spaceGirlSide.tif image from the chapter3\sourceimages directory on the DVD.

FIGURE 3.3
Use the View menu in the panel menu bar to add an image plane to the camera.

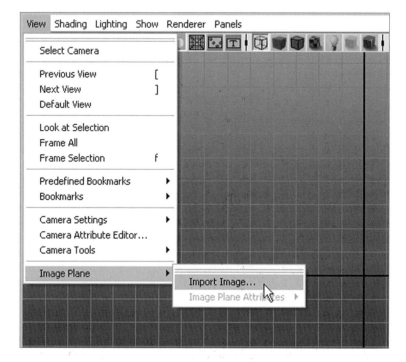

3. The side view opens and appears in the viewport. Select the side camera in the Outliner and open the Attribute Editor. Switch to the imagePlane1 tab (see Figure 3.4).

4. In the Image Plane Attributes section, you'll find controls that change the appearance of the plane in the camera view. Make sure the Display option is set to In All Views. This way, when you switch to the perspective view, the plane will still be visible.

5. You can set the Display mode to RGB if you want just color or to RGBA to see color and alpha. The RGBA option is more useful when the image plane has an alpha channel and is intended to be used as a backdrop in a rendered image as opposed to a modeling guide. There are other options such as Luminance, Outline, and None.

6. The Color Gain and Color Offset sliders can be used to change the brightness and contrast. By lowering the Color Gain and raising the Color Offset, you can get a dimmer image with less contrast.

7. The Alpha Gain slider adds some transparency to the image display. Lower this slider to reduce the opacity of the plane.

8. When modeling you'll want to set Image Plane to Fixed so the image plane does not move when you change the position of the camera. When using the image plane as a renderable backdrop, you may want to have the image attached to the camera.

FIGURE 3.4
The options for the image plane are displayed in the Attribute Editor.

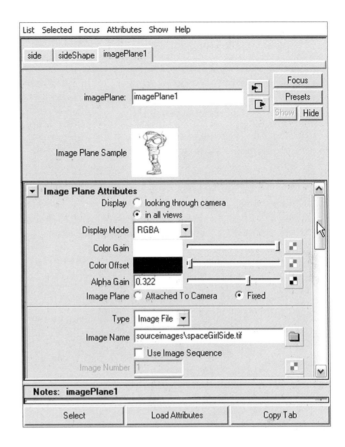

ARRANGING IMAGE PLANES

In this example the image plane is attached to Maya's side-view camera, but you may prefer to create a second side-view camera of your own and attach the image plane to that. It depends on your own preference. Image planes can be created for any type of camera. In some cases, a truly complex design may require creating orthographic cameras at different angles in the scene.

If you want to have the concept drawing or other reference images available in the Maya interface, you can create a new camera and attach an image plane using the reference image (you can use the spacegirlConcept.tif file in the chapter3\sourceimages directory on the DVD). Then set the options so the reference appears only in the viewing camera. Every time you want to refer to the reference, you can switch to this camera, which saves you the trouble of having the image open in another application.

Other options include using a texture or an image sequence. An image sequence may be useful when you are matching animated models to footage.

9. In the Placement Extras settings, you can use the Coverage sliders to stretch the image. The Center options allow you to offset the position of the plane in X, Y, and Z. The Height and Width fields allow you to resize the plane itself. In the Center options, set the Z file to **-1.8** to slide the plane back a little.

10. Switch to the front camera, and use the View menu in the viewport to add another image plane. Import the `spaceGirlFront.tif` image.

11. By default both image planes are placed at the center of the grid. To make modeling a little easier, move them away from the center. Set the Center X attribute of the side-view image (imagePlane1) to **-15** and the Center Z attribute of the front-view image (image-Plane2) to **-12**. In the perspective view, you'll see that the image planes are no longer in the middle of the grid (see Figure 3.5).

FIGURE 3.5

The image planes are moved away from the center of the grid by adjusting the Center attributes in the Attribute Editor.

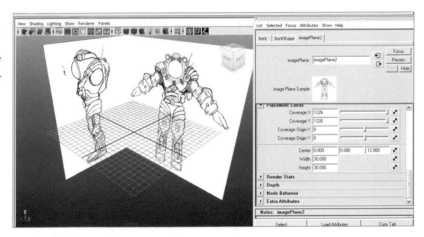

Reference Plane Display Layers

During the course of a modeling session, you may want to turn the image planes on and off quickly without taking the time to open the Attribute Editor for each and change the settings. To make things more convenient, you can put each plane on its own display layer.

1. Create a display layer in the Display Layer Editor and name it **frontView**. Select the image plane for the front view in the perspective window (drag a selection across the edge of the plane in the perspective view).

2. In the Display Layer Editor, right-click on the front-view layer and choose Add Selected Object. You can now toggle the visibility of the front view by clicking the V button for the layer in the Display Layer Editor.

3. Repeat steps 1 and 2 for the side-view image plane, and then name the new layer **sideView** (see Figure 3.6).

4. Save the scene as **spaceGirl_v01.ma**. To see a finished version of the scene, open spaceGirl_v01.ma from the `chapter3\scenes` directory.

Figure 3.6
The image planes are added to display layers so that their visibility can be turned on and off while working.

Copy Reference Images to Disk

You may want to copy the orthographic images and the concept drawing from the chapter3\sourceimages directory to a directory on your local disk so Maya can find them when you open the scene files. You will need to specify the location of the images in the Attribute Editor of the image plane node after moving the images.

Understanding NURBS

NURBS is an acronym that stands for Non-Uniform Rational B-Spline. A NURBS surface is created by spreading a three-dimensional surface across a network of NURBS curves. The curves themselves involve a complex mathematical computation that, for the most part, is hidden hidden from the user in the software. As a modeler you need to understand a few concepts when working with NURBS, but the software takes care of most of the advanced mathematics so that you can concentrate on the process of modeling.

Early in the history of 3D computer graphics, NURBS were used to create organic surfaces and even characters. However, as computers have become more powerful and the software has developed more advanced tools, most character modeling is accomplished using polygons and subdivision surfaces. NURBS are more ideally suited for hard-surface modeling; objects such as vehicles, equipment, and commercial product designs benefit from the types of smooth surfacing produced by NURBS models.

All NURBS objects are automatically converted to triangular polygons at render time by the software. You can determine how the surfaces will be tessellated (converted into polygons) before rendering and change these settings at any time to optimize rendering. This gives NURBS the advantage that their resolution can be changed when rendering. Models that appear close to the camera can have higher tessellation settings than those farther away from the camera.

One of the downsides of NURBS is that the surfaces themselves are made of four-sided patches. You cannot create a three- or five-sided NURBS patch, which can sometimes limit the kinds of shapes you can make with NURBS. If you create a NURBS sphere and use the Move tool to pull apart the control vertices at the top of the sphere, you'll see that even the patches of the sphere that appear as triangles are actually four-sided panels (see Figure 3.7).

To understand how NURBS works a little better, let's take a quick look at the basic building block of NURBS surfaces: the curve.

FIGURE 3.7
Pulling apart the control vertices at the top of a NURBS sphere reveals that all of the patches have four sides.

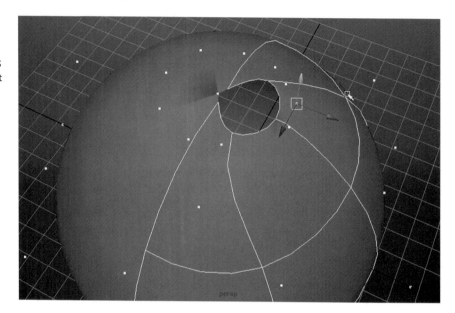

Understanding Curves

All NURBS surfaces are created based on a network of NURBS curves. Even the basic primitives, such as the sphere, are made up of circular curves with a surface stretched across them. The curves themselves can be created several ways. A *curve* is a line defined by points. The points along the curve are referred to as *curve points*. Movement along the curve in either direction is defined by its U coordinates. When you right-click on a curve, you can choose to select a curve point. The curve point can be moved along the U direction of the curve, and the position of the point is defined by its U parameter.

Curves also have *edit points* that define the number of spans along a curve. A *span* is the section of the curve between two edit points. Changing the position of the edit points changes the shape of the curve; however, this can lead to unpredictable results. It is a much better idea to use a curve's control vertices to edit the curve's shape.

Control vertices (CVs) are handles used to edit the curve's shapes. Most of the time you'll want to use the control vertices to manipulate the curve. When you create a curve and display its CVs, you'll see them represented as small dots. The first CV on a curve is indicated by a small box; the second is indicated by the letter U. The various components are displayed in Figure 3.8.

FIGURE 3.8
The top image shows a selected curve point on a curve, the middle image shows the curve with edit points displayed, and the bottom image shows the curve with control vertices (CVs) displayed.

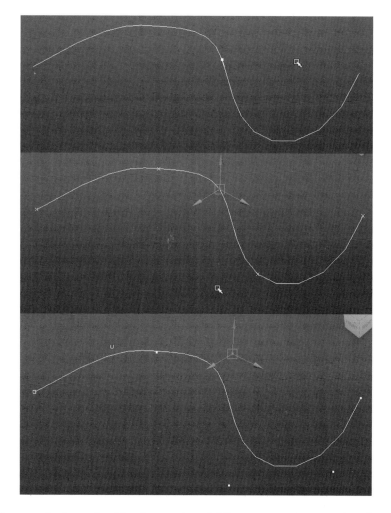

The degree of a curve is determined by the number of CVs per span minus one. In other words, a 3-degree (or cubic) curve has four CVs per span. A 1-degree (or linear) curve has two CVs per span (Figure 3.9). Linear curves have sharp corners where the curve changes directions; curves with two or more degrees are smooth and rounded where the curve changes direction. Most of the time you'll use either linear (1-degree) or cubic (3-degree) curves.

You can add or remove a curve's CVs and edit points, and you can also use curve points to define a location where a curve is split into two curves or joined to another curve.

Parameterization of a curve refers to the way in which the points along the curve are numbered. There are two types of parameterization: *uniform* and *chord length*. A curve with uniform parameterization has its points evenly spaced along the curve. The parameter of the last edit point along the curve is equal to the number of spans in the curve. You also have the option of specifying the parameterization range between 0 and 1. This method is available to make Maya more compatible with other NURBS modeling programs.

FIGURE 3.9
A linear curve has
sharp corners.

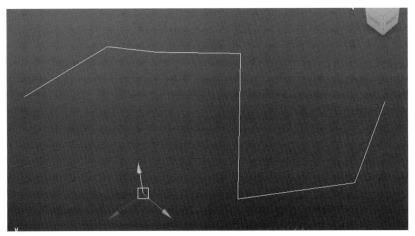

Chord length parameterization is a proportional numbering system that causes the length between edit points to be irregular. The type of parameterization you use depends on what you are trying to model. Curves can be rebuilt at any time to change their parameterization; however, this will sometime change the shape of the curve.

You can rebuild a curve to change its parameterization (Edit Curves ➢ Rebuild Curves). It's often a good idea to do this after splitting a curve or joining two curves together or when matching the parameterization of one curve to another. By rebuilding the curve, you ensure that the resulting parameterization (Min and Max Value attributes in the curve's Attribute Editor) is based on whole-number values, which leads to more predictable results when the curve is used as a basis for a surface. When rebuilding a curve you have the option of changing the degree of the curve so that a linear curve can be converted to a cubic curve and vice versa.

Understanding NURBS Surfaces

NURBS surfaces follow many of the same rules as NURBS curves since they are defined by a network of curves. A primitive, such as a sphere or a cylinder, is simply a NURBS surface lofted across circular curves. You can edit a NURBS surface by moving the position of the surface's CVs (see Figure 3.10). You can also select the *hulls* of a surface, which are groups of CVs that follow one of the curves that define a surface (see Figure 3.11).

NURBS curves use the U coordinates to specify the location of a point along the length of the curve. NURBS surfaces add the V coordinate to specify the location of a point on the surface. So, a given point on a NURBS surface has a U coordinate and a V coordinate. The U coordinates of a surface are always perpendicular to the V coordinates of a surface. The UV coordinate grid on a NURBS surface is just like the lines of longitude and latitude drawn on a globe.

SURFACES MENU SET

Many of the controls for editing NURBS surfaces and curves are found in the Surfaces menu set.

FIGURE 3.10
The shape of a NURBS surface can be changed by selecting its CVs and moving them with the Move tool.

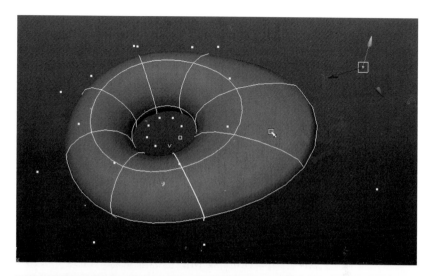

FIGURE 3.11
A hull is a group of connected CVs. Hulls can be selected and repositioned using the Move tool.

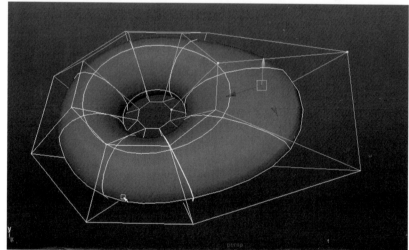

Just like NURBS curves, surfaces have a degree setting. Linear surfaces have sharp corners, and cubic surfaces (or any surface with a degree higher than 1) are rounded and smooth (see Figure 3.12). Oftentimes a modeler will begin a model as a linear NURBS surface and then either rebuild it as a cubic surface later on (Edit NURBS ➢ Rebuild ➢ Options) or convert the surface into polygons.

FIGURE 3.12
A linear NURBS
surface has
sharp corners.

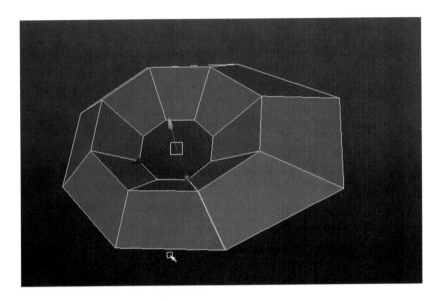

LINEAR AND CUBIC SURFACES

A NURBS surface can be rebuilt (Edit NURBS ➢ Rebuild ➢ Options) so that it is a cubic surface in one direction (either the U direction or the V direction) and linear in the other (either the U direction or the V direction).

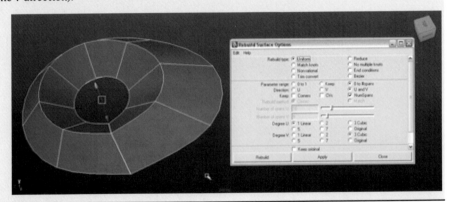

You can start a NURBS model using a primitive, such as a sphere, cone, torus, or cylinder, or you can build a network of curves and loft surfaces between the curves or any combination of the two. When you select a NURBS surface, the wireframe display shows the curves that define the surface. These curves are referred to as *isoparms*, which is short for isoparametric curve.

NURBS surfaces have implicit UV texture coordinates. This means that the UVs are not mapped as a separate process, as is the case with polygon models; rather the texture coordinates are defined by the parameterization of the surface itself. This offers less flexibility in the way textures are mapped on the surface, but at the same time you don't need to worry about creating a UV coordinate map once the model is complete.

A single NURBS model may be made up of numerous NURBS patches that have been stitched together. This technique was used for years to create CG characters. When you stitch two patches together, the tangency must be consistent between the two surfaces to avoid visible seams. It's a process that often takes some practice to master (see Figure 3.13).

FIGURE 3.13
A character is created from a series of NURBS patches stitched together.

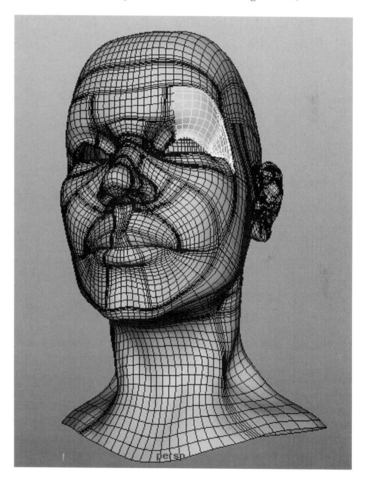

Surface Seams

Many NURBS primitives have a seam where the end of the surface meets the beginning. Imagine a piece of paper rolled into a cylinder. At the point where one end of the paper meets the other there is a seam. The same is true for many NURBS surfaces that define a shape. When you select a NURBS surface, the wireframe display on the surface shows the seam as a bold line. You can also find the seam by selecting the surface and choosing Display ➤ NURBS Surfaces ➤ Surface Origins (see Figure 3.14).

FIGURE 3.14
The point on a NURBS surface where the seams meet is indicated by displaying the Surface Origins.

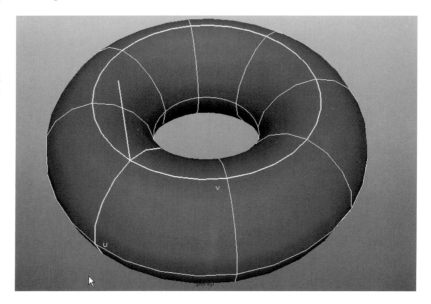

The seam can occasionally cause problems when you're working on a model. In many cases, you can change the position of the seam by selecting one of the isoparms on the surface (right-click on the surface and choose Isoparms) and selecting Edit NURBS ➤ Move Seam.

NURBS Display Controls

You can change the quality of the surface display in the viewport by selecting the surface and pressing 1, 2, or 3 on the keyboard. Pressing the 1 key displays the surface at the lowest quality, which makes the angles of the surface appear as corners. Pressing the 3 key displays the surface as smooth curves. The 2 key gives a medium-quality display. None of these display modes affect how the surface will look when rendered, but choosing a lower display quality can help improve Maya's performance in heavy scenes. The same display settings apply for NURBS curves as well. If you create a cubic curve that has sharp corners, remember to press the 3 key to make the curve appear smooth.

Modeling NURBS Surfaces

To start the model of the space girl, begin by creating the helmet from a simple NURBS sphere.

1. Continue with the scene from the previous section or open the spaceGirl_v01.ma scene from the chapter 3\scenes folder on the DVD. Make sure the images are visible on the image planes. The source files for these images are found in the chapter3\sourceimages folder.

2. Choose Create ➢ NURBS Primitives ➢ Sphere to create a sphere at the origin. If you have Interactive Creation active in the NURBS Primitives menu, you will be prompted to draw the sphere on the grid (personally I find Interactive Creation a bit of a nuisance and usually disable it).

3. In the Channel Box for the sphere, click the makeNurbsSphere1 node. If this node is not visible in the Channel Box, you need to enable Construction History and remake the sphere. Construction History needs to be on for this lesson. Make sure Sections is set to **8** and Spans is set to **4**.

4. Switch to the side view, select the sphere, and move it up along the Y axis so it roughly matches the shape of the helmet in the side view (see Figure 3.15). Enter the following settings in the Channel Box:

   Translate X: 0

   Translate Y: 9.76

   Translate Z: 0.845

   Rotate X: 102

   Rotate Y: 0

   Rotate Z: 0

   Scale X: 2.547

   Scale Y: 2.547

   Scale Z: 2.547

5. To see the sphere and the reference, you can enable X-ray mode in the side view (Shading ➢ X-Ray). Also enable Wireframe On Shaded so you can see where the divisions are on the sphere.

ARTISTIC JUDGMENT

Keep in mind that the main goal of this chapter is to give you an understanding of some of the more common NURBS modeling techniques. Creating a perfect representation of the concept image or an exact duplicate of the example model is not as important as gaining an understanding of working with NURBS. In some cases, the exact settings used in the example are given; in most cases, the instructions are slightly vague. In the real world, you would use your own artistic judgment when creating a model based on a drawing; there's no reason why you can't do the same while working through this chapter. Feel free to experiment as you work to improve your understanding of the NURBS modeling toolset. If you really want to know how the example model was created, take a look at the scene files used in this chapter and compare them with your own progress.

FIGURE 3.15
A NURBS sphere
is created and
positioned in
the side view to
match the drawing
of the helmet.

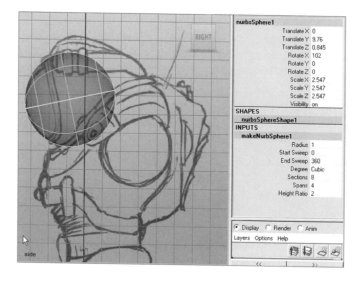

To create a separate surface for the glass shield at the front of the helmet, you can split the surface into two parts.

6. Right-click on the sphere and choose Isoparm. An isoparm is a row of vertices on the surface; sometimes it's also referred to as *knots*. Select the center line that runs vertically along the middle of the sphere.

7. Drag the isoparm forward on the surface of the sphere until it matches the dividing line between the shield and the helmet in the drawing (see Figure 3.16).

FIGURE 3.16
An isoparm is
selected to match
the place where
the glass shield
meets the rest of
the helmet.

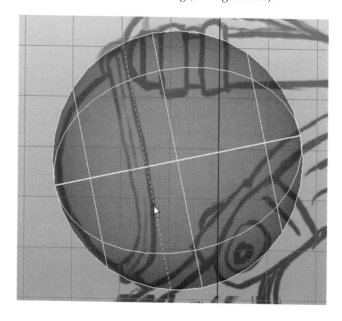

8. Choose Edit NURBS ➤ Detach Surfaces. This splits the surface into two parts along the selected isoparm. Notice the newly created node in the Outliner. Rename detached-Surface1 **shield**, as shown in Figure 3.17.

FIGURE 3.17

The area of the shield is detached from the rest of the sphere, creating a new surface node.

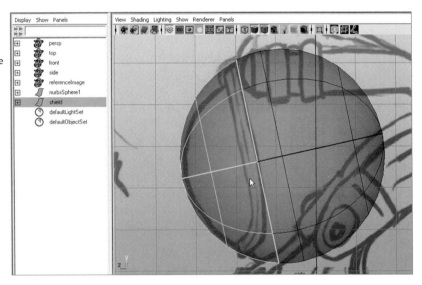

9. Select the front surface, and scale down and reposition it so that it matches the drawing. Enter the following settings in the Channel Box:

Translate X: 0

Translate Y: 9.678

Translate Z: 1.245

Rotate X: 102

Rotate Y: 0

Rotate Z: 0

Scale X: 2.124

Scale Y: 2.124

Scale Z: 2.124

10. Right-click on the rear part of the sphere and choose Control Vertex. You'll see the CVs of the helmet highlighted. Drag a selection marquee over the vertices on the back, and switch to the Move tool (hot key = w).

11. Use the Move tool to position these vertices so they match the contour of the back of the helmet. Select the Scale tool (hot key = r) and scale them down by dragging on the blue handle of the Scale tool. Adjust their position with the Move tool so the back of the helmet comes to a rounded point.

12. Select the group of vertices at the top of the helmet toward the back (third isoparm from the left), and use the Move tool to move them upward so that they match the contour of the helmet.

NURBS COMPONENT COORDINATES

When you select CVs on a NURBS surface, you'll see a node in the Channel Box labeled CVS (Click To Show). When you click this, you'll get a small version of the Component Editor in the Channel Box that displays the position of the CVs in local space—this is now labeled CVs (Click To Hide)—relative to the rest of the sphere. The CVs are labeled by number. In step 12, the vertices are labeled 2,0, 2,6, and 2,7 in the Channel Box. Notice also that moving them up in world space actually changes their position along the Z axis in local space. This makes sense when you remember that the original sphere was rotated to match the drawing.

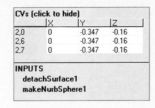

---

13. Select the group of vertices at the bottom of the helmet along the same isoparm. Move these upward to roughly match the drawing (see Figure 3.18).

14. Rename the back portion **helmet**.

15. Save the scene as **helmet_v01.ma**. To see a version of the scene to this point, open the helmet_v01.ma scene from the chapter 3\scenes directory on the DVD.

Lofting Surfaces

A *loft* creates a surface across two or more selected curves. It's a great tool for filling gaps between surfaces or developing a new surface from a series of curves. In this section, you'll bridge the gap between the helmet and shield by lofting a surface.

1. Continue with the scene from the previous section or open the helmet_v01.ma scene from the chapter 3\scenes folder on the DVD.

2. Switch to the side view. Right-click on the helmet surface and choose Isoparm. Select the isoparm at the open edge of the surface.

SELECTING NURBS EDGES

When selecting the isoparm at the edge of a surface, it may be easier to select an isoparm on the surface and drag toward the edge until it stops. This ensures that you have the isoparm at the very edge of the surface selected.

FIGURE 3.18
The CVs on the back portion of the helmet are selected and moved to match the drawing.

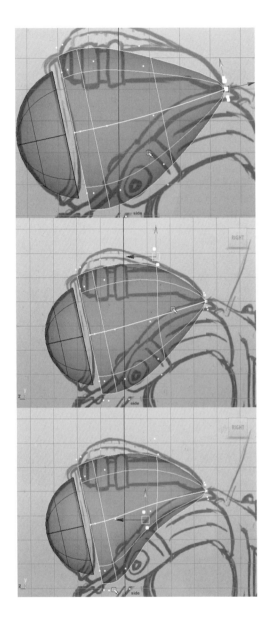

3. Right-click on the helmet's shield and choose Isoparm. Hold down the Shift key and select the isoparm at the edge of the surface so you have a total of two isoparms selected: one at the open edge of the helmet and the other at the open edge of the shield (sometimes this takes a little practice).

4. Select Surfaces ➢ Loft ➢ Options. In the options, choose Edit ➢ Reset Settings to set the options to the default settings. Set Surface Degree to Linear and Section Spans to **5**. Click Loft to create the surface (see Figure 3.19).

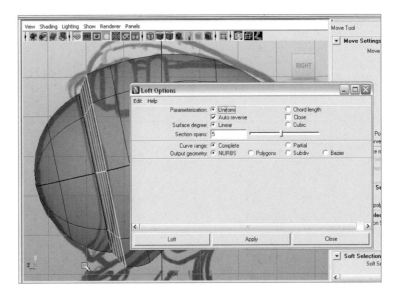

FIGURE 3.19
The options for the loft surface. Once created, the loft bridges the gap between the helmet and the shield.

By setting Surface Degree to Linear, you can create the hard-edge ridge detail along the helmet's seal depicted in the original drawing.

5. In the side view, zoom in closely to the top half of the loft. Right-click on the Loft and choose Hull.

6. Select the second hull from the left and choose the Move tool (hot key = w). Open the options for the Move tool, and set the Move Axis to Normals Average so you can easily move the hull back and forth relative to the rotation of the helmet.

7. Move the hull forward until it meets the edge of the shield (see Figure 3.20).

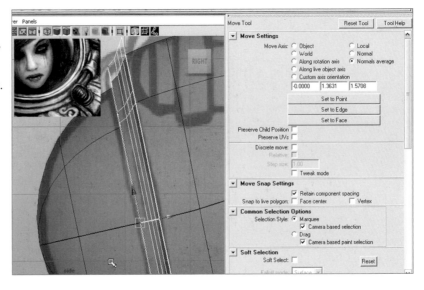

FIGURE 3.20
Select the hulls of the lofted surface, and use the Move tool to shape the contour of the loft.

8. Using the up-arrow key, select the next hull in from the left. Move this hull toward the back to form a groove in the loft.

PICK WALKING

Using the arrow keys to move between selected components or nodes is known as *pick walking*.

---

9. Use the Scale and Move tools to reposition the hulls of the loft to imitate some of the detail in the drawing.

10. Turn off the visibility of the image planes layers and disable X-ray mode so you can see how the changes to the loft look. Switch to the perspective mode and examine the helmet (see Figure 3.21).

FIGURE 3.21
The ridges in the surface between the helmet shield and the helmet are created by moving and scaling the hulls of the lofted surface.

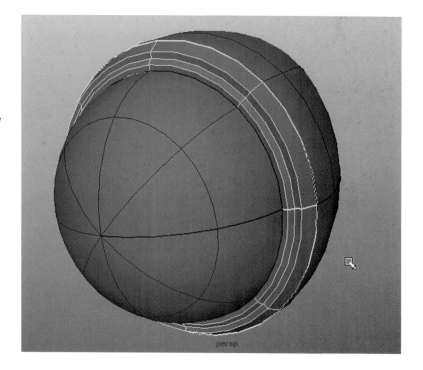

As long as the construction history is preserved on the loft, you can make changes to the helmet's shape, and the loft will automatically update. If you take a close look at the original concept sketch, it looks as though the front of the helmet may not be perfectly circular. By making a few small changes to the helmet's CVs, you can create a more stylish and interesting shape for the helmet's shield.

11. Select the helmet and the shield but not the loft. Switch to component mode. The CVs of both the helmet and the shield should be visible.

12. Select the four CVs at the bottom center of the shield and the four CVs at the bottom of the helmet. In the options for the Move tool, make sure the Move Axis is still set to Normals Average. Switch to the side view, and use the Move tool to pull these forward toward the front of the helmet.

13. Switch to the Rotate tool, and drag upward on the red circle to rotate the CVs on their local X axis. Switch back to the Move tool, and push along the red arrow to move them backward slightly.

14. These changes will cause some distortion in the shape of the shield and the loft. You can adjust the position of some of the CVs very slightly to return the shield to its rounded shape. Select the CVs from the side view by dragging a selection marquee around the CVs— so that the matching CVs on the opposite side of the X axis of the helmet are selected as well (as opposed to just clicking on the CVs). Use the move tool to adjust the position of the selected CVs.

15. Keep selecting CVs, and use the Move tool to reposition them until the distortions in the surface are minimized. Remember, you are only selecting the CVs of the helmet and shield, not the CVs of the lofted surface in between (remember to save often!).

This is the hardest part of NURBS modeling, and it does take practice, so be patient as you work. Figure 3.22 shows the process. Figure 3.23 shows the reshaped helmet and shield from the perspective view.

16. Save the scene as **helmet_v02.ma**. To see a version of the scene to this point, open the helmet_v02.ma scene from the chapter3\scenes directory.

Intersecting Surfaces

You can use one NURBS object to model another. Using a bit of ingenuity, you can find ways to create interesting shapes by carving a NURBS surface with a second surface. In this section, you'll prepare the helmet in order to create an opening at its bottom so the space girl can fit the helmet around her head.

1. Continue with the scene from the previous section, or open the helmet_v02.ma scene from the chapter3\scenes directory.

2. Create a new NURBS sphere. Position the sphere so it intersects the bottom of the helmet, and scale it in size so it covers most of the bottom of the helmet. Use the following settings in the Channel Box:

Translate X: 0

Translate Y: 8.491

Translate Z: -1.174

Scale X: 1.926

Scale Y: 2.671

Scale Z: 2.834

FIGURE 3.22
The CVs at the bottom of the shield and helmet are selected from the side view. Using the Move and Rotate tools, they are carefully positioned to match the shape of the helmet in reference drawings.

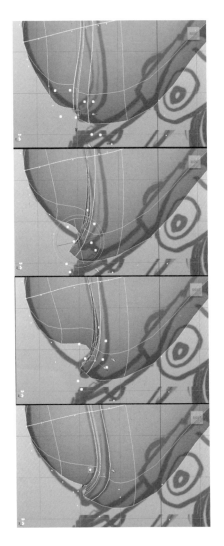

FIGURE 3.23
The reshaped helmet and shield from the perspective view

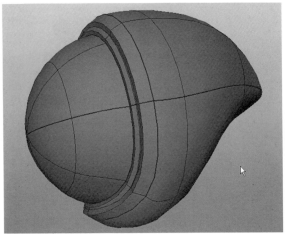

3. Select the helmet, and then Shift+click the sphere. Choose Edit NURBS ➤ Intersect Surfaces ➤ Options. In the options, choose Edit ➤ Reset Settings to return the options to the default settings. Set Create Curves For to First Surface. This creates a NURBS curve on the first selected surface. Click the Intersect button to perform the operation (see Figure 3.24).

4. In the viewport you'll see a new curve created on the helmet. Select the sphere you created for the intersection and hide it (Ctrl+h). You can see the curve drawn on the bottom of the helmet (see Figure 3.25).

Because of the helmet's construction history, if you move either sphere of the helmet, the curve will change positions. The curve on the surface can be selected and moved as well using the Move tool. As you reposition the curve on the surface, it will remain attached to the surface.

FIGURE 3.24
The options for the Intersect Surfaces operation

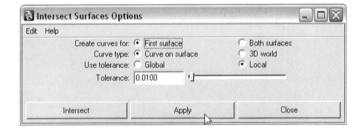

FIGURE 3.25
The Intersect Surfaces operation creates a curve on the surface where the two surfaces intersect.

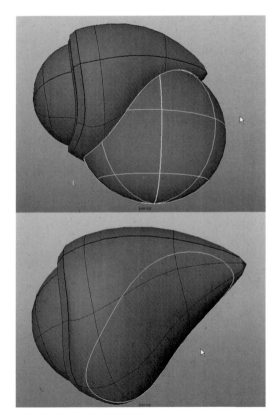

Trim Surfaces

When you *trim* a surface, you cut a hole in it. This does not actually delete parts of the surface; rather it makes the parts invisible as if they had been deleted. This is one way to get around the fact that NURBS surfaces must consist of only four cornered patches. To trim a surface, you must first create a curve on the surface, as demonstrated in the previous section.

1. Undo any changes made to the position of the two surfaces or the curve on the surface.

2. Select the helmet and choose Edit NURBS ➤ Trim Tool. When the Trim tool is activated, the surface appears as a white wireframe with the edges and curves on the surface highlighted in a bold solid line.

3. The Trim tool indicates which parts of the surface you want to remain visible when the Trim operation is completed. Use the tool to click on several parts of the helmet, but not within the area defined by the curve on the surface.

4. Wherever you click, a marker indicates the parts of the surface that will remain visible. When you have created five or six markers, press the Enter key to trim the helmet. A hole will appear at the bottom of the helmet. If it does not work, click Undo and try again (see Figure 3.26).

FIGURE 3.26
The Trim tool allows you to indicate which parts of the surface will remain visible when you execute the Trim operation.

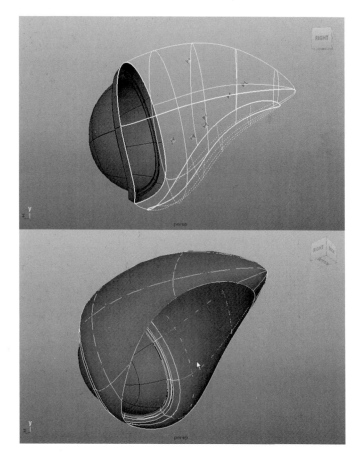

Just like with the curve on the surface, as long as the construction history is maintained for the surface, any changes you make to the intersecting spheres or the curve on the surface will change the position and shape of the hole in the helmet. You can animate the intersecting sphere to make the hole change size and shape over time; however, be aware that some changes may cause errors.

Working with Trim Edges

The edge of the trimmed surface can be used as a starting point for lofts or other NURBS surface types.

1. Right-click on the helmet and choose Trim Edge. This option appears only for trimmed surfaces (see Figure 3.27).

FIGURE 3.27
You can select the edges of a trimmed surface by choosing Trim Edge from the marking menu.

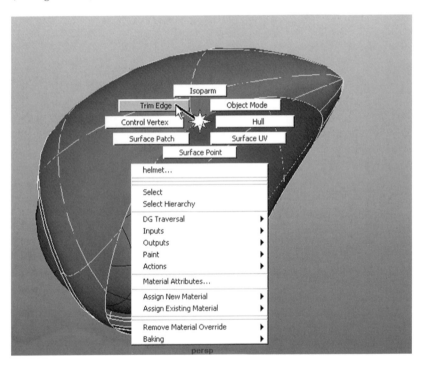

2. Select the trim edge (it should turn yellow when selected), and choose Edit Curves ➢ Duplicate Surface Curves. This creates a new curve that can be positioned away from the helmet.

3. Select the new curve and choose Modify ➢ Center Pivot so the pivot point of the new curve is at its center.

4. Use the Move tool to position duplicateCurve1 below the helmet. Scale it up in size a little as well. Use these settings:

    Translate X: 0

    Translate Y: -0.174

    Translate Z: 0

    Scale X: 1.275

    Scale Y: 1.275

    Scale Z: 1.275

5. With the curve selected, tumble the view so you can clearly see the bottom of the helmet. Right-click on the helmet and choose Trim Edge. Shift+click the trim edge at the bottom of the helmet so both the duplicate curve and the trim edge are selected.

6. Choose Surfaces ➢ Loft to create a loft using the same settings used to close the gap between the helmet and shield (see Figure 3.28).

7. Right-click on the new lofted surface and choose Hull. Use the Move and Scale tools to change the position and size of the hulls to create a couple grooves in the loft. This technique is similar to the one used to add detail to the loft between the helmet and the shield (see Figure 3.29).

8. Save the scene as **helmet_v03.ma**. To see a version of the scene to this point, open the helmet_v03.ma scene from the chapter 3\scenes folder on the DVD.

FIGURE 3.28
A loft surface is created between the trim edge and the duplicate curve.

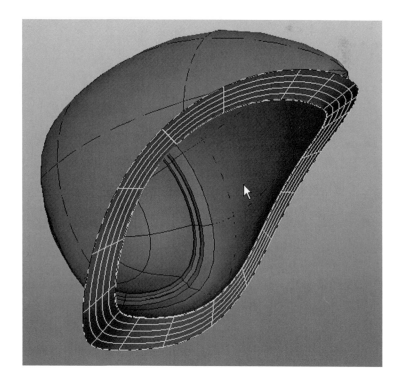

FIGURE 3.29
By repositioning the hulls of the loft, the surface around the helmet is shaped to resemble the concept drawing.

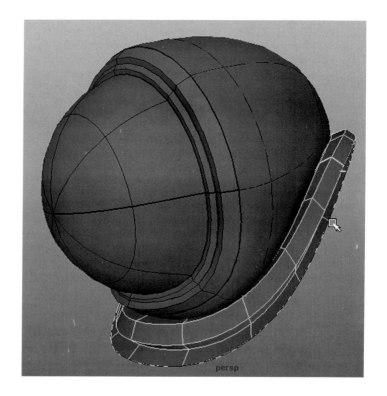

ORGANIZING SURFACES

When you're working with NURBS surfaces, the Outliner can quickly fill up with oddly named objects, such as detachedSurface23. When the scene gets big, this can get confusing. It's usually a good idea to occasionally take the time to rename the surfaces as you're working to help reduce clutter and confusion.

🌐 **Real World Scenario**

DUPLICATING TRIM EDGES OVER SEAMS

Sometimes you'll run into a situation where you want to create a curve from the edge of a trimmed surface. If the trim edge overlaps a seam in the model, you may find that the trim edge is broken into segments. This becomes apparent when you right-click on the opening in the surface and choose Trim Edge.

To make a single curve from the trim edges, use the following steps:

1. Shift+click each part of the trim edge until all the segments are highlighted.

2. Choose Edit Curves ➤ Duplicate Surface Curves.

3. Hide the NURBS surfaces so you can clearly see the curves.

4. Select two of the curves and choose Edit Curves ➤ Attach Curves ➤ Options. In the options, set the Attach Method to Connect and set Multiple Knots to Remove. Turn off Keep Originals.

5. Click Apply to attach the curves. When attaching curves, you may want to specify which end to attach by selecting a curve point at the end of the curve.

6. Repeat this process until you have a single curve.

7. Rebuild the curve using Edit Curves ➤ Rebuild Curve. You may also want to delete the construction history on the curve.

Extruding Surfaces: Distance Extrude

There are several ways to create NURBS surfaces by extruding from a curve. In this section, you'll see how these methods can be applied to create the lamps on the helmet and some of the other details.

1. Continue with the scene from the previous section, or open the helmet_v03.ma scene from the chapter3\scenes directory.

2. Create a NURBS sphere. Switch to the front view. Select the sphere, and use the Move and Scale tools to translate and scale the sphere so that it matches the lamp on the right side of the helmet. Use the following settings:

> Translate X: 2.175
>
> Translate Y: 11.785
>
> Translate Z: 1.621
>
> Rotate X: 90
>
> Rotate Y: 0
>
> Rotate Z: 0
>
> Scale X: 0.518
>
> Scale Y: 0.176
>
> Scale Z: 0.518

3. From the side view, select the center isoparm, and choose Edit NURBS ➤ Detach Surfaces. The front section of the sphere will be the glass casing of the lamp; the rear section will be the reflector inside the lamp.

4. Select the rear part of the sphere and name it **reflector**. Scale it up slightly and move it forward (see Figure 3.30).

FIGURE 3.30
The sphere is divided into two sections to create the lamp on the helmet. The rear section is scaled up and moved forward.

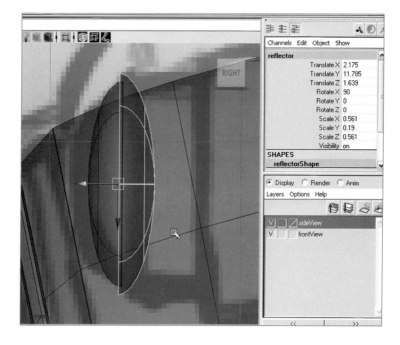

5. Select the front of the sphere and name it **lamp**. Create a loft to fill the gap between the lamp and the reflector. In the Loft Options, set Number Of Spans to **1**.

6. Select the isoparm at the edge of the reflector, and choose Edit Curves ➤ Duplicate Curve On Surface. Select the curve and center its pivot (Modify ➤ Center Pivot).

7. Move the curve back along the Z axis a little, and scale it up. Figure 3.31 shows the duplicated curve at its new position.

8. Select the curve and choose Surfaces ➤ Extrude ➤ Options. Choose Edit ➤ Reset Settings to reset the options. Set the Style to Distance and the Extrude Length to **2**. The Direction should be left at Profile Normal. Click the Extrude button to create the surface. Name the extruded surface **lampHousing** (see Figure 3.32).

FIGURE 3.31
A curve is created by duplicating the edge of the reflector. The curve is scaled up and moved back a little.

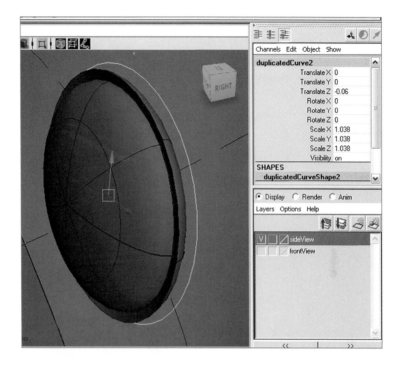

FIGURE 3.32
The housing for the lamp is created by extruding the duplicated curve.

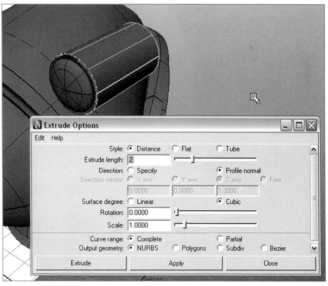

Extruding Surfaces: Profile Extrude

The distance extrude is the simplest type of extrusion you can create and requires only a single profile curve. To create the rounded surface between the helmet and the shield, you can use a profile curve extrusion. This requires two curves.

1. Right-click on the loft between the helmet and choose Isoparm. Select one of the isoparms that run around the loft at the edge, and drag it back toward the center of the loft.

2. Choose Edit Curves ➢ Duplicate Surface Curves to create a new curve that runs around the helmet's shield.

3. With the curve selected, choose Modify ➢ Center Pivot to center the pivot point on the curve (see Figure 3.33).

4. Switch to the top view and turn on Wireframe. To get a clear view of the grid, choose (from the viewport menu) Show ➢ NURBS Surfaces to temporarily hide the surfaces.

5. Turn on Grid Snapping and create a NURBS curve (Create ➢ CV Curve Tool). To create the curve, click once on the grid point two units to the left of center, and moving down one unit click twice on the grid point; this will give a harder edge to the curve while still retaining some roundness.

FIGURE 3.33
A curve is created by duplicating a selected isoparm on the shieldSeal.

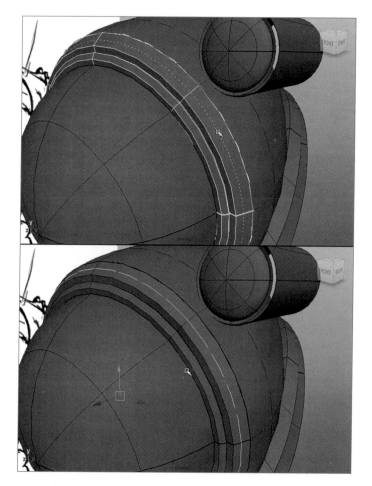

6. Click on the grid point one unit below the center; then click twice on the grid point one unit down and two units to the right of center. Finish the curve by clicking on the grid point two units to the right of center. Press the Enter key to complete the curve.

7. Scale the curve down to **0.12** units in X, Y, and Z.

8. Turn off Grid Snapping, and right-click on the curve. Select Control Vertex. Select the CV at the center of the line, and pull it down slightly to create a small arch in the curve (see Figure 3.34).

9. In the Outliner, select the newly created curve and Ctrl+click the curve created from the loft (make sure you Ctrl+click the second curve; Shift+click may produce different results). Choose Surfaces ➤ Extrude ➤ Options. In the Extrude Options, set the Style to Tube, the Result Position to At Path, the Pivot to Component, and the Orientation to Path Direction. Make sure Curve Range is set to Complete and Output Geometry is set to NURBS. Click Extrude to make the extrude (Figure 3.35).

FIGURE 3.34
A curve is drawn on the grid from the top view using Grid Snapping. It's then scaled down and shaped by pulling a CV.

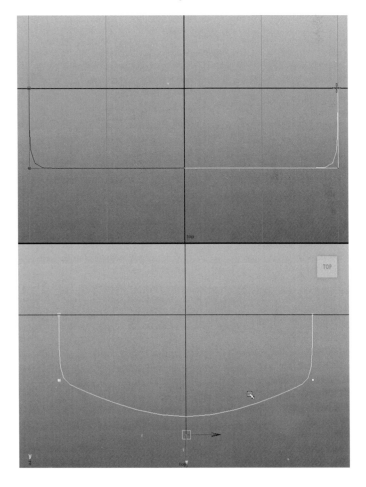

FIGURE 3.35
A surface is created by extruding a profile curve along a path that surrounds the seal between the glass shield and the helmet.

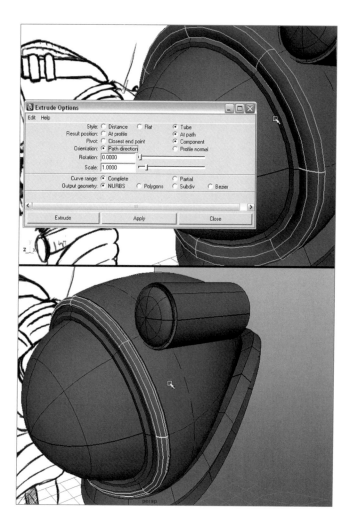

EXTRUSION SETTINGS

Often when creating an extrusion, you'll find that once you create it you need to adjust the options under the extrude node in the Channel Box to get the proper direction of the extrusion.

If you choose the Partial option under Curve Range, you'll find the subCurve1 and subCurve2 nodes in the Channel Box. By setting keyframes on the Min and Max values under these nodes, you can animate the surface extruding along the curve. This is a popular technique for animating tubes moving through space.

At the front of the helmet, you'll see a rounded tube surrounding the border of the helmet's shield. You can adjust the position of the duplicate curve and the position and shape of the profile curve to refine the shape of the extrusion.

10. To refine the shape of the extruded surface you can scale and reposition duplicateCurve3 (the path curve) and also scale and rotate curve1 (the profile curve you drew on the grid) along its Y axis about 45 degrees. Name the new surface **shieldSeal2**.

11. Save the scene as **helmet_v04.ma**. To see a version of the helmet to this point, open the helmet_v04.ma scene from the chapter3\scenes directory on the DVD.

Fillet Surfaces

A fillet surface is another method for bridging gaps between surfaces. You can create one to bridge the gap between the lamp and its housing.

1. Continue with the scene from the previous section, or open the helmet_v04.ma scene from the chapter3\scenes directory on the DVD.

2. Select the isoparms at the edge of the reflector and the lamp housing.

3. From the Surfaces menu, choose Edit NURBS ➤ Surface Fillet ➤ Freeform Fillet.

The freeform fillet creates a smooth, rounded surface between the two surfaces. Select the freeformFiletSurface1 node and open the Channel Box.

4. Set the Depth to **0.8** and the Bias to **-0.8**. The Depth adjusts the curvature of the surface and the Bias moves the influence of the curvature toward one end or the other of the fillet (see Figure 3.36).

FIGURE 3.36

A freeform fillet surface bridges the gap between the lamp and the lam-pHousing.

Next you'll add some additional fillets to the lamp housing to create more detail.

5. Select the isoparms at both ends of the lamp housing. Choose Edit NURBS ➤ Insert Isoparms ➤ Options. In the options, set the Insert Location to Between Selections, set # Isoparms To Insert to **4**. Click the Insert button to make the change. This creates four new isoparms evenly spaced along the housing (see Figure 3.37).

FIGURE 3.37

Four isoparms are
added to the lamp-
Housing surface.

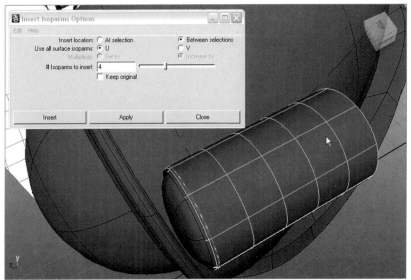

6. Select the four newly created isoparms, and choose Edit Curves ➤ Duplicate Surface Curves.

7. Select the four curves and center their pivots (Modify ➤ Center Pivot). Scale the curves up to **1.5** on the X and Y axis.

8. Create two lofts between the two pairs of curves. Make sure the lofts are cubic, and give them both two section spans.

9. Create a freeform fillet by choosing an isoparm at the front edge of the front loft and an isoparm on the lamp housing just ahead of the loft. Choose Edit NURBS ➤ Surface Fillet ➤ Freeform Fillet.

10. Repeat step 9 three more times to create fillets between the other edges of the two lofts and the lamp housing (see Figure 3.38).

11. Right-click on each loft and choose Hulls. Shift+click the outside hulls on the top of both lofts, and use the Move tool to pull them upward.

12. Switch to the Scale tool, and scale them along the X axis to flatten the tops of the lofts.

13. Shift+click the top-center hull on both lofts, and use the Move tool to pull them all down, closer to the housing.

14. Switch to the Rotate tool. Rotate the hulls along the X axis to give them a slight angle. Experiment with the shape of these surfaces by continuing to translate, rotate, and scale the hulls of the lofted surfaces. Because of construction history, the freeform fillet surfaces will update. You can also make changes by editing the curves duplicated from the lamp housing isoparms in step 5.

FIGURE 3.38
Four isoparms on
the lamp housing
are duplicated,
scaled, lofted,
and then con-
nected to the lamp
housing using a
freeform fillet.

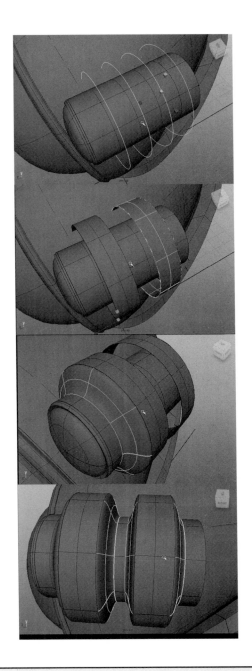

SELECTING AND MOVING HULLS

For some surfaces, selecting hulls can be tricky. If you're having trouble selecting a specific hull, try selecting a nearby hull that is more exposed, and then use the arrow keys to pick walk your way to the hull you need to select.

---

15. Select all the surfaces that make up the lamp and housing, the lofts, and the fillets. Delete history on these surfaces, and group them. Name the group **leftLamp** (it's on the character's left). Delete all the associated curves (see Figure 3.39).

FIGURE 3.39
The hulls of the lofted surface on the lamps are selected, moved, and scaled to shape the surfaces of the lamp casing.

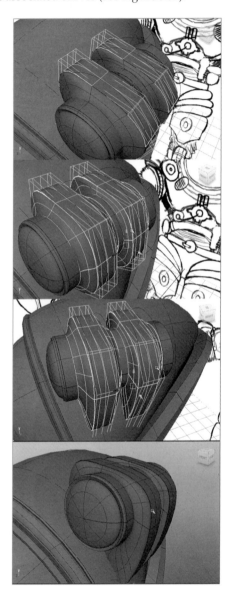

16. Select the leftLamp group and choose Edit ➢ Duplicate Special ➢ Options. In the options, set the X scale to **-1**. Click the Duplicate button. This creates a copy of the lamp on the opposite side of the helmet. Name the duplicate lamp **rightLamp** (see Figure 3.40).

17. Save the scene as **helmet_v05.ma**. To see the scene up to this point, open the helmet_v05.ma scene from the chapter3\scenes directory on the DVD.

FIGURE 3.40
The surfaces that make up the lamp are grouped. The group is mirrored to the right side by duplicating with a -1 setting in the Scale X attribute.

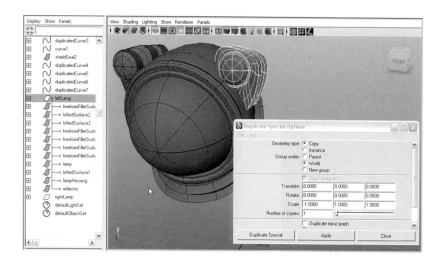

Creating Rail Surfaces

A rail surface uses at least one profile curve and two rail curves to create a surface.

1. Continue with the scene from the previous section or open the helmet_v05.ma scene from the chapter3\scenes directory on the DVD.

2. Select the leftLamp and rightLamp groups and hide them (hot key = Ctrl+h). Switch to the side-view camera. Switch to wireframe mode (hot key = 4).

3. Choose Create ➢ CV Curve tool (make sure you are in the side view). Place the first point of the curve near the front/top of the helmet. Create a curve as shown in Figure 3.41.

FIGURE 3.41
A curve is drawn in the side view.

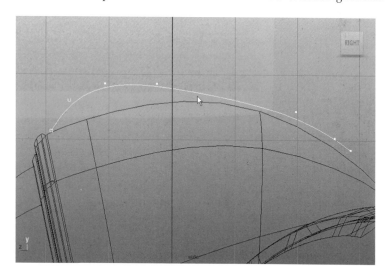

4. Switch to the front view. Select the curve and choose Modify ➤ Center pivot. Select the Move tool.

5. Press the d key on the keyboard to switch to pivot mode. Pull down on the Y axis of the Move tool. Reposition the pivot so that, from the front view, it is aligned with the center of the helmet's shield (see Figure 3.42).

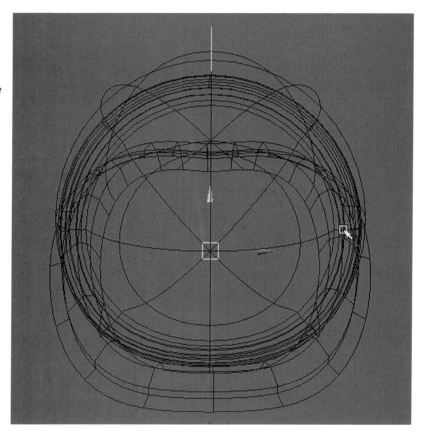

FIGURE 3.42
The pivot point of the new curve is placed at the center of the helmet's shield in the front view.

6. Switch to the Rotate tool (hot key = e). Rotate the curve -14 degrees on the Z axis.

7. Duplicate the curve (hot key = Ctrl+d) and rotate the duplicate -29 degrees on the Z axis.

8. Scale the duplicate curve to 0.95 on the Y axis. These two curves will become the rails for the birail surface.

9. Switch to the perspective view and turn shading mode back on.

10. Turn on Curve Snapping and select the EP Curve tool (Create EP Curve Tool). This will allow you to create a curve by clicking just twice.

11. Click on the first rail curve, and drag toward the end to make the first point of the curve.

12. Click on the second rail curve and drag toward its end (toward the back of the helmet) to make the second point of the curve. This might be easier to do if you rotate the view so the curves are not overlapping the surfaces. This helps avoid a situation in which Curve Snapping places one of the points of the EP curve on one of the isoparms of a visible surface (see Figure 3.43).

13. Select the curve between the two rails, choose Edit Curves ≻ Rebuild Curve ≻ Options. In the options, reset the settings. Set the Number Of Spans to **8** and the Degree to 1 Linear. Click Rebuild to rebuild the curve (see Figure 3.44).

14. Select the new curve and switch to component mode. Turn Curve Snapping off. Use the Move tool to drag some of the CVs to shape the profile. The profile will be swept along the curves to create grooves, similar to the detail on the top of the helmet in the drawing. You can keep it simple for now and add additional detail later.

FIGURE 3.43
With Curve Snapping enabled, each end point of an EP curve can be placed at the end of the two rail curves.

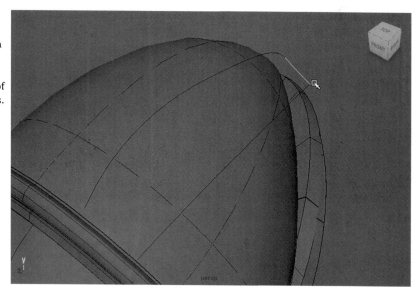

FIGURE 3.44
The options for the rebuilt curve

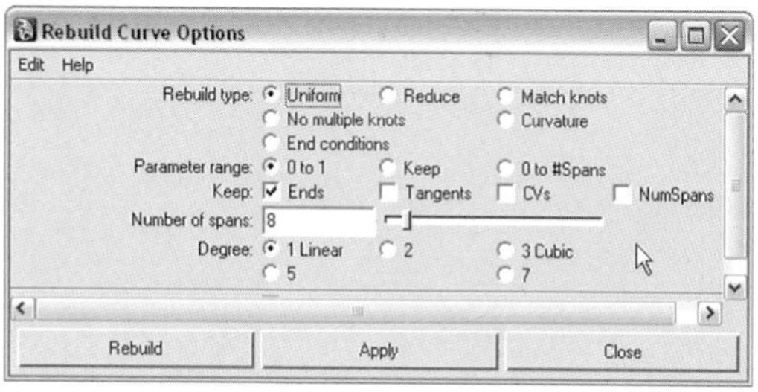

MOVING CVS AND OTHER COMPONENTS

While using the Move tool to edit the position of CVs, experiment with the different Axis settings in the Move tool options. Sometimes it's easier to use object mode, sometimes another mode. You can even use the position of a specific CV (or edge or face) to set the axis of the Move tool. To do this, switch the object to component mode, open the Move Tool Options box, click the Set To Point button, and then select a CV. The axis of the Move tool will be oriented to face the CV.

---

15. To create the birail, choose Surfaces ➤ Birail ➤ Birail1 Tool. (the options may open automatically; if they do, click the Create button to start using the tool). In the viewport, select the profile curve first and hit the Enter key. Then select the first and then the second rail curves. Hit the Enter key (see Figure 3.45).

FIGURE 3.45
The birail surface is created with the Birail1 tool. Select the profile first, hit Enter, and then select both rail curves.

16. You can change the shape of the surface by editing the position of the CVs on the profile curve. Be careful not to change the position of the rail curves. If the three curves no longer touch, the surface will disappear.

17. To make changes to the surface, select it, delete history, and then edit the surface by selecting the hulls and moving them with the Move tool.

18. When you're happy with the basic shape of the birail, select it and choose Duplicate Special ➢ Options. In the options, set Scale X to **-1**. Click Duplicate. This makes a copy of the surface on the opposite side of the helmet (see Figure 3.46).

19. Create a loft between the two inside edges of the birail surface. The loft should have nine divisions.

20. Use the Move tool to position the hulls of the loft to create the three curving bumps as shown in the concept sketch (see Figure 3.47). Select the surface and choose Edit ➢ Delete By Type ➢ History to remove the construction history from the object.

21. Save the scene as **helmet_v06.ma**.

FIGURE 3.46
The birail surface is adjusted by manipulating its hulls using the Move and Rotate tools. The surface is then mirrored to the opposite side of the helmet using Duplicate Special.

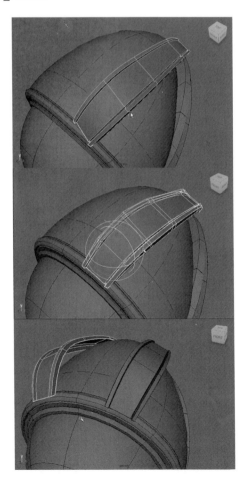

FIGURE 3.47
A loft is created between the two inner edges of the birail surfaces. The hulls are moved and scaled to match the concept drawing.

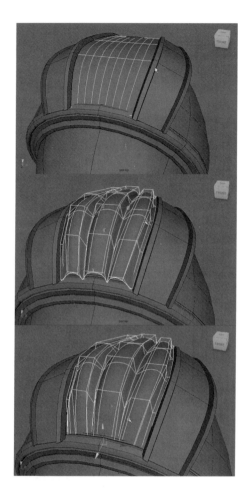

Lofting across Multiple Curves

To create the back of the helmet, you can loft a surface across multiple profile curves.

1. Continue with the scene from the previous section or open the helmet_v06.ma scene from the chapter3\scenes directory on the DVD.

2. Right-click on the rear of the housing for the leftLamp; select Isoparms. Select the isoparm at the very back end of the housing.

3. Choose Edit Curves ➢ Duplicate Surface Curves to create a curve based on the selected isoparm.

4. Choose Edit ➢ Duplicate Special ➢ Options. In the options, set Scale X to **-1**. Click the Duplicate button to make a mirror copy of the curve on the other side.

5. Select the first duplicate curve and chose Edit ➢ Duplicate (hot key = Ctrl+d) to make a standard duplicate of the curve. Set the rotation of this curve to 50 degrees in Y. Select the curve on the opposite side, and duplicate it as well. Set the Y rotation to **-50** degrees.

6. Starting from the helmet's left side, Shift+click each of the duplicate curves (this may be easier to do if you hide the NURBS surfaces using the Show menu in the panel menu bar). Choose Surfaces ➤ Loft ➤ Options. In the options, make sure the Degree of the loft is set to Cubic. Set the spans to **2**. Click the Loft button.

7. When the loft is created (turn the visibility of NURBS surfaces back on to see the loft), right-click on the new surface and choose Control Vertex to switch to component mode. Select pairs of CVSs at the back of the surface, and use the Move tool to reposition them to create a more interesting shape to the surface (Figure 3.48).

8. Name the new surface **helmetRear**. When you're happy with the result, save the model as **helmet_v07.ma**. To see a version of the scene to this point, open the helmet_v07.ma scene from the chapter3\scenes directory on the DVD.

FIGURE 3.48
The duplicated curves are selected in order from left to right, and then a loft surface is created. The CVs of the loft are selected and repositioned to match the reference images.

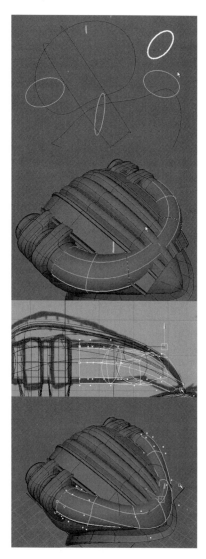

Live Surfaces

When you make a NURBS surface "live," you put it into a temporary state that allows you to draw curves directly on it. This is a great way to add detail that conforms to the shape of the object.

1. Continue with the scene from the previous section or open the `helmet_v07.ma` scene from the `chapter3\scenes` directory on the DVD.

2. Make sure that Wireframe On Shaded is enabled, and zoom into the model so you can see the birail surface you created in the previous section.

You're going to add some isoparms to the surface so that drawing clean curves on the surface will be a little easier. The isoparms will act as a guide for the curves that you draw.

3. Right-click on the birail surface and choose Isoparms. Add two isoparms that run along the length of the birail surface (in the options for Insert Isoparm, make sure Location is set to At Selection).

4. Add two additional isoparms just outside the isoparms created in step 3.

5. Add two additional isoparms that run across the surface as shown in the second image in Figure 3.49.

FIGURE 3.49
Four isoparms are added to the birail surface that runs along the length, and four isoparms are added that run across the surface. These will be used as guides for adding curves to the surface.

6. With the birail surface selected, choose Modify ➤ Make Live to make the surface live. You'll see the wireframe lines now appear green on the surface.

7. Enable Grid Snapping and choose Create ➤ CV Curve Tool ➤ Options. In the options, make sure the Curve is set to Linear.

8. With Grid Snapping enabled, the points of the curve will be snapped to the isoparms on the surface. Follow the guide in Figure 3.50 to add points to the curve.

9. Finish the curve by clicking one more time at the point where you started the curve. When you are finished, press the Enter key.

10. Repeat steps 8 and 9 to add another curve that surrounds the first. Make sure you add the same number of points in the same order and that you close the curve when finished.

FIGURE 3.50
Two linear curves are drawn on the live birail surface using the added isoparms as a guide. When Grid Snapping is enabled, a new curve will snap to the isoparms of a live surface.

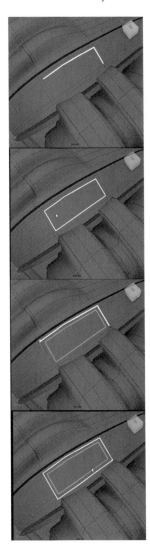

11. To select curves on a surface, turn off Surface Selection in the Selection Mask Options, and select the curves drawn on the surface. Select the outside curve and then Shift+click the inside curve.

12. Choose Surface ➢ Loft ➢ Options. In the options, make sure the Degree of the loft is Cubic and the Number Of Spans is set to **2**. Click Loft to make the loft.

13. When the loft is created, right-click on it and choose Hulls. Select the three central hulls of the loft. Switch to the Move tool. In the options, set the Axis to Normals Average and pull the hull up to create a raised surface (see Figure 3.51).

14. To make the birail surface "unlive," you can select it in the Outliner and choose Modify ➢ Live (alternatively you can select the shape node of the birail surface in the Outliner).

FIGURE 3.51
The hulls of the loft are selected and moved upward to create surface detail.

CONSTRUCTION HISTORY

As long as the Construction History option for the loft surface is enabled, you can experiment with the position of the loft by selecting the curves on the surface and moving them around using the Move tool.

Project Curves on the Surface

You can project a curve onto the surface as a way of devising interesting shapes. These shapes can be used for creating details, such as parting lines and seams on the surface.

1. Switch to the side view and turn on Grid Snapping.

2. Choose Create ➤ CV Curve Tool ➤ Options. In the options, make sure the Curve Degree is set to Linear.

3. Draw a simple square off to the side of the helmet using the grid as a guide. Use five points to make a complete square.

4. With the square curve selected, choose Edit Curves ➤ Open/Close Curves. This will close the curve so it is a loop.

5. Choose Modify ➤ Center Pivot to center the pivot on the square.

6. Turn off Grid Snapping, and switch to the perspective view. Use the Move tool to position the square on the helmet's left, as shown in Figure 3.52

7. Switch back to the side view. Make sure the square curve is overlapping the helmetRear surface. Select the curve and the helmetRear surface. Choose Edit NURBS ➤ Project Curve On Surface ➤ Options. In the options, choose Edit ➤ Reset to reset the settings. You want to project the curve from the active view, which is currently the side-view camera. Click Project to make the projection.

FIGURE 3.52
A square-shaped curve is created and positioned to the helmet's left side.

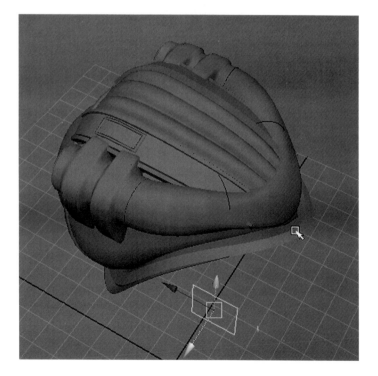

8. Switch to the perspective view again. You'll see the curve projected onto the back part of the helmet; it wraps around the surface. Any change you make to the square curve will change the shape of the curve on the surface.

9. Select the square projection curve and use the Move, Rotate, and Scale tools to reposition the curve until the projection resembles something like the projection shown in Figure 3.53.

FIGURE 3.53
The projected square curve is moved, scaled, and rotated. This changes the shape of the projected curve on the surface.

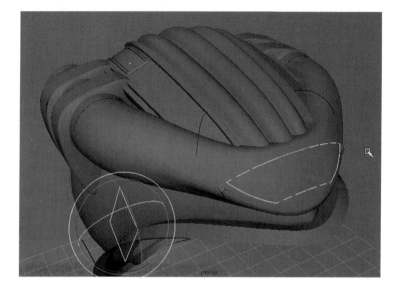

To create a raised panel from the curve on the surface, you'll trim the surface. You'll need two copies of the surface: one that has the hole and the other that has the raised portion of the surface.

10. Select the helmetRear surface, and choose Edit ➤ Duplicate Special ➤ Options. In the options, choose Duplicate Input Connections. This creates a duplicate of the surface with the same projected curve on the surface. Click Duplicate to make the copy.

11. In the perspective view, move the duplicate surface in X about -5 units. There is still a history connection between the curve and the curve on the surface for both copies of the surface, so try not to move the duplicate along any axis but X.

12. Select the original surface and choose Edit NURBS ➤ Trim Tool. Use the Trim tool to place markers in a few positions on the surface; don't place any markers in the area defined by the projected curve. Press the Enter key to make the trim.

13. Repeat step 12 for the duplicate surface; however, place the trim markers only in the area defined by the projected curve. You should be left with just the piece defined by the projected curve (Figure 3.54).

FIGURE 3.54
Both the original helmetRear and the helmetRear1 surfaces are trimmed based on the projected curve. However, one trim leaves a hole in the surface, and the other leaves the surface defined by the projected curve.

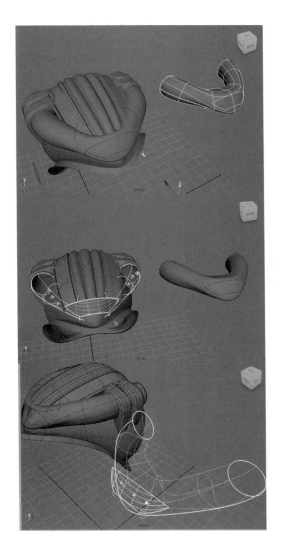

14. Select both copies of the helmetRear surfaces, and choose Edit ➢ Delete By Type ➢ History. Now you can move the surfaces without worrying about changing the shape of the opening. Change the name of helmetRear1to **panelTop**.

15. Center the pivot of panelTop. Set its Translate X back to **0,** and position it just above the opening in the helmetRear surface. Scale it down just slightly (see Figure 3.55).

16. To fill the gaps between the opening and the top of the panel, right-click on the original surface and choose Trim Edge. Select the edge, right-click over the panel top, and choose Trim Edge, and then Shift+click the second trim edge. You can then use a freeform fillet to close the gap (Edit NURBS ➢ Surface Fillet ➢ Freeform Fillet). Repeat this step for all of the edges around the panel (see Figure 3.56).

FIGURE 3.55
The panelTop surface is moved above the opening in the helmetRear surface and scaled down slightly.

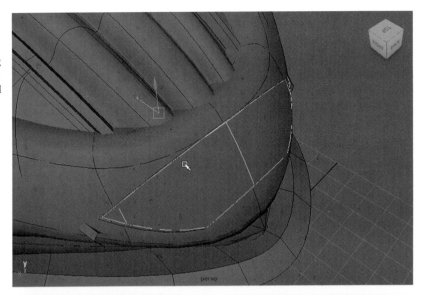

FIGURE 3.56
Freeform fillet surfaces are created to fill the gaps between the four sides of the panelTop and the opening in the helmetRear surface.

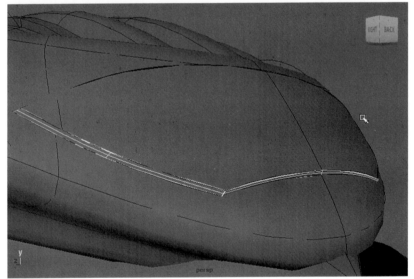

17. Take few minutes to rename the surfaces in the Outliner with descriptive names. Group the surfaces accordingly and delete history. Delete all of the curves created while modeling. Figure 3.57 shows how I have organized the surfaces in my version of the scene.

18. Save the scene as **helmet_v08.ma**. To see a version of the helmet to this point, open the helmet_v08.ma scene from the chapter3\scenes directory on the DVD.

FIGURE 3.57

The surfaces
have been renamed
and organized
using grouping.
History is deleted,
and the curves
are removed.

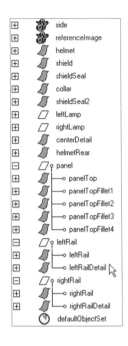

IMPORTING CURVES

You can create curves in Adobe Illustrator and import them into Maya for use as projections on the model. For best results, save the curves in Illustrator 8 format. In Maya, choose File ➤ Import ➤ Options, and choose Adobe Illustrator format to bring the curves into Maya. This is a great way to create even more intricate detailing on a surface.

Revolve

A *revolve* sweeps a surface generated by a curve around an axis. It's a very versatile modeling technique. In this section, you'll add a sensor to the lamp housing using a revolve operation.

1. Continue with the scene from the previous section or open the helmet_v08.ma scene from the chapter3\scenes directory on the DVD.

2. Switch to a front view and turn on Grid Snapping. Choose Create ➤ CV Curve Tool ➤ Options. In the options, set the Curve Degree to Linear.

You'll start by roughing out the curve on the grid. Using Grid Snapping is a good way to ensure that lines are straight. After the points of the curve are laid out on the grid, you'll turn Grid Snapping off and change their positions to refine the shape of the curve.

3. Starting from the center line, create a curve that looks like a blocky Y shape. Use Figure 3.58 as a reference. In total, click 14 times to create a 14-point curve. Press the Enter key when you have finished adding points to the curve.

4. Select the curve and choose Modify ➤ Center Pivot. This brings the pivot point up from the origin. Select the Move tool, hold the d key, and move the pivot so it snaps to the center line of the grid.

FIGURE 3.58
A revolve surface
is created from
a linear curve.
By adjusting the
points of the curve,
the revolve surface
is shaped into a
mechanical scope.

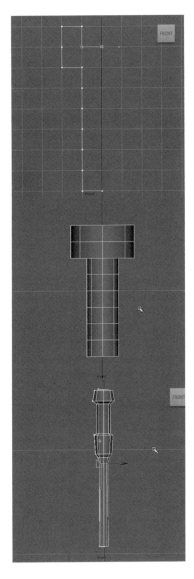

5. Turn off Grid Snapping and use the Scale tool to scale the curve down to **0.15** in X, Y, and Z.

6. With the curve selected, choose Surfaces ➢ Revolve. By default, the revolve will sweep around the Y axis.

7. Zoom in on the surface. Turn off Surface Selection in the Selection Mask Options on the status line. Select the curve and switch to component mode.

8. Use the Move tool to reposition the CVs of the Curve tool. You want to create a long, thin, mechanical-looking scope.

9. When you have a basic shape that you like, rename the surface **Sensor**. Select the revolved surface, center its pivot, and use the Move, Scale, and Rotate tools to position it next to the lamp on the spacesuit's left side; use Figure 3.59 as a guide.

10. Once you have it roughly in position, you can continue to edit the position of points on the original curve to change its shape. It may be easier to split the Maya interface into two windows. Use a front-view camera to make changes in the curve, and use the perspective camera to see the results of the changes.

11. Make the sensor extend a fair way toward the back of the helmet, as shown in Figure 3.60.

FIGURE 3.59
The sensor is moved, scaled, and rotated to fit next to the lamp on the left side of the helmet.

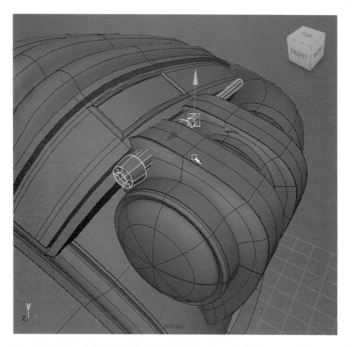

FIGURE 3.60
By editing the points of the original revolved curve, you can continue to change the shape of the sensor after it has been positioned.

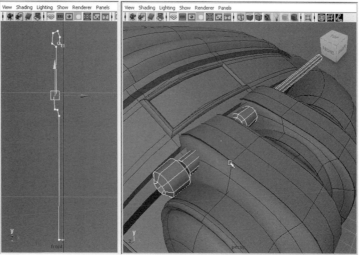

Using the Bend Deformer

Deformers are found under the Animation menu set, but they can be very useful as modeling tools. In this section, you'll add a slight bend to the end of the sensor created in the previous section. Small bends and curves created in mechanical parts can add a lot of style and realism to your model.

1. Select the sensor created in the previous section. Select an isoparm near the end of the tube, and Shift+click an isoparm about halfway down the back of the sensor.

2. To create a smooth bend at the end of the sensor, add additional isoparms to the surface. Choose Edit NURBS ➤ Insert Isoparms ➤ Options. In the options, set the Location to Between Selection and the Number Of Isoparms To Insert to **6**. You should see six new isoparms added to the back of the sensor (see Figure 3.61).

FIGURE 3.61
Six new isoparms are added at the back of the sensor.

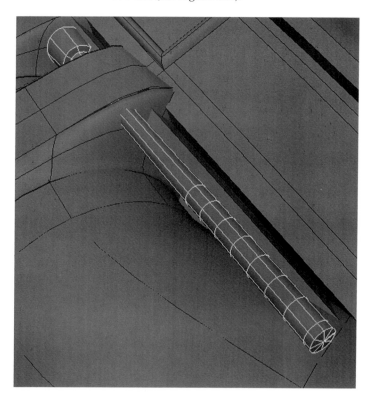

3. Switch to the Animation menu set. Select the sensor and choose Create Deformers ➤ Nonlinear ➤ Bend (see Figure 3.62). Select the bend1Handle in the Outliner. In the Channel Box, select the Bend1 node under INPUTS, and set the Curvature to **1**.

4. To restrict the bend to the back portion of the sensor, set High Bound to **0**. The Bounds determine the length of the bend deform.

5. In the Channel Box, set Rotate Z to **-90** so the sensor bends downward. Use the Move tool to move the Bend tool back along its Y axis (see Figure 3.63).

6. Select the sensor and choose Edit ➤ Delete By Type ➤ History to make the changes to the sensor permanent. This removes the bend handle from the scene.

7. Group all of the objects in the scene, and name the group **Helmet**. Delete history and any unused curves and surfaces.

8. Save the scene as **helmet_v09.ma**. To see a version of the scene up to this point, open the helmet_v09.ma scene from the chapter3\scenes directory on the DVD.

FIGURE 3.62

The bend deformer is applied to the sensor.

FIGURE 3.63

Using the settings in the Channel Box, edit the bend deformer to add a slight bend at the end of the sensor.

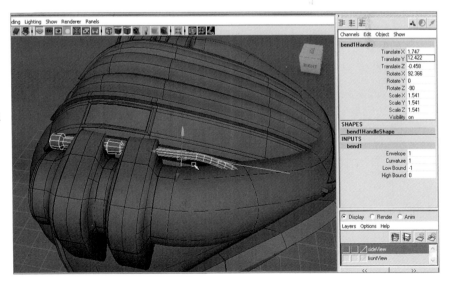

MIRROR OBJECTS

When you've completed changes on one side of the model, you can mirror them to the other side. Create a group for the parts you want to mirror; by default the pivot for the new group will be at the center of the grid. Select the group and choose Edit ➤ Duplicate Special. Set Scale X of the duplicate to **-1**. When you create the duplicate, you can freeze transformations on the objects and ungroup them if you like.

Creating Realism

The key to realistic modeling is in the details. Real, manufactured objects have seams, bolts, screws, weather stripping, and rubber gaskets. In any place two surfaces meet, try to create a believable transition using a surface fillet or a loft. By building from curves created on the surface, you can quickly add believable detail. In production, sometimes these details are modeled as part of the surface; sometimes they are created as part of the texture. In this example the details are modeled for the purpose of instruction.

Think about the possible use of the objects you model. In the case of the helmet, think about what parts of the object need to form a tight seal to protect the wearer from the harsh environment of space. Also think about which parts of the helmet may need to be manipulated by a person wearing heavy gloves. Think about things like servos and handles for the mechanical parts on the helmet.

Figures 3.64, 3.65, and 3.66 show the completed NURBS helmet from different views. Open the NURBShelmet.ma scene from the chapter3\scene directory on the DVD, and examine the model to see if you can figure out the techniques that were used to make it. All of the techniques used are just variations of the ones described in this section.

FIGURE 3.64
The completed NURBS helmet. Details were created using a combination of techniques described in the chapter.

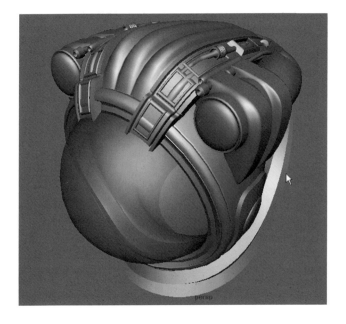

Figure 3.65
The completed
NURBS helmet
from the top.

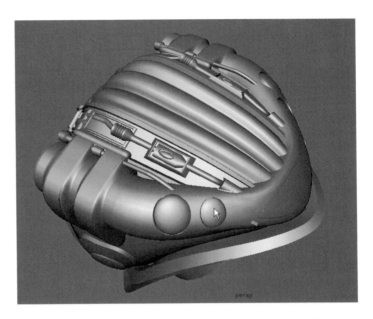

Figure 3.66
The completed
NURBS helmet
from the side.

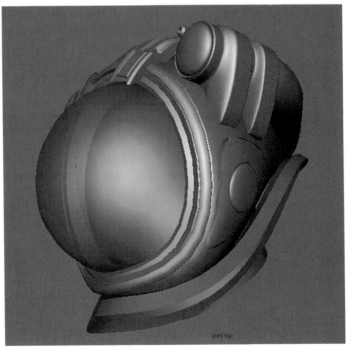

NURBS Tessellation

While working with NURBS surfaces, you may see small gaps or areas around the trim edge that do not precisely follow the curve. This is due to the settings found in the NURBS Display section of the surface's Attribute Editor. These settings adjust how the NURBS surfaces appear while working in Maya. They do not necessarily represent how the object will look when rendered. By increasing the precision of the NURBS surface display, you may find that the performance of Maya on your machine suffers. It depends on the amount of RAM and your machine's processor speed. The main thing to keep in mind is that changing these settings will not affect how the surface looks when rendered.

To preview how the surface will look in the render, you can enable Display Render Tessellation in the Tessellation rollout of the surface's Attribute Editor. A wireframe will appear on the surface, which represents the arrangement of triangles that will be used when the surface is converted to polygons by the renderer (note that the surface will remain as NURBS in the scene when you render).

Using the Tessellation settings found in the Simple or Advanced Tessellation Options, you can determine how the surface will look when rendered (see Figure 3.67). Keep in mind that increasing the precision of the tessellation will increase your render time. You can adjust the settings based on how close an object is to the rendering camera. The triangle count gives you precise numeric feedback on how many triangles a surface will contain based on its tessellation settings. Take a look at the NURBSdisplay.ma scene in the chapter3\scenes directory on the DVD.

The Advanced Tessellation settings give you even more control over how the object will be tessellated. Keep in mind that Advanced is not always better or appropriate. In some circumstances you may get better results using Simple Tessellation rather than Advanced. It depends on the model and the scene. If you're having problems with the scene, you can experiment using the two methods.

FIGURE 3.67
You can change the accuracy of the NURBS surface display and change the quality of the render tessellation in the Attribute Editor for the NURBS shape node. Three identical trimmed NURBS spheres have different settings applied.

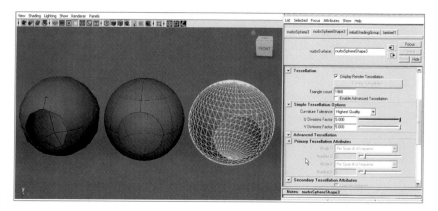

The Bottom Line

Use image planes.   Image planes can be used to position images for use as a modeling guide.

  Master it   Create image planes for side, front, and top views for use as a model guide.

Apply NURBS curves and surfaces.   NURBS surfaces are created by lofting a surface across a series of curves. The curve and surface degree and parameterization affect the shape of the resulting surface.

  Master it   What is the difference between a 1-degree (linear) surface, a 3-degree (cubic) surface, and a 5-degree surface?

Model with NURBS surfaces.   A variety of tools and techniques can be used to model surfaces with NURBS. Hard-surface/mechanical objects are well-suited subjects for NURBS surfaces.

  Master it   Create a NURBS model of a common object you own such as a cell phone, a computer monitor, or a particle accelerator.

Create realistic surfaces.   Manufactured objects usually have visible seams and parting lines that reveal how they are put together. Adding these details to your surfaces greatly increases the realism of your objects.

  Master it   Examine a manufactured object closely, and pay attention to the seams and parting lines. Look at weather stripping on the windows of vehicles; look at the trim around tail lights and openings in the surface. Look at the panels on the underside of electronic products such as a cell phone. Try to imitate these in your models even if the object does not exist in the real world.

Adjust NURBS render tessellation.   You can change how the rendering engine converts a NURBS surface into triangles at render time by adjusting the tessellation of the objects. This can impact render times and increase efficiency in heavy scenes.

  Master it   Test the tessellation settings on a row of NURBS columns. Compare render times and image quality using different tessellation settings.

Chapter 4

Polygon and Subdivision Surface Modeling

Maya's Polygon Modeling tool set has advanced significantly within the last two versions of the software. The addition of Smooth Mesh Polygon tools (also known as Smooth Mesh Preview Polygon tools) allows you to quickly and easily create and edit complex organic surfaces. The improvements to the Select and Move tools, such as the Soft Select and Reflection options, make modeling with polygons much more intuitive and sculptural.

There's a lot you can do with polygons in Maya. In this chapter, you'll use a wide range of tools and techniques to construct a character wearing a futuristic space suit. You'll also learn how to use polygons in conjunction with NURBS, Paint Effects, and subdivision surfaces.

In this chapter, you will learn to:

- ◆ Understand polygon geometry
- ◆ Work with smooth mesh polygons
- ◆ Model using deformers
- ◆ Combine meshes
- ◆ Use bevel tools
- ◆ Model polygons with Paint Effects
- ◆ Convert NURBS surfaces to polygons
- ◆ Use Booleans
- ◆ Sculpt polygons using Artisan
- ◆ Model a human head
- ◆ Create a character
- ◆ Use subdivision surfaces

Understanding Polygon Geometry

Polygon geometry refers to a surface made up of polygon faces that share edges and vertices. A polygon face is a geometric shape consisting of three or more edges. Vertices are points along the edges of polygon faces, usually at the intersection of two or more edges.

Polygons are simpler to understand and work with than NURBS surfaces. Polygon geometry is not restricted to four-sided patches as are NURBS surfaces. The many tools available allow you to make more arbitrary changes (such as splitting, removing, and extruding) to polygon faces. They are also versatile. They can be used to create hard-surface models, such as vehicles, armor, and other mechanical objects, as well as organic surfaces, such as characters, creatures, and other natural objects.

Modeling polygons generally means pushing and pulling the components (vertices, edges, and faces) of the geometry as well as extruding surfaces and edges, welding pieces together, and bridging gaps and holes with polygon faces.

In this chapter, you'll continue to use the space suit design as an example as you tour the various polygon modeling tools and techniques Maya has to offer. The chapter focuses on how various polygon tools and techniques can be used to create the model. If you were to create this model in the real world, you would rough out the major forms of the character and add detail only after the basic shapes of the model were complete. Since this chapter is organized by all the tools available, the order in which the model is created is a little more random. However, after you work through the chapter, you should understand the many ways the tools can be used.

Working with Smooth Mesh Polygons

Maya 2009 has enhanced the Smooth Mesh Polygon tools first introduced in Maya 2008. When you perform a standard Smooth operation on polygon geometry, the geometry is subdivided. Each level of subdivision quadruples the number of polygon faces in the geometry and rounds the edges of the geometry. This also increases the number of polygon vertices available for manipulation when shaping the geometry (Figure 4.1).

FIGURE 4.1
A polygon cube is
smoothed twice.
Each smoothing
operation quadru-
ples the number of
faces. increasing
the number of ver-
tices available for
modeling.

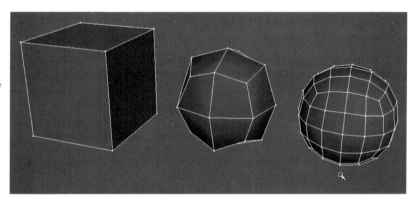

Smooth mesh polygons allow you to preview the geometry as if it has been subdivided. What's more, the number of vertices available for manipulation remains the same as the original geometry, which simplifies the modeling process. To create a smooth mesh polygon, select the polygon geometry and press the 3 key. To return to the original polygon mesh, press the 1 key. To see a wireframe of the original mesh overlaid on the smooth mesh preview, press the 2 key (Figure 4.2).

Smooth mesh polygons are also referred to as smooth mesh preview polygons (or just smooth mesh preview) in the Maya interface and in this chapter, because of the fact that you're essentially previewing the smooth polygons rather than actually subdividing the mesh.

FIGURE 4.2
This image shows the original cube, the smooth mesh preview with wireframe, and the smooth mesh preview.

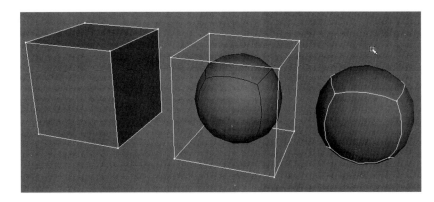

When you render polygon geometry as smooth mesh preview using mental ray, the geometry appears smoothed in the render without the need to convert the smooth mesh to standard polygons or change it in any way. This makes modeling and rendering smooth and organic geometry with polygons much easier than in previous versions of Maya.

Using Smooth Mesh Polygons

In this section, you'll create the basic shape of the torso for the space suit character introduced in Chapter 3 using smooth mesh polygon geometry.

1. Open the `torso_v01.ma` scene from the `chapter4\scenes` directory on the DVD.

In this scene, you'll see the NURBS helmet created in Chapter 3 as well as the image planes that display the reference images. If the reference images are not displaying correctly, select each image plane, open its Attribute Editor, and click the folder icon next to the Image Name field. The reference images are found in the `source images` subdirectory of the `Chapter 4` folder on the DVD.

To make the torso, you'll use a technique known as *box modeling*. This uses the polygon modeling tools to shape a basic cube into a more complex object.

2. Choose Create ➤ Polygon Primitives ➤ Cube. Switch to a side view and turn on X-Ray shaded mode (Shading ➤ X-Ray) so you can see the reference images through the geometry.

3. Select the cube and name it **torso**. Position and scale the torso so it roughly matches the position of the torso in the side view. Set the channels to:

Translate X: **0**

Translate Y: **6.375**

Translate Z: **-1.2**

Scale X: **8.189**

Scale Y: **6.962**

Scale Z: **6.752**

4. In the Channel Box, click the polyCube1 heading in the INPUTS section. Under the poly-Cube1 settings, set Subdivisions Width to **4** and Subdivisions Height and Depth to **3**, as shown in Figure 4.3.

5. With the torso selected, press the 3 key to switch to smooth mesh preview. The edges of the cube become rounded.

SMOOTH MESH PREVIEW SETTINGS

By default smooth mesh preview displays the smoothing at two divisions, as if you had applied a smoothing operation to the geometry twice. You can change the display settings on a particular piece of polygon geometry by selecting the object and choosing Display ➢ Polygons ➢ Custom Polygon Display. At the bottom of the options you'll find the Smooth Mesh Preview settings. Changing the value of the Division Levels slider sets the number of subdivisions for the smooth mesh preview. You can also enable the Show Subdivisions option to see the subdivisions on the preview displayed as dotted lines. The options are applied to the selected object when you click the Apply button. Be aware that a high Division Levels setting slows down performance of playback in Maya scenes.

Additional controls are available under the Extra Controls rollout. Lowering the Continuity slider decreases the roundness of the edges on the preview. You can also choose to smooth the UV Texture coordinates and preserve Hard Edges and Geometry Borders.

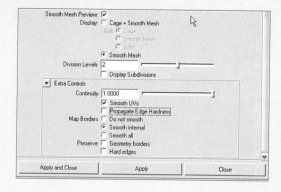

FIGURE 4.3

Place a polygon cube roughly in the position of the torso.

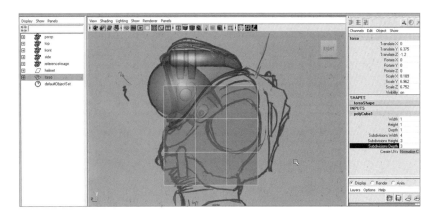

Selecting Components

The Selection and Move tools have been upgraded in Maya 2009 to make selecting and moving geometry components (vertices, edges, and faces) easier. Many of these options also work with NURBS surfaces and curves.

1. Switch to the perspective view and turn off X-Ray Shading so you can see the geometry more clearly.

2. Choose the Select tool (hot key = q) and open the Tool Options box.

3. Right-click on the torso and choose Face from the marking menu. As you hover the cursor over the torso, the face nearest the cursor is highlighted in red. If you switch to edge or vertex selection, the edges or vertices become highlighted as you hover over them.

4. Right-click on the torso and choose Multi from the marking menu. In this mode you can select any combination of faces, edges, or vertices (see Figure 4.4).

5. Select one of the vertices on the side of the torso. In the options for the Select tool, enable Soft Select. The wireframe display of the torso becomes colored. The coloring indicates the radius of the soft selection.

6. In the options for the Select tool, look at the Soft Selection section.

The colored ramp sets the coloring for the Soft Select option. By default components that are 100 percent selected are colored yellow. As the strength of the selection diminishes, the color coding of the components moves to orange and then to black. Areas beyond the black part of the radius are not selected.

7. Increase Falloff Radius to **8**. The radius of the color coding increases on the torso model.

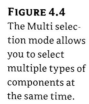

FIGURE 4.4
The Multi selection mode allows you to select multiple types of components at the same time.

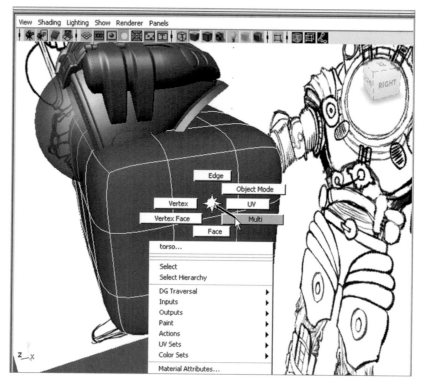

You can set Falloff Mode to Surface, Volume, or Global. In surface mode, the soft select radius selects components based on their position on the surface. If you selected a vertex on the upper lip of a character with a closed mouth, the vertices on the lower lip would not be selected, even if they are close to the center of the falloff radius in world space.

When you set Falloff Mode to Volume, any vertex within the falloff radius is selected. So if you select a vertex on the upper lip of the same character, vertices on the lower lip would also be selected if they fall within the falloff radius. Global mode works very similarly to Volume (Figure 4.5).

You can further refine the falloff using Falloff Curve. By adding points to the curve and changing their position, you can create selection shapes. A number of preset curve shapes are available. You can access these by clicking on any of the preset icons below Falloff Curve.

8. In the Reflection Settings section, enable Reflection. Reflection mirrors the selection of components across a specified axis. By default this is set to the X axis.

The Preserve Seam option protects components that lie along the center of the reflection axis from being moved away from the center. This ensures that the symmetry of the model is preserved.

9. Scroll to the top of the Select Tool Options box. Under Common Selection Options, you can choose to use Marquee selection or Drag selection.

FIGURE 4.5
Falloff Mode
determines how
the falloff radius
is applied to the
components of a
surface.

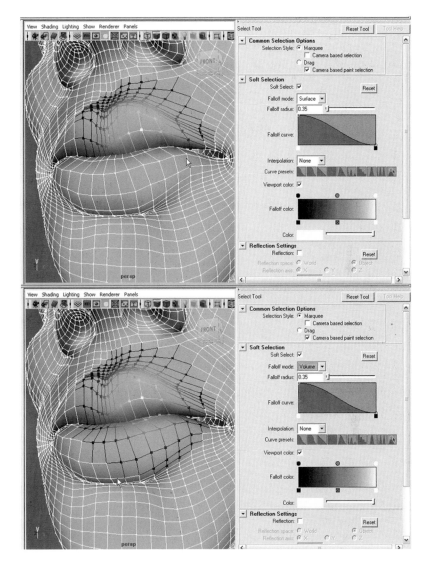

The Marquee selection option lets you select a component by dragging a rectangular selection box over the components you want to select.

In drag mode you can paint over the surface to select the components you want. This works similarly to the Paint Selection tool.

Both Marquee selection and Drag selection have a Camera Based Selection option. When this is on, only the components facing the current viewing camera will be selected. When this option is off, any components within the selected area will be selected, including those on the opposite side of the model.

Moving Components

Shaping geometry often involves using the Move tool to reposition the components of the surface. The same selection options are available for the Move tool. In fact, the same settings that you create for the Selection tool are automatically applied to the Move tool.

1. Turn X-Ray shaded mode back on and switch to a side view of the model. Open the options for the Move tool.

2. Set Move Axis to Local. Set Selection Style to Marquee mode and turn off Camera Based Selection. Enable Soft Select. Set Falloff Mode to Surface and Falloff Radius to **3**. Enable Reflection; the default Reflection setting should work.

3. From the side view, select vertices and use the Move tool to reposition the vertices of the torso to roughly match the sketch. The torso surface will serve as frame for the upper part of the space suit. At this time you want to keep the amount of detail fairly low.

4. Adjust the selection settings as you work. Align the four corners of one of the faces toward the rear with the arm socket opening in the sketch, as shown in Figure 4.6.

FIGURE 4.6
Use the Move tool to position the vertices of the torso to match the sketches on the image planes.

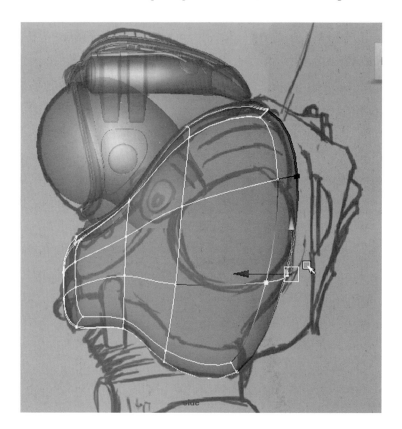

SMOOTH MESH VERTEX DISPLAY

As you select vertices using the Move tool, you'll notice that the handle of the Move tool is offset from the selected vertices. If you find this confusing, press the 2 key to see a wireframe cage of the original mesh. Then you'll see the actual positions of the vertices on the unsmoothed version of the surface.

---

5. Switch to the front view, and continue to shape the cube to roughly match the drawing. Remember, your goal is to create a rough shape at this point. Most of the details will be added as additional sections of armor later on (see Figure 4.7).

FIGURE 4.7
Shape the torso from the front view using the Move tool.

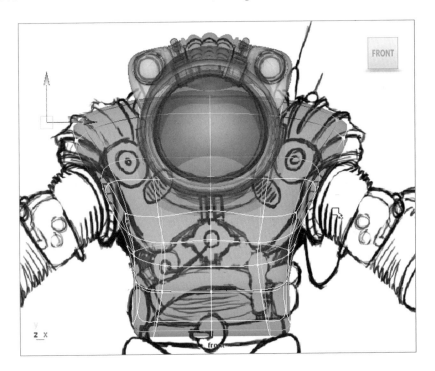

Since you've already shaped much of the profile in the side view, restrict the changes you make in the front view to movements along the X axis.

6. Finally, switch to the perspective view and shape the torso further. This requires some imagination and artistic judgment as to how the shape of the space suit looks in perspective. It may be easier to do this if you turn off X-Ray mode and set the helmet display layer to Template mode.

Don't forget to refer to the original sketch; if you switch to the referenceImage camera, you'll see the sketch on an image plane. Also remember to adjust your Move tool selection settings as needed. Always keep things as simple as possible and avoid getting lost in the details.

7. Save the scene as **torso_v02.ma**. To see a version of the scene to this point, open the torso_v02.ma scene from the chapter4\scenes directory on the DVD.

TWEAK MODE

You can activate tweak mode for the Move tool in the Move tool options. When this is on, any component you touch is nudged in the direction of the cursor movement. Combined with Soft Select, the Move tool feels much more like a sculpting tool and changes are more intuitive. Note that the Move tool manipulator is not displayed when tweak mode is activated.

Inserting Edge Loops

An edge loop is an unbroken ring of edges that traverses polygon geometry, similar to an isoparm in NURBS geometry. Think of the circular area around your lips and eyes. In 3D modeling, these areas are often defined using edge loops. You can insert edge loops into a model interactively using the Insert Edge Loops tool.

1. Continue with the scene from the previous section or open the torso_v02.ma scene from the chapter4\scenes directory on the DVD. Select the Polygons menu set from the upper-left menu in the interface.

2. Switch to the side view. Select the torso object, and choose Edit Mesh ➤ Insert Edge Loop Tool. The wireframe cage appears around the torso while the tool is active. Click on one of the cage's edges at the bottom row of the torso, as shown in Figure 4.8.

Edge loops are always added perpendicular to the selected edge. The loop continues to divide polygons along the path of faces until it encounters a three-sided or *n*-sided (more than four-sided) polygon (Figure 4.9).

3. Once you have inserted the edge loop, press Q to drop the tool (as long as the tool is active you can continue to insert edge loops in a surface). Select the vertices created by the new edge loop path, and continue to shape the torso using the Move tool (Figure 4.10).

BE STINGY WITH YOUR EDGE LOOPS

It's always tempting to add a lot of divisions to a surface to have more vertices available for sculpting detail. However, this often leads to a very confusing and disorganized modeling process. Keep the number of vertices in your meshes as low as possible. Add only exactly what you need, when you need it. If you are disciplined about keeping your models simple, you'll find the modeling process much easier and more enjoyable. Too many vertices too early in the process will make you feel like you're sculpting with bubblegum.

---

4. Save the scene as **torso_v03.ma**. To see a version of the scene to this point, open the torso_v03.ma scene from the chapter4\scenes directory on the DVD.

FIGURE 4.8
Add an edge loop at the base of the torso.

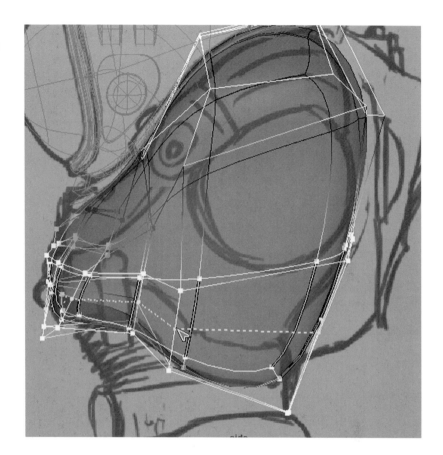

FIGURE 4.9
The Edge Loop tool divides along a path of four-sided polygons (left image). The path of the edge loop stops when a three-sided or *n*-sided polygon is encountered (right image).

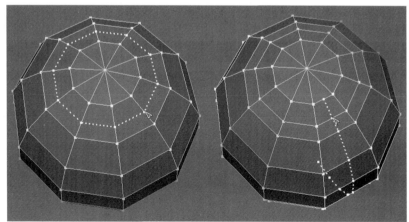

FIGURE 4.10
Shape the torso
using the new
vertices added
with the inserted
edge loop.

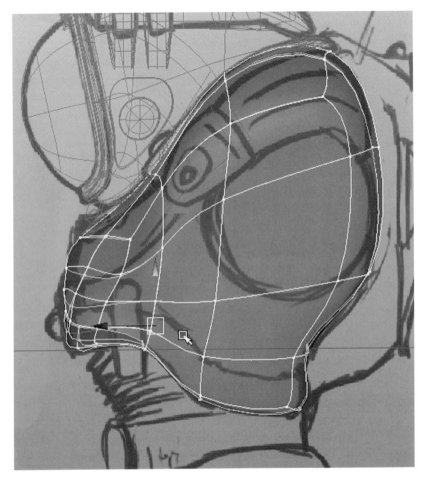

Extruding Polygons

Extruding a polygon face adds geometry to a surface by creating an offset between the extruded edge or face. New polygon faces are then automatically added to fill the gap between the extruded edge or face. In this section, you'll see a couple of the ways to use extrusions to shape the torso of the space suit.

1. Continue with the scene from the previous section or open the torso_v03.ma scene from the chapter4\scenes directory on the DVD.

2. Switch to the perspective view and turn off X-Ray Shading. Right-click on the model, and choose Face to switch to face selection mode. Select the face on the side that corresponds with the placement of the arm socket. Shift+click the matching face on the opposite side.

3. Choose Edit Mesh ➢ Extrude. A manipulator appears at the position of the new extruded face. Push inward on the blue arrow of the manipulator to push the extruded face toward the center of the torso. The extruded face on the opposite side should move into the center as well.

4. Open the Channel Box. Under the channels for the polyExtrudeFace1 node, scroll toward the bottom and set Divisions to **2**. This increases the number of polygons used to bridge the gap between the extruded face at the torso (Figure 4.11).

FIGURE 4.11
Extrude the face at the side of the torso inward. Set the divisions of the extruded faces to 2.

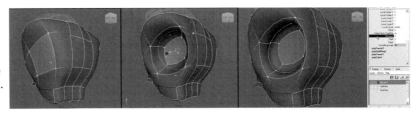

5. Select the six faces on the top of the torso that are directly beneath the NURBS helmet. It's a good idea to turn on Camera Based Selection in the Select Tool options. This prevents you from accidentally selecting faces on the opposite side of the torso. You can also turn off Soft Select.

6. Choose Edit Mesh ➢ Extrude. Click one of the scale cubes at the end of the manipulator handle (at the tip of one of the arrows). This switches the manipulator to scale mode. Drag to the left on the light blue cube at the center of the manipulator to scale down the extruded faces.

7. Set the Divisions of the polyExtrudeFace2 node to **2**. Push down on the blue arrow of the extrude manipulator to create a depression at the top of the torso (Figure 4.12).

FIGURE 4.12
Create a depression at the top of the torso using an extrude operation.

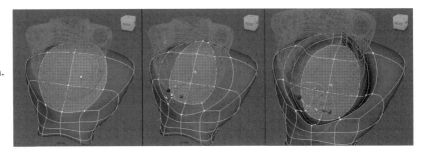

8. Turn Soft Select back on, and use the Move tool to shape the torso so it matches the design on the image planes. It may be helpful to set the HELMET display layer to Reference so you can close the gap between the neck opening and the bottom of the helmet. The base of the helmet should stay on top of the torso (Figure 4.13).

9. Save the scene as **torso_v04.ma**. To see a version of the scene to this point, open the torso_v04.ma scene from the chapter4\scenes directory on the DVD.

FIGURE 4.13
Shape the top of the torso with the HELMET layer visible. The NURBS helmet acts as a guide while modeling the torso.

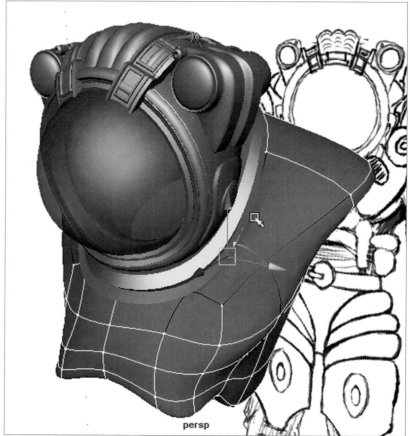

persp

Edge Creasing

One drawback to using the smooth mesh preview on polygon objects is that surfaces can look too smooth and almost pillowy. To add hardness to the edges of a smoothed object, you can use creasing.

In this section, you'll create the arm socket detail so you have a place to insert the arms into the torso (Figure 4.14).

1. Continue with the scene from the previous section or open the `torso_v04.ma` scene from the `chapter4\scenes` directory on the DVD.

2. Create a polygon sphere (Create ➢ Polygon Primitives ➢ Sphere). In the INPUTS section of the Channel Box, set Subdivisions Axis to **24** and Subdivisions Height to **12**.

3. Switch to a side view and zoom in on the sphere. Right-click on the sphere and choose Face.

FIGURE 4.14
The arm socket detail on the original sketch

4. In the Select Tool options, set Selection Style to Marquee and turn off Camera Based Selection. Select the top four rows on the sphere and delete them.

5. Select the bottom three rows on the sphere and delete them as well.

6. Switch to the perspective view. Select the sphere and name it **socket**. With socket selected, choose Edit Mesh ➢ Extrude. This extrudes all of the faces at the same time. Push in on the blue arrow of the extrude manipulator to add some thickness to the socket.

7. Use the Insert Edge Loop tool to insert edge loops on the upper side of the socket, as shown in the third image of Figure 4.15.

FIGURE 4.15
Add thickness to
the sphere using the
Extrude operation.

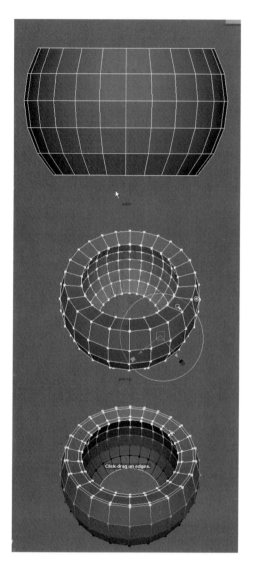

8. Rotate the view so you can clearly see the top of the socket. In the Select Tool options, set Selection Style to Drag and turn on Camera Based Paint Selection. The cursor turns into a paint brush icon. Paint a selection around the top of the socket. Select the middle row of polygon faces around the top.

If you select extra polygons by accident, you can hold the Ctrl key and paint on them to deselect them. To add to the current selection, hold the Shift key while painting the selection.

9. With the faces selected, choose Edit Mesh ➢ Extrude. Open the Channel Box for the poly-ExtrudeFace4 node. Toward the bottom, set Keep Faces Together to off.

10. Click on one of the scale cubes at the tip of the arrows on the extrude manipulator to switch to scale mode. Drag on the light blue cube at the center of the manipulator to scale down the extruded faces. Note that with Keep Faces Together turned off, each face is extruded individually.

11. With faces selected, create another extrusion (the g hot key repeats the last action). Push up on the blue manipulator to move the extruded faces upward. When you have finished creating the extrusion, press the q hot key or choose another tool to drop the Extrusion tool.

12. Select the socket object and press the 3 key to switch to smooth mesh preview. The extrusions at the top look like rounded bumps (Figure 4.16).

FIGURE 4.16
Extrude the faces upward to create detail on the socket.

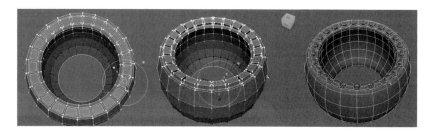

13. Use the Select tool to select each of the faces at the top of the rounded bumps. Hold the Shift key as you select each face.

14. Once you have all the faces selected, press Shift+> to expand the selection one time. The faces around each bump are now selected as well. Choose Select ➤ Convert Selection ➤ To Edges. Now the edges are selected instead of the faces.

15. Choose Edit Mesh ➤ Crease Tool. Drag to the right while holding the MMB. The edges become less round as you drag to the right, more round as you drag to the left. Set the creasing so the edges of the bumps are just slightly rounded.

16. Select the socket object and switch to edge selection mode. Double-click on the first edge loop outside the extruded bumps. Double-clicking on an edge selects the entire edge loop.

17. Use the Crease tool to create a crease on the selected edge loop.

18. Repeat steps 16 and 17 for the first edge on the inside of the socket just beyond the extruded bumps (Figure 4.17).

FIGURE 4.17
Crease the edges of the extruded bumps to create a more mechanical look.

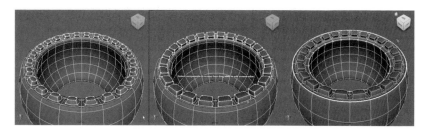

19. Select the socket and switch to the Move tool. Move, scale, and rotate the socket so it fits into the space on the side of the torso (Figure 4.18). Set these values in the Channel Box:

Translate X: **3.712**

Translate Y: **7.5**

Translate Z: **-2.706**

Rotate X: **11.832**

Rotate Y: **5.385**

Rotate Z: **-116.95**

Scale X: **1.91**

Scale Y: **1.91**

Scale Z: **1.91**

FIGURE 4.18
Position the socket
in the opening
at the side of the
torso.

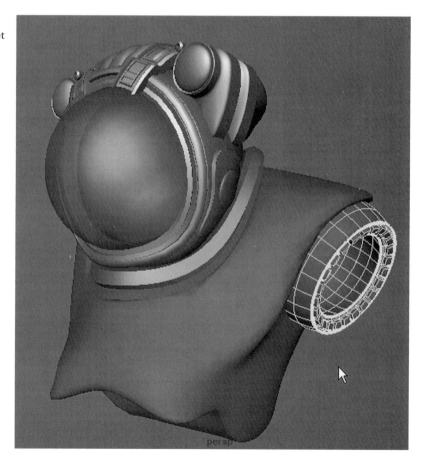

20. After placing the socket, spend a few minutes editing the position of the points on the torso so the socket fits more naturally.

21. Save the scene as **torso_v05.ma**. To see a version of the scene to this point, open the torso_v05.ma scene from the chapter4\scenes directory on the DVD.

CREASE SETS

If you create a crease for a number of selected edges that you will later readjust, you can create a crease set. A crease set saves the currently selected creased edges under a descriptive name. To create a crease set, select some edges that you want to crease or that already have a crease, and choose Edit Mesh ➤ Create Sets ➤ Create Crease Set ➤ Options. In the options, enter a descriptive name for the set. Any time you want to select the edges again to apply a crease, choose Edit Mesh ➤ Crease Sets, and choose the name of the set from the list. The edges will then be selected, and you can apply or adjust the creasing as needed.

Mirror Cut

The Mirror Cut tool creates symmetry in a model across a specified axis. The tool creates a cutting plane. Any geometry on one side of the plane is duplicated onto the other side and simultaneously merged with the original geometry.

The back side of the shoulder armor is not visible in the image (Figure 4.19), so we're going to assume that it's a mirror image of the geometry on the front side. You'll model the front side first and then use Mirror Cut for the geometry across the Z axis to make the back.

In this section, you'll model the geometry for the space suit's shoulder armor. You'll start by modeling the armor as a flat piece and then bend it into shape later on.

In the options for Mirror Cut, you can raise the Tolerance, which will help prevent extra vertices from being created along the centerline of the model. If you raise it too high, the vertices near the center may be collapsed. You may have to experiment to find the right setting.

1. Continue with the scene from the previous section or open the torso_v05.ma scene from the chapter4\scenes directory on the DVD.

2. Create a new display layer named **TORSO**. Add the torso and the socket geometry to this layer, and turn off the visibility of the layer. Turn off the visibility of the other layers as well so you have a clear view of the grid.

Use all capital letters in your display layer names so that you can add surface nodes that have the same name. Maya will not allow two nodes to share the same name; however, node names are case sensitive. By using all capital letters a layer and a node can have the same name without upsetting Maya.

FIGURE 4.19
The shoulder armor is the next object to model.

3. Create a polygon pipe by choosing Create ➢ Polygon Primitives ➢ Pipe. In the polyPipe1 node (under the INPUTS section of the Channel Box), set Height to **1**. Set Subdivisions Axis to **24** and Subdivisions Caps to **2**.

4. Switch to the top view. Choose the Move tool. In the Options box, set Selection Style to Marquee and turn off Camera Based Selection. This way you can select vertices on the top and bottom of the geometry from the top view. Turn off Soft Select and turn on Reflection. Make sure Reflection Axis is set to the X axis.

5. Right-click on the pipe and choose Vertex. Select the vertices on the outer edge of the pipe in the top half of the screen. Use the Scale and Move tools to move them away from the pipe (Reflection does not work for the Scale tool so you'll need to directly select all of the vertices you want to scale). Scale them up so the upper edge of the pipe has a shallow arc, as shown in the top image of Figure 4.20.

6. Select the vertices on the outer edge of the pipe at the bottom of the screen. Use the Move tool to shape these vertices so they are slightly closer to the center. Use the bottom image in Figure 4.20 as a reference.

7. Switch to the perspective view. Turn on Marquee and Camera Based Selection in the Select Tool options. Select the faces at the wide end of the pipe, shown in the first image in Figure 4.21.

FIGURE 4.20
Select, move, and
scale the vertices at
one end of the pipe.

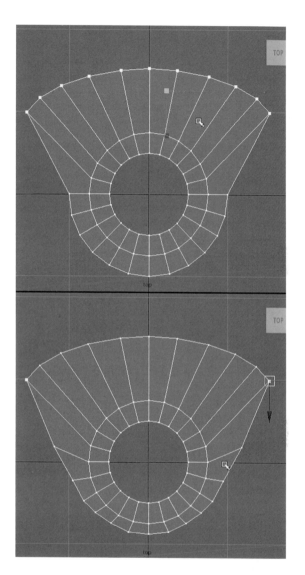

FIGURE 4.21
Extrude and scale
the faces at the long
side of the pipe.

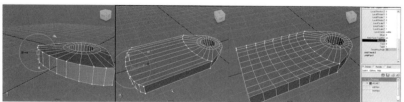

8. Choose Edit Mesh ➢ Extrude to perform an extrusion on these faces. Before you move the extrusion with the manipulator, click on the blue circle switch on the manipulator to switch to extrude in world space (second image in Figure 4.21).

9. Pull on the blue arrow of the manipulator to extend the face about three and a half units.

10. Use the blue scale handle of the extrude manipulator to flatten the arc in these extruded faces.

11. In the INPUTS section of the Channel Box, set Divisions for the polyExtrudeFace6 node to **8**.

12. Select the pipe and choose Mesh ➢ Mirror Cut. A plane appears at the center of the pipe. In the Channel Box, set the Y rotation of mirrorCutPlane1 to **0**. The pipe is now mirrored across the Z axis.

13. Set the Translate Z channel of mirrorCutPlane1 to **-3.42**. The mirrored geometry is extended.

In the Outliner, several new nodes have been created. These include the mirrorCutPlane1 and the mirroredCutMesh1 group. The pipe has been renamed polySurface1 (Figure 4.22).

FIGURE 4.22
Mirror the pipe across the Z axis using the Mirror Cut tool.

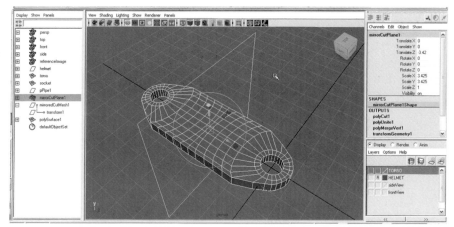

14. Select the polySurface1 node and choose Edit ➢ Delete By Type ➢ History. This removes the group nodes that were created. Select the mirrorCutPlane1 node and delete it.

15. Name the polySurface1 node **shoulderArmor1**.

16. Figure 4.23 shows some of the changes that were made to the shoulderArmor1 object to make it match the shoulder armor in the image using the Insert Edge Loop tool and the Extrude operation.

17. Save the scene as **torso_v06.ma**. To see a version of the scene to this point, open the torso_v06.ma scene from the chapter4\scenes directory on the DVD.

FIGURE 4.23
Additional changes
are made to the
shoulderArmor1
object.

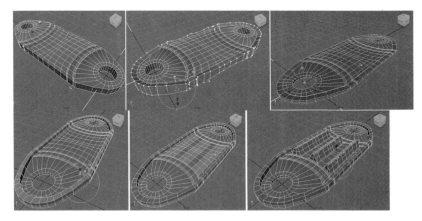

Modeling with Deformers

Deformers are used to bend, twist, and otherwise warp geometry. They are often used as Animation and Rigging tools but are quite helpful when modeling as well.

In this section, you'll use several deformers to bend the shoulder armor into a shape that matches the design in the original concept sketch.

Using a Lattice

The lattice creates a rectangular cage around a selected surface. You can move, scale, and rotate the points of the lattice to deform the selected object.

1. Continue using the scene from the previous section or open the `torso_v06.ma` scene from the `chapter4\scenes` directory on the DVD.

2. Select the shoulderArmor1 object. Choose Modify ➤ Center Pivot to place the pivot point at the center of the surface.

3. Turn on the TORSO and HELMET display layers so you can see the other parts of the model.

4. Move the shoulderArmor1 object roughly above the shoulder of the torso. Try the following settings:

   Translate X: **4.327**

   Translate Y: **10.364**

   Translate Z: **0.21**

   Scale X: **0.783**

   Scale Y: **0.177**

   Scale Z: **0.783**

The file `torso_v07.ma` in the `chapter4\scenes` directory has the armor placed above the shoulder (see Figure 4.24).

FIGURE 4.24
Position the armor
above the shoulder.

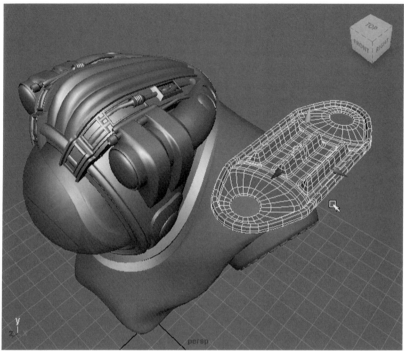

5. With the shoulderArmor1 object selected, press the 3 key to switch to smooth mesh preview.

6. Switch to the Animation menu set and choose Create Deformers ➤ Lattice.

LATTICE NODES

There are two nodes created when you make a lattice: ffd1Lattice node and ffd1Base node. The letters *ffd* stand for "free form deformer." The changes you make to the lattice are made to the ffd-1Lattice node. The changes in the shape of the ffd1Lattice cage are compared with the shape of the ffd1Base node, and the difference in the shape is transferred to the deformed object. If you need to move, scale, or rotate a lattice to match the position, size, and orientation of the object you want to deform, make sure you apply the transformations to both the ffd1Lattice and ffd1Base nodes. You can group them together and apply transformations to the group.

Before you edit the points of the lattice, you need to change the settings on the lattice so it's set up to deform the object correctly.

7. Select the ffd1Lattice node in the Outliner and open its Attribute Editor. Switch to the ffd1 tab and turn off the Local option. This makes the deformation of the object smoother.

When Local is on, changes to the lattice points affect only the object nearest the selected lattice point. When Local is off, changes made to the lattice points are applied more evenly to the entire object, resulting in a smoother deformation.

8. Switch to the ffd1LatticeShape tab. Set S Divisions to **9**, T Divisions to **2**, and U Divisions to **15**. This changes the way the lattice is divided.

9. Open the options for the Move tool. Turn off Soft Select and turn on Reflection. Set Reflection Space to Object and Reflection Axis to Z.

10. Right-click on the lattice and choose Lattice Point. (Sometimes this is tricky if you are right-clicking on both the lattice and the surface. Right-click on a corner of the lattice that has empty space behind it.)

11. Drag a marquee selection over the lattice points at the front of the lattice. Select the first six rows of lattice points, as shown in Figure 4.25. The points in the back of the lattice will be selected as well because of the Move tool Reflection settings.

FIGURE 4.25
Select the first six rows of lattice points.

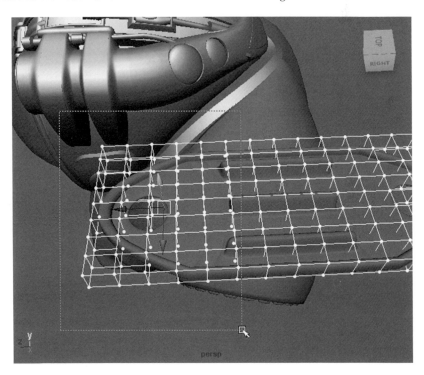

12. Switch to the Rotate tool, and drag on the red circle at the center of the tool to rotate the lattice points along the X axis. Use both the Rotate tool and the Move tool to position the lattice points so the shoulder armor has a bend at the front and back (see Figure 4.26).

FIGURE 4.26
Rotate the selected lattice points and move them into position to create a bend in the surface.

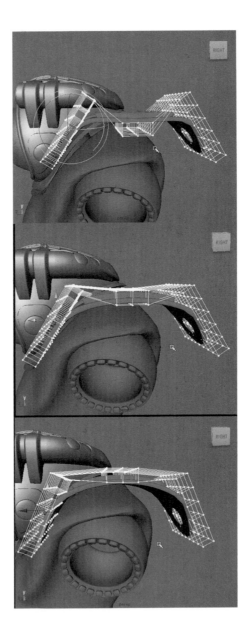

13. When you are happy with the bend created in the shoulderArmor1 object, select the object in the Outliner and choose Edit ➤ Delete By Type ➤ History. This deletes the lattice nodes and makes the changes to the object permanent.

14. Save the scene as **torso_v08.ma**. To see a version of the scene up to this point open the torso_v08.ma scene from the chapter4\scenes directory on the DVD.

Soft Modification Tool

The Soft Modification tool is a special deformer designed to help you sculpt objects. Using it is similar to activating the Soft Select option in the Move tool. In fact, the Soft Modification tool was the predecessor to the Soft Select option.

1. Continue with the scene from the previous section or open the `torso_v08.ma` scene from the `chapter4\scenes` directory on the DVD.

2. Select shoulderArmor1 in the Outliner, and select the Soft Modification icon in the toolbox. It's the icon that shows a red arrow pulling up the vertices of a blue surface.

3. When you activate the Soft Modification tool, the surface turns orange and yellow. The colors indicate the strength of the tool's falloff, similar to the color coding used by the Soft Select option on the Move tool.

When you activate the Soft Modification tool, you'll see options in the toolbox to edit the tool's falloff. However, when you edit the settings, you'll see no change in the tool that is currently active in the viewport window. What's happening is that these settings will be applied to the tool the next time you use it.

4. To edit the settings for the currently active Soft Modification tool, open the Attribute Editor and select the softMod1 tab. Set Falloff Radius to **3.3**.

5. Pull up on the green arrow of the Soft Modification tool to add a rounded warp to the surface. Use the scale handles to shape the surface of the armor. Switch to the Channel Box for the softMod1Handle and enter these settings (the result is shown in Figure 4.27):

    Translate Y: **1.526**

    Scale X: **1.513**

    Scale Z: **1.472**

6. In the toolbox, choose the Select tool. The Soft Modification handle and node disappear, and the changes are committed to the surface.

FIGURE 4.27
The Soft Modification tool adds a slight spherical bend to the surface.

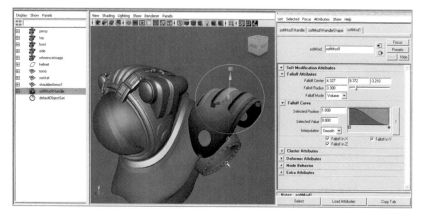

7. Select the shoulderArmor1 object, and use the Move, Rotate, and Scale tools to position it over the shoulder of the torso to match the concept sketch. Try these settings:

    Translate X: **4.327**

    Translate Y: **9**

    Translate Z: **0.775**

    Rotate X: **-3.379**

    Rotate Y: **4.324**

    Rotate Z: **-38.9**

    Scale X: **0.778**

    Scale Y: **0.176**

    Scale Z: **0.778**

8. Use the Move tool with Soft Select activated to move the vertices, and continue to shape the shoulderArmor1 object. Try using the Crease tool to add creases to some of the edges (see Figure 4.28).

9. Save the scene as **torso_v09.ma**. To see a version of the scene to this point, open torso_v09.ma from the chapter4\scenes directory on the DVD.

FIGURE 4.28
Shape the shoulderArmor1 object using the Move tool and the Crease tool.

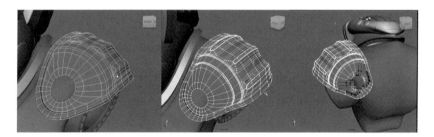

Combining Meshes

The Combine operation places two or more polygon meshes under a single transform node. Once they are combined, you can then use polygon editing tools to merge edges and vertices.

Creating the Bolt Detail

To create the large bolt detail on the shoulder armor, you'll combine several simple polygon primitives.

1. Continue with the scene from the previous section or open the torso_v09.ma scene from the chapter4\scenes directory on the DVD.

2. Choose Create ➢ Polygon Primitives ➢ Torus.

3. In the polyTorus1 node (under the INPUTS section of the Channel Box), set Subdivisions Axis to **20** and Subdivisions Height to **4**.

4. In the options for the Select tool, turn off Reflection and Soft Select. Right-click on the torus and choose Edge. Double-click on one of the edges on the top of the torus to select the edge loop.

5. Scale these edges inward, and move them down toward the center of the torus to create a beveled edge on the inner ring of the torus. See the upper-left image of Figure 4.29.

6. Use the Insert Edge Loop tool to create two new edge loops, one just outside the hole and one halfway down the top of the torus, as shown in the upper-right image of Figure 4.29.

7. Select the torus and press 3 to switch to smooth mesh preview.

8. Create a sphere and place it at the center on the torus. Rotate it 90 degrees on the Z axis, and use the Scale tool to flatten the sphere, as shown in the lower-left image of Figure 4.29.

9. To create the groove in the bolt, select two rows of faces at the top of the sphere. Extrude the selected faces once and scale the extrusion slightly inward; extrude again and push the faces of the second extrusion down into the sphere. This is shown in the lower-right image of Figure 4.29.

10. A smooth mesh preview surface can't be combined with a normal polygon object. Select the sphere and press 3 to switch to smooth mesh preview.

FIGURE 4.29
Create the bolt detail using a torus and a sphere. Create the groove in the sphere with an Extrude operation.

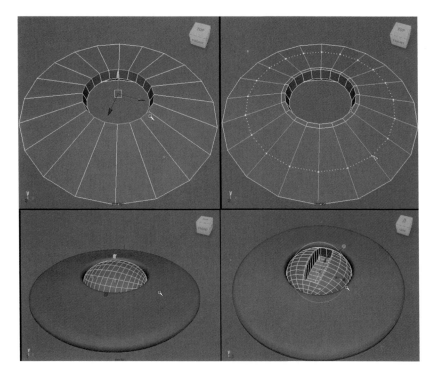

11. Shift+click the sphere and the torus, and choose Mesh ≻ Combine. The two surfaces now share the same transform and shape nodes; in the Outliner the combined surface is renamed polySurface1. Select this surface, and choose Edit ≻ Delete By Type ≻ History.

When the surfaces are combined, you'll see the original surface nodes appear as groups in the Outliner. Deleting history on the surface removes these groups. If you decide that you need to move a surface after combining it with another surface, you can select the transform node parented to these groups and use the Move tool to reposition the surface. Once you delete history, this is no longer possible.

12. Use the Crease tool to add creasing to the edges around the center ring of the torus and to the edges around the groove in the bolt. Use the Move tool to tweak the position of the edge loops (see Figure 4.30).

FIGURE 4.30
Refine the shape of the bolt by creasing and moving some of the edge loops on the surfaces.

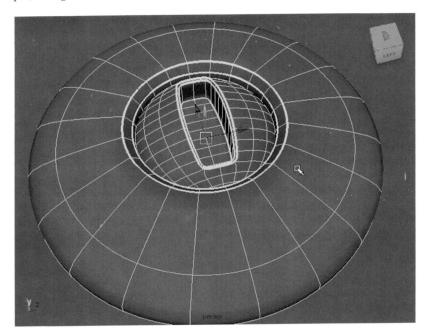

SELECTING PARTS OF COMBINED SURFACES

Double-click on a face to select all of the connected faces in a mesh. This is one way to select one of the parts of a combined mesh after you've deleted history on the object. You can then use the Move tool to reposition the selected faces.

---

13. Select the polySurface1 object, and use the Move, Rotate, and Scale tools to position it in the hole in the front of the shoulderArmor1 object. Try these settings in the Channel Box:

Translate X: **3.806**

Translate Y: **8.237**

Translate Z: **-.034**

Rotate X: **84.726**

Rotate Y: **13.881**

Rotate Z: **11.096**

Scale X: **0.291**

Scale Y: **0.291**

Scale Z: **0.291**

14. Duplicate polySurface1, and position the duplicate in the hole on the back side of the armor.

15. Shift+click the shoulderArmor1 and both polySurface objects, and choose Mesh ➢ Combine.

16. Delete history on the new combined surface, and rename it **shoulderArmor1**.

17. Select the vertices of the shoulderArmor1 object, and use the Move tool to close any gaps between the combined surfaces. Use the Crease Edges tool to create a crease in the edges around the bolts (see Figure 4.31).

18. Save the scene as **torso_v10.ma**. To see a version of the scene to this point, open the torso_v10.ma scene from the chapter4\scenes directory on the DVD.

FIGURE 4.31
Position the bolt detail and combine it with the shoulderArmor1 object.

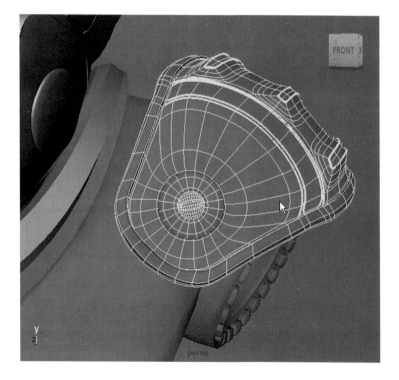

Using Bevel Plus and Bevel Edges

The Bevel Plus tool is normally used to create 3D text for logos, but it is actually very useful as a way to extrude shapes made with curves. In this section, you'll use Bevel Plus to create the design on the chest plate of the space suit.

Creating the Curves

To start the design, you'll create curve outlines that follow the pattern on the chest armor shown in Figure 4.32.

ANNOTATED GUIDES

Many of the steps used to create the space suit involve variations on the techniques already covered in the previous sections of the chapter. Because of the space limitations of the book, I can't describe every step used to create the suit in the text. However, I have included annotated files that briefly describe the steps left out of the text. Take a look at the chestarmorStart.ma file in the chapter4\ scenes directory to see how the chest armor plate was created for this section.

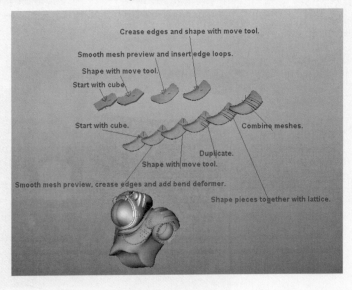

---

1. Open the chestdetail_v01.ma scene from the chapter4\scenes directory on the DVD. The chest armor has already been started in this scene using techniques described in previous parts of the chapter.

2. Switch to the front camera. Turn on Grid Snapping and make sure the grid is visible.

Figure 4.32

You'll create the curves to match the design on the chest armor in the sketch.

3. Choose Create ➢ CV Curve Tool ➢ Options. In the options, make sure Curve Degree is set to Cubic (see Figure 4.33, upper-left panel).

4. Draw an S curve as shown in the upper right of Figure 4.33. Snap each point to the grid as you go. The curve should have about 14 CVs total (resulting in 11 spans).

5. Turn Grid Snapping off, and use the Move tool to rearrange the points on the curve so that the spiral shapes are smoother (see Figure 4.33, upper-right panel).

6. Select the curve and switch to the Surface menu set. Choose Edit Curves ➢ Offset ➢ Offset Curve. This creates a second curve offset from the first.

7. Select the second curve and delete its history (Edit ➢ Delete By Type ➢ History).

8. Select the offset curve, and choose Edit Curves ➢ Rebuild Curve ➢ Options. In the options, set Number Of Spans to **11**. Click Rebuild.

9. Use the Move tool to shape the CVs of the second curve.

10. Shift+click both curves, and choose Edit Curves ➢ Attach Curves ➢ Options. In the options, set Attach Method to Blend and disable Keep Originals. Click Attach to perform the operation. One end of the two curves will be joined (see Figure 4.33, lower-left panel).

11. Select the curves, and choose Edit Curves ➢ Open/Close Curves. This closes the other end of the curves.

12. Delete history on the curve. Press the 3 key to smooth the display of the curve.

13. Use the Move tool to reposition the points of the curve to create the spiral S curve design (see Figure 4.33, lower-right panel).

14. Save the scene as **chestdetail_v02.ma**. To see a version of the scene to this point, open the chestdetail_v02.ma scene from the chapter4\scenes directory on the DVD.

FIGURE 4.33
Draw a curve in the front view (upper images). Create a duplicate curve using the Curve Offset operation (lower left). Join the duplicate to the original, and shape it with the Move tool (lower right).

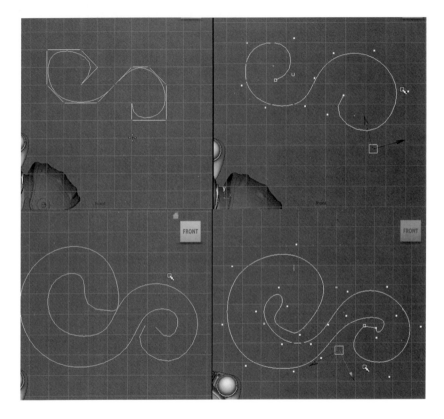

Bevel Plus

The Bevel Plus tool extrudes a curve and adds a bevel to the extrusion. The bevel can be shaped using the options in the Bevel Plus tool.

1. Continue with the scene from the previous section or open the chestdetail_v02.ma scene from the chapter4\scenes directory on the DVD.

2. Select the curve and switch to the Surfaces menu set. Choose Surfaces ➢ Bevel Plus ➢ Options.

Most of the options can be changed after the surface is created using the settings in the Attribute Editor. But you can specify the type of geometry Bevel Plus will create in the Output Options of the Options box.

3. Switch to the Output Options tab in the Bevel Plus Options dialog box (Figure 4.34). Make sure Output Geometry is set to Polygons. Tessellation Method should be set to Sampling. You can change the default Sampling Controls after you create the surface.

4. Click Bevel to make the surface.

FIGURE 4.34
The Output
Options for the
Bevel Plus tool

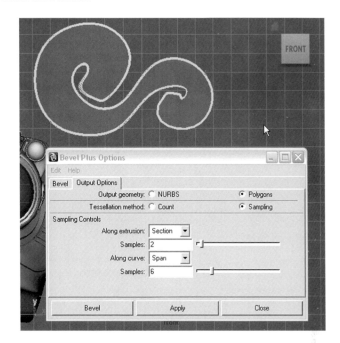

5. Switch to the perspective view, and select the bevelPolygon1 node in the Outliner. Open the Attribute Editor, and select the bevelPlus1 tab.

6. Only the front side of the surface is visible, so you can economize the geometry of the surface by turning off the Bevel At Start and Caps At Start options.

7. Set Bevel Width to **0.124**, Bevel Depth to **0.091**, and Extrude Distance to **1**.

8. Activate Bevel Inside Curves so the outside edge of the surface is defined by the shape of the curve.

9. To change the bevel style, click the arrow to the right of Outer Style Curve (or click the outerStyleCurve1 tab in the Outliner). You can choose a style from the style list. Choose Convex Out.

10. In the Polygon Output Options section in the bevelPlus1 tab, make sure Sampling is set to Extrusion Section in the top menu and Curve Span in the bottom menu. You can use these controls to edit the resolution of the surface. Set Curve Span to **9** (see Figure 4.35).

FIGURE 4.35
Edit the bevel surface using the controls in the Attribute Editor.

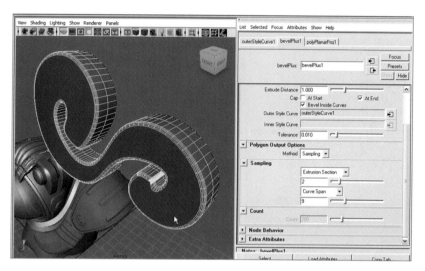

BEVEL PLUS TOOL TIPS

It's a good idea to create your own Bevel Plus presets when you establish a style that you know you'll use again. To create a preset, click the Presets button in the upper-right corner of the bevelPlus1 tab, and select Save bevelPlus Preset. Give your preset a descriptive name. When you create a similar surface using the Bevel Plus tool, you can apply the preset by clicking the Presets button. This will save you a lot of time and work.

If you are creating a number of bevels from several different curves, and some of the surfaces push out while others push in, try reversing the curve direction on the original curve used for the bevel operation. Select the curve and choose (from the Surfaces menu set) Edit Curves ➢ Reverse Curve Direction.

To create a hole in the beveled surface, select the outer curve first and then Shift+click the inner curve and apply Bevel Plus.

If surfaces are behaving strangely when you apply Bevel Plus, make sure there are no loops in the curves, and try deactivating Bevel Inside Curves to fix the problem. Sometimes it's just a matter of repositioning the CVs of the original curve.

Once you have the bevel style that you like, you can refine the shape of the object by moving the CVs of the original curve. The bevelPlus1 surface has a construction history connection to the original curve.

11. Select bevelPolygon1 in the Outliner and rename it **armorDetail1**. Center its pivot by choosing Modify ➢ Center Pivot.

12. Position the surface roughly above the chest armor plate. Try the following settings (your results may be different depending on the shape and size of your original curve):

Translate X: **-4.797**

Translate Y: **-8.926**

Translate Z: **0.782**

Rotate X: **-36.883**

Rotate Y: **19.96**

Rotate Z: **-15.679**

Scale X: **.08**

Scale Y: **.08**

Scale Z: **.08**

13. Once you have armorDetail1 roughly in position, switch to a front view and use the Move tool to shape the CVs of the original curve some more. The armorDesign1 object will update as you edit the curve.

It's a good idea to split the layout into two views while you work. Use the front view to edit the curve and the perspective view to observe the changes in the armorDetail1 surface as you work (Figure 4.36).

14. Switch to the Animation menu set. Select the armorDetail1 surface and choose Create Deformers ➢ Lattice.

FIGURE 4.36
When you edit the curve in the front view (right), you can observe changes to the armorDetail1 objects simultaneously in the perspective view (left).

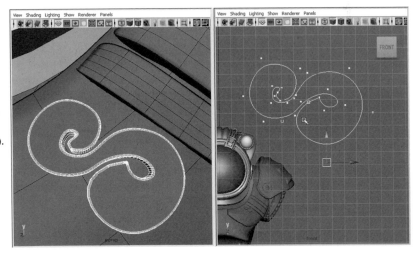

15. Set the lattice S Divisions to **5**, T Divisions to **5**, and U Divisions to **2**. In the Attribute Editor, turn off Local in the ffd1 tab.

16. Use the Move tool to edit the lattice points so the armorDetail1 object conforms to the surface of the chest armor.

17. Save the scene as **chestDetail_v03.ma**. To see a version of the scene to this point, open the chestDetail_v03.ma scene from the chapter4\scenes directory on the DVD.

KEEP YOUR HISTORY

You can build the other parts of the chest armor detail using the same techniques in this section. Don't delete history on your bevel objects until you have all the pieces in place. As long as you keep your construction history, you can easily edit the bevels using the CVs of the original curves. You may also find it easier to make the beveled objects conform to the surface of the armor if you deform all of the bevel surfaces using a single lattice. To see a finished version of the armor design, open the chestDetail_v04.ma scene from the chapter4\scenes directory on the DVD.

Bevel Edges

Adding a slight bevel to the edges of a surface makes an object look much more realistic in the final render. Perfectly sharp corners on an object make it look computer generated, which of course it is. For most manufactured objects, the smooth mesh preview is overkill. All you really need is the Bevel tool. In this section you'll create the detail at the center of the chest, as shown in Figure 4.37.

1. Open the chestDetail_v05.ma scene from the chapter4\scenes directory on the DVD. This scene has the completed chest armor plates (see Figure 4.38).

FIGURE 4.37
Create the detail at the center of the chest using the Bevel tool.

FIGURE 4.38
The armor has
been mirrored to
the opposite side
of the suit.

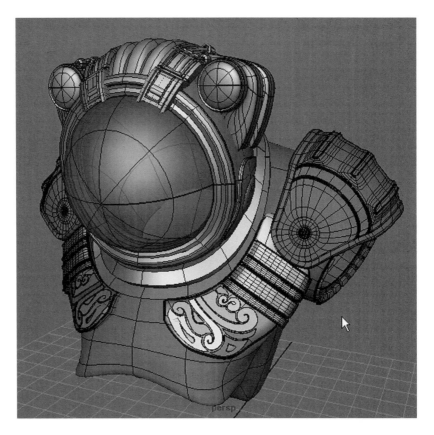

FIGURE 4.38
The armor has
been mirrored to
the opposite side
of the suit.

MIRROR OBJECTS

The shoulder armor, arm sockets, and chest armor have been mirrored to the opposite side of the model. To do this quickly, group the object so the pivot is at the center of the grid; choose Edit ➢ Duplicate Special ➢ Options. In the options, set the Scale X value to **-1**. After the object has been duplicated, you can freeze the transformations on the object and unparent it from the group.

2. Turn off the display of the TORSO and HELMET layers in the Display Layer Editor.

3. Create a polygon cube at the center of the grid (Create ➢ Polygon Primitives ➢ Cube). The cube should be scaled to **1** unit in the X, Y, and Z axes.

4. Right-click on the cube, and select Edges to switch to edge selection mode. Select the four edges that run vertically on each side of the cube.

5. Choose Edit Mesh ➤ Bevel. The edges are now beveled. Open the Channel Box and expand the polyBevel1 node in the INPUTS section. Set Offset to **0.4** to decrease the size of the bevel.

6. Rotate the view to the bottom of the cube. Select the face at the bottom and delete it.

7. Select the cube and create another bevel (Edit Mesh ➤ Bevel). When the object is selected, the bevel is applied to all the edges (see Figure 4.39, top panel).

8. Select the polyBevel2 node in the Channel Box. Set Segments to **3** and Offset to **0.3**.

Increasing the segments can make the bevel appear rounded. You can also control the roundness using the Roundness attribute.

9. Choose Create ➤ Polygon Primitives ➤ Cylinder to create a cylinder. Set the Translate Y channel to **0.344** and the Scale X, Scale Y, and Scale Z channels to **0.265**.

10. In the Channel Box under the polyCylinder1 node, type **1** in the Round Cap channel to add a rounded cap to the cylinder. Set Subdivisions Caps to **5**. Set Subdivisions Axis to **12**.

11. Set Scale Y to **0.157** and Translate Y to **0.448** (see Figure 4.39, middle panel).

12. Switch to a side view and turn on Wireframe. Right-click on the cylinder and choose Faces to switch to face selection mode.

13. Select all the faces on the rounded bottom of the cylinder and delete them (select the faces and press the Delete key).

14. In the perspective view, select each of the faces on the side of the cylinder that point toward the beveled corners of the cube, and extrude them as shown in Figure 4.39, lower panel. Use the extrude manipulator to scale the extruded faces down along their Y axis.

15. Switch to edge selection mode. Shift+click the edges that run along the top edge of each extruded section, and choose Edit Mesh ➤ Bevel to bevel these edges. In the options for the bevel node, set Offset to **0.1** (see Figure 4.39 bottom right panel).

16. Select both meshes and choose Mesh ➤ Combine. Delete history on the combined mesh, and name it **centerpiece**.

17. Move, rotate, and scale the centerpiece so it is positioned at the front of the torso, as shown in Figure 4.40. Try these settings:

    Translate X: **0**

    Translate Y: **5.667**

    Translate Z: **2.061**

    Rotate X: **80.678**

    Rotate Y: **13.293**

    Rotate Z: **42.411**

Scale X: **1**

Scale Y: **.608**

Scale Z: **1**

18. Save the scene as **chestDetail_v06.ma**. To see a version of the scene, open the chestDetail_v06.ma scene from the chapter4\scenes directory on the DVD.

FIGURE 4.39
Create the centerpiece from two polygon meshes that have been beveled and combined.

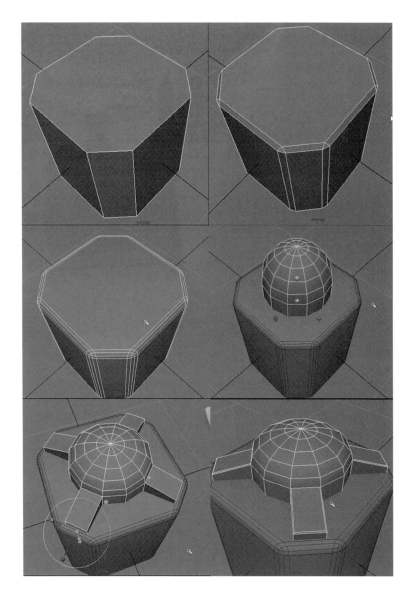

FIGURE 4.40
Place the center-
piece at the center
of the front of the
torso.

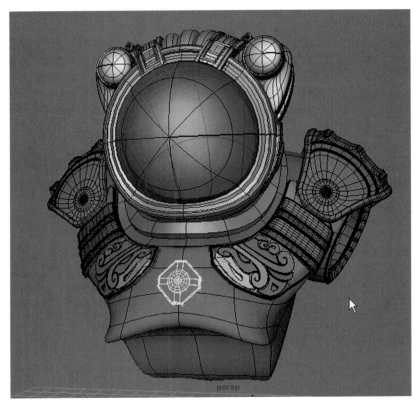

Polygon Modeling with Paint Effects

Paint Effects is most often used for creating large plants, trees, and other natural and organic objects. However Paint Effects is not limited to these types of objects by any means. You can easily adapt the procedural approach used to create Paint Effects strokes to create details, such as wires and hoses used for mechanical objects. You can convert the strokes into NURBS surfaces or polygons and incorporate them into your models.

Typically, modeling details, such as wires or hoses, involves extruding a circle along a path curve. The resulting NURBS surface can be used as is or converted to polygons.

One problem encountered with a typical extrusion is that the extruded tube can appear flattened or kinked if the extrusion path has sharp corners. When you apply a Paint Effects stroke to a curve and then convert the stroke to a NURBS surface or polygons, you'll encounter fewer problems at the corners of the curve. Figure 4.41 shows a typical NURBS extrusion at the top. The middle and bottom surfaces were created using a Paint Effects curve converted into a NURBS surface (middle) and polygons (bottom). Notice that the surface does not flatten out as it moves around the corners of the curve.

In addition, since the converted surface created from the Paint Effects stroke still has a connection to the original stroke, you can use the Paint Effects controls to add detail and even animate the surface (Figure 4.42).

FIGURE 4.41
A typical NURBS extrusion (top) produces kinks at the corners of the path. A Paint Effects stroke is converted to a NURBS surface (middle) and to polygons (bottom). There are fewer kinks in the converted surface.

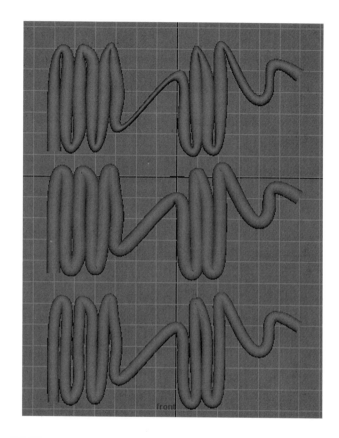

FIGURE 4.42
You can add details to the extrusion using the controls in the Paint Effects brush attributes.

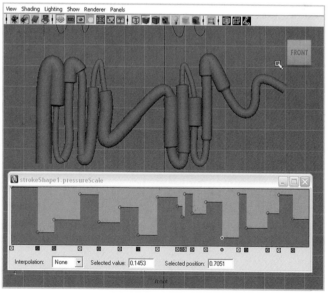

Attaching Strokes to Curves

Paint Effects is covered in detail in Chapter 8. In this section, you'll use some basic Paint Effects techniques to create some of the hoses and wires on the space suit.

1. Open the `paintEffectsHose_v01.ma` scene from the `chapter4\scenes` directory on the DVD.

This scene contains the torso and helmet as well as the armor created in previous sections. Two small connectors have been added to the space suit. These were created by extruding selected faces on a sphere and pipe primitive.

2. Switch to the front view and turn on wireframe display (hot key = 4). Choose Create ➢ CV Curve Tool. Make sure Curve Degree is set to Cubic. Create a short six-point curve that connects the two connector objects.

3. Switch to the perspective view. Select the curve and center its pivot (Modify ➢ Center Pivot). Use the Move tool to position the curve closer to the connectors on the suit.

4. Right-click on the curve and choose Control Vertex. Move the points of the curve. The curve should be shaped to look like a hose connecting parts of the suit (Figure 4.43).

5. Switch to the Rendering menu set, and choose Paint Effects ➢ Curve Utilities ➢ Attach Brush To Curves.

FIGURE 4.43
Create a curve between the two connector objects.

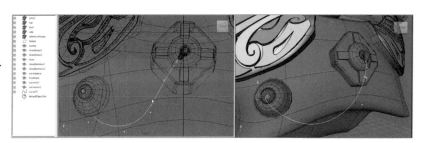

Step 5 attaches the currently selected stroke to a selected curve. Unless you have selected a stroke from the presets in the Visor, the default stroke is used for the curve. The default stroke works very well for simple hoses, although you'll notice that its default size is a little big.

6. In the Outliner, select the stroke1 node and choose Modify ➢ Convert ➢ Paint Effects To Polygons (see Figure 4.44).

7. In the Outliner, select stroke1 and hide it (Ctrl+h). Select the Brush2MeshGroup and choose Edit ➢ Ungroup. Rename brush2Main as **hose1**.

8. Select hose1 and choose Lighting/Shading ➢ Assign New Material ➢ Lambert.

9. Save the scene as **paintEffectsHose_v02.ma**. To see a version of the scene to this point, open the `paintEffectsHose_v02.ma` scene from the `chapter4\scenes` directory on the DVD.

Modifying the Converted Stroke

Now you are set to edit the stroke itself to define the shape of the hose. The settings required to do this are spread out between two tabs in the Attribute Editor. Paint Effects requires a bit of bouncing around between settings, which can be a little disconcerting at first. With some practice you'll get the hang of it. It helps to understand how Paint Effects brushes work. Creating and designing Paint Effects brushes is discussed in detail in Chapter 8.

1. Continue with the scene from the previous section or open the `paintEffectsHose_v02.ma` scene from the `chapter4\scenes` directory on the DVD.

FIGURE 4.44
Attach a stroke to the curve and convert it into polygons.

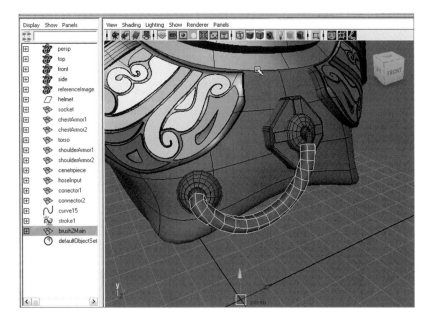

2. Select the stroke1 node in the Outliner, and open the Attribute Editor. Switch to the brush2 tab. Set Global Scale to **1**.

3. In the Twist section, activate Forward Twist. This setting automatically rotates leaves on Paint Effects plants so they continually face the camera. In some cases it can also remove unwanted twisting and other problems when creating simple hoses from strokes.

4. Switch to the strokeShape1 tab in the Attribute Editor. Set Sample Density to **4** (if the slider won't go beyond 1, type the number **4** in the field). This increases the divisions in the curve and makes it smoother.

5. Set Smoothing to **10**. This relaxes the shape of the hose somewhat.

6. Scroll down and expand the Pressure Scale settings in the Pressure Mappings rollout.

The Pressure Scale settings translate the recorded pressure applied while painting a Paint Effects stroke using a digital tablet into values applied to specified stroke attributes. Since you simply applied the stroke to a curve, no pressure was recorded; however you can still use these settings to modify the shape of the hose.

7. Set Pressure Map 1 to Width. Click the arrow to the right of the pressure scale curve. This expands the pressure scale curve into its own window.

Since the Pressure Map 1 is set to Width, changes made to the scale curve affect the width of the hose. You can add additional attributes using the Pressure Map 2 and Pressure Map 3 settings. This stroke does not use tubes, so settings like Tube Width and Tube Length have no affect on the shape of the hose.

8. Click on the curve in the curve editing window to add points. Observe the changes in the hose shape. Drag the points down to make the hose thinner (see Figure 4.45).

FIGURE 4.45
Create the shape of the hose by editing the settings of the Paint Effects brush.

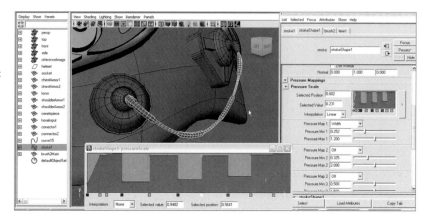

Interpolation sets the out tangent style of the selected point on the curve. Setting this to None creates a hard edge, Linear creates an angle, and Smooth and Spline create curved tangents. If you want to add a lot of detail, you'll need to increase the Sample Density value of the stroke. You can force the points of the curve to go beyond the range displayed in the Curve Editor by typing a value above 1 in the Selected Value field.

9. When you're happy with the shape of the curve, refine the shape of the hose by editing the CVs of the original curve.

10. Save the scene as **paintEffectsHose_v03.ma**. To see a version of the scene up to this point, open the paintEffectsHose_v03.ma scene from the chapter4\scenes directory on the DVD.

Drawing Curves on a Live Surface

Creating curves on a live surface is a quick way to create wires and hoses that conform to the shape of the object.

1. Continue with the scene from the previous section or open the paintEffectsHose_v03.ma scene from the chapter4\scenes directory on the DVD.

2. The TORSO display layer is set to Reference; click the R next to the label of the layer to set the display layer to normal editing mode.

3. Select the torso object and choose Modify ➢ Make Live.

4. Choose Create ➢ CV Curve Tool. Make sure Curve Degree is set to Cubic in the options.

5. Click on the surface to start drawing curves. Create a few short curves like the ones shown in Figure 4.46. Press the Enter key when you finish drawing each curve (in some cases you may have to switch to wireframe view to see the curve as you draw it on the surface). The curves may appear to float above or beneath the smooth mesh polygons. This is normal behavior when drawing curves on polygons. You can adjust the CVs of the curves later if necessary.

FIGURE 4.46
Draw curves directly on the live polygon surface.

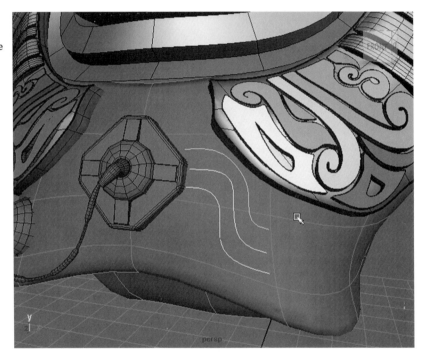

6. Select the stroke1 brush in the Outliner. Switch to the Rendering menu set, and choose Paint Effects ➢ Get Settings From Selected Stroke. This grabs the settings used for the stroke so they can be applied to the curves.

7. Select the curves drawn on the surface, and choose Paint Effects ➢ Curve Utilities ➢ Attach Brush To Curves.

8. Convert the strokes into polygons, and use the techniques described in the previous section to shape the curves into hoses and wires.

9. To make the torso unlive, select it in the Outliner and choose Modify ➢ Make Live. This will toggle the surface back to its normal state (see Figure 4.47).

10. Save the scene as **paintEffectsHoses_v04.ma**. To see a version of the scene to this point, open the paintEffectsHoses_v04.ma scene from the chapter4\scenes folder on the DVD.

FIGURE 4.47
Create hoses from the curves using Paint Effects Strokes.

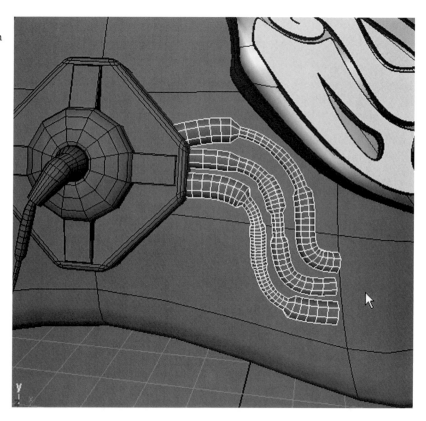

Converting NURBS Objects to Polygons

A NURBS surface can be used to start a polygon model. Using NURBS primitives and extruded and revolved surfaces, you can combine the strengths of both NURBS and polygon modeling tools and techniques in your projects.

If you are not familiar with NURBS modeling, review Chapter 3 before attempting the exercises in this section.

To convert NURBS objects to polygons, choose Modify ➢ Convert ➢ NURBS To Polygons ➢ Options, and then set the options to determine how the polygon mesh will be constructed from the NURBS surface.

Revolve

In the concept sketch by Chris Sanchez, a number of parts of the suit look like a pleated material. The arm sections and the area around the waist look like a good opportunity to use a revolved surface as a starting place for the model. In this exercise, you'll create the area below the torso. The same techniques can be applied to the arms (see Figure 4.48).

FIGURE 4.48
The area of the waist on the sketch looks like a good place to use a NURBS revolve.

1. Open the belly_v01.ma scene from the chapter4\scenes directory on the DVD.

2. Switch to a front view. Turn on Grid Snapping, and choose Create ➢ CV Curve Tool ➢ Options. In the options, set Curve Degree to Linear.

3. Use the Curve tool to create a sawtooth pattern running down the Y axis of the grid. Draw the curve four units away from the center line. Make the sawtooth pattern using six angles, as shown in Figure 4.49.

4. Switch to the Surfaces menu set and choose Surfaces ➢ Revolve. A new surface is created that looks like a pleated cylinder.

5. In the Channel Box, set Sections of the revolve1 node to **12**.

6. Turn Grid Snapping off. Select the curve, and use the Move and Scale tools to position it beneath the torso. The surface moves with the curve because of the construction history.

7. Select the curve, and switch to component mode. Select the CVs at the points of the curve, and move them inward to make the pleating less extreme.

8   Continue to move and shape the curve until the surface resembles the concept sketch.

9. Select revolvedSurface1, and choose Modify ➢ Convert ➢ NURBS To Polygons ➢ Options. In the options, set Type to Quads and Tessellation Method to General. This method works very well for making the polygon surface closely match the isoparms of the original surface.

10. Set U Type and V Type to Per Span # Of Iso Pararms. Set Number U and Number V to **1** (see Figure 4.50).

FIGURE 4.49
Create the pleated
surface by revolv-
ing a jagged curve.

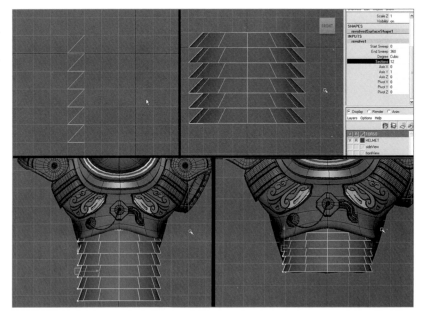

FIGURE 4.50
The options for
converting NURBS
to polygons

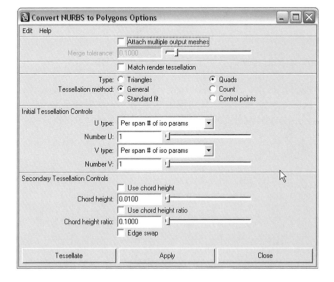

11. Click Tessellate to apply. In the Outliner, hide the original NURBS surface (Ctrl+h).

12. Select the new nurbsToPoly1 node and rename it **bellyPleats**.

13. Select bellyPleats, and press the 3 key to switch to smooth mesh polygons. Right-click on the surface and choose Vertex. Use the Move tool with Soft Select activated to move around the vertices of the pleated surface (see Figure 4.51).

FIGURE 4.51
You can model
irregularity
into the pleats
using the Move
and Crease tools.

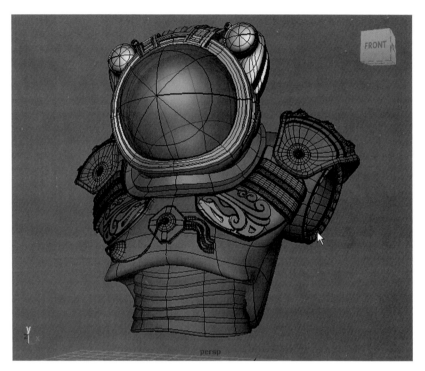

Create some irregularity in the pleated surface so it looks less perfect and more like a flexible material that has been used a lot. Use the Crease tool on a few of the edges.

14. When you are happy with the way the surface looks, delete history for the bellyPleats node, and delete the revolvedSurface1 node and the curve.

15. Save the scene as **belly_v02.ma**.

NURBS Extrusions

To create the rounded surface that surrounds the bottom of the torso, a NURBS extrusion con-verted to polygons may work better than a Paint Effects stroke. This is because the shape does not appear perfectly round. It might be easier to extrude an oval along a path curve to create this particular shape.

1. Continue with the scene from the previous section or open the belly_v02.ma scene from the chapter4\scenes directory on the DVD.

2. Make sure the TORSO display layer is not in reference mode.

3. Right-click on the torso, and choose Edge to switch to edge selection mode.

4. Double-click on one of the edges toward the bottom of the torso. The entire edge loop is selected when you double-click on an edge.

5. Choose Modify ➢ Convert ➢ Polygon Edges To Curves to create a curve based on these edges.

6. Select the newly created curve and delete its construction history.

7. The curve does not perfectly match the surface. Use the Move tool with Reflection on to reposition the CVs of the curve so they more closely resemble the shape of the torso.

8. Choose Create ➢ NURBS Primitives ➢ Circle. Rotate the circle 90 degrees on the X axis. Set the following values in the Scale channels:

    Scale X: **0.12**

    Scale Y: **0.725**

    Scale Z: **0.378**

9. Select the circle and Ctrl+click polyToCurve1. From the Surfaces menu, choose Surfaces ➢ Extrude ➢ Options. In the options, set Style to Tube, Result Position to At Path, and Pivot to Component. Set Orientation to Path Direction. Click the Extrude button to make the extrusion.

10. Select the new extrudedSurface1 node, and choose Modify ➢ Convert ➢ NURBS To Polygons. Use the same settings from the previous section (see Figure 4.52).

11. Hide the NURBS surface. Select the nurbsToPoly1 object and name it **torsoTrim**.

12. Press the 3 key to switch to smooth mesh preview mode.

FIGURE 4.52
Create a curve from the polygon edges. Extrude a circle along the curve.

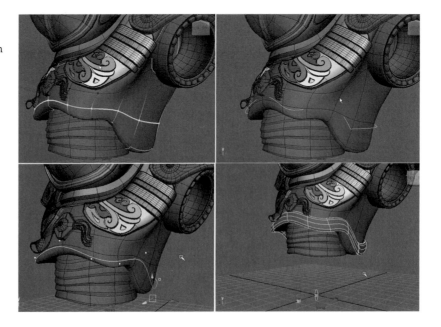

13. Select the polyToCurve1 curve, and use the Move tool to position its CVs so the torsoTrim surface fits snugly against the base of the torso.

14. When you are happy with the overall shape of the surface, delete history on torsoTrim. Delete the extruded surfaces and the curves.

15. Use the Move tool to further refine the vertices of the trim surface (see Figure 4.53).

16. Save the scene as **belly_v04.ma**. To see a version of the scene to this point, open the belly_ v04.ma scene from the chapter4\scenes directory on the DVD.

FIGURE 4.53
Use the Move tool to refine the shape of the torsoTrim object.

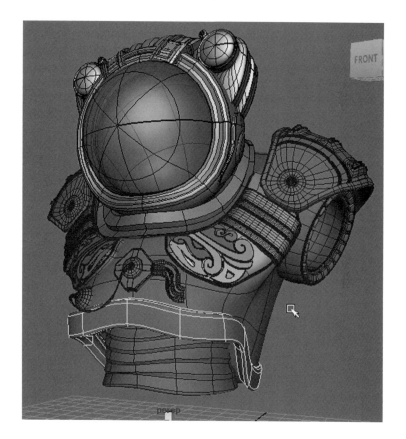

Boolean Operations

A Boolean operation in the context of polygon modeling creates a new surface by adding two surfaces together (union), subtracting one surface from the other (difference), or creating a surface from the overlapping parts of two surfaces (intersection). Figure 4.54 shows the results of the three types of Boolean operations applied to a polygon torus and cube.

The difference between using Combine to create a single mesh from two meshes and using a Boolean Union is that a Boolean Union operation removes all interior faces when the two surfaces are added together.

The geometry created using Booleans can sometimes produce artifacts in renders, so it's best to keep the geometry as simple as possible.

Using Booleans

In this section, you'll use Boolean operations to create detail for the space suit's torso.

1. Open the `torsoDetail_v01.ma` scene from the `chapter4/scenes` directory on the DVD.

2. Select the torsoTrim object in the Outliner.

Booleans don't always work well on smooth mesh preview objects, so it's a good idea to convert the smooth mesh preview to polygons.

3. Choose Modify ➤ Convert ➤ Smooth Mesh Preview To Polygons.

CONVERTING SMOOTH MESH PREVIEW TO POLYGONS

Converting a smooth mesh preview to polygons produces the same result as selecting the object, pressing the 1 key to deactivate smooth mesh preview, and then performing a Smooth operation (Mesh Smooth). However, if you have a creased edge on a smooth mesh preview surface, the crease will be carried over to the converted polygon model. The same is not true when you use the Smooth operation.

---

4. Create a polygon cylinder. Scale the polygon down to **0.5** in the X, Y, and Z axes. In the Channel Box, set Subdivisions Height to **3**. Make sure Subdivisions Axis is set to **20**.

5. Switch to a side view. Turn on face selection mode, select all of the polygons on the lowest subdivision, and scale them down as shown in Figure 4.55.

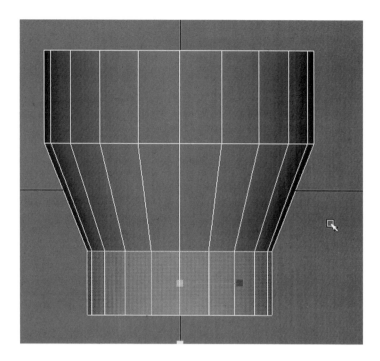

6. Select the cylinder and set its Scale Y to **0.165**.

7. Position the cylinder so it intersects with the front of the torsoTrim object. Try these settings in the Channel Box:

>Translate X: **0.418**
>
>Translate Y: **4.607**
>
>Translate Z: **2.575**
>
>Rotate X: **90.2**
>
>Rotate Y: **1.776**
>
>Rotate Z: **0.318**
>
>Scale X: **0.316**
>
>Scale Y: **0.104**
>
>Scale Z: **0.316**

8. Select the torsoTrim object, and Shift+click the cylinder. Choose Mesh ➢ Boolean ➢ Difference. The cylinder disappears, and a hole is now cut into the torsoTrim object (see Figure 4.56).

FIGURE 4.56
Cut a hole into the torsoTrim object using a cylinder.

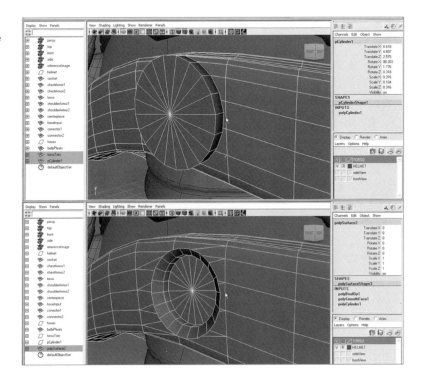

When using the Boolean ➤ Difference operation, Shift+click the object you want to cut into first and the cutting object second.

9. In the Outliner the pCylinder node is now a group. The mesh object no longer appears. You can adjust the position of the hole in the torsoTrim object by moving the pCylinder1 group (Figure 4.57). Once you delete history on the object, the position of the hole is permanent.

FIGURE 4.57
You can change the position of the hole by moving the pCylinder1 group.

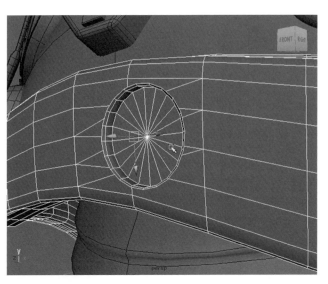

BEVEL THE CUTTING OBJECT

Applying a bevel to the edges created using a Boolean doesn't always work. Sometimes it's easier to create the bevel in the cutting object first. You did this when you scaled down the bottom section of the cylinder. You can then adjust the position of the cutting object after the Boolean operation to create the bevel in the edges.

---

10. Create a polygon sphere. Make sure the Subdivisions Axis and Height are set to **20**. Set the Scale X, Y, and Z of the sphere to **0.2**.

The sphere will be placed inside the hole created by the cylinder and then merged with the torsoTrim object using a Union. To keep the geometry produced by the Booleans as clean as possible, match the edges of the sphere with the edges of the hole created by the cylinder. One way to align the sphere involves creating a parent constraint between the pCylinder group node and the sphere.

11. In the Outliner, select the pCylinder1 group. Ctrl+click the sphere. Switch to the Animation menu set and choose Constrain ➢ Parent Options. In the options, turn off Maintain Offset. Turn on All for both Translate and Rotate (see Figure 4.58).

FIGURE 4.58

Constrain the polygon sphere to the position of the cylinder.

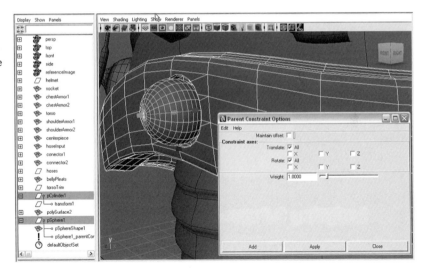

12. Once the sphere is constrained to the pCylinder1 group, it should appear in the hole. Expand the pSphere1 object in the Outliner, select the pSphere1_parentConstraint1 node, and delete it.

13. Select the pSphere1 node and the polySurface2 node in the Outliner, and choose Mesh ➢ Boolean ➢ Union. The objects are now merged into a single mesh.

14. Zoom in on the sphere (hot key = f). You'll see that the edges that wrap around the sphere match the position of the edges of the hole cut by the cylinder (see Figure 4.59). This is not always required when using Boolean operations, but it keeps the polygon geometry clean and reduces render artifacts.

15. Select the pSphere1 group in the Outliner. Scale it down on the Y axis a little. In the options for the Move tool, set Move Axis to Local and push the sphere back in the hole a little (see Figure 4.59).

16. Delete history on polySurface3 and rename it **torsoTrim**.

17. Save the scene as **torsoDetail_v02.ma**. To see a version of the scene to this point, open torsoDetail_v02.ma from the chapter4\scenes directory on the DVD.

FIGURE 4.59
Merge the sphere with the rest of the surface using a Union operation.

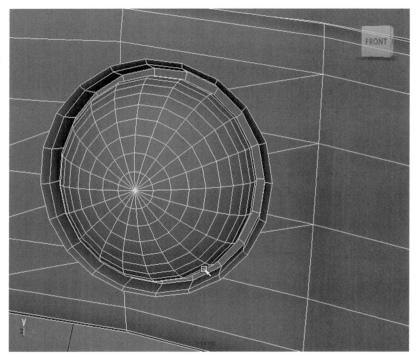

Sculpting Polygons Using Artisan

The Artisan interface is a Maya editing system that simulates using a brush to sculpt surfaces and paint attribute values. Artisan works best when used with a digital tablet and stylus, but it will also work with a standard mouse.

When used in modeling mode, Artisan can be used to sculpt polygon, NURBS, and subdivision surface geometry. In other parts of this book, you'll see how Artisan can also be used to paint weights for deformers, edit texture maps, and paint the strength of nParticle force fields emitted by surfaces.

For the most part, the Artisan modeling controls are the same whether you are working with polygons, NURBS surfaces, or subdivision surfaces. In this section, you'll be introduced to Artisan as you sculpt the fabric parts of the pants on the space suit.

Sculpting Polygons

The Artisan sculpting brushes work very well for creating details such as folds in fabric. In this section, you'll create the fabric portion of the legs between the armor plates and the thigh and the shin guards (see Figure 4.60).

FIGURE 4.60
We'll use the Artisan sculpting brushes to create the folds in the cloth parts of the pants shown in the drawing.

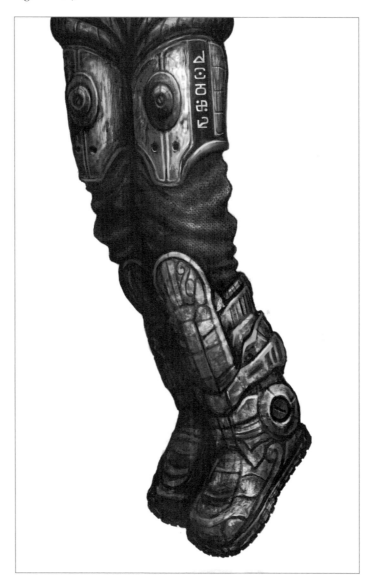

ANNOTATED LEG MODEL

In this section, the basic parts of the leg armor have already been modeled using the same techniques described in this chapter. To see a scene with an annotated guide describing the steps used to create these leg parts, open `legStart.ma` from the `chapter4\scenes` directory on the DVD.

---

1. Open the `pants_v01.ma` scene from the `chapter4\scenes` directory on the DVD. You'll see the helmet, torso, and parts of the legs have been modeled already.

2. Open the Outliner, select the rightBoot and rightThighGuard groups, and hide them (Ctrl+h). These groups are named based on the character's right side.

3. Create a polygon cube. Position the cube between the leftBoot and leftThighGuard groups. Try these settings in the Channel Box:

    Translate X: **2.018**

    Translate Y: **-6.384**

    Translate Z: **-1.689**

    Scale X: **2.3**

    Scale Y: **5**

    Scale Z: **2.4**

4. Set Subdivisions Width to **3**, Subdivisions Height to **6**, and Subdivisions Depth to **3**.

5. Select the cube, and press the 3 key to switch to smooth mesh preview. Right-click on the cube, and choose Vertex to switch to vertex editing mode.

6. Switch to the Move tool. In the options for the Move tool, turn on Soft Select. Use the Move tool to shape the cube into a loose cylinder. The upper part should fit inside the opening at the bottom of the leftThighGuard. The bottom of the cube should fit over the top of the leftBoot (Figure 4.61).

There's no need to be overly precise at this point; just try to imagine this surface as bulky, insulated fabric. It has to be flexible enough to bend but durable enough to protect the wearer in harsh environments, such as outer space. You'll refine the shape using Artisan.

7. Select the cube and name it **leftPants**. Choose Modify ➢ Convert ➢ Smooth Mesh Preview To Polygons.

8. Select leftPants and choose Mesh ➢ Sculpt Geometry Tool. Make sure the Tool Options window is open.

Choosing the Sculpt Geometry Tool activates the Artisan brush-based interface. The settings in the Options box control how the brush works as you sculpt the surface. At the top of the Options box are the basic controls:

Radius(U) and Radius(L) These settings define the range for the radius of the brush. If you are using a digital tablet and stylus, you can actually change the radius based on the amount of pressure you apply to the brush. The Radius(U) setting is the upper limit of the radius; Radius(L) is the lower limit of the radius. If you are using a mouse, only the Radius(U) value is used. You can also set the Radius(U) value interactively by holding the b key while dragging left or right on the surface in the viewport. The radius of the brush is represented by a red circle (Figure 4.62).

By default, the pressure you apply to the brush affects only the opacity of the stroke. If you want the pressure to control the radius of the brush, or both the radius and the opacity at the same time, scroll down to the Stylus Pressure settings and select from the choices in the Pressure Mapping menu.

FIGURE 4.61

Place a cube in the open area of the leg. Use the Move tool to roughly shape the vertices of the cube.

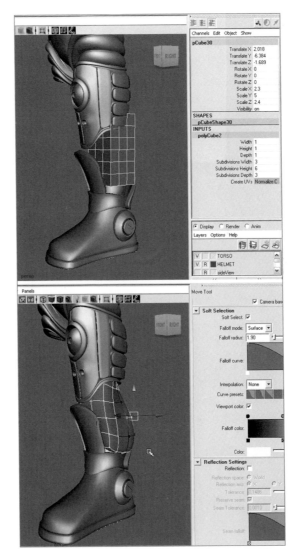

FIGURE 4.62
The settings for
the Artisan brush-
based sculpting
tool. The circle
represents the
radius of the
brush.

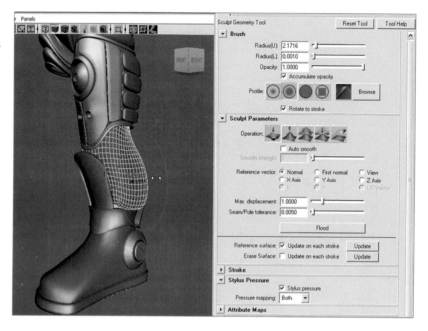

Opacity   This setting determines the strength of the change created by the brush. When using Artisan to sculpt geometry, Opacity modifies the Max Displacement setting found in the Sculpt Parameters section. If Max Displacement is set to 1 unit and Opacity is set to 0.1, each stroke displaces the surface 0.1 units. If Accumulate Opacity is activated, each time a single stroke passes over itself, the surface is displaced further. Setting Opacity to 0 means that the stroke has no effect on the surface.

Profile   This setting determines the shape of the brush tip. The first two icons on the left create a soft edge to the brush. This is more apparent when the geometry is very dense and has a lot of points that can be displaced. The second two icons produce a hard edge to the brush: one is circular, the other is square. By clicking the Browse button, you can load a grayscale image to use as the brush shape. The Rotate To Stroke option rotates the image as you draw so it always points in the direction of the stroke.

Sculpt Parameters   This section contains the settings for how the surface will react to the brush strokes. The Operation buttons cause the brush to push down, push up, smooth, relax, or erase the stroke. Smooth and relax are very similar. Smooth averages the position of the vertices on the surface. Relax averages the bumpiest areas of the surface while maintaining the overall shape of the surface.

Reference Vector   This setting determines the direction of the change sculpted on the surface. When set to Normal, the vertices are displaced in the direction of their normal. When set to First Normal, all the vertices are displaced in the direction of the normal of the first vertex affected by the stroke. View displaces the vertices based on the current view, and the X, Y, and Z Axis options restrict displacement to the specified axis.

NORMALS

A *normal* refers to the direction in which a vertex or face points in 3D space. Imagine a pin poking outward from a face on a polygon sphere. The direction the pin is pointing is the normal of the face. Vertices have normals as well. To display the normals of a polygon object, choose Display ➤ Polygons ➤ Face Normals or Vertex Normals. You can change the length of the normal display by choosing Display ➤ Polygons ➤ Normals Size.

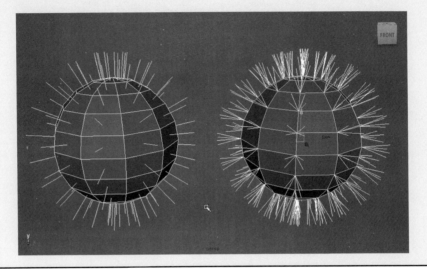

Flood This button fills the entire object based on the Operation, Reference Vector, Opacity, and Max. Displacement settings. You can use it to smooth or relax the whole object after making changes or to inflate or shrink the entire object.

Reflection These options, found in the Stroke section, are similar to the Reflection options found in the Move tool and are useful when sculpting symmetrical objects.

9. In the Sculpt Geometry Tool options, set Radius(U) to **0.25** and Opacity to **0.1**. Click the first icon in the Profile section and the first icon in the Operation section.

10. Set Reference Vector to Normal and Max. Displacement to **0.5**.

11. If you are using a digital tablet and a stylus, activate Stylus Pressure and set Pressure Mapping to Both.

12. In the Display section, turn on Draw Brush While Painting and Draw Brush Feedback, so you can see how the brush changes based on the amount of pressure applied to the pen on the tablet. You may also want to turn off Show Wireframe, so the wireframe display does not obscure your view of the changes made on the brush.

13. Paint some strokes on the leftPants object. Create folds in the clothing like the ones shown in the original sketch. You can hold the Ctrl key while you paint on the surface to invert the direction of the displacement. When you hold the Shift key while painting, the brush mode switches to smooth.

As you paint, experiment with the options for the Artisan brush settings. You can also activate smooth mesh preview on the surface by pressing the 3 key.

14. After you have created some folds, set Operation to Relax, and click the Flood button a few times to even out the lumps and bumps.

15. When you are happy with the surface, unhide the rightThighGuard and rightBoot groups. Create a mirror duplicate of the leftPants surface and rename it **rightPants**. Use the Artisan brushes to sculpt changes into this surface so it does not look like a copy of leftPants (see Figure 4.63). Remember to select the surface and choose Mesh ≻ Sculpt Geometry Tool.

16. Save the scene as **pants_v02.ma**. To see a version of the scene to this point, open the pants_v02.ma scene from the chapter4\scenes directory on the DVD.

FIGURE 4.63
Sculpt the fabric portions of the pants using the Artisan brush interface.

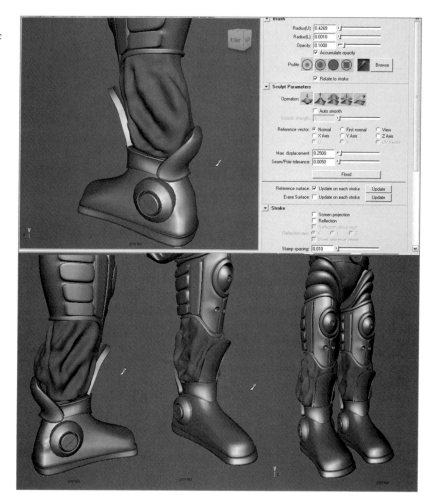

Advanced Polygon Modeling: The Head

Creating a believable character is one of the biggest challenges you can undertake. The face in particular is where most of the difficulty lies. This is because the human brain is a finely tuned face-reading machine. We are trained from the earliest age to recognize and read faces. When creating a character or a likeness in any artistic medium, if something is wrong with the face, it makes us uncomfortable, even if we can't articulate exactly what the problem is. Ironically, our understanding of the human face is often what gets in the way of creating a believable face in an artistic work. Creating a face in any medium takes practice, years of study, and more practice. That's part of what makes the face such an appealing subject.

In this section, we'll focus on using Maya tools to create a face. As you learn and practice, you'll develop your own techniques, which is what creating a personal style is all about. Even though the process is described in a step-by-step manner, in actuality modeling the face is much less straightforward and often involves going back and forth between levels of detail, changing and rearranging the topology of the polygons, and even sometimes bringing the model into a separate program, such as Autodesk's Mudbox or Pixologic's ZBrush, for further refinement.

Always save versions of the model as you work. This allows you to return to an earlier version if you need to make a fundamental change. As a general rule, keep the number of vertices as low as possible while you work to avoid becoming overwhelmed in detail.

Creating the Eye Socket

We'll incorporate this particular model into the space suit. As shown in the concept drawing, a young woman is wearing the suit. To keep things simple, you'll model the head in a separate scene and then import it with the rest of the suit when you have finished.

Reference images of the head have already been created. The reference images are low in detail and very generic; their main purpose is to act as a guide so the major forms of the head are placed correctly. You may prefer to work from a photograph or your own drawing.

There are many approaches to starting the head. Many modelers like using the box method approach, where a cube is gradually shaped into the form of the head, and faces are extruded to create holes for the eyes and the mouth. This approach works very well, but you may need to edit and reedit the topology (the arrangement of edges on the surface of the model) numerous times as you make changes to the model.

Another approach is to create parts of the face as separate pieces and then bridge the gaps between the pieces to form a complete head. The topology for the head is established early, and once the entire head has been created, the components are pushed and pulled until the face starts to resemble a character.

These approaches are equally valid. We'll use the second approach to create this head, but you're encouraged to try as many different methods as you can think of when creating your characters.

1. Open the head_v01.ma scene from the chapter4\scenes directory on the DVD. This scene has two image planes already placed. You should see a drawing of a simple head on each plane. If the drawings do not appear, select the image plane, open the Attribute Editor to the imagePlane tab, and click on the folder next to the Image Name field. Connect imagePlane1 to the headFront.tif file in the chapter4\sourceimages directory. Connect imagePlane2 to the headSide.tif file in the chapter4\sourceimages directory.

2. Choose Create ➤ Polygon Primitives ➤ Pipe. The pipe will be used to create the edge loops around the eyes. Rotate the pipe 90 degrees in X. Switch to a front view, and position the pipe over the eye in the drawing. Try the following settings:

    Translate X: **2.932**

    Translate Y: **1.429**

    Translate Z: **7.627**

    Rotate X: **90**

    Rotate Y: **0**

    Rotate Z: **0**

3. In the INPUTS section of the Channel Box, set Subdivisions Axis to **11**.

4. Switch to the perspective view. Right-click on the pipe and choose Face to switch to face selection mode. Select all of the faces except the face on the front and delete them (see the top image in Figure 4.64).

FIGURE 4.64

Shape the vertices of a polygon pipe, extrude the edges, and create the eye socket area.

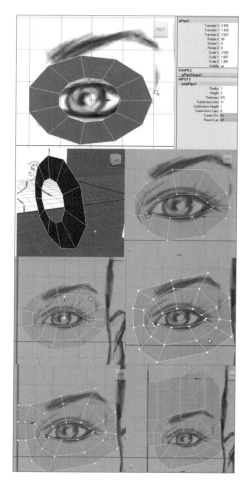

5. Switch back to the front view. Turn on X-Ray shaded mode. Use the Move tool to move around the vertices of the faces so they match the shape of the eye in the reference drawing.

6. Switch to edge selection mode. Double-click on one of the outer edges that circle the eye. Double-clicking will select the entire edge loop. Choose Edit Mesh ➤ Extrude.

7. Click on the blue circular switch on the extrude manipulator to change the Extrude tool out of local mode. Click on one of the scale handles on the extrude manipulator to activate scale mode. Scale the extruded edges out by dragging on the center of the manipulator.

8. Use the Move tool to move the vertices on the outer edge to roughly shape the brow and the area below the eye. Use the center images in Figure 4.64 as a guide.

9. Select the two outer edges closest to the center line (where the bridge of the nose will be), and create another extrusion.

10. Turn Grid Snapping on. From the front view, use the Move tool to snap each of the vertices of the extruded edge on the center line in the X axis (see Figure 4.64, bottom left).

11. Select the five edges on the top of the object, and create another extrusion. Pull these edges straight up with the extrude manipulator (Figure 4.64, bottom right).

12. Select the pPipe1 object in the Outliner, and switch to object selection mode. Choose Mesh ➤ Mirror Geometry ➤ Options. In the options, choose Edit ➤ Reset to set the options to their default values. Set Mirror Direction to -X. Click Mirror to mirror the geometry (Figure 4.65).

FIGURE 4.65
Mirror the eye socket area across the X axis.

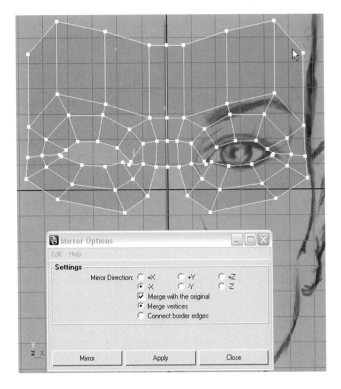

The default settings of the Mirror Geometry tool automatically combine the mirrored geometry and merge any vertices that are in the same position. The vertices that you snapped to the center line are merged with the vertices on the center line of the mirrored copy.

13. Select the nPipe1 object and rename it **upperFace**. Delete history on the object.

14. Save the scene as **head_v02.ma**. To see a version of the scene so far, open the head_v02.ma scene from the chapter4\scenes directory on the DVD.

Creating the Mouth Area

The mouth is very similar to the eye socket. It's basically a ring of polygons. You can start it the same way, using a pipe as a starting point.

1. Create another polygon pipe. Rotate it 90 degrees in X, and move it down to match the mouth in the front-view sketch. Try these settings:

   Translate X: **0**

   Translate Y: **-5.6**

   Translate Z: **7.696**

   Rotate X: **90**

   Rotate Y: **0**

   Rotate Z: **0**

   Scale X: **2.1**

   Scale Y: **1**

   Scale Z: **.931**

2. Set Subdivisions Axis to **16**.

3. Just as you did with the eye socket, delete all the faces except those on the front. Use the Move tool with Reflection turned on to shape the vertices of the polygons to roughly match the shape of the lips. Keep a slight opening at the center of the lips.

4. Shift+click the six edges on the top of the lips and extrude them. Pull the extruded edges straight up toward the bottom of the nose. Set the Divisions of the extrusion to **2**.

5. Shift+click the remaining edges around the outside of the mouth, and create another extrusion. Move these edges outward—in this case it may be easier to switch the Extrusion tool out of local mode (click the blue circular switch on the manipulator) and then scale the edges up so they move out from the center. Leave the Divisions on this extrusion set to 1.

6. Use the Move tool to reposition the vertices of this polygon object to roughly match the shape of the face; pull the vertices on the edge below the nose upward. This upper edge will form the lower planes of the nose, where eventually the nostrils will be placed. Use Figure 4.66 as a guide.

7. Select the pPipe1 object, and choose Edit Mesh ➤ Append Polygon Tool. The Append Polygon tool fills the gap between edges with a single polygon face. Select the edge on the right side of the polygon below the nose, and then select the opposing edge extruded from the lips. This closes the gap in this shape. Hit Enter to append the polygon. Refer to Figure 4.66.

8. Repeat step 7 for the opposite side of the face.

9. Use the Insert Edge Loop tool to insert an edge between the upper edge of the lip and the lower portion of the nose.

FIGURE 4.66
Create the mouth area from the faces of a polygon pipe. Extrude the edges and move the vertices to match the drawing.

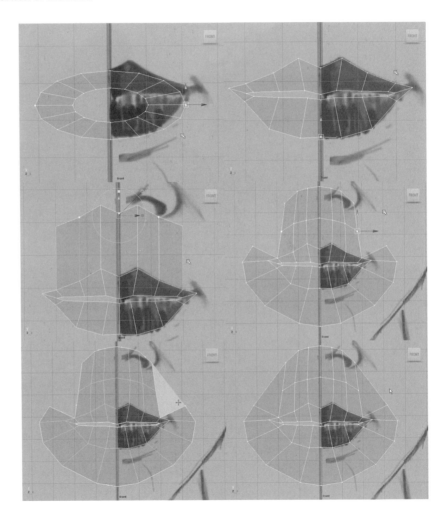

10. Use the Insert Edge Loop tool again to create another edge loop around the outside of the mouth (see Figure 4.67).

11. Rename pPipe1 as **lowerFace**. Save the scene as **head_v03.ma**. To see a version of the scene to this point, open the head_v03.ma scene from the chapter4\scenes directory on the DVD.

FIGURE 4.67
Insert two edge loops into the mouth object.

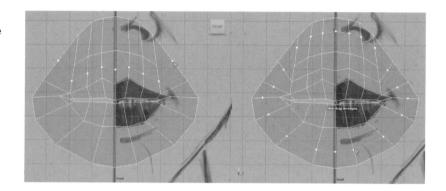

Shaping the Mouth and Eye Areas

At this point it's a good idea to start shaping the mouth and eye areas into something more three dimensional. You'll start by using a bend deformer to add some curvature to the face.

1. Continue with the scene from the previous section or open the head_v03.ma scene from the chapter4\scenes directory on the DVD.

2. Shift+click the upperFace and lowerFace objects. Switch to the Animation menu set, and choose Create Deformers ➤ Non-Linear ➤ Bend.

3. Select the bend handle, and set its Rotate X to **90** and Rotate Y to **-90**. In the INPUTS section of the Channel Box, set Curvature to **-1.5**.

4. Shift+click the upperFace and lowerFace objects, and choose Delete By Type ➤ History.

5. Switch to the side view. Turn on X-Ray Shading, and position the lowerFace object so it's closer to the front of the head (set its Translate Z to **9.31**).

6. Select the Move tool. Turn on Reflection and Soft Select. Set Soft Select Falloff Radius to **1.5**. Use the Move tool to drag back the corners of the mouth.

7. Use the Move tool to shape the mouth from the side to roughly match the drawing. Use Figure 4.68 (upper-right panel) as a reference. The vertices at the top of the lowerFace object should match the underside of the nose. As you work, you will need to adjust the radius of the Move tool's Soft Selection in the options and occasionally deactivate it so you can move individual vertices.

8. Switch to the front view, and continue moving the vertices to roughly match the drawing. Refer to Figure 4.68.

FIGURE 4.68
The vertices of the mouth are positioned from the side and front view.

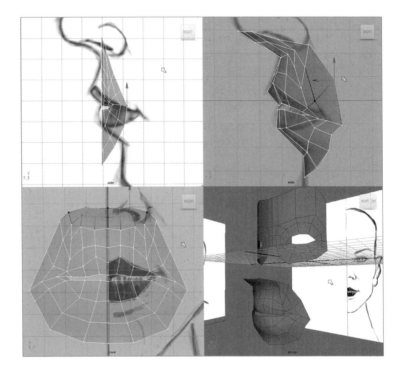

9. Switch to the side view, and position the upperFace object to match the drawing. Place the upperFace so the drawing of the eye in the side view can be seen in the hole for the eye on the mesh.

10. Move the vertices around the eye area to match the side view of the face.

11. Create a NURBS sphere. Rotate it 90 degrees in X. Position the sphere so it matches the eye in the drawing. Try the following settings:

    Translate X: **2.818**

    Translate Y: **1.549**

    Translate Z: **7.3**

    Rotate X: **90**

    Rotate Y: **0**

    Rotate Z: **0**

    Scale X: **1.252**

    Scale Y: **1.252**

    Scale Z: **1.252**

12. Switch to a perspective view. Turn off X-Ray Shading. Use the Move tool to position the vertices so the opening in the eye wraps around the surface of the eyeball. This will eventually become the eyelid.

LOSING SYMMETRY

Remember that if your model loses symmetry while working and the Reflection setting on the Move tool no longer seems to work, you can quickly restore symmetry using the Mirror Cut tool. See the "Mirror Cut" section earlier in the chapter. The Mirror Cut tool can sometimes create extra vertices along the center line of the model. Make sure you find any extra vertices along the center line and delete them.

---

13. Switch to the front view, and move the vertices of the upper face to match the drawing (see Figure 4.69).

14. Save the scene as **head_v04.ma**. To see a version of the scene to this point, open head_v04.ma from the chapter4\scenes directory on the DVD.

FIGURE 4.69
Shape the upper area of the face to match the drawing.

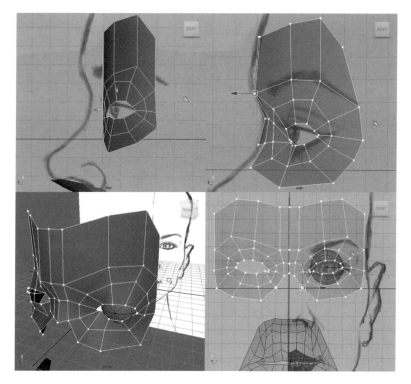

Creating the Nose

The nose is the most difficult part of the face to create—the nostril area in particular. The trickiest part is the naso-labial fold, which is the crease that appears starting from the area behind the nostril and moves down toward the sides of the mouth. This crease is very subtle in young faces when they are in a neutral expression; however, it becomes apparent when the face moves into an expression. Therefore, take great care to make sure that the edges in the face flow along the lines of the naso-labial fold so that when the face is animated it will deform correctly. The same is true for the areas at the bridge of the nose where skin bunches and wrinkles and the areas at the corners of the eyes and the forehead.

1. Continue with the scene from the previous section or open the head_v04.ma scene from the chapter4\scenes directory on the DVD.

2. Shift+click the top eight edges of the lowerFace object, the edges that define the area of the nose as shown in the upper left of Figure 4.70 (the edges are highlighted in the image for clarity).

3. Extrude these edges, and pull them straight up using the extrude manipulator (click on the blue circular switch of the manipulator to turn off local mode; this makes it easier to pull straight up).

FIGURE 4.70
Create the tip of the nose and the nostrils.

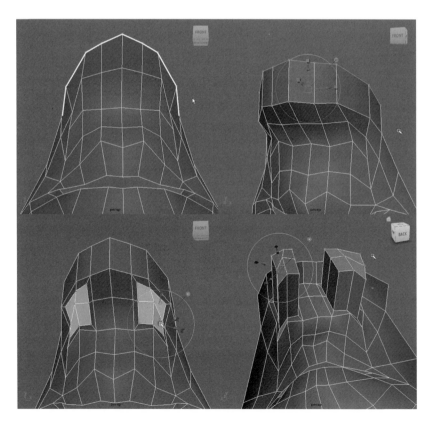

4. To create the nostrils, select the two sets of four faces on either side of the nose, as shown in the lower left of Figure 4.70.

5. Extrude these faces once, and scale them down slightly.

6. Extrude the faces again, and pull the second extrusion straight up (this is shown from the back of the lowerFace section in the lower right of Figure 4.70).

7. With the faces still selected, press the Delete key to delete the faces inside the nostril.

8. Select the lowerFace object, and choose Edit Mesh ➢ Split Polygon Tool ➢ Options. In the options, set Snapping Tolerance to **100**.

The Split Polygon tool lets you insert vertices and edges into the mesh by clicking directly on the edges of a mesh. By increasing the snapping tolerance, each time you click on an edge, the tool will snap to the center of the edge, making precision a little easier.

9. Start from the center of the middle polygon on the tip of the nose. Click each edge around the front of the nose, down the side, across the bottom, and up around the other side. To make this path, a triangle will be created in the outside corners of the nostril.

10. When you end up back at the first vertex created by the Split Polygon tool, click on it to complete the loop, and hit Enter to finish the tool. Make sure the line splits each polygon along the way; otherwise, when you press Enter, nothing happens. You can back up to the previous split by pressing the Backspace key.

11. Use the Split Polygon tool to split the polygon next to the triangle on the side of the nose, as shown in the lower-right image of Figure 4.71. Repeat this for the opposite side of the nose as well so that the geometry is symmetrical.

FIGURE 4.71
Divide the polygons around the tip of the nose using the Split Polygon tool.

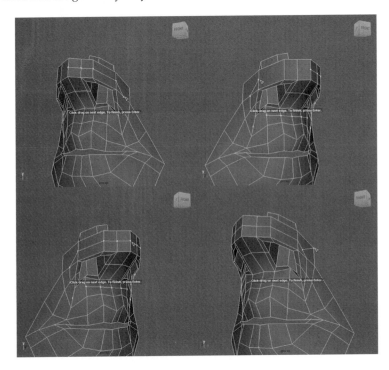

Connecting the Sections of the Face

Using the Append Polygon tool, you can connect the upper part of the face and the lower part of the face into a single mesh. Before you can use the Append Polygon tool to connect the two sections of the face, you must combine them under a single node.

1. Shift+click the lowerFace and upperFace objects. Choose Mesh ➤ Combine. Delete history on the combined mesh, and rename it **face**.

2. Select the face geometry and choose Edit Mesh ➤ Append Polygon Tool. Use the Append Polygon tool to attach the top part of the face to the bottom part. The two parts must be combined into a single mesh or the Append Polygon tool will not work. Connect the two pieces starting with the bridge of the nose; use Figure 4.72 as a guide.

3. Continue to use the Append Polygon tool to attach the upper part of the face to the lower part, as shown in Figure 4.72. Make sure you maintain symmetry by appending polygons on both sides of the face.

FIGURE 4.72
Use the Append Polygon tool to attach the upper part of the face to the lower part of the face.

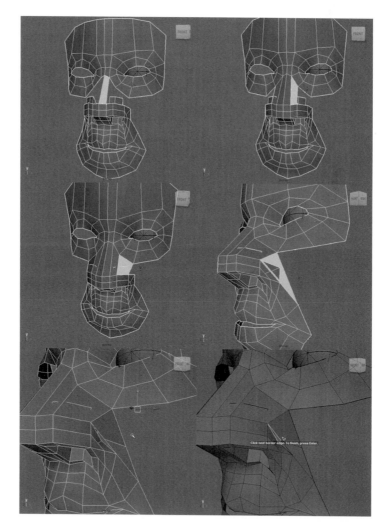

4. Notice in the middle right image of Figure 4.72 that the naso-labial fold is created by appending a polygon between the side of the nose and the area above the upper lip.

5. In the lower-left image of Figure 4.72, the appended polygon is split and the vertices are moved to bring the open edges into alignment.

BRIDGE TOOL

The Bridge tool appends multiple polygons between two opposing faces (polygon faces that are facing each other). Select the two faces you want to bridge, and choose Edit Mesh ➤ Bridge. In the options for the Bridge tool, you can specify the number of divisions created in the bridge. You must select an equal number of edges on each part of the mesh in order for the Bridge tool to work correctly.

6. In the lower-right image of Figure 4.72, the Merge Edge tool is used to close the open edges (Edit Mesh ➤ Merge Edge Tool). To use the tool, click on one of the open edges—the edge that you want to merge—and hit the Enter key. Don't forget to repeat these steps for the other side of the face.

BOWTIES

The term *bowtie* refers to a situation in which the Append Polygon tool creates a twisted polygon that resembles a bowtie. This happens when you combine two meshes that have opposing normals and then connect the meshes using the Append Polygon tool. To fix this, select the polygon meshes and use the Separate command to break them into two meshes (Mesh ➤ Separate). Then select one of the meshes and choose Normals ➤ Reverse. Combine the meshes again, and then try the Append Polygon tool. The resulting polygons should no longer be twisted.

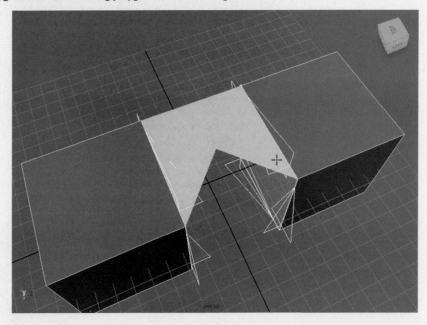

7. Select the border edges around the lower portion of the face that surround the mouth area, as shown in the upper-left image of Figure 4.73. Extrude these edges, and scale them out from the center using the extrude manipulator.

8. In the Channel Box for the extrude node, set Divisions to **2**.

9. Use the Move tool to position the vertices of the extruded faces so they match up with the upper portion of the face, as shown in the middle-left image of Figure 4.73.

10. Use the Merge Edge tool to close the gap between these edges.

11. Switch to a side view, turn on X-Ray mode, and move the vertices of the face so they match the contour of the drawing.

12. Spend a few minutes spacing out the edges on the nose. Look at the lower-left image in Figure 4.73. Notice how the vertices have been arranged to make smoother edge loops around the mouth area.

13. Switch to a front view, and use the Move tool to further shape the face to match the reference drawing.

14. Save the scene as **head_v05.ma**. To see a version of the scene to this point, open the head_v05.ma scene from the chapter4\scenes directory on the DVD.

FIGURE 4.73
Extrude the edges around the lower portion of the face. Close the gaps using the Merge Edge tool. Move the vertices to make the face match the reference sketch.

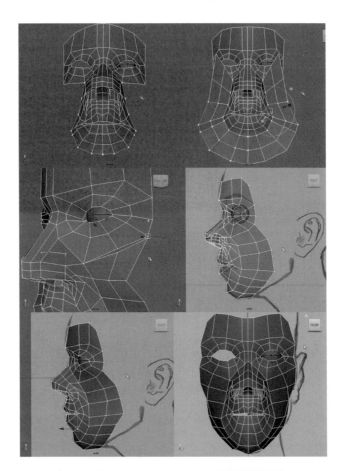

Enhancing Lips and Eyelids

At this point you can add some edge loops to the eyes and thicken the lips.

1. Continue with the scene from the previous section or open the head_v05.ma scene from the chapter4\scenes directory on the DVD.

2. Rotate the model so you can see the inside of the face. Zoom in on the back side of the mouth. Right-click on the model, and choose Edge to switch to edge selection mode.

3. Double-click on one of the border edges of the mouth to select the whole border.

4. Extrude these edges, and pull them straight back into the mouth.

5. Set Divisions to 2. Use the Move tool to select and move the vertices of the extruded edges. Pull them apart, as shown in Figure 4.74.

FIGURE 4.74
Extrude the edges on the inside of the mouth to create a simple throat.

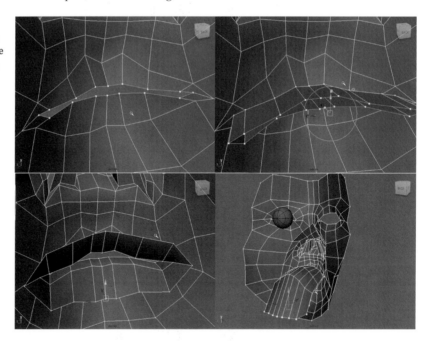

6. Double-click on the border edge again, and create another extrusion. Pull this extrusion back deeper into the area that will be the head. Set Divisions to **3**.

7. Shape the vertices into a tube that bends downward. You want to create a very simple throat.

8. Create the inside of the eyelids using a similar method. Extrude the inside edges of the character's left eyelid (on the character's left), hiding the eyeball while you work. A single-edge extrusion with two divisions should do the trick.

9. Pull the inside of the eyelids back far enough so the new edges do not intersect with parts of the face.

10. Select the face, and choose Mesh ➤ Mirror Cut so the extruded edges are duplicated to the opposite side of the face.

11. Delete history on the face, and delete the mirror cut plane nodes in the Outliner.

12. Right-click on the face, and choose Vertices so the face vertices are highlighted. Inspect the model for any extra vertices created along the center line by the mirror cut planes. Delete these vertices (an extra vertex appears on the edge of the nose in the lower-right image of Figure 4.75).

FIGURE 4.75
Extrude the edges on the inside of the eyelids. Mirror the face using the Mirror Cut tool. Select and delete any extra vertices.

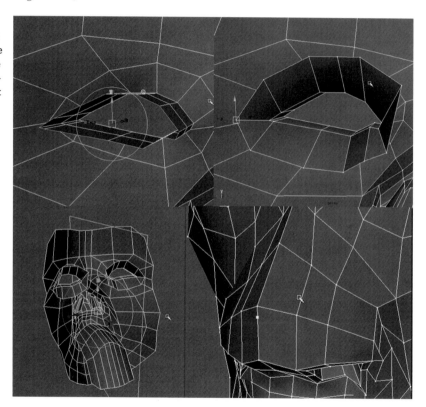

13. Delete history on the surface and rename it **face**.

14. Save the scene as **head_v06.ma**. To see a version of the model to this point, open the head_v06.ma scene from the chapter4\scenes directory on the DVD.

Creating the Cranium and Ear

We'll create the cranium by extruding the edges of the face, moving them back, and shaping the vertices to match the profile of the face. The techniques are very similar to the ones used to create the face. An annotated scene file named craniumStart.ma is included in the chapter4\ scenes directory on the DVD. Take a look at the scene to see how the rest of the head is created.

The ear is a tricky area that involves much study and experimentation. Take a look at the earStart.ma scene to see how the ear is created.

The geometry of the head is completed using the techniques described in earlier sections. For a detailed look at the steps used to finish the geometry, open the craniumStart.ma and earStart.ma scenes on the DVD (see Figure 4.76).

FIGURE 4.76
Complete the basic geometry of the head.

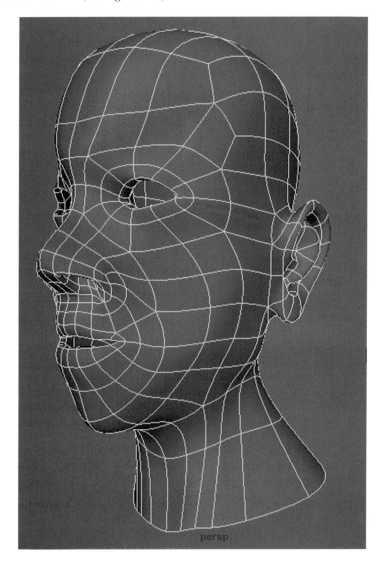

Creating a Character

At this point in the process, you should end up with a head that most likely is not terribly attractive or even feminine. Most artwork, CG or otherwise, goes through a very ugly stage, kind of like the awkward teenage phase people encounter when their bodies are developing. This part of the process usually inspires a fair amount of frustration, which is understandable. You've put a lot of work into the model already, and when you activate the smooth mesh preview, it still looks like some kind of rubbery alien.

If the topology of the head is good and it follows the flow of the facial muscles, you should be able to turn the rubbery alien into a believable character; it just takes a lot of hard work. This involves pushing and pulling vertices, using the Artisan brush interface, looking at the reference, and more pushing and pulling. Remember to keep things simple, move slowly, and save versions of the object as you go. Between this stage and the finished character, there are probably a thousand small changes you need to make. Modeling heads is more like learning the piano and less like assembling prefab furniture. It involves a lot of practice and study. Expect that the first few heads you make will not be perfect, but keep making them anyway!

In the example used in this chapter, you should need to add only a few more edge loops around the mouth and the eyes and maybe the ear. You should not need to split polygons or add edge loops anywhere else on the face. This section introduces a few more polygon-editing tools that should help you finish the model.

DIGITAL SCULPTING

Digital sculpting programs such as Autodesk's Mudbox and Pixologic's ZBrush are becoming a very important part of the character-creation pipeline. Because of their intuitive digital-sculpting tools and capacity for working with very dense meshes, they're often used to add changes and detail to models started in Maya. For more information, take a look at *Introducing ZBrush* by Eric Keller (Sybex, 2008) and *ZBrush Character Creation: Advanced Digital Sculpting* by Scott Spencer (Sybex, 2008).

Transform Component

The Transform Component tool is a manipulator that moves selected components relative to their local axes. It combines Move, Scale, and Rotate into a single manipulator. You've actually used the manipulator already; it appears whenever you extrude a polygon or edge.

1. Open the head_v07.ma scene from the `chapter4\scenes` directory on the DVD.

2. Right-click on the face object and choose Face. Select one of the faces behind the corner of the eye.

3. Transform Component does not have a mirror mode. If you want to keep the face symmetrical, you'll need to Shift+click the same face on the opposite side of the head.

4. Choose Edit Mesh ➤ Transform Component. The now-familiar manipulator will appear. Use the manipulator to move, scale, and rotate the selected face to create a more natural look for the eye area (see Figure 4.77).

FIGURE 4.77
The Transform Component moves components relative to their local space.

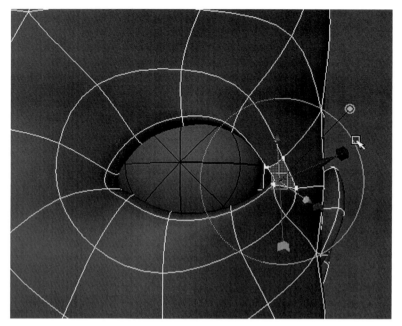

The advantage of the Transform Component manipulator is that it moves components relative to their local space. This is not always achievable with the Move tool. You can move any number of selected components using this tool. To toggle between local and global modes, click on the blue circular switch on the manipulator handle.

Offset Edge Loop Tool

The Offset Edge Loop tool will create a pair of parallel edge loops on either side of a selected edge.

1. Zoom in on one of the eyes, select the face object, and choose Edit Mesh ➤ Offset Edge Loop Tool.

2. Click on the edge of the eyelid. The tool inserts two edge loops on either side of the eyelid edge. By sliding the tool left or right, you can set the distance between the central edge loop and the offset edge loops (see Figure 4.78).

The Offset Edge Loop tool does not have a Reflection setting. After adding new edge loops on one side of the face, you'll use the Mirror Cut tool to restore symmetry to the other side of the face.

Slide Edge Tool

You can use the Slide Edge tool to change the position of an edge on the surface of the model.

1. Right-click on the face, and choose Edge to switch to edge selection mode. Select the three edges above the eyelid, as shown in Figure 4.79.

2. Choose Edit Mesh ➤ Slide Edge Tool. Drag with the middle mouse button toward the right to slide the edge up toward the brow.

To slide an edge loop, double-click on an edge to select the loop and then use the Slide Edge tool.

FIGURE 4.78
The Offset Edge Loop tool inserts a pair of edge loops parallel to a selected edge.

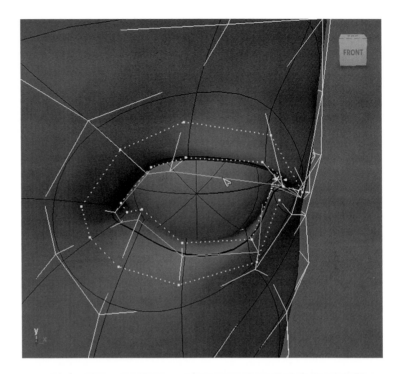

FIGURE 4.79
The Slide Edge tool slides edges on the surface of the model.

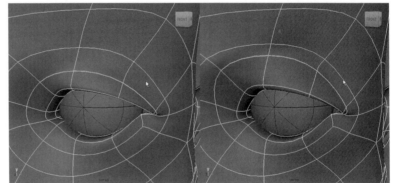

Flip Triangle Tool

You can use the Flip Triangle tool to change the direction of an edge shared by two triangles. This is helpful when rearranging the topology of a mesh.

1. Select the face object and choose Edit Mesh ➤ Split Polygon Tool. Use the tool to create a vertical split in the square polygon near the temple of the head, as shown in Figure 4.80. Hit Enter to finish the split operation.

2. Select the vertical edge and choose Edit Mesh ➤ Flip Triangle Edge. This changes the direction of the shared edge of the triangle.

FIGURE 4.80
You can use the Flip Triangle tool to flip the edge shared by two triangles.

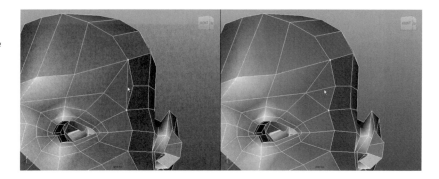

Sculpting the Head

To finish the head, add two edge loops around the lips and eyelids. Use the Move tool using both Reflection and Soft Select to push and pull the vertices to match the reference drawings. Use the Sculpt Geometry tool as well to smooth, create more volume in the cheeks, and relax the surface.

At a certain point, you'll need to increase the resolution of the mesh so you can create finer detail. The best way to do this is to switch out of smooth mesh preview mode (press the 1 key), select the head, and choose Mesh ➤ Smooth. Don't smooth more than one division at a time or you'll end up with a very dense model that is hard to work with. Don't forget to crease edges along the eyelids and within the ear.

You may also find that applying a Blinn texture to the model will help you visualize the contours of the geometry. The specular quality of the shader in the perspective view can help reveal the contours of the model.

To see an annotated guide that shows how the head was completed, open the headFinish.ma scene from the chapter4\scenes directory on the DVD (see Figure 4.81).

FIGURE 4.81
After many hours of tweaking, the model starts to look like a human female.

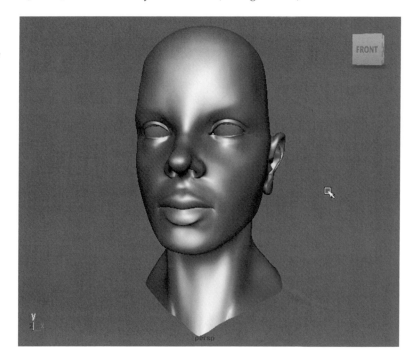

Real World Scenario

IMPORTING AND EXPORTING POLYGON GEOMETRY

As your character-modeling skills improve, you will depend more and more on using other programs, such as ZBrush and Mudbox, for creating character detail and texturing. It's important to understand the best way to move geometry in and out of Maya so you can use other 3D programs successfully. The most common file format supported by most 3D applications is the .obj format.

When importing and exporting .obj files from Maya, make sure that the point order does not change in the model. This ensures that the UVs are consistent and that you can use blend shapes correctly and subdivide the model in other programs successfully.

To export a model in the .obj format from Maya, use the following steps:

1. Make sure the objExport.mll plug-in is loaded in the Plug-in Manager. Go to Window ➤ Settings/Preferences ➤ Plug-in Manager, and check the Loaded box next to objExport.mll.

2. Select the polygon mesh you want to export, and choose File ➤ Export Selected ➤ Options. In the options, choose the obj format from the File Type menu. It's usually a good idea to set all the File Type options to Off.

3. Click the Export Selection button in the options, and use the dialog box to choose a location for the file on your hard drive.

To import a file back into Maya after editing it in another program, use the following steps:

1. In Maya, choose File ➤ Import ➤ Options. In the options, set File Type to obj. You should not need to worry about the Reference options if the file is not meant to be a reference (references are discussed in Chapter 1).

2. The Name Clash options help you to avoid problems that may occur when an object is imported into a scene that has another node that uses the same name. You can choose to append the filename to the imported object or a custom string using the options in the Resolve menus.

3. Under the File Specific options, make sure Create Multiple Objects is set to off. This prevents Maya from changing the point order in the imported object. This is the most important option in the Import options. If you remember to turn this option off, then you should be able to move the file back and forth between your other 3D editors without any problems.

Using Subdivision Surfaces

Maya's subdivision surfaces are very similar to the polygon smooth mesh preview that you have been working with throughout the chapter. The primary distinction between smooth mesh preview and subdivision surfaces (aka subDs) is that subdivision surfaces allow you to subdivide a mesh to add detail only where you need it. For instance, if you want to sculpt a fingernail at the end of a finger, using subDs you can select just the tip of the finger and increase the subdivisions. Then you have more vertices to work with just at the fingertip, and you can sculpt the fingernail.

Most subD models start out as polygons and are converted to subDs only toward the end of the modeling process. You should create UV texture coordinates while the model is still made of polygons. They are carried over to the subDs when the model is converted.

So why are subDs and smooth mesh preview polygons so similar, and which should you use? SubDs have been part of Maya for many versions. Smooth mesh preview polygons have only recently been added to Maya; thus the polygon tools have evolved to become very similar to subDs. You can use either type of geometry for many of the same tasks; it's really up to you to decide when to use one versus the other.

When you convert a polygon mesh to a subdivision surface, there are a few things you should keep in mind. Keep the polygon mesh as simple as possible; converting a dense polygon mesh to a subD significantly slows down Maya's performance. You can convert three-sided or *n*-sided (more than four-sided) polygons into subDs, but you will get better results and fewer bumps in the subD model if you stick to four-sided polygons as much as possible.

Working with SubDs

In this section, you'll build gloves for the space suit. These gloves will start as polygon models, and then they will be converted to subDs.

1. Open the gloveStart.ma scene from the chapter4\scenes directory on the DVD. You'll see that one of the gloves has been created using standard polygon modeling techniques (see Figure 4.82).

FIGURE 4.82
The glove has been created using standard polygon modeling techniques.

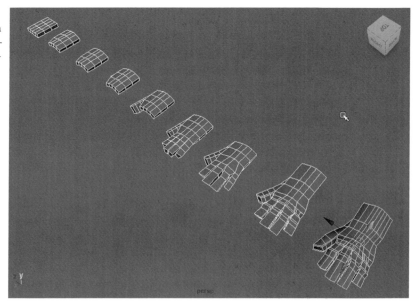

Each stage in the construction of the glove has been saved as a separate model so you can see the process involved. Since this is intended to be a big, bulky glove, there does not need to be a lot of detail.

2. Turn off the visibility of the GLOVE_CONSTRUCT display layer so the earlier versions of the glove are not visible.

3. Select glove10 and zoom in on the model (hot key = f).

4 With glove10 selected, choose Modify ➢ Convert Polygons To Subdiv.

5. Press the 3 key to switch to smooth display of the model.

6. Right-click on the model, and choose Vertex to display the vertices.

The vertices of a subD object behave very similarly to the CVs of a NURBS object. The vertices are offset from the surface much like NURBS CVs (Figure 4.83).

7. Right-click on the model and choose Edge. The edges appear as a cage around the object.

FIGURE 4.83
Convert the glove into a subdivision surface. Display the vertices of the model.

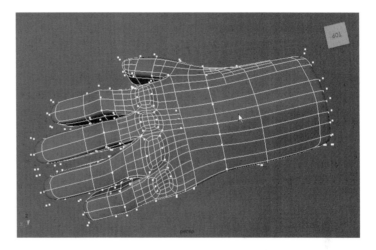

You can move the edges, vertices, or faces of the model. To add a crease to an edge, switch to the Surfaces menu set and expand the Subdivision Surfaces menu. At the top of the menu are options for adding a full crease, adding a partial crease, or removing a crease (Figure 4.84).

8. Select the polyToSubd1 object in the Outliner. Choose Subdivision Surfaces ➢ Polygon Proxy Mode. The edge appears as a cage around the model.

9. In the Outliner, expand the polyToSubd1 object. Under the transform node, you'll see two shape nodes: the polyToSubdShape1 node and the polyToSubdShape1HistPoly node.

Maya has created a duplicate polygon version of the model and placed it under the polyToSubd1 node. You can edit the polygon cage (by editing the polyToSubdShape1HistPoly node) using many of the polygon-editing tools, and the changes will be transferred to the subD version of the model (Figure 4.85).

10. To turn off the polygon proxy, select the model and choose Subdivision Surfaces ➢ Standard Mode.

11. Save the scene as **glove_v01.ma**. To see a version of the scene, open the glove_v01.ma scene from the chapter4\scenes directory on the DVD.

FIGURE 4.84

The creasing options appear at the top of the Subdivision Surfaces menu.

FIGURE 4.85

A polygon version of the model appears in the Outliner under the polyToSubd1 node when polygon proxy mode is activated.

SubD Poly Workflow

Many modelers prefer to switch between the polygon version of the model and the subD version while they work rather than use the Polygon Proxy. To do this, select the model and choose Modify ➢ Convert SubDiv To Poly ➢ Options. In the options, set Tessellation Method to Vertices and Level to **0**. If you want to switch back and forth between the two modes more quickly, you can download a script called zzToggleSubDee.mel from highend3d.com. This script allows you to toggle quickly between the two modes as you work. This script is available at this URL: www.highend3d.com/maya/downloads/mel_scripts/modeling/misc/1131.html.

SubD Levels

If you take a look at the area of the knuckles on the glove, you'll see that these parts of the model appear to have a higher number of divisions than the rest of the model. Subdivision surfaces have multiple levels of division. You can see this in the wireframe display when the object is selected. The knuckles and parts of the thumb have a higher level of subdivision than the rest of the glove. The different levels of subdivision are edited separately. So even though you can see that there are more divisions around the area of the knuckle, you need to switch to a higher subdivision level before you can edit these points directly. This exercise will show you how to do this.

1. Continue with the scene from the previous section or open the glove_v01.ma scene from the chapter4\scenes directory on the DVD.

2. Right-click on the glove and choose Vertex. The vertices are displayed for the model; notice that the top of each knuckle has six vertices.

3. Select the Move tool and open the Tool options. Activate Tweak Mode.

4. Spend a few minutes shaping the glove using the Move tool. In tweak mode, you can select each vertex and nudge it with the Move tool. The standard Move tool manipulator is not visible when you have tweak mode activated.

5. Right-click on the model and choose Display Finer (Figure 4.86). This moves you to the next higher level of subdivision. The knuckles have more vertices available for editing.

The lowest level of subdivision is labeled level 0 or the base level. The next level is 1, then 2, and so on.

6. Use the Move tool to reposition the vertices of the knuckle. If you are having trouble moving the vertices at the higher levels, try disabling Soft Select in the Move tool options. To switch back to level 0, right-click on the model and choose Display Coarser.

7. To add a level of subdivision to a specific area of the model, select a component and right-click on the model. Choose Refine Selected from the marking menu.

Notice that when you are working in level 1, if you change the position of a vertex that lies on the border of a level 0 region, the area near the edited vertex is subdivided automatically.

FIGURE 4.86
At the finer display level more vertices are available for editing the knuckles of the glove.

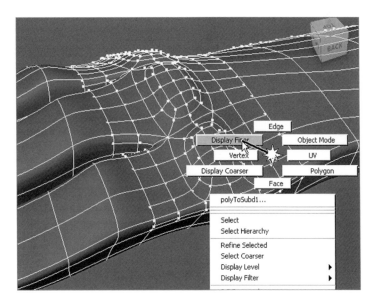

The glove has three levels of subdivision, 0 through 2. The level 2 area is found where the thumb meets the glove. Changes made at level 2 are best suited for details such as wrinkles and small folds. You can add up to 13 levels of subdivision to a model.

8. Select the Glove model and choose Subdivision Surfaces ➢ Sculpt Geometry Tool. You can use the Artisan brush interface to reshape the model. The Smooth operation is helpful for rounding the edges near the wrist.

9. When you are happy with the model, save the glove as **glove_v02.ma**. To see a version of the finished glove, open the glove_v02.ma scene from the chapter4\scenes directory on the DVD.

10. You can import the glove into your version of the space suit scene and scale, rotate, and position it to fit at the end of the arm. You can also use the armStart.ma scene from the chapter4\scenes directory on the DVD. Make a mirror copy of the glove, and position it at the end of the other arm (see Figure 4.87).

11. To see a finished version of the space suit character, open the spacesuitFinished.ma scene on the chapter4\scenes directory of the DVD (see Figure 4.88).

FIGURE 4.87
Import the gloves into the space suit scene and add them to the model.

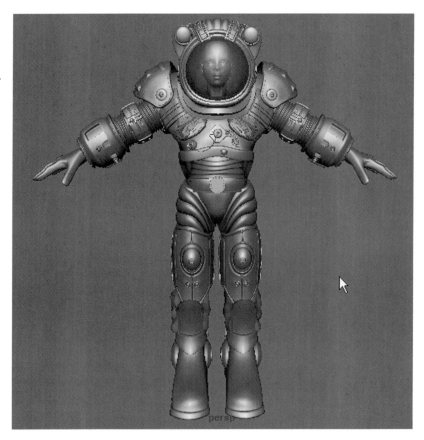

FIGURE 4.88
The completed
space suit model

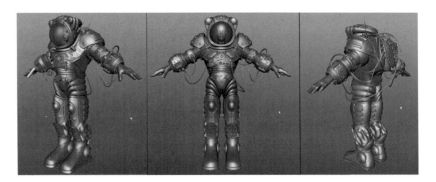

ARMS

If you'd like to see how the arms were created, open the `armStart.ma` scene in the `chapter4\` `scenes` directory on the DVD.

The Bottom Line

Understand polygon geometry. Polygon geometry consists of flat faces connected and shaped to form three-dimensional objects. You can edit the geometry by transforming the vertices, edges, and faces that make up the surface of the model.

Master it Examine the polygon primitives in the Create ➢ Polygon Primitives menu.

Work with smooth mesh polygons. The smooth mesh preview display allows you to work on a smoothed version of the polygon model while limiting the number of components needed to shape the model. You can use creasing to create hard edges in selected areas.

Master it Create a backpack for the space suit character.

Model using deformers. Deformers such as the lattice, non-linear deformers, and the Soft Modification tool can be used to help shape geometry and groups of objects.

Master it Create a number of small-detail objects for the belt of the space suit character. Shape the details so that they conform to the belt.

Combine meshes. Multiple meshes can be combined under a single shape node. When this is done, you can edit the components of the combined meshes as a single mesh.

Master it Combine two polygon spheres, and use the polygon-editing tools to join the faces of the spheres.

Use bevel tools. The Bevel tool can add a beveled edge to a polygon surface, creating more realism by smoothing the edges. The Bevel Plus tool is used primarily to create 3D logos from text curves, but it can be used to create interesting details and objects.

Master it Using the concept sketch as a guide, create the spiraling detail for the character's boots.

Model polygons with Paint Effects. Paint Effects strokes can be converted to NURBS and Polygon geometry. Using the default brush you can quickly create hoses and wires. Because construction history connects the converted objects to the strokes, you can use the stroke settings to edit the shape of the converted objects.

Master it Add additional hoses and wires to the space suit character.

Convert NURBS surfaces to polygons. NURBS surfaces are frequently used as a starting place to create polygon objects, giving you the power of both types of models.

Master it Convert the helmet object into polygons.

Use Booleans. Using Booleans you can use one polygon object to shape a second. The first object can be joined with the second or used to cut into it. An object can be created from the intersection of two objects.

Master it Create additional detail in the torso trim surface of the space suit character using Booleans.

Sculpt polygons using Artisan. The Artisan toolset is a brush-based modeling and editing tool. Using Artisan you can sculpt directly on the surface of geometry.

Master it Use Artisan to sculpt dents into a surface.

Model a human head. There are a variety of techniques you can use to create a human head. Modeling character heads is one of the most difficult challenges facing 3D artists. It takes a great deal of study and practice. This chapter demonstrates creating the head by connecting parts of the faces sculpted from polygon primitives.

Master it Take several photographs of yourself or a friend from the front and the side. Map these to image planes in a Maya scene, and create a polygon head using the photographs.

Create a character. Once you have the basic geometry for the head created, you can use the polygon editing and sculpting tools to shape the head into any number of characters.

Master it Use the geometry created for the head to make a different character. Try turning the head into an older man.

Use subdivision surfaces. Subdivision surfaces are similar to smooth mesh preview polygons except that specific parts of the model can be subdivided and edited as needed. You can traverse the subdivision levels while you work.

Master it Add wrinkles, seams, and other details to the glove model.

Chapter 5

Animation

Animation in Maya is accomplished through a variety of tools and techniques. The goal of this chapter is to show you how to use the tools in Maya to animate the attributes of various nodes. Gaining an understanding of how you can solve problems in Maya is essential to animating characters and scenes in a believable and entertaining way.

In this chapter you will learn to:

◆ Create a simple rig with joints and constraints

◆ Use Inverse Kinematics

◆ Animate with keyframes

◆ Use the Graph Editor

◆ Preview animations with Playblast

◆ Use driven keys

◆ Animate with expressions

◆ Animate with motion paths

◆ Use animation layers

Using Joints and Constraints

Most of this chapter is devoted to exercises that animate a simple mechanical bug model. Animation and rigging are closely related skills. Even if you don't intend to do much of your own rigging, you'll have an easier time understanding how to animate if you know what goes into creating a rig. Chapter 7 delves into more advanced rigging concepts; in this chapter you'll learn some basic tools and techniques for rigging to get you started.

When rigging mechanical objects and robots it's not always necessary to use joints; you can parent the parts of the object together in an organized fashion and then set keyframes directly on the geometry. However, because of the built-in hierarchy of joints as well as the many kinematic controls available, using joints can make rigging and animating mechanical objects easier, even if you don't intend to bind or skin the geometry so that it is deformed by the joints.

Joint Basics

You create joints using the Joint tool (from the Animation menu set choose Skeleton ➢ Joint Tool). A joint is represented by a simple wire sphere. When one joint is connected to another, the space between the two joints is bridged with a wireframe pyramid shape often referred to as a *bone*. The broad end of the bone is placed next to the parent joint, and the pointed end of the bone is pointed toward the child joint (see Figure 5.1).

FIGURE 5.1

Two joints are placed on the grid.

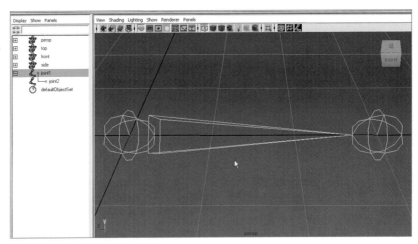

Joints are most often animated by rotating the parent joint or using *Inverse Kinematics*, which orients the joints based on the position of a goal called an *End Effector*. This is discussed later in this chapter. Joints can also be animated by placing keyframes on Translate or Scale channels; however, this is slightly less common.

Joints are usually placed in a hierarchical relationship known as a *joint chain*. Joint chains can have many branches and numerous controls depending on the complexity of the model.

A *joint* is a type of deformer that typically influences the shape of nearby components depending on how the components of the geometry are bound, or "skinned," to the joints. Since the bug in these examples is mechanical, the joints do not need to deform the geometry of the model. You can simply parent the pieces of the leg geometry to the individual joints. Skinning geometry to joints is explored further in Chapter 7.

Point Constraints

A point constraint uses the world space position of one object to control the world space position of another object. World space coordinates tell exactly where an object is in relation to the rest of the scene. This is different from object space coordinates, which are relative to the object's initial position.

For instance, if you move an object on the grid, the Translate channels in the Channel Box indicate where an object is in object space. If you freeze the transformations on an object (Modify ➢ Freeze Transformations) after moving the object, its Translate (and Rotate) channels become 0 in X, Y, and Z (Scale channels become 1 in X, Y, and Z), and its current position is now its starting position in object space.

If you create a joint in a scene and then reposition it and freeze transformations, you'll notice that the Rotate channels all become zero for its new orientation; however, the Translate channels are not affected by freeze transformations. If you want to place a joint exactly at the position of another object, you can't rely on the object's Translate channels as an accurate description of the object's location in world space. One way to get around this is to use a point constraint to position the joint according to the object's world space coordinates.

You'll use point constraints to place joints precisely at the pivot points of the leg parts. Once the joints are positioned you can delete the constraints.

1. Open the mechBugRig_v01.ma scene from the chapter5\scenes directory on the DVD.

The bug model is a combination of NURBS and polygon geometry. The bug's parts have already been parented in the Outliner to form a basic hierarchy (see Figure 5.2).

FIGURE 5.2

The mechanical bug is created from NURBS and polygon surfaces. Its various parts are organized in the Outliner.

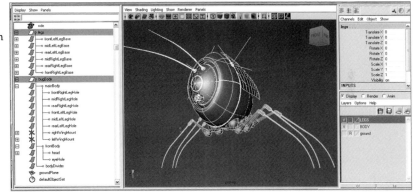

The model consists of two main groups: the legs and the bugBody. At the moment these two groups are separate. The legs and body are placed on two different display layers so their visibility can be turned off easily while working.

2. In the Layer Editor, turn off the BODY display layer so only the legs are visible.

3. Switch to the Animation menu set, and turn on Grid Snapping. Choose Skeleton ➤ Joint Tool. Draw three joints evenly spaced on the grid starting at the center. It doesn't matter in which direction you place the joints; they will be repositioned in a moment (see Figure 5.3).

4. In the Outliner, expand the legs group. Select the frontleftLegBase object. Ctrl+click joint1 and choose Constrain ➤ Point ➤ Options. In the Options box, make sure Maintain Offset is off and Constrain Axes is set to All (see Figure 5.4). Click Apply to create the constraint; the joints will snap to the position of the leg's base sphere.

When you create a constraint node, it appears in the Outliner parented to the constrained object. The icon looks like an exclamation point (see Figure 5.5). In this particular situation, you're only using the constraint to quickly position the joint at the same spot as the geometry, so once the joint is repositioned you can remove the constraint. This technique is a fast and easy way to make one object snap to the world space position of another. Using constraints as an animation tool is discussed later in the chapter.

5. In the Outliner, expand joint1. Select joint1_pointConstraint1, and press the Delete key to remove the constraint.

FIGURE 5.3
Place three joints
on the grid.

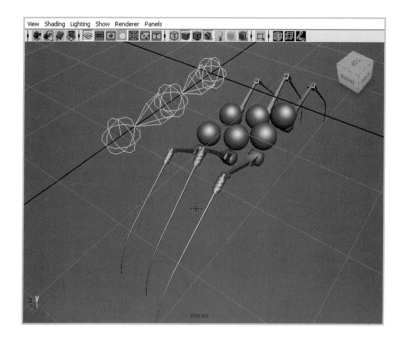

FIGURE 5.4
The options for the
point constraint

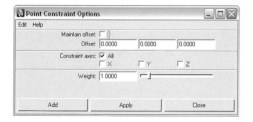

FIGURE 5.5
The point con-
straint appears
as an exclamation
point parented
to the constrained
object in the
Outliner.

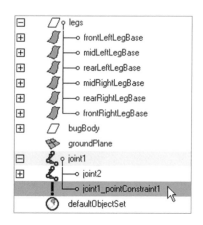

Real World Scenario

MEL IN ACTION: QUICK OBJECT-REPOSITION SCRIPT

You may find yourself frequently using a point constraint to snap one object to another. You can create a shelf button using a short MEL script so that, instead of repeating the same three steps over and over again, you can simply click a shelf button to instantly snap one object to another. This is an example of how learning just a little bit of MEL can make your workflow faster and easier.

Open a text editor such as Notepad (on Windows) or Text Edit (on the Mac). Type the following line.

```
string $mySelection[] = `ls -sl`;
```

This creates a variable array that holds a list of the currently selected objects. The list is numbered starting with zero, so once the list has been created from one or more selected objects, the first selected object is referred to as $mySelection[0], the second selected object is referred to as $mySelection[1], and so on.

The ls command stands for "list," and the -sl flag modifies the list command so it creates its list from the currently selected objects. The variable actually holds the result of the list command so the list command is contained within the accent marks. The accent mark key is the one below the ESC key on standard keyboards (not the apostrophe key). All commands in MEL must end in a semicolon.

Hit Enter (or Return) to start a new line. In this line type:

```
delete `pointConstraint $mySelection[0] $mySelection[1]`;
```

This command is actually two commands in a single line. The command within the accent marks creates a point constraint. The second object in the list, $mySelection[1], is constrained to the first, $mySelection[0]. When you create a constraint, you select the constraining object first and then the object that is constrained. The delete command then deletes the constraint immediately after it has been created, so that when you run the script the second object snaps to the first and you don't need to delete the constraint in the Outliner.

It may seem confusing to nest the point constraint command within the delete command and place them on a single line, but there's a good reason for using this convention. Let's say you wrote the script so that the point constraint command on one line creates the constraint—thus snapping one object to another—and then a second delete command deletes the constraint on another line. The delete command needs to know which point constraint it should delete. If you assume that the new point constraint will be named pointConstraint1, you run the risk of deleting a point constraint that already exists in the scene. You need a scripting strategy that creates a constraint, retrieves the correct name of the new constraint, and then deletes this new constraint. This involves many more lines of code. Hence it is much easier, and simpler, to nest the point constraint command within the delete command. Everything is taken care of within a single line of code. Select both lines in the Text Editor and copy them. In Maya, paste the script into the bottom half of the Script Editor (you can open the Script Editor by choosing Window ➢ General Editors ➢ Script Editor). In the Shelf tab, switch to the Custom shelf. Select both lines in the Script Editor, and choose File ➢ Save Script To Shelf. In the pop-up menu give the script a short, six-letter title such as **objSnp** (coming up with a descriptive six-letter title for a script is an art form unto itself).

CONTINUES

MEL IN ACTION: QUICK OBJECT-REPOSITION SCRIPT (*CONTINUED*)

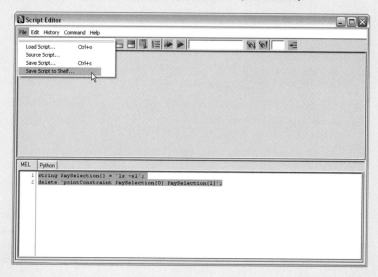

To the left of the shelf click the down-arrow button and choose Save All Shelves so this shelf button is available in future Maya sessions.

Create two objects in a Maya scene, select the constraining object first, then Shift+click the object to be constrained. Click the objSnp button in the Custom tab of the shelf to test the script. If you get an error, you can edit the command in the Shelf Editor. Click the down-arrow button to the left of the shelf, and choose Shelf Editor. Select the Custom shelf in the Shelf tab, switch to the Shelf Contents tab, and select the objSnp command in the Shelf Contents tab. Click the Edit Commands tab, and you'll see the script in the edit area. Correct any typos, and save the shelf.

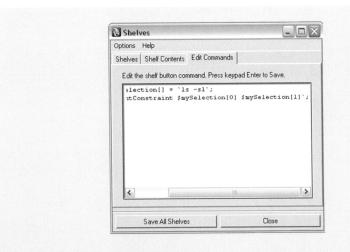

To see a version of the script open the objSnp.mel script in a text editor. The script is located in the chapter5\mel directory on the DVD.

6. Repeat steps 4 and 5 (or use the shelf button created in the "MEL In Action" section) to reposition joint2 to the frontLeftFoot object.

7. Turn on Point Snapping (turn off Grid Snapping), and position joint3 at the very tip of the frontLeftFoot.

8. Rename joint1 **frontLeftLegJoint**. Rename joint2 **frontLeftFootJoint**, and rename joint3 **frontLeftEndJoint**.

9. Make sure all point constraints on the joints have been deleted. Parent the frontLeftLeg-Base object to the frontLeftLegJoint, and parent the frontLeftFoot to the frontLeftFootJoint (see Figure 5.6).

FIGURE 5.6
Parent the parts of the leg to the leg joints.

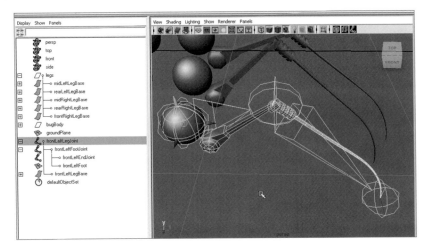

10. Create similar joint systems for the remaining five legs. Remember to rename your joints in a descriptive manner (see step 8) to avoid confusion when animating.

11. When you have finished creating all of the joints, place them in the legs group. To do this MMB-drag each of the top joints in the chain into the legs group in the Outliner (see Figure 5.7).

12. Save the scene as **mechBugRig_v02.ma**. To see a version of the scene to this point, open the mechBugRig_v02.ma scene from the chapter5\scenes directory.

FIGURE 5.7

Create joint chains for each of the legs.

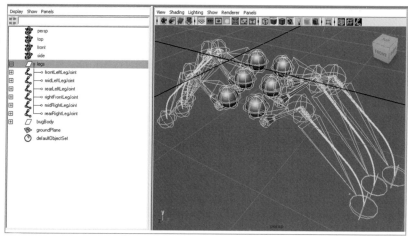

Aim Constraints

An *aim constraint* constrains the orientation of an object relative to the position of one or more other objects.

1. Continue with the scene from the previous section or open the mechBugRig_v02.ma scene from the chapter5\scenes directory on the DVD.

2. Turn on the display layer for BODY; turn off the LEGS layer so the legs are hidden and the body is displayed.

3. Create a locator and name it **eyeAimLoc**. Set the eyeAimLoc's Translate X, Y, and Z channels to **0, 0**, and **2**, respectively.

4. In the Outliner, expand the bugBodyGroup. MMB-drag eyeAimLoc into the bugBody group.

5. Select the eyeAimLoc and choose Modify ➤ Freeze Transformations so the Translate channels become 0, 0, and 0.

6. Expand the frontBody group, the head group, and the face group.

7. Select the eyeAimLoc and Ctrl+click the eyeBase group (see Figure 5.8). From the Animation menu set choose Constrain ➤ Aim Constraint ➤ Options.

8. In the options choose Edit ➤ Reset to return the settings to the default. Set the Aim Vector fields to **0, 0, 1**, so that the aim vector is set to the Z axis (see Figure 5.9). Click Apply to create the constraint.

FIGURE 5.8
Select the eyeAim-
Loc locator and the
eyeBase object in
the Outliner.

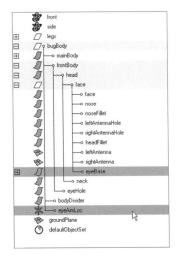

FIGURE 5.9
The Aim Con-
straint Options
window

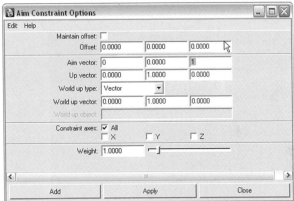

9. Move the locator around in the scene, and you'll see that the eyes follow it (see Figure 5.10). Because the locator is parented to the bug body, when you animate the bug, the locator will move with it.

FIGURE 5.10
The eyes follow the
position of the eye-
AimLoc locator.

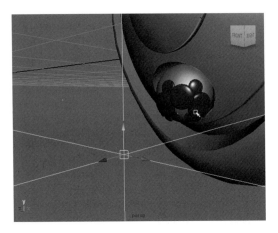

10. Create two new locators named **leftAntennaAimLoc** and **rightAntennaAimLoc**.

11. Set leftAntennaAimLoc's Translate X, Y, and Z to **1**, **0**, and **3**, respectively, and rightAntennaAimLoc's Translate X, Y, and Z to **-1**, **0**, and **3**.

12. Freeze transformations for both locators. Shift+click both locators and group them together. Name the group **antennaAim**. Leave the pivot point for the group at the center of the grid.

13. In the Outliner, MMB-drag antennaAim into the bugBody group.

14. Expand the antennaAim group. Expand the face group (in the bugBody/frontBody/head group). Aim constrain the leftAntenna to the leftAntennaAimLoc locator and the rightAntenna to the rightAntennaAimLoc locator.

When you move each antennaAimLoc locator, the antennae follow; when you rotate the antennaAim group, the locators move and the antennae follow. This gives you a way to animate the antennae separately and together (see Figure 5.11).

FIGURE 5.11
You can animate the antennae separately or together based on the grouping of the antennaAim-Loc locators.

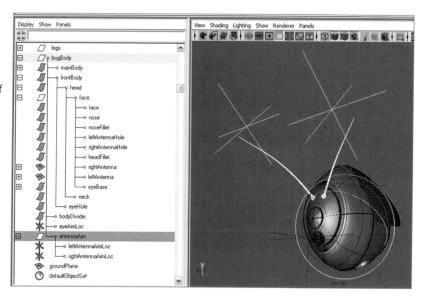

15. Save the scene as **mechBugRig_v03.ma**. To see a version of the scene to this point, open the mechBugRig_v03.ma scene from the chapter5\scenes directory on the DVD.

Inverse Kinematics

Kinematics is the study of the motion of objects. This is related to but distinguished from dynamics in that kinematics does not study the cause of the objects' motion, only the way in which the objects move. In 3D computer graphics the term *kinematics* describes how joints can be moved to animate objects and characters. There are two main types of kinematics: Forward Kinematics and Inverse Kinematics.

Forward Kinematics refers to a situation in which each joint in the chain inherits the motion of its parent joint. So if you have four joints in a chain, when you rotate the root, the three child joints move based on the rotation of the root. When you rotate the second joint, the third and fourth joints inherit the motion of the second (see Figure 5.12).

Forward Kinematics can be useful in many situations; for instance, it is often used for basic arm animation for characters. However, it can be tedious and difficult to work with for other types of animation, particularly when animating the legs of a character walking or jumping. Constant adjustments have to be made to ensure that as the root joints are animated, the limbs of the character do not penetrate the floor or slide during a walk cycle.

FIGURE 5.12
When using Forward Kinematics, each joint inherits the rotation of its parent.

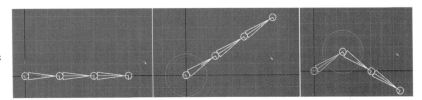

Inverse Kinematics (IK) causes the joints in a chain to orient themselves based on the position of a goal known as the *End Effector* (see Figure 5.13). Inverse Kinematics can be a more intuitive technique in many situations. When used on legs, the Sticky option for Inverse Kinematics can prevent joints from penetrating the floor or sliding during a walk cycle. When animating an IK chain, you can simply change the position of the End Effector using the Inverse Kinematics (IK) Handle, and all of the joints in the chain will orient themselves based on the position of the End Effector. The End Effector itself is positioned using the IK Handle; the End Effector is not actually visible or selectable in the viewport (it can be selected in the Hypergraph window).

FIGURE 5.13
Inverse Kinematics cause the joints in a chain to rotate based on the position of a goal.

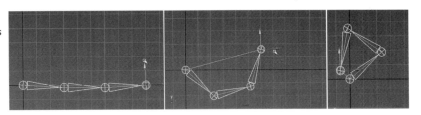

There are controls for blending between Forward and Inverse Kinematics known as FK/IK Blend. You can switch between Forward and Inverse Kinematics and even blend between the two.

Maya's kinematic controls work very well for many standard situations. Most professional riggers prefer to create their own custom controls and solutions. Creating custom controls is discussed in Chapters 6 and 7. In this section a very basic, simple IK technique is used on the legs of the mechanical bug. This makes animating the legs easier and more intuitive because you need only worry about the position of a single goal when animating all the parts of one of the legs.

IK Handle Tool

In this section you'll add Inverse Kinematics to each of the legs on the mechanical bug.

1. Continue with the scene from the previous section, or open the mechBugRig_v03.ma scene from the chapter5\scenes directory on the DVD. In the Layer menu, turn off Visibility for the BODY layer.

2. From the Animation menu set choose Skeleton ➢ IK Handle Tool ➢ Options. In the options, set the Current solver to ikSCsolver. This is the Single Chain solver that works well for simple joint chains, such as the legs in this bug.

The other option is the Rotate Plane solver (RPsolver). This solver has extra controls that can be used to solve joint-flipping problems, which can occur with more complex joint arrangements. If you create an IK Handle using the ikSCsolver and your joints behave unpredictably, try switching to the RPsolver (you can do this after creating the handle using the menu options in the IK Handle's Attribute Editor). The various types of IK solvers are discussed in Chapter 7.

In general, when adding Inverse Kinematics to a joint chain using the IK Handle tool, you don't want the joints to be aligned in a straight line. There should be a small bend in the joint chain. This helps the solver figure out how the joints should bend as they attempt to rotate based on the position of the End Effector. It's also a good idea to freeze transformations on the joints so their X, Y, and Z rotation channels are set to zero before adding the IK Handle (in the mechBug_v03.ma scene this has already been done).

3. Turn on Solver Enable and turn off Snap Enable. Snap Enable causes the IK Handle to snap back to the position of the end joint when you release it. You'll create a custom handle using a curve, so this option should be off.

4. Turn on Sticky. Sticky keeps the IK Handle's position constant as you pose the rest of the skeleton. This is very useful for keeping feet from moving through the floor when animating the other parts of the skeleton (see Figure 5.14).

FIGURE 5.14

The options for the IK Handle tool

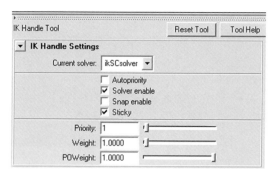

5. The other settings can be left at the default. With the IK Handle tool activated, click on the frontLeftLeg joint (the joint at the root of the front left leg); then click on the joint at the end of the frontLeftLeg chain. The IK Handle appears at the end of the joint chain (see Figure 5.15).

6. Try moving the IK Handle; you'll see the rest of the joint rotate based on the position of the handle.

7. Click Undo until the IK Handle returns to its original location.

It's usually a good idea to use a curve or another easily selectable object as a control for the IK Handle. This makes it easy to select the handle directly in the scene without having to hunt around in the Outliner.

8. Create a NURBS circle (Create ➢ NURBS Primitives ➢ Circle). Set the Scale channels of the circle to **0.4**.

FIGURE 5.15

The IK Handle tool creates an IK solver for the front left leg.

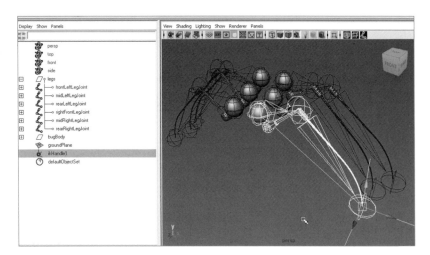

9. Use the objSnp shelf button created earlier in the chapter (see the "MEL in Action" section) to position the circle at the location of the IK Handle. To do this, select the ikHandle1 object, Ctrl+click the nurbsCircle1, and click the objSnp button in the Custom shelf.

10. Select the nurbsCircle1 and rename it **frontLeftFootCtrl**. Choose Modify ➢ Freeze Transformations so the current position of the curve becomes its home position.

11. Select the frontLeftFootCtrl, and Ctrl+click the ikHandle. Create a point constraint so the handle is constrained to the frontLeftFoot circle (Constrain ➢ Point).

12. You can turn off visibility of the ikHandle1 object. To animate the leg, select the frontleftLegCtrl circle and move it around. To reset its position, set its Translate X, Y, and Z channels to **0**.

13. Repeat steps 2 through 12 to create controls for the other five legs (the options for the IK Handle tool should already be stored, so you can just activate the tool and use it to add IK to the other legs).

14. When you have finished making the controls for the other legs, select the control circles and group them. Name the group **legsControlGroup**.

15. Select the legsControlGroup group, and choose Modify ➢ Center Pivot. This places the pivot of the group at the center of the controls.

16. Make another NURBS circle; name the circle **legsCtrl**. Use the objSnp button to place the circle at the position of the legControlGroup's pivot. Freeze transformations on the legsCtrl.

17. Select the legsCtrl circle, and Ctrl+click the legsControlGroup. Choose Constrain ➢ Parent ➢ Options. In the options make sure Maintain Offset is on and both Translate and Rotate are set to All. Click Apply to create the constraint. The Parent constraint constrains both the translation and the rotation of one object to another.

Now you have a selectable control for moving all of the legs as well as each individual leg. This will mean less time hunting around in the Outliner.

COLOR-CODING CONTROLS

You can create different colors for the NURBS curve you use as a control. To do this, open the Attribute Editor for the curve, and expand the Object Display rollout and then the Drawing Overrides rollout. Click Enable Overrides, and use the Color slider to choose a new color for the circles. This helps them stand out in the scene.

---

18. Finally, you can straighten up the Outliner by grouping the IK Handles. Name the group **feetIkhandles**. Group the legs and bugBody together, and name this group **bug**.

19. Save the scene as **mechBugRig_v04.ma**. To see a version of the scene to this point, open the mechBugRig_v04.ma scene from the chapter5\scenes directory on the DVD.

Create a Master Control

To finish the rig you can create a selectable control to animate the position and the rotation of the bug body and then group all of the parts of the bug together so that it can be easily moved or scaled in the scene.

1. Continue with the scene from the previous section or open the mechBugRig_v04.ma scene from the chapter5\scenes directory on the DVD.

2. Create a new display layer named **CONTROLS**. Turn off the visibility of the LEGS and BODY display layers, select the NURBS circles, and add them to the CONTROLS layer.

3. Turn off the Visibility of the CONTROLS layer so the scene is blank.

4. Turn on the Visibility of the grid. Turn on Grid Snapping. Choose Create ➢ CV Curve Tool ➢ Options. Set Curve Degree to Linear.

5. Switch to the top view, and use the curve to draw a shape like the one in Figure 5.16. The shape should be a cross with an arrowhead at each end of the cross. Press Enter to complete the curve.

FIGURE 5.16
Create a cross with an arrow at each end using a linear CV curve.

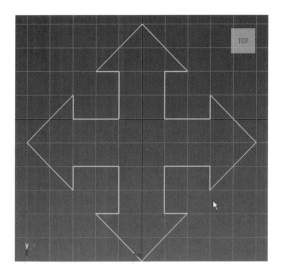

6. Center the pivot of the curve and name it **bodyCtrl**.

7. In the Outliner, expand the bug group. Click the objSnp button to snap the bodyCtrl curve to the center of the bugBody object. Scale the bodyCtrl curve in X, Y, and Z to **3.5**.

8. Freeze transformations on the curve.

Next, you want to move the curve above the body so you can easily select it. This curve controls the translation and rotation of the bugBody. However, you want to keep the pivot point of the control at the center of the bug body. Since you snapped the curve to the center of the bugBody, the pivot point of the curve is at the same position as the bugBody. So how do you move the curve without moving the pivot point? Simple—you move all of the CVs of the curve above the bug body. This moves the curve without changing its pivot point.

9. Select the bodyCtrl curve and switch to CV selection mode (right-click on the curve and choose CVs). Drag a selection marquee over all of the CVs of the curve. Switch to the Move tool, and drag up on the Y axis to position the CVs of the curve above the body. Since the pivot point has not changed, it doesn't matter how high you place the curve above the bug; it just has to be easily selectable (see Figure 5.17).

10. Select the bodyCtrl curve in the Outliner, and Ctrl+click the bug group. Choose Constrain ➢ Parent ➢ Options. In the options, make sure Maintain Offset is selected and Translate and Rotate are set to All. Create the constraint.

FIGURE 5.17
Move the CVs of the bodyCtrl curve above the bugBody; the pivot point of the curve remains at the center of the bugBody.

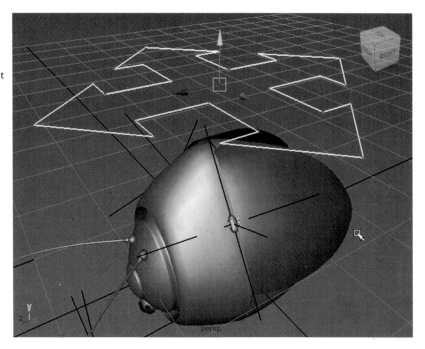

The parent constraint constrains both the translation and rotation of one object to another object.

11. Turn on the LEGS layer. Select the bodyCtrl curve and try moving and rotating it. The legs stay on the ground (within a certain range).

At this point you should have a nice set of simple controls for both the body and the legs of the bug. All this work will make animating the bug a much more pleasant experience.

12. Finally, select everything in the Outliner except the ground plane, and group them together. Name the group **mechanicalBug**.

13. Add the bodyCtrl curve and the three locators for the eyes and antenna controls to the CONTROLS layer.

14. Save the scene as **mechBugRig_v05.ma**. To see a version of the scene to this point, open the mechBugRig_v05.ma scene from the chapter5\scenes directory of the DVD (see Figure 5.18).

FIGURE 5.18
The completed bug rig is ready for animation.

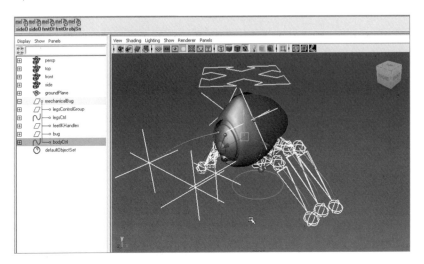

One last control you can add to the bug is a selectable rotational control for the antennaAim group. Use the same techniques used to create the bodyCtrl curve. The mechBug_v01.ma scene has an example of this control.

Keyframe Animation

The simplest way to animate an object in Maya is to use keyframes. A keyframe records the value of an attribute at a point in time on the timeline. When two keyframes are set for an attribute at different points in time, Maya interpolates the value between the two keyframes on the timeline, and the result is an animation.

Keyframes can be set on almost any attribute in Maya. You can use keyframes to animate an object's position, the color of the shader applied to the object, the visibility of the object, whether the object becomes dynamic, and so on.

Now that you have a rig for the mechanical bug that can be animated, you can get to work bringing him to life.

Creating Keyframes

In this exercise you'll see the various ways you can set and manipulate keyframes in the Maya interface.

1. Open the `mechBug_v01.ma` scene in the `chapter5\scenes` directory on the DVD.

The mechanical bug in this scene has been rigged using the techniques discussed in the first part of the chapter. The major difference is that a circle has been added between the two antenna controls that you can select and animate to control both antennae at the same time.

The controls are color coded so they are more organized visually. The visibility of the joints is turned off in the Show menu of the perspective view; however, they are still present in the scene.

FRAME RATE

When you begin an animation, it's always a good idea to set the frame rate in Maya's preferences. The default frame rate is 24 frames per second, which is standard for film. To change the frame rate, choose Window ➤ Settings/Preferences ➤ Preferences. In the Preferences window, select Settings from the list of Categories, and then choose Frame Rate from the Time menu.

Keyframes can be placed on the individual channels of an object using the Channel Box. It's usually a good idea to keyframe on the channels that need to be animated rather than all of the channels and attributes of an object. To keyframe individual channels, follow these steps:

2. In the perspective view, select the blue bodyCtrl curve above the bug (the curve that looks like a cross with an arrow on each end; see Figure 5.19).

FIGURE 5.19

Select the bodyCtrl curve above the bug.

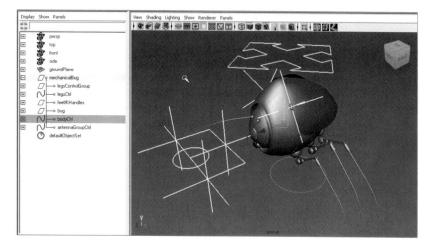

3. Move the current frame in the timeline to frame 20 by clicking and dragging the timeline until the marker is at frame 20. Alternatively, type **20** into the box to the far right of the timeline.

4. With the bodyCtrl selected, highlight the Translate Y channel in the Channel Box by clicking on it; then right-click and choose Key Selected from the pop-up menu (see Figure 5.20).

5. Set the timeline to frame 48. Use the Move tool to pull the bodyCtrl curve up to about two units, and set another keyframe on the Translate Y channel. The keys are represented on the timeline by a thin red vertical line (see Figure 5.21).

6. Rewind and play the animation; you'll see the bug start moving upward on frame 20 and stop on frame 48.

FIGURE 5.20

Set a keyframe on the Translate Y channel of the bodyCtrl.

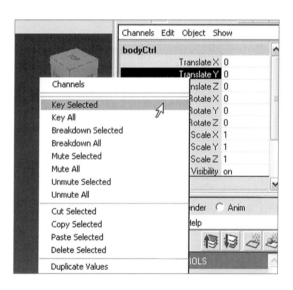

FIGURE 5.21

Keyframes are represented on the timeline by a thin red vertical line.

For the most part, setting keyframes is pretty straightforward. If you want to set a keyframe on all of the Translate channels at the same time, the hot key is W. To set a keyframe on all Rotate channels at once, use E. To set a keyframe on all the Scale channels at once use, use R.

PLAYBACK SPEED

You can change the playback speed of the animation in Maya in the Timeline Preferences window (you can also access these options quickly by right-clicking on the timeline and choosing a playback speed option from the pop-up menu). Open the options by choosing Window ➢ Settings/Preferences ➢ Preferences. Choose Timeline from the list of categories. The Playback Speed menu allows you to choose the playback speed.

You can choose Play Every Frame, Real-Time (24 frames per second), Half-Time (12 frames per second), or Twice (48 frames per second), or you can set a custom playback speed. Generally the most useful speeds are Play Every Frame and Real-Time. If there are dynamics in the scene (such as particles, nCloth, rigid bodies, and so on), set this option to Play Every Frame so the dynamics calculate correctly. You can set the Max Playback speed as well so the animation speed cannot exceed a certain rate. Setting Max Playback to Free means the animation will play back as fast as your processor allows, which can be faster than the final rendered animation.

Auto Keyframe

The Auto Keyframe feature automatically places keyframes on an object when a change is made to one of its attributes. For Auto Keyframe to work, the attribute must already have an existing keyframe. To turn Auto Keyframe on, click the key icon to the right of the timeline. This exercise shows you how to use Auto Keyframe.

1. On the timeline for the mechBug_v01.ma scene, set the current frame to **20**.

An easy way to do this is to use the Step Back One Key or Step Forward One Key buttons to the right of the timeline. The hotkeys for moving back and forth one key are Alt+comma and Alt+period.

2. Shift+click all six of the small purple leg control circles below the bug's feet (see Figure 5.22).

FIGURE 5.22
Select the leg control circles.

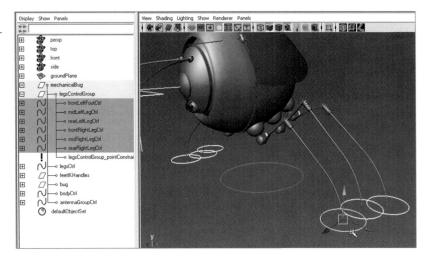

3. With the control circles selected, press the W hot key to place a keyframe on the Translate channels for all the selected curves.

4. Click the Key icon to the far right of the timeline to turn on Auto Keyframe.

5. Set the timeline to frame 40. Select each of the circles and move them in toward the center (see Figure 5.23).

6. When you play the animation, you'll see that the legs move inward without your having to set a keyframe in the Channel Box.

Using Auto Keyframe is certainly a matter of personal preference. You can easily set unwanted keys on an object by mistake using this feature, so remember to use it with caution.

7. Save the scene as **mechBug_v02.ma**. To see a version of the scene to this point, open the mechBug_v02.ma scene from the chapter5\scenes directory on the DVD.

FIGURE 5.23
Move the leg control circles in toward the center of the bug.

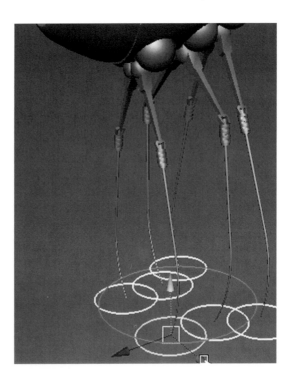

Move and Scale Keyframes on the Timeline

You can reposition keys on the timeline interactively by selecting the key markers and sliding them back and forth.

1. Continue with the scene from the previous section or open the mechBug_v02.ma scene from the chapter5\scenes directory on the DVD.

2. In the Perspective window, select the blue bodyCtrl curve. Hold the Shift key and drag a selection directly on the timeline. You'll see a red area appear as you drag. Keep dragging this area so it covers both keyframes set on the bodyCtrl curve (see Figure 5.24).

FIGURE 5.24

Hold the Shift key and drag on the timeline to select a range of keys.

3. To move the keys forward or backward in time, drag on the two arrows at the center of the selection. Drag on these arrows to move the keys so the first key is on frame 10.

To scale the keys, drag on one of the arrows on either side of the selection. The other end of the selection acts as the pivot for the scaling operation; you may need to reposition the keys on the timeline again after scaling.

4. Scale the keys down by dragging the arrow on the right side of the selection toward the left. After scaling the keys, drag on the arrows at the center to reposition the keys so the animation starts on frame 10.

SNAP KEYS

As you scale and move keys, you'll notice that a keyframe can be positioned on the fraction of a key. In other words, a key might end up on frame 26.68. You can fix this by choosing Edit ➢ Keys ➢ Snap Keys. In the options, set the value for Snap To to a multiple of 1 and set Snap Operation to Time. You can apply this to selected objects—or all objects, selected channels, or all channels—and define the time range. You can also right-click on selected keyframes on the timeline and choose Snap. This automatically snaps keyframes to the nearest integer value.

You can move an individual key by Shift+clicking the key marker on the timeline and then dragging on the arrows to move the key.

Repositioning and scaling keys directly on the timeline is usually good for simple changes. To make more sophisticated edits to the animation, you can use the Graph Editor discussed later in the chapter.

When you play the animation, you'll see that the bug jumps up fairly quickly and much sooner than before. You'll also notice that the animation of the legs has not changed.

5. Spend a few minutes practicing these techniques on each of the legBase objects. Changes made to the position of the keyframes affect selected objects. You can edit each legCtrl circle separately or all of them at the same time.

6. Save the scene as **mechBug_v03.ma**. To see a version of the scene to this point, open the mechBug_v03.ma scene from the chapter5\scenes directory on the DVD.

Copy, Paste, and Cut Keyframes

There are a number of ways you can quickly copy, paste, and cut keyframes on the timeline and in the Channel Box.

1. Continue with the scene from the previous section or open the mechBug_v03.ma scene from the chapter5\scenes directory on the DVD.

2. Select the bodyCtrl curve in the perspective view. On the timeline, Shift-drag a selection over both of the keyframes.

3. Right-click on the selection and choose Copy (see Figure 5.25).

4. Deselect the keys by clicking on the timeline, move to frame 70, right-click on the timeline, and choose Paste ➤ Paste.

FIGURE 5.25
You can copy keyframes directly onto the timeline.

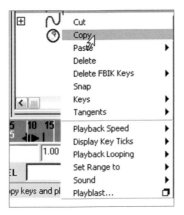

5. The keys for the Translate Y channel are pasted on the timeline at frame 70. If you play the animation, you'll see that the bug jumps up, moves back down, and then jumps up again.

Other options include the following:

Paste Connect pastes the copied key with an offset starting at the value of the previous key.

Cut removes the keyframes from the timeline but copies their values to the clipboard so they can be pasted anywhere on the timeline.

Delete removes the keys.

Delete FBIK deletes the Full Body IK keys.

You can copy and paste keys from two different channels by using the options in the Channel Box.

6. Select the bodyCtrl curve in the perspective view. In the Channel Box, right-click on the Translate Y channel. Choose Copy Selected (see Figure 5.26).

7. Highlight the Translate Z channel, right-click, and choose Paste Selected.

This pastes the values (including keyframes) copied from the Translate Y channel to the Translate Z channel. The starting point of the pasted keyframes is based on the current time in the timeline. When you play the animation, the bug moves forward as it moves up. The forward motion will be offset (in time) depending on the current frame in the timeline.

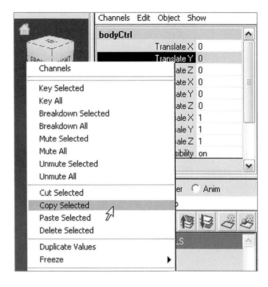

FIGURE 5.26
You can copy keyframes using the menu options in the Channel Box.

You can also cut and delete keyframes in the Channel Box. The Duplicate keyframe operation allows you to copy keyframes from one object to another.

8. Create a NURBS sphere and set its Translate X to **5**.

9. Select the sphere and then Shift+click the bodyCtrl curve. Right-click on the Translate Y channel, and choose Duplicate Values. This connects the keyframes on the Translate Y channel of the bodyCtrl curve to the NURBS sphere. If you change the values of these keys, both the bodyCtrl curve and the sphere will reflect the changes made to the keys.

When duplicating keyframes, the order in which you select the objects is important. Select the object you want to use as the source of the duplicate keyframes last. If you graph the objects on the Hypergraph, you'll see that the same keyframe nodes are attached to both objects.

The Graph Editor

The timeline and the Channel Box offer a few basic controls for creating and editing keyframes. However, when you're refining an animation, the controls in the Graph Editor offer greater flexibility as well as visual feedback on the interpolation between keyframes. To open the Graph Editor, choose Window ➢ Animation Editor ➢ Graph Editor. You can also set a viewport to the Graph Editor view.

THE GRAPH EDITOR AXES

The Graph Editor is a two-dimensional display of the animation in a scene. The Graph Editor has two axes: X and Y. The X, or horizontal, axis typically displays the time of the scene in frames. As you move from left to right on the graph, time moves forward. Moving from right to left means going backward. It is possible to go into negative keyframe values if you create keys to the left of the zero marker.

The Y, or vertical, axis displays the values of the keys in units for translation and scale and in degrees (or radians depending on the setting in the rotation settings in the preferences) for rotation. The higher you go on the Y axis, the higher the value of the key. Of course, anything below the zero line indicates negative values.

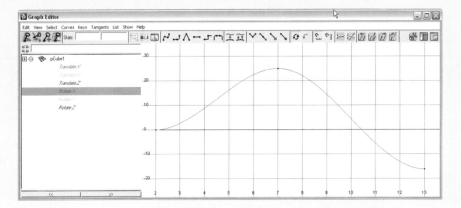

Animation Curves

Animation curves visually describe how the values between two keyframes are interpolated over time. A keyframe is represented by a point on the curve. The portion of the curve on the graph to the left of a keyframe represents the animation before the key, and the line and the portion on the right represent the animation after the key. The keys themselves have handles that can be used to fine-tune the shape of the curve and thus the behavior of the animation both before and after the key. The shape of the curve to the left of the key is known as the *incoming tangent* (or in tangent); the shape of the curve to the right of the key is known as the *outgoing tangent* (or out tangent), as shown in Figure 5.27.

Each animated channel has its own curve on the graph. You can use the menu in the Graph Editor to edit the keys and change the way the curves are displayed on the Graph Editor.

In this exercise, you'll use the Graph Editor to refine a simple animation for the mechanical bug. In this animation the bug will leap in the air, hover for two seconds, lean forward, and then fly off the screen in a gentle arc. You'll start by setting keys on the Translate channels of the bug. To make things easier you'll use Auto Keyframe.

FIGURE 5.27

The curves on the Graph Editor represent the interpolation of values between keyframes for a selected object.

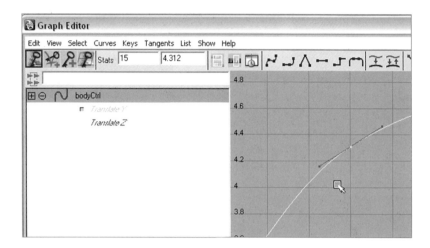

The setting applied to the tangents of the curves sets the overall shape of the curve before and after each key. You can apply a tangent setting to one or more selected keys on the graph, and the in and out tangents can also have their own setting.

The settings are listed in the Tangents menu in the Graph Editor and are also represented visually by the icons at the top of the Graph Editor. Clicking one of these buttons or applying a setting from the Tangents menu changes the interpolation of the selected key(s) or tangent handles (see Figure 5.28).

FIGURE 5.28

The icons for the tangent settings at the top of the Graph Editor

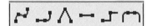

When blocking out an animation, it's common to use the Stepped tangent setting. The Stepped tangent setting creates no interpolation between keys, so an object's animated values do not change between keyframes; instead the animation appears to pop instantly from key to key. Using stepped keys when you block out the animation gives you a clear idea of how the object will move without the additional motion that can be added by curved tangents. Once you're happy with the blocking, you can switch to another tangent type and then refine the animation.

1. Open the mechBug_v01.ma scene from the chapter5\scenes directory on the DVD.

2. Open the Preferences window by choosing Window ➤ Settings/Preferences ➤ Preferences. Click the Animation category under Settings. Set Default In Tangent to Flat and Default Out Tangent to Stepped. You can't set Default In Tangent to Stepped in the Preferences window.

3. Make sure Auto Keyframe is enabled. Press Save to save the preferences (see Figure 5.29).

FIGURE 5.29
The animation preferences are established in the Settings/Preferences window.

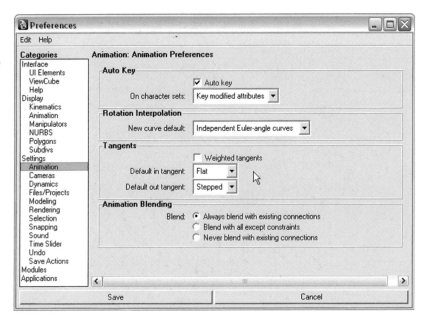

4. Set the length of the timeline to 120. Set the current frame to 20.

5. Select the blue bodyCtrl curve in the perspective view. Press W and E to set keyframes on the Translate and Rotate channels.

When blocking out the animation, the only object that needs to be keyframed at this point is the bodyCtrl curve.

6. Set the timeline to frame 25, and move the bodyCtrl curve down so the Translate Y channel is about -0.78.

7. Set the timeline to frame 35. Drag up on the bodyCtrl curve until the Translate Y channel is around 7 units.

8. Set the timeline to 45. Rotate the bodyCtrl slightly, and move the bug a little forward and to the side. This gives the bug a slight wobble as he hovers. Try these settings:

   Translate X: **-0.68**

   Translate Y: **4.968**

   Translate Z: **0.532**

   Rotate X: **-11**

   Rotate Y: **7**

   Rotate Z: **10**

Many of these values were arrived at by simply moving and rotating the bodyCtrl curve in the scene. You can use these exact values or something that's fairly close. Most of the time when blocking in the animation you'll move the objects in the scene rather than type in precise values, but the keyframe values are included here as a rough guide. Remember, right now the only object being keyframed is the bodyCtrl curve.

9. Set the frame to 60. The bug is starting to turn as he decides which way to fly. Rotate him to his left a little and add a bit more variation to his position. Try these settings:

Translate X: **-.057**

Translate Y: **4.677**

Translate Z: **-1.283**

Rotate X: **-18.137**

Rotate Y: **20.42**

Rotate Z: **-13.628**

10. Now the bug is starting to fly away. Rotate him so he is facing downward slightly. Try these settings:

Translate X: **1.463**

Translate Y: **3.664**

Translate Z: **-.064**

Rotate X: **31.488**

Rotate Y: **35.304**

Rotate Z: **1.545**

11. Set the time slider to frame 95. The bug is beginning his flight, so he turns more to the left and dips down a little. Try these settings:

Translate X: **4.421**

Translate Y: **3.581**

Translate Z: **1.19**

Rotate X: **1.593**

Rotate Y: **46.833**

Rotate Z: **1.935**

12. In the final keyframe on frame 120 the bug is flying away. Try these settings:

Translate X: **11.923**

Translate Y: **9.653**

Translate Z: **6.794**

Rotate X: **48.999**

Rotate Y: **62.691**

Rotate Z: **24.392**

13. Play back the animation a few times. You'll see the bug pop from one position to another. Make changes if you like, but try not to add any more keys just yet. It's best to use as few keys as possible; you'll let the curves do all the work in a moment.

14. Select the red legsCtrl circle, and keyframe its Translate channels so it follows the flight of the bug. To keep it interesting, place the keys at different frames than the bodyCtrl curve. Remember to set an initial keyframe before using Auto Keyframe.

You can set keys on the individual foot controls, but at this point let's keep things simple and focus on just the bodyCtrl curve and the translation of the legsCtrl curve.

15. In the Perspective View menu, choose Panels ➢ Saved Layouts ➢ Persp/Graph/Outliner so the interfaces are split between the perspective in the Outliner and the Graph Editor.

16. Select the bodyCtrl curve, and hold the cursor over the Graph Editor. Press the f hot key so you can see all the animation curves for the bodyCtrl object. Since the tangents are set to Stepped, they look like straight lines in a stepped pattern (Figure 5.30).

17. Save the scene as **mechBug_v04.ma**. To see a version of the scene to this point, open the mechBug_v04.ma scene on the chapter5\scenes folder of the DVD.

FIGURE 5.30
The Graph Editor is in its own panel in the interface; the keys for the bodyCtrl curve appear as straight lines.

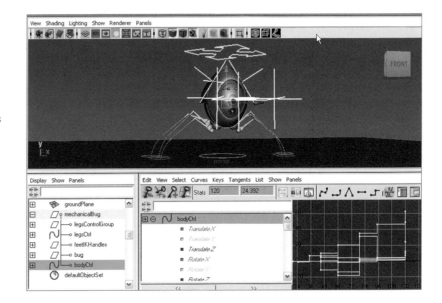

GHOSTING

Ghosting is a way to visualize how an object changes over time in space. It is analogous to "onion skinning" in traditional animation, where you can see how the object looks in the animation several steps before and/or after the current frame. To activate ghosting, select an animated object and choose Animate ➢ Ghost ➢ Options. In the options, you can specify the number of frames to display before and/or after the current frame. You can also choose to display specific frames. To remove the ghosting, select the object and choose Animate ➢ Unghost or Animate ➢ Unghost All.

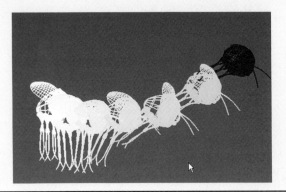

Editing Animation Curves

At this point you're ready to start refining the animation curves using the tangent tools. Keep things simple and add keys only when absolutely necessary.

1. Continue with the scene from the previous section or open the mechBug_v04.ma scene from the chapter5\scenes directory on the DVD.

2. In the Display Layers menu, turn off the visibility of the LEGS layer so you can just focus on the animation of the body.

3. Select the bodyCtrl curve, and in the Graph Editor drag a selection marquee over all the translation and rotation keys. Test how the animation looks when different tangent types are applied to the keys.

4. On the menu bar of the Graph Editor, click the first tangent icon or choose Tangents ➢ Spline. This changes all the selected key tangents to spline. Play the animation, and observe how the bug moves as it jumps, hovers, and flies away.

5. In the Graph Editor zoom in closely to the selected keys (MMB+Alt-drag).

You'll notice that spline tangents add a bit of overshoot to some of the keys, as shown in Figure 5.31, which results in a smooth, natural motion. However, in some cases this may add extra motion where you don't want it. It depends on how much precise control you want over the animation.

FIGURE 5.31
Switching to spline tangents adds a slight overshoot to the animation curves. Notice how the curve dips below the lowest value of some of the keyframes.

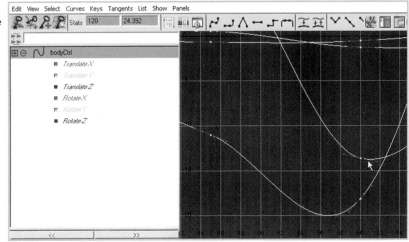

6. Try switching to the clamped-type tangent (second tangent icon, or choose Tangents ➢ Clamped).

Clamped tangents are very similar to spline tangents; in fact, you'll notice a difference between spline and clamped tangents only when two values in a curve are very close together. Clamped tangents remove any overshoot that may cause sliding or slipping in an object. In the current animation example, you won't see much a difference at all except for a couple keyframes (see Figure 5.32).

FIGURE 5.32
Clamped tangents are very similar to spline tangents except for values that are very close. In this figure spline tangents (left image) are converted to clamped tangents (right image).

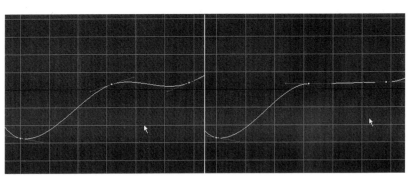

Aside from spline, clamped, and stepped tangents, you can also try using one of these tangent types. A single curve can use any combination of tangent types as well.

Linear tangents create straight lines between keyframes, resulting in a very sharp and direct motion.

Flat tangents make the tangents completely horizontal. Flat keyframes are very useful when you want to create a slow ramping effect to the values, known as "easing in" or "easing out."

"Easing in" means that the animation curve starts out flat and then gradually becomes steeper; "easing out" is the opposite.

Plateau tangents create smooth curves between keyframes. However, the overshoot that occurs with spline and clamped tangents is eliminated, so the peaks of each curve do not go beyond the values you set when you create the keyframes. Plateau tangents offer a good balance between smooth motion and control.

7. With all of the keys selected in the Graph Editor, click on the last tangent icon, or choose Tangents ➢ Plateau to switch to plateau-type tangents. Once an overall tangent type is established you can edit the tangents and values of individual keys.

A good place to start editing the animation is the initial leap that occurs at frame 20.

8. Make sure you can see both the Graph Editor and the body of the bug in the perspective view. The bugCtrl object should be selected so you can see its animation curves.

9. In the left column of the Graph Editor, highlight Translate Y to focus on just this individual curve.

The leap has a slight anticipation where the bug moves down slightly before jumping in the air. At the moment the motion is uniform, making it look a little uninteresting. You can edit the curve so the bug leaps up a little faster and sooner. Start by moving the third keyframe closer to the second.

10. Select the third keyframe, and click the move key icon (first icon on the far left of the menu bar) or use the w hot key. To move the key, hold the MMB and drag to the left (see Figure 5.33). To constrain the movement horizontally so its value is not changed (only its time), hold the Shift key while dragging with the MMB.

FIGURE 5.33
Move the third keyframe on the bodyCtrl's Translate Y channel to the left, closer to the second keyframe.

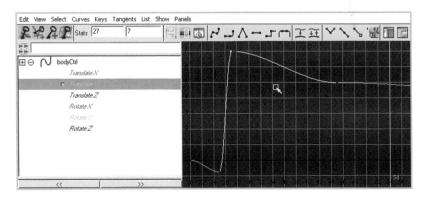

You can enter numeric values into the Stats field for precise control. The first field is the keyframe's time in frames; the second field is the value for the keyframe.

11. Slide the keyframe to the left so it is close to the second keyframe; the curve in between should become more of a straight line. If you want the keys to snap to whole values, select the key and choose Edit ➢ Snap.

There are two magnet icons on the menu bar of the Graph Editor (these may be visible only when the Graph Editor is maximized). These icons turn on horizontal and vertical snapping, respectively. The keyframes are then snapped to the grid in the Graph Editor (see Figure 5.34).

12. You can change the shape of the curves by editing the tangents directly. Drag a selection box around the handle to the right of the third key. Press the w hot key to switch to the Move tool. MMB-drag upward to add overshoot to the out tangent (see Figure 5.35).

FIGURE 5.34
The magnet icons turn on horizontal and vertical snapping.

FIGURE 5.35
MMB-drag on the tangent handles to directly edit the curve shape.

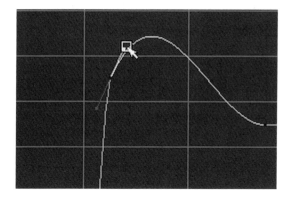

You'll notice that as you drag upward on the tangent handle, the handle on the opposite side of the key moves downward, maintaining the shape of the curve through the key. You can break the tangency of the curve handles if you want a different interpolation for the in and out tangents.

13. Drag a selection around both handles of the second key on the Translate Y channel. Choose Key ➤ Break Tangents to break the tangency of the handles. The in tangent is now colored gray and the out tangent is colored brown.

14. Drag a selection handle around the in tangent, and MMB-drag it upward so there is a slight bump and then a sharp dip in the curve (Figure 5.36).

When you play the animation, the bug moves up slightly, down quickly, and then leaps into the air. You can unify the tangents by choosing Keys ➤ Unify Tangents. The angle of the tangents will not change, but you won't be able to edit the in and out tangents independently until you break the tangents again.

15. Save the scene as **mechBug_v05.ma**. To see a version of the scene to this point, open the mechBug_v05.ma scene from the chapter5\scenes directory on the DVD.

FIGURE 5.36
When you break
the tangency of
the handles, you
can move the
tangent handles
on either side
of the keyframe
independently of
each other.

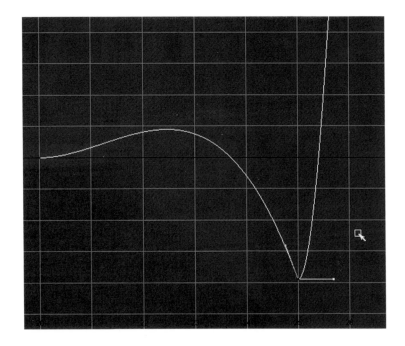

Weighted Tangents

You can convert the tangents to weighted tangents, which means you can further refine the in and out tangents by pulling on the tangent handles.

1. Continue with the scene from the previous section or open the mechBug_v05.ma scene from the chapter5\scenes directory on the DVD.

2. Select the bodyCtrl curve, and in the Graph Editor select the Translate Y channel to isolate the curve. Press the f hot key so the entire curve fits in the Graph Editor.

3. Drag a selection around the fourth key, and use the MMB to drag it down a little to create a slight dip in the curve (upper left of Figure 5.37).

4. With the key selected choose Curves ➤ Weighted Tangents. The ends of the handles turn into circles. When a key is converted to a weighted tangent, all the keys on the curve also become weighted tangents.

5. Select the handles and choose Keys ➤ Free Tangent Weight. The handles turn to small squares, indicating that the tangents can be pulled (upper-right image of Figure 5.37).

6. MMB-drag on the handles left or right to extend the length of the handles; notice the change in the shape of the curve (lower-left of Figure 5.37).

7. Break the tangents on the selected handles (Keys ➤ Break Tangents). Push the handle on the left of the fourth key toward the right to shorten the incoming tangent.

8. Pull the outcoming tangent of the fourth keyframe down and to the right (lower-right image of Figure 5.37).

9. Play the animation, and see how changing the length of the handles affects the way the bug jumps.

10. Save the scene as **mechBug_v06.ma**. To see a version of the scene to this point, open the mechBug_v06.ma scene from the chapter5\scenes folder on the DVD.

FIGURE 5.37
Weighted tangents allow you to edit the curves by pulling and pushing the tangent handles.

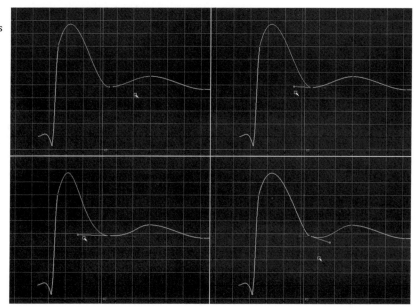

Additional Editing Tools

In addition to moving keyframes and tangents, you can also use the Scale tool to stretch and shrink a number of selected keys at once.

1. Continue with the scene from the previous section or open the mechBug_v06.ma scene from the chapter5\scenes directory on the DVD.

2. Select the bodyCtrl curve in the perspective view and open the Graph Editor. Press the f hot key so all the curves are visible on the editor.

3. Drag a selection marquee over all the keys to the right of the third key.

4. From the Graph Editor menu bar, choose Edit ➢ Transformational Tools ➢ Scale Key ➢ Options. In the options, turn on Manipulator. A box is drawn around the keys. You can stretch or shrink the box to change the distance between selected keys.

When the Scale Keys tool option is set to Gestural, the position of the cursor on the graph is the pivot for the scaling operation.

5. Hold the cursor over the fourth key. MMB-drag back and forth to scale the keys horizontally. Increasing the scale horizontally slows down the animation; decreasing the horizontal scale speeds up the animation (see Figure 5.38).

6. Drag the lower-left corner of the Scale Keys tool to the right a little to extend the animation and slow it down after the fourth keyframe.

FIGURE 5.38
The Scale Keys tool stretches or shrinks the distances between selected keys on the graph.

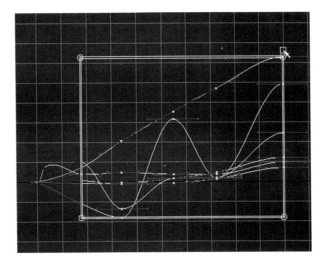

If you want to scale just the values, you can drag up or down. Small changes made with the Scale Key tool can have a large effect, so use this tool with caution.

Another way to edit the keys is to use the Lattice Deform Keys tool.

7. With the keys still selected, choose Edit ➤ Transformation Tools ➤ Lattice Deform Keys. This creates a lattice deformer around the selected keys. Click and drag on the points and lines of the lattice to change the shape of the lattice (see Figure 5.39). This is a good way to add a little variation to the animation.

FIGURE 5.39
The Lattice Deform Keys tool creates a lattice around selected keys to manipulate groups of selected keys.

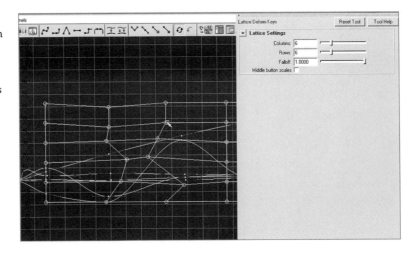

To change the number of rows and columns in the lattice, open the Tool Options box while the Lattice Deform Keys tool is active. If the lattice does not update properly when you change the settings in the Tool Options box, try reselecting the keys in the Graph Editor.

The Insert Keys tool inserts a key in one or more animation curves. To use this tool, first select one or more animation curves in the Graph Editor, click the Insert Key icon in the Graph Editor toolbar, and MMB-click on the curve.

The Add Key tool is similar to the Insert Keys tool except that wherever you click in the Graph Editor will be used as the value for the added key. Both tools require that you MMB-click in the Graph Editor (see Figure 5.40).

You can copy and paste keys on the graph; pasted keys are placed at the current location on the timeline. This means that if you select a group of keys that start at frame 40, then move the timeline to frame 60 and paste, the keys will be pasted at frame 60. For more precise copying and pasting, use the Copy and Paste options in the Graph Editor's Edit menu.

8. Practice editing the keys on the Graph Editor for the bodyCtrl curve (both Translate and Rotate channels). When you're happy with the animation, make the legs visible and edit the keys set on the legCtrl circle.

If you decide to use Auto Keyframe when refining the animation for other parts of the robot, switch the default in and out tangents to spline, clamped, or plateau in the preferences. Otherwise Maya inserts stepped keyframes while Auto Keyframe is on, which can be frustrating to work with at this point.

You can add natural-looking motion to the way the bug hovers by simply shifting the keys placed on the different channels back and forth in time so they don't occur on the same frame (see Figure 5.41).

9. To see a version of the scene where the keys have been edited, open the mechBug_v07.ma scene in the chapter5\scenes directory on the DVD.

FIGURE 5.40

The Insert Key tool (left) inserts a key into a selected curve when you MMB-click. The Add Key tool (right) adds a key to a selected curve wherever you click on the graph.

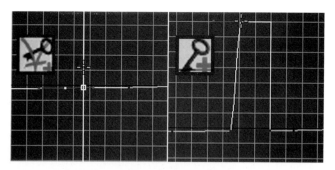

FIGURE 5.41

Shift the keys for the various channels back and forth in time so they don't occur on the same frame. This creates a more natural motion.

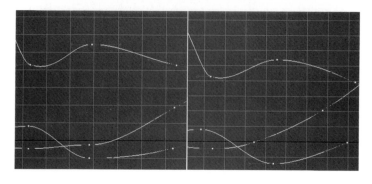

Breakdowns and In-Betweens

A *breakdown* is a special type of helper keyframe. The breakdown itself is just like a keyframe; what makes it special is how the breakdown affects the other keys on the curve. When you insert a breakdown and then move keys before or after the breakdown, the position of the breakdown moves as well to maintain a proportional relationship with the other keys on the curve. Normally when you move a keyframe, the other keys are not adjusted.

Try this short exercise to understand how breakdowns work.

1. Open the mechBug_v07.ma scene from the chapter5\scenes directory on the DVD.

2. Turn off the visibility of the LEGS layer so you can focus on just the bug body.

3. Select the blue bodyCtrl curve and open the Graph Editor. Select the Translate Y channel so it is isolated on the graph.

4. Drag a selection around the third key on the graph. Switch to the Move tool (hot key = w). Hold the Shift key and drag back and forth on the graph. The other keys on the graph do not move; this is the normal behavior for keys.

5. Drag a selection around the second key on the graph. From the menu in the Graph Editor, choose Keys ➢ Convert To Breakdown.

You won't notice any difference in the key itself or its tangent handles. The color of the key tick mark on the graph changes to green, but other than that it looks and acts the same.

6. Drag a selection around the third key on the graph, and try moving it back and forth.

This time you'll notice that the second key adjusts its position to maintain a proportional relationship in the shape of the curve with the changes made to the third key. The same behavior occurs if you change the first key (see Figure 5.42).

You can convert any key to a breakdown using the Edit menu. To insert a breakdown, set the timeline to the frame where you want the breakdown, right-click on one or more channels in the Channel Box, and choose Breakdown Selected. You can add a breakdown to all the channels by choosing Breakdown All.

FIGURE 5.42
Breakdowns are special keys that maintain the proportions of the curve when neighboring keys are edited.

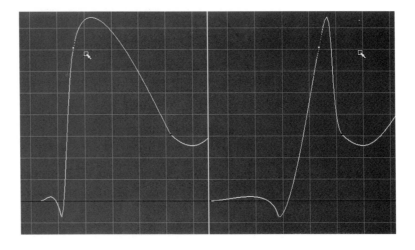

Breakdowns are useful for adding very precise animation to an object's channels without affecting the tangents of the surrounding keys. This can be important if you have perfected an animation but need to make a small change to a single key.

An *in-between* is a point on the curve that does not have a keyframe. In other words, each frame between two keys is known as an in-between. When you add an in-between, you shift all the keys to the right of the current point in the timeline one frame to the right. When you remove an in-between, you shift all the keys to the left.

Pre- and Post-Infinity

The Pre- and Post-Infinity settings can be used to quickly create simple repeating motions. To animate the flapping wings, you can set three keyframes and then set the Post-Infinity settings to Cycle.

1. Open the mechBug_v07.ma scene from the chapter5\scenes directory on the DVD.

2. Set the timeline to 10.

3. In the perspective view, zoom in closely to the body of the bug; on its left side, select the small piece of geometry that holds the wing to the body. The object is called leftWingMotor (see Figure 5.43).

4. Right-click on the Rotate X channel in the Channel Box, and choose Key Selected.

5. Set the frame in the timeline to frame 12. Set Rotate X to **60**, and create another keyframe.

6. Set the timeline to frame 14, set Rotate X to **0**, and create another keyframe.

7. With the leftWingMotor selected, open the Graph Editor. Select Rotate X in the column on the left, and press the f key so the editor focuses on the animation curve for this channel.

8. Select all the keys, and choose Tangents ➢ Linear to convert the curve to linear tangents.

FIGURE 5.43
Select the leftWingMotor on the side of the bug.

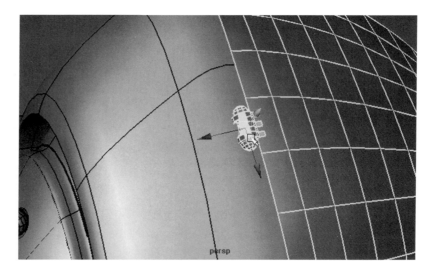

9. Zoom out a little in the Graph Editor (drag using Alt+RMB on the editor).

10. With the curve selected choose Curves ➤ Post Infinity ➤ Cycle.

11. Choose View ➤ Infinity in the Graph Editor. The cycling keyframes are shown as a dotted line on the graph (see Figure 5.44).

12. Play the animation in the perspective view. The wing starts flapping in frame 10; it continues to flap at the same rate for the rest of the animation.

FIGURE 5.44
You can view how the keyframes will cycle by choosing View ➤ Infinity. The animation curve after the last keyframe is shown as a dotted line.

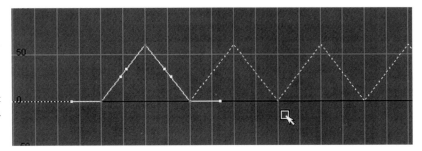

To make the wing flap faster, simply scale the keyframes.

13. Repeat steps 7 through 11 for the rightWingMotor.

14. Save the animation as **mechBug_v08.ma**. To see a version of the animation to this point, open the mechBug_v08.ma scene from the chapter5\scenes directory on the DVD.

The Pre-Infinity options work just like the Post-Infinity options, except the cycling occurs before the first keyframe. The Oscillate option cycles the keyframes backward and forward.

Cycle With Offset cycles the animation curve with an offset added to the cycle based on the value of the last keyframe (see Figure 5.45).

FIGURE 5.45
Cycle With Offset adds an offset to the cycle based on the value of the last keyframe.

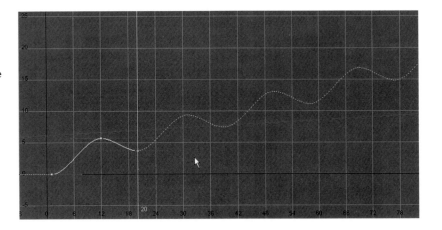

The Linear option extends the curve, based on the tangency of the final keyframe, into infinity. So if you wanted the bug to continue to fly upward forever, you can select the Translate Y channel and set Post Infinity to Linear.

Playblast and F Check

A *playblast* is a way to create an unrendered preview of an animation. When you create a playblast, Maya captures each frame of the animation. The frames can be stored temporarily or saved to disk. You should always use playblasts to get a sense of the timing of the animation. What you see in the Maya viewport window is not always an accurate representation of how the final animation will look.

F Check (or Frame Check) is a utility program that ships with Maya. This program plays back a sequence of images with some very simple controls. When you create a playblast you have the option of viewing the sequence in your operating system's media player or in F Check. F Check is usually the better choice because of its simplicity and support for a variety of image formats.

Create and View a Playblast

This exercise will show you how to preview an animation using Playblast and F Check.

1. Open the mechBug_v08.ma scene from the chapter5\scenes directory on the DVD.

2. Switch to the shotCam camera in the perspective view.

3. Choose Window ➤ Playblast ➤ Options. In the options, set Time Range to Time Slider. Set Viewer to Image Viewer (this option specifies F Check; the Movieplayer option uses the default movie viewer for your operating system).

4. Set Display Size to From Window and Scale to **0.75** (see Figure 5.46).

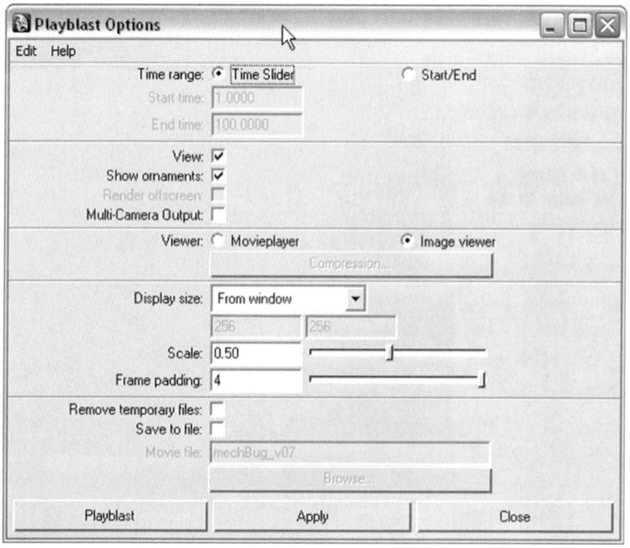

FIGURE 5.46
The options for
Playblast

5. Click Playblast to record the image sequence. In the case of the bug animation, this should take only a few seconds. A scene that has a lot of dynamics or a lot of geometry may take longer.

6. Once the playblast is complete, F Check should open automatically and play the sequence. You can also open a sequence in F Check by choosing (from the main Maya menu bar) File ➤ View Sequence.

The movie-viewing controls are at the top of the menu bar. The Alpha and Z Depth display options work only for rendered sequences that have alpha or Z Depth channels included.

In Windows, you can scrub back and forth in the animation by clicking and dragging directly on the image in F Check. You can also RMB-drag on the image to draw quick notes and annotations. The notes remain on the frame as long as F Check is open (see Figure 5.47). You can use F Check's File menu to save and load animation sequences.

The Mac version of F Check uses a separate control panel called Fcheck Info. You can scrub through the movie by dragging left or right in the window. In the Mac version you cannot draw on the images as you can with the Windows version. The Mac version may also display a blank image for a minute or so while it loads the sequence into memory. Once it has loaded, press the t hotkey to see the sequence play at the correct frame rate, otherwise the sequence may play too quickly.

FIGURE 5.47

F Check is a utility program that plays back image sequences. In Windows, you can draw on the frames displayed in F Check using the RMB.

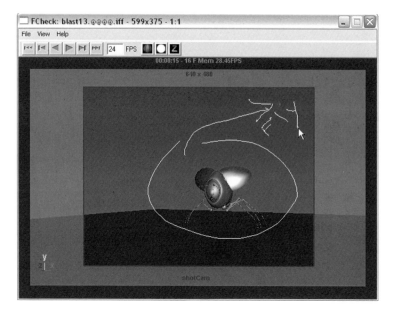

Driven Keys

Driven keys are keyframes that are driven by the attributes of another object rather than time. Standard keyframes describe a change for an object's attribute at two different points in time. For example, a cube may have a Translate Y value of 0 at frame 10 and a Translate Y value of 30 at frame 50. When the animation is played, the cube moves up 30 units between frames 10 and 50. When you create driven keys, you create a relationship between any two attributes. For example, you could have the Rotate X channel of a cone control the Translate Y channel of a cube. So when the cone's Rotate X is at 0 degrees, the Translate Y channel of the cube is at 0. When the Rotate X channel of the cone is 90 degrees, the Translate Y channel of the cube is at 50. The cone is referred to as the *driving object*, and the cube becomes the *driven object*. You can even have the attribute of one object drive one or more attributes on the same object.

Driven keys are often used in rigging to automate the animation of parts of the model, which saves a lot of time and tedious keyframing when animating the rest of the model.

Creating a Driven Key

In this section, you'll create driven keys to automate the walking motion of the mechanical bug's legs so that when the bug moves forward or backward on its Z axis, the legs automatically move.

1. Open the mechBugWalk_v01.ma scene from the chapter5\scenes directory on the DVD.

2. In the perspective view, use the Show menu to turn off visibility of the joints so it's easier to select the leg controls.

Driven keys are set through a separate interface. You'll set up the walk cycle for one leg and then copy and paste the keys to the others.

3. From the Animation menu set, choose Animate ➤ Set Driven Keys ➤ Set. The Set Driven Key window opens.

The upper part of the Set Driven Key window lists the driving object (there can be only one at a time) and its attributes. The bottom part of the window lists the driven object(s) (there can be more than one at a time) and their attributes. The first step is to load the driving and driven objects. Figure 5.48 shows the Set Driven Key window with objects loaded already; you'll load the objects and attributes in the next few steps.

FIGURE 5.48
The Set Driven Key interface lists the driver objects at the top and the driven objects on the bottom.

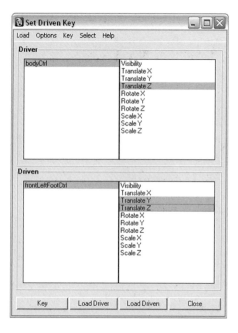

4. Select the bodyCtrl curve and click the Load Driver button.

5. Select the frontLeftFootCtrl curve and click Load Driven.

To create the walk cycle for the front left leg, the Z translation of the bodyCtrl curve will drive the Z translation of the front left foot (making it move forward) and the Y translation of the front left foot (making it move up as it moves forward). You need to create the first key to establish the starting position of the front left leg.

6. Select the frontLeftFootCtrl curve, and set its Translate Z channel to **-1**.

7. In the Set Driven Key window, select Translate Z in the upper-right corner (this indicates the Translate Z of the bodyCtrl curve as selected in the upper left of the box). Shift+click the Translate Y and Translate Z channels in the lower right (this indicates the Translate Z and Translate Y of the frontLeftFootCtrl curve (see Figure 5.48).

8. Click the Key button at the bottom of the Set Driven Key window.

When you click the Key button, the current value for the channel selected in the upper right is the driver for the values of the channels in the lower left. So in step 8, the Translate Z of bodyCtrl is set to 0, the Translate Z of frontLeftFootCtrl is set to -1, and the Translate Y of frontLeftFootCtrl is set to 0. A keyframe relationship is set up between the Translate Z of bodyCtrl and the Translate Z and Translate Y of frontLeftFootCtrl. When frontLeftFootCtrl is selected, its Translate Y and Translate Z channels are colored orange in the Channel Box, indicating a keyframe has been set on these channels.

9. Select the bodyCtrl curve again and set its Translate Z to **1**. Select the frontLeftFootCtrl curve, and set its Translate Z to **1** and its Translate Y to **0.8**.

10. Make sure that in the Set Driven Key window, the Translate Z channel is selected in the upper right and both the Translate Y and Translate Z channels are selected in the lower right. Click the Key button again to set another key.

11. Set the Translate Z of bodyCtrl to **2**. Set the Translate Z of frontLeftFootCtrl to **3** and the Translate Y to **0**. Click the Key button again.

12. Set the Translate Z of bodyCtrl to **4**. Don't change either setting for Translate Z or Translate Y of frontLeftFootCtrl. Set another key.

The IK applied to the front left leg keeps it stuck in place, which makes the walk cycle easy to animate.

13. In the perspective view try moving the bodyCtrl rig back and forth on the Y axis. You'll see the front left foot take a step.

14. Save the scene as **mechBugWalk_v02.ma**. To see a version of the scene to this point, open the mechBugWalk_v02.ma scene from the chapter5\scenes directory on the DVD.

Looping Driven Keys

To make the foot cycle you can simply use the Pre- and Post-Infinity settings in the Graph Editor.

1. Continue with the scene from the previous section or open the mechBugWalk_v02.ma scene from the chapter5\scenes directory on the DVD.

2. Select the frontLeftFootCtrl and open the Graph Editor (Window ➤ Animation Editors ➤ Graph Editor). In the left-hand column, select the Translate Y and Translate Z channels.

You'll see the animation curves appear on the graph. Since these are driven keys, the horizontal axis does not represent time; rather it is the Translate Z channel of the bodyCtrl curve. So as the graph moves from left to right, the value of the bodyCtrl's Translate Z channel increases. Moving from right to left, the value decreases.

3. In the Graph Editor menu, choose View ➤ Infinity. You can now see the Pre- and Post-Infinity values for the curves.

4. Select the green Translate Y curve. Choose Curves ➤ Pre Infinity ➤ Cycle. Then choose Curves ➤ Post Infinity ➤ Cycle.

By doing this you create a repeating cycle for Translate Y. The foot moves up and down in the same pattern as the bodyCtrl curve moves back and forth. The Translate Z channel is a little different. Since it is moving along the Z axis in space, you need to offset the value for each step so the foot continues to step forward.

5. Select the blue Translate Z curve and choose Curves ➤ Pre Infinity ➤ Cycle With Offset. Then choose Curves ➤ Post Infinity ➤ Cycle with offset. The dotted line on the graph shows how the Translate Z channel moves up in value with each cycle (see Figure 5.49).

6. Move the bodyCtrl curve back and forth on the Z axis, and you'll see that the front left leg now walks with the bug.

7. Save the scene as **mechBugWalk_v03.ma**. To see a version of the scene to this point, open the mechBugWalk_v03.ma scene from the chapter5\scenes directory on the DVD.

FIGURE 5.49
The Pre- and Post-Infinity values of the Translate Z channel are set to Cycle With Offset so it continually steps as the bug is moved back and forth.

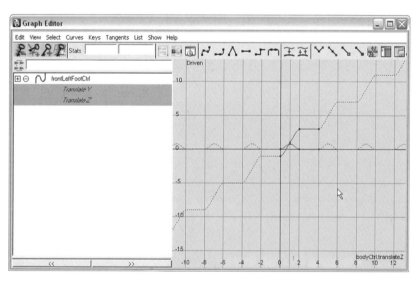

Copying and Pasting Driven Keys

The trick at this point is to create the same driven key arrangement for the other five legs in the easiest way possible. You can achieve this using Copy and Paste. The important thing to remember is that to paste driven keys from a channel on one object to another, you should have one driven key already created for the target objects.

1. Continue with the scene from the previous section or open the mechBug_v03.ma scene from the chapter5\scenes directory on the DVD.

2. From the Animation menu set, choose Animate ➤ Set Driven Key ➤ Set to open the Set Driven Key window.

3. Select the bodyCtrl curve and load it as the driver. Select all of the leg control curves except the frontLeftLegCtrl. Press the Load Driven button.

4. Make sure the Translate Z channel of the bodyCtrl curve is at **0**. Set the Translate Z of the five leg control curves to **-1**.

5. Select the Translate Z channel in the upper right of the Set Driven Key window. In the lower left, make sure all the leg control curves are selected.

6. Select the Translate Y and Translate Z channels in the lower right. Click the Key button to create an initial key for the five legs. You can close the Set Driven Key window (see Figure 5.50).

7. Make sure the bodyCtrl curve's Translate Z channel is at **0**. Select the frontLeftFootCtrl curve. In the Channel Box, highlight the Translate Y and Translate Z channels. Right-click and choose Copy Selected.

8. Shift+click the five other leg control curves. Highlight the Translate Y and Translate Z channels, right-click, and choose Paste Selected.

FIGURE 5.50

Set an initial driven key on the Translate Y and Translate Z channels of the five remaining legs.

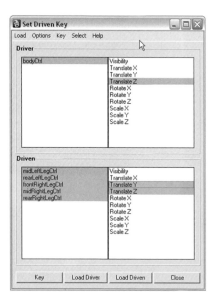

When you move the bodyCtrl curve back and forth, the other legs take one step. You need to loop the driven keys of the other legs in the Graph Editor.

9. Select the leg control circles for the five remaining legs, and open the Graph Editor. Ctrl+click the Translate Y channels of all the leg controls in the left column of the editor. Drag a selection over the keys on the graph, and choose Curves ➤ Pre Infinity ➤ Cycle and then Curves ➤ Post Infinity ➤ Cycle.

10. Ctrl+click the Translate Z channel for each of the leg controls in the Graph Editor. Drag a selection around the keys on the graph, and choose Curves ➤ Pre Infinity ➤ Cycle With Offset and then Curves ➤ Post Infinity ➤ Cycle With Offset.

11. Drag the bodyCtrl curve back and forth on the Graph Editor. All the legs take a step; however, they all do so at the same time, which looks a little silly.

12. To create a more convincing walk cycle for the bug, select each leg control, and open the Graph Editor. Select the keys on the graph and use the Move tool to slide them a little backward or forward in time so each leg has its own timing. See Figure 5.51.

13. As you change the position of the Translate Z keys on the Graph Editor, you may need to also slide the curves up or down a little to make sure that they remain within the proper leg length range as they step. You can generally figure out the proper setting through experimentation.

FIGURE 5.51
Add variation to the movement of the legs by sliding the keys for each leg control on the Graph Editor.

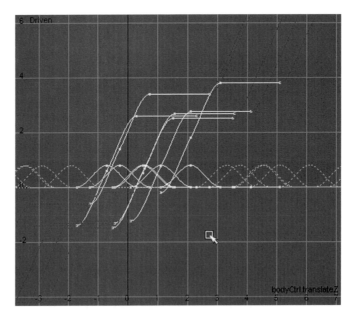

Creating a walk cycle this way is a little tricky and will take some practice. You can set keyframes on the Translate Z channel of the bodyCtrl curve so the bug walks forward and then adjust the position of the legCtrl curves as the animation plays. You can also change the position for the keyframes on the Graph Editor for pairs of legs so the midLeftLegCtrl, frontRightLegCtrl, and rearRightLegCtrl all move together, alternating with the remaining leg controls. Study the mechBugWalk_v04.ma scene in the chapter5\scenes directory on the DVD to see how this walk cycle was accomplished.

14. Save the scene as **mechBugWalk_v04.ma.** See Figure 5.52. To see a finished version of the walking bug, open the mechBugWalk_v04.ma scene from the chapter5\scenes directory on the DVD.

FIGURE 5.52
The completed walk cycle is completely automated for the bug.

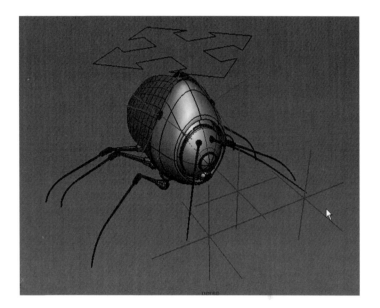

Animation Using Expressions

Mathematical expressions can be used to automate animation of an object's attributes. Expressions can be very simple or quite complex. There is almost an infinite variety of expression types and applications. In this section, you'll see how to add a few simple and common expressions to animate the bug's antennae.

1. Open the mechBugExpressions_v01.ma scene from the chapter5\scenes directory on the DVD. This scene has an animation of the mechanical bug walking.

2. Select the yellow circle in front of the bug. This is the antennaCtrl, which controls the rotation of the antenna control group.

3. In the menu above the Channel Box, select the Rotate Y channel so that it is highlighted. Choose Edit ➤ Expressions. This opens the Expression Editor.

4. In the Expression section type **rotateY=sin(time)**;. Click the Create button to add the expression to the antennaCtrl object (see Figure 5.53).

This expression creates a relationship where the rotation of the antennaCtrl group moves back and forth over time. The sin function creates a smooth curve using time as the input. The value of sin moves between -1 and 1. The value of the Rotate Y channel is expressed in degrees, so this expression does not create a very visible motion. It oscillates between -1 and 1 degrees. To fix this, you can add a multiplier to the expression.

FIGURE 5.53

Enter an expression for the antennaCtrl curve in the Expression Editor.

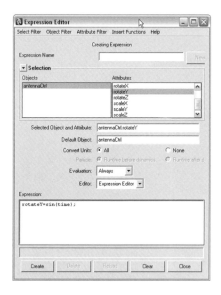

When you click the Create button, Maya fills in the detailed path to the antennaCtrl channel. The original expression is replaced with `antennaCtrl.rotateY=sin(time)`. As long as an object is selected when you open the Expression Editor, you can type the name of the channel, and Maya will understand that the channel is connected to the selected object. Otherwise, you must specify the path to the channel by typing **objectName.channelName**. Each statement in the expression should end with a semicolon.

5. In the Expression Editor, change the expression to read **antennaCtrl. rotateY=30*(sin(time));**. Click the Edit button to change the expression.

6. Rewind and play the animation. The antennae swing back and forth.

7. If you want the motion to move faster, create a multiplier for `time`. Change the expression so that it reads **antennaCtrl.rotateY=30*(sin(time*2));**. This makes the rotation occur twice as fast.

If you want to slow down the motion, multiply the time by a fraction. `time*0.5` makes the rotation move at half the original speed.

You can add an expression to the Translate Y of the antennaCtrl group to make the antenna move up and down.

8. Select the antennaCtrl and open the Expression Editor (if it's not still open). In the Expression section, type **translateY=cos(time);** below the first expression (see Figure 5.54). Click the Edit button to create the expression.

FIGURE 5.54

Add the expression for the Y translation as a second line in the Expression Editor.

This moves the antennaCtrl group up and down, making the antennae rotate upward and downward (recall that the locators in the antennaCtrl group are aim locators for the antennae geometry). The cos function (cosine) works like the sin function (sine) except the cosine is the opposite of sine, so when sine is at -1, cosine is at 1 and vice versa.

To make the motion more interesting, you can add a noise function to each of the locators in the antenna control group. The noise function creates a continuous random pattern that moves between -1 and 1 (as opposed to the rand function, which creates a discontinuous random motion between -1 and 1).

9. Select one of the yellow locators in the perspective view. In the Channel Box, highlight the Translate Y channel, and choose Edit ➤ Expressions to open the Expression Editor for the locator.

10. In the Expression section type **translateY=noise(time*4);**. Then click the Create button to make the expression. Play the animation; you'll see the antenna move somewhat randomly.

11. Add a similar expression to the Translate Y of the other yellow locator. To make the motion slightly different, try **translate=noise(time*5);**.

12. Save the scene as **mechBugExpressions_v02.ma**. To see a version of the scene, open the mechBugExpressions_v02.ma scene from the chapter5\scenes directory on the DVD.

Conditional Statements in Expressions

You can make expressions even more sophisticated by adding variables and conditional statements. A simple conditional statement looks like this in the Expression Editor:

```
if (x is true){
    Perform action;
}
else
{
    Perform a different action;

}
```

There are other ways to state conditionals, but this is the most common and simplest way to do it. To make the motion of the antennae more interesting, you'll make the antennae move faster when they are closer to the ground.

1. Continue with the scene from the previous section or open the mechBugExpressions_v02.ma scene from the chapter5\scenes directory on the DVD.

2. Select one of the yellow locators in front of the bug, and open the Expression Editor using the Edit menu in the Channel Box.

To create a condition, you'll make a variable that can hold a value. The value will be different depending on the outcome of the test performed by the conditional statement. In this case, the variable can hold a value, which will be a multiplier for time in the noise(time) statement applied to the locator's Translate Y channel. Before you can use the variable, you should declare it at the start of the expression. This lets Maya know what type of data the variable will hold. In this case, the variable can be an integer (a number without a decimal). The variable you will create is called $antSpeed, for antenna speed. All variables must be preceded by a dollar sign.

3. In the Expression Editor, select the text and press the Backspace or Delete key to clear the Expression field. Type **int $antSpeed;** in the field.

4. Press the Return key (the Return key on the keyboard, *not* the Enter key on the numeric keypad), and enter the following lines:

```
if (antennaCtrl.translateY<0){
    $antSpeed = 10;
}
else
{
    $antSpeed=2;
}
translateY = noise(time*$antSpeed);
```

Since the expression is testing to see the height of the antennaCtrl group, you need to specify the path to the antennaCtrl group's Translate Y channel. Expressions for channels are self-contained, so unless you specify the path to another object's channel, Maya won't understand what you're talking about. Figure 5.55 shows the expression in the Expression Editor.

FIGURE 5.55
Create a conditional statement as an expression to make the antenna move faster when it's closer to the ground.

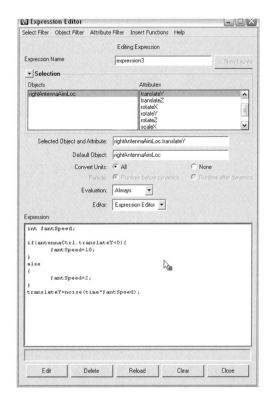

5. Add the same expression to the other locator in the group. Use different values for the $antSpeed variable so that the two antennae move in different ways.

6. Save the scene as **mechBugExpressions_v03.ma**. To see a finished version of the scene, open the mechBugExpressions_v03.ma scene from the chapter5\scenes directory on the DVD.

Motion Path Animation

You can animate the movement of an object by attaching the object to a curve and then sliding down the length of the curve over time. This is known as *motion path animation.*

Create a Motion Path

1. Open the mechBugPath_v01.ma scene from the chapter5\scenes directory on the DVD.

2. Turn on the grid display and choose Create ➢ CV Curve Tool ➢ Options. In the options, make sure Curve Degree is set to Cubic.

3. Draw a curve on the grid using any number of points; make sure the curve has some nice twisty bends in it.

4. Right-click on the curve and choose Control Vertex. Use the Move tool to move the CVs of the curve up and down so the curve is three-dimensional (see Figure 5.56).

5. In the Outliner, select the mechanicalBug group and Ctrl+click the curve. From the Animation menu set, choose Animate ➢ Motion Paths ➢ Attach To Motion Path ➢ Options.

FIGURE 5.56
Draw and shape a curve in the scene.

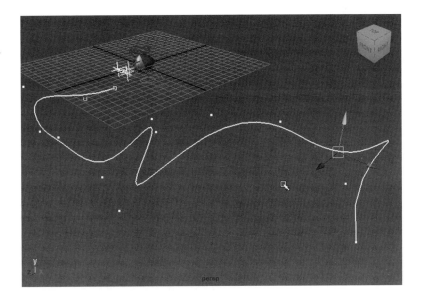

6. In the options, choose Edit ➤ Reset to reset the options. Set Front Axis to Z, turn on Follow, and enable Bank. Set Bank Limit to **30**. Click Attach to attach the bug to the curve (see Figure 5.57).

FIGURE 5.57
The options for Attach To Motion Path

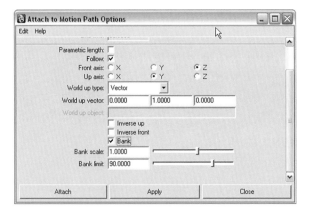

The default Time Range is set to Time Slider so the bug will travel the length of the curve based on the current length of the time slider (200 frames in this scene). You can change this after the motion path is created.

The Follow option orients the animated object so the front axis follows the bends in the curve. The Bank option adds a rotation on the Z axis around bends in the curve to simulate banking.

7. Play the animation. The bug follows the path (see Figure 5.58).

At this point the animation looks a little silly; the other parts of the bug need to be animated, which you can do using the techniques described in the chapter. By attaching the mechanicalBug group as opposed to the bodyCtrl group, you now have the option of adding additional animation to the bodyCtrl curve to add variation in the movement of the bug as it flies along the curve.

FIGURE 5.58
The bug is attached to the motion path curve. As the animation plays the bug travels along the length of the curve.

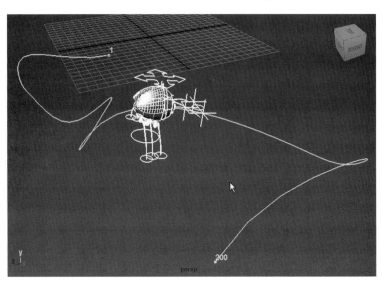

You can change the rate at which the bug flies along the curve by editing the motionPath1 node's U Value attribute on the Graph Editor.

8. In the Outliner, select the mechanicalBug group. In the Channel Box under Inputs, select motionPath1.

9. Choose Window ➤ Animation Editors ➤ Graph Editor to open the Graph Editor.

10. In the left-hand column, select the motionPath1 U Value attribute, and press the f hot key to focus the graph on its animation curve.

11. Use the graph-editing tools to edit the curve.

12. Save the scene as **mechBugPath_v02.ma**. To see a version of the scene to this point, open the mechBug_v02.ma scene in the chapter5\scenes directory on the DVD.

Animating Constraints

You can constrain an object to more than one node. The weighting of the constraint strength can be blended between the two nodes and even animated. This is a great technique for solving difficult animation problems, such as a character picking up and putting down an object.

Dynamic Parenting

Dynamic parenting refers to a technique in which the parenting of an object is keyframed. In this exercise, you'll animate the mechanical bug sitting on a moving object for a few moments before flying off along a motion path.

1. Open the mechBugConstrain_v01.ma scene from the chapter5\scenes directory on the DVD.

This scene has the bug rigged and sitting at the origin of the grid. A cattail is bobbing up and down in the breeze. Above the cattail, a curve defines a motion path (see Figure 5.59).

FIGURE 5.59

The scene contains an animated cattail and a motion path.

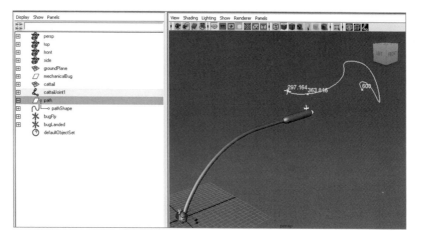

A locator named bugLanded is constrained to one of the joints of the cattail using a parent constraint. On the motion path is another locator named bugFly. To make the bug sit on the moving cattail, you'll create a parent constraint between the bug and the bugLanded locator.

2. In the Outliner, select the bugLanded locator and Ctrl+click the mechanicalBug group. From the Animation menu set, choose Constrain ➢ Parent ➢ Options. In the options, turn off Maintain Offset. Leave Translate and Rotate set to All. Click Add to make the constraint (see Figure 5.60).

FIGURE 5.60

The options for the parent constraint

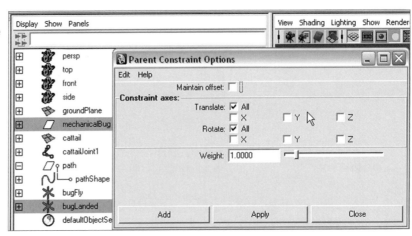

The mechanical bug now appears on the end of the cattail. You can reposition the bug on the cattail using the bodyCtrl and legCtrl curves.

3. In the Display Layers window, turn on the CONTROLS layer. Select the blue bodyCtrl curve, and pull it upward to move the bug up above the end of the cattail.

4. Turn on Wireframe view. Select the red legCtrl circle, and move it upward with the Move tool so the legs are positioned on the end of the cattail. (Use the Show menu in the viewport to turn off the visibility of Joints so that you can easily see the geometry.)

5. Position each of the small purple leg control circles so the bug's legs are posed on the end of the cattail geometry (see Figure 5.61).

6. Play the animation. You'll see the bug sticking to the cattail as it moves up and down.

7. Set the timeline to frame 320. In the Outliner, select the bugFly locator, and Ctrl+click the mechanicalBug. Create another parent constraint; the same options should be applied automatically when you create the constraint.

When you play the animation you'll see that the bug is floating between the two locators, thus inheriting a blend of their animation. This is because the strength of both constraints is at 1 (or full strength).

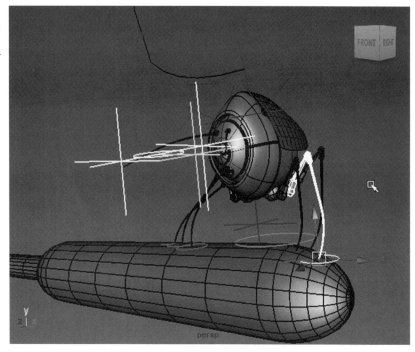

8. Set the timeline to frame 353. This is a point where the two locators are very close and a good time for the bug to start to fly off.

9. In the Outliner, expand the mechanicalBug group. Select the mechanicalBug_parentCon-straint1 node.

10. In the Channel Box, set Bug Fly W1 to **1** and Bug Landed W0 to **0**. The bug reorients itself to match the orientation of the bugFly locator.

11. Shift+click both the Bug Landed W0 channel and the Bug Fly W1 channel in the Channel Box (see Figure 5.62). Right-click and choose Key Selected.

FIGURE 5.62
Set the weights
of the parent con-
straint and key it
at frame 353.

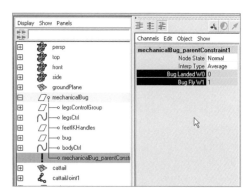

12. Set the timeline to 347. Reverse the values of the two weights so Bug Landed W0 is at **1** and Bug Fly W1 is at **0**. Set another keyframe.

13. Rewind and play the animation. You'll see the bug sitting on the cattail as it bobs up and down. At frame 347 the bug switches to the motion path and flies off.

14. With the mechanicalBug parentConstraint1 node selected, open the Graph Editor. Select the Bug Landed W0 and Bug Fly W1 channels on the left column of the Graph Editor, and press the f hot key to focus on their animation curves.

15. Use the curve-editing tools to fine-tune the animation so the transition between the cattail and the motion path is smoother. This usually takes a fair amount of experimentation (Figure 5.63).

In some cases you can create a smoother transition by extending the length of time between the keyframed weight values. It depends on what type of motion you are trying to achieve and your own personal taste.

16. Save the scene as **mechBugConstrain_v02.ma**. To see a version of the scene to this point, open the mechBugConstrain_v02.ma scene from the chapter5\scenes directory on the DVD.

You can also animate the bodyCtrl curve and the leg controls to create a more believable motion to the bug as he takes flight.

FIGURE 5.63
Edit the weights of the constraint on the Graph Editor.

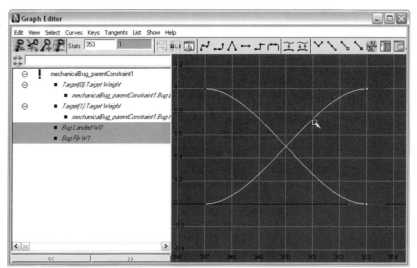

Animation Layers

Animation layers are a new feature in Maya 2009. Animation layers separate the keyframe data applied to objects in the scene so you can create variations of animation for approval from a director, blend different versions of an animation together for a higher level of control, or organize the animated parts of an animation. This section is a tour of how animation layers work and some of the ways they can be applied in a scene. There is a great amount of flexibility in how animation layers can be used; no doubt you will create your own preferred animation layer workflow after a little bit of practice.

Create an Animation Layer

In this section, you'll create a simple dancing motion for the mechanical bug. Animation layers take some getting used to, so you'll start with a very simple animation.

1. Open the mechBugLayers_v01.ma scene from the chapter5\scenes directory on the DVD.

2. Set the current frame on the timeline to 1. Select the blue bodyCtrl curve above the bug, and set its Translate Y channel to **-0.5**. Create a keyframe for this channel.

3. Set the current frame to 20, set Translate Y to **0.5**, and create another keyframe.

4. Create three more keyframes for the bodyCtrl curve:

   Frame 40 Translate Y: **-0.5**

   Frame 60 Translate Y: **0.5**

   Frame 80 Translate Y: **-0.5**

When you play the animation the bug bobs up and down.

5. In the Layer panel in the lower-right corner of the screen below the Channel Box, set the Mode to Anim. This switches the Layer Editor to Animation layers as opposed to Display or Render layers.

6. Choose Layers ➢ Create Empty Layer. Two layers appear. The new layer is AnimLayer1, and the default Base Animation layer is at the bottom.

In the perspective view nothing has changed regardless of which layer is selected.

7. Double-click on AnimLayer1 and rename it **bounce** (see Figure 5.64).

FIGURE 5.64
Create a new animation layer in the scene and rename it bounce.

8. Select the bodyCtrl curve. In the Animation Layer panel, select the bounce layer, RMB+click on it (or select it from the Layer menu), and choose Add Selected Objects. This adds just the bodyCtrl curve. Notice that all the channels in the Channel Box are now yellow. You'll also notice that in the INPUT section under the Channel Box for the bodyCtrl curve, bounce has been added to the list of inputs.

When creating an animation layer you have the option of creating the layer from selected objects in the scene or copying an existing layer (using the options in the Layers menu). When you copy a layer, the keyframes are also copied to the new layer. The Layers menu has a lot of options you'll explore as you go through the next few exercises.

9. Select the bounce layer, and a green circle appears on the right. This indicates that the layer is active.

10. Play the animation. It looks the same as before. Notice that there are no keyframe tick marks on the timeline. Select the BaseAnimation layer; the tick marks reappear. So what does this mean?

Each layer has its own set of keyframes for the objects in that particular layer. The bounce layer has no keyframes yet, so what you're seeing when you play the animation is the keyframes set on the BaseAnimation layer. The way in which the keyframes on one layer interact with the keys on another depends on the layer's Mode and Accumulation settings.

You can also use Extract ➢ Selected Object to create a new layer based on the selected objects. The keyframes set on the object are removed from the current selected layer and added to the new layer created from the Extract operation.

Layer Mode

The mode of a layer can either be Additive or Override. Additive layers blend the values of the keys together so the resulting animation is a combination of the two layers. Using the Additive mode you can add changes to the animation without affecting the original keyframes on the BaseAnimation layer.

When a layer is set to Override mode, the animation on that layer overrides the animation on the layers below it. Override mode is a good way to create different "takes" or versions of an animation without affecting the original BaseAnimation layer.

Follow the next steps to see how these modes work.

1. In the Layer Editor, select the bounce layer. Choose (from the menu in the Layer Editor) Layers ➢ Layer Mode ➢ Override. When you play the animation, the bug no longer moves.

2. If you switch to the BaseAnimation layer, you can see the keyframes on the timeline, but the bug still doesn't move. This is because even though the bounce layer is not selected, it is overriding the BaseAnimation layer.

3. In the Layer Editor, click the red Mute Layer button (see Figure 5.65). The Mute Layer button temporarily disables the layer; when you click Play, you'll see the bug move up and down again.

FIGURE 5.65

The Mute Layer button temporarily disables a layer.

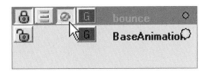

4. Turn the Mute Layer button off, and then play the animation. The bug should stop moving. Select the bounce layer, and drag the Weight slider slowly to the left as the animation plays (see Figure 5.66).

FIGURE 5.66
The Weight slider determines the amount of influence the layer has over the animation.

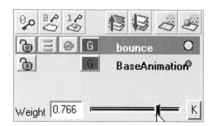

As you drag the Weight slider down, the influence of the overriding layer decreases, and you can see the bug start to move up and down again. When the weight is at zero the overriding layer has no more influence. The K button to the right of the Weight slider sets a keyframe on the Weight value so you can animate the strength of the weight over time.

5. Select the bounce layer. Set the Weight for the bounce Layer to **1**, and make sure the layer is not muted. When you play the animation you should see no motion. Select the bodyCtrl curve, and set the following keyframes on the Translate Y channel.

    Frame 1 Translate Y: **-0.05**

    Frame 10 Translate Y: **0.5**

6. With the bodyCtrl curve selected, open the Graph Editor and select the Translate Y channel. Drag a selection around the keys, and choose Curves ➤ Post Infinity ➤ Oscillate.

7. When you play the animation, the bug bounces a little faster. As you lower the Weight for the layer, you'll see the slower bouncing motion of the BaseAnimation layer.

If you turn off the Passthrough option in the Layers ➤ Mode menu, the animation of the lower layers does not pass through the upper layers, so as you lower the Strength you'll see the bouncing stop as the Weight approaches 0.

8. Set Layer Mode to Additive, as shown in Figure 5.67. Set the Weight of the bounce layer to **1**, and play the animation. You can see that the resulting animation is now a combination of the keyframe values on the bounce and BaseAnimation layers (the Passthrough option has no effect on additive layers).

9. In the Options menu of the Layer Editor, turn off Auto Ghost Selected Objects. Click on the red G in the Base Animation layer. This creates a ghost of the animated objects on this layer so you can compare it with the animation on other layers. In this case, you'll see a red copy of the bodyCtrl curve moving according to the keyframes set on the BaseAnimation layer.

10. Rewind the animation and select the bodyCtrl curve. In the Layer Editor, choose Create Layer From Selected. Name the new layer **rock** and set its mode to Override.

FIGURE 5.67
When Layer Mode is set to Additive, the animation of the two layers is combined.

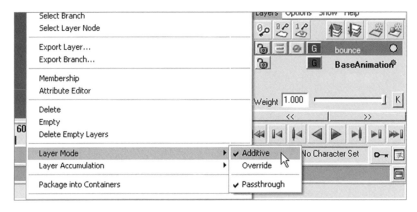

11. Select the rock layer. In the Channel Box, highlight the Rotate X, Y, and Z channels, and set a keyframe on these channels.

12. Turn on the Auto Keyframe feature by clicking the key icon to the right of the timeline.

13. Set the timeline to various points in the animation, and use the Rotate tool to rotate the bug, making him do a happy little dance.

14. Rewind and play the animation. You'll see him move around. Experiment with the weight of the rock layer; try setting its mode to Additive and observe the result.

By varying the weight, you get a pretty good dancing action (for a mechanical bug) fairly easily.

15. Save the scene as **mechBugLayers_v02.ma**. To see a version of the scene to this point, open the mechBugLayers_v02.ma scene from the chapter5\scenes folder on the DVD.

USE ANIMATION LAYERS FOR DRIVEN KEYS

Layers can be created for other types of keyframe animation such as driven keys. For instance, you can create a layer where driven keys make the legs of the bug appear to crawl forward as the bodyCtrl moves along the Z axis and then a second layer where a new set of driven keys makes the bug appear to crawl sideways as the bodyCtrl moves along the X axis.

Other Options in the Layer Editor

The Layer Editor includes other options as well. These are:

Lock Layer   Click the padlock icon to the left of the layer. When this is active, you cannot add keyframes to the layer. This is helpful if you use Auto Keyframe because it prevents you from accidentally changing the animation on a layer.

Solo Layer   Click the horizontal bar icon to left of the layer. This temporarily disables the animation of other layers so you can focus on just the soloed layer (more than one layer can be in solo mode).

Mute Layer   This button disables animation on the selected layer.

Ghost Layer   This button (G) creates a ghost of the animated objects on the layer. You can change the color of the ghost by right-clicking the G button and choosing a color from the pop-up window.

Zero Key Layer   The Zero Key Layer is a way to edit a small portion of an animation using an animation layer. Select an object in the layer, and click the Zero Key icon in the upper left of the Layer Editor to create a starting point on the timeline for the edit. Then move the Time slider to a later point in the animation, and click the Zero Key icon again. Any keyframes you set on the object between these two points in time will not be offset from the original animation.

You can change the order of layers by clicking the up and down arrows in the upper right of the Layer Editor window. The order of layers affects how the animation behaves. For instance, an override layer overrides animation on the layers below it but not above it. You can stack additive layers above, and Override Layer adjusts their weighting and rearranges their order to create different variations on the animation.

The Layer Accumulation settings determine how scaling and rotation are calculated when two or more layers that have animated scaling and rotation are combined.

The animated scaling on two layers can be added or multiplied depending on the Layer Accumulation setting.

Euler and quanternion are two different methods for calculating rotation. Euler is the standard method used in Maya. If the combination of rotation animation on two different layers leads to an unexpected result, try switching to quanternion in the Layer Accumulation settings.

EULER VERSUS QUANTERNION ROTATION

Euler rotation is calculated based on three angle values (X, Y, and Z) plus the order in which the angles are calculated. This is the standard method for calculating rotation in Maya, and it works in most cases. Euler rotation is prone to the problem of Gimbal Lock, where two of the axes overlap and lead to the same result.

Quanternion rotation uses a more complex algorithm that helps it avoid Gimbal Lock problems. When Rotation is set to Quanternion, Maya calculates the animation of rotation by using the X, Y, Z animation curves to create a fourth curve (W), which represents the rotation in quanternion units.

Layer Hierarchy

You can create a hierarchical relationship between animation layers. This is useful as an organizational tool and can speed up your workflow as you animate. Creating a hierarchy means parenting one or more animation layers to another. When you mute or solo the parent layer, all the child layers are also muted or soloed. Likewise the Weight and Mode settings of the parent can affect the child layers. When animation layering becomes complex, you can use the hierarchy to quickly enable, disable, and rearrange the layers.

1. Continue with the scene from the previous section or open the mechBugLayer_v02.ma scene from the chapter5\scenes folder on the DVD.

2. In the Animation Layer Editor, mute the rock and bounce layers. You'll notice that the bug still bounces. This is because of the keyframes set on the BaseAnimation layer.

3. Before creating a hierarchy for the layers, you can quickly move the animation on the BaseAnimation layer to its own new layer. To do this, select the bodyCtrl curve and the BaseAnimation layer. Right-click on the BaseAnimation layer and choose Extract Selected Objects.

Extracting the bodyCtrl object from the BaseAnimation layer creates a new animation layer that contains the bodyCtrl curve and its animation. At the same time, the keyframes from the bodyCtrl curve are removed from the BaseAnimation layer. If you mute all the layers except BaseAnimation, the bug no longer moves when you play the animation.

4. Name the new layer **bounce1**, and rename bounce as **bounce2**.

5. Make sure bounce1 is below bounce2. Mute all the layers (see Figure 5.68).

FIGURE 5.68
Copy the Base-Animation layer, renamed it bounce1, and move it below the other layers. Mute all layers.

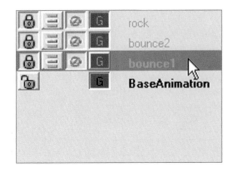

6. In the Layer Editor choose Layers ➤ Create Empty Layer. Name the new layer **legAnim**.

7. Select the circle under the front left leg. In the Layer Editor, choose Layers ➤ Create From Selected. Name the new layer **FLeftLegAnim**.

8. MMB drag FLeftLegAnim on top of the legAnim layer to make it a child of this layer. A small black triangle appears, and the FLeftLegAnim layer is indented above the legAnim layer (see Figure 5.69).

FIGURE 5.69
The FLeftLegAnim layer is parented to the legAnim layer.

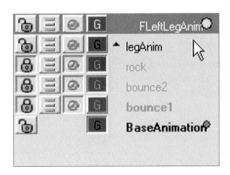

9. Repeat steps 7 and 8 for the front right leg circle. Name the new layer **FRightLegAnim**.

10. Select the FLeftLegAnim layer and, in the perspective view, select the circle under the front left leg. In the Channel Box, Shift+click all the channels except the Translate channels. Right-click and choose Remove From Selected Layers (see Figure 5.70).

FIGURE 5.70
Remove the Rotate and Scale channels from the animation layer.

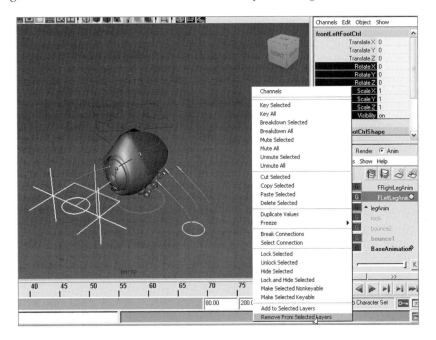

11. With the FLeftLegAnim layer selected, set a keyframe on the left leg control circle's Translate channels. Then use the Auto Keyframe feature to create an animation of the leg moving up and down as if it's tapping out a little beat.

12. Switch to the FRightLegAnim layer, and create a similar animation for the front right leg.

13. When you have a nice animation going for both layers, unmute the other layers and play the animation.

14. Click the black triangle on the legAnim layer to collapse the layer. Experiment with the Weight setting of the legAnim layer. The Weight value of the parent layer applies to both child layers as well. This is also true for the Layer Mode, Mute, and Solo settings.

You can create further nested layers within the hierarchy. Each child layer can have its own Mode setting. To keep things simple, you can use empty layers as parent layers. The empty parent layers can be used to set the Weight and Mode operation of the child layers. If the parent layer is empty, you don't have to worry about how the animation in a parent layer is blended with the child layers.

15. Save the scene as **mechBugLayers_v03.ma**. To see a version of the scene to this point, open the mechBugLayers_v03.ma scene from the chapter5\scenes folder on the DVD.

Merging Layers

You can merge the animation of two layers into a single animation layer.

1. Continue with the scene from the previous section or open the `mechBugLayers_v03.ma` scene from the `chapter5\scenes` folder on the DVD.

2. In the Animation Layers Editor, select the bounce2 and bounce1 layers.

3. Choose Layers ➤ Merge Layers ➤ Options. In the options, set the Merge To option to Bottom Selected Layer. Set Layers Hierarchy to Selected and Result Layer Mode to Additive.

4. Turn on the Smart Bake option.

When you merge two or more layers, the animation of the objects on the layers is baked. You can choose to sample the baked keyframes based on the Sample By value. For instance, if you set Sample By to 1, then the object on the resulting baked layer will have a keyframe placed on the animated channels for every frame of the animation. A setting of 2 creates a key on every other frame. The Smart Bake option creates a curve from the combined animation layers with fewer keyframes. The Increase Fidelity setting increases the accuracy of the resulting animation curve to better represent the combined animation of the two layers. The Sample By option is more accurate but creates a lot of keyframes, which can be hard to edit. The Smart Bake option works very well when there are fewer layers or the animation is simple.

You can bake a parent layer and all its child layers into a single layer. You can also choose to delete the original layers or keep them. Figure 5.71 shows the options for merging layers.

5. Click Apply to merge the layers. A new layer named Merged Layer is created. Rename the new layer **bounce**. Select the bounce layer. In the perspective view, select the bodyCtrl and open the Graph Editor. You'll see the merged animation curve in the Graph Editor (see Figure 5.72).

6. Save the scene as **mechBugLayers_v04.ma**. To see a version of the scene, open the `mechBugLayers_v04.ma` scene in the `chapter5\scenes` folder on the DVD.

FIGURE 5.71
The options for merging layers

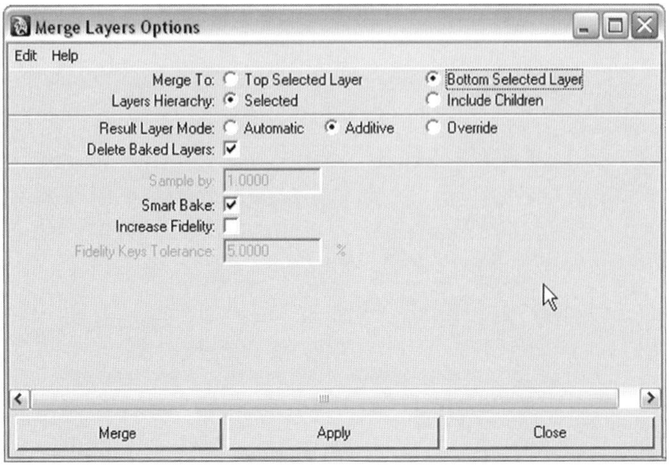

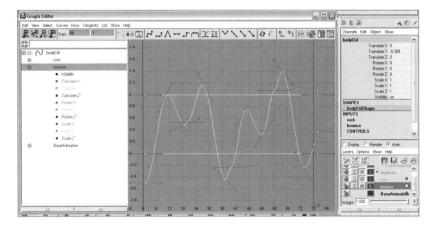

The Bottom Line

Create a simple rig with joints and constraints. Joints are a deformer commonly used in character animation. The hierarchical relationship makes them useful for rigging many types of characters. When creating robots and mechanical devices, you can build a skeleton using joints and then parent the parts of the robot to the joints.

Constraints are used to constrain the channels of one object to the world space coordinates of another object. Constraints are useful as rigging tools for snapping the pivot point of one object to another.

Master it Create a simple joint chain for a robot's arm. Use the joint chain to animate an arm made from simple polygon surfaces.

Use Inverse Kinematics. Inverse Kinematics creates a goal object, known as an End Effector, for joints in a chain. The joints in the chain orient themselves based on the translation of the goal. The IK Handle tool is used to position the End Effector.

Master it Create an Inverse Kinematic control for a simple arm.

Animate with keyframes. A keyframe marks the state of a particular attribute at a point in time on the timeline. When a second keyframe is added to the attribute at a different point in time, Maya interpolates the values between the two keyframes, creating animation. There are a number of ways to edit keyframes using the timeline and the Channel Box.

Master it Create a number of keyframes for the Translate channels of a simple object. Copy the keyframes to a different point in time for the object. Try copying the keyframes to the Scale channels. Try copying the keys to the Translate channels of another object.

Use the Graph Editor. More sophisticated animation editing is available using the animation curve editing tools on the Graph Editor.

Master it Create a looping animation for the mechanical bug model using as few keys as possible. The bug should leap up repeatedly and move forward with each leap.

Preview animations with Playblast.   Playblast is a tool for viewing the animation as a flip-book without having to actually render the animation. F Check is a utility program that is included with Maya. Playblasts can be viewed in F Check.

Master it   Create a playblast of the mechBugLayers_v04.ma scene.

Use driven keys.   A driven key is a keyframe that uses the attributes of one object as an input instead of time. Using driven keys you can automate many parts of an animation that might otherwise be tedious.

Master it   Create an alternate automated walk cycle for the mechanical bug so that when it walks sideways (along its Translate X), the legs automatically move in a crablike fashion.

Animate with expressions.   Expressions are a powerful way to automate the movement of an object. Using conditional statements you can create an expression that causes the animation to react to changes in the scene automatically.

Master it   Create an expression to randomly rotate the bug's eyes up and down. Make the rotation faster based on the height of the bodyCtrl curve.

Animate with motion paths.   Motion paths allow you to attach an object to a curve. Over the course of the animation the object slides along the curve based on the keyframes set on the motion path's U Value.

Master it   Make the bug walk along a motion path. See if you can automate a walk cycle based on the position along the path.

Use animation layers.   Animation layers are a new feature in Maya 2009. Using animation layers you can add new motion that can override existing animation or be combined with it.

Master it   Create animation layers for the flying bug in the mechBug_v08.ma scene in the chapter5\scenes directory on the DVD. Create two layers: one for the bodyCtrl curve and one for the legsCtrl curve. Use layers to make the animation of the wings start with small movements and then flap at full strength.

Chapter 6

Animating with Deformers

Deformers can be used for both modeling and animation and as part of an animation rig. In this chapter, you'll see some of the ways to animate geometry using deformers. From creating facial expressions to animating a jellyfish, there are thousands of ways you can apply deformers to bring your creations to life.

In this chapter you will learn to:

- ◆ Animate facial expressions
- ◆ Create Blend Shape sequences
- ◆ Use lattices
- ◆ Animate clusters
- ◆ Animate nonlinear deformers
- ◆ Use jiggle deformers
- ◆ Use the geometry cache

Animate Facial Expressions

Animating facial expressions for characters is usually accomplished through the use of Blend Shapes. While this is not the only way to animate expressions and speech, it is the most common because it is relatively straightforward to set up and animate. In this section, you'll learn how to create Blend Shape targets, paint Blend Shape weights, create a Blend Shape deformer, and build a simple facial animation rig.

A Blend Shape deformer uses one or more Blend Shape targets. These targets are duplicates of the original model that have been modified using a variety of modeling techniques. The Blend Shape deformer is created by selecting the targets and the original model and choosing Create Deformers ➢ Blend Shape. The deformer controls consist of sliders—one for each Blend Shape target. The original model is animated by moving and keyframing the sliders. As the value of a slider moves between 0 and 1, Maya interpolates the change, blending between the original shape and the target shape. The duplicate model is known as the Blend Shape target, and the original model is known as the base mesh.

There are a few things you should understand about how Blend Shapes work before you set up a facial animation rig.

First of all, Blend Shapes always move in a straight line when interpolating the change between the original model and the Blend Shape target. Think of how your eyelids move when you blink. Your eyelid is a flap of skin that moves over the spherical shape of your eyeball. If you make a dot on the edge of your eyelid with a marker (don't do this, just imagine it) and then follow the path of that dot from a side view, the dot moves in an arc as your eyelid closes.

If you have a model of a face with the eyes open and a Blend Shape target with the eyes closed, when you create the Blend Shape deformer and then animate the eyes closing, instead of moving in an arc, the eyelids will move in a straight line from the open position to the closed position. Most likely the eyelid geometry will pass through the eyeball geometry, creating a less-than-convincing blinking behavior (see Figure 6.1). Understanding that the Blend Shapes deformer moves in a linear direction from one state to the next is important if you are to develop a solution for this problem.

FIGURE 6.1
Blend Shape deformations move in a straight line, which can cause problems for certain types of facial movements, such as blinking eyelids.

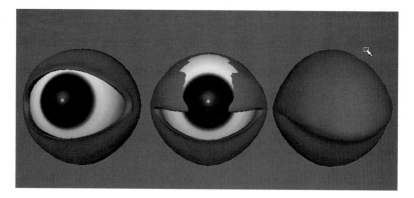

Second, a Blend Shape target should have the same number of vertices and the same point order as the original geometry. Vertices on polygons and CVs on NURBS geometry are numbered in a specific order. You can see the numbers listed in the Script Editor when the vertices are selected. If the number of points and the order of the points on a Blend Shape target do not match the original, the deformer will not be created or it will behave strangely (see Figure 6.2). It is possible to use a Blend Shape target that has a different number of vertices than the base mesh; however, this can lead to some unpredictable results.

POINT ORDER CHANGES ON IMPORT

It is a fairly common practice to export a polygon model from Maya as an .obj format file for editing in another 3D program such as Mudbox or ZBrush. When the edited object is imported back into Maya, the point order can change if the options are not set correctly in Maya's Import Options box. The model may have exactly the same number of points as the original, but when you use the imported model as a Blend Shape target and animate the deformer, the model suddenly becomes mangled.

When you import an .obj format model into Maya, always remember to uncheck the Create Multiple Objects option in the OBJ Import Options. This option should be off; otherwise the point order of the model can change, which would cause major problems when using the imported model as a Blend Shape target.

Third, when deforming a model with more than one Blend Shape target, the changes created by the targets are added together. So if you have one Blend Shape target in which a face is smiling and a second target in which the face is frowning, you may think that one target cancels out the other. In fact, setting both Blend Shape targets to Full Strength creates a strange result on the base mesh because the smile and the frown will be added together (see Figure 6.3).

FIGURE 6.2
When the point order of the base mesh and the Blend Shape target do not match, strange results can occur when the deformer is applied.

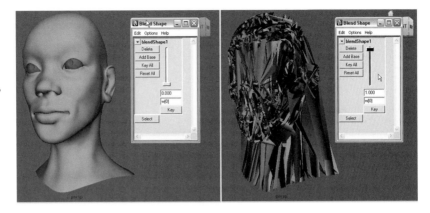

FIGURE 6.3
A smile shape and a frown shape are added together to create a very strange expression.

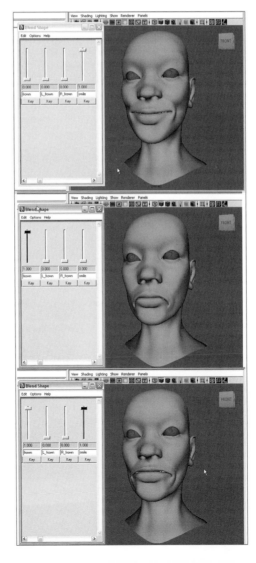

Blend Shape Targets

The first step in setting up a Blend Shape facial animation rig is to model the actual Blend Shapes based on the base mesh. The final rig works something like the controls for a puppet. Rather than animate a happy face model and a sad face model, you really want to isolate individual muscle movements. This will give you the most control when animating. When animating a smile, you'll have controls for the mouth, eyelids, eyebrows, cheeks, and more, so you have the option of animating a smile with brows up for a happy character and a smile with brows down for a menacing character. In addition, you want to isolate the sides of the face so the corner of one side of the mouth can be animated separately from the corner of the other side of the mouth.

When creating Blend Shape targets, it's best to think in terms of what the muscle is doing rather than a particular expression. The same targets are used to animate speech and emotion. So rather than creating a Blend Shape target for a smile and a Blend Shape target for the "eeeee" sound, you want to make a single Blend Shape target that pulls a corner of the mouth back. Then this Blend Shape target combined with muscle movements created for other targets can be used for smiling, saying "cheeeese," or both at the same time.

In this exercise, you'll create Blend Shape targets for a character's mouth that can be used for widening the lips as in a smile and narrowing the lips as in a kiss. These two shapes (mouthWide and mouthNarrow) will then be separated into four shapes (leftMouthWide, leftMouthNarrow, rightMouthWide, and rightMouthNarrow).

1. Open the nancy_v01.ma scene from the chapter6\scenes directory on the DVD. This scene shows a very basic polygon head. Simple shapes for the eyes, tongue, teeth, and hair are included.

It's a good idea to have these parts of the model included, even if they are just temporary versions. It makes modeling the shape changes easier. Teeth play a big role in the way the mouth is shaped when moving, so it's good to have some kind of guide available while making Blend Shape targets. A simple hair shape is useful as a visual indicator for the hairline starts when working on shapes for the brow.

2. Select the nancy model and duplicate it (Ctrl+d). Move the duplicate to the side, as shown in Figure 6.4. Name the duplicate **mouthWide**.

FIGURE 6.4
A duplicate of
the original head
model is created.

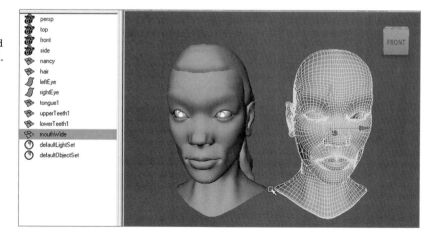

By default, Blend Shape deformers calculate only shape node–level changes. In other words, only changes made on the vertex level are considered. You can move, rotate, and scale the targets without affecting the base mesh—unless you specify otherwise in the Deformer options (this will be discussed further later on).

3. Select the Move tool and open the Options box for the tool. Under the Reflection Settings, activate Reflection, and set Reflection Axis to X.

4. Turn on Soft Select, and set Falloff Mode to Surface. Set Falloff Radius to **0.80** and add a point to the Falloff Curve. Adjust the curve to look like Figure 6.5. You'll be changing these options a lot, so keep the Move Tool window open while you work.

FIGURE 6.5

The options for the Move tool

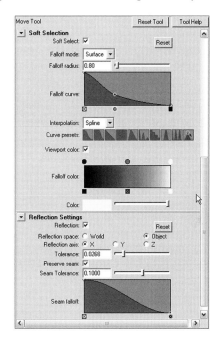

5. Right-click on the mouthWide geometry, and choose Vertex to switch to vertex selection mode.

6. Select a vertex at the corner of the mouth, as shown in Figure 6.6. You'll see the vertices colored, indicating the Soft Selection radius and falloff. Carefully start moving the corner to the side and back toward the ear.

The muscles in the face work in concert to create facial expressions. Most of the face muscles are designed to convey emotion, aid with speech, and keep food in your mouth while you eat. Muscles work in groups to pull parts of the face in various directions like a system of pulleys. When you smile or grimace, the corners of your mouth are pulled back toward the ears by several muscles working together.

FIGURE 6.6
The vertices are color coded to indicate the falloff strength and radius of the Move tool when Soft Selection is enabled.

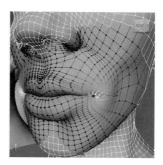

Cartoons often simplify the smile by drawing the corners of the mouth upward into a U shape. However, in reality the corners of the mouth actually move upward only a very small degree. The illusion of perspective makes it look as though the mouth is forming a U. The smile shape is not really a U shape, but rather the lips are stretched in a nearly a straight line across the teeth.

7. It will take a little work to form the smile shape on the face. Use a mirror for reference. Keep in mind that as the lips are pulled across the teeth, they are stretched and lose volume, giving them a thinner appearance (see Figure 6.7).

As you work, make adjustments to the settings on the Move tool, and change the Falloff Radius and Falloff Curve values as needed.

8. When the corners of the mouth are pulled back, adjust other parts of the face near the corners and on the lips, but don't go too far beyond the area of the mouth. Remember, you are making an isolated change in the shape of the mouth, not a complete facial expression.

In addition to the Move tool, the Artisan Brush is very useful for sculpting changes in the model. To activate this tool, select the mouthWide model, and choose (from the Polygon menu set) Mesh ➤ Sculpt Geometry. In the Options box, make sure the Reflection option is activated in the Stroke section so changes are mirrored to the opposite side of the head across the X axis.

FIGURE 6.7
Moving left to right, these images show some of the steps involved in creating a smile using the Move tool and the Artisan Brush tool.

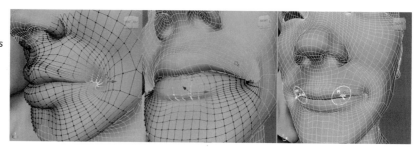

The final wide mouth shape should look like a fake smile because there are no changes in the other parts of the face. I tend to build a little overshoot into my Blend Shape targets so I have wider range to work with when animating (see Figure 6.8).

FIGURE 6.8
The base model (left) and the completed smile Blend Shape target (right)

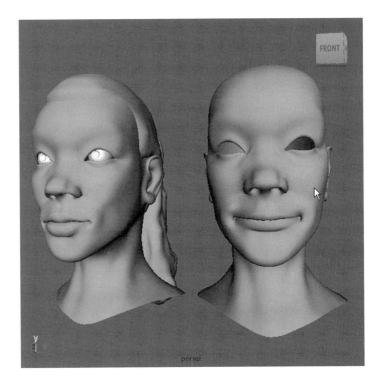

9. Save the scene as **nancy_v02.ma**.

10. Create another duplicate of the nancy model. Name the duplicate **mouthNarrow**. Move it to the model's right side. You may want to move the teeth with the model so you can use them as a guide.

11. Use the Move tool and the Artisan Brush to push the sides of the mouth toward the center of the face. The lips should bulge up in the center.

As the lips push together and bulge at the center, there is a slight curling outward. Those parts of the upper and lower lips that touch in the neutral pose become exposed and the flesh of the lips rolls outward (but just very slightly). You can use the Rotate tool to help create this rolling outward effect (see Figure 6.9). Figure 6.10 shows the finished narrow mouth Blend Shape target, the base mesh, and the smile Blend Shape target, respectively.

FIGURE 6.9
Moving left to right, the images show some of the steps involved in shaping the narrow lips using the Move tool, the Rotate tool, and the Artisan Brush tool.

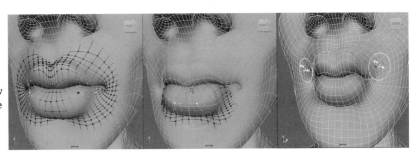

FIGURE 6.10
The completed
narrow mouth
Blend Shape
target is on the
left of the base
mesh and smile
Blend Shape
targets.

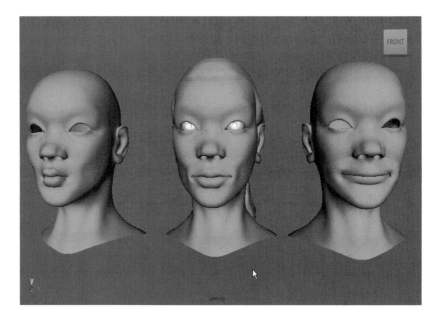

SURFACE VERSUS VOLUME SOFT SELECT

To move the vertices of the lips separately, use Soft Selection in surface mode. To move parts of the lips together, use Soft Selection in volume mode.

---

12. Once you are satisfied with the two mouth shapes, save the scene as **nancy_v02.ma**. To see a version of the scene up to this point, open the nancy_v02.ma scene from the chapter6\scenes folder on the DVD.

Create Blend Shapes

To create the Blend Shape deformer, select all of the targets first and then the base mesh. Next choose the Blend Shape deformer from the Deformers menu in the Animation menu set. In this section you'll create the deformer using the mouthWide and mouthNarrow shapes.

1. Continue with the scene from the previous section or open the nancy_v02.ma scene from the chapter6\scenes folder on the DVD.

2. Shift+click the mouthWide model and the mouthNarrow model; then Shift+click the nancy model.

3. Switch to the Animation menu set, and choose Create Deformers ➤ Blend Shape ➤ Options. In the Options box, choose Reset to set the options to the default settings. You want Origin set to Local; this means that only shape node–level changes will be used

on the deformer. If target can be moved, scaled, or rotated, it will not affect how the deformer is applied.

4. Name the Blend Shape deformer **nancyFace** (see Figure 6.11). Click Create to make the deformer.

5. To test the deformer, choose Window ➢ Animation Editors ➢ Blend Shape. A small pop-up window appears with two sliders. These are the controls for the Blend Shape deformers.

6. Move the sliders up and down, and see how they affect the model (see Figure 6.12). Try putting both sliders at 1 to see the shapes added together. Try setting the values to negative values or values beyond 1.

7. Save the scene as **nancy_v03.ma**. To see a version of the scene to this point, open the nancy_v03.ma scene from the chapter6\scenes directory on the DVD.

FIGURE 6.11
The options for the Blend Shape deformer

FIGURE 6.12
The Blend Shapes are controlled using the Blend Shape sliders.

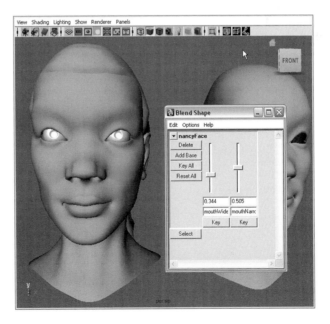

Paint Blend Shape Weights

At this point you have two Blend Shapes available for animating, mouthWide and mouthNarrow. You may decide you want additional Blend Shape targets for the same mouth shape but restricted to just one side of the mouth. This gives you more options for animating a wider variety of facial movement. One easy way to create these additional targets is to use Blend Shape weighting as a shortcut for making additional Blend Shape target models from the symmetrical facial poses you've already created.

1. Continue with the scene from the previous section or open the nancy_v03.ma scene from the chapter6\scenes directory on the DVD.

2. Select the nancy model, and choose Edit Deformers ➤ Paint Blend Shape Weights Tool ➤ Options.

3. The model turns completely white, and the options open in the Tool Options box on the right side of the screen.

In the Target box is the list of all the current Blend Shapes applied to the model. The white color on the model indicates that the Blend Shape weight is at full strength.

4. Open the Blend Shape control window by choosing Window ➤ Animation Editors ➤ Blend Shapes. Set the mouthWide slider to 1 so you can see the deformer applied to the model (see Figure 6.13).

5. In the Paint Blend Shape Weights Tool options, set Paint Operation to Replace and Value to **0**. Click the Flood button. This floods the model with a zero-weight value. The model turns black, and the mouthWide deformation disappears.

6. Set Value to **1,** and paint the area around the mouth on the model's left side. As you paint, you'll see the left side move into the mouthWide shape (see Figure 6.14).

7. When you feel that you have painted enough of one side of the mouth, select the nancy model and duplicate it (Ctrl+d). Move the duplicate up and off to the side and name it **mouthLeftWide** (remember to name the deformers based on the character's left or right side, not your left or right).

FIGURE 6.13
Activating the Paint Blend Shape Weights tool turns the model white, indicating that the selected target in the options is applied at full strength to all of the model's vertices.

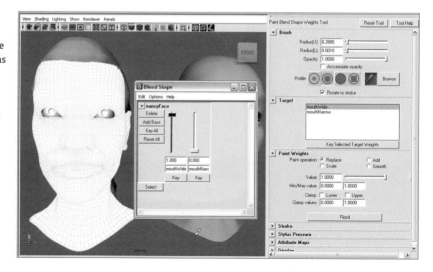

FIGURE 6.14
As the weights
are painted,
the side of the
mouth moves
into the mouth-
Wide shape.

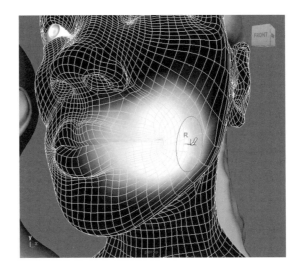

8. Select the nancy model again, and choose Edit Deformers ➤ Paint Blend Shape Weights.

9. Flood the model with a zero value again, set Value to **1**, and this time paint the mouth area on the model's right side.

10. Duplicate the model again, and move the duplicate model up and away from the nancy model. Name this duplicate **mouthRightWide**.

11. Select the nancy model again, and choose Edit Deformers ➤ Paint Blend Shape Weights. Set Value to **1**, and flood the model to return the weight for the mouthWide shape to 1.

The two duplicate models will look somewhat strange; this is a very unusual expression (see Figure 6.15). You can use the Artisan Brush and the Move tool to make the mouth look more natural, but try to restrict your edits to one side of the mouth or the other. Remember that this particular mouth movement will most likely be accompanied by other shape changes during animation, which will make it look more natural. Most likely these shapes will not be used at their full strength, but it's good to model a little overshoot into the shape to expand the range of possible movements.

FIGURE 6.15
Two new Blend
Shape targets have
been created using
the Paint Blend
Shape Weights tool.

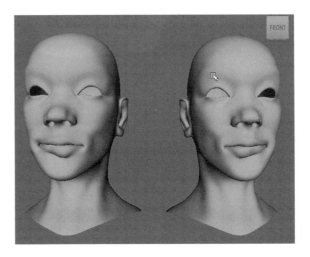

12. Open the Blend Shape control window (Window ➢ Animation Editors ➢ Blend Shapes). Set the mouthWide slider to 0 and the mouthNarrow slider to 1.

13. Select the nancy model, and choose Edit Deformers ➢ Paint Blend Shape Weights. Select the mouthNarrow shape in the Target options, and repeat steps 5 through 11 to create two more Blend Shape targets based on the mouthNarrow shape, one for each side of the mouth.

14. Name the two new targets **mouthRightNarrow** and **mouthLeftNarrow**. At this point, you should have a total of six Blend Shape targets (see Figure 6.16).

15. Save the scene as nancy_v04.ma. To see a version of the scene to this point, open the nancy_v04.ma scene from the chapter6\scenes directory on the DVD.

FIGURE 6.16
The scene is starting to fill up with Blend Shape targets.

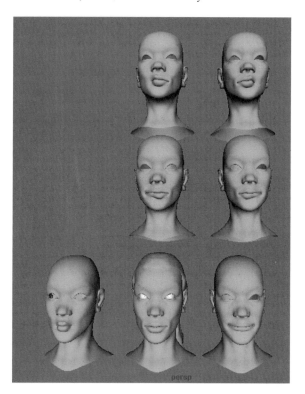

Adding Targets

You can add the new targets to the existing Blend Shape deformer.

1. Continue with the scene from the previous section or open the nancy_v04.ma scene from the chapter6\scenes directory on the DVD.

2. Select the nancy model, and choose Window ➢ Animation Editors ➢ Blend Shape to open the Blend Shape controls.

3. Choose the mouthRightWide target and Shift+click the nancy model. Choose Edit Deformers ➢ Blend Shapes ➢ Add. You'll see a new slider appear in the Blend Shape controls (see Figure 6.17).

4. Repeat step 3 for the mouthLeftWide, mouthRightNarrow, and mouthLeftNarrow targets.

5. Save the scene as **nancy_v05.ma**. To see a version of the scene to this point, open the nancy_v05.ma scene from the chapter6\scenes directory on the DVD.

FIGURE 6.17

Sliders are added to the Blend Shape control window as the additional targets are added to the deformer.

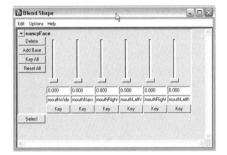

Test the slider controls in the Blend Shape window. You can continue to edit the Blend Shapes targets after they have been added to the deformer. You may want to make additional changes to improve the expressions and the movement between shapes. Remember that at this point it's fine to have some strange-looking expressions. The final rig may have dozens of Blend Shape targets that all work together to create various expressions and facial movement. As long as you have the Blend Shape targets available, you can continue to refine the expressions by editing the targets.

ADDING JOINTS

Some facial movements, such as opening and closing the jaw, blinking the eyes, and moving the tongue, are better suited for joint rigs than for Blend Shape targets. In the end, the final rig will use a combination of deformers to create the full range of facial movements.

Create a Custom Mouth Control Slider

You can animate the facial expressions by moving the sliders in the Blend Shape window and clicking the Key button beneath each slider. You can then use the Graph Editor to edit the animation curves. It is possible to animate this way, but you may find that as opposing shapes are animated, their animation curves start to overlap and create strange and unwanted facial movement.

There's a much better way to handle facial animation: create a set of intuitive interactive controls that you can move in the perspective view itself. These controls can be connected to the Blend Shape deformer using set driven keys. Animating the character will feel like moving a puppet, which will make your work easier and more enjoyable.

In this section, you'll see how to set up a basic interactive control to animate the Blend Shapes created in the previous section.

1. Continue with the scene from the previous section or open the nancy_v05.ma scene from the chapter6\scenes directory on the DVD.

2. Once you have the Blend Shape deformer set up, you can safely delete the Blend Shape targets. Save a version with the targets just in case you need to go back and make a change. Then select the target models and delete them.

3. Switch to a front view and turn on Grid Snapping. Choose Create ➤ CV Curve Tool ➤ Options. In the options, set Curve Degree to Linear. In the front view, create a rectangle that is one unit high and four units long.

4. Name the curve **wideNarrowCtrl**. Select it and choose Modify ➤ Center Pivot.

5. Use the Curve tool to create a triangle below the rectangle. Name the triangle **wideNarrow**. Center the pivot on the wideNarrow triangle (see Figure 6.18).

FIGURE 6.18
A rectangle and a triangle are created using a linear curve.

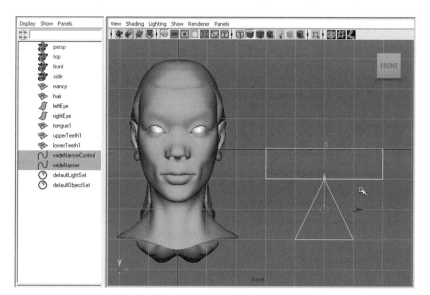

6. Scale the wideNarrowCtrl down along the Y axis to about **0.15**. Scale the wideNarrow triangle down to **0.3** in X and Y. Place the wideNarrow triangle just below the wideNarrowCtrl rectangle.

7. Make two duplicates of the triangle and name one **left** and the other **right**.

8. Scale the left and right triangles down to **0.1** in X and Y.

9. Arrange the left and right triangles so they fit in the bottom half of the wideNarrow triangle. The left and right triangles correspond to the character's left and right sides, so the left triangle should be on the right and the right triangle should be on the left. This may seem confusing, but in a 3D scene the camera can be anywhere, so it's important to keep left and right relative to the character's point of view.

10. Select the rectangle and the three triangles, and choose Modify ➤ Freeze Transformations. This will return them to this arrangement when their Translate and Rotate channels are set to 0.

11. Parent the left and right triangles to the wideNarrow triangle, and parent the wideNarrow triangle to the wideNarrowCtrl rectangle.

12. Select the wideNarrow triangle, and open its Attribute Editor to the wideNarrow tab. In the Limit Information rollout, expand the Translate controls. Check the boxes next to each Limit channel to turn on the translate limits. Set Trans Limit Y Min and Max to **0** and Trans Limit Z Min and Max to **0**. Set Trans Limit X Min to **-2** and the Trans Limit X Max to **2**.

13. Move the wideNarrow triangle back and forth along the X axis. It can travel the length of the wideNarrowCtrl rectangle but not beyond. This is one way to create a custom slider in Maya. When the Translate X channel of the triangle is set to 0, the triangle should be in the middle of the rectangle. Figure 6.19 shows the arrangement of the slider controls.

FIGURE 6.19

Limits are set on the movement of the slider controls.

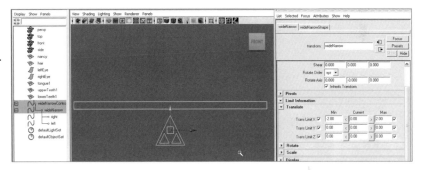

14. Use the same technique to set limits on the translation of both the left and right triangles. They should be restricted so they can move only between -1 and 1 on the X axis. Their Y and Z axis limits Min and Max should be set to **0**.

15. Save the scene as **nancy_v06.ma**. To see a version of the scene to this point, open the nancy_v06.ma scene from the chapter6\scenes directory on the DVD.

Connect the Slider to the Blend Shape

To make the slider functional, it will be connected to the Blend Shape using driven keys. The theory behind this arrangement is that you want to have opposing shapes on the opposite ends of a slider control. The mouthWide and the mouthNarrow shapes are connected to the X translation of the wideNarrow triangle, so the mouth is either wide or narrow but not both at the same time.

However, you also want to have enough freedom to control the sides of the mouth independently, so you'll connect the left and right triangles to the Blend Shapes for each side of the mouth. This way you still have the freedom to mix the Blend Shapes together to create a wide variety of possible mouth movements. This example uses only the wide and narrow controls. When you create similar controls for other mouth shapes, such as mouth corners down, lower lip curl, upper lip sneer, and so on, you end up with a very intuitive way to control the face by moving the sliders directly on the screen.

The next step in the process is creating the driven keys.

1. Continue with the scene from the previous section or open the nancy_v06.ma scene from the chapter6\scenes directory on the DVD.

2. Make sure the Translate X channels for all of the triangles are set to 0. Make sure all of the Blend Shape controls are set to **0** as well so the face is in a neutral pose.

3. From the Animation menu set choose Animate ➤ Set Driven Key ➤ Set to open the Set Driven Key window (see Figure 6.20)

FIGURE 6.20

Open the
Set Driven
Key window.

4. Select the wideNarrow triangle, and click the Load Driver button in the Set Driven Key window. In the upper left of the Set Driven Key window, select wideNarrow. Its animation channels will appear in the upper right.

5. From the Display menu in the Outliner, turn off the DAG Objects Only option so all of the nodes in the scene are visible. Select the nancyFace node, and click the Load Driven button in the Set Driven Key window.

You need to set a keyframe so that when the wideNarrow triangle's Translate X channel is at 0, the mouthWide Blend Shape setting is also at 0.

6. Select Translate X in the upper right of the Set Driven Key window and mouthWide in the lower right of the window, and click the Key button at the bottom of the Set Driven Key window (Figure 6.21).

7. Click the wideNarrow label in the upper left of the Set Driven Key window. Open the Channel Box and set Translate X to **-2**.

8. Select the nancyFace label in the lower left of the Set Driven Key window. In the Channel Box, set mouthWide to 1. Click the Key button at the bottom of the Set Driven Key window.

9. Zoom out in the front view so you can see the control and the nancy character. Move the wideNarrow triangle back and forth along the slider. You should see the mouth move between the neutral pose (when wideNarrow is at the center of the slider) and the mouth-Wide shape (when wideNarrow is moved all the way to the left of the wideNarrowCtrl slider).

FIGURE 6.21
The Set Driven Key window creates a keyframe relationship between the Translate X of wideNarrow and the mouthWide of nancyFace.

10. Set wideNarrow back to **0** in the Translate X channel of the Channel Box. In the lower right of the Set Driven Key window, select mouthNarrow and click the Key button.

11. Select wideNarrow in the upper left of the Set Driven Key window. In the Channel Box, set Translate X to **2**.

12. Select the nancyFace label in the lower left of the Set Driven Key window. In the Channel Box, set mouthNarrow to **1**. In the Set Driven Key window, click the Key button.

13. In the viewport, move the wideNarrow slider back and forth along the length of the wideNarrowCtrl. You'll see the face move between the mouthNarrow shape when the triangle is on the left side and the mouthWide shape when it's on the right side. Now the control is functional, and you can move between the two opposing mouth shapes using a single control.

14. Create set driven keys for the small triangles named left and right. Use the following settings:

        right Translate X = **0**, mouthRightWide = **0**

        right Translate X = **-1**, mouthRightWide = **1**

        right Translate X = **0**, mouthRightNarrow = **0**

        right Translate X = **1**, mouthRightNarrow = **1**

        left Translate X = **0**, mouthLeftWide = **0**

        left Translate X = **1**, mouthleftWide = **1**

        left Translate X = **0**, mouthLeftNarrow = **0**

        left Translate X = **-1**, mouthLeftNarrow = **1**

It seems a little tedious at first to create this kind of rig, but when you have the whole rig working, it's the easiest way to animate the face using blend shapes. Once you have all the driven keys created, spend some time moving the sliders back and forth. See how many mouth shapes you can create just by moving the sliders (see Figure 6.22).

FIGURE 6.22
A variety of mouth shapes can be created by moving the triangle controls.

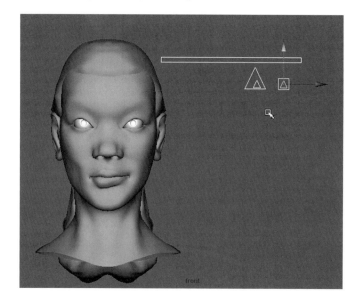

15. Save the scene as **nancy_v07.ma**. To see a finished version of the scene, open the nancy_v07.ma scene from the chapter6\scenes directory on the DVD.

There are many different ways to set up these types of controls. For a complex facial rig, try using curves to make controls that resemble a simplified face. This way you have a visual representation of how moving the controls affects the facial movements.

16. Open the nancy_rig.ma scene from the chapter6\scenes directory to see a more functional face and head rig. Play the animation to see the controls in action. Try moving various parts of the controls to see the resulting expressions (see Figure 6.23).

This rig uses a combination of Blend Shapes, joints, and a dynamic hair curve to create the various movements. A total of 49 Blend Shape targets were created for this rig. A more complete rig may use a hundred or more Blend Shape targets.

DEFORMER ORDER

When using Blend Shapes with joints or other deformers, you may have to change the position of the deformer in the deformer order. If you're getting strange results when you animate Blend Shapes, you may need to rearrange the deformer in the list of inputs. To do this, right-click on the base mesh and choose Inputs ➢ All Inputs from the marking menu. In the list of Input operations, you can MMB-drag any of the deformers up and down the list to change its position. You also have the option of setting the Blend Shape order in the Advanced tab of the options when you create the Blend Shape deformer.

FIGURE 6.23
A more complete
facial animation
rig. The controls
are positioned to
give visual clues
to the parts of the
face they control.

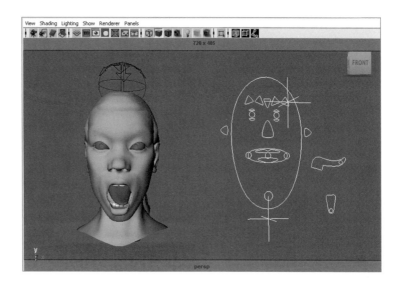

Create Blend Shape Sequences

When you choose the In Between setting in the Blend Shape options, the Blend Shape deformer deforms the base mesh based on a sequence created from multiple targets. The order in which you select the targets determines the sequence of the animation created when you move the Blend Shape slider. To understand this better, try this exercise, which uses a Blend Shape sequence to animate the growth of a snowflake crystal.

Create the Base Mesh

You'll start by creating the base mesh snowflake from a polygon prism using a series of polygon extrusions. It's important to name each extrude node as you create it so you can keep track of how it affects the shape of the snowflake.

1. Create a new scene in Maya. Make sure Construction History is enabled.

2. Switch to the Polygon menu set and choose Create ➤ Polygon Primitives ➤ Prism.

3. Open the Channel Box and select the polyPrism1 node from the INPUTS section. Set the Number Of Sides to **5** and the Length to **1** (see Figure 6.24).

FIGURE 6.24
Create a five-sided
prism.

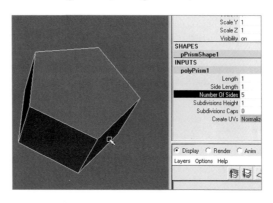

4. Right-click on the prism and choose Faces. Shift+click the five faces on the sides of the prism, but not the faces on the top or bottom.

5. Choose Edit Mesh ➤ Extrude. For the moment, do not pull on the extrude manipulator; you'll use the Channel Box to extrude the faces in the next steps. In the options for the polyExtrudeFace1 node in the Channel Box, set Keep Faces Together to Off.

6. Click the polyExtrudeFace1 label in the Channel Box, and rename the node **armRoot**. Since you'll be editing a number of extrude nodes later on in the process, it's good to give them descriptive names so you can keep track of each of the extrusions.

7. In the Channel Box, in the channels under the armRoot node, set Local Translate Z to **1.7** and Local Scale X and Local Scale Y to **0.5** (see Figure 6.25).

FIGURE 6.25
Extrude the faces on the sides of the prism, and rename the extrusion node armRoot.

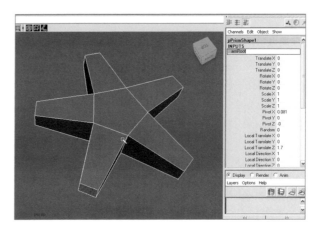

8. With the faces on the end of each extrusion still selected, press the g hot key to repeat the last action, which creates another extrusion.

9. Rename the new polyExtrudeFace1 node **firstArmSection**. Set its Local Translate Z channel to **1.5**. Set all the Local Scale channels to **0.5**. Set Number Of Divisions to **2**.

10. Shift+click the inside faces of the upper division on each of the arms of the snowflake, as shown in Figure 6.26. Press the g hot key to make another extrusion. Name this extrusion **firstBranch**.

11. Set the Local Translate Z channel of the firstBranch node to **1**. Set the Local Scale channels to **0.5**.

12. Select the face at the tip of each arm. Press the g hot key to create another extrusion. Name the extrusion **firstTipSection**. Set the Local Scale of firstTipSection to **2**.

13. Press the g hot key to make one last extrusion. Name the extrusion **secondTipSection**. Set the Local Translate Z channels of secondTipSection to **0.4** and the Local Scale channels to **0.4**. Figure 6.27 shows the final snowflake.

14. Rename the prism **snowflakeFinal**.

15. Save the scene as **snowflake_v01.ma**.

FIGURE 6.26
Using a series of extrude operations, form the arms of the snowflake.

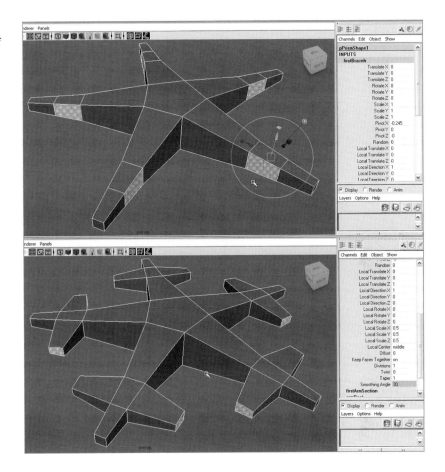

FIGURE 6.27
The final shape of the snowflake after the extrusions have been applied

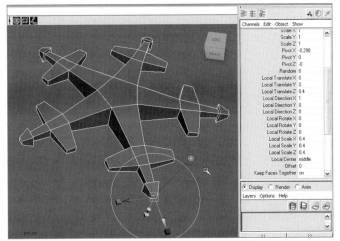

Create the Blend Shape Targets

The sequence of Blend Shapes will be created using duplicates of the snowflake. You'll make a duplicate for each growth stage in the sequence, working backwards from the final snowflake shape.

1. Continue with the scene from the previous section or open the snowflake_v01.ma scene from the chapter6\scenes directory on the DVD.

2. Select snowflakeFinal and choose Edit ➤ Duplicate Special ➤ Options. In the options, enable Duplicate Input Graph, and set Group Under to World. This makes a copy of the snowflake model, including all of the extrusion nodes (see Figure 6.28).

FIGURE 6.28

The options for
Duplicate Special

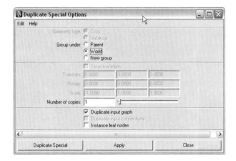

3. Name the duplicate **snowflakeTips**, and move it off to the side.

4. Select snowflakeTips and open the Channel Box. Select the secondTipSection1 node, and set the Local Scale channels to **1** and Local Translate Z to **0** so the tips disappear. Do the same for the firstTipSection1 node.

5. Select snowflakeTips and choose Edit ➤ Duplicate Special to make another copy. Name this copy **snowflakeBranches**, and move it off to the side.

6. In the Channel Box for snowflakeBranches, select the firstBranch2 node and set its Local Scale channels to **1** and its Local Translate Z to **0**.

7. Repeat this process until there are five duplicates of the snowflake. Each duplicate is a stage in the growth of the snowflake (see Figure 6.29). Name the last duplicate **snowflakeStart**. It should look just like the original five-sided prism.

8. Save the scene as **snowflake_v02.ma**. To see a version of the scene to this point, open the snowflake_v02.ma scene from the chapter6\scenes directory.

FIGURE 6.29

Create a duplicate
for each stage of
the snowflake's
growth.

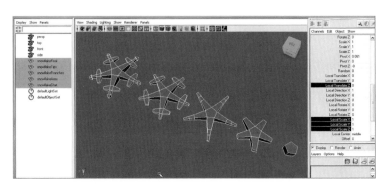

Create the Blend Shape Sequence

This process may seem a little strange, but it's important to remember that for the Blend Shape deformer to work correctly, the number of vertices and the point order of each model used in the Blend Shape deformer have to match. Therefore, it's best to work backwards from the finished model. You should be able to see at this point why naming each extrusion node is helpful. If the nodes do not have descriptive names, it's very hard to know which node corresponds to which part of a duplicate of the original snowflake, especially if you decide to make a more complex crystalline structure.

At this point the hard work is done; creating the Blend Shape sequence is very easy.

1. Shift+click the snowflake models in the order of their stage of growth, but don't select the snowflakeStart model.

2. With all of the models selected in the order of their growth stage, Shift+click the snow-flakeStart model and switch to the Animation menu set. Choose Create Deformers ➢ Blend Shape ➢ Options. In the options, enable In-between. Click Create to make the Blend Shape (see Figure 6.30).

FIGURE 6.30

Enable the In-between option in the Create Blend Shape Options.

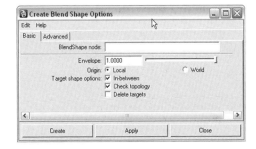

3. Choose Window ➢ Animation Editors ➢ Blend Shape to open the Blend Shape controls. Move the slider up and down, and the snowflakeStart model should grow into a snow-flake as you move the slider up.

4. If you decide to change the order of the sequence, swap targets. Select two of the Blend Shape targets, and choose Edit Deformers ➢ Blend Shapes ➢ Swap. This swaps the order of the selected targets in the Blend Shape sequence.

5. If you're happy with the final animation, delete all of the targets. Don't delete the snow-flakeStart model.

6. Save the scene as **snowflake_v03.ma**. To see a finished version of the scene, open the snowflake_v03.ma scene from the chapter6\scenes directory on the DVD.

LAYER BLEND SHAPES

A Blend Shape target can also be deformed using another Blend Shape deformer with a completely separate set of Blend Shape targets. You can create very complex effects by applying additional Blend Shape deformers (as well as other types of deformers) to your Blend Shape targets. These deformations can be animated, and that animation will carry on through to the base mesh.

Use Lattices

Lattices are the most versatile deformers available in Maya. A lattice is a cube-shaped cage that surrounds the object. When the points of the lattice are moved, the surface of the object becomes deformed. Chapter 4 shows how a lattice can be used as a modeling tool. In this chapter, you'll animate a lattice to add cartoonish movement to a simple character.

ENVELOPE

All deformers have an Envelope control that adjusts the overall strength of the deformer.

Create a Lattice

Lattices can deform all types of geometry, groups, particles, and even other lattices. When you create a lattice, two nodes are added to the scene: lattice node, which is labeled ffd1Lattice (the number 1 changes depending on how many lattices are in the scene), and ffd1Base. The letters *ffd* stand for free-form deformer. When you edit the shape of the ffd1Lattice, Maya compares the differences in the shapes of the ffd1Lattice and the ffd1Base and makes changes to the deformed object relative to the differences between these two nodes.

1. Open the mushroom_v01.ma scene from the chapter6\scenes directory on the DVD. This scene shows three cartoon mushrooms on a hill.

2. Select mushroom1Group in the Outliner, and choose Deformers ➤ Create Lattice. A cage appears around the pink mushroom. In the Outliner, there are two new nodes named ffd1Lattice and ffd1Base (Figure 6.31).

   The lattice is automatically sized and scaled to surround the deformed object.

3. Select the ffd1Lattice node and switch to the Move tool. Try moving the lattice; the entire mushroom1Group moves with it. The same is true as you scale or rotate the lattice.

FIGURE 6.31
The lattice deformer appears as a cage over the mushroom1Group.

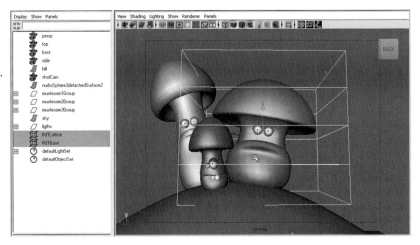

Since the lattice surrounds the entire group, moving it moves the whole mushroom. If you move the ffd1Base node, the mushroom character moves in the opposite direction and becomes mangled in the process. In most cases, you want to avoid moving the base node by itself (Figure 6.32).

FIGURE 6.32
Moving the ffd1Base node badly distorts the mushroom1Group.

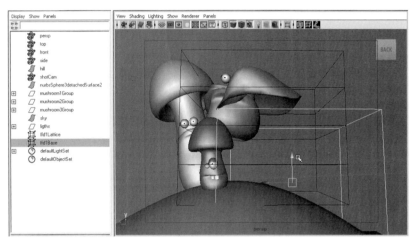

4. Undo any changes made to the ffd1Lattice and ffd1Base nodes. Shift+click both the ffd1Lattice and ffd1Base nodes, and move them together. When you move the nodes together, there's no change in the deformed object.

If you need to reposition a lattice over part of a model or scale it so it engulfs a larger portion of the scene, remember to select both the ffd1Base and ffd1Lattice nodes together and make the changes while both nodes are selected. You can even group the nodes if that makes it easier.

5. Right-click on the lattice and choose Lattice Point from the marking menu. Drag a selection marquee over some of the points and move them. The mushroom1Group becomes distorted again but in a more controllable manner (see Figure 6.33).

FIGURE 6.33
Moving selected lattice points deforms the mushroom.

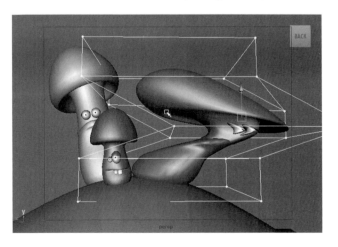

6. Select the ffd1Lattice node, and open its Attribute Editor to the ffd1 tab. Disable the Local option. This makes the lattice deformations much smoother.

7. Choose Edit Deformers ➤ Remove Lattice Tweaks to reset the lattice to its original state.

8. Switch to the ffd1LatticeShape tab in the Attribute Editor, and experiment with changing the settings in the sliders for the S, T, and U divisions. These control how many divisions are along each axis of the lattice.

The axes of the lattice are specified using the letters *S, T,* and *U,* kind of like the X, Y, and Z axes of an object. A lattice point is placed at the intersection of each division. Each point has a certain amount of influence over the deformed object. When the Local option is enabled in the ffd1 tab, each point can deform only the parts of the object that are nearby. When Local is off, any changes to a lattice point's position affect the entire object, resulting in a smoother deformation. When local mode is enabled, you can set the strength of the local influence using the Local S, T, and U sliders.

The Outside settings in the ffd1 tab specify the amount of influence the lattice has over parts of the deformed object that lie outside the lattice cage. When Outside Lattice is set to Inside, changes to the lattice affect only the parts of the model inside the lattice. When this is set to All, changes to the lattice affect the entire object regardless of whether the parts are inside or outside the lattice. The Falloff setting specifies a range of distance. Parts of the object that fall within this distance are affected by changes to the lattice, but the strength of influence diminishes as the space between the object and the lattice increases. Figure 6.34 shows the settings available in the ffd1LatticeShape and ffd1 tabs of the Attribute Editor.

FIGURE 6.34

Options for the lattice can be set in the tabs of the lattice's Attribute Editor.

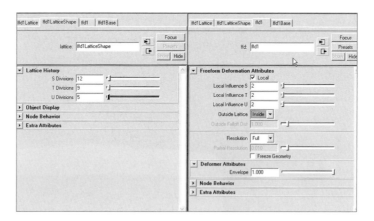

Animating Lattices

There are lots of ways to animate lattices. You can animate the transform node of the lattice or the individual points of the lattice; you can also apply deformers to the lattice and even bind a lattice to joints. In this example, a very simple animation is created by animating the transform node of the lattice.

1. Continue with the scene from the previous section. Delete the ffd1Lattice node in the Outliner. The ffd1Base node will also be deleted.

2. Select mushroomGroup1 and choose Deformers ➤ Create Lattice to create a new lattice.

3. Select the ffd1Lattice and ffd1Base nodes, and group them (hot key = Ctrl+g). Select the group, name it **lattice**, and center its pivot (Modify ➢ Center Pivot).

4. Select the lattice group, and in the Channel Box, set Scale Y to **5**.

5. Expand the lattice group in the Outliner; then select the ffd1Lattice node. In the Channel Box, set the T Divisions to **20**.

6. Switch to a side view, right-click on the lattice, and choose Lattice Point. Hold the Shift key, and drag a selection marquee over every other row of points on the lattice.

7. Switch to the Scale tool and push in the blue handle of the Scale tool to scale the lattice points along the Z axis. This creates an accordion shape in the lattice points (see Figure 6.35).

8. Switch to the front view, and push in the red handle of the Scale tool to scale the points along the X axis.

9. Select the lattice group and open the Channel Box. Highlight the Translate Y attribute. From the Channel Box menu, choose Edit ➢ Expressions.

10. In the Expression field, type **lattice.translateY=4*(sin(time));**.

FIGURE 6.35
A very tall lattice is created around the mushroom; the points of the lattice are scaled to create an accordion shape.

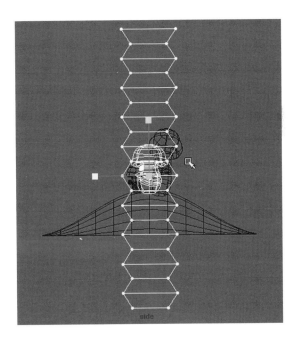

This expression moves the lattice group up and down along the Y axis, using the sin of the current time multiplied by 4.

11. Click the Create button to make the expression. Set the length of the timeline to **200**, and play the animation (see Figure 6.36).

FIGURE 6.36
Create an expression to automatically move the lattice up and down over time.

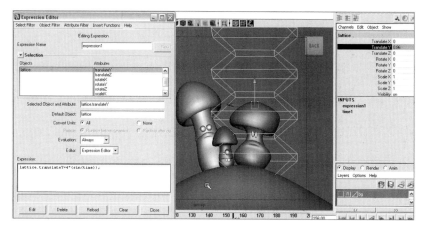

The movement of the lattice group causes a wave-type distortion in the mushroom. This is an extremely simple application of the lattice deformer, but it gives you a good idea of how it works. Lattices become even more powerful when you combine them with other deformers and techniques.

12. Save the file as **mushrooms_v02.ma**. To see a finished version of the scene, open the mushroom_v02.ma scene from the chapter6\scenes folder of the DVD.

FLOW PATH OBJECTS

You can make an object that has been attached to a motion path conform to the shape of the path using a Flow Path object. This automatically generates a lattice that matches the shape of the path. To create this effect, select an object that has been attached to a motion path, and choose (from the Animation menu set) Animate ➤ Motion Path ➤ Flow Path Object. You can specify in the options whether the lattice covers the entire curve or just the selected object.

If you apply the lattice to the entire curve, you can then edit the lattice points to add deformations to the object as it moves along the path. You can achieve similar results by rigging a lattice to a joint chain that is controlled by an IK spline. However, even though the Flow Path object offers less control than an IK spline, it is much easier and faster to set up.

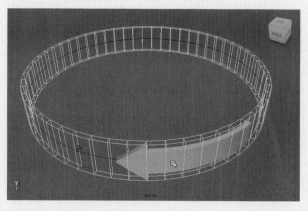

Animate Clusters

As deformers go, none are simpler or more useful than clusters. A cluster is a simple handle that can be applied to objects or components. Most often a cluster is applied to the vertices of an object. Think of a cluster as a way to group the vertices of one or more objects. You can then apply the cluster to animate the vertices.

KEYFRAMING COMPONENTS

It is possible to set keyframes on the components of geometry, such as the CVs of a curve or the points of a lattice. However, it's a better idea to create a cluster deformer for the component and then set keyframes on the cluster. Clusters are easier to work with in the viewport and on the Graph Editor, and you can easily return a cluster to its original position by setting all of its Translate and Rotate channels back to 0.

In this section, you'll see a few ways to create, edit, and animate clusters.

Cluster Objects

You'll start by placing a cluster on a group.

1. Open the `tree_v01.ma scene` from the `chapter6\scenes` directory on the DVD. This scene consists of a polygon palm tree model created by converting a Paint Effects stroke into polygons.

2. Select the palmTree group in the Outliner, and switch to the Animation menu set. Choose Create Deformers ➤ Cluster. A small *C* appears in the viewport, and you'll see the cluster1Handle node in the Outliner (see Figure 6.37).

FIGURE 6.37
The cluster appears as a small *C* in the viewport.

3. Select the Move tool and move the cluster around. The palmTree group moves with the cluster.

4. In the Outliner, select the cluster and Ctrl+click the palmTree group. Use the Move tool to move both objects.

The movement created using the Move tool is doubled for the tree. This is an example of a *double transform*. This occurs when you move the object and the deformer; the translation of the deformer is added to the translation of the cluster.

5. Undo all the changes you made with the Move tool. Try selecting the palmTree group and moving it. The cluster stays in its original position.

If you move the cluster now, it still works, but it has been offset from the deformed object. This is another situation you don't want. Once you cluster an object or part of an object, move the cluster by itself.

RELATIVE CLUSTERS

When you create a cluster deformer, in the Options box you can choose the Relative option. This option is also available in the Attribute Editor for the cluster node and can be turned on and off after you create the cluster deformer.

In a situation where you need to group a number of clusters with the object they deform and then translate the group node, you should turn on Relative. Otherwise, moving the group will create a double transform, which leads to unexpected results.

Paint Cluster Weights

The strength of cluster weights can be painted directly on an object.

1. Continue with the previous scene, and return the cluster and the objects to their original position.

2. Select the palmTree group, and choose Edit Deformers ➤ Paint Cluster Weights Tool. The palm tree turns white, indicating that the strength of the weight is at 1 (100 percent).

3. In the Tool Options box, set Paint Operation to Replace. Set Value to **0**.

4. Paint around the area of the trunk; it should turn black as you paint. The black color indicates that the strength values of the cluster at the trunk are now set to 0 (see Figure 6.38).

5. Set Paint Operation to Smooth, and click the Flood button a few times to smooth the transition between the white and black areas.

6. Select the cluster in the Outliner, and use the Move and Rotate tools to move it around. The trunk stays firmly planted in the ground (see Figure 6.39).

7. Save the scene as **tree_v02.ma**. To see a version of the scene to this point, open the tree_ v02.ma scene from the chapter6\scenes directory on the DVD.

FIGURE 6.38
The cluster weights at the bottom of the tree are reduced using the Paint Attributes tool.

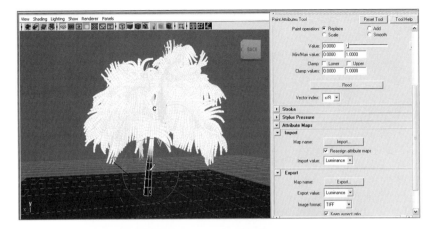

FIGURE 6.39
After you paint the weights of the cluster, the trunk stays in the ground when the cluster is moved.

Cluster Components

The most common use for clusters is to directly deform components of an object. Clusters are a great way to attach CVs of a curve to another object.

1. Create a new scene in Maya.

2. Turn on Grid Snapping, and choose Create ➢ EP Curve Tool. Click twice to make a curve about 10 units in length. Hit the Enter key to complete the Curve tool.

3. Right-click on the curve and choose Control Vertex so you can select the control vertices of the curve. Select one of the CVs at the end of the curve, and then Shift+click the other two CVs at the center of the curve.

4. Choose Create Deformers ➤ Cluster. The cluster will be named cluster1Handle.

5. Repeat steps 3 and 4, but this time select the CV at the opposite end of the curve as well as the two CVs in the middle. This is named cluster2Handle (be careful not to select cluster1Handle while you're selecting the middle CVs).

You should end up with two clusters. The two CVs in the middle of the curve are deformed by both clusters. You can adjust the amount of influence each cluster has on the vertices using the Component Editor.

6. Select the middle CV closest to cluster1Handle, and choose Window ➤ General Editors ➤ Component Editor.

7. In the Component Editor, switch to the Weighted Deformer tab. Set the weight for cluster1 to **0.75** and the weight for cluster2 to **0.25**. Together the weights add up to 1 (Figure 6.40).

8. Select the middle CV closest to cluster2Handle. In the Component Editor, set the weight for cluster1 to **0.25** and the weight for cluster2 to **0.75**.

9. Close the Component Editor. In the perspective view, switch to the Move tool. Select cluster1Handle, hold the d key on the keyboard to switch to pivot point editing mode. While holding the d key, snap the pivot point for cluster1Handle to the CV at the closest end (see Figure 6.41).

FIGURE 6.40
The weight for each cluster of the selected CV is entered numerically in the Component Editor.

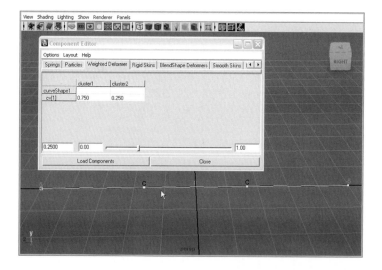

FIGURE 6.41
The pivot point for the cluster handle is moved to the end of the curve.

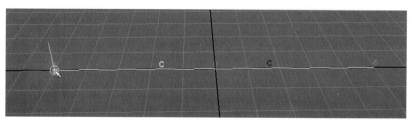

10. Repeat step 9 for cluster2Handle; snap its pivot point to the opposite end of the curve (closest to the cluster2Handle).

11. Select cluster1Handle and move it around. You can now easily move one end of the curve, and there is a built-in falloff in strength down the length of the curve (Figure 6.42).

FIGURE 6.42
Moving the cluster moves the end of the curve. The CVs in the middle of the curve are weighted to create a falloff in the strength of the clusters at either end.

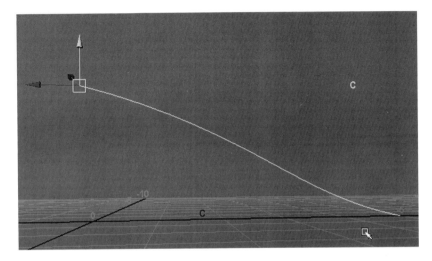

It may look like the cluster is offset from the curve, but in fact the C in the viewport is placed an average distance away from the deformed CVs. The display of the deformer handle is not important at this point because the actual handle has been snapped to the end of the curve. You can see this in the position of the Move tool manipulator.

12. Save the scene as **clusterCurve_v01.ma**. To see a version of the scene to this point, open the clusterCurve_v01.ma scene from the chapter6\scenes directory on the DVD.

Constraining Clusters

Clusters can be parented to other objects, but I actually prefer using constraints. Using a constraint means that you don't have to worry about whether the cluster is set to Relative or not, and it reduces the chance of accidentally creating a double transformation. As long as you animate only the constraining objects and not the clusters themselves, you should be fine.

1. Continue with the scene from the previous section or open the clusterCurve_v01.ma scene from the chapter6\scenes directory on the DVD.

2. Select both cluster handles, and make sure all of their Translate and Rotate channels are set to **0** in the Channel Box.

3. Create a NURBS sphere. Move the sphere so its surface is placed at the edge of the curve closest to cluster1Handle. If the sphere radius is 1 unit and Grid Snapping is enabled, the surface of the sphere should touch the edge of the curve when the sphere is placed one unit beyond the end of the curve.

4. In the Outliner, select the nurbsSphere1 node, and Ctrl+click cluster1Handle.

5. From the Animation menu set, choose Constrain ➢ Parent ➢ Options. In the options, enable Maintain Offset and set the axes for Translate and Rotate to All (see Figure 6.43).

FIGURE 6.43
A sphere is placed at one end of the curve. The cluster1Handle is constrained to the sphere.

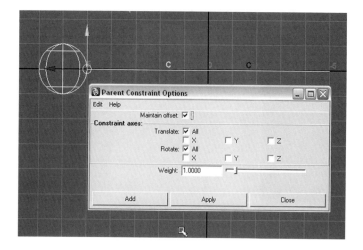

When you move or rotate the sphere, the curve travels with it.

6. Repeat steps 3 through 5, and create a sphere for the opposite end of the curve. Constrain cluster2Handle to this sphere (Figure 6.44).

FIGURE 6.44
The clusters are constrained to the spheres. A hose is created along the length of the curve using a Paint Effects curve that has been converted to polygons.

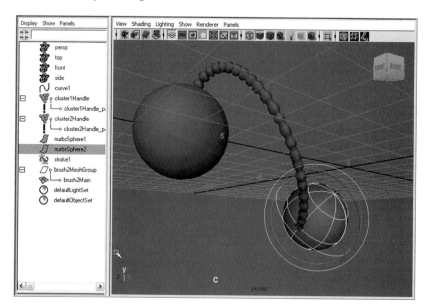

Try extruding a circle along the length of the curve, or attach a Paint Effects stroke to the curve (consult Chapter 3 for information on extruding along paths). Chapter 4 demonstrates how to model using Paint Effects. This is a great way to create a simple hose that connects two pieces of geometry. This technique works pretty well for many situations; however, you may experience some flipping of the curve when the spheres are rotated.

7. Save the scene as **clusterCurve_v02.ma**. To see a version of the scene to this point, open the clusterCurve_v02.ma scene from the chapter6\scenes directory on the DVD.

Nonlinear Deformers

The nonlinear deformers include the bend, flare, sine, twist, squash, and wave deformers. The names of the deformers give a pretty good indication of what they do. They work well for creating cartoonish effects and even do a decent job of faking dynamic effects, saving you from the extensive setup many dynamic simulations require. All of the nonlinear deformers work the same way. The deformer is applied to a surface, a lattice, components, or a group of surfaces, and then parameters are edited to achieve the desired effect. The parameters can be animated as well. You can use nonlinear deformers in combination with each other and other deformers.

In this section, you'll use nonlinear deformers to animate a jellyfish bobbing in the ocean. You'll use just a few of the deformers to create the scene, but since they all work the same way, you can apply what you've learned to the other nonlinear deformers in your own scenes.

The Wave

The wave deformer creates a ring of sine waves like a circular ripple in a puddle. To create the gentle bobbing up and down of a jellyfish, you'll animate the parameters of a wave deformer.

1. Open the jellyfish_v01.ma scene from the chapter6\scenes directory on the DVD.

This scene contains a very simple jellyfish model. The model consists of the body of the jellyfish and its tendrils. All the surfaces are NURBS. The tendrils, which were created by converting Paint Effects strokes to NURBS surfaces, are grouped together and then grouped again with the body (see Figure 6.45).

2. Select the jellyFish group in the Outliner. Switch to the Animation menu set, and choose Create Deformers ➤ Nonlinear ➤ Wave. The deformer appears as a wireframe wave. In the Outliner, you'll see that a new wave1Handle node has been created.

3. Select wave1Handle and open its Attribute Editor. Click the wave1 tab. The tab contains the parameters for the deformer.

4. Set Amplitude to **0.041**. The Amplitude increases the height of the sinusoidal wave. This is displayed in the wireframe deformer handle in the viewport. Notice that the jellyfish is now distorted.

5. Set Wavelength to **0.755**; this decreases the distance between the peaks and valleys of the sine wave, creating a long, smooth type of distortion (see Figure 6.46).

FIGURE 6.45
The jellyfish model
is created from
groups of NURBS
surfaces.

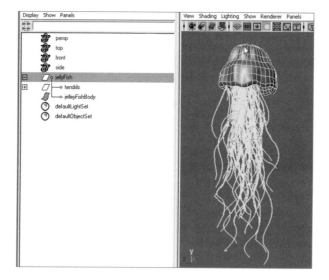

FIGURE 6.46
The settings on the
wave1 tab change
the shape of the
wave deformer.

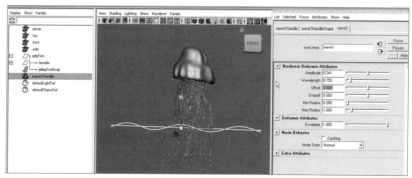

6. Select the wave1Handle node, and use the Move tool to position it at the center of the jellyfish body. Set the Translate coordinates as follows:

   Translate X: **0**

   Translate Y: **0.787**

   Translate Z: **-.394**

7. Set all three Scale channels to **30**.

8. To animate the bobbing motion, create a simple expression that connects the Offset value
   to the current time. Open the Attribute Editor for wave1Handle to the wave1 tab. In the
   field next to Offset, type **=time;** (see Figure 6.47), and press the Enter key.

FIGURE 6.47
The Offset attri-
bute is connected
to time.

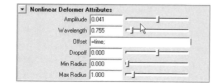

9. Set Min Radius to **0.1**. If you switch to wireframe display, you'll see that a circle has appeared at the center of the handle.

The deformer now affects only the areas between the edge of the min radius and the outer edge of the deformer. You can set a range of deformation by adjusting the Min and Max Radius sliders. Dropoff reduces the amplitude of the deformer at the outer edges of the range. Setting Dropoff to -1 reduces the amplitude at the center of the deformer.

10. Save the scene as `jellyfish_v02.ma`. To see a version of the scene up to this point, open the `jellyfish_v02.ma` scene from the `chaper6\scenes` directory on the DVD.

Squash

The squash deformer can actually both squash and stretch objects. It works well for cartoony effects. In this section, you'll add it to the jellyfish to enhance the bobbing motion created by the wave deformer.

1. Continue with the scene from the previous section or open the `jellyfish_v02.ma` scene from the `chapter6\scenes` directory on the DVD.

2. Switch to the Animation menu set. Select the jellyFish group in the Outliner, and choose Create Deformers ➤ NonLinear ➤ Squash. A node named squash1Handle appears in the Outliner. In the perspective view, the squash handle appears as a long line with a cross at either end.

3. Select squash1Handle in the Outliner, use the Move tool to position the handle at the center of the jellyfish. Set the Translate channels to the following:

   Translate X: **0**

   Translate Y: **1.586**

   Translate Z: **0**

4. Select the squash1Handle, and open the Attribute Editor to the squash1 tab. The Low and High Bound sliders set the overall range of the deformer. Leave Low Bound at -1, and set High Bound to **0.5** (see Figure 6.48).

You can animate any of the settings to add motion to the jellyfish. In this case, you'll add an expression to the Factor of squash1. Setting Factor to a positive value stretches the object; setting Factor to a negative value squashes the object. For the jellyfish, animating between squash and stretch helps make the model appear as though it's floating in water. You can use a sin function as part of an expression that smoothly animates the Factor value between positive and negative values.

5. In the field next to Factor, type `=0.25*(sin(time*2));` and hit the Enter key.

Multiplying time by 2 speeds up the animation of the values. Multiplying the entire expression by 0.25 keeps the range of values between -0.25 and 0.25. Going beyond this range deforms the jellyfish a bit too much.

Factor controls the vertical displacement created by the squash deformer; the Expand setting controls the horizontal displacement created by the effect.

6. Set Expand to **2**. Set Max Expand Pos to **0.78**. This places the vertical position of the center of the effect along the length of the deformer.

7. Save the scene as **jellyfish_v03.ma**. To see a version of the scene to this point, open the jellyfish_v03.ma scene from the chapter3\scenes directory on the DVD.

FIGURE 6.48

The squash deformer settings appear in the Attribute Editor.

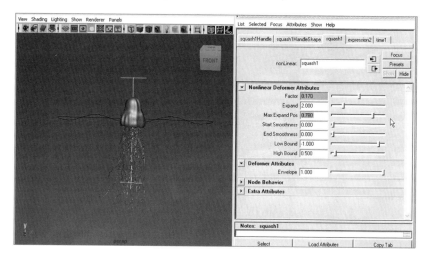

Twist

The twist deformer twists an object around a central axis. You'll add this to the jellyfish to create some additional motion for the tendrils.

1. Continue with the scene from the previous section or open the jellyfish_v03.ma scene from the chapter6\scenes directory on the DVD.

2. In the Outliner, expand the jellyFish group and select the tendrils group. Choose Create Deformers ➢ Nonlinear ➢ Twist. A new twist1Handle node will appear in the Outliner.

3. Select twist1Handle in the Outliner, and set the Translation channels to the following:

   Translate X: **0**

   Translate Y: **-18**

   Translate Z: **0**

4. Open the Attribute Editor for twist1Handle to the twist1 tab.

   Just like for the squash deformer, you can specify the range of the effect of the deformer using the Low Bound and High Bound sliders.

5. Set Low Bound to **-1** and High Bound to **0.825**.

   The Start Angle and End Angle values define the amount of twist created along the object. If you move the End Angle slider, the top of the tendrils spin around even if they are outside the High Bound range. Moving the Start Angle slider twists the tendrils at their ends, which is more like the effect you want. You can use a simple noise expression to create a smooth type of random oscillation between values. Since the Start Angle is specified in degrees, you can multiply the noise expression by 360 to get a full range of twisting motion.

6. In the Start Angle field, type **=360*(noise*(time*0.1));**. Multiplying time by 0.1 slows down the motion of the twisting.

7. Rewind and play the animation. You're on your way to creating an interesting jellyfish motion (see Figure 6.49).

8. Save the scene as **jellyfish_v04.ma**. To see a version of the scene to this point, open the jellyfish_v04.ma scene from the chapter6\scenes directory on the DVD.

Try adding additional nonlinear deformers to the jellyfish.

FIGURE 6.49
The jellyfish is animated using a number of nonlinear deformers.

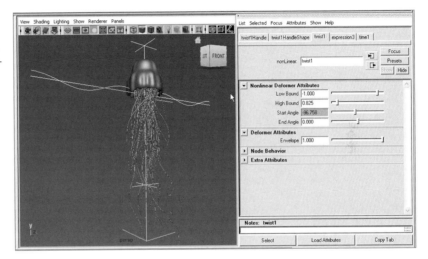

Real World Scenario

UNDULATING BACTERIA

While working on a creepy animation sequence for the closing titles of a feature film, I was asked to create hairy microbes floating in a cellular environment. The art director wanted the bacteria encased in an undulating membrane. To do this, I combined nonlinear deformers and a blend shape. Using a blend shape, I transferred the animation of the undulating membrane from a copy of the bacteria to the animated version of the bacteria. You can try this yourself using the following steps:

1. Create a model of a bacterium. Usually a rounded elongated cube with a lot of divisions does a good job.

2. Create a duplicate of the bacterium geometry.

3. Animate the original geometry floating in an environment or slinking along an animation path.

4. Apply a series of deformers to the duplicate geometry to make the surface undulate and throb.

5. Select the deformed duplicate and the animated original, and choose Create Deformers ➢ Blend Shape. Set the Value of the Blend Shape on the animated bacterium to **1**. The deformations applied to the duplicate are now transferred to the original.

Using this setup, you won't need to worry about grouping the nonlinear deformers or parenting them to the animated original. You can move the duplicate and its deformers out of camera view and continue to edit the animation by changing the settings on the duplicate's deformers.

Create Jiggle Deformers

A jiggle deformer is a very simple way to add a jiggling motion to deformed objects. Jiggle deformers do not have the same level of control as dynamic systems such as nucleus, fluids, or hair. Jiggle deformers are best used as a substitute for dynamics when the situation requires just a little jiggly motion.

Apply Jiggle Deformers

There aren't very many options for creating jiggle deformers. To apply a jiggle deformer, select the object you want to jiggle and create the deformer. In this section, you'll add the jiggle to the jellyfish.

1. Continue with the scene from the previous section or open the jellyfish_v04.ma scene from the chapter6\scenes directory on the DVD.

2. Select the jellyFish group in the Outliner. Choose Create Deformers ➤ Jiggle Deformer ➤ Options.

3. In the options, set Stiffness to **0.1** and Damping to **0.8**. A higher Stiffness setting creates more of a vibrating type of jiggle; lowering the Stiffness value makes the jiggle more jellylike.

4. Click Create to make the deformer. You won't see any new nodes appear in the Outliner because the Display option is set to DAG Objects Only.

If you turn off the DAG Objects Only option in the Outliner, you'll see that a jiggle deformer is created for each surface. A jiggle cache is created to aid in calculation and playback of the scene (Figure 6.50).

5. Rewind and play the scene; you'll see that the jellyfish has a jiggling motion, especially in the tendrils.

FIGURE 6.50
A node for each jiggle deformer applied to the surfaces appears in the Outliner

| layerManager |
| dof1 |
| dynController1 |
| expression1 |
| expression2 |
| expression3 |
| globalCacheControl |
| hardwareRenderGlobals |
| defaultHardwareRenderGlobals |
| ikSystem |
| jiggle1 |
| jiggle10 |
| jiggle11 |
| jiggle12 |
| jiggle13 |
| jiggle14 |
| jiggle15 |
| jiggle16 |
| jiggle17 |
| jiggle18 |
| jiggle19 |
| jiggle2 |
| jiggle20 |
| jiggle21 |
| jiggle22 |

If you want to edit the settings of all of the jiggle deformers at once (since there are so many tendrils, a lot of deformer nodes were created), disable the DAG Objects Only option in the Outliner's

Display menu, Shift+click all of the jiggle nodes, and then edit the settings in the Channel Box. When you have multiple objects selected, editing the settings in the Channel Box applies the settings to all of the selected objects. This is not true when working in the Attribute Editor.

Paint Jiggle Weights

The jiggle effect looks good in the area of the tendrils, but it's a little too strong on the top of the jellyfish body. You can edit the weights of the deformer interactively using the Paint Jiggle Weights Tool.

1. Select the jellyFishBody node in the Outliner, and choose Edit Deformers ➢ Paint Attributes Tool.

2. In the Options box, set Paint Operation to Replace and Value to **0**. Paint the area at the top of the jellyfish body.

3. Set Paint Operation to Smooth and click the Flood button a few times to smooth the overall weighting (see Figure 6.51).

FIGURE 6.51
Paint the weights of the jiggle deformer on the top of the jellyfish body and then smooth them using the Flood button.

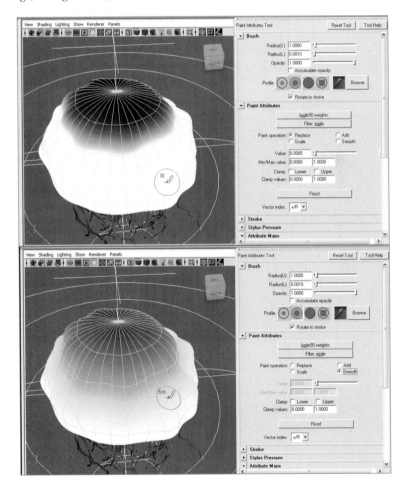

4. Rewind and play the animation. The jiggling is not quite as strong on the top of the jellyfish.

5. Save the scene as **jellyfish_v05.ma**. To see a version of the scene to this point, open the jellyfish_v05.ma scene from the chapter6\scenes directory on the DVD.

Use the Geometry Cache

When you create a geometry cache for animated geometry, a series of files are written to your computer's hard drive that store the position of each of the points of the specified geometry over time. Once you create a geometry cache, when you play the scene back the cached geometry will play much closer to real time. You can add more deformers and animation to the cached geometry, and you can also alter the playback speed of the cached geometry.

In this section, you'll cache the animation for the jellyfish and then use the geometry cache settings to slow the playback of the jellyfish so the floating motion looks more natural.

Create a Geometry Cache

The motion-deformed jellyfish looks pretty good as a simple animation. However, after all the deformers have been combined and the jiggle has been added, the motion looks a little too fast for a convincing deep sea environment. Obviously you can continue to edit the expressions used on the deformers, but in this section you'll take a shortcut by using a geometry cache.

1. Continue with the scene from the previous section or open the jellyfish_v05.ma scene from the chapter6\scenes directory on the DVD.

Unless you have a very powerful computer, most likely the playback of the jellyfish is not quite in real time. It may look alright in the scene view, but when you create a Playblast, you'll see that the overall motion is too fast.

2. In the viewport panel menu disable the display of deformers in the Show menu so you can clearly see the jellyfish.

3. Choose Window ➤ Playblast ➤ Options to open the Playblast Options. Set the Time Range to Time Slider. You can set the Viewer to Movieplayer if you want to see the playback in your computer's default media player, or to Image Viewer if you want to play the movie in FCheck (on a Mac the Quicktime option is offered instead of Movieplayer).

4. Set the Display Size to From Window, and use the Scale slider to determine the size of the movie.

5. Click the Playblast button in the options. Maya will play through the animation and take a screenshot of each frame as it plays. When it's finished, you can watch the movie play back in the default media viewer or in FCheck (see Figure 6.52).

To create a geometry cache, you need to select the geometry nodes; selecting group nodes or parents of the geometry nodes won't work.

6. In the Outliner, hold the Shift key and click the plus sign next to the jellyfish group to expand the group and the tendrils group at the same time.

FIGURE 6.52
The options
for creating a
Playblast

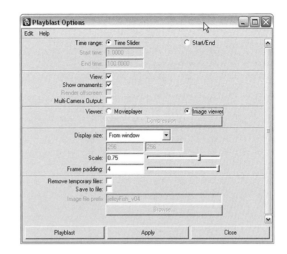

7. Shift+click all the tendril objects and the jellyFishBody surface.

8. From the Animation menu set, choose Geometry Cache ➢ Create New Cache ➢ Options.

9. In the options, you can use the Base Directory field to specify a directory for the cache. By default the cache is created in the **Data** folder for the current project. If you will be rendering across computers on a network, make sure all of the computers have access to the directory that contains the cache.

10. Name the cache **jellyfish**. Set the File Distribution to 1 file and the Cache Time Range to Time Slider.

11. Click Create to make the cache. Maya will play through the animation and write the cache files to disk.

12. When Maya has completed the cache, it should automatically be applied to the jellyfish. To prove this, you can select the deformers in the scene, delete them, and then play back the animation. The jellyfish should still bob up and down.

Editing the Cache Playback

Once the cache has been created, you can use the settings in the cache node to change the speed of the playback. This will create a more believable motion for the jellyfish.

1. Select any of the surfaces in the jellyfish (not the jellyfish group node), and open the Attribute Editor.

2. Switch to the jellyfishCache1 tab. Set the Scale attribute to **5**. This scales the length of the animation to be five times its original length, thus slowing down the speed of playback (see Figure 6.53).

3. Set the length of the timeline to **1000**. The original 200-frame animation has been scaled to 1000 frames.

4. Create a Playblast. You'll see that the jellyfish is now much slower and looks more like an undersea creature

Once you have created a cache you can add additional deformers, animate the movement of the jellyfish group, and even make animated copies.

5. Select the jellyFish group and choose Edit ➢ Duplicate Special ➢ Options. In the options, set the Geometry Type to Instance. Click Duplicate Special to create the copy.

6. Move the copy away from the original, and rotate it on its Y axis so it does not look exactly like the original.

7. Make a few more copies like this to create a small jellyfish army. Play back the animation to see the army in action (see figure 6.54).

FIGURE 6.53
The options for the geometry cache playback

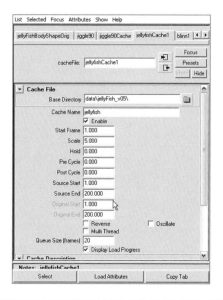

FIGURE 6.54
Duplicates of the original jellyfish are created to make a small jellyfish army.

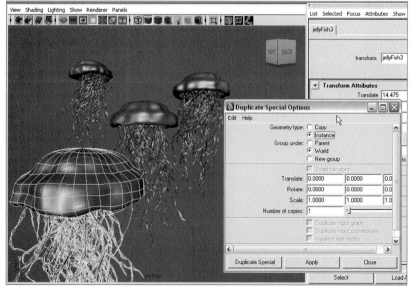

The Bottom Line

Animate facial expressions.   Animated facial expressions are a big part of character animation. It's common practice to use a Blend Shape deformer to create expressions from a large number of Blend Shape targets. The changes created in the targets can be mixed and matched by the deformer to create the expressions and speech for a character.

> **Master it**   Create Blend Shape targets for the nancy character. Make an expression where the brows are up and the brows are down. Create a rig that animates each brow independently.

Create Blend Shape sequences.   Blend Shapes can be applied in a sequential order to animate a sequence of changes over time.

> **Master it**   Create a Blend Shape sequence of a mushroom growing.

Use lattices.   Lattices are freeform deformers that create a 3D cage around an object. The differences between the lattice and the lattice base are used to deform geometry.

> **Master it**   Animate a cube of jelly squishing along a path.

Animate clusters.   Clusters are simple deformers that are most often used to animate the vertices of geometry.

> **Master it**   Create an animated garden hose using clusters.

Animate nonlinear deformers.   Nonlinear deformers apply simple changes to geometry. The deformers are controlled by animating the attributes of the deformer.

> **Master it**   Animate an eel swimming past the jellyfish we created in this chapter.

Use jiggle deformers.   Jiggle deformers add a simple jiggling motion to animated objects.

> **Master it**   Add a jiggling motion to the belly of a character.

Use the geometry cache.   Geometry caches store the animation information of each vertex of a piece of geometry. The Cache controls can be used to speed up or slow down the animation of a cached object.

> **Master It**   Create a slow-motion effect for an animation that uses a deformer.

Chapter 7

Rigging and Muscle Systems

A *rig* is an organized system of deformers, expressions, and controls applied to a surface so an animator can easily and efficiently animate the surface. A good rig should be easy to use so the animator can concentrate on the art of animation without the technical aspects of rigging getting in the way. In addition, a good rig should be well organized so it can easily be changed, repurposed, or fixed if there is a problem.

Rigging as a practice is continually evolving in the industry. New technologies, concepts, and approaches emerge every day and are widely debated and discussed among professional technical directors throughout the world. While this chapter will offer advice on how to best approach creating part of a character rig in Maya, its main purpose is to help you understand how the tools work so that you can approach creating your own rigs and adapting rigging practices from others.

In this chapter you will learn to:

◆ Understand rigging

◆ Create and organize joint hierarchies

◆ Use Inverse Kinematics rigs

◆ Apply skin geometry

◆ Use Maya Muscle

Understanding Rigging

The most common types of rigs are created using joint deformers. In character animation a skeleton system is created from joints to match the basic shape of the character. A joint is represented by a simple wireframe sphere. Joints are connected by bones, which are represented by a wireframe pyramid. When one joint is parented to another joint, the bone is aligned so the pointed end of the pyramid points to the child joint.

The geometry of the character is bound or skinned to the joints so the joints deform the geometry, making knees bend, wrists twist, fingers clench, and so on. Each joint in a hierarchy exerts influence over each vertex of the geometry, pushing or pulling it in one direction or another. The amount of influence exerted on a vertex by a joint is controlled through weighting (see Figure 7.1).

Once geometry has been skinned to a skeleton of joints, a system of controls is created to make animating the joints as simple as possible. Controls may be created from locators or curves or any other node which can be selected in the viewport. These nodes then control the movement of joints via expressions, constraints, or driven keys. You used a simple control system in Chapter 5 to rig a mechanical bug model.

FIGURE 7.1
Joints are positioned based on the shape of the object they are meant to deform.

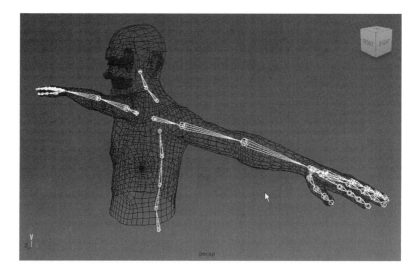

In addition, other types of deformers (such as the ones described in Chapter 6) are often applied to the geometry to compensate for the shortcomings of simple joint deformations. Joints by themselves will not maintain the volume of a surface properly when animated or create the impression of muscle, flesh, and bone beneath skin. Influence objects, lattice deformers, Maya Muscle, and other tools and techniques are often used to create believable motion and simulate the properties of flesh and tissue for characters. In addition, joints can be used to deform some types of other deformers such as lattices. A joint used as a deformer indirectly deforms geometry, or groups of objects, by deforming the lattice, which then deforms the geometry.

The first half of this chapter explores techniques for creating efficient character rigs. There are many approaches to rigging characters; the main focus of these lessons is to build an understanding of how the Maya toolset works so you can adapt it to your preferred rigging workflow. The lessons provide additional tips and tricks that can help you avoid common rigging pitfalls.

Although this chapter provides some background information for the techniques described, you should familiarize yourself with the fundamentals of how to create joints and to bind geometry to joints before attempting the exercises. Information on joint deformers is available in the Maya help files.

The second half of the chapter is devoted to Maya Muscle, which is a plug-in that has been fully integrated into Maya 2009. Maya Muscle is designed to create realistic deformations for character rigs. The muscle system works with skeletons to simulate the qualities of flesh and skin.

Creating and Organizing Joint Hierarchies

The Joint tool creates a joint each time you click on the scene. As long as the Joint tool is active, each time you click on the scene a new joint is added and parented to the previous joint, forming a simple hierarchy known as a *joint chain*. To exit the Joint tool, press the Enter key on the keyboard. This is useful if you need to finish one joint chain and then start another.

You can create branches of joints by parenting joint chains to intermediate joints in the initial chain. By parenting the branches and groups of joint chains, very sophisticated joint hierarchies, known as *skeletons*, can be created quickly.

Because many skeletons can become quite complex, they should be properly organized and labeled so animators and other riggers (referred to as technical directors in some instances) can easily access and understand the skeleton and all of its various parts.

The orientation of joints relative to their parent joints must be consistent throughout the skeleton to achieve proper functionality. The default orientation of a joint, established when the joint is added to a chain, is often incorrect and can lead to problems such as Gimbal Lock.

GIMBAL LOCK

Gimbal Lock is a situation in which a joint or object achieves a rotation that causes two of the rotation axes to overlap. When this occurs, the rotations for the overlapping axes are the same, which prevents the joint from rotating in three dimensions. In this image two of the rotational axes are so close that, when rotated along either axis, the resulting motion is the same.

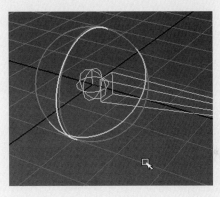

In this section you'll review how to create and organize a joint hierarchy for a character's arm and hand.

Create Joints

The Joint tool adds joints to a scene. When creating joints you want to visualize a simplified skeleton based on the shape of the geometry in the scene.

1. Open the `leftArm_v01.ma` scene from the `chapter7\scenes` folder on the DVD.

This scene has the arm of a human character created with polygons. To keep things simple, the rest of the body has been removed.

2. In the perspective view, switch to the top view.

3. Switch to the Animation menu set. Choose Skeleton ➤ Joint Tool.

4. Turn on Grid Snapping.

You'll create the arm's joint chain in front of the geometry and then reposition the joints after they have been created.

Rotate your wrist as if you were opening a door handle, you'll notice that this type of rotation originates not in the wrist, but in the middle of the forearm (the rotation is created by the two bones of the forearm: the radius and the ulna). To simulate this rotation, the forearm is split into two joints. These joints must be in a straight line or the arm will appear broken as it rotates. The best approach is to use Grid Snapping to create the joints along a straight line and then position and rotate them into place to match the arm geometry.

5. With the Joint tool active, click five times on the grid in a straight line in front of the arm, as shown in Figure 7.2. When you have created five joints, press the Enter key to complete the operation.

FIGURE 7.2
Initially place the arm joints in a straight line in front of the geometry.

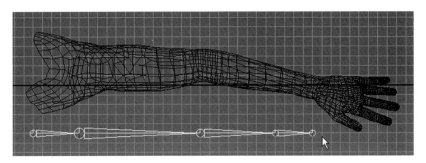

6. In the Outliner, Shift+click on joint1 to expand the joint chain hierarchy. The joints are labeled joint1, joint2, joint3, joint4, and joint5. You can see how they are parented in a simple chain (see Figure 7.3).

7. Turn off Grid Snapping and select joint1. In the options for the Move tool, set Move Axis to Local. In the top view, use the Move tool to position the joint near the center of the shoulder, as shown in the top image in Figure 7.4.

FIGURE 7.3
Expand the joint chain in the Outliner.

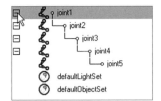

8. To position the other joints in the arm, you can either rotate the joint above the joint you want to position or use the Move tool while holding the d key. Do not move or rotate joint4 out of its alignment with joint3. Even a slight change in its position will cause problems later on.

9. At this point the best way to position joint5 is to rotate joint3 until joint5 is located near the position of the wrist. Use the middle image in Figure 7.4 as a guide as you position the joints. If you need to move joint5 closer to the center of the wrist, use the Move tool but move it only along the local X axis (the red handle of the Move tool) so it does not disturb the rotation of joint4.

JOINT DISPLAY SIZE

You can change the display size of the joints in the viewport window by choosing Display ➤ Animation ➤ Joint Size.

It's important to have a slight rotation for the elbow if you decide to use Inverse Kinematics later on. When you create Inverse Kinematics, Maya needs a hint as to how you want the joint to bend when the IK Handle is created and moved. Inverse Kinematics are discussed in more detail later in the chapter. For now, make sure there is an angle in the joint chain at the location of the elbow (joint3).

10. Switch to the front view. The joint chain is far below the arm geometry, close to the origin. Use the Move tool to move joint1 so the joints are in the center of the arm.

11. Use the Move tool to lower joint2 slightly to create a bend in the chain at the start of the upper arm. Rotate joint2 so the end of the chain is at the center of the wrist (see Figure 7.4, bottom image).

FIGURE 7.4
Carefully position the joints to match the shape of the arm.

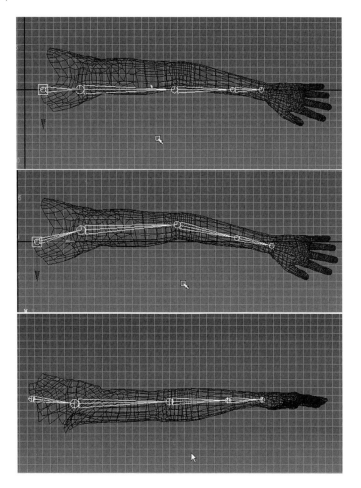

The joints for the fingers are created in a similar fashion. The easiest way to create the fingers is to make small joint chains, position them, and then parent them to the wrist.

12. Switch to the top view again, and turn on Grid Snapping. In front of the hand, make a small joint chain consisting of four joints.

13. Turn off Grid Snapping. Use the Move tool to position the root of the finger joint chain in the pointer finger. Rotate the root joint to match the finger. Use the Move tool to position the finger joints, but be careful to pull the joints only along the local X axis so the joint chain remains straight.

14. When you have the chain positioned, select the root (joint6) and duplicate the chain (Ctrl+d).

15. Move the duplicate into position in the middle finger. Repeat this process for the other fingers of the hand, but not the thumb.

16. To make the thumb, create a small joint chain of just three joints. Position it using Figure 7.5 as a guide.

FIGURE 7.5
Create joint chains
for each finger.

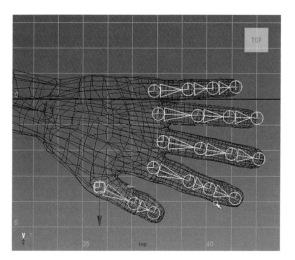

17. Create a single joint by clicking once on the grid in the top view and pressing the Enter key. Position this joint in the palm toward the pinky side of the hand, as shown in the top of Figure 7.6.

18. Duplicate this joint and move it down toward the center of the palm. Duplicate the joint one more time, and place this third joint at the bulge in the hand where the thumb starts (see the center image in Figure 7.6).

19. Select the root of the thumb chain and the free joint at the base of the thumb; then press the p hot key to parent the thumb chain to this joint. Parent both the pointer finger and the middle finger to the joint at the center of the palm. Parent the ring finger and the pinky to the free joint above the center of the palm (bottom image in Figure 7.6).

FIGURE 7.6
Create individual joints and position them in the hand.

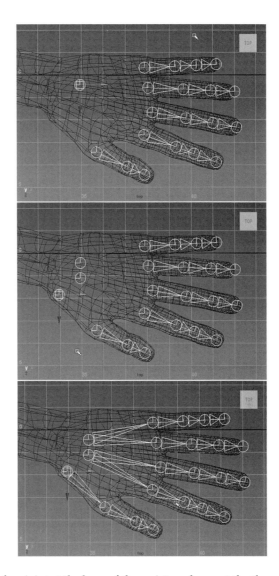

20. Create another free joint at the base of the wrist, and parent the three joint chains to this free joint (Figure 7.7, top image).

21. Switch to a front view, and move up the root of the finger joints (the joint created in step 20) so it fits in the hand. Parent this joint to the joint at the end of the arm (Figure 7.7, center image).

22. Switch to a perspective view. Carefully move and rotate the joints to match the bend in each finger. The safest way to position the finger joints is to use the Move tool and move the joints only along the X and Y axes (Figure 7.7, bottom image).

FIGURE 7.7
Move up the hand
joints to the hand
geometry and
parent them to
the arm.

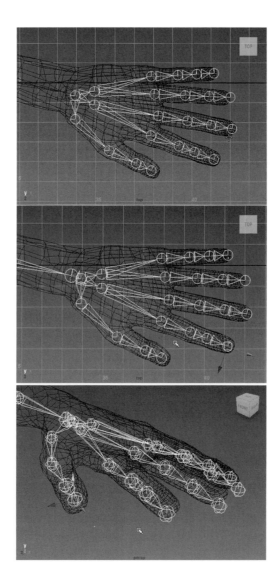

Note that the ring and pinky fingers use a separate joint chain from the index and middle fingers. This arrangement is used to allow the palm of the hand to roll inward so the character can grab objects.

23. Save the scene as **leftArm_v02.ma**. To see a version of the scene to this point, open the leftArm_v02.ma scene from the chapter7\scenes directory on the DVD.

Orient Joints

To ensure joints behave as expected when animated, establish proper joint orientation after the joints are placed in the geometry (but before the geometry is bound to the model).

Typically, each joint is oriented so the X axis of its rotation is aimed along the length of the joint. The axis points down toward the child joint. To see the rotation axis of a joint, select the joint and switch to component mode (hot key = F9), and press the question mark icon on the status line (see Figure 7.8).

FIGURE 7.8
The rotation axes of joints are displayed when the joint is in component mode.

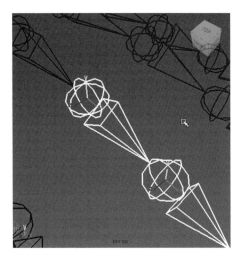

Once you've placed the joints in their correct position, freeze transformations so the Rotate X, Y, and Z channels are all at 0.

1. Continue with the scene from the previous section or open the leftArm_v02.ma scene from the chapter7\scenes directory on the DVD.

2. In the Outliner, select joint1. In the Channel Box, the Rotate X, Y, and Z channels are already 0. This is most likely true for most of the joints in the chain, but always double-check to make sure.

3. Press the down-arrow key, and observe the Rotate channels in the Channel Box. As you press the down-arrow key, you can pick walk through the joint chain and quickly see which joints have non-zero values in their Rotate channels.

Pick walking through the joint chain may not select the joints that branch from the main chain, so remember to check these joints as well. You can do this either by selecting them or by selecting the joints at the end of the branch and pressing the up-arrow key to pick walk in the reverse direction. Taking the time to perform this check saves work and aggravation later on.

4. As you can see, many of the joints do have non-zero values in the Rotation channels. To fix this, select joint1 and choose Modify ➤ Freeze Transformations. This sets the Rotate channels of all the children to 0. Double-check again by pick walking through the chain.

Another way to edit the orientation of the joint is to open the joint's Attribute Editor and enter values in the Joint Orient fields. These fields control the joint's local rotation; changing these values will not affect the Rotate channel values in the Channel Box (see Figure 7.9). You can also automatically orient the joints using the Skeleton ➤ Orient Joint command. You can specify in the options how the joint will be oriented.

FIGURE 7.9
The Joint Orient fields allow you to adjust the local rotation of a joint without affecting the Rotate channels in the Channel Box.

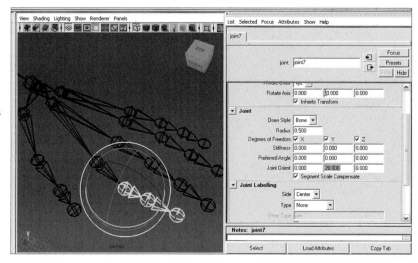

5. Select joint1 and choose Skeleton ➤ Orient Joint ➤ Options. In the options, set Orientation to XYZ and Second Axis World Orientation to -Y. Click Apply to orient the joints.

When you set the Second Axis World Orientation to -Y, the rotational axis of each joint is oriented so the red X axis points down the length of the bone, the blue Z axis points toward the back of the skeleton, and the green Y axis points downward. This type of orientation ensures that when rotating the elbow inward toward the chest, the Rotate Y values are positive and the finger joints use positive values on the Z axis when rotating in toward the palm. This behavior is ideal, especially if you decide to set rotation limits on the joint (a discussion of rotation limits appears later in this chapter).

The rotation axis of each joint should be consistent throughout the skeleton to ensure predictable behavior. Ideally, the red X axis should be pointing down the length of the joint, and the rotation of the green Y axis and blue Z axis should match throughout the skeleton as much as possible. For example, if the Y axis is pointing downward and the Z axis is pointing toward the rear of the skeleton throughout the arm, then when you rotate the elbow on the Y axis, positive Rotate Y values will cause the elbow to rotate inward, and negative values will cause it to rotate backward. Likewise this same arrangement will cause the fingers to use positive values in the Rotate Z channel when folding in toward the palm and to use negative values when rotating backward. The orientation of the joints at the very tips of the fingers doesn't usually matter since they won't need to be rotated or animated.

There will be exceptions to this based on the requirements of the skeleton or your own personal preference. For the most part, consistency is the most important aspect to watch out for. Figure 7.10 shows two joints that have different rotation axes.

The Joint Orient tool does a pretty good job of orienting the joints; however, it may have trouble orienting a joint at the root of a branch in the skeleton. In this case, you may need to manually edit the rotation of a joint. To manually change to the rotation axis of an individual joint, select the joint and switch to component mode. Right-click on the question mark selection mask icon on the status bar, and choose Local Rotation Axes (Figure 7.11). Select the axis icon, and use the Rotate tool to change the rotation axis. When you adjust the rotation axis, the wireframe sphere of the joint rotates, but the long pyramid bone shape should not move. If it does, undo the change, and make sure you are in component mode.

FIGURE 7.10

Two joints with different rotation axes

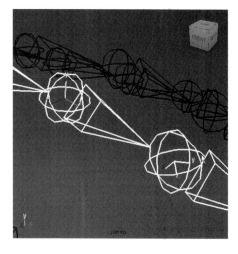

FIGURE 7.11

Enable the Local Rotation Axes selection mask.

You may decide you want a specific orientation at a point in the skeleton where a joint is a parent to two or more chains, or the joint may need to rotate on a different axis than the other joints in the chain to create a specialized type of rotation. In these cases you may need to manually rotate the local rotation axis.

If you need precise control over the rotation of the axis, select the axis icon and use a MEL command in the script editor like the following:

```
rotate -r -os 180 0 0;
```

This particular MEL command rotates the local rotation axis 180 degrees around its X axis relative to its current rotation. In other words, 180 is added to the X rotation axis of the selected joint. If you need to change the orientation for a large number of joints, this small snippet of code works well as a shelf button. To make a shelf button from this line of code, select the text in the Script Editor, and choose File ➤ Save Script To Shelf. Then you can select each joint that needs the same rotation applied, and press the shelf button.

6. Save the scene as **leftArm_v03.ma**. To see a version of the scene to this point, open the leftArm_v03.ma scene from the chapter7\scenes directory on the DVD.

Name Joints

When creating a skeleton you need to be extremely conscientious about how you name the joints. Clear, concise naming helps everyone involved in the animation understand how the rig is set up and how each joint is supposed to function. When naming joints, use a prefix such as L_ to indicate the left side and R_ to indicate the right side. If a joint is meant to be used as a control, use a suffix such as _CTRL. The advantage of being consistent with prefixes and suffixes is that you can easily search and replace the prefix or suffix if it needs to be changed on a large number of joints.

1. Continue with the scene from the previous section or open the `leftArm_v03.ma` scene from the `chapter7\scenes` folder on the DVD.

2. Select joint1 and group it. Name the group **L_ArmJoints**.

3. Shift+click the plus sign next to joint1 in the Outliner. Double-click on each joint in the Outliner, and rename each of the joints so the resulting skeleton hierarchy matches that in Figure 7.12.

4. Save the scene as **leftArm_v04.ma**. To see a version of the scene to this point, open the `leftArm_v04.ma` scene from the `chapter7\scenes` directory on the DVD.

FIGURE 7.12

Name each of the joints in the Outliner to make its purpose clear and to keep it organized.

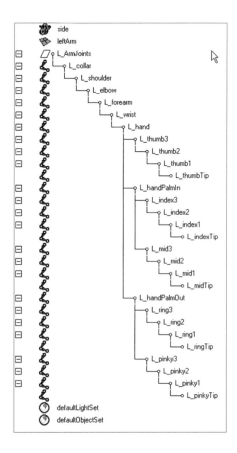

Rotation Limits

Rotation limits specify a range of rotation for any object. Using limits is particularly useful for joints. When creating a character you can use rotation limits to prevent an elbow joint from rotating backward. This helps the animator avoid mistakes and also helps the Inverse Kinematics system solve correctly. In this example you'll set rotation limits for the arm.

1. Continue with the scene from the previous section or open the leftArm_v04.ma scene from the chapter7\scenes folder on the DVD.

2. Select the L_forearm joint and open its Attribute Editor.

3. Under Limit Information, expand the Rotate rollout.

4. To set minimum and maximum limits for the joint, check the boxes next to Min and Max on either side of the Rot Limit fields.

5. For the X rotation, set the minimum to **-150** and the maximum to **150**. This range is beyond the range of realistic motion, but you should always build extra room into the range so the animator can keyframe overshoot (values beyond the normal range of motion) if necessary.

6. Activate the Min and Max ranges for Y and Z, but leave the fields set to zero (you can quickly transfer the current rotational value into the fields by clicking on the arrow buttons on either side of the Current field). This restricts the movement of the joint so it can't rotate on the Y or Z axis (see Figure 7.13).

FIGURE 7.13

Create rotational limits for the forearm.

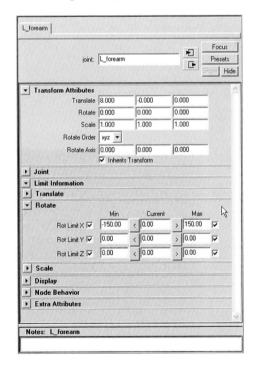

Setting a Min and Max range of 0 for a joint is preferable to locking the Rotate Y and Rotate Z channels in the Channel Box. If you lock the joint, you may run into problems later on when adding external controls via constraints.

7. Press the arrow key to move up one joint in the chain to the L_elbow joint.

8. Set Rot Limit X and Z Min and Max to **0**. Set Rot Limit Y Min to **-20** and Max to **180**.

Maya will not accept a maximum value that is lower than the minimum value, which is why it is important that the elbow uses positive values on the Y axis to rotate toward the chest. If the rotational axis for the elbow joint were flipped, you won't be able to set proper limits on the elbow to achieve the correct rotation.

9. Save the scene as **leftArm_v05.ma**. To see a version of the scene to this point, open the leftArm_v05.ma scene from the chapter7\scenes folder on the DVD.

Label Joints

Joint labels are another way you can organize the joints in a skeleton. You can use this as an alternative to naming the joints in the Outliner or in conjunction with it. The labels you apply to joints do not change the names of the joints. Labels are used to help Maya create a functional full-body IK system or when the animation from one skeleton is retargeted to another skeleton. If you are not using either of these solutions tools, joint labels are entirely optional. An example of Full Body IK appears later in the chapter.

1. Continue with the scene from the previous section or open the leftArm_v05.ma scene from the chapter7\scenes directory on the DVD.

2. Expand the L_Arm Joints group in the Outliner, and select the L_collar joint. Choose Skeleton ➢ Joint Labeling ➢ Label Based On Joint Names.

3. You need to enable the visibility of the labels to see them in the viewport window. Choose Skeleton ➢ Joint Labeling ➢ Show All Labels. The labels now appear in the viewport window (see Figure 7.14).

FIGURE 7.14
Joint labels appear in the perspective view.

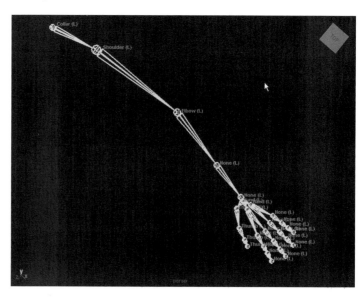

Maya automatically applies labels to the joints based on the names you give the joints. However, Maya has only a certain number of available labels. If Maya encounters a joint name for which it does not have a corresponding label, it leaves the joint label as "none." You need to create a custom joint label for these joints.

4. Select the L_forearm joint and open its Attribute Editor. Expand the Joint Labeling roll-out. Set the Type menu to Other. In the Other Type field, type **forearm** and hit the Enter key. The joint is now labeled forearm(L) (see Figure 7.15).

FIGURE 7.15
Use the Other Type option to give the forearm joint a custom label.

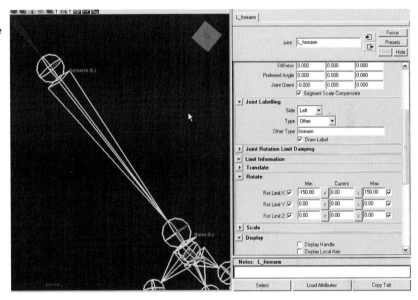

5. Label the other joints in the hand based on the names of the joints. Use the labels available in the Type menu, or create custom labels as needed.

The Side menu has options for labeling the joints based on Left, Right, or Center. You can also rename the joints based on labels by choosing Skeleton ➤ Joint Labeling ➤ Rename Joints Based On Labels.

6. Save the scene as **leftArm_v06.ma**. To see a version of the scene to this point, open the leftArm_v06.ma scene from the chapter7\scenes directory on the DVD.

Mirror Joints

The Mirror Joint command is used to instantly duplicate part of the skeleton across a specified axis. It's a time-saving device when creating symmetrical character skeletons. For example, if a joint chain is parented to part of the skeleton, or the collar bone is connected to the spine, the mirrored joint chain is parented to the same joint in the spine. In this example, you'll mirror the left arm skeleton to create a right arm.

1. Continue with the scene from the previous section, or open the leftArm_v06.ma scene from the chapter7\scenes directory on the DVD.

2. In the Outliner, expand the L_ArmJoints group and select the L_collar joint.

3. Choose Skeleton ➢ Mirror Joint ➢ Options. In the options, set Mirror Across Axis to YZ, and set Mirror Function to Behavior.

Behavior is usually the best option when building character skeletons. When this option is enabled, corresponding joints on either side of the central axis rotate the same way. So if both shoulder joints are selected and rotated, both arms will rotate forward toward the chest, producing a mirror image across the central axis (see the left image in Figure 7.16). The Orientation option means that when corresponding joints are rotated the same amount on the same axis, one of the arms will have the opposite behavior of the other (see the right image in Figure 7.16).

FIGURE 7.16
The left image shows how the Behavior option in the Mirror Joint options behaves when both joints are rotated 60 degrees in Y. The right image shows how the Orientation option behaves when both joints are rotated 60 degrees in Y.

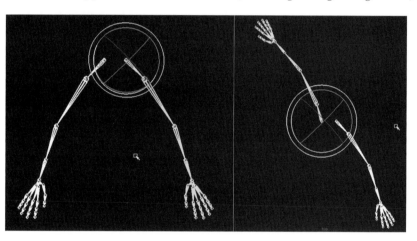

4. In the Replacement Names For Duplicate Joints section, set Search For to L and Replace With to R. This automatically renames the joint chains based on what you put in these fields. In this case, the arm joints on the character's right side use the prefix R_ instead of L_.

5. Click the Apply button to mirror the arm.

6. Select the new R_collar joint in the Outliner, and MMB-drag it out of the L_ArmJoints group. Group R_collar and name the group R_ArmJoints.

7. You'll notice that the mirrored joints use the same labels as the original, including the L prefix. To quickly change this, select the R_collar joint and choose Skeleton ➢ Joint Labeling ➢ Add Retargeting Labels ➢ Label Right (see Figure 7.17).

8. Save the scene as **arms_v01.ma**. To see a version of the scene, open the arms_v01.ma scene from the chapter7\scenes directory on the DVD.

FIGURE 7.17
FIGURE 7.17
Rename and relabel the mirrored arm joints appropriately to indicate they are on the right side of the body.

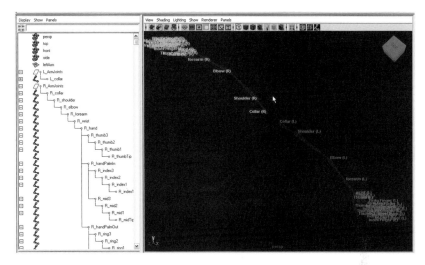

Inverse Kinematic Rigs

Inverse Kinematics (IK) was introduced in Chapter 5, where you created a very simple mechanical bug using IK Handles and basic techniques. In this section, you'll explore Inverse Kinematics a little further as well as some of the specialized IK rigging tools Maya offers.

As discussed in Chapter 5, *kinematics* is the study of the motion of objects. There are two main types of kinematics: Forward and Inverse Kinematics. Forward Kinematics refers to a situation in which each joint in the chain inherits the motion of its parent joint. Inverse Kinematics causes the joints in a chain to orient themselves based on the position of a goal known as the End Effector. In this section, you'll learn about how to set up and use Inverse Kinematics in more detail.

IK Solvers

Maya uses several types of solvers to calculate how the bones orient themselves based on the position of the End Effector. In Chapter 5 you used the Single Chain solver (ikSCsolver), which is a very simple solver with a few controls.

In this exercise, you'll practice applying each of these types of handles in a sample scene. You can then compare how each IK solver behaves.

The Single Chain solver (ikSCsolver) uses a single IK Handle to determine both the position and orientation of the End Effector based on the position and the orientation of the IK Handle. It's good for very simple joint chains; however, the rotation of the joints can be a little unpredictable.

1. Open the IKexamples_v01.ma scene from the chapter7\scenes directory on the DVD.

This scene has a number of joint chains already set up; each one is grouped and placed on its own display layer. The SC_example layer is currently visible (the other layers are invisible at the moment). The layer contains four joints.

2. From the Animation menu set, choose Skeleton ➤ IK Handle Tool ➤ Options. In the options, set the Current Solver to ikSCsolver, and leave the other settings at the default (see Figure 7.18).

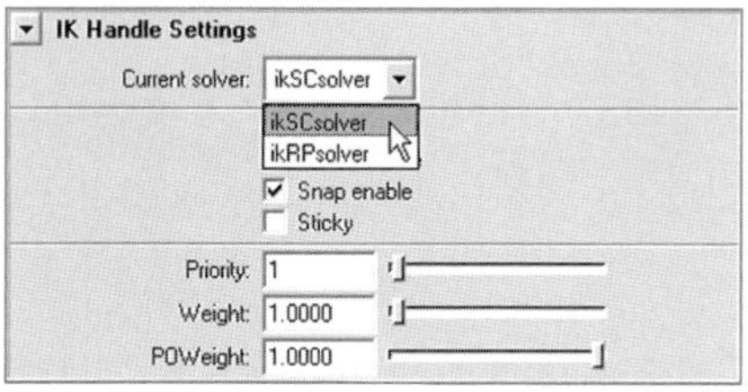

FIGURE 7.18

Choose the ikSCsolver in the IK Handle Settings options.

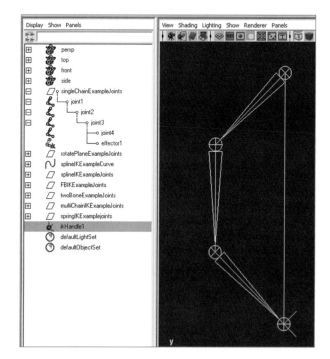

3. With the IK Handle tool active, click on the root joint of the chain (the top joint), and then click again on the bottom joint. You'll see a line drawn between the first joint you clicked on and the second joint. The line is known as the *IK Handle Vector*. You can also see a line that runs through the joint chain (this is not easy to see in the black-and-white image in this book); this line is the *Handle Wire* (see Figure 7.19).

Inverse Kinematics controls can be applied to any joints in the chain, not just between the root and the end joint.

FIGURE 7.19

Attach the IK Handle to the joint chain by clicking on the two end joints in the chain. Inverse Kinematics is indicated by a line between the two selected joints.

4. In the Outliner, expand the singleChainExampleJoints group. You'll see that a node named effector1 has been added at the end of the chain. Also, a node named ikHandle1 appears in the Outliner.

5. Switch to the perspective view, select ikHandle1 in the Outliner, and move it around. Notice how the joint chain reacts. Notice also that in some positions the joints flip around to try to match the position of the IK Handle.

The two main settings for the IK Handle are Sticky and Snap Enable. When Snap Enable is on, the IK Handle snaps back to the end joint. The Sticky setting keeps the joints oriented toward the goal when the root joint is moved. This is very useful for legs, as it keeps the feet from sliding on the floor.

To animate a joint chain with Inverse Kinematics, you set keyframes on the IK Handle, not the joints. In most situations, you'll want to constrain the IK Handle to a locator or another type of control object, such as a curve. The control is keyframed, and the IK Handle is constrained to the control so that it inherits the animation of the control. This is explained further later in the chapter; for now the exercise focuses on how to create the handles and edit their settings.

6. Select the ikHandle1 node and open its Attribute Editor. Set the Stickiness setting to Sticky. In the Outliner, select joint1 and move the joint around; note how the chain remains oriented toward the IK Handle.

The Rotate Plane solver (RP solver) differs from the Single Chain solver in that the End Effector matches the position of the IK Handle but not the rotation. Instead the rotation of the chain is controlled using a special disc-shaped manipulator that can be keyframed if needed. The RP solver is more predictable and used most often, especially when creating skeletons for characters.

7. Turn on the visibility of the RP_example layer. Repeat step 2 to create an IK Handle for this chain between the root and the tip. However, in the options for the IK Handle, set the solver to ikRPsolver.

The RP solver is similar to the SC solver except that an additional circular icon appears indicating the pole vector for the chain. The pole vector determines the direction of rotation for the joints as they attempt to reach the IK Handle (see Figure 7.20).

You can select the IK Handle (ikHandle2 in the example) and turn on the Show Manipulators tool. Using the tool you can rotate the blue disc to adjust the rotation of the chain, and you can change the numeric values in the Channel Box using the Twist channel (see Figure 7.21).

The Pole Vector of the chain is indicated by the white triangle in the rotate plane indicator at the start point of the IK chain. Changing the pole vector also changes the orientation of the chain. The Pole Vector determines the angle of the rotate plane for the RP solver. This can be used to control unwanted flipping while animating the IK Handle.

The Twist attribute is directly related to the Pole Vector. In general, you'll want to adjust the Pole Vector to properly orient the chain and then use the Twist attribute to solve any flipping problems you may encounter while animating.

FIGURE 7.20
The RP solver adds an additional control to determine how the chain rotates as it attempts to match the position of the IK Handle.

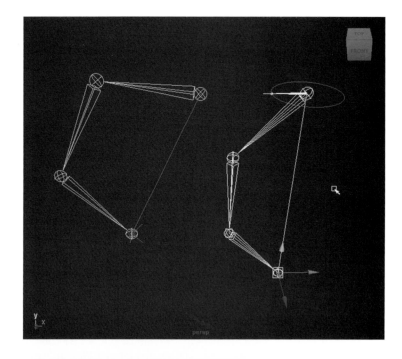

FIGURE 7.21
You can adjust the orientation of a joint chain using the ikRPsolver by changing the Pole Vector and the Twist settings in the IK Handle attributes.

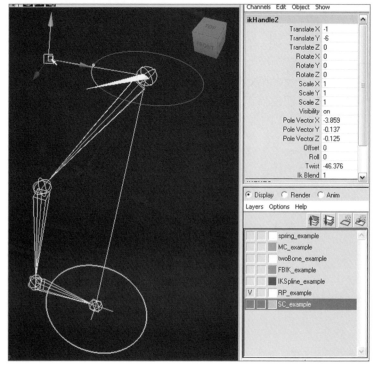

IK Spline Solver uses a curve to control the rotation of the joints. This is ideal for long snaking chains and tails. The solver can generate a curve or use an existing curve. The CVs of the curve become the manipulators for the joint chain. Usually it's a good idea to create clusters for the CVs of the curve and animate CVs of the curve indirectly using the clusters.

8. In the Outliner, select ikHandle1 and add it to the SC_example layer. Select ikHandle2 and add it to the RP_example layer. Turn off Visibility for both layers, and turn on Visibility for IKSpline_example layer. The ikSpline handle layer contains a joint chain and a curve.

9. Choose Skeleton ➤ IkSpline Handle Tool ➤ Options. In the options, turn off Auto Create Curve. You'll use the curve that already exists in the scene.

10. With the tool active, click on the first joint in the chain, the last joint in the chain, and then the curve. The joint chain jumps to the curve.

11. Right-click on the curve and choose CVs. Try moving the CVs of the curve around; the joint chain sticks to the curve, inheriting the changes you make to the curve.

12. Select the curve and switch to the Surfaces menu set. Choose Edit Curves ➤ Selection ➤ Cluster Curve. This automatically places clusters on each CV of the curve (see Figure 7.22). When animating the curve, you should keyframe the clusters and not the CVs of the curve. For more information on clusters, consult Chapter 6.

FIGURE 7.22
The ikSpline Handle tool attaches the joint chain to a curve. The CVs of the curve are animated using cluster deformers.

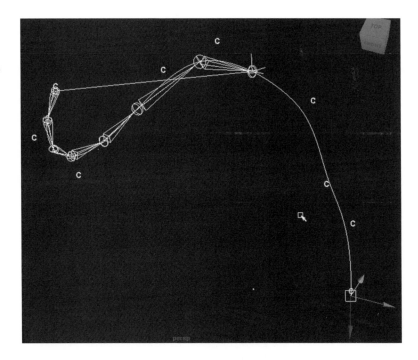

13. In the Outliner, select ikHandle3. This is the IK Handle for the ikSpline. In the Channel Box, adjust the Offset channel to slide the joint chain up and down the curve. Use Twist to twist the joints around the curve and Roll to change the rotation around the curve.

14. Select the clusters and ikHandle3. Add these to the IKSpline_example layer, and turn off this layer.

Full Body IK (FBIK) is used for Full Body IK skeletons. This system creates IK Handles that control an entire biped or quadruped skeleton rather than using multiple IK chains on individual limbs.

15. Switch back to the Animation menu set. Turn on the FBIK_example layer.

In this layer you'll see a simple skeleton. The joints of the skeleton have labels applied, which are displayed when you select the skeleton and choose Skeleton ➤ Joint Labeling ➤ Show All Labels.

16. In the Outliner, expand the FBIKExampleJoints group, and select the hips joint. Choose Skeleton ➤ Full Body IK ➤ Add Full Body IK.

When you add Full Body IK, a group called humanIK1 is added to the scene as well as a character node named fbikCharacter. The character node is used with the Trax Editor for non-linear animation. For more information on the Trax Editor consult the Non-Linear Animation PDF included on the DVD.

17. Expand the humanIK1 group, and select one of the Eff nodes, such as the LeftFootEff. Use the Move tool to drag the node around. You'll see that the entire skeleton reacts to the change in position (see Figure 7.23).

FIGURE 7.23
Full Body IK
creates Inverse
Kinematics for the
entire skeleton.

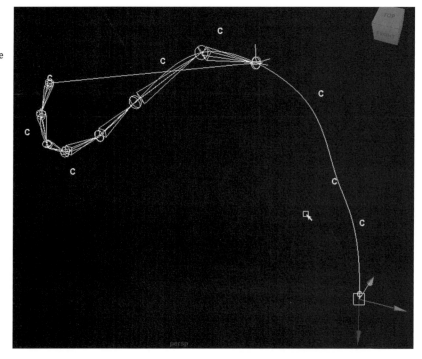

Maya has two examples of full rigged FBIK skeletons available in the Visor. Open the Visor window (Window ➤ General Editors ➤ Visor), and switch to the FBIK Examples tab. To load an example into a scene, right-click the icon and choose to import the example.

Two Bone solver (2B solver) is a variation of the Rotate Plane solver that is meant for chains consisting of two bones. Bones are the pyramid shapes between joints, so a two-bone chain uses three joints. The Two Bone solver needs to be loaded manually into Maya before it is available as an option in the IK Solver Attributes section.

18. Add the humanIK group to the FBIK_example display layer. Hide this layer and turn on the Visibility of the twoBone example.

19. Before you can add a Two Bone IK system to the joints, you need to load the ik2Bsolver. To do this, type **ik2Bsolver;** into the command line, as shown in Figure 7.24, and hit the Enter key.

20. Choose Skeleton ➤ IK Handle Tool ➤ Options. In the options, choose the ik2Bsolver from the list. In the perspective view, select the top joint in the two-bone chain and then select the bottom joint to create the two-bone IK Handle.

FIGURE 7.24
You must load the ik2Bsolver before it can be selected from the IK Handle Tool options.

The *Multi-Chain solver* is a series of single-chain solvers that can be used for complex skeleton rigs. Like the Two-Bone solver, it is not available in Maya unless you load it manually.

21. Turn on the Visibility for the MC_example layer. This layer has a long series of joints. In the command line, type **createNode ikMCsolver;** and press the Enter key.

When you create this node, it does not appear in the options for the IK Handle tool; instead you need to use a single-chain solver or an RP solver and then switch the solver type in the Attribute Editor.

22. Use the IK Handle tool to create three overlapping IK Handles in the series of joints, as shown in Figure 7.25.

23. Select each of the new IK Handles (they should be named ikHandle5, ikHandle6, and ikHandle7), and open their Attribute Editor. Set the solver for each of these to ikMCsolver1 (see left image, Figure 7.26).

The same ikMCsolver node is used to solve all three IK Handles. You can use the Priority and Weight settings in the IK Handle Attributes section of each handle's Attribute Editor to determine the amount of influence each handle has over the chain (see right image, Figure 7.26). This allows you to create complex motion using a few controls. If you use more than one Multi-Chain IK rig in a scene, you need to create more than one ikMCsolver and select the appropriate solver for each IK Handle in each chain.

FIGURE 7.25
Add three overlapping IK Handles to the joint chain.

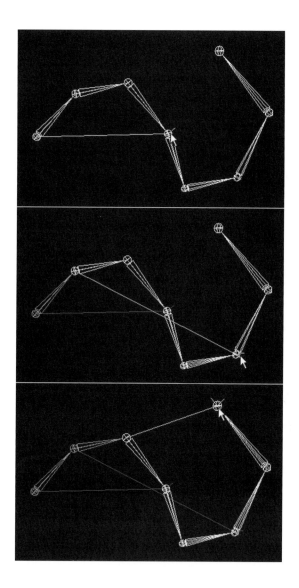

FIGURE 7.26
Select the ikMC-solver1 node in the Attribute Editor for the IK Handles. Then you can set Weight and Priority for each handle in the chain.

Spring IK solver creates a handle that adds a springlike motion to a series of joints. It accomplishes this by rotating each joint proportionally as the IK Handle is moved. You need to load this solver manually.

24. Add ikHandle5 through ikHandle7 to the MC_example display layer, and turn off Visibility for this layer. Turn on Visibility of the spring_example layer.

25. In the command line, type **ikSpringSolver;** and hit the Enter key. Choose Skeleton ➢ ikHandle ➢ Options. In the options, select the ikSpringSolver.

26. Click on the first joint in the chain and the last joint in the chain to create the handle.

27. Select ikHandle8 in the Perspective window and move it back and forth. The joint chain has an accordionlike behavior.

28. Select ikHandle8 and open its Attribute Editor. Expand the IK Spring Solver Attributes rollout. You'll see an edit curve, which allows you to adjust the bias for each joint in the chain (see Figure 7.27).

29. Save the scene as **ikExamples_v02.ma**. To see a version of the scene, open the ikExamples_v02.ma scene from the chapter7\scenes folder on the DVD.

FIGURE 7.27
You can change the bias for each joint in the ikSpring-Solver using the edit curve in the Attribute Editor for the IK Handle.

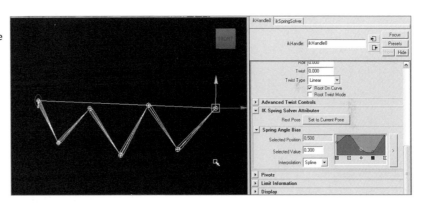

Creating a Custom Control

An ideal animation rig should be easy to understand and animate. This means the controls should be clearly labeled and easy to select directly in the viewport window. When using Inverse Kinematics, the animator should be able to enter 0 in all of the translation channels for the controls to return the rig to the start position if needed. IK Handles use world space coordinates, so setting their translation channels to 0 moves a handle to the origin. One common solution to this problem is to constrain the handle to a locator, which can then be used to animate the handle. You can set a start position for the control and then freeze transformations on it so that when the translation channels are set to 0, the control moves to the start position and brings the IK Handle along.

In addition, you can add custom controls to the locator to animate other attributes of the IK Handle so the animator does not need to hunt through the various nodes in the scene to animate the rig.

1. Open the leftArm_v07.ma scene from the chapter7\scenes directory on the DVD. This is the same left arm skeleton created earlier in the chapter.

You're going to create an IK Handle to control the arm. The arm has been created using a single bone for the upper arm and two bones for the forearm. Two bones are used for the forearm to simulate a realistic wrist rotation where the radius and ulna bones rotate around each other.

If you add an IK Handle from the upper arm joint to the wrist, the IK will interfere with your ability to properly rotate the forearm joints. To solve this problem, use an IK Handle to connect the upper arm to the forearm joint and then reposition the End Effector so that manipulating this IK Handle is natural.

2. Choose Skeleton ➢ IK Handle Tool ➢ Options. In the options, set the current solver to RP Solver or the ik2Bsolver if it is available (see the previous section for instructions on how to load the ik2Bsolver).

3. Click on the L_shoulder joint (the second joint in the chain) and the L_forearm joint (the fourth joint in the chain) to create the handle (see Figure 7.28).

FIGURE 7.28
An IK Handle connects the L_shoulder joint and the L_forearm joint.

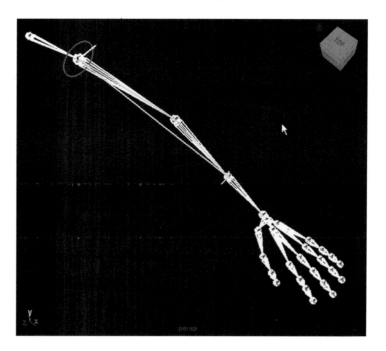

4. In the Outliner, Shift+click the L_ArmJoints group to expand the skeleton. In the skeleton, select effector1.

5. Turn on Point Snapping and select the Move tool. Hold the d key to switch to pivot-positioning mode. Snap the Effector to the L_wrist joint, as shown in Figure 7.29.

FIGURE 7.29
Snap the pivot point of the Effector to the wrist joint.

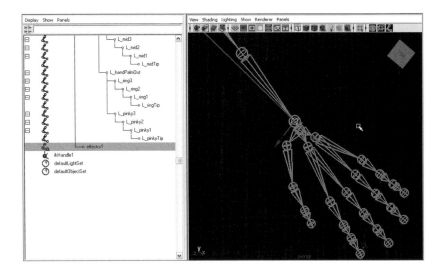

If you select the ikHandle1 node and move it around, the arm moves as if the IK Handle was placed at the wrist joint. However, if you rotate the L_forearm joint around the X axis and then move the IK Handle, the rotation of the forearm is not affected by the IK Handle as it would be if the IK Handle was connected to the wrist joint.

6. Undo any changes made to the position of IK Handle so the arm returns to the position it was in at the end of step 5. Create a locator in the scene, and name it **L_arm_CTRL**.

7. Turn on Point Snapping, and snap this locator to the L_wrist joint, the same joint where you placed the Effector.

8. In the Outliner, select the L_arm_CTRL and Ctrl+click the L_collar joint. Press the p hot key to parent L_arm_CTRL to the L_collar joint. Choose Modify ➢ Freeze Transformations to set this position as the start position for the L_arm_CTRL locator.

9. In the Outliner, select the L_arm_CTRL locator, and Ctrl+click ikHandle1. Choose Constrain ➢ Point to constrain ikHandle1 to the locator.

10. Try moving the L_arm_CTRL locator around the scene. You want to keyframe the locator, not the IK Handle, when animating the arm. To return it to the start position, set the Translate channels to 0.

To make things easier for animation you can add custom attributes to L_arm_CTRL to control the rotation of the forearm.

11. Select L_arm_CTRL and open its Attribute Editor. In the Attribute Editor menu, choose Attributes ➢ Add Attribute. In the Add Attribute window, set Long Name to **forearmRotate** (see Figure 7.30). Make sure the Make Attribute option is set to Keyable and the Data Type option is Float. Click OK to add the attribute.

12. Open the Channel Box for L_arm_CTRL, and you'll see the new channel named Forearm Rotate (Maya adds a space and capitalization to the channel names; see Figure 7.31).

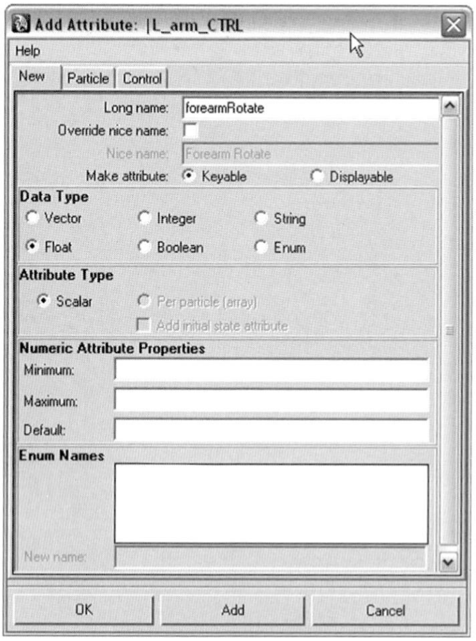

FIGURE 7.30
Use the Add Attribute window to create custom attributes for nodes.

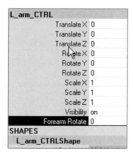

FIGURE 7.31
The custom attribute Forearm Rotate appears in the Channel Box.

13. Choose Window ➤ General Editors ➤ Connection Editor. Select L_arm_CTRL in the Outliner, and click the Reload Left button in the Connection Editor. Select the L_forearm joint, and click the Reload Right button.

14. On the left side of the Connection Editor, scroll to the bottom and choose forearmRotate from the list. On the right side of the Connection Editor, expand the rotate attributes and select rotateX (see Figure 7.32).

15. Close the Connection Editor. Select the L_arm_CTRL locator, and adjust the values for the Forearm Rotate Channel to test the attributes.

16. Save the scene as **leftArm_v08.ma**. To see a version of the scene, open the leftArm_v08.ma scene from the chapter7\scenes directory on the DVD.

FIGURE 7.32
Connect the forearmRotate attribute on the L_arm_CTRL to the rotateX of the L_forearm joint.

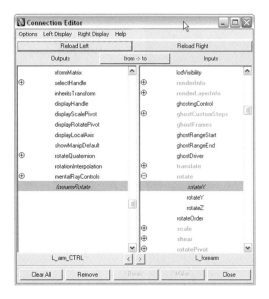

Pole Vector Constraint

A Pole Vector constraint can be used to constrain the Pole Vector of an IK chain to the position of a control such as a locator.

1. Continue with the scene from the previous section or open the leftArm_v08.ma scene from the chapter7\scenes folder on the DVD.

2. Create a locator and name it **L_armPV_CTRL**.

3. Point snap the locator to the position of the L_elbow joint. Once it is in position, use the Move tool to move the locator back along the Z axis one or two units, just enough so the locator is easy to see and select.

4. Parent L_armPV_CTRL to the L_collar joint, and then freeze transformations for L_armPV_CTRL.

5. In the Outliner, select L_armPV_CTRL and Ctrl+click ikHandle1. Choose Constrain ➢ Pole Vector.

A line appears between the IK Handle and L_armPV_CTRL, as shown in Figure 7.33.
If you select L_armPV_CTRL and move it up or down along the Y axis, you'll see the elbow adjust its position. Moving along the Z axis causes the joints to flip. You may want to set Translation Limits on the L_armPV_CTRL locator so it cannot be moved on the X axis and its range of movement is limited along the Y and Z axes.

6. Save the scene as **leftArm_v09.ma**. To see a version of the scene, open the leftArm_v09.ma scene from the chapter7\scenes directory on the DVD.

Figure 7.33
Use a Pole Vector constraint to control the Pole Vector of the arm's IK Handle.

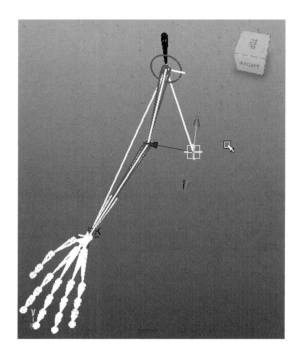

FK/IK Blending

You can use both Forward and Inverse Kinematics on the same rig and blend between the two types of controls using FK/IK blending. This short exercise demonstrates how.

1. Continue with the scene from the previous section or open the leftArm_v09.ma scene from the chapter7\scenes folder on the DVD.

2. Set the timeline to 100 frames; then set the current frame to frame1. Select L_arm_CTRL. In the Channel Box, Shift+click the Translate channels, right-click, and choose Key Selected.

3. Turn on Auto Keyframe by clicking the key icon to the right of the timeline.

4. Set the timeline to various frames, and reposition the L_arm_CTRL locator to create a short animation of the arm moving around.

Now that you have an animation created using Inverse Kinematics, you'll create another animation for the arm using Forward Kinematics.

5. Rewind the timeline to the start of the animation. In the Outliner, select the ikHandle1 node. Choose Skeleton ➤ Disable Selected IK Handles. This turns off the Inverse Kinematics for this handle. If you play the animation, you'll see the L_arm_CTRL locator move around, but the arm does not follow.

6. Select the L_shoulder joint and Shift+click the L_elbow joint.

7. In the Channel Box, set a keyframe for the rotation channels of both joints.

8. Set the timeline to various frames in the animation, and rotate the L_shoulder and L_forearm joints to create an animation. As long as Auto Keyframe is enabled, keyframes will automatically be generated each time you rotate the joints.

9. Rewind the scene and select the ikHandle1 node. Choose Skeleton ➤ Enable Selected IK Handles. Choose Skeleton ➤ Enable IK/FK Control.

In the Channel Box for the ikHandle1 node there is an attribute called IK Blend. When IK Blend is set to 1, the arm uses the animation created with Inverse Kinematics. When IK Blend is set to 0, the arm uses the animation created using Forward Kinematics. Values between 0 and 1 blend the two animations. When you play the animation you can see "ghosted" versions of the joints. The blue joints represent the FK animation, and the brown joints represent the IK animation (see Figure 7.34). This ghosting is visible only when the ikHandle node is selected.

10. Save the scene as **leftArm_v10.ma**. To see a version of the scene, open the leftArm_v10.ma scene from the chapter7\scenes directory on the DVD.

FIGURE 7.34
The IK Blend channel allows you to blend between animation created using Inverse Kinematics and animation created using Forward Kinematics.

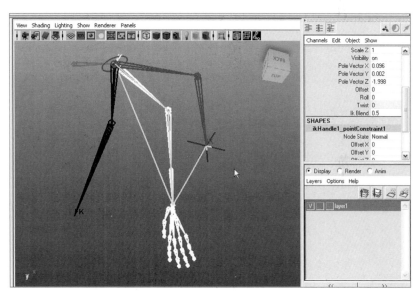

Skinning Geometry

Skinning geometry is the process in which geometry is bound to joints so that as the joints are rotated or translated, the geometry is deformed. The terms *skinning* and *binding* are interchangeable. There are two types of skinning: Smooth Binding and Rigid Binding. Although Rigid Binding is available as an option, it is rarely used, so this section focuses on Smooth Binding.

Polygon and NURBS geometry can be bound to skeletons; however, polygon geometry often produces more predictable results. In this section, you'll use polygon geometry.

When geometry is Smooth Bound to a skeleton, each vertex of the geometry receives a certain amount of influence from the joints in the skeleton. The amount of weight value of the joints determines the amount of influence each vertex receives from a joint. The values range from 0 to 1, where 0 is no influence and 1 is full (or 100 percent) influence. When you bind geometry to a skeleton, the vertex weights are set automatically based on the options you specify in the Smooth Bind command. In most situations the weights of the geometry require further editing after executing the Smooth Bind command.

When binding geometry to the skeleton, make sure the rotations of the joints in the skeleton are all at 0. This means that if an IK Handle has been added to the skeleton, you should select and disable the handle (choose Skeleton ➤ Disable Selected IK Handles) and then set the joint rotation channels to 0. Bind the skin to the joints and reenable the IK Handle (choose Skeleton ➤ Enable Selected IK Handles).

The pose the skeleton is in when you bind the geometry is known as the *bind pose*. If you need at some point to detach and reattach the geometry to edit the geometry, you will need to be able to easily return to the bind pose. Do this by selecting the skeleton's root joint and choosing Skin ➤ Go To Bind Pose.

Editing the skin weights is accomplished using the Paint Skin Weights tool, which employs the Artisan brush interface to interactively set weights. You can also edit the weight values directly for selected vertices using the Component Editor. Editing skin weights can be a difficult and occasionally frustrating process. In the following exercise you'll learn a few tips that can help make the process a little easier and faster.

Smooth Binding

Maya automatically assigns skin weights to each vertex of the geometry as it is bound to the joints. There are options for assigning these weights based on the vertices' proximity to the joints and the number of joints that can influence any particular vertex. Even so, after binding you'll need to edit the weights using the Paint Skin Weights tool. If the geometry is very dense, meaning it has a lot of vertices, this process can take a while.

There is a trick to make the process of skinning a little faster and easier. To accomplish this you will need a low resolution of the model. The low-resolution version can be extremely simple; in fact, you can reduce the number of edges on the model so there are edges only in the areas where the model bends (such as the shoulder, elbow, and wrist). Parts of the model between these areas can be reduced to just the edges needed to define the basic shape of the model (see Figure 7.35).

FIGURE 7.35
You can create a low-resolution copy of the arm geometry in the high-resolution version.

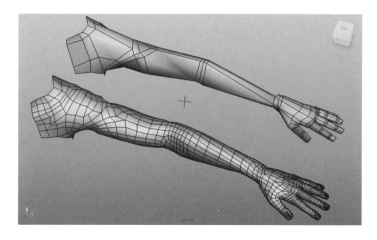

The process works like this: Skin the low-resolution version of the model to the joints, edit the weights on the low-resolution version of the model, skin the high-resolution version of the model to the joints, and then copy the joint weight from the low-resolution version to the high-resolution version. The weights copied to the high-resolution version require further editing, but in most cases the time spent editing these weights is less than if you had directly skinned the high-resolution version to the joints. To see this process in action, follow this exercise, which uses the arm joints as an example.

1. Open the `leftArm_v11.ma` scene from the `chapter7\scenes` directory on the DVD.

This version of the scene has both the low-resolution version of the arm and the same arm model that has been used in the other examples. The low-resolution version is on a display layer named lowResolutionMesh, and the other version of the arm is on the armMesh layer.

2. Turn off Visibility of the armMesh layer, and make sure the lowResolutionMesh layer is visible.

Before binding the joints to the geometry, double-check to make sure all the rotation channels of the joints are at 0.

3. In the Outliner, Shift+click the plus sign next to the L_armJoints group to expand it, and select the L_collar joint. Ctrl+click the leftArm_loResolution surface. From the Animation menu set, choose Skin ➤ Bind Skin ➤ Smooth Bind ➤ Options.

4. In the options, choose Edit ➤ Reset Options. The default options work just fine (see Figure 7.36).

FIGURE 7.36
Bind the low-resolution arm to the selected joint hierarchy.

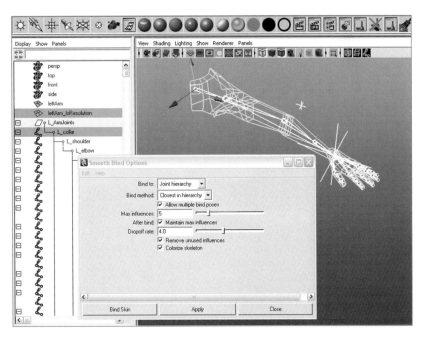

Notice that you can choose to bind the entire joint hierarchy or just selected joints. In this example you'll bind the entire hierarchy. Keep in mind that you also have the option of binding only selected joints. In some circumstances this can be quite useful. For example, if you set up what is known as a *broken-joint* skeleton, which uses additional bones outside of the main skeleton hierarchy as deformers, these additional joints are usually constrained to the main hierarchy using parent constraints. By using parent constraints the joints "float" outside of the main hierarchy, giving them a level of freedom of movement to create special deformation effects. (Sometimes floating joints are used for facial animation instead of or in addition to blendshape deformers.) When skinning a broken rig to the skeleton, select the floating joints along with the joints in the main hierarchy when the Smooth Bind operation is performed.

5. Once the skin is bound, select the IK Handle and move it around; the geometry should now move with the bones.

6. Save the scene as **leftArm_v12.ma**. To see a version of the scene, open the leftArm_v12.ma scene from the chapter7\scenes directory on the DVD.

FIGURE 7.37
Once you bind the geometry to the skin, it is deformed when you move the joints.

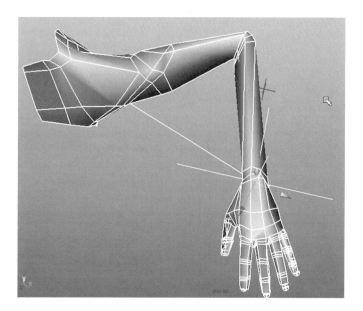

Paint Skin Weights

When the joints are moved it becomes immediately obvious that the geometry of the skin does not move in a realistic manner. To make the skin move properly, you need to edit the weight values of the vertices; this can be done with the Paint Weights tool. This exercise demonstrates techniques for painting weights on the low-resolution version of the arm.

1. Continue with the scene from the previous section or open the leftArm_v12.ma scene from the chapter7\scenes directory on the DVD.

2. In the viewport, switch to smooth-shaded mode (hot key = 6). Select the leftArm_loResolution and choose Skin ➢ Edit Smooth Skin ➢ Paint Skin Weights. Make sure the Tool Options window is open.

The geometry turns black except for the area around the joint listed in the Influence section of the Paint Skin Weights Tool window. The geometry is color coded. White indicates a joint weight value of 1 (100 percent), and black indicates a joint weight value of 0. Shades of gray indicate values between 0 and 1 (see Figure 7.38).

FIGURE 7.38
The Paint Skin Weights tool color-codes the geometry based on the amount of weight influence each joint has for each vertex of the skinned geometry.

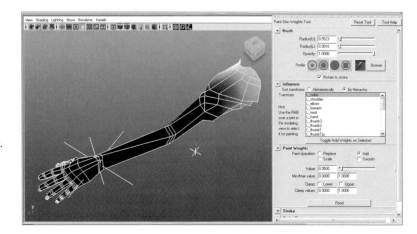

The Paint Skin Weights tool uses the Artisan brush interface. As you paint on the model, the operation selected in the Paint Weights section determines how the brush edits the weights. You can replace, add, smooth, or scale weights in the areas you paint on the model. The easiest way to approach weight painting is to stick to only the Add and Smooth operations.

Each vertex on the model receives up to a value of 1 from all the joints on the model. The total weight values must equal 1, so if a selected vertex receives a value of 0.8 from a particular joint, the remaining weight value (0.2) must come from another joint in the chain. Usually this remaining weight value comes from a joint close by the vertex as determined by Maya. This is where things can get tricky. If you paint on a vertex using the Replace operation with a value of 0.5 for a particular joint, the remaining 0.5 weight value is distributed among the other joints in the chain, which can lead to some strange and unpredictable results. If instead you use the Add operation with very low values, you can carefully increase a joint's influence over a vertex without worrying about Maya assigning the remaining weight values to other joints in the chain.

3. In the Influence section of the Paint Skin Weights Tool options, select the L_collar joint from the list. In the Paint Weights section, set Paint Operation to Add and Value to 0.**05** (Figure 7.39).

4. Lightly paint over the areas near the open end of the arm past the shoulder. As the color becomes brighter, the influence of the L_collar joint increases.

5. Select the L_arm_CTRL locator, and move it in to bend the arm. Select the arm geometry, and go back to the Paint Skin Weights tool.

You can continue to paint the skin weights with the joints posed. This is an excellent way to get visual feedback as you edit the weights.

6. To reduce the pinching in the elbow area, switch back and forth between the L_shoulder and L_elbow joints in the Paint Skin Weights Tool options. As you switch between the two, paint the vertices near the elbow. You'll see the vertices move as the influence from the joints increases as you paint (Figure 7.40).

FIGURE 7.39
The options for
the Paint Skin
Weights tool

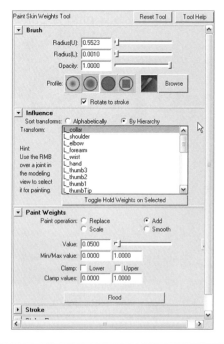

FIGURE 7.40
Pose the arm
while you edit the
skin weights with
the Paint Skin
Weights tool.

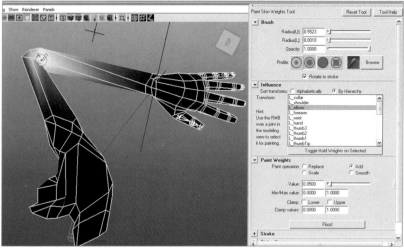

7. Continue to paint and adjust the weights of the low-resolution arm. Your goals are to reduce the compression of the geometry that occurs when the joints are rotated and to reduce movement at the open end of the geometry that occurs when the arm is repositioned (Figure 7.41). As much as possible, try to create a crease in the skin where a joint is at an extreme pose.

8. Save the scene as **leftArm_v13.ma**. To see a version of the scene to this point, open the leftArm_v13.ma scene from the chapter7\scenes directory on the DVD.

FIGURE 7.41
Paint the weights of the skin to create creases where the joints bend.

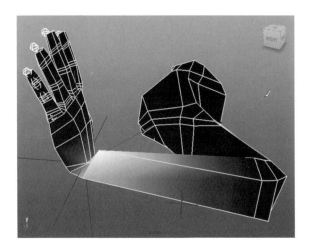

Edit Skin Weights in the Component Editor

In some cases you may want to edit the skin weights by entering a precise numeric value. To do this, switch to component mode and select the vertices you need to edit directly. Then choose Window ➢ General Editors ➢ Component Editor. In the Smooth Skins tab, you'll see a spreadsheet that lists each joint's influence for each of the selected vertices (Figure 7.42). You can change these values by directly entering numbers into the spreadsheet. Remember that each vertex must have a total weight value of 1, so if you set a value lower than 1, the remaining value will be assigned to a different joint. You can turn on the Hold option to lock a vertex's weight value so Maya will not change the value automatically.

FIGURE 7.42
You can use the Component Editor to enter numeric weight values for the joints.

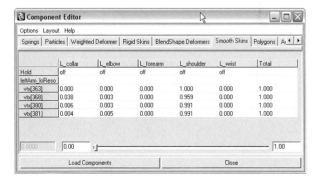

Copy Skin Weights

You can copy the weights from the low-resolution model to the high-resolution model. It does not matter that the vertices do not perfectly match because the overall weighting can easily be transferred. This reduces the difficulty of editing the initial weights on the high-resolution model.

1. Continue with the scene from the previous section or open the leftArm_v13.ma scene from the chapter7\scenes directory on the DVD.

2. Make sure that the L_arm_CTRL locator is back to its starting position (set the Translate channels to **0**). Make sure all Rotate channels for each joint are set to 0.

3. Turn on the armMesh layer's Visibility. Use Smooth Binding to skin the leftArm geometry to the arm joints using the same steps from the "Smooth Binding" section in this chapter.

4. Once the geometry is bound to the joints, select the leftArm_loResolution geometry, and then Ctrl+click the leftArm geometry. Choose Skin ➢ Edit Smooth Skin ➢ Copy Skin Weights ➢ Options.

5. In the Copy Skin Weights Options window, set Surface Association to Closest Point On Surface. Set Influence Association 1 to Label, Influence Association 2 to Name, and the Influence Association 3 to One To One (see Figure 7.43).

6. Click Apply to copy the weights. When the weights have been copied, you can hide the lowResolutionMesh display layer.

Use the Paint Weights tool to fine-tune the weights of the high-resolution mesh. The fingers will need some work to make them look more realistic as the finger joints rotate.

7. Switch to wireframe mode, and select the joints of the index finger (Shift+click L_index3, L_index2, and L_index1, in that order). Rotate the joints so they face inward toward the palm.

8. Use the Paint Skin Weights tool to adjust the weights on each section of the finger to create a more realistic behavior in the bent finger. The flesh should bulge slightly as the finger bends (Figure 7.44).

FIGURE 7.43
The options for the Copy Skin Weights operation

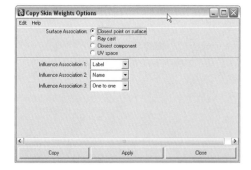

FIGURE 7.44
Paint the weights of the skin on the fingers to create realistic bulges in the flesh as the fingers bend.

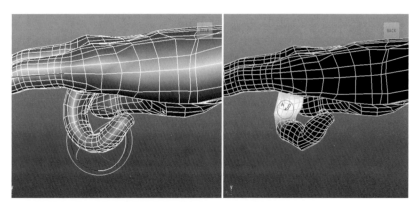

You can interactively change the size of the brush by holding the b hot key while dragging left and right. This helps when painting in tight spaces.

9. Save the scene as `leftArm_v14.ma`. To see a version of the scene to this point, open the `leftArm_v14.ma` scene from the `chapter7\scenes` directory on the DVD.

Mirror Skin Weights

You can copy weight values from one side of a symmetrical character to another using the Mirror Skin Weights command. This greatly reduces the amount of time spent painting weights and ensures consistency in weighting for both sides of a character. To do this, select the mesh and choose Skin ➢ Edit Smooth Skin ➢ Mirror Skin Weights ➢ Options. In the options you can choose which axis the weights are mirrored across.

 **Real World Scenario**

CREATE A DYNAMIC RIG FOR A PONYTAIL

Some stylized character models use geometry for hair instead of Maya's Paint Effects strokes. You can create a simple rig for parts of the hair, such as a ponytail, using an IK Spline curve and a Dynamic curve.

1. From a side view, create a joint chain that follows the shape of the character's pony tail. Start from the top of the pony tail, and draw the curve running down to the end of the pony tail.

2. Create a joint chain that follows the shape of the curve. To make it easy to follow the curve, turn on Curve Snapping. The joint chain should have between four and six joints.

3. Select the curve and switch to the Dynamics menu set. Choose Hair ➢ Make Selected Curves Dynamic.

When you convert a curve to a dynamic curve, a duplicate of the original curve is created. This curve is contained within a group named hairSystem1OutputCurves. You want to make sure that this duplicate curve is the one you use as the IK Spline handle, not the original curve you created from the side view.

4. Use the IK Spline tool to attach an IK Spline handle to the joint chain. In the options for the IK Spline tool, turn off Auto Create Curve. Select the root of the joint chain and then the last joint in the chain. In the Outliner, expand the hairSystem1OutputCurve group, and select the curve in this group.

5. Open the Attribute Editor for the dynamic curve, and switch to the follicleShape tab. Set Point Lock to Base.

6. Parent the root of the ponytail joint chain to a joint in the head.

7. Animate the head moving around; when you play the scene, the ponytail should flop around. You will need to adjust the settings in the Attribute Editor for the hairSystemShape1 node to change the way the ponytail moves.

For an example of this rig, open the `nancy_rig.ma` scene from the `chapter7\scenes` directory on the DVD.

Maya Muscle System

Maya Muscle is a new addition to the Maya rigging toolset. Maya Muscle (formerly known as cMuscleSystem) has been used in the industry for several years as a Maya plug-in for the realistic deformations of characters. Maya Muscle was first introduced as an extension to Maya 2008. The plug-in was originally developed by Michael Comet for his own company, Comet Digital LLC. Autodesk purchased the plug-in to integrate it into Maya. In Maya 2009 the integration is complete.

MICHAEL COMET AND THE DEVELOPMENT OF MAYA MUSCLE

In October 2007, Autodesk purchased the cMuscleSystem plug-in from Comet Digital LLC. Michael Comet, the developer of this plug-in, has developed many MEL scripts and plug-ins over the years. He is well known for his work in developing tools and sharing them with the Maya community. He is currently working at Pixar Animation Studios as a technical director generalist. Eric Allen interviewed Michael Comet for this edition of *Mastering Maya*.

When did you first come up with the idea of adding muscles to Maya?

I had thought about it and wanted to do some muscle rigging for a while, probably ever since movies like *Jurassic Park* came out, but the real motivation occurred when I was living in New York, probably between 2003 and 2004. At that point, I was working at Blue Sky and trying to find a way to supplement my income in order to make living on the East Coast more affordable. I really had a desire to write the software anyhow and decided it would make a lot of sense to try to do it right and make it a commercial product.

Part of it was a motivation to try to write something cool for Maya that wasn't yet available, and a large part of it was to try to write some basic deformation tools and a workflow that I felt would be the way I as an articulator wished to actually work: essentially taking what was there, extending it, and in a way writing my own dream rigging software.

I actually started the process middle-to-late 2003. I first sat down with a pencil and paper and wrote down the basic ideas I had about what I wanted the software do and how I thought I might accomplish it. I also started thinking about how I wanted to solve the problem of sliding surfaces under the skin and still allow them to push through beyond their center point. Once I had the basic gist worked out on paper I started coding. This was sort of my first real foray into the world of the Maya API, so I had to both learn that and develop the tools simultaneously.

At some point in early 2004 I got tired and took a three-month break from writing any of it. Then near the end of the year I started back up and finished it off in early 2005, finally releasing it in February to the public. It was quite interesting having to learn to deal with not only the development but also the business side of things. This included starting up and incorporating my own business, as well as things like software licensing. It was definitely a lot of work but a really good experience and fun as well.

What are some of your favorite characters that use this muscle system and why?

There have been several studios that used my software, some of which I probably don't even know about. It would probably be hard to pick a favorite, but I was very excited to see Framestore CFC use it for Aslan's body in the second of the *Chronicles of Narnia* movies. Tippett Studios also did some really cool work with it for the *Spiderwick Chronicles* on the Hobgoblin and smaller goblins.

Now that Autodesk is developing it, what would you like to see added, or what would you have added if you had had the time?

When the software was sold, all of my ideas and suggestions met with very good response from the Autodesk team. The future development work for the Maya Muscles software would fall under nondisclosure agreements, and therefore I can't really comment on this other than to say I have faith that they will keep improving their software for the end user.

How has your development background helped you at Pixar?

Being able to do technical work and software development is a big part of what I do. Pixar is a cool place in that a lot of the software is developed in house. This means that it's very easy to write additional scripts and tools to augment what is there. I've been able to write my own custom rigging deformers, tools, and interfaces while at Pixar that I and other people on the articulation team use. While I obviously enjoy modeling and point weighting, I do also enjoy the technical challenges of character setup. Being able to code and write new software means I've been able to work on some of the more technical rigs as well as make utilities to help streamline our process.

What are you working on now?

Right now I am working on a feature film titled *Up* that comes out in 2009. I'm one of several articulators working on the film. I've been able to update and maintain our main underlying rigs that are referenced by the entire team. I've also been able to work on several different characters and technical props. The modeling team at Pixar is somewhat different from those in other studios in that the members both model and articulate the characters, so I've been able to both model and articulate one of the secondary characters for the show. It has been great to be able to see it through a longer part of the pipeline and have more control over it. I've also modeled and articulated other characters and props as well.

Other than what is on your (very thorough and informative) website, www.comet-cartoons.com/, what would you tell those aspiring to be another "Michael Comet" developer and animator?

The main thing would be to practice, practice, practice, and be good at what you do. For a technical rigging artist I would recommend learning how to set up and create the technical parts of the rigs, basic things such as IK, spine setups, and so on, and then work on trying to develop your own techniques to solve various rigging problems. This would also include learning some basic programming languages such as Python, C++, or whatever scripting languages your software uses.

At the same time you should work on point-weighting deformation skills, and you should also work on modeling characters as well, because really these two things are the same when it comes to correcting shapes or targets for motion poses. The one thing I often see in rigging reels is that people need to remember to show both the technical side and the artistic side. Most studios look for articulators who can move points but also have some technical ability. Many times I have seen reels where it's more one or the other, and it leaves me wondering about the reel. Another thing is also to show extreme range of motion with the deformation, like legs doing the splits or farther, arms/shoulders up 90+ degrees, and such. And finally don't forget to work on facial rigging skills, and again be sure to show that in extreme ranges of motion. Facial rigging and setup is a good area also to experiment with for those with the more technical side to them, as far as working on and showing cool deformation ideas. If you are not as strong technically but want to be in rigging, I'd recommend focusing more on the modeling and point weighting, corrective shapes, and morph target creation. For the more technically focused, focus on the scripting and setup side mixed with problem solving. Being able to hunt down bugs, rig issues, shot problems, and so on is a large part of being one of the more technical artists. It can be difficult to get this experience outside of an actual production gig, but if you are the kind of person who takes to reading and learning software on your own, or has the ability to work on a small short with a team of people, it will show through when you interview.

Maya Muscles deform the surface of geometry much like other types of deformers. They simulate the behavior of actual muscles and can be driven by the rotation of joints or expressions. Muscles are similar to Maya's influence objects, but they offer better control for deforming the skinned geometry surface. Much of the purpose and functionality of influence objects are replaced by Maya Muscle so this edition of Mastering Maya does not discuss influence objects.

The Maya Muscle deformer is actually a surface that can be manipulated while connected to the deformed geometry. The muscle objects can create complex deformation by allowing for multiple end shapes per muscle.

Muscle objects can slide beneath the deformed geometry to create special effects, and muscles also have properties that allow movement such as jiggle, force, and collision.

The Maya Muscle System

The Maya Muscle system is a collection of deformation tools that can work independently or in concert to deform geometry so it looks like muscles are bulging and stretching beneath skin. The primary system has three main deformer types: capsules, bones, and muscles.

Capsules are very simple skin deformers used as replacement for Maya's joints. It is necessary to use capsules because standard Maya joints cannot work directly with the muscle deformer. Capsules are shaped like a simple pill. The basic capsule shape cannot be changed. However, it can be scaled to simulate the basic shape of muscles (see Figure 7.45).

Bones are skin deformers that have been converted from regular polygon geometry. Because of this, bones can be almost any shape you need. The term *bones* in this sense should not be confused with Maya's standard bones, which are the shapes that connect joints. The reason the Maya Muscle system uses the term *bones* is because these deformers are useful for simulating the movement of specially shaped bones—such as the scapula—beneath skin.

FIGURE 7.45
A capsule is a simple deformer that appears in the shape of a pill.

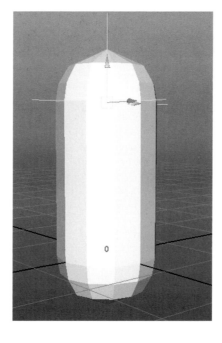

Muscles are skin deformers created from NURBS surfaces. The muscle deformers are designed to replicate the behavior of real-life muscles. To achieve this, they have two connection points at either end, which are attached to the character's rig. So, for example, when the character moves/bends his arm, the connection points move closer together, creating a bulging/squashing effect. When the character extends his arm, the connection points move farther apart, creating a stretching effect. The transition between squashing and stretching is automatically eased in and out, so the deformer's movements are very smooth.

Any of these muscle deformers can be bound to the character's skin geometry using one of the various types of weighting available. Weighting muscle deformers to geometry is similar to using Smooth Binding to connect geometry to Maya joints. The weighting types include Sticky, Sliding, Displacement, Force, Jiggle, Relax, and Smooth. The following sections demonstrate using muscle deformers with Sticky Weighting, which is very similar to Smooth Binding, discussed earlier in the chapter.

To use a muscle system you must first create the muscle objects (capsule, bone, or muscle), apply the muscle deformer to the character's skin, connect the specific muscle objects (capsule, bone, or muscle) to the deformer, and then use a weighting type to bind it to determine how the deformer affects the character's skin using one of the available weighting types.

It is important to understand that when you use the Maya Muscle system, the character's skin geometry must be bound to objects that have the cMuscleObject shape node. In other words, you must either replace or convert any existing joints with capsules or Maya Muscle bones. You can also transfer any existing skin weights created for Maya joints to the muscle system.

In the following exercises, you'll add the Maya Muscle system to the left arm rig created earlier in the chapter.

Using Capsules

Capsules are very similar to Maya joints except their shape can be used to influence the deformation of the character's skin geometry. It's also necessary to replace existing joints with capsules or polygon bones to use the Maya Muscle deformer.

1. Open the `leftArmCapsule_v01.ma` scene from the `chapter7\scenes` directory on the DVD.

This scene contains the left arm rig created earlier in the chapter. The geometry includes the left arm as well as part of the left side of a character's chest. The geometry is Smooth Bound to the rig, and the weights for the joints have been painted onto the model.

The Maya Muscle plug-in may not be loaded. If you do not see the Muscle menu in the Animation menu set, then you'll need to load the plug-in using the Plug-in Manager.

2. Choose Window ➤ Settings/Preferences ➤ Plug-in Manager. In the Plug-in Manager window, check the Loaded and Auto Load options next to `MayaMuscle.mll` (see Figure 7.46).

3. Once the plug-in is loaded, you should see the Muscle menu in the Animation menu set (the Muscle menu actually appears in all of the menu sets; for the moment though, you should be using the Animation menu set).

4. In the Outliner, expand the L_ArmJoints group. Select the root joint. Right-click on the root joint in the perspective view, and then from the pop-up window choose Select Hierarchy. This is a quick way to select all of the joints in the hierarchy (see Figure 7.47).

FIGURE 7.46
Load the Maya
Muscle plug-in
in the Plug-in
Manager.

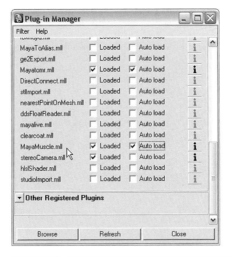

FIGURE 7.47
Use the pop-up
menu to select all
the joints in the
left-arm hierarchy.

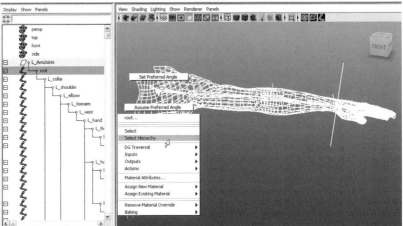

5. In the Outliner, Ctrl+click on any of the objects that are not joints, such as effector1, L_arm_ CTRL, and L_armPV_CTRL. By Ctrl+clicking on these objects, they become deselected without affecting the nodes that are selected in the hierarchy. You should end up with only joints selected in the Outliner.

6. With only the joints selected, choose Muscle ➤ Muscle/Bones ➤ Convert Surface To Muscle/ Bone. The joints automatically convert to capsules, and polygon geometry automatically converts to polygon bones. In this case you should not have any polygon geometry selected.

It is important to make sure that the joints are oriented properly. We discussed this earlier in the chapter in the section titled "Orient Joints." In the example scene, the joints have been oriented so the X axis points along the length of the bone toward the child joint.

7. When you execute the conversion command, you'll be asked to specify which axis points down the length of the joints. This is used to orient the capsules. Since the joint rig is set up to use the X axis, choose X-Axis from the pop-up window (see Figure 7.48).

FIGURE 7.48

Maya asks you to specify the axis that points down the length of the joint.

The joints are converted to capsules. You can clearly see them if you disable the Polygon option in the viewport's Show menu and switch to shaded view. The Inverse Kinematic controls still work just fine (see Figure 7.49).

8. Save the scene as **leftArmCapsule_v02.ma**. To see a version of the scene, open leftArmCapsule_v02.ma.

Converting joints to capsules is the easiest way to prepare an existing rig for use with Maya Muscle. The Convert Surface To Muscle/Bone command works only on selected joints and surfaces. You can also create individual capsules using the Muscle/Bones ➤ Make Capsule and Make Capsule With End Locator commands. You can add a capsule to a rig by parenting the capsule or its end locators to parts of the rig.

FIGURE 7.49

Convert the joints to capsules. The Inverse Kinematic controls created earlier still work.

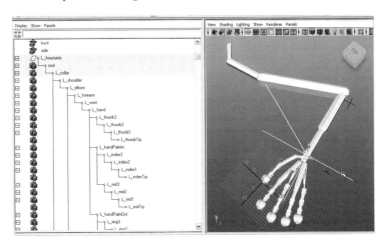

Edit Capsule Shape

You can edit the attributes of the capsule in the SHAPES section of the capsule's Channel Box.

1. Continue with the scene from the previous section or open the leftArmCapsule_v02.ma scene from the chapter7\scenes directory on the DVD.

2. In the Outliner, expand the L_ArmJoints group and select the L_collar node.

3. In the Channel Box, select the L_collarShape node in the SHAPES section. The channels here control how the capsule is displayed and behaves. Many of these options are also used for the other types of muscle deformers.

4. Set the Radius of the L_collarShape to **0.3** and the Length to **4.5**, as shown in Figure 7.50. These settings control how the capsule is displayed but do not affect how it behaves with regard to deforming the surface.

The settings at the bottom of the Channel Box determine the display quality of the capsule. The NSegs and NSides settings change the number of divisions in the capsule, but these settings do not affect how the capsule deforms the skin. NSegs sets the number of radial segments in the capsule; NSides sets the number of divisions around the radius of the capsule.

5. Spend a few minutes editing the size of capsules. Use a small radius size for the capsules. In the next sections you'll add more bone deformers. By using a small radius size you can clearly see how the parts work together.

6. Save the scene as **leftArmCapsule_v03.ma**. To see a version of the scene, open the leftArmCapsule_v03.ma from the chapter7\scenes directory on the DVD.

FIGURE 7.50
Adjust the size of the capsules using the settings in the Channel Box.

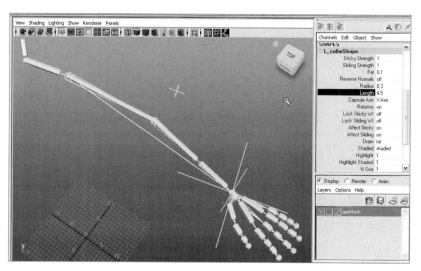

Create a Muscle Using Muscle Builder

The Muscle Builder interface is designed to make the creation of muscle deformers easy and fast. In this section, you'll create the bicep for the arm rig using the Muscle Builder window.

1. Continue with the scene from the previous section or open the leftArmCapsule_v03.ma scene from the chapter7\scenes directory on the DVD.

2. Choose Muscle ➤ Simple Muscles ➤ Muscle Builder to open the Muscle Builder interface.

This interface allows you to create and edit simple muscle shapes for the skeleton. To make the muscle, you'll first specify the Attach objects. These are the parts of the skeleton where each end of the muscle will be attached. Once you create the muscle, you can edit its shape using the controls in the Muscle Builder interface.

3. In the Outliner, Shift+click the plus sign next to L_ArmJoints to expand the L_ArmJoints group. Select the L_shoulder object.

4. In the Muscle Builder window, click the button labeled <<< to the right of the Attach Obj 1 field. This loads the L_shoulder capsule into this field.

5. In the Outliner, select the L_elbow capsule and load it into the Attach Obj 2 field (see Figure 7.51).

FIGURE 7.51
Specify the two
Attach objects in
the Muscle Builder
window.

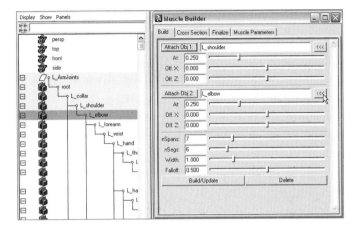

FIGURE 7.51
Specify the two
Attach objects in
the Muscle Builder
window.

The nSpans, nSegs, Width, and Falloff sliders determine the shape of the muscle's surface. The default settings should work fine for this demo. Usually you'll want to set these before creating the muscle surface. NSpans and nSegs determine the number of spans and segments that the NURBS muscle surface will use. Falloff determines how the ends of the muscle taper at each end; a lower setting creates less of a taper. Width determines the overall width of the muscle shape.

6. Click the Build/Update button to create the muscle.

The Muscle object appears in the perspective view attached to the skeleton, as shown in Figure 7.52. You'll see that a new NURBS surface named cMuscleBuilder_surf1 has been created along with two new cameras named MuscleBuilderCamera and MuscleBuilderCameraSide. The cameras are used in the Muscle Builder interface.

7. Save the scene as **leftArmMuscle_v01.ma**. To see a version of the scene, open the leftArmMuscle_v01.ma scene from the chapter7\scenes directory on the DVD.

FIGURE 7.52
The muscle surface
appears attached
to the skeleton.

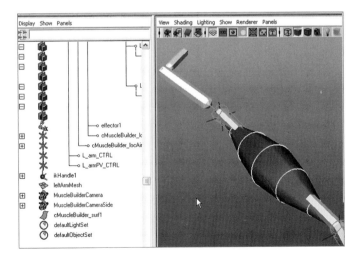

Edit a Muscle Using Muscle Builder

The settings in the Muscle Builder can be used to edit the placement and the shape of the muscle.

1. Continue with the scene from the previous section or open the leftArmMuscle_v01.ma scene from the chapter7\scenes directory on the DVD.

To properly place the bicep you should check an anatomy reference. Some experimentation is required to place the muscle and achieve realistic motion and deformation. The settings applied to the muscle may look exaggerated in Maya, but this may be necessary to create a realistic deformation. In this section you'll learn how to use the controls in the Muscle Builder interface to place the muscle.

2. In the Display Layer menu, set the display mode of the armMesh layer to Template so you can see the arm mesh while working on placing the bicep.

MUSCLE SURFACE NAME

Do not change the default name of the muscle surface (cMuscleBuilder_surf1) while working in the Muscle Builder interface. You'll have an opportunity to change the name when you convert the surface into a deformer. If you change the name of the surface before converting the surface to a muscle, the Muscle Builder will not be able to perform the conversion properly.

---

3. If the Muscle Builder is not already open, select the cMuscleBuilder_surf1 object and choose Muscle ➢ Simple Muscles ➢ Muscle Builder. In the Build tab, click the Attach Obj 1 button and switch to the Move tool.

4. Use the Move tool to place the Attach Obj 1 locator in front of the L_shoulder joint. Try to use the shape of the leftArmMesh geometry as a guide.

The sliders labels At, Off. X, and Off. Z in the Muscle Builder interface can be used to numerically position the attach points. The At slider is used to position the Y axis of the muscle attach point.

5. Click the Attach Obj 2 button to place the other end of the muscle. The bicep muscle attaches to the lower part of the arm just beyond the elbow (see Figure 7.53).

6. Switch to the Cross Section tab. In this section of the interface, the curves that control the shape of the muscle surface are listed on the left. Two camera views allow you to select the curves and move them to shape the overall muscle. To edit the position of one of the circles, select one of the curves listed on the left and then use the Move tool to reposition the curve. Movements of each control circle are limited to the X and Y axes.

You can move the circles in the perspective view as well as in the cross-section view of the Muscle Builder interface (see Figure 7.54).

FIGURE 7.53
Position the attach points at either end of the muscle using the Move tool and the sliders in the Muscle Builder interface.

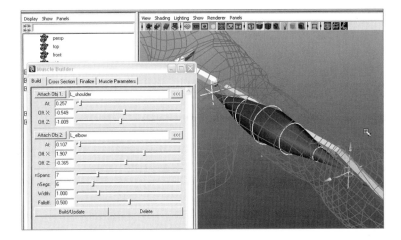

FIGURE 7.54
You can use the cross-section views to edit the shape of the muscle.

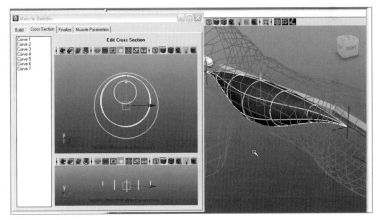

7. Right-click on one of the curves in the top cross-section view of the Muscle Builder interface, and choose Control Vertex. Use the Move tool to further customize the shape of the muscle by moving the CVs of the circles.

8. Save the scene as **leftArmMuscle_v02.ma**. To see a version of the scene to this point, open the leftArmMuscle_v02.ma scene from the chapter7\scenes directory on the DVD.

Finalize the Muscle

When you have finished editing the basic shape of the muscle, you are ready to convert it to a muscle deformer. This action is performed in the Finalize tab of the Muscle Builder window.

1. Continue with the scene from the previous section or open the leftArmMuscle_v02.ma scene from the chapter7\scenes folder on the DVD.

2. In the Outliner, select the cMuscleBuilder_surf1 object, and open the Muscle Builder window (Muscle ➤ Simple Muscles ➤ Muscle Builder).

The Finalize tab converts the surface into a muscle deformer—you have a choice between Muscle Spline Deformer and Muscle Stretch. Muscle Spline Deformer is the preferred option when creating a muscle because it has more controls and is therefore more useful than the Muscle Stretch option.

3. Leave Num Controls set to 3 and Type set to Cube (you can choose Curve or Null as well, whichever you prefer).

If you need to mirror the muscle to the opposite side of the body, you can choose a mirror axis from the Create Mirror Muscle options. You can use the Search and Replace fields to replace prefixes such as L (for left) with R (for right) on the mirrored objects.

4. Click the Convert To Muscle button to create the deformer. In the pop-up box, you will be warned that further changes cannot be made to the muscle using the interface controls. You'll also be prompted to name the muscle. Name it **L_bicep** (see Figure 7.55).

When you finalize the muscle, the original surface is grouped with its controls. Control cubes appear at either end of the muscle and in the center. These can be used to fix position and rotation problems. At this point you do not want to close the Muscle Builder window. You can test and edit settings using the controls in the Muscle Parameters tab.

FIGURE 7.55
You are prompted to name the muscle when you click the Convert To Muscle button.

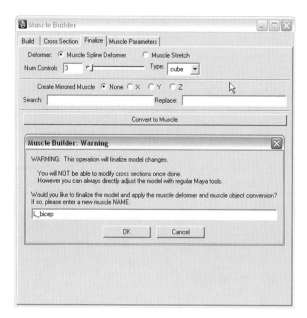

Edit Muscle Parameters

Muscle parameters determine how the muscle behaves as the joints are animated. If you select the L_arm_CTRL locator and move it around, you'll see that the muscle actually stretches and squashes.

Many of the settings in the Muscle Object Settings section can be changed in the Channel Box or Attribute Editor as well. Some of the settings, such as nSegs and nSides, apply only to the display of capsules. For this section, you'll be mostly concerned with settings related to Squash and Stretch.

1. In the Muscle Object Settings section, set Draw to Muscle. If this is set to Off, you'll see the deformer, but changes made to the Squash and Stretch settings will not be displayed.

The first step toward editing the muscle's behavior is to establish its default stretch and squash shapes based on the movement of the arm.

2. Currently the arm is slightly bent. You can use this pose to establish the relaxed, default shape of the bicep muscle. In the Spline Length Settings section, click the Set Current As Default button.

3. In the perspective view, select the L_arm_CTRL locator and pull it along the X axis to straighten the arm. This stretches the L_bicep muscle to its extreme pose. Click the Set Current As Stretch button.

4. Push the L_arm_CTRL locator toward the chest so the arm becomes completely folded. Click the Set Current As Squash button (see Figure 7.56).

5. In the Outliner, expand the grpMUSCLES group and the grpL_bicepRIG. Select the cMuscleSplineL_bicep node.

The settings in the Stretch Volume Presets section determine how the shape muscle deformer transitions between extreme poses. To set this properly, animate the arm so you can adjust the settings and see the results as the arm moves.

6. Set the Time slider to 100 frames. Select the L_arm_CTRL locator, and create a short animation where the locator moves back and forth, causing the arm to bend and straighten.

7. Play the animation, and make sure the Muscle Builder window is still open. Make sure the cMuscleSplineL_bicep node is selected in the Outliner. As the arm moves, you may see some jiggling in the muscle; that's part of the Jiggle settings, which we'll edit in the next few steps.

8. As the arm moves back and forth, click the Small, Medium, and Large buttons. Notice the change in the muscle's size and behavior as you switch between presets.

9. You can edit the numeric values in the START, MID, and END fields to fine-tune the behavior. It's usually easiest to start by loading one of the presets and then make small changes to the values.

When you're happy with how the muscle is shaped as it moves, you can move on to editing the Jiggle motion.

10. While the animation plays, click the Default, Light, Medium, Heavy, and OFF buttons in the Jiggle Presets section. Observe the difference in behavior as each preset is applied.

11. You can fine-tune the behavior of the jiggling by editing the numeric values in the START, MID, and END fields for Jiggle, Cycle, and Rest. Jiggle is the intensity of jiggle, Cycle is

the frequency of jiggle oscillation, and Rest is the time it takes for the muscle to come to a stop. The Dampen settings add a damping effect as the muscle reaches extreme poses.

12. Save the scene as **leftArmMuscle_v03.ma**. To see a version of the scene to this point, open the leftArmMuscle_v03.ma scene from the chapter7\scenes directory on the DVD.

FIGURE 7.56
Establish the Squash position for the L_bicep muscle.

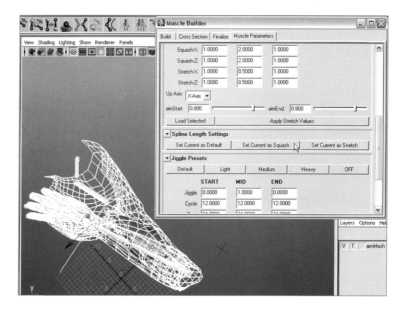

Convert the Smooth Skin to a Muscle System

Now that the muscle has been set up and is working properly, you can apply it to the arm geometry so it deforms the character's skin. Applying the deformer to the geometry involves weighting the skin to the muscles. This is very similar in concept to smooth binding geometry to Maya's joints. In fact you can actually convert the skin weights painted earlier in the chapter to the muscle system.

1. Continue with the scene from the previous section or open the leftArmMuscle_v03.ma scene from the chapter7\scenes directory on the DVD.

2. Select the L_arm_CTRL locator and delete the keyframes. Set the Translation Channels to **0**.

3. In the Layer Editor, set the Display mode of the armMesh to Normal (not Template or Reference).

4. In the Outliner, select leftArmMesh. Choose Muscle ➢ Skin Set Up ➢ Convert Smooth Skin To Muscle System. Maya asks if you want to delete or disable the skin weights applied to the arm. Choose Disable (you can delete the weights if you want to, but it may be a good idea to keep the weights in the scene in case they are needed later).

5. Maya asks you to choose the axis for the capsules. Choose the X-axis to match the orientation of the capsules. Converting the skin takes a few moments; you'll see a dialog box that displays the progress of the calculation.

This takes the smooth skin joint weights that were painted on the geometry and converts them to muscle weights. However, only the capsules in the L_armJoints hierarchy are included. If you move the L_arm_locator, you'll notice that the muscle does not yet deform the skin. It needs to be attached to the skin and weighted before it will work.

6. Select the L_bicep surface (in the Outliner expand the grpMUSCLES/grpL_bicepRIG/ grpL_bicepGEO hierarchy and select the L_bicep surface, or select the surface directly in the viewport window) and Ctrl+click the leftArmMesh object. Choose Muscle ➢ Muscle Objects ➢ Connect Selected Muscle Objects (see Figure 7.57).

FIGURE 7.57
Connect the L_bicep surface to the leftArmMesh geometry as a muscle deformer.

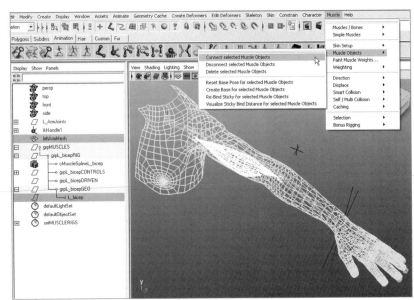

7. A dialog box asks you to set the Sticky Bind Maximum Distance. Choose Auto-Calculate.

The L_bicep surface is now connected to the skin geometry. However, it still will not affect the geometry until the weights are painted for L_bicep.

8. Switch to shaded view. Select leftArmMesh and choose Muscle ➢ Paint Muscle Weights. The geometry becomes color coded to indicate the weight strength of each of the muscles listed in the Muscle Paint window. Make sure the Weight type is set to Sticky.

9. Scroll to the bottom of the list in the Muscle Paint window and select L_bicep. The geometry turns black, indicating there is no weight for this muscle.

10. Set Weight to **0.1** and Operation to Add. Paint over the area of the bicep to start adding weights. Low-weight values are blue, and higher-weight values are green, orange, and red.

11. Use the L_arm_CTRL locator to pose the arm as you paint weight values for the bicep (see Figure 7.58).

FIGURE 7.58
Paint weight
values for the
L_bicep muscle.

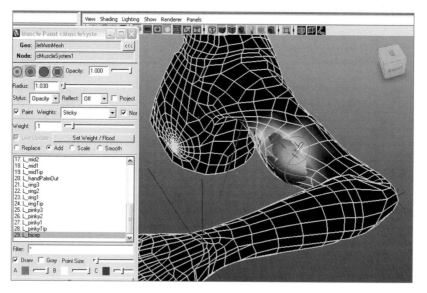

12. When you have finished painting the weights, close the window. Create another animation for the L_arm_CTRL locator so you can see the muscle in action as it deforms the skin.

13. If you need to change muscle parameters such as the Jiggle attributes, select the cMuscleSplineL_bicep node and choose Muscle ➤ Simple Muscle ➤ Set Muscle Parameters. Use the settings in the Muscle Parameters tab to adjust the muscle quality.

14. Save the scene as **leftArmMuscle_v04.ma**. To see a version of the scene, open the leftArmMuscle_v04.ma scene from the chapter7\scenes directory on the DVD.

Sliding Weights

Sliding weights are used to create the effect of bones sliding beneath the skin. In this example, you'll create a very simple elbow object that slides beneath the skin of the arm as the arm bends.

1. Continue with the scene from the previous section or open the leftArmMuscle_v04.ma scene from the chapter7\scenes directory on the DVD.

2. Create a polygon sphere object and name it **elbowBone**.

3. Position elbowBone at the end of the elbow in the arm; allow the elbowBone to protrude from the skin slightly. Scale elbowBone to **1**, **0.5**, and **0.5** in X, Y, and Z. See Figure 7.59.

4. Freeze transformations on the elbowBone. Select L_elbow joint and Ctrl+click elbowBone. Choose Constrain ➤ Parent ➤ Options. Make sure Maintain Offset is activated in the Parent Constraint options.

5. Select elbowBone and choose Muscle ➤ Muscle/Bones ➤ Convert Surface To Muscle/Bones.

FIGURE 7.59
Place the elbow-
Bone object at the
arm's elbow and
scale it.

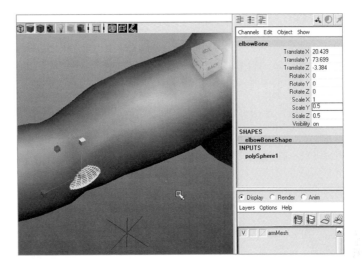

6. Select elbowBone and Ctrl+click the leftArmMesh. Choose Muscle ➤ Muscle Objects ➤ Connect Selected Muscle Objects.

7. Select leftArmMesh. In the Channel Box, select the cMuscleSystem1 node under INPUTS. Set Enable Sliding to On. This is an easy step to forget, but if you don't enable sliding weights on the character's skin, you won't see the sliding effect as the bone moves (see Figure 7.60).

FIGURE 7.60
Enable sliding
weights for the
leftArmMesh.

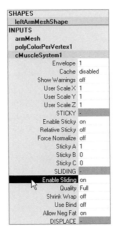

8. Select leftArmMesh and choose Muscle ➤ Paint Muscle Weights. Choose the elbowBone from the list of muscle objects. Set Weights to Sliding and the operation to Add. Set the Weight to **0.5**.

9. Paint a large area around the elbow. This does not have to be precise; you just need to cover the area the elbowBone will affect as it moves beneath the skin (see Figure 7.61).

FIGURE 7.61
Paint sliding weights in the elbow area of the arm geometry.

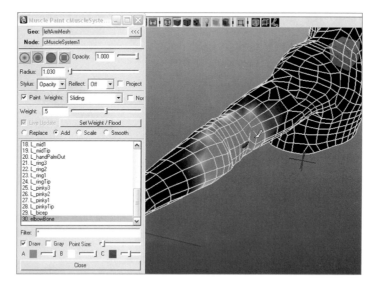

10. Close the Paint Weights window and play the animation. You can see that the geometry around the elbow is affected and the elbowBone object moves. It may be more obvious if you increase the resolution of the skin.

11. Select the leftArmMesh object. From the Polygon menu set, choose Mesh ➤ Smooth. This increases the resolution of the arm.

12. Select the elbowBone object. In the Channel Box, select the cMuscleObject_elbowBone-Shape1 node, and set Fat to **0.2**. This adds an offset to the deformation caused by the elbowBone shape.

The elbow object may penetrate the skin, but that's okay; you can disable its visibility so it does not appear in the render.

13. Play the animation and continue to make adjustments to the weighting of the elbowBone. Try adding a small amount of sticky weighting for the elbowBone (switch the Weight menu to Sticky in the Paint Weights window).

14. Select the leftArmMesh object and open its Channel Box. Under the cMuscleSystem1 node, you'll find additional settings to adjust the quality of sliding weights.

The Shrink Wrap feature helps when the bone has detail that you want to be visible in the character's skin. The skin should be dense enough to allow the detail to be visible.

There is still a ways to go before the arm deforms in a believable fashion. More muscles and bones can be added, and the weighting can be fine-tuned for each muscle to improve the deformations created by the muscle system. Setting up an entire character is even more work. It is no wonder why there are many artists who specialize in rigging. It's a difficult art to master, and it takes time, study, and practice.

15. Save the scene as **leftArmMuscle_v05.ma**. To see a version of the scene to this point, open the leftArmMuscle_v05.ma scene from the chapter7\scenes directory on the DVD.

The Bottom Line

Understand rigging.   A rig is a system of controls and deformers used to make the process of animating easier. Joints are the most common deformers used to create a character animation rig. Joints are bound directly to geometry or indirectly by skinning another deformer, such as a lattice, to the joints.

Master it   Create a rig using three bones and a lattice around a simple piece of geometry such as a sphere. Use the bones to animate the lattice.

Create and organize joint hierarchies.   A joint hierarchy is a series of joint chains. Each joint in a chain is parented to another joint, back to the root of the chain. Each joint inherits the motion of its parent joint. Organizing the joint chains is accomplished through naming and labeling the joints. Proper orientation of the joints is essential for the joints to work properly.

Master it   Create a joint hierarchy for a humanoid character. Label the joints and create names based on the labels. Orient the joints so the X axis points down the length of the joints.

Use Inverse Kinematics rigs.   A joint chain that uses Inverse Kinematics uses a goal called an End Effector to orient the joints in the chain. There are a number of solvers available in Maya, some of which need to be loaded into Maya using the command line.

Master it   Create an Inverse Kinematic rig for a character's leg. Use a separate control to position the knee of the character.

Apply skin geometry.   Skinning geometry refers to the process in which geometry is bound to joints so that it deforms as the joints are moved and rotated. Each vertex of the geometry receives a certain amount of influence from the joints in the hierarchy. This can be controlled by painting the weights of the geometry on the skin.

Master it   Paint weights on the hand model so that the padding of the thumb bulges when the thumb is rotated toward the palm of the hand.

Use Maya Muscle.   Maya Muscle is a series of tools designed to create more believable deformations and movement for objects skinned to joints. Capsules are used to replace Maya joints. Bones are deformers created from geometry, and muscles are NURBS surfaces that squash, stretch, and jiggle as they deform geometry.

Master it   Use Maya Muscle to create muscles for the forearm. Use the muscle system to reduce the amount of shrinking that occurs in the arm geometry when the forearm is rotated around its axis.

Chapter 8

Paint Effects and Toon Shading

Paint Effects is a special Maya module designed to allow artists to quickly build, animate, and render large amounts of organic and natural detail. Trees, grass, flowers, clouds, blood vessels, vines, rocks, and even small towns can be interactively painted into a scene in three dimensions. Paint Effects is both a dynamic particle-based system and a procedural modeling tool. There are many options for rendering the objects that you create using Paint Effects, giving you an astonishing amount of creative flexibility when incorporating natural elements into your projects.

Paint Effects is also a part of Maya's Toon Shading system, which is used to simulate the look of hand-drawn cartoons when rendering 3D animations. This chapter looks at how Paint Effects works through several short, experimental projects. By the end of the chapter, you'll understand how to design and apply your own custom Paint Effects objects in a scene.

In this chapter, you'll learn to:

- ◆ Use the Paint Effects canvas

- ◆ Paint on 3D objects

- ◆ Understand strokes

- ◆ Design a brush

- ◆ Create tubes

- ◆ Add growth

- ◆ Shape strokes with behaviors

- ◆ Animate strokes

- ◆ Render Paint Effects strokes

- ◆ Use Toon Shading

Using the Paint Effects Canvas

Maya actually contains a 2D paint program that can be used to paint illustrations, create textures, or experiment with Paint Effects brushes. The Paint Effects canvas works like a simplified version of a digital paint program such as Corel Painter. You can paint on the canvas using any of the Paint Effects brushes; it's a great way to test a brush before applying it in a 3D scene.

USING A TABLET

You don't have to use a digital tablet and pen to work with Paint Effects, but it makes things much easier. In this chapter, we assume that you'll be using a digital tablet. If you are using a mouse, understand that to paint with Paint Effects you can left-click and drag to apply a stroke. If you're using a digital tablet, you can drag the pen across the tablet to apply a stroke to the Paint Effects canvas or to a 3D scene.

The Paint Effects Window

The Paint Effects window is like a mini digital paint program inside Maya. In this section, you'll experiment with some basic controls to create simple images on the canvas.

1. Create a new scene in Maya.

2. In the view panel, choose Panel ➤ Paint Effects to open the Paint Effects window.

OPENING THE PAINT EFFECTS WINDOW

There are a number of ways to open Paint Effects. You can use the panel menu in a viewport, you can choose Window ➤ Paint Effects, or you can press 8 on the numeric keypad of your keyboard.

---

3. The viewport now appears white with some icons at the top. This white area is the Paint Effects canvas. If you see a 3D scene instead, choose Paint ➤ Canvas from the Paint menu (Figure 8.1).

4. Click and drag on the canvas; you'll see a black line resembling ink appear wherever you paint on the canvas. If you are using a digital tablet, vary the pressure as you paint: the line becomes thinner when less pressure is applied and thicker where more pressure is applied.

NAVIGATING THE PAINT EFFECTS WINDOW

You can use the same controls that you use in a 3D scene to zoom and pan while Paint Effects is open. To zoom, hold Alt and RMB-drag. To pan, hold Alt and MMB-drag. Since the canvas is two dimensional, holding Alt and LMB-dragging doesn't rotate the canvas but instead serves as another way to pan.

---

5. Click on the color swatch next to the C on the Paint Effects menu bar. This opens the Color Chooser. You can use this tool to change the color of the brush. Move the V slider to change the value (brightness) of the paintbrush color (see Figure 8.2).

6. The color swatch labeled with a T and the slider next to it control the transparency of the current stroke. Experiment with changing color and transparency as you paint on the canvas (see Figure 8.3).

FIGURE 8.1
Choosing Paint Canvas from the Paint menu switches Paint Effects to 2D paint mode.

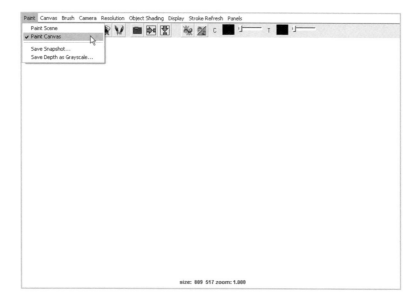

FIGURE 8.2
The Paint Effects canvas is a 2D paint program within Maya. Clicking on the C color swatch opens the Color Chooser, allowing you to change the brush color.

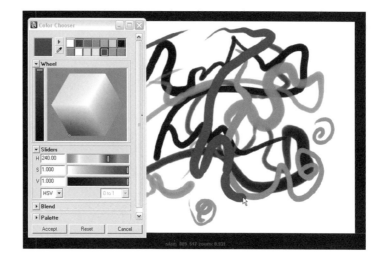

FIGURE 8.3
The icons on the menu bar of the Paint Effects window

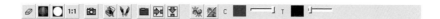

These are the other icons on the panel, from left to right, as shown in Figure 8.3:

◆ The eraser icon clears the canvas.

◆ The color icon displays the RGB channels (color) of the canvas.

◆ The white circle icon displays the alpha channel of the strokes on the canvas.

◆ The 1:1 icon displays the actual size of the canvas.

◆ The camera icon takes a snapshot of the canvas.

◆ The paintbrush icon opens the Attribute Editor for the current brush settings.

◆ The double paintbrush icon opens the Visor, which displays the available Brush presets.

◆ The folder icon opens the sourceimages folder. When this button is active, every time you make a change to the canvas, you'll be prompted to save the image in the sourceimages folder.

◆ The sideways arrow allows horizontal tiling. As you paint off one side of the canvas, this stroke is continued on the opposite side. This is useful when you want to create seamless tiling textures.

◆ The down arrow enables vertical tiling. Strokes that you paint off the top or bottom of the canvas are continued on the opposite side.

◆ The branching stroke icon enables tube painting. This will be discussed in more detail.

◆ The diagonally split icon flips tube direction. This will be discussed along with tubes.

7. Click the eraser icon to clear the canvas. Click the double brush icon to open the Visor (or choose Window ➢ General Editors ➢ Visor).

THE VISOR

The Visor is a central library within Maya that allows you to access presets, example files, and other assets. The tabs at the top of the Visor allow you to browse and then choose the various types of assets. Much of the time you'll use the Visor to select a Paint Effects brush.

---

8. In the Visor, make sure the Paint Effects tab is selected at the top. From the list of folders on the left side, open the flesh folder and select hands.mel. This switches the current brush to the hands brush—you'll see the current brush highlighted in yellow in the Visor (Figure 8.4).

9. Paint some strokes on the canvas. Instead of an inky line, you'll see numerous hands appear as you paint. The hands vary in color while you apply them to the canvas (Figure 8.5).

FIGURE 8.4
Select the
hands.mel
brush from
the Visor.

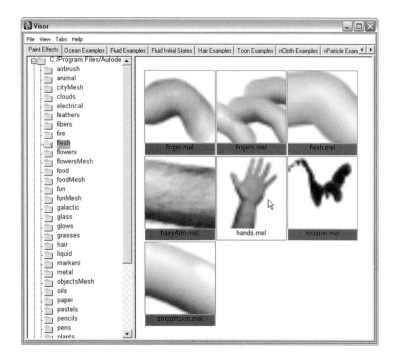

FIGURE 8.5
When the hands
.mel brush is
selected, paint-
ing on the canvas
produces a num-
ber of images of
human hands.

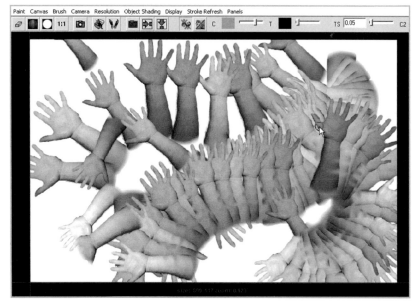

Note that when you switched to the hands brush, a new slider labeled TS appeared on the upper-right corner of the Paint Effects panel menu. This is the Tubes Per Step slider. Increasing this value raises the number of stamp images created when you paint on the canvas.

To interactively change the size of the hands as you paint, hold the B key and drag left or right on the canvas; you'll see the circular brush icon grow as you drag to the right and shrink as you drag to the left.

If you want to change the background color of the canvas, select Canvas ➤ Clear ➤ Options and change the Clear color. Clear the canvas. This removes strokes painted on the canvas and changes the background color at the same time.

10. Open the Visor and select some other brushes; make a mess on the canvas. Try the `defaultSmear.mel` brush found in the `airbrush` folder. When you paint on the canvas, the brush smears the strokes already painted.

Some Paint Effects brushes create colors and images, while others alter the colors and images painted on the canvas. And some, such as the `smearColor.mel` brush, smear the strokes and apply color at the same time (see Figure 8.6).

FIGURE 8.6
Some brushes, such as the smear brush, alter the strokes painted on the canvas.

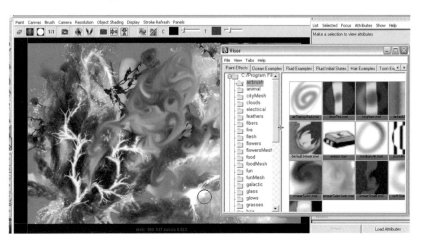

Painting in Scene Mode

You can use Paint Effects brushes to paint in 3D. The strokes actually produce three-dimensional images that are incorporated into the scene. While in the Paint Effects window, you can preview what strokes will look like in a 3D scene.

1. In the Paint Effects window, choose Paint ➤ Paint Scene. You'll be prompted by Maya to save or discard the current image on the canvas. You can click No to discard the image or Yes if you're really proud of it.

The Paint Effects window now displays a perspective view, but notice that the Paint Effects menu is still at the top of the canvas. You are now in scene mode of the Paint Effects window. You can switch cameras using the Panels menu in the Paint Effects menu bar.

2. Open the Visor and choose the `hands.mel` brush from the `flesh` folder. Paint some strokes on the grid.

3. The grid quickly becomes littered with dismembered hands (see Figure 8.7). Tumble around the scene. The hands switch to wireframe mode to help improve performance. If you'd like the hands to remain visible, choose Stroke Refresh ➤ Rendered. Whenever you stop moving the camera, the strokes on the grid will reappear.

FIGURE 8.7

Painting in scene mode allows you to paint strokes directly in a 3D scene.

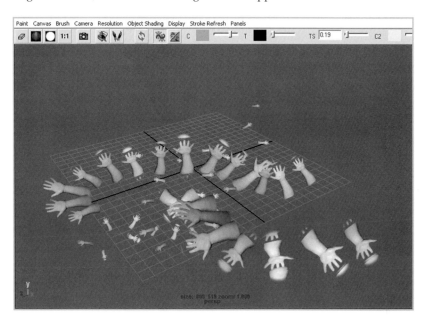

Notice that the brush icon appears as a 3D wireframe sphere. You can change its size interactively by holding the B key and dragging left or right in the perspective view.

Painting on 3D Objects

Once you are comfortable selecting and applying Paint Effects brushes, you're ready to actually paint on some 3D objects. Both NURBS and polygon objects can be painted on the canvas using Paint Effects. You can add grass and flowers to rolling fields, clouds in the sky, and whiskers on an old man's chin.

You're not limited to using the Paint Effects window when adding Paint Effects strokes to a scene. You can apply Paint Effects while working in any camera view in a standard Maya scene. However, if you'd like to see a more accurate preview of what the stroke will look like when rendered, then use the Paint Effects window in scene mode. For these exercises, you'll paint strokes in a scene using the standard Maya viewports.

1. Open the `skull_v01.ma` scene from the `chapter8\scenes` directory on the DVD.

This Maya scene consists of a polygon skull resting on a NURBS pedestal. The pedestal is resting on a polygon plane (see Figure 8.8). This scene will serve as your laboratory as you experiment with Paint Effects brushes.

FIGURE 8.8

The skull_v01.ma scene consists of a polygon skull on a NURBS pedestal.

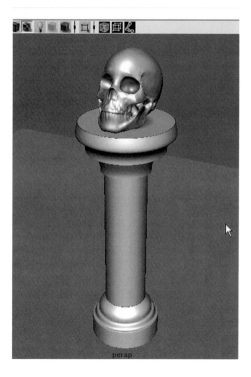

2. Choose Window ➢ General Editors ➢ Visor to open the Visor. Select the plants folder and choose the vineLeafy.mel brush. If you have a hard time reading the brush names, you can Alt+RMB-drag to zoom in on the icons or hold your cursor over one of the icons. The name of the brush appears as a pop-up (see Figure 8.9). Keep the Visor window open while working in this exercise.

3. In the scene, paint across the polygon floor and the pedestal. You'll see the vines appear on the floor but not on the pedestal.

What's actually going on here is that you're painting on the grid, not on any of the 3D objects (including the floor). To paint on an object, you need to make it "paintable."

4. Open the Outliner; you'll see two new nodes named strokeVineLeafy1 and curveVine-Leafy (see Figure 8.10). Select these nodes and press the Backspace button to delete them.

5. Switch to the Rendering menu set. In the Outliner, Shift+click the floor, the pedestal, and the skull; then choose Paint Effects ➢ Make Paintable. Try painting on the floor, the pedestal, and the skull with one or more continuous strokes. Paint across all three objects. Each time you let go of the mouse button or release the pen from the digital tablet, a stroke is created.

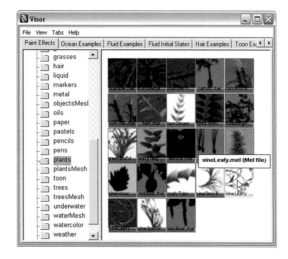

After you've painted a few strokes, you'll notice the vines are on the floor and the pedestal; some will even be stretched between the floor and the pedestal. However, there are no strokes on the skull itself (see Figure 8.11).

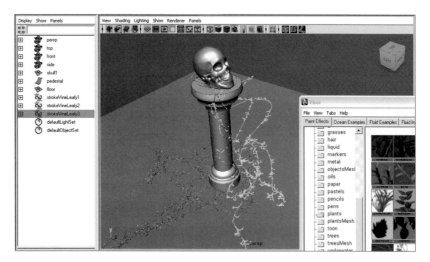

The reason for this is that the skull has no UV texture coordinates applied. This is a common problem when working with Paint Effects on polygon objects. Paint Effects strokes need UV coordinates to determine their position. If an object has no UVs or has poorly mapped UVs, the strokes will not appear or they will behave strangely. This is also true for animated objects that have UVs that move around (this occurs when you apply UVs but forget to delete history on the object). If your Paint Effects are behaving strangely when applied to a polygon object, double-check the UVs of the object.

6. Select the strokeLeafyVine nodes in the Outliner and delete them (notice that there is no curve node—we'll explain this a little further on).

7. Switch to the Polygon menu set and select the skull. Choose Create UVs ➢ Automatic Mapping. This will create a set of UV coordinates projected from six planes around the skull. It may take a few seconds to calculate (see Figure 8.12).

8. When the planes appear, select the skull in the Outliner, and choose Edit ➢ Delete by Type ➢ History. To see the UV coordinates for the skull, select the skull and choose Window ➢ UV Texture Editor.

FIGURE 8.12
UV texture coordinates are created for the skull using the Automatic Mapping method.

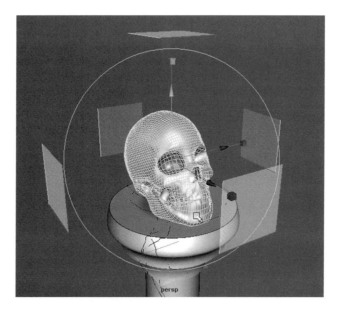

To learn more about creating and working with UV texture coordinates, consult Chapter 11. You can, and should, spend time creating a more efficient UV map for your models, but in a pinch automatic UVs should work well enough. Remember to delete history on the skull object after creating the UVs.

9. Now that the skull has UV coordinates, save the scene as **skull_v02.ma**.

10. Select the skull and choose Paint Effects ➢ Make Paintable. Try painting strokes on the skull; it should work just fine.

ATTACH TO A CURVE

Another way to add a stroke to a 3D object is to attach the stroke to a preexisting NURBS curve. To do this, select the stroke you want in the Visor to load it as the current stroke. Then select the curve and choose Paint Effects ➤ Curve Utilities ➤ Attach To Curve. The stroke appears on the curve without the need to paint it in the scene. Multiple strokes can be attached to the same curve.

Understanding Strokes

When you create a Paint Effects stroke in a scene, several nodes are automatically created and connected. Some of the nodes are visible and some are not. These nodes work together to produce the strokes you see in the scene.

The Anatomy of a Paint Effects Stroke

In this section, you'll look at the nodes created when you add a Paint Effects stroke to a scene. Some of these nodes you will most likely ignore; some of the nodes you will use to edit and animate the strokes.

1. Continue with the scene from the previous section or open the skull_v02.ma scene from the chapter8\scenes directory on the DVD.

2. Switch to the Rendering menu set. Select the skull and choose Paint Effects ➤ Make Paintable.

3. Choose Window ➤ General Editors ➤ Visor to open the Visor. Choose the Grasses folder and select the astroturf.mel brush; the icon turns yellow in the Visor.

4. Zoom in to the skull and start painting grass on the skull. It's a Chia-skull! Paint exactly three strokes. Each time you release the mouse button (or the pen from the tablet), a stroke node is added in the Outliner (see Figure 8.13).

The skull does not have to be selected to paint on it, but it must be made paintable (Paint Effects ➤ Make Paintable—see step 2 in this exercise).

FIGURE 8.13
Astroturf is painted on the surface of the skull.

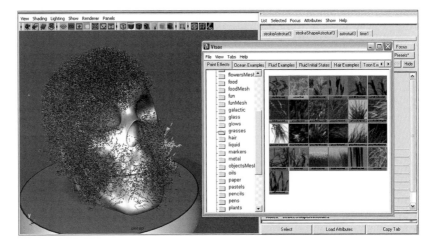

5. Once you have three strokes applied, look in the Outliner. You'll see that a stroke node was created each time you painted on a paintable surface.

Each stroke has a transform node and a shape node. Figure 8.14 shows the Outliner with one of the stroke nodes expanded, so you can see that the stroke's shape node is parented to the stroke's transform node (for more about transform and shape nodes consult Chapter 1).

FIGURE 8.14

The Astroturf nodes appear in the Outliner for each stroke painted on the skull. Each stroke has a transform node and a shape node.

The transform node contains information about the stroke's position, scale, and rotation. Most likely you'll almost never edit the transform node's attributes except maybe to hide the node by changing its Visibility attribute.

The shape node has a number of attributes specific to how the node appears and behaves.

6. Select the strokeAstroturf 1 node and open the Attribute Editor. You'll see a tab for the transform node labeled strokeAstroturf1. Open the Attribute Editor for the shape node by clicking on the strokeShapeAstroturf1 tab in the Attribute Editor.

7. The strokeShapeAstroturf1 node has attributes that control how the stroke is displayed in the scene, how it renders, the pressure settings, and other settings specific to the individual stroke (see Figure 8.15).

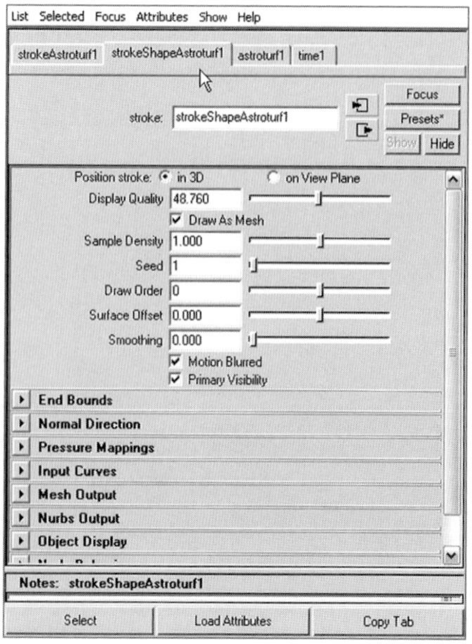

FIGURE 8.15

The strokeShape-Astroturf1 tab contains settings that control the stroke in the scene.

8. In the Attribute Editor, switch to the astroturf1 tab. This tab contains settings for the astroturf1 brush. Editing these settings also changes the way the stroke appears in the scene.

The relationship between the shape node (strokeShapeAstroturf1) and the brush node (astroturf1) can be a little confusing at first. Think of it this way: If you draw on a wall with a crayon, the mark on the wall is the stroke, and the shape node controls the appearance of that particular stroke. The crayon you used to make the mark on the wall is the brush (using Paint Effects terminology). Changing the settings on the brush would be like changing the crayon itself, which would affect the appearance and behavior of the strokes themselves. However, unlike in the real world where changing the crayon only affects each subsequent mark made by the crayon, there is a construction history connection between the stroke and the brush that made the stroke, so that changing the settings on the brush causes a change in the strokes already created in the scene that used that brush.

9. In the astroturf1 tab of the Outliner, set Global Scale to **0.1**. The size of strokeAstroturf1 shrinks. Notice that the other strokes are not affected (Figure 8.16).

FIGURE 8.16
Changing the Global Scale setting in the astroturf1 brush node affects only the size of one of the strokes painted on the skull.

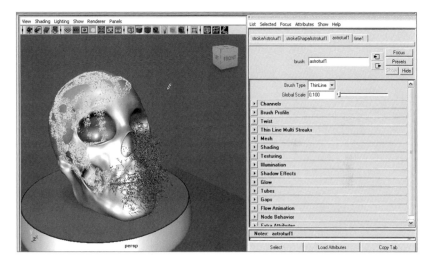

Brush Sharing

Another aspect of the relationship between the brush node (astroturf1) and the shape node (strokeShapeAstroturf1) is that even though you have the same brush selected when you create multiple astroturf strokes on the skull, Maya creates a new brush node for each stroke. It's as if you had a box of identical crayons, and each time you make a mark on the wall, you switch to a new crayon. This is confusing at first, but it means you have more options for varying strokes in a Maya scene. To understand this relationship further, let's take a closer look at the nodes in the scene.

1. In the Outliner, expand the Display menu and turn off DAG Objects Only. This causes the Outliner to display all of the nodes in the scene (for more on DAG nodes, consult Chapter 1).

2. In the Outliner, you'll see several astroturf brush nodes (the nodes with the brush icon; in some cases one of the nodes may be listed with the other astroturf nodes). These nodes are labeled astroturf, astroturf1, astroturf2, and astroturf3.

The first astroturf node is really an instance of the currently selected brush. If you change your current brush selection to a different brush, the node changes to match the name of the new brush. Think of this as a placeholder for the current brush settings. Each time a stroke is created in the scene, a copy of this node is created and associated with the stroke. Figure 8.17 shows how the node name changes when the grass ornamental brush is selected in the Visor (middle image); if the scene is reloaded in Maya, the brush is relabeled brush1.

3. Select astroturf2, and open the Attribute Editor to the astroturf2 node. Making a change to the settings—such as the Global Scale—affects only the associated stroke (in this case strokeAstroTurf2).

FIGURE 8.17
The name of the first brush node changes depending on the brush currently selected in the Visor.

The ability to change the brush settings associated with each stroke means that you can easily create variations of the brushes within the scene. However, let's say you have 200 brush strokes that all use the same brush and you need to change a setting, such as the Global Scale for all of them or maybe even just 99 of them. Instead of changing each brush stroke individually, you can enable brush sharing so that the same brush node affects all of the associated strokes.

4. In the Outliner, Shift+click strokeAstroturf1, strokeAstroturf2, and strokeAstroturf3. Choose Paint Effects ➢ Share One Brush. After a couple seconds, all of the brushes adopt the same Global Scale settings.

If you look in the Outliner, only one brush node is labeled astroturf3. The strokes adopt the brush settings of the last selected brush.

5. Select the astroturf3 node in the Outliner, and change its Global Scale slider. All three strokes update as you make the change.

6. Select the three strokeAstroturf nodes in the Outliner, and choose Paint Effects ➢ Remove Brush Sharing. At the bottom of the Outliner you'll see the three astroturf brush nodes reappear (the numbering of the brushes may change when you remove brush sharing). Now you can return to editing each brush individually.

If you find yourself in a situation in which you need to change 200 different brushes at once, you can select the strokes, enable brush sharing, make the change, and then remove brush sharing to return to a state where each brush can be edited individually. Note that turning on brush sharing applies only to changes made to the settings in the brush node. Each individual brush still has its own shape node. The settings in the shape node can't be shared among multiple brushes. We'll discuss this further in the section on creating custom brushes.

Brush Curve Nodes

When you paint a Paint Effects stroke in a scene, the stroke is attached to a curve that determines the overall shape of the stroke. The curve node itself may be visible or not depending on how the stroke is created. If you paint directly on the grid (Paint Effects ➤ Paint On View Plane), Maya creates a curve in the scene. The curve node is visible in the Outliner. This is demonstrated in steps 3 and 4 of the section "Painting on 3D Objects," earlier in this chapter.

If you select a NURBS object, choose Paint Effects ➤ Make Paintable, and then paint on the surface, Maya creates a curveOnSurface node. You can see the curve on surface if you hide or delete the stroke node after creating it. The curveOnSurface node is not visible in the Outliner, but you can see the connection to this node by selecting the stroke and graphing it in the Hypergraph, (Windows ➤ Hypergraph ➤ Connections), as shown in Figure 8.18.

FIGURE 8.18
A stroke painted on the NURBS pedestal is graphed in the Hypergraph. The node named curveBrushShape121 is the curveOnSurface node.

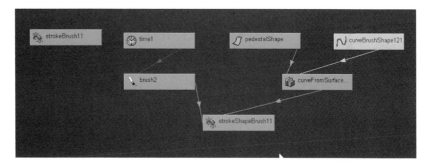

When you paint on a polygon surface, Maya creates a curveFromMeshCom node, which allows Maya to draw a curve on a polygon surface. When you graph a stroke painted on a polygon, you can see both the curve node and the curveFromMeshCom node. You can also see the curves parented to the shape node of the polygon geometry in the Outliner (see Figure 8.19).

FIGURE 8.19
A stroke painted on a polygon surface creates a curve node and a curveFromMesh-Com node.

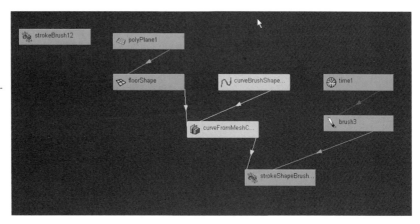

You may not be immediately concerned with the curve nodes Maya creates when you paint a stroke on a surface; however, a situation may arise in which you need to access the curve nodes to make some kind of change to the connection (for instance, if you decide you want to transfer a stroke from a regular curve to a dynamic hair curve). In these situations, it's good to have a basic understanding of how the paintbrushes are actually applied to 3D objects.

Designing Brushes

There's no better way to learn how to use Paint Effects than to get some hands-on training designing a custom brush. Once you have practical experience working with the many settings available for Paint Effects brushes, you'll have a much easier time working with the brushes listed in the Visor.

Most of the time when you create your own brushes you'll start with one of existing brushes available in the Visor and then edit its settings until you get the look and the behavior you want. For instance, if you want to create a creepy nerve growing in a test tube, you may start with a brush preset that looks similar to what you want, such as a tree branch, and then experiment with the settings in the Attribute Editor until the branch looks and acts like a creepy nerve.

Paint Effects is a procedural modeling and animation workflow—meaning that the objects created by Paint Effects and the animation applied to the models are derived from mathematical algorithms (as opposed to pushing and pulling vertices). The math involved is beneath the hood, so you don't need to worry about breaking out the slide rule. However, this does mean that you'll be working with a lot of interconnected sliders, settings, and controls. It's a very experimental process. Changing one setting affects a number of others. There's no particular order in how you edit the settings either; in fact, you'll find yourself bouncing around among the various controls and nodes in the Attribute Editor. Although this may seem overwhelming at first, after some practice you'll see that there's a lot to discover in Paint Effects, and you can create many very unusual and unexpected things, which is always a lot of fun.

Painting with the Default Paintbrush

You'll start by painting with the default paintbrush on the skull and pedestal in the skull scene. At this point there is no particular goal in mind; it's all about experimenting and seeing what happens.

1. Open the skull_v02.ma scene from the chapter8\scenes directory on the DVD. In this scene the polygon skull model already has UV texture coordinates applied, so you are ready to start painting brush strokes.

2. In the Outliner, Shift+click the skull1 and pedestal objects. Switch to the Rendering menu set, and choose Paint Effects ➤ Make Paintable.

3. Choose Window ➤ General Editors ➤ Visor to open the Visor. From the airbrush folder, choose the defaultPaint.mel brush.

4. Choose Paint Effects ➤ Paint Effects Tool ➤ Options. In the options, set the Pressure Mapping 1 setting to Width.

5. Rotate the perspective view so you can see part of the top of the skull. Paint a stroke starting at the top of the skull. Create a meandering stroke that moves down the skull onto the pedestal. If you are using a digital tablet, vary the pressure as you paint on the surfaces. The stroke will change in width, growing thicker when more pressure is applied.

6. Avoid painting around the back of the pedestal or on areas you can't see. This creates a long, stretched section of the stroke. You want a nice continuous stroke that moves down across the surface of the skull and pedestal. Use Figure 8.20 as a reference.

FIGURE 8.20

Create a meandering paint stroke, starting from the top of the skull and moving down to the floor. Changes in pressure applied to the pen on a digital tablet cause variations in the stroke width.

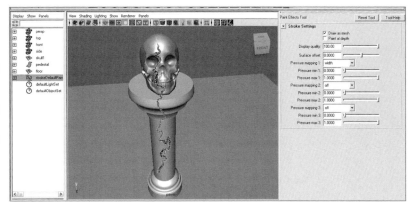

If you want the stroke to continue onto the floor, you can make the floor object paintable as well, but sometimes this can make painting the strokes trickier. When a NURBS surface has a paintable polygon object behind it in the perspective view, you may find that the stroke jumps from the pedestal to a point on a distant part of the floor. It may be easier to create a number of strokes on the skull and pedestal first and then make the floor paintable and paint new strokes to continue the lines drawn on the pedestal.

7. Use the same method to paint four or five more brush strokes. Start each stroke at the top and move down (see Figure 8.21).

8. Save the scene as **skull_v03.ma**. To see a version of the scene so far, open skull_v03.ma from the **chapter8\scenes** directory on the DVD.

FIGURE 8.21

Paint additional strokes on the surfaces.

Brush Types

In this section, you'll learn about the various brush types. You'll start at the top of the brush settings and work your way down. However, keep in mind that when working on your own brush designs, you will most likely not edit the settings in any particular order. A variety of brushes are available.

The **Paint** type brush creates strokes that are a series of dots stamped along the path of the stroke. The strokes look much smoother when a higher number of dots is used.

Smear and **Blur** type brushes distort or soften (respectively) the appearance of paint strokes applied to the canvas.

ThinLine/MultiStreak type brushes render strokes as groups of thin lines. This works well for hair and whisker effects.

The **Erase** type brush creates a black hole in the alpha channel of a scene. It can be used to paint holes in the rendered image.

The **Mesh** type brush actually creates geometry from the stroke. This type of brush works well for hard-edge objects that appear close to the camera, such as trees or buildings. There are several folders in the Visor that contain mesh type brush strokes. Using the mesh type stroke is not the same as converting a stroke to polygons. Mesh type strokes, like all of the other types, will not render in mental ray.

1. Continue with the scene from the previous section or open the skull_v03.ma scene from the chapter8\scenes directory. If you don't have a digital tablet, you may want to use the scene on the DVD so you can see the effect that variations in pressure have on the strokes.

2. Shift+click the strokes in the Outliner, and choose Paint Effects ➢ Share One Brush to enable brush sharing.

3. Select any of the brushes and open the Attribute Editor. Select the defaultPaint tab. (The name of the tab may vary depending on how many brushes you have in your scene. In the example scene this tab is labeled defaultPaint6.)

You can set the type of brush using the Brush Type drop-down list at the top of the settings. The brush types determine how the strokes are constructed (see Figure 8.22).

FIGURE 8.22

The type of brush is set using the menu at the top of the Attribute Editor for the brush node.

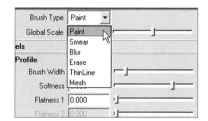

RENDERING BRUSH TYPES

Paint Effects brush strokes render only in Maya software. There are some workarounds that allow you to render Paint Effects in mental ray. These include converting the strokes to polygons or NURBS. However, this won't work for all brush types. For instance, the smear brush type will not smear pixels when rendered with mental ray.

The Global Scale slider sets an overall scale for the stroke. This can be adjusted to ensure that the stroke matches the scale of the other objects in the scene. When you use the b hot key to adjust the size of the brush, you are interactively setting its global scale.

4. Make sure the Brush Type is set to Paint and the Global Scale to 5.

Brush Profile

The settings in the Brush Profile area control how the brush looks when rendered.

1. Open the Render Settings Window (Window ➢ Rendering Editors ➢ Render Settings). Set the Renderer to Maya Software. In the Maya Software tab, set the Quality preset to Production.

2. Open the Render Preview window and create a test render of the scene. Store the image in the Render Preview window (choose File ➢ Keep Image In Render View).

Adjusting the Brush Width value changes the size of the area covered by the brush stroke. For simple strokes, such as the default stroke, it appears as though changing the Brush Width is similar to changing the Global Scale. However, with more complex brushes that use tubes, changing the Brush Width changes the amount of area covered by the tubes. For instance, paint a stroke using the astroturf brush; the Brush Width changes the width of the area covered by the grass. Changing the Global Scale changes the overall size of the stroke, including the size of each blade of grass. This is shown in Figure 8.23.

FIGURE 8.23
Three strokes are painted on the grid using the astroturf brush. The two strokes on the left have different Brush Width values; the stroke on the right has a larger Global Scale.

3. Increasing the brush Softness creates a fuzzy edge to the rendered stroke. Set Softness to **1**, and create an image (see Figure 8.24).

4. Store the image in the render view, set Softness to **0**, and create another test render. Store the image in the render view, and compare the two renders using the scroll bar at the bottom of the Render View window. Notice that the softer brush appears thinner than the brush in the render with 0 Softness.

Negative Softness values create a very unusual-looking brush.

5. Set Softness to **0.5**. Set Flatness1 to **0**.

FIGURE 8.24
Increasing brush Softness adds a fuzzy edge to the rendered strokes.

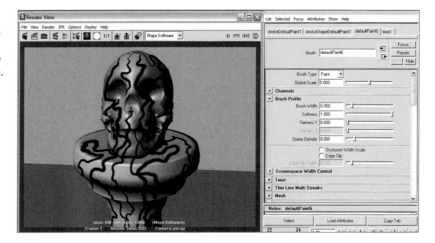

The defaultPaint brush is a rounded tube. Increasing the Flatness1 setting makes the brush appear as a flat strip. You can then use the Twist controls (under the Twist rollout a little farther down in the Attribute Editor) to rotate the stroke around its path curve. Increasing Twist Rate twists the stroke like a ribbon. Flatness2 is available only for strokes that use tubes (tubes are discussed later in the chapter).

Stamp Density controls how many dots are used to create the stroke when the Type is set to Paint. Increasing this setting creates a smoother stroke; decreasing the setting breaks the stroke into visible dots.

6. Set Stamp Density to **1** and create a test render. The strokes appear as dotted lines. This is shown in Figure 8.25.

7. Set Stamp Density to **8**.

If you want the brush size to remain constant regardless of how close the camera is to the stroke, you can use the Screen Space Width controls. These controls are very useful when working with toon lines. They will be discussed in more detail in the Toon Shading section later in the chapter.

FIGURE 8.25
When you decrease Stamp Density, the brush appears as a series of dots.

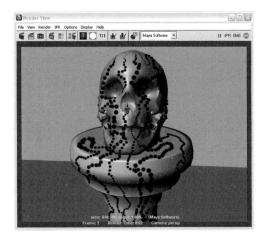

Coloring Strokes

In the Attribute Editor, scroll down to the Shading controls and expand the Shading rollout. This contains some basic controls to adjust the color of the strokes. These controls are very simple. The Color 1 slider applies a flat color to the stroke. This color is mixed with the color chosen in the Incandescence control. When the Transparency slider is increased, the incandescence has a stronger influence on the shading of the stroke. A transparent stroke with a bright incandescence setting creates a nice neon glow or laser beam effect.

1. Set Color to bright red, Incandescence to a very dim yellow, and Transparency to a very light gray.

2. Expand the Glow rollout. Set Glow to **0.256**. Set Glow Color to a dim red. Set Glow Spread to 2.

3. The Shader Glow setting adds a more realistic glow to the stroke. Set this to **0.074**.

4. Create a test render. A render using these settings is shown in Figure 8.26.

5. Save the scene as **skull_v04.ma**.

FIGURE 8.26
Add a glow to incandescent strokes. The Shader Glow setting adds a more realistic glow.

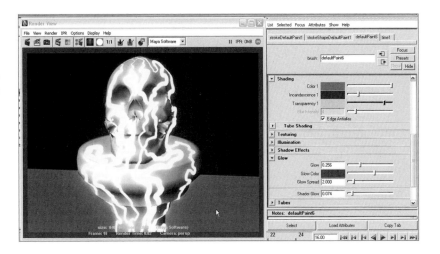

WORKING WITH THE SHADER GLOW NODE

To fine-tune the look of a glowing stroke, set the value for the Shader Glow slider above zero and select the shader glow node in the Hypershade. The shader glow node is a global control for all glowing shaders and strokes in the scene. You can spend a fair amount of time working with these settings to produce glowing effects. Be aware that when you render an animation that has glowing shaders, you may see a noticeable flickering. To remove the flickering, turn off the Auto Exposure setting. When you do this, the glows will appear blown out. You can lower the Glow Intensity slider in the Glow Attributes to eliminate the blown-out look in the render.

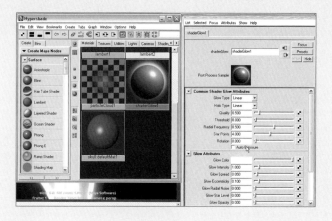

Texturing Strokes

To create variation in the surface of a stroke, you can apply textures to the color, opacity, and even the displacement of the strokes.

1. Continue with the scene from the previous section or open the skull_v04.ma scene from the chapter8\scenes directory.

2. In the Attributes for the defaultPaint node, set the Glow and Shader Glow settings to **0**. Set the Glow Color to black.

3. In the Shading rollout, set the Incandescence at **1** and Transparency color to black.

4. Expand the Texturing rollout. Click the box next to Map Color. This applies a texture to the color channel.

5. Scroll down in the Attribute Editor until you can see the Texture Type drop-down list. Leave this set to Checker. Create a test render (see Figure 8.27).

FIGURE 8.27
A checker pattern
is applied to the
color channel as a
texture.

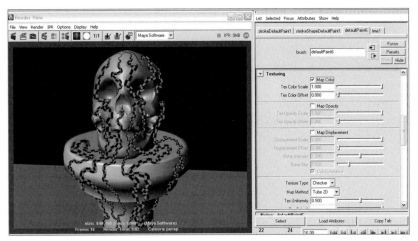

FIGURE 8.27
A checker pattern
is applied to the
color channel as a
texture.

Notice that the red color still appears in the texture. When Texture Color Scale is set to 1, the color chosen in the Shading section of the brush attributes overrides the colors chosen in the Tex Color 1 and Tex Color 2 sliders. Lowering Tex Color Scale to 0 replaces the red color in the checker pattern with the color chosen in Tex Color 1. The Tex Color Scale and Tex Color Offset sliders are similar to the Color Gain and Color Offset sliders found in the Color Balance section of a standard texture node. For more information on how the Color Balance and Color Offset controls work, consult Chapter 2.

The Map Method setting controls how the texture is applied to the strokes. Both the Tube 2D and Tube 3D methods wrap the texture around the stroke. However, when Map 2D is used, the texture is always centered on the stroke. This eliminates any visible seam as the texture wraps around the stroke. Using the Map 3D method may give better results if the view of the stroke is animated.

Using Full View maps the texture across the entire view scene in the viewport.

6. Set Texture Type to File. Scroll down and click the folder next to Image Name. Use the File Browser dialog box to select the metalPlate.tif file from the chapter8\ sourceimages directory on the DVD. Figure 8.28 shows the image.

FIGURE 8.28
The metal plate
texture that will
be applied to the
stroke

7. Set Map Method to Full View and Tex Color Scale to **0**. Create a test render. The image is revealed by the stroke. The image fills the viewable area. If this stroke covered most of the screen, you would see the entire metalPlate image (see Figure 8.29).

FIGURE 8.29
Full View maps the texture to the stroke based on the viewable area of the scene.

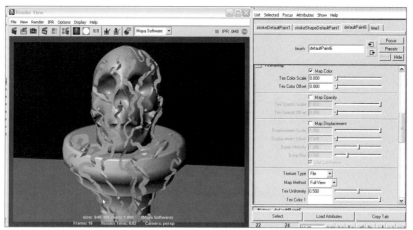

One possible use for this mapping method would be to animate a logo reveal by mapping an image file of a logo to the stroke using the Full View method. The stroke could then be animated by drawing on the screen to reveal the logo. Animating strokes will be covered a little later in the chapter.

The Brush Start method works similarly to the Full View method. However, the image is scaled to fit within the viewable area defined by the stroke.

You can map a texture to the opacity of the stroke and use a texture as a displacement. When using a displacement, Stroke Type should be set to Mesh, and you may need to increase the Tube Sections and Sub Sections settings in the Mesh controls. Setting Softness to 0 helps make the displacement more obvious. At this point you can see how designing strokes involves a lot of moving back and forth among settings in the Attribute Editor.

8. Disable Map Color and Map Opacity. Enable Map Displacement.

9. Scroll up to the top of the Attribute Editor, and set Brush Type to Mesh. Set Softness to **0**. In the Mesh rollout, set Tube Sections to **30** and Sub Sections to **20**.

10. Scroll back down to the Texturing section. Set Texture Type to Fractal.

11. At the bottom of the Texturing rollout, set Fractal Amplitude to **0.256**.

12. Expand the Illumination settings just below the Texturing rollout, and enable Illuminated and Real Lights.

13. Set Lighting Based Width to **0.68**. This causes lighter areas of the stroke to become thinner.

14. Create a test render. You can see that the fractal texture displaces the stroke, making it appear lumpy (see Figure 8.30).

15. Save the scene as **skull_v05.ma**. To see a version of the scene, open the skull_v05.ma scene from the chapter8\scenes directory on the DVD.

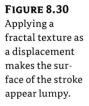

FIGURE 8.30
Applying a fractal texture as a displacement makes the surface of the stroke appear lumpy.

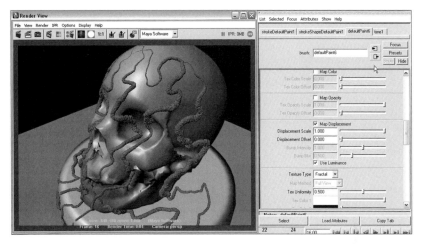

CONVERTING DISPLACED STROKES TO POLYGONS

The displacement created by the texture persists even when you convert the Paint Effects stroke to polygons (Modify ➤ Convert Paint Effects To Polygons). Converting strokes is covered later in the chapter.

Creating Tubes

Paint Effects brushes become much more interesting when you add tubes. Tubes are smaller brush strokes that radiate from the center of the area defined by the brush width. Using tubes, you can create a series of crawling vines as opposed to the long singular strands created by the default brush. The tubes themselves can grow branches, twigs, leaves, and flowers. A complex brush can create a row of trees. Each tree can have its own branches and leaves.

In this section, you'll create crawling vines over the surface of the skull and pedestal using the strokes painted in the first part of the chapter.

Tubes Controls

You'll start by adding tubes to the strokes in the skull_v04.ma scene. Tubes have a lot of controls. Rather than describe what every control does, this section uses hands-on exercises to get you used to using the controls. The goal is to add curling vines to the stroke.

The Maya documentation has descriptions for every control available for Paint Effects. Go to the help files and enter **Paint Effects** into the Search field. The page listed as Paint Effects Brush Settings provides you with brief descriptions of all of the controls found in the brush node for a Paint Effects stroke. In this exercise, you'll add tubes to the strokes painted on the skull and pedestal.

1. Open the skull_v04.ma scene from the chapter8\scenes directory on the DVD, or go back to your own version 4 of the scene.

2. Select the strokeDefaultPaint1 stroke in the Outliner, and open the Attribute Editor to the defaultPaint6 tab (the number of the stroke may be different in your version of the scene).

3. Under Brush Profile, set Softness to **0.1**.

4. In the Shading section, set Color to a dark brown. Set Incandescence to **1** and Transparency1 to **0**.

5. In the Glow section, set Glow to **0**, Glow Color to black, and Shader Glow to **0**.

6. Expand the Tubes section and activate Tubes. Immediately you'll see the strokes appear as long, thin spikes shooting from the stroke path (Figure 8.31). The thick central brush stroke is gone.

7. Turn off Tube Completion. When Tube Completion is off, tubes near the end of a Paint Effect stroke are not complete, just as younger branches at the top of a tree may be shorter than older branches toward the bottom.

8. Expand the Creation settings. These settings define how the tubes grow from the stroke. To set the number of tubes, adjust the Tubes Per Step. Set this to **0.8**.

FIGURE 8.31
Turning Tubes on creates long thin lines that grow from the original brush stroke.

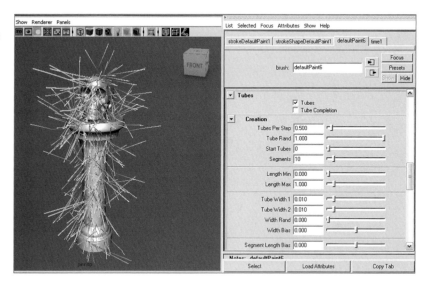

REVERSED TUBES

If you encounter a situation where you have painted a single stroke across multiple surfaces, and the tubes on one surface seem to face the opposite direction compared to the tubes on the other surface, you need to reverse the normals of one of the surfaces. This means going to the Polygon menu set and choosing Normals ➤ Reverse. If a NURBS surface is causing the problem, then go to the Surfaces menu set and choose Edit NURBS ➤ Reverse Surface. Unfortunately this may adversely affect your painted strokes. You may need to delete the strokes and repaint them across the reversed surfaces.

Tubes Rand randomizes the placement of tubes along the stroke. Start Tubes is useful if you want a single tube or a clump of tubes to appear at the start of the stroke. So if you want to precisely position a tree or a bolt of lighting, you can set Start Tubes to 1 and Tubes Per Step to 0 and draw a short stroke wherever you want the tree or lightning placed in the scene.

9. Set Segments to **60**.

Each tube is made up of segments. By increasing the number of segments per tube, the tube will appear smoother. This also exaggerates any curling or bending applied to the stroke. If the growth of the tube is animated, more segments will mean that the tube takes longer to reach its final length. We cover animation of tubes later in the chapter.

10. Length Min and Length Max define a range of lengths for the tubes. Setting these to the same value means all the tubes are at the same length. To create a more random look for the vines, set Length Min to **0.165** and Length Max to **0.579**.

11. Tube Width 1 controls the width of a stroke at its base; Tube Width 2 controls the width of the tube at the tip. Set Tube Width 1 to **0.02** and Tube Width 2 to **0**. This creates a pointy tip to the tubes.

The Width Rand slider randomizes the width of the tubes. It's a multiplier, so in some cases it increases the width of some of the tubes beyond the range specified by Tube Width 1 and Tube Width 2. The Width Bias slider helps bias the randomization of widths.

12. Set Width Rand to **0.65** and Width Bias to **-0.5**. The negative bias means the tubes are more likely to be thin than thick.

13. Set Segment Length Bias to **0.4**. This means that segments closer to the base of each tube will be longer. If you zoom in on a selected tube, you can see the segments in the wireframe display (Figure 8.32). Setting a negative Segment Length Bias would produce longer segments toward the tip of each tube.

FIGURE 8.32
Zooming in on a selected tube reveals its segmentation in the wireframe display.

14. Set Segment Width Bias to **0.175**. A positive Segment Width Bias makes longer segments thicker. A negative value would make shorter segments thicker.

You can also make tubes flatter at the base or tip using the Flatness 1 and Flatness 2 sliders. These controls are found in the Brush Profile section at the top of the Attribute Editor.

15. Save the scene as **skull_v06.ma**. To see a version of the scene to this point, open the skull_v06.ma scene from the chapter8\scenes directory on the DVD.

TUBE SEGMENTS FOR MESH TYPE STROKES

If you use the Mesh type brush, which renders strokes as geometry, as opposed to the Paint type brush, which renders stokes as dots, you can increase the number of segments using the sliders in the Mesh section toward the top of the attribute list.

Width Scale

If you want more precise control over the shape of the tubes, you can use the ramp curve in the Width Scale section of the Tube Creation controls.

1. Continue with the scene from the previous section or open the skull_v06.ma scene from the chapter8\scenes directory of the DVD.

The Width Scale controls modify the settings used to define the width of the tubes. To more easily see how the controls work, you can set the Width1 and Width2 sliders to the same value.

2. In the Creation rollout, set Width1 and Width2 to **0.02**.

3. You can edit the width curve in the Attribute Editor, but sometimes it is easier to edit it in a separate window. Click the arrow button to the right of the Width Scale curve. The curve opens in a new window (Figure 8.33).

4. Add points to the curve, and move them around to define a shape for the tubes.

FIGURE 8.33
Clicking the arrow button to the right of the curve opens a larger curve for editing.

The curve describes the profile of each tube, so to create a bulbous end to the tubes, make the points at the right end of the tube higher and the points on the left end lower. The Selected Position and Selected Value fields allow you to enter numeric values for each selected point. You can type values higher than 1 in the Selected Value slider to make parts of the profile even thicker (see Figure 8.34).

FIGURE 8.34

A test render is created after changing the profile of the tubes using the Width Scale Editor.

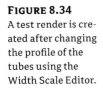

The Interpolation controls set the smoothness of the line to the right of the selected point. To make a more curved profile, set Interpolation to Smooth or Spline.

5. Create test renders as you make changes to the curve to see how the profile will look (Figure 8.34).

6. Save the scene as **skull_v07.ma**. To see a version of the scene to this point, open the skull_v07.ma scene from the chapter8\scenes directory on the DVD.

Tube Color

The controls for setting the color of tubes are found in the Shading section of the brush Attribute Editor under Tube Shading.

1. Open the skull_v06.ma scene from the chapter8\scenes directory, or return to your own saved version of the scene.

2. Select the strokeDefaultPaint1 brush in the Outliner, and open the Attribute Editor to the defaultPaint6 tab.

3. Under Shading, expand the Tube Shading section.

4. Click on the Color2 swatch, and use the Color Chooser to select a reddish-brown color.

The color at the base of the tube is determined by the settings in the Color1 control in the Shading section. The Color2 slider determines the color at the tip of the tube. You can also control incandescence and transparency at the tube tips using the Incandescence2 and Transparency2 controls.

To add variation to the tubes, you can use the Rand sliders. Hue Rand varies the hue of the tubes; the higher the value, the more variation in the colors of the tubes. Similarly the Sat Rand slider randomizes color saturation, and the Val rand slider randomizes value.

5. Set the Val Rand slider to **0.125**.

6. The Root Fade and Tip Fade sliders add transparency to the ends of the tubes. Set Root Fade to **0.025** and create a test render. Figure 8.35 shows the results of changing the Tube Shading settings.

FIGURE 8.35

Edit the tube colors by using the controls found in the Tube Shading section of the Attribute Editor.

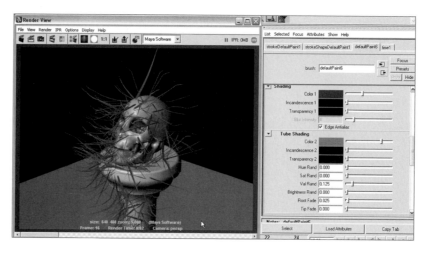

Tube Direction

The sliders in the Tube Direction section control the overall direction in which the tubes point. As you develop your own custom brushes, you're likely to return to this section a lot because changes further in the process may require you to tweak the tube direction.

You're likely to constantly experiment with these controls as you work, but it's good to have an understanding of what the controls actually do.

Setting Tube Direction to Along Normal makes the tubes point in a direction based on the normal of the path curve. Usually this means perpendicular to the curve itself. Setting Tube Direction to Along Path means the tubes point in the direction of the path.

Elevation refers to the direction the tubes point up and down, relative to the path. If you were lifting a flagpole to position it in the ground, the elevation of the pole at 0 would mean the flagpole is lying on the ground, and an elevation of 1 would mean the flagpole is sticking straight up out of the ground. Values above 1 push the flagpole over in the opposite direction.

Azimuth refers to the direction the tubes point as they rotate around their origin on the path. If you pointed a flashlight straight in front of you, the azimuth of the light beam would be 1. If you pointed it 90 degrees to the side, the azimuth would be 0.5. At 1.5 the flashlight would point in the opposite direction from 0.5 (see Figure 8.36).

FIGURE 8.36
The top image
demonstrates
changes in the
elevation of a
3D arrow. The
bottom image
demonstrates
changes in the
azimuth of a
3D arrow.

Together the sliders can be used to define a range of elevation and azimuth for the tubes. How these sliders work is affected by the setting used in Tube Direction. Keep in mind that if Elevation Min and Elevation Max are both set to 1, changing the azimuth will have no effect.

1. Set Tube Direction to Along Normal.

2. Set Elevation Min to **0.273**, Elevation Max to **0.843**, Azimuth Min to **-0.686**, and Azimuth Max to **0.256**, as shown in Figure 8.37.

3. Save the scene as **skull_v08.ma**.

FIGURE 8.37
The direction of
the tubes is con-
trolled using the
Elevation and
Azimuth sliders.

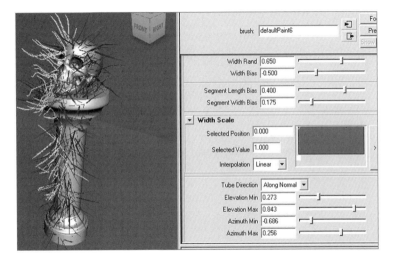

 **Real World Scenario**

PAINT EFFECTS CARDS

You may be required, at some point in your career, to create a very dense forest or a crowd of people that will fill the background of a scene. To maximize rendering efficiency, it's common practice to map images to flat pieces of geometry. These *flats* (also known as *billboards*) can be placed in the background to fill in spaces in the render. If they are far from the camera, in most cases no one will notice that they are not actually 3D objects. You can use Paint Effects to quickly paint these flats into the scene. Here are the steps to accomplish this:

1. Create a stroke in the scene. Paint it in the area where you want the flats to appear.

2. Turn on Tubes and Tube Completion for the stroke.

3. In the Stroke Profile section, set Flatness1 and Flatness2 to a value of 1.

4. In the Creation section, set Segments to 1. Lower the Tubes Per Step to increase the amount of space between flats.

5. Set the Tube Direction to Along Normal. Set the Elevation Min and Max and the Azimuth Min and Max to 1.

6. Make the tubes match the proportions of the image you want to map to the flats. Set Length Min and Length Max to the height value and TubeWidth1 and TubeWidth2 to the same value.

7. In the Texturing options, activate Map Color and Map Opacity. Set Texture Type to File, and use the Image Name field to select the image file. Use a file texture that has an alpha channel.

8. In the Twist controls, activate Forward Twist. This ensures that the tubes rotate to face the camera. Note that the automatic rotation occurs around only a single axis of the flats.

9. In the Shading section, you can add a slight randomization to the Hue, Saturation, and Value of the images to increase variety. Create several similar brushes that use different images, and overlap brush strokes to create a dense forest or thick crowd. Open the pfxFlatForest.ma scene from the chapter8\scenes folder on the DVD to see an example of this technique.

Add Growth

You can increase the complexity of the objects you create with Paint Effects by adding branches, leaves, twigs, flowers, and buds. These elements grow from tubes and can be used to create very natural-looking organic objects.

Paint Effects Tubes use L-systems to control the growth of tubes, branches, and twigs. An *L-system* is a mathematical language developed by the Hungarian botanist Aristid Lindenmayer in 1968 to describe the growth of plants. While using Paint Effects you won't need to work directly with L-systems, but if you're curious as to how Paint Effects creates such natural-looking objects, you may want to do some reading on L-systems.

The Growth Controls

The options for adding branches, twigs, leaves and other natural elements are found in the Growth rollout in the brush Attribute Editor (see Figure 8.38).

FIGURE 8.38
You can add branches, twigs, leaves, and other elements using the options in the Growth section of the Brush attributes.

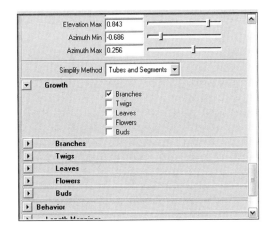

These options are:

Branches   Activating this option creates one or more splits in the growth of Paint Effects tubes.

Twigs   Activating Twigs creates additional tube sections that grow from both the tube and the tube branches.

Leaves   Leaves are a secondary set of tubes that grow off of the main tubes. There are controls available for coloring and shaping leaves that are very similar to the controls available for tubes.

Flowers   Flowers are similar to leaves in that they are another tube system that grows from the original tubes. A variety of controls allow you to simulate real flowers, such as roses, or to create your own unique flowers.

Buds   Buds are tiny tubes that are placed at the ends of branches and leaves.

These elements can be added in any combination. It's usually a good idea to start out by adding one element at a time to limit the amount of confusion that can be caused by working with so many controls.

The elements can be used to imitate real plants, and they can also be repurposed to create any number of custom objects. Flowers can be turned into eyeballs; leaves can become hands. The names given to these elements describe the basic idea behind how they work, but they are not limited to replicating just plants.

Adding Branches and Twigs

In this section, you'll continue to experiment by making edits to the tubes growing along the skull and pedestal.

1. Continue with the scene from the previous section or open the skull_v08.ma scene from the chapter8\scenes directory on the DVD.

2. Select strokeDefaultPaint1 in the Outliner, and open the Attribute Editor to the default-Paint6 tab.

3. Scroll down to the Creation rollout controls, and set Tubes Per Step to **0.25**. Reducing the number of tubes improves scene performance and makes it easier to see what's going on.

4. Scroll down to the Growth section, and activate the Branches option. Expand the Branches controls (see Figure 8.39).

FIGURE 8.39
Adjusting the Branches controls defines how the tubes split into branches.

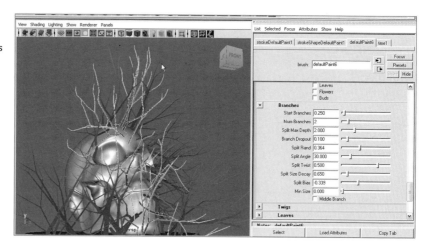

5. Set these attributes for the controls:

Start Branches: **0.25**. This defines the number of branches at the tube root.

Num Branches: **2**. This specifies the number of branches at each split.

Split Max Depth: **2**. This sets a limit to the number of branches that can be created.

Branch Dropout: **0.1**. This prunes the number of branches to create a more natural look.

Split Rand: **0.364**. This randomizes branch spacing.

Split Angle: **30**. This sets the angle where the branches split.

Split Twist: **0.5**. This rotates the branches relative to the root.

Split Size Decay: **0.65**. As this value approaches 1, the branches become closer in size to the original tube. Making this value larger than 1 produces branches that are larger than the root.

Split Bias: **-0.339**. This moves the split closer or farther from the root. Positive values move the branch split closer to the tip.

Min Size: **0**. This sets a minimum size for the pruning created using the Branch Dropout control.

Middle Branch: Off. When this is on, the tube continues to grow through the middle of the split.

6. Save the scene as **skull_v09.ma**.

Twigs are very similar in concept to branches, and their controls are similar to those used in the Creation section of the Attribute Editor. Experiment using twigs with and without branches. Sometimes they can be used to extend branches; sometimes they work well as an alternative to branches.

Adding Leaves and Flowers

Leaves create another set of tubes that grow from tubes, twigs, and branches. You can shape and color them to create some interesting Paint Effects objects.

1. Continue with the scene from the previous section or open the skull_v09.ma scene from the chapter8\scenes directory on the DVD.

2. Select strokeDefaultPaint1 in the Outliner, and open the Attribute Editor to the default-Paint6 tab.

3. In the Growth section, activate Leaves. Immediately the leaves look huge compared to the rest of the Paint Effects brush.

4. Scroll down to the Leaves controls. Set Leaf Length to **0.022**, Leaf Base Width to **0.058**, and Leaf Tip Width to **0.05**.

5. The leaf size and shape can be edited using the Leaf Width Scale curve. This is similar to the Tube Width controls discussed earlier in the chapter. Expand the curve control by clicking the arrow button to the right of the curve, and make changes.

If you shape the leaf using the profile curve, you'll need to set Brush Type to Mesh; otherwise the changes made using the curve won't show up in the render.

You can map an image to the leaves to increase the realism of the Paint Effects brush. A leaf is used in this example, but keep in mind that you can use anything you want.

6. Set Leaf Color 1 and 2 to white. Scroll down and uncheck the option for Leaf Use Branch Tex. Click the folder next to Image Name, and use the file browser to find the leaf.tif image in the chapter8\sourceimages folder on the DVD.

The leaf image has an alpha channel, which can be used to define the shape of the leaf.

7. Remove any changes made to the Leaf Width Scale curve so it appears as a solid gray box.

8. Create a test render of the image (see Figure 8.40).

FIGURE 8.40

Map an image to the leaves to create more realism.

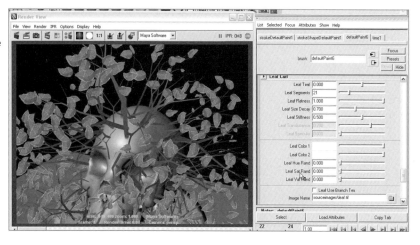

LEAF RENDER QUALITY

If you notice that the edges of the leaf image look a little jagged, you can improve the render quality by opening the Render Settings window. In the Maya Software tab, you can scroll to the bottom, expand the Paint Effects Rendering options, and enable Oversampling.

---

9. Set Brush Type to Mesh. Images will work on both Mesh and Paint brush types, but some of the deformations you can apply to the leaves look better when Brush Type is set to Mesh.

10. Try experimenting with different settings for Leaf Curl, Leaf Twirl, Leaf Hue Rand, Leaf Sat Rand, Leaf Bend, and Leaf Val Rand. Increasing the Leaf Segments value will improve the quality when you increase the Leaf Bend settings.

Lowering the Leaf Flatness setting creates a more three-dimensional shape. This works well when you shape the profile of the leaf using the Leaf Width Scale curve editor.

Activating Leaf Forward Twist ensures that the leaf always faces the rendering camera.

11. Save the scene as skull_v10.ma. To see a version of the scene to this point, open the skull_v10.ma scene from the chapter8\scenes directory on the DVD.

Flowers are very similar to leaves. To add flowers, activate the Flowers options under Growth. To change the size of the flowers, use the Petal Length, Petal Base Width, and Petal Tip Width sliders in the Flowers section of the Attributes.

PAINT EFFECTS DISPLAY CONTROLS

As you add more elements to the scene, it may slow down the performance of Maya. You can reduce the display quality of the strokes in the scene or disable Display As Mesh. This makes working in the scene much more responsive.

The display quality controls are found on the Shape node of each stroke—not in the brush controls. So you need to set each one individually. However, if you have a lot of strokes in the scene, you can Shift+click them all in the Outliner and then change the display settings in the SHAPES section of the Channel Box.

Reducing the Display Percent makes it look as though parts of the stroke are being removed, but this will not actually affect how the stroke looks when rendered. Turning off Draw As Mesh makes the brush appear as a curve in the scene.

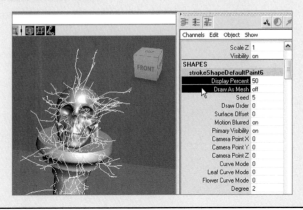

Shaping Strokes with Behavior Controls

The controls found in the Behavior section of the brush attributes are similar to deformers that you apply to models. You can use behaviors to shape the strokes and control how they appear in the scene.

Forces

You'll continue using the skull-and-pedestal scene to see how the stroke can be further shaped using the settings in the Behavior section of the brush node.

1. Continue with the scene from the previous section or open the skull_v10.ma scene from the chapter8\scenes directory on the DVD.

2. Select strokeDefaultPaint1 in the Outliner, and open the Attribute Editor to the default-Paint6 tab.

3. In the Growth section, deactivate Leaves so that you can clearly see the tubes and branches crawling on the skull.

4. Scroll down, and expand the Behavior rollout.

The order in which these settings are placed in the Attribute Editor is not exactly intuitive. Displacements are listed above Forces, but I have found that it's easier to work with the Forces settings first to establish a shape to the strokes and then use the Displacement settings to add detail to the shape of the strokes.

5. Expand the Forces rollout.

The various controls in the Forces rollout offer different ways of pushing and pulling the strokes. They can be used separately or in combination. Once again, applying these settings is an experimental process.

6. Increase the Path Follow slider—this causes the strokes to grow along the length of the path used to define the stroke. A setting of 1 causes the strokes to cling to the original path. A negative value makes the strokes grow in the opposite direction.

7. Set Path Follow to **0** and try adjusting Path Attract. This slider causes the original stroke to influence the growth of the tubes and branches. Increasing this value makes the tubes bend toward the path; decreasing this value makes the tubes bend away.

8. Set Path Follow to **0.256** and Path Attract to **-0.4**.

The Curve Follow and Curve Attract settings work the same way as Path Follow and Path Attract; however, they use a separate control curve rather than the original path curve. If there is no control curve present, these settings have no effect.

To add a control curve, draw a curve in the scene. Select the strokes in the Outliner and the curve, and choose Paint Effects ➢ Curve Utilities ➢ Set Control Curves. More than one curve can be used. The Max Distance slider sets a maximum distance for the influence the control curve has on the stroke. A control curve can be attached to an animated object or character so that when the character comes close to the strokes, they bend away from or toward the character. Control curves can be used to more precisely define the overall shape of the strokes. For instance, if you need ivy to grow in a very specific way over the arched doorway of a building, you can use multiple control curves to shape the ivy strokes.

9. Set Random to **0.5** to add some additional randomization to the direction in which the strokes grow.

The Uniform Force and Gravity controls apply a force to the strokes along a specified axis. You can define the axis of influence by entering numeric values in the Uniform Force fields. By increasing the Gravity slider, the force is applied in the negative Y direction.

10. Set Gravity to **0.5**.

When applying forces, you may find that the strokes are getting pushed through the surface they have been painted on. You can use deflection to fix this.

11. Turn Deflection on and set Deflection Max to **0.107**. If you zoom into the pedestal surface, you can see the stroke is raised above the surface when Deflection is activated. The settings are shown in Figure 8.41.

FIGURE 8.41
Forces are used to push the strokes along the original stroke path.

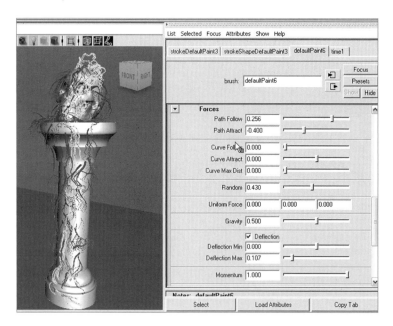

Displacement, Spiral, and Bend

You can add details to the stroke shape using the sliders in the Displacement section. It is sometimes easier to add displacements after adding forces.

Displacement Delay causes the changes made with the Displacement controls to be stronger toward the ends of the tubes. Setting this to 0 means that displacements are applied along the length of the tube.

The Noise, Wiggle, and Curl sliders add tiny bends to the tubes and branches to create randomness. A larger Frequency value adds more detail to the changes. The Offset sliders are used when animating these attributes. Keyframing the offset over time will make the strokes appear to wiggle, curl, or move randomly. We'll discuss other stroke-animation techniques later on in the chapter. The following example shows how you can change the shape of the strokes using Displacement, Spiral, and Bend.

1. Try the following settings:

> Displacement Delay: **0.074**
>
> Noise: **1**
>
> Noise Frequency: **0.1**
>
> Wiggle: **0.3**
>
> Wiggle Frequency: **2**
>
> Curl: **0.326**
>
> Curl Frequency: **5**

Figure 8.42 shows the result.

The Spiral and Bend settings toward the bottom of the Displacement controls are an additional set of controls that define the shape and behavior of the strokes.

FIGURE 8.42
You can add detail to the stroke shape using the controls in the Displacement settings.

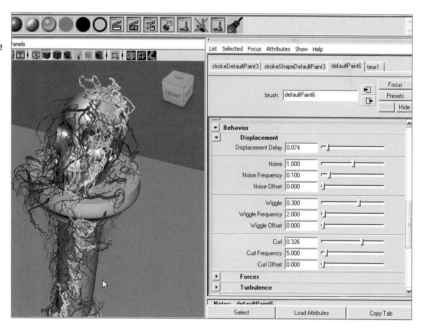

Spiral and Bend are similar except that increasing the Spiral attribute creates a curve in the tubes, leaves, and flowers that bends the stroke around the stroke normal, whereas increasing the Bend attribute curves the stroke bend along the direction of the path. Once again, the best way to understand these behaviors is through experimentation.

2. Set Spiral Min to **0.107** and Spiral Max to **0.355**. Set Spiral Decay to **0.5**.

Positive Spiral Decay values create tighter spirals; negative values create looser spirals.

Set Spiral Min and Spiral Max back to **0**. Set Bend to **3.4** and Bend Bias to **0.554**.

Bend Bias determines where, along the length of the tube, the bend starts. A Bias value of 0 makes the bend start at the base. Higher values cause the bend to be closer to the tip.

4. Set Spiral Min to **0.107** and Spiral Max to **0.355**. Turn Leaves back on and create a test render (Figure 8.43).

LEAF STIFFNESS

If you find that the Displacement settings distort the shape of the leaves, you can increase the Leaf Stiffness setting in the Leaf controls to force the leaves back into their original shape.

---

5. Save the scene as **skull_v11.ma**.

FIGURE 8.43
The vines are bent and twisted around after the Spiral and Bend settings are applied.

Animating Strokes

There are a number of ways that Paint Effects strokes can be animated. Animation creates the sense that the strokes are alive and organic. Even a small amount of animation can have a major impact on the mood of a scene. In this section, you'll learn some of the techniques available for animating Paint Effects.

PRESSURE MAPPINGS

When you paint strokes in a scene using a digital tablet as an input device, variations in pressure are recorded as you paint the stroke. You can actually edit these recorded pressure values in the Attribute Editor for each stroke's shape node and change which attributes are affected by pressure after the stroke has been painted.

In the shape node for a Paint Effects stroke, the recorded pressure values are listed in a table found under Pressure Mappings ➤ Pressure in the Attribute Editor. When you expand this list, you can select values and change them by typing in new values. To scroll down the list, select the lowest displayed value and press the down-arrow key on the keyboard.

You can select up to three stroke attributes that can be controlled by the recorded pressure values. Select the stroke attribute you want pressure to affect from the menu next to Pressure Map 1, 2, and 3.

The Pressure Scale section provides you with a ramp curve that can be used to fine-tune how the pressure modifies the stroke attribute values.

You can use the Pressure Mappings to further refine the shape and the animation of a brush stroke. Note that since the Pressure Mappings are part of the stroke shape node, they are not included when Brush Sharing is enabled.

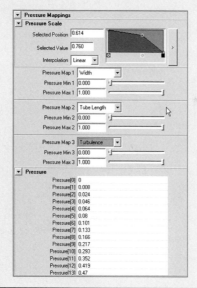

Animating Attribute Values

As you have no doubt noticed, a Paint Effects brush has a large number of attributes. Almost every single one of these can be animated using keyframes, expressions, driven keys, and textures. There's almost no limit to the number of wild effects that you can achieve by animating attribute values. This section demonstrates just a couple creative ways to keyframe the attributes.

1. Open the skull_v07.ma scene from the chapter8\scenes directory on the DVD. In this version of the scene, the strokes are shaped using the Width Scale curve so their ends are bulbous.

2. Select the strokeDefaultPaint1 stroke in the Outliner, and open the Attribute Editor to the defaultPaint6 tab. Scroll down to the bottom of the Attributes section, and expand the Behavior controls.

3. Expand the Displacement rollout, and set Wiggle attribute to 0.12.

4. In the field next to Wiggle Offset, type `=time;`. This creates a very simple expression that sets the Wiggle Offset value equal to the current time (in seconds). See Figure 8.44.

FIGURE 8.44

Add a simple expression to the Wiggle Offset attribute.

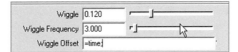

5. Set the timeline to **200** and play the animation. The strokes wiggle as a sinusoidal pattern moves along the length of the stroke.

6. Rewind the animation. Scroll up to the Tube Shading section, and set the color of the tubes to a bright red.

7. Set the Hue Rand value to **0.5**. Right-click this value and choose Set Key.

8. Move the timeline to frame 20. Set Hue Rand to **1**, and set another key.

9. Open the Graph Editor (Window ➤ Animation Editors ➤ Graph Editor). Select default-Paint6.HueRand on the left-hand side, and press f to focus the graph on its animation curve.

10. Select the keyframes on the graph, and choose Tangents ➤ Flat to add an easing in and out of the keyframes (see Figure 8.45).

11. Select the animation curve, and choose Curves ➤ Post Infinity ➤ Oscillate.

12. Close the Graph Editor, rewind, and play the animation. The colors of the tubes now change over time.

FIGURE 8.45

Edit the animation curve for the Hue Rand attribute in the Graph Editor.

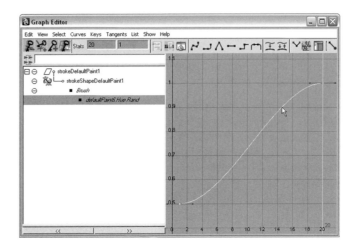

Adding Turbulence

Paint Effects strokes have built-in Turbulence controls that are similar to the fields used with a dynamic system, such as nCloth and nParticles. Adding turbulence is very simple, and you can choose among several types of turbulence.

1. Open the skull_v11.ma scene from the chapter8\scenes directory.

2. Select the strokeDefaultPaint1 stroke in the Outliner, and open the Attribute Editor to the defaultPaint6 tab.

3. In the Creation controls, set Tubes Per Step to **0.1**. Under Growth, turn off Leaves.

4. Toward the bottom of the Attribute Editor, expand the Behavior rollout. Within the Behavior settings, expand the Turbulence settings. Take a look at the options in the Turbulence Type menu.

The options are Off, Local Force, World Force, Local Displacement, World Displacement, Grass Wind, and Tree Wind.

Turbulence as a *force* causes the ends of the tubes to move back and forth as though the turbulence is moving laterally through a field of tubes. Turbulence as a *displacement* causes the tubes to bob up and down so the strokes are being displaced based on the normal of the stroke.

You can choose to have the turbulence force or displacement applied in local or world space. World space is generally a better option if you want a number of separate strokes to appear as though they are all affected by the same turbulence.

Grass Wind and Tree Wind are similar in that the turbulence affects the ends of the tubes more than the roots so it appears as though the strokes are blowing in the wind. Grass Wind affects the tips of the tubes; Tree Wind affects the tips of branches. Both forces are applied using world space coordinates. The options are shown in Figure 8.46.

The interpolation adjusts the quality of the turbulence. A linear setting causes a jerkier, random motion; Smooth Over Time and Smooth Over Time And Space create a more natural motion. Smooth Over Time And Space offers the highest quality, while Linear and Smooth Over Time work better for higher turbulence speeds.

5. Set Turbulence Type to Tree Wind and Interpolation to Smooth Over Time.

6. Set Turbulence to **1**, Frequency to **0.405**, and Turbulence Speed to **0.174**.

7. Play the animation. To get a sense of how the branches behave, create a Playblast.

8. Save the scene as **skull_v12.ma**.

FIGURE 8.46

You can choose from a number of different types of turbulence.

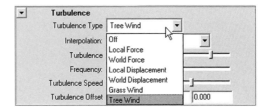

Animating Growth

The most interesting way to animate a stroke is to animate its growth using the Flow Animation controls. Flow animation animates the growth of tubes, branches, leaves, twigs, and flowers along the path of the stroke.

1. Continue with the scene from the previous section or open the skull_v12.ma scene from the chapter8\scenes directory on the DVD.

2. Select the strokeDefaultPaint1 stroke in the Outliner, and open the Attribute Editor to the defaultPaint6 tab.

3. Scroll to the bottom of the attribute list, and expand the Flow Animation controls. Set Flow Speed to **1**.

4. Turn on the options for Stroke Time and Time Clip. When Time Clip is enabled, the display of the strokes automatically converts to wireframe; this does not affect how the strokes appear in the render.

If Stroke Time is on, the tubes at the start of the stroke will grow first, and the tubes at the end of the stroke will grow last, so that the growth moves along the path of the stroke. If Stroke Time is off, all of the tubes grow at the same time.

Time Clip enables the growth animation. If this option is off, the strokes will not grow. However, if Texture Flow is on and Time Clip is off, textures applied in the Texturing section appear to move along the tubes. This is a great way to animate things like blood cells moving through blood vessels.

Time Clip uses the Start and Time values to establish the beginning and end of the animation. These values refer to seconds. So if your animation is set to 24 frames per second and you enter 2 for the start time, the growth will not begin until frame 48 (24×2).

The End time is usually set to a high value, but you can create very interesting effects by lowering this setting. If the End time is within the range of the animation, the strokes will appear to fly off of the path as they disappear from the root of each tube. This is great for creating the look of fireworks or solar flares.

5. Play the animation and observe the growth of the vines. The Flow Animation controls combined with turbulence give a very creepy look to the animation.

6. Try setting the End time to **1**, and play the animation.

7. Save the scene as **skull_v13.ma**.

END BOUNDS

You can also animate the growth of strokes by keyframing the Min and Max Clip attributes found in the End Bounds controls in the Attribute Editor of the stroke's shape node.

Modifiers

Modifiers can be used to affect specified regions of a stroke. A modifier appears as a sphere or a cube. The modifier's position, rotation, and scale can be animated. You can use this when an object or character moves past Paint Effects strokes and you'd like the strokes to react to the object or character's movement. The modifier can be attached to the object or character.

To add a modifier, select one or more strokes, and choose Paint Effects ➤ Create Modifier. In the Attribute Editor for the modifier, you can set the range and fall off for the modifier as well as which stroke attributes are affected by the modifier.

Rendering Paint Effects

When Maya renders Paint Effects strokes, they are added to the image after the rest of the image has been created. This is known as *post-process*. Because the strokes are rendered after the rest of the scene elements have been rendered, very complex Paint Effects objects can render very quickly. However, it takes a little work to smoothly integrate Paint Effects into a realistic rendering.

Paint Effects are rendered normally using Maya Software. At the bottom of the Maya Software Tab in the Render Settings window are a number of options specific to Paint Effects. Strokes will not render unless Stroke Rendering is enabled. You can improve the quality of rendered strokes by enabling Oversampling, and you can also choose to render only the strokes by themselves.

Illumination

There are two ways to light Paint Effects strokes in the scene. You can use the scene lights or a default Paint Effects light. In the Illumination section of the Brush attributes, you'll find the controls for these options.

If the Illumination option is not checked, the strokes render as a flat color using the color specified in the Shading options of the Brush attributes. If the Real Lights option is not selected, then you can specify the direction of the default Paint Effects lights numerically using the Light Direction fields.

The Lighting Based Width option alters the width of the tubes based on the amount of light they receive.

There are a number of options, including Translucence and Specular, that affect the shading of the strokes and tubes when they are lit (see Figure 8.47).

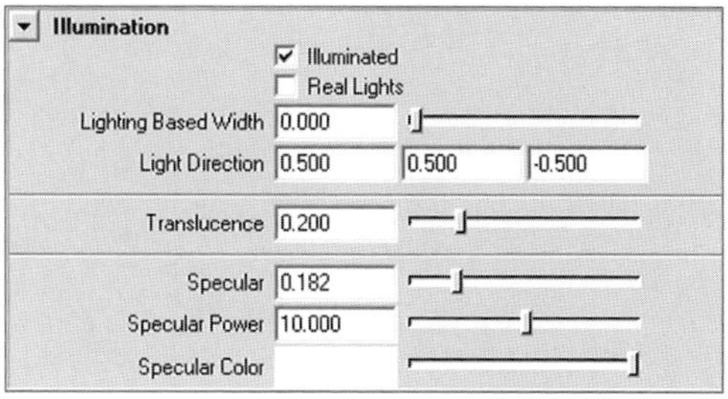

FIGURE 8.47
The Illumination options determine how strokes react to lighting.

Shadow Effects

Paint Effects strokes can cast shadows in a number of different ways. The options are set in the Shadow Effects controls in the Brush attributes.

If you want the shadows to be cast based on the actual lights in the scene, activate Real Lights in the Illumination options, set the Fake Shadow option to None, and activate the Cast Shadows option at the bottom of the Shadow Effects section. To change the quality of the shadows, you should use the Shadow controls for the lights in the scene (see Figure 8.48). The other options in the Shadowing section of the Brush attributes will have no effect on the render. Paint Effects works only with Depth Map shadows (shadows are covered in Chapter 9).

LIGHT LINKING PAINT EFFECTS

Light Linking will not work with Paint Effects. If you want only specific lights to illuminate Paint Effects strokes, use render layers to separate the strokes and shadows from the other scene elements, and then use compositing software to merge the passes. Render Layer techniques are discussed further in Chapter 12.

Paint Effects also has a number of controls for creating fake shadows. You can use 2D Offset to create a simple drop shadow, much like a drop-shadow effect created in a paint program such as Photoshop. You can also create fake 3D cast shadows. When you select 3D Cast in the Fake Shadows menu, Paint Effects creates an invisible plane beneath the surface of the stroke. Shadows are cast onto this plane and rendered in the scene (see Figure 8.49).

FIGURE 8.48
To cast shadows from scene lights, activate the Real Lights and the Cast Shadows options in the Brush attributes.

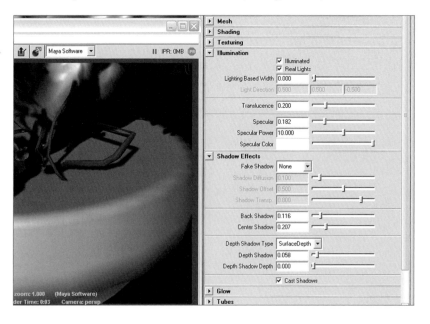

Some of the options available include the following:

Shadow Diffusion   Increasing this setting softens the edge of the shadows.

Shadow Offset   This determines the distance between the stroke and the 2D Offset fake shadow type. This option is not available for 3D cast shadows.

Shadow Transparency   Increasing this value makes the fake shadow more transparent.

Back Shadow   This darkens the areas of the stroke that face away from the light source.

Center Shadow   This is useful when painting a clump of strokes, such as tall grass. The areas inside the clump are shaded darker than the areas that are more exposed to light. This makes a clump of strokes look more realistic.

Depth Shadow   This darkens the tube based on its distance from the surface or path. When you increase this setting, you can fine-tune the look by choosing Path Dist or Surface Depth from the Depth Shadow Type menu. Path Dist darkens the parts of the stroke that are closer to the path; Surface Depth darkens parts of the stroke that are close to the surface.

Depth Shadow Depth   If the distance between the stroke and the shadow-receiving surface is greater than this setting, the shadow will not appear.

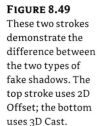

FIGURE 8.49
These two strokes demonstrate the difference between the two types of fake shadows. The top stroke uses 2D Offset; the bottom uses 3D Cast.

Rendering Strokes with mental ray

If you need to render Paint Effects strokes using mental ray, the best way to accomplish this is to convert the Paint Effects strokes into geometry. You can convert strokes into polygons or NURBS geometry. When you do this, Maya automatically creates a shader and applies it to the converted surface. The shader attempts to replicate any shading and texturing applied to the stroke in the brush panel. However, you'll most likely need to tweak the shader a little (or replace the shader with one of your own) to get the best results. A new shader is created for each stroke, so if you have a grass lawn made up of 30 strokes, Maya creates 30 identical shaders. You may want to apply one shader to all of the strokes and then delete the unused shaders.

To convert the stroke to polygons, select it and choose Modify ➢ Convert Paint Effects To Polygons (see Figure 8.50).

FIGURE 8.50
A Paint Effects tree is converted into a polygon model. Shaders for the model are automatically generated and appear in the Hypershade.

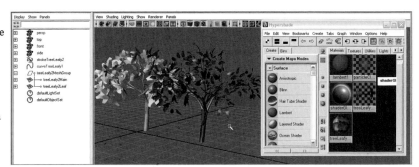

When you convert strokes to polygons, there is a limit to the number of polygons that Maya can generate. This limit can be adjusted in the options for Convert Paint Effects To Polygons. If the conversion exceeds the polygon limit, you'll see a warning, and the resulting geometry will be incomplete.

To convert the stroke to NURBS, select the stroke and choose Modify ➢ Convert Paint Effects To NURBS. The resulting geometry will be created from a group of NURBS surfaces.

When converting Paint Effects to geometry, you can choose to hide the original strokes in the scene; this option is on by default. There is a history connection between the converted stroke and the geometry, so any animation applied to the stroke will be carried over to the geometry.

If you convert a stroke that uses flow animation into polygons, you may find that at some point during the growth of the stroke the polygon limit is exceeded. To avoid this, set the timeline to the end of the stroke's growth when it has reached its full length, and then convert the Paint Effects to polygons. You'll get a warning if the limit is exceeded. You can then take measures such as reducing the number of tubes or re-creating the animation using a number of shorter strokes.

Toon Shading

You can make your 3D objects and characters look as though they are hand-drawn cartoons using Toon Shading. Toon Shading is simple to apply and use, and it generally renders very quickly.

Toon Fills

A toon fill is simply a ramp shader that you apply to the objects in a scene. There are several Fill presets you can apply from the Maya Rendering menu set. Each one is a ramp shader with different settings designed to give you a starting point from which you can design your own custom look.

1. Open the toon_v01.ma scene from the chapter8\scenes folder on the DVD. The scene consists of several cartoon mushrooms on a hill. There is also a directional light in the scene.

2. In the perspective view, switch to the shotCam camera. Switch to the Rendering menu set, and choose Toon ➢ Set Camera Background Color ➢ Shot Cam (Figure 8.51). The Color Chooser appears; choose a sky blue color.

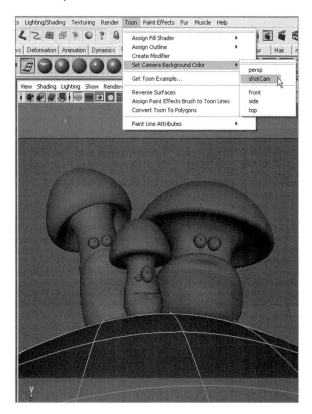

3. To use the preset fills, select an object and choose Toon ➢ Assign Fill Shader; then choose one of the presets from the list. Apply a solid color fill to the hill, Light Angle Two Tone to mushroomGroup1, Shaded Brightness Two Tone to mushroomGroup2, and Shaded Brightness Three Tone to mushroom Group3.

4. Create a test render using Maya software (choose Production Quality from the Quality presets). Compare the look of the different shaders (see Figure 8.52).

5. Open the Hypershade to see the newly created shaders. Select one of the shaders and change its settings in the Attribute Editor.

6. Try some of the other presets, such as Dark Profile and Rim Light.

All of the Fill presets are created from ramp shaders. Ramp shaders use ramps to apply a color to the surface based on an input, such as light angle, facing angle, or brightness. You can add or remove colors from the various ramps by clicking them in the Attribute Editor. The Interpolation option determines the smoothness of the transition between each color in the ramp (see Figure 8.53).

RAMP SHADER PRESETS

A number of additional presets can be applied and even blended together. In the Attribute Editor for any of the ramp shaders, click the Preset button in the upper-right-hand corner, select a preset from the list, and choose to replace the current shader settings using the presets or blend the current settings with one of the presets.

FIGURE 8.52
You can apply fills to objects using the presets in the Toon menu.

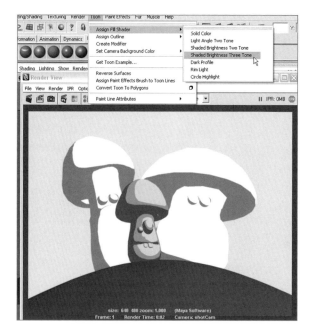

FIGURE 8.53
Toon fills are created from ramp shaders. The settings can be adjusted in the Attribute Editor to customize the look of the fill.

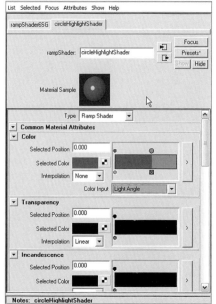

Toon Outlines

Toon outlines are a special type of Paint Effects stroke. When you add a Paint Effects toon outline to an object and then rotate the object or the camera, the outline adjusts its position automatically so that it always remains on the contour of the object regardless of the viewing angle.

1. Open the `toon_v02.ma` scene from the `chapter8\scenes` directory on the DVD. This version of the scene has the same mushrooms as `toon_v01.ma`. In this case, fill shaders have already been applied to the mushroom characters.

2. In the Outliner, Shift+click the hill and each mushroom group. Choose Toon ➢ Assign Outline ➢ Add New Toon Outline. In the Outliner, you'll see a new pfxToon1 node.

3. Select the pfxToon1 node in the Outliner, and open the Attribute Editor. Select the pfxToonShape1 tab. This is where you'll find all of the settings for tuning the look of toon lines. The toon lines are visible in the viewport window as well.

4. Expand the Common Toon Attributes, and set Line Width to **0.025**. Create a test render in the render view from the shotCam camera.

5. Save the scene as **toon_v03.ma**. To see a version of the scene to this point, open the `toon_v03.ma` scene from the `chapter8\scenes` directory (see Figure 8.54).

FIGURE 8.54
Toon lines are applied to the contours of the mushroom characters.

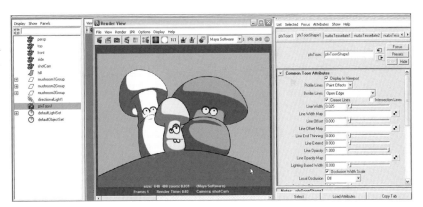

There are a large number of settings you can use to control the look of the toon lines. Some of the more important settings are listed here:

Profile Lines   A profile line is the line that is attached to the contours of the geometry. If you draw an apple on a piece of paper, the line that describes the outside edge of the apple is the profile line. Profile lines can be Paint Effects strokes or an offset mesh. An offset mesh is a copy of the surface that is scaled slightly larger than the original. The faces of the offset mesh are inverted to create the look of toon lines. This technique can be used when rendering with mental ray.

Border Lines   These lines can be set to appear at the open edge of geometry, such as the lip of a cup. They can also appear at the border between two shaders that have been applied to the geometry or both.

Crease Lines   These lines appear at the hard edges of geometry, such as the corner edge of a cube.

Intersection Lines   These appear at the intersection of two pieces of geometry. In the mushroom scene, the base of each mushroom character intersects with the geometry of the hill. If intersection lines are activated, a line will appear where these two surfaces meet.

In the lower section of the Attribute Editor there are settings available to control how each of these types of lines appears. You can edit their color, width, and specific attributes that apply to these types of lines.

CREATING A TOON WIREFRAME

You can create the look of a wireframe object in a render by turning on crease lines. In the Crease Lines settings, turn on Hard Creases Only and lower the Crease Angle Min slider until you get the look that you want.

Using Paint Effects Presets for Toon Lines

You can replace the toon lines assigned to a model with a Paint Effects preset. You can use any brush available in the Visor or any brush that you create. The process for doing this is very simple.

1. Continue with the scene from the previous section or open the `toon_v03.ma` scene from the `chapter8\scenes` directory on the DVD.

2. Choose Window ➢ General Editors ➢ Visor. Select the Toon folder from the Visor.

3. Choose the `brokenWiggle.mel` brush from the Toon presets. The icon should turn yellow when its selected, indicating that it's the currently loaded brush.

4. Select the pfxToon1 node in the Outliner, and choose Toon ➢ Assign Paint Effects Brush To Toon Line.

5. Create a test render of the scene. You may want to increase the Line Width setting in the pfxToon1 node to see the line more clearly.

The brokenWiggle brush now replaces the original toon lines (see Figure 8.55). You can edit the settings on the pfxToon1 node to change how the toon lines behave. You also now have the brokenWiggle1 brush attributes available. These attributes work just like any other Paint Effects brush.

To edit the settings for the brokenWiggle brush, select the pfxToon1 brush and open the Attribute Editor. You may need to click the right arrow in the upper-right corner of the Attribute Editor about a dozen or so times to find the brokenWiggle1 tab. Alternatively, you can turn off the DAG Objects Only option in the Display menu of the Outliner and select the brokenWiggle1 node.

The Bottom Line

Use the Paint Effects canvas.   The Paint Effects canvas can be used to test Paint Effects strokes or as a 2D paint program for creating images.

   Master it   Create a tiling texture map using the Paint Effects canvas.

Paint on 3D objects.   Paint Effects brushes can be used to paint directly on 3D objects as long as the objects are either NURBS or polygon geometry. Paint Effects brushes require that all polygon geometry have mapped UV texture coordinates.

   Master it   Create a small garden or jungle using Paint Effects brushes.

Understand strokes.   A Paint Effects stroke has a number of associated nodes that are created and connected when the stroke is painted in the scene. These include the stroke's transform node, shape node, brush node, and curve node. Most of the time you'll edit settings on the stroke's shape node and brush node. You can use brush sharing to connect all of the strokes in the scene to the settings on a single brush node.

   Master it   Use the Leafy Vine stroke to add a series of vine strokes to a simple wall model. Change the Global Scale setting of all the strokes at the same time.

Design a brush.   Custom Paint Effects brushes can be created by using a preset brush as a starting place. You can alter the settings on the brush node to produce the desired look for the brush.

   Master it   Design a brush to look like a laser beam.

Create tubes.   Tubes are short strokes that grow outward from the main path of the stroke. They can assume a variety of shapes and sizes to create any number of objects.

   Master it   Create a paintbrush that resembles the strokes used in Vincent Van Gogh's painting "Starry Night."

Add growth.   Branches, twigs, leaves, flowers, and buds can be added to Paint Effects tubes. You can use these to simulate plants or apply them creatively to design unique shapes.

   Master it   Create a mushroom tree using the Cortinarius Mushroom stroke found in the plantsMesh folder of the Visor.

Shape strokes with behaviors.   Behaviors are settings that can be used to shape strokes and tubes, giving them wiggling, curling, and spiraling qualities. You can animate behaviors to bring strokes to life.

   Master it   Add tendrils to a squashed sphere to create a simple jellyfish.

Animate growth.   Paint Effects strokes can be animated by applying keyframes, expressions, or animated textures directly to stroke attributes. You can animate the growth of strokes by using the Time Clip settings in the Flow Animation section of the Brush attributes.

Master it   Animate blood vessels growing across a surface. Animate the movement of blood within the vessels.

Render Paint Effects strokes.   Paint Effects strokes are rendered as a post process using Maya software. To render with mental ray, you should convert the strokes to geometry.

Master it   Render an animated Paint Effects tree in mental ray.

Use Toon Shading.   Toon Shading uses Paint Effects to create lines around the contours of an object and a ramp shader to color the surface of the object to replicate the look of a hand-drawn cartoon.

Master it   Add glowing contour lines to a futuristic vehicle to imitate the look of a vector-style rendering in a computer display.

Chapter 9

mental ray Lights

To achieve professional-quality, realistic renders in Maya, you need to master the mental ray render plug-in that comes with Maya. mental ray is a complex rendering system that is incorporated through the Maya interface. Learning how to use it properly and efficiently takes time, study, and practice. Chapters 9 through 12 discuss various aspects of working with mental ray, starting with how to set up mental ray light nodes.

In this chapter you will learn to:

- Use shadow-casting lights
- Render with Global Illumination
- Render with Final Gathering
- Use Image-Based Lighting
- Render using physical sun and sky
- Understand mental ray area lights
- Work with mental ray light shaders
- Create Participating Media

Shadow-Casting Lights

There are two types of shadows that can be created in mental ray and several methods for creating them. The two shadow types are cast shadows and ambient occlusion. Any combination of cast shadows and ambient occlusion can be used in a mental ray scene.

Cast shadows are created when an object blocks the rays of light coming from a light source from reaching one or more other surfaces. Cast shadows are the most familiar type of shadow, and they are often a good indication of the type, location, and orientation of the light source casting the shadow.

Ambient occlusion occurs when indirect light rays are prevented from reaching a surface. Ambient occlusion is a soft and subtle type of shadowing. It's usually found in the cracks and crevices of 3D objects and scenes.

In this section, you'll create and tune cast shadows using lights in mental ray. Ambient occlusion is discussed later in the chapter in the "Indirect Lighting" section.

REVIEW MAYA LIGHTS

Before starting this chapter, you should be familiar with the basics of using lights in Maya. You should understand how to create, position, and edit standard Maya lights (spotlight, directional light, point light, area light). Using Maya Software as a renderer is not covered in this book. Maya Software settings have not changed significantly in several years, while mental ray's implementation in Maya continues to develop and to expand. In a professional setting, you will be expected to understand how to render with mental ray, so this book is devoted to helping you achieve the necessary understanding of and skill with mental ray.

A light source in a Maya scene casts either ray trace or depth map shadows. When you create a light in Maya, its shadows are turned off by default. To activate shadow casting, you can open the Attribute Editor for the light's shape node and activate either depth map or ray trace shadows. You can use both depth map and ray trace shadows together in the same scene, but each light can only cast one or the other type of shadow.

Shadow Preview

When you create a shadow-casting light in a Maya scene, you can preview the position of the shadow in the viewport window.

1. Open the car_v01.ma scene from the chapter9\scenes directory on the DVD.

This scene shows a futuristic three-wheeled vehicle on a simple, flat plane. The shaders used for the vehicle are very simple. When setting up lights for a scene, it's usually a good idea to use simple shaders as you work. This makes test rendering faster and also keeps the focus on how the lighting will work within the composition. Later on, as you refine the lighting of the scene, you can add more complex shaders and textures.

2. Create a spotlight by choosing Create ➤ Lights ➤ Spot Light.

To position the spotlight, use the Move and Rotate tools. You can also look through the light as if it were a camera, which is often a faster and easier way to place the light in the scene.

3. Select the spotlight, and from the pPanels menu choose Panels ➤ Look Through Selected. Use the Alt+MMB and the Alt+RMB key combinations to move the view so you can see the camera from above (Figure 9.1).

4. The green circle at the center of the view represents the cone angle of the spotlight. Open the Attribute Editor for the spotLight1 object, and click the spotLightShape1 tab. Set the cone angle to **90**. The light from the spotlight now covers more area in the scene.

5. Switch to the renderCam view in the viewport (from the viewport Panels menu choose Panels ➤ Perspective ➤ renderCam).

6. In the viewport Panels menu, choose Lighting ➤ Use All Lights. You'll see a preview of the light cast by the spotlight on the ground plane.

FIGURE 9.1
View the scene
from the position
of the spotlight.

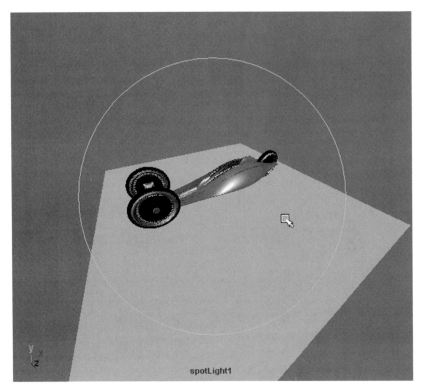

spotLight1

At the moment, the preview of the light looks very blocky. You can improve the quality of the light preview by selecting the ground plane and increasing its subdivisions.

7. Select the ground plane and open the Channel Box. In the INPUTS section, set Subdivisions Width and Height to **30**.

8. In the Panels menu, choose Lighting ➤ Shadows (it may already be activated).

You won't see any shadows until you activate shadows for the lights in the scene.

9. Select the spotLight1 object and open its Attribute Editor and click on the spotLight-Shape1 tab. Expand the Shadows section and activate Use Depth Map Shadows. A preview of the shadow appears on the ground plane. The preview looks the same regardless of whether you use depth map or ray trace shadows (Figure 9.2).

10. Select the spotlight, and use the Move and Rotate tools to change its position and rotation. Observe the changes in the preview. The preview will most likely slow down the performance of Maya, so use this feature only when you are positioning lights.

11. Scroll to the top of the spotlight attributes and set Type to Directional. Notice the difference in the shape of the shadow.

FIGURE 9.2
Activate a preview of the spotlight's shadow in the scene.

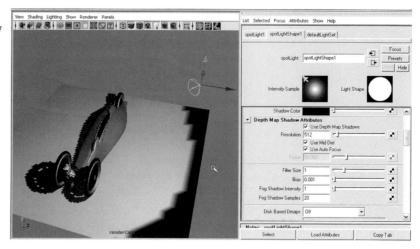

The shadow preview works only for spotlights and directional-type lights.

12. Switch Type back to Spotlight. With the spotlight selected, click on the Show Manipulators tool at the bottom of the toolbar.

The Show Manipulators tool has both aiming and positional manipulators that can help you set up your lights. Click on the small switch to the right of the spotlight to cycle through the different manipulators (Figure 9.3). If you want to know what each manipulator does, click on its handle, and you'll see a short description in the help line at the lower left of the Maya interface.

FIGURE 9.3
The Show Manipulators tool displays interactive control handles for the spotlight.

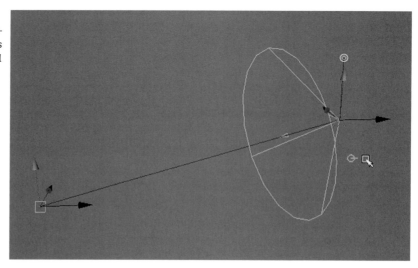

Depth Map Shadows

Depth map shadows (also known as shadow maps) are created from data stored in a file that is generated at render time. The file stores information about the distance between the shadow-casting light and the objects in the scene from the light's point of view. Depth map shadows usually take less time to render than ray trace shadows and produce excellent results in many situations.

When using mental ray, you can choose to use Maya's native depth map shadows or to use mental ray's own depth map format. In this exercise, we will compare the results produced using various depth map shadow settings.

USING THE MENTAL RAY PLUG-IN

The implementation of mental ray in the Maya interface is admittedly not intuitive. Remember that mental ray is a separate program that is integrated into Maya, which is why it seems very scattered. Understanding this can help you cope with the strangeness of mental ray's Maya integration. Be prepared for some convoluted workflow practices as well as a certain level of redundancy, as mental ray has its own version of many common Maya nodes.

---

1. Open the car_v02.ma scene from the chapter9\scenes directory on the DVD. In this version of the scene, the car has a simple white Lambert shader applied.

Using a simple flat shader speeds up the render and allows you to focus on how the shadows look on the surfaces without the distraction of reflections and specular highlights.

2. Open the Render Settings window (Window ➢ Rendering Editors ➢ Render Settings), and choose mental ray from the Render Using menu. Switch to the Quality tab, and make sure the Quality Presets drop-down is set to Production (see Figure 9.4).

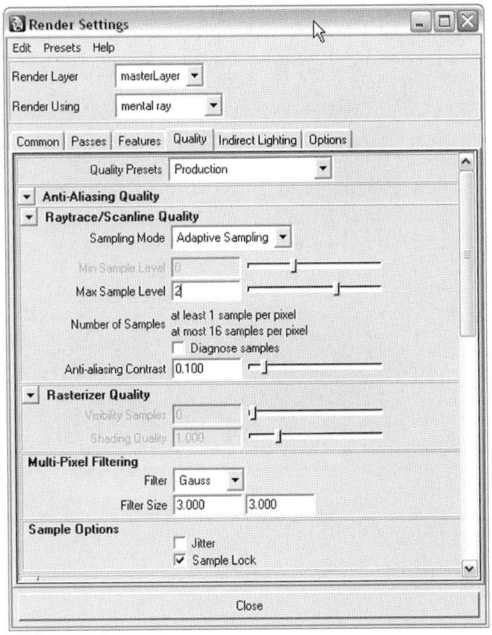

FIGURE 9.4

Choose the Production preset in the mental ray Quality tab.

LOADING MENTAL RAY

If mental ray does not appear in the Render Using list, you'll need to load the plug-in listed in the preferences; this happens from time to time. Open Window ➢ Settings/Preferences ➢ Plug-in Manager. In the list of plug-ins make sure there's a check in the box next to Mayatomr.dll in the Loaded And AutoLoad column. You'll see that mental ray now appears in the Render Using drop-down menu.

---

3. Choose Create ➢ Lights ➢ Spot Light. Select the spotlight, position it above the car, and aim the light toward the car at an angle.

4. Open the Attribute Editor for spotLight1, and click the spotLightShape1 tab. Set Cone Angle to **90**. Scroll down to the Shadows section and activate Use Depth Map Shadows.

5. Choose Window ➢ Rendering Editors ➢ Render View to open the Render View window.

The Render View window is where you can preview your renders as you work. As you create renders, you can store the images and compare them with previous renders. You can also create Interactive Photorealistic Renders (IPRs), which update interactively as you change certain scene elements. IPR is discussed in more detail in Chapter 10.

6. From the Render View menu, choose Render ➢ Render ➢ RenderCam.

You'll see the render appear in the window after a few seconds. By default, the quality of depth map shadows is pretty poor. With some tweaking you can greatly improve the look of the shadows.

The shadow is generated using a special depth file, which is an image. As such, the image has a resolution that is controlled by the Resolution slider. When the resolution is low, you can see a visible grainy quality in the shadows, as shown in Figure 9.5.

FIGURE 9.5
The default depth map shadows have a grainy quality.

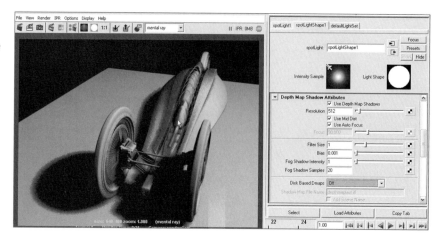

VIEW DEPTH MAP FILES

You can view the depth map files created by the lights in the scene using FCheck. However this works only for depth map files generated when rendering with Maya Software. Follow these steps to view a depth map file:

1. Create a scene using a light with Use Depth Map Shadows activated.

2. Set the Renderer to Maya Software.

3. In the Attribute Editor for the light's shape node, set the Disk Based Dmaps menu to Overwrite Existing Dmap(s). In the field, type a name for the file and use the **.iff** extension.

4. Create a render of the scene using Maya Software in the Render View window.

5. Open FCheck (you can choose File ➢ View Image in Maya to do this).

6. In FCheck, use the File menu to browse to the renderData\Depth folder in the current project. Open the file labeled depthmaptest.iff_spotLightShape1.SM.iff. FCheck will appear blank until you enable the Z Depth.

7. In FCheck, click the Z button to enable a preview of the Z Depth file.

You'll see the scene from the point of view of the shadow-casting light. The resolution of the image should match the resolution setting in the light's Attribute Editor.

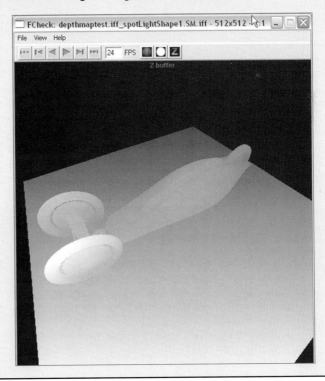

To improve the look of the shadow, you can balance the resolution with the filter size.

7. Set Resolution to **2048** and Filter Size to **0**. Create a test render in the render view, and store the image in the Render View window (in the Render View menu choose File ➢ Keep Image In Render View). The shadow is very crisp and relatively free from artifacts.

8. Set Resolution to **512** and the Filter Size to **5**. Create a test render, store the render in the Render View window, and use the scroll bar at the bottom of the render view to compare the two images (Figure 9.6).

FIGURE 9.6
Two renders using depth map shadows. The left side uses a high-resolution map with no filtering; the right side uses a low-resolution map with high filtering.

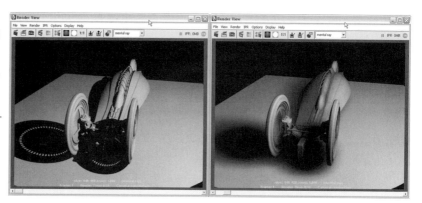

Using a low resolution (such as 512) and a high filter size (such as 5) creates soft shadows, the kind you might expect on an overcast day. One weakness in using a high filter size is that the blurring is applied to the entire shadow. In reality, shadows become gradually softer as the distance increases between the cast shadow and the shadow-casting object.

The Use Mid Dist feature is enabled by default. This option corrects banding artifacts that can occur on curved and angled surfaces (Figure 9.7). The Mid Dist Map is a second image file that records the points midway between the first surface encountered by the light and the second surface encountered by the light. The second image is used to modify the depth information of the original depth map file to help eliminate banding artifacts.

FIGURE 9.7
When Use Mid Dist is disabled, artifacts can appear on the surface.

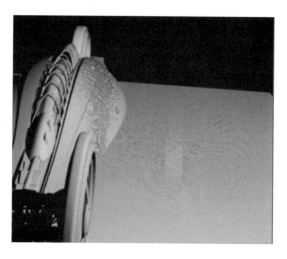

The Bias slider provides a similar function for eliminating artifacts. The slider adjusts the depth information in the depth map file. Increasing the bias pushes surface points closer to the shadow-casting light to help eliminate artifacts. This transformation of surface points occurs in the depth map file, not in the actual geometry of the scene.

If you are encountering artifacts on the surface of objects and Use Mid Dist is enabled, you can use the Bias slider to reduce the artifacts. Change the bias values in small increments as you create test renders. If the bias is too high, you'll see a gap between the shadow-casting object and the shadow.

The Use Auto Focus setting automatically adjusts the objects within the field of the light's viewable area to the maximum size of the shadow map resolution. So if, from the light's point of view, an object is surrounded by empty space, the light will zoom into the object in the depth map image. This helps optimize the use of the pixels within the depth map image so that none are wasted. It's usually a good idea to leave this setting enabled when using spotlights; however, you may encounter a different situation with other types of lights.

9. Set Resolution of the depth map to **512** and Filter Size to **0**.

10. Scroll up in the Attribute Editor, and set Light Type to Directional. Create a test render and store the image.

11. Select the ground plane object, and set its Scale X and Scale Z values to **500**. Create another test render, and compare it to the last render created.

The shadow is very blocky when the size of the ground plane is increased (see Figure 9.8).

FIGURE 9.8
When the size of the ground plane is increased, depth map shadows cast by directional lights appear very blocky.

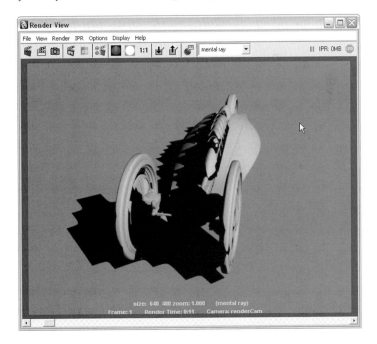

When using spotlights, the size of the viewable area from the light's point of view is restricted by the cone angle and the distance between the light and the subject. When using directional lights, the size of the viewable area is always adjusted to fit all of the objects in the scene. This is because directional lights do not factor in their position in the scene when calculating shadows, only their orientation.

In this situation you may need to create a separate shadow pass for your lights or use ray trace shadows. Render passes are covered in Chapter 12.

mental ray Shadow Map Overrides

The mental ray overrides offer settings that are similar to the standard Maya shadow maps. In addition to the Resolution setting, there are also Samples and Softness settings. The Softness setting is similar to the Filter Size attribute for Maya shadow maps. You can click the Take Settings From Maya button to automatically load the settings created for standard Maya shadow maps into the mental ray attributes.

1. Open the car_v02.ma scene from the chapter9\scenes directory on the DVD. In the Render Settings window, set Render Using to mental ray. On the Quality tab, set Quality Presets to Production.

2. Select the spotlight, and open the Attribute Editor to the spotlightShape1 tab. In the Shadows section, turn on Use Depth Map Shadows.

3. Scroll down to the Attribute Editor, expand the mental ray rollout, and expand the Shadows section under mental ray.

4. Check the Use mental ray Shadow Map Overrides box. This activates the Shadow Map Overrides section, giving you access to mental ray controls for shadow maps.

5. Set Resolution to **2048** and Softness to **0.025**. Create a test render. Store the image in the Render View window. The render is very similar to the results seen before, very grainy.

6. Set Samples to **64**, and create another test render. The graininess is reduced without significantly impacting the render time. Store the image in the render view.

Detail shadow maps are a more advanced type of shadow map that stores additional information about the surface properties of shadow-casting objects. This information includes surface properties such as transparency. In the current scene, enabling Detail Shadow Map can reduce the shadow artifacts visible on the surface of the car (see Figure 9.9).

7. Set Shadow Map Format to Detail Shadow Map, and create another render. Use the scroll bar at the bottom of the render view to compare this render with the previous two renders (Figure 9.10).

Detail shadow maps are more sensitive to changes in the Softness setting. There are also additional Samples and Accuracy settings that can be used to tune the quality of the maps. You can use the Shadow Map File Name field to set a name for saved shadow maps and then reuse the shadow maps to improve render time. The settings for saving shadow maps are found in the Shadows section of the Render Settings window under the Quality tab.

8. Save the scene as **car_v03.ma**. To see a version of the scene to this point, open the car_v03.ma scene from the chapter9\scenes directory on the DVD.

FIGURE 9.10
The car is rendered
with Samples set
to 1 (left image),
Samples set to 64
(middle image),
and Detail Shadow
Map enabled (right
image).

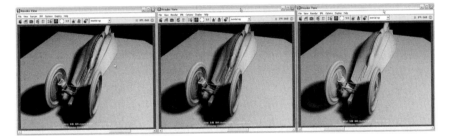

Ray Trace Shadows

Ray trace shadows are created by tracing the path of light rays from the light source to the rendering camera. Using ray trace shadows produces more accurate results but often takes a little more time and processor power to calculate.

Some advantages ray trace shadows have over shadow maps include the following:

◆ Ray trace shadows created with area lights become softer and lighter as the distance increases between the shadow and the shadow-casting object.

◆ Ray trace shadows can be accurately cast from transparent, refractive, and colored objects.

To activate ray trace shadows, make sure Raytracing is enabled in the Quality tab of the mental ray Render Settings window, and enable Use Ray Trace Shadows for the light. When you choose the Production Quality preset for mental ray, Raytracing is enabled by default (see Figure 9.11).

Ray trace shadows are typically very crisp when enabled. To add softness to the shadow, increase the Shadow Rays and the Light Radius values in the Raytrace Shadow Attributes section. In Figure 9.12 you can see how increasing the Light Radius and the Shadow Rays values adds softness to the shadow. The render in the left image uses a Light Radius of 0 and a Shadow

Rays setting of 1. The render in the right image has a Light Radius of 1, and Shadow Rays is set to 40. Notice that the blurring on the shadow increases as the distance between the shadow and the shadow-casting object increases.

FIGURE 9.11
Raytracing is enabled in the mental ray Render Settings window, and Use Ray Trace Shadows is enabled for the light.

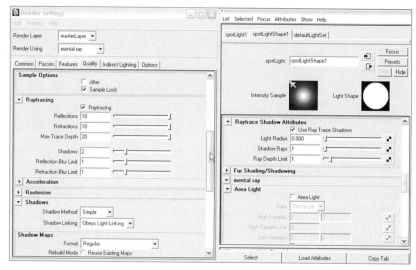

FIGURE 9.12
Add softness to ray trace shadows by increasing the Light Radius and Shadow Rays settings.

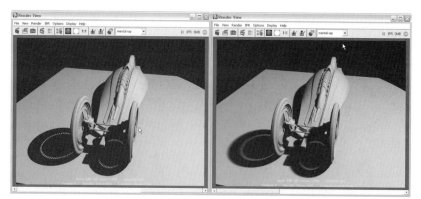

Increase the Ray Depth Limit value when you need a shadow to be visible in reflections. Each level of the Ray Depth Limit corresponds to the number of transparent surfaces between the light and the shadow (Figure 9.13).

UMBRA AND PENUMBRA

The *umbra* of a shadow is the area that is completely blocked from the light source. The *penumbra* is the transition from a lighted area to the umbra. Crisp shadows have a very small penumbra; soft shadows have a large penumbra.

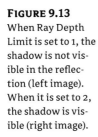

FIGURE 9.13
When Ray Depth Limit is set to 1, the shadow is not visible in the reflection (left image). When it is set to 2, the shadow is visible (right image).

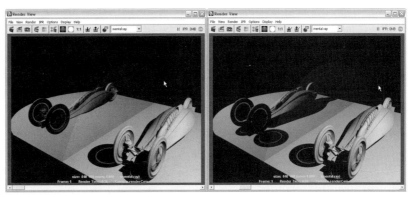

Indirect Lighting: Global Illumination

In reality, when a ray of light hits an opaque surface, it is either absorbed or reflected (or a little of both) by the surface. If the light ray is reflected, it reenters the environment and continues to bounce off reflected surfaces until it is absorbed by another surface. Objects illuminated by reflected light are thus lit indirectly.

mental ray has several methods for simulating indirect lighting: Global Illumination, Final Gathering, and Ambient Occlusion shaders. These can be used separately or together depending on what you are trying to achieve in your render.

In this section, you'll get some hands-on experience working with the Global Illumination and Final Gathering. Using ambient occlusion will be discussed in Chapter 10.

SUBSURFACE SCATTERING

Technically, subsurface scattering—a phenomenon in which light rays are reflected within a surface—also qualifies as a type of indirect lighting. Using subsurface scattering is discussed in Chapter 11.

Global Illumination

Global illumination simulates photons of light bouncing off geometry in a Maya scene. It is actually a two-step process. The photon-emitting light shoots out photons into a scene. A photon map is created that records the position of the photons and their intensities in three-dimensional space. Then the area is searched for surfaces that intersect the photons, the surfaces are illuminated based on the intensities of the intersecting photons, and the diffuse value of the shader is applied to the surface.

Glossy, black, or reflective surfaces with no diffuse value will not be affected by global illumination; a diffuse value must be present. The second part of the process is the actual rendering of the image. The photon map is stored in a data structure known as a *Kd-Tree*. During rendering, the energy values are averaged over a given radius in the Kd-Tree, and these values are interpolated to create the look of light bouncing off the diffuse surfaces. The great thing about this method is that once you have perfected the look of the global illumination, if the elements of the scene are fairly static, you can save the photon map and reuse it in the scene, cutting down on the amount of time required to render each frame.

In this exercise, you'll use global illumination to light a simple temple scene. There are no textures or color in the scene, so you can focus specifically on how global illumination reacts with surfaces.

1. Open the temple_v01.ma scene from the chapter9\scenes directory on the DVD. In the scene a camera named renderCam has already been created and positioned.

2. Create a directional light and place it outside the window; rotate the light so it's shining in the window (the position of a directional light does not affect how it casts light—only the rotation does—but it's convenient to have it outside the window). Use these settings in the Channel Box:

   Translate X: **0**

   Translate Y: **21**

   Translate Z: **-16.85**

   Rotate X: **143.7**

   Rotate Y: **3.5**

   Rotate Z: **180**

3. In the Attribute Editor, switch to the directionalLightShape1 tab. Turn on Use Depth Map Shadows. Set the Resolution slider to **1024**, and set Filter Size to **0**.

4. Create a test render in the render view using the renderCam camera. The image should look very dark except for the outline of the window on the floor.

5. Open the Render Settings window, and switch to the Indirect Lighting tab. Expand the Global Illumination rollout, turn on Global Illumination, and use the default settings (see Figure 9.14).

6. In the Attribute Editor settings for directionalLightShape1, expand the mental ray rollout and, under Caustic and Global Illumination, activate Emit Photons. Create another test render. The resulting render should look pretty horrible.

FIGURE 9.14

Activate Global Illumination in the Render Settings window, and use the default settings for the light.

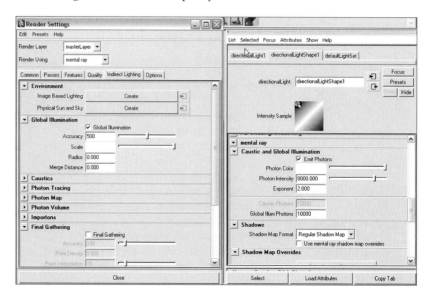

Using a directional light is a perfectly reasonable choice for creating the look of light coming through a window. The light rays cast by a directional light are parallel, which simulates the way light from a distant source, such as the sun, behaves. However, directional lights tend to have an overexposed quality when used as photon-casting lights (see Figure 9.15). This is because the photons cast from a photon-emitting light need to have both a direction and a position. Directional lights have only a direction (based on the rotation of the light), so the light often casts too many photons, and artifacts can result. It's a good practice to avoid directional lights altogether as photon-casting light. The best types of lights to use are area, spot, and point. Area lights tend to work the best since they cast light from a sizeable area as opposed to a point in space.

FIGURE 9.15

When a directional-type light is used to cast photons, the result is a blown-out image.

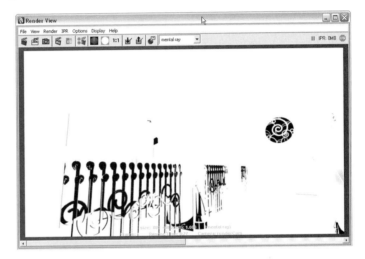

The photon-casting properties of a light are completely separate and unrelated to the light's intensity. In practice, it's often a good idea to use one light to cast direct light as well as to create cast shadows, and another light to create the indirect light.

If you are in a situation where the same light is casting direct and indirect illumination, raising the intensity can cause the area around the light to become overexposed. In this situation, you may want to use two lights placed near each other. One light should cast only direct light (that is, Cast Photons is disabled), and the other light should have 0 Intensity but Cast Photons should be enabled.

7. In the Attribute Editor for the directional light, turn off Emit Photons in the Caustic And Global Illumination settings. Rename the light **Sun**.

8. Create an Area Light (Create ➤ Lights➤ Area Light). Place the light on the floor of the temple near the positions where the sunlight hits the floor. Name the light **Bounce**. You can use these settings in the Channel Box:

    Translate X: **-1.816**

    Translate Y: **-0.227**

    Translate Z: **11.555**

    Rotate X: **90**

    Scale X: **3**

    Scale Y: **3**

    Scale Z: **3**

9. Open the Attribute Editor for Bounce. Turn off Emit Diffuse and Emit Specular. Set Intensity to **0**.

10. In the mental ray rollout, turn on Emit Photons. Create a test render of the scene, and store the image in the Render View window.

The render is a big improvement, although clearly the default settings are not adequate and require some tuning, but it looks less like a nuclear blast.

11. The image looks a little weird because there is sunlight coming through a black window. To create a quick fix for this, select renderCam and open its Attribute Editor. In the Environment tab, set the background color to white. Create another test render. (Figure 9.16).

12. Save the scene as **temple_v02**. To see a version of the scene to this point, open the temple_v02.ma scene from the chapter9\scenes directory on the DVD.

FIGURE 9.16
Photons are cast from an area light placed on the floor of the temple. When the background color for the camera is set to white, the area outside the window is white.

Tuning Global Illumination

Adjusting the look of the global illumination requires editing the settings in the area light's Attribute Editor and in the Render Settings window. The settings work together to create the effect. Often you'll tune the lighting of the scene by adjusting and readjusting the various settings until you get the best result you can.

1. Continue with the scene from the previous section or open the temple_v02.ma file from the chapter9\scenes directory on the DVD.

2. Select the Bounce light, and open its Attribute Editor to the bounceShape tab. Expand the mental ray rollout in the Attribute Editor. Under Area Light activate Use Light Shape. Set Type to Disc. This will match the shape of the sunlight cast on the floor.

3. Take a look at the settings under Caustics And Global Illumination:

Emit Photons turns on the photon-casting property of the light.

Photon Color adds color to the actual photons.

Photon Intensity controls the energy of the photons as they are shot into the room and how they are reflected from various sources.

Exponent controls the photon decay rate. A setting of 2 is consistent with the inverse square law, which states that the intensity of light is inversely proportional to the square of the distance from the source. A setting of 2 would be analogous to setting a light's Decay rate to Quadratic. This simulates how light actually works in the real world. Setting Exponent to 1 is analogous to setting a light's Decay setting to Linear, which is closer to how light from distant bright sources, such as the sun, decays.

Global Illum Photons is the number of photons cast into the room by the photon-casting light. Increasing this value often aids in the look of the effect. The more photons you add, the longer the render can take in some cases.

4. The indirect lighting looks a little blown out. Lower Photon Intensity to **5000**.

The blotchy quality on the wall is caused because there are not enough photons being cast by the light. Increasing the number of photons creates more overlapping and thus smoothes the look of the light as it reflects from the surface.

5. Set Global Illum Photons to **80000**. Create a test render (Figure 9.17).

FIGURE 9.17
By decreasing Photon Intensity and increasing Global Illum Photons, the lighting is improved.

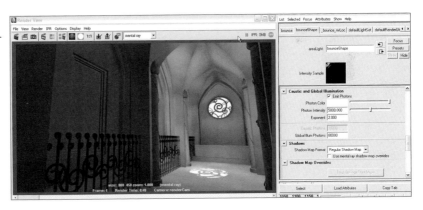

6. Open the Render Settings window, and click the Indirect Lighting tab. Take a look at the Global Illumination settings.

Global Illumination turns on global illumination calculations. Some mental ray presets, such as Preview Global Illumination, activate this option when chosen. Notice the Caustics check box above. This activates the caustics calculations, which are separate from Global Illumination; this will be explained further on in the chapter.

Accuracy sets an overall level of accuracy in the Global Illumination calculations. If this is set to 1, the photons are not blended together at all, and you can see the individual photons (Figure 9.18). Generally it's a good idea to keep Accuracy between 250 and 800 for most situations.

Scale can act as a global brightness control for the global illumination effect.

Radius controls the radius of the actual photons. When this is set to 0, mental ray determines the radius of the photons based on the requirements of the scene. The radius is not actually 0. Increasing the radius can smooth the photons; however, too large an area can cause a loss of detail in the shadows and color bleeding, which leads to a blurry, undefined sort of look.

Merge Distance specifies a distance in world space within which overlapping photons are merged. This is used to reduce the size of photon maps and increase render times. You should raise this setting by very small increments. It can increase the blotchy look of the render.

7. Click on the color swatch next to Scale to open the Color Chooser. Set the value (V) to **1.2** and create another test render. This is a good way to brighten the overall global illumination effect without raising the Photon Intensity value on one or more lights (Figure 9.19).

8. Save the scene as **temple_v03.ma**. To see a version of the scene to this point, open the temple_v03.ma scene from the chapter9\scenes directory on the DVD.

Working with Global Illumination requires a lot of testing and tuning. At a certain point, you'll need to combine the techniques with other indirect lighting tools such as Final Gathering to perfect the look.

FIGURE 9.19
Raising the Scale value brightens the overall effect of Global Illumination.

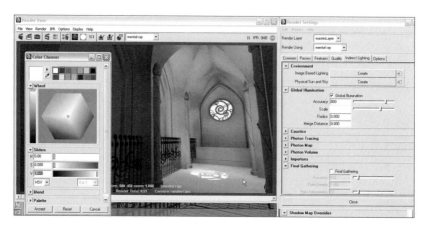

Working with Photon Maps

Photon maps are generated during a mental ray render using Global Illumination. They store the position, energy, color, and other data associated with the photons cast during render. The map can be saved to disk and reused to cut down on render time. This, in fact, eliminates the first stage of rendering with Global Illumination on subsequent renders.

Of course, if there is a lot of animation in the scene, reusing the same map will not always work, but in a scene such as the current one it can be quite helpful.

To save a photon map, type a name for the map in the Photon Map File field (found in the Photon Map section in the Indirect Lighting tab of the Render Settings window), and create a render (do not add a file extension to the name). When you want to reuse the same map, uncheck Rebuild Photon Map. The map is stored in the `renderData\mentalRay\photonMap` directory with the `.pmap` extension. When you want to overwrite the map, simply check Rebuild Photon Map.

Remember to turn on Rebuild Photon Map when you make changes to the scene. Otherwise the scene will not update correctly as you create test renders.

The Enable Map Visualizer option is a way to visualize how the photons are cast in the scene. When you enable this and create a Global Illumination render, you'll see dots spread about the scene in Maya's camera view, representing the distribution of photons cast by the light.

1. Type **test** into the Photon Map File field in the Photon Map section of the Indirect Lighting tab in the Render Settings window.

2. Check Rebuild Photon Map and Enable Map Visualizer.

3. Open the render view, and create a test render from the renderCam.

4. Close the render view when the render is complete. Look at the perspective view in Maya. You should see the geometry covered in dots representing the distribution of photons created by the bounce light.

5. Choose Window ➢ Rendering Editors ➢ mental ray ➢ Map Visualizer. The options in the box allow you to customize the look of the Visualizer in the perspective window (see Figure 9.20).

6. To remove the dots, select the mapViz1 node in the Outliner and delete it. This will not affect the render or the saved photon map.

FIGURE 9.20
The map Visualizer allows you to see how the photons are cast in the scene.

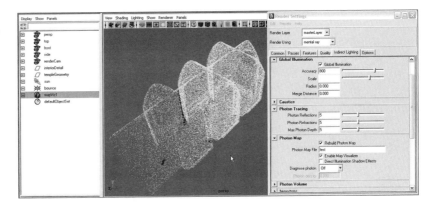

The dots in the scene can be colored based on the Photon Color of the light; you can use this to diagnose how each photon-casting light is affecting the scene. Also, if you save more than one photon map, you can load and view them using the Enable Map Visualizer option. Use the Map File Name dialog box to load saved maps.

Another way to visualize the photons in the scene is to use the Diagnose Photon menu. When you choose a setting from this menu and create a render, the shaders in the scene are replaced with a single shader colored to indicate either the photon density or the irradiance of surfaces in the scene (irradiance is discussed a little later in this chapter).

Color Bleeding

When light is reflected from a colored surface, the color can mix with the indirect light. mental ray's Global Illumination can simulate this property.

1. Open the `temple_v04.ma` scene from the `chapter9\scenes` directory on the DVD. This scene has a globe model added close to where the sunlight strikes the floor.

2. The model has a Lambert shader applied with bright yellow set for the color. Create a test render. You'll see the yellow color bleed onto the surrounding area of the temple.

Color bleeding is a part of Final Gathering and occurs automatically when colored objects are near the photon-emitting lights.

IRRADIANCE

The Irradiance controls can be found under the mental ray rollout in standard Maya shaders applied to objects. The slider is a multiplier used to adjust how a particular surface responds to the total amount of incoming light energy (or radiant power) from the surroundings.

By raising the value of Irradiance, the surface is affected by the color in the Irradiance Color slider. You can lower the value of the Irradiance Color slider to eliminate any areas on the shader that may appear too bright or blown out. You can also change the hue of the irradiance color to change the color of the indirect lighting on all surfaces that have the shader applied. Remember to keep these settings as consistent as possible between shaders in a given scene to avoid incoherence in the lighting.

Importons

Importons are very similar to photons. Importons are emitted from the camera and bounce toward the light. Photons, on the other hand, are emitted from the lights and bounce toward the camera, so importons actually move in the opposite direction of photons. You can use importons to improve the quality of global illumination maps.

The Importons controls are found under the Indirect Illumination tab in the Global Illumination Controls of the Render Settings window. Importons are available only when Global Illumination is enabled.

When you render using importons, mental ray first calculates the importon emission and then renders the scene. The importons are discarded when the render is completed.

The Density value of the importons controls how many importons are emitted from the camera per pixel. Generally this value does not need to be higher than 1. The Merge setting works very similarly to the Merge setting used for photons. The Traverse feature maximizes the number of importons in the scene; it's generally a good idea to leave this option on.

You can improve the quality of Global Illumination renders by activating the Importons option. The option must be turned on in the Indirect Lighting tab in the Render Settings window and also in the Features tab of the Render Settings window. The right image in Figure 9.21 shows the temple scene rendered using Global Illumination, with Importons turned off. The left image shows the same render with Importons turned on. The default settings are used for the Importons controls.

FIGURE 9.21
The right image is rendered without impor-tons; the left image is the same render with Importons activated.

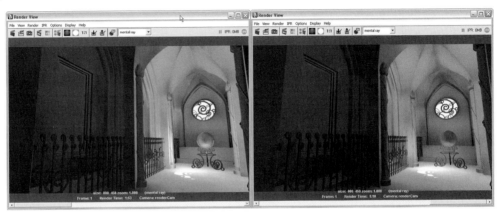

Caustics

Global Illumination simulates light reflected from diffuse surfaces. Caustics simulate light reflected from glossy and reflective surfaces as well as light that passes through refractive trans-parent materials. Caustics are calculated completely independently from Global Illumination; however, the workflow is very similar.

This exercise will show you how to set up and render using Caustics.

1. Open the crystalGlobe_v01.ma scene from the chapter9\scenes directory on the DVD.

The scene contains a globe with crystalline structures emanating from the top. The globe is set on top of a metal stand. At the moment all the objects in the scene use a simple Lambert shader.

2. In the Outliner, expand the Globe group and select the crystal object. Assign a Blinn shader to the crystal (from the Rendering menu set choose Lighting/Shading ➢ Assign Material ➢ Blinn). Open the Attribute Editor for the Blinn material and name it **crystalShade**.

3. Set the Color of crystalShade to red and Transparency to a very light gray—almost white.

4. In the Specular Shading section of the Attribute Editor, set Eccentricity to **0.05**. Set Specular Roll Off to **1** and Specular Color to white. Set Reflectivity to **0.25**.

5. Expand the Raytrace Options rollout and activate Refractions; set Refractive Index to **1.2** (Figure 9.22).

FIGURE 9.22

The settings for the crystalShade shader

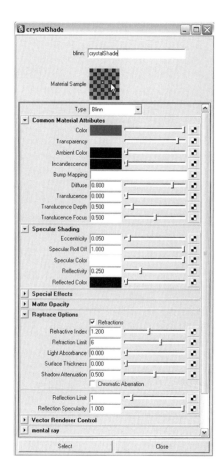

6. Create a spotlight. Select the spotlight and choose Look Through Selected. Aim the spotlight so it's looking down at the globe and stand. Position the light so the globe fits inside the cone angle radius (the circle at the center of the screen). Figure 9.23 shows this.

7. Switch to the perspective view. Open the Render Settings window, and set Render Using to mental ray. In the Quality tab, set Quality Presets to Production.

8. In the Attribute Editor for the spotlight, turn on Use Ray Trace Shadows. Create a test render of the scene.

At the moment Caustics have not been activated. Keep this image in the render view so you can compare it with the Caustics render.

9. Open the Render Settings window, and switch to the Indirect Lighting tab. Under Global Illumination, turn on Caustics. Leave Global Illumination unchecked.

10. Select the spotlight. In the Attribute Editor for the spotlight, scroll down to the mental ray section. Under Caustics And Global Illumination, turn on Emit Photons.

11. Create another test render in the render view. Immediately you can see a dramatic difference in the two renders (Figure 9.24).

FIGURE 9.23
The scene is viewed from the spotlight. Position the light so the cone angle fits around the globe and stand.

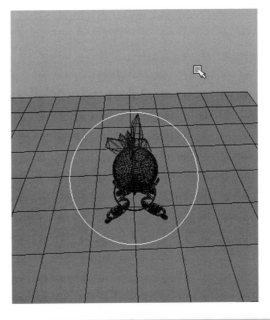

FIGURE 9.24
The image on the left is rendered without Caustics enabled; the image on the right has Caustics enabled.

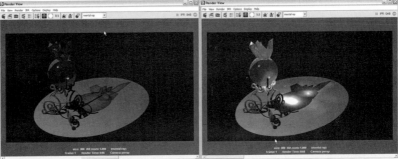

The light passing through the refractive surface produces a white highlight in the shadow on the floor. You can also see some of the red color of the globe reflected on the floor in a few spots. Notice, however, that the shadow is no longer transparent. The light that passes through the transparent globe is bent by the globe's refractive properties. This results in the hot spot seen at the center of the shadow. mental ray adds the bright spot on top of an opaque shadow.

12. The Caustics settings are similar to the Global Illumination settings. In the spotlight's Attribute Editor, lower Photon Intensity to **3000**. Set Caustic Photons to **80000**.

You can adjust the color of the caustic highlight by changing the caustic photon color or by changing the color of the transparency on the crystal shader. It's probably a better idea to change the transparency color on the shader; that way, if one light is creating caustics on two different objects that are shaded with different colors, the color of the caustic photons won't clash with the color of the objects.

The Exponent setting for Caustics works just like the Exponent setting for Global Illumination.

13. Select the crystal object, and open the Attribute Editor. Click the Crystal Shade tab. Set the Transparency color to a light pink.

14. Open the Render Settings window, and click the Indirect Lighting tab. Set Accuracy of the Caustics to **32**. Create a test render of the scene (Figure 9.25).

FIGURE 9.25
The scene is rendered after lowering the Accuracy and the Photon Intensity settings.

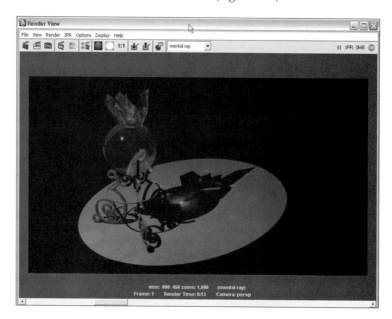

A lower Accuracy value produces sharper caustic highlights at the risk of some graininess. A higher value removes the grainy quality but softens the look of the caustics. You can also soften the look a little by setting Filter to Cone.

The Radius value can be left at 0 if you want Maya to determine the proper radius at render time. Settings below 1 make individual photons more visible. The Merge Distance setting merges all photons within the specified distance, which can decrease render times but remove the detail in the caustic patterns.

Caustic Light Setup

In practice spotlights are usually the best choice for creating caustics. Area lights don't work nearly as well. The cone angle of the spotlight is reduced so no photons are wasted; they are concentrated on the globe and stand. However, you may not want the visible edge of the spotlight cone on the floor. To fix this you can use two spotlights—one to create the caustic photons and the other to light the scene.

1. Select the spotlight and duplicate it (Ctrl+d).

2. Open the Attribute Editor for spotlight1. Under Spotlight Attributes, turn off Emit Diffuse. Under Shadows, turn off Use Ray Trace Shadows.

3. Select spotlight2 and open its Attribute Editor. Under Spotlight Attributes, turn off Emit Specular.

4. Set Cone Angle to 90. Turn on Use Ray Trace Shadows and turn off Emit Photons under Caustics And Global Illumination.

5. Create a test render of the scene. The scene looks pretty much the same, but the area of light cast by the spotlight has been widened.

6. In the Outliner, select the Stand group and apply a Blinn shader. Name the shader **standShader**.

7. Open the Attribute Editor for the standShader. Set Color to a light, bright yellow. Set Diffuse to **0.25**.

8. Under Specular Shading, set Eccentricity to **0.1**. Set Specular Roll Off to **1**, Specular Color to white, and Reflectivity to **0.85**. Create another test render. You can clearly see the light reflected off the stand and onto the floor.

When working with Caustics, you'll get more interesting results when the caustic light patterns are created from complex objects. You'll also find that the patterns created by transparent objects vary greatly when you change the Refractive Index value of the transparent shader (Figure 9.26).

9. Save the scene as **crystalGlobe_v02.ma**. To see a version of the scene to this point, open the crystalGlobe_v02.ma scene from the chapter9\scenes directory on the DVD.

FIGURE 9.26
Apply a reflective shader to the stand, creating intricate patterns of reflected light on the floor.

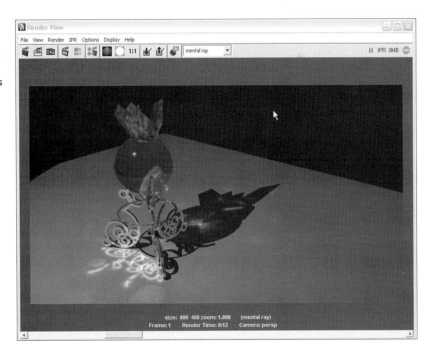

Indirect Illumination: Final Gathering

Final Gathering is another method for calculating indirect lighting. It can be used on its own or in conjunction with Global Illumination. Final Gathering uses irradiance sampling and ambient occlusion to create the look of ambient and indirect lighting. When Final Gathering is enabled, rays are cast from the camera into the scene. When a ray intersects with a surface, a Final Gathering point is created that samples the irradiance value of the surface and how it is affected by other scene elements, such as nearby objects, lights, and light-emitting surfaces.

Final Gathering uses ray tracing rather than photon casting. Each Final Gathering point that the camera shoots into the scene lands on a surface and then emits a number of Final Gathering primary rays, which gather information about the irradiance values and proximity of other scene elements. The information gathered by the rays is used to determine the shading of the surface shading normal at the location of the Final Gathering point. Imagine a hemispherical dome of rays that are emitted from a point on a surface; the rays gather information about other surfaces in the scene. Like Global Illumination, this allows it to simulate color bleeding from nearby surfaces.

The effect of ambient occlusion is created when ambient or indirect light cannot reach a surface point because it is blocked by a nearby surface. Simply put, ambient occlusion is basically a type of ambient light shadowing. Think of the dark areas you see in the cracks and crevices between objects or parts of an object on an overcast day. Final Gathering creates ambient occlusion as part of its calculation. You can also use the Ambient Occlusion shader to create this look. The Ambient Occlusion shader is discussed in Chapter 10.

Light-Emitting Objects

One of the most interesting aspects of Final Gathering is that you can use objects as lights in a scene. An object that has a shader with a bright incandescent or ambient color value actually casts light in a scene. This works particularly well for situations in which geometry needs to cast light in a scene. For example, a cylinder can be used as a fluorescent light bulb (Figure 9.27). When a shader is assigned to the cylinder with a bright incandescent value and Final Gathering is enabled, the result is a very convincing lighting scheme. In a scene like the one in this chapter, you can strategically place bright objects in areas around the room and then disable their visibility in the render. The light will be cast from the object, but the object itself will not be seen.

In this exercise, you'll light the car model used earlier in this chapter using only objects with incandescent shaders. Polygon planes will be used as so-called light cards to simulate the look of diffuse studio lighting. You'll find that it's easy to get a great-looking result from Final Gathering rendering while still using very simple, standard Maya shaders.

1. Open the car_v04.ma scene from the chapter9\scenes directory on the DVD.

2. Open the Render Settings window and click the Common tab. Scroll to the bottom of the window and expand the Render Options rollout. Make sure the Enable Default Light option is not checked.

FIGURE 9.27
A cylinder with
an incandescent
shader actually
casts light in
the scene when
Final Gathering is
enabled.

The Enable Default Light option is normally on so that when you create a test render in a scene with no lights, you can still see your objects. When you add a light to the scene, the default light is overridden and should no longer illuminate the objects in the scene. However, since you won't be using actual lights in this scene, you need to disable Enable Default Light.

3. Click the Quality tab and set Quality Presets to Production.

4. Create a quick test render using the renderCam camera. The scene should appear completely black, confirming that no lights are on in the scene.

5. Switch to the Indirect Lighting tab, scroll down, and activate Final Gathering. Do another test render. The scene should still be black.

6. Select the renderCam camera in the Outliner, and open its Attribute Editor. Switch to the renderCamShape tab, scroll down to the Environment section, and set Background Color to white. Create another test render. Make sure the renderCam is chosen as the rendering camera.

You'll see the car appear as the scene renders. There are no lights in the scene. However, the white color of the background is used in the Final Gathering calculations. You'll notice that the scene renders twice.

The Final Gathering render takes place in two stages, much like Global Illumination. In the first pass, Final Gathering projects rays from the camera through a hexagonal grid that looks like a low-resolution version of the image. In the second stage, the Final Gathering points calculate irradiance values, and the image is actually rendered and appears at its proper quality. You'll often notice that the first pass appears brighter than the final render.

The car has a simple white Lambert shader applied. The shadowing seen under the car and in the details is an example of ambient occlusion that occurs as part of a Final Gathering render (Figure 9.28).

FIGURE 9.28
The car is rendered with no lights in the scene. The background color is used to calculate the Final Gathering points.

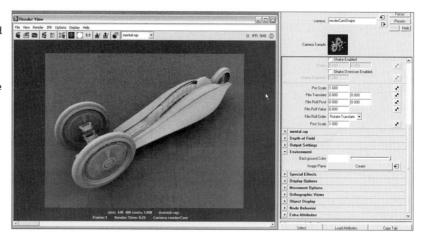

7. Set Background Color of the renderCam back to black. Create a polygon plane, and apply a Lambert shader to the plane.

8. Set the Incandescence of the plane's Lambert shader to white.

9. Use the Move and Rotate tools to position the plane above the car at about a 45-degree angle. Use the following settings in the Channel Box for the plane:

   Translate X: **-.431**

   Translate Y: **25.793**

   Translate Z: **14.072**

   Rotate X: **45**

   Rotate Y: **0**

   Rotate Z: **0**

   Scale X: **40**

   Scale Y: **20**

   Scale Z: **20**

10. Select the plane, and open the Attribute Editor to the pPlaneShape2 tab. Expand the Render Stats rollout and turn off Primary Visibility. This means that the plane still influences the lighting in the scene and can still be seen in reflections and refractions, but the plane itself is not seen by the rendering camera.

Color Gallery

On the following pages, you will find color versions of some of the renders created from the example scenes in this book. In addition you'll find examples of work by Maya users.

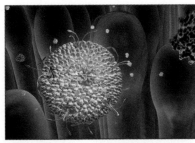

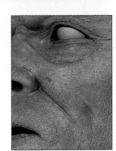

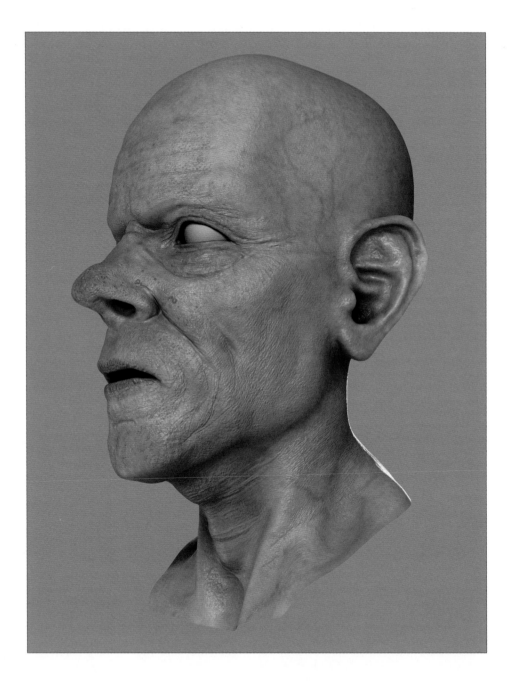

The old man model from Chapter 11 is rendered with displacement maps, painted textures, and subsurface scattering to create a very realistic skin texture.

ABOVE: The Physical Sun and Sky network is used to generate realistic outdoor lighting. Rotating the sunDirection light changes the time of day. This technique is explained in Chapter 9. **BELOW:** Reflection Occlusion is used to increase the realism of the reflections seen in the chrome wheels of the car. This technique is explained in Chapter 10.

ABOVE: The car is rendered using a studio lighting rig. **BELOW:** The same car is rendered in the same scene on a different render layer using outdoor lighting and different textures. This technique is explained in Chapter 12.

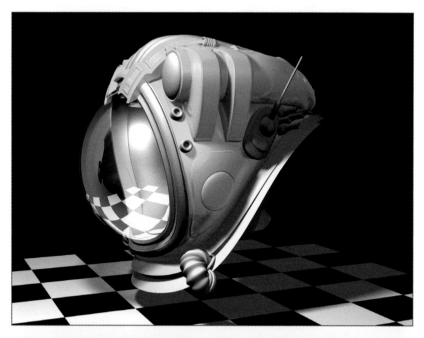

ABOVE: mental ray base shaders can be used to create realistic metal for the space helmet. These techniques are discussed in Chapter 10. **BELOW:** mental ray architectural shaders are used to create realistic materials for the helmet. These techniques are discussed in Chapter 10.

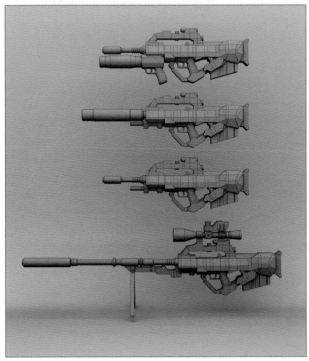

ABOVE: "The Boiler Room" by Ara Kermanikian.
BELOW: Gun model designs by Ara Kermanikian
(www.kermaco.com).

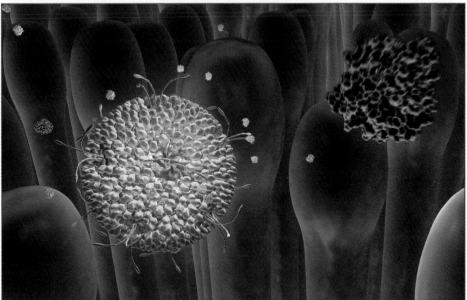

ABOVE: "VW Beetle" by Michael Walberg (www.walbergstudios.com). **BELOW:** The *A. reovirus* particle (yellow/red) floating in the human gut is attacked by trypsin digestive enzymes (pink/grey). The virus structure is an accurate reconstruction using both cryo-electron microscopy and X-ray crystallography 3D coordinates. By Gael McGill, Digizyme (www.digizyme.com).

"The Pit" by Eric Keller

11. Create another test render from the renderCam. The car appears much darker this time.

12. Select the pPlane2 shape and open the Attribute Editor. Select the tab for the plane's shader, and click on the swatch next to Incandescence to open the Color Chooser. Set the value slider (V) to 4. Create another test render. The car should be more visible now (Figure 9.29).

FIGURE 9.29
Raising the value of the incandescence on the shader's plane makes the car more visible.

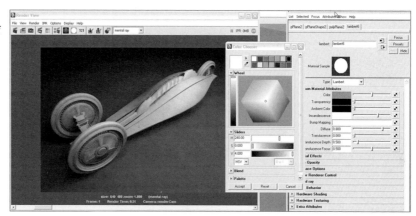

Using incandescent objects is a great way to simulate the diffuse light boxes used by photographers. You can easily simulate the lighting used in a studio by strategically placing incandescent planes around the car. However, you'll notice that the lighting is somewhat blotchy. You can fix this using the Final Gathering settings in the Indirect Lighting tab of the Render Settings window.

The Final Gathering options in the render settings set the global quality of the Final Gathering render. Here is a brief description of what these settings do.

Accuracy   This value determines the number of Final Gathering rays shot from the camera. Higher values increase render time. A value of 100 is fine for testing; a high-quality render typically uses 500 to 800 rays.

Point Density   This setting determines the number of Final Gathering points generated by the rays. Increasing this value also increases quality and render time.

Point Interpolation   This setting smoothes out the point calculation. Increasing this value improves the quality of the result without adding too much to render time. However, as with any smoothing operation, detail can be lost at higher values.

Primary Diffuse Scale   Just like with Global Illumination and caustics, this scale brightens the resulting Final Gathering render.

Secondary Diffuse Bounces   Enabling this option allows Final Gathering rays to bounce off a second diffuse surface before terminating. This increases realism as well as render time. Final Gathering rays do most of their work on the first or second bounce; beyond that the calculations don't yield a significant difference.

Secondary Diffuse Scale   Increasing the value of Secondary Diffuse Scale increases the influence of the Secondary Diffuse Bounces.

PER-SURFACE FINAL GATHERING SETTINGS

Individual surfaces can have their own Final Gathering settings located in the mental ray rollout in the surface's shape node. These settings will override the render settings and can be used as needed for optimizing renders.

---

13. Set Accuracy to **400**, Point Density to **2**, and Secondary Diffuse Bounces to **1**.

14. In the Outliner, expand the Car group. Select the leftBody, and Ctrl+click the rightBody. Open the Hypershade and assign the metal shader to these two groups. Create another test render (Figure 9.30).

The white polygon is reflected in the surface of the car. The shader that is applied to the body is a very simple Phong-type shader, and it looks pretty good.

15. Save the scene as **car_v05.ma**. To see a version of the scene to this point, open the car_v05.ma scene from the chapter9\scenes directory on the DVD.

FIGURE 9.30
Apply a reflective material to the body, enhancing the realism of the lighting.

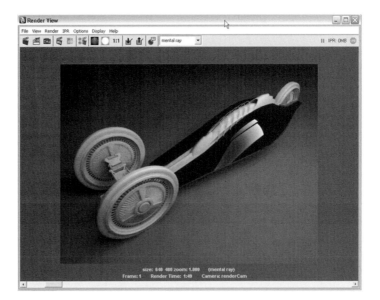

Final Gathering Maps

Setting the Rebuild option to Off causes mental ray to reuse any saved Final Gathering maps generated from previous renders. This saves a great deal of time when creating a final render. However, if the camera is moving and Final Gathering requires additional points for interpolation, new points are generated and appended to the saved map.

When Rebuild is set to Freeze, the scene is rendered with no changes to the Final Gathering map regardless of whether the scene requires additional points. This reduces flickering in animated sequences, but you need to make sure the scene has enough Final Gathering points generated before using the Freeze option.

Real World Scenario

NEON LIGHTS

You can create convincing neon lights using light-emitting objects. Add a glow effect to your incandescent shaders, and render with Final Gathering to make realistic neon lighting that lights a scene. Follow these steps:

1. Create a series of curves to build the neon light geometry. Shape them into letters or decorative elements.

2. Apply a Paint Effects brush to the curves to build the neon tubes.

3. Convert the brush strokes into NURBS or polygon geometry.

4. Apply a Blinn shader to the neon tube geometry. In the incandescence channel of the shader, add a ramp texture.

5. To make the center of the tube brighter than the edges, connect a Sampler Info node to the ramp. Use the Connection Editor to connect the Facing Ratio attribute of the Sampler Info node to the V Coordinate attribute of the ramp. Make sure the ramp is set to V Ramp.

6. Edit the ramp so the top of the ramp (which corresponds to the center of the neon tube) is brighter than the bottom of the ramp (which corresponds to the edges of the neon tube).

7. In the Special Effects rollout of the shader, increase the Glow Intensity setting. A value of 0.1 should be sufficient.

8. In the Hypershade, select the shaderGlow1 node and open its Attribute Editor. Turn off Auto Exposure. This eliminates flickering problems that may occur if the scene is animated.

9. Turning off Auto Exposure causes the glow effect to be overly bright. In the Glow Attributes section of the shaderGlow node, lower the Glow Intensity setting. Finding the proper value takes some experimentation on a number of test renders.

There is only one shaderGlow node for each Maya scene. This node applies the same settings to all the glowing objects within a scene. The glow effect is a post-process effect, so you won't see the glow applied in the render until all the other parts of the image have been rendered.

10. In the Render Settings window, make sure Renderer is set to mental ray. In the Indirect Lighting tab, turn on Final Gathering. Click the swatch next to Primary Diffuse Scale to open the Color Chooser. Raise the Value above 1. A setting between 2 and 4 should be sufficient.

Surfaces near the neon tubes should have a high diffuse value so they reflect the light emitted by the tubes. To see an example of neon lighting using Final Gathering, open the vegas.mb scene from the chapter9\scenes directory on the DVD.

If a scene has an animated camera, you can generate the Final Gathering map by rendering an initial frame with Rebuild set to On and moving the Time slider until the camera is in a new position, then setting Rebuild to Off and rendering again. Repeat this procedure until the path visible from the camera has been sufficiently covered with Final Gathering points. Then create the final render sequence with Rebuild set to Freeze. This short exercise demonstrates this technique.

1. Open the `car_v06.ma` scene from the `chapter9\scenes` directory on the DVD. In this scene, a camera named FGCam is animated around the car.

The first 10 frames of the animation have been rendered using Final Gathering. In the Final Gathering Map section of the Render Settings window, the Rebuild attribute is set to On, so new Final Gathering points are calculated with each frame.

2. View the rendered sequence by choosing File ➢ View Sequence. The 10-frame sequence is found in the `chapter9\images` directory on the DVD. The sequence is labeled carFG_test1. You can clearly see flickering in this version of the animation.

3. In the Final Gathering Map section, turn on Enable Map Visualizer. Set the timeline to frame 1, and create a test render using the FGCam camera.

4. When the render is complete, switch to the perspective view. In the viewport window, disable NURBS Surfaces and disable Polygons in the View menu. You can clearly see the Final Gathering points outlining the surface of the car.

Notice there are no points on the surfaces that have the metal texture applied. This is because they are reflective surfaces with a very low diffuse value—remember that Final Gathering is used for rendering diffuse surfaces, such as the surfaces with the white Lambert shader applied (see Figure 9.31).

5. In the Render Settings window, set Rebuild to Off. Set the timeline to 4, and create another test render using the FGCam camera.

FIGURE 9.31
The Final Gather points are visible in the scene after creating a test render.

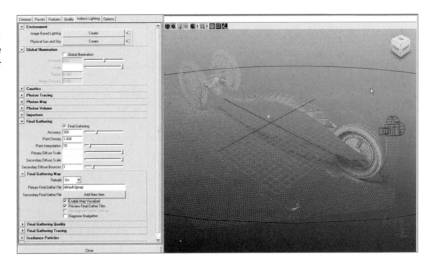

You'll notice it takes less time to render, and the display of the Final Gathering points in the perspective view is updated. More points have been added to correspond with the FGCam's location on frame 4. The Final Gathering points are saved in a file named `default.fgmap`.

6. Make three more test renders from frames 6, 8, and 10.

7. Render a sequence of the first 10 frames of the animation, and compare this to the `carFG_test1` sequence. You can also view the `carFG_test2` sequence in the `chapter9\images` directory on the DVD.

The flickering in the new sequence is greatly reduced using this technique.

8. Save the scene as **car_v07.ma**. To see a version of the sequence, open the car_v07.ma scene from the `chapter9\scenes` directory on the DVD (see Figure 9.32).

This system does not work if there are animated objects in the scene. If the Final Gathering map is generated and saved while an object is in one position, the same irradiance values are used on a subsequent frame after the object has moved to a new position. This can lead to a strange result. You can enable the Optimize For Animations option in the Final Gathering Tracing section to help reduce Final Gathering flickering in scenes with animated objects.

FIGURE 9.32
Additional Final Gathering points are added to the existing map file each time a test render is created.

FINAL GATHERING PASS

Maya 2009 introduces the ability to render a Final Gathering Map pass. The purpose of this pass is to create a Final Gathering map for the entire scene before rendering the images. This can save time on subsequent renders if you do not need to change the lighting or if you need to recompute Final Gathering points for a specific set of frames or render layers. Once the Final Gathering Map pass is created, you can specify the files generated by the pass in the Final Gathering Map section in the Indirect Lighting section of the Render Settings window. For more information on creating render passes, consult Chapter 12.

The Diagnose Final Gathering option color codes the Final Gathering points so you can easily distinguish the initial points created with the first render from points added during subsequent renders.

Other Final Gathering quality controls are found in the Final Gathering Quality and Final Gathering Tracing sections in the Indirect Lighting tab of the Render Settings window.

Optimize For Animations   This option essentially automates the system described previously. It reduces flickering but at the expense of accuracy.

Use Radius Quality Control   This setting has been largely replaced by the Point Interpolation setting. However, it can still be used if you prefer. If this option is enabled, the Point Interpolation setting is automatically disabled and vice versa. Use Radius Quality Control corresponds to the Accuracy setting. It basically sets the sampling range for Final Gathering rays to search for irradiance information from nearby surfaces. The typical practice is to set Max Radius to 10 percent of the overall scene size and Min Radius to 10 percent of Max Radius. You also have the option of specifying the radius in terms of pixel size. These settings help to reduce artifacts.

Filter   This attribute relates to using High Dynamic Range (HDR) images and will be discussed in Chapter 10.

Falloff Start and Stop   These settings limit the distance Final Gathering rays can travel. This is especially important in a large scene where objects may be far apart. You can optimize render time by setting a range for these values. When a Final Gathering ray has reached its maximum distance as set by Falloff Max, it samples any further irradiance and color values from the environment and uses them to shade the surface. The falloff start begins a linear transition to the environment sampling, and the falloff stop is the end point for this transition as well as the farthest point a Final Gathering ray can travel. Think of the start and stop points as the beginning and end of a gradient. At the start portion of the gradient, surface sampling is at 100 percent and environment sampling is at 0 percent. At the stop point of the gradient, the surface sampling is at 0 percent and the environment sampling is at 100 percent.

This can reduce render times even in an indoor scene. By default the scene background color is black. If you set Falloff Start to 15 and Falloff Stop to 20 and render, the frame takes less time to render but comes out very dark in shadowed areas that are 15 to 20 units from a Final Gathering point. This is because the default black background is being blended into the surface color. If you feel too much detail is lost to the darkness, you can create an environment dome with a constant color or an HDR image, or you can simply set the render camera's background to a value above 0. Setting the value too high reduces contrast in the scene, similar to adding an ambient light. A low value between 0.25 and 0.5 should work well.

Reflections, Refractions, and Max Trace   These sliders set the maximum number of times a Final Gathering ray can be reflected (create a secondary ray) or refracted from reflective, glossy, or transparent surfaces. The default values are usually sufficient for most scenes.

MIDEFAULTOPTIONS NODE

You can access even more options for Global Illumination and Final Gathering settings by selecting the miDefaultOptions node. To find this node, open the Outliner, and under the Display menu, uncheck DAG Options Only. Scroll down and select the miDefaultOptions node from the list, and open the Attribute Editor. You'll see the options described above as well as some options not otherwise available, such as the FG Diffuse Bounces field, which you can use to set the number of diffuse bounces above 2 (which of course you rarely need to do).

Using Lights with Final Gathering

The previous exercises demonstrated how Final Gathering can render a scene without lights by using only incandescent objects. However, for many situations you'll want to combine Final Gathering with lights so that specular highlights and clear shadows are visible in the render. If you take a look outside on a sunny day, you'll see examples of direct lighting, cast shadows, indirect lighting, and ambient occlusion working together. Likewise, a typical photographer's studio combines bright lights, flash bulbs, and diffuse lights to create a harmonious composition. You'll also find that combining lights and Final Gathering produces a higher-quality render. In the car_v08.ma scene found in the chapter9\scenes directory on the DVD, light-emitting planes are used as fill lights in conjunction with a shadow-casting spotlight (Figure 9.33).

In many cases the look of indirect lighting can be improved and rendering times can be reduced by using Final Gathering and Global Illumination at the same time. Final Gathering usually works fairly well on its own, but Global Illumination almost always needs a little help from Final Gathering to create a good-looking render. When Global Illumination and Final Gathering are enabled together, the Final Gathering secondary diffuse bounce feature no longer affects the scene; all secondary diffuse light bounces are handled by Global Illumination.

FIGURE 9.33
A spotlight is combined with light-emitting planes and rendered using Final Gathering.

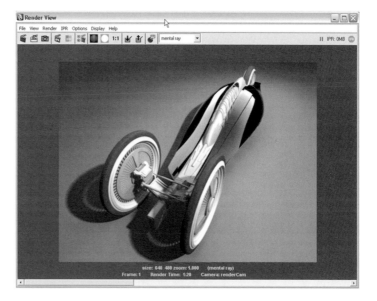

Image-Based Lighting

Image-Based Lighting (IBL) uses the color values of an image to light a scene. This can often be done without the help of additional lights in the scene. When you enable IBL, you have the choice of rendering the scene using Final Gathering, IBL with Global Illumination, or IBL with the mental ray Light Shader. This section will describe all three methods.

You can use both High Dynamic Range (HDR) images and Low Dynamic Range (LDR) images with IBL. HDR differs from LDR in the number of exposure levels stored in the format. An LDR image is typically a standard 8-bit or 16-bit image file, such as a TIFF. An HDR image is a 32-bit floating point format image that stores multiple levels of exposure within a single image. Both 8-bit and 16-bit image formats store their color values as integers (whole numbers), while a 32-bit floating point file can store colors as fractional values (numbers with a decimal). This means that the 8-bit and 16-bit formats cannot display a full range of luminance values, whereas the 32-bit floating point images can. Multiple levels of exposure are available in HDR 32-bit floating images, which can be used to create more dynamic and realistic lighting in your renders when you use IBL.

HDR images come in several formats including .hdr, OpenEXR (.exr), Floating Point TIFFs, and Direct Draw Surface (DDS). Most often you'll use the .hdr and .exr image formats when working with IBL.

OPENEXRLOADER

To view and use OpenEXR images in Maya, you'll need to enable the openEXRLoader.mll plug-in. It should be on by default, but occasionally it does not load when you start Maya. To load this plug-in, go to Window ➤ Settings/Preferences ➤ Plug-in Manager. From the list of plug-ins, check the Loaded and Auto Load boxes next to the openEXRLoader.mll plug-in.

When an HDR image is used with IBL, the lighting in the scene looks much more realistic, utilizing the full dynamic range of lighting available in the real world. When integrating CG into live-action shots, a production team often takes multiple HDR images of the set and then uses these images with IBL when rendering the CG elements. This helps the CG elements to match perfectly with the live-action shots.

The downside of HDR images is that they require a lot of setup to create. However, you can download and use HDR images from several websites, including Paul Debevec's website (www .debevec.org/Probes/). Paul Debevec is a pioneer in the field of computer graphics and virtual lighting. He is currently a researcher at the University of Southern California's Institute for Creative Technologies.

Several companies, such as Dosch Design (www.doschdesign.com/), sell packages of HDRI images on DVD, which are very high quality.

HDR images are available in several styles including angular (light probe), longitude/latitude (spherical), and vertical cubic cross. mental ray supports angular and spherical. You can convert one style to another using a program like HDRShop.

Enabling IBL

To use IBL in a scene, open the Render Settings window, and make sure mental ray is chosen as the renderer. Switch to the Indirect Lighting tab, and click the Image Based Lighting Create button at the top of the window. This creates all the nodes you need in the scene to use IBL.

You can have more than one IBL node in a scene, but only one can be used to create the lighting.

IBL and Final Gathering

Using IBL with Final Gathering is similar to the concept of using light-emitting objects. When you enable IBL, a sphere is created, and you can map either an HDR or a LDR image to the sphere (HDR is the most common choice). The scene is rendered with Final Gathering enabled, and the luminance values of the image mapped to the sphere are used to create the lighting in the scene. You can use additional lights to create cast shadows and specular highlights or use IBL by itself. The following exercise takes you through the process of setting up this scenario.

1. Open the `car_v09.ma` scene from the `chapter9\scenes` directory on the DVD.

2. Open the Render Settings window, and make sure the Render Using option is set to mental ray.

3. Switch to the Indirect Lighting tab, and click the Create button next to Image Based Lighting. This creates the mentalrayIbl1 node, which is a sphere scaled to fit the contents of the scene.

4. Select the mentalrayIbl1 node in the Outliner, and open its Attribute Editor. Click the folder icon next to the Image Name field. Go to www.debevec.org/Probes/ and download the `building_probe.hdr` image to the sourceimages directory of the current project. Connect this image to the mentalrayIbl node in the scene.

This image was downloaded from Paul Debevec's website, where you can find many other examples of HDR images.

5. The image is in the Angular mapping style, so set Mapping to Angular.

6. In the Render Settings window, enable Final Gathering. Create a test render using the renderCam camera.

In this case you'll see that the image is blown out. You can also see the HDR image in the background of the scene.

7. In the Attribute Editor for the mentalrayIblShape1 node, scroll down to Render Stats. Turn off Primary Visibility.

8. Enable Adjust Final Gathering Color Effects. This enables the Color Gain and Color Offset sliders. Set the Color Gain slider to a light gray.

9. Create another test render (Figure 9.34).

10. Save the scene as **car_v10IBL_FG.ma**. To see a version of the scene, open the car_v10IBL_FG.ma scene in the `chapter9\scenes` folder on the DVD.

FIGURE 9.34
The settings on the mentalrayIbl-Shape1 node are adjusted in the Attribute Editor. The scene is lit using the HDR image and Final Gathering.

You can see the car is now lit entirely by the HDR image. The HDR image is also visible in the reflection on the surface of the car. If you want to disable the visibility of the reflections, turn off Visible As Environment.

If you need to adjust the size and position of the IBL sphere, turn off the Infinite option at the top of the node's Attribute Editor.

The quality of the lighting can be adjusted using the Final Gathering controls in the Render Settings window.

IBL and Global Illumination

The IBL node can be used to emit photons into the scene, both Global Illumination and Caustics. This can be used in conjunction with Final Gathering or with Global Illumination alone.

1. Open the car_v09.ma scene from the chapter9\scenes directory on the DVD.

2. Follow steps 2 through 5 in the "IBL and Final Gathering" section to set up the IBL node.

3. In the Render Settings window, enable Global Illumination.

4. In the mentalrayIbl1 node, under Photon Emission, enable Emit Photons. Turn off Primary Visibility in the Render Stats section. Create a test render from the scene.

5. The render most likely looks very blown out. In the mentalrayIbl1 node's Attribute Editor, enable Adjust Photon Emission Color Effects and set Color Gain to a light gray color.

6. Increase the Global Illumination value to **150000** Photons, and set Accuracy in the Render Settings window to **1200**. Create a test render (Figure 9.35).

7. Save the scene as **car_v10IBL_GI.ma**. To see a version of the scene, open the car_v10IBL_GI.ma scene in the chapter9\scenes folder on the DVD.

The render looks pretty good, but you'll get better results combining Global Illumination with either Final Gathering or the IBL Light Shader. You can also turn on Caustics in the Render Settings window if you want create caustic light effects from a surface reflecting the IBL.

You can use the Global Illumination settings in the Render Settings window as well as the Photon Emission settings in the mentalrayIbl1 node to tune the look of the photons. By default, photons emitted from the IBL node are stored in the map at the moment they hit a surface. This makes the Global Illumination render fast and works well if Global Illumination is used by itself.

FIGURE 9.35
The IBL node emits photons into a scene rendered using Global Illumination.

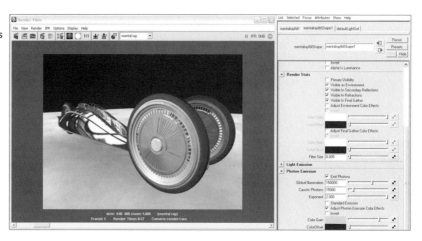

If you are using the IBL node to emit light (covered in the next section) or you are emitting caustic photons alone, turn on Standard Emission.

The Adjust Photon Emission Color Effects option allows you to adjust the brightness of the IBL's photon emission using the Color Gain and Color Offset sliders.

IBL Light Shader

When the Emit Light option is enabled in the mentalrayIbl1 node, the image used for the IBL node emits light as if the image itself were made up of directional lights. Each directional light gets a color value based on a sampling taken from the image mapped to the sphere. This technique tends to work best with images that have large areas of dark colors.

1. Open the car_v09.ma scene from the chapter9\scenes directory on the DVD.

2. Follow steps 2 through 5 in the "IBL and Final Gathering" section to set up the IBL node.

3. In the Attribute Editor for the mentalrayIbl1 node, turn on Emit Light in the Light Emission rollout.

4. Turn on Adjust Light Emission Color Effects, and set the Color Gain value to a dark gray. Create a test render of the scene. The render will take a while to create (15 minutes on my machine), but it should look pretty good (Figure 9.36).

5. Save the scene as **car_v10IBL_LS.ma**. To see a version of the scene, open the car_v10IBL_LS.ma scene in the chapter9\scenes folder on the DVD.

The Quality U and Quality V sliders adjust the sampling of the image. Higher values increase precision but add to render time. The image mapped to the IBL is converted into a control texture by the shader. Every pixel in the control texture is converted to a directional light. The Quality sliders control the resolution of the control texture.

FIGURE 9.36

The IBL node acts as a series of directional lights that sample their color values from the HDR image.

To optimize render times, the light shader node samples the image and assigns a certain number of lights as key lights based on the color values of the image. The other parts of the image are randomly sampled and used as fill lights. This saves mental ray time because it does not need to use every single light created by the control texture, which would make rendering prohibitively slow. The values in the Samples field represent the number of key lights (first value) and fill lights (second value) used during rendering.

The Low Samples setting is used when both Emit Light and Final Gathering are used in combination. This value specifies the number of samples taken when using Final Gathering. By default it is set to 1/8 the Samples setting.

The Vary Focus setting randomly alters the rotation of each directional light, which can improve quality.

The Disable Back Lighting option should be used when the scene does not need backlighting to create subsurface scattering effects. Leaving this option on optimizes sampling of the scene.

To get the best-quality rendering using IBL, it's probably a good idea to combine methods for rendering the image. Use both Emit Light and Final Gathering (Figure 9.37), or use Final Gathering with Global Illumination. In many cases you may need to lower the Color Gain value of the image to keep the lighting from appearing blown out.

FIGURE 9.37
The IBL is used with both the light shader and Final Gathering.

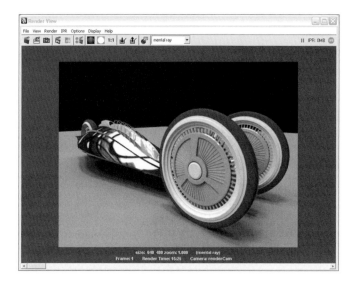

Physical Sun and Sky

mental ray provides a special network of lights and shaders that can accurately emulate the look of sunlight for outdoor scenes. Using the Physical Sun and Sky network requires rendering with Final Gathering. It's very easy to set up and use.

Enable Physical Sun and Sky

To create the Physical Sun and Sky network, use the controls in the Indirect Lighting tab of the Render Settings window.

1. Open the car_v10.ma scene from the chapter9\scenes directory on the DVD.

2. Open the Render Settings window and make sure Render Using is set to mental ray.

3. Switch to the Indirect Lighting tab in the Render Settings window, and click the Create button for Physical Sun And Sky.

Clicking the Create button creates a network of nodes that generates the look of sunlight. These include the mia_physicalsun, mia_physicalsky, and mia_exposure simple nodes. You'll notice that there is a directional light named sunDirection that has been added to the scene. To control the lighting of the scene you'll change the orientation of the light. The other light attributes (position, scale, intensity, color, and so on) will not affect the lighting of the scene. To change the lighting you need to edit the mia_physicalsky node in the Attribute Editor.

4. Select the sunDirection light in the Outliner, and use the Move tool to raise it up in the scene so you can see it clearly. The position of the sun will not change the lighting in the scene.

5. In the Render Settings window, make sure Final Gathering is enabled. It should be turned on by default when you create the physical sun nodes.

6. Open the Render View window, and create a test render from the renderCam camera. Store the rendered image in the Render View window.

The rendered image includes cast shadows from the sun, ambient occlusion created by Final Gathering, and a sky gradient in the background that is reflected in the body of the car.

7. Select the sunDirection light, and set its Rotate X value to **-150**. Create another test render and compare it with the first.

When you change the orientation of the sunDirection light, it affects the color of the lighting as well to accurately simulate the lighting you see at different times of day.

8. Select the sunDirection node, and use the following settings:

Rotate X: **329**

Rotate Y: **12**

Rotate Z: **-51.8**

Create another test render. With these settings the sun itself is actually visible in the sky (see Figure 9.38).

9. Save the scene as **car_v11.ma**. To see a finished version of the scene, open the car_v11.ma scene from the chapter9\scenes directory on the DVD.

FIGURE 9.38
Changing the rotation of the sunDirection light changes the lighting to emulate different times of the day.

Editing the Sky Settings

To change the look of the sky in the scene, use the settings found on the mia_physicalsky node.

A number of settings in the Attribute Editor for the sunDirection node help define the color and quality of the sky and the sun in the render. Here is a brief description of some of these settings (Figure 9.39):

Multiplier   This setting adjusts the overall brightness of the sky.

R, G, and B Unit Conversions   These setting adjust the coloring of the sky in the R (red), G (green), and B (blue) channels when these values are changed incrementally.

Haze   This setting adds haziness to the sky.

Red/Blue Shift   Use this option to shift between warm and cool lighting in a scene. Negative numbers shift colors toward blue; positive numbers shift colors toward red. The value range should be kept between -1 and 1.

Horizon Height and Blur   These settings change the position and blurriness of the horizon line visible in the renders behind the geometry.

Ground Color   This option changes the color of the area below the horizon. Note that the horizon does appear in reflective shaders applied to the geometry in the scene.

Night Color   This option affects the color of the sky when the sun is rotated close to 180 degrees.

Sun Direction   This setting rotates the sunDirection light in the scene to change the sun direction. Fields should be left at 0.

Sun   This option connects the sun settings to a different light in the scene.

Sun Disk Intensity, Sun Disk Scale, and Sun Glow Intensity   These settings affect the look of the sun when it is visible in the render.

Use Background   This option adds a texture for the environment background. Use this setting as opposed to the standard Maya environment shaders.

FIGURE 9.39

The settings for changing the look of the physical sky in the render

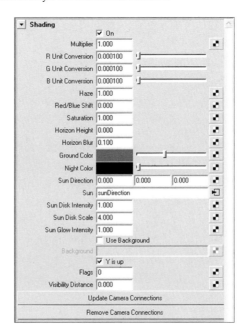

Update Camera Connections   This button adds a new renderable camera to the scene after you create the Physical Sun and Sky network. The network applies specific shaders to all of the renderable cameras in the scene when it is first created. Any new cameras added to the scene will not have these connections enabled by default.

Remove Camera Connections   This option removes all cameras from the Physical Sun and Sky network.

If you need to delete the Physical Sun and Sky network from the scene, open the Render Settings window, and click the Delete button for the Physical Sun and Sky attribute.

mental ray Area Lights

mental ray area lights are designed to create a simulation of light sources in the real world. Most lights in Maya emit light rays from an infinitely small point in space. In the real world, light sources are three-dimensional objects, such as a light bulb or a window, that have a defined size.

Lighting a scene using standard lights, such as the point and spot lights, often require additional fill lighting to compensate for the fact that these lights do not behave like real-world light sources. Area lights are designed as an alternative to this approach. A mental ray area light is essentially an array of spot lights. The array creates a 3D light source, which results in more realistic light behaviors, especially with regard to shadow casting. The downside is that area lights often take longer to render, so they are not always ideal for every situation.

Using Area Lights

Follow the steps in this exercise to understand how to use area lights in mental ray:

1. Open the `crystalGlobe_v01.ma` scene from the `chapter9\scenes` directory on the DVD.

2. Create an area light (Create ➢ Lights ➢ Area Light). Position the light using the following settings:

   Translate X: **-2.848**

   Translate Y: **4.826**

   Translate Z: **0.745**

   Rotate X: **-33.259**

   Rotate Y: **-90**

   Rotate Z: **0**

   Scale X: **2.5**

   Scale Y: **2.5**

   Scale Z: **2.5**

3. In the Attribute Editor, enable Use Ray Trace Shadows in the light's Shadows rollout.

4. Open the Render Settings window, and set Render Using to mental ray. In the Quality tab, set the Quality Presets option to Production.

5. Open the Render View window, and create a test render from the renderCam camera. Store the image in the render view.

The render looks very blown out and grainy. As you know, you can reduce the grainy quality by increasing the shadow rays used on the light. However, there is something important and potentially confusing about using a standard Maya area light with mental ray. The light as it stands right now is not actually taking advantage of mental ray area light properties. To make the light a true mental ray area light, you need to enable the Use Light Shape attribute in the Attribute Editor. Until you enable this attribute, you'll have a hard time getting the area light to look realistic.

6. Open the Attribute Editor for areaLight1. Switch to the AreaLightShape1 tab. In the mental ray ➤ Area Light rollout, activate Use Light Shape and create another test render.

The new render is less blown out, and the shadows are much softer (although still grainy).

7. To brighten the light, set Intensity to 2; create another test render (see Figure 9.40).

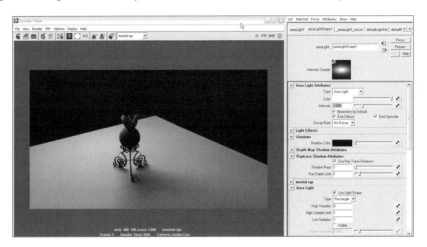

FIGURE 9.40
The mental ray area light is enabled when Use Light Shape is activated in the Attribute Editor.

Unlike Maya area lights, the intensity of mental ray area lights is not affected by the scale of the light. To change the intensity, use the Intensity slider at the top of the Attribute Editor. The shape of the shadows cast by mental ray area lights is affected by the shape chosen in the Type menu and the scale of the light.

You can make the light visible as a light source in the scene by choosing the Visible option.

To improve the quality of the shadows, increase the High Samples setting. The High Samples and Low Samples settings control the quality of the shadow in reflected surfaces. These can be left at a low value to improve render efficiency.

8. Set Light Shape Type to Sphere, and increase High Samples to **32**. Scale the light down to **0.6** in X, Y, and Z, and turn on the Visible option.

9. Create a test render, and compare the render to the previous versions (Figure 9.41).

A standard Maya spotlight can also be converted into a mental ray area light.

10. Scroll up in the Attribute Editor for areaLight1, and set the light Type to Spotlight. Set Cone Angle to **60**.

11. Scroll down to the mental ray section. Notice that Area Light is still activated. In the scene you can see that the area light is attached to the spotlight. It may be still set to the sphere type.

FIGURE 9.41
The area light
is visible in the
render.

12. There are now two fields available for High Samples and Low Samples. These represent the distribution of samples in U and V space within the area light shape. Set both High Samples to **8**.

13. Create another test render (Figure 9.42).

The light quality and shadow shape remain the same as in the previous renders. However, switching the light Type to Spotlight adds the penumbra shape you expect from a spotlight. This allows you to combine the properties of spotlights and mental ray area lights. The Visible option in the mental ray settings does not work when using a spotlight as the original light.

FIGURE 9.42
The shape of the
spotlight creates
shadows based
on the area light
settings.

Spotlights and area lights are the only kinds of lights that can be converted to mental ray area lights. In older versions of Maya, point lights also had this ability.

POINT LIGHT AREA LIGHTS

There is a cheat for turning a standard Maya point light into an area light. Set the light Type (at the top of the Attribute Editor) to Spotlight, enable the Area Light feature in the mental ray section, and then create your sampling and light shape settings. Then scroll to the top of the Attribute Editor and set Type to Point Light. You won't have access to the area light settings in the Attribute Editor, but the shadows cast by the point light and the quality of the light will match the area light settings.

---

14. Save the scene as **crystalGlobe_v03.ma**. To see a version of the scene, open the crystal-Globe_v03.ma scene from the chapter 9\scenes directory on the DVD.

Light Shaders

mental ray has a number of light shaders that can be applied to lights in a scene. The purpose of these shaders is to extend the capabilities of Maya lights to allow for more lighting options. When a mental ray shader is applied to a Maya light, specific attributes on the original light node are overridden. The light's attributes can then be set using the controls on the light shader node.

Some shaders, such as the Mib_blackbody and Mib_cie_d shaders, are very simple. These two shaders translate the color of the light as temperature specified in Kelvin. Other shaders are more complex, providing a number of attributes that can be used in special circumstances.

This section will discuss some of the light shaders and how they can be used in Maya scenes.

Physical Light Shader

The Physical Light shader is used primarily with indirect lighting (Final Gathering, Global Illumination) to create more physically accurate light behavior. There are also certain materials, such as the mental ray Architectural materials (mia), that are designed to work with physical lights. Physical lights always cast ray trace shadows, and the falloff rate for the light obeys the inverse square law just like lights in the real world. This law states that the intensity of light is inversely proportional to the square of the distance from the source. So the light intensity decreases rapidly as the light travels from the source.

Physical lights are easy to set up and use. Once you are comfortable with them, consider using them whenever you use indirect lighting, such as Global Illumination and Final Gathering. This exercise will show you how to create a physical light.

1. Open the rotunda_v01.ma scene from the chapter9\scenes directory on the DVD.

2. Create a point light, and position it using these settings:

Translate X: **0**

Translate Y: **52**

Translate Z: **26**

3. Open the Attribute Editor for the point light, and switch to the pointLightShape1 tab. Scroll down, and expand the mental ray settings.

4. Expand the Custom Shaders rollout. Click on the checkered box to the right of the Light Shader field. From the Create Render Node pop-up, switch to the mental ray tab and expand the MentalRay Lights section. Click the Physical_light icon to add the Physical Light shader (Figure 9.43).

5. Click the physical_light1 tab in the Attribute Editor. Click on the color swatch next to the Color settings. The Color Chooser appears. You'll notice that the value is set to 1000 by default. This value represents the intensity of the light; set this value to **10000**.

6. Create a test render from the renderCam camera (see Figure 9.44). Store the render in the Render View window.

FIGURE 9.43
Apply the Physical Light shader to the point light.

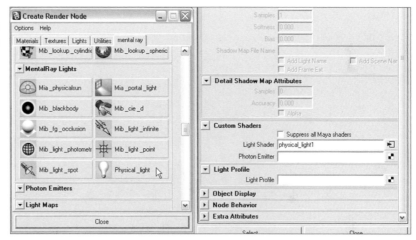

FIGURE 9.44
Render the scene using a physical light.

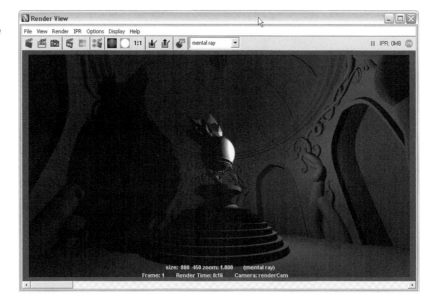

The Cone setting is used when the Physical Light shader is applied to mental ray spot and area spotlights to define the cone angle and penumbra.

The Threshold setting defines a minimum illumination value. When you increase the threshold, the lighting in the scene is contracted around the brighter areas, giving you more control over the precise areas of light in the scene.

The Cosine Exponent attribute is similar to the Cone setting and works only when the shader is applied to mental ray area lights. It contracts the area of light cast when this shader is applied to mental ray area lights. As value of Cosine Exponent increases, the light cast by the area light becomes more focused.

You can see in the test render that, even though shadows are not enabled for the light, ray trace shadows are cast in the scene.

7. Switch to the pointLightShape1 tab, and enable Emit Photons. Set Photon Intensity to **25000**.

8. In the Render Settings window, enable Global Illumination and Final Gathering. Create another test render, and compare it to the render stored in the Render View window (Figure 9.45).

FIGURE 9.45
Physical Light shaders create realistic lighting and work well with Final Gathering and Global Illumination.

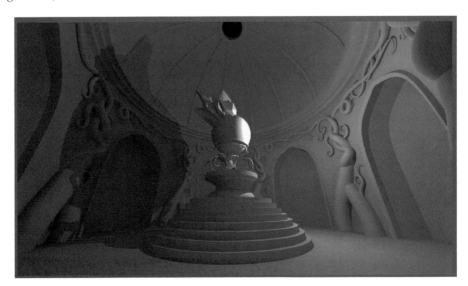

TONE MAPPING

Rendering using physical lights often results in a very blown out image. This is because computer monitors are unable to display the full range of luminance values created by physical lights. To correct this, you may need to apply a tone-mapping lens shader to the rendering camera (mia_exposure_photographic or mia_exposure_simple). This technique is discussed in Chapter 10.

Photometric Lights and Profiles

Photometric lights allow you to attach light profiles created by light manufacturers so you can simulate specific lights in your scenes. These profiles are often available on light manufacturers' websites. The profile itself is a text file in the `.ies` format.

The profiles simulate the qualities of the light, such as falloff, and the influence of the light fixture. A light profile can include the sconces and fixtures attached to the light itself. This is most helpful in creating accurate architectural renderings.

To use a photometric light, you can attach the Pmib_light_photometric shader to a point light and then attach the profile to the light using the Profile field in the shader's attributes. You can also skip using the shader altogether and attach the `.ies` profile directly to the point light in the Light Profile field available in point lights.

In many cases, you'll need to adjust the shadows cast by lights using a profile to make them more realistic. Use ray trace shadows and adjust the Shadow Rays and Light Radius values to improve the look of the shadows.

If you'd like to experiment using light profiles, you can download `.ies` format light profiles from www.lsi-industries.com/products.asp.

Portal Light

The purpose of the Portal Light shader is to correct for common problems encountered when rendering a scene in which the light is entering a room from the outside through a window or opening. Oftentimes, when rendering such a scene without the Portal Light shader, the number of Final Gathering rays emitted by the camera needs to be very high so they can find the light entering the room from the window. The Portal Light shader helps focus the Final Gathering rays on the opening itself, so fewer rays need to be used and render time can be more reasonable.

This exercise will demonstrate how to use the Portal Light shader.

1. Open the `temple_v07.ma` scene from the `chapter9\scenes` directory in the DVD.

In this version of the scene a Physical Sun and Sky network has been added. The sunDirection light is oriented so the sunlight enters the temple through the window on the far side. Final Gathering, which is normally on when the Physical Sun and Sky network is created, is disabled.

2. Create a test render from the renderCam camera, and store the render in the Render View window.

In this render, you can see the light coming through the window, casting shadows on the floor. The light has a slight amber quality; notice that the sky in the window is a cool blue. These colors are based on the orientation of the light, which simulates a late afternoon or early morning type of lighting.

3. Open the Render Settings window, and enable Final Gathering. Use the default Accuracy of 250 and a Point Density of **0.8**. Create another test render (Figure 9.46).

The lighting in the scene is very dark and blotchy. It can be improved by increasing the accuracy and the scale but at the cost of render time. The Final Gathering points emitted by the rendering camera are not being used efficiently. The next step is to set up an area light that uses the Portal Light shader. This shader works only with mental ray area lights (or spotlights that have Area Light activated in the mental ray section of the Attribute Editor).

FIGURE 9.46
Even with Final
Gathering enabled,
the render is very
dark, and there is
significant noise.

4. Create an area light, and position it in front of the window—on the inside. Use the following settings in the Channel Box:

Translate X: **0**

Translate Y: **19.63**

Translate Z: **-11.194**

Rotate X: **180**

Rotate Y: **0**

Rotate Z: **0**

Scale X: **2.88**

Scale Y: **2.88**

Scale Z: **2.88**

5. Open the Attribute Editor for the area light. In the mental ray section, turn on Use Light Shape and activate the Visible option.

The visibility of the area light must be enabled in these options for the Portal Light shader to work. The actual visibility of the light can be controlled in the shader's attributes once it has been applied to the light.

6. Scroll down to the Custom Shaders rollout. Click on the checkered box to the right of the Light Shader field. In the Create Render Node pop-up, switch to the mental ray tab, and click on the Mia_portal_light shader.

7. The Create Render Node window closes, and the Attribute Editor switches to the mia_portal_light1 tab. Select areaLight1 in the Outliner to switch the Attribute Editor back to the area light settings.

8. Scroll down to the Custom Shaders section. In the Photon Emitter field type `mia_portal`
`_light1`, and hit the Enter key (Figure 9.47). Both the Light Shader and Photon Emitter
attributes must be connected to the Portal Light shader; otherwise it will not work. This is
true even if the light does not emit photons.

FIGURE 9.47

Connect the
mia_portal_light1
shader to both
Light Shader and
Photon Emitter
in the area light's
Attribute Editor.

Notice that shadows were not enabled for the area light. Shadows, intensity, and the visibility
of the area light are now controlled by the settings in the mia_portal_light1 tab.

9. In the Render Settings window, switch to the Indirect Lighting tab. Disable both Final
Gathering and Global Illumination. Create another test render. Compare this render with
the one created in step 2.

You'll see more of the light coming through the window, the cool coloring of the sky, and the
amber color of the bounced light on the walls. However, if indirect lighting is disabled, where is
the bounced light coming from? The shader is using the area light to intensify the light (and the
colors of the light) coming from the physical sun and sky seen outside the window. The shader
makes the area light block Final Gathering points from going outside the window and converts
the light outside the window (created by the Physical Sun and Sky network) into direct light.

10. In the mia_portal_light1 tab of the Attribute Editor, set Intensity Multiplier to **5**. Create
another test render (Figure 9.48, top-right image).

The higher intensity increases the light coming through the window.

11. In the Render Settings window, enable Final Gathering and set Secondary Diffuse
Bounces to **3**. Create another test render (Figure 9.48, lower-left image).

The lighting in the temple is significantly brighter. To help smooth the noise of the temple
walls, enable Global Illumination. Note that when you enable Global Illumination, the Secondary
Bounce setting in the Final Gathering Settings section no longer affects the lighting of the scene.
Global Illumination takes care of light bounces in the scene.

12. In the Render Settings window, enable Global Illumination.

13. Click the areaLight1 node and enable Emit Photons. Set Photon Intensity to **20000** and the
number of Global Illum Photons to **15000** (lower-right image, Figure 9.48).

The noise pattern on the walls is decreased, and the render takes several minutes less to complete. The render itself can be improved by increasing Accuracy on the Final Gathering Settings.
Try turning off the Enable Sky Portal option in the mia_portal_light1 node's Attribute Editor,
and create a test render using the same settings. You can clearly see how the sky portal shader
helps boost the lighting of the room and reduce the amount of noise in the indirect lighting.

FIGURE 9.48
The upper-left image shows the lighting without the portal shader applied. The portal shader boosts the light coming in from the window (upper right). The lower-left image shows the portal light with Final Gathering. The lower-right image shows the portal light with both Final Gathering and Global Illumination.

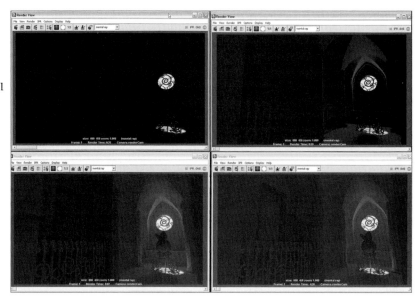

Here is a brief description of some of the other settings available on the Portal Light shader:

Intensity Multiplier   This setting controls the intensity of the portal light.

Color Multiplier   This adjusts the color of the portal light. Remember that the color of the portal light is also affected by the colors of the lights coming through the window (colors created by physical sun and sky shaders, IBL, light cards, and so on).

Transparency   This slider acts as a multiplier for the color of the light transmitted by the area light. Adjusting the Transparency slider reduces the blown-out quality of the light as well as adjusts the color of the light.

Shadows   The option turns shadow casting on or off for the area light. This overrides the Shadow Casting setting on the area light node.

Shadow Ray Extension   This setting determines where shadow casting starts for the light. If this value is 0, shadow casting starts at the location of the area light. If it is a positive value, shadow casting starts behind the area light as if the shadow starts outside the window.

Emit Direct Photons   This option turns off the direct light properties of the portal light. In this case the light emits photons but no direct light.

Use Custom Environment   This option uses colors from a specified environment shader. When this setting is off, the shader takes colors from the environment outside the window.

Visible   This setting enables the visibility of the area light itself. This overrides the visibility setting in the area light's Attribute Editor.

Look Up Using FG Rays   Enable this setting when using the physical sky shader to color the environment of the scene.

Portal Shader   Use this option with IBL as well as light cards placed outside the window. If the area light is placed outside the window, an increase in graininess may result.

14. Save the scene as **temple_v08.ma**. To see a version of the scene, open the temple_v08.ma scene from the chapter9\scenes directory on the DVD.

Participating Media

Participating Media (PM) refers to the phenomenon of light reflecting off particulate matter suspended in air. This is also known as *volumetric lighting.* mental ray has the ability to simulate extremely realistic participating media effects. These techniques are processor intensive, so you should use them wisely to avoid extremely long render times.

The setup for creating PM light effects involves a number of nodes and takes a little practice to get used to. This exercise demonstrates how to create a basic PM light rig.

1. Open the `temple_v09.ma` scene from the `chapter9\scenes` directory on the DVD.

2. Create a directional light, and place it outside the window of the temple (even though the location of the light doesn't matter for directional lights, placing it outside the window helps you visualize where the light is coming from).

3. Set the Rotate X value of the light to **-150**.

4. Open the Attribute Editor for directionalLight1, and switch to the directionalLightShape1 tab. Expand the mental ray section and, in the Custom Shaders section, click on the checkered box to the right of the Light Shader field.

5. In the Create Render Nodes window, switch to the mental ray tab. Under MentalRay Lights, click the Physical_light button to apply a Physical Light shader to the directional light.

6. Switch to the physical_light1 tab, and click on the color swatch. The Color Chooser opens up. By default, Value is set to 1000, which works well with point, area, and spotlights but is too high for directional lights. Set this value to **10**.

The PM effect needs a defined volume within which it can create the medium for the volumetric light. To create this you can use a polygon cube.

7. Switch to the perspective view. Create a polygon cube. Scale it up so it encompasses the entire structure and the light (Figure 9.49). Name the cube **volumeCube**.

8. Open the Hypershade window. Switch to the Create mental ray Nodes tab. From the Materials section, choose the Transmat material. The Transmat material is essentially a transparent material that disables the visibility of connected surfaces in the render. To create the Participating Media, apply this material to the surface that contains the volumetric light.

FIGURE 9.49
Create a cube and scale it so it fits around the geometry of the scene.

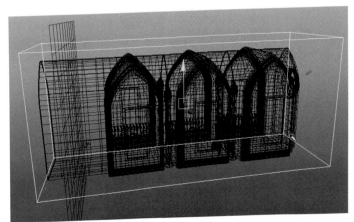

9. Apply the Transmat material to the volumeCube (select the volumeCube, and in the Hypershade, right-click on the transmat1 material and choose Assign transmat1SG To Selection).

10. Open the Attribute Editor for the volumeCube. In the Render stats, turn off the Casts Shadows and Receive Shadows options.

The Transmat material causes the cube to be invisible. However, unless you turn off the Casts Shadows and Receive Shadows options, the cube will block the physical light from entering the scene (this is because the light is a directional light, and as you saw before, the position of the directional light has no bearing on how it casts light, only its rotation; even when the light is inside the cube, the surface of the cube can still cast shadows and block the light).

You'll notice that the Transmat material has no options. The volumetric shader is actually applied to the shader group node connected to the Transmat material. This is often the case with mental ray shaders, as you'll see in Chapter 10.

11. In the Hypershade, select the Transmat material and display the upstream and downstream connections.

12. From the Create mental ray Nodes section, expand the Volumetric Materials rollout, and click the parti_volume node to create the volumetric shader.

13. Open the Attribute Editor for the transmat1SG node. Expand the mental ray section, and MMB-drag the parti_volume1 node from the Hypershade Work Area into the slot for the Volume Shader in the Custom Shaders section. This connects it to the Transmat material's shading group (Figure 9.48).

14. Open the Attribute Editor for the parti_volume1 node. Initially the two most important settings are the Scatter and Extinction settings.

15. Scatter controls the color and intensity of the effect. This usually does not have to be set very high. Click on the Scatter color swatch, and set the value to **0.15**.

FIGURE 9.50

Connect the parti_volume1 node to the Volume Shader slot of the transmat1SG node.

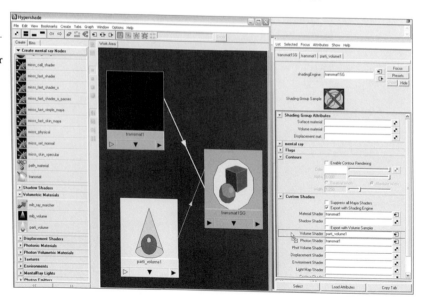

Extinction controls the falloff for the effect. If this is set to a high value, it can actually affect how far the light travels in the scene from the physical light, creating the look of very dense fog (see Figure 9.51).

FIGURE 9.51

The Scatter and Extinction settings are the most important controls for the parti_volume1 node. They should be set to low values.

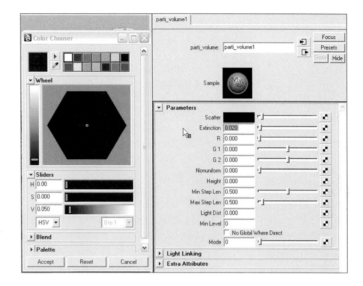

16. Set the Extinction value to **0.02**.

The Scatter, Extinction, and Physical Light values work together to create the effect. When using PM in your own scenes, you'll find that you'll have to spend some time experimenting with these settings to get the exact look you want.

17. The Min Step Len and Max Step Len attributes contribute to the sampling quality of the effect. Lowering these values produces higher-quality renders and longer render times. Set the minimum to **1** and the maximum to **5**.

The result is grainy, but it gives you a general idea of how the PM will look. When you're ready for a high-quality render, set the minimum to a value of 0.**1** and the maximum to **5**.

18. Open the Render Settings window, and switch to the Features tab. Under Extra Features, enable Auto Volume. If this is not enabled, the PM effect will not appear in the render. This is a change from previous versions of Maya.

19. Select the Globe group in the Outliner, open the Hypershade, and apply the globeShader to the Globe group. Create a test render of the scene from the renderCam camera. You do not need to turn on Final Gathering or Global Illumination when using Participating Media.

Participating Media adds a fair amount of time to the render. The white color outside the window is created by setting the Environment of the renderCam camera to white. The red color of the transparent shader applied to the globe is seen in the light rays that travel through the globe (Figure 9.52).

20. Save the scene as **temple_v10.ma**. To see a finished version of the scene, open `temple_v10.ma` from the `chapter9\scenes` directory on the DVD.

FIGURE 9.52
Participating
Media adds a
lot of drama to
the scene.

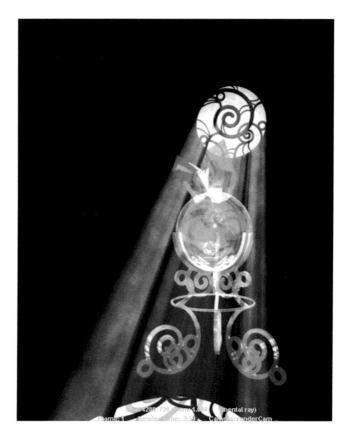

Tuning Participating Media

Once you have the Participating Media rig working, you can adjust the settings on the parti_
volume1 node to tune the effect.

R, G1, and G2 sliders These sliders control the intensity of the scattered light based on the
scatter direction (forward or backward scattering). These sliders are based on the physical
properties of how light scatters in a particulate medium and the incidence angle at which
the light is viewed. The values should typically range between -1 and 1. Combinations of
different values can be used to achieve very specific results; however, some research will be
required to obtain the values you need. For more detailed information on how these work
refer to *Mental Ray for Maya, 3dsMax, and XSI* by Boaz Livny (Sybex, 2008).

Height This setting controls the height of the effect in the scene. If you would like to create the look of a low, dense fog clinging to the surface of a lake, you would set the height
of the fog using this value. The Height value works only when the Mode slider is set to 1.
Furthermore, the Mode slider has only two options, 0 and 1. The only reason you would need
to change the mode to 1 is to activate the Height value.

Light Dist This value optimizes sampling from area lights when they are used to illuminate the PM.

Light Linking controls   These controls restrict the PM effect to the light listed in the field. If this is left blank, the PM effect will use all the lights in the volume. You can optimize render times by connecting only the lights you need.

Nonuniform slider   This slider adds turbulent noise to the PM effect.

Rendering Participating Media with Indirect Lighting

PM effects can be very expensive to render, and when indirect lighting is added to the scene, the render times become unreasonable for production. There are two approaches that can optimize render times:

You can disable PM and render the scene with indirect lighting (Final Gathering, Global Illumination), save the maps created for the indirect lighting, and then reuse the maps (set the Rebuild function to Freeze). You can then enable PM and render using the stored maps for Final Gathering and Global Illumination.

The other approach is to render the PM effects as a separate pass and then composite the PM pass together with the indirect lighting pass in your compositing software.

You can use Participating Media with any physical light, including the Light Portal arrangement discussed earlier in the chapter. You may need to increase the Multiplier value on the mia_physicalsky1 node (see Figure 9.53).

FIGURE 9.53
The temple scene rendered with the Portal Light shader and Participating Media

The Bottom Line

Use shadow-casting lights.   Lights can cast either depth map or ray trace shadows. Depth map shadows are created from an image projected from the shadow-casting light, which reads the depth information of the scene. Ray trace shadows are calculated by tracing rays from the light source to the rendering camera.

Master it   Compare mental ray depth map shadows to ray trace shadows. Render the crystalGlobe.ma scene using soft ray trace shadows.

Render with Global Illumination.   Global Illumination simulates indirect lighting by emitting photons into a scene. Global Illumination photons react with surfaces that have diffuse shaders. Caustics use photons that react to surfaces with reflective shaders. Global Illumination works particularly well in indoor lighting situations.

   Master it   Render the rotunda_v01.ma scene using Global Illumination.

Render with Final Gathering.   Final Gathering is another method for creating indirect lighting. Final Gathering points are shot into the scene from the rendering camera. Final Gathering includes color bleeding and ambient occlusion shadowing as part of the indirect lighting. Final Gathering can be used on its own or in combination with Global Illumination.

   Master it   Create a fluorescent light bulb from geometry that can light a room.

Use Image-Based Lighting.   Image-Based Lighting (IBL) uses an image to create lighting in a scene. High Dynamic Range Images (HDRI) are usually the most effective source for IBL. There are three ways to render with IBL: Final Gathering, Global Illumination, and with the light shader. These can also be combined if needed.

   Master it   Render the car scene using the Uffizi Gallery probe HDR image available at www.debevec.org/Probes/.

Render using physical sun and sky.   The Physical Sun and Sky network creates realistic sunlight that's ideal for outdoor rendering.

   Master it   Render a short animation showing the car at different times of day.

Understand mental ray area lights.   mental ray area lights are activated in the mental ray section of an area light's shape node when the Use Light Shape option is enabled. mental ray area lights render realistic, soft ray trace shadows. The light created from mental ray area lights is emitted from a three-dimensional array of lights as opposed to an infinitely small point in space.

   Master it   Build a lamp model that realistically lights a scene using an area light.

Work with mental ray light shaders.   mental ray has a number of shaders that can be applied to lights to extend their capabilities in a scene. One of these shaders is the Portal Light shader, which helps focus Final Gathering points around light entering a room through an opening.

   Master it   Render the rotunda_v01.ma scene using the Portal Light shader.

Create Participating Media.   Participating Media (PM) refers to particulate matter suspended in the air. Light is reflected from PM, creating the streaming beams of light known as volumetric lighting. Several shaders can be set up to create the look of PM in a mental ray render.

   Master it   Render a beam of light coming from a flashlight model.

Chapter 10

mental ray Shaders

mental ray is a rendering plug-in that is included with Maya. It is a professional-quality photo-realistic renderer used throughout the industry in film, television, architectural visualization, and anywhere photorealism is required.

Learning mental ray takes time and practice. Even though it's a plug-in, you'll find that it is as deep and extensive as Maya itself. mental ray includes a library of custom shading nodes that work together to extend the capabilities of mental ray. There are a lot of these nodes, many more than can be covered in this book.

In this chapter you will learn to:

- ◆ Use ambient occlusion
- ◆ Understand shading concepts
- ◆ Apply reflection and refraction blur
- ◆ Use basic mental ray shaders
- ◆ Apply the car paint material
- ◆ Use the MIA materials
- ◆ Control exposure using tone mapping
- ◆ Render contours

Ambient Occlusion

Ambient occlusion refers to a type of shadowing that occurs when the ambient light in an environment is occluded (blocked) from reaching a surface by other nearby objects or other parts of the same object. You can see ambient occlusion effects in the photograph in Figure 10.1. The darkness that occurs in the cracks and crevices in the plaster design on an overcast day is a perfect example of ambient occlusion.

Ambient occlusion effects are seen in many renders created using Final Gathering. However, you may have noticed while working through the exercises in Chapter 9 that the ambient occlusion that occurs in a Final Gathering render lacks a certain amount of detail. Unless you increase the number of Final Gathering rays, detailed ambient occlusion shadows are difficult to achieve, and the more rays you emit into a scene, the longer the render time will be.

FIGURE 10.1
Ambient occlusion occurs when photons of light are unable to reach the cracks and crevices of a surface.

mental ray has a special ambient occlusion texture node that you can use to create detailed ambient occlusion shadowing while maintaining reasonable render times. The texture is usually used in one of two ways. You can connect it as part of a shader network to include ambient occlusion within a rendered image, or you can use the material to create a separate ambient occlusion pass. This ambient occlusion render pass can then be used in a composite to add the shadowing effects to the color pass.

This latter method is the most common approach and offers the most flexibility: the occlusion pass can easily be modified in the compositing software (such as Adobe After Effects or Autodesk Toxic), eliminating the need to re-render the entire scene if a change needs to be made. In this way you can use the ambient occlusion texture to augment the shadowing of a render pass that uses Final Gathering or as a substitute for rendering with Final Gathering.

Reflection occlusion is similar to ambient occlusion. Reflection occurs when light rays are reflected off a surface. If fewer light rays can reach a reflective surface because of nearby occluding surfaces, then reflection occlusion is the result. Areas of a surface within crevices or near other objects are less reflective than the fully exposed parts of the surface. Reflection occlusion is available as a mode of the ambient occlusion texture.

In this section you'll learn how to use the ambient occlusion node.

Create an Ambient Occlusion Shader

In this exercise you'll apply the ambient occlusion texture to the out color of a surface shader that is applied to all the objects in a scene. You can apply the shader to all the objects in a scene and place the objects on a separate render layer to create your own custom occlusion pass. Using Render layers is discussed in Chapter 12.

1. Open the carScene_v01.ma scene from the chapter10\scenes directory on the DVD. The scene has the three-wheeled vehicle in a futuristic setting created by Anthony Honn.

2. Create a render from the renderCam (make sure mental ray is chosen as the current renderer).

Understanding mental ray Shader Nodes

When approaching mental ray as a rendering option, you can become quickly overwhelmed by the number of shading nodes in the mental ray section of the Hypershade. When these shading nodes are coupled with the mental ray–specific attributes found on standard Maya nodes, it can be very difficult to know what to use in a particular situation. Think of mental ray as a large toolkit filled with a variety of tools that can be used in any number of ways. Some tools you'll use all the time, some you'll need only for very specific situations, and some you may almost never use. You'll also find that over time, as your understanding and experience with mental ray grows, you may change your working style and use particular nodes more often. As you work with mental ray, expand your knowledge and experience through study and experimentation.

In this chapter you'll be introduced to the more commonly used nodes, which will make you more comfortable using them in professional situations. There should be enough information in this chapter to give the everyday Maya user a variety of options for shading and rendering using mental ray. If you decide that you'd like to delve deeper into more advanced techniques, I recommend reading the mental ray shading guide that is part of the Maya documentation as well as Boaz Livny's excellent book *Mental Ray for Maya, 3ds Max, and XSI* (Sybex, 2008).

Before starting this chapter, make sure you are familiar with using and applying standard Maya shaders, such as the Lambert, Blinn, Phong, Ramp, Surface, and Anisotropic shaders. You should be comfortable making basic connections in the Hypershade and creating renders in the Render View window. You should understand how to use Maya 2D and 3D textures, such as Fractal, Ramp, and Checker. Review Chapter 9 for background on lighting with mental ray. Many of the issues discussed in this chapter are directly related to lighting and mental ray lighting nodes.

Currently there is a basic white Lambert shader applied to the car and a gray Lambert shader applied to the scenery. The default light is enabled in the Render Settings window.

3. Open the Outliner, and Shift+click all of the group nodes and the glass object. From the Rendering menu set choose Lighting/Shading ➢ Assign New Material ➢ Surface Shader (Figure 10.2).

FIGURE 10.2

Apply a surface shader to the geometry in the scene.

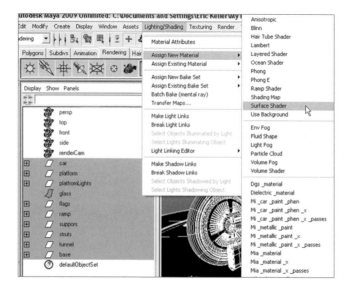

4. Open the Hypershade window (Window ➤ Rendering Editors ➤ Hypershade). Select the surfaceShader1 material, and MMB-drag it down to the Work Area.

5. On the left column of the Hypershade, set the mode of the Create tab to Create mental ray Nodes. Expand the Textures rollout, and click the mib_amb_occlusion button to create an ambient occlusion texture. It should appear in the Work Area of the Hypershade.

6. In the Work Area of the Hypershade, MMB-drag the mib_amb_occlusion1 node on top of the surfaceShader1 node, and choose Default from the pop-up. This connects the ambient occlusion node to the outColor channel of the surface shader (see Figure 10.3).

Surface shaders are the simplest of all shaders. They do not react to the lighting in the scene at all. The outColor channel applies a flat color to all the geometry that uses the shader. By connecting the ambient occlusion texture to the out color, you'll see only the effects of the ambient occlusion node on the geometry. Any lighting or other surface properties in the scene will be overridden by the ambient occlusion texture.

FIGURE 10.3
Apply a surface shader to the geometry in the scene.

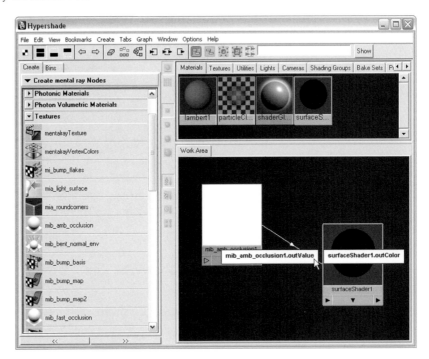

7. In the render view, create a test render of the scene from the renderCam camera (see Figure 10.4).

The render takes a while (two minutes on my machine), partly because of the car's complex geometry and partly because the occlusion texture needs to be tuned to maximize efficiency. You'll also notice the image is very grainy. To fix these problems, let's look at how ambient occlusion is calculated.

FIGURE 10.4
Render the scene using a surface shader with an ambient occlusion node connected to the outColor channel.

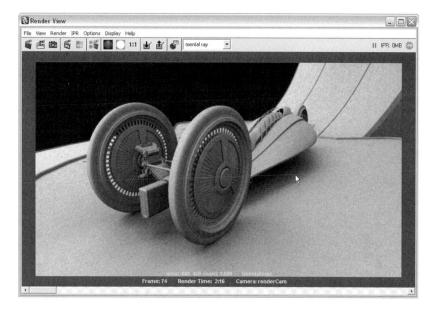

Ambient occlusion uses ray tracing to determine how the shading of a surface is colored. When a ray from the camera intersects with geometry that has the ambient occlusion texture applied, a number of secondary rays are shot from the point of intersection on the surface back into the scene. Imagine all the secondary rays as a hemisphere above each point on the surface that receives an initial ray from the camera. If the secondary ray detects another object (or part of the same object) within a given distance from the original surface, that point on the original surface has a dark color applied. If no other nearby surfaces are detected, then a light color is applied. The level of dark or light color is determined by the proximity of nearby surfaces.

8. In the Render View window, store the current image so you can compare it with future renders. Select the mib_amb_occlusion node in the Hypershade, and open its Attribute Editor.

9. The Samples attribute adjusts the overall quality of the ambient occlusion shading. Raising this setting improves quality but also increases render times. Set this to **32**.

The bright and dark colors determine how a surface is shaded based on the proximity of other surfaces or parts of the same surface. If you reverse these colors, you'll see the negative image of the previous render.

The Max Distance attribute determines how much of the scene is sampled. Think of this as the distance the secondary rays travel in the scene as they search out nearby surfaces. If a nearby object is beyond the Max Distance, then it will not affect how ambient occlusion is calculated because the secondary rays will never reach it. When Max Distance is set to 0, the entire scene is sampled; the Max Distance is essentially infinite.

One of the best ways to increase efficiency in the scene is to establish a value for Max Distance. This decreases the render time and improves the look of the image. Determining the proper value for Max Distance often takes a little experimentation and a few test renders. You want to find the value that offers the type of shadowing you need within a reasonable render time.

Spread determines the distance of the shading effect across the surface. Think of this as the size of the shadow. Higher values produce larger areas of shadowing on the surface; lower values produce tighter shadows.

10. Set Max Distance to **20** and create another test render; compare this with the previous render.

The render takes about half the time as the original render, and there is less noise in the lighter areas. The overall image is brighter because fewer objects are within the range of Max Distance, and thus there are fewer objects creating shadows on the surface.

The Falloff attribute modifies Max Distance. Lowering this value will produce darker shadows in crevices and softer shadows at the edges of the Max Distance. In practice, use Spread, Max Distance, and Falloff together to tune the look of the ambient occlusion shading (see Figure 10.5).

FIGURE 10.5

The attributes for the ambient occlusion texture

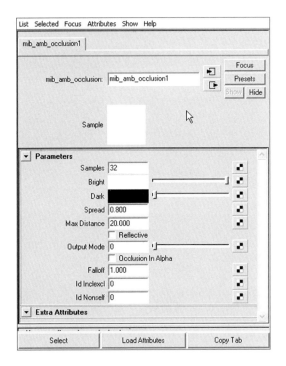

The Id Incexcl and Id Nonself attributes are two ways in which you can segregate occlusion shading by surface. If you have a scene in which there are multiple ambient occlusion textures applied to different objects, setting the Id Incexcl setting to a non-zero value either includes or excludes the surfaces from the effects of ambient occlusion.

If you set Id Incexcl to a positive value, the object is excluded from ambient occlusion; if you set it to a negative value, the object is included. A value of zero means that the object is always included in the ambient occlusion calculation.

11. Save the scene as **car_scene_v02.ma**. To see a version of the scene, open carScene_v02.ma from the chapter10\scenes directory on the DVD.

AMBIENT OCCLUSION AND INVISIBLE SURFACES

If a surface in a scene has its primary visibility disabled in the Render Stats section of its Attribute Editor, it can still influence the ambient occlusion of objects in the scene. If you have light cards or geometry that's used as an environment dome or any surfaces that you don't want to influence the ambient occlusion, either remove them from the current render layer or set their Visibility in the Channel Box to off.

Ambient Occlusion and Bump Textures

One drawback to using a surface shader to create the ambient occlusion effect is that surface shaders do not have a bump channel. You may want to include a bump texture in the ambient occlusion calculation. In this situation it may be desirable to use a Lambert shader instead of a surface shader.

1. Continue with the scene from the previous section or open the carScene_v02.ma file from the chapter10\scenes directory on the DVD.

2. In the Outliner, expand the platform group and select the platformSurface object. Apply a Lambert shader to this object (Lighting/Shading ➤ Assign Material ➤ Lambert).

3. Open the Attribute Editor for the new Lambert material, and click on the checkered box to the right of the Bump Mapping field. From the Create Render Node pop-up, click the Textures tab and choose SolidFractal from the 3D Textures section.

4. Open the Hypershade, and switch to the Textures tab. With the new Lambert shader open in the Attribute Editor, MMB-drag the mib_amb_occlusion1 node from the Textures section of the Hypershade on top of the Incandescence channel of the Lambert shader.

5. Set the Color of the Lambert Shader to black so lighting from the scene does not affect the shader. Create a test render of the scene; the bump texture appears on the platform as part of the ambient occlusion shading (see Figure 10.6). This will also work for displacement maps and normal maps.

FIGURE 10.6

Render the scene using a surface shader with an ambient occlusion node connected to the outColor channel.

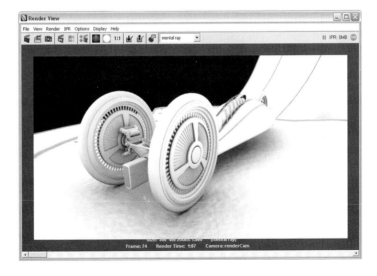

By using the same ambient occlusion texture for the surface shader and the Lambert shader, you only have to worry about changing the setting on one ambient occlusion node.

6. Save the scene as **carScene_v03.ma**. To see a version of the scene to this point, open the carScene_v03.ma file from the chapter10\scenes directory on the DVD.

Reflection Occlusion

By default the ambient occlusion node creates ambient occlusion shading for diffuse surfaces. You can use the same texture node to create occlusion for reflective surfaces. As stated before, if fewer light rays reach a reflective surface because of occluding surfaces (surfaces that block the light rays), the surface appears less reflective. The cracks and crevices on the vehicle's wheels provide a good example of this situation.

1. Open the carScene_v04.ma file from the chapter10\scenes directory on the DVD.

In this version of the scene, a Physical Sun and Sky network has been added to the scene, and Final Gathering is enabled. A Blinn texture named wheelShader has been applied to the wheels of the car. The Reflectivity of the Blinn is at 1 (or 100 percent), so the wheels will resemble chrome when rendered.

2. Create a render from the renderCam camera in the Render View window.

The wheels are 100 percent reflective, which makes them appear somewhat unrealistic (see Figure 10.7). You can tone down the reflectivity in the crevices of the wheel geometry, which will help make them appear more realistic and the details more visible.

FIGURE 10.7
The wheels are 100 percent reflective, making them appear less realistic. Much of the detail of the wheels is lost in the reflection.

3. Open the Hypershade window, and MMB-drag the wheelShader from the Materials library down to the Work Area.

4. Set the Create column on the left side of the Hypershade window to Create mental ray Nodes. Expand the Textures section, and click the mib_amb_occlusion button to create an ambient occlusion node.

When you connect the ambient occlusion texture to a shader, you want to use the outColor attribute of the texture as the output. The outColor attribute is a vector, meaning it has three components (the red channel, the blue channel, and the green channel). To modify the Blinn texture, connect the color output of the ambient occlusion texture into the Reflectivity attribute of the wheelShader. However, the Reflectivity channel accepts only an input that has a single component, not a vector. To make the two channels compatible, you can use the Luminance color utility. This converts the vector output of the ambient occlusion texture into a single value, which can then be connected to the Reflectivity channel of the wheelShader.

5. In the Create column on the left of the Hypershade, set the mode to Create Maya Nodes.

6. Scroll down to the Color Utilities section, expand it, and click the Luminance button to create the Luminance utility.

7. In the Work Area of the Hypershade, MMB-drag the mib_amb_occlusion1 node on top of the luminance node. Choose Value from the pop-up window.

8. MMB-drag the luminance node on top of the wheel shader. Choose Other from the pop-up window. This opens the Connection Editor.

9. In the Connection Editor, select outValue on the left and the Reflectivity channel on the right (you may need to scroll to the bottom of the list; see Figure 10.8).

10. Open the Attribute Editor for the mib_amb_occlusion1 node. Set Samples to **32** and Max Distance to **20**, and activate the Reflective option.

11. Create a test render from the renderCam camera, and compare it to the original render created at the start of the section (see Figure 10.9).

FIGURE 10.8
Connect the ambient occlusion texture to the Reflectivity channel of the wheelShader using a Luminance color utility node.

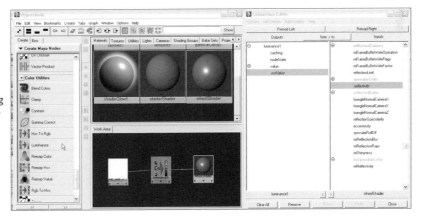

FIGURE 10.9
The reflection occlusion helps bring out the detail of the wheels and makes much more realistic-looking chrome.

The ambient occlusion texture makes the wheels look more realistic by controlling the amount of reflectivity in the cracks and crevices of the surface to bring out the detail. The wheels are now a bit closer to looking realistic.

You can use a reflection occlusion texture to create a separate render pass the same way that you created an ambient occlusion pass at the start of the chapter. All you need to do is use an ambient occlusion texture with the Reflective option activated for reflective surfaces and a standard ambient occlusion texture for diffuse surfaces. Render them all out in a single pass, or split them into separate passes and use the images to modify the render in your compositing software.

12. Save the scene as **carScene_v05.ma**. To see a version of the scene to this point, open the carScene_v05.ma file from the chapter10\scenes folder on the DVD.

Additional Ambient Occlusion Techniques

There are several additional ambient occlusion nodes and techniques that you can use to increase efficiency or for special circumstances.

Fast Occlusion

The mib_fast_occlusion texture can be used to increase the speed of an occlusion pass. This shader utilizes the ambient occlusion shading that is built into the mental ray renderer. This is a new feature of mental ray for Maya, which is part of the redesigned render pass workflow discussed in Chapter 12.

For the most part, the setup and attributes are very similar to those of the standard ambient occlusion shader. However, there are several options that need to be enabled in the Render

Settings window; otherwise you won't see any results when you use the shader. In the Features tab of the Render Settings window, make sure the Ambient Occlusion option is enabled. If this is not enabled, you'll see a flat white color or no effect from the occlusion texture.

In the Indirect Lighting section of the Render Settings window, enable Ambient Occlusion; then use the Cache settings to determine the number of rays and cache points used to calculate ambient occlusion. A higher number of points creates a smoother render but also results in less detail. The Cache Points attribute on the mib_fast_occlusion texture overrides the Cache Points setting in the Indirect Illumination tab of the Render Settings window.

The difference in quality between the mib_fast_occlusion shader and the standard mib_occlusion shader should be negligible in most situations. However, your own results may vary. You should experiment with both shaders and compare the results in terms of both quality and render time.

Ambient Occlusion and Transparency

If you're using a shader that has a texture in the Transparency channel, you'll find that the standard ambient occlusion textures will not calculate the transparency correctly. To fix this you can create a custom shader network and render with Final Gathering. This exercise demonstrates the technique.

1. Open the occlusionTransparency_v01.ma scene from the chapter10\scenes directory on the DVD. This scene has two planes, one on top of the other.

2. Open the Render Settings window, and make sure the Renderer is set to mental ray. In the Quality tab, set the Quality Presets option to Production. In the Indirect Lighting tab, turn on Final Gathering and set Accuracy to **400**.

3. Create a Lambert shader and apply it to the upperPlane object. Name the shader **transparentOcclusion**.

4. Open the Hypershade window, and MMB-drag the transparentOcclusion shader from the Materials tab into the Work Area of the Hypershade.

5. Create a grid texture (under 2D textures in the Create Maya Nodes mode of the left-hand column).

6. Set the Create tab in the left-hand column to Create mental ray Nodes. Expand the MentalRay Lights section, and choose mib_fg_occlusion to create an mib_fg_occlusion node.

7. Expand the Sample Compositing section lower in the left column, and create an mib_transparency node (see Figure 10.10).

The mib_transparency node allows for the correct calculation of the Final Gathering rays as they pass through the transparent parts of the texture. The mib_fg_occlusion shader is a simple switch. If Final Gathering (FG) is on in the Render Settings window, the shader renders ambient occlusion shadowing effects much like the ambient occlusion texture. If Final Gathering is off, it returns the Color When Off value set in its Attribute Editor.

FIGURE 10.10
Create the grid texture, mib_fg_ occlusion, mib_ transparency, and transparent- Occlusion shader nodes, and place them in the Work Area of the Hypershade.

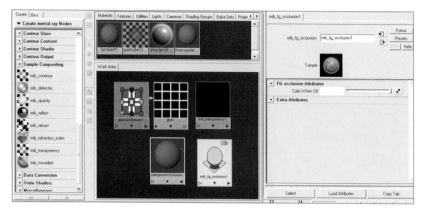

You can connect an ambient occlusion texture to the Color When Off value so that the shader acts as a switch. When FG is on, you get ambient occlusion shading as calculated by Final Gathering points. When FG is off, you get standard ambient occlusion shading, courtesy of the mib_amb_occlusion texture connected to the Color When Off attribute.

The mib_transparency node will allow for the correct calculation of the Final Gathering rays as they pass through the transparent parts of a texture.

8. In the Work Area of the Hypershade, connect the outColor channel of the grid texture to the Transparency channel of the mib_transparency1 node.

9. Open the grid texture's Attribute Editor, and set U Width and V Width to **0.5**. This makes the squares of the grid smaller so it's easier to see the effect of the occlusion shading.

10. Connect the mib_fg_occlusion node's outValue to the mib_transparency1 node's Input channel.

11. Select the transparencyOcclusion shader, and graph its input and output connections. Select the shading group node, and open its Attribute Editor. Expand the mental ray section, and find the Custom Shaders section.

The shading group node is the node labeled lambert2SG. It is the node that serves as an interface between the shader, the geometry, and the lights in the scene. It's also where you'll find many of the connections for mental ray override shaders. Every Maya shader that has been applied to geometry in a scene has an associated shading group node. When working with mental ray nodes, you'll be using the shading group node a lot.

12. Drag the mib_transparency1 shader from the Utilities tab of the Hypershade to the Material Shader slot in the lambert2SG node (see Figure 10.11).

This completes the shader for the upper plane. However, you'll need a custom shader for the lower plane so the ambient occlusion shadowing effect is calculated correctly for both surfaces.

13. Create a surface shader, and apply it to the lowerPlane object.

14. Connect the mib_fg_occlusion1 node (the same one that's connected to the network applied to the upper plane) to the outColor channel of the surface shader.

15. Create a test render to see the result; it should look like Figure 10.12.

16. To see a version of the scene with the network set up, open the `occlusionTransparency_` `v02.ma` scene from the `chapter10\scenes` directory on the DVD.

FIGURE 10.11
Connect the mib_ transparency1 node to the lambert2SG node's Material Shader attribute.

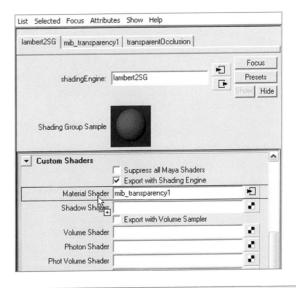

FIGURE 10.12
The transparency on the upper plane is calculated correctly showing the proper ambient occlusion shading for the two panes.

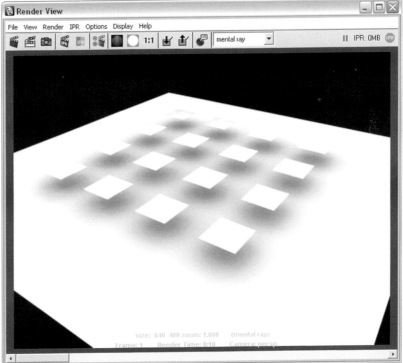

Shading Concepts

Shaders are sets of specified properties that define how a surface reacts to lighting in a scene. A mental ray material is a text file that contains a description of those properties. In Maya, the Hypershade provides you with a graphical user interface so you can edit and connect shaders without writing or editing the text files themselves. The terms *shader* and *material* are synonymous; you'll see them used interchangeably through the book and the Maya interface. mental ray also uses shaders to determine properties for lights, cameras, and other types of render nodes.

Three key concepts that determine how a shader makes a surface react to light are diffusion, reflection, and refraction. Generally speaking, light rays are reflected or absorbed or pass through a surface. Diffusion and reflection are two ways in which light rays bounce off a surface and back into the environment. Refraction refers to how a light ray is bent as it passes through a transparent surface.

Diffusion

Diffusion describes how a light ray is reflected off of a rough surface. Think of light rays striking concrete. Concrete is a rough surface covered in tiny bumps and crevices. As a light ray hits the bumpy surface, it is reflected back into the environment at different angles, which diffuse the reflection of light across the surface (see Figure 10.13).

You see the surface color of the concrete mixed with the color of the lighting, but you generally don't see the reflected image of nearby objects. A sheet of paper, a painted wall, and clothing are examples of diffuse surfaces.

In standard Maya shaders, diffusion is controlled using the Diffuse slider. A Lambert shader, named for the eighteenth-century Swiss physicist Johann Heinrich Lambert, is commonly used for diffuse surfaces that have no specular reflectivity.

FIGURE 10.13
Light rays that hit a rough surface are reflected back into the environment at different angles, diffusing light across the surface.

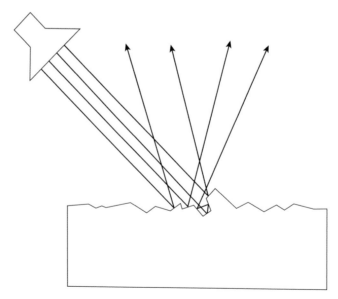

Reflection

When a surface is smooth, light rays bounce off the surface and back into the environment. The angle at which they bounce off the surface is equivalent to the angle in which they strike the surface—this is the incidence angle. This type of reflection is known as a *specular* reflection. You can see the reflected image of surrounding objects on the surface of smooth, reflective objects. Mirrors, polished wood, and opaque liquids are examples of reflective surfaces. A specular highlight is a reflection of the light source on the surface of the object (see Figure 10.14).

Logically smoother surfaces, or surfaces that have a specular reflectivity, are less diffuse. However, many surfaces are composed of layers (think of glossy paper) that have both diffuse and specular reflectivity.

A glossy reflection occurs when the surface is not perfectly smooth, but not so rough as to completely diffuse the light rays. The reflected image on a surface is blurry and bumpy and otherwise imperfect. Glossy surfaces can represent those surfaces that fit between diffuse reflectivity and specular reflectivity.

FIGURE 10.14
Light rays that hit a smooth surface and are reflected back into the environment at an angle equivalent to the incidence of the light angle

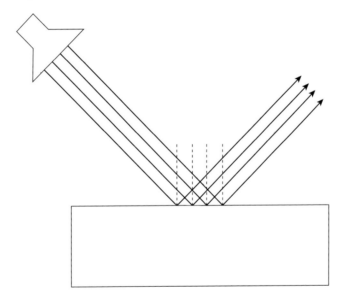

Refraction

A transparent surface can change the direction of the light rays as they pass through the surface (Figure 10.15). The bending of light rays can distort the image of objects on the other side of the surface. Think of an object placed behind a glass of water. The image of the object as you look through the glass of water is distorted relative to an unobstructed view of the object. Both the glass and the water in the glass bend the light rays as they pass through.

The refraction index is a value that describes the amount in which the speed of the light rays is reduced as it travels through a transparent medium, as compared to the speed of light as it travels through a vacuum. The reduction in speed is related to the angle in which the light rays are bent as they move through the material. A refraction index of 1 means the light rays are not bent. Glass typically has a refraction index between 1.5 and 1.6; water has a refraction index of 1.33.

FIGURE 10.15
Refraction changes
the direction of light
rays as they pass
through a transpar-
ent surface.

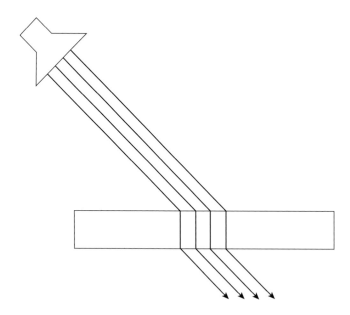

If the refracting surface has imperfections, this can further scatter the light rays as they pass through the surface. This creates a glossy/blurry refraction.

Refraction in Maya is available only when ray tracing is enabled (mental ray uses ray tracing by default). The controls for refraction are found in the Raytrace section of the Attribute Editor of standard Maya shaders. A shader must have some amount of transparency before refraction has any visible effect.

The Fresnel Effect

The *Fresnel effect* is named for the nineteenth-century French physicist Jean Agustin Fresnel (pronounced with a silent *s*). This effect describes the amount of reflection and refraction that occurs on a surface as the viewing angle changes. The glancing angle is the angle at which you view a surface. If you are standing in front of a wall, the glancing angle is 0 and the wall is per-pendicular. If you are looking across the ocean, the glancing angle of the surface of the water is very high. The Fresnel effect states that as the glancing angle increases, the surface becomes more reflective than refractive. It's easy to see objects in water as you stare straight down into water (low glancing angle); however, as you stare across the surface of water, the reflectivity increases, and the reflection of the sky and the environment makes it increasingly difficult to see objects in the water.

Opaque, reflective objects also demonstrate this effect. As you look at a billiard ball, the envi-ronment is more easily seen reflected on the edges of the ball as they turn away from you than on the parts of the ball that are perpendicular to your view (see Figure 10.16).

FIGURE 10.16

A demonstration of the Fresnel effect on reflective surfaces: the reflectivity increases on the parts of the sphere that turn away from the camera.

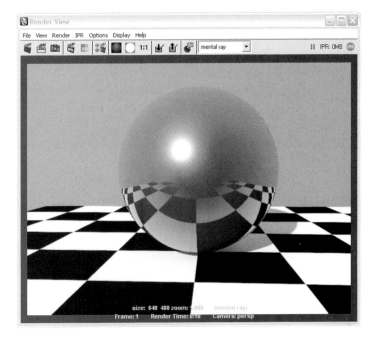

Real World Scenario

ADD FRESNEL REFLECTIONS TO A STANDARD MAYA SHADER

You can use a ramp node to add Fresnel reflections to a standard Maya shader. The ramp controls the amount of reflectivity on the surface. Using the Sampler Info node to determine the position of the colors on the ramp controls the reflectivity of the shader so the parts of the object that face away from the camera are more reflective than the parts that face toward the camera. Use the following workflow to create this setup:

1. Create a Blinn material (any standard Maya material that has a Reflectivity channel, such as Phong, Layer, or Anisotropic, will work).

2. Assign the material to an object such as a sphere.

3. In the Hypershade, create a ramp texture and a Sampler Info Utility node. These are found in the Create tab on the left side of the Hypershade. Set the mode of the Create tab to Create Maya Nodes.

4. Use the Connection Editor to connect the Out Alpha of the ramp to the Reflectivity of the Blinn material.

5. Use the Connection Editor to connect the facingRatio of the Sampler Info node to the V Coordinate channel of the uvCoord attribute of the ramp.

6. Open the Attribute Editor for the ramp texture; make sure the Ramp Type is set to V Ramp.

7. Set the color at the bottom of the ramp to white and the color at the top of the ramp to black; delete the center color.

CONTINUES

 **Real World Scenario**

ADD FRESNEL REFLECTIONS TO A STANDARD MAYA SHADER *(CONTINUED)*

8. Set the mental ray render quality to Production to ensure that ray tracing is enabled.

9. Increase the Specular Color of the Blinn and the Specular Rolloff settings, and render the scene.

To tune the amount of reflectivity on the edges, you can adjust the positions of the color on the ramp.

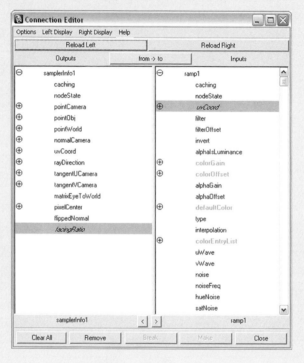

BSDF, BRDF, AND BTDF

The acronyms BSDF, BRDF, and BTDF refer to shading models used in CG to simulate how light interacts with surfaces. Different shaders, such as Lambert, Phong, Blinn, Ward, and Cooke-Torrance, employ these shading models in different ways to deal with the problem of light and surface interaction. BSDF stands for Bidirectional Scattering Distribution Function. BRDF (Bidirectional Reflectance Distribution Function) and BTDF (Bidirectional Transmittance Distribution Function) are two components of BSDF.

Using Reflections and Refraction Blur

Standard Maya shaders, such as the Blinn and Phong shaders, take advantage of mental ray reflection and refraction blurring to simulate realistic material behaviors. These options are available in the mental ray section of the shader's Attribute Editor. Blurry reflective and refractive surfaces are also referred to as *glossy* surfaces.

INTERACTIVE PHOTOREALISTIC RENDER PREVIEW

Interactive Photorealistic Render (IPR) preview is a mode that can be used in the Render View window. When you create a render preview using the special IPR mode, any change you make to a shader or the lighting, or even some modeling changes in the scene, automatically updates the Render View window, allowing you to see a preview of how the change will look interactively. IPR works very well with mental ray; in fact, it supports more rendering features for mental ray than for Maya Software. The workflow for creating an IPR render in mental ray is slightly different than the one for creating a Maya Software IPR. To create an IPR render, follow these steps:

1. Open the Render View window.

2. Set the current camera for the Render View window (Choose Render ➤ Snapshot ➤ *camera name*).

3. Click the IPR button at the top of the Render View window. The image will not actually render, but a message tells you to select a region to start tuning. Information about the scene is collected by mental ray. This may take a few seconds for complex scenes.

4. Select a region in the Render View window by drawing a rectangle over the parts of the image you want to tune; you'll see this part of the image update.

5. Make changes to the materials and the lighting; you'll see the image in the selected area update as you make the changes.

Most, but not all, mental ray features are supported by IPR. Occasionally you'll need to click the IPR button to update the render if IPR gets out of sync (or choose IPR ➤ Refresh IPR Image from the menu in the Render View window). The IPR render is a close approximation of the final render; be aware that what you see in the IPR render may look slightly different in the final render.

Reflection Blur

Reflection blur is easy to use and is available for any of the reflective shaders, such as Blinn, Phong, Anisotropic, and Ramp. This exercise demonstrates how to add reflection blur to a Blinn shader.

1. Open the crystalGlobe_v01.ma file from the chapter10\scenes directory on the DVD.

The scene shows the crystal globe and stand. The scene uses the Physical Sun and Sky network to create simple lighting.

2. Select the ground plane and apply a Blinn material. Set the Reflectivity of the Blinn material to **1** and the Diffuse value to **0**. Then render the scene in the render view from the renderCam camera.

3. Open the Attribute Editor for the Blinn shader that is applied to the ground. Expand the mental ray section and increase Mi Reflection Blur to **3**. Create another test render, and compare this to the render in the previous step (Figure 10.17).

FIGURE 10.17
Add a blurred reflection to the ground plane (right image).

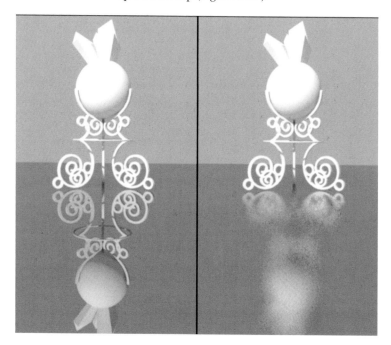

Reflection Blur Limit sets the number of times the reflection blur itself is seen in other reflective surfaces. Increasing the Reflection Rays value increases the quality of the blurring, making it appear finer. Notice that the reflection becomes increasingly blurry as the distance between the reflective surface and the reflected object increases.

Many surfaces are more reflective than you may realize. A wooden tabletop or even concrete can have a small amount of reflection. Adding a low reflectivity value plus reflection blurring to many surfaces increases the realism of the scene.

Refraction Blur

Refraction blur is similar to reflection blur. It blurs the objects that appear in a refracted surface. This gives a translucent quality to the object.

1. Continue with the scene from the previous section. In the Outliner, expand the globe group and select the crystal object. Assign a Blinn shader to the object.

2. Set Reflectivity of the new Blinn texture to **0** so you can clearly see the refractions.

3. Set Transparency of the object to light gray.

4. Expand Raytrace Options, and activate the Refractions option. Set Refractive Index to **1.4**.

5. Render the scene from the renderCam camera, and store the image in the Render View window.

6. Expand the mental ray section in the Blinn's Attribute Editor. Set Mi Refraction Blur to **5**, and create another test render (Figure 10.18).

7. Save the scene as **crystalGlobe_v02.ma**. To see a version of the scene, open the `crystal-Globe_v02.ma` file from the `chapter10\scenes` directory on the DVD.

Refraction Blur Limit sets the number of times the refraction blur itself will be seen in refractive surfaces. Increasing the value of Refraction Rays increases the quality of the blurring, making it appear finer.

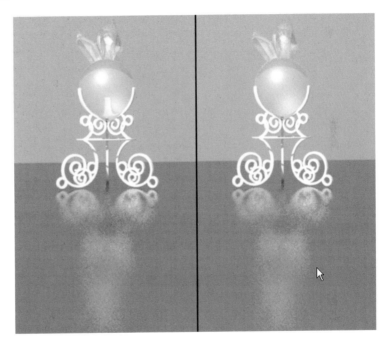

FIGURE 10.18
Add a blurred refraction to the surface of the crystal globe (right image).

Basic mental ray Shaders

mental ray has a number of shaders designed to maximize your options when creating reflections, glossy reflections, and refractions. Choosing a shader should be based on a balance between the quality of the material you want to create and the amount of time and processing power you wish to devote to rendering the scene. This section looks at a few of the shaders available for creating various types of reflections and refractions. These shaders are by no means the only way to create reflections and refractions. As discussed in previous sections, standard Maya shaders also have a number of mental ray–specific options for controlling reflection and refraction.

DGS Shaders

Diffuse Glossy Specular (DGS) shaders have very simple controls for creating different reflective qualities for a surface as well as additional controls for transparency and refraction. The reflections and refractions created by this shader are physically accurate. In this exercise you'll apply the material to the helmet model created in Chapter 3.

1. Open the `helmet_v01.ma` scene from the `chapter10\scenes` directory on the DVD.

2. Open the render view, and create a render using the renderCam camera. Store the render in the Render View window.

The scene has a very simple light setup. The key lighting is provided by a mental ray area light, which can be seen as a specular highlight on the orange metal of the helmet and on the glass face shield. The fill lighting is supplied by two directional lights; these lights have their specularity turned off so they are not seen as reflections on the surface of the helmet (see Figure 10.19).

The helmet uses standard Maya shaders. The metal of the helmet uses an orange Blinn, the face shield uses a transparent Blinn, and the helmet details and the woman's head use Lambert shaders. The grainy quality of the shadows results from the low sampling level set for the area light. By keeping the samples low, the image renders in a fairly short amount of time (under a minute on my machine). The reflection of the checkerboard plane beneath the helmet is clearly seen in the metal of the helmet and on the face shield.

3. Open the Hypershade window. In the Create tab on the left column, switch the mode to Create mental ray Nodes. Under Materials, click the dgs_material twice to create two DGS material nodes. Name the first one **helmet_dgs** and the second **shield_dgs**.

FIGURE 10.19
The space helmet rendered with simple lighting and standard Maya shaders

4. In the Outliner, select the group labeled helmetSurfaces. In the Hypershade, right-click the helmet_dgs shader and choose Assign dgs_material1SG from the marking menu. This assigns the material to all the objects in the group.

5. In the Outliner, select the shield surface. In the Hypershade, right-click the shield_dgs material, and choose Assign dgs_material2SG from the marking menu.

6. In the Hypershade, select the helmet_dgs material and open its Attribute Editor. Set the Diffuse color to bright orange. Set Glossy to black and Specular to white.

7. In the Hypershade, select the shield_dgs material. Set Transparency to **0.8**. Set Glossy to black and Specular to white.

8. In the render view, render the scene from the renderCam camera. Compare this render to the previous render. Immediately you'll notice a lot of strange things going on with the materials you just applied (see Figure 10.20).

If you compare Figure 10.20 with Figure 10.19, you should notice a few details:

◆ The surfaces are reflective; however, there is no specular highlight (reflection of the light source) on either the helmet surfaces or the glass shield.

◆ The shadow of the face shield that falls on the checkered floor is not transparent in Figure 10.20, but it is transparent in Figure 10.19.

FIGURE 10.20
The helmet and face shield surfaces have DGS shaders applied.

Let's look at how to solve these problems. The shader is meant to be physically accurate. The Specular attribute refers to the reflectivity of the shader. In standard Maya shaders, reflectivity and specularity are separated (however, increasing one affects the intensity of the other). In the DGS shader, the Specular channel controls the reflection of visible objects, so a light source must be visible to be seen in the specular reflections.

9. Select the area light in the Hypershade and open its Attribute Editor. In the areaLight-Shape1 tab, expand the mental ray attributes and activate the Visible option.

10. Render the scene again. This time you can see a reflection of the light in the surfaces. You can clearly see that the light is square shaped.

Glossy reflections, on the other hand, automatically render the reflection of a light source regardless of whether the light source is set to visible or not. The Glossy attribute on the DGS shader controls how reflections are scattered across the surface of an object. The term *specular highlight* with regard to shading models implies a certain amount of glossiness. Understandably, it's confusing when talking about specular reflections and specular highlights as two different things. The bottom line is this: To make a specular highlight appear in a DGS shader, either the light has to be visible when the Specular attribute is above zero and Glossy is set to zero *or* the Glossy setting must be above zero.

Glossy reflections can be blurry or sharp. To control the blurriness of a glossy reflection, you need to adjust the Shiny setting. Lower Shiny values create blurry reflections; higher Shiny values create sharp reflections.

11. Select the helmet_dgs shader and open its Attribute Editor. Set Glossy to a medium gray; set the Specular color to black. Set Shiny to **10** and create another render. This time the surface of the helmet appears more like painted metal and less like a mirror (upper-left image in Figure 10.21).

The Shiny U and Shiny V settings control the blurriness of the glossy reflection when Shiny is set to 0. Using these settings you can create an anisotropic type of reflection. Anisotropic reflections appear on surfaces that have a directionality to their roughness. When you look at the surface of a compact disc, the tiny grooves that are created when data is written to the disk create the satinlike anisotropic reflections. Brushed metal, hair, and satin are all examples of materials that have anisotropic specular reflections.

The U and V values control the direction of the anisotropic reflections across the surface. For best results set one value higher than the other.

12. Set Shiny to **0**. Set the Shiny U value to **3** and the Shiny V value to **10**, and create another render; the helmet now appears more like brushed metal (upper-right image in Figure 10.21).

The Shiny U and Shiny V settings simulate the anisotropic reflections on the material by stretching the reflection along the U or V direction. In this case this is not physically accurate and does not simulate how tiny grooves in the surface affect the reflection.

ISOTROPIC AND ANISOTROPIC SPECULAR REFLECTIONS

Isotropic and anisotropic both refer to a glossy specular highlight caused by microfacets on a surface. These tiny imperfections scatter reflected highlights, giving a glossy or blurry edge to highlights. Isotropic surfaces have a random order to the direction of the microfacets on the surface; anisotropic surfaces have microfacets that all run in a similar direction, which spread the specular highlights in a particular direction.

When rendering transparent surfaces using the DGS shader, the Specular, Glossy, Transparency, and Refraction settings all work together to create the effect. For transparency to work, the shader must have a Transparency setting higher than zero and either a Specular or a Glossy setting above zero. If Transparency is set to 1 and both Specular and Glossy are set to black, the surface will render as opaque, the same as if Transparency were set to 0.

The Specular color can be used to color the transparent surface, and the Glossy setting can be used (along with the Shiny settings) to create the look of a translucent material, such as plastic, ice, or frosted glass.

13. Select the shield_dgs material. Set the Specular color to a light green, and set Transparency to **0.8**.

14. Set Index Of Refraction to **1.1**. This makes the glass appear thicker as the light rays are bent as they pass through the glass.

15. Create another test render. Notice that the green specular color tints both the objects behind the glass as well as the reflections on the surface (lower-left image in Figure 10.21).

16. To create the look of frosted glass, set Diffuse to light gray, Specular to black, Glossy to light gray, Shiny to 20, Transparency to 0.8, and Index Of Refraction to **1.2**.

17. Create another test render to see the result (lower-right image in Figure 10.21).

FIGURE 10.21
Rendering using different settings for the DGS materials applied to the helmet metal and face shield.

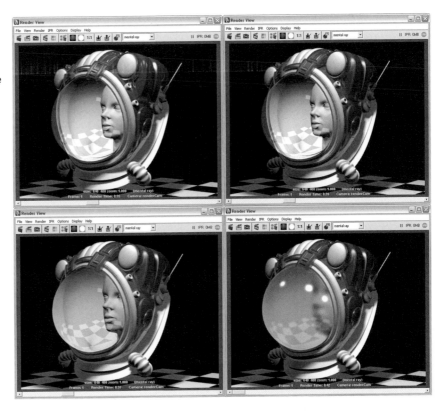

A few details are worth noting about using the Glossy settings:

- Specular reflections of all the lights in the scene are visible on the surface when Glossy is above zero. Notice that the highlights of the two directional lights are visible in the glass even though the Specularity option for both lights is disabled. To avoid this, consider using Global Illumination or Final Gathering to create fill lighting in the scene.

- Glossy reflections and refractions are physically accurate in that objects close to the refractive or reflective surface will appear less blurry than objects that are farther away.

- To make an object look more metallic, tint the Glossy color similar to the Diffuse color.

- Try using textures in the Glossy and Specular channels to create more interesting materials.

- When using the shader on scenes that employ Global Illumination, you need to create a dgs_material_photon node (found in the Photonic Materials section of the mental ray render nodes of the Hypershade). Attach this shader to the shading group of the original DGS material in the Photon Shader slot, and then use the settings on the dgs_material_photon to control the shader.

- You can increase realism further by rendering a separate reflection occlusion pass to use in a composite or plug occlusion textures into the specular and glossy attributes (enable Reflection on the occlusion textures).

18. Save the scene as **helmet_v02.ma**. To see a finished version of the scene, open the helmet_v02.ma scene from the chapter10\scenes directory on the DVD.

CASTING TRANSPARENT SHADOWS USING DGS SHADERS

The most accurate way to render transparent shadows when a DGS shader is applied is to render with caustic photons enabled. Using Caustics is covered in detail in Chapter 9.

If caustic photons are not practical, you can use this simple workaround; however, this method is really a "hack." It's not accurate and may not work in every situation:

1. Create a duplicate object, and apply a standard Blinn shader to the duplicate. If the original object is animated, the duplicate should be parented to either the original or an instance of the original so that it follows the animation of original object exactly.

2. Open the Attribute Editor for the original object. In the Render Stats, turn off Casts Shadows.

3. Open the Attribute Editor for the duplicate object. In the Render Stats, turn off Primary Visibility and Visible In Reflections And Refractions.

4. Assign a Blinn material to the duplicate. Set its Transparency and Index Of Refraction to the same value as the DGS material on the original object.

Another option would be to plug a mib_shadow_transparency node (found in the Shadow Shaders section of the mental ray nodes) into the Shadow Shader slot on the shading group node of the material. Using this node you can add transparency to the cast shadow created by the object by changing the color and transparency values on the shadow transparency node. The result is very simple and not physically accurate.

The downfall of this workflow is that the cast shadow will not be seen through transparent parts of the DGS material. Another option would be to create a separate shadow pass using transparent standard materials.

Dielectric Material

The purpose of the Dielectric material is to accurately simulate the refraction of light as it passes through transparent materials. Use the Dielectric material for glass, water, and other fluids. The term *Dielectric* refers to a surface that transmits light through multiple layers, redirecting the light waves as they pass through each layer.

If you observe a fish in a glass bowl, the light rays that illuminate the fish in the bowl transition from air to glass, then from glass to water, then again from water back to glass, and finally from glass out into the air on the other side. Each time a light ray makes a transition from one surface to another, the direction of the light ray changes. The index of refraction describes the change in the light ray's direction.

Most standard materials in Maya use a single index of refraction value to simulate the change of direction of the light ray as it is transmitted through the surface. This is not accurate, but it's usually good enough to create a believable effect. However, if you need to create a more physically accurate refractive surface, the Dielectric material is your best choice.

The material is most appropriately used to simulate glass and transparent liquids. This is because it has two settings for the index of refraction that describes the change of the light's ray's direction as it makes a transition from one refractive surface to the next.

In this exercise you'll create a physically accurate rendering of a glass of blue liquid using the Dielectric material. In this example, light will move from the air into glass and then from the glass into the water. The glass is open at the top, so you'll also need to simulate the transition from air to water. This means you'll need to use three dielectric materials: one for air to glass, one for glass to water, and one for air to water. This tutorial is based on Boaz Livny's discussion of the Dielectric material in *Mental Ray for Maya, 3ds Max, and XSI* by Boaz Livny (Sybex, 2008).

1. Open glass_v01.ma from the chapter10\scenes directory on the DVD.

In this scene a simple glass has been modeled and split into four surfaces. Each surface represents one of the three transitions that will be simulated using the Dielectric material. To make this easier to visualize, each surface each has a colored Lambert shader applied. The scene is lit using a single spotlight that casts ray trace shadows.

The four surfaces are named air_glass1, air_glass2, liquid_glass1, and liquid_air1.

2. Open the Hypershade window. Set the Create tab on the left to Create mental ray Nodes.

3. Expand the Materials section, and click the dielectric_material button. Name the new dielectric_material1 node **air2GlassShader**.

4. Create two more materials and name one **glass2LiquidShader** and the other **liquid2AirShader**.

5. Apply the air2GlassShader to both the airGlass1 and airGlass2 objects. Apply glass2LiquidShader to the liquid_glass1 object and liquid2AirShader to liquid_air1.

6. Select the air2glassShader and open its Attribute Editor.

The Index Of Refraction (IOR) for glass is typically 1.5, and the IOR for air is 1. Look at the settings for the air2Glass shader. The Index Of Refraction setting defines the IOR for the material; the Outside Index Of Refraction setting defines the IOR for the medium outside the material. The default settings for the Dielectric material are already set to the proper glass-to-air transition. Index Of Refraction should be set to **1.5**, and Outside Index of Refraction should be set to **1**.

7. Set Phong Coefficient to **100** and turn on Ignore Normals.

The Phong Coefficient creates a specular reflection on the glass. The Dielectric material uses the surface normals of the object to create the refraction effect. If you activate the Ignore Normals option, the shader bases the normal direction on the camera view. For a basic glass model such as this one, you can safely use the Ignore Normals feature.

8. Select the glass2LiquidShader and open its Attribute Editor. Set Index Of Refraction to **1.33** (the IOR of water is 1.33) and Outside Index Of Refraction to **1.5**. Set Phong Coefficient to **100**, and turn on Ignore Normals.

9. Click on the color swatch next to the Col attribute. This determines the color of the shader (why spell out Index Of Refraction in the interface but at the same time abbreviate Color? One of the many mysteries of Maya). In the Color Chooser set Hue (H) to **180**, Sat (S) to 0.**45**, and Value (V) to **1**.

10. Select the liquid2AirShader. Set Index Of Refraction to **1.33** and leave Outside Index Of Refraction at 1. Set Phong Coefficient to **100**, and turn on Ignore Normals.

11. Select the Col swatch, and use the same HSV values in the Color Chooser that you set in step 9.

12. Open the Render View window, and create a test render from the renderCam camera (see Figure 10.22).

FIGURE 10.22
Render the glass using the Dielectric material (left image). Add transparent shadows by rendering with caustics (right image).

You can see that there are differences between the refractions of the various surfaces. Just like the DGS shader, the Dielectric material fails to cast transparent shadows (Figure 10.22, left image). The best solution for this problem is to enable Caustics. When using caustics with the Dielectric shader, you need to connect a dielectric_material_photon material to the Photon Shader slot of the Shading Group node and enable Caustics. The settings for the dielectric_material_photon material should be the same as the settings for the Dielectric material. To see an example of this setup, open the `dielectricCaustics.ma` scene in the `chapter10\scenes` directory of the DVD. The image on the right of Figure 10.22 shows the glass rendered with Caustics enabled.

mental ray Base Shaders

A number of shaders available in the Hypershade are listed with the prefix *mib* (mental images base): mib_illum_cooktor, mib_illum_blinn, and so on. These are the mental ray base shaders. You can think of these nodes as building blocks; you can combine them to create custom shaders to create any number of looks for a surface. There are far too many to describe in this chapter, so it's more important that you understand how to work with them. Descriptions of each node are available in the mental ray user guide that is part of the Maya documentation.

In this exercise you'll see how a few of these shaders can be combined to create a custom material for the helmet.

1. Open the helmet_v03.ma scene from the chapter10\scenes folder on the DVD. This scene currently uses standard Maya shaders applied to the geometry.

2. Open the Hypershade window, and set the mode of the Create tab to Create mental ray Nodes.

3. Expand the Materials section; you'll see a number of mib materials toward the bottom (see Figure 10.23).

MIB _ ILLUM _ BLINN, MIB _ ILLUM _ PHONG, AND MIB _ ILLUM _ LAMBERT SHADERS

The mib_illum_blinn, mib_illum_phong, and mib_illum_lambert shaders use the same shading models as the standard Maya Blinn, Phong, and Lambert shaders with the exception that they have no reflection or refraction settings. If you are comfortable with the standard Maya Blinn, Phong, and Lambert shaders you won't gain very much from using the mental ray versions, so there is no reason to use these shaders if you don't want to.

---

4. Click the mib_illum_cooktorr button to create a Cook-Torrance material, and open its Attribute Editor.

FIGURE 10.23
Some of the mental ray base shaders are available in the Materials section of the Create mental ray Nodes menu.

The Cook-Torrance shader creates physically accurate isotropic specular highlighting, meaning that the specular highlights on surfaces are scattered as if the surface was covered with tiny microfacets arranged randomly.

The look of the highlight is created by setting the Specular color to a value above zero. The Roughness slider determines the spread of the highlight. The shader has three separate controls to determine the Index Of Refraction for each color channel (red, green, and blue). When light is reflected from the tiny bumps on an isotropic surface, the directionality of each light wave changes. The three IOR sliders allow you to specify this directional change for each color channel. This gives the specular highlight the appearance of "color fringing"—a slight tint on the edge of the highlight (this appears as blue fringe in the shader's preview). The color fringing around the highlight make this shader very useful for creating realistic-looking metals.

The Ward (mib_illum_ward) material is similar to the Cook-Torrance but offers more options for creating realistic anisotropic specularity. The Ward material works best on NURBS surfaces; the mib_illum_ward_deriv shader is a little easier to use, giving you two simple sliders to control the direction of the anisotropy along the U and V coordinates of the surface.

5 In the Outliner, select the helmetSurfaces group. In the Hypershade, right-click on the mib_illum_cooktorr1 shader, and choose Assign Material To Selection from the marking menu.

6. In the Attribute Editor, set the Diffuse color to light orange. Set the Specular channel to light gray.

7. Set Roughness to **0.19**.

8. To create an orange fringe around the highlight, set Index Of Refraction, Red to **80**, Index Of Refraction, Green to **10**, and Index Of Refraction, Blue to **8**.

9. In the Render View window, create a test render using the renderCam camera (Figure 10.24).

FIGURE 10.24

The Cook-Torrance shader creates fairly realistic metallic highlights.

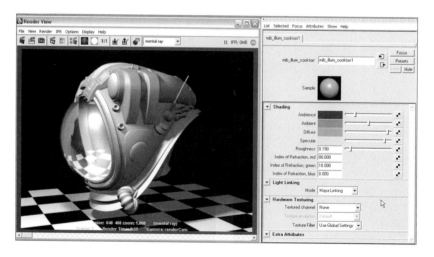

The helmet has a very convincing metallic look, but you'll notice there are no reflections. To add reflections you can combine the Cook-Torrance shader with a glossy reflection node.

10. In the Create tab of the Hypershade, click the mib_glossy_reflection button. Assign the new mib_glossy_reflection1 node to the helmet surfaces group. This overwrites the Cook-Torrance shader that has been applied.

11. Open the Attribute Editor for the mib_glossy_reflection1 node. From the Hypershade window, MMB-drag the mib_cook_torr1 node from the Hypershade to the Base Material slot of the mib_glossy_reflection1 node (see Figure 10.25).

FIGURE 10.25
Connect the Cook-Torrance shader to the Base Material slot of the mib_glossy_ reflection1 node.

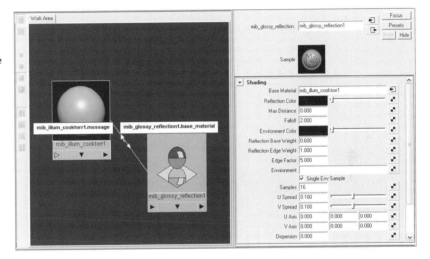

12. Set Reflection Color to white (white sets the shader to maximum reflectivity; darker shades create a less-reflective material), and create another render.

13. The default settings create a glossy reflection in the helmet surfaces. To adjust the quality and glossiness of the reflections, increase the Samples value to **32**.

The U Spread and V Spread sliders control the glossiness of the reflections, much like the Shiny U and Shiny V settings on the DGS shader. Higher values produce glossier reflections. Using a different value for U than V creates anisotropic specular highlights. Ideally you want to match the glossiness of the reflections on the mib_glossy_reflection1 shader with the glossiness of the highlight on the mib_cooktorr shader.

You can blend between a reflection of the objects in the scene and an environment reflection. To do this, you first need to create an environment reflection node.

14. Open the Attribute Editor for the mib_glossy_reflection1 node. Click on the checkered box to the right of the Environment field. From the mental ray tab of the Create Render Node window, scroll down to the Environments section. Click the mib_lookup_back-ground button.

This connects a mib_lookup_background node to the Environment slot of the mib_glossy_reflection1 node. You can use any of the environment nodes to map an image to the reflection of the environment. Mib_lookup_background works with standard rectangular images. The node sizes the background image to fit the resolution of the rendering camera.

15. The Attribute Editor should open to the mib_lookup_background1 node. Click on the checkered box next to the Texture tab to add a mental ray texture node. This allows you to map an image to the background.

16. In the Attribute Editor for the mentalRayTexture1 node, click on the folder next to Image Name. Load the `desert.jpg` image found in the `sourceimages` directory in the `Chapter10` folder on the DVD.

17. Select the mib_glossy_reflection1 node, and in its Attribute Editor, set Environment Color to medium gray. This sets the strength of the reflectivity of the environment.

The shader can create a smooth transition from the reflections of objects in the scene and the environment reflections. The Max Distance attribute sets a limit in the scene for tracing reflections. When reflection rays reach this limit, they stop sampling reflections of objects in the scene and start sampling the image mapped to the environment. The Falloff value determines the smoothness of the transition. The Falloff value is a rate of change. A setting of 1 creates a linear falloff; higher values create a sharper transition.

18. Set Max Distance to **5** and Falloff to **2**. Turn off Single Env Sample, and create another test render. You can see the blue sky of the desert image reflected in the metal of the helmet.

To increase the realism of the reflections, you can add an ambient occlusion node to decrease the intensity of the reflections in the crevices of the model.

19. Open the Attribute Editor of the mib_glossy_reflection node. Click on the checkered box next to Reflection Color. From the Create Render Node pop-up, switch to the mental ray tab, and click on the Mib_amb_occlusion node in the Textures section.

20. Open the Attribute Editor for the mib_mab_occlusion node, set Samples to **32**, Bright Color to medium gray, and Dark Color to a very dark gray (but not black). Set Max Distance to **5**, and turn on Reflective.

21. Create another test render of the scene. Now the reflections on the model look much more believable (see Figure 10.26).

FIGURE 10.26
The Cook-Torrance shader is combined with a glossy reflection shader (left image). An environment is added to the reflectivity (center image), and an ambient occlusion node is used to modify the reflectivity (right image).

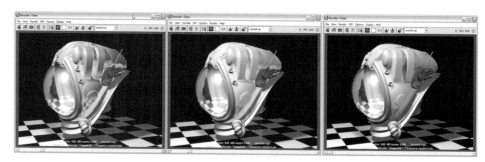

Figure 10.27 shows the shader network for this material.

This gives you a basic idea of how to work with the mental ray base materials. Of course, you can make many more complex connections between nodes to create even more realistic and interesting surface materials. Experimentation is a good way to learn which connections work best for any particular situation.

22. Save the scene as **helmet_v04.ma**. To see a version of the scene to this point, open the helmet_v04.ma scene from the chapter10\scenes directory on the DVD.

FIGURE 10.27
The mental ray base shaders are connected to create a realistic painted metal surface for the helmet.

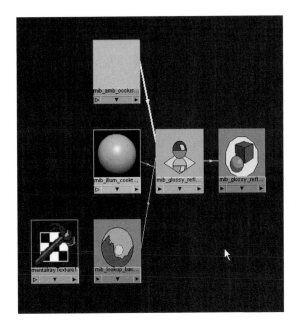

Car Paint Materials

Simulating the properties of car paint and colored metallic surfaces is made considerably easier thanks to the special car paint phenomenon and metallic paint mental ray materials.

In reality car paint is made up of several layers; together these layers combine to give the body of a car its special, sparkling quality. Car paint uses a base-color pigment, and the color of this pigment actually changes hue depending on the viewing angle. This color layer also has thousands of tiny flakes of metal suspended within it. When the sun reflects off these metallic flakes, you see a noticeable sparkling quality. Above these layers is a reflective clear coat, which is usually highly reflective (especially for new cars) and occasionally glossy. The clear coat itself is a perfect study in Fresnel reflections. As the surfaces of the car turn away from the viewing angle, the reflectivity of the surface increases.

The metallic paint material is very similar to the car paint phenomenon material. In fact, you can re-create the car paint material by combining the mi_metallic_paint node with the mi_glossy_reflection node and the mi_bump_flakes node.

Using the Car Paint Material

In this exercise you'll apply the car paint material to the three-wheeled vehicle created by Anthony Honn.

1. Open the carScene_v06.ma scene from the chapter10\scenes directory on the DVD. This scene uses the Physical Sun and Sky network for lighting.

2. Open the Hypershade window, and set the mode of the Create column on the left to Create mental ray Nodes. Expand the Materials section, and click on the mi_car_paint_phen_x shader (see Figure 10.28).

FIGURE 10.28

The car paint materials are found in the Materials section of the Create mental ray Nodes column in the Hypershade.

MENTAL RAY EXTENDED MATERIALS

The mental ray nodes that use the x suffix are more advanced (extended) versions of the original shader. Most of the advancements are in the back end; the interface and attributes of mi_car_paint_phen and mi_car_paint_phen_x are the same. It's safe to use either version. You can upgrade the mi_car_paint_phen material by clicking the buttons in the Upgrade Shader section of the material's Attribute Editor. The x_passes materials are meant to be used with render passes. This topic is covered in Chapter 12.

---

3. Open the Outliner and select the carBody group; apply the mi_car_paint_phen1 material to this group. This group consists of the surfaces that make up the body of the car.

4. Open the Attribute Editor for the mi_car_paint_phen1 material.

The Diffuse Parameters section determines the color properties of the base pigment layer. As the color of this layer changes depending on the viewing angle, the various settings determine all of the colors that contribute to this layer.

5. Set Base Color to dark navy blue; this is the main color of the base layer. If you wanted to add a texture map to apply decals to the car, you would use this channel.

6. Set Edge Color to a similar shade of blue, but lower the Value so it is almost black. The Edge Color is apparent on the edges that face away from the camera. Newer cars and sports cars benefit from a dark Edge Color.

Edge Color Bias sets the amount of spread seen in the Edge Color. Lower values (0.1 to 3) create a wider spread; higher values (4 to 10) create a narrower band of Edge Color.

7. Lit Color is the color seen in the surface areas that face the light source. Set this color to a bright purplish-blue.

Lit Color Bias works on the same principle as Edge Color Bias. Lower values (above zero) create a wider spread in the Lit Color.

8. Diffuse Weight and Diffuse Bias set the overall strength of the Diffuse colors. A lower Diffuse Bias value (0 to 1) flattens the color; higher values (1 to 2) increase intensity toward the lit areas. Set Diffuse Bias to **2**.

The Specular Parameters settings define the look of the specular highlight on the surface. The highlight has two components: a bright center highlight and a surrounding secondary highlight. The Spec Glazing feature adds a polished shiny quality to the highlight, which works well on new cars. Turn this feature off when you want to create the look of an older car with a duller finish.

Spec Weight and Spec Sec Weight are multipliers for the primary specular and secondary specular colors (respectively). Spec Exp and Spec Sec Exp determine the tightness of the highlight; higher values (30 and higher) produce tighter highlights. Generally Spec Sec Exp should be lower than Spec Exp.

The Flake Parameters settings are the most interesting components of the shader. These determine the look and intensity of the metallic flakes in the pigment layer of the car paint.

Flake Color should usually be white for new cars. Flake Weight is a multiplier for Flake Color; higher values intensify the look of the flakes; usually 1 is a good setting for most situations.

Flake Reflect adds ray-tracing reflectivity to the flakes. This means that the flakes contribute to reflections of objects in the scene. For most situations a value of 0.1 is sufficient.

Flake Exp is the specular exponent for the flakes. Much like Spec Exp, higher values create a tighter highlight.

Flake Density determines the number of flakes visible in the paint. The values range from 0.1 to 10. In many situations a high value actually means that the individual flakes are harder to see.

Flake Decay optimizes rendering times by setting a limit to the visibility of the flakes. Beyond the distance specified by this value the Flakes are no longer rendered, which can keep render times down and reduce render artifacts, especially if Flake Density is set to a high value.

Flake Strength varies the orientation of the flakes in the paint. Setting this to 0 makes all the flakes parallel to the surface; a setting of 1 causes the flakes to be oriented randomly, making the flakes more reflective at different viewing angles.

Flake Scale sets the size of the flakes. It's important to understand that the size of the flakes is connected to the scale of the object. If you notice that the size of the flakes is different on one part of the car than another part of the car, select the surface geometry and freeze the transformations so that the Scale X, Y, and Z values are all set to 1. This will correct the problem and ensure that the flakes are a consistent size across all the parts of the car.

9. Set Flake Density to **0.6**, Flake Strength to **1**, and Flake Scale to **0.08**.

The Reflection Parameters settings are similar to those for the reflection parameters on the glossy reflection material. The reflectivity of the surface is at its maximum when Reflection Color is set to white. When this is set to black, reflections are turned off.

Edge Factor determines the transition between the reflection strength at glancing angles and the reflection strength at facing angles.

Reflection Edge Weight sets the strength of reflectivity at glancing angles, and Reflection Base Weight sets the reflectivity at facing angles. Generally the base weight should be lower than the edge weight to create a proper Fresnel reflection effect.

Samples sets the sampling for glossy reflections. Unless you want to create glossy reflections, which are best used for older, duller cars, you can leave Samples at 0.

Glossy Spread defines the glossiness of the reflections. Max Distance sets the point where reflection rays start sampling environment shaders and stop sampling the geometry in the scene.

The Dirt Parameters settings allow you to add a layer of dirt to the surface of the car. Dirt Weight specifies the visibility strength of the dirt. For best results you can connect a painted texture map to Dirt Color if you want to add splashes of mud and grime.

10. Set Edge Factor to **4**, and leave the other settings at their defaults (see Figure 10.29).

FIGURE 10.29

The settings for the car paint shader

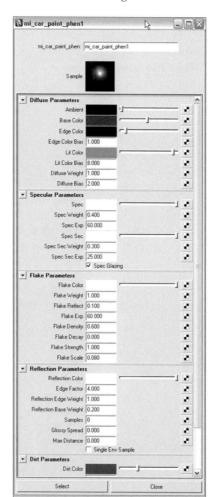

FIGURE 10.30

The car paint material is applied to the body of the car and rendered with the physical sun and sky lighting.

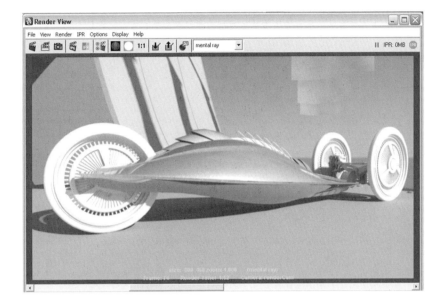

11. In the Render View window, create a test render from the renderCam camera (Figure 10.30).

12. Save the scene as **carScene_v07.ma**. To see a finished version of the scene, open the carScene_v07.ma file from the chapter10\scenes directory on the DVD.

The MIA Material

The MIA material is the Swiss army knife of mental ray shaders. It is a monolithic material, meaning that it has all the functionality needed for creating a variety of materials built into a single interface. You don't need to connect additional nodes into a specific network to create glossy reflections, transparency, and the like.

MIA stands for mental image architectural, and the shaders (mia_material, mia_material_x, mia_material_passes) and other lighting and lens shader nodes (mia_physicalsun, mia_portal, mia_exposure_simple, and so on) are all part of the mental images architectural library. The shaders in this library are primarily used for creating materials used in photorealistic architectural renderings; however, you can take advantage of the power of these materials to create almost anything you need.

The MIA material has a large number of attributes that at first can be overwhelming. However, there are also presets available for the material. You can quickly define the look you need for any given surface by applying a preset. Then you can tune specific attributes of the material to get the look you need.

Because of the physical-based nature of the materials, the dynamic range of their output can exceed what is visually pleasing on a standard computer monitor. To correct for this you can apply a lens shader to the rendering cameras to control the exposure. The lens shaders are explored later in the chapter. For this section, the exercise uses the Physical Sun and Sky network. When you add this network to a scene, the rendering cameras automatically have a lens shader applied, which means the materials will look correct when rendering.

In this section you'll get some practice working with the MIA material presets.

Using the MIA Material Presets

The presets that come with the MIA material are the easiest way to establish the initial look of a material. Presets can also be blended to create novel materials. Furthermore, once you create something you like, you can save your own presets for future use in other projects. You'll work on defining materials for the space suit helmet. This version of the scene uses the mia_physical-sunsky lighting network and Final Gathering to light the scene.

1. Open the helmet_v05.ma scene from the chapter10\scenes directory on the DVD. The surfaces in the model have been grouped by material type to make it easier to apply shaders.

2. Open the Hypershade window, and set the mode of the Create column on the left to Create mental ray Nodes. Expand the Materials section, and click the mia_material_x button to create a material. Name the material **metalShader**.

3. In the Outliner, select the helmetMetalSurfaces group, and apply the metalShader material to this group (right-click on the material in the Hypershade, and choose Assign mia_material_x1SG To Selection).

4. Open the Attribute Editor for the metalShader. Click the Presets button in the upper right, and choose Copper ➤ Replace.

5. Open the Render View window, and create a render from the renderCam camera. It really looks like copper. Save the render in the render view.

6. The material could use a little tweaking to make it look less like a kitchen pot. Click the Presets button again, and choose SatinedMetal ➤ Blend 50%. This will add some anisotropy to the highlights on the helmet.

7. In the Attribute Editor, set Color to a medium grayish-blue (the color should be fairly unsaturated; otherwise the helmet will look very disco!). In the Reflection section, set Color to a light blue and turn on Metal Material—this adds a bluish tint to the reflections.

8. Create another test render and compare it with the previous render (Figure 10.31).

You can tweak many of the settings to create your own custom metal, but already it looks pretty good. The Glossiness setting adds blur to the reflections. Turning on Highlights Only creates a more plastic-like material—with this option activated the Reflection settings apply only to specular highlights.

9. Next you can add chrome to the helmet. Create a new mia_material_x shader, and name it **chromeShader**. Select the chromeParts group in the Outliner, and apply the chromeShader to the group.

10. Open the Attribute Editor for the chromeShader material. Click the Presets button, and apply the Chrome preset to the shader.

11. Create another mia_material_x shader. Name it **rubberShader**. Apply this shader to the rubberParts group. Use the Presets button to apply the rubber preset.

12. Create another test render and compare it to the previous renders.

The rubber shader can use a little tweaking. A slight bump can increase the realism.

FIGURE 10.31

The MIA material comes with a number of presets that can be blended together to create novel materials.

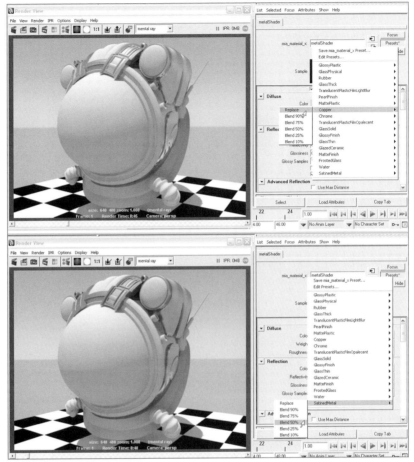

13. Scroll down in the Attribute Editor, and click on the checkered box next to Standard Bump. In the Create Render Nodes pop-up, switch to the Textures tab, and select the Leather texture. The Attribute Editor opens to the leather node. Use the following settings (Figure 10.32):

Cell Color: light gray

Crease Color: dark gray

Cell Size: **0.074**

If the bump seems too strong, you can either adjust the cell and crease colors so that the shades of gray are closer together or switch to the Bump3D1 node and lower the Bump Depth value.

When you use the mia_material_x shader, you have a choice of bump styles. When Standard Bump is enabled and No Diffuse Bump is activated, the bump appears only in the specular and reflective parts of the material, which can be useful for creating the look of a lacquered surface. Standard Bump works much like a typical bump shader on a standard Maya shader.

FIGURE 10.32
The Leather tex-
ture is added as a
bump to the rubber
MIA material.

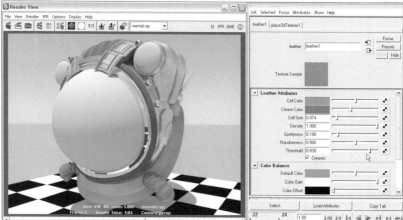

3D TEXTURES

The Leather texture is a 3D texture. It does not use UV coordinates to determine the texture's placement on the surface; the texture exists in 3D space. This means that if the object is animated, the texture will appear stationary as the object moves, creating a very strange swimming effect in the texture. To fix this you must either parent the 3D texture node to the animated object or, if the object is deformed, create a texture reference object. To do this, select the object and choose Texturing ➤ Create Texture Reference Object. This makes a duplicate of the original object that is not seen in the render. You can hide the texture reference object, and the texture on the original object should move with the animated object just fine. To remove the texture reference object, select the original and choose Texturing ➤ Delete Texture Reference Object.

The Overall Bump shader can be used for bump textures as well (the No Diffuse Bump setting has no effect on textures used for the Overall Bump shader); however, the Overall Bump slot is really intended for use with the mia_roundcorners texture. The mia_roundcorners texture adds a slight bevel to the edges of a surface in the render. This means you do not need to create beveled edges directly in the geometry. A very slight edge bevel can improve the realism of the model (sharp edges on surface are often a tell-tale sign that the object is computer generated). Let's take a look at the roundcorners texture in action by applying it to the chrome material. You can apply the roundcorners texture to the Overall Bump shader and another texture to the Standard Bump shader.

14. In the Hypershade, select the chromeShader and open its Attribute Editor. Scroll down to the Bump section, and click on the checkered box to the right of Overall Bump. In the Create Render Nodes pop-up, switch to the mental ray tab and expand the Textures section. Click the Mia_roundcorners button to create this node.

15. In the Attribute Editor for the mia_roundcorners1 node, set Radius to **0.1**. Create another test render and compare it to the previous renders. You'll see that the chrome trim around the helmet has a light roundness to it, making it look a little more believable (see Figure 10.33, right image).

FIGURE 10.33
Adding the mia_roundcorners texture to the chromeShader's Overall Bump channel creates a slight beveled edge to the geometry in the render (right image).

Creating Thick and Thin Glass and Plastic

Another feature of the mia_material shader is the ability to simulate thickness and thinness in the material itself without creating extra geometry. This can be very useful, especially for glass surfaces.

1. In the Hypershade, create two new mia_material_x nodes. Name one **thinGlass** and the other **thickGlass**.

2. Apply the thinGlass shader to the glassShield object in the Outliner. Apply the thickGlass material to the lampShields group in the Outliner.

3. In the Attribute Editor for the thinGlass material, use the Preset button to apply the glassThin preset. In the Attribute Editor for the thickGlass shader, apply the glassThick preset.

4. Create another test render.

The thin glass of the face shield looks extremely believable, especially with regard to the shading on the inside of the helmet. The lamps at the top of the helmet have a chrome reflector behind the thick glass, which adds to the reflectivity of the material. The settings to control thickness are found under the Advanced Refractions controls. Along with the standard Index Of Refraction setting, there is an option for making the material either thin walled or solid. You also have the option of choosing between a transparent shadow and a refractive caustic that is built into the material (the caustics render when caustic photons are enabled and the light source emits caustic photons; for more information on caustics, consult Chapter 9).

5. Open the Hypershade window, and create another mia_material_x node. Name this one **plasticShader**. Apply this shader to the plasticParts in the Outliner.

6. Open the Attribute Editor for the plasticShader, and apply the translucentPlasticFilm-LightBlur preset. Create another test render.

This preset creates very translucent plastic using glossy refractions. In this situation it seems a little too transparent. Use the following settings to make the plastic look a little more substantial.

◆ In the Diffuse section, set Color to a dim pale blue.

◆ In the Reflection section, set Color to a dark gray, and set Glossiness to **0.35**.

◆ In the Refraction section, set Color to a dark blue and Glossiness to **0.52**.

◆ Scroll down to the Ambient Occlusion section, and activate Ambient Occlusion. Set Ambient Light Color to a light gray.

7. Create another test render (see Figure 10.34).

8. Save the scene as **helmet_v06.ma**. To see a finished version of the scene, open the helmet_v06.ma scene from the chapter10\scenes directory on the DVD.

FIGURE 10.34
Apply the glass and plastic presets to parts of the helmet.

Other MIA Material Attributes

The ambient occlusion can be subtle on some materials, especially reflective material. This is because using Final Gathering creates a certain amount of ambient occlusion already. The Ambient Occlusion option on the material acts as a multiplier for existing ambient occlusion created by the indirect lighting (Final Gathering/Global Illumination). The Use Detail Distance option can be used to enhance fine detailing when set to On. When set to With Color Bleed, Ambient Occlusion factors the reflected colors from surrounding objects into the calculation.

The Translucency setting is useful for thin-walled objects, such as paper. This option works only when the material has some amount of transparency. The Translucency Weight setting determines how much of the Transparency setting is used for transparency and how much is used for translucency. So if Transparency is 1 (and the transparency color is white), and Translucency Weight is 0, the object is fully transparent (Figure 10.35, left). When Translucency Weight is at 0.5, the material splits the Transparency value between transparency and translucency (Figure 10.35, center). When Translucency Weight is set to 1, the object is fully translucent (Figure 10.35, right).

FIGURE 10.35
Three planes with varying degrees of translucency applied

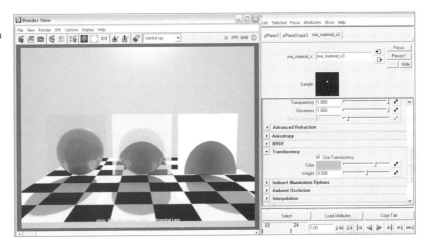

Translucency can be used for solid transparent objects to create a simple version of subsurface scattering; however, it is not as realistic as the misss shaders discussed in Chapter 11. Notice that you can also create translucent objects by experimenting with the glossiness in the Refraction settings. This can be used with or without activating the Use Translucency option.

The MIA materials have a wide variety of uses beyond metal and plastic. The materials offer an excellent opportunity for exploration. For more detailed descriptions of the settings, read the mental ray for Maya Architectural Guide in the Maya documentation.

Controlling Exposure with Tone Mapping

Tone mapping refers to a process in which color values are remapped to fit within a given range. Computer monitors lack the ability to display the entire range of values created by physically accurate lights and shaders. This becomes apparent when using HDRI lighting, MIA materials, and the physical light shader. Using tone mapping, you can correct the values to make the image look visually pleasing when displayed on a computer monitor.

Lens shaders are applied to rendering cameras in a scene. Most often they are used for color and exposure correction. You've already been using the mia_physicalsky lens shader, which is created automatically when you create the Physical Sun and Sky network using the controls in the Indirect Lighting section of the Render Settings window.

Using Exposure Shaders

The mia_exposure_photographic and mia_exposure_simple shaders are used to correct exposure levels when rendering with physically based lights and shaders. The mia_exposure_photographic lens shader has a lot of photography-based controls that can help you correct the exposure of an image. The mia_exposure_simple lens shader is meant to accomplish the same task; however, it has fewer controls and is easier to set up and use. In this exercise, you'll use the mia_exposure_simple lens shader to fix problems in a render.

The scene you'll use is the space helmet scene. This version of the scene uses the same mia_ materials as the previous section. In the previous section the problems with the exposure were not noticeable because lens shaders were already applied to all the cameras when the Physical Sun and Sky network was created. In this section you'll learn how to apply the lens shader manually.

1. Open the helmet_v07.ma scene from the chapter10\scenes directory in the DVD. Currently this scene has no lighting. All the materials on the helmet are the same MIA materials described in the previous section.

2. Open the Render Settings window, and switch to the Indirect Lighting tab. Click the Create button next to Image Based Lighting.

3. In the Attribute Editor for the mentalrayibl1 node, click on the folder next to Image Name. Select the building_probe image from the chapter10\sourceimages directory on the DVD. This is a typical, high-dynamic range image.

4. Set Mapping to Angular. In the Render Stats section, turn off Primary Visibility so that the IBL sphere is not visible in the render.

5. Enable Final Gathering in the Indirect Lighting tab of the Render View window, and set Accuracy to **200**.

6. Create a test render in the Render View window using the renderCam camera, and store the image in the Render View window.

The rendered image looks very underexposed; the dark parts are very dark.

7. In the Outliner, select the renderCam camera and open its Attribute Editor. Expand the mental ray section and click on the checkered box to the right of Lens Shader.

8. In the Create Render Nodes window, switch to the mental ray tab, expand the Lenses section, and click the button labeled Mia_exposure_simple.

This applies the mia_exposure_simple lens shader to the rendering camera. You need to remember to apply this shader to any of the cameras you'll use for rendering the scene.

9. Create another test render from the renderCam camera. You'll see a big improvement in the image using the default settings of the mia_exposure_simple lens shader (see Figure 10.36).

10. Save the scene as **helmet_v08.ma**. To see a finished version of the scene open the helmet_v08.ma scene from the chapter10\scenes directory on the DVD.

Following is a brief description of the shader's attributes.

Pedestal adds lightness to the black areas of the image; a negative value will "crush the blacks" by adding contrast to the image.

Gain increases the brightness of the lighter areas in the image.

The **Knee** value sets the point where overbright values (values that go beyond the 0–1 range) are brought down within the normal range.

The **Compression** setting applies compression to the overbright values as defined by the Knee setting.

Gamma applies the overall color correction to the image so it appears correct on the computer monitor. A typical value for Windows displays is 2.2. It's important to make sure that if you set the Gamma value in the lens shader, additional Gamma correction does not take place in the rendering and compositing pipeline.

For a more in-depth discussion of tone mapping, consult the mental ray for Maya Architectural Guide included in the Maya documentation.

FIGURE 10.36
The image on the left appears under-exposed; adding a lens shader to control exposure fixes the problem, as seen in the image on the right.

Rendering Contours

mental ray has a special contour rendering mode that enables you to render outlines of 3D objects. This is a great feature for nonphotorealistic rendering. You can use it to make your 3D animations appear like drawings or futuristic computer displays. The end title sequence of the film *Iron Man* is a great example of this style of rendering.

Enable Contour Rendering

Rendering contours is easy to set up, but it requires activating settings in several different places.

1. Open the `carContour.ma` scene from the `chapter10\scenes` directory on the DVD. This scene shows the car modeled by Anthony Honn. A simple Lambert material is applied to the car.

2. Open the Render Settings window, and select the Features tab. Expand the Contours section, and click Enable Contour Rendering. This makes contour rendering possible, but you won't see any results until you activate a few more options.

3. Expand the Draw By Property Difference section. These settings define how the contours will be drawn. One of these options must be activated or contour rendering will not take place. Click Between Different Instances. This means lines will be drawn around each piece of geometry in the scene (see Figure 10.37).

FIGURE 10.37
To render contour lines, you must check Enable Contour Rendering and choose a Draw By Property Difference option.

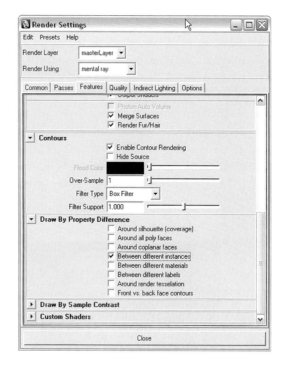

4. Open the Hypershade window, select the whiteLambert material, and graph its input and output connections. In the Work Area of the Hypershade, select the whiteLambertSG node that is attached to the whiteLambert shader, and open its Attribute Editor.

5. In the Contours section of the mental ray rollout in the Attribute Editor, check the Enable Contour Rendering option. Set Color to red (Figure 10.38).

FIGURE 10.38
Contour Rendering also needs to be enabled in the shader's shading group node settings.

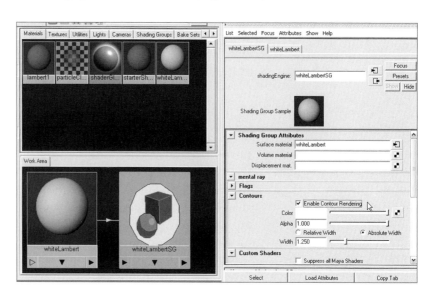

6. Create a test render in the Render View window from the renderCam camera. The contours are added after the scene renders, on top of the shaded view of the geometry.

7. Open the Render Settings window. In the Features tab, in the Contours section, activate Hide Source, and set Flood Color to a dark blue. Create another test render (see Figure 10.39).

This time the original geometry is hidden, and only the contours are rendered. Flood Color determines the background color when Hide Source is activated. Oversampling sets the quality and antialiasing of the contour lines.

You can adjust the width of the contours using the controls in the Contours section of the shading group. Absolute Width ensures that the contours are the same width; Relative Width makes the width of the contours relative to the size of the rendered image.

Since each shading group node has its own contour settings, you can create lines of differing thickness and color for all of the parts of an object. Just apply different materials to the different parts, and adjust the settings in each material's shading group node accordingly.

FIGURE 10.39
Contour rendering creates lines on top of the rendered surface. In the bottom image the source has been hidden so only the lines render.

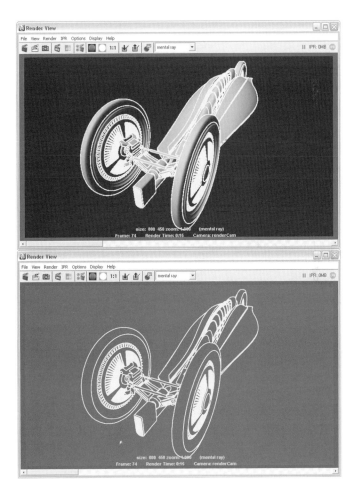

Experiment using different settings in the Draw By Property Difference section of the Render Settings window. More complex contour effects can be created by plugging one of the contour shaders available in the Create mental ray Node section of the Hypershade into the Contour Shader slot under the Custom Shaders section of the shading group node.

The Bottom Line

Use ambient occlusion. Ambient occlusion describes the dark shadowing that occurs when ambient light rays are prevented from reaching part of a surface by another nearby surface. You can use the mib_amb_occlusion node in mental ray to fake the look of indirect lighting or augment the ambient occlusion shadowing that occurs when rendering with Final Gathering.

Master it   Create an ambient occlusion shader from a standard Maya shader.

Understand shading concepts.   Light rays are reflected, absorbed by, or transmitted through a surface. A rough surface diffuses the reflection of light by bouncing light rays in nearly random directions. Specular reflections occur on smooth surfaces; the angle at which rays bounce off a smooth surface is equivalent to the angle at which they strike the surface. Refraction occurs when light rays are bent as they are transmitted through the surface. A specular highlight is the reflection of a light source on a surface. In CG rendering this effect is often controlled separately from reflection; in the real world specular reflection and highlights are intrinsically related.

Master it   Create a standard Maya shader that is more reflective on parts of the shader that face away from the camera.

Apply reflection and refraction blur.   Reflection and Refraction Blur are special mental ray options available on many standard Maya shading nodes. You can use these settings to create glossy reflections when rendering standard Maya shading nodes with mental ray.

Master it   Create the look of translucent plastic using a standard Maya Blinn shader.

Use basic mental ray shaders.   The DGS and Dielectric shaders offer numerous options for creating realistic reflections and transparency. The mib (mental images base) shader library has a number of shaders that can be combined to create realistic materials.

Master it   Create a realistic CD surface using the mib shaders.

Apply the car paint shader.   Car paint consists of several layers, which creates the special quality seen in the reflections on car paint. The mi_carpaint_phen shader can realistically simulate the interaction of light on the surface of a car model. The diffuse, reflection, and metallic flakes layers all work together to create a convincing render.

Master it   Design a shader for a new and an old car finish.

Use the MIA materials   The MIA materials and nodes can be used together to create realistic materials that are always physically accurate. The MIA materials come with a number of presets that can be used as a starting point for your own materials.

Master it   Create a realistic polished-wood material.

Control exposure using tone mapping.   Tone mapping corrects images that appear improperly exposed when rendering. This frequently occurs when HDRI lighting is used, when physical lights are used, and especially when physical lights are combined with MIA materials.

> **Master it**   Create a scene that uses physical light shaders on the lights. Apply MIA materials to the objects in the scene, and correct the exposure using tone mapping.

> **scene. Adjust the settings on the lens shader to correct for exposure problems.**

Render contours.   mental ray has the ability to render contours of your models to create a cartoon drawing look for your animations. Rendering contours requires that options in the Render Settings window and on the shading group for the object are activated.

> **Master it**   Render the space suit helmet using contours.

Chapter 11

Texture Mapping

The use of two-dimensional images to add color and detail to three-dimensional objects has been a big part of computer modeling and animation from the very start. This is known as *texture mapping*, and it is practically an art form all its own. A well-painted texture map can add an astonishing degree of realism, especially when combined with good lighting and a well-constructed 3D model. In this chapter you'll see how to use texture mapping to create photorealistic skin for a character.

In this chapter you will learn to:

- ◆ Create UV texture coordinates
- ◆ Create bump and normal maps
- ◆ Create displacement maps
- ◆ Use the PSD network node
- ◆ Create a misss_fast_skin shader
- ◆ Create texture maps for NURBS surfaces

UV Texture Layout

No matter what software you use or what type of object you're trying to model, UV texture mapping is not fun. It's a chore, and like most things in life that are tedious and difficult, it has to be done. Someday soon advances in rendering technology may make UV texture mapping unnecessary; however, until that day comes you'll have to embrace the arcane art of UV mapping. Fortunately Maya provides you with some advanced, yet simple-to-use tools to create UV texture coordinates for your models.

What Are UV Texture Coordinates?

Just as x-, y-, and z-coordinates tell you where an object is located in space, u- and v-coordinates tell you where a point exists on a surface. Imagine a dot drawn on a cardboard box. The u- and v-coordinates specify the location of that dot on the surface of the box. If you unfold the box and then place a grid over the flattened box, you can plot the position of the dot using the grid. One axis of the grid is the u-coordinate; the other axis is the v-coordinate. 3D software uses u- and v-coordinates to determine how textures should be applied to 3D objects. *UV mapping* refers to the process of determining these coordinates for polygon objects. *UV layout* is a term that refers to the 2D configuration of the UVs on a surface, such as a picture of the unfolded box on a grid taken from above (see Figure 11.1). In the UV Texture Editor, u-coordinates are plotted along the horizontal axis, and v-coordinates are plotted along the vertical axis.

FIGURE 11.1

UV coordinates appear as an unfolded version of the model. They determine how textures are applied to 3D models. In this image the coordinates tell Maya where to place the black dot on the cube.

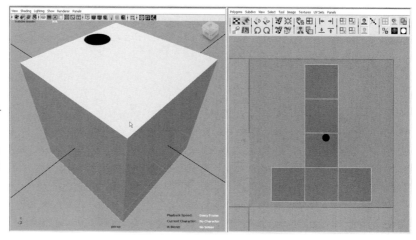

NURBS surfaces have implicit UVs; this means that the coordinates are built into the parameterization of the surface. UV texture coordinates do not have to be created for NURBS surfaces; only polygon and subdivision surfaces require mapped UVs. With regard to subdivision surfaces, it's usually best to map the UVs on a polygon version of the model and then convert that model to subdivision surfaces. The mapped UV coordinates will be converted along with the polygon object (a discussion of texturing NURBS surfaces is at the end of the chapter).

Most of the time you are creating UV coordinates so that the colors applied to the object can be painted in a two-dimensional digital paint program, such as Photoshop. The UV map acts as a guide in Photoshop that tells you where to paint the various colors. Figure 11.2 shows a typical Photoshop texture-painting session using a snapshot of the UVs, created in Maya, as a guide. So for a character's head, a good UV layout may look a little strange, but you should be able to make out where the eyes, nose, mouth, ears, and other features are located. This is often referred to as a *human readable* UV layout as opposed to an automatically tiled layout that functions just fine but is impossible to decipher when trying to paint a 2D map in Photoshop (see Figure 11.3).

A good UV layout will also minimize stretching, warping, and the appearance of seams between the parts of the UV map. As you go through the exercise in this chapter, you'll learn about strategies that can help you avoid, or at least reduce, many of the problems that can arise when painting two-dimensional textures that will be applied to a three-dimensional model.

Even if you intend to create texture maps in a program such as BodyPaint 3D or ZBrush, which allow you to paint directly on a 3D model, it's a good idea to make sure you have human readable UVs. This is especially true when working in a production pipeline. The textures you create in ZBrush or BodyPaint may need to be mapped or enhanced in Photoshop. If the UVs are not human readable, this will be impossible.

FIGURE 11.2
UV coordinates are used as a guide for painting 3D model textures in digital paint programs such as Photoshop.

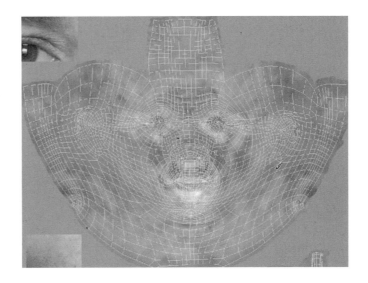

FIGURE 11.3
Human readable UVs bear some resemblance to the original 3D object (top) so that an artist can easily paint textures. Automatically tiled UVs (bottom) will function but are impossible for artists to decipher.

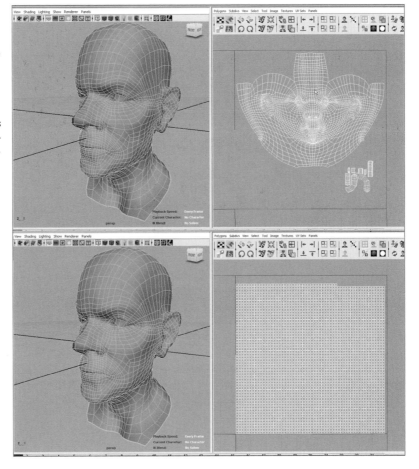

Creating UV Texture Coordinates

This exercise uses a human head as an example. You can learn almost everything you need to know about creating UV coordinates for characters just from the head. Most of the rest of the body is pretty straightforward, and you can apply the techniques you learn here to most other objects.

There are many approaches to mapping the head, depending on what you need to achieve in your final render. In this example the goal is to create neat UVs that will maximize the texture space reserved on the face.

1. Open the UVMap_v01.ma file from the chapter11\scenes folder on the DVD. You'll see a polygon head of an older man, as shown in Figure 11.4.

2. In the perspective view choose the UV layout panel arrangement by choosing Panels ➤ Saved Layouts ➤ Persp/UV Texture Editor. This splits the screen so that the perspective view is on the left and the UV Texture Editor is on the right (Figure 11.4). If the UV Texture Editor is already open as a separate panel, you'll get a warning, and the right side of the screen will be something other than the UV Texture Editor.

The interface of the UV Texture Editor is a 2D graph with menus and an icon bar at the top. Many of the icon commands are duplicated in the menu selections. The graph is divided into four quadrants. The upper-right quadrant (shaded darker gray) is typically where you'll keep your texture coordinates. Notice the numbers on the graph; the upper-right quadrant has the positive U and V values. The values range from 0 to 1. It is possible to have coordinates existing outside this range, and this may be useful in some circumstances, but most of the time you want to keep the coordinates within this range.

FIGURE 11.4
The workspace is divided between the perspective view on the left and the UV Texture Editor on the right. Currently the selected head object has no UV texture coordinates.

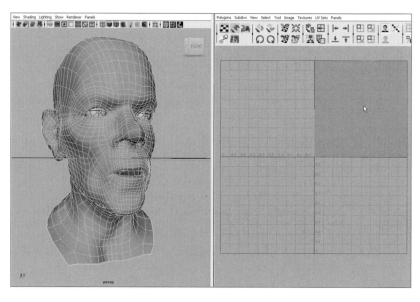

NAVIGATION IN THE UV TEXTURE EDITOR

You can move about in the UV Texture Editor just as you can in the perspective view, except that you can't tumble around, since by its nature UV texturing is a 2D process. Use Alt+RMB to zoom and Alt+MMB to pan.

Mapping the Scalp

When creating coordinates for a large complex object, it's best to break it into its simplest components. The model has a large bald head; you'll start by making coordinates for just this part of the model.

Creating and editing UV coordinates is a lot like modeling, and you'll use many of the same tools and selection modes. The best time to create UV coordinates for a model is when you've finished editing the model itself. Inserting edges, subdividing, and extruding will alter the coordinate layout and produce undesirable effects.

1. Click on the head model in the perspective view, and press the F key to center the model.

2. Select the model and apply a Lambert shader. Name the shader **oldManShader**.

3. Open the Attribute Editor for oldManShader. Click the checkered box next to the color slider to open the Create Render Node panel, as shown in Figure 11.5. Make sure that Normal is selected in the 2D Textures rollout, and click Checker. This will apply the checker texture to the color of the model. The checker pattern will not appear since the model has no texture coordinates.

FIGURE 11.5
Select the checker texture in the Create Render Node panel.

4. In the perspective view, select the model and press the 6 key to switch to shaded view.

5. From the toolbar, select the Paint Selection tool, and the model will switch to vertex component mode. Right-click on the model, and choose Face to switch to face selection mode.

6. Open the Paint Selection Tool options (see Figure 11.6). In the Stroke rollout, choose Reflection, and set Reflection Axis to X. When you use the tool to select faces, the faces on the opposite side will also be selected.

FIGURE 11.6
The options for the Paint Selection tool

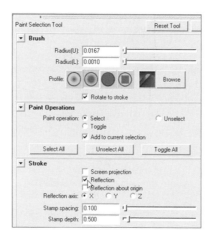

7. Switch back to shaded view (hot key = 5). Paint across the top of the head on one side of the model. To adjust the radius of the Paint Selection tool interactively, hold the b key and drag on the model; the red circle indicates the radius of the selection brush.

8. Use the Paint Selection tool to select the area of the head that corresponds to the scalp; use Figure 11.7 as a guide. You want to select just the top of the head. If you need to deselect some faces, just hold the Ctrl key while painting on the model. Switch to wireframe view, and make sure only the faces of the scalp are selected. By default the Paint Selection tool adds to the current selection, so you do not need to hold the Shift key while painting.

FIGURE 11.7
Use the Paint Selection tool to select the faces of the scalp. The Reflection settings in the tool options allow the faces on the opposite side to be selected automatically.

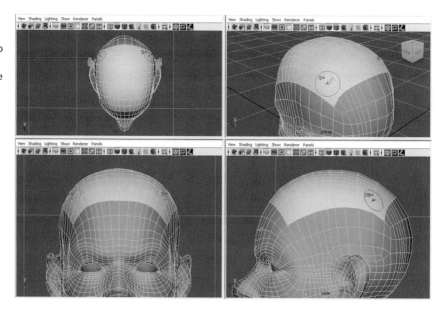

QUICK SELECT SETS

Creating a Quick Select set is a great way to store your component selections. To make a Quick Select set, choose Create ➤ Sets ➤ Quick Select Set. You'll be prompted to name the set and asked if you want to save the set to the currently selected shelf. When you want to select the components in the Quick Select set, you can choose Edit ➤ Quick Select Set and choose the name of your set from the menu, or you can click the shelf button if you create one with the set. The components selected when you created the set will be reselected. This is very helpful, especially when the model is complex and you've spent a long time selecting specific components.

9. Once you have the faces of the scalp selected, you'll map the UVs using one of Maya's preset mapping primitives. The cylinder works well to match to the rounded surface of the scalp. With the faces still selected, switch to the Polygon menu set, and choose Create UVs ➤ Cylindrical Mapping. Switch back to textured shading to see the pattern on the scalp (hot key = 6).

By default the cylindrical mapping manipulator appears aligned on the Y axis; you'll notice that the checker pattern in Figure 11.8 now appears on the scalp, since now the selected faces have UV coordinates. However, the pattern on the top of the head is distorted. The goal is to create as even and undistorted a checker pattern as possible on the entire head. Doing this requires some manipulation of the UV mapping manipulator and, later on, the UV points themselves.

FIGURE 11.8
The checker pattern appears on the top of the head, where coordinates have been mapped using the cylindrical mapping manipulator.

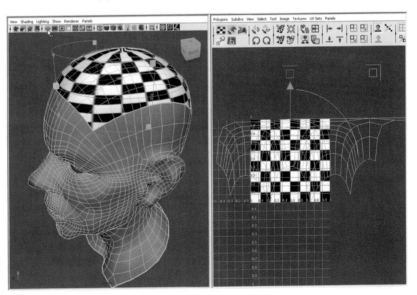

In the perspective view you can see the UV mapping manipulator and its position relative to the model; in the UV Texture Editor you can see a wireframe representation of the flattened model indicating how the mapping is being applied. You can also see the checkerboard pattern on the UV grid. The texture you have applied to the model will appear on the grid. This can be helpful in some cases, especially if you are trying to match the UVs to a prepainted texture map. In this case it's not helping much.

10. Choose Image ➤ Display Image (uncheck this option in the UV Texture Editor's menu bar) to turn off the texture preview. The checkerboard disappears in the UV Texture Editor.

DIM IMAGE

Note: you can use the Dim Image button just below the Display Image button to lower the opacity of the image in the UV Texture Editor.

---

11. In the perspective view, tumble around the model and find the red T in the lower corner of the cylindrical mapping manipulator. Click on this to switch to the translate/rotate/scale mode of the manipulator (see Figure 11.9).

12. Click on the blue circle of the manipulator to switch to rotate mode. Gently drag upward on the red circle of the manipulator to rotate it along the X axis. If you accidentally click somewhere and lose the manipulator, you can press Ctrl+z to undo and bring the manipulator back.

FIGURE 11.9
Clicking on the T at the lower corner of the mapping manipulator switches to the translate/rotate/scale mode of the manipulator.

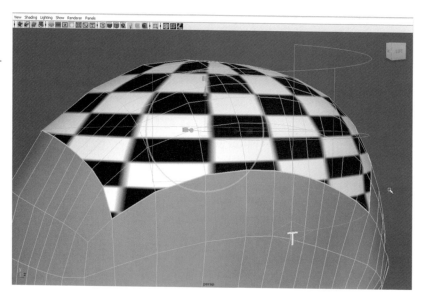

RESELECTING THE TEXTURE MAPPING HANDLE

Another way to reselect the manipulator handle is to select the model, look in the Channel Box under inputs, and find the projection node (usually named something like polyCylProj1). Select this node in the Channel Box, and the manipulator should reappear in the perspective view. Note that if you delete history on the model, this node will no longer exist.

---

13. You want to rotate the manipulator so that the cylinder is positioned like a curved hat above the head. You can rotate the manipulator numerically by opening the Channel Box and entering **-90** in the Rotate X channel of the polyCylProj1 node.

14. Notice that as you rotate the manipulator, the wireframe depiction of the UV coordinates in the UV Texture Editor also changes. The goal here is to create an undistorted, flat representation of the scalp that can easily be used as a guide in Photoshop for painting the scalp texture.

15. In the perspective view, carefully click on the blue arrow at the center of the cylindrical mapping manipulator to switch to translate mode. Drag downward on the manipulator to reposition it. You want to remove as much of the distortion in the checker pattern seen on the top of the head as possible. The checker pattern on the sides of the head will become stretched. That's okay; it can be fixed later. You can also enter **0.690** in the Y field of the Projection Center coordinates in polyCylProj1's Attribute Editor or in the Channel Box.

16. Switch to scale mode by clicking on the green box at the end of the arrow that points to the back of the head. Scale the manipulator along its Y axis until the squares of the checker pattern are no longer stretched. Note that since the manipulator has been rotated -90 degrees, the Y axis scale handle (colored green) is now facing the back of the head and not the top. Alternatively it may be easier to edit the scale numerically (see Figure 11.10). Enter **1.829** in the Projection Height field of the polyCylProj1 Channel Box.

17. In the UV Texture Editor, drag on the red arrow, and move the wireframe view of the scalp off to the right.

Notice that as you move the UV coordinates off the grid in the UV Texture Editor, the checker pattern moves but does not disappear. This is because the pattern repeats infinitely beyond the 0 to 1 range of the grid (where the image preview is seen when the Display Image button is activated). Eventually you'll move the scalp back to the grid, but for now you just want to move it out of the way while you work on the rest of the head.

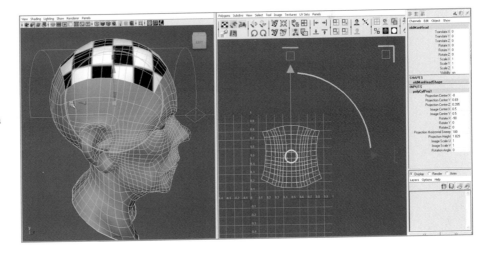

FIGURE 11.10
The cylindrical projection manipulator is translated, rotated, and scaled until the checker pattern on the scalp is even.

Creating UV Shells

The sections of the mapped head (such as the scalp coordinates mapped in the previous section) are referred to as *UV shells*. You'll continue by creating a UV shell for the back of the head.

1. Tumble around to the back of the head in the perspective view. Deselect the selected faces, select the object, then switch to the Paint Selection tool and select the faces on the back of the head (take a peek at Figure 11.11 to see which faces you need to select).

2. When the faces are selected, switch to wireframe view (hot key = 4), and make sure no faces on the model other than those on the back of the head are selected. If there are extra faces selected, remember that you can deselect faces by holding the Ctrl key while painting on the model with the Paint Selection tool.

3. Switch back to textured view (hot key= 6). Click on the view cube in the upper-right corner of the perspective view, and switch to the back view (this may require clicking on the triangles just outside the view cube a couple times until the back view appears).

4. Zoom out a little so you can see the entire back of the head. With the faces of the back of the head still selected, choose Create UVs ➢ Planar Mapping ➢ Options. Set Fit Projection to Bounding Box and Project From to Camera. Click Project to create the projection and close the Options dialog box.

5. In the UV Texture Editor, drag on the green arrow to push the wireframe representation of the UV coordinates on the back of the head downward and out of the way of the main grid.

FIGURE 11.11
The faces on the back of the head are mapped using a planar projection.

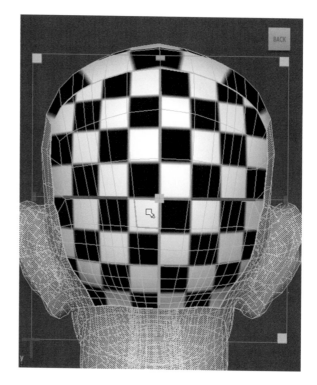

6. In the perspective view, right-click on part of the model, and choose Select from the marking menu. In the UV Texture Editor you can see the wireframe of both the scalp and the back of the head. If you deselect the head, the coordinates disappear; to bring them back, just reselect the head object.

7. In the toolbar at the top of the UV Texture Editor, click the Move UV Shell tool icon (see Figure 11.12). This is the icon at the upper-right corner in the first section of icons at the upper-left of the UV Texture Editor toolbar.

ICON HELP

Remember that if you hover over an icon with the mouse, the name of the tool will appear in the help line at the lower left of the screen. This is useful when the icon for the tool is less than intuitive.

FIGURE 11.12
The icon for the
Move UV Shell tool

8. Click on any point in the shell for the back of the head. The points of the shell turn green, indicating that you are in UV selection mode—each green point is a single UV coordinate.

9. Use the Move tool to reposition the shell above the scalp shell.

10. Switch to the Scale tool (hot key = r), and drag on the yellow box at the center of the Scale tool in the UV Texture Editor to scale the back-of-the-head shell down so that the checker pattern on the scalp and the back of the head roughly match.

11. Save your scene. To see an example of the scene so far, open the UVMap_v02.ma file from the chapter 11\scenes folder on the DVD.

Flipped and Overlapping UVs

When creating UV texture coordinates, you need to make sure that the direction is consistent among all of the UVs; otherwise, strange artifacts can appear when the model is textured and rendered. Likewise, it is extremely important that UVs are not overlapping, tangled, or folded improperly. Overlapping UVs can cause a render to crash. Maya's UV Texture Editor has tools that can help you detect and eliminate overlapping UVs. In this next section you'll see these tools in action as you continue to create UV shells for the sides of the head.

1. Continue with the scene from the previous exercise or open the UVMap_v02.ma file from the chapter 11\scenes folder on the DVD.

2. In the perspective view, use the Paint Selection tool to select the faces on the side of the head down to the jawline, just above the neck. Select all of the faces of the ears as well. Match the selection of faces, as shown in Figure 11.13.

SELECTING FACES IN THE UV TEXTURE EDITOR

If you select faces that have already been mapped, you'll see the faces highlighted in the UV Texture Editor. You can Ctrl-drag a selection marquee around these faces in the UV Texture Editor to deselect them. The UV Texture Editor can be used as an aid to selecting and deselecting polygons in tricky spots.

3. Make sure the selection on each side of the face is identical; even when the Paint Selection tool is set to Reflection, sometimes the selection on each side can be slightly different. This particular model is not perfectly symmetrical.

4. Turn on wireframe view, and make sure only the sides of the face and the ears have been selected. Look for stray selections on other parts of the head. You can deselect extra faces by holding Ctrl while painting over them using the Paint Selection tool.

CAMERA BASED SELECTION

In the options for the Select tool, you can activate Camera Based Selection, which restricts component selection to the camera view. This option prevents you from selecting components on the opposite side of the model by mistake.

5. From the Polygon menu set, choose Create UVs ➤ Planar Mapping ➤ Options. In the options, choose to project from the X axis; this is similar to projecting from the side view using a camera projection.

FIGURE 11.13
Use the Paint Selection tool to select the unmapped faces on either side of the head.

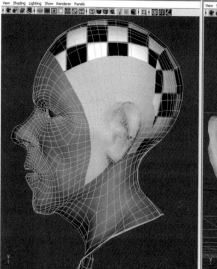
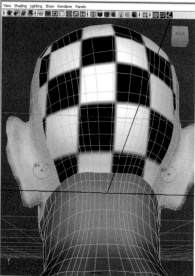

6. In the UV Texture Editor you'll see only one UV shell. If you zoom in, though, you'll see that there are actually two shells on top of each other. The slight asymmetry in the model reveals the difference in the wireframe of the two shells.

7. In the UV Texture Editor, right-click on the UV shell created from the projection in step 6, and choose UV to switch to UV selection mode. Select a single UV point on one of the shells. Right-click on the selected UV, and choose Select ➤ Shell to select all of the UVs that are contained within the same shell, as shown in Figure 11.14.

8. Press the w key to switch to the Move tool. Move the selected shell to the left so that it is no longer on top of the other shell. You could use the Move UV Shell tool as well; this is just an alternate workflow.

9. Repeat steps 7 and 8 to select the other matching shell; move it to the left and below its twin.

These two shells are on top of each other because they were created from the same side view camera that projected through the model. One of these shells needs to have its direction flipped so that it is consistent with the other shells. You can easily figure out which one by turning on the shaded UV mode.

10. Click the Toggle Shaded UV Mode button on the UV Texture Editor toolbar. The icon is shown in Figure 11.15. When shaded UV mode is activated, the UV shells are colored according to their direction.

FIGURE 11.14
Zooming in on the UVs reveals that there are two UV shells, one on top of the other. The slight asymmetry in the model makes selecting a UV of one of the shells a little easier.

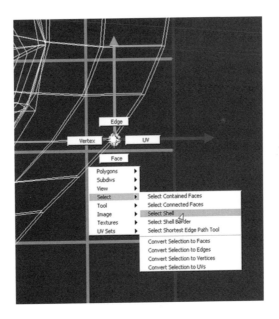

FIGURE 11.15
The icon for the shaded UV display mode

If you zoom out on the editor, you'll see that the shells created in the previous section are colored blue. Likewise, one of the side-of-the-face shells is blue and the other is red. The red shell needs to be flipped to make it consistent with the other shells (Figure 11.16).

FIGURE 11.16

The shell shaded in red (light gray in this figure) needs to be flipped so its UV direction is consistent with the other shells.

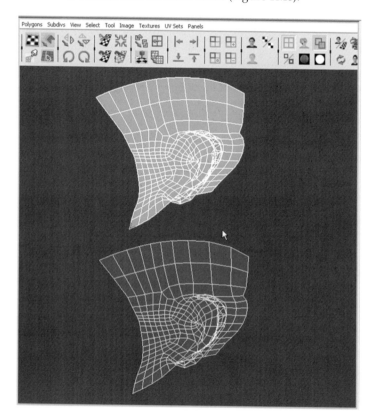

11. Switch to UV selection mode (right-click on the UVs and choose UV from the marking menu). Select the red side-of-the-face shell (right-click and choose Select ➢ Shell, or just drag a selection over the entire shell, making sure that every point in the shell is selected).

12. Click either the Flip UV button in the second section of the UV Texture Editor toolbar or choose Polygons ➢ Flip from the UV Texture Editor menus. The shell will flip either horizontally or vertically; since it will be repositioned anyway, it doesn't matter which way it flips. What does matter is that the shell is now shaded blue and not red, indicating that the UVs are running in the same direction as the other shells.

13. Zoom in to a part of the shell that corresponds with the ear. You'll notice that some of the shell is shaded dark blue, purple, and red. These parts of the shell are overlapping each other as well as reversing direction as the ear curls around (see Figure 11.17). This is a situation you want to avoid at all costs. Maya has several tools that can help solve this problem.

FIGURE 11.17
When shaded UV mode is activated, overlapping UVs are a darker shade than nonoverlapping UVs

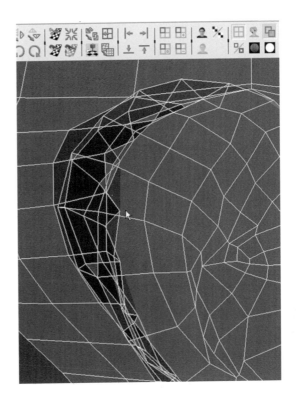

Smooth UV Tool

The ears are a little tricky since they are a convoluted shape. However, since they are most likely going to have very simple colors applied, you may be able to get away with some stretching and warping of the coordinates. You can smooth out the overlapping UVs interactively using Maya 2009's new Smooth UV tool.

1. In the UV Texture Editor, right-click on one of the shells, and choose UV to switch to UV selection mode.

2. Drag a rectangular selection marquee over one of the shells to select all of its UVs.

3. From the menu bar in the UV Texture Editor choose Tools ➤ Smooth ➤ Options. In the Options box, make sure Pin Borders is selected—it should be by default.

4. In the UV Texture Editor, you'll see a handle with two text boxes: one labeled Unfold, the other labeled Relax. Click and drag over the word *Relax* (drag back and forth). This smoothes the UVs by averaging their distances. By dragging back and forth, you can interactively set the level of relaxation. Keep an eye on the model in the perspective view to see how relaxing the UVs affects the texture mapping. Relax the UVs so the overlapping disappears, as shown in Figure 11.18. The position of the tool in the UV Texture Editor does not affect its operation.

FIGURE 11.18
The Smooth UV tool allows you to relax or unfold the UVs interactively in the UV Texture Editor.

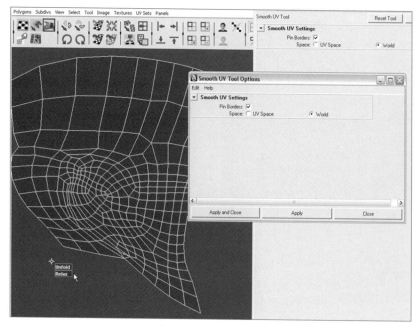

5. With the same UV shell selected, drag over the word *Unfold*. The Unfold operation untangles the UVs while trying to match the shape of the 3D surface. This fixes the warping caused by the Relax operation.

6. Repeat these steps for the other side-of-the-face shell. You don't have to use both Relax and Unfold depending on the situation; sometimes you can get away with using just Unfold.

UV Smudge and UV Lattice Tools

Two additional tools that can help fix warped and stretched areas are the UV Smudge and Lattice tools.

1. Use the Paint Selection tool to select the faces of the neck; use Figure 11.19 as a guide for selecting the polygon faces. The selection on the sides of the neck and the back of the neck should extend up to the previously mapped areas.

2. Use cylindrical mapping to create coordinates for these areas (Create UVs ➤ Cylindrical Mapping).

3. In the UV Texture Editor, move the neck shell down off the grid.

4. Convert the current selection to UVs. From the Polygon menu set choose Select ➤ Convert Selection ➤ To UVs.

The UV Smudge tool works on selected UVs. The icon looks like a finger pulling a grid of UVs (see Figure 11.20). It's the first icon on the bottom row on the left side of the UV Texture Editor toolbar.

FIGURE 11.19
Select the faces
of the neck.

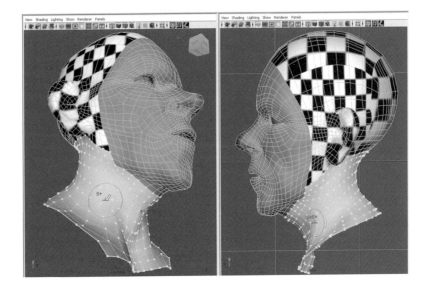

FIGURE 11.20
The icon for the UV
Smudge tool

5. Click the icon for the UV Smudge tool. A red circle will appear, as shown in Figure 11.21. If you zoomed in too closely to the UVs, you may have to zoom out to see it. The red circle is the radius of the UV Smudge tool; you can resize it interactively by MMB-dragging while holding the B key.

6. Drag the selected UVs in the UV Texture Editor window to reposition them. Watch the results in the perspective window; see if you can remove some of the warping in the checker pattern on the spaces on the bottom edges of the neck. There's no Reflection option for this tool, so try your best to make both sides of the neck shell consistent in shape.

FIGURE 11.21
The UV Smudge
tool allows you to
push around the
selected UVs.

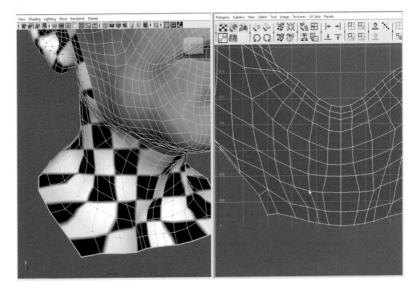

7. You'll need to occasionally resize the smudge radius as you work to move more or fewer UV points. It may be difficult to eliminate all warping in the texture.

8. When you have the warping under control, select the UVs in the shell, and activate the UV lattice by clicking the UV Lattice tool icon (the icon shown in Figure 11.22). A red grid will appear over the selected UVs in the shell, as shown in Figure 11.23.

FIGURE 11.22

The icon for the UV Lattice tool

FIGURE 11.23

You can use the UV Lattice tool to refine the arrangement of the selected UVs.

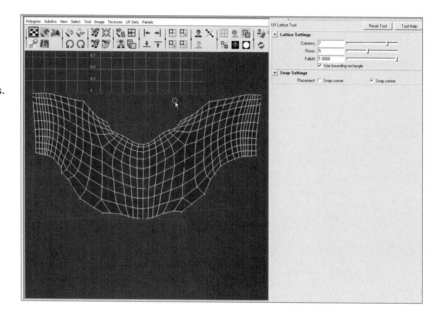

9. To change the number of rows and columns in the UV Lattice, open the Lattice Settings panel and change the settings in the Columns and Rows sliders. Set Columns to **7** and Rows to **5**.

10. Move the points of the lattice around to help reduce the stretching and warping seen in the checker pattern on the model in the perspective view.

11. Reselect the UVs of the shell with the UV Lattice button, and a new lattice replaces the older one. You can use this technique to apply multiple iterations of the UV Lattice tool when fine-tuning the shape of the UV shell.

12. Select small portions of the shell with the UV Lattice tool to fix those areas.

13. When the overall warping in the neck shell has been reduced, use the Smooth UV tool to relax and unfold the neck UV shell.

14. Save the scene. To see a version of the scene so far, open the UVMap_v03.ma file from the chapter 11\scenes folder on the DVD.

Automatic Mapping

Before tackling the face, there's one last bit that you can quickly map. You'll use automatic mapping to quickly generate UVs for the geometry that makes up the throat. Since this geometry will rarely be seen, if at all, you can get away with automatically generating UVs.

1. Continue with the model from the previous section or open UVMap_v03.ma from the chapter11\scenes folder on the DVD. Tumble around the model in the perspective view until you can see the throat geometry inside the head from the bottom of the neck.

2. Use the Paint Selection tool to select the ring of polygons at the bottom end of the throat geometry, as shown in Figure 11.24. Remember to double-check in wireframe mode to make sure no extra faces have been selected.

FIGURE 11.24
Select the ring of faces at the end of the throat inside the head.

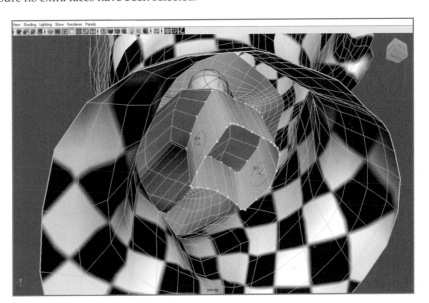

3. Once you've selected this ring, press the Shift+> keys to expand the selection. Repeat this six more times to add polygons to the selection, but stop just short of selecting the polygons that make up the outside of the lips (see Figure 11.25). It's easier to see what's going on if you switch to wireframe view in the viewport window (hot key = 4).

4. Choose Create UVs ➤ Automatic Mapping. The UV mapping texture manipulator will appear as six planes arranged around the selection. You can alter the arrangement if you need to change the attributes in the polyAutoProj1 node; however, the default arrangement should work just fine.

5. In the UV Texture Editor you'll see the UVs of the throat geometry broken into several shells (see Figure 11.26). Select these shells and move them out of the way for now. You can take the time to sew them together, but it's not necessary since they won't really be seen.

Generating UVs automatically works when you need some texture coordinates made quickly or as a starting point for mapping out UVs on a complex object.

FIGURE 11.25
The faces of the throat are selected. The edges of the selected faces are enhanced in this image to make it easier to see in black and white.

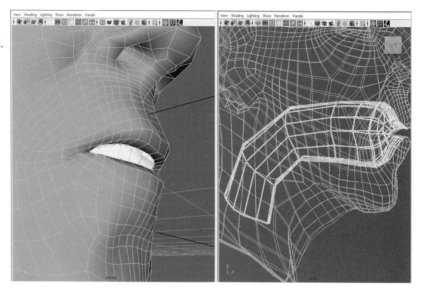

FIGURE 11.26
Automatic mapping creates a number of UV shells from the selected area.

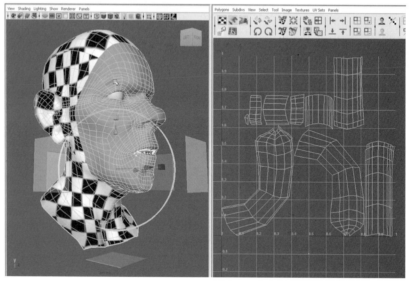

UV Mapping the Face

Generating UVs for the face is the hardest part, primarily because this is where the majority of the texture will be visible. You want to minimize warped or stretched UVs as much as possible, especially on the nose, where the tiny pores you paint as dots in Photoshop can become stretched, making the model appear less believable. The following exercise is one approach to mapping the face.

1. In the perspective view, use the Paint Selection tool to paint the remaining unmapped faces of the face. Don't select the faces at the bottom of the chin.

2. Turn off the visibility of NURBS objects in the perspective window to hide the eyes; make sure all the faces inside the eye sockets and the inside of the nostrils are selected.

3. Zoom the camera inside the model, and make sure none of the polygons on the throat geometry are selected. Brush while holding the Ctrl key to deselect specific faces.

USE THE UV TEXTURE EDITOR TO REFINE SELECTION

If any previously mapped faces are selected by accident, you'll see them highlighted in the UV Texture Editor. You can switch to face selection mode and Ctrl-drag over the faces you want to deselect in the UV Texture Editor.

---

4. Zoom inside the mouth so that you're viewing the lips from inside the mouth cavity behind the face. Make sure everything is selected except the polygon faces inside the mouth. Inspect the inside of the nose from within the head as well as the back of the eye sockets for any unselected polygon faces; this is shown in Figure 11.27.

5. When you are satisfied that only the polygons that make up the face are selected, create a cylindrical UV texture coordinate projection by choosing Create UVs ➢ Cylindrical Mapping.

6. Click on the red T at the corner of the cylindrical mapping manipulator to activate the translate, rotate, scale manipulator for the cylindrical projection.

7. Drag the blue arrow (the Z axis) of the manipulator toward the back of the head until the mapping becomes fairly even, as shown in Figure 11.28. The checker pattern on the nose will still be a little stretched. You can also set the Z coordinates of the Projection Center of the Attribute Editor to **0.721** to numerically position the manipulator.

FIGURE 11.27
Zooming inside the face allows you to make sure the eye sockets and nostril interior faces are selected.

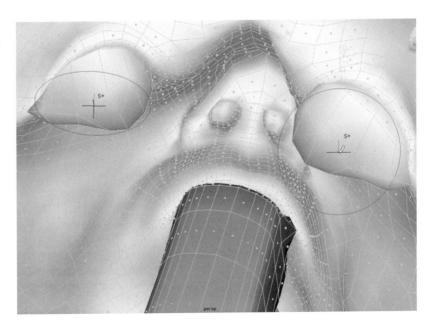

FIGURE 11.28
Apply cylindrical mapping to the face.

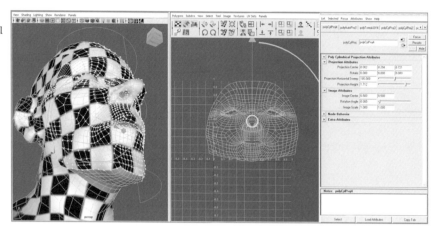

For the most part the projection is pretty good. There are a few areas that will need tweaking. For one thing, the UVs in the eye sockets and nostrils are overlapping.

8. In the perspective view zoom in so that you are inside the head and can view the eye sockets from behind the eyes.

9. Right-click on the model, and choose UV to switch to UV selection mode.

10. Select the four UV points at the back of the eye socket. Click the Shift+> hot key three times to expand the selection until only the UVs within the eye socket are selected, as shown in Figure 11.29 (you may want to turn off textured view so the UV points are easier to see: hot key = 5).

11. In the UV Texture Editor choose Tools ➢ Smooth UV Tool. Use the Smooth UV tool to relax the UVs in the eye sockets, as shown in Figure 11.30.

12. Repeat steps 8 through 11 to relax the UVs inside the nostrils. It's very important that all overlapping UVs are eliminated.

FIGURE 11.29
Select the UVs on the back of the eyes.

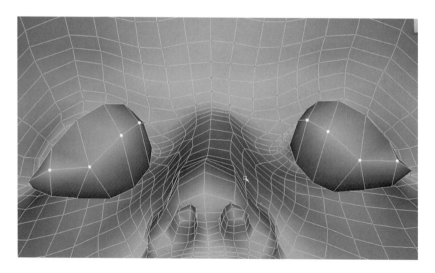

FIGURE 11.30
The UVs on the inside of the eye socket are selected and relaxed to remove overlapping.

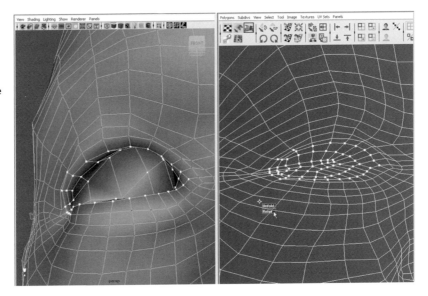

13. Use the UV Smudge tool to remove any overlapping on the lips as well.

14. Save your scene. To see a version of the scene so far, open the UVMap_v04.ma scene from the chapter 11\scenes folder on the DVD.

Sewing UV Shells

The separate UV shells of the head and face will be joined into a single shell (with the exception of the shells on the neck and the interior of the mouth). The goal is to create an arrangement that minimizes UV stretching and seams. It should also be easy to determine the features of the face in the flattened UV arrangement so it will be easy to paint textures in a paint program. Before joining the shells, you need to map the chin.

1. Select the unmapped faces on the chin, and use a planar projection on the Y axis to map these faces. If the resulting shell appears shaded red in the UV Texture Editor, flip it so it's consistent with the other shells (in the Polygon Texture Editor menu choose Polygons ➤ Flip).

2. Position this shell below the shells of the face, and scale down the projection in the UV Texture Editor, as shown in Figure 11.31.

3. In the UV Texture Editor, select the shell for the top of the head and move it above the face shell.

4. In the UV Texture Editor, right-click on the bottom edge of the top-of-the-head shell, and choose Edge to switch to edge-selection mode.

5. Select an edge at the bottom of the top-of-the-head shell; you'll see that a corresponding edge on the top-of-the-face shell is selected as well. This is a single edge shared by the two shells, as shown in Figure 11.32. In the perspective view, you can see the edge selected on the model. The shared edge indicates how the shells should be arranged before they are sewn together.

FIGURE 11.31
Map the faces of
the chin using a
planar projection.

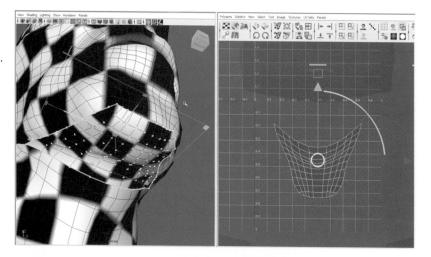

FIGURE 11.32
Select the edge
shared by the face
shell and the top-
of-the-head shell
(enhanced in this
image).

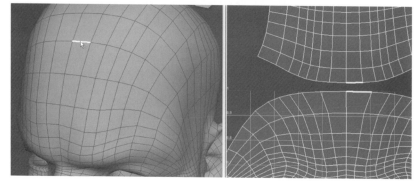

6. Select the other edges at the bottom of the top-of-the-head shell.

7. Click the icon for the Move and Sew Selected Edges tool (shown in Figure 11.33) to join the face and the top of the head. Some warping will result, but you can fix it (see Figure 11.34).

8. Use the same technique from steps 4 through 7 to attach the shells for the sides of the head to each side of the face shell. Be careful to select only the edges shared by the face and the side-of-the-head shells. If you select too many edges, the neck shell will be sewn to the face as well.

9. Select the chin shell. Click the Rotate Selected UVs icon (clockwise or counterclockwise) four times to rotate the shell 180 degrees. These buttons (shown in Figure 11.35) rotate UVs 45 degrees each time you click them. The UV layout is shown in Figure 11.36.

FIGURE 11.33
The icon for the
Move and Sew
Selected Edges tool

FIGURE 11.34
Sew the top-of-the-head shell and the face shell together.

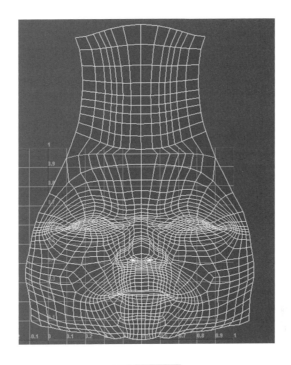

FIGURE 11.35
The icons for the Rotate Selected UVs tools

FIGURE 11.36
The chin shell is positioned below the face shell.

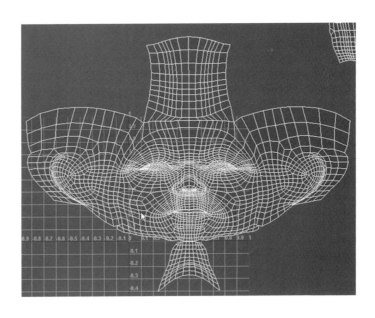

10. Select the edges shared by the bottom of the face and the chin shells; these should run all along the jawline.

11. Click the Sew Selected Edges tool to sew these together (the icon shown in Figure 11.37). You can see in Figure 11.38 that there will be a lot of stretching along the jaw; once again, you'll fix this shortly.

12. Find the back-of-the-head shell in the UV Texture Editor. Switch to edge-selection mode, and carefully select the edges that go straight down the middle of the shell.

13. Click the Separate UVs Along Selected Edges tool to split this shell into two parts. When you click the icon for the tool (shown in Figure 11.39), it looks as though nothing has happened until you select one of the halves and move it away from the other, as shown in Figure 11.40.

14. Move each half of the back-of-the-head shell to its matching side-of-the-face shell, and sew them to the face shell to complete the UV mapping for the face and head (see Figure 11.41).

15. To see a version of the scene so far, open UVMap_v05.ma from the chapter 11\scenes folder on the DVD.

FIGURE 11.37
The icon for Sew
Selected Edges tool

FIGURE 11.38
Sew the chin shell
to the face shell.

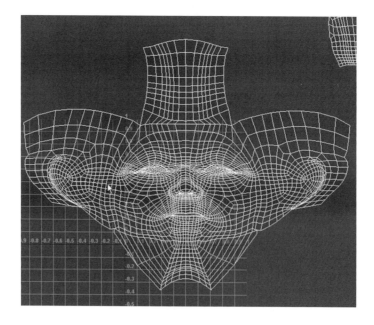

FIGURE 11.39
The icon for the
Separate UVs
Along Selected
Edges tool

FIGURE 11.40
Split the shell for the back of the head into two shells.

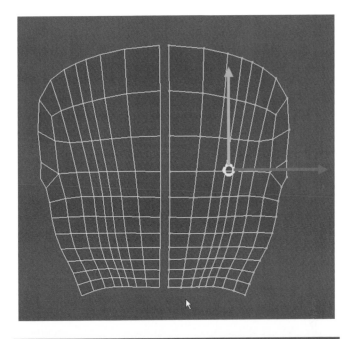

FIGURE 11.41
Sew the shells for the back of the head onto the face shell.

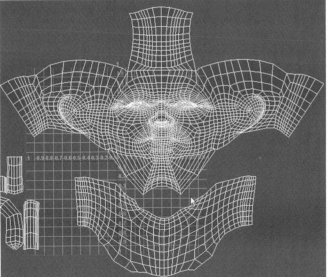

Unfolding UVs

Once you have the basic UV layout created for the model, you can use Maya's UV Unfold command to remove any remaining overlapping UVs as well as to reduce distortion on the model. Unfold UVs can be used at any time during the process on entire shells or just selected UVs. The Unfold command tries to make the UVs conform to the three-dimensional shape of the object.

At this point, prioritize the areas of the face in terms of how much texture space needs to be reserved for detail. If your primary concern is to maintain a consistent level of detail across the entire model or to reduce seams between shells, you may want to attach the face, head, and ear shells into one piece. If you want to reserve as much texture space as possible for the face, you may want to keep the face as its own separate shell and scale larger than the other shells that make up the head.

1. Select the face and neck shells, and choose Polygons ➢ Unfold ➢ Options.

2. In the options leave the Weight Solver set to 0. There are two types of solvers, Local and Global. The slider determines a bias setting toward one or the other. A setting of 0 means that the Local solver will be used, a setting of 1 means that the Global solver will be used, and any setting in between blends the two solvers.

LOCAL VERSUS GLOBAL UNFOLD SOLVER

The Local Unfold solver is faster than the Global solver, and in most cases, such as with this head model, it works just fine. If you experience an undesirable tapering effect on parts of a UV layout when using UV Unfold, try raising the slider value to increase the bias toward the Global solver. It will take longer to solve but may help with problem areas.

---

3. You can uncheck Pin UV Border and Pin UVs so that the entire shell can be unfolded without pins. If you want to unfold only part of the shell, you can use the Pinning settings to constrain the unselected UVs or the UV border so that they remain unaltered while the selected UVs are unfolded.

4. You can set Unfold Constraint to None so the UVs can be moved in both U and V.

5. The Unfold calculations are iterative, much like the Relax feature. The unfolding process will continue until the maximum iterations have been reached or the stopping threshold has been met. Maya makes its calculations based on a comparison between the original model and the unfolded result. For some models this process can take awhile. The face is simple enough that you can set the Stopping Threshold to **0** and the Maximum Iterations to **10**.

6. The Rescale feature is useful when you are unfolding multiple shells that need to have a consistent size. Check this option so the face and neck shells have a consistent size when the unfold operation is performed. Set the Scale Factor to **1** so the shells remain about the same size.

7. Click the Apply button, and observe the results in the perspective view. You can keep clicking Apply to repeat the unfold process until most of the checker pattern is relatively even.

8. If the shells end up on top of one another, select each shell and move it aside so that they no longer overlap, as shown in Figure 11.42.

9. Select the shared edges at the bottom of the face and top-of-the-neck shells, and sew the two shells together.

10. Select the joined shells, and run another unfold operation a few times to smooth the border along the jawline, as shown in Figure 11.43.

FIGURE 11.42
Unfold the face shell and the neck shell, creating a nice, even UV mapping for each shell.

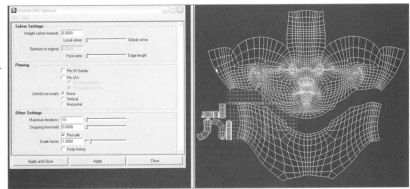

FIGURE 11.43
The face shell and the neck shell are joined and unfolded a few more times.

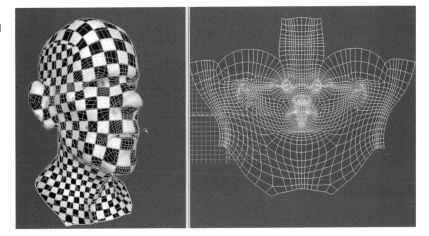

Overall it looks pretty good: the checker pattern is mostly even with minimal warping, and most of the seams are on the back of the head or in places that can be hidden with hair. The only problem is that most of the texture space is devoted to the neck and the sides of the head and not to the face, where it will be needed the most. Wherever the checks are smaller and more numerous, that part of the model has more texture space. To fix this, you can use the UV Lattice tool.

11. Select the face shell and use the UV Lattice tool to stretch out the UVs on the face so that more of the texture space can be devoted to it. This will take several applications of the UV Lattice tool, the UV Smear tool, Relax, UV Unfold, and a lot of tweaking. Try to get more of the checker pattern to appear on the nose. However, be careful not to introduce too much warping into the pattern. Remember to double-check areas such as the mouth for overlapping UVs.

Figure 11.44 shows the updated UV layout. Notice that the checker pattern on the face is smaller than in Figure 11.43. This means more texture space is devoted to it so that these regions can support more detail in the painted texture maps.

FIGURE 11.44
Tweak the UV shell so that more texture space is available for the face.

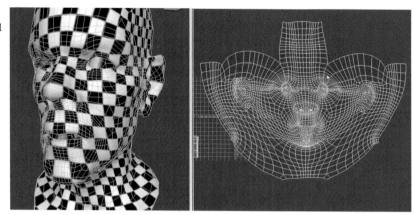

Arranging UV Shells

When you are satisfied with the overall job you've done on the UVs, you'll want to arrange the shells so they all fit within the 0 to 1 range on the UV Texture Editor grid. In this example, the face shell will be the largest of all the shells.

1. The UV Layout command will automatically place all selected shells within an ideal arrangement on the UV Texture Editor grid. Just select the shells and choose Polygons ➢ Layout.

2. In some cases you may choose to arrange the shells manually so you can prioritize texture space yourself. You can use the Move, Scale, and Rotate tools to position each shell within the upper-right quadrant of the grid. The main things to keep in mind are to:

   ◆ Arrange the shells so they all fit within the upper-right quadrant; this keeps them within the 0 to 1 range in U and V.

   ◆ Arrange the shells efficiently, minimize the space between shells, but at the same time keep enough space so the textures are easy to paint.

   ◆ Reserve more space for those parts of the object that will require more detail.

   ◆ Avoid overlapping shells (at all costs), and keep a little space between the edges of the shells and the grid border.

3. Once you are happy with the final layout, remember to delete history on the object! Otherwise, when you move or deform the object the UVs may not update correctly, and suddenly the textures will become distorted or behave in strange ways. Figure 11.45 shows the final UV layout for the head.

UV MAPS FOR CHARACTERS

Arranging UV shells for a head is pretty simple since there's basically just one piece you need to worry about. For a full figure things get a bit more complicated when you need to arrange all the shells for the entire body in the 0 to 1 range. In this case you want to prioritize the head and hands, which should get about 25 percent of the space, over the shells for the rest of the body, which should get about 75 percent of the space.

FIGURE 11.45
The final UV layout
for the character

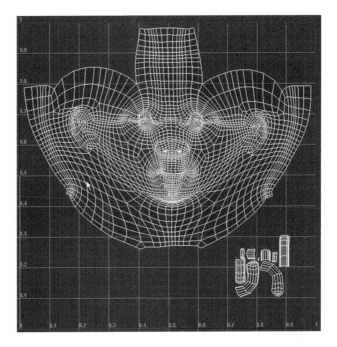

FIGURE 11.45
The final UV layout
for the character

UV Snapshot

You can generate a snapshot of the UVs that will serve as a guide for painting the textures in Photoshop.

1. In the UV Texture Editor window choose Polygons ➢ UV Snapshot.

2. In the options, use the browse button to choose the directory where you want to save the file.

3. Set the size of the texture file. In this case choose 2048. You can resize the document in Photoshop if you decide you need higher or lower resolution for the texture. Since this is a single head model that will be seen close up, you may eventually want to increase the resolution as high as 4096. It's usually best to keep these dimensions the same size in X and Y so the texture is square.

4. Keep Color Value white so the UV texture guide appears as white lines on a dark background. In Photoshop you can set the UV texture snapshot on a separate layer above all the other layers and set the bending mode to Screen so that the UV texture lines appear on top of the painted textures.

5. Set the image format to .tiff, and click OK to generate the snapshot.

6. Open the snapshot in Photoshop or your favorite paint program, and use the UVs as a guide for painting the textures. Refer to the section on the PSD texture node for more information.

7. To see a finished version of the head with complete UV maps, open the UVMap_v06.ma file from the chapter11\scenes folder on the DVD.

Additional UV Mapping Considerations

Proper UV mapping is essential for the creation and application of painted textures to your polygon and subdivision surface models. However, UV mapping can also affect how your models work with other aspects of Maya. Since displacement maps are essentially textures that deform geometry, it's important that UV coordinates are properly created in order for the displacements to deform the geometry properly.

2D procedural nodes, such as ramps, fractals, and (obviously) checker patterns, are affected by UV mapping. When you apply a fractal to a polygon model, the seams between UV coordinates can be very obvious if the UVs are not carefully mapped, as shown in Figure 11.46. Likewise, paint effects, hair, and fur all rely on UV coordinates to function properly.

UVs can also be animated using keyframes. You can use this to create some interesting effects, especially in games where it may be more efficient to create a repeating animated loop of UV texture coordinates than to create an animated sequence of images. To animate UVs, select the UVs in the UV Texture Editor, press the s hot key to create a keyframe, change their positions, and set another keyframe by pressing the s hot key again. You can refine the animation using the Graph Editor.

FIGURE 11.46
The UV seams on this object can be seen in the 2D fractal texture applied to the Color channel of the object's shader.

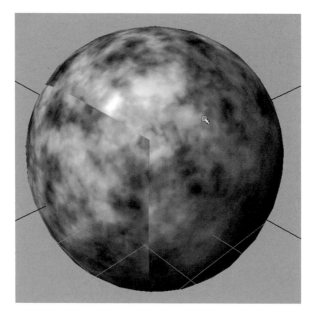

Transferring UVs

UVs can be transferred from one object to another. This is usually done between two versions of the same object and can be useful as a tool for quickly creating UVs on a complex object. This workflow might go something like this:

1. Create a duplicate of a complex object.

2. Smooth the duplicate using an operation such as Average Vertices or the sculpting brush.

3. Generate UV coordinates for the smoothed version using any combination of methods. Smoothing out the detail makes applying UV coordinates a little easier.

4. Select the smoothed version, and then Shift+click the original and choose Mesh ➤ Transfer Attributes ➤ Options. Set the options so the UVs are copied from the smoothed version to the original.

Multiple UV Sets

An object can actually have more than one version of the UV coordinates. These are known as *UV sets*. For instance, for a character's head you may use one UV set to control how color information is applied to the face and another set to control how the hair or fur is applied to the head. To create multiple sets you can use the UV Set Editor (Create UVs ➤ UV Set Editor). You can copy UVs from one set to another and link textures to different sets using the Relationship Editor (Window ➤ Relationship Editors ➤ UV Linking).

UV Mapping Alternatives

As mentioned at the start of the chapter, the process of mapping UVs is often tedious and technical. It's a necessary evil. Consider how much time you've just spent on the head of a character; now consider how much more work and time would be required to do a full body. Creating UV texture coordinates can bog down a production pipeline as well as hamper your creativity. Maya's UV mapping tools are powerful and easy to use, but there are also alternatives to consider that may make your life even easier. If you find yourself doing this kind of work a lot, you may want to consider a third-party UV coordinate-mapping program such as UV Layout by Headus (www.uvlayout.com), as shown in Figure 11.47.

FIGURE 11.47
UV Layout by Headus is an application devoted to making UV mapping faster and easier.

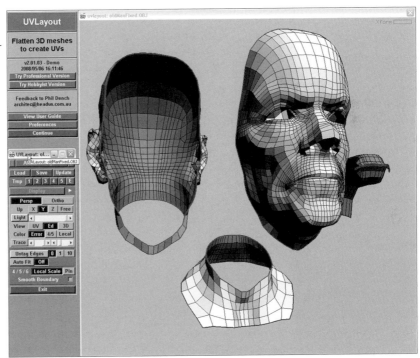

UV Layout is a simple, inexpensive program that allows you to interactively split up a 3D model and create UVs using a process similar to Maya's UV Unwrap feature. However, the tools are much easier and faster to use, and you may find yourself spending much less time on UV mapping and more time creating your models. Headus has student and hobbyist pricing for UV Layout as well as a professional version.

There are also UV mapping scripts available on websites, such as www.highend3d.com, which can help you save time creating UV coordinates. Pelting Tools is a powerful script created by Sunit Parekh. The script actually uses particle springs to stretch a polygon mesh such as a fur pelt. The UVs are then projected onto the stretched version of the mesh and copied to the original polygon object.

 Real World Scenario

UV PROJECTING ACROSS MULTIPLE OBJECTS

Once while working on a television commercial for a major bank, I was required to take a film sequence that was shot by a camera crew and break it up into hundreds of logos, which then flew toward the screen. I solved the problem of mapping the footage onto the logos by creating a single planar projection. Here's a rough breakdown of this technique:

1. I arranged the logos in their starting position (all of the logos I worked with were polygon objects). The camera was placed above them facing directly downward.

2. I switched to component mode and carefully selected all the top faces of all the polygon logos.

3. With all the top faces of all the logos selected at once, I created a planar projection along the Y axis.

4. I applied a single shader to these faces that contained the footage as an animated sequence in the Color channel.

5. I deleted history on all the logos to keep the UVs from moving when the logos were animated; then all I had to worry about was animating the logos.

Bump and Normal Mapping

Bump maps, normal maps, and displacement maps are three ways to add surface detail to a model using textures. In this section you'll learn about bump and normal maps. A discussion concerning displacement maps appears later on in the chapter.

Bump maps and normal maps are similar in that they both create the impression of surface detail by using color information, stored in a 2D texture map, to alter the surface normal of an object. When the light in a scene hits the surface of an object, the color values in the texture tell the rendering engine to alter the surface normal so the light creates a highlight or shading/shadowing. The surface geometry itself is not changed; however, the altered normal makes it look as though the geometry has more detail than it actually does. This saves the modeler the trouble of sculpting every single wrinkle, fold, bump, screw, or scratch into a model as well as keeps the geometry resolution of the model down to a level the computer's processor can handle.

Bump and normal maps do not actually alter the surface geometry. This means that the part of the surface that faces the camera will appear as though it has bumps and depressions, but as the surface of the geometry turns away from the camera, it becomes apparent that the silhouette of the geometry has not actually been changed by the bump or normal map. Figure 11.48 demonstrates this principle.

FIGURE 11.48
This sphere has
a fractal texture
applied as a bump
map. It looks lumpy
from the front, but
the silhouette of the
sphere is not altered
by the bump map.

Bump and normal maps are mutually exclusive, meaning that you'll use either one or the other but not both at the same time. Normal maps are a more recent development and are gaining in popularity over bump maps. This is because normal maps are calculated very quickly, which makes them popular for use in real-time game engines. The shadows they create are also more accurate than those bump maps create. However, normal maps need to be generated automatically by software and can't easily be painted or edited by a texture artist in Photoshop.

PROCEDURAL BUMP MAPS

Any texture can be used as a bump map, including the 2D and 3D procedural textures such as Fractal, Ramp, Grid, Crater, Water, Brownian, and so on. When you place a texture in the Bump Mapping channel of a standard Maya shader, a connection is made between the outAlpha attribute on the texture and the Bump value of the shader.

Bump Maps

Bump maps are simply grayscale textures, usually painted in a 2D paint program such as Photoshop. Bump maps are best used for fine detail, such as tiny wrinkles, pores, small rivets, scratches, small dents, wood grain, and so on. When texturing highly detailed characters, you can best use bump maps with displacement maps, and you'll see how to combine them later on in the chapter. In this section, you'll apply a bump map to the old man character.

1. Open the bump_v01.ma file from the chapter 11\scenes folder of the DVD. You'll see the same old man character from the previous part of this chapter; his UV texture coordinates have already been created.

LINKING TEXTURE FILES

The project files in this chapter are linked to texture files found in the chapter11\sourceimages directory on the DVD. It's possible that these links may break when working with the scenes on the DVD. You may want to copy the Chapter 11 project to your local hard drive and make sure that the current project is set to Chapter 11. This way, when you load a premade scene and render it, the scenes should render properly.

2. A camera (renderCam) and basic three-point lighting arrangement have been created, and the renderer is set to mental ray, Production Settings.

3. Select the old man's head, and open the UV Texture Editor (Window ➤ UV Texture Editor).

4. In the UV Texture Editor's menu, choose Polygons ➤ UV Snapshot. The options for the snapshot will open.

5. Use the browse button to set the location of the snapshot file and its name. Name the file **oldManUV**. The sourceimages directory of the current project is usually a good place to store textures since this is the default location Maya uses for texture files.

6. Set Size X and Size Y to 2048, leave Color Value as white, and leave Image Format as .tiff.

7. Leave the UV Range option set to Normal (0 to 1). Click OK. Maya will create the snapshot and save it in the directory you chose. Figure 11.49 shows the options.

8. Start Photoshop or your favorite digital painting program (this exercise assumes you are familiar with and are using Photoshop).

9. Open the oldManUV.tif file you created in Maya.

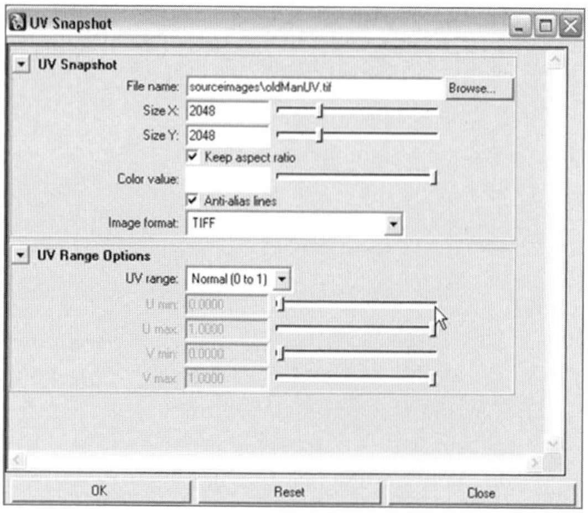

FIGURE 11.49

The options for creating a UV snapshot

10. The image will appear black with the UVs outlined in white.

11. In Photoshop open the Layers panel. Select the Background layer and duplicate it.

12. Create a new layer and fill it with gray (RGB = 128, 128, 128).

13. Place the duplicate background layer above the gray layer, and set its mode to Screen. The UV lines will now appear as a guide over whatever is painted on the gray layer (see Figure 11.50).

FIGURE 11.50
Open the UV snapshot in Photoshop. Arrange the layers so that the UV lines appear as a guide above the painted bump texture.

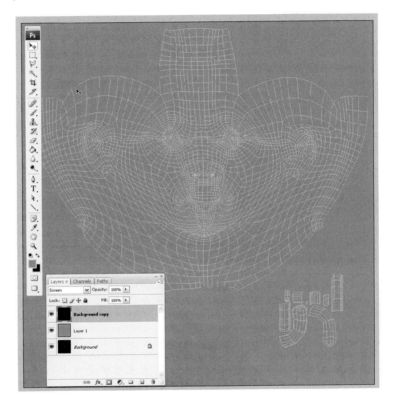

14. The gray color serves as the baseline bump value. Anything darker than the gray value will appear as a depression in the bump map; anything lighter will appear as a raised bump. The value 128 is halfway between 0 (black) and 255(white). The following list provides some tips for painting a believable skin bump map:

◆ Get as much reference material as you can, and keep it nearby as you work. Online reference sites, such as www.3d.sk, are pretty good. Fine art photography books and magazines are also quite helpful.

◆ Take photographs of skin and scans of images from books and magazines, and bring them into Photoshop as texture swatches; use the Clone tool to paint the texture into the areas outlined by the UVs. A number of skin texture samples are included in the chapter 11\scenes folder on the DVD.

◆ Pay attention to how skin changes over the face. The skin on the end of the nose is very different from the skin between the eye and the brow.

◆ Older people are not raisins; don't create a bunch of random wrinkles. Pay close attention to how wrinkles appear on the face. Some older people have very smooth skin with wrinkles in very specific places; others have wrinkles all over. Skin tells the story of how a person has lived, which is what makes it interesting to study.

◆ Use references from real people, not 3D characters created by other artists; otherwise you risk repeating someone else's mistakes or bad habits.

◆ Use layers and blending modes to your advantage. Build up the skin bumps by layering textures and varying the opacity.

◆ Use the Clone tool to blend textures across the seams.

◆ A good texture map should take a long time to create—don't rush it!

15. Save your painting and all its layers as an unflattened Photoshop file; you want to keep this version in case you need to make changes. The finished bump map is shown in Figure 11.51.

16. Hide the UV snapshot layer so the UV lines are no longer visible. Hide any other layers you don't want visible in the texture.

17. Select the entire image by choosing Select ➢ All. Select one of the visible layers and choose Edit ➢ Copy Merged; this copies all the visible layers into a single layer on the clipboard.

18. Create a new file; by default the new file should be 2048 × 2048. Paste the contents of the clipboard into the new file. Flatten the file and save it as oldManBump.tif in the source-images directory. In the TIFF Options panel, make sure the file is set to Uncompressed.

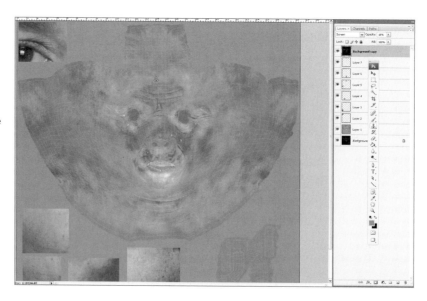

FIGURE 11.51
The bump map is painted in Photoshop using the UV snapshot as a guide. You can use photographs as a source for the clone brush.

Applying the Bump Texture to the Model

Applying the bump texture to the model is very simple; you can even preview the bump texture in the perspective window.

1. Start Maya and open the bump_v01.ma file from the chapter 11\scenes folder on the DVD.

2. Create a new Blinn texture. Name it **oldManShader**, and apply it to the old man character.

3. Open oldManShader in the Attribute Editor. In the Bump Mapping channel, click on the checker pattern next to the Bump Mapping field. From the Create Render Node pop-up, choose File from the 2D Textures rollout (as shown in Figure 11.52).

4. In the bump2d1 tab of the Attribute Editor, set Bump Depth to **0.5**. This controls the intensity of the bump map (see Figure 11.53). Most of the time a value of 1 is too strong.

FIGURE 11.52
Create a file node for the Bump channel in the oldManShader.

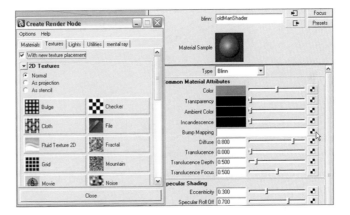

FIGURE 11.53
The Bump Depth slider controls the strength of the bump texture.

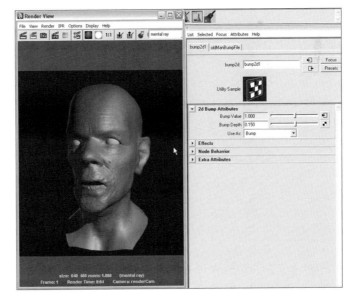

5. Click the file1 tab in the Attribute Editor. In the File field rename the node **oldManBumpFile**.

6. Click the folder icon next to the Image Name field; browse your computer and find the `oldManBump.tif` file.

7. When the file is loaded, turn on High Quality Rendering in the toolbar of the camera view. The bump map will preview in the viewport window (see Figure 11.54).

8. Switch to the renderCam in the perspective view, and create a test render.

9. The bump is still a bit strong, so try lowering the strength of the bump to somewhere between 0.1 and 0.2, as shown in Figure 11.53.

FIGURE 11.54
Activating High Quality Rendering allows you to preview the bump map in the viewport.

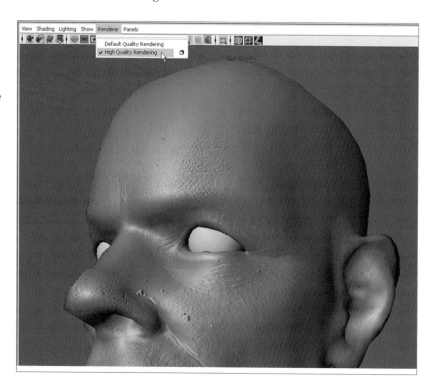

HIGH-QUALITY RENDER PREVIEW

To preview the bump map on the model in the perspective view, select High Quality Rendering from the Renderer menu in the camera view (Figure 11.54), and press 6 on the keyboard to switch to shaded view. If your graphics card supports it, you should see the bump applied to the model. Note that the bump in the perspective view is not quite as strong as in the rendered version.

3D Paint Tool

If you can see seams along the hairline or other bad spots, you may need to continue to work on the bump texture. You can do this interactively using the 3D Paint tool in Maya.

1. Select the oldMan head, and switch to the Rendering menu set.

2. Choose Texturing ➢ 3D Paint Tool. You'll get the following warning in the status line: Some Surfaces Have No File Texture Assigned To The Current Attribute. You can ignore this warning.

The 3D Paint tool needs to have a texture assigned to the current channel before you can paint on the model. By default the tool is set up to paint in the Color channel. The oldMan-Shader has no texture in the Color channel, just in the Bump channel.

3. Open the settings for the 3D Paint tool, scroll down to the File Textures rollout, and set Attributes to Paint To BumpMap.

4. Switch to hardware texturing (press the 6 key). After a few seconds you'll see the bump map appear on the model as a color texture.

5. Zoom into an area that has bad spots or visible seams.

6. Reduce the size of the brush by holding the b key while MMB-dragging in the window.

7. You can sample colors on the surface by clicking on the swatch next to the Color slider in the Color rollout, then using the eyedropper to select a color from the model's surface. You can also lower the opacity of the color with the Opacity slider.

8. The Paint Operations rollout allows you to change the operation of the brush. You can switch to a Clone tool (see Figure 11.55). When Clone is active, you can click the Set Clone Source button, click on the model near the area you need to fix, and then paint on the problem area. Just like in Photoshop, the Clone tool copies the sampled area to the area below the brush.

FIGURE 11.55
Use the 3D Paint tool to fix problems in the bump map.

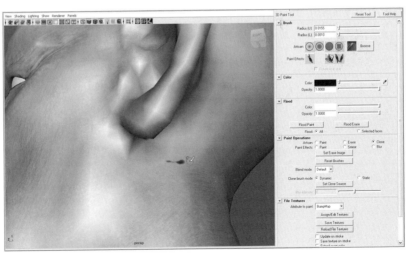

9. Use the 3D Paint tool to touch up the bump map texture if needed. The painting action will probably be fairly slow, which is why 3D Paint is best used for touch-ups rather than creating a map from scratch.

10. When you've finished, click the Save Textures button to save the changes you've made to the bump texture.

3D PAINT TEXTURES DIRECTORY

The new bump texture is saved to the 3DPaintTextures directory of the current project. You may need to copy the updated texture from here to your sourceimages directory when you have finished. It's saved as an 8-bit .tif file. If you get an error while rendering with mental ray, open the file in Photoshop, convert it to a 16-bit file (Image ➤ Mode), and resave it as a .tif with no compression.

---

11. Do a test render of the model.

12. To see a finished version of the model with the bump texture, open the bump_v02.ma file from the chapter 11\scenes folder on the DVD.

If you look at Figure 11.53, you'll see that bump maps can only get you so far. To create believable characters, you must combine bump maps with displacement maps and well-painted diffuse and specular maps. You should also keep in mind how close the object will be to the camera; close-ups of an object require higher-resolution texture maps.

Rendering Textures Using the Optimized Format

Maya offers an optimized format that is used at render time. Textures using standard image file formats such as .tif are loaded into memory before rendering begins, which can slow down the rendering and lead to instability. Maya can convert the file texture to an optimized, uncompressed, OpenEXR format that allows Maya/mental ray to load the texture as needed during render, which not only increases stability but also allows for the use of much larger textures.

The original file textures, such as the .tif used for the bump map, are still used in the scene and stored in the sourceimages directory and referenced when you work in the scene. The conversion takes place automatically, and the converted files are stored in the sourceimages/cache directory by default. When you render the scene, you'll see your file textures listed there with the .map extension. In versions of Maya prior to 2008, you had to convert file texture images to the .map format manually using the imf_copy utility.

To enable this feature choose Window ➤ Settings/Preferences ➤ Preferences. In the Rendering section enable the check box for Use Optimized Textures (Auto-conversion). This is shown in Figure 11.56. You can choose to use the default sourceimages/cache directory for the current project or specify a custom location. If you are rendering on a network, make sure that all render nodes on the farm can see the directory where you store the optimized file. You can also choose to convert all textures or just the ones that have been assigned to shaders. To update the files, click the Update Optimize Cache Textures Now button. The files should update automatically at render time, but just in case they don't for some reason, you can use this button to force a refresh.

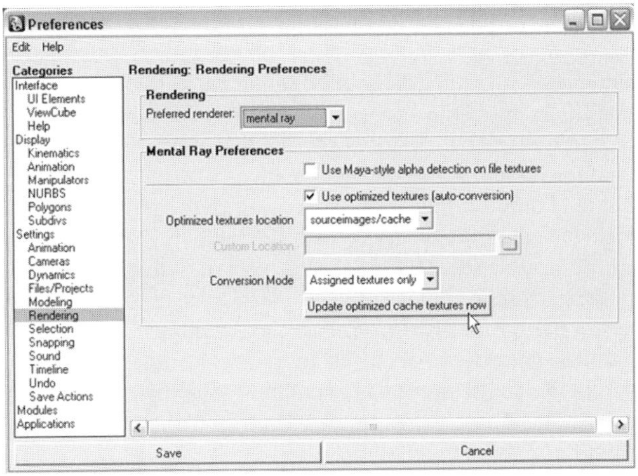

FIGURE 11.56
Enable the Use
Optimized Tex-
tures feature in
the Preferences
window.

Normal Maps

A bump map displaces a surface normal either up or down (relative to the surface normal) based on the value of the texture. Normal maps, on the other hand, replace the normal direction with a vector stored in the RGB colors of the map. In other words, rather than pulling out a bump or pushing in a depression, the colors of the normal map change the X, Y, Z of the normal based on the RGB color of the map (see Figure 11.57).

FIGURE 11.57
The diagram shows
how bump maps and
normal maps affect
the surface normals
of a polygon in dif-
ferent ways.

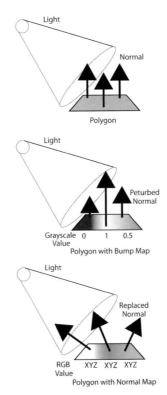

When viewed as a 2D texture in a paint program, normal maps have a psychedelic rainbow color. These colors tell Maya how the normal on the surface of the geometry should be bent at render time. It's very difficult for an artist to paint a normal map because the RGB values are not intuitively applied.

There are two types of normal maps: object space and tangent space. Object space maps are used for nondeforming objects, such as walls, spaceships, trashcans, and the like. They are calculated based on the local object space of the object. *Up* in object space means toward the top of the object. If the object is rotated upside down in world space, the top is still the top—so a robot's head is still the top of the object in object space even if it's hanging upside down.

Tangent space maps are used for deforming objects, such as characters. Tangent space maps record the normal's vector relative to the object's surface. In tangent space, *up* means up away from the surface of the object. Tangent space maps appear more blue and purple since the direction in which the normal is being bent is always relative to the surface along the tangent space Z axis. The Z axis corresponds with the blue channel (XYZ = RGB). Object space maps, on the other hand, have more variation in color.

In practice, most artists use tangent space maps for everything. In fact, prior to Maya 2008, tangent space maps were the only type of normal maps that Maya supported. Tangent space maps actually work well for both deforming and nondeforming objects.

The most common way to create a normal map is to use a high-resolution, detailed version of the model as the source of the normal map and a low-resolution version of the model as the target for the map. The difference between the two surfaces is recorded in the colors of the map, which is then used to alter the appearance of the low-resolution model. This is a typical process when creating models for games where low-resolution models are required by the real-time rendering engine, but the audience demands realistically detailed objects.

Creating Normal Maps

In this exercise you'll create a normal map for the old man character. A high-resolution version of the model will be used as the source of the map. To create a normal map in Maya, you'll use the Transfer Maps tool. This tool can be used to create a number of different texture map types, including normal maps.

1. Open the normal_v01.ma file from the chapter 11\scenes folder of the DVD.

2. Look at the familiar old man model. If you look in the Display Layer panel, you'll see two layers: one labeled loRes, the other hiRes. Turn off the loRes layer and turn on the hiRes layer. You'll see a higher-resolution detailed version of the head, as shown in Figure 11.58.

3. Turn on both layers. Select loResMan in the Outliner, and switch to the Rendering menu set.

4. Choose Lighting/Shading ➢ Transfer Maps to open the Transfer Maps interface.

5. Expand the Target Meshes rollout. The loResManShape object will be listed since loResMan was selected when you opened the interface. If it does not appear, select it in the Outliner and click the Add Selected button. No other objects should be listed; if they are, select them in the list and click the Remove Selected button.

6. Expand the Source Meshes rollout, select the hiResMan object in the Outliner, and click the Add Selected button to add it to the list.

FIGURE 11.58
The scene contains
a high-resolution
model of the old
man's head on a
separate display
layer.

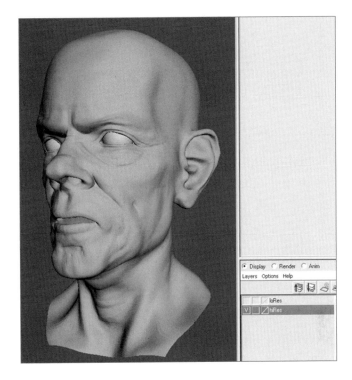

7. Expand the Output Maps section; you'll see icons representing all of the different types of maps that can be created. Click the Normal button to add *normal map* to the list. If other types of maps are listed, click the Remove Map button in the section for the map you want to remove.

8. Click on the folder next to the Normal Map field, and set the location and filename for the location of the map that will be created. Choose the sourceimages directory of the current project. Name the file **oldManNormal**.

9. There are a number of file format options to choose from. The two best choices are Maya IFF and EXR. Both are 32-bit formats that will ensure a detailed smooth map. Choose EXR; this way you can open the map in Photoshop (CS1 and higher) for viewing if you need to. If the file format in the name of the file is something other than .exr, it will be automatically updated.

OPEN EXR LOADER PLUG-IN

When using the EXR format in Maya, you'll need to make sure the OpenEXRLoader plug-in is currently loaded; otherwise you'll get an error when you try to connect the file to a shader. Choose Window ➢ Settings And Plug-ins ➢ Plug-in Manager. In the list of plug-ins make sure OpenEXRLoader.mll is currently checked.

10. The Include Materials check box is extremely useful if you want to include a bump map as part of the normal map. For now, uncheck it since there is no bump map applied to the hi-res mesh material. However, make a note of this option—you can add more detail to your normal map, such as pores and fine wrinkles, by applying a bump texture to the shader for the hi-res mesh object and then activating this option when using the Transfer Maps tool.

BAKING BUMP MAPS

When baking a bump map into the normal map using the Include Materials option, the Bump Depth setting on the shader of the source mesh will determine the intensity of the bump as it's baked into the normal map. If you need to change this later, you'll need to adjust Bump Depth on the source mesh and rebake the normal map.

---

11. Set Map Space to Tangent Space. You should always use tangent space maps for characters. Actually, as stated before, you can use them for any type of object.

12. The Use Maya Common Settings check box makes the tool use the settings specified in the Maya Common Output. If this is unchecked, sliders will appear that will allow you to set the size of the map in this section. For now, keep this box checked.

13. In the Connect Output Maps settings, you can connect the map to a shader automatically; you can uncheck the Connect Maps To Shader option for now. Later on you'll learn how to make the connection manually. Once you understand how the connection is made, you can use this option in the future to make things more convenient.

14. In the Maya Common Output settings, set the size of the map to **2048** in width and height, set Transfer In to Object Space, Sampling Quality to Low, Filter Size to **1**, and Filter Type to Gaussian. Leave Fill Texture Seams at 1 and the remaining three check boxes (Ignore Mirrored Faces, Flip U, and Flip V) unchecked. The settings are shown in Figure 11.59.

USE LOW-QUALITY SETTINGS WHEN TESTING

Normal maps can take a while to calculate, so it's a good idea to create a few test maps at lower quality and then raise the quality settings once you're happy that the map is free of errors.

---

15. Keep the scene and the Transfer Maps window open for the next section.

The Transfer In option has three choices: World Space, Object Space, and UV Space. These specify how the map will be calculated and transferred from the high-resolution version to the low-resolution version. If the models were different sizes, then World Space would be appropriate and the models would need to be directly on top of each other. The objects used in this tutorial are the same size and very similar except for their resolutions and level of detail, so Object Space is more appropriate. The UV Space option works best for objects of fairly similar but not exactly the same shape, such as a female human character and a male human character.

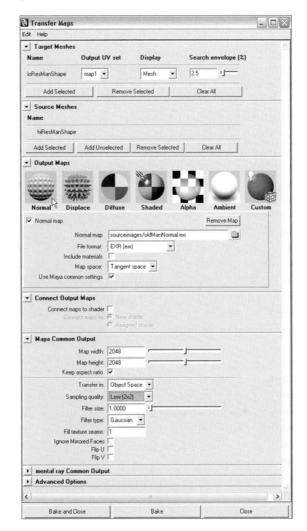

The Search Envelope

The search envelope is the most important aspect of this tool. It specifies the volume of space that Maya will use to search when creating the transfer map. Maya compares the target geometry (the low-resolution map) with the source geometry (the high-resolution map) and records the difference between the two as color values in the normal map. The search envelope sets the

limits of the distance Maya will search when creating the map. The envelope itself is a duplicate of the target geometry that's offset from the original. The offset distance is specified by the
Search Envelope slider in the Target Meshes section of the Transfer Maps tool. What's more, you
can edit the Target Mesh geometry itself to improve the results of the final map.

1. Continue with the scene from the previous section. In the Target Meshes options, set the
   Search Envelope slider to **2.5**.

2. Set Display to Envelope. The target mesh will be hidden, and you'll see a bloated ver-
   sion of the target appear around the hiResManShape mesh. This is the search envelope.
   It has a semitransparent shader applied so you can see the source mesh inside it (see
   Figure 11.60).

FIGURE 11.60
The search enve-
lope is an offset
polygon copy of
the model that
defines the range
Maya uses when
calculating the
normal map.

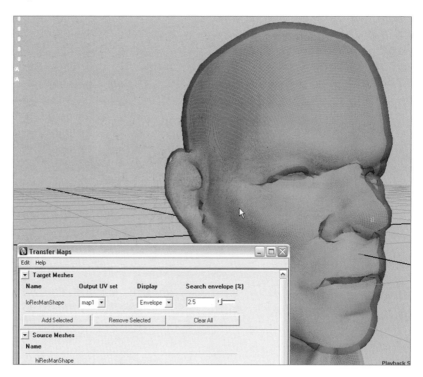

3. Changing the Search Envelope slider changes the volume of the search envelope and thus
   the distance Maya searches when creating the map.

4. Expand the loResManShape in the Outliner; you'll see that the shape node of the original
   model is hidden (when the name of the object appears in blue, it means the object is not
   visible). A second shape node labeled loResManShapeEnvelope has been created; this is
   the shape node for the envelope. Select this node and open the Channel Box.

5. Select the polyMoveFace1 node and find the localTranslateZ value. If you change this
   value, the offset of the envelope will change just as if you had changed the Search
   Envelope percent value.

6. If you ever need to generate a new envelope while still creating settings for the Transfer Maps tool, you can delete the loResManShapeEnvelope node for the Outliner, set the display menu to Mesh and then back to Envelope (or to Both if you want to see the target mesh and the envelope), and a new envelope will be created.

7 Undo any changes you've made to the envelope, and return to its state from step 2. Inspect the envelope and see if there are any parts of the source mesh poking through the envelope. There should be such a spot at the tip of the nose as well as on the ear. If you select the hi-res mesh in the Outliner, these spots will be more obvious.

8. Right-click on the envelope, and choose Vertex to switch to vertex-selection mode. Use the Move tool to gently edit the envelope mesh so that no portions of the source mesh are poking through it.

9. Select the envelope, and choose (from the Polygon menu set) Mesh ➤ Sculpt Geometry Tool. Use the Artisan Brush tool to carefully smooth sections of the envelope that intersect with itself; this occurs mostly in the mouth area. This is one reason why a model with a slightly open mouth is easier to create maps for than one with a closed mouth (see Figure 11.61).

FIGURE 11.61
You can edit the search envelope geometry using the Artisan Brush tool. Overlapping areas in the mouth are removed by smoothing.

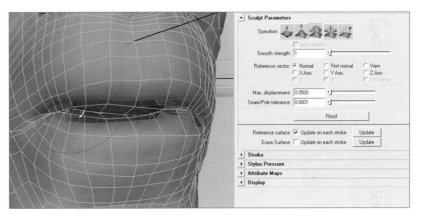

10. Smooth out the corners of the eyes as well. Don't overdo it; just separate the overlapping parts of the envelope as best you can. Depending on the complexity of the model, this may take a few tries before you get the hang of it.

11. Scroll to the bottom of the Transfer Maps Advanced options. Uncheck Delete Envelopes On Bake so you can reuse this envelope if you need to.

USING CUSTOM ENVELOPE GEOMETRY

If you want to use a custom object as an envelope, you can add it to the Target Meshes section, then right-click over the object's name in the Transfer Maps options, and choose Use Selected As Envelope from the pop-up menu.

---

12. Set Max Search Depth to **0**. This means Maya uses an unlimited search depth. If you keep getting errors in the map on complex objects, adjust this value when creating a map.

13. Set Match Using to Geometry Normals; this option is best for organic surfaces such as characters. The Surface Normals option works better for hard-edge geometry like space-ships and vehicles.

14. Set the Search method to Inside Envelope Then Outside Envelope. This setting deter-mines how the map will be made. You can experiment using different settings to see if you get different results.

15. Click Bake to make the map. The status of the process will appear in the help line. Depending on the complexity of the high-resolution mesh and the quality settings, this can take a fair amount of time, anywhere from a minute to several minutes. When it's done, the baked map should appear in the `sourceimages` directory. The next section cov-ers how you can connect the map to the shader.

Applying Normal Maps

Normal maps are applied to an object's shader in the Bump channel, and they can be viewed in the perspective window. In this section, you'll see how the map looks when it's applied to the model as well as a few suggestions for fixing problems.

1. Continue with the scene from the previous section.

2. Open the Hypershade window (Window ➢ Rendering Editors ➢ Hypershade).

3. In the Display Layer panel, turn off the visibility of the HiRes layer so only the low-resolution mesh is visible. The Envelope mesh is either hidden or deleted depending on the settings, once the normal map-generation process is complete.

4. Select the low-resolution version of the old man. In the Work Area of the Hypershade, right-click and choose Graph Materials On Selected.

5. Select the Old Man shader and open the Attribute Editor.

6. Click on the checkered box next to the Bump Mapping channel, and choose a file from the Create Render Node pop-up.

7. When you add the file node, the Attribute Editor will open to the bump2D node. Set the Use As option to Tangent Space Normals. This tells Maya the texture you're applying is a normal map and not a bump map. You can leave the Bump Depth at 1; it has no effect on the strength of the normal map.

8. Switch to the file1 node, and click on the folder next to the Image Name field. Browse your computer's file directory and find the `oldManNormal.exr` file; it should be in the `source-images` directory (if you get an error when loading the plug-in, make sure the openEXR-Loader plug-in is checked in the preferences).

9. Once the file is loaded, you should see a preview in the texture sample icon. The texture should appear mostly blue and purple. If it is completely flat blue, then there was an error

during the creation process—most likely the source mesh was not selected in the Transfer Maps options, so you'll need to remake the map.

10. In the perspective view, choose High Quality Rendering from the Renderer menu at the top of the panel. After a few seconds you should see a preview of the normal map in the perspective view, as shown in Figure 11.62. (Make sure you have Texture Shaded activated; press the 6 key to switch to this mode.)

FIGURE 11.62
The low-resolution model (left) has the same detail as the high-resolution model (right).

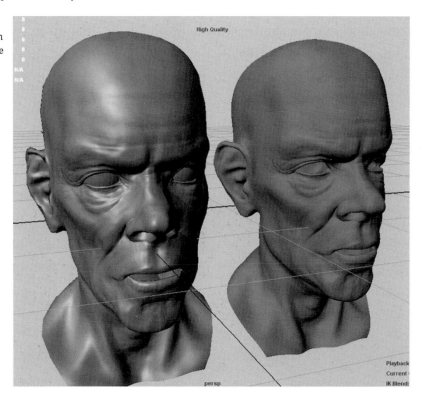

The normal map should make the low-resolution model look very similar to the high-resolution model. You can see in the silhouette of the geometry that the blockiness of the profile indicates that geometry is still low resolution, but those areas facing the camera look highly detailed. This workflow is very popular when creating models for games. The models end up looking much more realistic and detailed without taxing the processor of the game console.

11. Inspect the model for errors in the texture. Most likely you'll find some errors around the lips, ears, and eyes. If large portions of the model look wrong, you'll need to try creating the map again. Sometimes just editing the geometry of the search envelope can fix the errors when you regenerate the map. Other times you may need to change the actual generation settings such as the Search Method and Max Search Depth in the Advanced settings (see Figure 11.63).

FIGURE 11.63
Small errors appear on the model in some parts of the map.

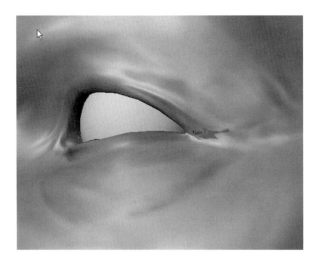

Normal maps are difficult but not impossible to edit in a 2D paint program such as Photoshop. If the normal map has just a few small glitches, you may be able to open it in Photoshop and very carefully use the Clone tool and Paint tool to eliminate small problems. This is faster than trying to regenerate a whole new map just to fix a tiny spot.

12. Open the Attribute Editor for the normal map file node, and click the View button below the Image Name field. The normal map will open in either FCheck or whatever image-editing program you have set in the preferences. You can inspect the map for errors. Errors behind the eyeballs and deep inside the nose can usually be safely ignored.

13. In the Render settings, set the Render Using field to mental ray and the Preset to Production Quality. Create a test render, and compare it with what you see in the perspective view (see Figure 11.64).

14. For a completed version of the scene open the normal_v02.ma file from the chapter 11\ scenes folder on the DVD.

FIGURE 11.64
Two versions of the completed normal map. The right image shows the normal map with the bump texture baked in using the Include Materials option.

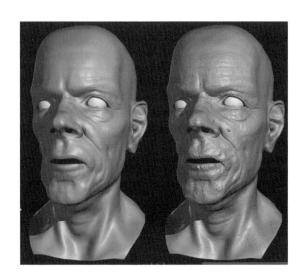

Displacement Mapping

Displacement maps are like bump maps in that they use a grayscale texture to add detail to a model. However, rather than just perturb the normal of the surface, displacement maps actually alter the geometry at render time. Unlike normal and bump maps, the silhouette of the geometry reflects the detail in the map. Displacement maps can be used with NURBS, polygon, and subdivision surfaces and can be rendered in both mental ray and Maya software. The best results are usually achieved by rendering displacement maps on a polygon surface in mental ray using metal ray's Approximation Editor to subdivide the surface appropriately during render.

VIEWING DISPLACEMENTS

Displacement maps can be viewed only in a software render; they can't be previewed in the perspective window.

Displacement maps are tricky to use and require some practice to master; however, the results are often worth the time invested. Recent advances in digital sculpting programs such as ZBrush and Mudbox have enabled modelers to bring an unprecedented amount of realism and detail to digital characters. The detail created in these high-density meshes is often brought into Maya in the form of displacement maps (and normal maps as well).

In addition to aiding in creating detail on creatures, displacement maps have a wide variety of creative applications and innovations. You can use animated displacements to simulate rolling waves on an ocean surface, fissures opening in the earth, or veins crawling beneath the skin. In this section you'll see some basic applications of displacement maps as well as how they can be applied to the old man character from the previous sections.

Creating Terrain with Displacement Maps

In this exercise you'll create detailed animated terrain using a simple Hypershade network and displacement mapping.

1. Create a new scene in Maya.

2. Create a polygon plane (Create ➢ Polygon Primitives ➢ Plane).

3. In the polyPlane1 shape node attributes, set the values to **24** units in Width and Height. Set the Subdivisions Width and Height to **24**. Increasing the subdivisions will help ensure a smooth displacement.

4. Create a Blinn shader and assign it to the plane; set the Reflectivity of the shader to **0**.

5. Click on the checkered box next to the Color channel to create a render node. You'll preview the displacement texture in the Color channel before applying it as a displacement (see Figure 11.65).

6. Select Crater from the Create Render Node panel. Press the 6 key to switch to shaded mode so that you can see the texture.

FIGURE 11.65
Placing the crater
texture in the Color
channel allows you
to preview the look
of the texture as
you fine-tune it.

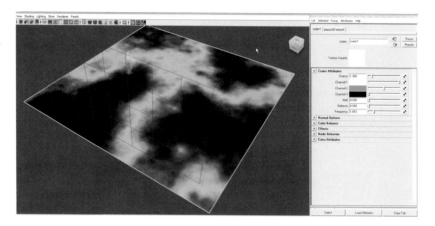

7. Set the following attributes in the crater's Attribute Editor:

Shaker = **1.98**

Channel 1 = White

Channel 2 = Gray

Channel 3 = Black

Melt = **0**

Balance = **0**

Frequency = **1.653**

8. Switch the Attribute Editor to the place3dTexture1 tab, and set the Scale values for X, Y, and Z to **10**.

9. Set the render to mental ray. In the Quality tab of the Render settings, set the Quality preset to Production Settings and create a test render.

10. Select the Blinn shader in the Hypershade and graph it. On the Create Maya Nodes rollout on the left side of the Hypershade, expand the Displacement rollout and click on the Displacement texture to create a displacement node.

11. In the Work Area of the Hypershade, MMB-drag the new displacement node on top of the blinnSG1 node, and then choose Default from the pop-up menu. This will automatically connect the displacement node to the shading group in the Displacement channel.

12. In the Hypershade, MMB-drag the crater texture on top of the displacement shader node; then choose Default from the pop-up menu. This will connect the crater texture to the displacement shader. The connection is made between the crater's outAlpha attribute and the displacement shader's Displacement attribute, as shown in Figure 11.66.

13. Open the Attribute Editor for the crater node, and check the box that says Alpha Is Luminance. This converts the luminance of the texture into the alpha output of the texture so that the displacement is correct. Disconnect the crater texture from the Color channel of the Blinn shader.

FIGURE 11.66
The displace-
ment shader is
connected to the
Blinn's shading
group node. This
figure shows a typ-
ical Hypershade
network for a dis-
placement shader.

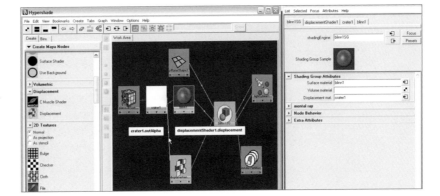

14. Create a test render of the scene using mental ray Production Settings (see Figure 11.67).

15. To see a version of the scene, open the `terrainDisplace.ma` file from the `chapter 11\` `scenes` folder of the DVD.

INCREASING THE HEIGHT OF THE TERRAIN

To increase the height of the terrain, set Alpha Gain to a value above 1; to increase the depth, set Alpha Offset to a value below zero. Both of these attributes can be animated to create the appearance of emerging terrain.

When you use simple geometry and procedural textures, the default settings for the displacement are usually just fine. There's no need to create an approximation node or change the settings in the plane's Displacement Map rollout in its shape node. More complex geometry requires a few more steps, as you'll see when a displacement is added to the old man character.

FIGURE 11.67
The crater texture
can create a very
realistic-looking
terrain quickly.
You can increase
the height of the
terrain by setting
Alpha Gain to 4
and Alpha Offset
to -4.

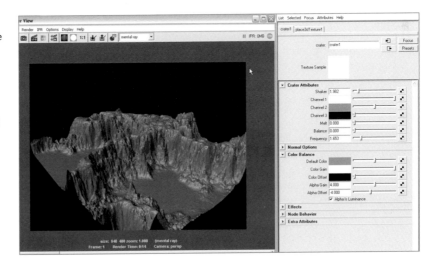

Converting Displacement to Polygons

If you decide you want actual geometry to be created from the displacement, you can convert the displacement to a polygon object. This might be helpful as a stand-in object if you need to position objects in the scene near the displaced plane or if you want to model terrain using a procedural texture.

1. Select the plane and choose Modify ➤ Convert ➤ Displacement To Polygons. There are no options for this action. A second object will be created based on the original displaced plane. Any animation of the texture will not be reflected in the converted object; it derives its displacement from the current state of the displacing texture.

2. To increase the resolution of the converted object, increase the subdivisions in Height and Width on the original plane. The conversion will take longer to calculate, and the resulting geometry will be denser.

Displacement Maps for Characters

Using displacement maps to add detail to characters is becoming increasingly common. This allows a low-resolution version of the model to be rigged and animated and then converted into a highly detailed mesh at render time. The end result can be quite spectacular. The render time involved, however, makes this workflow useable only for film and television; game engines are not nearly fast enough to render displacements in real time.

Since a displacement map is a grayscale texture, it can be painted much like a bump map. A displacement map should be used for larger details that need to be seen in the silhouette of the geometry, such as large folds and wrinkles in the flesh, bumps on the nose, and large veins. Smaller details, such as pores, should be reserved for bump or normal maps that can be used in conjunction with displacement maps. Furthermore, with characters and complex objects, the geometry to be displaced should be fairly close in shape to the displaced version and have just enough subdivisions to allow for the additional detail. The base mesh of the old man's head used in this chapter is a good example of how geometry should be organized to support displacement.

Maya's Transfer Maps tool also allows for the creation of displacement maps. The Transfer Maps tool works very well for normal maps but not nearly as well for displacement maps. Generating a workable displacement map using this tool takes a lot of time and effort, and the results are often disappointing. It does well for simple objects, but you should avoid it when creating displacement maps for complex objects such as characters.

The best possible way to generate a displacement map for a character or creature is to use a digital sculpting program such as ZBrush or Mudbox. Although it involves learning another application, the results are excellent. This is becoming the workflow of choice for many major studios. This lesson will demonstrate how to render the old man character using a displacement map generated in Pixologic's ZBrush 3.1.

When generating maps in a third-party application, it's always best to create 32-bit floating point maps. This will ensure that the displacement is smooth and free of the stair-stepping artifacts that can appear in 16-bit maps. Use the Optimized File Texture feature with displacement maps to ensure stability (see the section titled "Rendering Textures Using the Optimized Format," earlier in the chapter).

Mental ray's Approximation Editor is used in this section.

1. Open the `displace_v01.ma` scene from the `chapter 11\scenes` folder on the DVD. You'll see the same old man character from the previous sections complete with UV texture coordinates.

2. Create a Blinn texture and name it **oldManShader**; then apply it to the character.

3. In the Blinn shader, set Reflectivity to **0**.

4. Select the character's head and create an approximation node. Choose Window ➢ Rendering Editors ➢ mental ray ➢ Approximation Editor (if mental ray does not appear in the list, you'll need to load the `Mayatomr.mll` plug-in using the Plug-in Manager).

5. In the Approximation Editor, click the Create button in the Subdivisions (Polygon And Subd. Surfaces) section. You do not need to create a displacement approximation node; the default settings will work just fine.

6. In the Attribute Editor for the mentalRaySubdivApprox1 node, leave Approx Method set to Parametric, and set N Subdivisions to **3**. This subdivides the model so the detail created by the displacement texture is more refined. Higher values allow more of the detail in the map to come through. A setting higher than 5 may cause mental ray to crash. The settings are shown in Figure 11.68.

7. Set the renderer to mental ray, and use the Production Quality preset. Create a test render of the head. It should look nice and smooth.

8. In the Hypershade, create a displacement shader node and attach it to the Blinn shader. Review steps 10 and 11 of the section "Creating Terrain with Displacement Maps" to see how to do this.

9. In the Attribute Editor for the displacementShader1 node, click on the checker pattern next to the Displacement attribute and choose File from the Create Render Node pop-up.

10. Name the new file1 node **oldManDispFile**. Click on the folder next to the Image Name field, and use the computer's browser to locate the `oldManDisplace.map` file from the `sourceimages` directory in the `chapter 11\scenes` folder on the DVD.

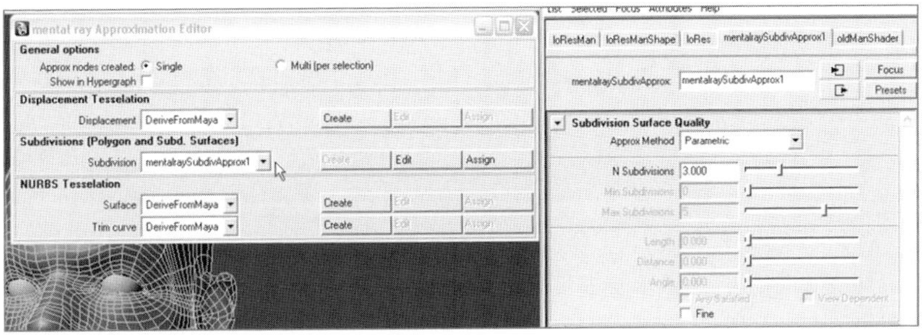

FIGURE 11.68
The subdivision approximation node will subdivide the polygon model at render time to allow more detail in the displacement to come through.

11. Expand the Color Balance section of the oldManDispFile node, set Alpha Gain to **2.2** and Alpha Offset to **-1.1**.

12. Turn on Alpha Is Luminance and create a test render. The old man should look nice and detailed (see Figure 11.69). You can try increasing the number of subdivisions on the Approximation Editor node to allow more detail to come through, but don't move the value past 5.

FIGURE 11.69
The displacement map adds very realistic detail to the rendered character.

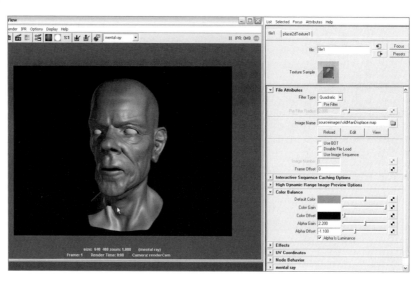

ZBRUSH DISPLACEMENT MAPS

This displacement texture was created in ZBrush using the Multi Displacement Exporter plug-in. It's a 32-bit floating point map that has already been flipped vertically. By default, textures created in ZBrush are upside down when imported into Maya.

Displacement textures created in ZBrush using the Multi Displacement Exporter plug-in will always use 2.2 for Alpha Gain and -1.1 for Alpha Offset unless the object has been scaled in Maya, in which case Alpha Gain should be set to 2.2 times the scale of the object, and Alpha Offset should be negative one-half of the Alpha Gain.

If your object looks bloated or distorted, double-check the Alpha Gain and Alpha Offset settings for the file texture used for the displacement, or check to see if Alpha Is Luminance has not been checked.

Combined Displacement and Bump Maps

1. Open oldManShader in the Attribute Editor. Add a file node to the Bump Mapping channel by clicking on the checkered box.

2. Set the Bump2d1 Use As option to Bump Map. Set Bump Depth to **0.12**.

3. Rename the connected file node **oldManBumpFile**. Use the Image Name field to open the File Browser dialog box. Add the oldManBump.tif file from the sourceimages directory in the chapter 11\scenes folder on the DVD.

4. To see a completed version of the model with displacement, open the displace_v02.ma scene from the chapter 11\scenes folder on the DVD. A rendered version is shown in Figure 11.70.

At this point the character looks very detailed, and you can move on to the next section to add a more lifelike color to the skin using a Photoshop file node.

FIGURE 11.70
The displacement and bump maps are used together to create realistic detail in the model.

FILTER

Textures have an attribute called Filter, which is found in the Special Effects rollout in the file texture node. The Filter is a blur that Maya adds to the texture to reduce artifacts in the render. Oftentimes this blur can reduce detail that is carefully painted into the map or can even create new artifacts. If you find your texture maps are not rendering correctly, try setting both the Filter and Filter Offset sliders to 0.01 as a possible solution. Setting the value to 0 may cause artifacts in some situations.

PSD Networks

The PSD network is a quick and easy way to set up a single, layered Photoshop file that can be applied to multiple channels of a shader. In this section you'll create a PSD network to create the file textures for the color, diffuse, and specular channels of the character's skin texture. You will need to have a recent version of Photoshop (Photoshop 7 or higher) installed on your computer to use a PSD network.

1. Open the PSDnetwork_v01.ma scene from the chapter 11\scenes folder on the DVD. The scene contains the old man's head with a shader already applied. The shader has both a displacement map and a bump map applied.

2. Select the old man's head, and switch to the Rendering menu set. Choose Texturing ➢ Create PSD Network. An Options box will open automatically.

3. In the Image Name field you can set the location where the PSD file will be saved. It's best to store this in the sourceimages directory of the current project.

4. Check the Open Adobe(R) Photoshop(R) option so that Photoshop opens automatically when the shader is created.

5. Set the Size X and Size Y values to **2048**. Check the option Include UV Snapshot and set Position to Top. Leave UV Set as map1 (the model only has one set), and leave Color Value at white so the UV snapshot is drawn as white lines in the Photoshop file. The UV lines will serve as a guide for painting the texture.

6. The Attributes Selection box shows the shader channels available for use in the network. The Bump and Displacement channels have icons next to them indicating that there's already a texture in these channels. Click Color from the list on the left side of the panel, and then click the arrow in the middle pointing to the right. The Color channel will now be listed on the right, meaning that a layer will be created in the final Photoshop file for the Color channel.

7. Add Bump, Diffuse, and SpecularColor to the left-hand side. When you add a channel that already has a texture, the texture will be included as part of the Photoshop file (see Figure 11.71). By adding the Bump channel to the Photoshop network, the texture for the Bump channel will be placed into a layer in the Photoshop file. You can then copy the detail you painted for this texture into the other layers and use them as a basis for the other texture channels.

FIGURE 11.71
The options for the PSD network

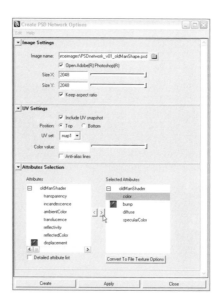

DETAILED ATTRIBUTE LIST

Clicking the Detailed List Attribute at the bottom reveals a more complete list of attributes for the model's shader. These can be included in the Photoshop network as well.

8. Click Create to make the network. Photoshop will start (if it's not running already), and a Photoshop file will open. Each channel of the shader is stored as a layer group, and the UV snapshot is visible at the top.

9. When working with the file in Photoshop, don't change the names of the layer groups or their configuration. Try to keep a single layer in each group when you've finished with the file.

10. Turn on the visibility of the upper layers to see the lower layers; just remember to restore the visibility of all the layers when you save the file before updating the network in Maya. Here are some tips for working with each layer:

    ◆ Use the Bump layer as the basis for the other textures to help keep things consistent. For instance, you can duplicate the Bump layer and move the duplicate into the diffuse layer folder. Set its Blending Mode to Multiply and reduce its Opacity. Adjust the levels of the duplicate to make it lighter. Merge this with the gray color in the diffuse group, and you have a diffuse texture ready to go. You can use this layer to darken the areas under the eyes and brighten areas close to the cheekbone. The layer should remain grayscale.

    ◆ The Specular layer can be painted quickly and roughly. Paint brighter areas where you think the skin should be shiny, such as on the tip of the nose and the lips. Darker areas should be matched with less-shiny regions, such as the cheeks. Add as much noise as possible to this layer to help break up the highlights on the skin.

    ◆ The Color layer is a good place for freckles, blotchy red areas, veins, capillaries, zits, and lip color. Use photographs and reference skin close-ups when creating this texture. You can clone the pores in the bump texture to this layer so that they will show up better on the face.

11. When you've finished painting each texture, make sure that there is one layer for each group and that they are all visible; then save the file (see Figure 11.72). In Maya, select the head and choose Texturing ➤ Update PSD Network. The file will reload and the shader channels will update.

12. You can make further adjustments to each texture without going back into Photoshop. To do this, adjust the Color Gain and Color Offset settings on textures that are connected through the outColor attribute of the texture (color, skin color), and the Alpha Gain and Alpha Offset settings of the textures that are connected using outAlpha (diffuse).

13. In the Specular Shading section of the oldManShader, set Eccentricity to **0.5** and Specular Rolloff to **0.859**.

FIGURE 11.72
Painting textures
in Photoshop
requires time,
effort, and lots of
reference materi-
als. Each layer
group in the file
corresponds to a
designated chan-
nel in the shader.

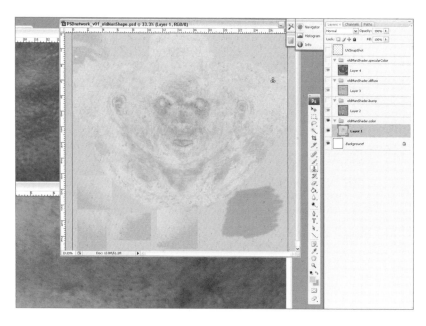

14. Create a test render of the model. Continue to tweak the textures in the shader as well as in Photoshop (see Figure 11.73).

15. To see a finished version up to this point, open the PSDNetwork_v02.ma scene from the chapter 11\scenes folder on the DVD.

FIGURE 11.73
The old man char-
acter with Bump,
Displacement,
Color, Specular,
and Diffuse chan-
nels textured.

Subsurface Scattering

Subsurface scattering refers to the phenomenon of light rays bouncing around just beneath the surface of a material before being reflected back into the environment. It's the translucent quality seen in objects such as jade, candle wax, and human skin (actually almost every material except metal has some amount of subsurface scattering). Subsurface scattering adds an amazing level of realism to CG objects and characters. It takes practice to master, but the results are worth it.

Fast, Simple Skin Shader Setup

In Maya there are several ways to create the look of subsurface scattering ranging from simple to complex. The Translucence, Translucence Depth, and Translucence Focus sliders included on standard Maya shaders offer the simplest way to create translucency. These sliders work fine for an object made of a single material, such as candle wax. Likewise the Scatter Radius slider and related attributes in the mental ray section of Maya shaders add a quick-and-dirty subsurface quality to simple objects. However, these options fall far short when you're trying to create a complex material such as human skin.

Since Maya 2008, the mental ray simple subsurface scattering shaders have become much easier to set up and use. Many of the connections that needed to be created manually in previous versions of Maya are now set up automatically when you create the shader.

There are several subsurface scattering shaders. These include:

misss_call_shader

misss_fast_shader

misss_fast_shader_x

misss_fast_shader_x_passes

misss_fast_simple_maya

misss_fast_skin_maya

misss_physical

misss_set_normal

misss_skin_specular

With the exception of misss_physical, these shaders are all similar and use the same basic technique for creating the effect of subsurface scattering. Some of the misss shaders are really combined versions of others. For instance, misss_fast_skin_maya is actually a combination of misss_fast_shader and misss_skin_specular with an extra layer of subsurface scattering. In this chapter, you'll focus on using the misss_fast_skin_maya shader.

MISSS SHADERS

The prefix *misss* stands for Mental Images Subsurface Scattering.

The misss_physical shader is a more complex, physically accurate shader meant to be used with photon casting lights. For complete information on this shader refer to *Mental Ray for Maya, 3ds Max, and XSI* by Boaz Livny (Sybex, 2008). This shader also works best for objects that require a deep level of scattering, such as thick candles and marble.

1. Open the `sss_v01.ma` scene from the `chapter 11\scenes` folder on the DVD. You'll see the old man character with a custom light rig. The light rig uses area lights to cast soft shadows. The soft shadows created by the area lights will add to the realism of the render.

2. Switch to the render camera and do a quick test render. Store the image in the render view so you can compare it with the subsurface scattering renders.

You'll see that the character has a Blinn texture applied along with the skin, bump, displacement, and specular textures used in the previous section. These same file textures (along with a few others) will be plugged into the simple skin shader. The colors of the textures seem very extreme; however, once they are plugged into the misss_fast_skin_maya shader, you'll see that the variations in color become more subtle and even (see Figure 11.74).

3. Open the Hypershade and, on the left side, switch to the Create mental ray Nodes section. From the Materials section, create a misss_fast_skin shader. Name the shader **oldManSkinShader.**

4. Select the old man character and apply the oldManSkinShader (right-click the shader's icon in the Hypershade, and choose Assign Material To Selection). He'll turn red in the perspective view, and that's okay. Maya just can't preview some of the mental ray nodes using hardware rendering.

5. Select the misss_skin_mayaSG1 node (it resides in the shader hierarchy above the misss_fast_skin_shader node) in the Hypershade, and right-click the shader. Choose Graph Network.

FIGURE 11.74
The old man character rendered without subsurface scattering

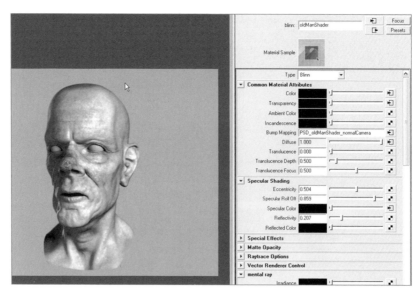

You'll see that Maya has automatically created the necessary light map and texture nodes (misss_fast_Imap_maya and mentalRayTexture1). If you select the mentalrayTexture1 node, you'll see that the File Size Width and File Size Texture attributes are both highlighted in purple, indicating an expression is controlling their values. The expression is tied to the render size automatically, so you don't have to set these as you did in previous versions of Maya.

LIGHT MAPS

A light map (lmap) is a special mental ray node used to calculate the influence of light across the surface based on the camera's position in the scene. Light maps are used to emulate the subsurface effect without having to perform physically based calculations. They render quickly and do a pretty good job of faking the subsurface scattering phenomena.

---

6. In the Image Name field you can type a name for the light map texture file and a location for the file as well. It's a good idea to do this if you have more than one surface using a light map. You can leave this field blank for now. All other attributes can be left at their default settings. Likewise, there's no need to change anything in the misss_fast_lmap node.

7. Select oldManSkinShader and open its Attribute Editor. At the top you'll see the diffuse layer. This layer controls the basic color of the object, much like the Color and Diffuse settings in a standard shader but with a couple of differences.

Diffuse Weight controls the overall contribution, or lightness, of the combined diffuse channels. The Overall Color channel is a multiplier for the Diffuse Color channel, so you'll want to put your color textures in the Diffuse Color channel and then modify it using the Overall slider. That said, you can actually do the reverse in some cases; you may want to experiment by putting a color texture map in the Overall Color channel.

8. In the Hypershade, switch to the Textures tab and find the PSD_oldManShader_color texture. MMB-drag it down to the Attribute Editor on top of the Diffuse Color channel. This texture file is the skin color used in the previous section.

The Overall Color channel is also a good place for dirt or cavity maps. In this case you'll hook up an ambient occlusion node.

9. In the left side of the Hypershade under the Create mental ray nodes, expand the Textures section and choose the mib_amb_occlusion node. An ambient occlusion texture node will appear in the Work Area. Reselect the misss_fast_skin shader, and MMB-drag the ambient occlusion node from the Hypershade Work Area over the Attribute Editor for the oldManSkinShader . Drop it on top of the overall color node.

10. Set Diffuse Weight to **0.5**; you'll probably want to adjust this more later.

11. In the Textures area of the Hypershade, find the PSD_oldManShader_normalCamera (this is the texture used to create the bump) texture, and MMB-drag it to the Work Area. Expand the Bump Shader rollout in the oldManSkinShader, and MMB-drag the PSD_old-ManShader_normalCamera texture on top of this channel.

MISSS _ FAST _ SKIN BUMP MAPS

Since Maya 2008, you no longer need to create a bump 2d2 node manually; the Bump channel works just like any standard Maya shader.

---

12. Select the bump2d node and set the Bump Depth to **0.15**.

13. In the Materials tab of the Hypershade, find the oldManDisplacement shader. MMB-drag this shader on top of the shading group labeled misss_fast_skin_maya1SG node, and choose Default. These are the same displacement node, file texture, and settings created earlier in the chapter (see Figure 11.75).

FIGURE 11.75
The shading network for the misss_fast_skin shader has several file textures connected to it.

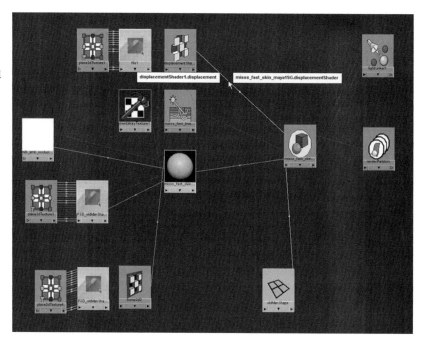

14. Select the oldMan head in the perspective view, and switch to the renderCam. The old-Man head already has an approximation node attached, and the renderer has been set to mental ray. Create a test render to see how he looks so far.

15. He has a very interesting look, kind of like a plastic doll. Compare the render with the previously stored version; notice how the color texture is not nearly as strong. The sub-surface settings need to be tuned to create a more realistic-looking skin. Save your scene.

16. To see a version of the scene so far, open the sss_v02.ma file from the chapter 11\scenes folder on the DVD. The render is shown in Figure 11.76.

Figure 11.76
At this point a render of the character looks grainy and plastic.

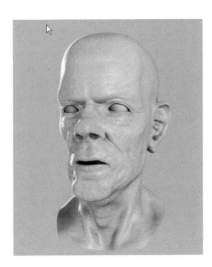

Subsurface Scattering Layers

The three channels listed under the Subsurface Scattering Layers control three different levels of subsurface scattering. Their controls are the same except for one additional attribute slider in the back scattering layer.

The Scatter Weight slider for each channel controls its overall contribution to the shader. Scatter Radius controls how light scatters across the surface of the object, and Scatter Depth (found only on Back Scatter Color in the misss_fast_skin_maya shader) controls how deeply light penetrates into the object. The Color value for each controls the color of the subsurface scattering; you can apply textures to all of these values.

The Epidermal layer is the topmost layer, where you'll find freckles and moles; the Subdermal layer is just beneath the skin, where you'll find veins and capillaries; and the back scatter color is the deepest layer, where bone and cartilage allow different amounts of backlighting to show through the skin.

1. To remove the grainy quality you can expand the Lightmap rollout in the oldManSkinShader and increase Samples to **256**. Raising this value does not actually increase render times much, but it will remove the graininess.

2. Select the Ambient Occlusion node connected to Overall Color. Set its Samples value to **32** and its Max Distance to **1**. This limits the amount of distance mental ray uses to calculate Ambient Occlusion.

3. Select the oldManSkinShader, and connect the PSD_oldManShader_color texture to the Epidermal Scatter Color channel (MMB-drag the texture node on top of the Epidermal Scatter Color slider in the Attribute Editor). It's common practice to use the same texture for both the diffuse color and the uppermost layer of subsurface scattering.

4. In the Textures tab of the Hypershade, drag the subdermalScatterColor and backScatterColor file texture nodes down into the Work Area. Connect them to their respective channels in the oldManSkinShader.

5 Set the following values for the Subsurface Scattering Layer channels:

Epidermal Scatter Weight = **0.5**

Epidermal Scatter Radius = **0.25**

Subdermal Scatter Weight = **0.5**

Subdermal Scatter Radius = **1**

Back Scatter Weight = **1.5**

Back Scatter Radius = **1**

Back Scatter Depth = **0.2**

These values are often arrived at through experimentation. The lighting, size of the scene, and objects, along with the desired look, all affect how these values are set. In general when working with them you'll want to set all of the weight values to 0 to turn them off and then raise the weight value of each one, starting with the back scattering layer, and set their values by tweaking and test rendering. If you arrive at settings you like, save the preset for reuse in other scenes. You can use the Scale Conversion attribute under the Algorithm Control rollout as a global scale adjuster for scenes and objects of different sizes.

Select the file node for backScatterColor, and click the View button to see the texture. Notice how deep the color is, yet it's quite subtle in the final render. Take a look at the subdermal file texture as well. The philosophy behind the arrangement of the colors in the file is based on the typical color zones of the face. Faces, both male and female and across races, generally have cooler colors around the mouth and eyes and in the recesses of the neck and ears. Warmer colors appear on the nose, cheeks, and forehead, and some yellows are seen in places where bone is close to the surface of the skin, such as in the temples and cheekbones.

Subsurface Specularity

The Subsurface Specularity attributes provide a number of ways to control how the skin of your character reflects the lights in the scene.

1. Overall Weight adjusts how much the combined specularity settings affect the object. Setting this to 0 turns off the specularity altogether. Set this value to **1.5.**

2. Edge Factor controls the Fresnel effect of the specular reflection. Areas of the surface that turn away from the camera reflect more light than those that face the camera. This value controls the width of this effect. A higher value creates a thinner edge for the highlight on the skin. Set this value to **2.**

The specularity for the skin shader has two layers to simulate the broad, overall specularity of the skin as well as the shiny quality of oily or wet skin. The Primary specularity controls the broad specular reflection and should usually have lower values than the Secondary specularity values. The sliders themselves work the same way. Weight controls the overall contribution; Color controls the color or texture. Edge Weight is a multiplier for the edge of the highlight, and Shininess controls the size and intensity of the highlight (lips will have a higher shininess than the cheeks).

3. In the Hypershade, switch to the Textures tab and find the PSD_oldManShader_diffuse node. This texture shares much of the same detail as the bump node, so it should work pretty well for the primary specularity. MMB-drag this node on top of the Primary

Specular Color slider. Set Primary Weight to **0.2**, Primary Edge Weight to **0.8**, and Primary Shininess to **5**.

4. Use the same technique to connect the PSD_oldmanShader_specularColor node to the Secondary Specular Color. This texture contains a lot of noise and fine detail, so it should do a good job of breaking up the brighter highlights on the shinier parts of the face.

5. Set Secondary Weight to **0.8**, Secondary Edge Weight to **0.1**, and Secondary Shininess to **50**.

6. The reflection settings work much like the specular values. If Reflect Environment Only is selected, only environment maps will be used for reflection and no reflection rays will be generated for the object. Skin is not terribly reflective, so for this scene you can leave Reflect Weight at 0 or put it at an extremely low value such as **0.005**, and set Reflect Edge Weight to **0.1**. The final settings are shown in Figure 11.77.

7. Create a test render of the scene. To see a completed version, open the `sss_v03.ma` scene from the `chapter 11\scenes` folder on the DVD. Compare the image (shown in Figure 11.78) with the render from the PSD network section. Subsurface scattering does a great deal toward adding realism to a character.

FIGURE 11.77
The settings for the final oldManSkinShader

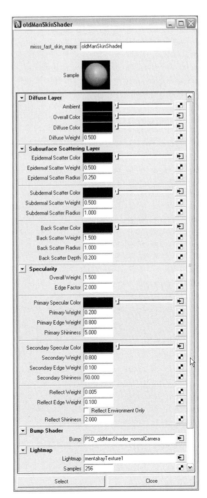

FIGURE 11.78
The final render of
the character with
displacement,
bump, painted skin
textures, and sub-
surface scattering

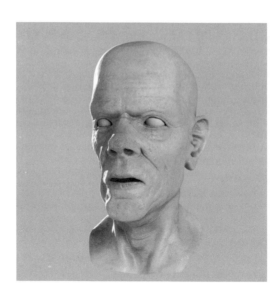

SUBSURFACE SCATTERING TIPS

When creating a complete character, remember to add subsurface scattering to the teeth and eyeballs to make a truly realistic character.

Texture Mapping NURBS Surfaces

NURBS surfaces use their own parameterization to determine texture coordinates. In other
words, you don't need to map u- and v- coordinates using the UV layout tools. This makes
NURBS easier to work with but less flexible. You can project a texture onto a NURBS surface
similarly to the way you project UV coordinates onto a polygon. In this section, you'll see a
couple common ways to map UVs onto NURBS surfaces.

Convert Texture to File Texture

Painting a texture map for a NURBS surface can be made easier by creating a visual guide that
you can use in Photoshop. In this example you'll create a tire tread for a NURBS tire and use the
image created in Photoshop as a displacement map.

1. Open the carTexture_v01.ma scene from the chapter11\scenes directory on the DVD.

The tires on Anthony Honn's car model are revolved NURBS surfaces. You can try painting a
tread pattern in Photoshop and then apply it to the model using the Texture Placement tool, but
you'll probably get very frustrated when you try to precisely place the tread. Instead, you can
first create a guide texture that can be used in Photoshop when you create the tread pattern.

2. Select the rear wheel surface of the car in the perspective view, and apply a Lambert texture. Name the texture **rubberTireShader**.

3. Open the Attribute Editor for rubberTireShader. Click on the checkered swatch next to the Color channel, and apply a ramp texture.

4. Open the Attribute Editor for the new ramp, and set the Type to U Ramp so the colors of the ramp wrap around the tire (Figure 11.79).

5. In the Attribute Editor for the ramp, set Interpolation to None.

6. Change the colors of the ramp so the top and bottom are black and the middle is white.

7. Move the positions of the color markers on the ramp so the center strip, where the tread pattern will be, is white and the sides are black. Use the numeric inputs in the Ramp's Attribute Editor to precisely position the color markers. Set the bottom marker's Selected Position to **0**, the middle marker's Selected Position to **0.35**, and the top marker's Selected Position to **0.65** (see Figure 11.80).

FIGURE 11.79
Set the ramp texture to U Ramp so the colors of the ramp wrap around the tire.

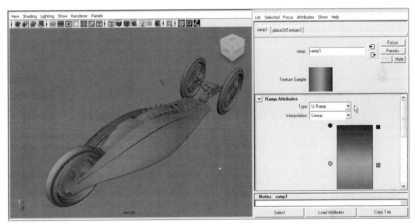

FIGURE 11.80
The ramp colors are modified to black and white to define the limits of the tread.

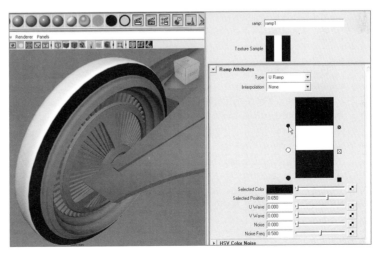

Once you have the ramp positioned to indicate the placement of the tread, you can convert the ramp into a file texture that can be opened in Photoshop.

8. Open the Hypershade window. In the perspective view, select the rear tire, and Shift+click the rubberTireShader in the Hypershade. From the Hypershade drop-down menu, choose Edit ➤ Convert To File Texture ➤ Options. In the Options box, reset the settings to the defaults. Set the X and Y Resolutions to **1024**. Set the format to TIFF. Click the Convert And Close button.

9. A new rubberTireShader appears in the Hypershade. A file texture node is connected to this new shader. Select the new file1 texture, and open its Attribute Editor. In the Image Name field, you'll see the path to the directory where the image is stored (it should be stored in the sourceimages directory of the current project).

FIGURE 11.81

The ramp texture is converted into a file texture and attached to a duplicate of the original shader.

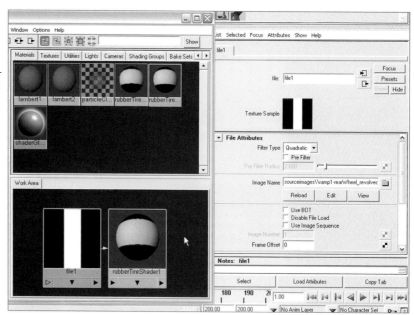

The file texture can be opened in Photoshop and used as a guide to create the tread. The tricky part of the tread is making a repeating pattern that does not have visible seams at the top and bottom. The tread pattern should stay within the white area on the original texture. Make the tread pattern white and the black areas gray. Remember that in a displacement map a gray value of 0.5 means no displacement. Black creates a recess, and white creates a bump. So the parts of the tread that stick out should be white. I added dark gray areas in my version for the tread to create recesses. The sides of the tire can be gray so that the texture does not alter the model of the tires.

You can create a pattern along the entire strip or make a section that can be repeated in Maya. In this example, I chose the latter method (see Figure 11.82).

FIGURE 11.82

The treadTexture .tif file was created based on the converted ramp texture. It has been carefully cropped so the texture repeats exactly on the top and bottom.

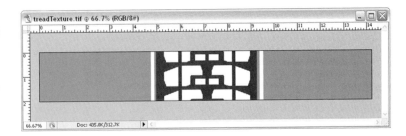

10. In the carTexture_v01.ma scene, open the Hypershade window and select the rubberTireShader1 shader. This is the duplicate that was created when you converted the ramp into a file texture. It has automatically been applied to the tire surface.

11. Select the file1 node and open its Attribute Editor. Click on the folder next to the Image Name field and browse your computer to find the tread file you created, or use the treadTexture.tif file found in the chapter11\sourceimages directory on the DVD.

12. When you use the treadTexture.tif file, you'll notice it is stretched on the tire. To fix this you need to attach a file texture placement node. In the Create column of the Hypershade window, set Mode to Create Maya Nodes. Scroll down to the General Utilities section, and click 2d Placement Node to create a placement node.

13. In the Hypershade window, MMB-drag the new 2dTexture Placement node on top of the file1 texture node, and choose Default from the pop-up menu. This makes the default connections between the placement node and the file texture.

14. Open the Attribute Editor for the 2d Texture Placement node, and set the V field of the Repeat UV attribute to **88**. In the perspective window, you'll see that the texture is now repeating on the tire (I arrived at the number 88 through trial and error). See Figure 11.83.

FIGURE 11.83

The treadTexture file repeats around the tire, creating the texture pattern.

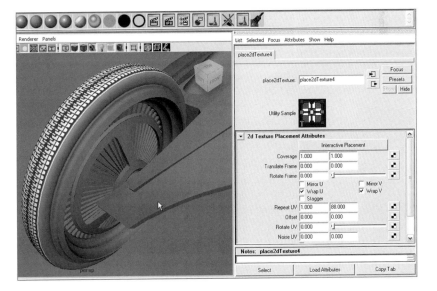

15. To make the texture a displacement map, graph the rubberTireShader1 shader in the Hypershade. Disconnect the connection between the texture and the Color channel of rubberTireShader1. Select the shading group node attached to the rubberTireShader1 node (it should be named lambert3SG1).

16. Open the Attribute Editor for lambert3SG1. MMB-drag the file1 texture node on top of the Displacement Mat. slot to make the texture a displacement material.

17. Open the file1 node in the Attribute Editor and, under the Color Balance rollout, set Alpha Gain to **0.1** and Alpha Offset to **-0.05** (for more information on these settings review the "Displacement Mapping" section in this chapter).

18. Create a test render. You may need to adjust the Alpha Gain value to create the height for the tread pattern. The Alpha Offset option should be set to -1/2 of the Alpha Gain if you want the black parts of the texture to push into the tire.

19. Zoom in on the tire, and create a test render of the scene (see Figure 11.84).

20. Save the scene as carTexture_v02.ma. To see a finished version of the scene, open the carTexture_v02.ma scene from the chapter11\scenes directory on the DVD.

FIGURE 11.84
The treadTexture.tif file is used as a displacement map for the tire.

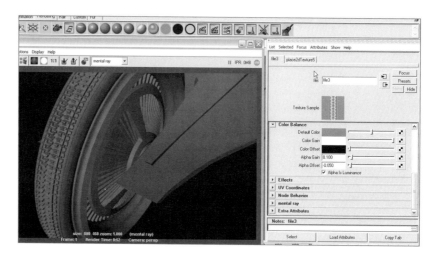

REVERSED DISPLACEMENT MAPS ON NURBS SURFACES

If you find that the texture appears inverted, you may need to reverse the NURBS surface so the normals face outward. To do this, select the NURBS surface, switch to the Surfaces menu set, and choose Edit NURBS ➤ Reverse Surface Direction.

Another way to map a texture onto a NURBS surface is to use a projection node. To project a texture on a NURBS surface, make sure the As Projection option is selected in the 2D Textures section of the Create Maya nodes. You can then use the projection manipulator to place the texture in the perspective view.

The Bottom Line

Create UV texture coordinates. UV texture coordinates are a crucial element of any polygon or subdivision surface model. If a model has well-organized UVs, painting texture and displacement maps is easy and error free.

> **Master it** Map UV texture coordinates for a character's hand; then try a complete figure.

Create bump and normal maps. Bump and normal maps are two ways to add detail to a model. Bump maps are great for fine detail, such as pores; normal maps allow you to transfer detail from a high-resolution mesh to a low-resolution version of the same model as well as offer superior shading and faster rendering than bump maps.

> **Master it** Paint a bump map for a character. Create high-resolution and low-resolution versions of the model, and try creating a normal map using the Transfer Maps tool. See if you can bake the bump map into the normal map.

Create displacement maps. A displacement map is a grayscale texture that can actually alter the geometry of a model. There are a wide variety of uses for displacement maps.

> **Master it** Create some terrain using a procedural texture, such as the crater texture, as a displacement map for a plane. Try animating the depth of the map so that canyons form in the ground over time.

Use the PSD network node. A PSD network automatically creates a multilayer Photoshop file with a layer group for each designated channel of a shader.

> **Master it** Create a PSD network for a shader that includes layers for transparency, incandescence, and reflected color.

Create a misss_fast_skin shader. The misss_fast_skin shader can create extremely realistic-looking skin. The secret is using painted texture maps for the Subsurface and Specularity channels.

> **Master it** Change the look of the old man character by making his skin paler or tanner; see if you can get the backlight to make his ears glow from behind.

Create texture maps for NURBS surfaces. NURBS models have UV texture coordinates built into the parameterization of the surface. You can convert a ramp into a texture to use as a guide for painting texture maps in Photoshop.

> **Master it** Create a texture for a tire that includes the text for the tire brand on the side of the tire.

Chapter 12

Rendering for Compositing

Maya offers a number of options for separating the individual elements of a render into separate passes. These passes can then be reassembled and processed with additional effects using compositing software, such as Adobe After Effects or Autodesk Toxic. In this chapter, you'll learn how to use Maya's Render Layers and mental ray's Render Passes features to split rendered images into elements that can then be used in your compositing software.

In this chapter you will learn to:

- ◆ Use render layers
- ◆ Use render passes
- ◆ Perform batch renders
- ◆ Use mental ray quality settings

Render Layers

The Render Layers feature is best used to isolate geometry, shaders, and lighting to create different versions of the same animation. Render Layers can be used to create a balance between efficiency and flexibility.

If you've used Render Layers in previous versions of Maya, you'll find that much has been changed in Maya 2009. Render Layers now offers the ability to create multiple render passes for each individual layer. This means it is no longer necessary to create separate render layers for ambient occlusion, reflection, beauty, shadows, and so on. Instead these separate renders can be created for each layer using Render Passes. Render Passes is discussed later in this chapter. To avoid confusion, it's best to forget what you know about Render Layers and start over from the beginning.

There is an enormous amount of creative flexibility using Render Layers. This chapter explains the more typical workflow; however, you may develop your own way of using Render Layers over time.

MAYA 2008 LAYERS IN MAYA 2009

If you open a Maya 2008 scene (or any scene with Render Layers), the layers will still appear and behave the same way they did in older versions of Maya. If you really want to, you can continue to use your old workflow; however, you may notice that the Render Layer presets no longer appear or work the same way. They have been replaced with Render Pass presets. This takes a little getting used to if you've been using older versions of Maya.

Render layers are created and managed using the Render Layer Editor. This is found in the Layer Editor in the lower-right corner of the default interface layout, just below the Channel Box. The Layer Editor has three modes: display, animation, and render. You change the mode by clicking one of the radio buttons at the top of the Layer Editor. These are the three types of layers you can create in Maya. Figure 12.1 shows the Layer Editor in render mode. The example shows a scene that has two custom render layers and the default render layer.

FIGURE 12.1
The Render Layer Editor is a mode of the Layer Editor found below the Channel Box on the lower right of the default interface.

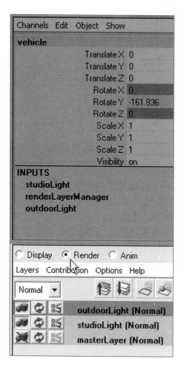

By default, every Maya scene has at least one render layer labeled masterLayer. All the lights and geometry of the scene are included in the master layer. When you create a new render layer, you can specify precisely which lights and objects are included in that layer. As you add additional render layers, you can create alternate lights for each layer, use different shaders on each piece of geometry, render one layer using mental ray and another using Maya Software, use indirect lighting effects on one layer and not on another, and so on. A render layer can be rendered using any camera, or you can specify which camera renders which layer. In this section, you'll use many of these techniques to render different versions of the same scene.

Creating Render Layers

In this exercise, you'll render Anthony Honn's vehicle model in a studio environment and in an outdoor setting. Furthermore, the car is rendered using a different shader on the body for each layer. The first step is to create a new render layer for the scene.

1. Open the carComposite_v01.ma scene from the chapter12\scenes directory on the DVD. Open the Render View window, and create a test render using the renderCam camera. It may take a minute or so to create the render (Figure 12.2).

FIGURE 12.2

The carComposite _v01.ma scene shows a typical studio lighting and shading arrangement for the car.

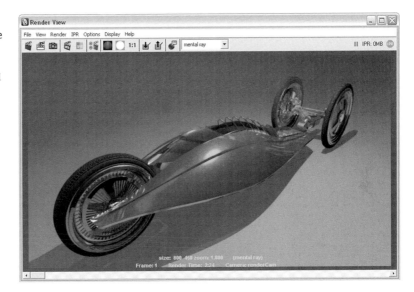

The scene is set up in a studio environment. The lighting consists of two point lights that have mental ray Physical Light shaders applied. These lights create the shadows and are reflected in the body of the car. An Area light and a Directional light are used as simple fill lights.

The car itself uses several MIA materials for the metallic, glass, chrome, and rubber parts. The body uses a shading network that combines the mib_glossy_reflection shader and a mi_metallic_paint_x shader. An HDRI image is used to create some reflections on the surface. The HDRI image is mapped to an mib_lookup_sphere node. This same texture is used to create reflections on some of the other metallic parts.

CHEATING REFLECTIONS

If you take a look at images of CG cars in advertisements and books, you'll notice many artists cheat the reflections in a studio environment, adding HDRI images that are completely unrelated to the background. The reason they do this is to create reflections and highlights on the surface that show off the contours of the car design even if it means creating a less realistic render.

The shader used for the car body is named blueCarBody. You can select it in the Hypershade and graph the input and output connections in the Work Area to see how the shader is arranged (select the shader in the Hypershade and choose Graph ➢ Input And Output Connections from the Hypershade menu bar). Figure 12.3 shows the graphed network.

FIGURE 12.3
The blueCarBody shader is graphed in the Work Area of the Hypershade.

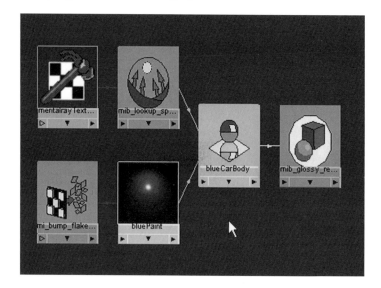

The renderCam camera has a lens shader applied to correct the exposure of the image. As you learned in Chapter 10, MIA materials and physical lights are physically accurate, which means their range of values does not always look correct when displayed on a computer screen. The mia_exposure_simple lens shader is applied to the camera to make sure the scene looks acceptable when rendered.

To create two alternative versions of the scene, you'll want to use two separate render layers. The first render layer will look exactly like the current scene; the second render layer will use a different shader for the car body and the Physical Sky and Sun network to create the look of outdoor lighting. Generally when you start to add render layers, the master layer is not rendered; only the layers that you add to the scene are used for rendering.

2. Set the Layer Editor mode to Render.

3. You can quickly add all the scene elements to a new layer by simply copying the layer. Select the masterLayer label in the Layer Editor, right-click, and choose Copy Layer. This creates a duplicate of the layer in the editor using all the same settings. See Figure 12.4, left image.

4. In the Layer Editor, double-click on the label for the new layer and rename it **studioLighting**. This is shown in the second image from the left in Figure 12.4.

5. In the menu bar for the Render Layer Editor, select Options and make sure Render All Layers is not activated (click on this option until the check mark disappears). This is shown in the second image from the right in Figure 12.4.

Right now you're interested in rendering only a single layer at a time. If this option is on, Maya will render all the layers each time you create a test render in the render view.

6. Click on the blue sphere and cube icon to the left of the masterLayer label so a red X appears. This deactivates this render layer so it is not renderable. This is shown in the right image in Figure 12.4.

7. Select the studioLighting layer in the Layer Editor so it is highlighted in blue. Open the Render View window and create a test render using the renderCam camera. It should look exactly the same as the render from step 1.

FIGURE 12.4

Graph the blueCar-Body shader in the Work Area of the Hypershade, then copy masterLayer (top left image) and rename it studioLighting (top right). Deactivate the Render All Layers option (bottom left), and turn off the masterLayer render option (bottom right).

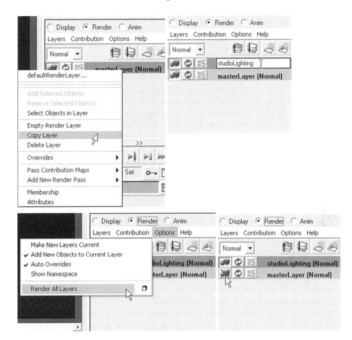

Copying a layer is a fast and easy way to create a render layer. You can also create an empty layer by choosing Create Empty Layer from the Layers menu in the Render Layer Editor. You can then select objects in the scene, right-click on the new layer, and choose Add Selected Objects from the pop-up menu. Another way to create a new layer is to select objects in the scene and choose Create Layer From Selected from the layers Menu. A new render layer containing all of the selected objects is created.

You can add new objects at any time by right-clicking on the render layer and choosing Add Selected Objects. Likewise, objects can be removed by selecting the objects and choosing Remove Selected Objects. You can delete a render layer by right-clicking on the layer and choosing Delete Layer. This does not delete the objects, lights, or shaders in the scene, just the layer itself.

8. Save the scene as **carComposite_v02.ma**. To see a version of the scene to this point, open the carComposite_v02.ma scene from the chapter12\scenes directory on the DVD.

An object's visibility can be on for one render layer and off for another. Likewise, if an object is on a display layer and a render layer, the display layer's visibility affects whether or not the object is visible in the render layer. This is easy to forget, and you may find yourself unable to figure out why an object that has been added to a render layer is not visible. Remember to double-check the settings in the Display Layer Editor if you can't see a particular object.

You can use the Relationship Editor to see which layers an object belongs to. Choose Window ➤ Relationship Editors ➤ Render Layers.

Render Layer Overrides

To create a different lighting and shading setup for a second layer, you'll use Render Layer Overrides. An override changes an attribute for a specific layer. So, for example, if you wanted Final Gathering to calculate on one layer but not another, you would create an override in the Render Settings window from the Final Gathering attribute. To create an override, right-click next to an attribute and choose Create Layer Override. As long as you are working in a particular layer that has an override enabled for an attribute, you'll see the label of the attribute highlighted in orange. Settings created in the master layer apply to all other layers unless there is an override.

This next section shows how to use overrides as you create a new layer for the outdoor lighting of the car.

1. Continue with the scene from the previous section or open the carComposite_v02.ma scene from the chapter12\scenes directory on the DVD.

2. In the Outliner, select the Vehicle group. Shift+click the ground object. In the Render Layer Editor, choose Layers ➤ Create Layer From Selected.

3. Select the new layer so it is highlighted in blue, and rename it **outDoorLighting**.

If a group such as the Vehicle group is added to a render layer, all of its children are part of that layer. If you want to add just a part, such as the wheels, select the geometry (or subgroup) and add that to the render layer rather than the entire group.

Currently this layer has no lighting, so if you render it the layer will appear dark (the default light in the render settings is off). That's fine because at this point you want to create a Physical Sky and Sun network for this layer.

4. Make sure the outDoorLighting layer is selected in the Render Layer Editor. This ensures that you are currently in this layer and that any changes you make to the lighting or shading will appear in this layer.

5. Click the small clapboard icon just to the left of the outDoorLighting label. This opens the render settings for this layer.

In the Render Settings window, you'll notice outDoorLighting is selected in the Render Layer menu at the top. You can use this menu to switch between settings for the different layers.

6. Switch to the Indirect Lighting tab, and click the Create button for the Physical Sun and Sky.

This button creates a series of nodes including the Sun Direction light, the Physical Sky node, and a mia_exposure lens shader for all the lights in the scene. It also enables Final Gathering in the Render Settings window.

7. In the Render Settings window, RMB-click *over* the label Final Gathering and choose Create Layer Override (Figure 12.5). You'll see that Final Gathering turns orange, letting you know this setting has an override for the current layer (outDoorLighting).

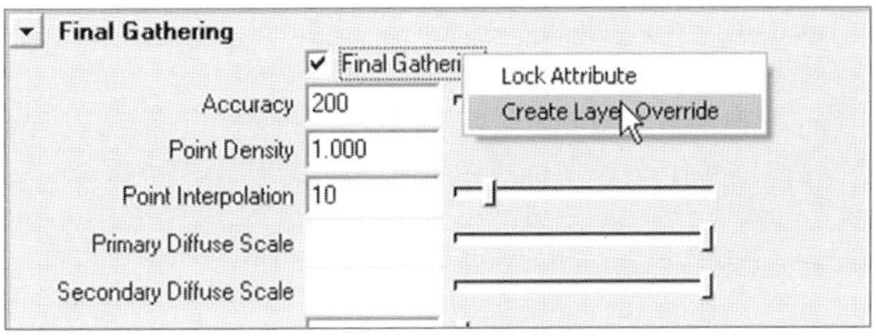

FIGURE 12.5
Create a layer over-
ride for Final Gath-
ering in the Render
Settings window
for the outDoor-
Lighting layer.

Final Gathering

☑ Final Gatheri   Lock Attribute

Accuracy 200   Create Laye Override

Point Density 1.000

Point Interpolation 10

Primary Diffuse Scale

Secondary Diffuse Scale

8. You want Final Gathering only for the outDoorLighting layer. In the Render Settings window, select masterLayer from the Render Layer drop-down menu. Turn off Final Gathering while this layer is selected.

9. Select the studioLighting layer from the Render Layer menu in the Render Settings window. Final Gathering should now be off for this layer as well. Select outDoorLighting, and you'll see that Final Gathering is enabled and the label is still orange.

This is the basic workflow for creating a render layer override. How do you know which settings can be overridden? Most attributes related to lighting and shading can be overridden on most nodes. You can always right-click next to the attribute layer and see if the Create Layer Override setting is available.

10. In the Render View window, create a test render, but make sure outDoorLighting is still the selected render layer. The render will take four or five minutes (depending on your computer's speed and available RAM).

The render is obviously quite different from the render created for the studioLighting layer (Figure 12.6).

11. Store the render in the Render View window (from the File menu in the Render View window choose Keep Image In Render View). In the Render Layer Editor, select the studioLighting layer and create another test render.

FIGURE 12.6
The lighting in the
outDoorLighting
layer is very dif-
ferent from the
lighting in the stu-
dioLighting layer.

Something has gone wrong because the lighting has changed for this layer. Final Gathering is not calculating, but you'll see that the render takes a long time and the lighting no longer matches the original studioLighting render. The reason for this is not because of render layers per se but because of the Physical Sun and Sky network that was added to the scene. Remember from Chapter 9, when you add a Physical Sun and Sky network, a number of nodes are added to the scene, including the renderable cameras. Normally this feature saves time and work, but in this case it's working against the scene.

The easiest way to fix the problem is to create a duplicate render camera. One camera can be used to render the studioLighting layer; the other can be used to render the outDoorLighting layer. You can make sure that the correct lens shaders are applied to both cameras. You can use overrides to specify which camera is available from which layer.

12. Select the renderCam camera in the Outliner. Rename it **outdoorCam**.

13. Duplicate outdoorCam and rename the duplicate **studioCam**. Open the Attribute Editor for studioCam. Switch to the studioCamShape tab and expand the mental ray section.

You'll see there are no lens or environment shaders attached to the studioCam camera. If you switch to the outdoorCam camera, you'll see the mia_physicalsky1 shader in the Environment Shader slot and the mia_exposure_simple2 shader in the Lens Shader slot. The original render-Cam camera had a mia_exposure_simple1 node in the Lens Shader slot, but this was replaced by mia_exposure_simple2 when the Physical Sun and Sky network was added to the scene. The solution here is to reattach the mia_exposure_simple1 node to the lens shader of studioCam.

14. Open the Hypershade window and switch to the Utilities tab. MMB-drag mia_exposure_simple1 (you can see the full name if you hold the cursor over the icon) down to the Lens Shader slot for studioCam (Figure 12.7).

15. In the Hypershade, select the mia_physicalsky1 node from the Utilities tab, and open its Attribute Editor to the mia_physicalsky1 tab. Right-click next to the On attribute and choose Create Layer Override. The attribute label should turn orange.

16. After adding the override, deselect the checkbox for this attribute to turn it off for this layer.

FIGURE 12.7
Attach the mia_exposure_simple1 node to the Lens Shader slot of studioCam.

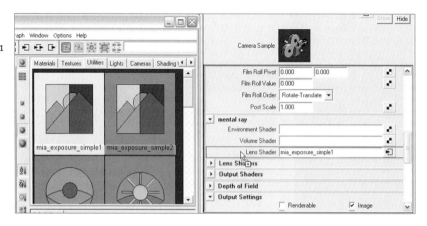

17. Create a test render in the Render View window, and make sure that studioCam is chosen as the rendering camera. The render now looks like it did at the start of the section.

18. Save the scene as **carComposite_v03.ma**. To see a version of the scene to this point, open the carComposite_v03.ma scene from the chapter12\scenes directory on the DVD.

ANIMATED CAMERAS

You can use a parent constraint to attach the duplicate camera to the original if the original camera is animated. To do this, select the original camera, Shift+click the duplicate, switch to the Animation menu set, and choose Constrain ➢ Parent ➢ Options. In the options, turn off Maintain Offset and turn on All for both Translate and Rotate. Animation constraints are covered in Chapter 5.

Creating Overrides for Rendering Cameras

Notice that you do not need to add cameras to render layers when you add them to a scene. You can if you want, but it makes no difference. The cameras that render the scene are listed in the Common tab of the Render Settings window.

If you're rendering an animated sequence using two cameras with different settings as in the carComposite example, you'll want to use overrides so you don't render more images than you need.

1. Continue with the scene from the previous section or open the carComposite_v03.ma scene from the chapter12\scenes directory on the DVD.

2. Open the Render Settings window. Set the Render Layer menu at the top of the Render Settings window to studioLighting.

3. Switch to the Common tab and expand the Renderable Cameras section.

4. Use the Renderable Camera menu to choose the studioCam camera. Right-click next to the menu and choose Create Layer Override (Figure 12.8).

5. Set the Render Layer drop-down at the top of the Render Settings window to outDoorLighting.

6. From the Renderable Camera menu choose outdoorCam. Right-click next to the menu and choose Create Layer Override (in some cases Maya may create the override for you if you already have an override for the same setting on another layer).

7. Switch between the studioLighting layer and the outDoorLighting layer, and make sure the correct camera is selected for each layer.

8. Save the scene as **carComposite_v04.ma**. To see a version of the scene to this point, open the carComposite_v04.ma scene from the chapter12\scenes directory on the DVD.

After creating the overrides for the cameras, it is still possible to render with either camera in the render view. The overrides ensure the correct camera is used for each layer during a batch render.

FIGURE 12.8
Create a layer over-
ride for the render-
ing camera on the
studioLighting
layer.

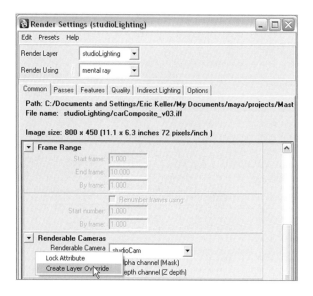

Using Different Shaders on Render Layers

The flexibility of render layers becomes even more apparent when you apply different shaders
to the same object on different layers. This allows you to render alternate versions of the same
animation.

1. Continue with the scene from the previous section or open the carComposite_v04.ma
   scene from the chapter12\scenes directory on the DVD.

2. In the Render Layer Editor, select the outDoorLighting layer. Open the Hypershade.

3. In the Outliner, expand the Vehicle group and select the carBody subgroup (Figure 12.9).

4. In the Hypershade, find the stripedCarBody shader (its icon is the same as for the
   mib_glossy_reflection shader). Right-click on the shader and choose Assign Material
   To Selected Objects.

FIGURE 12.9
Apply the striped-
CarBody shader to
the carBody group.

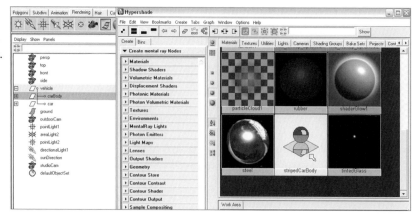

This shader uses a projected texture map to color the surfaces in the carBody group. The projection node is already placed in the carBody group.

   5. With the outDoorLighting render layer selected, create a test render in the Render View window. Make sure the outdoorCam camera is selected as the rendering camera (Figure 12.10).

FIGURE 12.10
The outDoorLighting layer uses a different shader to color the body of the car.

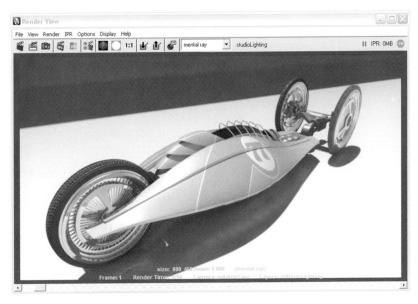

The car renders with a different material applied to the body. If you render the studioLighting layer (using the studioCam camera), you'll see the car is still blue. The new shader appears only when the outDoorLighting layer is rendered.

You don't need to create overrides to apply different materials on different render layers; however, you can create overrides for the attributes of render nodes used on different layers (for instance, one shader could have different transparency values on different render layers).

Shaders applied to the components of a surface, such as selected polygon faces, can differ from one render layer to the next.

   6. Save the scene as **carComposite_v05.ma**. To see a finished version of the scene, open the carComposite_v05.ma scene from the chapter12\scenes directory on the DVD.

Material Overrides

A material override applies a material to all of the objects within a particular layer. To create a material override, right-click on one of the layers in the Render Layer Editor and choose Overrides ➢ Create New Material Override. You can then select a material from the list. A material override is a good way to apply a specialized ambient occlusion shader—like one of the the shaders described in Chapter 10—to all the objects in a render layer.

Render Layer Blend Modes

Render layers can use blend modes, which combine the results of the render to form a composite. You can preview the composite in the Render View window. Typically you render each layer separately, import the render sequences into compositing software (such as Adobe After Effects or Autodesk Toxic), and then apply the blend modes using the controls in the compositing software. Maya gives you the option of creating a very simple composite using render layers, which you can view in the Render View window.

Blend modes use simple algorithms to combine the numeric color values of each pixel to create a composite. A composite is created by layering two or more images on top of each other. The image on top is blended with the image below. If both images are rendered as Normal, then the top image covers the bottom image completely. If the blend mode is set to Multiply, then the light pixels in the top image are transparent and the darker pixels of the top image darken the pixels in the bottom image. This technique is often used to add shadowing to a composite. If the blend mode of the top image is set to Screen, then the darker pixels are transparent and the lighter pixels brighten the pixels of the lower image. You can use this to composite glowing effects.

The blend modes available in Maya are Lighten, Darken, Multiply, Screen, and Overlay:

Lighten   This mode compares the layered images and uses the lightest pixel value of the two layers to determine the resulting color. For example, the lower image has a pixel in a particular spot with an RGB value of 0, 125, 255, and the pixel at the same location in the top image has an RGB value of 0, 115, 235. The resulting RGB value for that pixel will be 0, 125, 255.

Darken   This is the opposite of Lighten, and the darker value is used. In the example cited previously, the resulting RGB value for the pixel would be 0, 115, 235.

Multiply   The pixel values of the top image are multiplied by the pixel values of the bottom image and then divided by 255 to keep the values within the range of 0 to 255. The lighter pixels in the top image are semitransparent, and the darker values of the top image result in a darkening of the lower image.

Screen   A slightly more complex algorithm is used for this mode. The formula is 255-[(255-top color RGB pixel value)*(255-bottom color RGB pixel value)/255]= blended RGB pixel value. This has the effect of making darker pixels in the top image semitransparent and lighter, resulting in a lightening of the lower image.

Overlay   This combines Multiply and Screen modes so the lighter pixels of the top image brighten the bottom image and the darker pixels of the top image darken the bottom image.

In this exercise, you'll use blending modes to create soft shadows for the render of the car in the studio lighting scenario.

1. Open the carComposite_v06.ma scene from the chapter12\scenes directory on the DVD.

This scene shows the car in the studio lighting scenario. A single render layer exists already. Using the technique in this exercise, you'll eliminate the harsh cast shadows that appear on the ground in the rendered image (see Figure 12.2) and replace them with soft shadows created using ambient occlusion. First you'll remove the shadows cast on the ground by the physical lights in the scene (note that physical lights always cast shadows; there is no option for turning shadows off when you use these lights).

2. Select the ground object in the Outliner. Open its Attribute Editor and switch to the groundShape tab. Expand the Render Stats section in the Attribute Editor and deactivate Receive Shadows (see Figure 12.11). Note that, for some attributes, changing a setting on a render layer automatically creates a layer override.

FIGURE 12.11
Disable Receive Shadows for the ground surface.

3. In the Options menu of the Render Layer Editor, deactivate Render All Layers. Select the studioLighting layer, and create a test render in the Render View window using the renderCam camera (see Figure 12.12).

4. In the Outliner, Shift+click the vehicle group and the ground surface. In the Render Layer Editor, choose Layers ➢ Create Layer From Selected. Name the new layer **AOShadow**.

5. Open the Hypershade window. Make sure the AOShadow layer is selected in the Render Layer Editor. Create two new surface shaders in the Hypershade (from the Hypershade menu bar choose Create ➢ Materials ➢ Surface Shader).

6. Name one of the surface shaders **shadowShader** and the other **whiteMask**.

FIGURE 12.12
In this version of the render the ground does not receive cast shadows from the car.

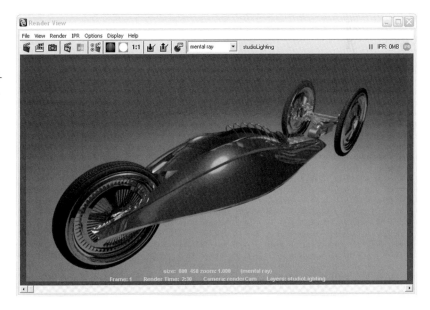

7. In the Outliner, select the vehicle group and apply the whiteMask shader to this group. Select the ground object and apply the shadowShader to this surface.

8. Open the Attribute Editor for the whiteMask node, and set Out Color to white.

9. Open the Attribute Editor for the shadowShader. Click the checkered box to the right of Out Color. Switch to the mental ray tab, and from the Textures section click Mib_amb_ occlusion (Figure 12.13).

10. Open the Attribute Editor for the Mib_amb_occlusion1 node and set Samples to **64**.

11. Make sure the AOShadow is selected in the Render Layer Editor; then create a test render using the renderCam camera.

The car appears as flat white, but you can see the soft shadows created on the ground by the ambient occlusion node (Figure 12.14).

FIGURE 12.13
Create an ambient occlusion texture and connect it to the shadow-Shader's Out Color channel.

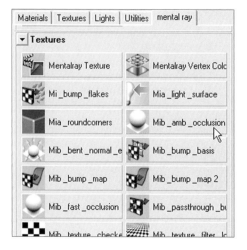

FIGURE 12.14
The soft shadows created by the ambient occlusion texture appear on the ground while the car is masked in flat white.

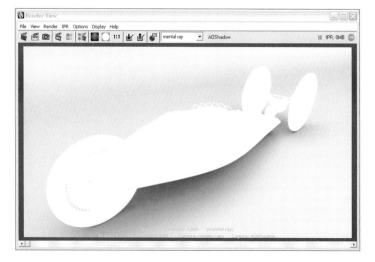

FIGURE 12.15
Set the blend mode
of the AOShadow
layer to Multiply.

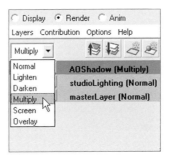

12. Now you are ready to preview the composite in the Render View window. In the Render Layer Editor, set the mode of the AOShadow layer to Multiply (see Figure 12.15).

Because the car in this render layer is flat white, when the pixels of the AOShadow layer are multiplied by the pixels of the studioLight layer, only the soft shadows appear in the composite.

13. In the Render Layer Editor, select Options ➤ Render All Layers ➤ Options. In the Options box, set Keep Image Mode to Composite Layers.

This setting renders both layers and then composites them in the Render View window. The Composite And Keep Layers setting create the composite, but it also keeps the rendered image of each individual layer available in the Render View window. The Keep Layers option will not composite the layers; instead it renders all renderable layers and keeps them as individual images in the Render View window.

14. After choosing the Composite Layers option, click Apply And Close. Double-check and make sure that Render All Layers is now checked in the Options menu of the Render Layer Editor (Figure 12.16).

FIGURE 12.16
Select the Render
All Layers option in
the Options menu.

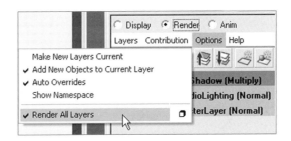

15. In the Render Layer Editor, click the blue sphere and cube icon next to masterLayer so that a red X appears. You don't need this layer to be included in the composite. Select the AOShadow layer.

16. Open the Render View window, and create a test render using the renderCam camera. You'll see the studioLighting layer render first, and then the AOShadow layer will render on top of it. Figure 12.17 shows the composited image.

17. Save the scene as **carComposite_v07.ma**. To see a finished version of the scene, open the carComposite_v07.ma scene from the chapter12\scenes directory on the DVD.

FIGURE 12.17
The two images are composited in the Render View window.

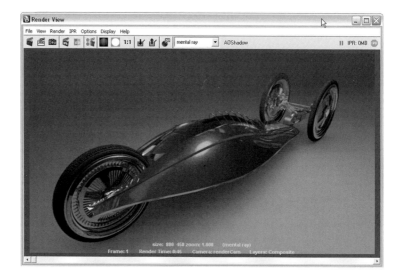

This is a good way to preview basic composites; however, in practice you will most likely want more control over how the layers are composited. To do this you should use more advanced compositing software such as Adobe Photoshop (for still images) or Adobe After Effects or Autodesk Toxic (for animations). Autodesk is working toward automating the Maya to Toxic workflow so render layers can be imported into Toxic while maintaining their respective blend mode settings.

 Real World Scenario

COMPOSITE HARDWARE PARTICLES USING RENDER LAYERS

If you have a scene that involves a large number of nParticles, you may want to use hardware rendering to reduce the render time. If the scene also contains geometry that you want to render with Maya Software or mental ray, you can use render layers to composite the hardware-rendered nParticles with the software-rendered geometry in Maya.

1. In your scene, create a new render layer and add the geometry to this new layer. Name the layer **geometryRL**.

2. Create a second render layer above the geometry layer; then add the nParticles and the geometry to this layer. Name the layer **nParticleRL**.

3. Open the Render Settings window for geometryRL, and set Render Using to mental ray.

4. Open the Render Settings window for nParticlesRL. Right-click on Render Using and choose Create Layer Override. Set the Render Using menu to Maya Hardware.

5. In the Maya Hardware tab of the Render Settings window, turn on Enable Geometry Mask.

6. In the Render Layer Editor, make sure both the nParticlesRL and geometryRL layers are set to Renderable. In the Options menu, turn on Render All Layers. Set the mode of the nParticlesRL layer to Screen.

7. Create a test render of a frame in which nParticles and the geometry are visible.

Render Passes

Render passes divide the output created by a render layer into separate images or image sequences. Using Render Passes you can separate the reflections, shadows, diffuse color, ambient occlusion, specular highlights, and so on into images or image sequences, which can then be reassembled in compositing software. By separating things like the reflections from the diffuse color, you can then exert maximum creative control over how the different images work together in the composite. This also allows you to easily make changes or variations or fix problems in individual elements rather than re-rendering the entire image or sequence every time you make a change.

Render Passes replaces the technique of using multiple render layers to separate things like reflections and shadows in older versions of Maya. (Render Passes also replaces the layer presets; more on this in a moment.) In Maya 2009, each layer can be split into any number of render passes. When render passes are created, each layer is rendered once, and the passes are taken from data stored in the Frame Buffer. This means each layer needs to render only once to create all the necessary passes. Render time for each layer increases as you add more passes.

THE FRAME BUFFER

When Maya renders an image it collects data from the scene and stores it in a temporary image known as the Frame Buffer. When rendering is complete, the data from the Frame Buffer is written to disk as the rendered image. The images created by Render Passes are extracted from the render, which is why the layer needs to render only once to create a number of render passes.

A typical workflow using passes is to separate the scene into one or more render layers, as demonstrated in the first part of this chapter, and then assign any number of render passes to each render layer. When you create a batch render, the passes are stored in subfolders in the Images directory of the current project. You can then import the images created by Render Passes into compositing software and assemble them into layers to create the final composite.

Render passes work only with mental ray; they are not available for any other renderer. To create render passes for Maya Software, the best approach is to use separate render layers.

It's also crucial to understand that at this point not all materials will work with render passes. If you find that objects in your scene are not rendering correctly, double-check that you are using a material compliant with render passes.

The materials that work with Render Passes are Anisotropic, Blinn, Lambert, Phong, Phong E, Environment Fog, Fluid Shape, Light Fog, Particle Cloud, Volume Fog, Volume Shader, Hair Tube Shader, Ocean Shader, Ramp Shader, Hair, Fur, Image Plane, Layered Shader, Shading Map, Surface Shader, Use Background, mi_metallic_paint_x_passes, mi_car_phen_x_passes, mia_material_x_passes, and misss_fast_shader_x_passes.

Note that the mental ray DGS, Dielectric, mib_glossy_reflection, and mib_glossy_refraction shaders, and the other mib shaders, are not yet supported by Render Passes. Even if you use a supported shader (such as mi_metallic_paint_x_passes) as a base material for these shaders, it will not render correctly. When using these shaders you may need to devise an alternate workflow involving render layers and material overrides.

Creating an Ambient Occlusion Pass

As an example you'll start by creating an ambient occlusion render pass for the space helmet scene. In previous versions of Maya you could create a render layer and use the Ambient
Occlusion preset. The preset would automatically shade all of the objects in the layer with a
custom ambient occlusion shader network. In Maya 2009 the mental ray renderer has a built-in
ambient occlusion pass, which creates ambient occlusion shadowing in a render pass without
the use of a shader network. This gives you another option for creating ambient occlusion
passes. Ambient occlusion passes are frequently used in compositing, so you'll start with this
type of pass.

1. Open the helmetComposite_v01.ma scene from the chapter12\scenes directory on
   the DVD.

This scene shows the space helmet constructed in Chapter 3. All of the shaders applied
to the helmet are variations of the MIA Materials shader. The lighting in the scene is created
using a point light with a Physical Light shader applied. The fill lighting is created using Final
Gathering and an HDRI probe image (see Figure 12.18).

The scene has a single render layer named helmet. This layer is a duplicate of the master-
Layer. You can create render passes for the masterLayer, but for the sake of simulating a production workflow, you'll use a render layer in this demonstration.

FIGURE 12.18
The helmet scene
has been lit and
shaded and is
ready to render
using Render
Passes.

The mia_material_x shader is not compliant with Render Passes. To make the material compliant, it must be upgraded to an mia_material_x_passes shader. This process is necessary only when using the mental ray shaders.

2. Open the Hypershade window and select the chromeShader. Open its Attribute Editor to the chromeShader tab.

3. Scroll to the bottom of the Attribute Editor. Expand the Upgrade Shader rollout. Click the button labeled Upgrade Shader To mia_material_x_passes (see Figure 12.19).

4. Repeat step 3 for the metalShader, plasticShader, rubberShader, thickGlass, and thinGlass shaders.

FIGURE 12.19

Upgrade the chrome-Shader to the mia_material_x_passes shader.

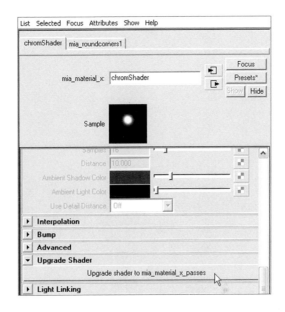

The attributes of the shader won't change save for the addition of the Frame Buffer Contribution attribute. This can usually be left at the default settings.

At this point you're ready to add the ambient occlusion pass.

5. Open the Render Settings window and choose the Passes tab. At the top of the Render Settings window, make sure Render Layer is set to Helmet.

The upper portion of the Render Passes area is the Scene Passes section. This holds all the passes available for the scene. This section is blank until you add a pass.

6. Click the top icon to the right of the Scene Passes section to open the Create Render Passes window. From Pass List, select Ambient Occlusion (Figure 12.20).

7. Click Create And Close to add the pass to the Scene Passes section.

8. You'll now see the Ambient Occlusion pass listed in the Scene Passes section as AO. Select the AO pass and open the Attribute Editor (if the pass settings don't appear in the Attribute Editor, double-click AO in the Passes tab of the Render Settings window).

FIGURE 12.20
Select the Ambient
Occlusion preset
from the list of
available Render
Passes presets.

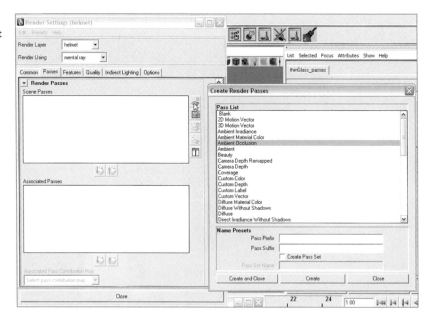

The settings for the pass are listed in the Attribute Editor. These include the number of channels used for the pass and the bit depth. The available settings may differ depending on the selected pass preset.

When Channels is set to 3, the pass will contain the red, green, and blue channels (RGB). When Channels is set to 4, an Alpha channel is also included (see Figure 12.21) along with the red, green, and blue channels.

FIGURE 12.21
The settings for the
render pass are dis-
played in the Attri-
bute Editor when
the pass is selected
in the Passes tab
of the Render Set-
tings window.

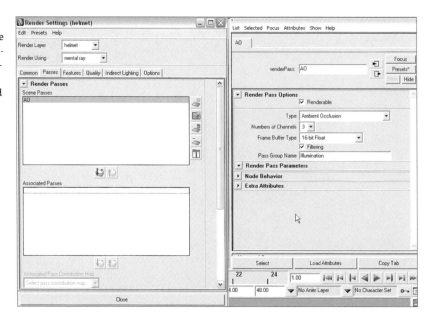

The pass is now available for the scene, but it needs to be associated with the current render layer.

9. Select AO in the Scene Passes section. Click the icon with the downward-pointing arrow between the Scene Passes and Associated Passes sections to associate the pass with the current render layer.

Once the pass is associated with the current layer, it is included in the Frame Buffer when the scene renders and saved as a separate image after rendering is complete. The Scene Passes and Associated Passes interface is a little confusing at first; just remember that only the passes listed in the Associated Passes section will be rendered for the current render layer. If you switch to another render layer, you'll see all the passes listed in the Scene Passes section. To disassociate a pass from a render layer, select the pass in the Associated Passes section and click the up-arrow icon between the two sections. This moves the pass back to the Scene Passes section. To delete a pass from either section, select the pass and press the Backspace key.

The Ambient Occlusion pass will not calculate correctly until you enable Ambient Occlusion in the Features section of the Render Settings window.

10. Click the Features tab of the Render Settings window. Under Secondary Effects, select the Ambient Occlusion option.

This activates mental ray's built-in ambient occlusion. This is calculated without the need to create a shader network with an mib_amb_occlusion node.

11. To set the quality of the ambient occlusion, click the Indirect Lighting tab in the Render Settings window. Expand Ambient Occlusion at the bottom. Make sure the Ambient Occlusion option is activated, and use the Rays field to specify how many rays will be used to calculate the effect. Set Rays to **256** (see Figure 12.22).

FIGURE 12.22
For the Ambient Occlusion pass to calculate, you must activate Ambient Occlusion in the Features tab. Quality is determined by the settings in the Indirect Lighting tab.

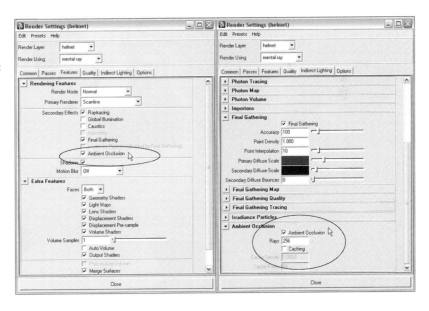

12. Open the Render View window and create a render using the renderCam camera. The render will not look any different from Figure 12.18.

The render will take three or four minutes to calculate depending on the speed of your hardware and available RAM. When it's finished, you'll most likely be wondering where the Ambient Occlusion pass is. The pass is stored in a temporary folder in the project's Images directory. If the scene uses layers, each layer has its own subfolder where the passes are stored.

13. To see the Ambient Occlusion pass, use the File menu in the Render View window. Choose File ➢ Load Render Pass ➢ AO. The image opens in a separate image view window (see Figure 12.23).

14. Save the scene as **helmetComposite_v02.ma**. To see a finished version of the scene, open the helmetComposite_v02.ma scene from the chapter12\scenes directory on the DVD.

AMBIENT OCCLUSION OPTIONS

The Ambient Occlusion pass technique described in this section is not the only way to render ambient occlusion. If you prefer to have more direct control over how ambient occlusion is rendered, you can create a separate render layer and apply the mib_amb_occlusion texture to the objects in the layer and render without passes. This technique is described in Chapter 10.

FIGURE 12.23
You can load the Ambient Occlusion pass from the File menu in the Render View window.

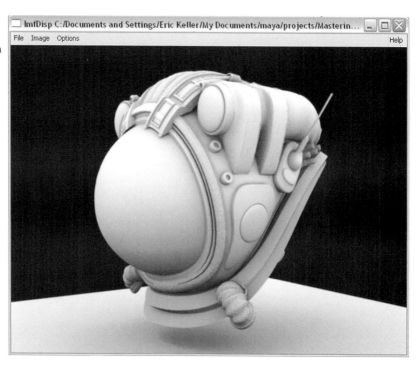

Creating Reflection, Specular, Depth, and Shadow Passes

The previous example demonstrated how to create a single render pass. In this example, you'll create multiple passes for reflection, specular, depth, and shadow.

Depth passes are particularly helpful in compositing. They can be used to add, among other things, camera depth of field in the composite. For example, using Adobe After Effects's Lens Blur filter, you can apply a depth pass to control the focal region of the render based on the luminance of the depth pass. There are also plug-ins available for After Effects, such as Lens Care by Frischluft, which create realistic lens effects far superior to the standard After Effects blurs. Using a depth pass for depth of field in After Effects dramatically reduces Maya render times, because mental ray's depth of field can take a long time to calculate. Furthermore any changes you make to the depth of field, such as the focal region, are done in After Effects and do not require re-rendering the entire scene. The same is true for motion blur. You can create a 2D or 3D motion vector pass and then use a plug-in such as Reel Smart Motion Blur to add motion blur in the composite rather than in the initial render. This is a huge time-saver.

1. Continue with the scene from the previous section or open the helmetComposite_v02.ma scene from the chapter12\scenes directory on the DVD.

2. Open the Render Settings window and choose the Passes tab. Select AO in the Associated Passes section, and click the up-arrow icon to move this pass back to the Scene Passes section. This means the AO pass will not be rendered with the layer.

3. Click the Create Render Passes icon to the right of the Scenes Passes section. From the Pass List select Camera Depth, and click the Create button to add this pass to the Scene Passes section.

4. Add reflection, shadow, and specular passes as well. You can find complete descriptions of each Render Pass preset in the Maya documentation.

5. Close the Create Render Pass window. In the Passes tab of the Render Settings window, select the depth, reflection, shadow, and specular passes, and use the down arrow to move them to the Associated Passes section.

6. Double-click the depth pass in the Associated Passes list, and open the Attribute Editor. Turn on Remap Depth Values, and set the Far Clipping plane to **20**.

The scene size for this scene is 20 units in Z; by setting the Far Clipping Plane to 20, any parts of a surface beyond 20 units are clipped to a luminance value of 1 (meaning they are white).

7. Double-click Reflection to open its settings in the Attribute Editor. Raise Maximum Reflection Level to **10**.

8. Create another test render from the Render View window using the renderCam camera. You can use the File ➢ Load Render Pass menu in the Render View window to see each of the render passes (Figure 12.24).

9. Save the scene as **helmetComposite_v03.ma**. To see a finished version of the scene, open the helmetComposite_v03.ma scene from the chapter12\scenes directory on the DVD.

You can add render passes to a render layer in the Render Layer Editor. To do this, right-click on the layer and choose Add New Render Pass. You can choose the type of pass from the pop-up list (Figure 12.25). The pass then automatically appears in the Associated Passes section in the Passes tab of the Render Settings window.

FIGURE 12.24
Clockwise from the upper left are the reflection, depth, specular, and shadow passes for the helmet scene. The elements of the passes appear dark because they have been separated and rendered against black.

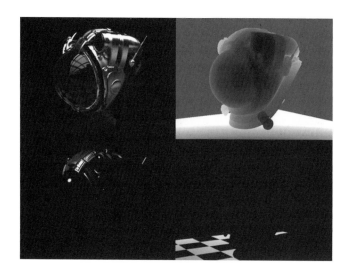

FIGURE 12.25
You can add render passes to a render layer by right-clicking on the layer in the Render Layer Editor.

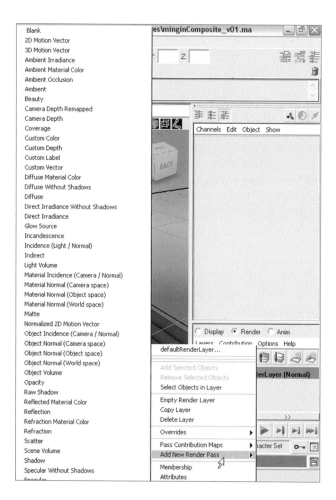

Render Pass Contribution Maps

Render Pass Contribution Maps can be used to further customize the render passes for each layer. A contribution map specifies which objects and lights are included in a render pass. By default when you create a render pass and associate it with a particular render layer, all the objects on the layer are included in the pass. Using a contribution map you can add only certain lights and objects to the render pass. The whole point is to give you even more flexibility when rendering for compositing. This exercise demonstrates how to set up contribution maps.

1. Open the minigunComposite_v01.ma scene from the chapter12\scenes directory on the DVD.

2. This scene contains a model of a minigun, a simple backdrop, and some directional lights.

The scene also uses an HDRI image to create reflections on the metal of the gun. The shader applied to the gun is a standard Maya anisotropic shader. An ambient occlusion texture is connected to the Reflectivity of the material, and the texture is set to Reflective Occlusion mode.
A single render layer named miniGun contains all of the lights and surfaces in the scene.

3. In the Outliner, expand the turret object. Select the right_mount1 subgroup. In the Render Layer Editor, right-click on the miniGun layer and choose Pass Contribution Maps ➤ Create Pass Contribution Maps and Add Selected Objects (see Figure 12.26).

4. A small arrow is added to the miniGun render layer label. Click this label to expand the layer. You'll see the contribution map listed as passContributionMap1. Double-click on this and change the name to **rightGun** (see Figure 12.27).

FIGURE 12.26
Create a render pass contribution map from the selected objects in the Outliner.

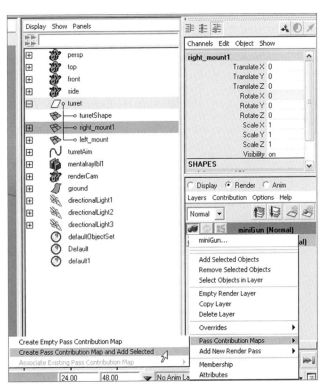

FIGURE 12.27
Rename the new
map rightGun.

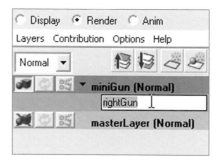

5. Repeat steps 3 and 4 for the left_mount group. Name the new contribution map **leftGun**.

6. Select the miniGun render layer, open the Render Settings window, and switch to the Passes tab. Click the Create New Render Pass icon to the right of the Scene Passes section, and add Reflection and Specular pass presets.

7. Select both the Reflection and Specular passes in the Scene Passes section. Click the down arrow to move them to the Associated Passes section.

8. Below the Associated Passes section you'll see the Associated Pass Contribution Map section. Set the Associated Passes Contribution Map drop-down menu to rightGun.

9. Select the Reflection pass in the Associated Passes section, and click the down arrow below this section to move the Reflection pass preset to the Passes Used By Contribution Map section.

This means that only the objects in the rightGun contribution map (the right_mount1 group) appear in the Reflection pass created for the miniGun layer.

10. Repeat steps 8 and 9, but this time set the Associated Pass Contribution Map drop-down menu to leftGun, and move the Specular preset down to the Passes Used By Contribution Map section (Figure 12.28).

11. Open the Render View window, and create a render using the renderCam camera. Once again the render looks the same as if you had not added any render passes.

12. When the image has finished rendering, use the File menu in the Render View window to load the Specular and Reflection passes.

Notice that in these passes only one part of the gun appears. In the Specular pass, the left_mount1 group appears; in the Reflection pass, the right_mount1 group appears (Figure 12.29). The rest of the gun and the backdrop are absent from each pass. Although this is not a practical application of contribution maps, it demonstrates clearly that the point of a contribution map is to specify exactly which objects appear in a render pass.

13. Save the scene as **minigunComposite_v02.ma**. To see a version of the scene to this point, open the minigunComposite_v02.ma scene from the chapter12\scenes directory on the DVD.

FIGURE 12.28
Associate the
Specular pass with
the leftGun contri-
bution map.

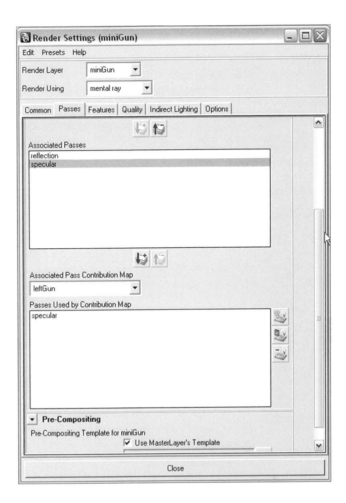

FIGURE 12.29
After you render
the image, the
Reflection and
Specular passes
show only the
objects added to
the contribution
map for each pass.

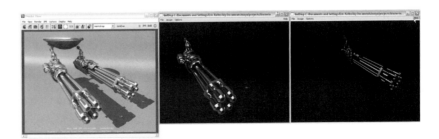

Lights and Contribution Maps

Lights can also be included in contribution maps. If no lights are specified, all of the scene lights are added. In the minigun scene the directional light is the only light that casts shadows; the other two lights have shadow casting turned off. You can use pass contribution maps to create a shadow pass just for this light.

1. Continue with the scene from the previous section or open the minigunComposite_v02.ma scene from the chapter 12/scenes directory on the DVD.

2. In the Outliner, Shift+click ground and directionalLight1. In the Render Layer Editor, right-click on the miniGun render layer, and choose Pass Contribution Maps ➢ Create Pass Contribution Map and Add Selected.

3. Double-click passContributionMap1 and rename it **groundShadow**.

4. Open the Render Settings window and switch to the Passes tab. Select Reflection and Specular in the Associated Passes section, and use the up arrow to move them to the Scene Passes section. Doing this prevents the passes from being included in the render.

5. Click the Create New Render Pass button, and add a Raw Shadow pass to the Scene Passes section.

6. Move shadowRaw from the Scene Passes section to the Associated Passes section (make sure miniGun is the currently selected render layer when you do this).

7. Set Associated Pass Contribution Map to groundShadow. Use the down-arrow button to move shadowRaw into the Passes Used By Contribution Map section.

8. Double-click the shadowRaw pass to open its Attribute Editor. In the Attribute Editor, disable Hold-Out (see Figure 12.30).

FIGURE 12.30
Associate the shadowRaw preset with the groundShadow contribution map. In the settings for shadowRaw, disable the Hold-Out option.

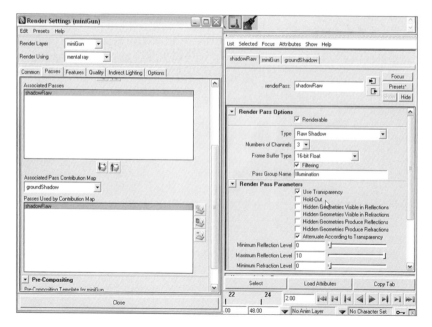

The Hold-Out setting creates a geometry mask for geometry that is not included in the render pass. By disabling this, you'll see only the ground surface and the cast shadow in the render.

9. Open the Render View window, and create a test render from the renderCam camera (see Figure 12.31).

In the composite, the shadow pass should be inverted and color corrected. When creating a shadow pass contribution map, you may want to include just the shadow-casting lights. In some cases including all of the lights can produce strange results.

10. Save the scene as **miniGun_v03.ma**. To see a finished version of the scene, open the miniGun_v03.ma scene from the chapter12\scenes directory on the DVD.

FIGURE 12.31
The ground-Shadow contribution map shows only the directionalLight, the ground, and the shadow cast by the gun geometry.

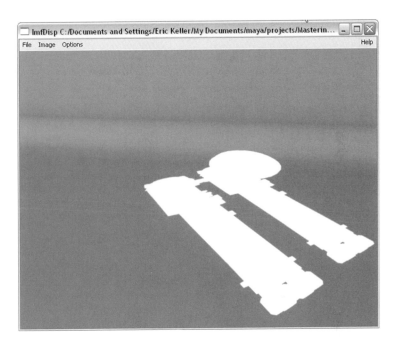

MENTAL RAY SHADERS AND CONTRIBUTION MAPS

mental ray shaders such as the mia_material_x_passes will always use all of the lights assigned to the render layer regardless of which lights have been added to the contribution map.

Render Pass Sets

Render pass sets are simply a way to organize large lists of render passes in the Passes tab of the Render Settings window. You can create different groupings of the passes listed in the Scene Passes section, give them descriptive names, and then associate the set with the render layer or the associated contribution maps. If you have a complex scene that has a large number of passes, you'll find it's easier to work with the pass sets rather than all of the individual passes.

You can create a render pass set as you create the render passes or add them to the set later. In the Create Render Passes window, check the box that says Create Pass Set, and give the pass set a descriptive name (Figure 12.32). The new pass set appears in the Scene Passes section in the Render Settings window along with all of the newly created passes (Figure 12.33). To associate a render layer with the new pass set, you only have to move the pass set to the Associated Passes section. All of the passes included with the set will be associated with the layer even though they do not appear in the Associated Passes section.

FIGURE 12.32
You can create a pass set in the Create Render Passes window using the options at the bottom.

FIGURE 12.33
Associating the set with the current render layer associates all of its contained passes with the layer. You can use the Relationship Editor to add and remove passes from the set.

To verify which passes are included in the set, open the Relationship Editor for Render Passes (Window ➤ Relationship Editor ➤ Passes). When you highlight the pass set on the left, the passes in the set are highlighted on the right. You can add or remove passes from the set by selecting them from the list on the right of the Relationship Editor (Figure 12.33).

You can add a new set in the Passes tab of the Render Settings window by clicking the Create New Render Pass Set icon. You can then use the Relationship Editor to add the passes to the set. A render pass can be a member of more than one set.

PRECOMPOSITING FOR TOXIC

You can use the Precompositing template when exporting renders and cameras from Maya to Autodesk Toxic. More options are available in the Render menu in the Maya menu toolbar (you must select the Rendering menu set).

Batch Rendering

Batch rendering is the process of translating a Maya animation into a sequence of images. The images are processed and saved to disk. The rendered image sequences can then be brought into compositing software, where they can be layered together, edited, color corrected, combined with live footage, and have additional effects applied. The composite can then be converted to a movie file or a sequence of images for distribution or imported to editing software for further processing.

Generally you want to render a sequence of images from Maya. You can render directly to a movie file, but this usually not a good idea. If the render stops while rendering directly to a movie file, it may corrupt the movie, and you will need to restart the whole render. When you render a sequence of images and the render stops, you can easily restart the render without re-creating any of the images that have already been saved to disk.

When you set up a batch render, you can specify how the image sequence will be labeled and numbered. You also set the image format of the final render, which render layers and passes will be included and where they will be stored, and other aspects related to the rendered sequences. You can use Maya's Render Settings window to determine these properties or perform a command-line render using your operating system's terminal. In this section you'll learn important features of both methods.

Batch rendering is also accomplished using render farm software, which distributes the render across multiple computers. This subject is beyond the scope of this book.

File Tokens

File tokens are a way to automate the organization of your renders. If your scene has a lot of layers, cameras, and passes, you can use tokens to specify where all the image sequences will be placed on your computer's hard drive, as well as how they are named.

The image sequences created with a batch render are placed in the Images folder of the current project or whichever folder is specified in the Project Settings window (see Chapter 1 for information regarding project settings). Tokens are placed in the File Name Prefix field found in the Common tab of the Render Settings window. If this field is left blank, the scene name is used to label the rendered images (Figure 12.34).

Render Settings
Edit Presets Help
Render Layer masterLayer
Render Using mental ray
Common Passes Features Quality Indirect Lighting Options
Path: C:/Documents and Settings/Eric Keller/My Documents/maya/projects/
File name: untitled.iff
Image size: 640 x 480 (8.9 x 6.7 inches 72 pixels/inch)
File Output
File name prefix: (not set; using scene name)
Image format: Maya IFF (iff)
Compression...
Frame/Animation ext: name.ext (Single Frame)
Frame padding: 1
Frame Buffer Naming: Automatic

FIGURE 12.34 The File Name Prefix field in the Common tab of the Render Settings window is where you specify the image name and tokens.

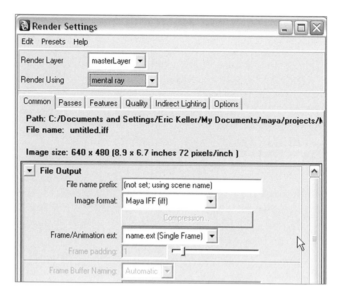

By default if the scene has more than one render layer, Maya creates a subfolder for each layer. If the scene has more than one camera, a subfolder is created for each camera. For scenes with multiple render layers and multiple cameras, Maya creates a subfolder for each camera within the subfolder for each layer.

You can specify any directory you want by typing the folder names into the File Name Prefix field. For example if you want your image sequences to be named `marshmallow` and placed in a folder named `chocolateSauce`, you can type **`chocolateSauce/marshmallow`** into the File Name Prefix field. However, explicitly naming a file sequence lacks the flexibility of using tokens and runs the risk of allowing you to overwrite file sequences by mistake when rendering. You can see a preview of how the images will be named in the upper portion of the Render Settings window (Figure 12.35).

The whole point of tokens is to allow you to change the default behavior and specify how subfolders will be created dynamically for a scene. To use a token to specify a directory, place a slash after the token name. For example, to create a subfolder named after each camera, type **<camera>/** into the File Name Prefix field. To use a token to name the images, omit the slash. For example **<scene>/<camera>** results in a folder named after the scene containing a sequence of images named `camera.iff`.

Common Passes Features Quality Indirect Lighting Options
Path: C:/Documents and Settings/Eric Keller/My Documents/maya/projects/
File name: chocolateSauce/marshmallow.iff
Image size: 640 x 480 (8.9 x 6.7 inches 72 pixels/inch)
File Output
File name prefix: chocolateSauce/marshmallow
Image format: Maya IFF (iff)

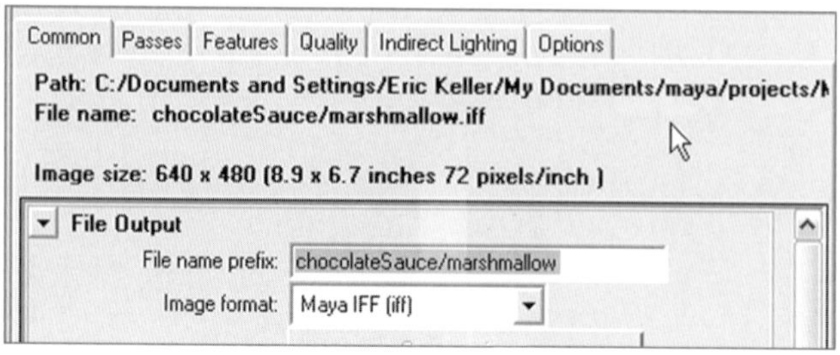

FIGURE 12.35 A preview of the image name appears at the top of the Common tab of the Render Settings window.

Here are some of the more common tokens:

<Scene>   This token names the images or subfolder after the scene name.

<Camera>   This token names the images or subfolders after the camera. For example, in a scene with two cameras named renderCam1 and renderCam2, <Scene>/<Camera>/<Camera> creates a single folder named after the scene, within which are two subfolders named render-Cam1 and renderCam2. In each of these folders is a sequence named renderCam1.ext and renderCam2.ext.

<RenderLayer>   This token creates a subfolder or sequence named after each render layer. If there are passes associated with the layer, then the pass names are appended to the layer name. For example if you have a layer named spurtsOfBlood and an associated specular pass, the folder or image sequence would automatically be named spurtsOfBlood_specular.

<RenderPass>   This token creates a subfolder or sequence named after the render pass. Since render passes are available only for mental ray renders, this token applies only when using mental ray.

<RenderPassType>   This token similar to <RenderPass> except it abbreviates the name of the render pass. A reflection pass, for example, would be abbreviated as REFL.

<RenderPassFileGroup>   This adds the name of the render pass file group. The file group name is set in the Attribute Editor of the render pass node (see Figure 12.36). Render pass file groups are assigned by mental ray, but you can create your own name for the group by typing it in the Pass Group Name field of the render pass node.

FIGURE 12.36
You can set the render pass group name in the Attribute Editor of the render pass node.

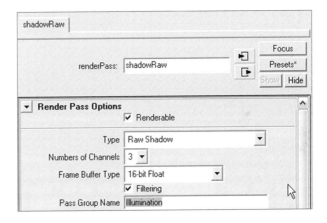

<Extension>   This adds the file format extension. It is usually added to the end of the filename automatically, but you can also use this token to label a directory based on the image format.

<Version>   This adds a custom label specified by the Version Label field in the Render Settings window (Figure 12.37).

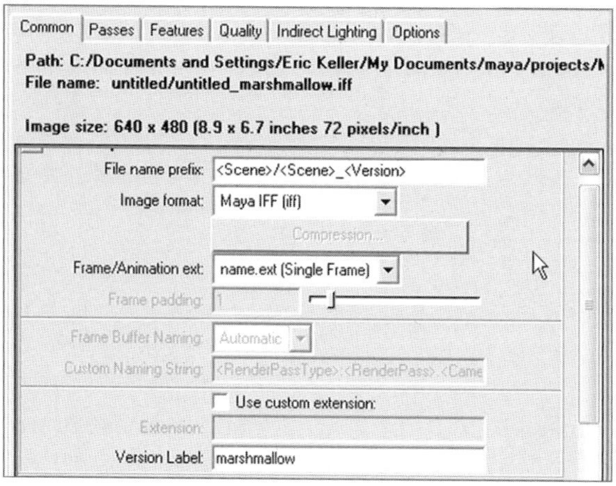

FIGURE 12.37
The <Version>
token adds the
label specified in
the Version Label
field in the Render
Settings window.

Note that the capitalization of the token name does matter. If you had a scene named choco-lateSauce that has a render layer named banana that uses a specular and diffuse pass with two cameras named shot1 and shot2, and you want to add the version label v05, the following tokens specified in the File Name Prefix field

```
<Scene>/<RenderLayer>/<Camera>/<RenderPass>/<RenderPass>_<Version>
```

will create a file structure that looks like this:

```
chocolateSauce/banana/shot1/specular/specular_v05.#.ext
chocolateSauce/banana/shot1/diffuse/diffuse_v05.#.ext
chocolateSauce/banana/shot2/specular/specular_v05.#.ext
chocolateSauce/banana/shot2/diffuse/diffuse_v05.#.ext
```

Use underscores or hyphens when combining tokens in the directory or image name. Avoid using periods.

TOKENS FOR OPENEXR FILES

The OpenEXR format can create multiple additional channels within a single image. Each channel can contain an image created from a render pass. If a scene has one or more render passes and you choose the OpenEXR image format, you can use the Frame Buffer Naming field to specify the name of each pass. This feature is available only when OpenEXR is chosen as the file format and the scene has one or more render passes. You can use the automatic naming setting or enable the Custom option in the Frame Buffer Naming drop-down menu. You can then use the Custom Naming String field to choose the token you want to use.

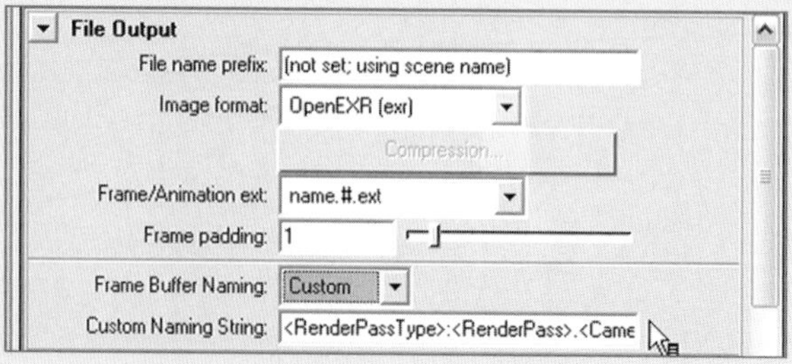

Specifying Frame Range

For multiframe animations, you have a number of options for specifying the frame range and the syntax for the filenames in the sequence. These settings are found in the Common tab of the Render Settings window. To enable multiframe rendering, choose one of the presets from the Frame/Animation Ext menu. When rendering animation sequences the safest choice is usually the name.#.ext option. This names the images in the sequence by placing a dot between the image name and the image number and another dot between the image number and the file extension. The Frame Padding option allows you to specify a number of zeros between the image number and the extension. So a sequence named marshmallow using the Maya IFF format with a Frame Padding of 4 would look like `marshmallow.0001.iff`.

The Frame Range settings specify which frames in the animation will be rendered. The By Frame setting allows you to render each frame (using a setting of 1), skip frames (using a setting higher than 1), or render twice as many frames (using a setting of 0.5, which renders essentially at half speed).

It is possible to render backwards by specifying a higher frame number for the Start Frame value than the End Frame value and using a negative umber for By Frame. You would then want to use the Renumber Frames option so the frame numbers move upward incrementally.

The Renumber Frames option allows you to customize the labeling of the image sequence numbers.

Renderable Cameras

The rendering cameras are specified in the Renderable Camera list. To add a camera, expand the Renderable Camera menu and choose Add Renderable Camera. To remove a rendering camera, click the trash can icon next to the renderable camera. As noted earlier in the chapter, you can use a layer override to include a specific camera with a render layer.

Each camera has the option of rendering alpha and Z depth channels. The Z depth channel stores information about the depth in the scene. This is included as an extra channel in the image (only a few formats such as Maya IFF support this extra channel). Not all compositing software supports Maya's Z depth channel. You may find it easier to create a camera depth pass using the custom passes (passes are described earlier in this chapter). The render depth pass can be imported into your compositing software and used with a filter to create depth of field effects.

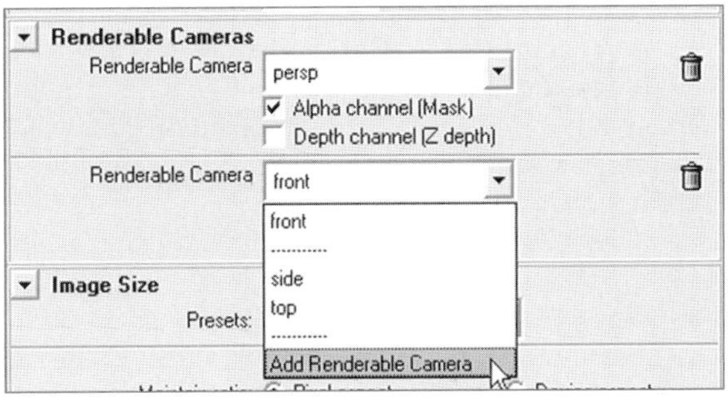

FIGURE 12.38

You can add and remove renderable cameras using the Renderable Camera menu.

File Formats and the Frame Buffer

When Maya renders a scene, the data stored in the Frame Buffer is converted into the native IFF format and then translated to the file type specified in the Image Format menu. So if you specify the SGI format, for example, Maya translates the SGI image from the native IFF format.

Most popular compositing packages (such as Adobe After Effects and Autodesk Toxic) support the IFF format, so it's usually safe to render to this file format. The IFF format uses four 8-bit channels by default, which is usually adequate for most viewing purposes. If you need to change the file to a different bit depth or a different number of channels, you can choose one of the options from the Data Type menu in the Framebuffer section in the Quality tab. This is where you will also find the output options, such as Premultiply (see Figure 12.39).

Render passes uses the secondary Frame Buffer to store the image data. You can specify the bit depth of this secondary buffer in the Attribute Editor for each render pass.

A complete list of supported image formats is available in the Maya documentation. Note that Maya Software and mental ray may support different file formats.

FIGURE 12.39
Specify bit depth and other output options using the Framebuffer settings in the Quality tab of the Render Settings window.

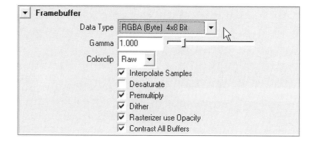

IMAGE SIZE SETTINGS

The Image Size settings are discussed in Chapter 2.

Starting a Batch Render

When you are satisfied that your animation is ready to render, and all the settings have been specified in the Render Settings window, you're ready to start a batch render. To start a batch render, set the main Maya menu set to Rendering and choose Render ➤ Batch Render ➤ Options. In the options, you can specify memory limits and multithreading, as well as local and network rendering.

One of the most useful options is the Verbosity Level. This refers to the level of detail of the messages displayed in the Maya Output window as the render takes place. On the Mac, progress messages should be displayed in the Console Window (Window ➤ Console Window). You can use these messages to monitor the progress of the render as well as diagnose problems that may occur while rendering. The Progress Messages setting is the most useful option in most situations (Figure 12.40).

FIGURE 12.40
Detailed progress
messages for each
frame can be dis-
played in the Out-
put Window.

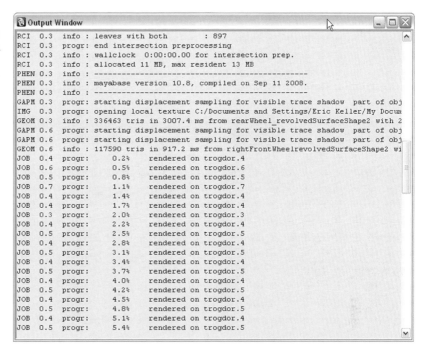

To start the render, click the Batch Render (or the Batch Render And Close) button. As the batch render takes place, you'll see the Script Editor update (Figure 12.41). For detailed information on the progress of each frame, you can monitor the progress in the Output Window.

To stop a batch render, choose Render ➢ Cancel Batch Render. To see how the current frame in the batch render looks, choose Render ➢ Show Batch Render.

When the render is complete, you'll see a message in the Script Editor that says Rendering Completed. You can then use F Check to view the sequence (File ➢ View Sequence) or import the sequence into your compositing software.

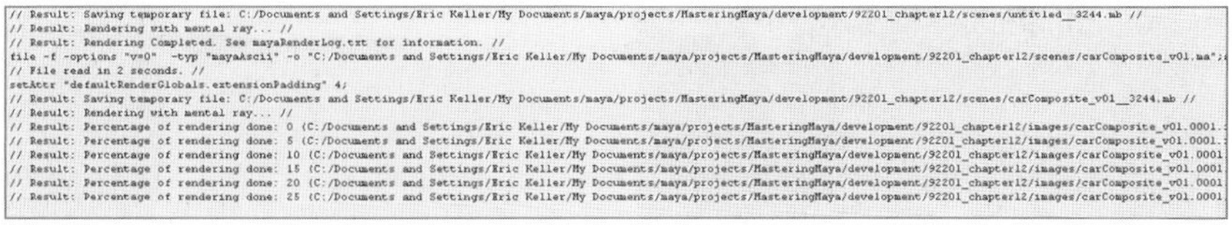

FIGURE 12.41
The Script Edi-
tor shows the
progress of the
batch render.

MONITORING A RENDER IN THE SCRIPT EDITOR

The Script Editor is not always completely reliable when it comes to monitoring the progress of a render. If the messages stop updating as the render progresses, it may or may not indicate that the render has stopped. Before assuming the render has stopped, use your computer's operating system to browse to the current image directory, and double-check to see if images are still being written to disk. This is especially true when using Maya on a Mac.

Command-Line Rendering

A batch render can be initiated using your operating system's command prompt or terminal window. This is known as a command-line render. A command-line render takes the form of a series of commands typed into the command prompt. These commands include information about the location of the Maya scene to be rendered, the location of the rendered image sequence, the rendering cameras, image size, frame range, and many other options similar to the settings found in the Render Settings window.

Command-line renders tend to be more stable than batch renders initiated from the Maya interface. This is because when the Maya application is closed, more of your computer's RAM is available for the render. You can start a command-line render regardless of whether Maya is running or not. In fact, to maximize system resources, it's best to close Maya when starting a command-line render. In this example you can keep Maya open.

In this exercise you'll see how you can start a batch render on both a PC and a Mac. You'll use the solarSystem_v01.ma scene, which is a very simple animation showing two planets orbiting a glowing sun.

1. From the DVD, copy the solarSystem_v01.ma scene to the scenes directory of your current project on your computer's hard drive.

2. Open the scene in Maya.

This scene has a masterLayer render layer, which should not be rendered, and two additional layers. The solarSystem layer contains the sun and planets, which have been shaded. It uses the mental ray renderer. If you open the Render Settings window to the Passes tab, you'll see this scene uses two render passes: diffuse and incandescence. The second layer is named orbitPaths. It contains Paint Effects strokes that illustrate the orbit paths of the two planets (Figure 12.42).

In the Common tab of the Render Settings window, no filename prefix has been specified and a frame range is not set. Maya will use the default file structure when rendering the scene, and the frame range will be set in the options for the command line.

FIGURE 12.42
The solarSystem
_v01.ma scene has
been prepared for
rendering.

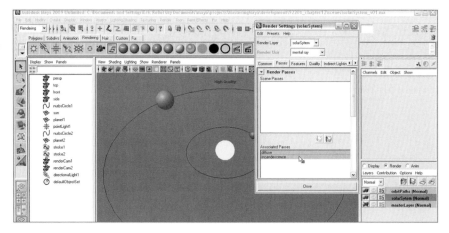

WINDOWS COMMAND-LINE RENDER

The first example starts a command-line render using Windows.

1. Go to the Windows Start menu and choose Start ➤ All Programs ➤ Accessories ➤ Command Prompt to open the Command Prompt shell.

2. Use Windows Explorer to browse your computer's directory (right-click the Start button and choose Explore to open Windows Explorer), open the scenes folder in your current project where you placed the solarSystem_v01.ma scene.

3. Select the Address line at the top of Windows Explorer, and choose Edit ➤ Copy to copy the path to the scenes directory to the Clipboard.

4. At the command prompt, type **cd ..\..** and hit Enter. This sets the command prompt to the root directory.

5. Type **cd,** space, and then right-click the command line and select Paste. This pastes the path to the scenes directory in the command prompt. Press the Enter key to set the current directory to the scenes directory (Figure 12.43).

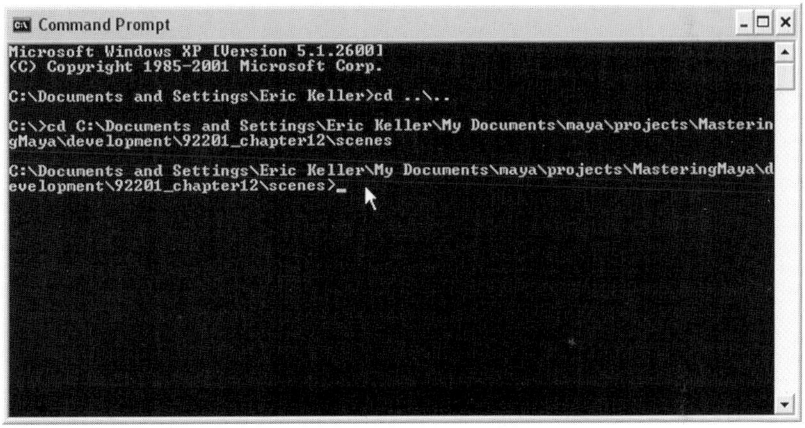

FIGURE 12.43
Set the command prompt to the current directory where the solar System_v01.ma scene is stored (the exact directory path will look different on your machine).

When starting a batch render, you can either specify the path to the scenes directory in the command-line options or set the command prompt to the directory that contains the scene.

To start a batch render, use the render command in the command prompt followed by option flags and the name of the scene you want to render. The option flags are preceded by a hyphen. The flags are followed by a space and then the flag setting. For example, to start a scene using the mental ray renderer, you would type **render -r mr myscene.ma.** The render command starts the batch renderer, the -r flag specifies the renderer, and mr sets the -r flag to mental ray. The command ends with the name of the scene (or the directory path to the scene if you're not already in the directory with the scene).

There are a large number of options, but you don't need to use them, except if you want to specify an option that's different from what is used in the scene. If you want all the layers to render using mental ray regardless of the layer setting in the scene, then you specify mental ray using the -r mr flag. If you omit the -r flag, then Maya uses the default renderer, which is Maya

Software. If you have a scene with several layers that use different renderers (as in the case of the solarSystem_v01.ma scene), then you would type -r file. This sets the renderer to whatever is specified in the file, including what is specified for each layer.

Other common flags include:

-s <float> sets the start frame (replace <float> with the starting frame, for example -s 120 would set the start frame to 120. A float is number with a decimal point).

-e <float> sets the end frame.

-x <int> sets the X resolution of the image (an integer is a whole number without a decimal point).

-y <int> sets the Y resolution of the image.

- cam <name> sets the camera.

-rd <path> specifies the directory for the images (if this is not used, the directory in the project settings is used).

-im <filename> sets the name of the rendered image.

-of <format> sets the image format.

There is a complete list of the flags in the Maya documentation. You can also print a description of commands by typing **render -help**. To see mental ray–specific commands, type **render -help -r mr**.

6. For example, if you want to render the scene using renderCam1, starting on frame1 and ending on frame 24, type the following in the command prompt (Figure 12.44):

   render -r file -s 1 -e 24 -cam renderCam1solarSystem_v01.ma

FIGURE 12.44
Enter the render command with options and the scene name in the Command Prompt window.

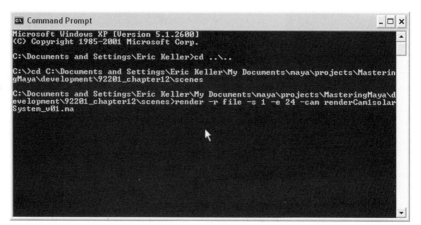

You'll see the render execute in the command prompt. When it's finished, you can use F Check to view each sequence. In the Images folder, you'll see two directories named after the layers in the scene. The orbitPath directory has the Paint Effects orbit paths rendered with Maya Software. The solarSystem directory has the rendered sequence of the planets and sun as well as subdirectories for the diffuse, incandescence, and MasterBeauty passes (the MasterBeauty pass is created by default when you add passes to a scene).

7. Let's say you want to render only the orbitPaths layer using renderCam2 for the frame range 16 to 48. You want to specify Maya Software as the renderer. You may want to name the sequence after the camera as well. Type the following into the command prompt (use a single line with no returns):

```
render -r sw -s 16 -e 48 -rl orbitPaths -cam renderCam2 -im
solarSystemCam2 solarSystem_v01.ma
```

MAC COMMAND-LINE RENDER

For a Mac, the Maya command-line render workflow is similar except that instead of the command prompt you use a special Terminal window that is included when you install Maya. This is an application called Maya Terminal.term and it's found in the Applications ➤ Autodesk ➤ Maya 2009 folder (Figure 12.45). It's probably a good idea to add this application to the Dock so you can easily open it whenever you need to run a batch render.

FIGURE 12.45
The Maya Terminal window is installed with Maya in the Maya 2009 folder.

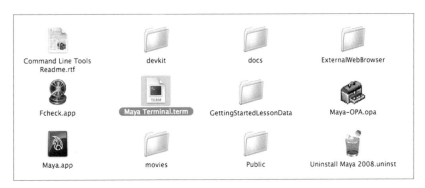

You need to navigate in the terminal to the scenes directory that contains the scene you want to render.

1. Copy the solarSystem_v01.ma scene from the DVD to the scenes directory of your current project on you computer's hard drive.

2. In the Finder, open the current project directory.

3. Start the Maya Terminal application, and type **cd** at the prompt.

4. In the Finder, drag the scenes folder from the current project on top of the Maya Terminal. This places the path to the scenes directory in the Terminal.

5. Press the Enter button. The Terminal window is now set to the project's scenes folder, which contains the solarSytem_v01.ma scene.

The commands for rendering on a Mac are the same as they are for Windows. You can continue starting with step 6 in the previous exercise.

Creating a Batch Script

It's possible to create a text file that can initiate a series of batch renders for a number of different scenes. This can be useful when you need a machine to perform several renders overnight or over a long weekend. This can save you the trouble of starting every batch render manually. This section describes how to create a batch script for Windows and Mac.

WINDOWS BATCH RENDER SCRIPT

1. Move the scenes you want to render into the renderScenes directory of the current project. Give them a name that distinguishes them from the original scenes in the scenes directory just to avoid confusion.

2. Create a new plain-text file using Notepad.

3. In the text file, type out the render commands exactly the same way you would initiate a batch render. Use a new line for each render. For example:

   ```
   render -r file -s 20 -e 120 -cam renderCam1 myScene.mb
   render -r file -s 121 -e 150 -cam renderCam2 myScene.mb
   render -r file -s 1 -e 120 -cam renderCam1 myScene_part2.mb
   ```

4. Save the scene as a .bat file, and save it in the same directory as the scenes you wish to render, usually the renderScenes directory. The file can be named anything, but it should end in .bat. Make sure the format is plain text, for example, weekendRender.bat.

5. When you are ready to render, double-click on the batch script (for example, weekendRender .bat) (see Figure 12.46).

You'll probably want to close Maya to maximize system resources for the render. Maya will render each scene in the order it is listed in the batch file. Be very careful in naming the files and the image sequences so one render does not overwrite a previous render. For example, if you render overlapping frame sequences from the same file, use the -im flag in each batch render line to give the image sequences different names.

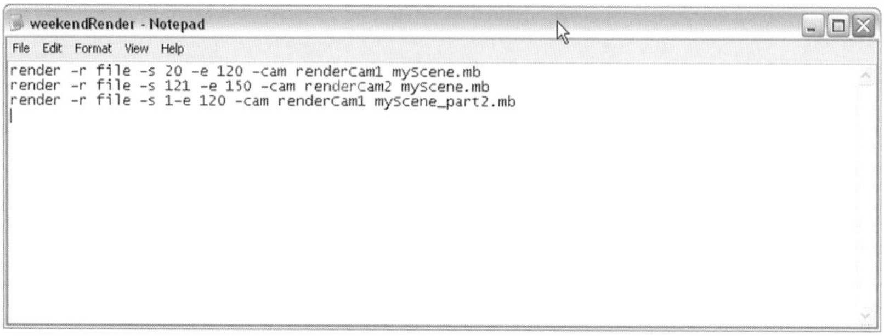

FIGURE 12.46

An example of a batch script file

Mac Batch Render Script

There are a few extra steps involved in creating a Mac batch render script, but for the most part it is similar to the Windows workflow.

1. Move the scenes you want to render into the `renderScenes` directory of the current project. It's a good idea to give the scenes a name that distinguishes them from the original scenes in the `scenes` directory just to avoid confusion.

2. Create a new plain-text file using TextEdit.

3. In the text file, type out the render commands exactly the same way you would initiate a batch render. Use a new line for each render. For example:

```
render -r file -s 20 -e 120 -cam renderCam1 myScene.mb
render -r file -s 121 -e 150 -cam renderCam2 myScene.mb
render -r file -s 1-e 120 -cam renderCam1 myScene_part2.mb
```

4. Save the scene as a `.batch` file, and save it in the same directory as the scenes you wish to render, usually the `renderScenes` directory. The file can be named anything, but it should end in `.batch`. Make sure the format is plain text, for example, `weekendRender.batch`.

5. In the Maya Terminal window, navigate to the location of the batch file (in the `renderScenes` folder of the current project). Convert the batch file to an executable by typing **chmod 777 weekendRender.batch**.

6. In the Maya Terminal window, navigate to the location of the batch file and type **./weekendRender.batch**.

The scenes will render in the order in which they are listed in the batch file.

mental ray Quality Settings

The quality of your render is determined by a number of related settings, some of which appear in the Render Settings window and some of which appear in the Attribute Editor of nodes within the scene. Tessellation, anti-aliasing, sampling, and filtering all play a part in how good the final render looks. You will always have to strike a balance between render quality and render time. As you raise the level of quality, test your renders and make a note of how long they take. Five minutes to render a single frame may not seem like much until you're dealing with a multilayered animation that is several thousand frames long. Remember that you will almost always have to render a sequence more than once as changes are requested by the director or client (even when you are sure this is the absolute final render!).

In this section, you'll learn how to use the settings in the Quality tab as well as other settings to improve the look of the final render.

Always Test Short Sequences

A single rendered frame may not reveal all of the quality problems in a scene. Remember to test a short sequence of rendered frames for problems such as flickering or crawling textures before starting a full batch render.

Tessellation and Approximation Nodes

At render time, all the geometry in the scene, regardless of whether it is NURBS, polygons, or subdivision surfaces, is converted to polygon triangles by the renderer. *Tessellation* refers to the number and placement of the triangles on the surface when the scene is rendered. Objects that have a low tessellation will look blocky compared to those with a high tessellation. However, lower-tessellation objects take less time to render than high-tessellation objects (Figure 12.47). Tessellation settings can be found in the shape nodes of surfaces. In Chapter 3, the settings for NURBS surface tessellation are discussed. The easiest way to set tessellation for NURBS surfaces is to use the Tessellation controls in the shape node of the surface. You can also set tessellation for multiple surfaces at the same time by opening the Attribute Spreadsheet (Window ➤ General Editors ➤ Attribute Spreadsheet) to the Tessellation tab.

You can also create an approximation node that can set the tessellation for various types of surfaces. To create an approximation node, select the surface and choose Window ➤ Rendering Editor ➤ mental ray ➤ Approximation Editor.

FIGURE 12.47
In the top image, the background structure has a low tessellation setting. In the bottom image, the same geometry is rendered with a high tessellation setting.

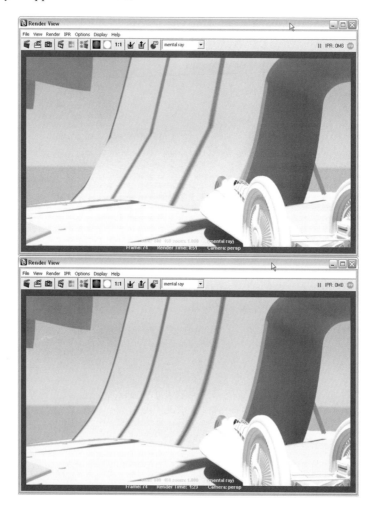

The editor allows you to create approximation nodes for NURBS surfaces, displacements (when using a texture for geometry displacement), and subdivision surfaces.

To create a node, click the Create button. To assign the node to a surface, select the surface and select the node from the drop-down menu in the Approximation Editor; then click the Assign button. The Unassign button allows you to break the connection between the node and the surface. The Edit button allows you to edit the node's settings in the Attribute Editor, and the Delete button removes the node from the scene (see Figure 12.48).

You can assign a subdivision surface approximation node to a polygon object so the polygons are rendered as subdivision surfaces, giving them a smooth appearance similar to a smooth mesh or subdivision surface. In Figure 12.49 a polygon cube has been duplicated twice. The cube on the far left has a subdivision approximation node assigned to it. The center cube is a smooth mesh. (The cube is converted to a smooth mesh by pressing the 3 key. Smooth mesh polygon surfaces are covered in Chapter 4.) The cube on the far right has been converted to a subdivision surface (Modify ➢ Convert ➢ Polygons To Subdivision Surfaces). When the scene is rendered using mental ray, the three cubes are almost identical. This demonstrates the various options available for rendering smooth polygon surfaces.

FIGURE 12.48
The Approximation Editor allows you to create and assign approximation nodes.

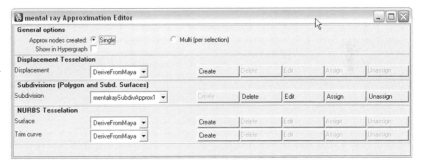

FIGURE 12.49
Three duplicate cubes are rendered as smooth surfaces using an approximation node, a smooth mesh, and a subdivision surface.

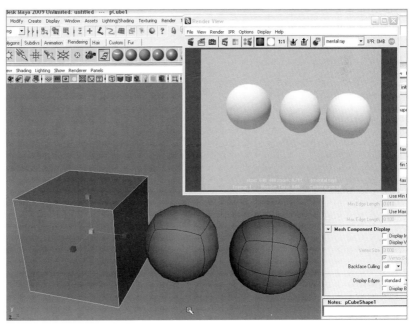

When editing the settings for the subdivision approximation node, the Parametric Method option is the simplest to use. You can use the N Subdivisions setting to set the smoothness of the render. Each time you increase the number of subdivisions, the polygons are multiplied by a factor of four. A setting of 3 means that each polygon face on the original object is divided 12 times.

Anti-Aliasing and Sampling

The anti-aliasing settings in the Quality tab of the Render Settings window are used to control and reduce flickering and artifacts that can appear along the edges of 3D objects or within the details of high-contrast or detailed textures applied to surfaces. Flickering in high-contrast textures is not noticeable in still frames, only when a sequence of frames is rendered and played back. This is why it's often important to test short sequences of your animations when adjusting the quality.

To minimize flickering and artifacts, you can adjust the settings found in the Anti-Aliasing Quality section of the Render Settings window (see Figure 12.50).

FIGURE 12.50

You can control the anti-aliasing quality in the Anti-Aliasing Quality section of the Quality tab in the Render Settings window.

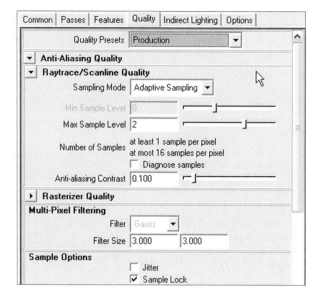

The two main controls are the Sample Levels and Anti-Aliasing Contrast. When adjusting the sampling level, you can choose among Fixed, Adaptive, and Custom sampling modes.

Sampling refers to how mental ray determines the color of a pixel in a rendered image of a 3D scene. A camera emits a number of rays into the scene (known as Primary Eye Rays) to determine the initial color value that will be created for the individual pixels in the final image. After sampling occurs, filters are applied to average the color values for each pixel in the final image. Secondary rays may be cast into the scene to determine raytracing effects such as reflections and refractions.

The type of Primary Eye Ray is determined by the Primary Renderer setting in the Features tab of the Render Settings window. Usually this is set to Scanline for most renders. Secondary rays are specified by the options in the Secondary Effects section of the Features tab (see Figure 12.51).

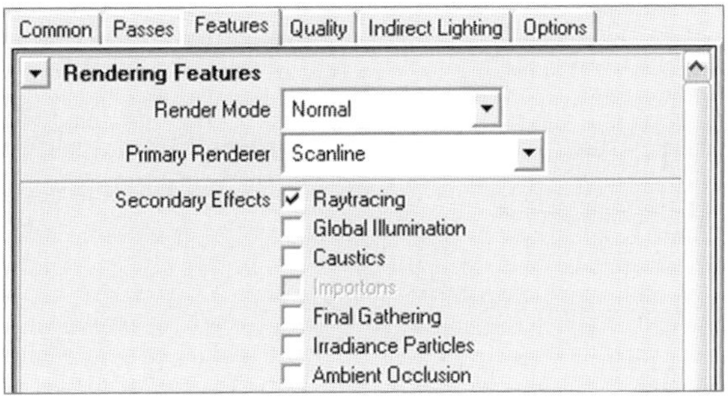

FIGURE 12.51

The settings in the Features tab determine the type of Primary Eye Ray cast by the rendering cameras to sample a 3D scene.

mental ray evaluates the render using tiles. A *tile* is a square section of what will become the rendered image. As mental ray renders the image, it stores the samples for each tile in the sampling Frame Buffer. Once the samples have been collected for a tile, filters are applied to average the colors. The filtered samples are translated into color values and then stored in the image buffer. A tile defines a region of samples that will become pixels in the final image.

The Min and Max Sample Levels determine the sampling range. mental ray uses the Min Sample Level as a starting point and then evaluates the scene and determines whether any parts of the scene require additional samples. If so, more samples are taken. The number of additional samples is determined by the Max Sample Level.

Sample levels increase by a factor of 4. A Sample Level of 0 means that each pixel in the image receives 1 sample. A sample level of 1 means 4 samples per pixel. A sample level of 2 means 16 samples per pixel and so on.

Negative values mean that each sample contains a number of pixels. A sample level of -2 means that one sample is used for an area of 16 pixels in the rendered image. Again, the number of pixels in negative sampling increases by a factor of 4. As you change the sampling, the number of samples that will be used is displayed in the Render Settings window under Number Of Samples (see Figure 12.52).

As the sampling rate is increased, the render time increases significantly. The Sampling Mode option can be used to increase the efficiency of the sampling process. When Sampling Mode is set to Fixed, mental ray uses the sampling level specified by Max Sample Level. This is often useful for rendering with Motion Blur. When Sampling Mode is set to Adaptive Sampling, mental ray uses one level below the Max Sampling Level as the minimum and one level above the Max Sampling Level as the maximum. In other words, when Max Sampling Level is set to 2, the minimum becomes 1 sample per pixel and the maximum becomes 16 samples per pixel. When Sampling Mode is set to Custom Sampling, you can enter your own values for Min Sample Level and Max Sample Level.

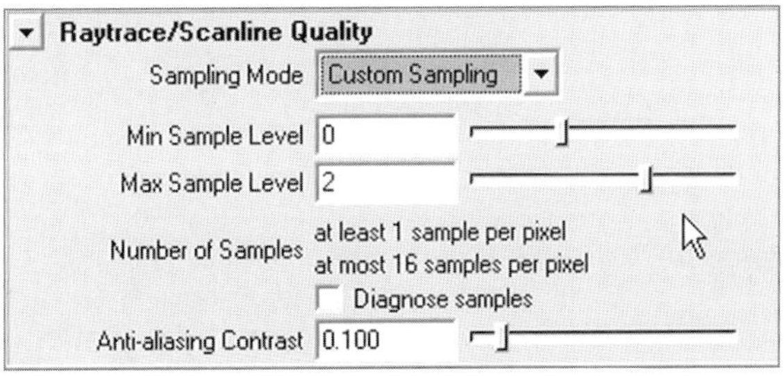

FIGURE 12.52

As you adjust the Min Sample and Max Sample Levels, the range of samples is displayed next to Number Of Samples.

So how does mental ray know when a pixel requires more sampling? Mental ray uses the Anti-Aliasing Contrast value to determine if a pixel requires more sampling. Lower Anti-Aliasing Contrast values increase the likelihood that addition sampling will be required.

The best approach to take when setting the sampling level is to adjust Anti-Aliasing Contrast gradually before increasing the Min and Max Sampling Levels. You'll notice that the Production Quality preset uses Adaptive Sampling with a Max Sampling Level of 2 and an Anti-Aliasing Contrast setting of 0.1. If you find this is not sufficient, try lowering the Anti-Aliasing Contrast setting. Try a setting of 0.05. If your image still has artifacts, you may then consider raising the Max Sample Level.

If you image has large blank areas and only small portions of detail, try setting a Min Sampling Level of 0 or -1 and a Max Sampling Level of 2. This way sampling is not wasted in areas where it is not needed.

Other options include adjusting the textures, applying filtering to the textures, or using the mental ray overrides on individual surface shape nodes to adjust the sampling for whichever surface is causing problems.

You can get a sense of how the sampling is being applied in a render by activating the Diagnose Samples option (found in the Raytrace/Scanline Quality section in the Quality tab of the Render Settings window) and performing a test render. The rendered image will show areas of higher sampling in white and lower sampled areas in black (Figure 12.53).

FIGURE 12.53
You can visualize areas of high sampling in a test render when Diagnose Samples is activated.

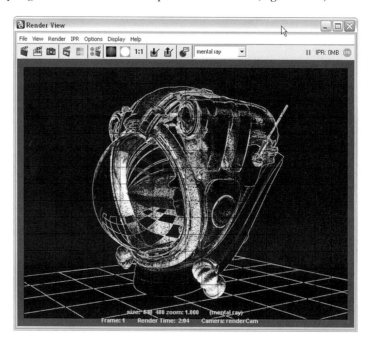

MENTAL RAY DEFAULT OPTIONS

If you'd like more control over each channel of the Anti-Aliasing Contrast (RGB and Alpha), open the miDefaultOptions node in the Attribute Editor, and use the settings under the Sampling Quality section. To access this node, turn off DAG Objects Only in the Display menu of the Outliner and select the miDefaultOptions node. The settings will become available in the Attribute Editor.

Filtering

Filtering occurs after sampling as the image is translated in the Frame Buffer. There are a number of different filters you can apply, found in the menu in the Multi-Pixel Filtering section of the Render Settings Quality tab. Some filters blur the image while others sharpen the image. The Filter Size fields determine the height and width of the filter as it expands from the center of the sample across neighboring pixels. A setting of 1×1 covers a single pixel, and a setting of 2×2 covers four pixels. Most of the time the default setting for each filter type is the best one to use.

The Box filter applies the filter evenly across the image's height and width. Triangle and Gauss filters both add a small amount of blurring to the pixels, while Mitchel and Lanczos both sharpen the image.

The Jitter option reduces flickering or banding artifacts. Jittering offsets the sample location for a given sample block in a random fashion.

The Sample Lock option locks the sampling pattern. This reduces flickering by forcing mental ray to sample the scene the same way for each frame. It can be useful in animated sequences and when using Motion Blur. If Sample Lock does not reduce flickering, try Jitter as an alternative.

Rasterizer

The Rasterizer is an alternative to the Scanline and Raytrace renderers that uses a different sampling algorithm. You can choose Rasterizer as your Primary Renderer in the Features tab of the Render Settings window. Rasterizer is most often used for scenes with motion blur or scenes with hair. It handles large amounts of overlapping thin surfaces (such as hair) quite well.

When Rasterizer is chosen as the Primary Renderer, the options for Raytrace/Scanline Quality sampling in the Quality tab become unavailable. Instead you can use the Visibility Samples and Shading Quality settings in the Rasterizer Quality section of the Quality tab (see Figure 12.54).

Visibility Samples works much like the Max Sample Level setting in the Raytrace/Scanline Quality options; however, the Rasterizer is not adaptive. The default setting of 0 means that one sample is used for anti-aliasing. Shading Quality sets the number of shading samples per pixel. The Rasterizer caches the samples with the geometry in the scene, so sampling actually travels with moving geometry. This is why it is an ideal algorithm for use with motion blur. Motion blur is discussed in Chapter 2.

FIGURE 12.54
When you choose Rasterizer as the Primary Renderer, the Rasterizer Quality options become available.

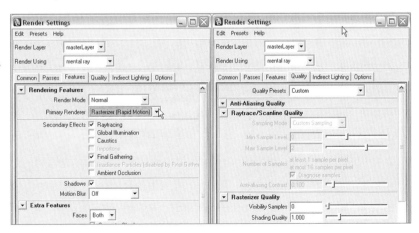

Raytrace Acceleration

Raytrace Acceleration settings are found in the Raytrace settings in the Render Settings Quality tab. The purpose of these settings is to improve the speed of your renders when raytracing is enabled. Changing the settings does not affect how the image looks, only how fast it renders.

Raytracing is a process where rays are shot into a 3D scene from the rendering camera. When Raytracing is used as the Primary Renderer (this is set in the Features tab), each ray shot from the camera is compared with every triangle face of every piece of geometry in the scene to determine if additional rays are required for reflection or refraction (recall that all geometry is tessellated into polygon triangles when the scene is rendered).

To reduce the number of comparisons made between each ray and each triangle, mental ray offers several versions of the Binary Space Partition (BSP) algorithm (see Figure 12.55), which is meant to accelerate the process. The BSP algorithm divides the scene into sections; each section is a 3D container known as a *voxel*. The number of calculations required for each ray is limited to the number of triangles within a section of the scene as defined by the algorithm. In the Acceleration Method menu, you'll find Regular BSP, Large BSP, and BSP2. The Large BSP method is meant for use with large scenes; it does a better job of managing memory through disk swapping than Regular BSP. The BSP2 method does not allow you to set the Size and Depth options. BSP2 is also useful for large scenes and whenever a large number of instances are present.

The voxels created by the BSP method are adaptive. If needed, a voxel can be subdivided into smaller voxels. The lowest level of division is a voxel that contains only triangles; such voxels are known as *leaf nodes*.

You can set Bsp Size and Bsp Depth. Bsp Size refers to the maximum number of triangles a voxel can contain before it is subdivided. Bsp Depth sets a limit on the number of times a voxel can be subdivided. When tuning the performance of raytrace acceleration, you want to balance the size of the voxels against the voxel depth. A large voxel size means that each ray must make a large number of comparisons as it enters a voxel. A large depth value requires more memory to store the calculations for each voxel as well as more time for determining the placement and division of the voxels. Voxel depth has a larger impact on render time than voxel size.

You can use a separate BSP tree (a *BSP tree* is the hierarchy of voxels created in the scene) to calculate raytraced shadows. This is activated by turning on Separate Shadow Bsp.

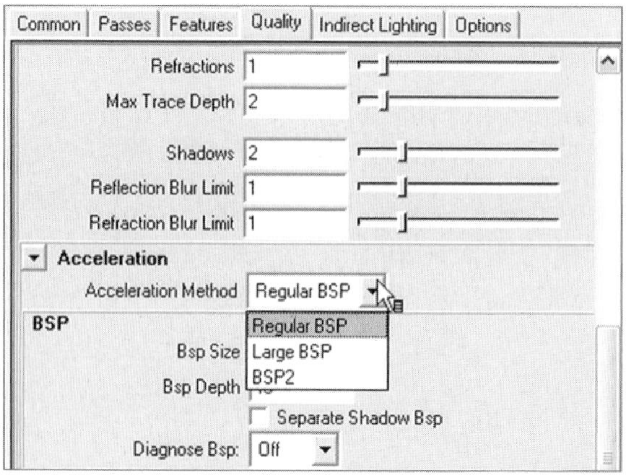

FIGURE 12.55

mental ray offers three versions of the BSP Acceleration Method for improving the speed of raytrace calculations.

Diagnose BSP

Tuning BSP settings often takes a fair amount of testing, trial, and error. You can create a visual representation of how BSP is calculated by activating the Diagnose Bsp setting. This allows you to see a color-coded version of the scene based on the BSP size or depth.

1. Open the `carSceneBSP_v01.ma` scene from the `chapter12\scenes` directory on the DVD.

This scene uses very simple standard Maya shaders to create reflective materials on the car and the structure behind it.

When diagnosing acceleration, you can speed up the process by lowering the sampling in the scene and, in the case of this scene, turning off Final Gathering.

2. In the Indirect Lighting tab, deactivate Final Gathering. In the Quality tab, set Sampling Mode to Fixed and the Max Sample Level to **-3**.

3. In the Acceleration section, set Diagnose Bsp to Depth. Then open the render view, and create a test render using the renderCam camera.

The scene renders in a very low quality, but this is perfectly fine; you want to pay attention to the colors in the image. Areas that are red indicate that the maximum number of subdivisions for the voxels that contain those triangles has been reached. You'll see this around the detailed wheel section and on parts of the structure. Ideally you want to see orange and yellow in these areas and less red. To fix this, raise the Bsp Depth setting.

4. Set Bsp Depth to **45** and create another test render (Figure 12.56).

5. Set the Diagnose Bsp menu to Size and create another test render.

For the most part the scene appears in blue, indicating that the voxel size is more than adequate. You can try lowering this value, but for this particular scene a size of 10 is fine. If you prefer to have a more detailed report of the impact of the BSP Acceleration settings, set the Verbosity of the output messages to Progress Messages (you can do this in Render Current Frame ➢ Options) and observe the report in the Output window.

FIGURE 12.56

The Diagnose Bsp option color codes the render based on the voxel depth set in the Acceleration options.

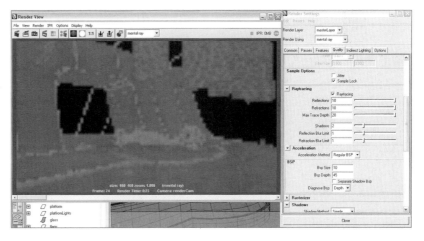

The Bottom Line

Use render layers.   Render layers can be used to separate the elements of a single scene into different versions or into different layers of a composite. Each layer can have its own shaders, lights, and settings. Using overrides you can change the way each layer renders.

Master it   Use render layers to set up alternate versions of the space helmet. Try applying contour rendering on one layer and Final Gathering on another.

Use render passes.   Render passes allow you to separate material properties into different images. These passes are derived from calculations stored in the Frame Buffer. Each pass can be used in compositing software to efficiently rebuild the rendered scene. Render Pass Contribution Maps define which objects and lights are included in a render pass.

Master it   Create an Ambient Occlusion pass for the minigun scene.

Perform batch renders.   Batch renders automate the process of rendering a sequence of images. You can use Maya's Batch Render options in the Maya interface or choose Batch Render from the command prompt (or Terminal) when Maya is closed. A batch script can be used to render multiple scenes.

Master it   Create a batch script to render five fictional scenes. Each scene uses layers with different render settings. Set the frame range for each scene to render frames 20 through 50. Each scene is named myScene1.ma through myScene5.ma.

Use mental ray quality settings.   The settings in the Quality tab of the Render Settings window allow you to adjust the anti-aliasing quality and the raytrace acceleration of a scene (among other things). Sampling improves the quality of the image by reducing flickering problems. Raytrace acceleration does not affect image quality but improves render times when raytracing is activated in a scene.

Master it   Diagnose both the sampling and the BSP depth of the helmetComposite_v04.ma scene.

Chapter 13

Introducing nParticles

This chapter introduces Maya's new nParticle dynamics and shows you how they can be used creatively to create a wide variety of visual effects. The example scenes demonstrate the fundamentals of working with and rendering particles. The subsequent chapters on Maya dynamics build on these techniques.

nParticles are new to Maya 2009. These nParticles are connected to the Nucleus solver system, a difference from traditional Maya particles. Nucleus is a unified dynamic system first introduced in Maya 8.5 as part of nCloth. The Nucleus solver is the brain behind the nDynamic systems in Maya.

In this chapter you will learn to:

- ◆ Create nParticles
- ◆ Make nParticles collide
- ◆ Create liquid simulations
- ◆ Emit nParticles from a texture
- ◆ Move nParticles with nucleus wind
- ◆ Use the Hardware Render Buffer
- ◆ Use force fields
- ◆ Render nParticles with mental ray

Creating nParticles

nParticles can do just about everything that traditional Maya particles can do plus a lot more. Furthermore, they can create much more sophisticated simulations without relying on complex expressions. For this reason, the exercises in this book focus on nParticles and the nDynamic systems. The traditional particle and rigid body systems have not changed since older versions of Maya and aren't as powerful as the Nucleus systems. If you're familiar with traditional Maya particles, you'll see some similarities when using nParticles.

When you create an nParticle object or an nCloth object, or both, in a scene, a Nucleus solver is created. The same solver is used to calculate the dynamics and interactions within the nParticle system and the nCloth system. A scene can have more than one Nucleus solver, but nDynamic systems using two different solvers can't directly interact. However, two separate nParticle objects using the same Nucleus solver can interact.

In this chapter, several exercises demonstrate the possibilities of nParticle systems. Other Nucleus systems are covered in Chapters 14 and 15.

There are a number of ways to create nParticles in a scene. You can draw them on the grid, use an emitter to spawn them into a scene, use a surface as an emitter, or fill a volume with nParticles. When you create an nParticle object, you also need to specify the nParticle's style.

Choosing a style activates one of a number of preset settings for the nParticle's attributes, all of which can be altered after you add the nParticle object to the scene. The nParticle styles include balls, points, cloud, thick cloud, and water. The following exercises take you through the process of using the different nParticle creation methods and introduce you to working with the Nucleus solver.

NDYNAMICS

The Nucleus dynamic systems (aka nDynamics) are distinguished from the traditional dynamic systems by the letter *n*. So nParticles, nCloth, and nRigids are part of the new nDynamics system, and particles and rigid bodies are part of traditional Maya dynamics.

Drawing nParticles Using the nParticle Tool

The simplest way to create nParticles is to draw them on the grid using the nParticle tool.

1. Create a new scene in Maya. Switch to the nDynamics menu set.

2. Choose nParticles ➢ Create nParticles, and set the style to Balls (see Figure 13.1).

3. Choose Create nParticles ➢ nParticle Tool. Click six or seven times on the grid to place individual particles.

4. Press the Enter key on the numeric keypad to create the particles.

You'll see several circles on the grid. The ball-type nParticle style automatically creates blobby surface particles. Blobby surfaces are spheres rendered using Maya Software or mental ray. Blobby surfaces use standard Maya shaders when rendered and can be blended together to form a gooey surface.

FIGURE 13.1
Use the nParticle menu to specify the nParticle style.

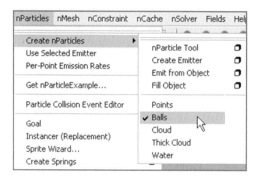

5. Set the length of the timeline to 600. Rewind and play the animation. The particles will fall in space.

6. Open the Attribute Editor for the nParticle1 object, and switch to the nucleus1 tab. The settings on this tab control the Nucleus solver, which sets the overall dynamic attributes of the connected nDynamic systems (see Figure 13.2).

7. By default a Nucleus solver has Gravity enabled. Enable Use Plane in the Ground Plane settings (Figure 13.3). This creates an invisible floor that the nParticles can rest on. Set the Plane Origin's Translate Y to **-1**.

FIGURE 13.2

The settings on the nucleus1 tab define the behavior of the environment for all connected nDynamic nodes.

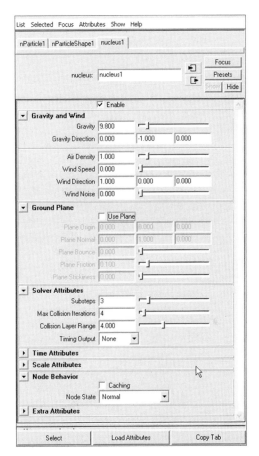

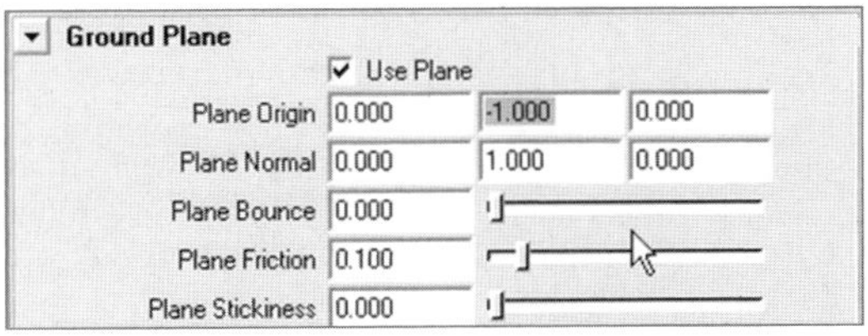

FIGURE 13.3

The ground plane creates an invisible floor that keeps the nParticles from falling.

8. The Nucleus solver also has wind settings. Set Wind Speed to **3** and Wind Noise to **4**. By default Wind Direction is set to 1, 0, 0 (Figure 13.4). The fields correspond to the X, Y, and Z axes, so this means that the nParticles will be blown along the positive X axis. Rewind and play the animation. Now the nParticles are moving along with the wind, and a small amount of turbulence is applied.

FIGURE 13.4

The settings for Air Density, Wind Speed, Wind Direction, and Wind Noise are found under the Nucleus solver's attributes.

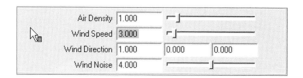

By increasing the Air Density value, you adjust the atmosphere of the environment. A very high setting is a good way to simulate an underwater environment. Using wind in combination with a high air density pushes the nParticles with more force; this makes sense since the air is denser.

The Solver Attributes section sets the quality of the solver. The Substeps setting specifies how many times per frame the solver calculates nDynamics. Higher settings are more accurate but can slow down performance. Increasing the Substeps value may alter some of the ways in which nDynamics behave, such as how they collide with each other and other objects, so when you increase this value, be aware that you may need to adjust other settings on your nDynamic nodes.

The Scale Attributes section has sliders for adjusting both Time Scale and the Space Scale. Use Time Scale to speed up or slow down the solver. Values below 1 slow down the simulation; higher values speed it up. If you increase Time Scale, you should increase the number of substeps in the Solver Attributes section to ensure that the simulation is still accurate. Time Scale can be keyframed to create the "bullet time" effect made famous in *The Matrix* movies.

Space Scale scales the environment of the simulation. By default nDynamics are calculated in meters even if the Maya scene unit is set to centimeters. You should set this to 0.1 if you need your nDynamics simulation to behave appropriately when the Maya scene units are set to centimeters. This is more noticeable when working with large simulations. You can also use this setting creatively to exaggerate effects or when using more than one Nucleus solver in a scene. For the following examples, leave Space Scale set to 1.

Spawning nParticles from an Emitter

An emitter shoots nParticles into the scene, like a sprinkler shooting water onto a lawn. When a particle is emitted into a scene it is "born" at that moment, and all calculations based on its age begin from the moment it is born.

1. Continue with the scene from the previous section. Add an emitter to the scene by choosing nParticles ➢ Create nParticles ➢ Create Emitter. An emitter appears at the center of the grid.

2. Open the Attribute Editor for the emitter1 object, and set Rate to **10**. Set Emitter Type to Omni.

3. Rewind and play the scene. The omni emitter spawns particles from a point at the center of the grid. Note that after the particles are born, they collide with the ground plane and are pushed by the nucleus wind in the same direction as the other particles (see Figure 13.5).

The new nParticles are connected to the same Nucleus solver. If you open the Attribute Editor for the nParticle2 object, you'll see the tabs for nucleus1 and nParticle2, as well as the tab for nParticle1. If you change the settings on the nucleus1 tab, both nParticle1 and nParticle2 are affected.

FIGURE 13.5

A second nParticle system is spawned from an emitter. These nParticles also collide with the ground plane and are pushed by the wind.

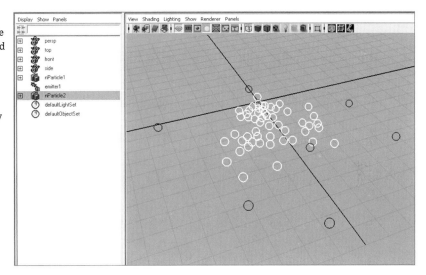

NPARTICLE TABS IN THE ATTRIBUTE EDITOR

The tabs for each nParticle connected to a Nucleus solver appear at the same time at the top of the Attribute Editor. Thus it is easy to make the mistake of editing the settings for the wrong nParticle object. To avoid this mistake, pay attention to which nParticle object is listed in the tab at the top of the Attribute Editor while you are changing settings!

---

4. Select nParticle2 and choose nSolver ➤ Assign Solver ➤ New Solver. Rewind and play the scene. NParticle2 now falls in space, whereas nParticle1 continues to slide on the ground plane.

5. Open the Outliner and, in the Outliner's Display menu, turn off DAG Objects Only. This allows you to see all the nodes in the scene. If you scroll down, you'll see nucleus1 and nucleus2 nodes (see Figure 13.6).

6. Select nParticle2 and choose nSolver ➤ Assign Solver ➤ nucleus1. This reconnects nParticle2 with nucleus1.

FIGURE 13.6
The nucleus nodes
are visible in the
Outliner.

7. Select emitter1 and set Emitter Type to Volume. In the emitter's Attribute Editor, set
   Volume Shape in the Volume Emitter Attributes section to Sphere. Use the Move tool to
   position the emitter above the ground plane. The emitter is now a volume, which you can
   scale up in size using the Scale tool (hot key = r). nParticles are born from random locations within the sphere (see Figure 13.7).

The directional emitter type is similar to the omni and volume emitters in that it shoots
nParticles into a scene. The directional emitter emits the nParticles in a straight line. The range
of the directional emitter can be altered using the Spread slider, causing it to behave more like a
sprinkler or fountain.

FIGURE 13.7
Volume emitters
spawn nParticles
from random loca-
tions within the
volume.

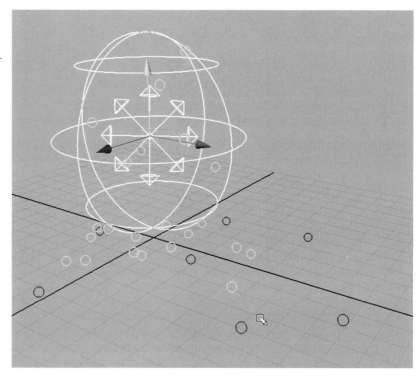

8. Open the Attribute Editor to the nParticleShape1 tab. This is where you'll find the attributes that control particle behavior, and there are a lot of them. As an experiment, expand the Force Field Generation rollout and set Point Force Field to Worldspace.

9. Rewind and play the animation. As the emitter spawns particles in the scene, a few nParticles from nParticle2 are attracted to nParticle1. NParticle1 is emitting a force field that attracts individual nParticles from nParticle2 like a magnet. You can also make the nParticles attract themselves by increasing the Self Attract slider (see Figure 13.8).

This is an example of how the Nucleus solver allows particles from two different particle objects to interact. The Force Field settings will be further explored in the section "Working with Force Fields" later in this chapter. If you switch nParticle2 to the nucleus2 solver, you will lose this behavior; only nParticles that share a solver can be attracted to each other. Be careful when using force fields on large numbers of nParticles (more than 10,000), as this will slow the performance of Maya significantly.

FIGURE 13.8
The Force Field settings cause one nParticle object to attract other nDynamic systems like a magnet.

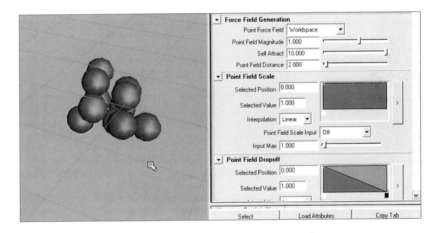

Emitting nParticles from a Surface

Polygon and NURBS surfaces can be used to generate nParticles as well.

1. Create a new Maya scene. Create a polygon plane (Create ➢ Polygon Primitives ➢ Plane).

2. Scale the plane 25 units in X and Z.

3. Switch to the nDynamics menu set. Set the nParticle style to Balls (nParticles ➢ Create nParticles ➢ Balls).

4. Choose nParticles ➢ Create nParticles ➢ Emit From Object ➢ Options. In the options, set Emitter Type to Surface and Rate to **10**. Set Speed to **0**. Click Create to make the emitter. Figure 13.9 shows the options for the surface emitter.

FIGURE 13.9
The options for
creating a surface
emitter

SURFACE EMITTERS

When you create a surface emitter, the emitter node is parented to the emitting geometry in the Outliner.

5. Set the timeline to 600.

6. Open the Attribute Editor to the nucleus1 tab, and set Gravity to **0**.

7. Rewind and play the animation. Particles appear randomly on the surface.

8. Open the Attribute Editor to the nParticle Shape tab. Expand the Particle Size rollout. Set Radius to **1**.

9. Click on the right side of the Radius Scale ramp to add a point. Adjust the position of the point on the left side of the ramp edit curve for Radius Scale so that it's at 0 on the left side and moves up to 1 on the right side (see Figure 13.10).

FIGURE 13.10
The Radius Scale
ramp curve adjusts
the radius of the
nParticles.

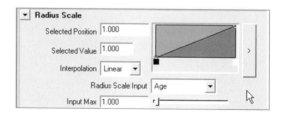

10. Rewind and play the animation. The particles now scale up as they are born (by default Radius Scale Input is set to Age). Notice that adjacent particles push each other as they grow. The ball-style particle has Self Collision on by default, so the particles will bump into each other (see Figure 13.11).

11. Set Radius Scale Randomize to **0.5**. The balls each have a random size. By increasing this slider, you increase the random range for the maximum radius size of each nParticle.

12. Set Input Max to **3**. This sets the maximum range along the X axis of the Radius Scale ramp. Since Radius Scale Input is set to Time, this means each nParticle takes 3 seconds to achieve its maximum radius, so they slowly grow in size.

FIGURE 13.11
The balls scale up as they are born and push each other as they grow.

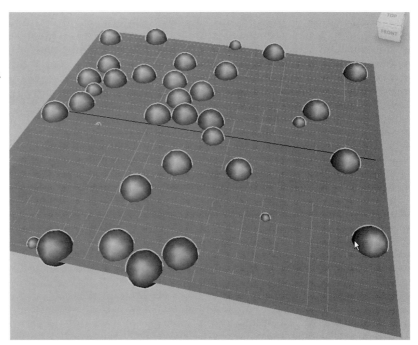

Filling an Object with nParticles

An object can be instantly filled with particles. Any modeled polygon mesh can hold the nParticles as long as it has some kind of depression in it. A flat plane, on the other hand, can't be used.

1. Open the forge_v01.ma scene from the chapter13\scenes folder on the DVD. You'll see a very simple scene consisting of a tub on a stand. A bucket is in front of the tub. The tub will be used to pour molten metal into the bucket.

2. Set the nParticle style to Water by choosing nParticles ➢ Create nParticles ➢ Water.

3. Select the tub object and choose Create nParticles ➢ Fill Object ➢ Options (see Figure 13.12). In the options, turn on Close Packing and click the Particle Fill button.

FIGURE 13.12
Select the tub object is selected, and it will be filled with nParticles.

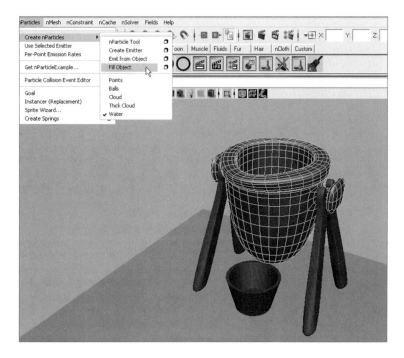

IF NO NPARTICLES ARE CREATED

If no nParticles are created at all, open the options for the Particle Fill command, reset the options, and turn on Close Packing. The problem occurs when Maya can't figure out how to fill the surface.

---

4. Set the display to Wireframe. You'll see a few particles stuck in the rim of the tub. If you play the scene, the particles fall through space.

There are two problems. The first problem is that the object has been built with a thick wall, so Maya is trying to fill the inside of the surface with particles rather than the well in the tub. The second problem is that the tub is not set as a collision surface (see Figure 13.13).

5. Select the nParticle1 object in the Outliner and delete it. Note that this does not delete the nucleus1 solver created with the particle, and that's okay; the next nParticle object you create will be automatically connected to this same solver.

There are a couple solutions to this problem. When you create the nParticle object, you can choose Double Walled in the Fill Object options, which in many cases solves the problem for objects that have a simple shape, such as a glass. For more convoluted shapes the nParticles may try to fill different parts of the object. For instance, in the case of the tub, as long as the Resolution setting in the options is at 10 or below, the tub will fill with nParticles just fine (increasing Resolution increases the number of nParticles that will fill the volume). However, if you create a higher-resolution nParticle, you'll find that nParticles are placed in the well of the tub and on the handles where the tub is held by the frame.

FIGURE 13.13
The nParticles
lodge within the
thick walls of
the tub.

FIGURE 13.13
The nParticles
lodge within the
thick walls of
the tub.

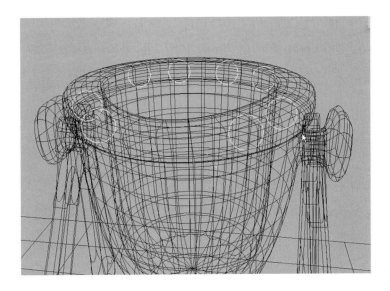

Another solution is to split the polygons that make up the object so that only the parts of the tub that actually collide with the nParticles are used to calculate how the nParticles fill the object.

6. Switch to shaded view. Select the tub object, and move the view so you can see the bottom of its interior.

7. Chose the Paint Selection tool, right-click on the tub, and choose Face to switch to face selection. Use the Paint Selection tool to select the faces at the very bottom of the tub (see Figure 13.14).

FIGURE 13.14
Select the faces at
the bottom of the
tub with the Paint
Selection tool.

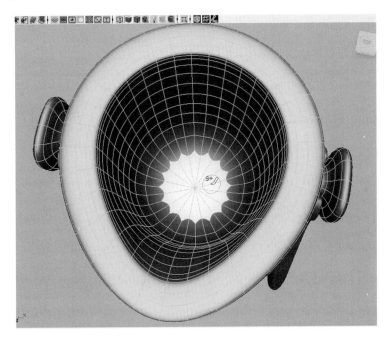

FIGURE 13.15
Expand the selection to include all the faces up to the rim of the tub.

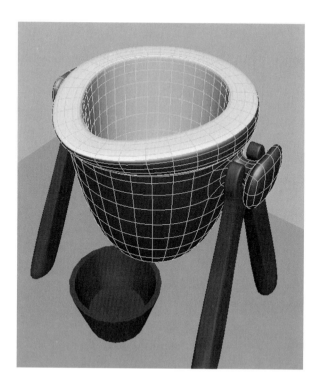

8. Hold the Shift key and press the > key on the keyboard to expand the selection. Keep pressing the > key until all the interior polygons are selected up to the edge of the tub's rim (see Figure 13.15).

9. Switch to wireframe mode, and make sure none of the polygons on the outside of the tub have been selected by accident. Hold the Ctrl key and select any unwanted polygons to deselect them.

10. Switch to the Polygon menu set and choose Mesh ➤ Extract. This splits the model into two parts. The selected polygon becomes a separate mesh from the deselected polygons. In the Outliner, you'll see that the tub1 object is now a group with two nodes: polySurface1 and polySurface2 (see Figure 13.16).

11. Select the polysurface1 and polysurface2 nodes, and choose Edit ➤ Delete By Type ➤ History.

12. Name the interior mesh **insideTub** and the exterior mesh **outsideTub**.

13. Switch to the nDynamics menu set. Select the insideTub mesh, and choose nParticles ➤ create nParticles ➤ Fill Object ➤ Options.

14. In the options, set Solver to nucleus1, and set Resolution to **15**.

The Fill Bounds settings determine the minimum and maximum boundaries within the volume that will be filled. In other words, if you want to fill a glass from the middle of the glass to the top, leaving the bottom half of the glass empty, set the minimum in Y to 0.5 and the maximum to 1 (the nParticles would still drop to the bottom of the glass if Gravity were enabled, but for a split second you would confuse both optimists and pessimists).

FIGURE 13.16
Split the tub into two separate mesh objects using the Extract command.

15. Leave all the Fill Bounds settings at the default. Turn off Double Walled and Close Packing. Click Particle Fill to apply it. After a couple seconds you'll see the tub filled with little blue spheres (see Figure 13.17).

16. Rewind and play the animation. The spheres drop through the bottom of the tub. To make them stay within the tub, you'll need to create a collision surface.

FIGURE 13.17
The inside of the tub is filled with nParticles.

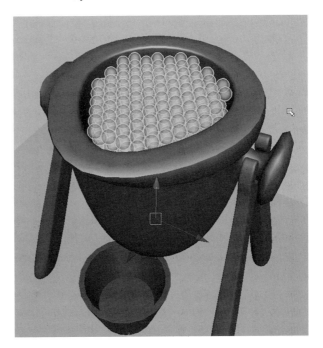

nParticle Collisions

nParticles collide with nCloth objects, passive collision surfaces, and other nParticle objects. They can also be made to self-collide; in fact, when the ball-style nParticle is chosen, Self Collision is on by default. To make an nParticle collide with an ordinary rigid object, you need to convert the collision surface into a passive collider. The passive collider can be animated as well.

Passive Collision Objects

Passive collision objects, also known as nRigids, are automatically connected to the current Nucleus solver when they are created.

1. Rewind the animation and select the insideTub mesh. Choose nMesh ➤ Create Passive Collider. By default the object is assigned to the current Nucleus solver. If you want to assign a different solver, use the options for Create Passive Collider.

2. Play the animation. You'll see the nParticles drop down and collide with the bottom of the tub. They'll slosh around for awhile and eventually settle.

CREATING NRIGID OBJECTS

When you create a passive collider object (aka nRigid object), any new nDynamic system you add to the scene that is connected to the same Nucleus solver will collide with the nRigid, as long as the new nDynamic node has Collisions enabled.

When creating a collision between an nParticle and a passive collision surface, there are two sets of controls you can tune to adjust the way the collision happens. Collision settings on the nParticle shape control how the nParticle reacts when colliding with surfaces, and collision settings on the passive object control how objects react when they collide with it.

For example, if you dumped a bunch of basketballs and Ping-Pong balls on a granite table and a sofa, you would see that the table and the sofa have their own collision behavior based on their physical properties, and the Ping-Pong balls and basketballs also have their own collision behavior based on their physical properties. When a collision event occurs between a Ping-Pong ball and the sofa, the physical properties of both objects are factored together to determine the behavior of the Ping-Pong ball at the moment of collision. Likewise a basketball has its own physical properties that are factored in with the same sofa properties when a collision occurs between the sofa and a basketball.

The nDynamics systems have a variety of ways to calculate collisions as well as ways to visualize and control the collisions between elements in the system.

3. Select the nRigid node in the Outliner, and switch to the nRigidShape1 tab in the Attribute Editor. Expand the Collisions rollout.

The Collide option turns collisions on or off for the surface. It's sometimes useful to temporarily disable collisions when working on animating objects in a scene using nDynamics. Likewise the Enable option above the Collisions rollout disables all nDynamics for the surface when it is unchecked.

4. Set the Solver Display option to Collision Thickness. Turning this option on creates an interactive display so you can see how the collisions for this surface are calculated (see Figure 13.18).

5. Switch to wireframe view (hot key = 4). Move the Thickness slider back and forth, and the envelope grows and shrinks, indicating how thick the surface will seem when the dynamics are calculated.

FIGURE 13.18
You can display the collision surface thickness using the controls in the nRigid body shape node.

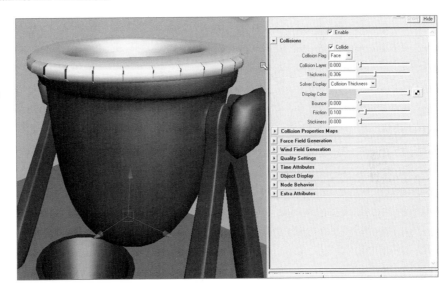

The thickness will not change its appearance when rendered, only how the nParticles will collide with the object. A very high Thickness value makes it seem as though there is an invisible force field around the object.

6. Switch back to smooth shaded view (hot key = 5). Collision Flag is set to Face by default, meaning that collisions are calculated based on the faces of the collision object. This is the most accurate but slowest way to calculate collisions.

7. Set Collision Flag to Vertex. Rewind and play the animation. You'll see the thickness envelope drawn around each vertex of the collision surface.

The nParticles fall through the bottom of the surface, and some may collide with the envelopes around the vertices on their way through the bottom. The calculation of the dynamics is faster, though. This setting may work well for dense meshes, and it will calculate much faster than the Face method.

8. Set Collision Flag to Edge; rewind and play the animation. The envelope is now drawn around each edge of the collision surface, creating a wireframe network (see Figure 13.19).

The calculation is much faster than when Collision Flag is set to Face, but the nParticles stay within the tub. You may notice some bumping as the nParticles collide with the wireframe. Many times this may not be noticeable at all, which makes the Edge method useful for calculating collisions.

FIGURE 13.19
When Collision Flag is set to Vertex, the nParticles collide with each vertex of the collision surface, allowing some to fall through the bottom. When the flag is set to Edge, the nParticles collide with the edges and the calculation speed improves.

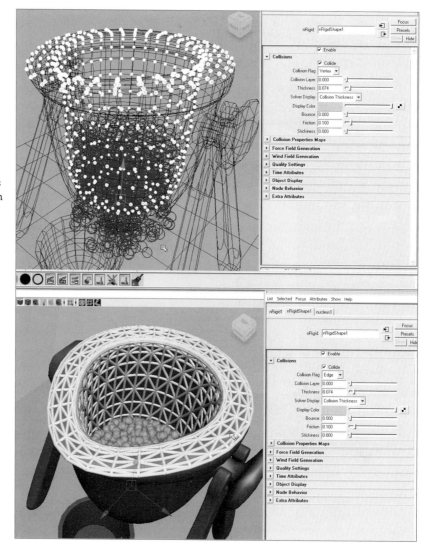

The other settings in the Collisions section include:

Bounce   Controls how high the nParticles bounce off the surface. Think of the Ping-Pong balls hitting the granite table and the sofa. The sofa would have a much lower Bounce setting than the granite table.

Friction   A smooth surface has a much lower Friction setting than a rough one. nParticles will slide off a smooth surface more easily. If the sofa was made of suede, the friction would be higher than for the smooth granite table.

Stickiness   Pretty self explanatory—if the granite table were covered in honey, the Ping-Pong balls would stick to it more than to the sofa, even if the friction is lower on the granite table. The behavior of the nParticles sticking to the surface may be different if Collision Flag is set to Face than if it is set to Edge or Vertex.

9. Make sure that Collision Flag is set to Edge and that Bounce, Friction, and Stickiness are set to 0. Set Collision Thickness to 0.**05.**

10. Select the nParticle1 object, and open the Attribute Editor to the nParticleShape1 tab. Expand the Collisions rollout for the nParticle1 object. These control how the nParticles collide with collision objects in the scene.

11. Click on the Display Color swatch to open the Color Chooser, and pick a red color. Set Solver Display to Collision Thickness. Now the nParticles each have a red envelope around them. Changing the color of the display makes it easier to distinguish from the nRigid collision surface display.

12. Set Collide Width Scale to **0.25**. The envelope becomes a dot inside each nParticle. The nParticles have not changed size, but if you play the animation, you'll see that they fall through the space between the edges of the collision surface (see Figure 13.20).

FIGURE 13.20
Reducing the Collide Width Scale value of the nParticles causes them to fall through the spaces between the edges of the nRigid object.

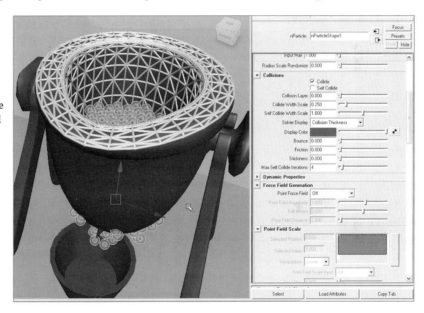

13. Scroll down to the Liquid Simulation tab and uncheck Enable Liquid Simulation. This makes it easier to see how the nParticles behave when self-collision is on. The Liquid Simulation settings alter the behavior of nParticles; this is covered later in the chapter.

14. Turn on Self Collide and set Solver Display to Self Collision Thickness.

15. Set Collide Width Scale to **1** and Self Collide Width Scale to **0.1**. Turn on wireframe view (hot key = 4) and play the animation; watch it from a side view.

The nParticles have separate Collision Thickness settings for collision surfaces and self-collisions. Self Collide Width Scale is relative to Collide Width Scale. Increasing Collide Width Scale also increases Self Collide Width Scale (see Figure 13.21).

FIGURE 13.21
Reducing the Self Collide Width Scale value causes the nParticles to overlap as they collide.

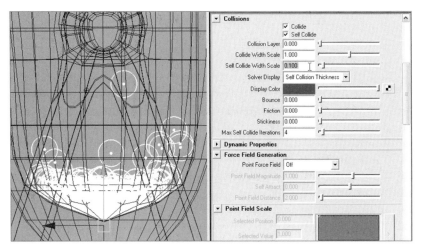

16. Scroll up to the Particle Size settings and adjust the Radius; set it to **0.8**. Both Collide Width Scale and Self Collide Width Scale are relative to the radius of the nParticles. Increasing the radius can cause the nParticles to pop out of the top of the tub.

17. Set Radius to **0.4** and Collide Width Scale to **1**, and turn off Self Collide. Turn Enable Liquid Simulation back on.

The nParticles also have their own Bounce, Friction, and Stickiness settings. The Max Self Collide Iterations slider sets a limit on the number of calculated self-collisions per substep when Self Collide is on. This keeps the nParticles from locking up or the system from slowing down too much. If you have a lot of self-colliding nParticles in a simulation, lowering this value can increase performance.

The Collision Layer setting sets a priority for collision events. If two nDynamic objects using the same Nucleus solver are set to the same Collision Layer value, they will collide normally. If they have different layer settings, those with lower values will receive higher priority. In other words, they will be calculated first in a chain of collision events. Both nCloth and passive objects will collide with nParticles in the same or higher collision layers. So if the passive collision object has a Collision Layer setting of 10, an nParticle with a Collision Layer setting of 3 will pass right through it, but an nParticle with a Collision Layer value of 12 won't.

18. Save the scene as **forge_v02.ma**. To see a version of the scene so far, open forge_v02.ma from the chapter13\scenes folder on the DVD.

Liquid Simulation

You can make nParticles simulate the behavior of fluids by enabling the Liquid Simulation attribute in the particle's shape node or by creating the nParticle as a water object. In this exercise you'll use a tub filled with nParticles. The tub will be animated to pour out the nParticles, and their behavior will be modified to resemble hot molten metal.

Creating Liquid Behavior

Liquid simulations have unique properties that differ from other styles of nParticle behavior. This behavior is actually amazingly easy to set up and control.

1. Continue with the scene from the last section or open the forge_v02.ma scene from the chapter13\scenes folder on the DVD. In this scene the tub has already been filled with particles, and collisions have been enabled.

2. Select nParticle1 in the Outliner and name it **moltenMetal**. Open its Attribute Editor to the moltenMetalShape tab. Expand the Liquid Simulation rollout (Figure 13.22).

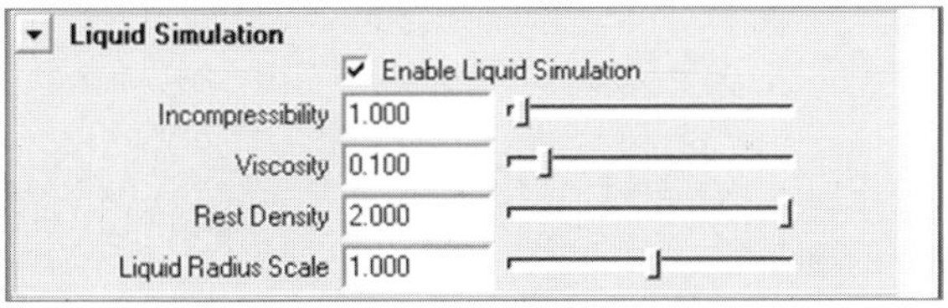

FIGURE 13.22

Turning on Enable Liquid Simulation causes the nParticles to behave like water.

Liquid simulation has already been enabled because the nParticle style was set to Water when the nParticles were created. If you need to remove the liquid behavior from the nParticle, you can uncheck the Enable Liquid Simulation checkbox; for the moment, leave the box checked.

3. Switch to a side view and turn on wireframe mode. Play the animation and observe the behavior of the nParticles.

If you look at the Collisions settings for moltenMetal, you'll see that the Self Collide attribute is off, but the nParticles are clearly colliding with each other. This type of collision is part of the liquid behavior defined by the Incompressibility attribute (this is discussed a little later in the chapter).

4. Play the animation back several times; notice the behavior when:

   Enable Liquid Behavior is off.

   Self Collide is on (set Self Collide Width Scale to **0.7**).

   Both Liquid Behavior and Self Collide are enabled.

5. Turn Liquid Behavior back on and turn Self Collide off. Open the Particle Size rollout, and set Radius to **0.25**; play the animation. There seems to be much less fluid for the same number of particles when the radius size is lowered.

6. Play the animation for about 140 frames until all the nParticles settle. With the moltenMetal shape selected, choose nSolvers ➤ Initial State ➤ Set From Current. Rewind and play the animation; the particles start out as settled in the well of the tub (see Figure 13.23).

7. Select moltenMetal. At the top of the Attribute Editor, uncheck Enable to temporarily disable the nParticle simulation so you can easily animate the tub.

8. Select tub1 in the Outliner and switch to the side view. Select the Move tool (hot key = w). Hold the d key on the keyboard, and move the pivot for tub1 so it's aligned with the center of the handles that hold it in the frame (see Figure 13.24).

FIGURE 13.23
Setting Initial
State makes the
nParticles start out
from their settled
position.

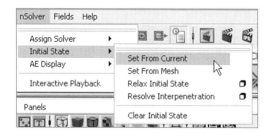

FIGURE 13.24
Align the pivot
point for the tub
group with the
handles from the
side view.

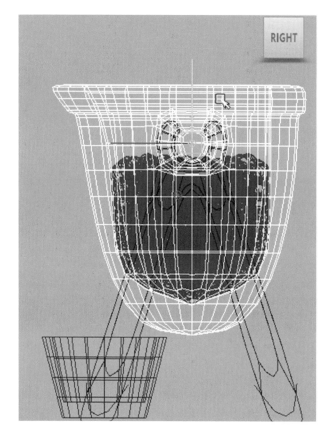

9. Set the timeline to frame 20. In the Channel Box, select the Rotate X channel for the tub1 group node, right-click, and set a keyframe.

10. Set the timeline to frame 100. Set the value of tub1's Rotate X channel to **85**, and set another key. Move the timeline to frame 180, and set another keyframe.

11. Set the timeline to 250, set Rotate X to 0, and set a fourth key.

12. Select moltenMetal, and in the Attribute Editor, check the Enable checkbox. Rewind the animation and play it. The nParticles pour out of the tub like water (see Figure 13.25).

FIGURE 13.25
When you animate the tub, the nParticles pour out of it like water.

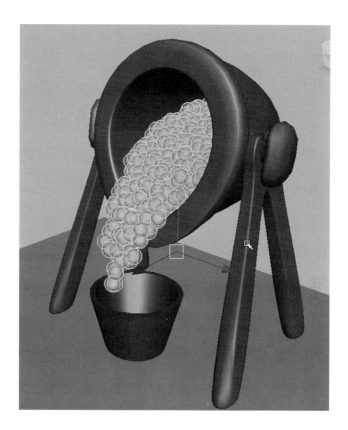

13. Switch to the perspective view. When you play the animation, the water goes through the bucket and the floor. Select the bucket and Choose nMesh ➤ Create Passive Collider. Switch to the nucleus1 tab and turn on Use Plane. Set the PlaneOrigin's Y Translate to **-4.11** to match the position of the floor. Now when you play the animation, the nParticles land in the bucket and on the floor.

SET THE COLLISION FLAG TO EDGE

You can improve the performance speed of the playback by selecting the nRigid node connected to the bucket and setting Collision Flag to Edge instead of Face.

---

14. By default the liquid simulation settings approximate the behavior of water. To create a more molten metal–like quality, increase Viscosity to 10. Viscosity sets the liquid's resistance to flow. Sticky, gooey, or oily substances have a higher viscosity.

VISCOSITY AND SOLVER SUBSTEPS

Increasing the number of substeps on the Nucleus solver will magnify viscosity.

---

15. Set Liquid Radius Scale to **0.5**. This sets the amount of overlap between nParticles when Liquid Simulation is enabled. Lower values create more overlap. By lowering this setting, the fluid looks more like a cohesive surface.

The other settings in the Liquid Simulation rollout can be used to alter the behavior of the liquid:

Incompressibility This setting determines the degree to which the nParticles resist compression. Most fluids use a low value (between 0.1 and 0.5). If you set this value to 0, all the nParticles will lie at the bottom of the tub in the same area, much like a nonliquid nParticle with Self Collide turned off.

Rest Density This sets the overlapping arrangement of the nParticles when they are at rest. It can affect how "chunky" the nParticles look when the simulation is running. The default value of 2 works well for most liquids, but compare a setting of 0.5 to a setting of 5. At 0.5 fewer nParticles overlap, and they flow out of the tub more easily than when Rest Density is set to 5.

16. To complete the behavior of molten metal, set Rest Density back to **2**, and set Incompressibility to **0.5**. In the Collisions rollout, set Friction to **0.5** and Stickiness to **0.25**. Expand the Dynamic Properties rollout and increase Mass to **6**. Note that you may want to reset the initial state after changing the settings because the nParticles will now collapse into a smaller area (see Figure 13.26).

17. Save the scene as **forge_v03.ma**. To see a version of the scene to this point, open forge_v03.ma from the chapter13\scenes folder.

FIGURE 13.26
Adjusting the settings under Liquid Simulation, Collisions, and Dynamic Properties makes the nParticles behave like a heavy, slow-moving liquid.

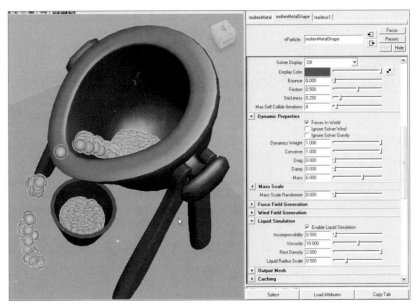

Converting nParticles to Polygons

Maya 2009 introduces a way to convert nParticles into a polygon mesh. The mesh updates with the particle motion to create a smooth blob or liquidlike appearance, which is perfect for rendering fluids. In this section, you'll convert the liquid nParticles created in the previous section into a mesh to make a more convincing molten metal effect.

1. Continue with the scene from the previous section or open the `forge_v03.ma` scene from the `chapter13\scenes` folder on the DVD.

2. Play the animation to about frame 160.

3. Select the moltenMetal object in the Outliner, and choose Modify ➤ Convert ➤ nParticle To Polygons (see Figure 13.27).

If you look at the particles, you'll see they are still there but a polygon mesh has been added to the scene. You can adjust the quality of this mesh in the Attribute Editor of the nParticle object used to generate the mesh.

4. Select the moltenMetal object in the Outliner, and open the Attribute Editor to the moltenMetalShape tab. Expand the Shading rollout and set Opacity to 0.

FIGURE 13.27
Converting an nParticle into a polygon creates a polygon mesh around the nParticle object.

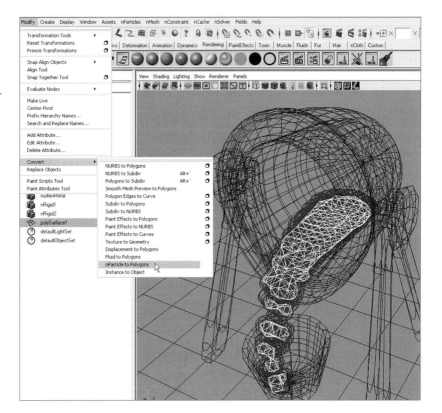

Lowering the opacity of the nParticles makes it easier to see the mesh. If you hide the nParticles or disable nParticles in the View menu of the viewport, the polygon mesh will not animate with the nParticles. The simulation has to be visible, so the easiest workaround is to make the nParticles completely transparent.

5. In the Render Stats section of the Attribute Editor, turn off all the checkboxes. This ensures that the nParticles are not seen in the render.

6. Expand the Output Mesh section. Set Threshold to **0.8** and Blobby Radius Scale to **1.8**.

These settings smooth the converted mesh. Higher Threshold settings create a smoother but thinner mesh; increasing Blobby Radius Scale does not affect the radius of the original nParticles. Rather it uses this value as a multiple to determine the size of the enveloping mesh around each nParticle. Using the Threshold and Blobby Radius Scale settings together you can fine-tune the look of the converted mesh.

7. Set Motion Streak to **0.5**. This stretches the mesh in areas where there is motion in the direction of the motion to create a more fluid-like behavior.

8. Mesh Triangle Size determines the resolution of the mesh. Lowering this value increases the smoothness of the mesh but also slows down the simulation. Set this value to **0.3** for now, as shown in Figure 13.28. Once you're happy with the overall look of the animation, you can set it to a lower value. This way the animation continues to update at a reasonable pace.

Max Triangle Resolution sets a limit on the number of triangles used in the nParticle Mesh. If the number is exceeded during the simulation, Max Triangle Size is raised automatically to compensate.

FIGURE 13.28
Adjust the quality of the mesh in the Output Mesh section of the nParticle's shape node attributes.

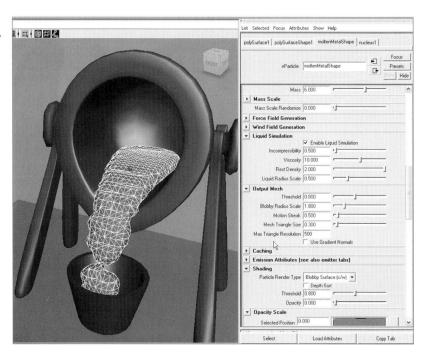

ADJUST MAX TRIANGLE SIZE NUMERICALLY

Be careful when using the slider for Mesh Triangle Size. It's easy to move the slider to a low value by accident, and then you'll have to wait for Maya to update, which can be frustrating. Use numeric input for this attribute, and reduce the value by 0.05 at a time until you're happy with the look of the mesh.

Use Gradient Normals smoothes the normals of the mesh.

Mesh Method determines the shape of the polygons that make up the surface of the mesh. The choices are Cubes, Tetrahedra, Acute Tetrahedra, and Quads. After setting the Mesh Method option, you can create a smoother mesh around the nParticles by increasing the Max Smoothing Iterations slider. For example, if you want to create a smoother mesh that uses four-sided polygons, set Mesh Method to Quads and increase the Max Smoothing Iterations slider. By default, the slider goes up to 10. If a value of 10 is not high enough, you can type values above 10 into the field.

Shading the nParticle Mesh

To create the look of molten metal you can use a simple Ramp shader as a starting point.

1. Select the polySurface1 node in the Outliner. Rename it **metalMesh**.

2. Right-click on the metalMesh object in the viewport. Use the pop-up menu to assign a ramp material. Choose Assign New Material ➤ Ramp Shader (see Figure 13.29).

FIGURE 13.29
Assign a Ramp shader to the metalMesh object.

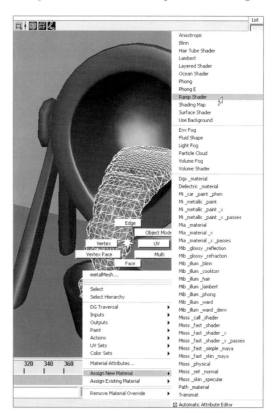

3. In the Common Materials Attributes section, set the Color Input to Facing Angle.

4. Click on the color swatch, and use the Color Chooser to pick a bright orange color.

5. Click on the right side of the ramp to add a second color. Make it a reddish orange.

6. Create a similar but darker ramp for the Incandescence channel.

RAMP SHADER COLOR INPUT SETTINGS

Each of the color channels that use a ramp will use the same Color Input setting as the Color rollout. So, in the case of this ramp, Incandescence will also use Facing Angle as the input.

---

7. Set Specularity to **0.24** and the specular color to a bright yellow. Raise the Glow intensity in the Special Effects rollout to **0.15**.

8. Back in the moltenMetal particle Attribute Editor, decrease the Mesh Triangle Size to **0.1** (it will take a couple minutes to update), and render a test frame using mental ray. Set the Quality preset in the Quality tab to Production.

9. Save the scene as **forge_v04.ma**. To see a version of the finished scene, open forge_v04.ma from the chapter13\scenes folder on the DVD (see Figure 13.30).

FIGURE 13.30
Render the molten metal in mental ray.

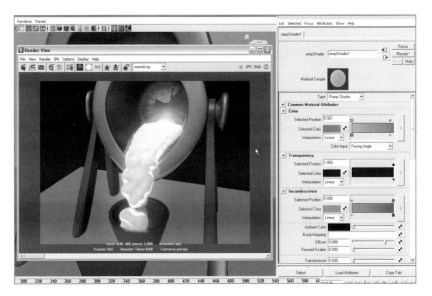

Texture Emission Attributes

The behavior of nParticles is often determined by their many dynamic properties. These control how the nParticles react to the settings in the Nucleus solver as well as fields, collision objects, and other nParticle systems. In the following section, you'll get more practice working with these settings.

If you have used standard particle systems in previous versions of Maya, you'll be pleased to see how Maya 2009 has streamlined the workflow for creating particle effects. Many of the attributes that required custom connections, expressions, and ramps are now automated.

Surface Emission

In this exercise you'll use nParticles to create the effect of flames licking the base of a space capsule as it reenters the atmosphere. You'll start by emitting nParticles from the base of the capsule and use a texture to randomize the generation of the nParticles on the surface.

1. Open the capsule_v01.ma scene from the chapter13\scenes directory on the DVD. You'll see a simple polygon capsule model. The capsule is contained in a group named space-Capsule. In the group there is another surface named capsule emitter. This will serve as the surface emitter for the flames (see Figure 13.31).

FIGURE 13.31
The capsule group consists of two polygon meshes. The base of the capsule has been duplicated to serve as an emitter surface.

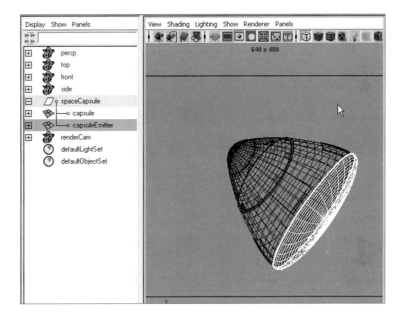

CREATING AN EMITTER SURFACE FROM A MODEL

The capsule emitter geometry was created by selecting the faces on the base of the capsule and duplicating them (Edit Mesh ➤ Duplicate Face). A slight offset was added to the duplicate face operation to move it away from the capsule surface. The idea is to have the nParticles generated by the bottom of the capsule. By creating an object separate from the bottom of the model, you can make the process much easier and faster.

---

2. Play the animation. The capsule has expressions that randomize the movement of the capsule to make it vibrate. The expressions are applied to the Translate channels of the group node. To see the Expressions, open the Expression Editor (Window ➤ Animation

Editors ➤ Expression Editor) and choose Select Filter ➤ By Expression Name. Select expression1, expression2, or expression3, and you'll see the expression in the box at the bottom of the editor (see Figure 13.32).

FIGURE 13.32
Create the vibration of the capsule using random function expressions applied to each of the translation channels of the capsule.

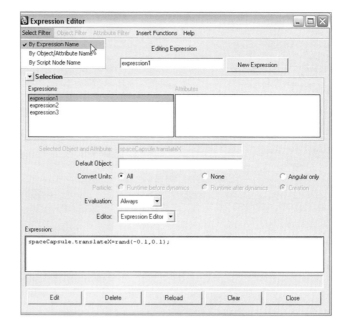

3. In the viewport, choose to look through the renderCam. The camera has been set up so the capsule looks as though it's entering the atmosphere at an angle.

4. In the Outliner, expand the spaceCapsule and choose the capsuleEmitter object. Switch to the nDynamics menu set and choose nParticles ➤ Create nParticles ➤ Points to set the nParticle style to Points.

5. Select the capsuleEmitter and choose nParticles ➤ Create nParticles ➤ Emit From Object ➤ Options. In the options, choose Edit ➤ Reset to clear any settings that remain from previous Maya sessions. Set Emitter Name to flameGenerator. Set Emitter Type to Surface and Rate to **150**. Leave the rest of the settings at the default, and click the Apply button to create the emitter.

6. Rewind and play the animation. The nParticles are born on the emitter and then start falling through the air. This is because the Nucleus solver has Gravity activated by default. For now this is fine; leave the settings on the Nucleus solver where they are.

To randomize the generation of the nParticles, you can use a texture. To help visualize how the texture creates the particles, you can apply it to the surface emitter.

7. Select the capsuleEmitter and open the UV Texture Editor. The base already has UVs projected on the surface.

8. Select the capsuleEmitter, right-click on the surface in the viewport, and use the pop-up menu to create a new Lambert texture (Assign New Material ➤ Lambert) for the capsuleEmitter surface. Name the shader **flameGenShader**.

9. Open the Attribute Editor for flameGenShader, and click on the checkered box to the right of the Color channel to create a new render node for color. In the Create Render Node window, click Ramp to create a ramp texture.

10. Open the Attribute Editor for the ramp (it should open automatically when you create the ramp). Name the ramp **flameRamp**. Make sure texture view is on in the viewport so you can see the ramp on the capsuleEmitter surface (hot key = 6).

11. Set the ramp's Type to Circular Ramp, and set Interpolation to None. Remove the blue color from the top of the ramp by clicking on the blue box at the right side at the top of the ramp. Click on the color swatch and use the Color Chooser to change the green color to white and then the red color to black.

12. Set Noise to **0.5** and Noise Freq to **0.3** to add some variation to the pattern (see Figure 13.33).

13. In the Outliner, select the nParticle node and hide it (hot key = Ctrl+h) so you can animate the ramp without having the nParticle simulation slow down the playback. Set the renderer to High Quality display.

FIGURE 13.33
Apply the ramp to the shader on the base capsuleEmitter object.

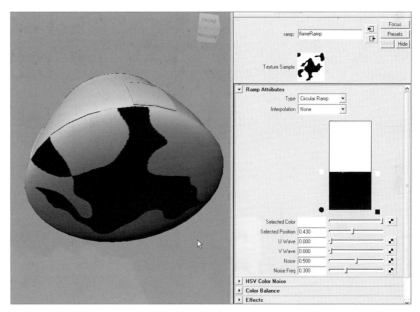

14. Select the flameRamp node and open it in the Attribute Editor (select the node by choosing it from the Textures area of the Hypershade). Rewind the animation and drag the white color marker on the ramp down toward the bottom. Its Selected Position should be at .05.

15. Right-click Selected Position and choose Set Key (see Figure 13.34).

FIGURE 13.34
Position the white color marker at the bottom of the ramp and keyframe it.

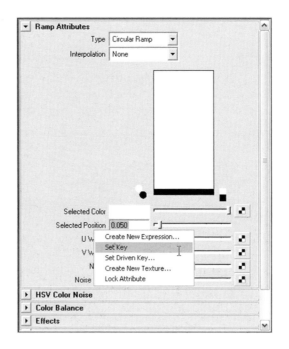

16. Set the timeline to frame 100, move the white color marker to the top of the ramp, and set another key.

17. Play the animation; you'll see the dark areas on the ramp grow over the course of 100 frames.

18. Open the Graph Editor (Window ➤ Animation Editors ➤ Graph Editor. Click the Select button at the bottom of the ramp's Attribute Editor to select the node; you'll see the animation curve appear in the Graph Editor. Select the curve, switch to the Insert Keys tool, and add some keyframes to the curve. Use the Move tool to reposition the keys to create an erratic motion to the ramp's animation (see Figure 13.35).

FIGURE 13.35
Add keyframes to the ramp's animation on the Graph Editor to make a more erratic motion.

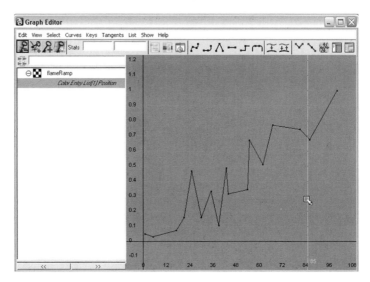

ANIMATE U WAVE AND V WAVE WITH EXPRESSIONS

To add some variation to the ramp's animation, you can animate the U and V Wave values or create an expression. In the U Wave field, type **=0.5+(0.5*noise(time));**. The noise(time) part of the expression creates a random set of values between -1 and 1 over time. Noise creates a smooth curve of randomness values as opposed to the rand function, which creates a discontinuous string of random values (as seen in the vibration of the capsule). By dividing the result in half and then adding 0.5, the range of values is kept between 0 and 1. To speed up the rate of the noise, multiply time by 5 so the expression is =0.5+(0.5*noise(time*5));. You can use an expression to make the V Wave the same as the U Wave; just type **=flameRamp.uWave;** in the field for the V Wave attribute. When you play the animation, you'll see a more varied growth of the color over the course of the animation.

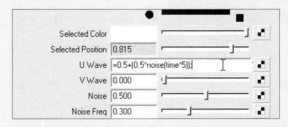

19. In the Outliner, select the capsuleEmitter node and expand it. Select the flameGenerator emitter node and open its Attribute Editor. Scroll to the bottom of the editor and expand Texture Emission Attributes.

20. Open the Hypershade to the Textures tab. MMB-drag flameRamp from the Textures area onto the color swatch for Texture Rate to connect the ramp to the emitter (see Figure 13.36). Select Enable Texture Rate and Emit From Dark.

21. Increase Rate to **2400**, unhide the nParticle1 node, and play the animation. You'll see that the nParticles are now emitted from the dark part of the ramp.

FIGURE 13.36
Drag the ramp texture with the middle mouse button from the Hypershade onto the Texture Rate color swatch to make a connection.

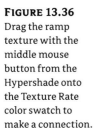

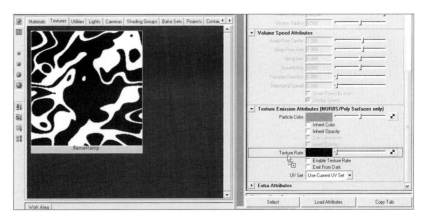

INHERIT COLOR AND OPACITY

You can make the particles inherit the color of the texture. To do this, first add a per-particle color (RGB PP) attribute to the particle, place the texture in the Particle Color color swatch, and then enable Inherit Color. You can do the same for Opacity, but you have to first add an OpacityPP attribute to the particle. To add a color or opacity attribute, expand the Add Dynamic Attributes rollout in the particle's shape tab, and click Opacity or Color. Then choose Add Per Particle from the pop-up window.

---

22. Select the capsuleEmitter shape and hide it. Save the scene as **capsule_v02.ma**. To see a version of the scene to this point, open capsule_v02.ma from the chapter13\scenes folder on the DVD.

23. Disable High Quality Renderer in the viewport to improve playback speed—make sure nParticles is enabled in the viewport's Show menu.

Using Wind

The Nucleus solver contains settings to create wind and turbulence. These can be used with nParticles to create snow blowing in the air, bubbles rising in water, or flames flying from a careening spacecraft.

The Wind Settings

Now that you have the basic settings for the particle emission, the next task is to make the particles flow upward rather than fall. You can do this using either an air field or the Wind settings on the Nucleus solver. Using the Wind settings on the Nucleus solver applies wind to all nDynamic nodes (nCloth, nRigid, nParticles) connected to the solver. For this section you'll use the Nucleus solver. We'll discuss fields later in this chapter.

1. Continue with the scene from the previous section or open the capsule_v02.ma file from the chapter13\scenes directory. Make sure High-Quality Rendering is disabled in the viewport in order to improve playback speed (nParticles should be enabled in the viewport's Show menu as well). Select the capsule emitter and hide it; this also improves performance.

2. Select the nParticle1 object. Rename it **flames**. Open the Attribute Editor and choose the nucleus1 tab.

3. Set Gravity to **0** and play the animation. The particles emerge from the base of the capsule and stop after a short distance. This is because by default the nParticles have a Drag value of 0.01 set in their Dynamic Properties settings.

4. Switch to the flamesShape tab, expand the Dynamic Properties rollout, and set Drag to **0**. Play the animation, and the nParticles emerge and continue to travel at a steady rate.

5. Switch back to the nucleus1 tab. Set the Wind Direction fields to 0, 1, 0 so the wind is blowing straight up along the Y axis. Set Wind Speed to **5** (see Figure 13.37). Play the animation—there's no change; the nParticles don't seem affected by the wind.

FIGURE 13.37
The settings for
the wind on the
nucleus tab

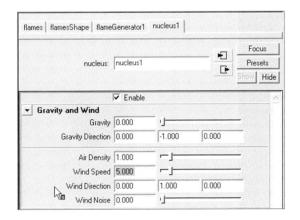

For the Wind settings in the Nucleus solver to work, the nParticle needs to have a Drag value, even a small one. This is why all the nParticle styles except Water have drag applied by default. If you create a Water-style particle and add a Wind setting, it won't affect the water until you set the Drag field above 0. Think of drag as a friction setting for the wind. In fact, the higher the Drag setting, the more the wind can grab the particle and push it along, so it actually has a stronger pull on the nParticle.

6. Set the Drag value to **0.01** and play the animation. The particles now emerge and then move upward through the capsule.

7. Switch to the nucleus1 tab; set Air Density to **5** and Wind Speed to **25**. The Air Density setting also controls, among other things, how much influence the wind has on the particles.

A very high air density acts like a liquid, and a high wind speed acts like a current in the water. It depends on what you're trying to achieve in your particular effect, but you can use drag or air density or a combination to set how much influence the Wind settings have on the nParticle. And of course another attribute to take into consideration is the particle's mass. Since these are flames, presumably the mass will be very low.

8. Set Air Density back to **1**. Play the animation. The particles start out slowly but gain speed as the wind pushes them along. Set the Mass attribute in the Dynamic Properties section to **0.01**. The particles are again moving quickly through the capsule (see Figure 13.38).

9. Switch to the nucleus1 tab and set Wind Noise to **10**. Because the particles are moving fast, Wind Noise needs to be set to a high value before there's any noticeable difference in the movement. Wind noise adds turbulence to the movement of the particles as they are pushed by the wind.

FIGURE 13.38

Set the Mass and Drag attributes to a low value, enabling the nParticle flames to be pushed by the wind on the Nucleus solver.

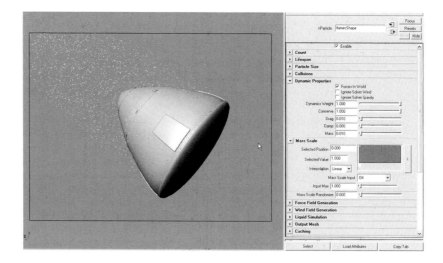

SOLVER SUBSTEPS

The Substeps setting on the Nucleus tab sets the number of times, per frame, the nDynamics are calculated. Increasing this value increases the accuracy of the simulation but also slows down performance. It can also change how some aspects of nDynamics behave. If you change the Substeps setting, you may need to adjust Wind Speed, Noise, Mass, and other settings.

---

10. To make the nParticles collide with the capsule, select the capsule node and choose nMesh ➢ Create Passive Collider. The nParticles now move around the capsule.

11. Select the nRigid1 node in the Outliner, and name it **flameCollide**.

12. Expand the Wind Field Generation settings in the flameCollideShape node. Set Air Push Distance to **0.5** and Air Push Vorticity to **1.5** (see Figure 13.39).

A passive object can generate wind as it moves through particles or nCloth objects to create the effect of air displacement. In this case, the capsule is just bouncing around, so the Air Push Distance setting helps jostle the particles once they have been created. If you were creating the look of a submarine moving through murky waters with particulate matter, the Air Push Distance setting could help create the look of the particles being pushed away by the submarine, and the Air Push Vorticity setting could create a swirling motion in the particles that have been pushed aside. In the case of the capsule animation, it adds more turbulence to the nParticle flames.

FIGURE 13.39

The Wind Field Generation settings on the flame-CollideShape node

▼	**Wind Field Generation**		
	Air Push Distance	0.500	
	Air Push Vorticity	1.500	
	Wind Shadow Distance	0.000	
	Wind Shadow Diffusion	0.000	

The Wind Shadow Distance and Diffusion settings block the effect of the Nucleus solver's Wind setting on nParticles or nCloth objects on the side of the passive object opposite the direction of the wind. The Wind Shadow Diffusion attribute sets the amount at which the wind curls around the passive object.

Air Push Distance is more processor intensive than Wind Shadow Distance, and the Maya documentation recommends that you do not combine Air Push Distance and Wind Shadow Distance.

nParticles have these settings as well. You can make an nParticle system influence an nCloth object using the Air Push Distance setting.

13. Save the scene as **capsule_v03.ma**. To see a version of the scene to this point, open capsule_v03.ma from the chapter13\scenes folder on the DVD.

Shading and Hardware Rendering nParticles

Shading and rendering nParticles has been made much easier in Maya 2009. Many of the color and opacity attributes that required manual connections are now automatically set up and can easily be edited using the ramp in the nParticle's Attribute Editor.

1. Continue with the same scene from the previous section or open capsule_v03.ma from the chapter13\scenes folder on the DVD.

2. Select the flames nParticle node in the Outliner, and open the Attribute Editor to the flamesShape node. Expand the Lifespan Attributes rollout, and set Lifespan to Random Range. Set Lifespan to **3** and Lifespan Random to **3**.

This setting makes the average lifespan for each nParticle 3 seconds with a variation of half the Lifespan Random setting in either direction. In this case the nParticles will live anywhere between 0.5 and 4.5 seconds.

3. Scroll down to the Shading rollout and expand it; set Particle Render Type to MultiStreak. This makes each nParticle a group of streaks and activates attributes specific to this render type.

4. Set Multi Count to **5**, Multi Radius to **0.8**, and Tail Size to **0.5** (see Figure 13.40).

FIGURE 13.40
Change Particle Render Type to MultiStreak to better simulate flames.

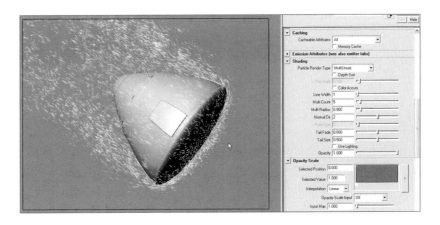

5. In the Opacity Scale section, set Opacity Scale Input to Age. Click on the right side of the Opacity Scale ramp curve to add an edit point. Drag this point down. This creates a ramp where the nParticle fades out over the course of its life (see Figure 13.41).

If you've used standard particles in older versions of Maya, you know that you normally have to create a per-particle Opacity attribute and connect it to a ramp. If you scroll down to the Per Particle Array Attributes section, you'll see that Maya has automatically added the Opacity attribute and connected it to the ramp curve.

FIGURE 13.41

The opacity and color ramps in the nParticle's attribute replace the need to connect ramps manually.

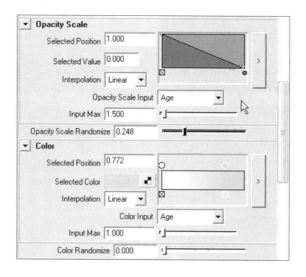

FLASHING NPARTICLE COLORS

If the opacity of your nParticles seems to be behaving strangely or the nParticles are flashing different colors, make sure that the renderer in the viewport is not set to High Quality Rendering. Setting it to Default Quality Rendering should fix the problem.

---

6. Set Input Max to **1.5**. This sets the maximum range along the X axis of the Opacity Scale ramp. Since Opacity Scale Input is set to Age, this means that each nParticle takes 1.5 seconds to become transparent, so the nParticles are visible for a longer period of time.

INPUT MAX VALUE

If the Input Max value is larger than the particle's lifespan, it will die before it reaches zero opacity, making it disappear rather than fade out. This is fine for flame effects, but you should be aware of this behavior when creating an effect. If Opacity Scale Input is set to Normalized Age, then Input Max has no effect.

7. To randomize the opacity scale for the opacity, set Opacity Scale Randomize to **0.5**.

8. Expand the Color rollout. Set Color Input to Age. Click on the ramp just to the right of the color marker to add a new color to the ramp. Click on the color swatch and change the color to yellow.

9. Add a third color marker to the right end of the ramp, and set its color to orange.

10. Set Input Max to **2** and Color Randomize to **0.8**.

11. In the Shading section, enable Color Accum. This creates an additive color effect, where denser areas of overlapping particles appear brighter.

12. Save the scene as **capsule_v04.ma**. To see a version of the scene to this point, open capsule_v04.ma from the chapter13\scenes folder on the DVD.

Creating an nCache

Before rendering it's always a good idea to create a cache to ensure that the scene renders correctly.

1. Continue with the scene from the previous section or open the capsule_v04.ma file from the chapter13\scenes folder on the DVD.

2. Set the timeline to 200 frames.

3. In the Outliner, expand the capsuleEmitter section, and select the flameGenerator emitter. Increase Rate (Particle/Sec) to **25,000**. This will create a much more believable flame effect.

4. Select the flames node in the Outliner. Switch to the nDynamics menu set, and choose nCache ➤ Create New Cache ➤ Options. In the options you can choose a name for the cache or use the default, which is the name of the selected node (flameShape in this example). You can also specify the directory for the cache, which is usually the project's data directory. Leave File Distribution set to One File Per Frame and Cache Time Range to Time Slider. Click Create to make the cache (see Figure 13.42).

FIGURE 13.42
The options for creating an nCache

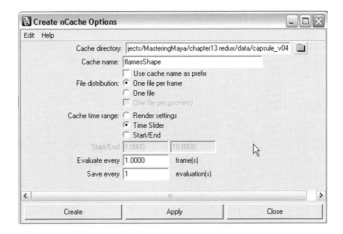

5. The scene will play through, and the cache file will be written to disk. It will take a fair amount of time to create the cache, anywhere from 5 to 10 minutes depending on the speed of your machine.

6. You can use the options in the nCache menu to attach an existing cache file to an nParticle or to delete, append, merge, or replace caches.

PARTICLE DISK CACHE

nParticles do not use the Particle Disk Cache settings in the Dynamics menu set. A normal Particle Disk Cache works only for standard particles. Create an nCache for nParticles and any other nDynamic system.

Using the Hardware Render Buffer

One of the fastest and easiest ways to render flames in Maya is to use the Hardware Render Buffer. The results may need a little extra tweaking in a compositing program, but overall it does a very decent job of rendering convincing flames. The performance of the Hardware Render Buffer depends on the type of graphics card installed in your machine. If you're using an Autodesk-approved graphics card, you should be in good shape.

THE HARDWARE RENDER BUFFER VERSUS MAYA HARDWARE

There are two ways to hardware render in Maya: You can use the Hardware Render Buffer, which takes a screenshot of each rendered frame directly from the interface, or you can batch render with Maya Hardware. Maya Hardware is chosen in the Render Settings window. The Hardware Render Buffer uses its own interface.

The Blobby Surface, Cloud, and Tube nParticle render styles can only be rendered using software (Maya Software or mental ray). All nParticle types can be rendered in mental ray, although the results may be different than those rendered using the Hardware Render Buffer or Maya Hardware.

NETWORK RENDERING WITH HARDWARE

If you are rendering using a farm, the render nodes on the farm may not have graphics cards, so using either the Hardware Render Buffer or Maya Hardware won't actually work. You'll have to render the scene locally.

---

1. To render using the Hardware Render Buffer choose Window ➤ Rendering Editors ➤ Hardware Render Buffer. A new window opens showing a wireframe display of the scene. Use the Cameras menu in the buffer to switch to the renderCam.

2. To set the render attributes in the Buffer, choose Render ≻ Attributes. The settings for the buffer appear in the Attribute Editor.

The render buffer renders each frame of the sequence and then takes a screengrab of the screen. It's important to deactivate screen savers and keep other interface or application windows from overlapping the render buffer.

3. Set Filename to **capsuleFlameRender** and Extension to name.0001.ext. Set Start Frame to **1** and End Frame to 200. Keep By Frame set to 1.

4. Keep Image Format set to Maya IFF. This file format is compatible with compositing programs like Adobe After Effects.

5. To change the resolution, you can manually replace the numbers in the Resolution field or click the Select button to choose a preset. Click this button and choose the 640 × 480 preset.

6. In the viewport window, you may want to turn off the display of the resolution or film gate. The view in the Hardware Render Buffer updates automatically.

7. Under Render Modes, turn on Full Image Resolution and Geometry Mask. Geometry Mask renders all the geometry as a solid black mask so only the nParticles will render. You can composite the rendered particles over a separate pass of the software-rendered version of the geometry.

8. To create the soft look of the frames, expand the Multi-Pass Render Options rollout. Enable Multi-Pass Rendering and set Render Passes to **36**. This means the buffer will take 36 snapshots of the frame and slightly jitter the position of the nParticles in each pass. The passes will then be blended together to create the look of the flame. For flame effects, this actually works better than the buffer's Motion Blur option. Leave Motion Blur at 0 (see Figure 13.43).

FIGURE 13.43
The settings for the Hardware Render Buffer

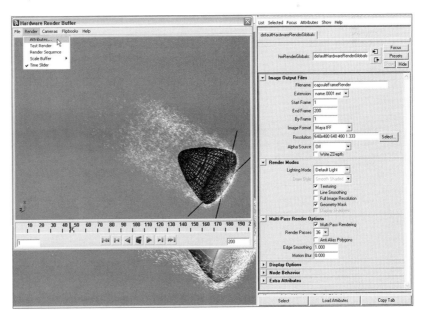

9. Play the animation to about frame 45. In the Hardware Render Buffer, click the clapboard icon to see a preview of how the render will look (see Figure 13.44). If you're happy with the look, choose Render ➤ Render Sequence to render out the 200-frame sequence. It should take five or ten minutes depending on your machine. You'll see the buffer render each frame.

10. When the sequence is finished, choose Flipbooks ➤ capsuleFlameRender1-200 to see the sequence play in FCheck.

11. Save the scene as **capsule_v05.ma**. To see a version of the scene to this point, open the capsule_v05.ma scene from the chapter13\scenes directory on the DVD.

FIGURE 13.44
When Geometry Mask is enabled, the Hardware Render Buffer renders only the nParticles.

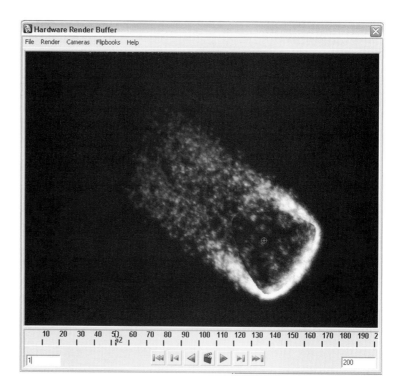

nParticles and Fields

The behavior of nParticles is most often controlled by using fields. There are three ways to generate a field for an nParticles system. You can connect one or more of the many fields listed in the Fields menu. These include Air, Gravity, Newton, Turbulence, Vortex, and Volume Axis Curve. You can use the fields built into the Nucleus solver—these are the Gravity and Wind forces that are applied to all nDynamic systems connected to the solver. And you can use the Force field and the Air Push fields that are built into nDynamic objects. In this section you'll experiment using all of these types of fields to control nParticles.

Using Multiple Emitters

When you create the emitter, an nParticle object is added and connected to the emitter. An nParticle can actually be connected to more than one emitter.

1. Open the generator_v01.ma scene in the chapter13\scenes folder on the DVD. You'll see a device built out of polygons. This will act as your experimental lab as you learn how to control nParticles with fields.

2. Switch to the nDynamics menu set, and choose nParticles ➤ Create nParticles ➤ Cloud to set the nParticle style to Cloud.

3. Choose nParticles ➤ Create nParticles ➤ Create Emitter ➤ Options. In the options, set Emitter Name to **energyGenerator**. Leave Solver set to Create New Solver. Set Emitter Type to Volume and Rate (Particles/Sec) to **200** (see Figure 13.45).

FIGURE 13.45
The settings for the volume emitter

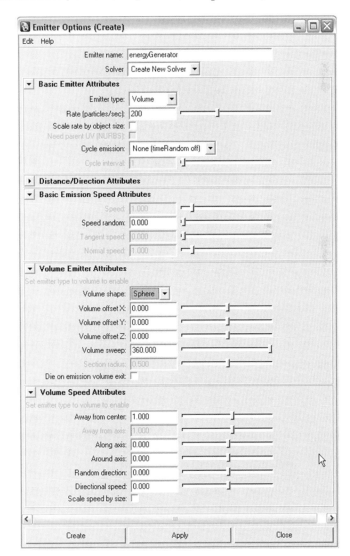

4. In the Volume Emitter Attributes rollout, set Volume Shape to Sphere. You can leave the rest of the settings at the default. Click Create to make the emitter.

5. Select the energyGenerator1 emitter in the Outliner. Use the Move tool (hot key = w) to position the emitter around one of the balls at the end of the generators in the glass chamber. You may want to scale it up to about 1.25 (Figure 13.46).

FIGURE 13.46
Place the volume emitter over one of the balls inside the generator device.

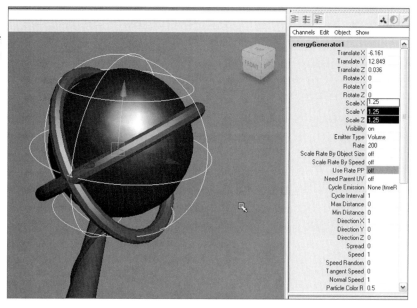

6. Set the timeline to 800, and play the animation. The nParticles are born and fly out of the emitter.

Notice that the nParticles do not fall even though Gravity is enabled in the Nucleus solver and the nParticle has a mass of 1. This is because in the Dynamic properties for the Cloud style of nParticle, the Ignore Solver Gravity checkbox is enabled.

7. Select the energyGenerator1 emitter and duplicate it (hot key = Ctrl+d). Use the Move tool to position this second emitter over the ball on the opposite generator.

If you play the animation, the second emitter creates no nParticles. This is because duplicating the emitter did not create a second nParticle object, but that's okay; you're going to connect the same nParticle object to both emitters.

8. Select nParticle1 and rename it **energy**. Select energy and choose Window ➤ Relationship Editors ➤ Dynamic Relationships. A window opens showing the objects in the scene; energy is selected on the left side. On the right side, click the Emitters radio button to switch to a list of the emitters in the scene. EnergyGenerator1 is highlighted, indicating that the energy nParticle is connected to it. Select energyGenerator2 so both emitters are highlighted (see Figure 13.47).

FIGURE 13.47
Use the Dynamic
Relationships Edi-
tor to connect the
energy nParticle to
both emitters.

9. Close the Dynamic Relationships Editor, and rewind and play the animation. You'll see both emitters now generate nParticles—the same nParticle object actually.

10. Select the energy object and open the Attribute Editor. Switch to the nucleus tab and set Gravity to **1**.

11. In the energyShape tab, expand the Dynamic Properties rollout and turn off Ignore Solver Gravity, so the energy nParticles slowly fall after they are emitted from the two generator poles (see Figure 13.48).

FIGURE 13.48
The energy nPar-
ticles are emitted
from both emit-
ters. Gravity is
set to a low value,
causing the nPar-
ticles to slowly fall.

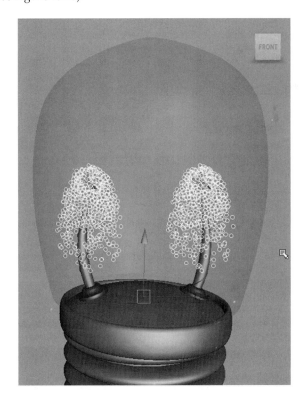

Volume Axis Curve

The volume axis curve is a new type of dynamic field that has been added to Maya 2009. You can use this field with any of the dynamic systems (traditional and nDynamic) in Maya. In this section you'll perform some tricks using the field inside a model of an experimental vacuum chamber.

1. Select the energy nParticle node in the Outliner. In the Attribute Editor, open the Lifespan rollout, and set the Lifespan mode to Random Range. Set Lifespan to **6** and Lifespan Random to **4**. The nParticles will now live between 4 and 8 seconds each.

2. With the energy nParticle selected, choose Fields ➢ Volume Curve. By creating the field with the nParticle selected, the field is automatically connected.

DYNAMIC RELATIONSHIP EDITOR

You can use the Dynamic Relationship Editor to connect fields to nParticles and other dynamic systems. Review the previous section on using multiple emitters to see how the Dynamic Relationship Editor works.

---

3. Select curve1 in the Outliner, and use the Move tool to position it between the generators. The field consists of a curve surrounded by a tubular field.

4. Use the Show menu to disable the display of polygons so the glass case is not in the way. Select curve1 in the Outliner and right-click on the curve; choose CVs to edit the curve's control vertices. Use the Move tool to position the CVs at the end of the curve inside each generator ball. Use the Move tool to add some bends to the curve (see Figure 13.49).

5. Rewind and play the animation. A few of the nParticles will be pushed along the curve. So far, it's not very exciting.

FIGURE 13.49
Position the CVs of the Volume Axis curve to add bends to the curve. The field surrounds the curve, forming a tube.

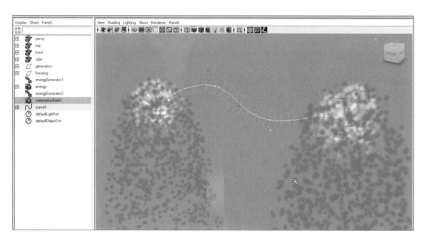

6. Select the volumeAxisField1 node in the Outliner, and open its Attribute Editor. Use the following settings:

The default Magnitude and Attenuation settings (5 and 0) are fine for the moment.

Leave Use Max Distance off.

In the Volume Control Attributes rollout, set Section Radius to **3**.

Set Trap Inside to **0.8**. This keeps most of the nParticles inside the area defined by the volume radius (the Trap Inside attribute is available for other types of fields such as the Radial field).

Leave Trap Radius set to 2. This defines the radius around the field within which the nParticles are trapped.

Edit the Axial Magnitude ramp so each end is at about 0.5 and the middle is at 1, as in Figure 13.50. Set the Interpolation of each point to Spline. This means that the area at the center of the curve has a stronger influence on the nParticles than the areas at either end of the curve.

Edit the Curve Radius ramp, add some points to the curve, and drag them up and down in a random jagged pattern. You'll see the display of the field update; this creates an interesting shape for the curve.

In the Volume Speed Attributes rollout, set Away From Axis and Along Axis to **0**, and set Around Axis to **4**. This means that the nParticles are pushed in a circular motion around the curve rather than along or away from it. If you zoom into the field, you'll see an arrow icon at the end of the field indicating its direction. Positive numbers make the field go clockwise; negative numbers make it go counterclockwise.

Set Turbulence to **3** and leave Turbulence Speed at 0.2. This adds noise to the field, causing some nParticles to fly off (see Figure 13.50).

7. Play the animation. You'll see the nParticles move around within the field. Faster-moving particles fly out of the field.

FIGURE 13.50
The settings for the Volume Axis Curve field

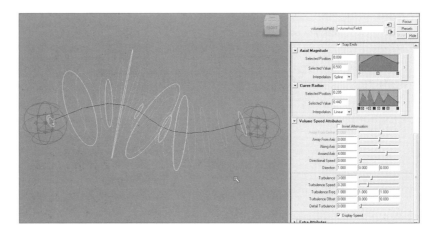

This is interesting, but it can be improved to create a more dynamic look.

8. In the Attribute Editor for the Volume Axis Curve field, remove the edit points from the Curve Radius ramp. Edit the curve so it has three points. The points at either end should have a value of 1; the point at the center should have a value of 0.1.

9. Select the edit point at the center, and in the Selected Position field type **=0.5+(0.5* (noise(time*4)));**. This is similar to the expression that was applied to the ramp in the "Surface Emission" section of this chapter. In this case, it moves the center point back and forth along the curve, creating a moving shape for the field (see Figure 13.51).

10. Save the scene as **generator_v02.ma**. To see a version of the scene to this point, open the generator_v02.ma scene from the chapter13\scenes folder on the DVD.

FIGURE 13.51
Create an expression to control the Selected Position attribute of the Curve Radius ramp's center point. The numeric field is not large enough to display the entire expression.

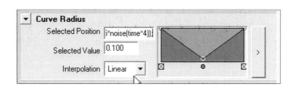

USING A DYNAMIC HAIR CURVE WITH A VOLUME AXIS CURVE

For an even more dynamic look, you can animate the curve itself using hair dynamics. Hair is discussed in Chapter 15, but here is a quick walk-though of how to set this up. In addition to making the volume curve dynamic, this workflow demonstrates how to change the input curve source for the volume curve:

1. Select the curve1 object in the Outliner. Switch to the Dynamics menu set and choose Hair ➤ Make Selected Curves Dynamic.

2. Open the Attribute Editor for the hairsystem1 node, and switch to the hairSystem-Shape1 tab.

3. In the Dynamics rollout, set Stiffness to **0** and Length Flex to **0.5**. Set Gravity to **0**, Turbulence Intensity to **4**, Turbulence Frequency to **2**, and Turbulence Speed to **1.5**.

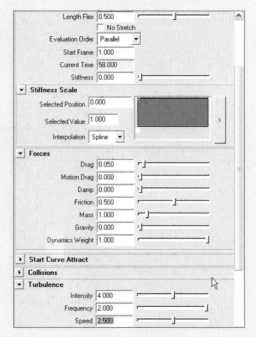

4. If you play the animation, you'll see two curves; the original Volume Axis curve is unchanged, but a second curve is now moving dynamically. You need to switch the input curve for the Volume Axis curve from the original curve to the Dynamic Hair curve.

5. In the Outliner, expand the hairSystem1OutputCurves group, and select the curveShape2 node. Open the Connection Editor (Window ➤ General Editors ➤ Connection Editor). The curveShape2 node should be loaded on the left side.

6. In the Outliner, select the VolumeAxisField1 and click Reload Right on the Connection Editor. Select worldSpace from the list on the left and inputCurve from the list on the right to connect the Dynamic Hair curve to the Volume Axis field.

7. Play the animation; the Volume Axis field now animates in a very dynamic way. This technique can be used to swap any curve you create for the input of the Volume Axis field.

You can use the Hypergraph to view connections between nodes. In your own animations, you may need to do some detective work to figure out how to make connections like this. If you graph the Volume Axis field in the Hypergraph, you can hold your mouse over the connection between curveShape1 and the Volume Axis field to see how the worldSpace attribute of the curve is connected to the input curve of the field. It's a simple matter of making the same connection between the shape node of a different curve to the Volume Axis field to replace the input curve for the field.

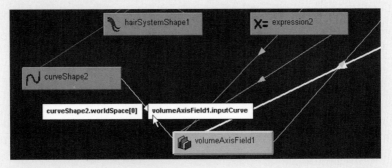

Working with hair curves is discussed in detail in Chapter 16.

Real World Scenario

ANIMATING BLOOD CELLS

Blood cells flowing through a tubular-shaped blood vessel are a common challenge facing many animators. In previous versions of Maya, the solution has been to use the Curve Flow Effect, which uses a series of goals, or emitters, placed along the length of a curve. With the introduction of the Volume Axis curve in Maya 2009, the solution to this animation problem is much easier to set up and edit.

To create this effect:

1. Add an omni emitter and an nParticle to a scene using the Water nParticle style.

2. Draw a curve that defines the shape of the blood vessel.

3. Extrude a NURBS circle along the length of the curve to form the outside walls of the vessel.

4. Place the emitter inside the blood vessel at one end of the curve.

5 Select the nParticle and add a Volume Axis Curve field.

6. Use the Connection Editor to attach the worldSpace attribute of the blood vessel curve's shape node to the inputCurve attribute of the Volume Axis Curve.

7. In the Volume Axis field's attributes, set Trapped to **1**, and define the trapped radius so it fits within the radius of the vessel.

8. Adjust the Along Axis and Around Axis attributes until the nParticles start to flow along the length of the curve.

9. Adjust the Drag attribute of the nParticles to adjust the speed of the flow.

10. Set the lifespan of the nParticles so they die just before reaching the end of the blood vessel.

You can use the Blobby Surface render type to make the nParticles look like globular surfaces or try instancing modeled blood cells to the nParticles. Instancing is covered in Chapter 14.

Working with Force Fields

nParticles, nCloth, and passive collision objects (also known as nRigids) can all emit force fields that affect themselves and other nDynamic systems attached to the same nucleus node. In this example, the surface of the glass that contains the particle emitters will create a field that controls the nParticle's behavior.

1. Continue with the scene from the previous section or open the generator_v02.ma scene from the chapter13\scenes folder on the DVD.

2. Expand the Housing group in the Outliner. Select the dome object and choose nMesh ➤ Create Passive Collider. In the Outliner, rename the nRigid1 node **domeCollider**.

3. To keep the particles from escaping the chamber, you'll also need to convert the seal and base objects to passive collision objects. Select the seal object and choose nMesh ➤ Create Passive Collider. Name the new nRigid node **sealCollide**. Do the same for the base and name it **baseCollide**.

FIGURE 13.52
Parts of the generator device are converted to collision objects, trapping the nParticles inside.

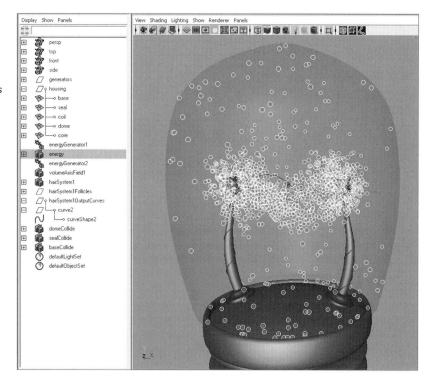

FIGURE 13.52
Parts of the generator device are converted to collision objects, trapping the nParticles inside.

4. Play the animation. As some of the nParticles are thrown from the Volume Axis field, they are now contained within the glass chamber (see Figure 13.52).

5. Open the settings for the energyShape node in the Attribute Editor. Set Radius Scale Input to Age. Edit the Radius Scale ramp so it slopes up from 0 on the left to 1 in the middle and back down to 0 on the left. Set Input Max to **3** and Radius Scale Randomize to **0.5** (see Figure 13.53).

6. Select the domeCollide node, and open the Attribute Editor to the domeCollideShape tab. Expand the Force Field Generation settings, and set Force Field to Single Sided. This generates a force field based on the positive normal direction of the collision surface.

FIGURE 13.53
Edit the Radius Scale settings to create a more randomized radius for the nParticles.

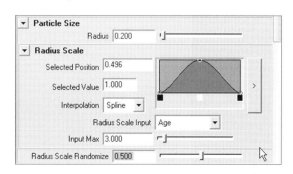

Along Normal generates the field along the surface normals of the collision object. In this case the difference between Along Normal and Single Sided is not noticeable. Double Sided generates the field based on both sides of the collision surface.

7. The normals for the dome shape are actually pointing outward. You can see this if you choose Display ➤ Polygons ➤ Face Normals. To reverse the surface, switch to the Polygons menu set and choose Normals ➤ Reverse (see Figure 13.54).

8. Set Field Magnitude to **100** and Field Distance to **4**, and play the animation. The particles are repelled from the sides of the dome when they are within four field units of the collision surface. A lower field magnitude will repel the particles with a weaker force, allowing them to collide with the dome before being pushed back to the center. If you set Magnitude to **1000**, the nParticles never reach the collision surface.

9. Set Field Magnitude to **-100**. The nParticles are now pulled to the sides of the dome when they are within four field units of the collision surface, much like a magnet. Setting a negative value of -1000 causes them to stick to the sides.

10. The Field Scale Edit ramp controls the strength of the field within the distance set by the Field Distance value. The right side of the ramp is the leading edge of the field—in this case four field units in from the surface of the dome. The left side represents the scale of the force field on the actual collision surface.

FIGURE 13.54
Reverse the normals for the dome surface so they point inward.

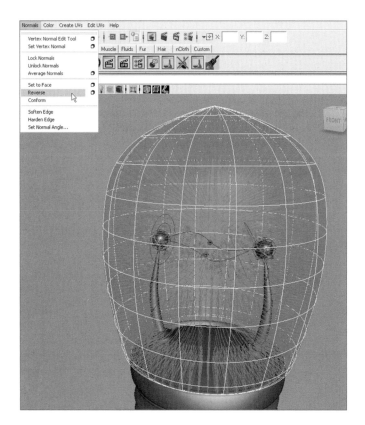

You can create some interesting effects by editing this curve. If Field Magnitude is at a value of -100 and you reverse the curve, the nParticles are sucked to the dome quickly when they are within four units of the surface. However, they do not stick very strongly to the side, so they bounce around a little within the four-unit area. Experiment creating different shapes for the curve, and see how it affects the behavior of the nParticles. By adding variation to the center of the curve, you get more of a wobble as the nParticle is attracted to the surface.

11. Save the scene as **generator_v03.ma**. To see a version of the scene to this point, open the generator_v03.ma scene from the chapter13\scenes folder on the DVD.

Painting Field Maps

The strength of the force field can be controlled by a texture. The texture itself can be painted onto the collision surface.

1. Continue with the scene from the previous section or open the generator_v03.ma scene from the chapter13\scenes folder on the DVD.

2. In the Attribute Editor for domeCollide, set the Field Scale ramp so it's a straight line across the top of the curve editor. Set Field Magnitude to **1**.

3. Select the dome object and choose nMesh ➢ Paint Texture Properties ➢ Field Magnitude. The dome turns white, and the Artisan Brush tool is activated.

4. Open the tools options for the Artisan Brush. The color should be set to black, and Paint Operation should be set to Paint. Use the brush to paint a pattern on the surface of the dome. Make large, solid lines on the surface; avoid blurring the edges so the end result is clear (see Figure 13.55).

FIGURE 13.55
Use the Artisan Brush tool to paint a pattern for the field magnitude on the collision surface.

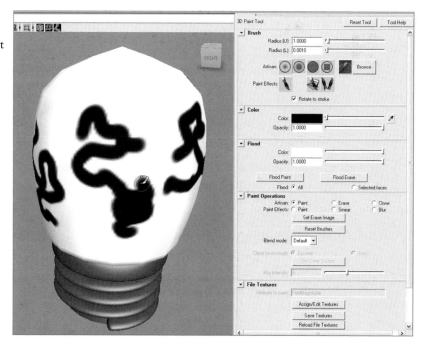

5. When you've finished, click the Select tool in the toolbox to close the Artisan Brush options. Open the Hypershade. In the Textures tab, you'll see the texture map you just created. You can also use file textures or even animated sequences for the map source.

6. Select the dome in the scene. In the Work Area of the Hypershade, right-click and choose Graph ➤ Graph Materials On Selected Objects. MMB-drag the file1 texture from the texture area of the Hypershade down onto the shader, and choose Color. Connecting the texture to the color does not affect how the field works, but it will help you to visualize how the map works (see Figure 13.56).

FIGURE 13.56
Connect the newly painted texture to the color of the dome shader.

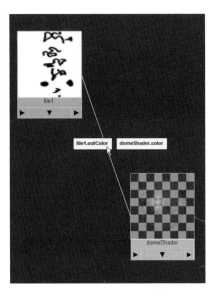

7. If you play the animation, you won't see much of a result. The reason is that the values of the map are too weak and the movement of the nParticles is too fast to be affected by the field.

8. In the Hypershade, select the file1 texture and open its Attribute Editor. The outAlpha of the texture is connected to the field magnitude of the collision surface. You can see this when you graph the network in the Hypershade. To increase the strength of the map, expand the Color Balance section. Set Alpha Gain to **1000** and Alpha Offset to **-500**. Chapter 2 has a detailed explanation of how the Alpha Gain and Alpha Offset attributes work. Essentially this means that the light areas of the texture cause the force field magnitude to be at a value of 500, and the dark areas cause it to be at -500.

9. Play the animation. You'll see that most of the nParticles stay in the center of the dome, but occasionally one or two nParticles will fly out and stick to the side. They stick to the areas where the texture is dark (see Figure 13.57).

TEXTURE MAPS FOR DYNAMIC ATTRIBUTES

You can create texture maps for other attributes of the collision surface, including stickiness, friction, bounce, and collision thickness.

FIGURE 13.57
The painted force field texture causes most of the nParticles to remain hovering around the center, but a few manage to stick to the dark areas.

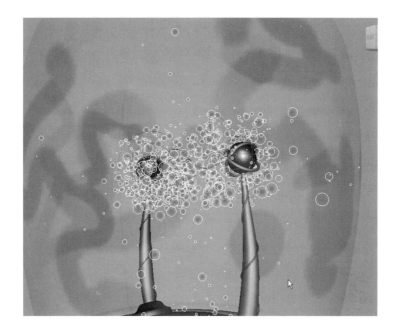

Vertex maps assign values to the vertices of the surface using the colors painted by the brush; texture maps use a file texture. One may work better than the other depending on the situation. You can paint vertex maps by choosing nMesh ➤ Paint Vertex Properties. In the Map properties, set Map Type to Vertex or Texture, depending on which one you are using.

When using a texture or vertex map for the force field, the Force Field Magnitude setting acts as a multiplier for the strength of the map.

10. Back in the domeCollide node, set Field Magnitude to **10** and play the animation. You'll see more nParticles stick to the surface where the texture has been painted.

11. To smooth their motion, you can adjust the Field Scale ramp.

12. Save the scene as **generator_v04.ma**. To see a version of the scene to this point, open generator_v04.ma from the chapter13\scenes folder on the DVD.

Using Dynamic Fields

The traditional set of dynamic fields is found in the Fields menu. They have been included as part of Maya since version 1.

Fields such as Air and Gravity are similar to the wind and gravity forces that are part of the Nucleus system. But that is not to say you can't use them in combination with the Nucleus forces to create a specific effect.

Drag is similar to the Drag attribute of nParticles; it applies a force that in some cases slows an nParticle down; in other cases it actually pulls the nParticle in a direction determined by the force. You can use the Inherit Transform slider on the Drag field to create wakelike effects in a cloud of particles, similar to the wind field generation on nDynamic objects.

Radial fields are similar to force fields emitted by nRigids and nParticles; they push or pull particles, depending on their Magnitude settings.

A Uniform force is similar to Gravity because it pushes a particle in a particular direction. The Volume Axis field is similar to the Volume Axis curve used earlier in the chapter. It has a built-in turbulence and affects particles within a given volume shape (by default).

ATTENUATION AND MAX DISTANCE IN DYNAMIC FIELDS

Attenuation with dynamic fields can be a little difficult to wrap your head around when you start using fields with dynamic simulations because many fields have both Attenuation and a Max Distance falloff curve, which, at first glance, appear to do very similar things.

Using traditional Maya particles, the exercise in this sidebar illustrates how Attenuation and Max Distance work on particles. Their effect is the same when used on nParticle systems.

The Maya documentation defines Attenuation with regard to an air field as a value that "sets how much the strength of the field diminishes as distance to the affected object increases. The rate of change is exponential with distance; the Attenuation is the exponent. If you set Attenuation to 0, the force remains constant over distance. Negative numbers are not valid." Before you break out the calculator, you can get a visual guide of how Attenuation affects the application of a field by using the Show Manipulators tool on a field. Try this experiment:

1. Start a new scene in Maya.

2. Switch to the nDynamics menu set, and choose Create nParticles ➢ nParticle Tool ➢ Options. In the options, select the Create Particle Grid checkbox and With Text Fields under Placement.

3. In the Placement options set the Minimum Corner X, Y, and Z values to -10, 0, -10 and the Maximum Corner X, Y, and Z to 10, 0,10. Press Enter on the numeric keypad to make the grid.

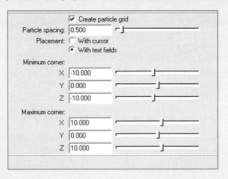

4. Select the grid and choose Fields ➢ Air. An air field is placed at the center of the grid.

5. Select the air field and open the Attribute Editor. You'll see that the air field is at the default settings where Magnitude is 4, the air field is applied along the Y axis (Direction = 0, 1, 0), and Attenuation is set to 1. Under the Distance settings, Use Max Distance is on, and Max Distance is set to 20.

6. Play the animation, and you'll see the grid move upward; the strength of the air field is stronger at the center than at the edges, creating a semi-spherical shape as the particles move up. You may need to extend the length of the timeline to something like 500 frames to see the motion of the particles.

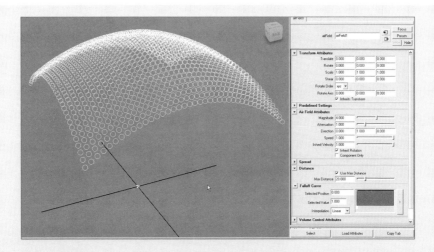

4. Rewind the animation, turn Use Max Distance off, and play the animation again. Now the entire grid moves uniformly. For air fields, Attenuation has no effect when Use Max Distance is off.

5. Rewind the animation. Turn Use Max Distance back on. Select the air field, and choose the Show Manipulator tool from the toolbox.

6. Drag the blue dot connected to the attenuation manipulator handle in toward the center of the manipulator, and play the animation. You'll see that the shape of the field resembles the attenuation curve on the manipulator.

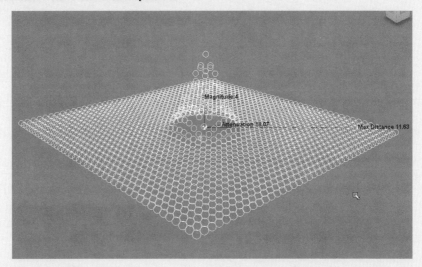

7. If you turn off Use Max Distance, you'll see the Attenuation slider flatten out as it no longer has an effect on the field.

CONTINUES

ATTENUATION AND MAX DISTANCE IN DYNAMIC FIELDS *(CONTINUED)*

8. Turn Use Max Distance on, and set Attenuation to 0. In the Attribute Editor, find the falloff curve for the air field. Click at the top-left corner of the falloff curve to add a control point. Drag the new control point downward, and play the animation. The falloff curve appears to work much like Attenuation. You can create interesting shapes in the field motion by adding and moving points on the falloff curve, and you can also change the interpolation of the points on the curve.

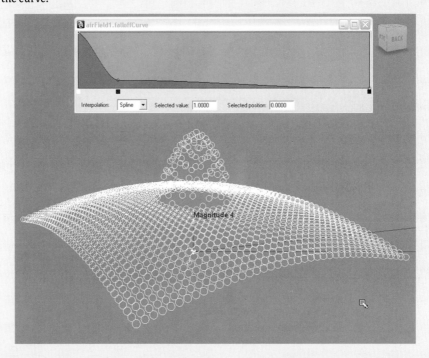

The difference between Attenuation and the Max Distance falloff curve is often subtle in practice. Think of it this way: Attenuation affects how the force of the field is applied; the falloff curve defines how the maximum distance is applied to the force. It's a little easier to see when you lower the Conserve value of the nParticle. By default Conserve is at 1, meaning that particles do not lose any energy or momentum as they travel. Lowering the Conserve even a little (say a value of 0.95) causes the nParticle to lose energy or momentum as it travels; the effect is that the nParticle slows down when it reaches the boundary of the force. In practice the best approach is to set Attenuation to 0 when you first apply the field to a particle system and then adjust Attenuation and/or the Max Distance setting and falloff until you get the behavior you want.

Some fields have unique properties that affect how they react to Attenuation settings. With some fields, such as Turbulence, the Attenuation attribute will affect the dynamic simulation even when Use Max Distance is off. Once again, it's a good idea to start with Attenuation at 0 and then add it if needed.

The behavior of Attenuation and Max Distance is the same for both nDynamic systems and traditional Maya dynamics.

The Turbulence field creates a noise pattern, and the Vortex field creates a swirling motion. Newton fields create a Newtonian attraction to dynamic objects.

1. Open the generator_v04 scene from the chapter13\scenes folder on the DVD.

2. Select the energy nParticle object and choose Fields ➢ Turbulence to connect a Turbulence field to the nParticle.

3. In the Attribute Editor for the Turbulence field, set Magnitude to **100**, Attenuation to **0**, and Frequency to **0.5**.

4. Attach a Vortex field to the energy nParticle. By default the vortex travels around the Y axis, which works well for this scene. Set the Magnitude of the vortex to **25** and the Attenuation to **0.5**.

5. To see the particles behave properly, you'll probably want to create a playblast. Set the timeline to 300, and choose Window ➢ playblast. A flip book will be created and played in FCheck. For more about creating playblasts, consult Chapter 4.

6. Save the scene as **generator_v05.ma**. To see a version of the scene to this point, open generator_v05.ma from the chapter13\scenes folder on the DVD.

Rendering Particles with mental ray

All particle types can be rendered using mental ray software rendering, and particles will appear in reflections and refractions. In this section you'll see how easy it is to render different nParticle types using mental ray.

Setting nParticle Shading Attributes

In this exercise you'll render the nParticles created in the generator scene.

1. Open the generator_v05.ma scene from the chapter13\scenes folder on the DVD.

2. Select the energy nParticle node in the Outliner, and open its Attribute Editor to the energyShape1 tab.

3. Expand the Shading attributes in the bottom of the editor. Set Opacity to **0.8**.

4. Set Color Input to Age. Make the left side of the ramp bright green and the right side a slightly dimmer green.

5. Set Incandescence Input to Age. Edit the ramp so the far-left side is white followed closely by bright green. Make the center a dimmer green and the right side completely black (see Figure 13.58).

6. Select each of the emitter nodes, and raise the Rate value to **1000**.

7. Select the domeShader node in the Hypershade, and break the connection between the color and the file texture (don't delete the file texture—it still controls the force field magnitude). Set the color of the domeShader to a dark gray.

8. Play the animation for about 80 frames. Open the render settings, and set the renderer to mental ray. In the Quality tab, set the Quality preset to Production.

FIGURE 13.58
The shading attributes for the energy nParticle

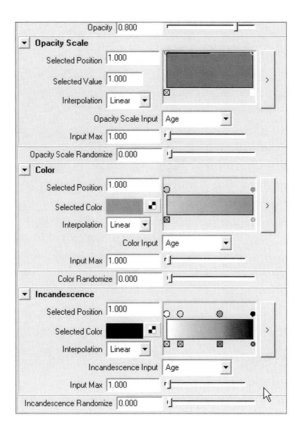

9. Select the energy nParticle, and in the Render Stats section of the energyShape tab, check the boxes for Visible in Reflections and Refractions.

10. Create a test render of the scene. You can see in the glass of the chamber and the metal base that the nParticles are reflected. Open the Hypershade and select the metal shader. Increase Reflectivity in the Attribute Editor to **0.8**. The nParticles are more visible in the reflection on the base (see Figure 13.59).

11. Select the dome shader, and in its Attribute Editor under Raytrace Options, activate Refractions and set the Refractive Index to **1.2**. Under the Specular Shading rollout, increase Reflectivity to **0.8**. Create another test render. You can see the effect refraction has on the nParticles.

You can render the point, multipoint, streak, and multiStreak render types using mental ray. They will appear in reflections and refractions as well; however, you'll notice that in the Render Stats section for these nParticle types, the options for Reflections and Refractions are unavailable.

12. In the Hypershade select the npCloudVolume shader. This shader is created with the nParticle. Graph the network in the Hypershade Work Area (see Figure 13.60).

FIGURE 13.59
The nParticles are visible in reflections on the surfaces.

FIGURE 13.60
Shaders are automatically created for the nParticles. The particleSamplerInfo node connects the attributes of the nParticle to the shader.

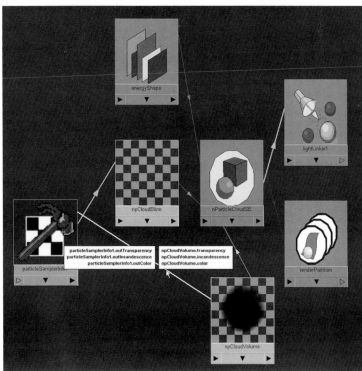

You can see that a particleSampler node is automatically connected to the volume shader. This node transfers the settings you create in the nParticle's Attribute Editor for color, opacity, and transparency to the shader. An npCloudBlinn shader is also created. This shader is applied when you switch the Particle Type to Points. You can further refine the look of the nParticles by adjusting the settings in the npCloudVolume shaders Attribute Editor.

You can add a shader glow to the particles by increasing Glow Intensity in the npCloudVolume shader; however, the glow does not appear behind refractive surfaces with standard Maya shaders.

13. When you are happy with the look of the render, you can create an nCache for the energy nParticle and render the sequence using mental ray.

14. Save the scene as **generator_v06.ma**. To see a finished version of the scene, open the generator_v06.ma file from the chapter13\scenes directory.

The Bottom Line

Create nParticles.   nParticles can be added to a scene in a number of ways. They can be drawn using the tool or spawned from an emitter, or they can fill an object.

Master it   Create a spiral shape using nParticles.

Make nParticles collide.   NParticles can collide with themselves, other nParticles, and polygon surfaces.

Master it   Make nParticles pop out of the top of an animated volume.

Create liquid simulations.   Enabling Liquid Simulations changes the behavior of nParticles so they act like water or other fluids.

Master it   Create a flowing stream of nParticles that ends in a waterfall.

Emit nParticles from a texture.   The emission rate of an nParticle can be controlled using a texture.

Master it   Create your own name in nParticles.

Move nParticles with nucleus wind.   The wind force on the nucleus node can be used to push nParticles.

Master it   Create the effect of bubbles pushed back and forth under water.

Use the Hardware Render Buffer.   The Hardware Render Buffer is a quick way to render nParticles using your machine's graphics card. It works well for creating flame effects.

Master it   Render a small fire using the Hardware Render Buffer.

Use force fields.   Force fields can be emitted by nParticles and collision objects, creating interesting types of behavior in your scenes.

Master it   Add a second nParticle object emitted from the base of the generator. Enable its force field so that it attracts some of the original energy nParticle.

Render nParticles with mental ray.   mental ray can be used to render all nParticle styles using raytraced features such as reflections and refractions.

Master it   Create and render a snowglobe effect.

Chapter 14

Advanced nDynamic Effects

In this chapter, you'll delve deeper into Maya dynamics to understand how the various dynamic systems, such as nCloth, nParticles, and Rigid Bodies, can be used together to create spectacular effects. You'll also use more advanced particle expressions to control the motion of particle instances.

In this chapter you will learn to:

- ◆ Use nCloth

- ◆ Combine nCloth and nParticles

- ◆ Use nCloth for rigid body simulations

- ◆ Use traditional Maya rigid body dynamics

- ◆ Instance geometry to nParticles

- ◆ Create nParticle expressions

- ◆ Create smoke effects

nCloth

nCloth uses the Nucleus solver to create soft body dynamics. Typically nCloth is used to make polygon geometry behave like clothing, but nCloth can actually be used to simulate the behavior of a wide variety of materials. Everything from concrete to water balloons can be achieved by adjusting the attributes of the nCloth object. nCloth uses the same dynamic system as nParticles and applies it to the vertices of a piece of geometry. An nCloth object is simply a polygon object that has had its vertices converted to nParticles. A system of virtual springs connects the nParticles and helps maintain the shape of nCloth objects. nCloth objects automatically collide with other nDynamic systems (such as nParticles and nRigids) that are connected to the same Nucleus solver, and an nCloth object collides with itself.

In this section you'll see how to get up and running fast with nCloth using the presets that ship with Maya as well as get some background on how the Nucleus solver works. The examples in this chapter illustrate a few of the ways nCloth and nParticles can be used together to create interesting effects. These examples are only the beginning; there are so many possible applications and uses for nCloth that a single chapter barely scratches the surface. The goal of this chapter is to give you a starting place so you feel comfortable designing your own unique effects. Chapter 15 demonstrates techniques for using nCloth to make clothing for an animated character.

Creating nCloth Objects

Any polygon mesh you model in Maya can be converted into an nCloth object; there's nothing special about the way the polygon object needs to be prepared. The only restriction is that only polygon objects can be used. NURBS and subdivision surfaces can't be converted to nCloth.

There are essentially two types of nCloth objects: active and passive. Active nCloth objects are the ones that behave like cloth. They are the soft, squishy, or bouncy objects. Passive objects are solid pieces of geometry that react with active objects but do not have their own dynamic properties. For example, to simulate a tablecloth sliding off a table, the tablecloth would be the active nCloth object and the table would be the passive nCloth object. The table prevents the tablecloth from falling in space. You can animate a passive object, and the active object will react to the animation. So you can keyframe the table tilting, and the tablecloth will slide off the table based on its dynamic settings.

The first lesson in this chapter shows how to create the effect of a dividing cell using two nCloth objects.

1. Create a new scene in Maya.

2. Create a polygon cube at the center of the grid. The cube should have one subdivision in width, height, and depth. Scale the cube up eight units in each axis.

3. Select the cube, switch to the Polygon menu set, and choose Mesh ➢ Smooth. In the Channel Box, select the polySmoothFace1 node and set Divisions to **3**. This creates a sphere. Unlike a regular polygon sphere, the smoothed cube has no poles at the end, which prevent unwanted pinching when the cube is converted to an nCloth object (Figure 14.1).

4. Switch to a side view. Right-click on the cube and choose Vertices to switch to component mode.

FIGURE 14.1
Create a sphere by smoothing a polygon cube.

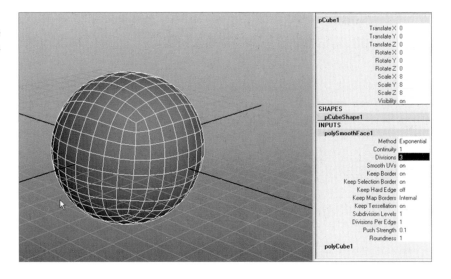

5. Switch to wireframe view (hot key = 4). Select all the vertices on the right-side center line of the grid but not the vertices on the center line.

6. Select the Scale tool (hot key = r), and scale the vertices along the Z axis so they are flat. Turn on Grid Snapping, and use the Move tool (hot key = w) to snap these vertices on the center line. You should end up with a rounded cube with one flattened side (Figure 14.2).

FIGURE 14.2

Select, scale, and snap the vertices of the right half of the cube along the center line in the side view.

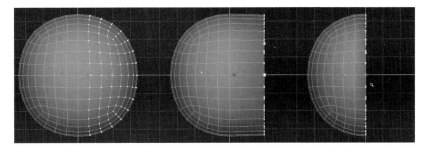

7. Name the cube **cellLeft**.

8. Turn off Grid Snapping. Select cellLeft and move it just to the left of the center line; set the Translate Z channel to 0.**08**.

9. Turn Grid Snapping on; hold the d key and use the Move tool to position the pivot point at the center of the grid. Be careful not to move the geometry, only the pivot point.

MOVING THE PIVOT POINT

You can also press the Insert key on your PC keyboard (or Home key on a Mac keyboard) while the Move tool is active. This switches to pivot point editing mode. You can then reposition the pivot point without holding the d key. To exit the mode, just press the Insert key again.

---

10. Select cellLeft and choose Modify ➢ Freeze Transformations. The Translate and Rotate channels should now be at 0 and the Scale channels at 1.

11. Select cellLeft and duplicate it (hot key = Ctrl+d). Set the Scale Z channel of the duplicate to **-1**. Choose Modify ➢ Freeze Transformations. A warning appears in the Script Editor that says "Freeze transform with negative scale will set the 'opposite' attributes for these nodes." You can safely ignore this warning.

12. Name the duplicate **cellRight** (see Figure 14.3). Select both sides and delete history (Edit ➢ Delete By Type ➢ History).

13. Switch to the nDynamics menu set. Select both objects and choose nMesh ➢ Create nCloth. In the Outliner, you'll see that two nCloth nodes have been added.

FIGURE 14.3
Create the second half of the cell by duplicating and scaling the first.

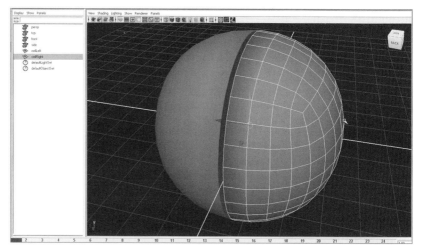

14. Switch to the wireframe node and select nCloth1. One of the cell halves turns purple, indicating the nCloth node is an input connection to that particular piece of geometry. Rename the nCloth1 and nCloth2 nodes **cellLeftCloth** and **cellRightCloth** according to which piece of geometry they are connected to (Figure 14.4).

15. Set the timeline to 400 frames and play the scene. You'll see both pieces of geometry fall in space. This is because Gravity is turned on by default in the Nucleus solver.

16. Save the scene as **cellDivide_v01.ma**. To see a version of the scene to this point, open cellDivide_v01.ma from the chapter14\scenes directory on the DVD.

FIGURE 14.4
Add two nCloth nodes to the Outliner, one for each side of the cell, and rename them cellLeftCloth and cellRightCloth.

nCloth Nodes

When you create an nCloth object or any nCloth dynamic system (nParticles, nRigids), several additional nodes are created and connected. You can see this when you graph the cellLeft shape on the Hypergraph, as shown in Figure 14.5.

FIGURE 14.5
The input and output connections for the cellLeft shape are graphed on the Hypergraph.

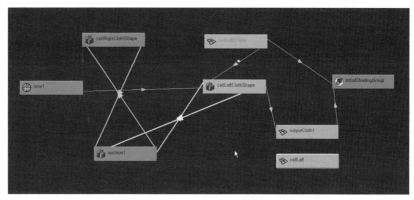

Each nCloth object consists of the original geometry, the nCloth node, and the Nucleus solver. By default, any additional nDynamic objects you create are attached to the same Nucleus solver. Additional nodes include the original cellLeftShape node, which is connected as the inputMesh to the cellLeftClothShape node. This determines the original starting shape of the nCloth object.

1. Continue with the scene from the previous section or open cellDivide_v01.ma from the chapter14\scenes folder on the DVD. Select the cellLeftCloth node and open the Attribute Editor. Switch to the cellLeftClothShape tab, as shown in Figure 14.6. This node was originally named nCloth1. The tabs found here include the following:

   cellLeftCloth   This tab contains the settings for the nCloth1 transform node. Most of the time you won't have a reason to change these settings.

   cellLeftClothShape   This tab contains the settings that control the dynamics of the nCloth object. There are a lot of settings in this tab, and this is where you will spend most of your time adjusting the settings for this particular nCloth object.

   nucleus1   This tab contains all the global settings for the Nucleus solver. These include the overall solver quality settings but also the Gravity and Air Density settings. If you select the cellRightCloth node in the Outliner, you'll notice it also has a nucleus1 tab. In fact, this is the same node as attached to the cellLeftCloth object.

It's possible to create different Nucleus solvers for different nDynamic objects, but unless the nDynamic objects are connected to the same Nucleus solver, they will not directly interact.

NAME YOUR NCLOTH NODES

Because the nCloth objects are connected to the same Nucleus solver, when you open the Attribute Editor for the nucleus node, you'll see tabs for each node that's connected to the solver. To reduce confusion over which nCloth object is being edited, always give each nCloth node a descriptive name as soon as the node is created.

---

2. Select the nucleus1 tab and set Gravity to **0**. When you rewind and play the scene, nothing happens because there are no forces acting on the cells.

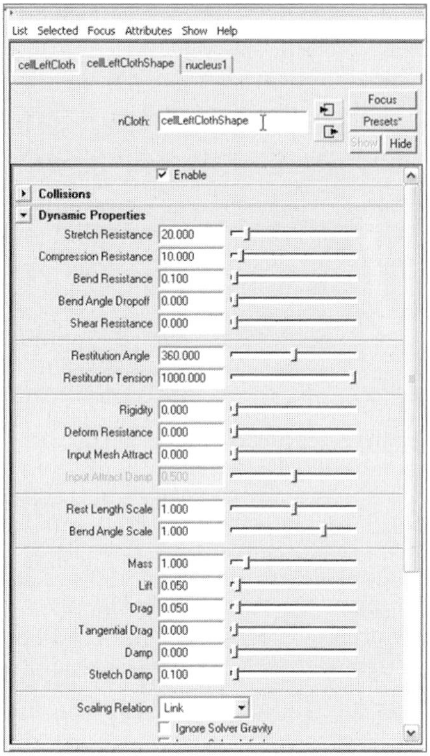

FIGURE 14.6
The Attribute Editor
for the cellLeftCloth-
Shape node has tabs
for the transform
and shape nodes as
well as the nucleus1
solver.

nCloth Presets

The concept behind this particular example is that both halves of the cell together form a single circular spherical shape. To make the cells separate, we'll adjust the nDynamic settings so that each half of the cell inflates and pushes against the other half, moving them in opposite directions. Creating the right settings to achieve this action can be daunting simply because there is a bewildering array of available settings on each nCloth shape node. To help you get started, Maya includes a number of presets that can act as a template. You can apply a preset to the nCloth objects and then adjust a few settings until you get the effect you want.

1. Continue with the scene from the previous section.

MAYA PRESETS

You can create a preset and save it for any Maya node. For instance you can change the settings on the nucleus1 node to simulate dynamic interactions on the moon and then save those settings as a preset named moonGravity. This preset will be available for any Maya session. Some nodes, such as nCloth and fur nodes, have presets already built in when you start Maya. These presets are created by Autodesk and other Maya users and can be shared between users. You'll often find new presets available on the Autodesk Area website (http://area.autodesk.com).

---

2. Select the cellLeftCloth node, and open the Attribute Editor to the cellLeftClothShape1 node. At the top of the editor, click and hold the Presets button in the upper right. The asterisk by the button label means that there are saved presets available for use.

3. From the list of presets, scroll down and find the waterBalloon preset. A small pop-up appears; from this pop-up choose Replace (see Figure 14.7). You'll see the settings in the Attribute Editor change, indicating the preset has been loaded.

4. Repeat step 2 for the cellRightCloth node.

5. Rewind and play the animation. Immediately you have a decent cell division going.

FIGURE 14.7
Using a preset selected from the Presets list is a quick way to start a custom nCloth material.

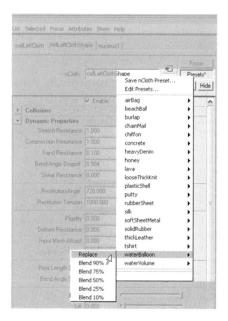

OVERLAPPING NCLOTH OBJECTS

Initially it might seem like a good idea to have two overlapping nCloth objects that push out from the center. However, if the geometry of the two nCloth objects overlaps, it can confuse the Nucleus solver and make it harder to achieve a predictable result.

The next task is to create a more realistic behavior by adjusting the setting on the nCloth objects.

6. Switch to the nucleus1 tab and set Air Density to **35**. This makes the cells look like they are in a thick medium, such as water (see Figure 14.8).

FIGURE 14.8
Increasing the Air
Density setting on
the nucleus1 tab
makes it appear as
though the cells are
in a thick medium.

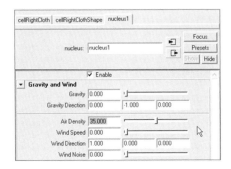

7. You can blend settings from other presets together to create your own unique look. Select cellLeftCloth, and in its shape node tab click and hold the Presets button in the upper right. Choose Honey ➢ Blend 10%. Do the same for the cellRightCloth.

8. Play the animation. The two cells separate more slowly.

9. You can save these settings as your own preset so it will be available in other Maya sessions. From the Presets menu, choose Save Maya Preset. In the dialog box, name the preset **Cell** (see Figure 14.9).

10. Save the scene as **cellDivide_v02.ma**.

FIGURE 14.9
You can save your
own custom pre-
sets to the Presets
list so they will be
available in other
Maya sessions.

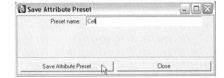

SAVING MAYA PRESETS

When you save a Maya preset, it is stored in a subfolder of maya\2009\presets\attrPresets. Your custom nCloth presets will appear in the nCloth subfolder as a MEL script file. You can save nCloth presets created by other users to this folder, and they will appear in the Presets list. If you save a preset using the same name as an existing preset, Maya will ask you if you want to overwrite the existing preset.

Stickiness

At this point, you can start to adjust some of the settings on the nCloth tabs to create a more interesting effect. To make the cells stick together as they divide, you can increase the Stickiness attribute.

1. Continue with the scene from the previous section or open the cellDivide_v02.ma scene from the chapter14\scenes directory on the DVD.

2. Select the cellLeftCloth node, and open the Attribute Editor to its shape node tab. Expand the Collisions rollout, and set Stickiness to 1 (see Figure 14.10). Do the same for the cell-Right object.

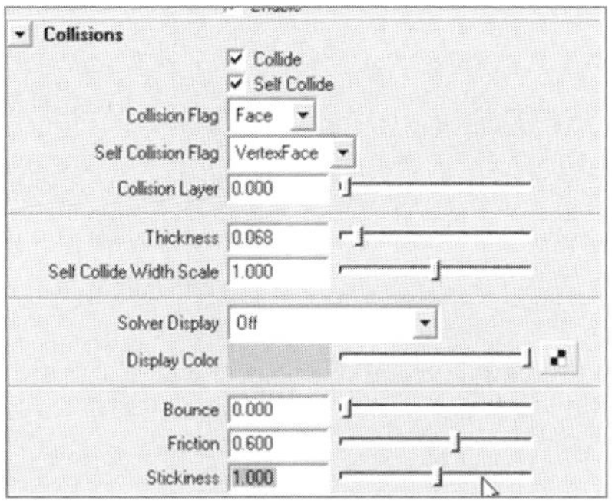

FIGURE 14.10
Increase the Sticki-ness attribute in the cellLeftCloth-Shape tab of the Attribute Editor.

Notice that many of the settings in the Collision rollout are the same as the nParticle Collision settings. For a more detailed discussion of how nucleus collisions work, consult Chapter 13.

3. Play the animation; the cells remain stuck as they inflate. By adjusting the strength of the Stickiness attribute, you can tune the effect so the cells do eventually come apart. Try a setting of 0.8 for both cells.

USE PRESETS TO COPY ATTRIBUTES

To save time when working with two identical nCloth objects, you can overwrite the nCloth preset and then apply it to the other nCloth object. This has the advantage of saving your settings so that if your computer crashes before you save the scene, you won't need to re-create the settings from scratch.

---

4. Save the nCloth settings as **stickyCell**. Save the scene as **cellDivide_v03.ma**.

CREATE PLAYBLASTS OFTEN

It's difficult to gauge how the dynamics in the scene work using just the playback in Maya. You may want to create a playblast of the scene after you make adjustments to the dynamics so you can see how effective your changes are. For more information on creating playblasts, consult Chapter 5.

---

nConstraints

nConstraints can be used to attach nCloth objects together. The constraints themselves can be broken depending on how much force is applied. In this example nConstraints will be used as an alternative technique to the Stickiness attribute. There are some unique properties of nConstraints that can allow for more creativity in this effect.

1. Continue with the scene from the previous section or open the cellDivide_v03.ma scene from the chapter14\scenes directory on the DVD.

2. Shift+click both the cellLeftCloth and cellRightCloth nodes in the Outliner. Open the Channel Box and, with both nodes selected, set Stickiness to **0** to turn off this attribute.

EDIT MULTIPLE OBJECTS USING THE CHANNEL BOX

By using the Channel Box, you can set the value for the same attribute on multiple objects at the same time. This can't be done using the Attribute Editor.

---

3. Switch to the side view. In the Outliner, Shift+click the cellLeft and cellRight polygon nodes. Set the selection mode to Component. By default the vertices on both objects should appear.

4. Drag a selection down the middle of the two objects so the vertices along the center line are selected (see Figure 14.11).

FIGURE 14.11

Create nConstraints between the vertices along the flattened side of each cell.

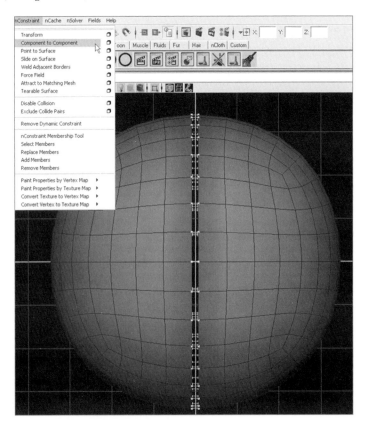

5. In the nDynamics menu set, choose nConstraint ➤ Component To Component. This creates a series of springs that connect the two objects.

6. Rewind and play the scene. The two sides of the cell are stuck together.

7. In the Outliner, a new node named dynamicConstraint1 has been created. Select this node and open the Attribute Editor.

TRANSFORM CONSTRAINTS

A transform node can be created between nCloth objects and the transform node of a piece of geometry. You can create the constraint between the vertices and another object such as a locator. Then you can animate the locator and have it drag the nCloth objects around in the scene by the nConstraint attached to the selected vertices.

A wide variety of settings are available in the Attribute Editor for the dynamicConstraint node; each one is described in detail in the Maya documentation. For the moment your main concern is adjusting the constraint strength.

8. Strength determines the overall strength of the constraint. Tangent Strength creates a resistance to the tangential motion of the constraint. In this example you can leave Strength at 20 and set Tangent Strength to **0**.

9. Glue Strength is the setting that determines whether the constraint will break when force is applied. It is calculated in world space based on the size of the objects. A value of 1 means the constraint can't be broken; a value of 0 turns the constraint off altogether. Set this attribute to **0.25**.

10. Glue Strength Scale modifies the Glue Strength based on the world space distance between the constraints. Set this value to **0.6**.

11. Rewind and play the animation. The two sides of the cell start to separate but fail to part completely. There are a few techniques you can use to separate the cells.

    Keyframe the Glue Strength Scale to diminish over time.

    Create a radial field with a negative magnitude for each cell. A field can be applied independently of the Nucleus solver. You can apply a radial field to one cell and not the other. When you apply a radial field to each cell, the radial fields pull the two cells apart.

    Create a passive rigid object in the shape of a wedge that divides the two cells along the center line.

    Use the Force attribute on the dynamic constraint.

For this exercise, you'll use the Force attribute that is built into the dynamic constraint node. The Force attribute determines the level of attraction between the constraints. Positive values cause the constraints to repel each other after they break; negative values cause the constraints to attract each other. In this scene, very small values can create a big difference.

12. Set the Force attribute on the dynamic constraint node to 0.**01**. Rewind and play the scene.

13. The cells now push each other apart and keep going. To halt their motion after separation, adjust the Dropoff Distance value. Set this to **3**. Adjust the Strength Dropoff curve so that there is a sharp decline to 0 on the left side of the curve. The strength of the force drops to 0 as the distance between the constraints approaches 3 units (Figure 14.12).

14. You can fine-tune the effect by adding a small amount of motion drag. Set Motion Drag to 0.**01**. If the cells can't quite separate, try raising Force to 0.**012**.

FIGURE 14.12
Add a small value to the Force attribute, and lower the Dropoff Distance to a value of 3. By adjusting the Strength Dropoff ramp you can fine-tune the field.

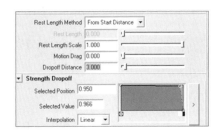

THE CONSTRAINT FORCE ATTRIBUTE

Using the Force attribute you can make constraints repel each other after they break. This would work well for a situation like a shirt splitting under pressure as buttons fly off. Setting the Force attribute to a small negative value causes the constraints to attract each other. This works well for gelatinous or gooey substances that reform after being sliced by a passive collision object.

Working with the Nucleus solver quickly becomes a very experimental process much like cooking; you adjust the sliders and season to taste until the effect looks like what you want. Since many of the attributes are interconnected, it's best to adjust one at a time and test as you go. You can move an nCloth object after it has been constrained. However, the results of the simulation may not behave they way you expect. It's usually best to make sure your nCloth objects and their constraints are positioned where you want them. Avoid setting keyframes on the translation or rotation of the nCloth object itself.

Rest Length attributes significantly affect how the simulation behaves. Rest length refers to the length of each constraint when no tension is applied (imagine an unattached spring sitting on a table; its length at rest is its rest length). If Rest Length Method is set to Start Frame, then the rest length of each constraint is equal to its length at the first frame of the animation. If this is set to Constant, then the rest length is determined using the Rest Length numeric input.

Rest Length Scale applies a scaling factor to the constraints. If this is set to 1 and Rest Length Method is set to From Start Distance, then the constraints have no initial tension. In other words, at frame 1 the scale is equal to the rest length. Lowering this value increases the tension on the constraint and makes it harder to break.

15. Rewind the animation and set Rest Length Scale to **0.5**.

16. Play the animation to frame 40 and set a keyframe on Rest Length Scale.

17. Play the animation to 50 and set Rest Length Scale to **1**. Set another keyframe. Rewind and play the animation. This is one way in which you can control the timing of the cell division. You can also control this attribute using an expression or Set Driven Key.

REST LENGTH SCALE

The nCloth nodes also have a Rest Length Scale attribute that can be adjusted to alter the behavior of the cells. The stickyCell preset created by blending the waterBalloon and Honey presets has a Rest Length Scale of 0.73. Lowering this value causes the cells to push against each other with more force. Setting this value to 1 reduces the tension, making the cells more relaxed and less likely to divide.

---

18. Save the scene as **cellDivide_v04.ma**. To see a version of the scene to this point, open the cellDivide_v04.ma scene from the chapter14\scenes folder on the DVD.

 Real World Scenario

CONNECTING NCLOTH OBJECTS TO DYNAMIC CURVES

In a recent scientific animation I created for Harvard Medical School, I attached a chromosome made of an nCloth object to a spindle fiber created from a dynamic curve. The technique I used involved these steps:

1. Create a standard CV curve. This will be used to drag the nCloth chromosome around the scene.

2. Select the curve and switch to the Dynamics menu set. Choose Hair ➢ Make Selected Curves Dynamic. When you convert a curve to a dynamic curve, a duplicate of the original curve is created. This curve is contained within a group named hairSystem1OutputCurves. Curves are discussed in detail in Chapter 15.

3. Attach a locator to the output curve of the hair system using a motion path. In the options for the Motion Path set the Time Range to Start.

4. Delete the keyframes on the motion path's U Value, and set the U Value so the locator is at one end of the curve. This way the locator is attached to the curve.

5. Use a transform nConstraint to attach the vertices at the center of the nCloth chromosome (known in biology circles as the *centromere* of the chromosome) to the locator.

Once this setup is complete, you can use the hair curve to drag the nCloth object all over the scene.

Pressure

One of the more significant attributes that creates the motion of the nCloth objects used in this example is pressure. Using pressure you can inflate a piece of geometry like a balloon, or in the case of this example, make it appear as though the geometry is filled with fluid.

There are two ways to calculate pressure: Manual Pressure Setting and Volume Tracking Model.

Manual Pressure Setting is very simple—the Pressure slider and Pressure Damping slider are the only two controls (see Figure 14.13). These can be keyframed to make it appear as though the nCloth object is being filled with air. If you set Pressure at 0 and create a keyframe, then play the animation to frame 100, set Pressure to 1, and set another keyframe, the nCloth object will grow in size over those frames.

Volume Tracking Model, which is used by the waterBalloon preset originally applied to the cell geometry, is a more accurate method for calculating volume and has more controls (see Figure 14.14).

FIGURE 14.13

Manual Pressure Setting has very simple controls for adding internal pressure to nCloth objects.

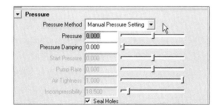

FIGURE 14.14

Volume Tracking Model has more controls and produces a more accurate internal pressure simulation for nCloth objects.

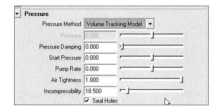

When Volume Tracking Model is selected as the Pressure Method, you have access to additional controls, such as Pump Rate, Air Tightness, and Incompressibility. The Pump Rate value determines the rate at which air is added within the volume. Positive values continue to pump air into the volume; negative values suck the air out. The Start Pressure value sets the initial pressure of the air inside the volume at the start of the animation.

The Air Tightness value determines the permeability of the nCloth object. Lower settings allow the air to escape the volume. The Incompressibility setting refers to the air within the volume. A lower value means the air is more compressible, which slows down the inflation effect of the cell. Activating Seal Holes causes the solver to ignore openings in the geometry.

As you may have noticed, after the cells divide they don't quite return to the size of the original dividing cell. You can use the Pump Rate attribute to inflate the cells.

1. Continue with the scene from the previous section or open the cellDivide_v04.ma scene from the chapter14\scenes directory on the DVD.

2. Select the cellLeftCloth shape and open its Attribute Editor. Expand the Pressure settings. Note that Pressure Method is already set to Volume Tracking Model. These settings were determined by the waterBalloon preset originally used to create the effect.

3. Set Pump Rate to **50** for each cell and play the animation (Figure 14.15). Each cell starts to grow immediately and continues to grow after the cell divides.

4. Try setting keyframes on the start Pump Rate of both cells so that at frame 15 Pump Rate is 0, at frame 50 it's 50, and at frame 100 it's 0.

CONNECT ATTRIBUTES USING THE CONNECTION EDITOR

You can save some time by using the Connection Editor to connect the Pressure attributes of one of the cells to the same attributes of the other. This way you need only keyframe the attributes of the first cell. For more information on using the Connection Editor, consult Chapter 1.

---

5. To give an additional kick at the start of the animation, set Start Pressure to 0.**25**.

FIGURE 14.15
Setting Pump Rate to 50 on the cellLeftCloth object causes it to grow as it separates from the right side.

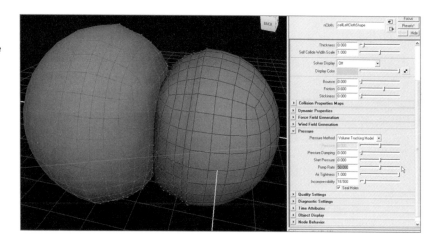

Additional Techniques

To finish the animation, here are some additional techniques you can use to add some style to the behavior of the cells.

1. Increase the Stickiness of each cell to a value between 0.8 and 1. You can also try painting a Stickiness texture map. To do this select the cells and choose nMesh ➤ Paint Texture Properties ➤ Stickiness. This activates the Artisan Brush, which allows you to paint specific areas of stickiness on the cell surface (refer to Chapter 13 to see how a similar technique is used to paint the strength of a force field on geometry).

2. If you want the objects to start out solid and become soft at a certain point in time, set keyframes on each cell's Input Mesh Attract attribute. The input mesh is the original geometry that was converted into the nCloth object. Setting the Input Mesh Attract attribute to 1 or higher causes the nCloth objects to assume the shape of the original geometry. As this value is lowered, the influence of the nucleus dynamics increases, causing the objects to become soft.

3. Try adding a turbulence field to both nCloth objects to add a little more interesting motion.

4. To see a finished version of the scene, open the `cellDivide_v05.ma` scene from the `chapter14\scenes` folder on the DVD.

COMBINE TECHNIQUES

In practice you'll most likely find that the best solution when creating a complex effect is to combine techniques as much as possible. Use Dynamic Fields, Force, Wind, nConstraints, Air Density, Stickiness, and Pressure together to make a really spectacular nCloth effect.

Create an nCache

At this point you'll want to cache the dynamics so that playback speed is improved and the motion of the cells is the same every time you play the animation. This also ensures that when you render the scene the dynamics are consistent when using multiple processors.

1. Shift+click the cellLeft and cellRight objects in the Outliner.

2. Choose nCache ➢ Create New Cache ➢ Options. In the options, you can specify where the cache will be placed. By default the cache is created in a subfolder of the current project's Data folder. If the scene is going to be rendered on a network, make sure the cache is in a subfolder that can be accessed by all of the computers on the network.

3. In the options, you can specify if you want to create a separate cache file for each frame or a single cache file. You can also create a separate cache for each geometry object; this is not always necessary when you have more than one nCloth object in a scene (Figure 14.16).

FIGURE 14.16
The options for creating an nCache

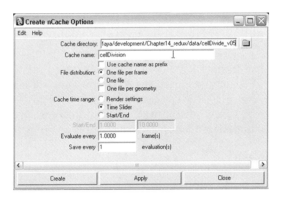

4. The default settings should work well for this scene. Click the Create button to create the cache. Maya will play through the scene.

When the cache is complete, the scene will play much faster. If you make changes to the nCloth settings, you won't see the changes reflected in the animation until you delete or disable the nCache (nCache ➢ Delete nCache). Even though the geometry is using a cache, you should not delete the nCloth nodes. This would disable the animation.

5. You can select the cellLeft and cellRight objects and move them so they overlap at the center. This removes the seam in the middle and makes it look as though there is a single object dividing into two copies.

6. You can also select the cellLeft and cellRight objects and smooth them using the Smooth operation in the Polygon ➢ Mesh menu, or simply select the nCloth object and activate Smooth Mesh Preview by pressing the 3 key on the keyboard.

Using nCloth with nParticles

Creating dynamic interaction between nParticles and nCloth objects is quite easy because both systems can share the same Nucleus solver. The collision properties of nDynamics make effects that were extremely difficult to create in previous versions of Maya very simple to create. Before continuing this section, review Chapter 13 so you understand the basics of working with nParticles.

nParticles and Goals

Goal objects attract nParticles like a magnet. A goal can be a locator, a piece of geometry, or even another nParticle. In Chapter 13 you worked with force fields, which are similar to goals in some respects in that they attract nParticles dynamically. Deciding whether you need to use a goal or a force field generated by an nDynamic object (or a combination of the two) depends on the effect you want to create. This section will demonstrate some uses of goal objects with some simple examples.

1. Create a new, empty scene in Maya.

2. Create a locator (Create ➢ Locator).

3. Switch to the nDynamics menu set, and choose nParticles ➢ Create nParticles ➢ Balls to set the nParticle style to Balls.

4. Choose nParticles ➢ Create nParticles ➢ Create Emitter. By default an omni emitter is created at the center of the scene. Use the Move tool to position the emitter away from the locator (set Translate X, Y, and Z to **20**).

5. Set the length of the timeline to 300. Play the animation. Balls are emitted and fall through space because of the Gravity settings on the nucleus node.

6. Select the nParticle object and Ctrl+click locator1. Choose nParticles ➢ Goal ➢ Options. In the options, set Goal Weight to **1** (see Figure 14.17).

FIGURE 14.17
Convert the locator into a goal for the nParticles.

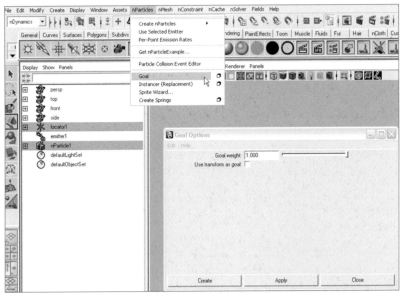

7. Rewind and play the scene. The nParticles appear on the locator and bunch up over time. Since Goal Weight is set to 1, the goal is at maximum strength and the nParticles move so quickly between the emitter and the goal object that they cannot be seen until they land on the goal. Since the Balls-style nParticles have Collision on by default, they stack up as they land on the goal.

8. Select the nParticle object. In the Channel Box, set Goal Weight to **0.25**. Play the animation. You can see the nParticles drawn toward the locator. They move past the goal and then move back toward it, where they bunch up and start to collide, creating a swarm (see Figure 14.18).

FIGURE 14.18
Lower the Goal Weight for the nParticle in the Channel Box, causing the nParticles to swarm around the locator.

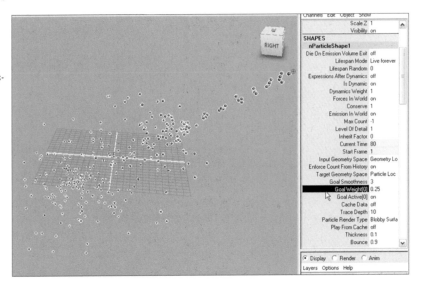

9. Create a second locator. Select the nParticle and Ctrl+click locator2. Make it a goal with a weight of **0.25** as well.

10. Position locator2 ten units above locator1.

11. Play the scene. The nParticles swarm between the two goals (Figure 14.19)

MULTIPLE GOALS

As goals are added to an nParticle, they are numbered according to the order in which they are added. The numbering starts at 0, so the first goal is referred to as Goal Weight[0], the second goal is referred to as Goal Weight[1], and so on. It's a little confusing; sometimes it's best to name the goal objects themselves using the same numbering convention. Name the first goal locator **locatorGoal0**, and name the second **locatorGoal1**. When adding expressions or when creating MEL scripts, this technique will help you keep everything clear.

FIGURE 14.19
By adding two goals with equal weights the nParticles swarm in between them.

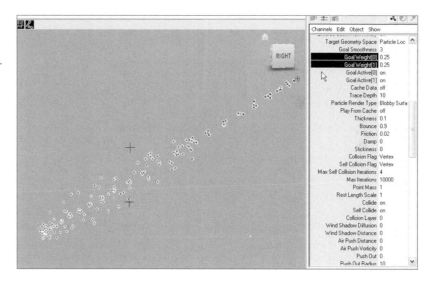

12. Select one of the locators and choose nSolver ➤ Interactive Playback. You can move the locator in the scene while it's playing and watch the nParticles follow. They are always drawn to the midpoint between the two goals (Figure 14.20).

13. Open the Attribute Editor for the nParticle, and switch to the nParticleShape1 tab. Try lowering the Conserve value on the nParticles. This causes the nParticles to lose energy as they fly through the scene.

14. Try these settings: Conserve = **0.98**, Drag = **0.05**. Set Wind Speed on the nucleus tab to **8** and Wind Noise to **25**. You can edit these settings in the Attribute Editor or in the Channel Box for the nParticleShape1 node. Suddenly a swarm of particles buzzes between the goal. By animating the position of the goals, you control where the swarm goes.

FIGURE 14.20
Using Interactive Playback, you can move the goals around and watch the nParticles follow.

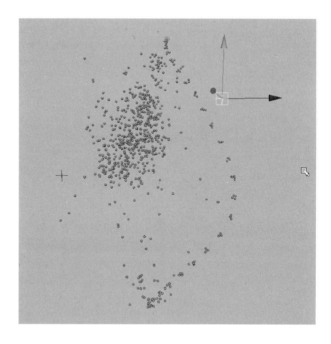

15. Set Point Force Field on the nParticle node to World Space. Set Point Field Magnitude to **8**, Self Attract to **-10**, and Point Field Distance to **10**. Now the motion of the nParticles is controlled by the goals, gravity, wind, wind noise, and a force field generated by the nParticles themselves. You can quickly create complex behavior without the need for a single expression (see Figure 14.21).

16. To see an example version of this scene, open the swarm.ma file from the chapter14\ scenes folder on the DVD.

FIGURE 14.21
Combining goals, forces, dynamic attributes, and wind noise creates some very complex nParticle behaviors.

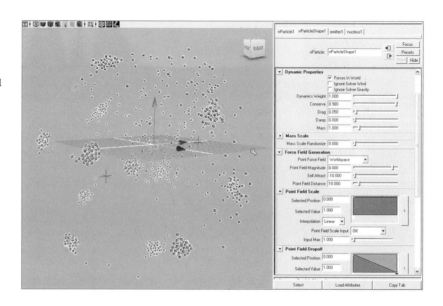

Using nCloth as a Goal

In this example an nCloth object will be used as a goal. The nParticles will be attracted to the nCloth surface and collide with it at the same time to create a very interesting effect.

1. Create a new, empty Maya scene.

2. Create a polygon cube at the center of the grid. The cube should have one subdivision in width, height, and depth. Scale the cube up eight units in each axis.

3. Select the cube, switch to the Polygon menu set, and choose Mesh ➤ Smooth. In the Channel Box, select the polySmoothFace1 node and set Divisions to 3. This creates a sphere. Unlike a regular polygon sphere, the smoothed cube has no poles at the end, which prevent unwanted pinching when the cube is converted to an nCloth object.

4. Select the cube and switch to the nDynamics menu set. Choose nMesh ➤ Create nCloth to make the object an nCloth.

5. Open the Attribute Editor for the nCloth object, and use the Presets menu to apply the solidRubber preset to the nCloth object (see Figure 14.22).

6. Set the length of the timeline to 500 frames. Switch to the nucleus tab, and activate the Use Plane option to create an invisible ground plane. Set the Plane Origin's Y axis to **-4**. Play the animation. The nCloth object falls and then bounces on the invisible floor.

7. Choose nParticles ➤ Create nParticles ➤ Balls to set the nParticle style to Balls. Choose nParticles ➤ Create nParticles ➤ Create Emitter to create an emitter. By default the emitter should be set to Omni and the rate should be at 100.

FIGURE 14.22
Apply the solidRubber preset to the nCloth object.

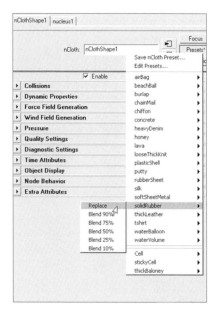

8. Select the nParticle and Ctrl+click the nCloth object. Choose nParticles ➤ Goal ➤ Options. In the options, set the Goal Weight to **1**. Click Create to make the goal.

9. Select the nParticle object and, in the Channel Box, set Goal Weight to **0.5** (see Figure 14.23).

10. Position the emitter away from the nCloth object. Rewind and play the scene. The nParticles fly toward the nCloth object and attack it. Each nParticle is attracted to a vertex on the nCloth object. The nParticles will stack up when they can't reach a vertex.

11. Set Mass of the nParticles to **10**. The attack is much more violent.

12. To see an example of the scene described, open the nClothGoal.ma scene from the chapter14\scenes directory.

FIGURE 14.23

Set Goal Weight of the nParticle object to 0.5 in the Channel Box.

FIGURE 14.24

When an nCloth object is used as a goal, the nParticles are attracted to the nCloth object and collide with it at the same time, making it appear as though the nParticles are attacking the nCloth object.

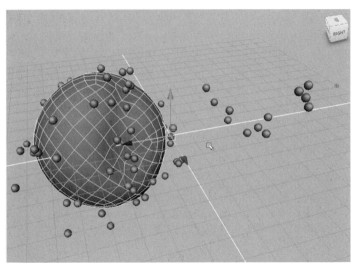

Collision Events

Using the Collision Event Editor you can specify what happens when a collision between an nParticle and a goal object occurs.

1. Continue with the scene from the previous section or open the nClothGoal.ma scene from the chapter14\scenes directory.

2. Select the nParticle and choose nParticles ➤ Particle Collision Event Editor.

3. In the Editor window, select the nParticle. Leave the All Collisions check box enabled. You can use the slider to specify the collision number. Each collision event is tracked with a specific number. Using the slider you can specify that the event occurs only on the collision with the specific number.

4. Set Event Type to Emit. The difference between Emit and Split is fairly subtle, but when Emit is selected new particles are emitted from the point of collision, and you can specify that the original colliding nParticle dies. When you choose Split, the option for killing the original nParticle is unavailable.

5. Set Num Particles to **5** and Spread to **0.5**. Set Inherit Velocity to **0.5**. Check the Original Particle Dies option. Click Create Event to make the event (Figure 14.25).

Note that the collision event will create a new nParticle object.

6. Rewind and play the scene. You'll see small particle explosions occur wherever the nParticles collide with the goal object.

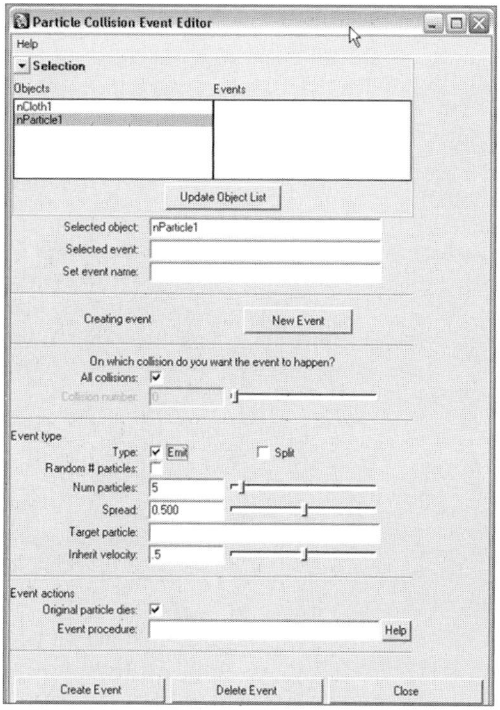

FIGURE 14.25

The Collision Event Editor allows you to create an event wherever the nParticle collides with a surface.

Tearable nConstraints

This short example demonstrates how to create a bursting surface using nParticles and an nCloth surface.

1. In a new Maya scene, create a polygon cube at the center of the grid. The cube should have one subdivision in width, height, and depth. Scale the cube up eight units in each axis.

2. Select the cube, switch to the Polygon menu set, and choose Mesh ≻ Smooth. In the Channel Box, select the polySmoothFace1 node and set Divisions to 3. This creates a sphere. Unlike a regular polygon sphere, the smoothed cube has no poles at the end, which prevent unwanted pinching when the cube is converted to an nCloth object.

3. Select the cube and switch to the nDynamics menu set. Choose nMesh ≻ Create nCloth to make the object an nCloth.

4. Open the Attribute Editor for the nCloth object, and use the Presets menu to apply the rubberSheet preset to the nCloth object.

5. Switch to the nucleus1 tab and set Gravity to **0**.

6. Choose nParticles ≻ Create nParticles ≻ Balls to set the nParticle style to Balls.

7. Choose nParticles ≻ Create nParticles ≻ Create Emitter to create a new emitter. By default the emitter is placed at the origin inside the nCloth object.

8. Select the nParticles; in the Attribute Editor for the nParticleShape1 tab, expand the Particle Size rollout and set Radius to **0.5**.

9. Set the Timeline to 800. Rewind and play the animation. The nParticles start to fill up the surface, causing it to expand (see Figure 14.26). If some nParticles are passing through the surface, switch to the Nucleus solver and raise the Substeps value to 8.

FIGURE 14.26
Placing the emitter inside the nCloth object causes it to fill with nParticles.

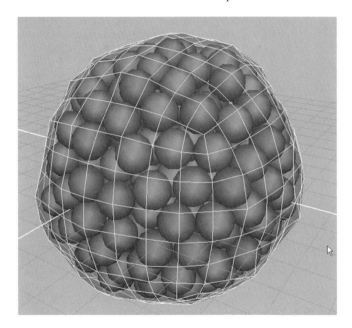

10. Select the pCube1 object in the Outliner.

11. Choose nConstraint ➤ Tearable Surface. This applies a new nConstraint to the surface.

12. If you play the scene, you'll see the surface burst open (Figure 14.27). Open the Attribute Editor for the nDynamic constraint. Set Glue Strength to 0.3 and Glue Strength Scale to 0.8; this will make the nConstraint more difficult to tear, so the bursting will not occur until around frame 500.

13. To see two examples of Tearable Surface nConstraints, open `burst.ma` and `burst2.ma` from the `chapter14\scenes` directory on the DVD.

FIGURE 14.27
Adding a Tearable Surface nConstraint allows the surface to rip when a certain amount of force is applied.

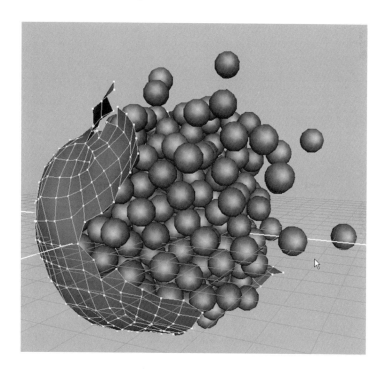

DESIGNING TEARING SURFACES

You can specify exactly where you'd like the tearing to occur on a surface by selecting specific vertices before applying the Tearable Surface nConstraint.

---

nCloth and Rigid Body Simulations

A rigid body object is a piece of geometry that simulates the behavior of hard or rigid objects. They are best used to create the basis of an animation that would be difficult to create using keyframes alone. Bowling pins, pool balls, collapsing bridges, and colliding cars are examples of the types of scenes that benefit from rigid body simulations.

Maya has included a Rigid Body system as part of its dynamics since version 1. However, you can also simulate some rigid body dynamics using nCloth.

In this tutorial you'll use nCloth to simulate a small stone tower exploding, and this will be compared with using traditional Maya rigid bodies.

Rigid nCloth Objects

In Maya 2009, the process of creating an active rigid nCloth object is no different from creating a soft nCloth object; the difference is the settings used in the nCloth tab. In fact, the concrete nCloth preset is a perfect place to start. A passive rigid nCloth (nRigid) is the same type of passive collision object you've used in the previous tutorials.

1. Open the tower_v01.ma scene form the chapter14\scenes directory on the DVD. The scene contains a small stone tower on top of a hill.

2. Open the Outliner and expand the tower group. There are three subgroups named static, passive, and active (Figure 14.28).

FIGURE 14.28
The bricks of the small tower have been divided into groups.

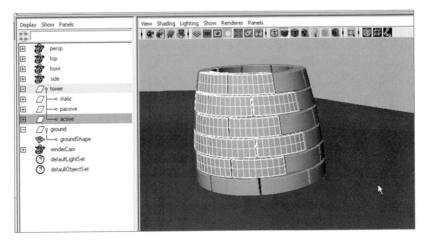

The scene is designed so only one side of the tower will explode. Only a few stone bricks will be pushed out from the explosion; these bricks have been placed in the active group. The bricks in the passive group will be converted to passive colliders; they won't move but they will support the active brick. The bricks in the static group will be left alone. Since they won't participate in the explosion, they won't be active or passive, just plain geometry. This will increase the efficiency and the performance of the scene.

3. Select the ground object and choose nMesh ➤ Create Passive Collider. In the Outliner, select the new nRigid node and name it **groundRigid**.

4. In the Outliner, expand the passive group and Shift+click all of the passive bricks in the group. Choose nMesh ➤ Create Passive Collider. In the Outliner, select the new nRigid nodes in the Outliner and group them. Name the group **nRigidBricks**.

5. Expand the active group and Shift+click all of the active objects. Select nMesh ➤ Create nCloth. In the Outliner, select the new nCloth nodes, group them, and name the group **nClothBricks**.

6. Rewind and play the scene. You'll see the active bricks sag and collapse in on themselves (see Figure 14.29).

7. Expand the nClothBricks group and select the nCloth1 node. Open the Attribute Editor to the nClothShape1 tab. Use the Presets menu to apply the Concrete preset to this node (click the Presets button in the Attribute Editor and choose Concrete ➤ Replace). Repeat this step for each of the bricks in the nCloth bricks group.

FIGURE 14.29
Converting the active bricks to nCloth objects causes them to sag when the animation is played.

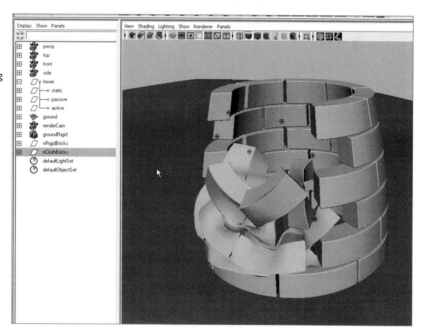

APPLYING PRESETS WITH MEL

Anytime you need to repeat the same action in Maya is an opportunity to practice some MEL scripting. In this case, you can write a very simple loop to apply the concrete preset to all of the active bricks.

1. Rewind the scene and select the nCloth1 object in the nClothBricks group.

2. Open the Script Editor window and choose History ➤ Echo All Commands so you can see all the commands Maya performs. This will help you see the syntax for applying the Concrete preset, which you can use in your loop.

CONTINUES

APPLYING PRESETS WITH MEL *(CONTINUED)*

3. In the Attribute Editor, click the nClothShape1 tab. Click the Presets button and choose Concrete ➢ Replace.

4. In the Script Editor, look for the line that applies the preset. It should read: `applyPresetToNode` `"nclothBricks|nCloth1|nClothShape1" " " " " "C:/Program Files (x86)/Autodesk/` `Maya 2009/presets/attrPresets/nCloth/concrete.mel" 1;`

The actual MEL command you use to apply the preset in a script is `applyAttrPreset`. You can find the proper MEL command by looking in the Mel command reference in the Maya documentation. Many times the command you use in the script is different from the command you see Maya use in the Script Editor. Writing MEL scripts usually takes a little detective work and trial and error. The path to your `presets` folder may look different depending on how your directory structure was created when you installed Maya. Likewise, if you are using a Mac, the path to the presets may look something like this: `/Applications/Autodesk/maya2008/Maya.app/Contents/presets/` `attrPresets/nCloth/concrete.mel`

5. Open a text editor and type the following (make sure the format in the text editor is set to Plain Text;

do not use a word processor such as Microsoft Word to write your MEL scripts):

```
//Create variable to hold selection
string $selectedNcloth[] = ls-sl`;

//Create loop based on size of the selection
For($i=0;$i<size($selectedNcloth);$i++){

/*
apply the preset to the selected nodes
the exact path to your preset directory may be different from what appears in
the applyAttrPreset command
if this is the case, replace the text in quotes in the next line with the
correct path*/
applyAttrPreset $selectedNcloth[$i] "C:/Program Files (x86)/Autodesk/Maya 2009/
presets/attrPresets/nCloth/concrete.mel " 1;
//close loop
}
```

The `applyAttrPreset` command takes at least three arguments—the node to which you want to apply the preset, the location of the preset, and the blend value. A blend value of 1 means 100 percent. To blend 50 percent, you would specify a blend value of 0.5.

In Maya, expand the nClothBricks group. Make sure the shape nodes are visible in the Outliner, and Ctrl+click the shape node for each nCloth node except nCloth1, which already has the preset applied. Copy the text from the Text Editor into the Script Editor and hit the Enter key on the numeric keypad to run the script. If you get no errors, the script should be applied to all of the selected nodes. If you do get an error message, double-check the script of the text and make sure you did not mistype or leave anything out.

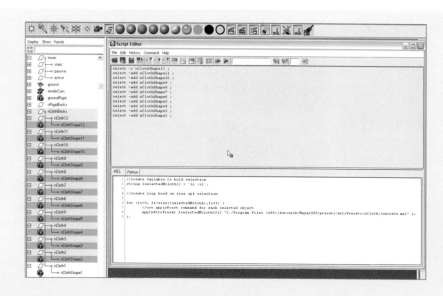

Common mistakes include leaving the semicolon off the end of command lines, forgetting to close loops with the curly braces, or leaving the double slashes off comment lines. Don't get too frustrated if it doesn't work; it takes a while to get used to using MEL scripts. However, you'll thank yourself for taking the time to learn MEL when you're faced with applying a preset to 200 objects in a scene.

8. Rewind and play the scene. The bricks don't sag, but they do collapse, and there is a fair amount of interpenetration problems. Fix this by adjusting some of the collision properties on the active objects and passive objects.

9. Select the nRigid1 node in the Outliner in the nRigidBricks group, and open its Attribute Editor to the nRigidShape1 tab. Set Solver Display to Collision Thickness. Do the same for the nCloth1 object so you can see the collision thickness of both objects in the perspective view (for more information on collision properties, consult Chapter 13).

10. There is a small gap between the bricks that could be closed up by raising the thickness of both objects. Set the collision thickness of both the nRigid1 node and the nCloth1 node to **0.05**. This closes the gap, which reduces the amount of movement at the start of the animation (see Figure 14.30).

11. In the Outliner, expand the nRigid group and Shift+click all of its members. Open the Channel Box and find the Thickness channel. Set it to **0.5**. Using the Channel Box allows you to quickly set the value of the same channel on multiple selected objects at the same time. Do the same for the nodes in the nClothBricks group (see Figure 14.31).

12. Select any one of the nCloth or nRigid nodes and, in the Channel Box, select the nucleus1 node in the Inputs section. Scroll to the bottom and set the Substeps channel to **6**. This increases the accuracy of the simulation by increasing the number of times the Nucleus solver calculates each frame.

FIGURE 14.30
Raising the collision thickness for both nCloth and nRigid bricks closes the gap between bricks.

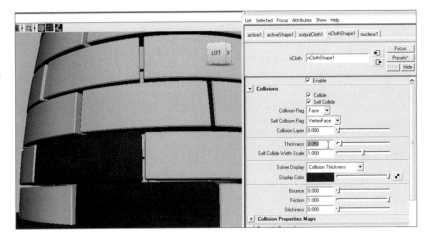

FIGURE 14.31
You can increase the collision thickness for all selected nCloth and nRigid objects in the Channel Box.

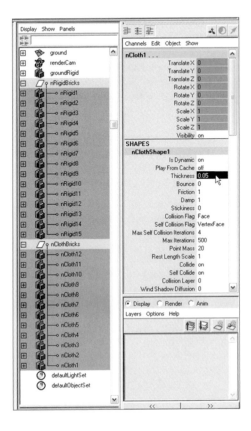

13. Since the nCloth objects are too stiff to bend or fold, you can turn off Self Collide in the Channel Box for the selected objects. This improves performance slightly.

14. Set Friction for all of the nCloth and nRigid objects to **5** and Stickiness to **1**. This prevents the bricks from sliding out at the start of the animation.

15. Rewind and play the scene. There is still movement, but the bricks should no longer collapse and penetrate each other.

Set nCloth Start Frame

To remove the movement of the bricks at the start of the animation, you can continue to tweak the thickness and solver settings until it's perfect. However, there are a few easier methods you can use to set the start time of the simulation.

For this particular scene, the explosion will occur at frame 20. From frames 1–19 you want the bricks to remain motionless. So, one way to postpone the evaluation of the nCloth dynamics is to set the Start Frame of the nCloth evaluation to frame 20.

The Start Frame attribute can be found in the Attribute Editor for the Nucleus solver. If you set Start Frame to 20, the Nucleus solver will not begin evaluating until frame 20. This works pretty well, except this means any other nDynamic nodes attached to this solver won't evaluate until frame 20 either. As one solution, you can add additional Nucleus solvers to the scene as you add additional nDynamic objects. Another solution is to break the connection between the individual nCloth objects and the Start Frame attribute on the nucleus nodes. The following steps demonstrate how to do this:

1. In the Outliner, expand the nClothBricks group and select nCloth1. Open its Attribute Editor.

2. In the Attribute Editor, expand the Time Attributes rollout. Notice that the Start Frame attribute is in yellow, indicating it has an incoming connection. This connection is coming from the nucleus1 node. Right-click on the Start Frame field and choose Break Connection (see Figure 14.32).

3. Enter the value **20** in this field.

4. Repeat these steps for the other nCloth nodes in the nClothBricks group (this attribute is not found in the Channel Box or the Attribute Spreadsheet, so unfortunately you need to repeat these steps for all of the nCloth objects). This is another opportunity to create a MEL script loop.

5. Save the scene as **tower_v02.ma**. To see a version of the scene to this point, open the tower_v02.ma scene from the chapter14\scenes folder on the DVD.

FIGURE 14.32

Break the connection for the Start Frame attribute in the Attribute Editor for the nClothShape1 node.

ANIMATE INPUT MESH ATTRACT

An alternative way to animate the activation of the nCloth behavior is to keyframe the Input Mesh Attract attribute found in the Dynamics Properties rollout. The input mesh is the original polygon object that was converted into the nCloth object. If you graph an nCloth object on the Hypergraph, you can see that there is an input connection coming from a hidden mesh object; this is the input mesh. By setting an Input Mesh Attract value of 1 or higher for the nCloth object, you're forcing the nCloth object to assume the shape of the original mesh. You can keyframe this value, moving from 1 to 0 so the nCloth dynamics take over as the Input Mesh Attract value is reduced over time. The nCloth object should inherit any animation placed on the original input mesh. This way you can animate a rigid object turning into a soft object over time. You can also paint textures to control which parts of a surface are more attracted to the input mesh than others.

nCloth and Fields

To create the explosion you can add a radial field to the nCloth objects.

1. Continue with the scene from the previous section or open the tower_v02.ma scene from the chapter14\scenes directory.

2. In the Outliner, expand the active group and Shift+click its members (when applying a field to nCloth objects, select the polygon objects, not the nCloth nodes—it seems arbitrary but that is how it works).

3. From the nDynamics menu set choose Fields ➢ Radial. This attaches the field to the selected objects (see Figure 14.33).

FIGURE 14.33
Apply a radial field
to the selected
active bricks.

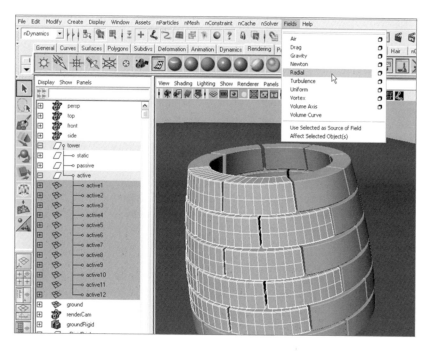

APPLY FIELDS TO SELECT NCLOTH OBJECTS

Fields are not connected to the Nucleus solver, so a field can affect only specific nCloth objects if you like. Again, this opens up many possibilities for creative exploration of dynamic simulations.

---

4. Switch to wireframe mode. In the Outliner select the field and use the Move tool to position it just behind the active bricks in the tower. Set the Translate X of the field to **-2** and the Translate Y to **1.654**.

5. Select the radial field. In the Channel Box, set Magnitude to **100**, Attenuation to **0**, and Max Distance to **5**. Rewind and play the animation. At frame 20 the bricks will fly out. The field does not affect the bricks until they become dynamic at frame 20.

This works pretty well; however, the movement of the bricks is a little too uniform and boring. You can make it more interesting by changing the shape of the force exerted by the radial field.

6. Select the radial field and set Magnitude to **400**, Attenuation to **0.5**, and Max Distance to **5**.

The Attenuation setting creates a falloff in the strength of the radial field so that force at the center of the field is stronger than at the edges. By raising the Magnitude value, you can counteract the weakening of the field caused by adding attenuation. Setting Max Distance to 3 makes the field more focused. For a discussion of the Attenuation and Max Distance settings, consult Chapter 13.

7. Rewind and play the animation. At this point the explosion looks pretty good. If the bricks appear to stick together too much, you can lower the Stickiness value to 0.5.

8. If you find that some bricks still penetrate each other after landing, you can activate the Trapped Check attribute and set a Crossover Push value of 0.1. These attributes are found in the Channel Box for the active bricks in the tower (Figure 14.34). These settings check for penetration between nCloth objects and then force the penetrating objects apart by a small distance.

9. To reduce sliding on the ground, you can select the groundRigid object and increase Friction to **1**. If the bricks appear to be floating above the ground, lower Collision Thickness on the groundRigid object to **0.01**.

10. Save the scene as **tower_v03.ma**. To see a version of the scene to this point, open tower_v03.ma from the chapter14\scenes folder on the DVD (see Figure 14.35).

11. Before leaving this section, create an nCache of the motion of the bricks (that is, select all the nCloth bricks and to go nCache ➤ Create New Cache). Later in the chapter, you'll create the look of an explosion by adding nParticles to the animation. By caching the dynamic systems as you add them, you'll improve the performance of the scene during playback, which will make working with the dynamics a more pleasant experience.

FIGURE 14.34
The Trapped Check and Crossover Push settings reduce unwanted interpenetration problems.

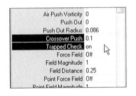

FIGURE 14.35
The nCloth bricks are a good start to a convincing explosion.

Traditional Rigid Body Dynamics

For larger scenes with more complex dynamics, using traditional rigid body dynamics may be a better alternative than using nCloth. Setting up rigid body dynamics is fairly straightforward. In this example, you'll use the same stone tower so you can compare the differences in workflow when using nCloth and traditional rigid body dynamics.

1. Starting from the `tower_v01.ma` scene in the `chapter14\scenes` directory, expand the active group and select all of the brick nodes in this group. Switch to the Dynamics menu set and choose Soft/Rigid Bodies ➢ Create Active Rigid Body.

2. Expand the passive group, Shift+click all of the bricks in this group, and choose Soft/Rigid Bodies ➢ Create Passive Rigid Body.

3. Select the ground and choose Soft/Rigid Bodies ➢ Create Passive Rigid Body.

4. By default, there is no gravity attached to the active rigid bodies; to add gravity, you need to create a gravity field. Shift+click all of the members of the active group and choose Fields ➢ Gravity.

5. If you play the scene, you'll see the bricks sag slightly. To animate their dynamics state, Shift+click the members of the active group, and set the Active attribute in the Channel Box to Off. Keyframe this value at frame 19 (see Figure 14.36); then move the timeline to frame 20, set Active to On, and set another keyframe.

6. To make the bricks explode, select the members of the active group and add a radial field. Position the radial field behind the active bricks and set Magnitude to **400**, Attenuation to **0.5**, and Max Distance to **5**.

7. Select the active bricks and set their Mass value to **20** (see Figure 14.37). When you play the scene, the action of the bricks is very similar to the nCloth version, although you may notice that the performance on your machine is a little better compared to using nCloth.

FIGURE 14.36
You can keyframe the Active state of the rigid bodies.

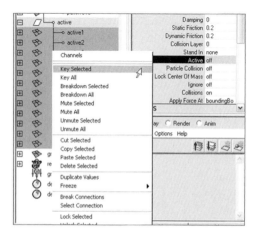

FIGURE 14.37
Increase the Mass value of the rigid bodies to make the bricks appear heavier.

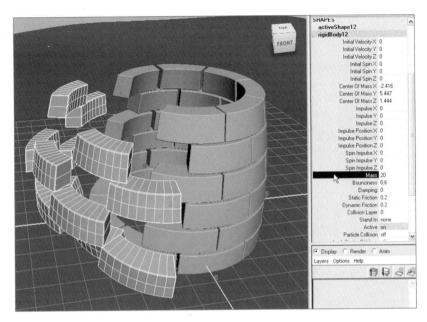

INTERPENETRATION ERRORS

Interpenetration errors occur when the geometry passes through each other in such a way as to confuse Maya. Only one side of the surface is actually used in the calculation based on the direction of the surface normals—there are no double-sided rigid bodies. The surface of two colliding rigid bodies (active + active or active + passive) need to have their normals pointing at each other to calculate correctly.

You can increase the Tessellation Factor value in the Performance Attributes rollout of each of the rigid body objects to improve accuracy, or you can adjust the settings on the rigidSolver node.

The solvers used to calculate traditional rigid body dynamics are in the Attribute Editor for the rigidSolver node. The three rigid solver types are Mid-Point, Runge Kutta, and Runge Kutta Adaptive. Mid-Point is the fastest but least accurate type, Runge Kutta is more accurate and slower, and Runge Kutta Adaptive is the most accurate and slowest method. You can leave the setting on Ringe Kutta Adaptive.

8. Select the ground plane, and set both the Static and Dynamic Friction attributes in the Channel Box to **1**.

9. Shift+click the active bricks and, in the Channel Box, set Dynamic Friction to **0.5**. Lower Bounciness to **0.1**.

Static Friction sets the level of resistance for a resting dynamic object against another dynamic object. In other words, if an object is stationary, this means how much it resists starting to move once a force is applied.

Dynamic Friction sets how much a moving dynamic object resists another dynamic object, such as a book sliding across a table.

Other settings to take note of include Damping and Collision Layer. Damping slows down the movement of the dynamic objects. If the simulation takes place under water, you can raise this setting to make it look as though the objects are being slowed down by the density of the environment.

The collision layer specifies which objects collide with other objects. By default all rigid bodies are on collision layer 0. However if you set just the active bricks to collision layer 1, they react only with each other and not the ground or the passive bricks, which would still be on collision layer 0.

Rigid Body Constraints

Rigid body constraints can be used to connect rigid bodies together. The nail, hinge, pin, spring, and barrier constraints are different ways of attaching rigid bodies to each other or to static objects in the scene. You can use hinge constraints to attach a door to a building or a spring constraint to power the throwing arm of a catapult. A nail constraint acts as a solid bar that connects the object to the constraint position. You can use this to create the effect of a ball swinging on a cord. A barrier constraint creates a very simple collision object.

---

10. Save the scene as **rigidBodyTower_v01.ma**. To see a version of the scene to this point, open rigidBodyTower_v01.ma from the chapter14\scenes directory.

Baking Simulations

It's common practice to bake the motion of traditional rigid bodies into keyframes once you're satisfied that the simulation is working the way you want. This improves the performance of the scene as well as allows you to adjust parts of the animation by hand. Be aware that the number of keyframes affects the size of the scene (the memory space needed for storage on disk).

1. In the Outliner, Shift+click the active bricks, and choose Edit ➢ Keys ➢ Bake Simulation ➢ Options.

2. In the Channel Box, Shift+click the Translate and Rotate channels.

3. In the Bake Simulation Options section, set Time Range to Time Slider. Set the Sample By option to **1** so a keyframe is created for each frame of the animation.

4. Set the Channels option to From Channel Box. Keyframes are created for just the channels currently selected in the Channel Box. This eliminates the creation of extra, unnecessary keys.

5. Turn on Smart Bake. This setting tells Maya to create keyframes only where the animation requires it instead of creating a keyframe on every frame of the animation.

The Increase Fidelity option improves the accuracy of the smart bake. Fidelity Keys Tolerance specifies the baking tolerance in terms of a percentage. Higher percentages produce fewer keyframes but also allow for more deviation from the original simulation.

Other important options include Keep Unbaked Keys, Sparse Curve Bake, and Disable Implicit Control. The Keep Unbaked Keys option keeps any key outside the baked range. Sparse Curve Bake keeps the shape of connected animation curves when baking. Since the bricks are using dynamics, this option does not apply. Disable Implicit Control is useful when the object's animation is being driven by Inverse Kinematic handles and other controls. Again this is not necessary when baking rigid body dynamics.

6. Activate Increase Fidelity and set Fidelity Keys Tolerance to **1** percent. See Figure 14.38.

7. Click the Bake button to bake the simulation into keyframes. The animation will play through as the keys are baked.

8. When the animation is finished, select Edit ➢ Delete All By Type ➢ Rigid Bodies to remove the rigid body nodes. Select the active bricks and open the Graph Editor (Window ➢ Animation Editors ➢ Graph Editor) to see the baked animation curves for the bricks (see Figure 14.39).

9. Save the scene as **rigidBodyTower_v02.ma**. To see an example of the scene that uses traditional rigid bodies, open the rigidBodyTower_v02.ma scene from the chapter14\scenes folder on the DVD.

FIGURE 14.38
The options for baking keyframes

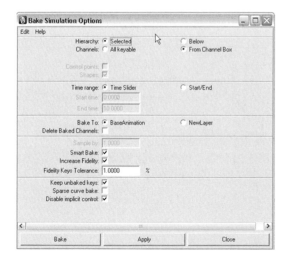

FIGURE 14.39
The Graph Editor shows the animation curves for the baked simulation of the active bricks.

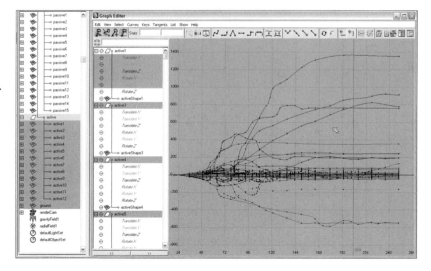

DUPLICATING TRADITIONAL RIGID BODIES

When duplicating rigid bodies that have fields connected, do not use Duplicate Special ➤ Duplicate Input Connections or Duplicate Input Graph. These options do not work well with rigid bodies. Instead, duplicate the object, convert it to an active rigid body, and then use the Relationship Editor to make the connection between the rigid bodies and the fields.

---

nParticle Instancing

nParticle instancing attaches one or more specified pieces of geometry to a particle system. The instanced geometry then inherits the motion and much of the behavior of the particle system. For this example, you'll instance debris and shrapnel to a particle system and add it to the current explosion animation. In addition, you'll control how the instance geometry behaves through expressions and fields.

Particle Debris

The goal for this exercise is to add bits of flying debris to the explosion that behave realistically. This means you'll want debris of various sizes flying at different speeds and rotating as the particles move through the air. The first step is to add an nParticle system to the scene that behaves like debris flying through the air.

1. Open the tower_v03.ma scene from the chapter14\scenes directory. Expand the tower group and the active subgroup. Switch to the nDynamics menu set. In the Outliner, select the members of the nClothBricks group and choose nCache ➤ Create New Cache.

   It's easier to work in the scene if you create an nCache on your local hard drive. The scene will play through, and the animation of the bricks will be stored in the data folder of the current project.

2. Rewind the scene and play it. The animation should play faster, and the bricks should fly out from the tower starting at frame 20.

EDITING CACHED NDYNAMICS

If you change the settings on any of the nucleus nodes or the radial field, you won't see a change in behavior for the bricks until you disable the cache. If the link between an nCloth object and its nCache is broken, the nDynamics may not calculate as expected. A link can become broken if the cache or the scene is moved to a different directory. You can relink the nCache using the Base Directory field in the Attribute Editor for the nCache.

---

3. Choose nParticles ➤ Create nParticles ➤ Balls to set the nParticle style to Balls.

4. Choose nParticles ➤ Create nParticles ➤ Create Emitter ➤ Options. In the Options, leave Solver set to nucleus1. Set Emitter Type to Volume and Rate to **800**. In the Distance/Direction Attributes rollout, set Direction X and Direction Z to **0** and Direction Y to **1** so the nParticles initially move upward.

5. In the Volume Emitter Attributes rollout, set Volume Shape to Cylinder.

6. In the Volume Speed Attributes rollout, set Away From Axis to **1**, Along Axis to **0.5**, Random Direction to **1**, and Directional Speed to **4**. Click Create to make the emitter (see Figure 14.40).

7. Switch to wireframe mode. Select emitter1 in the Outliner, and use the Move and Scale tools to position the emitter at the center of the stone tower (set Translate Y to **3.1** and all three Scale channels to **2**).

8. Rewind and play the animation.

FIGURE 14.40

The options for the volume emitter

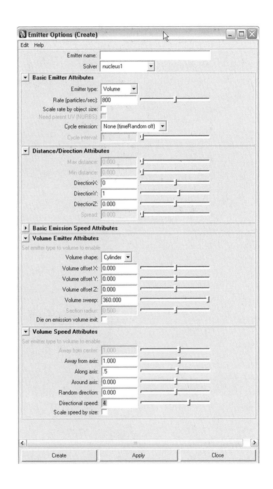

The nParticles start pouring out of the emitter. They collide with the active and passive bricks but pass through the bricks in the back, which are not dynamic at all (see Figure 14.41). You can convert the static bricks to passive colliders; however, this adds a large number of new nRigid nodes to the scene, which may slow down the performance of the scene. These nodes may also have attributes that need to be set. Instead, you can create a single, simple collider object to interact with the nParticles. This object can be hidden in the render.

FIGURE 14.41
The nParticles pass through the nondynamic bricks at the back of the tower.

9. Switch to the Polygon menu set and choose Create ➢ Polygon Primitives ➢ Cylinder.

10. Select the nParticle node, and in the Attribute Editor for the shape nodes set Enable to Off to temporarily disable the calculations of the nParticle while you create the collision object.

11. Set the timeline to frame 100 so you can easily see the opening in the exploded tower.

12. Select the cylinder and switch to face selection mode; delete the faces on the top and bottom of the cylinder and in the opening of the exploded tower (Figure 14.42).

FIGURE 14.42
Delete the faces on the top and bottom of the cylinder. Select the faces near the opening of the exploded tower and delete them.

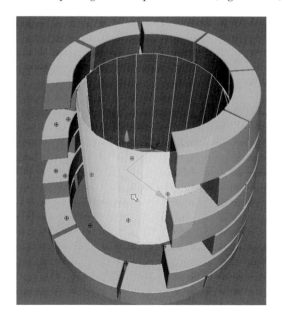

13. Set the scale and position of the cylinder so it blocks the nParticles from passing through the back of the tower (set Translate Y to **2.639**, Scale X and Scale Z to **2.34**, and Scale Y to **3.5**.)

14. Rename the cylinder **collider**. Switch to the nDynamics menu set and choose nMesh ➢ Create Passive Collider.

15. Select the nParticles and turn Enable back on. Rewind and play the animation; the nParticles now spill out of the front of the tower once it breaks open (Figure 14.43).

FIGURE 14.43
With the collision surface in place, the nParticles pour out of the opening in the front of the stone tower.

nParticles and Fields

The effects so far look like a popcorn popper gone bad. To make it look as though the nParticles are expelled from the source of the explosion, you can connect the radial field to the nParticle.

1. Select nParticle1 and rename it **particleDebris**.

2. Open the Attribute Editor for particleDebris. Under the Time Attributes section, right-click on Start Frame and choose Break Connection. This removes the connection between the nParticle shape and the nucleus1 solver's Start Frame attribute. Type **20** into this field. The particle debris won't start emitting until frame 20.

It's not necessary to have the debris continually spewing from the tower. You need only a certain number of nParticles. You can either set keyframes on the emitter's rate or set a limit to the number of nParticles created by the emitter. The latter method is easier to do and to edit later.

3. In the Attribute Editor for particleDebris, expand the Emission Attributes rollout. Max Count is set to -1 by default, meaning that the emitter can produce an infinite number of nParticles. Set this value to **1200** (see Figure 14.44). After the number of nParticles reaches 1200, the emitter stops creating new nParticles. Select the emitter and set the rate to **2400**. This means that the emitter will create 1200 nParticles in half a second, making the explosion faster and more realistic.

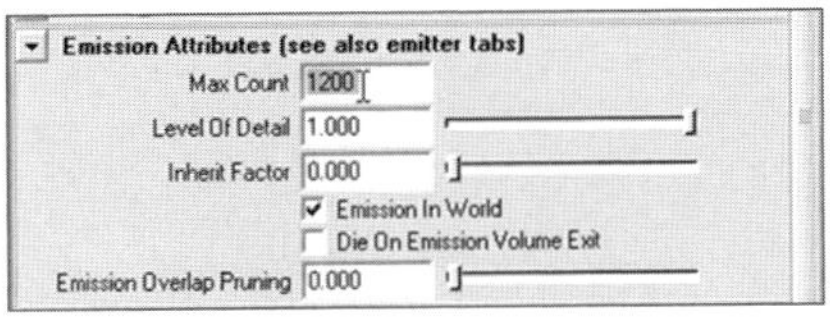

FIGURE 14.44

Set Max Count to 1200, limiting the number of nParticles created by the emitter.

MAX COUNT AND NPARTICLE DEATH

This method works well as long as the nParticles do not have a finite life span. If there is a life span set for the nParticles or if they die from a collision event, the emitter creates new nParticles to make up the difference.

---

4. To connect the radial field to the particle debris, select the particle debris object and Ctrl+click radialField1 in the Outliner. Choose Fields ➤ Affect Selected Object(s).

MAKING CONNECTIONS WITH THE RELATIONSHIP EDITOR

You can also connect the field to the nParticle using the Dynamic Relationship Editor. This is discussed in Chapter 13.

---

5. Rewind and play the animation. Not all of the nParticles make it out of the tower; many of the nParticles are pushed down on the ground and toward the back of the collider object. To fix this, reposition the radial field.

Because the animation of the bricks has been cached, changing the position of the field won't affect their movement. However, if you decide to change the animation of the bricks later on, the edited radial field will change the way the bricks move. In this case you can create a new radial field, disconnect the bricks from the original field, connect them to the new field, and make your changes.

6. Set the Translate X of the field to **1.347** and the Translate Y to **0.364**. (See Figure 14.45.)

7. Save the scene as **tower_v04.ma**. To see a version of the scene to this point, open the tower_v04.ma scene from the chapter14\scenes folder on the DVD.

FIGURE 14.45
Once you reposi-
tion the radial
field, the nParticles
are sent flying out
of the tower.

If the nCloth bricks do not play back as expected, you may need to relink the nCache. Select one of the nCloth bricks, and open its Attribute Editor to the stoneTowerCache1 tab (the tab may have a different name depending on what name you used when creating the nCache). Use the Base Directory and Cache Name fields to relink the nCache.

nParticle Size and Mass

Next, to create a more interesting behavior for the nParticles you can randomize the mass. Creating randomized mass for an nParticle system using the ramps can be very confusing since the controls all work together. It's much easier to see what's going on if you adjust the Radius Scale settings and then transfer these settings to the Mass Scale settings. This way you get instant visual feedback that tells you how the controls work.

1. To speed up playback of the scene, Shift+click all of the nRigid bricks and all of the nCloth bricks. Set the Is Dynamic channel to Off.

2. Select the particleDebris object. In the Attribute Editor for the particleDebrisShape node expand the ParticleSize rollout. In the Particle Size attributes, set Particle Radius to **1**. When you play the scene, all the nParticles should be the same size.

3. In the Radius Scale attributes, set Radius Scale Input to Randomized ID. This random-izes the size of the particles based on their individual ID. If you play the animation, you'll notice that the nParticles are still the same size (see Figure 14.46). This is because the Radius Scale ramp has a value of 1 across the horizontal axis of the ramp. This is like picking a random lottery ball from a bin of balls all labeled 1.

4. Create a new marker on the right side of the scale, and drag it down to 0.1. Play the ani-mation; now the nParticles are all different sizes. The radius varies between 1 and 0.1. Now the available sizes vary between 0.1 and 1. This is like picking a random lottery ball from a bin of balls with values between 0.1 and 1 (see Figure 14.47).

FIGURE 14.46
Even though Radius Scale is set to Randomized ID, the size of each nParticle is still the same.

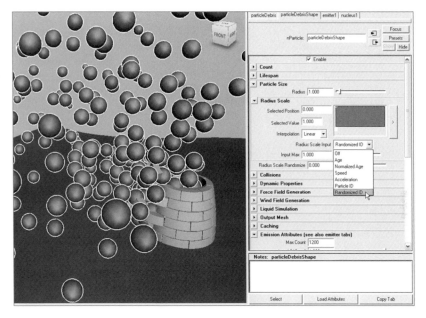

FIGURE 14.47
Once you edit the Input Scale ramp, the size of the nParticles becomes randomized.

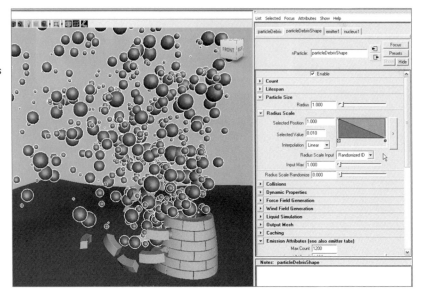

5. The size for each nParticle is randomized using its particle ID number as a seed value. This is still difficult to visualize. Set Radius Scale Input to Particle ID. The randomization factor is now removed. Play the animation. Each nParticle is progressively smaller.

As the emitter creates nParticles, the Particle ID value increases. As the value increases, the downward slope of the ramp causes nParticles with higher ID values to be smaller. Once the particle ID value is larger than the Max Input value, the nParticles remain at a radius of 0.1.

6. Set Input Max to **0.5**. The nParticles get smaller faster (see Figure 14.48).

7. Set Radius Scale Randomize to **1**. This acts as a multiplier; the larger nParticles at the start of the sequence have a random radius range added to their initial radius. The smaller nParticles are still small, but their sizes within that range are randomized.

8. Set Radius Scale Input back to Randomize ID and play the animation. The radius is now very random.

FIGURE 14.48
Reducing Input Max while Radius Scale Input is set to Particle ID reduces the number of larger particle sizes.

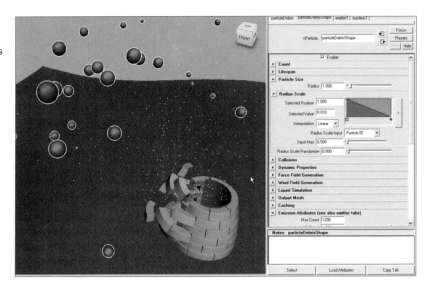

What is interesting is that when Radius Scale Input is set to Randomize ID, you can alter the range of variation by adjusting either or both Input Max and Radius Scale Randomize. If you think of the ramp as representing possible random ranges, lowering Input Max shrinks the available number of random scales available to the randomize function, thus forcing the randomizer to have more "contrast" between values. Increasing Input Max makes more data points available to the randomize function, making a smoother variation between random values and producing less contrast.

On top of this you can edit the ramp, adding points randomly or bias one side of the ramp to produce more larger radii or vice versa.

Now we can take this information and apply it to the mass of the nParticles to create a more interesting behavior for the explosion.

9. Set Radius Scale Randomize to **0**, and remove the edits from the radius settings. Set the radius on the nParticles to **0.2**.

10. In the Dynamic Properties section, expand the Mass Scale rollout. Leave Mass at 1. Add a control point to the right side of the ramp, and drag it down so the selected value is 0.1.

11. Set Mass Scale Input to Randomize ID.

12. Set Input Max to **0.5**.

13. Set Mass Scale Randomize to **1**.

14. Play the animation. It looks pretty good, but you may notice that some nParticles get stuck in the air (see Figure 14.49).

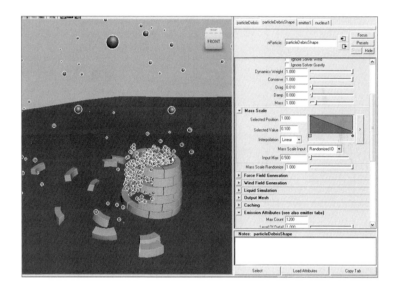

The Balls-style nParticle has a very small Drag value applied by default. nParticles with a very low or zero mass get stuck in the air because of this low value. The low end of the Mass Scale ramp is 0.1. Mass Scale Randomize acts as a multiplier, which in some cases causes the mass of a few nParticles to be 0. This causes them to be strongly affected by the Drag setting. To fix this, you can either set Drag to 0 or lower the Mass Scale Randomize value so that even the nParticles with the smallest mass never approach 0. The downside of removing the drag is that you lose some of the realism of the simulation. It's probably a better idea to lower Mass Scale Randomize.

15. Set Mass Scale Randomize to **0.05**.

16. Save the scene as **tower_v05.ma**. To see a version of the scene to this point, open tower_v05.ma.

Instancing Geometry

To create the debris, you'll need to instance some premade geometry to each nParticle. This means that a copy of each piece of geometry will follow the motion of each nParticle.

1. Continue using the scene from the previous section or open the tower_v05.ma scene from the chapter14\scenes directory.

2. The debris is contained in a separate file, which will be imported into the scene. Choose File ➤ Import and select the debris.ma scene from the chapter14\scenes directory on the DVD.

3. The debris scene is simply a group of seven polygon objects in the shape of shards. Expand the debris group in the Outliner, Shift+click all of the members of the group, and choose nParticles ➤ Instancer (Replacement) ➤ Options.

In the Options window, all of the debris objects are listed in the order in which they were selected in the Outliner. Notice that each one has a number to the left in the list. This number is the index value of the instance. The numbering starts with 0.

4. In the Particle Object To Instance drop-down menu, choose the particleDebrisShape object. This sets the instance to the correct nDynamic object (see Figure 14.50).

5. Leave the rest of the settings at the default, and choose Create to instance the nParticles. In the Outliner a new node named instance1 has been created.

6. Play the scene. Switch to wireframe mode, and zoom in closely to the nParticles so you can see what's going on.

You'll notice that each nParticle has the same piece of geometry instanced to it, and they are all oriented the same way (see Figure 14.51). To randomize which objects are instanced to the nParticles and their size and orientation, you'll create need to create some expressions.

FIGURE 14.50

The selected objects appear in the Instanced Objects list. Select the particleDebris-Shape node in the Particle Object To Instance options.

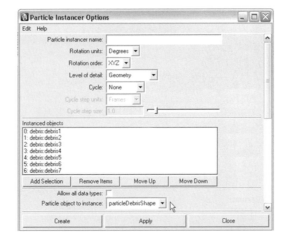

FIGURE 14.51

Each nParticle has the same piece of geometry instanced to it.

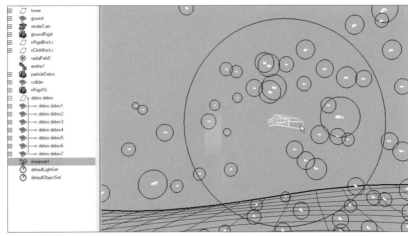

TIPS FOR WORKING WITH NPARTICLE INSTANCES

Geometry that is instanced to nParticles inherits the position and orientation of the original geometry. If you place keyframes on the original geometry, this is inherited by the instanced copies.

If you're animating flying debris, it's a better idea to animate the motion of the instances using expressions and the dynamics of the nParticles rather than setting keyframes of the rotation or translation of the original instanced geometry. This makes animation simpler and allows for more control when editing the effect.

It's also best to place the geometry you want to instance at the center of the grid and place its pivot at the center of the geometry. You'll also want to freeze transformations on the geometry to initialize its translation, rotation, and scale attributes.

In some special cases, you may want to offset the pivot of the instanced geometry. To do this, position the geometry away from the origin of the grid, place the pivot at the center of the grid, and freeze transformations.

If you are animating crawling bugs or the flapping wings of an insect, you can animate the original geometry you want to instance, or you can create a sequence of objects and use the Cycle feature in the instance options. The Cycle feature causes the instance to progress through a sequence of geometry based on the index number assigned to the instanced geometry. The Cycle feature offers more flexibility than simply animating the instanced geometry. You can use expressions to randomize the start point of the cycle on a per-particle basis. Particle expressions are covered in the next section.

You can add more objects to the Instanced Objects list after creating the instance using the options in the Attribute Editor for the instance node.

---

nParticle Expressions

The new features of nParticles allow you to create more interesting particle effects than in previous versions of Maya without relying on expressions. However, in some situations expressions are still required to achieve a believable effect. If you've never used particle expressions, they can be a little intimidating at first, and the workflow is not entirely intuitive. Once you understand how to create expressions, they can unleash an amazing level of creative potential; combined with the power of the Nucleus solver, there's almost no effect you can't create. Expressions work the same way for both nParticles and traditional Maya particles.

There are two types of expressions you can create for a particle object: creation and runtime. The difference between creation and runtime is that creation expressions evaluate once when the particles are created (or at the start of the animation for particles that are not spawned from an emitter), and runtime expressions evaluate on each frame of the animation for as long as they are in the scene.

A good way to think of this is that a creation expression is like a trait determined by your DNA. When you're born, your DNA may state something like "your maximum height will be 6 feet 4 inches." So your creation expression for height would be maximum height = 6 feet 4 inches. This has been set at the moment you are created and will remain so throughout your life unless something changes.

Think of a runtime expression as an event in your life. It's calculated each moment of your life. If for some reason during the course of your life your legs were replaced with bionic extend-o legs that give you the ability to automatically change your height whenever you want, this would be enabled using a runtime expression. It happens after you have been born and can override the creation expression. Thus, at any given moment (or frame in the case of particles) your height could be 5 feet or 25 feet, thanks to your bionic extend-o legs.

If you write a creation expression for the particles that says radius = 2, each particle will have a radius of 2, unless something changes. If you then add a runtime expression that says something like "if the Y position of a particle is greater than 10, then radius = 4," then any particle that goes beyond 10 units in Y will instantly grow to four units. The runtime expression overrides the creation expression and is calculated at least once per frame as long as the animation is playing.

Randomizing Instance Index

The first expression you'll create will randomize which instance is copied to which nParticle. To do this you'll need to create a custom attribute. This custom attribute will assign a random value between 0 and 6 for each nParticle, and this value will be used to determine the index number of the instance copied to that particular particle.

1. Select the particleDebris object and expand the Add Dynamic Attributes rollout. Click the General button (see Figure 14.52); a pop-up dialog box appears. This dialog box offers you options to determine what type of attribute will be added to the particle shape.

2. In the Long Name field type **debrisIndex**. This is the name of the attribute that will be added to the nParticle. You can name it anything you want (as long as the name does not conflict with a preexisting attribute name). It's best to use concise names that make it obvious what the attribute does.

3. Set Data Type to Float. A float is a single numeric value that can have a decimal. Numbers like 3, 18.7, and -0.314 are examples of floats.

4. Set Attribute Type to Per Particle (Array). A Per Particle attribute contains a different value for each particle in the particle object. A Scalar attribute holds the same value for all of the particles in the particle object.

FIGURE 14.52
The General button in the Add Dynamic Attributes section allows you to create your own custom attributes.

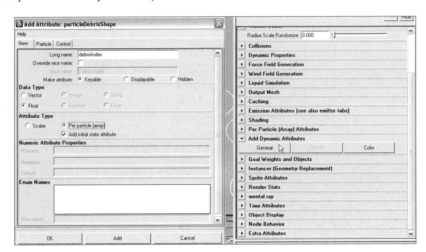

5. Click OK to add the attribute.

6. Now that you have an attribute, you need to create the expression to determine its value. Expand the Per Particle (Array) Attributes rollout, and you'll see Debris Index listed. Right-click on the field next to Debris Index and choose Creation Expression (see Figure 14.53).

7. The Expression Editor opens, and debrisIndex is selected in the Attributes list. Notice that the Particle mode is automatically set to Creation.

8. In the Expression field type **debrisIndex=rand(0,6);**. Remember that the list of instanced objects contains seven objects, but the index list starts with 0 and goes to 6 (see Figure 14.54).

FIGURE 14.53
The new Debris Index attribute appears in the list of Per Particle (Array) Attributes. To create an expression, right-click and choose Creation Expression.

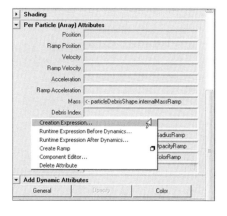

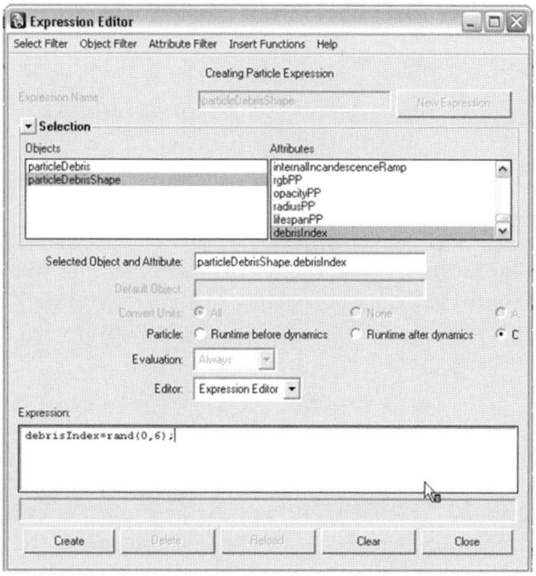

FIGURE 14.54
Add an expression to randomize the value of the debrisIndex attribute for each nParticle.

This adds a random function that assigns a number between 0 and 6 to the debrisIndex attribute of each nParticle. The semicolon at the end of the expression is typical scripting syntax and acts like a period at the end of a sentence.

9. Click the Create button to create the expression. Rewind and play the animation; nothing has changed at this point—the same piece of debris is assigned to all the nParticles. This is because even though you have a custom attribute with a random value, you haven't told Maya how to apply the attribute to the particle.

10. Expand the Instancer (Geometry Replacement) rollout in the Attribute Editor. In the General Options section, expand the Object Index menu and choose debrisIndex from the list (see Figure 14.55). Now when you rewind and play the animation, you'll see a different piece of geometry assigned to each nParticle.

FIGURE 14.55

Assign the new debrisIndex attribute as the input for the Object Index attribute in the Instancer section of the nParticle's Attribute Editor.

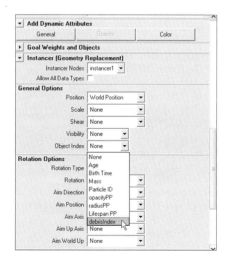

Connecting Instance Size to nParticle Mass

Next you'll create an expression that determines the size of each nParticle based on its mass. This way larger pieces of debris will move slower than smaller ones.

The size of instances is determined by their Scale X, Scale Y, and Scale Z attributes, much like a typical piece of geometry that you work with when modeling in Maya. This is different from a Balls-type nParticle that uses a single radius value to determine its size.

The size attributes for instanced geometry are contained in a vector. A vector is an attribute with a three-dimensional value, as opposed to an integer or a float, which has only a single-dimensional value.

1. Select the particleDebris object, and in the Attribute Editor, click the General button to create a new attribute. Set the Long Name value to **debrisScale**. Set Data Type to Vector and Attribute Type to Per Particle (Array). See Figure 14.56.

2. In the Per Particle (Array) Attributes section right-click on the field next to debrisScale and choose to create a creation expression.

FIGURE 14.56
Create another
attribute and name
it debrisScale; this
time set Data Type
to Vector.

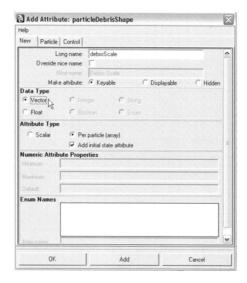

REFRESH THE ATTRIBUTE LIST

If the new attribute does not appear in the list, click on the Load Attributes button at the bottom
of the Attribute Editor to refresh the list.

---

3. In the Expression field of the Expression Editor you'll see the debrisIndex expression
   (note that the name debrisIndex has been expanded; it now says particleDebrisShape.
   debrisIndex=rand(0,6);. Maya does this automatically when you create the expression.

4. Below the debrisIndex expression type **debrisScale=<<mass,mass,mass>>;**. Click Edit to
   add this to the expression (see Figure 14.57).

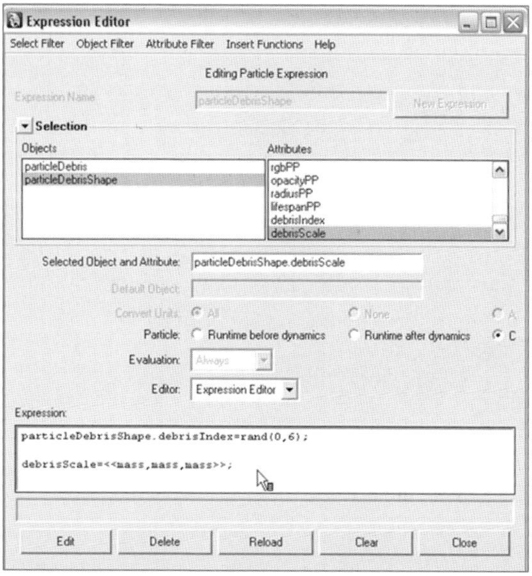

FIGURE 14.57
Set the debris-
Scale attribute to
be equivalent to
the mass of each
nParticle. Add the
expression in the
Expression Editor.

The double brackets are the syntax used when specifying vector values. Using mass as the input value for each dimension of the vector ensures that the pieces of debris are uniformly scaled.

5. In the Instancer (Geometry Replacement) attributes of the particleDebris object, set the Scale menu to debrisScale (see Figure 14.58).

6. Rewind and play the animation. The pieces of debris are now sized based on the mass of the nParticles, but of course the mass of some of the particles is so small that the instanced particles are invisible. To fix this you can edit the expression.

FIGURE 14.58
The size of the debris is determined by the mass of each nParticle. In some cases the mass is so small the instanced geometry can't be seen.

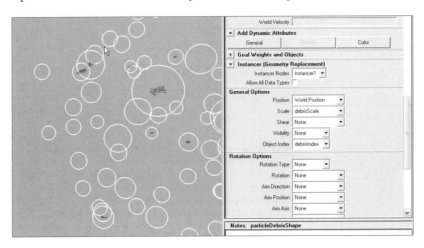

7. In the Per-Particle (Array) Attributes section, right-click on debrisScale and choose Creation Expression to open the Expression Editor. In the Expression field, add the following text above the debris scale expression:

```
float $massScale = mass*3;
```

8. Now edit the original debrisScale expression, as shown in Figure 14.59, so it reads:

```
debrisScale = <<$massScale, $massScale, $massScale>>;
```

By using the float command in the Expression Editor, you're creating a local variable that is available to be used only in the creation expressions used by the nParticle. The same variable and its value are not available for use in runtime expressions. The variable is preceded by a dollar sign. The $massScale variable is assigned the mass multiplied by three.

9. Click Edit to implement the changes to the expression. Rewind and play the animation. It's an improvement; some debris pieces are definitely much bigger, but some are still too small. You can fix this by adding a clamp function. Make sure you click the Edit button in the editor after typing the expression.

A clamp sets an upper and lower limit to the values generated by the expression. The syntax is clamp(lower limit, upper limit, input);.

10. Edit the expression for the massScale variable so it reads float $massScale=clamp (2,5,mass*10);. Make sure you click the Edit button in the editor after typing the expression (Figure 14.60).

11. Play the animation. Now you have a reasonable range of sizes for the debris, and they are all based on the mass on the particles.

12. In the Attribute Editor for the particleDebris, set Shading Type to Point so you can see the instanced geometry more easily.

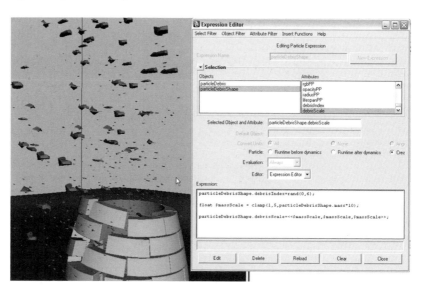

Rotation Expressions

Next you'll add some expressions to animate the rotation of the nParticles. The first task is to establish an initial random rotation, and then a runtime expression can be added to tie the velocity of the nParticles to their rotation as they move through space.

1. Create a new Per Particle vector attribute and name it **debrisRotate**. Follow steps 1 and 2 from the previous section to do this.

2. Make a creation expression for debrisRotate. In the Expression Editor, add these lines. Make sure you click the Edit button in the editor after typing the expression (Figure 14.61):

```
float $randX = rand(0,180);
float $randY = rand(0,180);
float $randZ = rand(0,180);

debrisRotate = <<$randX, $randY, $randZ>>;
```

Notice that for this expression you want to have a different value for each dimension of the debrisRotate vector, so each piece of debris is rotated randomly on each axis as opposed to the debrisScale attribute, which needed the same value applied to each dimension of the vector. Each variable produces a different random value between 0 and 180 for each particle.

To add a little more realism to the movement of the instances, you can have them rotate as they fly through the air. There are a number of ways to do this. For this example you can create a simple runtime expression that increments the rotation of each piece by the magnitude of its velocity.

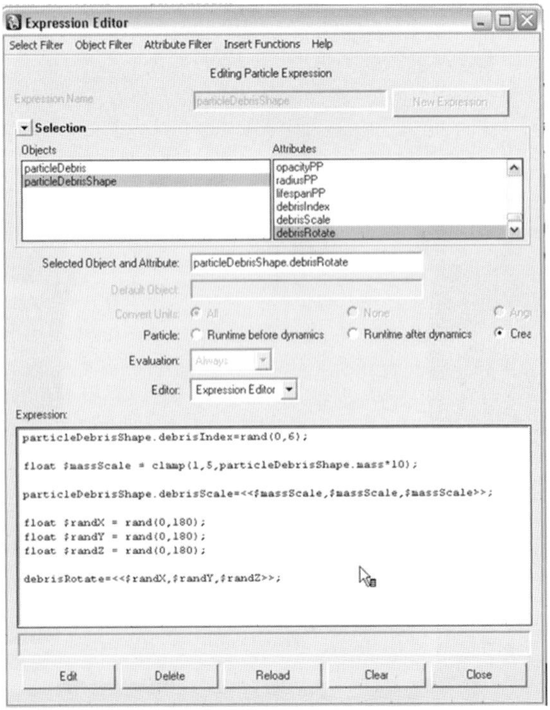

FIGURE 14.61

Add an expression to randomize the rotation of each instance.

The mag function is a simple way to convert a vector value into a float by giving you the length of the vector. Magnitude (not to be confused with the magnitude of a field in this sense) is the square root of the sum of the square of each coordinate in the vector. It sounds more complicated than it is. The formula looks like this:

$$mag = \sqrt{x^2 + y^2 + z^2}$$

In this expression, you'll take the magnitude of the velocity of the particle and add it to the rotation of the instances. This is done in a runtime expression so it executes each frame. When you add a float to a vector, Maya returns the result as a vector. So the question you may be asking now is, why would you want to convert the velocity, which is a vector, into a float, and then add the float to the rotation, which is also a vector, only to get a vector as the result? In other words, why not just add velocity to rotation and keep them all vectors? Well, the reason is that when you add a float to a vector, the same value is added to each coordinate of the vector. In other words:

```
n + <<x,y,z>> = <<n+x,n+y,n+z>>
```

which gives you a different result than adding the velocity and rotation, which looks more like this:

```
<<x1,y1,z1>>+<<x2,y2,z2>>= <<x1+x2,y1+y2,z1+z2>>
```

The upshot is that adding velocity as a vector to rotation gives you a wobbly type of motion as opposed to the constant rotation you get by adding the magnitude of the velocity to rotation.

The reason you want to use the magnitude of the velocity is so the instance stops rotating when it stops moving (that is, when velocity = 0).

3. In the Expression Editor click the radio button to switch to Runtime After Dynamics mode.

4. In the Expression field type (see Figure 14.62):

debrisRotate=debrisRotate+mag(velocity);

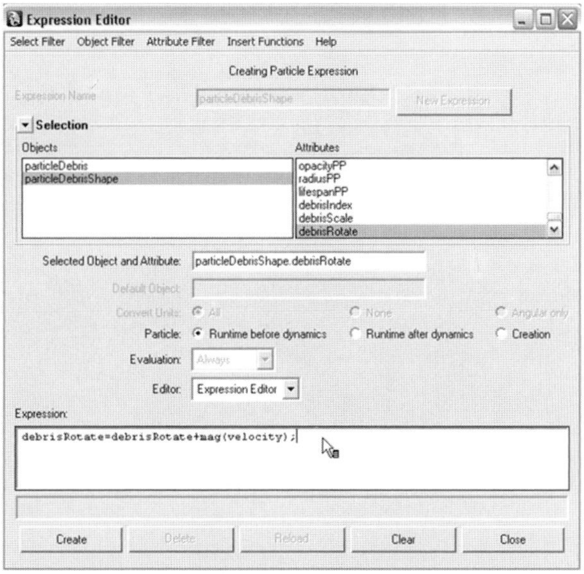

FIGURE 14.62
Add a runtime expression to increment the rotation of each nParticle by the magnitude of its velocity.

5. Click Create to make the expression. In the Instancer (Geometry Replacement) section of the Attribute Editor, set Rotation to debrisRotate (see Figure 14.63). Leave the other settings at the default. Rewind and play the animation.

6. Set the timeline to 300 and create a playblast of the animation so you can see the explosion in real time.

7. Save the scene as **tower_v06.ma**.

Overall it's a pretty respectable start to an explosion effect. In the next section you'll add some smoke trails to the debris.

FIGURE 14.63
The rotation of each instance is now randomized and animated according to the velocity of the nParticle.

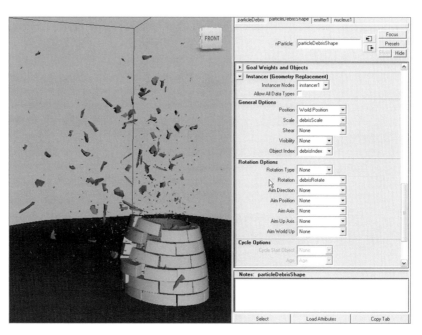

Creating Smoke Effects

To complete the look of the explosion you can use the cloud nParticle type to add a smoke trail to each of the pieces of debris. The cloud nParticle type uses a special shader to create the look of smoke in a software render. The thick cloud nParticle uses a special fluid shader to create a realistic-looking cloud. It takes longer to calculate and render than the standard cloud nParticle. Fluids are discussed in Chapter 16.

Using the Cloud nParticle Style

To add a smoke trail to the debris you can actually make each nParticle of the particleDebris object an emitter.

1. Continue with the scene from the precious section or open the tower_v06.ma scene from the chapter14\scenes directory.

2. Choose nParticles ➢ Create nParticles ➢ Cloud to set the nParticle style to Cloud.

3. In the Outliner, select the particleDebris object. Choose nParticles ➢ Create nParticles ➢ Emit From Object ➢ Options. In the options, set Emitter Type to Omni and Rate to **40**. You can leave the other settings at their default. Click Create to add the emitter.

4. In the Outliner a new nParticle node has been added to the scene. Rename this node **smokeParticle**. If you expand the particleDebris object, you'll see that an emitter has been parented. This is the emitter for the smokeParticle (Figure 14.64).

Since there are a total of 1200 particleDebris objects that will be emitted in the scene, each one of these will emit 40 cloud nParticles per second. This quickly adds up to a lot of nParticles. To avoid bogging the scene down, set a short life span on the smokeParticles.

FIGURE 14.64
Add a new nParticle to the scene and rename it smokeParticle. Parent the emitter for this nParticle to the debrisParticle node.

NPARTICLES EMITTING NPARTICLES

The smokeParticle object won't appear in the scene until the debrisParticle is emitted at frame 20.

---

5. Select the smokeParticle object. Set Life Span to Random Range. Set Life Span Value to **2** and Life Span Random to **2**. This means each cloud particle lasts between 1 and 3 seconds.

6. Set Radius in the Particle Size rollout to **1.3**. Expand the Radius Scale attributes and set Radius Scale Input to Age. Add two control points to the Radius Scale ramp, and edit the position of the points so that the ramp starts at 0.1 and slopes up smoothly to the right.

7. Set Radius Scale Randomize to **0.1**.

DOUBLE-CHECK YOUR SELECTED NPARTICLE

Since both the debrisParticle and the smokeParticle are connected through the nucleus1 solver, its very easy to accidentally edit the attributes for the wrong particle while working in the Attribute Editor. Make sure you double-check which tab is selected when working in the Attribute Editor!

---

8. In the Dynamic Properties section set Drag to **0.1**, and make sure Ignore Solver Gravity is activated (see Figure 14.65). The smoke particles should not fall to the ground.

9. Scroll down to the Emission Attributes section and set Inherit Factor to **0.5**. This causes the smoke particle to inherit some of the motion of the particleDebris object, giving it a more believable motion as it flies out from each piece of debris.

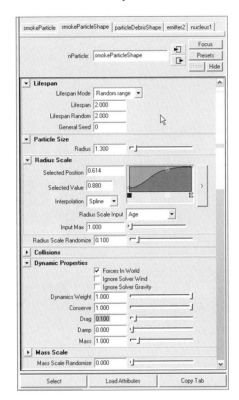

FIGURE 14.65
Edit the Dynamic Properties settings for the smokeParticle object in the Attribute Editor.

10. Scroll down to the Opacity Scale attributes in the Shading rollout. Set Opacity Scale Input to Age. Edit the Opacity Scale ramp so it starts at 0.7 on the left and slopes down to 0 on the right, as shown in Figure 14.66.

11. Expand the Color attributes. Set Color Input to Age. Edit the Color ramp so it is bright yellow on the left side, fading quickly to light gray and then gradually to dark gray on the right of the ramp. This makes each smoke trail bright yellow on the end closest to the flying debris, fading out to dark gray over time.

12. Expand the Incandescence section. Set Incandescence Input to Age. Edit the ramp so there is a small sliver of bright yellow on the left side that quickly fades to black.

FIGURE 14.66
The shading
settings for the
smokeParticle

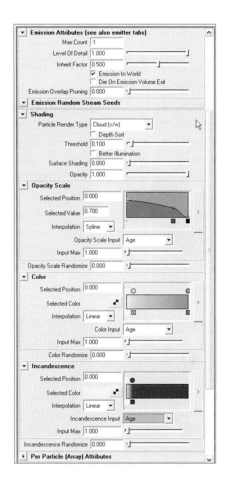

13. Select the emitter attached to the debris particle. Set a keyframe on the Rate attribute on frame 90. Move the timeline to frame 120, and set Rate to **0**; set another keyframe.

14. To create the effect of the smoke drifting upward, add some wind to the Nucleus solver. First select the particleDebris object and activate the Ignore Solver Wind option in the Dynamic Properties rollout so that the debris is not affected by the wind.

15. Open the Nucleus solver and set Wind Speed to **3**. Set Wind Direction to **0, 1, 0** so it pushes upward. Set Noise to **0.5** to add some turbulence.

16. Save your scene. Rewind the animation and create a playblast to see the explosion in action (Figure 14.67). It should take anywhere from 5 to 10 minutes to create the playblast.

17. Save the scene as **tower_v07.ma**. To see a finished version of the scene open tower_v07.ma from the chapter14\scenes folder on the DVD.

FIGURE 14.67
A playblast of the animation reveals a very dramatic explosion worthy of an episode of *Mythbusters*.

The Bottom Line

Use nCloth.   nCloth can be used to make polygon geometry behave dynamically to simulate a wide variety of materials. Using the presets that come with Maya, you can design your own materials and create your own presets for use in your animations.

Master it   Create the effect of a cube of gelatinous material rolling down the stairs.

Combine nCloth and nParticles.   Because nCloth and nParticles use the same dynamic systems, they can be easily combined to create amazing simulations.

Master it   Make a water balloon burst as it hits the ground.

Use nCloth for rigid body simulations.   nCloth can be used to simulate rigid dynamics as well as soft surfaces. The Concrete preset is usually the best place to start when creating an nCloth rigid body. nCloth objects have a large number of settings that can give you more control over their behavior than you would get using traditional rigid bodies.

Master it   Animate a wrecking ball destroying a wall of nCloth bricks.

Use traditional Maya rigid body dynamics.   Traditional rigid body dynamics are not quite as powerful as nCloth objects, but they do calculate much faster and work better for simulations involving a large number of interacting pieces.

Master it   Animate a series of dominoes falling over.

Instance geometry to nParticles.   Modeled geometry can be instanced to nParticles to create a wide variety of effects.

Master it   Create the effect of a swarm of insects attacking a beach ball.

Create nParticle expressions. nParticle expressions can be used to further extend the power of nParticles. Using expressions to automate instanced geometry simulations is just one of the ways in which expressions can be used.

> **Master it** Improve the animation of the insects attacking the beach ball by adding different types of insects to the swarm. Randomize their size, and create expressions so that larger insects move more slowly.

Create smoke effects. Using the cloud nParticle type, smoke can be added to a simulation. nCloth objects and nParticles can be turned into emitters to emit the smoke.

> **Master it** In the explosion scene from this chapter, make the nCloth bricks emit a smoke trail as they fly out from the tower.

Chapter 15

Fur, Hair, and Clothing

Maya offers a number of tools for adding fur, hair, and clothing to characters. Creative use of these tools adds believability and originality to your animated characters. In addition, many of these tools can be used to create engaging visual effects. This chapter takes you through a number of techniques that can be used to add fur, hair, and clothing to characters.

In this chapter you will learn to:

- ◆ Add fur to characters
- ◆ Add dynamic motion to fur
- ◆ Render fur with mental ray
- ◆ Create dynamic curves
- ◆ Add hair to characters
- ◆ Style hair
- ◆ Use hair constraints
- ◆ Render hair
- ◆ Create clothing for characters
- ◆ Paint nCloth properties

Add Fur to Characters

In this section you'll add Maya Fur to a model of a hound dog's head. Maya Fur can be used on NURBS, polygon, and subdivision surfaces. There are some limitations when using NURBS and subdivision surfaces. For instance, rendering fur on trimmed NURBS surfaces can add to render time, and many of the paintable fur attributes do not work when using subdivision surfaces. For this reason, it's recommended that you use polygon geometry whenever possible.

Maya Fur works best for short-haired characters. Think about using fur for hair that is two inches or shorter in the real world. If your character's hair is longer than that, then consider using Maya Hair or Paint Effects.

Prepare Polygons for Maya Fur

Polygon models need to have properly mapped UV coordinates that lie within to 0 to 1 range in texture space. You should make sure that there are no overlapping UVs. This can cause problems and may even crash Maya when rendering.

Try as best as you can to maintain consistency in texture space as you create UV coordinates. Seams between separate UV shells and between parts of the model's texture coordinates are easily seen in the distribution of fur across the surface, and they can be very difficult to eliminate. Figure 15.1 shows an example of a visible seam in the fur attached to the hound dog model. This seam appears because the end of the nose is a separate shell from the rest of the hound's head. In some cases it may be impossible to eliminate all seams.

The best strategy is to place UV seams on parts of the surface that are less noticeable than others. Once you have an understanding of how fur works after completing this chapter, you should test a simple fur preset (such as the duckling preset) on your models as you map the UV texture coordinates. You'll see where the problem areas are before you spend a great amount of time perfecting the fur itself. Props, such as clothing, can also be used strategically to hide UV seams.

Chapter 11 has detailed information on how to create UV texture coordinates for polygon models.

FIGURE 15.1
A seam is visible in the fur on the nose of the hound.

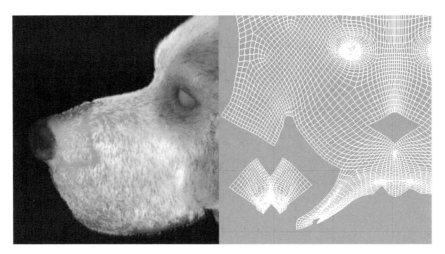

USING THE EXAMPLE SCENES

Maya Fur relies heavily on file textures that are saved in the Fur subfolders of the current project. If you intend to use the example scenes in this chapter, you should copy the entire Chapter 15 project folder from the DVD to your local disk. This should ensure that the results you get when you test the example scenes are consistent with what is presented in the figures in this book.

In this example the hound model has been created and the UVs have been properly prepared.

1. Open the hound_v01.ma scene from the chapter15\scenes folder.

2. Select the houndHead model and choose Window ➢ UV Texture Editor.

The UVs for the houndHead model are displayed in the UV Texture Editor (see Figure 15.2).

If you are applying fur to a subdivision surface, you may want to convert the model to polygons first and prepare the UVs before applying the fur. You can convert the model back to subdivision surfaces after the fur has been applied. Working with subdivision surfaces and polygons is covered in Chapter 4.

FIGURE 15.2
The UV texture coordinates have already been created for the houndHead model.

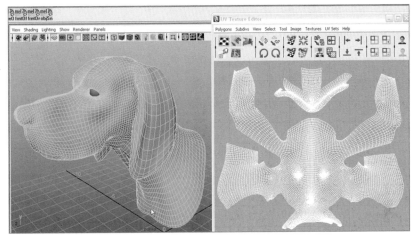

Create a Fur Description

The fur description node contains all the settings for the fur, such as length, color, width, density, and so on. A single fur description node can be applied to more than one surface.

A number of preset fur descriptions are available on the Fur shelf or in the Presets button in the Attribute Editor for the fur description node. You can use a preset as a starting point. In this exercise, you'll build the fur description from the default fur settings.

1. Select the houndHead model. Switch to the Rendering menu set, and choose Fur ➢ Attach Fur Description ➢ New.

The houndHead surface is covered in long spikes. These spikes are a preview that approximates how the fur will look on the surface. This approximation is a visual aid you can use while editing the fur. If you do not see the spikes (Figure 15.3), the display of locators may have been disabled in the Viewport window. To fix this, choose Show ➢ Locators from the menu in the Viewport window.

The controls for the fur preview are found in the Attribute Editor for the houndHead_FurFeedbackShape node. This node is parented under the FurFeedback node in the Outliner.

2. In the Outliner, expand the FurFeedback group and select the houndHead_FurFeedback node. Open the Attribute Editor and click the houndHead_FurFeedbackShape tab.

3. To increase the number of fur strands displayed in the viewport, set U Samples and V Samples to **128**.

FIGURE 15.3
The fur is displayed as long spikes on the surface. Locators must be visible in the perspective view in order to display the spikes.

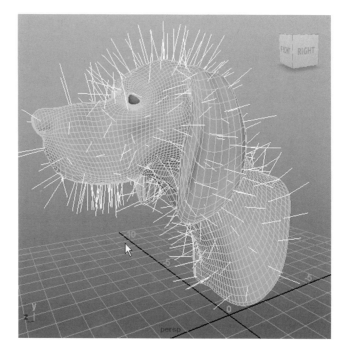

You can set these values higher for a more accurate display; however, higher settings will slow the performance of Maya on your computer. The U and V Samples affect only how the fur is displayed in Maya; they do not affect how it will look when rendered.

4. Switch to the FurDescription1 tab in the Attribute Editor. Here you'll find the settings that determine how the fur will look when rendered.

5. In the Fur Description field, rename FurDescription1 as **houndFur**.

6. Save the scene as **hound_v02.ma**. To see a version of the scene to this point, open the houndFur_v02.ma scene from the chapter15\scenes folder on the DVD.

Edit the Fur Description: Baldness

There are several ways to design the look of fur applied to your model. You can adjust the slider settings in the fur description node to create an overall look for the fur, or you can apply texture maps to the fur settings. These texture maps can be procedural nodes (such as ramp, fractal, checker), or they can be file textures painted in other programs. You can also use the Artisan Brush tool to paint settings directly on the model. In this section, you'll use Artisan to determine where fur grows on the model.

Fur is applied uniformly across the surface of a model. In order to control exactly where the fur grows, you'll use the Baldness attribute. The Baldness value ranges between 1 and 0. The confusing aspect about the Baldness setting in particular is that a setting of 1 means fur covers the surface. A setting of 0 means the fur does not grow at all. This is confusing because intuitively more baldness (higher values) should mean less fur. In Maya the settings are reversed, so higher Baldness values mean more fur. Fortunately this is the only setting that suffers from this counterintuitive behavior.

Settings between 0 and 1 determine the sparseness of the fur. Using a low Baldness setting, such as 0.1 or 0.2, might work well when creating whiskers for a man's face.

In this exercise, you'll apply Baldness values so that fur does not grow on the end of the nose, in the eye sockets, or on the inside of the mouth.

1. Open the hound_v02.ma scene from the chapter15\scenes directory.

2. In the Outliner, select the houndHead_FurFeedback node parented to the FurFeedback group. In the Attribute Editor, select the houndFur tab.

3. Set the Base and Tip Color attributes to bright red. This makes it easier to see the fur as you paint attribute maps. If the fur does not turn red when you adjust the sliders, make sure Color Feedback Enabled is turned on in the houndHead_FurFeedbackShape node.

4. Switch to the houndFur tab. To make it easier to see what's going on, set the Length slider to 0.1. This reduces the overall length of the fur. Later on you'll fine-tune the length of the fur on the model using Artisan.

5. Move the Baldness slider back and forth between a value of 1 and 0. You'll see the fur become sparser when the value is lower.

FUR GLOBAL SCALE

You can also reduce the length of the fur by reducing the Global Scale value. However, refrain from adjusting this slider when you first edit a new fur description because the slider should be used to keep all of the fur settings consistent when the model itself is scaled. For example, if this model and its fur are imported into a scene that requires the model to be resized, you can adjust the Global Scale of the fur based on the scaling values applied to the model, and the look of the fur should remain consistent when rendered. If you adjust Global Scale before designing the fur, it may make it hard to adjust the settings properly if the model is scaled.

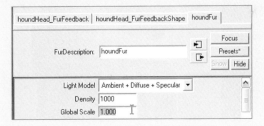

The slider works well to establish an overall value. For precise control you'll paint Baldness values directly on the model.

6. Set the Baldness slider to 1 so that the fur covers the entire model evenly.

7. In the Outliner, select the houndHead object. Choose Fur ➢ Paint Fur Attributes Tool ➢ Options. The Attribute Editor switches to the Tool Options view at the same time a small pop-up menu appears. If Maya stops for a moment, don't be alarmed; it is preparing the model for painting.

8. In the Paint Fur Attributes Tool Settings pop-up, make sure Fur Attribute is set to Baldness and Fur Description is set to houndFur. Set Attribute Map Width and Height to **1024**.

The Attribute Map Width and Height determine the resolution of the baldness map that will be created when you use the Paint Fur Attributes tool. In the case of the hound model, you'll need a higher resolution so that you can more precisely paint Baldness values around the tight areas of the eyes, nose, and lips. If the attribute you are painting does not require precision, you can use lower values for Height and Width.

9. In the options for the Artisan Brush, set Paint Operation to Replace and Value to 0. Wherever you paint on the surface of the model, fur will be removed.

10. In the Tool Options section, under the Display rollout, activate Color Feedback. This colors the model according to the values you paint on the fur. The colors act as a guide as you paint.

11. Zoom in on the nose of the model. Hold the cursor over the nose of the hound. Hold the b key and drag left or right to interactively adjust the width of the brush.

12. Start painting in the nose; you'll see the spikes start to disappear as you paint. The area where you paint also turns black (see Figure 15.4).

Sometimes you need to paint over a spike a couple times to get it to update. If you need more detail in the Fur Feedback, you can increase the U and V Samples values in the houndHead_FurFeedbackShape tab.

FIGURE 15.4
The surface of the hound turns black as you paint the Baldness value on the model. The fur spikes disappear in the black areas.

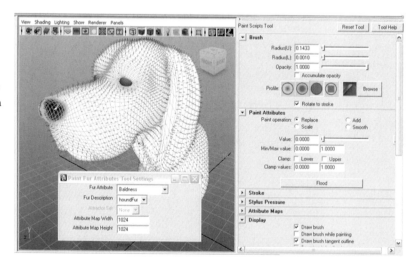

MAP FILE UPDATE

As you paint, Maya creates a temporary map file for the Baldness attributes. Occasionally Maya pauses as it updates the file. Hopefully this should not happen too often. If Maya appears to freeze while working, don't be alarmed. Give it a few moments to think while it's updating the fur file.

If you get no reaction from the Paint Fur Attributes tool at all, try unselecting and reselecting the houndHead surface in the Outliner. The Paint Fur Attributes tool works only when the surface object is currently selected, so it won't work if just the fur nodes are selected.

13. Paint on the nose and the inside folds of the nose until all the fur spikes are gone. You'll edit the Baldness values more later, so don't stress out if it's not absolutely perfect.

14. When you have finished the nose, use the Show menu in the perspective view to turn off the visibility for NURBS surfaces. The eyes disappear. Paint inside the eye sockets to remove the fur from inside of the eye (see Figure 15.5).

15. To remove fur from the lips, you can move the perspective view inside the model and paint on the backside of the surface (Figure 15.6).

FIGURE 15.5
Use the Paint Fur Attributes tool to remove fur from inside the eye sockets.

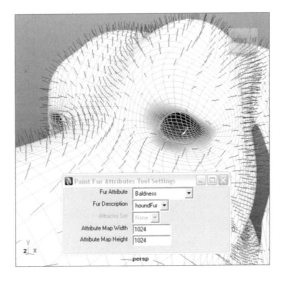

FIGURE 15.6
Remove fur from the lips by painting from the inside of the model.

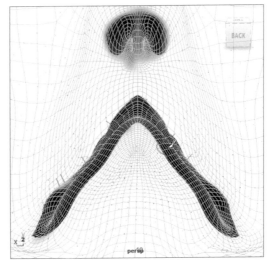

16. In the Attribute Editor for the houndFur node, scroll down and expand the Details section. Find the Baldness rollout and expand the Maps section. This lists the maps painted for the houndHeadShape. Currently the baldness map is listed as UNNAMED. This refers to the map you have been painting on the hound. It exists as a temporary file until you save the scene (see Figure 15.7).

17. Save the scene as **hound_v03.ma**.

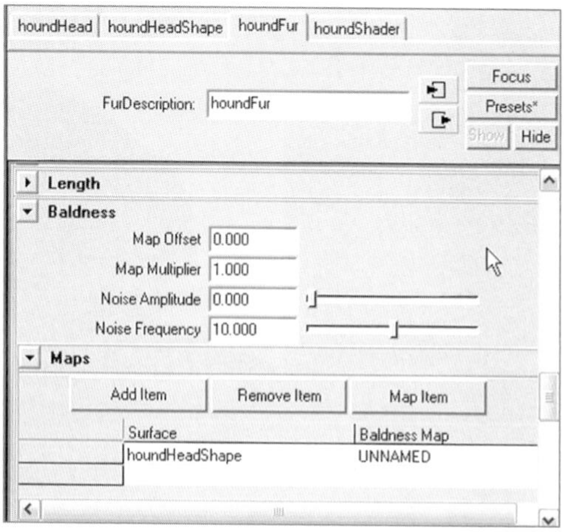

FIGURE 15.7
An unnamed map is listed in the Maps section for the Baldness attribute.

When you save the scene, the maps that you have painted for the fur attributes are saved to disk. They can be found in the current project's `fur\furAttrMap` directory. The maps are saved in the Maya `.iff` format (see Figure 15.8).

If you reopen the scene, the UNNAMED label is replaced in the Maps section of the Attribute Editor for the houndFur node with the path to the baldness map that has been saved to disk (Figure 15.9).

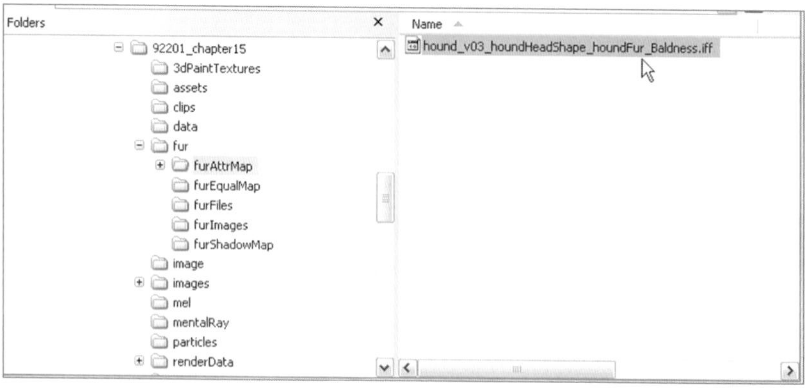

FIGURE 15.8
When you save the scene, the baldness map is written to disk.

FIGURE 15.9

When you reopen the scene, the UNNAMED label is replaced with the path to the baldness map that has been written to disk.

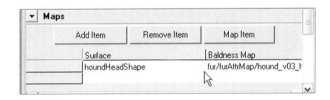

 Real World Scenario

EDITING MAP FILES

Maps listed in the Details section of the fur node are always image files (as opposed to procedural textures such as ramp, fractal, or checker). You can edit these images in other programs such as Photoshop.

To edit a map in Photoshop follow these steps:

1. Open FCheck (Choose File ➢ View Image, browse to the fur\furAttrMap folder in the current project, and open the image).

2. Use FCheck to save the image in a format Photoshop can read; a TIFF image should work fine. From the File menu in FCheck, choose Save Image. Save the image as **houndBaldnessMap.tif**.

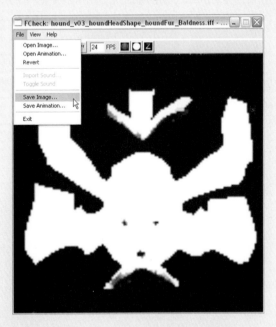

3. Open the houndBaldness.tif map in Photoshop, and edit the image with the standard Photoshop paint tools. Make sure you paint only grayscale values on the map. Lighter colors mean more fur; darker colors mean less fur.

CONTINUES

EDITING MAP FILES *(CONTINUED)*

4. When you have finished editing the file, save the image with no compression.

5. In Maya, open the Attribute Editor for the houndFur node. In the Details section under Baldness, expand the Maps section. Select the label under the Surface heading, click the Map Item button, and use the dialog box to select the image edited in Photoshop.

You can activate the Paint Fur Attributes tool to continue editing the map in Maya. You'll see the changes made to the map appear on the model if Color Feedback is enabled in the Artisan options. Remember that Maya may take a few moments to update the display on the model.

Other programs that have advanced 3D texturing tools, such as BodyPaint, ZBrush, or Mudbox, can be used to paint and edit maps for fur attributes. Save the image as a Tiff format file and apply it to the model using the instructions in step 5. Some programs such as ZBrush invert the vertical dimensions of the texture map. You may need to flip the vertical scaling of texture maps painted in ZBrush before applying them to a fur attribute in Maya.

Edit the Fur Description: Direction

You can use the Artisan Brush interface to comb the fur by painting the Direction attribute.

1. Continue with the scene from the previous section or open the hound_v03.ma scene from the chapter15\scenes directory on the DVD.

You'll notice that there is no Direction or Comb attribute listed in the attributes for the houndFur node. Painting the Direction attribute is the same as painting the Polar attribute.

2. In the houndFur node's Attribute Editor, set Inclination to 1 and move the Polar slider back and forth. The Polar slider determines the direction in which the fur strands face, but you'll notice that the direction is not uniform across the surface.

Inclination sets the angle at which the hair stands from the surface. A value of 0 is perpendicular to the surface; a value of 1 causes the fur to lie flat against the surface. If the value is 0, then the fur strand sticks straight up, so changing its direction has no visible effect.

Roll rotates the fur around its root. A value of 0 is -90 degrees; a value of 1 is 90 degrees.

Base Curl and Tip Curl determine the amount of curling applied to the base and tip of the hair. A value of 0.5 produces straight hair; a value of 0 or 1 curls the hair from one side or the other.

The change in direction created by the Polar attribute is based on the direction of the UV texture coordinates. This means that a value applied to fur on one part of the model has a different result than a value applied on another part of the model. In order to comb the hair correctly, you use the Direction attribute in the Paint Fur Attributes tool to apply a Polar value based on the direction that you drag across the surface. So when you choose to paint the Direction attribute in the Paint Fur Tool options, you're really painting values for the Polar attribute but in a way that is a bit more intuitive.

When painting the direction, set Inclination to a value other than 0, and the Roll value must be something other than 0.5. The Base Curl and Tip Curl values must be something other than 0.5 as well. If these values are not set properly, painting the Direction has no effect. In addition, Color Feedback has no bearing on the direction of the fur, so you can turn this option off in the options for the Artisan tool.

3. Open the Attribute Editor for the houndFur node. Set Inclination to **0.8**, and set Roll to **0.2**. Set Base Curl to **0.7** and Tip Curl to **0.3**.

4. Select the houndHead surface. Choose Fur ➤ Paint Fur Attributes Tool ➤ Options. Wait a few moments for Maya to update.

5. In the Options box for the Artisan tool, scroll to the bottom. In the Display options, turn off Color Feedback.

6. In the pop-up options for the Paint Fur Attributes Tool settings, set Fur Attribute to Direction. Make sure Fur Description is set to houndFur and the Attribute Map Width and Height are set to **1024**.

7. Drag across the surface to push the fur in the general direction you want it to go. Use Figure 15.10 for reference. Figure 15.11 shows how the paint stroke influences the direction of the fur on the model.

Paint lightly and slowly using repeated strokes to make the fur point in the desired direction. Combing the fur requires some patience and practice. It's helpful to increase the U and V samples on the FurFeedback node so that you can see more fur as you are painting. It can be difficult to maintain a consistent direction across UV seams. The fewer seams you have in your UV texture coordinates, the easier it will be to paint the direction of the fur.

The Direction attribute responds to the direction in which you move the cursor over the surface. The Paint Operation or Value settings in the Artisan options do not affect how the fur is combed.

8. Save the scene as **hound_v04.ma**. To see a version of the scene to this point, open the hound_v04.ma scene from the chapter15\scenes directory.

FIGURE 15.10
Observe the direction of the fur in this photo of an American foxhound.

FIGURE 15.11
Paint the direction of the fur on the surface of the hound. Increase the U and V Samples in the fur feedback node to 256 to make it easier to see details in the fur direction.

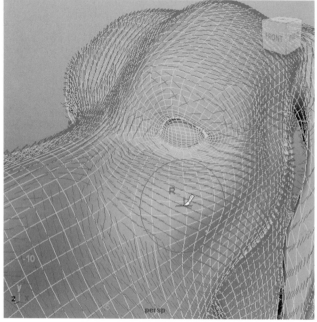

PAINTING ACROSS UV TEXTURE BORDERS

As you paint across UV borders on the model, you'll see the hair suddenly flip around. Since fur relies on UV texture coordinates to determine how the Polar attribute affects direction, as you move from one part of the texture space to another the polarity of the fur can suddenly change (a good example of this occurs on the back of the hound's head). This may drive you crazy. Here are some tips you can follow to help deal with these problems. Select the model and choose Display ➤ Polygons ➤ Texture Border Edges. This makes the border edges of the UV coordinates visible as bold lines on the surface of the model. Reduce the size of the brush so that you can more easily paint specific areas along the border. With some patience and work you'll be able to make the direction of the fur consistent across the UV texture border.

Edit the Fur Description: Length

The Length attribute can be edited using the Paint Attributes tool as well. When editing lengths you need to pay attention to the values used in the options for the Artisan Brush. For the hound, the fur is shorter near the end of the nose, medium length on the face, and long on the back of the head and neck.

1. Continue with the scene from the previous section or open the hound_v04.ma scene from the chapter15\scenes directory.

2. Select the houndHead object and choose Fur ➤ Paint Fur Attributes Tool.

3. In the houndHead_furFeedbackShape tab, set U and V Samples to **128**.

4. In the pop-up menu for the Paint Fur Attributes Tool settings, set Fur Attribute to Length. Make sure Fur Description is set to houndFur and Attribute Map Width and Height are set to **1024**.

5. In the options for the Artisan Brush, set Paint Operation to Replace and Value to **0.5**.

6. Paint around the area of the neck. You'll see the fur become longer as you paint (Figure 15.12).

7. Set Value to **0.25** and paint on the ears, under the ear, the top of the head, and the upper part of the throat.

8. Set Value to **0.1** and paint the area near the nose and the front of the snout near the lips.

9. To even out the transition between the fur lengths, set Paint Operation to Smooth, and paint the areas on the border between the different lengths of fur.

After painting fur lengths you may decide to touch up the Direction attribute of the fur as well. You can change the paint operation mode (from Length to Direction, for example) in the Paint Fur Attributes Tool Settings pop-up whenever you need to, but remember that Maya may pause for a few moments to update the maps when you change attributes.

10. Save the scene as **hound_v05.ma**. To see a version of the scene to this point, open the hound_v05.ma scene from the chapter15\scenes.

FIGURE 15.12
Edit the length of the hair by painting on areas of the houndHead surface.

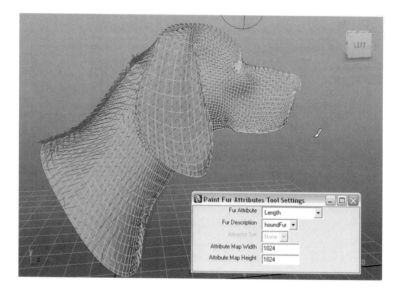

Real World Scenario

BAKING TEXTURES INTO MAPS

You can use a procedural texture node (such as a ramp, fractal, or checker) as a starting place for a fur attribute map. This works well when you are painting fur applied to a NURBS surface, since the UV texture coordinates are based on the parameterization of the surface itself. The following steps demonstrate how to do this.

1. Create a new scene in Maya.

2. Create a NURBS sphere.

3. Select the sphere and choose Fur Attach ➢ Fur Description ➢ New.

4. Open the Attribute Editor for the FurDescription1 node.

5. Right-click on the field next to Baldness, and choose Create New Texture.

6. From the Create Texture Node window, choose the ramp texture. The fur on the Sphere disappears.

7. Open the Attribute Editor for the ramp texture. Change the colors of the ramp so that the top is black and the bottom is white. Delete the color marker in the center. The fur display returns.

8. If you move the markers on the ramp up and down, you'll notice that the fur display does not change. In order to use the ramp values to affect the Baldness setting, you need to bake the ramp.

9. In the Attribute Editor for the FurDescription node, set Bake Attribute to Baldness, and leave Map Width and Height set to 256. Click the Bake button.

The fur becomes sparse on part of the sphere. This sparse area corresponds to the black part of the ramp. You can select the ramp texture in the Hypershade and connect it to the Color channel of the sphere's shader if you'd like to see a visual representation of the placement of the ramp on the sphere.

10. Open the Attribute Editor for the ramp texture, and set Interpolation to None.

11. Move the Black color marker down. The fur on the sphere will not update until you bake the texture again.

12. In the Attribute Editor for Fur Description, click the Bake button. The fur on the sphere updates. To see this example, open the `rampBaldness.ma` scene from the `chapter15\scenes` directory on the DVD.

Test Render Fur

Now that you have the basic fur description created for the houndHead, you may want to see what it looks like when rendered. You can render the scene using either mental ray or Maya Software. The results should be fairly similar. In this example, you'll use mental ray.

1. Continue using the scene from the previous section or open the hound_v05.ma scene from the chapter15\scenes folder.

2. Open the Render Settings window, and set the Render Using menu to mental ray.

3. In the Quality tab, set Quality Presets to Production: Rapid Fur (see Figure 15.13). This preset uses the Rasterizer as the primary renderer instead of raytracing. For more information on rendering with mental ray, consult Chapter 12.

4. Open the Render View window, and create a test render using the perspective camera.

FIGURE 15.13

Choose the Rapid Fur preset in the Quality tab of the Render Settings window.

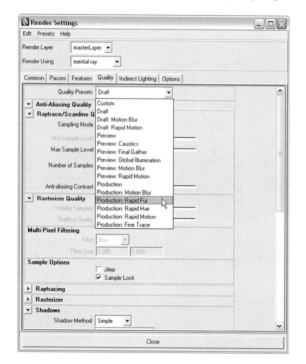

You'll notice immediately that the fur does not look very realistic (see the upper-left image in Figure 15.14). It is very sparse and bright red. You need to increase the Density setting of the fur so that enough hair covers the surface of the model.

5. Set Density in the houndFur tab to **100,000**, and create another test render (see the upper-right image in Figure 5.14).

The fur is much denser without adding too much to the render time. To improve the look of the fur, you can edit the base and tip widths as well as the basic color.

6. In the houndFur tab in the Attribute Editor, click on the color swatch next to Base Color, and use the Color Chooser to set the color to a dark brown.

7. Set Tip Color to a light brown.

8. Make sure Base Opacity is set to **1**. Set Tip Opacity to **0.1**. Set Base Width to **0.01** and Tip Width to **0.005**.

9. Create another test render (see the lower-left image in Figure 5.14).

10. Raise Density to 500,000, and create another test render (see the lower-left image in Figure 5.14).

11. Save the scene as **hound_v06.ma**. To see a version of the scene, open the hound_v06.ma scene from the chapter15\scenes directory.

The fur should cover the model completely; however, you will notice that some attributes, such as the baldness map and the direction, may require further editing.

FIGURE 15.14
Create test renders of the fur as you adjust the settings.

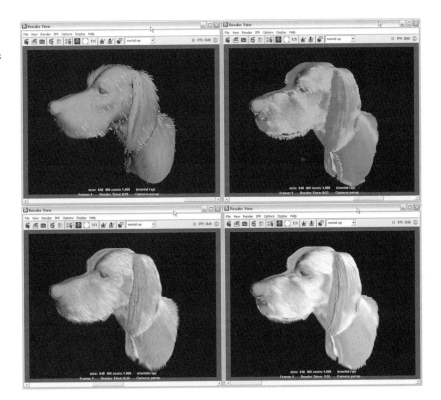

Apply a Color Map

Adding a texture map to the color greatly helps the realism of the fur. You can increase the efficiency of the render by applying the same file texture to the fur color and the shader as applied to the model. This technique should work as long as the model does not get extremely close to the camera.

A texture map that has been carefully painted in Photoshop or in a 3D texturing program works better than a map created by painting color on the fur. In this case ZBrush was used to create the color texture map for the hound model.

1. Continue with the scene from the previous section or open the hound_v06.ma scene from the chapter15\scenes directory on the DVD.

2. Open the Hypershade, select the houndShader material, and open its Attribute Editor.

3. Click on the checkered button next to the Color channel to open the Create Texture Node window. Click the File button to create a file texture node.

4. In the Attribute Editor for the file node, click the folder icon next to File Name. Use the browser to select the houndBaseColor file texture from the chapter15\sourceimages directory on the DVD. Press the 6 key to switch to textured view so you can see how the color is placed on the model.

5. Keep the Hypershade window open. In the Outliner, expand the FurFeedback group and select the houndHead_FurFeedback node. In the Attribute Editor, select the hound-Fur tab.

6. In the Hypershade, switch to the Textures tab. MMB-drag the file1 texture onto the Base Color swatch in the Attribute Editor for houndFur (see Figure 15.15).

7. In the Hypershade, create a second file texture node (Create 2D Texture ➢ File). In the Attribute Editor for file2, load the houndTipColor texture. This is a lighter, less-saturated version of the base color. Attach this file to the Tip Color channel in the houndFur node.

FIGURE 15.15
Drag the file1 node from the Textures tab of the Hypershade onto the Base Color channel of the hound-Fur node.

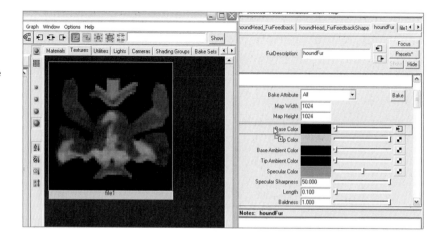

8. Lower Specular Color to a dark gray, and set Specular Sharpness to **80**. This makes the specular highlight on the fur smaller and less reflective.

9. Set the Density value of the fur to **250,000** in the houndFur tab, and create a test render (see the left image in Figure 15.16).

10. To increase the realism of the fur, turn on shadows for the scene lights. Select the spot-light1 object and open its Attribute Editor. Under Shadows, turn on Use Depth Map Shadows. Set Resolution to **1024** and turn off Use Auto Focus. Create another test render (see the right image in Figure 15.16).

11. Save the scene as **hound_v07.ma**. To see a version of the scene, open the hound_v07.ma scene from the chapter15\scenes directory.

FIGURE 15.16
Add a color map to the fur description (left image) and render the scene shadows (right image).

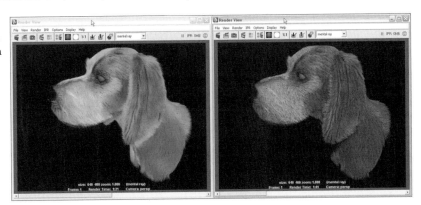

Map Offsets and Multipliers

In the Details section of the houndFur node, you'll notice each attribute has Map Offset, Map Multiplier, Noise Amplitude, and Noise Frequency settings. These sliders can apply an additional adjustment to the fur map attributes.

The Map Offset and Multiplier attributes are used to change the range of values for any of the attributes. Most of the attributes are limited to a range between 0 and 1, which corresponds to the grayscale values painted on the surface with the Paint Fur Attributes brush. If you would like to change the range so that it can go beyond 1, you can use Map Offset or Map Multiplier.

Offset adds a number to the overall range. If you want to offset the range for an attribute so that instead of a range of 0 to 1 the range becomes 2 to 3, set Offset to **2**.

If you want to expand or diminish the range of values use Multiplier. For example if you want the range of a value to be between 0 and 10 instead of 0 to 1, set Multiplier to **10**.

The Noise Amplitude and Frequency sliders add randomness to the map values.

1. Continue with the scene from the previous section or open the hound_v07.ma scene from the chapter15\scenes directory.

The fur for the hound is a little too long to be appropriate for a typical foxhound. Rather than repaint the Length values, you can simply adjust Multiplier for the Length attribute.

2. Open the Attribute Editor for the houndFur node. Expand the Details ➤ Length rollout. Set Map Multiplier to **0.5**.

3. Expand the Tip Ambient Color attribute, and set Noise Amplitude to **0.5** and Noise Frequency to **25**. This adds variation to the brightness of the fur tips.

4. Create a test render from the perspective camera (Figure 15.17).

5. Save the scene as **hound_v08.ma**. To see a version of the scene, open the hound_v08.ma scene from the chapter15\scenes directory.

FIGURE 15.17
Shorten the overall length of the hair by reducing the Multiplier value for the Length attribute. Add variation to the tip color by adding noise to the Tip Ambient Color attribute.

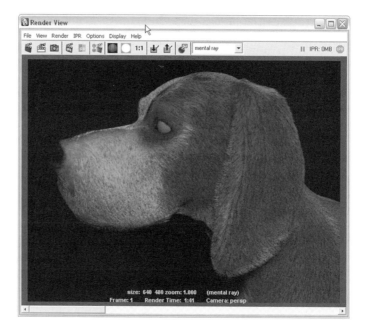

Additional Fur Attributes

The basic fur description for the hound has been created, but to make it look realistic a fair amount of editing still needs to be done. There are many additional attributes you can use to help accomplish this. This section describes how these attributes work. As with the Baldness, Length, Direction, and Color attributes, you can use a single value to determine the overall setting for each attribute, paint values for the attribute on selected areas, or use a texture map to determine the strength of the selected values.

Inclination, Roll, and Polar are attributes that determine the direction the fur is pointing along the surface of the model. As noted before, Inclination determines whether the hair points straight up from the surface (at values closer to 0) or lies along the surface (at values closer to 1). The Roll setting rotates each hair around the base, and the Polar attribute determines the direction the fur points along the surface. Roll and Polar can be used together to fine-tune the direction of the hair. If you have painted a map for the Direction attribute using the Paint Fur Attributes tool, changing the Polar setting has no effect.

After painting a map for the Direction attribute using the Paint Fur Attributes tool, you may want to paint values for the Inclination and Roll attributes. This can help define more exactly the direction in which the fur points along the surface. You may find yourself switching back and forth among Direction, Inclination, and Roll as you edit the fur on the surface. If you need precise control over the styling of the fur, be prepared to spend some time working with these attributes.

Base Opacity and Tip Opacity are self-explanatory attributes. The base of the fur is the part of the fur strands closest to the surface; the tip is the part of the fur farthest from the surface. Opacity is applied as a gradient across the length of the fur. To create the look of soft, fine fur, set Base Opacity to **1** and Tip Opacity to a very low setting or even **0**. You can experiment with these values to create special effects; try a low Base Opacity and a high Tip Opacity.

Base Width and Tip Width establish the shape of the fur strands. A small Tip Width coupled with a large Base Width produces a pointy shape for the fur. A very low Tip Width helps to create the look of soft, fine fur.

The Base Curl and Tip Curl attributes add curl to the fur strands at the base or tip. A value of 0.5 produces no curling. A value of 1 or 0 produces curling in one direction or the other.

The Scraggle, Scraggle Frequency, and Scraggle Correlation attributes add random kinks to the hair to create a messy appearance. The Scraggle setting determines the strength of the scraggle. Scraggle Frequency determines how many kinks appear in each strand of fur. Scraggle Correlation determines how the Scraggle value of one strand affects another. A setting of 0 for Scraggle Correlation creates random kinks throughout the fur strands, and a Scraggle Correlation of 1 means all the fur strands kink the same way, creating a wavy appearance for the fur.

The Clumping, Clumping Frequency, and Clump Shape settings cause the fur strands to attract each other into bunches on the surface. This is useful for making a surface appear wet or matted. The Clumping setting sets the strength of the clumping, and Clumping Frequency determines the number of clumps created across the surface. Clumping Frequency ranges between 0 and 100; higher values take longer to render. Clump Shape determines whether the clumps themselves are convex or concave. Settings closer to -10 produce concave clump shapes, while settings closer to 10 produce convex clumps (Figure 15.18).

FIGURE 15.18
Clumping is demonstrated on two planes. The plane on the left has a Clump Shape value of -10; the plane on the right has a Clump Shape value of 10.

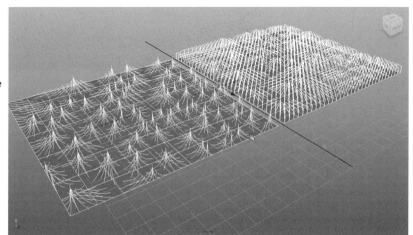

Add Dynamic Motion to Fur

Creating dynamic motion for fur is actually quite easy. A fur description node uses dynamic hair curves to control the movement of the fur.

Attach a Fur Description to Hair Curves

In this example, you'll add a hair system to a simple NURBS sphere that already has fur applied. The hair curves will then be used to add dynamic motion to the fur.

1. Open the furBall_v01.ma scene from the chapter15\scenes directory on the DVD.

The Baldness attribute of the fur has been created using a ramp texture that has been baked into the fur description.

2. Right-click on the sphere and choose Surface Point. Hold the Shift key and select 10 or 12 surface points at the top of the sphere (see Figure 15.19).

3. Switch to the Dynamics menu set. Choose Hair ➤ Create Hair ➤ Options. In the Create Hair Options box, set Output to NURBS Curves and choose At Selected Points Faces. Leave the other settings at their default values.

FIGURE 15.19
Select surface points at the top of the sphere.

ADDING HAIRS TO POLYGONS

If fur is applied to a polygon surface, select the faces of the surface before adding the hair curves. If you want to add hair curves all over the surface rather than at specific points/faces, choose the Grid option on the Create Hair Option box.

---

4. Click the Create Hairs button to make the hairs. The hair curves appear as longer curves coming out of the surface of the sphere.

5. Open the Outliner and select the hairSystem1 node. Switch to the Rendering menu set and choose Fur ➢ Attach Hairsystem To Fur ➢ FurDescription1.

6. Set the timeline to 200 and play the scene. As the hair curves fall, the strands of fur follow. Try animating the sphere so that it moves around the scene (see Figure 15.20).

To keep the hair from penetrating the NURBS sphere, you need to make the sphere a collision object for the hair curves. This along with other dynamic properties of hair curves is discussed later in the chapter. Essentially, any dynamics added to the hair curves are inherited by the fur.

7. Save the scene as **furBall_v02.ma**. To see a version of the scene, open the furBall_v02.ma scene from the chapter15\scenes folder on the DVD.

FIGURE 15.20
The strands of fur follow the motion of the hair curves.

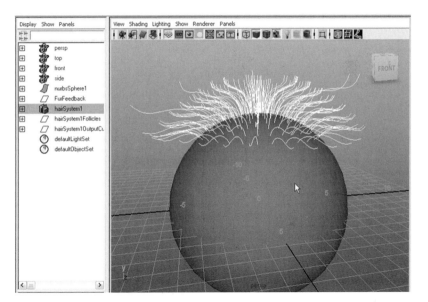

Render Fur Using mental ray

You can render fur using mental ray or Maya Software. When rendering with Maya Software, you'll need to add a fur shadowing node to the lights in the scene. In this section, you'll learn how to render fur with mental ray, which generally produces a more realistic result than Maya Software.

If you plan to use depth map shadows, use the Production: Rapid Fur preset. If you plan to use ray trace shadows, use the Production: Fine Trace Render preset. If you need the fur to appear in reflections or refractions, use raytracing.

Fur renders use indirect lighting techniques such as Final Gathering. Be aware that the render times for dense fur descriptions when Final Gathering is enabled can be quite long.

Render Fur Using Raytracing

To create a realistic render of the hound using raytracing, follow these steps:

1. Open the hound_v08.ma scene from the chapter15\scenes directory.

2. Open the Hypershade and select the houndShader material. In the attributes for the material, set the Diffuse attribute to **1**. Increasing the Diffuse quality of the shader can sometimes help blend the surface material with the color of the fur.

3. Open the Render Settings window and select the Quality tab. Set Quality Presets to Production: Fine Trace.

4. In the Outliner, select the spotlight and open its Attribute Editor. Under Shadows, turn on Use Ray Trace Shadows.

The Fur/Shadowing attributes listed below the Use Ray Trace Shadows settings are used specifically when rendering with Maya Software, which requires that the shadow-casting lights be connected to the fur description. This is not necessary when rendering with mental ray.

5. Create a directional light. Rotate the light so that it is shining toward the camera. This creates nice fill lighting as well as a fringe of light along the edge of the fur. In the settings for the directional light, turn off Emit Specular and set Intensity to **0.8**.

6. In the Outliner, expand the FurFeedback group and select the houndHead_FurFeedback node. In the Attribute Editor, click the houndFur node.

7. Set Density to **500,000**. Scroll down to the list of Attributes. Set Tip Opacity to **0** and Base Opacity to **0.5**. This helps soften the look of the fur.

8. Set Base Width to **0.008** and Tip Width to **0.001**.

9. Create a test render from the perspective camera. The scene takes between 5 and 8 minutes to render depending on your machine (see Figure 15.21).

FIGURE 15.21
Render the hound using ray trace shadows.

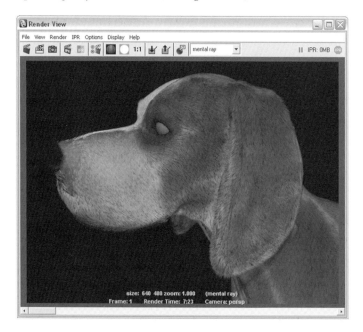

You can continue to improve the look of the fur by improving the texture maps applied to the fur description as well as by improving the lighting in the scene.

10. Save the scene as **hound_v09.ma**. To see a finished version of the scene, open the hound_v09.ma scene from the chapter15\scenes directory on the DVD.

Maya Fur does a pretty good job creating fur effects for many typical situations. For truly stunning fur and hair effects, you may want to consider using the Shave and a Haircut plug-in developed for Maya by Joe Alter. This plug-in has been used for many feature films and television shows. For more information visit www.joealter.com.

Dynamic Curves

Dynamic curves are NURBS curves that have dynamic properties. The primary use of dynamic curves is to drive the dynamics of hair systems applied to characters. However, the usefulness of dynamic curves goes far beyond creating hair motion. Curves used to loft or extrude surfaces, curves used for Paint Effects strokes, curves projected on NURBS surfaces, curves used as IK Splines, curves used as particle emitters, and so on can be made dynamic, thus opening up a large number of possibilities for creating additional dynamic effects in Maya. Furthermore, dynamic curves calculate fairly quickly compared to nCloth, making surfaces created from lofted dynamic curves a useful alternative to nCloth for some situations.

While working through the scenes in this chapter, you may want to set the timeline preferences to loop so that you can see the hair update continuously as you adjust its settings. To do this, choose Window ➤ Settings/Preferences ➤ Preferences. Choose the Time Slider category in the Preferences box, and set Looping to Continuous.

DYNAMIC CURVES VERSUS NUCLEUS

As you learn about dynamic curves you'll immediately notice many similarities between the interfaces for dynamic curves and Nucleus, yet dynamic curves are not part of nDynamics. This is because the introduction of dynamic curves predates the introduction of nDynamics and the Nucleus solver. It's a safe bet that in a future version of Maya, Autodesk will most likely incorporate the Hair system, and thus dynamic curves, into nDynamics.

Use Dynamic Curves with IK Splines

In Chapter 7 you learned about the IK Spline tool, which uses a curve to control the Inverse Kinematics (IK) of a joint chain. The curve itself can be converted into a dynamic curve that can be used to drive the IK Spline tool. This is a great way to add dynamic motion to a rig used for tails or tentacles.

In this example, you'll use a dynamic curve to control a segmented armored tail. The armored tail consists of polygon pieces, each of which has been parent-constrained to a joint in a chain. The first step is to create a curve (see Figure 15.22).

1. Open the armoredTail_v01.ma scene from the chapter15\scenes folder on the DVD.

2. Switch to a side view and turn on Point Snapping.

FIGURE 15.22
The armored tail consists of polygon pieces constrained to a joint chain.

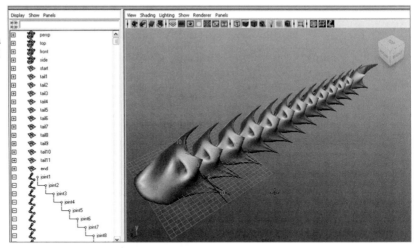

3. In the viewport's Show menu, turn off the visibility of polygons so only the joints are visible. Choose Create ➢ EP Curve Tool. Click on the first joint in the chain on the far left and the last joint in the chain on the far right.

4. Press the Enter key to complete the curve.

The EP Curve tool creates a curve that has four CVs. Using the EP Curve tool is an easy way to create a straight curve. If you want to add more vertices, you can use the Edit Curves ➢ Rebuild Curve command. In the options, specify how many spans you want to add to the curve. In this example, the curve should work fine with only four CVs.

5. Switch to the perspective view. Turn off the visibility of Joints in the Show menu, so only the curve is visible.

6. Switch to the Dynamics menu set. Select curve1 and choose Hair ➢ Make Selected Curves Dynamic. In the Outliner, a new hairSystem1 node is created as well as two groups: hairSystem1Follicles and hairSystem1OutputCurves (see Figure 15.23).

The hairSystem1 node controls the dynamics of the curve; it is similar to the Nucleus solver when using nDynamics.

The hairSystem1Follicles group contains the follicle1 node and the original curve1. The follicle node contains settings to control the dynamics of the individual follicles. Some of these settings can override the hairSystem settings. If you selected a number of curves before issuing the Make Selected Curves Dynamic command, the hairSystem1Follicles group would contain a follicle node for each curve. This is explored later on when creating hair for a character.

The hairSystem1OutputCurves group creates a duplicate curve named curve2. This curve is a duplicate of the original curve. The output curve is the dynamic curve; the curve in the follicle group is the original, nondynamic curve. The purpose of the nondynamic curve is to serve as an attractor for the dynamic curve if needed. The dynamic curve gets its shape from the follicle curve.

7. Set the timeline to 200 and click the Play button. You'll see the dynamic curve move a little (it can be a little hard to see; this will be more obvious in the next step).

8. Stop the playback and switch to the hairSystem1 tab. In the Dynamics rollout, set the Stiffness Scale Selected value to 0 and play the scene. You'll see the dynamic curve droop a little. As the scene is playing, increase Length Flex.

FIGURE 15.23
A number of nodes are added to the scene when a curve is made dynamic.

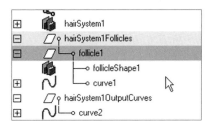

The Stiffness setting controls the rigidity of the curve. A higher Stiffness setting makes the curve less flexible. Lowering the Stiffness value makes the curve bend easily.

As you increase the Length Flex value, the curve stretches as much as it needs to in order to accommodate the dynamic forces applied to the curve. You'll notice the curve droop downward, indicating that it has weight. The hairSystem1 shape has a Gravity setting built in, much like the Nucleus solver discussed in Chapter 13.

You'll notice that both ends of the curve appear to be attached to the original curve (Figure 15.24).

9. Stop the playback and rewind the animation. Set Length Flex to **0.5** and Stiffness to **0.1**. Select the follicle1 node in the Outliner, and switch to the Move tool (turn off Grid or Point Snapping if it is still on).

10. Choose Solvers ➢ Interactive Playback. The animation starts playing automatically. As it is playing, move the follicle around in the scene; you'll see the dynamic curve follow the movements.

FIGURE 15.24
The dynamic curve droops as if it is attached at both ends to the original curve.

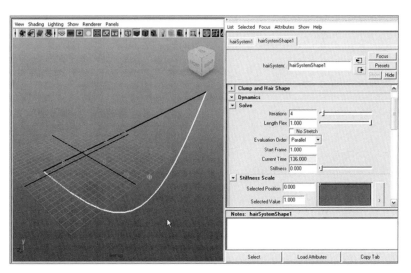

11. Stop the animation and switch to the follicleShape1 tab in the Attribute Editor.

12. Set the Point Lock menu to Base. Turn on Interactive Playback and move the follicle around again. You'll see that the dynamic curve is attached at only one end.

If you wanted the curve to be attached to the other end, you'd set Point Lock to Tip. To detach the curve entirely, set Point Lock to No Attach.

KEYFRAME POINT LOCK

The Point Lock attribute can be keyframed in the Channel Box for the follicle node. To animate a dynamic curve detaching from one end, set Point Lock to Both Ends, create a keyframe (right-click on the Point Lock channel in the Channel Box, and choose Key Selected), change the current frame on the timeline, set Point Lock to Tip or Base (the opposite end will become detached), and then set another keyframe. This is a good way to create the effect of a cable or rope snapping.

---

13. Stop the animation and rewind the playback. Select the follicle node, and set the Translate channels to 0 to return the curve to its start position.

14. With the follicle selected, turn on Point Snapping. Hold the d key, and use the Move tool to move the pivot point of the follicle to the end of the curve on the side where the dynamic curve is still attached, as shown in Figure 15.25. (As you are moving the pivot point, the curve should not move; sometimes it takes a couple of tries to get Maya to properly switch to move pivot mode. An alternative to the d hotkey is to press the Insert key (on a PC, the Home key on a Mac) on the keyboard while the Move tool is activated—not every keyboard has an Insert key, however.)

15. When the pivot point is repositioned, Shift+click the Translate and Rotate channels in the Channel Box, right-click, and choose Key Selected from the pop-up menu.

FIGURE 15.25
Move the pivot point of the follicle to the end of the curve.

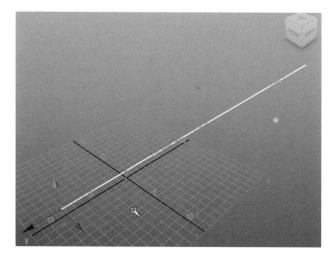

16. Turn on Auto Keyframe; go to various points in the animation and move and rotate the follicle. While Auto Keyframe is on, a keyframe is placed on all of the Translate and Rotate channels as you make changes to the position of the follicle. The dynamic curve may not update correctly as you make changes; don't worry about that at the moment.

You want to create an animation where the curve moves about in the scene like a sword slashing through the air.

17. Rewind and play the animation; you'll see the dynamic curve follow the movements of the follicle as it moves through the air.

18. Save the scene as armoredTail_v02.ma. To see a version of the scene, open the armoredTail_v02.ma scene from the chapter15\scenes directory.

Create an IK Spline Handle from the Dynamic Curve

In this section, you'll create an IK Spline handle for the armored tail and attach it to the dynamic curve. The dynamics of the curve will be edited to change the behavior of the tail.

1. Continue with the scene from the previous section or open the armoredTail_v02.ma scene from the chapter15\scenes directory. In the perspective view, turn on the visibility of joints in the Show menu.

2. In the Outliner, select and hide the follicle1 node. This prevents you from selecting the wrong curve when creating the IK Spline handle.

3. Switch to the Animation menu set and choose Skeleton ➤ IK Spline Handle Tool ➤ Options. In the options, make sure Auto Create Curve and Snap Curve To Root are both off.

4. With the IK Spline Handle tool active, select the first joint in the chain and the last joint in the chain. Zoom in closely, and carefully select the blue curve that runs down the center of the chain.

If the operation is successful you'll see the ikHandle1 node appear in the Outliner. The Dynamic curve (curve2) will move out of the hairSystem1OutputCurves group. That should not affect how the curve behaves.

5. Rewind and play the scene. The joints follow the motion of the curves.

6. In the Show menu of the perspective view, turn the visibility of polygons back on, and play the scene. The armored tail thrashes around when you play the animation.

7. In the Outliner, select the hairSystem1 node, and open its Attribute Editor to the hair-SystemShape1 tab. Scroll down and expand the Dynamics section.

The Stiffness Scale edit curve changes the stiffness of the curve along the length of the curve. The left side of the curve corresponds to the stiffness at the base; the right side of the curve corresponds to the stiffness at the tip.

8. Add a point to the Stiffness Scale edit curve by clicking on the left side of the curve and dragging downward.

9. Play the animation, and you'll see the end of the tail lag behind the motion more than the front of the tail. You should be able to edit the curve while the animation is playing and observe the changes (see Figure 15.26).

The Stiffness setting creates the overall stiffness value for the dynamic curve. Stiffness Scale modifies that value along the length of the curve. Both settings, like almost all of the dynamic curve settings, can be animated.

10. Save the scene as **armoredTail_v03.ma**. To see a version of the scene, open the armoredTail_v03.ma file from the chapter15\scenes directory.

FIGURE 15.26
Editing the Stiffness Scale curve changes the stiffness along the length of the dynamic hair.

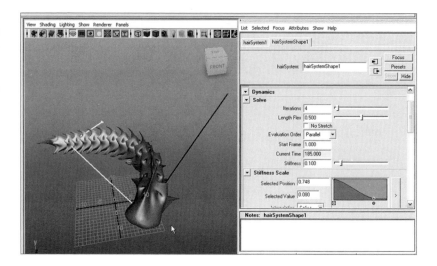

Use Forces

The settings in the Forces section add additional levels of control for the curve's motion. Play the animation in the armoredTail_v03.ma scene and adjust these settings while the scene loops so you can see how they affect the motion of the tail.

The Iterations setting affects how the hair responds to stiffness and dynamics. Iterations refers to the number of times the hair solver calculates per time step, similar to the Substeps setting on the Nucleus node. Raise this to improve the accuracy of the hair motion; higher values slow down Maya's playback.

Drag creates friction between the dynamic curve and the air. Increasing this is a good way to simulate the motion of hair in thick fluids.

Motion Drag is similar to Drag; however, it is affected by the Stiffness Scale attribute. In other words, the Drag setting creates a drag in the motion across the length of the dynamic curve, whereas Motion Drag creates a drag along the length of the curve that is influenced by the Stiffness Scale curve. This can be used to fine-tune the motion of the dynamic curve.

Damp is most often used to control erratic motion of dynamic curves. Higher Damp values decrease the momentum of the curve as it follows the motion of the follicle.

Friction reduces the motion of dynamic curves when they collide with surfaces. This won't produce a visible effect unless the curve comes in contact with a collision surface. Collisions are discussed in more detail later in the chapter.

Mass affects the motion of the curve only when additional fields (created from the Dynamics menu set) are applied to the curve, for example, a Turbulence or a Drag field. Mass does not change how the curve responds to forces created in the hairSystem1 shape node. Increasing Mass increases the simulated weight of each CV on the curve as the curve moves through a dynamic field.

Dynamics Weight is used to control the amount of overall influence external dynamic fields (such as Turbulence and Drag) have over the dynamic curve. It does not affect how the Forces settings in the hairSystem node affect the dynamic curve.

Start Curve Attract creates an attraction between the original curve (curve1 in the armored-Tail example) and the dynamic curve. This can be used to blend between the dynamic curve and animation created through the use of deformers on the original curve. The Attraction Scale curve can be used to edit the strength of the attraction along the length of the curve, similar to the Stiffness Scale.

Add Hair to a Character

Hair is created by attaching follicle nodes to a surface. Each follicle node controls a number of hairs. The follicles themselves are styled using a combination of control curves and forces. Follicles and control curves are connected to a hair system node. A single hair system node can control hair connected to any number of surfaces, and a single surface can be attached to multiple hair systems.

When you create hair you have to consider how you plan to render it. You have the choice of creating Paint Effects strokes for the hair or curves that can be used to render in third-party rendering engines such as Render Man, or you can create both Paint Effects strokes and curves. Even though hair uses Paint Effects, it renders using mental ray without the need to convert the hair to polygons.

In this section, you'll create and style hair for a character.

Apply Hair to a Surface

When you want to apply hair to a character, you can either apply the hair uniformly to the entire surface or paint the hair selectively on parts of the surface.

It is common practice to create a nonrendering scalp surface that can be parented to a character's head and then apply the hair to the scalp surface rather than directly to the character's head. This allows flexibility because scalp surfaces and their attached hair can easily be swapped between characters. It also speeds up playback in the animation because the hair dynamics are not factored into the calculations required to deform the character's surface if it has been skinned to a skeleton or to other deformers.

Some animators like to apply separate hair systems to each part of the scalp to control the various sections of a particular hairstyle. For instance, one hair system may be applied to the bangs that hang over the character's forehead, while another system is used for the hair on the back of the head. In this exercise, you'll keep things simple by using a single hair system for the character's hairstyle. Both methods are valid, and as you become comfortable working with hair, you may want to experiment with different techniques to see which approach works best for you.

1. Open the nancyHair_v01.ma scene from the chapter15\scenes directory.

This scene contains the rigged nancy character used in Chapter 6. The head is rigged to a series of joints. You can select and rotate the headCtrl curves above the head to change the position of the head. A scalp surface has been created by duplicating part of the head geometry. This scalp geometry is parent-constrained to one of the joints in the head rig.

You can apply hair to NURBS or polygon surfaces. When using polygon surfaces, the UV texture coordinates must be mapped so that none of the UVs overlap and the coordinates fit within the 0 to 1 range in the UV Texture Editor. As with fur, you'll get better results from your hair system if the UV coordinates have been carefully mapped. Remember to delete history for the surface once you have created UV texture coordinates to keep the coordinates (and attached hair) from moving unpredictably during animation.

2. In the Outliner, select the scalp surface and open its Attribute Editor. In the scalpShape tab, expand the Render Stats section; then turn off Casts Shadows, Receive Shadows, Motion Blur, and Primary Visibility so the surface will not render or affect any other geometry in the render.

There are a number of ways to add hair to a surface. You can paint hair on the surface using the Artisan Brush interface, you can select faces on polygons or surface points on NURBS surfaces and apply hair to the selected components, or you can create a uniform grid of follicles on a surface. Once you attach follicles to a surface, you can add more follicles later to fill in blank areas by painting them on the surface. For the scalp you'll create a simple grid and then add additional follicles if needed later.

3. Select the scalp surface, switch to the Dynamics menu set, and choose Hair ➤ Create Hair ➤ Options. In the Create Hair Options box, choose Edit ➤ Reset to reset the options to the default settings.

4. Set the Output to Paint Effects and choose the Grid option. Set U and V Count to **24** and Points Per Hair to **20**. Set Passive Fill to **1**. Set Randomization to **0.1**.

Follicles can be dynamic, passive, or static. Dynamic follicles react to forces and dynamic fields based on the settings in the hairSystem node or on any dynamic overrides created in the follicle shape node. Dynamic follicles can collide with surfaces. Passive follicles inherit the dynamic motion of nearby dynamic follicles, which can reduce computational overhead, especially when collisions are involved. Static follicles have no dynamic motion but can be used to style parts of the hair. You can change the mode of a follicle after creating the hair system if you decide to make a passive follicle dynamic, a dynamic follicle static, or any other of the three modes.

The Randomization setting randomizes the arrangement of the grid to make the hair placement look less even.

By increasing the Passive Fill option, a number of the follicles created when the hair is attached to the surface will be passive rather than dynamic. If the Passive Fill option is set to 1, every other row and column of the follicles based on the settings for U and V Count will be passive follicles. If the setting is 2, every two rows and every two columns of follicles will be passive.

When you first create a hair system, you can create a number of passive follicles using this setting. This speeds up the dynamics as you create the initial hairstyle. Later you can convert the follicles to dynamic or static follicles as needed.

5. Turn on the Edge Bounded and Equalize options.

When the Grid method is used, the follicles are placed uniformly on the surface based on the U and V coordinates. If Edge Bounded is on, the follicles are placed up to and including the edge of the UV coordinates. In the case of the example, this means hairs are placed along the edge of the scalp surface. The Equalize option evens out the spacing of the follicle placement to compensate for areas of the U and V coordinates that may be stretched or squashed.

6. Set Points Per Hair to **20** and Length to **5**.

Hairs that have more points per curve are more flexible and have more detail in their motion as they respond to dynamics; they also slow down the playback speed of Maya in the scene. The Length attribute can be modified after creation.

The Place Hairs Into option should be set to New Hair System. If a hair system exists in the scene already, you can use this option to add the newly created hairs into the existing system by selecting it from the list. Figure 15.27 shows the settings for the new hair.

7. Click Create Hairs to make the hair. The hairs appear as long spikes coming out of the head.

8. Click Play on the scene, and the hairs start to fall. After a few moments, the hairs start to settle. In the next section you'll learn how to style the hair (see Figure 15.28).

9. Save the scene as **nancyHair_v02.ma**. To see a version of the scene, open the nancyHair_v02.ma scene from the chapter15\scenes directory.

FIGURE 15.27
The Create Hair Options area

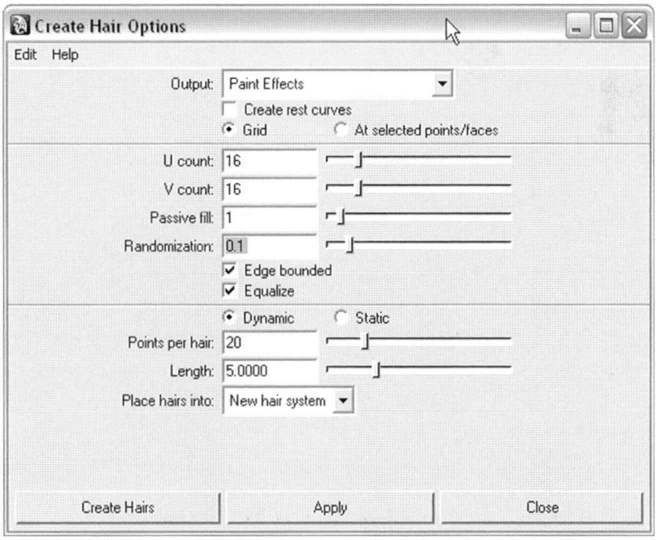

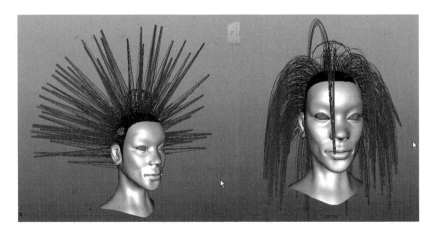

FIGURE 15.28
The hairs appear as long spikes on the top of the head. When you click the Play button, the hairs fall and settle into a basic hair shape.

HAIR TRANSPLANTS

An existing hair system can be moved from one surface to another surface using the Transplant command. To use this command, select the hair system you want to move, and Ctrl+click the destination surface. From the Dynamics menu set choose Hair ➤ Transplant Hair. If the surfaces have very similar UV texture coordinates, you can choose to move the hair based on the UV coordinates in the Transplant options. Otherwise you can choose to move the hair based on the closest points in the surface. In this case, make sure the destination surface is placed and scaled to match the existing hair system and its source.

Hair Collisions

Polygon and NURBS surfaces can collide with hair, and there are a number of settings on the hairSystemShape node that can affect how the collisions are calculated as well as how the hair behaves when it collides with a surface.

To understand how to create collisions between surfaces and hair, you'll follow an example that is a slight detour from working with characters.

1. Open the undeseaPlants_v01.ma scene from the chapter15\scenes directory. This scene contains a very simple NURBS plane that has been sculpted to look like the floor of the ocean.

2. Switch to the Dynamics menu set and choose Hair ➤ Paint Hair Follicles. The Options box for the Artisan Brush interface opens along with a pop-up box for the Paint Hair Follicles settings.

3. In the Paint Hair Follicles Settings box, make sure Hair System is set to Create New, and set Output to NURBS Curves.

4. Set Follicle Density U and V to **6**, leave Points Per Hair set to **6**, and set Hair Length to **3**.

5. Paint on the surface to add a few follicles. The interaction may be faster if the shaded mode is set to wireframe or if Color Feedback is turned off in the Display section of the Artisan Tool options.

6. When you have 15 to 20 curves painted on the surface, you can close the Paint Hair Follicle Settings box and switch to the Select tool.

7. In the Outliner, select the hairSystem1 node and open its Attribute Editor.

8. In the hairSystemShape1 tab enter the following settings:

   Stiffness: **0.03**

   Drag: **0.7**

   Gravity: **0**

9. In the Turbulence settings, set Intensity to **0.8**, Frequency to **1**, and Speed to **1**.

10. Set the timeline to **300** and play the scene. The curves appear to move a bit like some undersea plant life (see Figure 15.29).

11. Create a polygon sphere. Animate the sphere moving around randomly through the hair curves in such a way that the sphere contacts the hair curves.

12. When you are happy with the animation, select the polySphere and Ctrl+click the hair-System node in the Outliner. Choose Hair ➢ Make Collide.

13. Play the scene.

You may not see much of a collision just yet, or the sphere may appear to collide with some but not all of the hairs.

14. Select the hairSystem node and open its Attribute Editor. Scroll down to the Collisions section.

FIGURE 15.29
Paint a hair system on a model of the ocean floor. Set the dynamics to simulate undersea plant life.

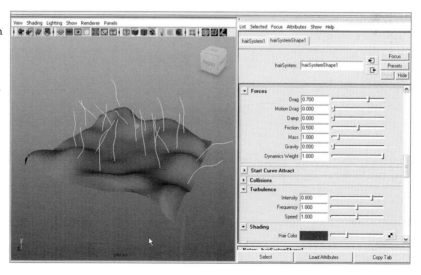

15. Play the animation. As the animation is playing, increase the Collide Over Sample value. This setting adjusts how often collisions are calculated per time step. Higher values increase accuracy but slow down playback in Maya. Set the value to **6**.

You'll notice that the hair sticks to the sphere as it passes. This is a common problem when using geometry to collide with hair. There are some techniques you can use to reduce this problem.

16. Turn on Draw Collide Width and increase the Collide Width Offset value.

The Draw Collide Width setting creates circles around the hair curve that represent the collision width. Increasing Collide Width Offset increases the collision boundary, making the collision thickness of each hair larger (Figure 15.30).

To reduce the stickiness of the hair, you can lower the Friction setting in the hairSystem's Dynamics settings as well as increase the Iterations value and lower the Stiffness value. Increasing Friction makes the hair stick to the surface longer, which may work well when animating the tendrils of a jellyfish.

Ultimately, if you are unable to eliminate the hair sticking to the collision surface, you may need to consider some alternative techniques. Some models experience more or fewer sticking problems than others.

One technique for eliminating the stickiness is to attach a radial field to the hair and parent the field to the collision object. The max distance of the field can be adjusted to reach just beyond the edge of the sphere.

The best way to eliminate the sticking problem is to use hair collision constraint primitives. This is a special type of hair constraint that uses simple primitives as collision objects. The collision constraints can be parented to objects, and collisions between the hairs and the constraints are faster and more accurate than collisions between geometry and hair. In addition, a collision constraint can be made to collide only with specific follicles. Collision geometry, on the other hand, collides with all of the hairs in a hair system.

FIGURE 15.30
The collision width of the hair is displayed as circles around each hair.

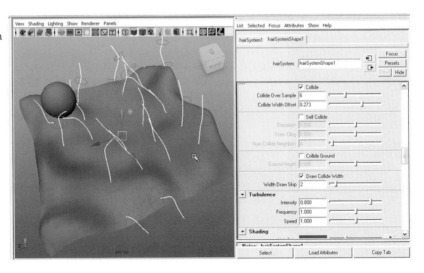

In the next section, you'll use collision constraints to control how the hair interacts with the character's head. The collision example used in this section is available in the `chapter15\scenes` directory as the `underseaPlants_v02.ma` scene.

ADDITIONAL COLLISION PROPERTIES

Additional hair collision options include Self-Collide, which enables collisions between the hair follicles of a system. The Static Cling option can be used to make the hairs stick together when they collide, while the Repulsion option increases the tendency for hairs to repulse each other.

An invisible collision plane can be created by enabling the Collide Ground option. This setting creates an infinite plane parallel to the X and Z axes in the scene. The height of the ground is set using the Ground Height slider.

Hair Collision Constraints

Hair collision constraints are simple spherical and cubical primitives that can be used to collide with dynamic hair. The accuracy and speed of collision constraints is superior to collision geometry. Multiple collision constraints can be added to a hair system and scaled to approximate the surface of colliding objects in the scene. In this section, you'll add collision constraints to the nancy character's hair.

1. Open the `nancyHair_v02.ma` scene from the `chapter15\scenes` directory.

2. In the Outliner, select the hairSystem1 node and open its Attribute Editor. To improve the playback of simulations during animation, set Display Quality at the top of the editor to **1** and set Simulation Method to Dynamic Follicles Only.

3. In the Outliner, expand the hairSystemFollicles group. Select the top node in the group, hold the Shift key, scroll down, and select the bottom node in the group. From the Dynamics menu set, choose Hair ➤ Create Constraint ➤ Collide Sphere.

4. In the Perspective window, switch to wireframe mode. Select the hairConstraint1 node, represented by a wire sphere, and position it roughly in the center of the head. Use the Scale tool to scale the sphere to match the size of the cranium (see Figure 15.31).

FIGURE 15.31
Scale the collision constraint to match the size of the cranium.

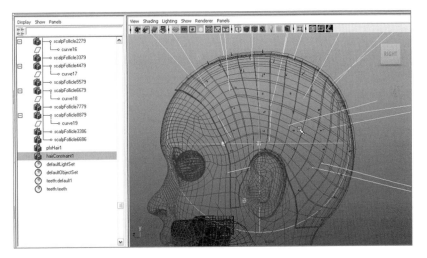

5. Switch to the front view and scale the constraint in a little to match the head.

6. Repeat steps 3 through 5 to create additional collide spheres. Position these to match the jaw, neck, and ears.

7. When you have positioned the collide spheres to match the basic shape of the head, turn off the visibility of polygons in the perspective view and turn on the visibility of joints.

8. Use a parent constraint to connect the collide sphere in the head, jaw, and ears to the large joint that runs down the center of the head. (Select the joint first and then the collide sphere to be constrained. In the options for the parent constraint, make sure the Translate and Rotate channels are selected as well as Maintain Offset.)

9. Use a parent constraint to connect the collide sphere in the neck to the middle neck joints.

10. Play the scene. The hairs should not penetrate the head, thanks to the constraints. This is more obvious if you lower the Stiffness attribute to a low value such as 0.03 in the hair shape node so that the hairs droop more (see Figure 15.32).

11. Save the scene as **nancyHair_v03.ma**. To see a version of the scene, open the nancyHair_ v03.ma scene from the chapter15\scenes directory.

FIGURE 15.32

Parent constrain the collide spheres to the joints in the head rig. When you lower the Stiffness value and play the scene, the hairs are prevented from moving through the collide spheres.

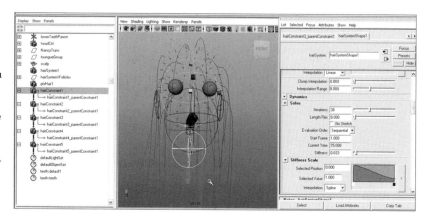

Hair Shape

There are a number of settings in the hair system node that determine the look of the hair. These are found in the Clump And Hair Shape section of the hair system's attributes.

1. Open the nancyHair_v03.ma scene from the chapter15\scenes directory.

2. Select hairSystem1, and open its Attribute Editor to the hairSystemShape1 tab.

3. Set Display Quality to **100** so you get a more accurate preview of the hair. Leave Simulation Method set to Dynamic Follicles Only.

This improves performance while working in the scene. Keep in mind, though, that you are viewing about half the hair that is actually on the head. If you look at the scalp surface, you'll see the small colored spikes indicating the position of the follicles. Red follicles indicate dynamic follicles; blue follicles indicate passive follicles. The passive follicles are hidden until you switch Simulation Method to All Follicles.

The hair appears as groups bunched around long spikes that shoot out from the scalp. Each group of hairs is a clump. The movement of each clump of hair is driven by the movement of the follicles. This way Maya can create dynamics for thousands of hairs using a much smaller number of follicles.

4. The hair remains as long spikes until you play the simulation and let the hair fall down. For the moment, leave the animation at frame 1. It's easier to see how the clumps work when the hair is in its spiky state.

5. In the Clump And Hair Shape section, increase the Hairs Per Clump number to **60** to increase the fullness of the hair.

The Baldness Map field allows you to apply a texture to control where the hair grows on the head. The texture must be a black and white, 2D texture. The texture itself does not need to be baked as it does with fur. Just like with fur, black areas of the map indicate no hair (or baldness), and white areas indicate places where the hair grows. Texture maps can also be used, much like the texture maps created for fur baldness.

The Sub Segments attribute improves the details of the hair (such as curls and kinks) when rendered. Increasing this setting does not affect the dynamics of the hair.

Increasing Thinning shortens a number of hairs per clump to create a thin and wispy look to the hair.

Clump Twist rotates each clump around the base of the follicle. Positive values rotate the clump in one direction; negative values rotate it in the opposite direction.

Bend Follow determines how closely the rotation of the clump affects the shape of the hair clumps. This is most noticeable at the end of each clump.

6. Play the animation until frame 20 and then stop the animation. Zoom in to the end of a clump, and move the Bend Follow slider back and forth.

When Bend Follow is at 0, the end of the clump appears flat if the follicle is curved. When Bend Follow is 1, the clump shape is more tubular toward the end of the clump. This attribute should be used to fine-tune the look of your hair as you develop the overall shape.

7. Rewind the animation and set Clump Width to **0.7**. This expands the overall width of the clumps, which helps fill out the hairstyle without the need to add more follicles.

Hair Width adjusts the width of the hairs. This can be used to thicken or thin the hair. The effect of changing hair width is seen when the hair is rendered. This is a setting you'll probably want to return to when you are setting up your hair for a render.

Below the Clump And Hair Shape setting sliders are a number of edit curves that can be used to further refine the hair shape. The left side of each curve represents the area of the clump closest to the root; the right side represents the area closest to the tip. Each scale uses the setting in the sliders in the Clump And Hair Shape section as a starting point, so each scale is a modifier for the settings you have already created.

You can exaggerate or reduce the amount of tapering in the clumps by changing the Clump Width Scale edit curve. Hair Width Scale modifies the width of the hairs based on the setting in the Hair Width slider.

The Clump Curl edit curve can be used to twist the clumps around the central axis of the follicle. By default the graph is set so that the value of the curling is at 0.5. By moving a point on the curve up (moving up creates values closer to 1; moving down creates values closer to 0) or down, the curling twists in one direction or the other (see Figure 15.33).

FIGURE 15.33
Adding and moving points along the various edit curves can shape the overall look of the hair.

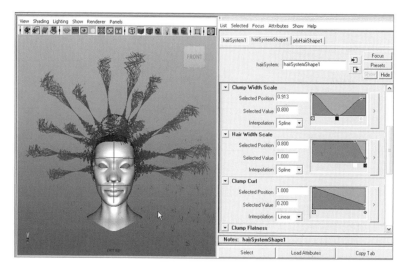

8. Play the animation to frame 50 and stop. Remove any extra points you may have placed on the Clump Width Scale and Clump Curl so that there are only two points on the scales, one on the far right and one on the far left.

9. Set the value of the point on the left side of the Clump Width Scale to **1**; set the point on the far right to **0.32**.

10. Set the point on the far right of the Clump Curl curve to **0.6**.

The Clump Flatness scale can be used to make the clumps appear as flat planks of hair. Higher values along the curve flatten out the clumps. This setting works well for creating the shape of wet hair.

11. Set the point on the far left of the Clump Flatness scale to **0.5**. Add a point to the far right side of Clump Flatness and move it to **0.7**. This helps the roots of the hair to lie closer to the head, creating less of a "poufy" shape.

Increasing the Clump Interpolation slider spreads the hair out between clumps. This can be used to even out the shape of the hair so that the clumping is much less obvious. Dynamics are calculated based on the position of each clump. If you set a high Clump Interpolation value, you may find that hairs do not appear to collide correctly. This is because the interpolation can push hairs outside the boundary of the original clump width, and thus their placement exceeds the collision width of their clump.

Interpolation Range sets the limits for how far a hair can move out of the width of the clump when Clump Interpolation is increased. The value set in Interpolation Range is multiplied against the Clump Width setting.

12. Set Clump Interpolation to **0.3**. Leave Interpolation Range set to the default value of 8.

13. Rewind and play the animation, and make any changes you'd like to the shape of the hair. The length, color, and other properties are further defined in the next section.

14. To get a better sense of the overall look of the hair, set Simulation Method to All Follicles; then rewind and play the animation (see Figure 15.34).

15. Save the scene as **nancyHair_v04.ma**. To see a version of the scene, open the nancyHair_v04.ma scene from the chapter15/scenes folder.

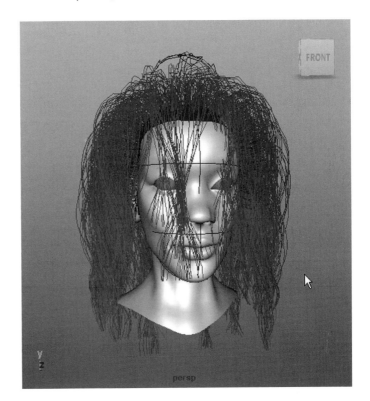

FIGURE 15.34
Establish the basic shape of the hair using the settings in the hairSystem1 node.

FOLLICLE OVERRIDES

Many of the settings found in the hairSystemShape node are also found on the nodes for individual follicles in the Per Follicle Overrides section of each follicle's Attribute Editor. You can use these overrides to refine the hair shape for individual follicles. Dynamic overrides are available only for dynamic follicles; these settings are grayed out for passive or static follicles.

Style Hair

Once the hair has been set up, there are a number of tools you can use to style the hair. You can use dynamic fields as a hair styling tool, paint follicle properties on the hair, or even manipulate the CVs of control curves.

HAIRSTYLE PRESETS

Maya comes with a number of preset hairstyles in the Visor. You can open these by choosing (from the Dynamics menu set) Hair ➤ Get Hair Example. To use a hairstyle, right-click one of the icons, and choose to import the file into your scene. Each preset style comes with hairline geometry that can be parented to your character's head. Or you can copy the style using the Transplant Hair option.

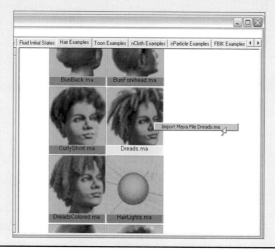

Start and Rest Positions

Before styling the hair properly, you should create a start position for the hair so that the animation does not start with the hair sticking straight out of the head. This makes styling much easier.

The start position represents the shape of the hair at the start of the simulation. The rest position represents the hair's shape when no forces are acting upon it. These are very similar, but you can distinguish between the two by thinking of it like this: Imagine an animation where a character is jumping up and down and then stops. The animation starts with the character in midair. You want to set the start position to represent what the hair looks like when the character is in midair. Once the character stops jumping and the hair settles, the hair assumes its rest position. For some animations the start and rest positions may look exactly the same; other times, such as in the example described, the start and rest positions look different.

1. Continue using the scene from the previous section or open the nancyHair_v04.ma scene from the chapter15\scenes directory.

2. Select the hairSystem1 node, and open its Attribute Editor to the hairSystemShape1 node. Set Simulation Method to Dynamic Follicles Only and Display Quality to **50**.

3. Play the animation until the hair has completely settled.

4. Once the hair has settled, expand the hairSystem1Follicles group in the Outliner, and Shift+click all of the follicle nodes. Choose Hair ➤ Set Start Position ➤ From Current.

5. Set the rest position by choosing Hair ➤ Set Rest Position ➤ From Current.

Notice that you can set the start position from the rest position and vice versa. These positions can be changed at any time as you continue to work on the hair and any animations. Notice also that the start and rest positions are applied to the follicles themselves rather than to the hair system. This means you can set start and rest positions for individual follicles if needed.

6. Rewind the animation. The hair should now be down and relatively motionless at the start of the animation.

The start and rest positions are actually determined by two sets of curves that drive the follicles. You can activate the visibility of these curves in the Perspective window.

7. In the Viewport menu, use the Show menu to turn off the visibility of Strokes. This hides the Paint Effects hair.

8. Select the hairSystem1 node, and choose Hair ➤ Display ➤ Start Position. A series of curves appears in blue, representing the hair's start position.

9. Choose Hair ➤ Display ➤ Rest Position. The rest position curves appear in red. If the start and rest positions for the hair system are different, each set of curves will have a different shape.

10. Save the scene as **nancyHair_v05.ma**. To see a version of the scene, open the nancyHair_v05.ma scene from the chapter15\scenes directory on the DVD.

Paint Follicle Attributes

Using the Artisan Brush interface you can paint follicle attributes. Before doing this you must make sure that the hair is in its rest or start position. Some attributes, such as Inclination, require that the animation be on frame1.

1. Continue with the scene from the previous section or open the nancyHair_v05.ma scene from the chapter 15\scenes directory.

2. Select the hairSystem1 node and open its Attribute Editor. Switch to the hairSystemShape1 tab, and set Simulation Method to All Follicles. The Display Quality value can be raised to **50**.

3. In the Outliner, select the hairSystem1 node (or the scalp surface). From the Dynamics menu set choose Hair ➤ Paint Hair Follicles.

4. The Tool Options area for the Artisan Brush interface opens as well as the Paint Hair Follicles Settings pop-up box.

5. Set Paint Mode to Trim Hairs. This setting allows you to reduce the length of the hair as you paint across the follicles.

In order for the dynamics to remain consistent, you must adjust the number of points on the hair as you paint. When you created the hair originally, the Points Per Hair attribute was set to **10**, so to trim the length of a hair to half, set Points Per Hair to **5**. The Points Per Hair setting is the setting that actually determines how the hair will be trimmed. Whether you set Hair Length to **1,000** or **0.1** and set Points Per Hair to **5**, the hair will be trimmed to half the original length regardless of the Hair Length setting.

6. Set Points Per Hair to **5**, and paint across the follicles in the front of the scalp to create bangs for the nancy character (Figure 15.35).

7. Once you have trimmed the hair, select the follicles in the Outliner (it's easiest just to Shift+click all the follicles rather than figure out which ones were painted) and choose Hair ➢ Set Rest Position ➢ From Current. You may also want to reset the start position as well.

QUICK SELECT FOLLICLES

Repeatedly selecting all the follicles or certain follicles whenever you need to set the rest or start position gets tedious rather quickly. You can speed up the process by creating a quick select set for the follicles.

1. Shift+click the follicles in the Outliner.

2. Choose Create ➢ Sets ➢ Quick Select Set.

3. Name the set **NancyFolliclesAll**. You have the option to create a shelf button for this set. To do this, click Add Shelf Button.

4. The button appears in the shelf. Every time you need to select all of the follicles, just click the button.

If you want to take it a step further, try writing a MEL script that selects the follicles and sets the rest and/or start position all in one click. Creating MEL scripts is discussed in Chapter 17.

5. If you want the button to appear on the shelf the next time you start Maya, click on the downward-facing black triangle next to the shelf and choose Shelf ➢ Save All Shelves.

Be aware that this selection set is specific to this scene. If you click the button in another scene, you will get an error.

---

8. To extend the hair, set Paint Mode to Extend Hair, and increase Points Per Hair to a number larger than 10. Remember to reset the rest and start positions after extending the hair.

The Hair ➢ Scale Hair tool can be used to apply global scaling to the hair. To use this tool, select it from the Hair menu and drag left or right. This tool will scale all aspects of the hair, so some adjustment to the shape and dynamics settings maybe required after using the tool.

To paint other attributes set Paint Mode to Edit Follicle Attributes, and choose an attribute from the Follicle Attribute menu. When painting these attributes, the Value setting in the Brush Options area determines the value painted on the follicles.

9. Save the scene as **nancyHair_v06.ma**. To see a version of the scene, open the nancyHair_ v06.ma scene from the chapter15\scenes directory.

FIGURE 15.35
Trim the hair at the front of the head using the Paint Hair Follicles tool.

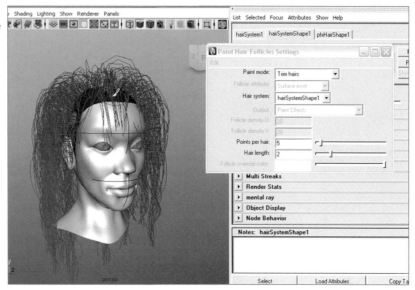

Style Hair with Fields

You can use dynamic fields to style hair. To do this, simply apply a field to a hair system, run the simulation, and then set the rest and/or start position once the hair assumes the desired shape. Follow these steps to create a unique hairstyle for the nancy character.

1. Continue with the scene from the previous section or open the nancyHair_v06.ma scene from the chapter15\scenes directory.

2. In the Outliner, select hairSystem1. From the Dynamics menu set choose Fields ➢ Newton.

3. Move the icon for the Newton field above the head, and open its Attribute Editor. In the Attribute Editor, set Magnitude to **100** and Attenuation to **0** (Figure 15.36).

4. Play the animation. The hair should be sucked up into the field.

5. After about 100 frames or so, stop the animation. Shift+click the follicles in the Outliner, and choose Hair ➢ Set Rest Position ➢ From Current. Then choose Hair ➢ Set Start Position ➢ From Current.

6. Delete the Newton field and rewind the scene.

7. Select the hairSystem1 node and open its Attribute Editor. In the Dynamics section, set the Start Curve Attract attribute to **0.3**. This helps the hair maintain its shape when the scene is played.

If motion continues in some of hairs after the field has been deleted and the start and rest position have been set, try lowering the Stiffness value and raising Iterations. Also changing the Attraction Scale for specific follicles in the Dynamics Override section of the follicle's Attribute Editor can help fix problem areas.

8. Save the scene as **nancyHair_v07.ma**. To see a version of the scene, open the nancyHair_v07.ma scene from the chapter15\scenes directory on the DVD.

FIGURE 15.36

Style the hair using a Newton field.

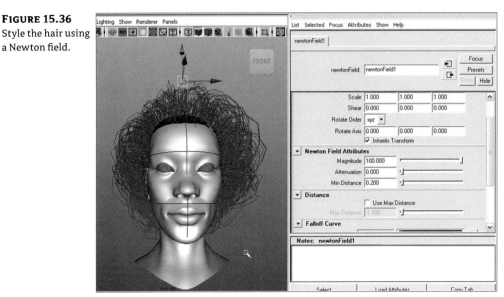

Modify Curves

You can modify curves directly by moving their CVs or by using the tools in the Hair ➤ Modify Curves menu. By modifying curves directly, you can fine-tune a style.

You can modify only start or rest curves. To do this, disable the visibility of Strokes in the scene and choose Hair ➤ Display Rest Curves (or Start Curves). Select the curve (or right-click on the curve and choose Control Vertex to work just on selected CVs) and apply the actions in the Hair ➤ Modify Curves menu. You can also use the Move tool to change the position of CVs on the curve (see Figure 15.37).

As you are editing the curve, you can lock the length so that the changes you make do not stretch the curve beyond its original length. Select the curve and choose Hair ➤ Lock Length (or use the l hot key). Conversely, you can unlock the curve if you want to change its length.

FIGURE 15.37
Modify the CVs of
a start curve using
the Move tool.

Curling, Noise, Sub Clumping, and Braids

Curling, Noise, and Braids all work best when the Sub Segments attribute in the Clump And Hair Shape section of the hair system node is increased. The Curling and Noise settings are found in the Displacement section of the hair system node.

The Sub Clumping setting causes the hair within clumps to bunch together. This helps when creating wet or kinky hair.

The Braid option is available as an attribute for individual hair follicle nodes. For a braid to work successfully, you may need to alter the clump shape and the hairs per clump. Often it may be a good idea to use a separate hair system to create a detailed braid.

Hair Constraints

Hair constraints are another way to shape hair and are a useful tool for making hair follow other objects in the scene, such as rubber bands or ribbons.

Create a Constraint

Constraints are applied to selected follicles, and they work only with active follicles. If you try to apply a constraint to a passive follicle, you get a warning that says no hair curves have been selected for the constraint.

You've already used the collision constraint. When you create a constraint, the position of the constraint is indicated by a locator. The locator's position at the start of the animation determines the constraint's starting position. The position of the constraint on subsequent frames of the animation determines how it pulls the hair relative to its position at the start of the animation.

This exercise demonstrates how to add a constraint to a hair system. The example demonstrates the constraint in a simplified scene, making it easier to see how the different types of constraints affect a hair system.

1. Open the constraintsStart_v01.ma scene from the chapter15\scenes directory.

This scene has a simple hair system applied to the top of a polygon sphere. The output of the system is curves.

2. Play the scene until about frame 60. The hair curves at the center of the bunch should be visible and easy to select. Select all the curves at the center, as shown in Figure 15.38.

3. Rewind the animation while the curves are still selected. Choose Hair ➤ Create Constraint ➤ Rubber Band to create a constraint. A locator appears at the center of the bunch. Use the Move tool to move the locator above the top of the hair.

FIGURE 15.38
You can easily select the hair curves at the center of the bunch when the animation is played.

When you move the locator, blue lines appear connecting the hairs to the locator. Since the animation is at frame1, the current position of the locator is the start position of the constraint.

4. With the Move tool still active, choose Solvers ➤ Interactive Playback. While the scene plays, move the locator around and watch how the hairs react (see Figure 15.39).

5. Rewind the animation and change the position of the locator. Start Interactive Playback again. The position of the locator at the start frame affects how the blue lines are attached to the hairs as well as how the constraint pulls the hairs on subsequent frames.

6. Select the hairConstraint1 node in the Outliner, and open its Attribute Editor.

You can change how the constraint is attached to the hairs (the position of the blue lines that attaches the constraint to the hairs) by changing the Point Method setting.

The Nearest setting uses the closest distance along the hair to the locator at the start frame of the animation to determine where the constraint is connected to the hairs.

The U Parameter setting allows you to specify the precise U parameter along the length of the curve as the connection point between the constraint and the hairs. The U parameter of the curve ranges between 0 and 1.

FIGURE 15.39
As you move the locator, the hairs react to its new position.

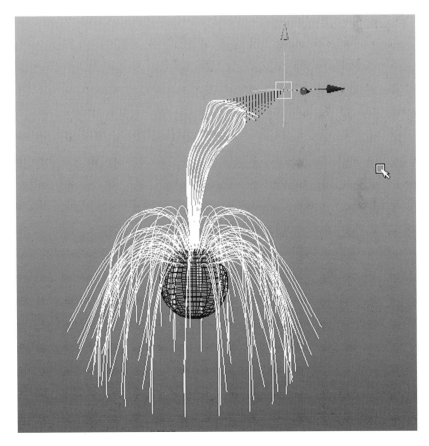

The U Distance setting defines the distance between the start of the curve and the connection point in U space. So if the curve is six units long, the U distance ranges between 0 and 6.

The two primary controls for hair constraints are Glue Strength and Stiffness. Setting Glue Strength to a value below 1 allows the constraint to be broken depending on the amount of force applied to it during the simulation.

The Stiffness value can be used to determine the amount of influence the constraint has over the hair curves.

You can add as many constraints as you need to a hair system. You can also change which curves are connected by selecting the curves, Ctrl+clicking the constraint, and choosing Hair ≻ Assign Hair Constraint. You can change the type of constraint after you create it. Here is a brief description of the different constraint types.

Rubber band constraints are somewhat stretchy. The distance between the constraint and the hair on the first frame of the animation establishes the length of the rubber band. If the constraint is moved beyond this length later in the animation, the hairs are pulled toward the constraint.

The stick constraint maintains the initial length of the constraint throughout the animation. If the constraint is moved away from the hairs, it pulls them, and if the constraint is moved closer to the hairs, it pushes the hairs.

Transform is similar to stick in that the constraint both pulls and pushes the hairs. The rotation of transform constraints also affects the hairs.

Hair-to-hair constraints create a clump. To use this constraint properly, play the simulation until some of the hairs are close together; then select the hair curves and create a hair-to-hair constraint. Rewind and play the animation. The hairs are connected by blue lines and should react as if they are bound together. Moving the locator changes the position of the constraints along the hair curves depending on the setting used for Point Method in the constraint properties. Moving the constraint locator around after the initial frame has no effect on how the constraint behaves (see Figure 15.40).

FIGURE 15.40

Use a hair-to-hair constraint to bind the ends of selected hairs together.

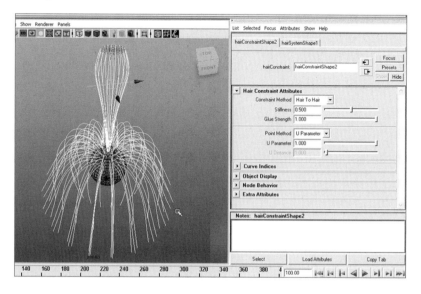

Hair bunch is a method of simulating self-collision between hairs that is more computationally efficient than the built-in Self Collide feature available in the Collision section of the hairSystem node. This constraint is meant to keep hairs from intersecting one another.

To see a version of the scene with an attached hair constraint, open the `constraintsStart_v02.ma` scene from the `chapter15\scenes` directory on the DVD.

Render Hair

Rendering hair can be done using Maya Software or mental ray. The hair should be either Paint Effects strokes or Paint Effects strokes converted to geometry. Paint Effects strokes are discussed in detail in Chapter 7.

Color Hair

If you decide to render hair as Paint Effects strokes, you can change the Hair Color, Translucence, and Specular properties using the settings in the hairSystemShape tab's Shading section.

Tips for Rendering Hair

Rendering hair is a very straight-forward process. If you're not familiar with Paint Effects, you should review Chapter 8 before reading this section.

When you convert hair to geometry, the Hair Tube shader is automatically applied. You can render Paint Effects hair using mental ray without the need to convert the hair to geometry.

When you are ready to render the hair, you'll want to increase the Hair Sub Segments setting in the hairSystem's Attribute Editor, as well as the Hairs Per Clump, Hair Width, and Hair Width Scale, in order to create fuller hair. You can always add additional follicles as well using the Paint Follicles tool.

In the Render Stats section of the hairSystem node, you can enable Receive Shadows, Visible In Reflections, and Visible In Refractions when rendering with mental ray.

In the Quality tab of the mental ray render settings, you can use the Rapid Motion Hair preset to render hair without raytracing or the Production: Fine Trace preset for rendering with raytracing.

If the hair will not render using mental ray, make sure the Render Fur/Hair setting is activated in the Features tab of the mental ray Rendering section.

1. Open the `renderHair.ma` scene from the `chapter15\scenes` folder on the DVD.

In this scene the `dreads.mel` preset, found in the Hair Examples tab of the Visor, is applied to the nancy model. The `hairLights.mel` file has also been imported from the Visor and applied to the scene.

2. Switch to the quarterSide camera, and create a test render in the Render View window. The scene is set up to render using mental ray. The render will take a couple minutes (see Figure 15.41).

Most standard lights will render hair nicely. When you're testing out the look of the hair, using the `hairLights.mel` preset makes it easy to see how the hair will look when rendered.

FIGURE 15.41
Apply the dreadlocks preset hair to the nancy model and render it with mental ray.

size: 720 405 zoom: 1.000 (mental ray)
Frame: 101   Render Time: 4:02   Camera: quarterSideCam

Create Clothing for Characters

Chapter 14 introduced the nCloth dynamic simulation tools in the context of creating advanced simulations with nParticles. As the name suggests, nCloth was originally developed to simulate the dynamic properties of clothing. In this section, you'll explore techniques for using nCloth to add dynamic motion to a character's clothes. The example files are simple, but the same techniques can be used for more complex characters and models.

Before starting this section you should review Chapters 13 and 14 so that you understand how nDynamics and the Nucleus solver work.

Model Clothes for nCloth

The models you create for use with nCloth must be polygon meshes. Beyond that, there is nothing special about how you model your clothing. Smooth mesh polygons work just as well as standard polygons. You'll start by taking a look at an example scene.

1. Open the simpleMan_v01.ma scene from the chapter15\scenes directory on the DVD (see Figure 15.42).

FIGURE 15.42
The simpleMan_
v01.ma scene
contains a simple
cartoon character.
Clothes have been
modeled using
polygons.

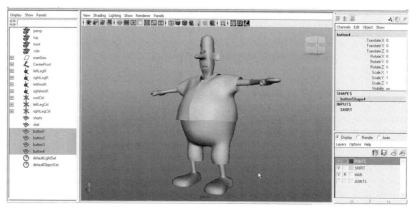

This scene has a very simple cartoon character who has been rigged and animated. He has a shirt and pants that have both been created using standard polygon modeling techniques. Both objects are currently smooth mesh polygons. The scene has been arranged so that the display layers contain the major components of the model and the animation rig.

2. Turn off the visibility of the SHIRT and PANTS layers and play the scene. Starting at frame 50 you'll see the man has been animated so that he moves up and down. This is just a simple animation cycle suitable for testing basic nCloth properties.

3. Rewind and restore the visibility of the PANTS layer. If you select the pants geometry, you'll see it's a basic polygon mesh. Press the 1 key and you'll see the pants as standard nonsmoothed polygons.

Convert Smooth Mesh Polygons to nCloth

You can convert smooth mesh polygons to nCloth objects. When you do this, the smooth mesh polygons switch to standard polygon mode automatically. You can then switch them back to smooth mesh polygons.

1. Continue with the simpleMan_v01.ma scene from the previous section.

2. Switch the nDynamics menu set. Select the pants and choose nMesh ➤ Create nCloth. The pants switch to standard polygon mode.

3. Select the pants and press the 3 key to switch back to smooth mesh polygons.

4. Play the scene. You'll see the pants fall down (this kind of thing can be embarrassing, but it happens a lot to cartoon characters; see Figure 15.43).

The first step in preventing the pants from falling is to make the character's body a Passive Collider object. It does not matter that the character is already rigged and animated. However, it's a good idea to convert the polygons to nCloth objects (both nCloth and Passive Collider objects) when the character is in the default pose and there are no intersections between the nCloth and Passive Collider geometry.

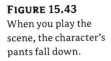

FIGURE 15.43
When you play the
scene, the character's
pants fall down.

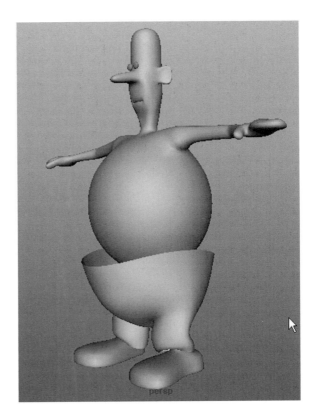

5. Rewind the animation. In the Display Layer Editor, click the R next to the MAN layer to turn off Reference mode so you can directly select the man geometry.

6. Select the man geometry and choose nMesh ➢ Create Passive Collider.

The geometry used for the man is fairly simple. If you have a very complex character, you may want to use a lower-resolution copy of the geometry as a collision object. This lower-resolution copy should have its Primary Visibility setting turned off in the Render Stats section of its Attribute Editor, and the geometry should be skinned to joints or deformers in a way that matches the deformations of the higher-resolution objects.

7. Rewind and play the scene. The pants still fall down, but they are stopped from falling indefinitely by the character's feet. In the next section you'll create a constraint that will keep his pants from falling down.

8. Save the scene as **simpleMan_v02.ma**. To see a version of the scene, open the simpleMan_v02.ma scene from the chapter15\scenes directory.

Add a Transform Constraint

The simplest way to keep the character's pants on is to create a transform constraint. A transform constraint attaches the selected vertices on an nCloth object to the pivot point of another object without affecting the position of the nCloth vertices. When the constraining object is translated or rotated, the vertices follow along, dragging the rest of the nCloth object with them.

1. Continue with the scene from the previous section or open the simpleMan_v02.ma scene from the chapter15\scenes directory on the DVD.

2. Turn off the visibility of the MAN layer, and turn on the visibility of the JOINTS layer.

3. At the center of the pelvis you'll see a locator. This is the rootControl locator used to animate the character's skeleton. You can use this locator as the constraining object for the nCloth pants.

4. Right-click on the pants, and choose Edges to switch to edge selection mode.

5. Double-click on one of the edges at the top of the pants. This selects all the edges that run around the top of the pants (left image, Figure 15.44).

6. Hold the mouse over the selected edges, press the Ctrl key, and RMB-drag to the left; then select the To Vertices label from the marking menu. This converts the selection to vertices (center image, Figure 15.44).

7. With the vertices selected (they should be highlighted in yellow) in the Outliner, Ctrl+ click the rootCtrl locator and choose nConstraint ➤ Transform. The vertices should turn green, indicating that they are constrained. In the Outliner, you'll see a new dynamicConstraint1 node has been created.

8. Turn the visibility of the MAN layer back on, and play the animation. The pants should now stay in place, and when the man starts moving, they should collide with the character's legs (right image, Figure 15.44).

9. Save the scene as **simpleMan_v03.ma**. To see a version of the scene, open the simpleMan_ v03.ma scene from the chapter15\scenes directory on the DVD.

FIGURE 15.44
Select the edges at the top of the pants (left image). Convert the edge selection to vertices (center image). When you constrain the vertices to the rootCtrl locator, the pants stay up and collide with the animated character (right image).

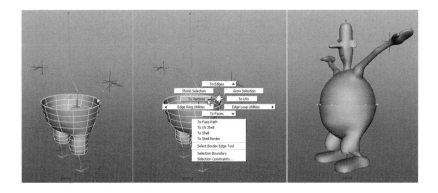

Use Component Constraints

Components of nCloth objects, such as vertices, can be used as constraints. Using this technique, you can easily simulate the effect of buttons holding a shirt together.

1. Continue with the scene from the previous section or open the `simpleMan_v03.ma` scene from the `chapter 15\scenes` directory.

2. In the Display Layer Editor, turn on the visibility of the SHIRT layer.

3. Before converting the shirt to an nCloth object, make sure it does not intersect with the pants. Rotate the view so you can see the back of the character; here you can see that the shirt is intersecting the pants (top image, Figure 15.45).

4. Right-click on the faces near the intersection and choose Faces. Use the Move tool to move the faces outward just enough that they do not intersect the pants (bottom image, Figure 15.45).

FIGURE 15.45
The surface of the shirt intersects the pants in the back of the character. Use the Move tool to move the faces of the shirt outward to fix the problem.

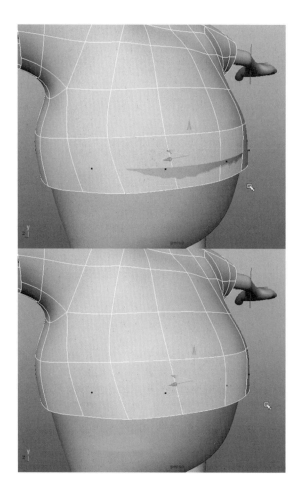

5. Select the shirt and choose nMesh ➤ Create nCloth. The shirt switches back to standard polygon mode; press the 3 key to return to smooth mesh.

6. Rewind and play the animation. The shirt falls until it collides with the character geometry. It moves as the character moves; however, you can see the front of the shirt fly open (see Figure 15.46).

FIGURE 15.46
As the character moves, the front of the shirt flies open.

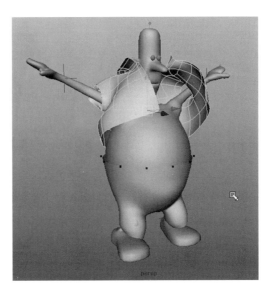

7. Zoom in to the front of the shirt. Turn off the visibility of the MAN and PANTS display layers. Right-click on the shirt and choose Vertices.

8. Switch to wireframe mode. Select the two vertices at the top of the shirt close to the collar (Figure 15.47, top image).

9. Choose nConstraints ➤ Component To Component. This creates a constraint between the two vertices.

10. Repeat step 8 and 9 to create constraints for the other three pairs of vertices running down the shirt. You don't need to constrain the two at the very bottom. You should end up with four constraints running down the front of the shirt (Figure 15.47, bottom image).

11. Switch to shaded mode, turn on the MAN and PANTS layers, and rewind and play the scene. The front of the shirt is now bound as if it has buttons (see Figure 15.48).

12. Save the scene as **simpleMan_v04.ma**. To see a version of the scene, open the simpleMan_v04.ma scene from the chapter15\scenes directory on the DVD.

FIGURE 15.47
Select vertices near the collar and turn them into a constraint (top image). Then create four pairs of constraints on the front of the shirt (bottom image).

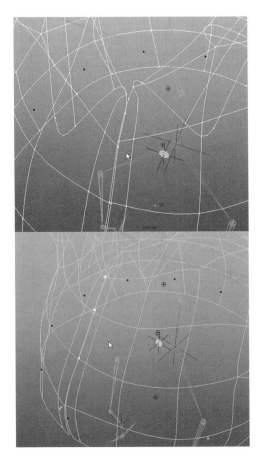

FIGURE 15.48
When you play the animation, the shirt stays closed as if it has buttons.

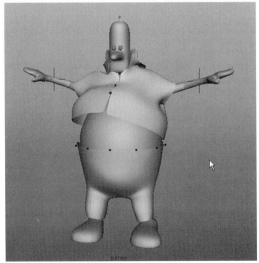

Connect Buttons to the Shirt

There is an interesting technique that you can use to attach objects to polygons. This involves converting a polygon edge to a NURBS curve. The object can then be connected to the curve using a motion path. As long as history is not deleted on the shirt, the curve and the connected object will move with the shirt.

1. Continue with the scene from the previous section or open the simpleMan_v04.ma scene from the chapter15\scenes directory on the DVD.

2. Zoom in to the front of the shirt.

3. Right-click on the shirt and choose Edge. Select the edge closest to the top constraint on the shirt.

4. With the edge selected, choose Modify ➤ Convert ➤ Polygon Edges To Curve (top image, Figure 15.49).

A small curve is created at the position of the selected edge. The curve is listed as polyTo-Curve1 in the Outliner.

5. Select the polyToCurve1 curve and choose Modify ➤ Center Pivot.

6. Use the Move tool to move the curve out just slightly in front of the shirt.

7. In the Outliner, select polyToCurve1 and Ctrl+click button1. Switch to the Animation menu set and choose Animate ➤ Motion Paths ➤ Attach To Motion Path ➤ Options.

8. In the options, set Time Range to Start. Click Attach to make the motion path. The button appears at the position of the curve (center image, Figure 15.49).

Why not parent constrain the button to the curve? The reason a motion path works better than a constraint in this situation is that the curve's transform node does not update as the shirt animates. The history that connects the shirt to the curve acts only on the curve's shape node. So if you constrain the button to the curve, the button will not move with the shirt even though the curve appears to.

Rewind and play the animation. The button moves with the shirt, but notice that the rotation of the button is incorrect. To fix this you can use a normal constraint.

9. Select the shirt and Ctrl+click button1. From the Animation menu set choose Constrain ➤ Normal ➤ Options.

10. In the Options box for the normal constraint, choose Edit ➤ Reset to reset the settings to the default. Set the Aim Vector fields to **0, 0, 1** so that the aim vector is aligned with the button's Z axis.

11. Click Apply to create the constraint.

12. Rewind and play the animation. The button now moves with the shirt and rotates to align itself correctly with the surface of the shirt.

This method works pretty well. However, if the camera is close, you may need to make some adjustments to the position of the curve, as the button may intersect with the shirt from time to time.

13. Repeat these steps to attach the other buttons to the shirt (bottom image, Figure 15.49).

14. Save the scene as **simpleMan_v05.ma**. To see a version of the scene, open the simpleMan_v05.ma scene from the chapter15\scenes directory on the DVD.

FIGURE 15.49
Convert an edge of the shirt geometry into a curve (top image). Attach a button to the curve using a motion path (center image). Then add more buttons to the shirt (bottom image).

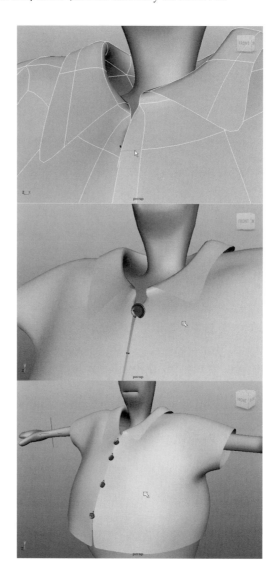

Paint nCloth Properties

nCloth properties, such as Bounce, Stretch, and Wrinkle, can be painted onto an nCloth object. There are two ways to do this: vertex property maps and texture property maps.

When you paint a vertex property map, you paint property values directly onto the vertices of the object, similar to painting smooth skin weights for joints. The more vertices you have in your object, the more detail you can create for your vertex property map. The vertex map values are saved with the object, so you do not need to link to external map files.

Texture property maps are independent of the number of vertices in the object, but they do require that UVs are properly created for the object, meaning that the UVs do not overlap and remain within the 0 to 1 range in the UV Texture Editor. Texture property maps for nCloth objects are very similar to texture property maps created for fur (this was demonstrated earlier in the chapter). However, you do not need to bake the maps after applying them.

When you paint a vertex or texture map, the map is listed in the Attribute field in the Dynamic Properties section of the nCloth shape node's Attribute Editor.

Paint a Vertex Property Map

In this example you'll paint Wrinkle attributes for the simple man character's pants. A wrinkle map displaces an nCloth object to create folds in the surface. You can paint detailed wrinkles into objects with a lot of vertices. In this example, the wrinkle map will be used to add cartoonish embellishments to the pants, which have a fairly low number of vertices.

When applying a Wrinkle attribute, positive values push the nCloth outward, while negative values push inward. There are a few peculiarities about painting Wrinkle values, which we'll explore in this lesson.

1. Continue with the scene from the previous section or open the simpleMan_v05.ma scene from the chapter15\scenes directory.

2. Turn off the visibility of the SHIRT and JOINTS layers.

3. Rewind and play the animation. The pants maintain their shape until they start to collide.

4. Rewind the animation again, select the pants object, and choose (from the nDynamics menu set) nMesh ➤ Paint Vertex Properties ➤ Wrinkle.

The pants turn white, indicating that a value of 1 is applied to the vertices of the pants for the Wrinkle property.

5. Rewind and play the animation. The pants suddenly bloat outward, even though you have not made any changes. What just happened (left image, Figure 15.50)?

When you start to create the wrinkle map, Maya applies a value of 1 to all the vertices of the object at the moment the map is created. Prior to creating the wrinkle map, no Wrinkle value is applied to the pants, so they do not bloat outward until the map is made. This behavior is specific to the wrinkle map.

6. Open the Tool Options box and set the value to **0**. Click the Flood button and rewind the animation.

The pants turn black and the bloating disappears. The wrinkle values are now set to 0 for all the vertices of the pants geometry (right image, Figure 15.50).

FIGURE 15.50
When you create the wrinkle map and play the animation, the pants bloat outward. When you apply the value 0 to all the vertices, the pants turn black and the shape returns to normal.

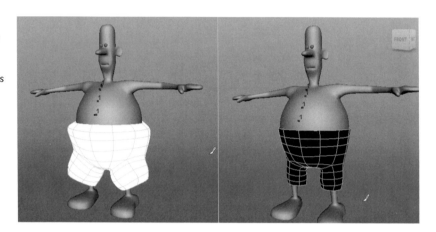

At this point you'll paint the area where the pant legs emerge from the pants with a value of -0.2 so that the pant legs shrink inward. Notice, however, that the Value slider in the Artisan Tool options only goes from 0 to 1.

7. In the Tool Options box, set Min Value to **-1** and Max Value to **1**.

Now it is possible to paint negative numbers, but you'll notice that since the black color on the pants indicates a value of 0, there is no color feedback for negative numbers. This can be changed as well.

8. Scroll down to the bottom of the Tool Options box and expand the Display rollout. Make sure Color Feedback is on. Set Min Color to **-1** and Max Color to **1** (see Figure 15.51).

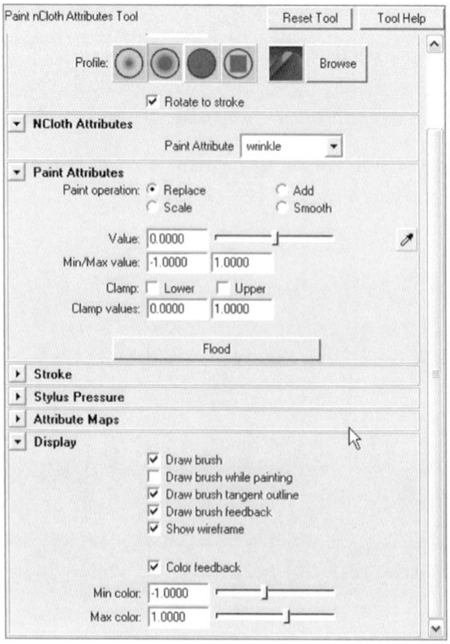

FIGURE 15.51
The Min/Max value fileds can be adjusted to allow for a wider range of values for the Paint nCloth Attributes tool. Adjusting the Min Color and Max Color sliders allows you to visualize the new values painted on the surface.

The pants turn gray, indicating that the current value applied to the vertices (0) is in the middle range of colors between black and white. As you paint negative values on the pants, you'll see darker areas appear.

9. Set the Value slider to -0.2, and paint around the area where the pant legs meet the pants (see Figure 15.52).

FIGURE 15.52
Paint a value of -0.2 around the belt area of the pants. Paint positive values near the pant cuffs to create flares.

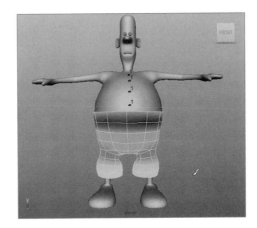

10. Rewind and play the scene. You'll see the tops of the pant legs shrink in a little.

11. To create flares (flares on shorts are apparently all the rage now), set the value to **0.4**, and paint the cuffs of the pants.

12. To create the impression of a drawstring, paint a value of **-1** around the area of the pants where a belt would go.

13. Press the q hot key to switch to the Select tool. Doing this will close the Artisan tool; the pants return to green. Rewind and play the animation. Experiment making more changes by painting various Wrinkle values on the pants.

14. Save the scene as **simpleMan_v06.ma**. To see a version of the scene, open the simpleMan_v06.ma scene from the chapter15\scenes directory.

The Bottom Line

Add fur to characters. Maya Fur is a rendering module that adds realistic short hairs to the surface of characters to simulate fur. Fur can be rendered using both Maya Software and mental ray. The placement, length, and other attributes of fur can be controlled by painting on the surface with the Artisan tool interface. When adding fur to polygons, the success of the fur is largely dependent on how well the UV texture coordinates have been mapped.

Master it   Create furry whiskers for the old man model used in Chapter 11.

Add dynamic motion to fur.   Using hair curves as a control, fur can be made to react to dynamic forces.

> **Master it**   Create a field of grass that blows in the wind.

Render fur with mental ray.   Fur can be rendered using mental ray or Maya Software. The Rapid Fur mental ray Quality preset works well when rendering fur with depth map shadows. The Fine Trace mental ray Quality preset works well when rendering with mental ray and ray trace shadows and reflections.

> **Master it**   Add a Physical Sun and Sky network to the hound dog scene, and render with mental ray.

Create dynamic curves.   A standard Maya curve can be made dynamic by using the Make Dynamic Curves action in the Hair menu. A copy of the curve is created that will respond to dynamic motion and forces. The curve can be used in skeletons for IK Spline tools, as a source for Paint Effects strokes, as a modeling tool, or for any other effect that requires curves.

> **Master it**   Create a flag using dynamic curves.

Add hair to characters.   Hair is created using Paint Effects strokes that are controlled by follicles. The follicles are dynamic curves that respond to forces and movement. Follicles can be applied to polygon or NURBS surfaces as a grid or by painting on the surface. The Visor contains a number of hair presets that can be imported into a scene.

> **Master it**   Add hair to the old man character from Chapter 9.

Style hair.   Hair can be styled by painting attribute values on follicles, by using dynamic fields, or by directly editing the CVs of start or rest curves.

> **Master it**   Create an avant-garde hairdo for the nancy character using fields.

Use hair constraints.   Hair constraints can be used to control the motion of hair or to connect the hair to props, such as hair ties and scrunchies.

> **Master it**   Use a constraint to create a ponytail for a character.

Render hair.   Hair can be rendered using mental ray or Maya. You can render as Paint Effects strokes or convert the strokes to geometry. Either method works in both Maya Software and mental ray (in spite of the fact that Paint Effects cannot normally render in mental ray).

> **Master it**   Apply the Hair preset examples found in the Visor to a character, and render with mental ray.

Create clothing for characters.   Clothing is created by converting polygon geometry to an nCloth object. The object can be attached to a character using constraints.

> **Master it**   Create sweatpants and a sweatshirt with a hood for the simple man character.

Paint nCloth properties.   Properties such as Bounce, Stretch, and Wrinkle can be painted onto nCloth objects using either texture or vertex painting techniques. When painting properties, the Min and Max Value ranges in the Artisan interface may need to be altered to allow for values beyond the range of 0 to 1. Vertex maps have the advantage that the values are not stored in an external texture file.

> **Master it**   Add starch to the simple man's shirt by painting a Rigidity value on the shirt geometry.

Chapter 16

Maya Fluids

Maya Fluids is a suite of tools designed to create a number of fluid-based effects. The tools available in Fluids consist of containers and emitters, which are designed to simulate gaseous effects like clouds, smoke, flames, explosions, galactic nebulae, and so on, as well as dynamic geometry deformers and shaders, which can be used to simulate rolling ocean waves, ripples in ponds, and wakes created by boats.

In this chapter you will learn to:

◆ Use fluid containers

◆ Create a reaction

◆ Render fluid containers

◆ Use fluids with nParticles

◆ Create a pond

◆ Create an ocean

Use Fluid Containers

Fluid containers can be thought of as mini scenes within a Maya scene. Fluid containers are best used for gaseous and plasma effects like clouds, flames, and explosions. The effect itself can exist only within the container. Fluids can be generated inside the container using an emitter or by painting the fluid inside the container. Dynamic forces then act on the fluid within the container to create the effect.

There are two types of containers: 2D and 3D. They work the same way. Two-dimensional containers are flat planes that generally calculate faster than 3D containers, which are cubical volumes. If you do not need an object to fly through a fluid effect or if the camera angle does not change in relation to the fluid, you might want to try a 2D container instead of the 3D container, which can take a much longer time to calculate and render. Two-dimensional containers are also a great way to generate an image sequence that can be used as a texture on a surface.

FLUIDS VERSUS nPARTICLES

When should you use fluids and when should you use nParticles? There's no hard-and-fast rule for choosing one over the other. However, if you need to create a dense cloud and you find yourself setting the rate of an nParticle emitter above 100,000 nParticles/second, you should really consider switching to Fluids. Fluids and nParticles can work together as well, as you'll see later in the chapter.

Fluids are not part of the Nucleus system so they are not influenced by settings on the Nucleus solver.

Use 2D Containers

In this first exercise, you'll work with fluid basics to create a simple but interesting effect using 2D containers. When you set up a container, you can choose to add an emitter that generates the fluid within the container, or you can place the fluid inside the container using the Artisan Brush interface. You'll start your experimentation using the latter method. Later in the chapter, as you work with 3D containers, you'll use emitters.

1. Create a new scene in Maya. Switch to the Dynamics menu set.

2. Choose Fluid Effects ➤ Create 2D Container. A simple plane appears on the scene.

The simple plane is the 2D container. If you play the scene, nothing happens because currently there are no fluids within the container. In the Outliner you'll see a new node named fluid1. The fluid1 object, like many Maya objects, consists of a transform node (named fluid1) and a shape node (fluidShape1).

3. Select fluid1 and choose Fluid Effects ➤ Add/Edit Contents ➤ Paint Fluids Tool. This activates the Artisan Brush interface.

4. Open the Tool options, and make sure Paintable Attributes is set to Density and Value is set to 1. Paint a few strokes on the container.

5. Clumps of green dots appear if you are in wireframe mode. Press the 5 key on the keyboard to switch to shaded mode. The clumps appear as soft, blurry blobs (see Figure 16.1).

6. Set the timeline to 200. Rewind and play the scene. The fuzzy blobs rise and distort like small clouds. They mix together and appear trapped by the edges of the container.

FIGURE 16.1
Use the Artisan Brush to paint areas of density in the 2D fluid container.

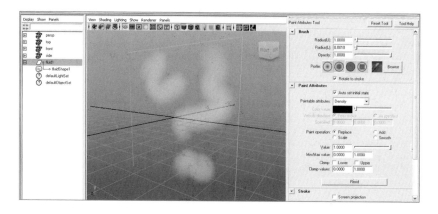

PLAYING FLUID SIMULATIONS

Like many of Maya's dynamics modules, Fluids evaluates each frame based on what occurs in the previous frame. Therefore you need to have your playback preferences set to Every Frame in order for Fluids to calculate correctly.

The properties that govern how the fluid exists within the container and how it behaves are controlled using the settings on the fluidShape1 node. When you painted in the container using the Paint Fluid tools, you painted the density of the fluid. By creating areas of density, you position the fluid in an otherwise empty container.

Before you start to edit the other properties of the fluid (such as Buoyancy, Temperature, and Color), you can create a much more interesting effect using some of the controls available in the Paint Fluids tool. You can use a file texture to determine the density of the fluid within the container, which is a great way to create an unusual effect.

7. Rewind the scene. In the options for the Artisan Brush, set Value to **0** and click the Flood button. This clears the container of any existing fluid density.

8. Set Value back to **1**. Scroll down in the options and expand the Attribute Maps rollout. Expand Import and click the Import button.

9. The File Import dialog box opens. Browse your computer and find the JollyRoger.tif file located in the chapter16\sourceimages folder on the DVD. Select this file and click Import.

When you import the file you'll see a very blocky skull and crossbones appear in the container. The blocky quality of the image is because the resolution of the fluid container is very low, so the resolution of the image is not displayed correctly.

10. In the Outliner, select the fluid1 node and open the Attribute Editor.

The resolution for the 2D container is represented by two fields corresponding to the X and Y dimensions of the container. The original JollyRoger.tif texture is 1024´1024. You can raise the resolution of the fluid container to match; however, the higher the resolution, the longer it takes Maya to calculate the simulation.

One advantage of 2D containers over 3D containers is that 2D containers can tolerate a much higher Resolution setting than 3D containers. Depending on the effect you are trying to create, this fact may influence your choice of one over the other. Three-dimensional containers are explored further later in the chapter.

11. Set the two Resolution fields to 512 × 512. When you do this, the image still appears blocky. To fix this you can re-import the image.

12. Switch to the Tool Options box, and click the Import button in the Attribute Maps ➢ Import section of the Artisan Brush options. Choose the same JollyRoger file again.

13. After a few seconds the image updates. Now you can see much more detail in the fluid density.

14. Rewind and play the scene. The Jolly Roger starts to break apart and rise to the top of the container (see Figure 16.2, left image).

15. Save the scene as **jollyRoger_v01.ma**. To see a version of the scene, open the jollyRoger_v01.ma scene from the chapter16\scenes directory on the DVD.

Fluid containers are subdivided into a grid. Each subdivision is known as a *voxel*. When Maya calculates fluids, it looks at each voxel and how the fluid particles in one voxel affect the particles in the next voxel. As you increase the resolution of a fluid container, you increase the number of voxels and the number of calculations Maya has to perform in the simulation. When setting the resolution of a 2D container, you can use much higher values than with a 3D container. If you make a 3D container with a resolution of 512 in each dimension (X, Y, and Z), you'll find that Maya grinds to a halt unless your machine is very powerful and has a lot of memory. You'll gain a deeper appreciation for the Resolution setting later in the chapter.

FIGURE 16.2
A file texture image of the Jolly Roger determines the density of the fluid. The image becomes clearer when you increase the resolution of the container. When you play the animation, the image distorts over time like smoke.

Use Fields with Fluids

Fluids can be controlled using dynamic fields such as Turbulence, Drag, and Vortex. In this section, you'll distort the image of the Jolly Roger using Radial fields.

1. Continue with the scene from the previous section or open the jollyRoger_v01.ma scene from the chapter16\scenes folder on the DVD.

As demonstrated in the previous section, when you play the scene, the image immediately starts to rise to the top of the container like a gas that is lighter than air. In this exercise you want the image to remain motionless until a dynamic field is applied to the fluid. To do this you'll need to change the Buoyancy property of the fluid.

2. In the Outliner, select the fluidShape1 node and open the Attribute Editor.

3. Scroll down to the Content Details rollout, and expand the Density section. Set Buoyancy to **0**.

4. Rewind and play the animation. The image of the Jolly Roger should remain motionless.

5. Stop the animation and rewind. Select fluidShape1 and choose Fields ➤ Radial. By selecting the fluid first and then creating a field, the field is automatically connected to the fluid.

If you need to connect a field to a fluid after it has been created, you can use the Dynamic Relationships Editor. This editor is discussed in Chapter 13.

6. Select the Radial field and open its Attribute Editor. Enter the following settings:

   Magnitude = **200**

   Attenuation = **0**

   Max Distance = **1** (Use Max Distance should be on by default.)

7. On frame 1 of the animation, set the Translate Z of the Radial field to **5** and set a keyframe.

8. Set the Timeline to frame 50. Set the Translate Z of the Radial field to **-5** and set another keyframe.

9. Rewind and play the animation (or create a playblast). As the Radial field passes through the container, it pushes the fluid outward like a cannonball moving through smoke (see Figure 16.3).

10. Add two more Radial fields to the container with the same settings. Position them so they pass through the image at different locations and at different frames on the keyboard.

11. Create a playblast of the scene. Watch it forward and backward in FCheck.

12. Save the scene as **jollyRoger_v02.ma**. To see a version of the scene, open the jollyRoger_v02.ma scene from the chapter16\scenes directory on the DVD.

Now that you have had a little experience working with containers, the next section explores some of the settings more deeply as you create an effect using 3D fluid containers and emitters.

FIGURE 16.3
The Radial field pushes the smoke as it moves through the field.

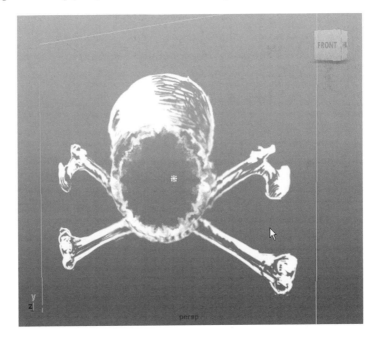

Fluid Examples

Maya comes with a number of Fluids examples located in the Visor. To use one of these examples, choose Fluid Effects ➢ Get Fluid Example. The Fluid examples are found under the Ocean Examples, Fluid Examples, and Fluid Initial States tabs (see Figure 16.4). To use an example, right-click on the example icon and choose Import Into Maya Scene. Information about the examples is stored in the Notes section of the fluid shape node's Attribute Editor. These notes explain how the example was created and how it can be edited. Much of the information in the notes makes more sense after you have some experience using Fluids.

FIGURE 16.4

The Visor contains numerous Fluids examples.

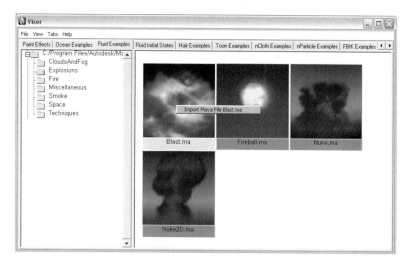

Use 3D Containers

Three-dimensional Fluids containers work just like 2D containers except they have depth as well as width and height. This does mean that they are computationally much more expensive. If you double the resolution in X and Y for a 2D container, the number of voxels increases by a factor of 4 (2×2); if you double the resolution of a 3D container, the number of voxels increases by a factor of 8 ($2 \times 2 \times 2$). A good practice for working with 3D containers is to start at a low resolution, such as $20 \times 20 \times 20$, and increase the resolution gradually as you develop the effect.

1. Start a new Maya scene and switch to the Dynamics menu set.

2. Choose Fluid Effects ➢ Create 3D Container.

You'll see the 3D container appear in the scene. On the bottom of the container you'll see a small grid. The size of the squares in the grid indicates the resolution (in X and Z) of the container.

3. Select the fluidShape1 node in the Outliner, and open its Attribute Editor. Expand the Display section under the fluidShape1 tab. Set Boundary Draw to Reduced. This shows the voxel grid along the X, Y, and Z axes (see Figure 16.5). The grid is not drawn on the parts of the container closest to the camera, so it's easier to see what's going on in the container.

FIGURE 16.5

The voxel resolution of the 3D container is displayed as a grid on the sides of the container.

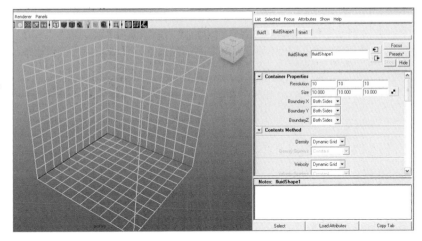

At the top of the Attribute Editor for the fluidShape1 node, you'll see the Resolution and Size fields for each of the three axes. These two settings are proportionally related. If you create a container with a Size of 10, 40, 10, then you should keep the Resolution values proportionally the same; for example, use 20, 80, 20 or 5, 10, 5. Otherwise, the voxels appear stretched along one axis, giving a stretched look to the fluid simulation (there are some instances where this may be desirable; for example, when creating the elongated glow of the aurora borealis).

You can use the Scale tool to resize the fluid container, but it's a better idea to use the Size setting in the fluid's shape node. This Size setting affects how dynamic properties (such as Mass and Gravity) are calculated within the fluid. Using the Scale tool does not affect these calculations, so increasing the scale of the fluid using the Scale tool may not give you the results you want. It depends on what you're trying to accomplish, of course. If you look at the Blast.ma example in the Visor, the explosion effect is actually created by animating the Scale X, Y, and Z channels of the fluid container.

Create a Reaction

There's no better way to gain an understanding of how fluids work than by directly designing an effect. In this section you'll learn how emitters and fluid settings work together to create flame and smoke. You can actually simulate a reaction within the 3D container as if it were a miniature chemistry lab.

Fluid Emitters

There are a number of ways to add contents to a fluid container. In the previous section you saw how to paint density directly into a container. You can also use an emitter to inject contents (such as density) into a container over time. Fluid emitters are very similar to particle emitters in that you can use an omni emitter, which is a single point in space, a volume, a curve, or a surface. The main difference between particle emitters and fluid emitters is that a fluid emitter has to be within the bounds of the fluid container to emit.

The contents that you can inject into a container by a fluid emitter are density, fuel, and temperature. You can use an emitter to inject any combination of the three. The settings on the fluid container's shape node determine how these contents behave within the container. You can use more than one emitter within a container and can create reactions by the interaction of anything within the container. For instance, you can use one emitter to add fuel and another to add temperature. The contents of two separate fluid containers can't interact.

In this example, you'll use an animated surface to emit temperature into a container that will appear as a flame. The simplest way to create flames or explosions is to add temperature. However, as you'll see later on, more interesting effects result when fuel and density are combined with temperature.

1. Open the reaction_v01.ma scene from the chapter16/scenes directory on the DVD.

2. This scene contains a spiral curve. Play the animation. You'll see a tube animate along the length of the curve.

The surface was created by converting an animated Paint Effects stroke into a NURBS surface. The surface is named emitterSurface (see Figure 16.6).

3. Switch to the Dynamics menu set, and choose Fluid Effects ➢ Create 3D Container. A 3D grid appears in the scene.

4. Select fluid1 in the Outliner and open its Attribute Editor. Switch to the fluidShape1 tab. Set the Resolution fields to **20**, **40**, **20**. Set Size to **20**, **40**, **20**.

5. Select fluid1 and use the Move tool to reposition it so that the animated spiral is near the bottom of the container. Set the Translate Y of fluid1 to **19**.

6. In the Outliner, select the emitterSurface and Ctrl+click fluid1. Choose Fluid Effects ➢ Add/Edit Contents ➢ Emit From Object ➢ Options.

7. In Emit From Object Options window, choose Edit ➢ Reset to set the options to their default values. Set Emitter Type to Surface.

FIGURE 16.6
An animated tube is created by converting a Paint Effects stroke into a NURBS surface.

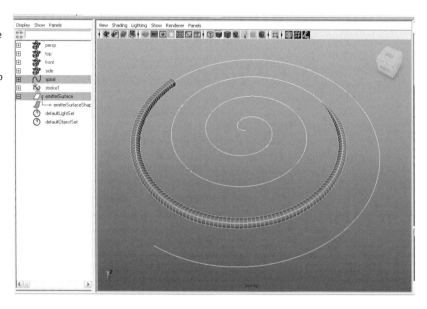

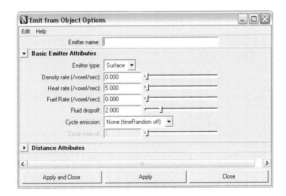

FIGURE 16.7

The options for the fluid emitter

8. Set Density Rate (/Voxel/Sec) to **0**. Set Heat Rate (/Voxel/Sec) to **5**. Set Fuel Rate (/Voxel/Sec) to **0** (see Figure 16.7). This emitter emits only temperature (heat) into the container, nothing else.

9. Click Apply And Close to create the emitter.

In the Outliner you'll see that the emitter node is parented to the emitterSurface node. If you play the animation, you'll see no change. You need to edit the fluid container itself so that it can properly display the temperature emitted by the surface.

10. Select the fluid container (fluid1) and open the Attribute Editor to the fluidShape1 tab.

11. In the Contents Method section, set Temperature to Dynamic Grid.

There are several options for adding temperature (as well as velocity, density, or fuel) to a 3D container. These are Static Grid, Dynamic Grid, and Gradient. If you don't need to calculate a particular content, you can set these to Off.

Static Grid is used for elements of the simulation that are placed within the container using the Paint tool or emitters. The values created for these elements are not changed by the simulation. For example, if you wanted to create a simple cloud, you could set Density to Static Grid, paint the cloud in the container, and then animate the container moving across the sky.

Dynamic Grid is used when the element and its values will change over time as a result of the simulation. Most of the examples in this section use dynamic grids.

Gradients create a static range of values between 0 and 1. The values affect the simulation but are not changed by it. For example, a container can be set so that the velocity at one end is higher than the velocity at the other end, which causes the fluid to move steadily faster as it approaches the higher range of values in the gradient. When you choose the Gradient option, a menu becomes available that allows you to determine the direction of the gradient.

12. Scroll down to the Shading section. Set Transparency to a very light gray color, almost white. In the Color section, click on the color swatch and choose a black color.

13. The Incandescence ramp is already set to Temperature. By setting Color to black, you'll be able to see how the colors of the ramp represent the temperature of the fluid.

14. In the Opacity section, set Opacity Input to Temperature.

15. Expand the Display section and set the Shaded Display option to As Render.

16. Press the 6 key to switch to shaded mode. Rewind and play the animation. The animation will play more slowly, but you'll see some yellow flames start to rise from the emitter surface (see Figure 16.8).

17. Save the scene as **reaction_v02.ma**. To see a version of the scene, open the reaction_v02.ma scene from the chapter16\scenes folder on the DVD.

FIGURE 16.8
When you play the animation, yellow frames rise from the animated surface.

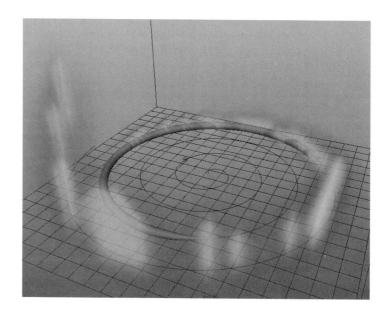

Add Velocity

Velocity is used to push fluids around within a container. You can add velocity as a constant force to push fluids in a particular direction, or you can use an emitter. The Swirl setting adds rolling and swirling motion to the contents of a container. In the current example, the flames are already rising to the top of the container because of the Buoyancy setting, so you'll use Velocity to add swirl.

1. Continue with the scene from the previous section or open the reaction_v02.ma scene from the chapter16\scenes folder on the DVD.

Before editing the simulation, you can improve the detail of the fluid by increasing the resolution. Be aware that this will slow down the playback of the simulation. You may want to create playblasts occasionally as you work so that you can see the fluid play in real time.

2. Open the Attribute Editor to the fluidShape1 tab, and set Resolution to **40, 80, 40**.

3. In the Contents Method section, make sure Velocity is set to Dynamic Grid. Expand the Contents Details rollout and the Velocity subsection. Raise Swirl to **10**.

4. Rewind and play the animation. The fluid looks more like a swirl; however, the fluid does not last very long before disappearing. Expand Temperature and set Temperature Scale to **3**. Stop the animation at frame 80.

VELOCITY DRAW

You can activate the Velocity Draw option in the Display rollout of the fluid shape node. This creates a number of arrows within the container that indicate the direction of the fluid velocity. Longer arrows indicate areas of faster motion.

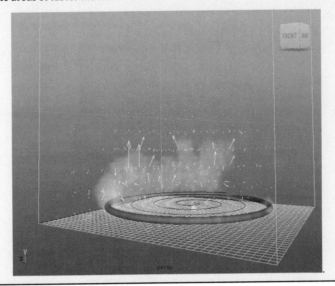

Temperature Scale is a global control for increasing the overall temperature of the container. This increases the size of the flame and keeps it around a little longer.

5. Scroll down to the Shading section. Move the orange color marker to the left slightly, and move the yellow color marker also slightly to the left. The left side of the Incandescence ramp is used to color lower temperatures; the right side colors higher temperatures.

6. Click on the right side of the Incandescence ramp to add another color marker. Set the color of the new marker to a light bluish-white.

7. Set Input Bias to **0.4**. This moves the bias of the incandescence so that more of the fluid receives more color.

8. Edit the Opacity ramp by adding points to the curve. Just like the Incandescence ramp, the left side of the curve controls opacity based on lower temperatures, while the right side controls the opacity of higher temperatures.

You can experiment with this ramp to shape the way the flames look (see Figure 16.9).

9. Save the scene as **reaction_v03.ma**. To see a version of the scene, open the reaction_v03.ma scene from the chapter16\scenes directory on the DVD.

FIGURE 16.9
The flame is colored and shaped using the Incandescence and Opacity ramps based on temperature.

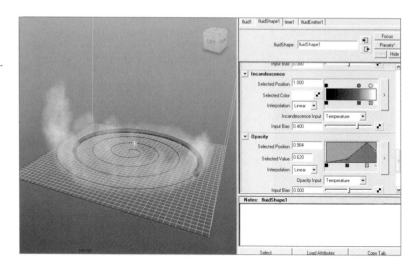

Add Fuel

Once you have a flame in your container, you can create a dramatic reaction by adding fuel. As with velocity, density, and temperature, you can add fuel using an emitter, or by painting fuel with Artisan, or by using a gradient. In this exercise you'll use a second emitter to add fuel.

1. Continue with the scene from the previous section or open the reaction_v03.ma scene from the chapter16\scenes directory on the DVD.

2. Select fluid1 and choose Fluid Effects ➤ Add Edit Contents ➤ Emitter ➤ Options. In the Options, set Emitter Type to Volume. Set Density Rate and Heat Rate to 0. Set Fuel Rate to **10**. In the Volume Emitter Attributes section, set Volume Shape to Sphere.

3. Click Apply And Close to create the emitter. The emitter appears as a sphere at the center of fluid1.

4. In the Outliner, expand fluid1 and select fluidEmitter2. Use the Move tool to move the emitter down closer to the bottom of fluid1. Set its Translate Y to -16.

You can think of the fuel emitter as a gas leak inside the container. As the temperature and the fuel come within close proximity of each other, a reaction takes place. The fuel burns until the fuel is exhausted or the temperature is lowered. Since the fuel is injected into the container, the flame keeps burning. If you play the scene at this point, no reaction will take place. You must set the fuel to Dynamic Grid in the fluid shape node before the temperature can react with the fuel in the emitter.

5. Open the fluidShape1 node in the Attribute Editor, and set Fuel in the Contents Method section to Dynamic Grid.

6. Scroll down to the Contents Details section and expand Fuel. Use the following settings:

   Reaction Speed: **1**

   Ignition Temperature: **0.1**

   Max Temperature: **100**

   Heat Released: **100**

   Light Released: **1**

7. Rewind and create a playblast of the scene.

The emitter surface acts like a fuse—when the temperature it emits gets close to the fuel emitter a reaction takes place, and suddenly a plume of flame and gas rises dramatically from the center. You'll also notice that after the initial reaction the fuel coming from the emitter continues to burn. This is because a small piece of the emitter surface continues to emit heat below the fuel emitter.

Reaction Speed determines how fast the reaction takes place once the heat ignites the fuel. Higher values produce faster reactions.

Ignition Temperature sets the minimum temperature required to ignite the fuel. If you want to create a reaction that occurs regardless of temperature, set this value to a negative number such as -0.1.

Heat Released causes the reaction to add more temperature to the fluid container.

Light Released adds value to the current Incandescent value of the fluid, which causes the fluid to glow brightly when rendered.

You'll notice that as the simulation plays, the flame and smoke appear trapped within the walls of the 3D container. This is because, by default, containers have boundaries on all sides. You can remove these boundaries to let the contents escape. Be aware that as the contents leave the container they will disappear, since fluid simulations cannot exist outside the fluid container (2D or 3D).

8. Select the fluid1 node and open its Attribute Editor. In the Container Properties section at the top of the fluidShape1 tab, set the Boundary Y option to -Y Side. This means that there is a boundary on the bottom of the container but not on the top (see Figure 16.10).

9. Create another playblast of the simulation. The explosion is no longer trapped at the top of the container.

10. Save the scene as **reaction_v04.ma**. To see a version of the scene, open the reaction_v04 .ma scene from the chapter16\scenes directory on the DVD.

FIGURE 16.10
Boundaries keep the simulation within the container (left image). When you set the Y boundary to -Y Side, the explosion can escape out the top (right image).

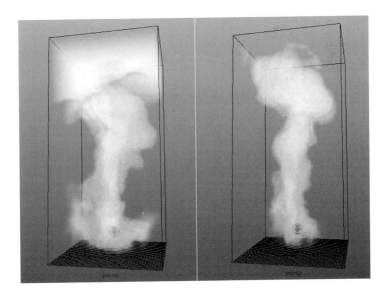

Render Fluid Containers

Fluid simulations can be rendered using Maya Software or mental ray, and they will be identical for the most part. Since fluids have an incandescent value, they can be used as light-emitting objects when rendering with Final Gathering. If you want the fluid to appear in reflections and refractions, you need to turn on the Visible In Reflections and Visible In Refractions options in the Render Stats section of the fluid's shape node.

This section demonstrates some ways in which the detail and the shading of fluids can be improved when rendered.

Texturing Fluids

You can add more detail to a fluid simulation by increasing the resolution of the fluid container; however, this makes playback of the scene slower as well as increases render times. Fluids have a set of built-in procedural texturing options that can help add more detail to the fluid without the need to change the resolution of the fluid container.

1. Continue with the scene from the previous section or open the reaction_v04.ma scene from the chapter16\scenes directory on the DVD.

2. Play the scene to about frame 200 and stop the animation.

3. Open the Render Settings window and set the Renderer to mental ray. In the Quality tab, set Quality Preset to Production.

4. Open the Render View window, and create a render from the perspective camera. Store the render in the Render View window.

5. Select fluid1 and open the Attribute Editor to the fluidShape1 tab. In the Shading section, set Dropoff Shape to Y Gradient and Edge Dropoff to **0.1**.

Dropoff Shape fades the edges of the simulation as the contents approach the edge of the container. Choosing Y Gradient means that the top of the simulation fades out as it leaves the top of the container. The Edge Dropoff value sets the range of the fading effect.

6. Scroll down and expand the Textures section. Turn on Texture Opacity and Texture Incandescence. Notice that the cloud appears to have more detail even in the perspective view.

7. By default, Texture Type should be set to Perlin Noise. You can also choose Billow, Volume Wave, Wispy, or Space Time. Perlin Noise is good for creating random detail in the cloud.

The settings for Perlin Noise are very similar to the settings found in the 3D noise texture that you create in the Hypershade.

8. Set Frequency to **4** to add more detail.

9. Create a test render and compare this with the previously saved render.

The fluid now looks as though it is more detailed. This can help to add a sense that the fluid simulation is much larger.

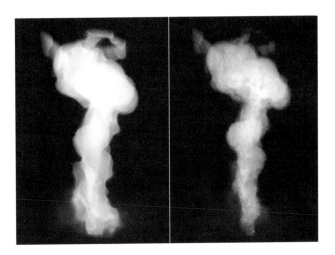

FIGURE 16.11
Render the simulation using mental ray (left image). Adding a Perlin Noise texture adds detail to the simulation without changing the fluid resolution (right image).

10. You can animate the texture using the Texture Time attribute. In the field next to Texture Time type **= time*0.1;**. This creates an expression where the texture is animated based on the current time of the animation.

11. Save the scene as **reaction_v05.ma**. To see a version of the scene, open the reaction_v05 .ma scene from the chapter16\scenes directory on the DVD.

THICK CLOUD NPARTICLES

When you create an nParticle using the Thick Cloud particle style, a fluid node is created. This fluid node does not contain a simulation but is used to determine how the nParticles will look when rendered. Using the texturing and shading settings on the fluid node, you can change the look of the nParticle. For more information on using nParticles, consult Chapters 13 and 14.

Glowing Fluids

Fluid simulations can benefit from using shader glow. This creates the impression that the bright parts of the fluid are emitting light in the scene.

1. Continue with the scene from the previous section or open the reaction_v05.ma scene from the chapter16\scenes directory on the DVD.

2. Rewind and play the scene to about frame 200.

3. Select fluid1 and open the Attribute Editor to the fluidShape1 tab. In the Shading section, set Glow Intensity to **0.1**.

The Glow Intensity attribute works exactly like the Glow Intensity slider found in the Special Effects section of standard Maya shaders. This boosts the incandescent values of the fluid as a post-render effect, making the fluid appear to glow. Just like all glow effects in the scene, the quality of the glow is controlled using the shader glow node found in the Hypershade. When rendering a sequence using a glow, you should always turn off the Auto Exposure setting in the shader glow node to eliminate flickering that may occur when the animation is rendered.

4. Open the Hypershade, select shaderGlow1, and open its Attribute Editor.

5. Turn off Auto Exposure.

Whenever Auto Exposure is disabled, the glows become much more intense in the render. To fix this you can adjust the Glow Intensity value in the Glow Attributes section of the shader glow node.

6. In the Common Shader Glow Attributes area, set Threshold to **0.1**. In the Glow Attributes section, set Glow Intensity to **0.05** (Figure 16.12).

The Threshold setting sets the minimum value required to create a glow effect in the final image. In other words, if Threshold is 0, then the glow is applied to all the visible pixels in the image, although black pixels do not produce much of a glow. When you raise Threshold to a value such as 0.1, then very dim pixels will not glow; only pixels above the Threshold value will glow in the final render. The higher the Threshold value, the less glow you'll see, and the glow itself will be localized to the brighter areas of the image.

7. Create a test render to see the fluid with the glow applied.

8. Save the scene as **reaction_v06.ma**. To see a version of the scene, open the reaction_v06 .ma scene from the chapter16\scenes directory on the DVD.

FIGURE 16.12
Edit the Shader Glow settings to reduce flickering and overexposure in the render.

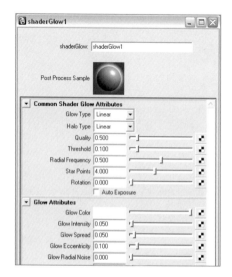

GLOW SETTINGS IN THE OUTPUT WINDOW

Auto Exposure is used to control the exposure for any particular frame in the scene. As the camera and objects in the scene move, Auto Exposure adjusts the shader glow to prevent overexposure. This is what leads to flickering when Auto Exposure is enabled on the shader glow node in rendered sequences. The glow settings appear in the Output Window when you render a test frame (as long as Verbosity is set to Progress Messages in Render Current Frame ➢ Options). If you want to match the settings used by Auto Exposure, you can render a test frame with Auto Exposure on, note the values in the Output Window, turn Auto Exposure off, and then adjust the other settings in the shader glow node based on the values listed in the Output Window. Set Glow Intensity to the Glow: Normalization value listed in the Output Window. Set Halo Intensity to the Halo: Normalization value.

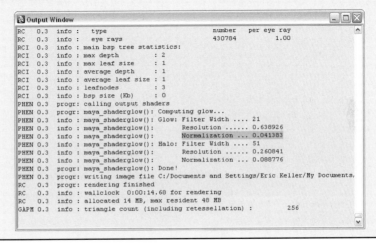

Lighting Fluids

Fluids can react to lighting in the scene, and you can apply self-shadowing to increase the realism. As an example of how to light fluids, a scene with simple clouds has been created for you to experiment with.

1. Open the `simpleCloud_v01.ma` scene from the `chapter16\scenes` directory on the DVD.

2. Play the animation to frame 100. A simple cloud appears in the center of the scene.

The scene contains a fluid container, an emitter, a plane, and a light. The scene is already set to render using mental ray at production quality.

3. Open the Render View window, and render the scene from the perspective camera. A puffy white cloud appears in the render. Store the render in the Render View window (Figure 16.13, left image).

4. Select the fluid1 node, and open the Attribute Editor to the fluidShape1 tab. Scroll down to the Lighting section at the bottom of the editor.

The Lighting section contains two settings: Self Shadow and Real Lights. When Real Lights is off, the fluids are lit from a built-in directional light. The three fields indicate the direction the light is pointing in X, Y, and Z. Rendering with Real Lights off tends to be much faster than rendering with Real Lights on, even when the real light is a directional light.

5. Turn on Self Shadowing. You'll see that the cloud now has dark areas at the bottom in the perspective view. The Shadow Opacity slider controls the darkness of the shadows. Create a test render, and store the render in the Render View window (Figure 16.13, middle image).

6. Select the directional light and open its Attribute Editor. Under Shadows, turn on Use Ray Trace Shadows.

7. Select fluid1, and in the Lighting section under the fluidShape1 tab turn off Self Shadows. Turn on Real Lights.

8. In the Render Stats section, make sure Casts and Receive Shadows are on.

9. Create another test render from the perspective camera (Figure 16.13, right image).

When rendering using Real Lights, the fluid casts shadows onto other objects as well as itself. When rendering using real shadow casting lights, make sure that Self Shadow is disabled to avoid calculating the shadows twice. You can see that rendering with Real Lights does take significantly longer than using the built-in lighting and shadowing. Take this into consideration when rendering fluid simulations.

FIGURE 16.13
Render the cloud with built-in lights (left image). Enable Self Shadows (center image). Then render the cloud using a directional light that casts ray trace shadows (right image).

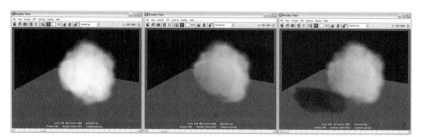

Fluids and nParticles

Fluids and nParticles use separate dynamic systems but they can be made to work together indirectly to create effects. A fluid system can be used to influence the movement of nParticles, like a field.

Add Sparks to a Flame

In this section, you'll create sparks using nParticles. The motion of the sparks will be controlled using a flame within a 3D container. To keep things simple you'll use one of the flame examples in the Visor.

1. Create a new scene in Maya. Choose Window ➤ General Editors ➤ Visor. Click the Fluid Examples tab in the Visor window, and choose the Fire folder.

2. Right-click the Flame.ma example, and choose Import Maya File Flame.ma. This imports the 3D container, emitter, and all of its settings into the scene.

3. Select the flame container and open its Attribute Editor to the flameShape tab. In the display options, set Shaded Display to Temperature. This does not affect how the flame looks when rendered, but it makes it easier to see the simulation in the perspective view.

4. Press the 6 key to switch to shaded view. Set the timeline to 800 and play the scene. You'll see the flame simulation play at the center of the 3D container (see Figure 16.14).

5. Switch the menu set to nDynamics. Choose nParticles ➢ Create nParticles ➢ Points to set the nParticle style to Points.

6. Choose nParticles ➢ Create nParticles ➢ Create Emitter ➢ Options. In the options, set Emitter Type to Volume and Rate to **40**. In the Volume Emitter Attributes section, set Volume Shape to Cylinder. Click Create to make the emitter.

7. Select the emitter, and use the Move tool to position the emitter at the base of the flame.

8. When you play the scene, the nParticles fall out of the emitter. Select nParticle1 in the Outliner, open its Attribute Editor, and switch to the Nucleus1 tab. Set Gravity in the Gravity And Wind section to **0**.

9. In the Outliner, select nParticle1 and Ctrl+click on the flame shape. Choose Fields ➢ Affect Selected Objects. This connects the fluid simulation to the nParticles.

10. Rewind and play the scene. You'll see the nParticles that are closest to the center of the flame shoot out of the top of the simulation. This may be easier to see if you set the Display option in the flameShape tab back to As Render.

Once the nParticles leave the fluid container, they continue to move at a constant rate. You can edit the settings on the nParticle shape node to make the movement more interesting.

FIGURE 16.14
Import the flame example into the scene. A flame burns at the center of the container when you play the scene.

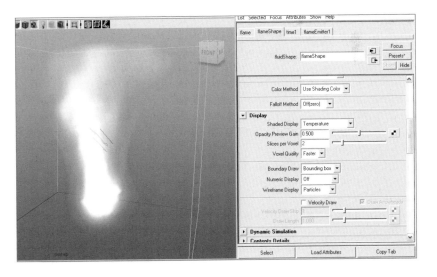

11. Select nParticle1, and open its Attribute Editor to the nParticleShape1 tab. In the Lifespan section, set Lifespan Mode to Random Range. Set Lifespan to **2** and Lifespan Random to **1**. As explained in Chapter 13, this means that the nParticles have a lifespan between 1 and 3 seconds.

12. In the Dynamic Properties section, set Drag to **0.3**. This causes the nParticles to slow down as they move away from the flame.

13. Rewind and play the animation.

The nParticles follow the movement of the flame fairly well, but they stop outside the fluid container, which looks rather odd. You can use the opacity settings to make slower-moving particles fade out and disappear, which really helps them to look like sparks.

14. Scroll down and expand the Shading rollout. Set Opacity Scale Input to Speed. Click on the ramp to add a new point. Edit the ramp so it looks like Figure 16.15. This causes slower-moving particles to become completely transparent.

15. In the Color section, set Color Input to Speed. Edit the Color ramp so that the left side is black, the center is orange, and the right side is yellow.

16. In the Shading section, set Particle Render Type to Streak. Set Tail Size to **0.2**, Tail Fade to **-1**, and Opacity to **0.5**.

17. Rewind and play the animation. You should have some nice-looking sparks that fly upward with the motion of the flame. If the scene is rendered using mental ray, the sparks and the flame appear together (Figure 16.16).

18. Save the scene as **sparkingFlame.ma**. To see a version of the scene, open the sparkingFlame.ma file from the chapter16\scenes directory on the DVD.

FIGURE 16.15
Edit the Opacity Scale edit curve so slower-moving particles disappear.

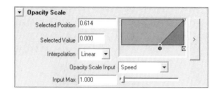

FIGURE 16.16
When you render the scene with mental ray, the sparks and the flame appear to interact.

Create a Pond

A pond is a special type of 2D fluid container that uses a Height field and a Spring Mesh solver to convert the 2D fluid container into a 3D surface. Ponds, as the name suggests, are suitable for simulating the surface of small bodies of water.

The Spring Mesh solver is one of the two solvers used by fluid effects. Up until this point you have been using the Navier-Stokes solver, which is a more accurate and computationally intense solver. The Spring Mesh solver is simpler, similar to dynamic springs used with soft body dynamics.

All of this sounds fairly complicated. However, most of the tricky parts of the effect are handled by Maya behind the scenes. Creating and using the pond effect is actually quite simple.

Set Up the Pond

In this example you'll use the pond effect to create the milky surface of a bowl of cereal, like something you might see in a commercial.

1. Open the `bowl_v01.ma` scene from the `chapter16\scenes` directory on the DVD. This scene contains a simple NURBS bowl, a polygon spoon, and a piece of cereal made from a NURBS torus.

2. Switch to the Dynamics menu set, and choose Fluid Effects ➢ Pond ➢ Create Pond. A blue plane appears inside a 2D fluid container. In the Outliner the Pond1 node appears; this is the 2D fluid container.

3. Select Pond1 and open its Attribute Editor to the PondShape1 node. Scroll down to the Surface section and expand these attributes.

The pond is set to a Surface render. All the previous examples in this chapter used a Volume render. Volume renders create clouds and flames. Surface renders generate a mesh. The Hard Surface option creates a mesh with hard edges useful for creating liquids such as water or milk. The Soft Surface option creates a surface with a fuzzy edge. This can be useful for certain types of clouds that require detailed self-shadowing effects. If you are creating thick clouds like what you might see in a nuclear blast, and you're not satisfied with the results you get with Volume render, you may want to try using a Surface render with the Soft Surface option.

4. Scroll down to the shading options and expand the Opacity section.

This attribute actually controls the height of the pond surface, which, admittedly, seems a little strange. The surface of the pond is displaced by the outAlpha channel value of the pondShape. The outAlpha value is controlled by the Opacity curve.

5. To move the field up or down you can adjust the points of the curve on the left or right side, or you can use the Input Bias slider (Figure 16.17).

At the moment the opacity settings cause the surface of the pond to remain at the middle of the container, which should work just fine for this example. Adding points to the curve will not distort the surface. To do that you can use the Textures section.

6. Scroll down to the Textures section and activate the Texture Opacity option. Set Texture Type to Billow.

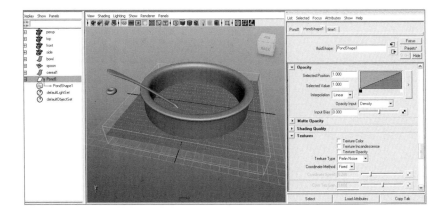

The Textures settings distort the surface of the pond. By adjusting the settings for the texture, you can create a lumpy surface on the pond, which might work well for creating mud or slime (see Figure 16.18).

7. In the Textures options, turn off Texture Opacity so that the surface is smooth again. In the Color section, edit the ramp so that the color of the surface is white. Edit the Incandescence ramp so that the incandescence is black (see Figure 16.19).

FIGURE 16.18
Applying a texture
to the opacity of the
fluid distorts the
surface of
the pond.

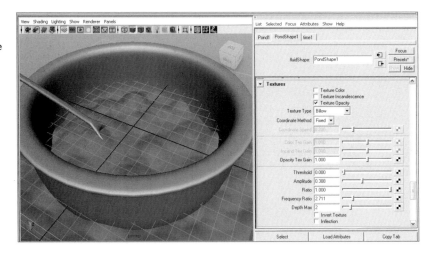

FIGURE 16.19
Edit the Color and
Incandescence
ramps so that the
surface is white but
does not emit light.

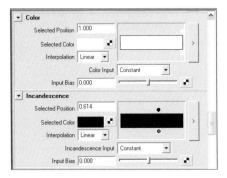

Right now the milk surface extends beyond the edges of the bowl. Later on you'll fix this using a texture, but for now you can leave it the way it is.

8. Save the scene as **bowl_v02.ma**. To see a version of the scene, open the bowl_v02.ma scene from the chapter16\scenes directory on the DVD.

Create a Wake

To make the simulation of the cereal bowl a bit more exciting, you can add ripples using a wake.

1. Continue with the scene from the previous section or open the bowl_v02.ma scene from the chapter16\scenes directory on the DVD.

2. Set the timeline to 500. Select the spoon in the Outliner, and keyframe its Translate and Rotate channels.

3. Create an animation of the spoon moving back and forth rapidly inside the bowl as if it is stirring the milk. Try animating the spoon moving in and out of the surface of the milk as well.

4. Select Pond1 in the Outliner. Choose Fluid Effects ➢ Pond ➢ Create Wake.

5. In the Outliner, you'll see a new PondWakeEmitter1 node, and a volume emitter appears in the pond. Select and hide Pond1 (Ctrl+h) and position the emitter around the end of the spoon. Scale and rotate the emitter so that it surrounds the end of the spoon.

6. Parent the PondWakeEmitter1 node to the spoon (see Figure 16.20).

7. Select and unhide Pond1 (Ctrl+H on a PC; Shift+H on a Mac)

FIGURE 16.20
Position Pond-WakeEmitter1 around the end of the spoon. In the Outliner parent it to the spoon.

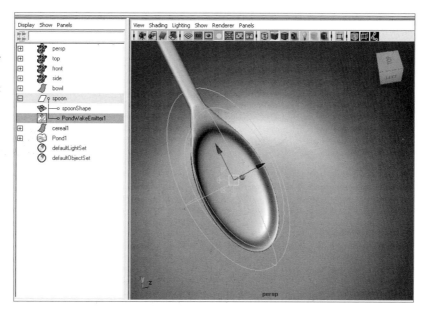

8. Rewind and play the animation. The pond responds to the wake, although the motion is rather violent.

9. Select PondWakeEmitter1 and open its Attribute Editor. In the Fluid Attributes section, set Density Rate (/Voxel/Sec) to **-1**. Negative values cause the wake to push down on the surface; positive values cause the wake to push up.

10. Select the Pond1 node, and open its Attribute Editor to PondShape1. In the Dynamic Simulation section, set Damp to 0.**08** and Viscosity to **1**.

11. Rewind and play the animation to see the spoon stir the milk (see Figure 16.21).

You can simulate various types of fluids by increasing the Damp and Viscosity settings. If you wanted to animate whipping cream turning from liquid to a stiffer substance, you could animate the Damp value using keyframes.

12. Save the scene as **bowl_v03.ma**. To see a version of the scene, open the bowl_v03.ma scene from the chapter16\scenes directory on the DVD.

FIGURE 16.21
Parent the emitter to the animated spoon to create the effect of the spoon stirring the milk.

Use Boats

Boats are simply locators that ride on the surface of the pond. An object can be parented to the locator to make it look as though the object is floating on the surface.

1. Continue with the scene from the previous section or open the bowl_v03.ma from the chapter16\scenes directory on the DVD.

2. In the Outliner, select Pond1 and choose Fluid Effects ➤ Pond ➤ Add Boat Locator. This creates a new locator, named locator1, that rests on the surface of the milk.

3. In the Outliner, select cereal1 and parent it to Locator1. You can do this by MMB-dragging cereal1 on top of Locator1.

4. Expand Locator1 in the Outliner and select cereal1. In the Channel Box, set cereal1's Translate X, Y, and Z values to **0**. This places cereal1 at the same location as Locator1.

5. Rewind and play the animation. You'll see the cereal bob up and down with the surface of the milk.

6. Select Locator1. You'll see that, in the Channel Box, the Translate Y, Rotate X, and Rotate Z channels are all colored purple, indicating that they are controlled by an expression.

7. Set Translate X to **-4.5** and Translate Z to **-1**. If you want to animate the cereal moving around, you can keyframe these channels.

8. Open the Attribute Editor for Locator1, and switch to the locatorShape1 tab. Expand the Extra Attributes section. This section contains a number of sliders that can be used to control the motion of the locator.

9. Set Buoyancy to **0.4**. Lowering this value makes the cereal sink a little in the fluid, and it also appears to bob a bit slower, making it look heavier.

10. Set Start Rot X to **90**. This causes the boat to start out on its side at the beginning of the animation. It will roll over to right itself. To control the speed at which it rolls, set the Roll value to **0.2**. The Start Y and Start Rot Z attributes create the same effect on a different axis. Pitch controls the speed at which the boat rights itself on the Z axis.

11. Set Boat Length to **2** and Boat Width to **1** to match the size of the cereal. By matching the size of the cereal, the simulation should be more accurate (see Figure 16.22).

Since the cereal geometry is parented to the locator, you can animate its local rotation as well if you need to make the cereal rotate in a specific fashion.

12. Save the scene as **bowl_v04.ma**. To see a version of the scene, open the bowl_v04.ma scene from the chapter16\scenes folder on the DVD.

FIGURE 16.22
Adjusting the settings in the Extra Attributes section of the locator's shape node allows you to change the behavior of the cereal floating on the surface.

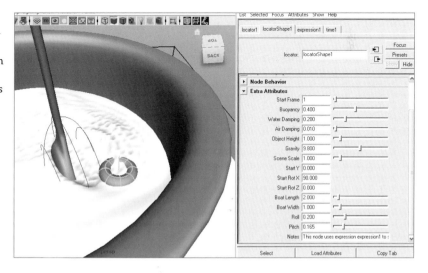

MOTOR BOATS

The Make Motor Boats command creates a locator like the boat locator; however, it has additional throttle, rudder, and other settings that allow you to drive the locator around on the surface of the water.

Convert Fluids to Polygons

To solve the problem of the milk surface extending past the edges of the bowl, you can convert the pond into a polygon object and then use the transparency of a shader to hide the protruding edges of the milk surface.

1. Continue with the scene from the previous section or open the bowl_v04.ma scene from the chapter16\scenes folder on the DVD.

2. Select Pond1 in the Outliner, and choose Modify ➢ Convert Fluid To Polygons. This creates a polygon surface named polySurface1 in the Outliner. Rename this surface **milk**.

3. Select Pond1 and hide it (Ctrl+h).

4. Create and assign a Blinn material to Milk. Make the color of the Blinn white. Name the shader **milkShader**.

5. Rewind and play the animation. You'll see that the milk surface is animated based on the fluid settings, but the playback speed is much slower.

6. Open the Hypershade window and select milkShader. Open its Attribute Editor.

7. Click on the checkered box next to Transparency to open the Create Render Node window. In the 2D Textures section, make sure As Projection is checked at the top (Figure 16.23).

The milk surface does not have UV coordinates. You can create UV coordinates, but this is a little risky. As the surface moves, the UV coordinates could slide around. It's safer to simply project the transparency texture onto the surface using a projection node, which does not require UV coordinates.

8. Click Ramp to create a new ramp texture.

FIGURE 16.23

Create a texture as a projection for the transparency of the milk surface.

9. In the Outliner, you'll see a new place3DTexture1 node. Select this node and set its Rotate X channel to **-90** so that it projects down from above the surface.

10. Open the Attribute Editor for place3DTexture1, and click the Fit To Group BBox button. This sizes the projection to match the surface (see Figure 16.24).

11. Open the Hypershade and switch to the Textures tab. Click on ramp1 and open its Attribute Editor.

12. In the Attribute Editor for Ramp1, set Ramp Type to Circular Ramp and Interpolation to None.

13. Edit the ramp so that there are two color markers: one at the bottom and one in the middle. The color marker at the bottom should be black, and the one in the middle should be white.

14. Create a test render of the scene. You'll notice that the edges of the surface are still visible. This is because the Specularity channel of the Blinn texture is reflecting light on both the opaque and transparent parts of the surface.

15. Open the Hypershade window and graph the milkShader in the Work Area. In the Create Maya Nodes column, scroll down to the General Utilities section, and create a Reverse Node.

16. In the Hypershade, connect the output of projection1 into the input of reverse1. Connect the output of reverse1 into the specular color of the milkShader (see Figure 16.25).

FIGURE 16.24
Size the Projection node to match the milk surface.

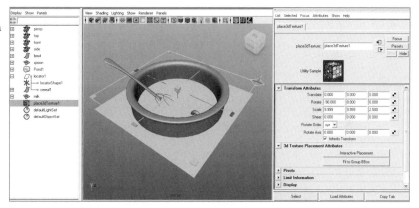

FIGURE 16.25
Use a reverse node to connect the inverted colors of the ramp to the specular color of the milkShader.

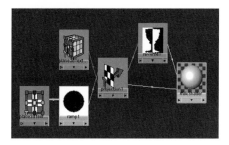

By using a reverse node, you can invert the colors of ramp1 and use it to color the Specularity channel of the milkShader. This allows the milk surface to still appear reflective and wet, but it prevents the edges that extend beyond the bowl from reflecting light, thus making them invisible in the render. Figure 16.26 shows the milk surface rendered using mental ray.

17. Save the scene as **bowl_v05.ma**. To see a finished version of the scene, open the bowl_v05 .ma scene from the chapter16\scenes folder on the DVD.

FIGURE 16.26
Render the scene using mental ray.

⊕ Real World Scenario

FILL AN OBJECT WITH A FLUID

NURBS and polygon surfaces can be used as collision objects in fluid containers. You can fill an object with a fluid using these steps:

1. Create a 3D fluid container with an emitter.

2. Set the buoyancy of the fluid to a negative value so that it falls.

3. Create a NURBS or polygon surface in the shape of a cup.

4. Place the geometry below the emitter.

5. Select the geometry and choose Fluid Effects ➢ Make Collide.

6. Run the simulation, and edit the fluid to generate the desired behavior.

Filling an object like this can take some time. In some cases you may get better results using nParticles, as demonstrated in Chapter 13. To make the object appear like a solid, set Surface to a Hard Surface render type in the fluid shape node. For an example scene, open the `fluidCollision.ma` scene in the `chapter16\scenes` directory on the DVD.

Create an Ocean

The ocean fluid effect uses a surface and a special Ocean shader to create a realistic ocean surface that can behave dynamically. The Ocean shader uses an animated displacement map to create the water surface. Ocean surfaces can take a while to render, so you should take this into consideration when planning your scene.

The Ocean Shader

All of the controls needed to create the ocean are found on the ocean shader node. This node is created and applied automatically when you make an ocean. In this example, you'll create the effect of a space capsule floating on the surface of the ocean.

1. Open the `capsule_v01.ma` scene from the `chapter16\scenes` directory on the DVD. This scene has the simple space capsule model used in Chapter 13.

2. Switch to the Dynamics menu set, and choose Fluid Effects ➤ Ocean ➤ Create Ocean.

When you create an ocean, you'll see a large NURBS surface appear. This represents the surface of the ocean. At the center is a preview plane, which gives an approximation of how the ocean will behave when the scene is played.

3. Rewind and play the scene. You'll see the preview plane move up and down. This demonstrates the default behavior of the ocean (Figure 16.27).

4. In the Outliner, select the node labeled Transform1, and open the Attribute Editor. Switch to the Ocean Shader tab.

FIGURE 16.27
The ocean effect
uses a preview
plane to indicate
the behavior
of the ocean.

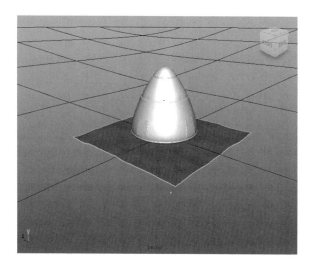

All the controls you need to change the way the ocean looks and behaves are found in the Ocean Shader controls. Each control is described in the Maya documentation. This section demonstrates how to use some of these controls. Many of the controls are actually self-explanatory (possibly a first for Maya).

5. To slow down the ocean, set Wave Speed to **0.8**. Observer Speed can be used to simulate the effect of the ocean moving past the camera without the need to animate the ocean or the camera. Leave this at 0.

6. To make the ocean waves seem larger, increase Wave Length Max to **6**. The wave length units are measured in meters.

To make the ocean seem a little rougher, you can adjust the Wave Height edit curve. The Wave Height edit curve changes wave height relative to the wave length. If you edit the curve so that it slopes up to the right, then the waves with longer wavelengths will be proportionally taller than the waves with shorter wavelengths. A value of 1 means that the wave is half as tall as it is long. When you edit this curve, you can see the results in the preview plane.

Wave Turbulence works the same way, so by making the curve slope up to the right, longer waves will have a higher turbulence frequency.

Wave Peaking creates crests on top of areas that have more turbulence. Turbulence must be a non-zero value for wave peaking to have an effect.

7. Experiment with different settings for the Wave Height, Wave Turbulence, and Wave Peaking edit curves (Figure 16.28). Create a test render from the perspective camera to see how these changes affect the look of the ocean.

8. To make the capsule float in the water, select the capsule and choose Fluid Effects ➤ Ocean ➤ Float Selected Objects. You can also create boat locators just like the ones created for the pond effect in the previous section.

9. In the Outliner, select Locator1 and open its Attribute Editor. In the Extra Attributes section, set Buoyancy to **0.01** and Start Y to **-3**.

10. Select the capsule, and rotate it a little so that it does not bob straight up and down.

FIGURE 16.28

You can shape the ocean by editing the Wave Height, Wave Turbulence, and Wave Peaking edit curves.

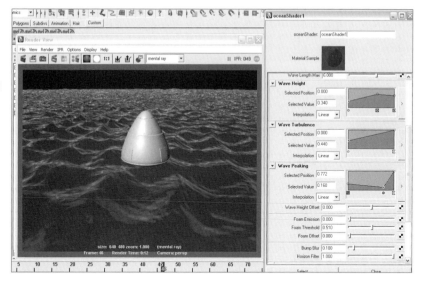

11. Select the transform1 node, and open the Attribute Editor to the Ocean Shader tab. In the Common Material Attributes section, set Transparency to a dark gray color. This allows you to see some of the submerged parts of the capsule through the water. The oceanShader already has a refraction index of 1.3, so the water will refract light.

12. Set Foam Emission to **0.355**. This shades the peaks of the ocean with a light color, suggesting whitecaps.

13. Create a test render of the scene from the perspective camera (see Figure 16.29).

14. Save the scene as **capsule_v02.ma**. To see a finished version of the scene, open the capsule_v02.ma scene from the chapter16\scenes directory on the DVD.

This is a good start to creating a realistic ocean. Take a look at some of the ocean examples in the Visor to see more advanced effects.

FIGURE 16.29

Render the capsule floating in the water.

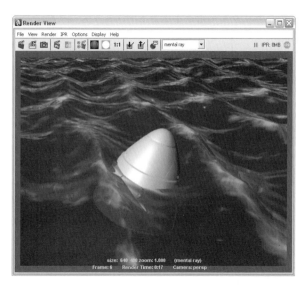

The Bottom Line

Use fluid containers. Fluid containers are used to create self-contained fluid effects. Fluid simulations use a special type of particle that is generated in the small subunits (called voxels) of a fluid container. Fluid containers can be 2D or 3D. 2D containers take less time to calculate and can be used in many cases to generate realistic fluid effects.

Master it Create a logo animation that dissolves like ink in water.

Create a reaction. A reaction can be simulated in a 3D container by combining temperature with fuel. Surfaces can be used as emitters within a fluid container.

Master it Create a chain reaction of explosions using the Paint Fluids tool.

Render fluid containers. Fluid containers can be rendered using Maya Software or mental ray. The fluids can react to lighting, cast shadows, and self-shadow.

Master it Render the TurbulentFlame.ma example in the Visor so that it emits light onto nearby surfaces.

Use fluids with nParticles. Fluid simulations can interact with nParticles to create a large array of interesting effects.

Master it nCloth objects use nParticles and springs to simulate the behavior of cloth. If fluids can affect nParticles, it stands to reason that they can also affect nCloth objects. Test this by creating a simulation where a fluid emitter pushes around an nCloth object.

Create a pond. A pond uses a 2D fluid container and the Spring Mesh solver to create a pond surface. You can float objects in the pond and use wake emitters to create ripples. The pond can be converted to a polygon mesh to allow for more advanced shading techniques.

Master it Open the swamp.ma scene in the chapter16\scenes directory, and create a pond. Add ripples to the surface.

Create an ocean. Ocean effects are created and edited using the Ocean shader. Objects can float in the ocean using locators.

Master it Create an ocean effect that resembles stormy seas. Add the capsule geometry as a floating object.

Chapter 17

MEL and Python

MEL is a powerful scripting language that can be used to automate many tasks within Maya. As a matter of fact, The Maya interface itself is actually the result of many MEL scripts working together. Using MEL you can create your own scripts, which can save you time and labor and extend the capabilities of Maya. If you already know the popular scripting language Python, then you can use Python to run MEL commands, which makes Maya more compatible with other software packages that use Python.

In this chapter you will learn to:

◆ Use a MEL command

◆ Use MEL scripting techniques

◆ Create a procedure

◆ Use Python

Use a MEL Command

MEL stands for Maya Embedded Language. MEL is a scripting language similar to a programming language such as C++ or Java. An important difference between a programming language such as Java and a scripting language such as MEL is that a programming language must be compiled into an executable program, whereas a scripting language already resides within a program and does not need to be compiled.

A scripting language uses a series of commands that tell a running program what to do. What you may not realize is that you already use MEL all the time. The entire Maya interface is created using MEL commands. When you choose an option from a menu in Maya, Maya actually executes a command. To demonstrate this, try the following exercise.

MEL Interfaces

There are a number of ways to enter MEL commands. You can use the command shell, the command line, or the Script Editor.

1. Open Maya to a new, empty scene. Choose Window ➢ General Editors ➢ Command Shell (the command shell is not available on the Mac). The command shell opens as a blank window. The word `mel:` appears in the upper left. This is the command prompt.

2. Type **sphere** and press the Enter key on the keyboard.

A NURBS sphere appears at the center of the grid; you'll also see some text in the command shell describing the result of the command. This text includes the nurbsSphere1 node and the history node named makeNurbsSphere1 (see Figure 17.1).

3. With the sphere selected, type **delete** in the command shell and press the Enter key; the sphere disappears. Close the command shell.

FIGURE 17.1
Entering the sphere command in the command shell creates a sphere on the grid.

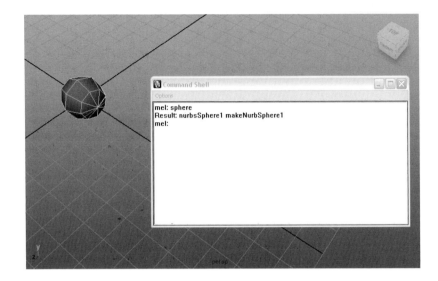

At the bottom of the Maya interface on the left side you should see the label MEL and a blank line. This is the command line; it is another place where you can enter MEL commands. If you don't see this, choose Display ➤ UI Elements ➤ Command Line. If the label reads Python instead of MEL, click the label itself to switch to MEL.

4. Type **sphere** in the command line and press the Enter key (Figure 17.2). Once again, a new sphere appears on the grid.

5. With the sphere selected, type **delete** and press the Enter key to delete the sphere.

6. On the bottom, far-right side of the Maya interface, click the Script Editor button to open the Script Editor. This is another interface you can use to enter MEL commands.

FIGURE 17.2
Enter the **sphere** command in the command line at the bottom left of the Maya interface.

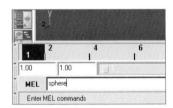

The Script Editor has two stacked windows. The top half of the editor shows the history of the commands entered and executed while Maya is open. This persists even when you close the scene file and open a new one. The bottom half of the Script Editor is an area where you can enter and edit MEL scripts. The two tabs in the bottom half of the editor allow you to switch between MEL and Python (see Figure 17.3).

7. Make sure the MEL tab is active in the bottom half of the Script Editor. Type **sphere** and press the Enter key on the keyboard.

FIGURE 17.3
The Script Editor is divided into the upper area, which lists the command history, and the lower area, where you can enter multiline scripts.

When you press the Enter or Return key on the keyboard, instead of executing the command, the Script Editor moves to a new line. This may be confusing at first. The Script Editor is designed to allow you to create multiline scripts. The Enter key on the keyboard starts a new line. To execute the commands in the Script Editor, press the Enter key on the numeric keypad of the keyboard. Some computers, such as laptops, do not have numeric keypads. If this is the case, use the Ctrl+Return key combination, or look to see if there is a smaller, separate Enter key on another part of the keyboard.

8. Press the Enter key on the numeric keypad to execute the script. A sphere should appear on the grid once again.

ENTER VERSUS RETURN

For the remainder of this chapter, when the instruction "Press the Enter key" is given, press the Enter key on the numeric keypad (or use Ctrl+ Return if your computer keyboard does not have a numeric keypad). If the instruction "Press the Return key" is given, press the Return (or Enter) key on the main part of the keyboard.

You'll notice in the history of the Script Editor that a semicolon is appended at the end of the sphere command. In practice, you should always place a semicolon at the end of each command. This lets Maya know that the command should be executed and, if the Script Editor contains a second line of commands, Maya needs to move on to execute the next line of the script. A semicolon in MEL is analogous to a period at the end of a sentence in English. Get into the habit of adding a semicolon to the end of each command or line in your scripts. In most cases, if you leave the semicolon off the end of a line, you'll get an error message and the script will not execute.

The Script Editor has a number of features available in the Script Editor menu bar. You can save selected lines of code to the shelf as a button. The buttons execute the lines of code whenever you click them, which is useful for commands that you repeat a lot. You can use the File menu to load MEL scripts that have been saved to text files. Any plain text file saved using the .mel extension can be loaded as a MEL script. You can also save selected lines of code in the Script Editor as a MEL script.

The File ➢ Source menu option is used to load a MEL script into current memory so it is available as a command in the current Maya session. This is explained later in this chapter.

The options in the Edit menu can be used to copy and paste MEL commands as well as to clear the history visible in the top section of the Script Editor. Search and replace features are also available here.

The Command menu lets you create new tabs in the Script Editor in case you want to enter new commands without disturbing any of the commands entered in another tab. This is useful as a testing area.

To keep things simple, you'll use the Script Editor for most of this chapter as opposed to the command shell or the command line. Many of the common features found in the Script Editor menus, such as creating shelf buttons, loading scripts, and sourcing scripts, are used in the examples in this chapter.

MEL Scripting Techniques

You can become an accomplished Maya animator without ever writing a single MEL script. If this is the case, why should you concern yourself with learning MEL? MEL is a way to save time and labor. You may not be interested in advanced MEL scripting features, such as creating custom plug-ins or your own Maya interfaces, which are certainly possible using MEL. But sooner or later you'll run into a situation in which you need to perform the same complex task multiple times, which can quickly become tedious and time consuming.

Consider the following scenario, which is very common in a production environment. You just spent the better part of a week setting up a complex nParticle simulation. Variations of this simulation are used in ten different shots, each shot has its own scene and each scene contains five or six separate nParticle objects that have similar attributes. The particle motion has been approved, but suddenly the client requests that, instead of simple colored spheres, all the shots now need to use animated logos. The client also wants to see the new version using the logos first thing on Monday morning. It's now Friday and you have planned a weekend getaway with your friends. You realize that the best way to turn the colored nParticle balls into animated logos is to use sprites.

A *sprite* is a special type of particle that places a flat, rectangular plane at the position of each nParticle. The plane is always oriented so it is perpendicular to the camera. Using a shader and expressions, an image is mapped to the plane. The images can be animated to create particle effects that would be difficult to generate using the other particle types. For instance, an animated sequence of flames can be mapped to the sprites to generate realistic fire. Since sprites are two-dimensional planes, they do not have a Radius attribute, instead they use Scale X and Scale Y. Likewise, sprites rotate only around the Z axis. This rotation is controlled using the Sprite Twist attribute. Custom attributes and expressions need to be created for each of the nParticle objects so the sprite images animate correctly.

You can choose to go into each scene and manually add attributes and expressions for each nParticle object, which will most likely destroy your weekend plans, or you can create a MEL script that automates the conversion of all particle objects in each scene, which may only take a few hours. In this situation, having even a basic understanding of simple MEL commands can save your weekend and your sanity.

In this section of the chapter, you'll add custom attributes and expressions to an nParticle object so it renders as sprites as the basis for creating your own MEL script. You'll save this script as a shelf button and also as a separate MEL file. You'll gain an understanding of some useful MEL tricks and hopefully an appreciation for MEL that inspires you to learn more about MEL scripting.

Learning From the Script Editor

One of the best MEL scripting resources available is the Script Editor itself. As you execute commands in Maya using the menu, the Script Editor prints a history of the commands and their results in the history section of the Script Editor. By observing the feedback in the history section, you can learn common commands, and you can then use these commands in your scripts.

You need to be aware of two important concerns about the way Maya lists the command history: The first is that by default, Maya does not list every single command in the history section. If you'd like to see every command executed during a Maya session, go to the Script Editor window and choose History ➢ Echo All Commands. The resulting history list becomes very long very quickly, but in some cases this is the best way to find out how Maya executes certain commands that are otherwise hidden from view. Second, the commands that Maya uses to perform a task are not always phrased the same way as the commands you use in the scripts that you write. Experimentation and experience teach you how to translate commands listed in the history into commands you can use in your scripts.

The example used in this chapter is a hypothetical commercial spot. Your task is to create a script that makes converting the existing particles into sprites easier so you can simply select one or more of the existing nParticle systems, run a script, and automatically create the necessary attributes and expressions. Let's look at the first shot in the commercial.

1. Open the shot1_v01.ma scene from the chapter 17\scenes directory on the DVD. Switch to the renderCam camera in the perspective view. Rewind and play the scene.

The scene starts with dark blue nParticle spheres appearing inside a cylindrical volume emitter. A vortex field pushes the nParticles along in circular motion. The dark blue nParticles are sucked into a volume axis curve field, which spirals upward. As the camera tracks upward, a second set of pink nParticles is being born. They are sucked into a second spiraling volume axis curve field (see Figure 17.4).

FIGURE 17.4
Pink and blue
nParticles follow
along the spiral
paths created by
two volume axis
curve fields.

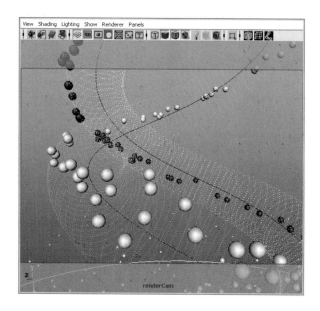

The script you will write automates the process of converting the nParticle spheres into sprites and attaching attributes and expressions to alter their behavior. To learn how to create the script, you'll perform actions as you normally would. In this case, you'll convert the blue_nParticle into sprites, and then you'll observe what happens in the Script Editor and use this to build a script. You'll then use the script to convert the pink_nParticle into sprites.

2. Open the Script Editor window (Window ➢ General Editors ➢ Script Editor), and move it off to the side so you can see it and the Attribute Editor.

3. Choose Edit ➢ Clear All from the Script Editor menu. This clears both parts of the Script Editor so you have a fresh view of what's going on. Make sure Echo All Commands is not selected in the History menu.

4. Select the blue_nParticle node in the Outliner, and open its Attribute Editor to the blue_nParticleShape tab. Scroll to the Shading section and set the Particle Render Type menu to Sprites.

The Script Editor displays a number of lines in the history section. The first line says select -r blue_nParticle ;. This is the command that was executed when you selected the blue_nParticle object in the first part of step 4. The command is followed by many additional commands, each of which sets up the basic sprite nParticle type attributes (see Figure 17.5).

FIGURE 17.5
Changing the
nParticle type to
sprites produces a
number of lines of
code in the Script
Editor.

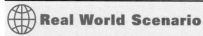

Real World Scenario

THE SELECT COMMAND

The `select` command is one of the most frequently used commands in a MEL script. If you Shift+click on a number of objects in the Outliner, the command as listed in the history of the Script Editor looks like this:

```
select -r object1 object2 object3;
```

In this case the `select` command syntax replaces the current selection with the objects listed after the `-r` flag. What is interesting is that if you Shift+click on objects in the perspective view instead of in the Outliner, then the commands listed in the Script Editor history consist of several lines that look like this:

```
select -r object1;
select -tgl object2;
select -tgl object3;
```

Here the first line replaces the current selection with the newly selected object (`object1` in this example), and then the toggle flag is used to add more selected objects to the list (`object2` and `object3`).

However, if you Ctrl+click on objects in the Outliner, the list of commands in the Script Editor history looks like this:

```
select -r object1;
select -add object2;
select -add object3;
```

In this case, the `-add` flag is used instead of the `-tgl` flag. The first line replaces the current selection with `object1`, and then each subsequent `select` command uses the `-add` flag to add another object to the selection (`object2` and `object3`).

This demonstrates that the context in which commands are executed often affects which flags are used.

The command syntax for many commands is `command flag nodeName;`, so the command in this case is `select`. The flag is `-r`, the node is `blue_nParticle`, and the command is ended using a semicolon. Most of this is fairly straightforward except for the command flag. What does `-r` mean? Flags are preceded by a hyphen and often abbreviated, so you have to find out what the r flag stands for. You can find out what a flag does by opening the help files and doing a search for the particular command in question, or you can type **help** and the name of the command directly in the Script Editor.

5. Type **help select;** in the lower half of the Script Editor, and press the Enter key. In the history section of the Script Editor you'll see a list of flags (see Figure 17.6).

According to the help on the `select` command, the `-r` flag stands for *replace*. The `-r` flag tells the `select` command to replace the current selection with the object specified in the command. So, as you select objects in the scene, the `-r` flag is used each time the selection is changed. The other flags listed in the Script Editor can be used with the `select` command as well. For example, if you wanted to create a script in which all DAG (directed acyclic graph) objects are selected, you can use the -ado flag. The command looks like this: select -ado;. Executing this command using this syntax selects all DAG nodes in the scene at once.

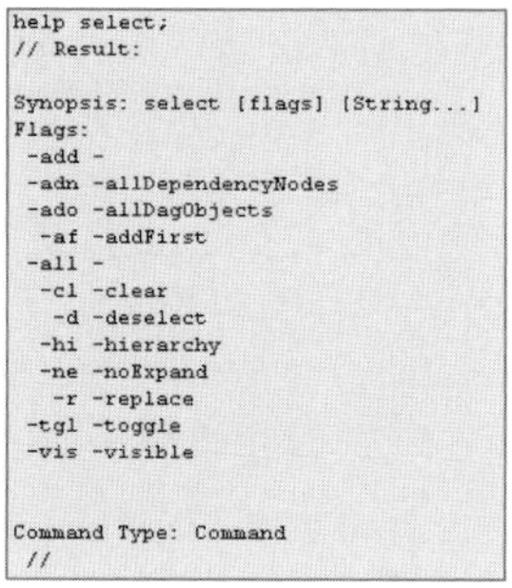

FIGURE 17.6

Typing help and the name of the command you need help with into the Script Editor displays a list of available flags.

```
help select;
// Result:

Synopsis: select [flags] [String...]
Flags:
  -add -
  -adn -allDependencyNodes
  -ado -allDagObjects
   -af -addFirst
  -all -
   -cl -clear
    -d -deselect
   -hi -hierarchy
   -ne -noExpand
    -r -replace
  -tgl -toggle
  -vis -visible


Command Type: Command
 //
```

The second line in the Script Editor history reads setAttr blue_nParticleShape.particleRenderType 5;. In this line the command being executed is setAttr, which sets an attribute for a particular node. The node receiving the setAttr command is the blue_nParticleShape node, which was selected in the first line of the Script Editor history. The attribute being set on the blue_nParticleShape is the particleRenderType and the value applied to the particleRenderType is 5. So what does this mean?

When accessing a node's attribute the dot syntax is used. To set the particle render type of the blue_nParticle shape node, you must specify the syntax using nodeName.attributeName. Hence you have blue_nParticleShape.particleRenderType specified in the setAttr command. The value of the setting depends on the attribute. In this case, particleRenderType requires a numeric setting to convert the nParticle from a sphere into a sprite.

Maya uses a numbered sequence for some attributes, such as particleRenderType. The way in which an attribute setting is listed in a menu in the Maya interface gives a clue as to how Maya numbers the attribute's settings. Take a look at the Particle Render Type menu in the shading section of the particle shape node. The menu options are MultiPoint, MultiStreak, Numeric, Points, Spheres, Sprites, Streak, BlobbySurface, Cloud, and Tube. The numbers Maya uses in the command are not listed, but if you change the particle render type to one of the choices in the menu and observe the script history, you'll see a different number applied at the end of the setAttr blue_nParticleShape.particleRenderType line. The particleRenderType attribute uses 0 for MultiPoint, 1 for MultiStreak, 2 for Numeric, 3 for Points, and so on. Hence, to change the particle render type to sprites, the command is setAttr blue_nParticleShape.particleRenderType 5;.

The next few lines in the Script Editor use the addAttr command. This command adds attributes to the selected node. The syntax is the same as the setAttr command; however, in this case there are a few flags as well. These flags specify the settings that will be used for the added attribute. In the history section of the Script Editor the third line says:

```
addAttr -is true -ln "spriteTwist" -at "float" -min -180 -max 180 -dv 0.0
    blue_nParticleShape;
```

In this case the attribute being added is the spriteTwist command, which is used only by the sprite particle type (and not by any of the other types such as sphere, blobby surface, or point).

The -is flag means "internal set." This is an internal flag used for updating the user interface. This is not something you need to specify every time you use this command. In fact, many flags that Maya lists in the history section can be left out when you use them in your own scripts. This is another aspect of scripting that you'll understand more with experience.

To find out what's going on with the four addAttr commands and their various flags that appear in the Script Editor, you can do a little detective work. The lines read:

```
addAttr -is true -ln "spriteTwist" -at "float" -min -180 -max 180 -dv 0.0
    blue_nParticleShape;
addAttr -is true -ln "spriteScaleX" -dv 1.0 blue_nParticleShape;
addAttr -is true -ln "spriteScaleY" -dv 1.0 blue_nParticleShape;

addAttr -is true -ln "spriteNum" -at long -dv 1 blue_nParticleShape;
```

Take a look at the Attribute Editor for the blue_nparticleShape node. If you scroll down to the Sprite Attributes rollout and expand this section, you'll see there are Sprite Num, Sprite Scale X, Sprite Scale Y, and Sprite Twist attributes.

6. Rewind the animation, and then play it for 50 frames and click Stop. Experiment with changing the values for the Sprite Twist, Sprite Scale X, and Sprite Scale Y settings in the Attribute Editor, and observe the results in the camera view (see Figure 17.7).

Sprite Num changes the image used for the sprite itself. Since no image is assigned, currently this attribute has no effect. Sprite Twist changes the rotation of the sprites around the sprite's local Z axis. Sprite Scale X changes the horizontal size of the sprites, and Sprite Scale Y changes the vertical size.

7. Select the pink_nParticle object in the Outliner and open its Attribute Editor. You'll notice that under Sprite Attributes these settings do not exist. Therefore, you can surmise that these attributes were added to the blue_nParticle shape when Maya executed the four addAttr commands when the particle render type was changed to sprites in step 4.

FIGURE 17.7

The four attributes listed in the Sprite Attributes section of the Attribute Editor were added using the addAttr command. These settings change the behavior of the sprites.

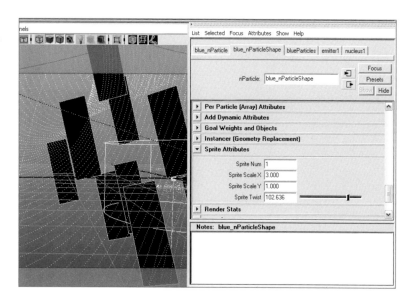

The point of this exercise is to give you an understanding of what happens behind the scenes when you change settings for various node attributes in Maya. What you've learned from these observations is that changing the particle render type to sprites in the Attribute Editor not only sets the particle type to sprites but also executes several lines of code, which adds several attributes specific to sprites.

The Sprite Num, Sprite Twist, Sprite Scale X, and Sprite Scale Y attributes added to the blue_nparticleShape node affect all blue nParticles equally. In the animation you're creating, you'll want to override these settings with Per Particle, Num, Twist, and Scale attributes so each individual nParticle has its own behavior. This means that in the script you're creating you won't need to use the four `addAttr` commands listed in the Attribute Editor.

8. Undo any changes made to the Sprite Attributes settings for blue_nParticle. Save the scene as **shot1_v02.ma**. To see a version of the scene so far, open the shot1_v02.ma scene from the chapter17\scenes directory on the DVD.

COMMAND REFERENCE

The Maya documentation includes a searchable command reference. Perusing these descriptions of commands will help you to understand MEL and solve problems you may be experiencing in your scripts. Open the help files and choose Commands from the Technical Documentation section on the left side of the Maya Help interface.

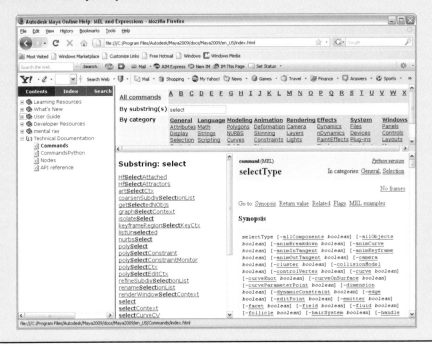

Create a MEL Script File

The term *MEL script* refers to the lines of commands typed and executed in the Script Editor or a series of commands saved in a text file that uses the `.mel` extension. You can create MEL scripts in the Script Editor, but it is often a better idea to create your scripts in a separate text editor program. One reason for this is that whenever you type a MEL command into the bottom half of the Script Editor and press the Enter key, the text disappears (as long as there are no errors). This means you have to hunt through the history to find the commands that were executed. Another argument for creating your scripts in a second file is that keeping the script open in a text editor prevents you from losing your work if Maya crashes.

COMMAND HISTORY IN THE SCRIPT EDITOR

If you select text in the work area of the script editor and then press the Enter key, the command is executed but the text will remain in the work area, allowing you to repeat the command again without having to retype the text.

When creating a MEL script file, use a standard text editor such as Notepad or WordPad (in Windows, or TextEdit on the Mac) and make sure the encoding is set to plain text. If you use a word processor such as Microsoft Word, hidden characters copied and pasted from Word into the Script Editor can cause errors in your script, so do not use Microsoft Word to create MEL scripts!

1. Continue with the scene from the previous section or open the `shot1_v02.ma` scene from the `chapter17\scenes` directory on the DVD.

2. Open a text editor such as Notepad or TextEdit. In a blank text file type the following:

```
//set the particle render type of the current selection to sprite

setAttr blue_nParticleShape.particleRenderType 5;
```

These are the first two lines of your first MEL script, the script that will convert a selected nParticle's render type from spheres to sprites. The first line of the script starts with the double slash followed by some descriptive text. This is a comment line. Maya ignores everything on this line of the script that follows the double slash. The text is a comment that tells you what the next line in the script does. It's a good practice to use comment lines as much as possible to help you keep track of what's going on in the script, especially if you may be returning to the script later on and might forget what the script does.

The second line is the command that sets the particle render type to sprites. This line is copied from the Script Editor. You may have guessed at a potential problem in the way this line is written. Since the command specifies that the particle render type of blue_nParticleShape will be set to 5, only nodes named exactly blue_nParticleShape will be affected by the command. You'll need to edit the script so any nParticleshape that is selected will be affected by the `setAttr` command. To accomplish this you'll use an array.

An *array* is a list contained within a variable. Array variables are often used to hold a list of the currently selected nodes in a scene.

3. Edit the script so it says the following:

```
//create an array containing the current selection
string $mySelection[] = `ls -selection`;
```

```
//set the particle render type of the current selection to sprite
```

```
//setAttr blue_nParticleShape.particleRenderType 5;
```

Notice that the double slash has been added to the `setAttr` command. This turns this line into a comment so it is ignored when the script is run. This is a way to save the commands you know you'll be using later in the script.

The command that creates the array is the second line, which reads `string $mySelection[]` `= `ls -selection``;. The first part of the command to the left of the equal sign creates the array variable. The variable type is a string. String variable types contain letters as opposed to float or integer variable types, which contain numeric values. The variable is named `$mySelection[]`. Variables are preceded by dollar signs. You can name a variable anything you want, but it's best to make the name descriptive of what the variable contains. The square brackets indicate that the variable is an array. Think of the double brackets as a box that holds the list.

The equal sign is used to assign data to the variable. Notice the slanted accent (`) marks. This symbol is created using the key below the Esc key and to the left of the number keys on most keyboards. It is not an apostrophe. If you used an apostrophe in your script, change it to the accent mark; otherwise you'll get an error when you run the script. The text between the two accent marks is the `list` command. In this case the selection flag (`-selection`) is added to the `list` command (`ls`), so the list that will be created is the currently selected objects in the scene. Hence the command is written as `ls -selection`;. The `-selection` flag is often abbreviated as `sl`. At the start of many scripts you'll see a line that reads `ls -sl`;. This means "list selected objects."

So why is the `list` command contained within the accent marks? The second line of the script creates a variable array named `$mySelection[]` and then, using the `list` command, it places all of the selected objects in the scene into `$mySelection[]`. The accent marks are used to assign the results of an executed command to a variable. The order of the selected objects in the list is based on the order in which they were selected before the script is executed.

4. Edit the script so that it says the following:

```
//create an array containing the current selection
string $mySelection[] = `ls -selection`;
```

```
//set the particle render type of the current selection to sprite
```

```
setAttr ($mySelection[0]+".particleRenderType") 5;
```

It may look as though the `setAttr` command has been drastically changed, but in reality it has only been edited slightly. The text has been changed, so `blue_nParticleShape` has been replaced with the variable `$mySelection[0]`. The 0 contained in the square brackets of `$mySelection[]` refers to the first item listed in the `$mySelection[]` array. The numbering of lists in Maya always begins with 0, not 1.

Since a variable is being used instead of a node, the syntax must be changed so Maya does not search for a node named $mySelection[0]. The proper syntax for accessing the attribute of a node contained within a variable requires that the variable name is placed within parentheses and that the attribute name is appended with a plus sign and surrounded by quotes. So instead of $mySelection[0].particleRenderType, you have to type **($mySelection + ".particleRenderType").**

5. At this point you can test the code. Select the code in the text editor and copy it. Switch to Maya. In the Outliner, select the pink_nParticle object.

6. Paste the copied text into the work area of the Script Editor, and press the Enter key (Figure 17.8).

If all goes well, you'll see no error messages and the pink_nParticle node will display as sprites. If there are error messages, double-check your script for typos and make sure only pink_nParticle is selected when the script is run.

FIGURE 17.8
Copy the text from the text editor and paste it into the Script Editor. Select pink_nParticle and execute the script.

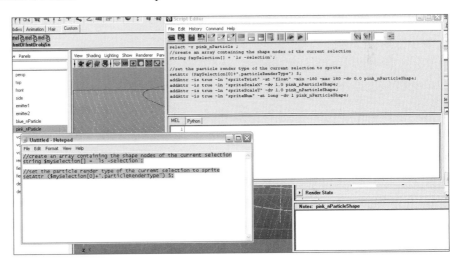

Notice that if you select the pink_nParticleShape node, Maya also adds the four addAttr lines to the script, creating the spriteTwist, spriteScaleX, spriteScaleY, and spriteNum attributes automatically.

7. Save the text file as **mySpriteScript.mel**. Make sure the encoding is plain text and that the extension is .mel. Some text editors will ask you if you want to append .txt to the end of the filename; do not do this.

8. Save the scene as **shot1_v03.ma**. To see a version of the scene, open the shot1_v03.ma scene from the chapter17\scenes directory on the DVD.

Add Attributes with MEL

If you recall from the section on nParticle expressions in Chapter 14, expressions can be used to control the behavior of individual nParticles within an nParticle object. In the simulation you are editing, you need to create a random rotation and size for the nParticles (based on the hypothetical client's request). To do this you'll create a per-particle twist attribute and per-particle Scale X and Scale Y attributes.

1. Continue with the scene from the previous section or open the shot1_v03.ma scene from the chapter17\scenes directory on the DVD. Continue editing the mySpriteScript.mel file in your text editor.

Once again, we can use the Script Editor to find out the precise syntax for adding these attributes.

2. In the Outliner, select the blue_nParticle object, and open its Attribute Editor to the blue_nParticleShape tab. Scroll down and expand the Add Dynamic Attributes section below the Per Particle Array Attributes list. Click the General button to open the Add Attribute window.

3. In the Add Attribute window, switch to the Particle tab. Scroll toward the bottom of the list, and Ctrl+click on spriteNumPP, spriteScaleXPP, SpriteScaleYPP, and spriteTwistPP. The *PP* indicates that each attribute is a per-particle attribute (see Figure 17.9).

FIGURE 17.9
Select the per-particle sprite attributes in the Add Attribute menu.

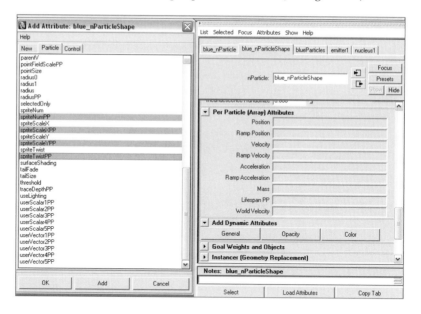

4. Click the Add button to add these attributes. The new attributes should appear in the Per Particle (Array) Attributes list. If they do not, click the Load Attributes button at the bottom of the Attribute Editor to refresh the window.

5. Open the Script Editor and take a look at the history. At the top you'll see that the addAttr command is used to add the attributes to the blue_nParticleShape object. Notice that each attribute uses two addAttr commands to add the attribute (see Figure 17.10).

You can copy these lines of code and adapt them to the script based on what you've learned so far.

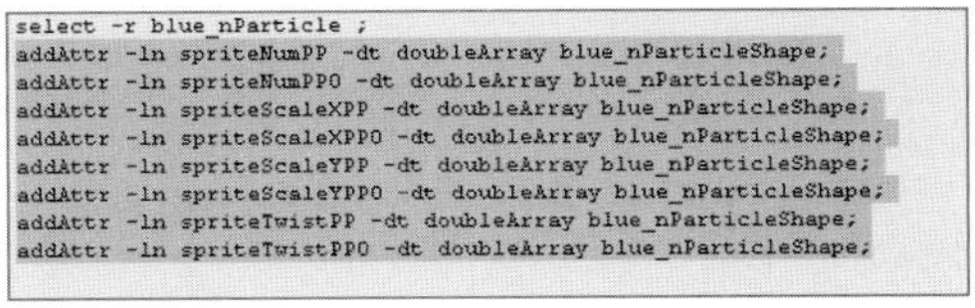

FIGURE 17.10

The Script Editor reveals the syntax for adding the per-particle array attributes.

```
select -r blue_nParticle ;
addAttr -ln spriteNumPP -dt doubleArray blue_nParticleShape;
addAttr -ln spriteNumPPO -dt doubleArray blue_nParticleShape;
addAttr -ln spriteScaleXPP -dt doubleArray blue_nParticleShape;
addAttr -ln spriteScaleXPPO -dt doubleArray blue_nParticleShape;
addAttr -ln spriteScaleYPP -dt doubleArray blue_nParticleShape;
addAttr -ln spriteScaleYPPO -dt doubleArray blue_nParticleShape;
addAttr -ln spriteTwistPP -dt doubleArray blue_nParticleShape;
addAttr -ln spriteTwistPPO -dt doubleArray blue_nParticleShape;
```

6. Edit the mySpriteScript.mel file so it says:

```
//create an array containing the current selection
string $mySelection[] = `ls -selection`;

//set the particle render type of the curremt selection to sprite
setAttr ($mySelection[0]+".particleRenderType") 5;

//add per-particle spriteNum, scale, and twist attributes

addAttr -ln spriteNumPP -dt doubleArray $mySelection[0];
addAttr -ln spriteNumPPO -dt doubleArray $mySelection[0];

addAttr -ln spriteScaleXPP -dt doubleArray $mySelection[0];
addAttr -ln spriteScaleXPPO -dt doubleArray $mySelection[0];

addAttr -ln spriteScaleYPP -dt doubleArray $mySelection[0];
addAttr -ln spriteScaleYPPO -dt doubleArray $mySelection[0];

addAttr -ln spriteTwistPP -dt doubleArray $mySelection[0];
addAttr -ln spriteTwistPPO -dt doubleArray $mySelection[0];
```

In this case the pasted code from the Script Editor was changed so that blue_nParticleShape is now the variable $mySelection[0];.

7. Test the script. First, save the mySpriteScript.mel file in the text editor. Save the Maya scene as **shot1_v04.ma**. Go back to an earlier version of the Maya scene, before pink_nParticle was converted to a sprite, so you can test the entire script. Open the shot_v02.ma scene for the chapter17\scenes folder on the DVD.

8. In the Outliner, select pink_nParticle. Copy all the text in the mySpriteScript.mel file and paste it into the work area of the Script Editor. Click the Enter key to run the script.

When you run the script, you should have no error messages. If you do see an error in the Script Editor, double-check the text of the script and make sure there are no mistakes.

Even though there are no errors, you may have noticed that something is not quite right. Select pink_nParticle and open its Attribute Editor to the pink_nParticleShape tab. In the Per Particle (Array) Attributes section you'll notice that the per-particle attributes do not appear, even when you click the Load Attributes button at the bottom of the Attribute Editor. What happened?

9. In the Attribute Editor, click the pink_nParticle tab to switch to the nParticle's transform node. Expand the Extra Attributes section. Here you'll find the per-particle attributes. They have been added to the wrong node (see Figure 17.11).

FIGURE 17.11

The per-particle array attributes have been added to the transform node by mistake.

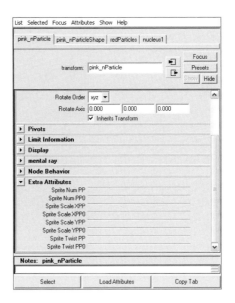

This is a common mistake that is easy to make. When you write a MEL script, you must keep in mind the potential problems that can occur when you or another user applies the script in a scene. In this case the MEL script did exactly what you asked it to: It added per-particle attributes to the selected node, which in this case is the pink_nParticle node. Your intent is to add the attributes to the shape node. You have two options: You can make sure that you—and anyone else who uses the script—remember to always select the shape nodes of the nParticles every time you use the script, or you can build in a command that ensures that the attributes are applied to the shape node. The second option is more desirable and actually involves little coding.

10. Edit the text at the top of the script in the mySpriteScript.mel file so it says:

```
//create an array containing the shape nodes of the current selection
pickWalk -d down;

string $mySelection[] = `ls -selection`;
```

A new line has been added to the top of the script using the pickWalk command. This command moves the current selection down one node (notice the -d flag, which stands for direction, and that the flag is set to down) in the node hierarchy, which means that if a user selects the nParticle node, the pickWalk command at the top of the script will move the selection down to the shape node and then load the selected shape node into the $mySelection[] array variable. If the user has already selected the shape node before running the script, it will still function properly since there are almost always no other nodes below the shape node in the node hierarchy. Later on you'll see how to add a conditional statement so the user will get an error if he or she picks anything other than an nParticle object. Anticipating user errors is a big part of becoming an accomplished MEL script author.

11. Repeat steps 7 and 8 to test the script. This time the new attributes should appear in the Per Particle (Array) Attributes list of the pink_nParticleShape node, as shown in Figure 17.12.

12. Save the mySpriteScript.mel file.

FIGURE 17.12
When you correct the script, the new attributes are added to the Per Particle (Array) Attributes section of the pink_nParticleShape tab.

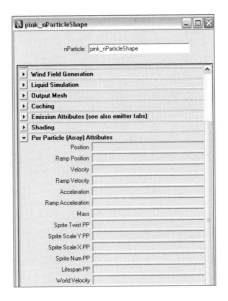

Add an Image Sequence to the Sprites

At this point you can apply the animated image sequence of the logos to the blue_nParticle sprites.

1. Open the shot1_v04.ma scene from the chapter17\scenes folder on the DVD.

2. Open the Hypershade window and create a new Lambert shader. Name the shader **spriteShade**.

3. Select blue_nParticle in the Outliner. In the Hypershade, right-click on spriteShade and choose Assign Material To Selection.

4. Rewind and play the animation to frame 50. The sprites appear as blue squares.

5. Open the Attribute Editor for spriteShade. Add a file texture node to the Color channel by clicking on the checkered box next to Color and choosing File from the Create Render Nodes window.

6. In the options for the file node, click on the folder next to File Name, and select the logo.1.iff file from the chapter17\sourceimages folder on the DVD.

The image appears as a small pentagon with a hole in it. When you rewind and play the scene, each of the blue_nParticles should look like the small pentagon. The image has an alpha channel that is automatically used in the Transparency channel of spriteShade. This image is actually the first in an animated sequence of 60 frames. The process for adding image sequences to sprites is a little odd. The next steps explain how this is done.

7. Open the Attribute Editor for the file1 node that has been applied to the Color channel of spriteShade. Expand the Interactive Sequence Caching options.

8. Turn on Use Interactive Sequence Caching. Set Sequence Start to **1**, Sequence End to **60**, and Sequence Increment to **1**.

9. Turn on the Use Image Sequence option above the Interactive Sequence options (Figure 17.13 shows this). Rewind and play the scene. The sprites don't look any different, and you'll see a warning in the Script Editor complaining that images cannot be found once the animation passes frame 60.

FIGURE 17.13

Turn on Use Interactive Sequence Caching and Use Image Sequence to apply the animated images to the spriteShade material.

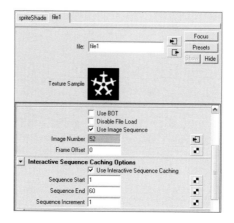

The spriteNumPP attribute controls how the image sequence is applied to each sprite. Until you create an expression for this attribute, you won't see the image sequence properly on the sprites.

10. Open the Attribute Editor for the blue_nParticleShape node. In the Per Particle (Array) Attributes section, right-click on the field next to spriteNumPP, and choose Creation Expression to open the Expression Editor.

11. In the Expression section of the Expression Editor type the following:

```
spriteNumPP=1;
```

12. Click the Create button to make the expression.

13. In the Expression Editor, click the Runtime Before Dynamics button to switch to runtime expression mode. Type the following:

```
spriteNumPP=spriteNumPP+1;
```

14. Click the Create button to make the expression.

15. Rewind and play the animation. Now you'll see each of the blue logos appears as a small pentagon that grows into the snowflake logo as it is born (see Figure 7.14).

16. Save the scene as **shot1_v05.ma**. To see a version of the scene to this point, open the shot1_v05.ma scene from the chapter17\scenes folder on the DVD.

FIGURE 17.14
The snowflake logo is animated as each sprite nParticle is born into the scene.

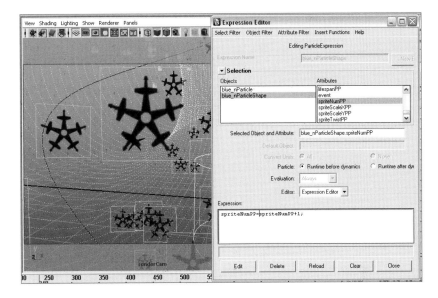

Add Expressions Using MEL

The previous section described the standard manner in which the spriteNumPP attribute is used to animate sprite images. In this section you'll add commands to your MEL script that will apply the same expressions to selected nParticles. In addition, you'll add expressions to control the twist and scale of the nParticles.

1. Continue with the scene from the previous section or open the shot1_v05.ma scene from the chapter17\scenes directory on the DVD. Open the mySpriteScript.mel file in a text editor.

If you look in the Script Editor when you add the creation expression for blue_nParticle's spriteNumPP, you'll see the following command:

```
dynExpression -s "blue_nParticleShape.spriteNumPP=1;" -c blue_nParticleShape;
```

The runtime expression looks like this:

```
dynExpression -s "blue_nParticleShape.spriteNumPP=blue_nParticleShape.
spriteNumPP+1;"

    -rbd blue_nParticleShape
```

The expression is added using the dynExpression command. The -s flag specifies a string that is the expression itself surrounded by quotes. You'll see that the creation expression uses the -c flag, and the runtime before dynamics expression uses the -rbd flag.

2. Edit the text in the mySpriteScript.mel file so it reads:

```
//create an array containing the shape nodes of the current selection
pickWalk -d down;
string $mySelection[] = `ls -selection`;
```

```
//set the particle render type of the curremt selection to sprite
setAttr ($mySelection[0]+".particleRenderType") 5;

//add per-particle twist, scale, and spriteNum attributes

addAttr -ln spriteNumPP -dt doubleArray $mySelection[0];
addAttr -ln spriteNumPP0 -dt doubleArray $mySelection[0];

addAttr -ln spriteScaleXPP -dt doubleArray $mySelection[0];
addAttr -ln spriteScaleXPP0 -dt doubleArray $mySelection[0];

addAttr -ln spriteScaleYPP -dt doubleArray $mySelection[0];
addAttr -ln spriteScaleYPP0 -dt doubleArray $mySelection[0];

addAttr -ln spriteTwistPP -dt doubleArray $mySelection[0];
addAttr -ln spriteTwistPP0 -dt doubleArray $mySelection[0];

//add expressions for per-particle attributes

dynExpression -s "spriteNumPP=1;" -c $mySelection[0];

dynExpression -s "spriteNumPP=spriteNumPP+1;" -rbd $mySelection[0];
```

You'll notice that in the expression text itself, within the quotes, you can print just the name of the attribute spriteNumPP without adding the array variable. Maya understands that the expression will be added to the selected particle object.

3. Test the script by selecting the pink_nParticle object in the Outliner. Copy all the text in the text file, and paste it into the work area of the Script Editor. Press the Enter key.

4. In the Hypershade, select spriteShade and apply it to the pink_nParticle object.

5. If there are no error messages, rewind and play the scene.

You'll see the pink_nParticle object now has the animated sprites applied. The sprites are pink thanks to the pink color that was originally applied to the spheres in the first version of the scene.

6. Select the blue_nParticle object and edit the creation expression. Add the following and click the Edit button (see Figure 17.15):

```
spriteTwistPP=rand(360);

spriteScaleXPP=rand(0.5,2);
spriteScaleYPP=spriteScaleXPP;
```

7. Edit the runtime before dynamics expression. Add the following line and click the Edit button:

```
spriteTwistPP=spriteTwistPP+1;
```

8. Rewind and play the scene. The blue_nParticles are rotated randomly as they fly through the scene. They are also sized randomly.

FIGURE 17.15

Edit the creation
expression for the
blue_nParticleShape
in the Expression
Editor.

FIGURE 17.15

Edit the creation
expression for the
blue_nParticleShape
in the Expression
Editor.

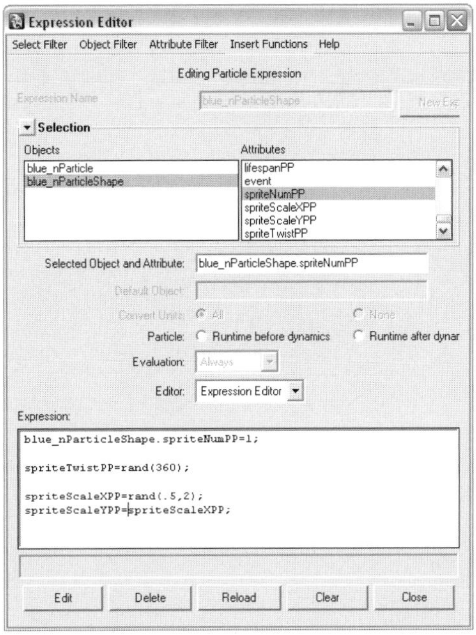

Note that when you set a scaleXPP value for a sprite, you should then set the scaleYPP attribute equal to the scaleXPP attribute. This way the sprites are scaled uniformly and remain square shaped.

9. To add these changes to the script, edit the text in the mySpriteScript.mel file so the expressions look like this (the expressions printed in this book span more than one line; when you place them in your script, you should paste them onto a single line without adding returns):

```
//add expressions for per-particle attributes

dynExpression -s "spriteNumPP=1; \r\n\r\nspriteTwistPP=rand(360);
    \r\n\r\nspriteScaleXPP=rand(.5,2);
    \r\nspriteScaleYPP=spriteScaleXPP;" -c $mySelection[0];

dynExpression -s "spriteNumPP=spriteNumPP+1;
    \r\n\r\nspriteTwistPP=spriteTwistPP+1;"
    -rbd $mySelection[0];
```

Figure 17.16 shows the script text in a text editor. The \r and \n that you see in the expression stand for "return" (\r) and "newline" (\n). Adding these to the expressions in your MEL script creates spaces between the expressions in the Expression Editor, which makes the expressions organized and easy to read.

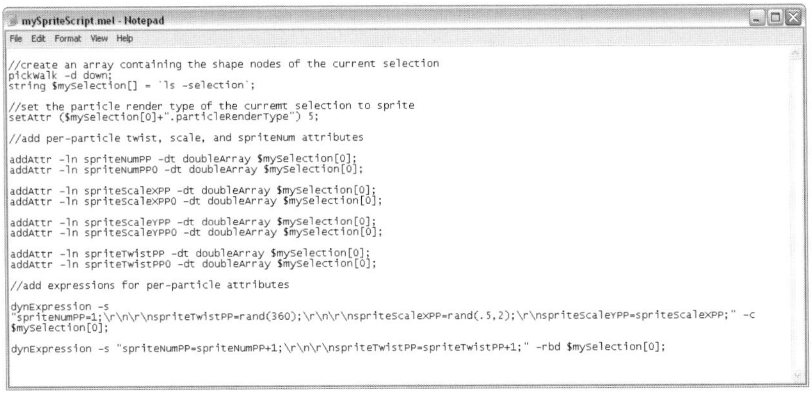

FIGURE 17.16

Edit the text in the MEL script to update the expressions.

10. Edit the text and save the mySpriteScript.mel file. Select pink_nParticle. Copy and paste the text from the text file into the work area of the Script Editor, and press the Enter key.

11. To see a version of the scene, open the shot1_v06.ma scene from the chapter17\scenes folder on the DVD.

Create a Conditional Statement

Conditional statements are used to direct the commands of a script toward one action or another. If a certain condition is met, then the script performs an action; if not, the script does something else. Conditional statements work very well for error detection. In the case of the current example, you'll use a conditional statement to make sure the script works only when an nParticle object is selected. This can prevent errors from occurring in the script or in the scene.

You will add a conditional statement to the mySpriteScript.mel file that tests to make sure the selected object is an nParticle object. If it is, then the script will run and perform all the commands you've created in the previous section. If it is not, the script will print an error message that says that the selected object is not an nParticle.

There are several types of conditional statements. In this example you'll use the most common if/then conditional. The syntax for this type of conditional looks like this:

```
If (condition to test is true)
    {
    Execute commands;
    }
else
    {
    Print error message or execute a different set of commands;

    }
```

The statement within the parentheses at the start of the conditional is the statement that needs to be tested. If this statement is true, then the commands within the first set of curly braces are executed. Notice that these commands are indented. Using indentation in your script makes the script appear organized and legible.

If the statement within the parentheses is false, then Maya skips down to the else statement and executes the set of commands in the second set of curly braces. This can be an error message or even additional conditional statements. In this section you'll add a conditional statement that uses the objectType command to test whether the selected object is an nParticle.

1. Open your most recent version of the mySpriteScript.mel file.

2. At the top of the script, edit the text so that it says the following:

```
//create an array containing the shape nodes of the current selection
pickWalk -d down;
string $mySelection[] = `ls -selection`;

//make sure selected object is an nParticle

if (`objectType -isType "nParticle" $mySelection[0]`){
```

The objectType command uses the isType flag to test whether $mySelection[0] is an nParticle. Notice that this command is surrounded by the accent marks within the parentheses. These accent marks are used whenever one command is nested within another. Compare this line with the line that creates the $mySelection[] array variable and assigns it to a list of the selected objects. How is the use of the accent marks similar in these two lines?

When you use the if statement, the condition within the parentheses is tested to be either true or false. If the statement is true, a value of 1 is returned. If the statement is false, a value of 0 is returned.

3. Use the Tab key to indent the commands you created in the previous section. Add the else statement and the error message at the bottom. The entire script should look like this:

```
//create an array containing the shape nodes of the current selection
pickWalk -d down;
string $mySelection[] = `ls -selection`;

//make sure selected object is an nParticle
if (`objectType -isType "nParticle" $mySelection[0]`){

    //set the particle render type of the current selection to sprite
    setAttr ($mySelection[0]+".particleRenderType") 5;

    //add per-particle twist, scale, and spriteNum attributes

    addAttr -ln spriteNumPP -dt doubleArray $mySelection[0];
    addAttr -ln spriteNumPP0 -dt doubleArray $mySelection[0];

    addAttr -ln spriteScaleXPP -dt doubleArray $mySelection[0];
    addAttr -ln spriteScaleXPP0 -dt doubleArray $mySelection[0];

    addAttr -ln spriteScaleYPP -dt doubleArray $mySelection[0];
    addAttr -ln spriteScaleYPP0 -dt doubleArray $mySelection[0];

    addAttr -ln spriteTwistPP -dt doubleArray $mySelection[0];
    addAttr -ln spriteTwistPP0 -dt doubleArray $mySelection[0];
```

```
//add expressions for per-particle attributes

dynExpression -s "spriteNumPP=1;\r\n\r\nspriteTwistPP=rand(360);
    \r\n\r\nspriteScaleXPP=rand(.5,2);
    \r\nspriteScaleYPP=spriteScaleXPP;" -c $mySelection[0];

dynExpression -s "spriteNumPP=spriteNumPP+1;
    \r\n\r\nspriteTwistPP=spriteTwistPP+1;"
    -rbd $mySelection[0];


}
else
{
    error "Sorry, you must select an nParticle to use this script";

}
```

4. To test the script, open the shot2_v01.ma scene from the chapter17\scenes directory on the DVD. This is the second shot in the commercial spot. It uses five nParticle objects.

5. Select the orange_nParticle object in the Outliner.

6. Select and copy all of the text in the mySpriteScript.mel file, and paste it into the Script Editor.

7. Press the Enter key to run the script. If there are no errors, the orange_nParticle object will turn into a sprite.

8. Select the emitter1 object in the Outliner. Copy and paste the script into the Script Editor, and run the script again. This time you should see an error message that says, Sorry, you must select an nParticle to use this script.

9. Save the mySpriteScript.mel file in your text editor.

Create a Loop

As it stands, the script is designed to convert one nParticle object at a time. By adding a simple loop to the script, running the script a single time will convert all of the selected nParticles at the same time.

There are many types of loop statements you can use in MEL. One of the most common and easiest to create is the for loop. It uses the following syntax:

```
for ($i=0;$i<length of loop;$i++){ loop commands }
```

There are three commands within the parentheses separated by semicolons. The first command creates a variable named $i. The new $i variable is set to equal 0, which is the starting value of the loop. The second command in the parentheses sets the limit of the loop. So long as the variable $i is less than a particular value, the loop continues to run. The third statement in the parentheses increases the variable $i by increments of 1. Another way of saying $i = $i + 1 is to use $i++.

The commands that will be executed each time the loop runs are contained within curly braces, just like the conditional statement. Once again, using the Tab key to indent statements within the braces can help you keep the script visually organized, especially if multiple nested loops are used.

1. Open the mySpriteScript.mel file in your text editor. Edit the script so it matches the following:

```
//create an array containing the shape nodes of the current selection
pickWalk -d down;
string $mySelection[] = `ls -selection`;

//create a loop based on the number of selected object
for ($i=0;$i<size($mySelection);$i++){

    //make sure selected object is an nParticle
    if (`objectType -isType "nParticle" $mySelection[$i]`){

        //set the particle render type of the curremt selection to sprite
        setAttr ($mySelection[$i]+".particleRenderType") 5;

        //add per-particle twist, scale, and spriteNum attributes

        addAttr -ln spriteNumPP -dt doubleArray $mySelection[$i];
        addAttr -ln spriteNumPP0 -dt doubleArray $mySelection[$i];

        addAttr -ln spriteScaleXPP -dt doubleArray $mySelection[$i];
        addAttr -ln spriteScaleXPP0 -dt doubleArray $mySelection[$i];

        addAttr -ln spriteScaleYPP -dt doubleArray $mySelection[$i];
        addAttr -ln spriteScaleYPP0 -dt doubleArray $mySelection[$i];

        addAttr -ln spriteTwistPP -dt doubleArray $mySelection[$i];
        addAttr -ln spriteTwistPP0 -dt doubleArray $mySelection[$i];

        //add expressions for per-particle attributes

        dynExpression -s "spriteNumPP=1;\r\n\r\nspriteTwistPP=rand(360);
            \r\n\r\nspriteScaleXPP=rand(.5,2);
            \r\nspriteScaleYPP=spriteScaleXPP;" -c $mySelection[$i];

    dynExpression -s "spriteNumPP=spriteNumPP+1;
        \r\n\r\nspriteTwistPP=spriteTwistPP+1;"
        -rbd $mySelection[$i];

    }
    else
    {
        error "Sorry, you must select an nParticle to use this script";
    }
}
```

The loop is set to run as long as $i is less than the size of $mySelection. The size of $mySelection is based on the number of items selected before the script is run. For each iteration of the loop $i is increased by an increment of 1.

The first time the loop runs $i is equal to 0, the second time the loop runs $i is equal to 1, the third time the loop runs run $i is equal to 2, and so on until $i is equal to the number of items selected in the scene.

Notice that the 0 in the brackets of the $mySelection variable is now changed to the $i variable throughout the script. Recall that the items in the list contained in the $mySelection array variable are numbered based on the order in which they are selected and that this numbering starts with 0. By changing the code so that $mySelection[0] is now $mySelection[$i], the commands are run on each of the objects contained in the array variable.

Before completing the script there is one final line of code you can add to the loop. This line simply turns on the Depth Sort option for sprites, which is usually off by default. Depth Sort ensures that the sprites closest to the camera appear in front of the sprites farthest from the camera.

2. In the script add a line after the command that sets the particle render type to sprites but before the lines that add the per-particle render attributes. The new line should read:

```
//Turn on Depth Sort

setAttr ($mySelection[$i]+".depthSort") 1;
```

Figure 17.17 shows the final script as it appears in Notepad.

FIGURE 17.17
The screen grab shows the final script as it appears in Notepad.

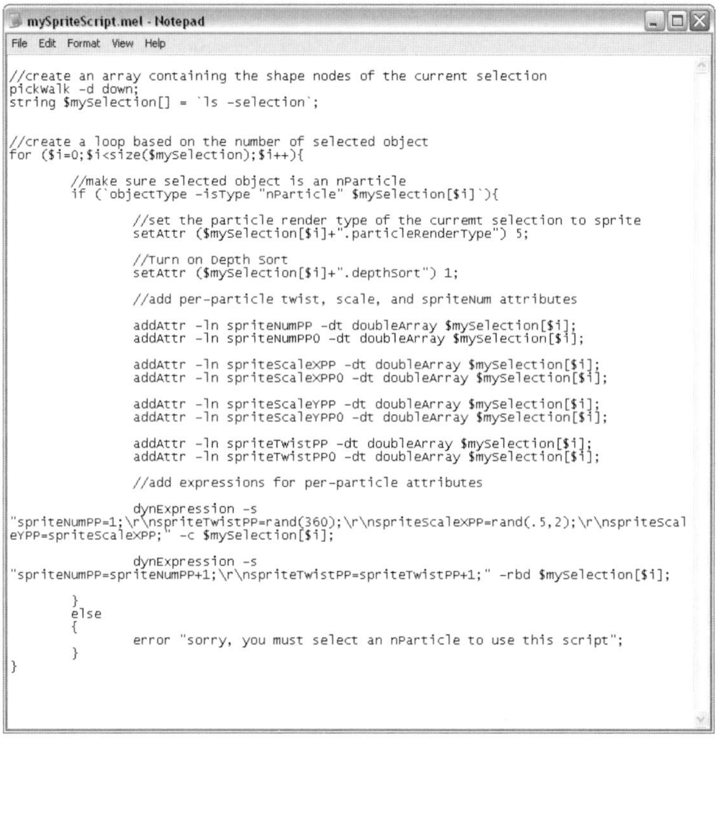

3. Save the mySpriteScript.mel file to your local directory. Save the script in the Maya\
scripts directory found in the My Documents folder.

Scripts are usually saved in the My Documents\Maya\scripts folder on your local drive. You
may also save scripts to the My Documents\Maya\2009\scripts directory, or if they are specific
to your project, you can save them in the mel folder of the current project.

You can compare your version of the script with the mySpriteScript.mel file in the chapter17\
mel directory on the DVD.

4. To test the script, open the shot2_v01.ma scene from the chapter17\scenes folder on the
DVD. If it is already open, reload the scene.

5. In the Outliner, Shift+click on the green_nParticle, red_nParticle, yellow_nParticle,
purple_nParticle, and orange_nParticle objects.

6. Open the Script Editor and choose File ➤ Load Script. Find the script on your local drive
and choose it.

7. The script loads in the work area of the Script Editor window. Press the Enter key to run
the script. If there are errors, open the mySpriteScript.mel file from the chapter17\mel
folder on the DVD. Compare your code with the code in this file; keep a sharp eye for
typos, because even the smallest mistake can cause an error. Unfortunately, debugging
scripts for small errors is a rite of passage for beginning MEL scripters.

8. Select the nParticle objects, open the Hypershade, and apply the spriteShade material to
the selected nParticle objects.

9. Save the scene as **shot2_v02.ma**. To see a finished version of the scene, open the shot2_
v02.ma scene from the chapter17\scenes folder on the DVD.

If everything works, congratulations on creating your first MEL script. With more practice
and study you'll find that creating scripts saves you a great deal of time and labor.

CREATE A SHELF BUTTON FOR A SCRIPT

You can create a shelf button from selected code in the Script Editor. If the script is something you
think you'll use fairly often in a scene, a shelf button can save even more time. Whenever you need
to run the script, you simply click the shelf button. To create a shelf button, switch to the Custom
Shelf tab, select the code you want to make into a button, and choose File ➤ Save Script To Shelf.
Give the shelf a name as descriptive as you can within the six-character limit. Remember to save the
shelves before quitting Maya so that the buttons appear the next time you open Maya. To do this,
click the black down-arrow button to the left of the shelves, and choose Save All Shelves.

Procedures

A complex MEL script is often made up of procedures. A *procedure* is a small section of code that
may be called upon by the script one or more times. You can think of a procedure as a mini-
MEL script within a script. Procedures are a useful and efficient way to organize a script.

Make a Procedure from a Script

In this example you'll create a procedure from a script.

1. In your text editor, open the shakeMe.mel file from the chapter17\mel folder on the DVD.

The shakeMe.mel script is a very simple loop that attaches an expression to the Translate channels of selected objects. Take a look at the code:

```
string $mySel[] = `ls -sl`;

for ($i=0;$i<size($mySel);$i++){

    makeIdentity -apply true -t 1 -r 1 -s 1 -n 0 $mySel[$i];

    expression -s "translateX=rand(-1,1);"  -o $mySel[$i] -ae 1 -uc all ;
    expression -s "translateY=rand(-1,1);"  -o $mySel[$i] -ae 1 -uc all ;
    expression -s "translateZ=rand(-1,1);"  -o $mySel[$i] -ae 1 -uc all ;


};
```

The script starts by making an array of the selected objects in the scene (the -sl flag is an abbreviation for *selection*). The loop then uses the makeIdentity command to freeze all of the transformations for the selected objects. The three expression commands attach an expression to each of the Translate channels, which randomizes the position of the translation between -1 and 1.

The flags in the expression command are -s (string), -o (object), -ae (always evaluate), and -uc (unit conversion).

2. To test the script, make a new blank scene in Maya. Create a number of polygon cubes, and place them randomly in the scene.

3. Select the cubes and open the Script Editor. Copy and paste the code from the shakeMe. mel file into the work area of the Script Editor, and then press the Enter key.

4. Rewind and play the scene. The cubes should shake randomly around their original location.

5. To turn the script into a procedure, edit the text file so it looks like the following:

```
proc shakeMe(){

    string $mySel[] = `ls -sl`;

    for ($i=0;$i<size($mySel);$i++){

        makeIdentity -apply true -t 1 -r 1 -s 1 -n 0 $mySel[$i];

        expression -s "translateX=rand(-1,1);"  -o $mySel[$i] -ae 1 -uc all ;
        expression -s "translateY=rand(-1,1);"  -o $mySel[$i] -ae 1 -uc all ;
        expression -s "translateZ=rand(-1,1);"  -o $mySel[$i] -ae 1 -uc all ;


    }
}
```

At the start of the script, the text `proc shakeMe()` is added. This creates a new procedure named shakeMe. The procedure is contained within the set of curly braces.

6. Create a new scene in Maya. Create a number of randomly placed polygon cubes.

7. Copy and paste the edited text into the Script Editor. Select the cubes and press the Enter key. Nothing happens.

Nothing happens because instead of executing a script, you've actually *sourced* the procedure. In other words, you've made this snippet of code available as part of Maya.

8. With the cubes selected, type **shakeMe** into the command line and press the Enter key. The script is now applied to the selected cubes.

This is useful because you can run the script any number of times on any number of selected objects by selecting the objects and then typing shakeMe into the command line.

9. Save this file as **shakeMeProc.mel**. To see a version, open the shakeMeProc.mel file from the chapter17\mel folder on the DVD.

Use a Procedure within a Script

The real usefulness of a procedure is when it is contained as part of a script. The procedure can be called on within the script at any time, which is a way of reusing the same bit of code whenever it is needed. Procedures should always appear at the start of the script so that, when the script is run, the procedures are sourced into Maya's memory before the rest of the script executes.

As a simple example, suppose that instead of randomly moving the selected objects between a value of -1 and 1, you wanted to create a range for the expression that itself is based on a random value.

1. Open a text editor to a new file and type in the following:

```
//create a random number between 0 and 3

float $randVal = rand(3);
```

This is an extremely simple script that generates a random number between 0 and 3.

2. Copy the text shakeMe proc from the shakeMeProc.mel file in the chapter17\mel folder. Paste this text above the lines you have typed in the text editor so the script looks like the following:

```
proc shakeMe(){

    string $mySel[] = `ls -sl`;

    for ($i=0;$i<size($mySel);$i++){

        makeIdentity -apply true -t 1 -r 1 -s 1 -n 0 $mySel[$i];

        expression -s "translateX=rand(-1,1);"  -o $mySel[$i] -ae 1 -uc all ;
        expression -s "translateY=rand(-1,1);"  -o $mySel[$i] -ae 1 -uc all ;
```

```
expression -s "translateZ=rand(-1,1);"  -o $mySel[$i] -ae 1 -uc all ;

      }
  }

  //Create a random number between 0 and 3

  float $randVal = rand(3);
```

3. Edit the first line of the script to read **proc shakeMe($num){**. This adds a variable that allows the script to pass information to the procedure.

4. Even though the variable is stated in the procedure, you still need to declare its type as a float. Edit the first three lines of the script like this:

```
proc shakeMe(float $num){

    float $num;


    string $mySel[] = `ls -sl`;
```

5. Within the loop, below the makeIdentity command, add two new lines:

```
            float $lowRange = -0.5*$num;

            float $highRange = 0.5*$num;
```

These lines create two new variables that represent the low and high ranges of the random value that will be used in the next lines of the script. So if the initial $num is equal to 3, the low range will be -1.5 and the high range will be 1.5. Thus, the object will move randomly within a total range of three units when the expression is applied.

6. Edit the expression lines of the script:

```
    expression -s ("translateX=rand(" + $lowRange + "," + $highRange +");")
     -o $mySel[$i] -ae 1 -uc all ;
    expression -s ("translateY=rand(" + $lowRange + "," + $highRange +");")
     -o $mySel[$i] -ae 1 -uc all ;
    expression -s ("translateZ=rand(" + $lowRange + "," + $highRange +");")

     -o $mySel[$i] -ae 1 -uc all ;
```

It is very important to pay attention to how these lines are written because it illustrates an important aspect of using MEL to create expressions. On the surface it may seem logical to place the $lowRange and $highRange variables directly into the expression so that the line looks like this:

```
    expression -s "translateX=rand($lowRange, $highRange );"

     -o $mySel[$i] -ae 1 -uc all ;
```

But this will not work. If you run the script using this syntax, you will get an error that says that $lowRange and $highRange have not been declared as variables. At first this makes no sense—clearly you declared the variables in the two lines added before the expression lines. So why is Maya complaining about undeclared variables?

You have to understand what the expression command actually does. When you use the expression command, it is like you are telling MEL to write the expression for you in the Expression Editor. Variables within the Expression Editor are local. They have no relationship or connection to the variables created within MEL scripts (one alternative is to declare the variables as global variables, however, for the sake of understanding how to write expressions with MEL, let's pretend global variables do not exist). When you run the script, MEL creates the expressions exactly as they appear between the quotes in the expression command. Therefore, if you place variables within these quotes that have not been declared *in the expression itself*, Maya won't understand where these variables came from. To work around this, you concatenate the expression using the plus sign. This is the same syntax you used earlier in the chapter when you set an attribute for an object contained within a variable. The syntax looks like this:

```
Expression -string "The first part of the expression text" +
    the variable created in mel +

    "the second part of the expression text";
```

7. Finally, at the very end of the script add a line that calls the procedure so the entire script, with procedure, looks like this:

```
proc shakeMe(float $num){

    float $num;

    string $mySel[] = `ls -sl`;

    for ($i=0;$i<size($mySel);$i++){

        makeIdentity -apply true -t 1 -r 1 -s 1 -n 0 $mySel[$i];

        float $lowRange = -0.5*(0.5+$num);
        float $highRange = 0.5*(0.5+$num);


        expression -s ("translateX=rand(" + $lowRange + "," + $highRange +");")
          -o $mySel[$i] -ae 1 -uc all ;
        expression -s ("translateY=rand(" + $lowRange + "," + $highRange +");")
          -o $mySel[$i] -ae 1 -uc all ;
        expression -s ("translateZ=rand(" + $lowRange + "," + $highRange +");")
          -o $mySel[$i] -ae 1 -uc all ;

    }
};

//Create a random number between 0 and 3
float $randVal = rand(3);

shakeMe($randVal);
```

When you select objects in a scene and run the script, the shakeMe procedure is loaded into memory. This is everything within the curly braces. Then the variable $randVal is created and assigned a number between 0 and 3 randomly. The last line of the script calls the shakeMe procedure and passes the procedure the random value held in the $randVal variable. In the procedure, the $num variable is set to be equivalent to the $randVal value, and the procedure is executed.

8. To see a finished version of the script, open the shakeMeProc_v02.mel file from the chapter17\mel folder on the DVD.

Global Procedures

The procedure created in the previous section is a *local* procedure. The procedure is available only within the script that uses it. A *global* procedure is one that can be called upon by any script in Maya. Maya uses global procedures to create the interface and perform the tasks necessary to make Maya functional. To make a procedure global, you simply start the procedure using the text **global proc** instead of just **proc**.

You should be very careful when creating your own global procedures. It is possible to overwrite one of Maya's own global procedures, which can disrupt the way Maya works. The safest bet is to name the global procedure using your own name or initials in a way that will most likely not interfere with one of Maya's global procedures.

Scripts containing global procedures can be saved in the My Documents\Maya\Scripts folder on your local drive. These scripts should load automatically when Maya starts, making the procedures available for use within a Maya session.

You can source a procedure using the File menu in the Script Editor. This loads the procedures contained within a MEL script file into memory so they are available when working in Maya. You can then run the procedure by typing the name of the procedure on the command line. The author of the procedure will usually include instructions on how to use the procedure within comment tags at the top of the procedure. When you source a procedure, you won't notice an immediate change in Maya until you actually call the procedure in a script or on the command line. It's usually a good idea to open the script file that contains the procedure and read the instructions at the top before trying to source and run the procedure.

Use Python

Python is a scripting language developed independently of Maya. Python is used for a wide variety of computing tasks well beyond 3D animation and modeling. In recent years, Python has been incorporated into a number of 3D animation packages, making it easier for the various software programs to work together within a studio pipeline.

Use Maya Commands within Python

If you are familiar with Python, you can use Python to run MEL commands within a Python script. To run or write a Python script within Maya, switch to the Python tab in the Script Editor. This tells Maya to interpret any commands as Python and not MEL. Likewise, you can switch the command line and the command shell to Python mode.

Before you can use Maya commands within Python scripts, you must first import the Maya commands into Python. To do this, switch to the Python tab in the Script Editor and type:

```
import maya.cmds
```

Press the Enter key to execute the command.

You can test a Maya command by typing the following:

```
maya.cmds.sphere (radius=1, name='myBall')
```

Note that the syntax for the Python command is different from the MEL syntax. Apostrophes are used around the myBall variable instead of quotes or accent marks, and the line does not end in a semicolon.

The Bottom Line

Use a MEL command.   MEL commands are used to perform many tasks within Maya. There are numerous ways to enter MEL commands in the Maya interface. These include the command shell, the command line, and the Script Editor.

> **Master it**   Create a polygon cube using the command shell. Create a NURBS cone using the command line. Create a polygonSphere using the Script Editor.

Use MEL scripting techniques.   Many basic MEL techniques can be used to reduce the number of repetitive tasks performed during a Maya session. Using commands, conditional statements, and loops, you can make simple scripts that make working in Maya faster and more efficient.

> **Master it**   Write a more efficient version of the mySpriteScript file that automatically selects all of the nParticle objects in a scene without the need for a conditional statement to test the type of the selected nodes.

Create a procedure.   Procedures are sections of code that can be called upon at any time within a script. Procedures can help make longer scripts more efficient by eliminating the need to repeat sections of code.

> **Master it**   Write a procedure that adds an expression to selected objects that use the noise function to randomly scale objects over time.

Use Python.   Python can be used within the Script Editor to execute Python commands or to execute MEL commands within a Python script. The Maya commands must be imported at the start of Python script if you want to incorporate MEL into the Python code.

> **Master it**   Use Python to make a NURBS torus.

Appendix A

The Bottom Line

Each of The Bottom Line sections in the chapters suggest exercises to deepen skills and understanding. Sometimes there is only one possible solution, but often you are encouraged to use your skills and creativity to create something that builds on what you know and lets you explore one of many possible solutions.

Chapter 1: Working in Maya

Understand transform and shape nodes.   DAG nodes have both a transform and a shape node. The transform node tells where an object is located; the shape node describes how it is made. Nodes can be parented to each other to form a hierarchy.

Master it   Arrange the nodes in the miniGun_v03.ma file in a hierarchical structure so the barrels of the guns can rotate on their Z axis, the guns can be aimed independently, and the guns rotate with the turret.

Solution   In the Outliner, MMB-drag the left_gunBarrels node onto the left_housing node. MMB-drag the left housing node onto left_mount, then MMB-drag left mount onto the turret node. Do the same for the right gunBarrels, housing, and mount nodes. Graph the node structure on the Hypergraph, and examine the network.

Create a project.   Creating a project directory structure keeps Maya scene files and connected external files organized to ensure the animation project is efficient.

Master it   Create a new project named Test, but make sure the project has only the scene, source images, and data subfolders.

Solution   Use the Options box in the Create New Project command to make a new project named Test; leave all the fields blank except for scenes, source images, and data. Name the folders in these fields **scenes**, **sourceImages**, and **data**, respectively.

Use assets.   An asset is a container in which the contained nodes have specific attributes published to the top level of the container. This means that members of each team in a pipeline have easy access to the attributes they need, thus streamlining production.

Master it   Create an asset from the nodes in the miniGun_v04.ma scene in the chapter1\ scenes folder. Make sure that only the Y rotation of the turret, the X rotation of the guns, and the Z rotation of the gun barrels are available to the animator.

Solution   Create a container that holds the turretAim curve and turret nodes (and their child nodes). Use the Asset Editor to publish the Rotate Y, Rotate X, and Barrel Spin attributes of the turretAim curve node to the container. Set the container to black box mode so the animator can't access any of the attributes of the contained nodes.

Create file references. File references can be used so that as part of the team works on a model, the other members of the team can use it in the scene. As changes to the original file are made, the referenced file in other scenes will update automatically.

Master it Create a file reference for the miniGun_v04.ma scene; create a proxy from the miniGun_loRes.ma scene.

Solution Create a new scene and reference the miniGun_v04.ma file in the chapter1\ scenes directory. Use the Reference Editor to make a proxy from the miniGun_loRes .ma scene in the same folder on the DVD.

Chapter 2: Maya Cameras

Determine image size and resolution. The final image size of your render should be determined at the earliest possible stage in a project. It will affect everything from texture resolution to render time. Maya has a number of presets that can be used to set the image resolution.

Master it Set up an animation that will be rendered to be displayed on a high-definition progressive-scan television.

Solution Open the Render settings and choose the HD 1080 preset under the Image Size presets on the Common tab. Progressive scan means the image will not be interlaced (rendered as alternating fields), so you can render at 24 frames per second. Open the Preferences/Settings window and set the Time setting under Settings to Film (24 FPS).

Work with camera settings. The settings found in the Attribute Editor for a camera enable you to replicate real-world cameras as well as add effects such as camera shaking.

Master it Create a camera setting where the film back shakes back and forth in the camera. Set up a system where the amount of shaking can be animated over time.

Solution Enable the Shake Overscan attribute on a camera. Attach a fractal texture to the Shake Overscan attribute and edit its amplitude settings. Create an expression that sets the Alpha Offset to minus one-half of the Alpha Gain. Set keyframes on the Alpha Gain to animate the shaking of the Shake Overscan attribute over time.

Create custom camera rigs. Dramatic camera moves are easier to create and animate when you build a custom camera rig.

Master it Create a camera in the car chase scene that films from the point of view of chopperAnim3 but tracks the car as it moves along the road.

Solution Create a two-node camera (Camera and Aim). Attach the camera to a NURBS curve using a motion path, and parent the curve to chopperAnim3. Parent the aim of the camera to the vehicleAnim group. Create an asset for the camera so that the position of the camera around the helicopter can be changed as well as the position of the aim node relative to the vehicleAnim group.

Use Depth of Field and Motion Blur. Depth of Field and Motion Blur replicate real-world camera effects and can add a lot of drama to a scene. Both are very expensive to render and should be applied with care.

Master it Create a camera asset with a built-in focus distance control.

Solution   Create the same camera and focus distance control as shown in this chapter. Select the camera, camera shape node, and distance controls, and place them within a container. Publish the Z Translation of the distToCam locator to the container. Publish the F Stop and Focus Region Scale attributes as well.

Create orthographic and stereoscopic cameras.   Orthographic cameras are used primarily for modeling because they lack a sense of depth or a vanishing point. A stereoscopic rig uses three cameras and special parallax controls that enable you to render 3D movies from Maya.

Master it   Create a 3D movie from the point of view of the driver in the chase scene.

Solution   Create a stereo camera rig, and parent it to the car in the chase scene. Use the center camera to position the rig above the car's cockpit.

Chapter 3: NURBS Modeling In Maya

Use image planes.   Image planes can be used to position images for use as a modeling guide.

Master it   Create image planes for side, front, and top views for use as a model guide.

Solution   Create reference drawings or use photographs taken from each view. Save the images to your local disk. Create image planes for the front, side, and top views, and apply the corresponding reference images to each image plane. Use the settings in each image plane's Attribute Editor to position the image planes in the scene. Use display layers for each plane so their visibility can be turned on and off easily.

Apply NURBS curves and surfaces.   NURBS surfaces are created by lofting a surface across a series of curves. The curve and surface degree and parameterization affect the shape of the resulting surface.

Master it   What is the difference between a 1-degree (linear) surface, a 3-degree (cubic) surface, and a 5-degree surface?

Solution   The degree of the surface is determined by the number of CVs per span minus one, so a 1-degree surface has two CVs per span, a 3-degree surface has four CVs per span, and a 5-degree surface has six CVs per span. Linear and cubic surfaces are the ones used most frequently.

Model with NURBS surfaces.   A variety of tools and techniques can be used to model surfaces with NURBS. Hard-surface/mechanical objects are well-suited subjects for NURBS surfaces.

Master it   Create a NURBS model of a common object you own such as a cell phone, a computer monitor, or a particle accelerator.

Solution   Start with drawings or photographs of the object and place them on image planes. Use whichever techniques described in this chapter work best for you to create the object. Remember to combine tools and techniques and use the construction history to your advantage.

Create realistic surfaces.   Manufactured objects usually have visible seams and parting lines that reveal how they are put together. Adding these details to your surfaces greatly increases the realism of your objects.

Master it   Examine a manufactured object closely, and pay attention to the seams and parting lines. Look at weather stripping on the windows of vehicles; look at the trim around tail lights and openings in the surface. Look at the panels on the underside of electronic products such as a cell phone. Try to imitate these in your models even if the object does not exist in the real world.

Solution   Use intersecting surfaces, curves projected or drawn on a surface, and the Trim tool to create parting lines and seams around panels. Use lofts and freeform fillets to bridge gaps between surfaces. Manipulate the hulls on the lofts and fillets to change the shape of the surfaces.

Adjust NURBS render tessellation.   You can change how the rendering engine converts a NURBS surface into triangles at render time by adjusting the tessellation of the objects. This can impact render times and increase efficiency in heavy scenes.

Master it   Test the tessellation settings on a row of NURBS columns. Compare render times and image quality using different tessellation settings.

Solution   Create a row of identical NURBS Greek columns using a revolve surface. Place a camera in the scene that looks down the row of columns. Compare render times and quality when you lower or raise the tessellation of surfaces far away and close to the camera. Use the Display Render Tessellation feature, the Attribute Editor, or the surfaces so that you can visualize the difference in tessellation.

Chapter 4: Polygon and Subdivision Surface Modeling

Understand polygon geometry.   Polygon geometry consists of flat faces connected and shaped to form three-dimensional objects. You can edit the geometry by transforming the vertices, edges, and faces that make up the surface of the model.

Master it   Examine the polygon primitives in the Create ➢ Polygon Primitives menu.

Solution   Create an example of each primitive shown in the menu. Adjust their settings in the INPUTS section of the Channel Box. Switch to vertex selection mode, and move the vertices of each primitive to create unique shapes.

Work with smooth mesh polygons.   The smooth mesh preview display allows you to work on a smoothed version of the polygon model while limiting the number of components needed to shape the model. You can use creasing to create hard edges in selected areas.

Master it   Create a backpack for the space suit character.

Solution   Create a polygon cube and activate smooth mesh preview. Use the Insert Edge Loop tool, extrude faces, and crease edges to create a backpack that fits on the back of the space suit character.

Model using deformers.   Deformers such as the lattice, non-linear deformers, and the Soft Modification tool can be used to help shape geometry and groups of objects.

Master it   Create a number of small-detail objects for the belt of the space suit character. Shape the details so that they conform to the belt.

Solution   Create a number of small objects suitable for detailing the belt. Line up the objects in the front view. Group the objects, and use a combination of lattices and bend deformers to shape the objects so they conform to the circular shape of the belt.

Combine meshes.   Multiple meshes can be combined under a single shape node. When this is done, you can edit the components of the combined meshes as a single mesh.

Master it   Combine two polygon spheres, and use the polygon-editing tools to join the faces of the spheres.

Solution   Create two polygon spheres. Combine the spheres (Mesh ➢ Combine). Use the Bridge tool to connect faces between the spheres. Select a face on each sphere, and choose Edit Mesh ➢ Bridge.

Use bevel tools.   The Bevel tool can add a beveled edge to a polygon surface, creating more realism by smoothing the edges. The Bevel Plus tool is used primarily to create 3D logos from text curves, but it can be used to create interesting details and objects.

Master it   Using the concept sketch as a guide, create the spiraling detail for the character's boots.

Solution   Draw some spiral curves, or reuse the curves created earlier in the chapter. Use the Bevel Plus tool to create geometry from the curves. Group the geometry together, and use deformers to make the geometry conform to the shape of the boot.

Model polygons with Paint Effects.   Paint Effects strokes can be converted to NURBS and Polygon geometry. Using the default brush you can quickly create hoses and wires. Because construction history connects the converted objects to the strokes, you can use the stroke settings to edit the shape of the converted objects.

Master it   Add additional hoses and wires to the space suit character.

Solution   Make the torso object live, and draw curves directly on the surface. Select the curves, and choose Paint Effects ➢ Curve Utilities ➢ Attach Brush To Curves. Open the Attribute Editor for the stroke nodes, and edit the settings to shape the wire detail. Choose Modify ➢ Convert Paint Effects To Polygons to turn the strokes into polygons.

Convert NURBS surfaces to polygons.   NURBS surfaces are frequently used as a starting place to create polygon objects, giving you the power of both types of models.

Master it   Convert the helmet object into polygons.

Solution   Select the NURBS objects and convert each to polygons. You will need to adjust the conversion options for many of the surfaces as you create them. Once you have converted all the objects, combine them into a single surface.

Use Booleans.   Using Booleans you can use one polygon object to shape a second. The first object can be joined with the second or used to cut into it. An object can be created from the intersection of two objects.

Master it   Create additional detail in the torso trim surface of the space suit character using Booleans.

Solution   Use cylinders, spheres, and cubes to cut holes and create details in the torso trim object. Experiment with combinations of the different Boolean operations.

Sculpt polygons using Artisan.   The Artisan toolset is a brush-based modeling and editing tool. Using Artisan you can sculpt directly on the surface of geometry.

Master it   Use Artisan to sculpt dents into a surface.

Solution   Create a polygon surface with fairly dense geometry. Choose Polygons ➤ Sculpt Geometry to activate Artisan. Open the options for the tool while working, and then use the brush to make small dents in the surface of the geometry. Try this technique on parts of the space suit character.

Model a human head.   There are a variety of techniques you can use to create a human head. Modeling character heads is one of the most difficult challenges facing 3D artists. It takes a great deal of study and practice. This chapter demonstrates creating the head by connecting parts of the faces sculpted from polygon primitives.

Master it   Take several photographs of yourself or a friend from the front and the side. Map these to image planes in a Maya scene, and create a polygon head using the photographs.

Solution   Using the image planes as a reference, start by building simple geometry around the mouth and eyes. Use the polygon tools to create the features, and then connect them together into a single mesh. Once you have the basic geometry created, sculpt the geometry of the head to match the photographs using the Move tool and the Artisan tool set.

Create a character.   Once you have the basic geometry for the head created, you can use the polygon editing and sculpting tools to shape the head into any number of characters.

Master it   Use the geometry created for the head to make a different character. Try turning the head into an older man.

Solution   Use the Artisan tool set, the Transform Component, and other tools to push and pull the vertices of the head until it resembles a different character.

Use subdivision surfaces.   Subdivision surfaces are similar to smooth mesh preview polygons except that specific parts of the model can be subdivided and edited as needed. You can traverse the subdivision levels while you work.

Master it   Add wrinkles, seams, and other details to the glove model.

Solution   Convert the subdivision surface version of the glove into polygons, and insert edge loops to create lines around the perimeter of the glove. Convert the glove back into subdivision surfaces. Add creasing to the inserted edge loops, and use the Move tool in tweak mode to add detail to the model. Move up to higher subdivision levels to create finer detail.

Chapter 5: Animation

Create a simple rig with joints and constraints.   Joints are a deformer commonly used in character animation. The hierarchical relationship makes them useful for rigging many types of characters. When creating robots and mechanical devices, you can build a skeleton using joints and then parent the parts of the robot to the joints.

Constraints are used to constrain the channels of one object to the world space coordinates of another object. Constraints are useful as rigging tools for snapping the pivot point of one object to another.

Master it   Create a simple joint chain for a robot's arm. Use the joint chain to animate an arm made from simple polygon surfaces.

Solution   Create a joint chain using three joints—one for the upper arm, one for the forearm, and one for the wrist. Create two cylinders and a sphere. Parent each cylinder to the upper arm and forearm joints; parent the sphere to the wrist joint.

Use Inverse Kinematics.   Inverse Kinematics creates a goal object, known as an End Effector, for joints in a chain. The joints in the chain orient themselves based on the translation of the goal. The IK Handle tool is used to position the End Effector.

Master it   Create an Inverse Kinematic control for a simple arm.

Solution   Create a simple arm using three joints—one for the upper arm, one for the forearm, and one for the wrist. Rotate the forearm slightly so the Inverse Kinematic solver understands which direction the joint should rotate. Freeze transformations on the joints. Activate the IK Handle tool, click on the first joint (known as the root), and then click on the wrist joint. Move around the IK Handle to bend the joint.

Animate with keyframes.   A keyframe marks the state of a particular attribute at a point in time on the timeline. When a second keyframe is added to the attribute at a different point in time, Maya interpolates the values between the two keyframes, creating animation. There are a number of ways to edit keyframes using the timeline and the Channel Box.

Master it   Create a number of keyframes for the Translate channels of a simple object. Copy the keyframes to a different point in time for the object. Try copying the keyframes to the Scale channels. Try copying the keys to the Translate channels of another object.

Solution   After creating keys for the object, Shift-drag a selection on the timeline. Use the arrows in the selection box to move or scale the keys. Right-click on the keys and choose Copy. Move to a different point in time on the timeline and paste the keys. Copying, pasting, and duplicating keys to another object can be accomplished by selecting the channels in the Channel Box and using the options that appear when you right-click on the channels.

Use the Graph Editor.   More sophisticated animation editing is available using the animation curve editing tools on the Graph Editor.

Master it   Create a looping animation for the mechanical bug model using as few keys as possible. The bug should leap up repeatedly and move forward with each leap.

Solution   Create keyframes on the bug's Translate Y and Translate Z channels. Set four keys on the Translate Y channel so the bug is stationary, then moves up along the Y axis, moves back down to zero, and then holds for a number of frames. In the Graph Editor, set the Post-Infinity option for the Translate Y channel to Cycle. Create a similar set of keyframes for the Translate Z channel on the same frames. Set the Post-Infinity option for Translate Z to Cycle With Offset.

Preview animations with Playblast.   Playblast is a tool for viewing the animation as a flip-book without having to actually render the animation. F Check is a utility program that is included with Maya. Playblasts can be viewed in F Check.

Master it   Create a playblast of the mechBugLayers_v04.ma scene.

Solution   Open the mechBugLayers_v04.ma scene from the chapter5\scenes directory on the DVD. Rewind the animation and create a playblast by choosing Windows≻Playblast. Watch the playblast in FCheck.

Use driven keys.   A driven key is a keyframe that uses the attributes of one object as an input instead of time. Using driven keys you can automate many parts of an animation that might otherwise be tedious.

Master it   Create an alternate automated walk cycle for the mechanical bug so that when it walks sideways (along its Translate X), the legs automatically move in a crablike fashion.

Solution   Use the same techniques used to create the walk cycle described earlier in the chapter. Use the Translate X channel of the bodyCtrl curve to drive the Translate X and Translate Y channels of one of the legs. Use the Pre- and Post-Infinity options to cycle the leg animation. Copy the animation to the other legs, and then use the Graph Editor to offset the animation for each leg.

Animate with expressions.   Expressions are a powerful way to automate the movement of an object. Using conditional statements you can create an expression that causes the animation to react to changes in the scene automatically.

Master it   Create an expression to randomly rotate the bug's eyes up and down. Make the rotation faster based on the height of the bodyCtrl curve.

Solution   Create an expression on the Translate Y channel of the eyeAimLoc locator in the mechanicalBug rig. The expression should read as follows:

```
eyeAimLoc.translateY = (bodyCtrl.translateY*noise(time));
```

Animate with motion paths.   Motion paths allow you to attach an object to a curve. Over the course of the animation the object slides along the curve based on the keyframes set o n the motion path's U Value.

Master it   Make the bug walk along a motion path. See if you can automate a walk cycle based on the position along the path.

Solution   Draw a curve in a scene with the fully rigged mechanical bug. Attach the bodyCtrl curve to the curve using Animate ≻ Attach To Motion Path. Create set driven keys for the leg animation, but instead of using the Translate Z of the bodyCtrl curve, use the U Value of the motion path node.

Use animation layers.   Animation layers are a new feature in Maya 2009. Using animation layers you can add new motion that can override existing animation or be combined with it.

Master it   Create animation layers for the flying bug in the mechBug_v08.ma scene in the chapter5\scenes directory on the DVD. Create two layers: one for the bodyCtrl curve and one for the legsCtrl curve. Use layers to make the animation of the wings start with small movements and then flap at full strength.

Solution Open the mechBug_v08.ma scene. Select the bodyCtrl curve. In the animation layers create an empty layer. Select the BaseAnimation layer, select the bodyCtrl curve, and choose Layers ➤ Extract Selected. Do the same for the legsCtrl curve and the wing motors. Set keyframes on the weight of the layer that contains the wing motors. Keyframe the weight from a value of 0 to a value of 1 over 20 frames.

Chapter 6: Animating with Deformers

Animate facial expressions. Animated facial expressions are a big part of character animation. It's common practice to use a Blend Shape deformer to create expressions from a large number of Blend Shape targets. The changes created in the targets can be mixed and matched by the deformer to create the expressions and speech for a character.

Master it Create Blend Shape targets for the nancy character. Make an expression where the brows are up and the brows are down. Create a rig that animates each brow independently.

Solution Create two duplicates of the neutral nancy character. Use the modeling tools to model raised eyebrows on one copy and lowered eyebrows on the other. Add these targets to the nancy model. Use the Paint Blend Shape tool to make four additional targets: leftBrowUp, leftBrowDown, rightBrowUp, and rightBrowDown. Add these new targets to the nancy model. Create a custom slider using the Curve tool. Connect the slider to the Blend Shape controls using driven keys.

Create Blend Shape sequences Blend Shapes can be applied in a sequential order to animate a sequence of changes over time.

Master it Create a Blend Shape sequence of a mushroom growing.

Solution Create a model of a mushroom. Create a duplicate of the model, and edit each duplicate to represent stages in the growth of the mushroom. Work backwards from the formed mushroom to the very beginning. Select the mushroom stage models in order of their growth stages, and apply them to the first stage of the mushroom group as a Blend Shape. Check the In-between setting in the Blend Shape Options.

Use lattices Lattices are freeform deformers that create a 3D cage around an object. The differences between the lattice and the lattice base are used to deform geometry.

Master it Animate a cube of jelly squishing along a path.

Solution Create a polygon cube with a lot of divisions. Apply a lattice deformer to the cube. Scale the lattice and the base node together so they encompass the path of the cube. Use the Move tool to select and move the lattice points. Animate the cube moving through the lattice.

Animate clusters Clusters are simple deformers that are most often used to animate the vertices of geometry.

Master it Create an animated garden hose using clusters.

Solution   Create a NURBS curve. Create cluster deformers for each CV of the curve. Extrude a NURBS circle along the curve path. Keyframe the translation of the clusters as you move them in the scene.

Animate nonlinear deformers.   Nonlinear deformers apply simple changes to geometry. The deformers are controlled by animating the attributes of the deformer.

Master it   Animate an eel swimming past the jellyfish we created in this chapter.

Solution   Model a simple eel using your favorite tools and techniques. Apply a sine deformer to the eel. Create an expression that animates the offset of the sine. Group the eel and the deformer, and animate the group moving past the jellyfish.

Use jiggle deformers   Jiggle deformers add a simple jiggling motion to animated objects.

Master it   Add a jiggling motion to the belly of a character.

Solution   Create a rotund character. Animate the character moving. Add a jiggle deformer to the character. Use the Paint Jiggle Weights tool to mask the jiggle weights on the entire character except for the belly.

Use the geometry cache.   Geometry caches store the animation information of each vertex of a piece of geometry. The Cache controls can be used to speed up or slow down the animation of a cached object.

Master It   Create a slow-motion effect for an animation that uses a deformer.

Solution   Animate an object using deformers. Create a geometry cache. In the attributes for the geometry cache, increase the scale. Try animating the Scale attribute using keyframes.

Chapter 7: Rigging and Muscle Systems

Understand rigging.   A rig is a system of controls and deformers used to make the process of animating easier. Joints are the most common deformers used to create a character animation rig. Joints are bound directly to geometry or indirectly by skinning another deformer, such as a lattice, to the joints.

Master it   Create a rig using three bones and a lattice around a simple piece of geometry such as a sphere. Use the bones to animate the lattice.

Solution   Create a polygon sphere and apply a lattice deformer to the sphere. Create three joints at the center of the lattice running along its vertical axis. Select the joints and the lattice, and use Smooth Binding to bind the lattice to the joints. Move the joints, and the lattice should update.

Create and organize joint hierarchies.   A joint hierarchy is a series of joint chains. Each joint in a chain is parented to another joint, back to the root of the chain. Each joint inherits the motion of its parent joint. Organizing the joint chains is accomplished through naming and labeling the joints. Proper orientation of the joints is essential for the joints to work properly.

Master it   Create a joint hierarchy for a humanoid character. Label the joints and create names based on the labels. Orient the joints so the X axis points down the length of the joints.

Solution   Create a joint chain with the root of the chain at the character's pelvis. Create a leg and an arm on one side of the body. Use the Label feature to create labels for these joints; then use the Create Names From Labels feature to automatically name the joints after the labels. Orient the joints, and then mirror the legs and arms from one side to the other.

Use Inverse Kinematics rigs.   A joint chain that uses Inverse Kinematics uses a goal called an End Effector to orient the joints in the chain. There are a number of solvers available in Maya, some of which need to be loaded into Maya using the command line.

Master it   Create an Inverse Kinematic rig for a character's leg. Use a separate control to position the knee of the character.

Solution   Create an Inverse Kinematic Handle for a simple leg using the RP Solver. Create a locator and place it in front of the knee. Apply a Pole Vector constraint to the leg's IK Handle using the locator as a handle.

Apply skin geometry.   Skinning geometry refers to the process in which geometry is bound to joints so that it deforms as the joints are moved and rotated. Each vertex of the geometry receives a certain amount of influence from the joints in the hierarchy. This can be controlled by painting the weights of the geometry on the skin.

Master it   Paint weights on the hand model so that the padding of the thumb bulges when the thumb is rotated toward the palm of the hand.

Solution   Bind the joints created in the left arm example files to the arm geometry. Use the Paint Weights tool to paint the weights for each joint on the arm. Rotate the thumb joints so that the thumb points toward the palm of the hand. Carefully paint the weights on the inside of the hand so that they are distributed between the hand joints and the thumb joints.

Use Maya Muscle.   Maya Muscle is a series of tools designed to create more believable deformations and movement for objects skinned to joints. Capsules are used to replace Maya joints. Bones are deformers created from geometry, and muscles are NURBS surfaces that squash, stretch, and jiggle as they deform geometry.

Master it   Use Maya Muscle to create muscles for the forearm. Use the muscle system to reduce the amount of shrinking that occurs in the arm geometry when the forearm is rotated around its axis.

Solution   Use the Muscle Builder to make a surface that is attached to the wrist and elbow. Convert the surface into a muscle, and use the Squash and Stretch presets to deform the muscle so that it reduces the shrinking that occurs when the upper part of the forearm is twisted.

Chapter 8: Paint Effects and Toon Shading

Use the Paint Effects canvas.   The Paint Effects canvas can be used to test Paint Effects strokes or as a 2D paint program for creating images.

Master it   Create a tiling texture map using the Paint Effects canvas.

Solution   Choose a brush from the Visor, such as the downRedFeathers.mel brush from the feathers folder. On the canvas toolbar, enable the Horizontal and Vertical Wrap options. Paint feathers across the canvas; strokes that go off the top or sides will wrap around to the opposite side. Save the image in the Maya IFF format, and try applying it to an object in a 3D scene.

Paint on 3D objects.   Paint Effects brushes can be used to paint directly on 3D objects as long as the objects are either NURBS or polygon geometry. Paint Effects brushes require that all polygon geometry have mapped UV texture coordinates.

Master it   Create a small garden or jungle using Paint Effects brushes.

Solution   Model a simple landscape using a polygon or NURBS plane. Create some small hills and valleys in the surface. Make the object paintable, and then experiment using the Brush presets available in the Visor. The plants, plantsMesh, trees, treesMesh, flowers, and flowersMesh folders all have presets that work well in a garden or jungle setting.

Understand strokes.   A Paint Effects stroke has a number of associated nodes that are created and connected when the stroke is painted in the scene. These include the stroke's transform node, shape node, brush node, and curve node. Most of the time you'll edit settings on the stroke's shape node and brush node. You can use brush sharing to connect all of the strokes in the scene to the settings on a single brush node.

Master it   Use the Leafy Vine stroke to add a series of vine strokes to a simple wall model. Change the Global Scale setting of all the strokes at the same time.

Solution   Create a wall model from a polygon cube. Make sure the wall model has UV texture coordinates properly applied. Make the wall paintable, and select the Leafy Vine stroke from the Plants folder of the Visor. Paint strokes directly on the wall to create a series of vines. Select all of the vine strokes, and choose Paint Effects ➤ Shape One Brush. In the Attribute Editor for one of the brushes, adjust the Global Scale setting. All the other strokes will update at the same time.

Design a brush.   Custom Paint Effects brushes can be created by using a preset brush as a starting place. You can alter the settings on the brush node to produce the desired look for the brush.

Master it   Design a brush to look like a laser beam.

Solution   Use one of the neonGlow brushes found in the glows folder in the Visor. Paint the brush in a 3D scene, paint as straight a line as possible, or attach the stroke to a straight curve using the options in the Paint Effects ➤ Curve Utilities menu. Open the Attribute Editor for the neon brush, and adjust the Color and Glow settings in the Shading section of the Brush attributes. Set the Stamp Density in the Brush Profile to a low value to create a series of glowing dots.

Create tubes.   Tubes are short strokes that grow outward from the main path of the stroke. They can assume a variety of shapes and sizes to create any number of objects.

Master it   Create a paintbrush that resembles the strokes used in Vincent Van Gogh's painting "Starry Night."

Solution   Choose the Blue Oil brush from the `oils` folder of the Visor. Paint a stroke in a scene. Increase the Brush Width, and activate Tubes. Increase the Tubes Per Step, and then see if you can fine-tune the brush to look like an Impressionist stroke. Use the Hue Rand, Sat Rand, Val Rand, and other Randomization options in the Shading and Tube Shading sections of the Brush attributes.

Add growth.   Branches, twigs, leaves, flowers, and buds can be added to Paint Effects tubes. You can use these to simulate plants or apply them creatively to design unique shapes.

Master it   Create a mushroom tree using the Cortinarius Mushroom stroke found in the `plantsMesh` folder of the Visor.

Solution   Use the Cortinarius brush to paint some mushrooms in the scene. In the Growth section of the Brush attributes, activate Branches. Increase the Length Min and Length Max sliders in the Creation section of the Brush attributes to extend the height of the tree and the length of the branches. Adjust the settings in the Flowers section of the attributes to change the shape of the mushroom cap.

Shape strokes with behaviors.   Behaviors are settings that can be used to shape strokes and tubes, giving them wiggling, curling, and spiraling qualities. You can animate behaviors to bring strokes to life.

Master it   Add tendrils to a squashed sphere to create a simple jellyfish.

Solution   Use the slimeWeed brush in the `grasses` folder of the Visor. Paint on the bottom of the sphere. Adjust the look of the tendrils by modifying the Noise, Curl, Wiggle, and Gravity forces in the Behavior section of the Brush attributes.

Animate growth.   Paint Effects strokes can be animated by applying keyframes, expressions, or animated textures directly to stroke attributes. You can animate the growth of strokes by using the Time Clip settings in the Flow Animation section of the Brush attributes.

Master it   Animate blood vessels growing across a surface. Animate the movement of blood within the vessels.

Solution   Use any of the Branching Tree presets as a starting point for the blood vessels. Use the Shading attributes to add a red color. Animate the growth of the vessels by activating Time Clip in the Flow Animation attributes. To animate the blood in the vessels, set the Texture type to Fractal for the color in the Texturing section and activate Texture Flow in the Flow Animation attributes.

Render Paint Effects strokes.   Paint Effects strokes are rendered as a post process using Maya software. To render with mental ray, you should convert the strokes to geometry.

Master it   Render an animated Paint Effects tree in mental ray.

Solution   Choose the Tree Sparse stroke from the `Trees` folder of the Visor. Draw the tree in the scene, and add animation using the Turbulence controls (choose Tree Wind turbulence). Convert the tree to polygons and render with mental ray.

Use Toon Shading.   Toon Shading uses Paint Effects to create lines around the contours of an object and a ramp shader to color the surface of the object to replicate the look of a hand-drawn cartoon.

Master it   Add glowing contour lines to a futuristic vehicle to imitate the look of a vector-style rendering in a computer display.

Solution   Add Paint Effects outlines to a vehicle. Select one of the neon brush strokes from the Glows folder of the Visor, and apply it to the toon lines (Toon ➢ Apply Paint Effects Brush To Toon Lines).

Chapter 9: mental ray Lights

Use shadow-casting lights.   Lights can cast either depth map or ray trace shadows. Depth map shadows are created from an image projected from the shadow-casting light, which reads the depth information of the scene. Ray trace shadows are calculated by tracing rays from the light source to the rendering camera.

Master it   Compare mental ray depth map shadows to ray trace shadows. Render the crystalGlobe.ma scene using soft ray trace shadows.

Solution   Depth map shadows render faster and are softer than ray trace shadows. Ray trace shadows are more physically accurate. Create a light and aim it at the crystalGlobe. Enable Ray Trace Shadows and increase the Shadow Rays and the Light Radius settings.

Render with Global Illumination.   Global Illumination simulates indirect lighting by emitting photons into a scene. Global Illumination photons react with surfaces that have diffuse shaders. Caustics use photons that react to surfaces with reflective shaders. Global Illumination works particularly well in indoor lighting situations.

Master it   Render the rotunda_v01.ma scene using Global Illumination.

Solution   Create a photon-emitting area light, and place it near the opening in the top of the structure. Set its Intensity to 0. Create a shadow-casting direct light, and place it outside the opening in the ceiling. Turn on Emit Photons for the area light, and enable Global Illumination in the Render Settings window. Increase Photon Intensity and the number of photons emitted as needed.

Render with Final Gathering.   Final Gathering is another method for creating indirect lighting. Final Gather points are shot into the scene from the rendering camera. Final Gathering includes color bleeding and ambient occlusion shadowing as part of the indirect lighting. Final Gathering can be used on its own or in combination with Global Illumination.

Master it   Create a fluorescent light bulb from geometry that can light a room.

Solution   Model a fluorescent light bulb from a polygon cylinder. Position it above objects in a scene. Apply a Lambert shader to the bulb, and set the incandescent channel to white. Enable Final Gathering in the Render Settings window, increase the Scale value, and render the scene. Adjust the settings to increase the quality of the render.

Use Image-Based Lighting. Image-Based Lighting (IBL) uses an image to create lighting in a scene. High Dynamic Range Images (HDRI) are usually the most effective source for IBL. There are three ways to render with IBL: Final Gathering, Global Illumination, and with the light shader. These can also be combined if needed.

Master it Render the car scene using the Uffizi Gallery probe HDR image available at `www.debevec.org/Probes/`.

Solution Create an Image-Based Lighting node in the car scene using the settings in the Render Settings window. Download the Uffizi Gallery light probe image from `www .debevec.org/Probes/`. Apply the image to the IBL node in the scene (use Angular mapping). Experiment using Final Gathering, Global Illumination, and the IBL light shader. Use these in combination to create a high-quality render.

Render using physical sun and sky. The Physical Sun and Sky network creates realistic sunlight that's ideal for outdoor rendering.

Master it Render a short animation showing the car at different times of day.

Solution Add the Physical Sun and Sky network to the car scene using the settings in the Render Settings window. Make sure Final Gathering is enabled. Keyframe the sunDirection light rotating on its X axis over 100 frames. Render a sequence of the animation.

Understand mental ray area lights. mental ray area lights are activated in the mental ray section of an area light's shape node when the Use Light Shape option is enabled. mental ray area lights render realistic, soft ray trace shadows. The light created from mental ray area lights is emitted from a three-dimensional array of lights as opposed to an infinitely small point in space.

Master it Build a lamp model that realistically lights a scene using an area light.

Solution Build a small lamp with a round bulb. Create an area light, and place it at the center of the bulb. In the area light's shape node settings, enable Use Shape in the mental ray settings, and set the shape Type to Sphere. Scale down the light to fit within the bulb. Enable Ray Trace Shadows and render the scene.

Work with mental ray light shaders. mental ray has a number of shaders that can be applied to lights to extend their capabilities in a scene. One of these shaders is the Portal Light shader, which helps focus Final Gather points around light entering a room through an opening.

Master it Render the `rotunda_v01.ma` scene using the Portal Light shader.

Solution Open the `rotunda_v01.ma` scene and add a Physical Sun and Sky network using the settings in the Render Settings window. Create a mental ray area light, and place it near the opening in the ceiling. Make sure the Visible option is enabled. Add the Portal Light shader to the Light Shader and the Photon Emitter slots in the area light's Custom Shader section. Enable Final Gather and render the scene. Use the settings on the portal shader node to adjust the look of the lighting.

Create Participating Media. Participating Media (PM) refers to particulate matter suspended in the air. Light is reflected from PM, creating the streaming beams of light known as volumetric lighting. Several shaders can be set up to create the look of PM in a mental ray render.

Master it   Render a beam of light coming from a flashlight model.

Solution   Model a simple flashlight. Parent a spotlight to the end of the flashlight. Create a polygon cube to surround the area around the flashlight, and attach the Transmat shader to the cube. In the Transmat shader's shading group node, attach a parti_volume shader to the Volume Material slot in the mental ray section. Enable Auto Volume in the Features section of the Render Settings. Attach a Physical Light shader to the spotlight, and render the scene. Adjust the settings on the parti_volume shader to improve the brightness and quality of the PM.

Chapter 10: mental ray Shaders

Use ambient occlusion.   Ambient occlusion describes the dark shadowing that occurs when ambient light rays are prevented from reaching part of a surface by another nearby surface. You can use the mib_amb_occlusion node in mental ray to fake the look of indirect lighting or augment the ambient occlusion shadowing that occurs when rendering with Final Gathering.

Master it   Create an ambient occlusion shader from a standard Maya shader.

Solution   Create a surface shader, connect an mib_amb_occlusion node to the Out Color channel of the surface shader. Use the Sampling, Spread, and Max Distance settings to tune the quality of the effect.

Understand shading concepts.   Light rays are reflected, absorbed by, or transmitted through a surface. A rough surface diffuses the reflection of light by bouncing light rays in nearly random directions. Specular reflections occur on smooth surfaces; the angle at which rays bounce off a smooth surface is equivalent to the angle at which they strike the surface. Refraction occurs when light rays are bent as they are transmitted through the surface. A specular highlight is the reflection of a light source on a surface. In CG rendering this effect is often controlled separately from reflection; in the real world specular reflection and highlights are intrinsically related.

Master it   Create a standard Maya shader that is more reflective on parts of the shader that face away from the camera.

Solution   Connect a black and white ramp texture to the Reflectivity of a standard Maya shader such as Blinn or Phong. Create a Sampler Info node and connect the facingRation of the smaplerInfoNode to the V coordinates of the ramp texture using the Connection Editor. Apply the shader to a surface and render using mental ray.

Apply reflection and refraction blur.   Reflection and Refraction Blur are special mental ray options available on many standard Maya shading nodes. You can use these settings to create glossy reflections when rendering standard Maya shading nodes with mental ray.

Master it   Create the look of translucent plastic using a standard Maya Blinn shader.

Solution   Apply a Blinn shader to an object. Increase transparency and reflectivity. Enable Refractions in the Raytrace Options settings. In the mental ray section, increase the Mi Reflection and Mi Refractions settings. Render with mental ray.

Use basic mental ray shaders.   The DGS and Dielectric shaders offer numerous options for creating realistic reflections and transparency. The mib (mental images base) shader library has a number of shaders that can be combined to create realistic materials.

> **Master it**   Create a realistic CD surface using the mib shaders.

> **Solution**   Attach a mib_illum_ward_deriv shader to the base shader slot of the mib_glossy_reflection node. Apply this material to the top of a disc. Use the settings on the mib_illum_ward_deriv shader to create anisotropic specular highlights.

Apply the car paint shader.   Car paint consists of several layers, which creates the special quality seen in the reflections on car paint. The mi_carpaint_phen shader can realistically simulate the interaction of light on the surface of a car model. The diffuse, reflection, and metallic flakes layers all work together to create a convincing render.

> **Master it**   Design a shader for a new and an old car finish.

> **Solution**   Apply the mi_carpaint_phen_x shader to a model, and add lighting to the scene (using a Physical Sun and Sky network is a fast way to create realistic lighting). For the new car, make sure that the reflections have a Glossy setting of 1, and increase the strength of the flakes. For the older car, lower the Glossy setting on the reflections and the strength of the flakes; add a dirt layer to the shader.

Use the MIA materials   The MIA materials and nodes can be used together to create realistic materials that are always physically accurate. The MIA materials come with a number of presets that can be used as a starting point for your own materials.

> **Master it**   Create a realistic polished-wood material.

> **Solution**   Create a mia_material_x shader for an object in a scene that uses physical sky and sun lighting. Use the Glossy finish as a starting place to create the material. In the Color channel of the Diffuse settings, add the Wood 3D texture from the standard Maya 3D texture nodes. Add glossiness to the reflections and the highlight (remember that lower settings spread out the reflection, whereas higher settings create a more defined reflection).

Control exposure using tone mapping.   Tone mapping corrects images that appear improperly exposed when rendering. This frequently occurs when HDRI lighting is used, when physical lights are used, and especially when physical lights are combined with MIA materials.

> **Master it**   Create a scene that uses physical light shaders on the lights. Apply MIA materials to the objects in the scene, and correct the exposure using tone mapping.

> **Solution**   Add an mia_exposure_simple lens shader to the rendering cameras in the scene. Adjust the settings on the lens shader to correct for exposure problems.

Render contours.   mental ray has the ability to render contours of your models to create a cartoon drawing look for your animations. Rendering contours requires that options in the Render Settings window and on the shading group for the object are activated.

> **Master it**   Render the space suit helmet using contours.

> **Solution**   Open one of the versions of the helmet scene in the `chapter10\scenes` directory. Apply a material to the helmet geometry. Enable Contour Rendering in the material's shading group node and in the Features tab of the Render Settings window.

Chapter 11: Texture Mapping

Create UV texture coordinates.   UV texture coordinates are a crucial element of any polygon or subdivision surface model. If a model has well-organized UVs, painting texture and displacement maps is easy and error free.

Master it   Map UV texture coordinates for a character's hand; then try a complete figure.

Solution   Start by using the UV map projection utilities to project coordinates onto the surfaces of the model. Then use the tools in the UV Texture Editor to stitch the coordinates together to create as few shells as possible. Apply a checker texture to the model so that you can spot areas where the texture is warped.

Create bump and normal maps.   Bump and normal maps are two ways to add detail to a model. Bump maps are great for fine detail, such as pores; normal maps allow you to transfer detail from a high-resolution mesh to a low-resolution version of the same model as well as offer superior shading and faster rendering than bump maps.

Master it   Paint a bump map for a character. Create high-resolution and low-resolution versions of the model, and try creating a normal map using the Transfer Maps tool. See if you can bake the bump map into the normal map.

Solution   To include a bump map in the normal map calculation, first apply the bump texture to the object's material and then activate the Include Materials option in the settings of the Transfer Maps tool.

Create displacement maps.   A displacement map is a grayscale texture that can actually alter the geometry of a model. There are a wide variety of uses for displacement maps.

Master it   Create some terrain using a procedural texture, such as the crater texture, as a displacement map for a plane. Try animating the depth of the map so that canyons form in the ground over time.

Solution   Start the animation with the Alpha Offset of the crater texture set to 1. Keyframe the Alpha Offset value over time so that after 60 frames or so, the Alpha Offset is at -2. Keep the Alpha Gain value at 1 throughout the animation.

Use the PSD network node.   A PSD network automatically creates a multilayer Photoshop file with a layer group for each designated channel of a shader.

Master it   Create a PSD network for a shader that includes layers for transparency, incandescence, and reflected color.

Solution   When you create the network, use the PSD Network dialog box to select Transparency, Incandescence, and Reflected Color from the left side of the dialog and move them to the right.

Create a misss_fast_skin shader.   The misss_fast_skin shader can create extremely realistic-looking skin. The secret is using painted texture maps for the Subsurface and Specularity channels.

Master it   Change the look of the old man character by making his skin paler or tanner; see if you can get the backlight to make his ears glow from behind.

Solution   Increase the weighting for the back-scattering challenge, and reposition the back light so that it shines from directly behind the character. Adjust the weights on the other channels, and try changing the Color Gain and Color Offset sliders on each of the textures used in the network.

Create texture maps for NURBS surfaces. NURBS models have UV texture coordinates built into the parameterization of the surface. You can convert a ramp into a texture to use as a guide for painting texture maps in Photoshop.

Master it Create a texture for a tire that includes the text for the tire brand on the side of the tire.

Solution Create a ramp texture for the tire, and use the ramp's color as a guide so you can see where the tread should go as well as which parts of the texture correspond to the sides of the tire. Convert the ramp into a file texture. In Photoshop, import the file texture, and create a tread pattern for the length of the center of the tire. Create text for the tire brand, and rotate it 90 degrees vertically. Use the texture as a displacement map for the tire.

Chapter 12: Rendering for Compositing

Use render layers. Render layers can be used to separate the elements of a single scene into different versions or into different layers of a composite. Each layer can have its own shaders, lights, and settings. Using overrides you can change the way each layer renders.

Master it Use render layers to set up alternate versions of the space helmet. Try applying contour rendering on one layer and Final Gathering on another.

Solution Open the `helmetComposite_v01.ma` scene from the `chapter12\scenes` directory on the DVD. Add a second render layer by copying the helmet layer. In the render settings for the helmet layer, create a Layer Override for the Enable Contours setting, and turn this on (remember to activate one of the Draw By Property Difference options). Create a Layer Override for the Final Gathering option in the Indirect Illumination tab, and turn Final Gathering off. Apply a Lambert texture to all the helmet surfaces while in the helmet layer, and activate Contours in the Lambert's shading group node attributes. The helmet2 layer should still have Final Gathering activated. Test render both layers, and see if contours render correctly on the helmet layer and if Final Gathering renders on the helmet2 layer.

Use render passes. Render passes allow you to separate material properties into different images. These passes are derived from calculations stored in the Frame Buffer. Each pass can be used in compositing software to efficiently rebuild the rendered scene. Render Pass Contribution Maps define which objects and lights are included in a render pass.

Master it Create an Ambient Occlusion pass for the minigun scene.

Solution Open the `minGunComposite_v01.ma` scene. In the Passes tab of the Render Settings window, create an Ambient Occlusion pass. Move the AO (Ambient Occlusion) pass from the Scene Passes section to the Associated Passes section. In the Features tab, enable Ambient Occlusion. In the Indirect Lighting tab, set Ambient Occlusion Rays to **64**. Render a test from the renderCam camera in the Render View window. Use the File menu in the Render View window to load the Ambient Occlusion pass (if the Load Render Pass option is not available, use the File menu to browse to the `images` directory of the current project; you'll find the pass in a folder called `miniGun/AO`).

Perform batch renders.   Batch renders automate the process of rendering a sequence of images. You can use Maya's Batch Render options in the Maya interface or choose Batch Render from the command prompt (or Terminal) when Maya is closed. A batch script can be used to render multiple scenes.

Master it   Create a batch script to render five fictional scenes. Each scene uses layers with different render settings. Set the frame range for each scene to render frames 20 through 50. Each scene is named myScene1.ma through myScene5.ma.

Solution   Create a text file in plain-text format. Each line should be a command-line render script that looks like this:

```
Render -r file -s 20 -e 50 myScene1.ma
```

Save the text file as **batchRender.bat** (or **.batch** on a Mac) in the same directory as the scenes. On a Windows machine, you can double-click the .bat file. On a Mac, you need to use the Terminal to change the mode of the file into an executable (chmod 777). On the Mac, type **./batchRender.batch** to start the render.

Use mental ray quality settings.   The settings in the Quality tab of the Render Settings window allow you to adjust the anti-aliasing quality and the raytrace acceleration of a scene (among other things). Sampling improves the quality of the image by reducing flickering problems. Raytrace acceleration does not affect image quality but improves render times when raytracing is activated in a scene.

Master it   Diagnose both the sampling and the BSP depth of the helmetComposite_v04 .ma scene.

Solution   Open the helmetComposite_v04.ma scene on the chapter12\scenes directory on the DVD. In the Render Settings window, activate Diagnose Samples and perform a test render (turn off Final Gathering). The areas of light gray and white indicate the areas where most of the sampling occurs. Turn off Diagnose Sampling, and in the Acceleration options, set the Diagnose Bsp option to Depth. Set the sampling of the scene to -3 and perform a test render. The orange and red portions of the test render indicate areas where BSP voxels are approaching or have reached maximum depth.

Chapter 13: Introducing nParticles

Create nParticles.   nParticles can be added to a scene in a number of ways. They can be drawn using the tool or spawned from an emitter, or they can fill an object.

Master it   Create a spiral shape using nParticles.

Solution   Create a polygon helix and fill it with nParticles. Make the surface transparent, and set Gravity to **0** in the Nucleus solver.

Make nParticles collide.   NParticles can collide with themselves, other nParticles, and polygon surfaces.

Master it   Make nParticles pop out of the top of an animated volume.

Solution   Create a polygon cube and remove the top. Animate the cube shrinking along the X or Z axis. Fill the cube with nParticles (make the nParticle style balls or water with an Incompressibility value of 1), and make the cube a collision surface.

Create liquid simulations.   Enabling Liquid Simulations changes the behavior of nParticles so they act like water or other fluids.

> **Master it**   Create a flowing stream of nParticles that ends in a waterfall.

> **Solution**   Model a trough in a polygon plane that slopes downward and ends at a cliff. Create a volume emitter set to the water nParticle style. Set Incompressibility to **0.5**.

Emit nParticles from a texture.   The emission rate of an nParticle can be controlled using a texture.

> **Master it**   Create your own name in nParticles.

> **Solution**   Use a digital paint program to create a texture using your name (black letters on a white surface work best). Import the texture into Maya using a file texture node. Create a surface emitter using a plane. Attach the file node to the Texture Emission Rate attribute of the emitter, and check Emit From Dark.

Move nParticles with nucleus wind.   The wind force on the nucleus node can be used to push nParticles.

> **Master it**   Create the effect of bubbles pushed back and forth under water.

> **Solution**   Create an emitter using the ball-style nParticles. Set Gravity Direction to **1** in the Y axis field so the nParticles are pulled upward. Set the Air Density above **20**. Create an expression that randomizes the wind speed using the `noise` function, such as `nucleus1.windSpeed=2*(noise(time));`, and set the Wind Noise attribute to **5**.

Use the Hardware Render Buffer.   The Hardware Render Buffer is a quick way to render nParticles using your machine's graphics card. It works well for creating flame effects.

> **Master it**   Render a small fire using the Hardware Render Buffer.

> **Solution**   To create the soft look of the frames, use the Multi Pass Render options in the Hardware Render Buffer Attributes section. Enable Multi Pass Rendering, and set Render Passes to a high value such as **20**.

Use force fields.   Force fields can be emitted by nParticles and collision objects, creating interesting types of behavior in your scenes.

> **Master it**   Add a second nParticle object emitted from the base of the generator. Enable its force field so that it attracts some of the original energy nParticle.

> **Solution**   Create a surface emitter from the base object in the generator. In the options, set Min Distance to **1** and Max Distance to **1.5**; this ensures that the new particle is not trapped by the base surface (it is a collision object). Set Emission Rate to **10**, and lower the Emission Rates on the other emitters so the scene plays back at a reasonable rate. Set the Point Force field to World Space. Set Magnitude to **10**.

Render nParticles with mental ray.   mental ray can be used to render all nParticle styles using raytraced features such as reflections and refractions.

> **Master it**   Create and render a snowglobe effect.

> **Solution**   Create a sphere and fill it halfway with point-style nParticles. Make the sphere a collision surface. Paint a texture map so that the base of the sphere has a high Stickiness value. Add a Wind setting to the Nucleus tab with an Air Density of 25. Add a Vortex field and a Turbulence field to the nParticle snow. Create reflective and refractive shaders for the sphere (or use the mia shader with the thick glass preset), and render using mental ray.

Chapter 14: Advanced nDynamic Effects

Use nCloth. nCloth can be used to make polygon geometry behave dynamically to simulate a wide variety of materials. Using the presets that come with Maya, you can design your own materials and create your own presets for use in your animations.

Master it Create the effect of a cube of gelatinous material rolling down the stairs.

Solution Model a cube and some stairs. Position the cube above the stairs and convert it into an nCloth object. Apply the Putty preset and try blending Water Balloon, Solid Rubber, and other presets until you get a nice gelatinous motion. Try raising the stickiness on the material to counteract some of the bounciness.

Combine nCloth and nParticles. Because nCloth and nParticles use the same dynamic systems, they can be easily combined to create amazing simulations.

Master it Make a water balloon burst as it hits the ground.

Solution Create a polygon balloon and convert it to an nCloth object. Place it above a floor object. Apply the Water Balloon preset to the nCloth. Fill the nCloth balloon with water nParticles. Add a tearable constraint to the nCloth balloon. Play the animation and adjust the settings until you get the effect you want.

Use nCloth for rigid body simulations. nCloth can be used to simulate rigid dynamics as well as soft surfaces. The Concrete preset is usually the best place to start when creating an nCloth rigid body. nCloth objects have a large number of settings that can give you more control over their behavior than you would get using traditional rigid bodies.

Master it Animate a wrecking ball destroying a wall of nCloth bricks.

Solution Model a polygon ball and a simple polygon rope. Convert the ball and rope to nCloth objects. Apply the Concrete preset to the wrecking ball and the Chain Mail preset to the rope. Use the component nConstraint to attach the end of the rope to the vertices at the top of the wrecking ball. Create a wall of polygon bricks and convert them to nCloth objects; apply the Concrete preset to the bricks. Position the ball so it swings toward the bricks. Adjust the settings as needed to create a believable effect.

Use traditional Maya rigid body dynamics. Traditional rigid body dynamics are not quite as powerful as nCloth objects, but they do calculate much faster and work better for simulations involving a large number of interacting pieces.

Master it Animate a series of dominoes falling over.

Solution Create a large number of polygon cubes, and arrange them in a line on a floor that is a passive rigid body. Convert the cubes into active rigid bodies. Add a gravity field to all of the active bodies. Apply a small radial field to the first rigid body so it falls over and collides with the second rigid body, creating a chain reaction of toppling dominoes.

Instance geometry to nParticles. Modeled geometry can be instanced to nParticles to create a wide variety of effects.

Master it Create the effect of a swarm of insects attacking a beach ball.

Solution Model a single insect. Place the model at the origin of the grid, and freeze transformations on the model. Animate the insect's wings flapping at a high rate of speed. Add an nCloth sphere and an nParticle emitter to the scene. Instance the insect to the nParticles, and make the nCloth sphere a goal for the nParticles. To make the insects face the correct direction, set the aim direction in the nParticles' Instance attributes to Velocity.

Create nParticle expressions. nParticle expressions can be used to further extend the power of nParticles. Using expressions to automate instanced geometry simulations is just one of the ways in which expressions can be used.

> **Master it** Improve the animation of the insects attacking the beach ball by adding different types of insects to the swarm. Randomize their size, and create expressions so that larger insects move more slowly.

> **Solution** Model several types of insects; place them all at the origin. Add the new geometry to the instance node in the swarm scene. Make a creation expression to randomize the index number of the instances so more than one type of insect is included in the swarm. Use the Mass Scale ramp to randomize the mass of the insect nParticles. Create an expression that bases the scale in X, Y, and Z of each instance on the mass of each nParticle.

Create smoke effects. Using the cloud nParticle type, smoke can be added to a simulation. nCloth objects and nParticles can be turned into emitters to emit the smoke.

> **Master it** In the explosion scene from this chapter, make the nCloth bricks emit a smoke trail as they fly out from the tower.

> **Solution** Select the active bricks and convert them to surface emitters. Set the nParticle type to Cloud. Use the nParticle ramps to make the cloud nParticles grow and fade in opacity as they are emitted from the nCloth bricks. Make sure the nParticles have a defined life span.

Chapter 15: Fur, Hair, and Clothing

Add fur to characters. Maya Fur is a rendering module that adds realistic short hairs to the surface of characters to simulate fur. Fur can be rendered using both Maya Software and mental ray. The placement, length, and other attributes of fur can be controlled by painting on the surface with the Artisan tool interface. When adding fur to polygons, the success of the fur is largely dependent on how well the UV texture coordinates have been mapped.

> **Master it** Create furry whiskers for the old man model used in Chapter 11.

> **Solution** Open the UVMap_v06.ma scene from the chapter11\scenes directory on the DVD. Attach fur to the model and paint a baldness map so that nonwhiskered areas are at a value of 0 and whiskered areas have a low value, such as 0.3, to create sparse whiskers.

Add dynamic motion to fur. Using hair curves as a control, fur can be made to react to dynamic forces.

> **Master it** Create a field of grass that blows in the wind.

> **Solution** Model some rolling hills and apply the Grass Fur preset to the hills. Make the length of the grass fairly long. Apply a grid of hair follicles to the field, and apply forces to the hair follicles (you may want to lower the gravity in the hairSystem node). Attach the hairSystem to the grass fur description.

Render fur with mental ray. Fur can be rendered using mental ray or Maya Software. The Rapid Fur mental ray Quality preset works well when rendering fur with depth map shadows. The Fine Trace mental ray Quality preset works well when rendering with mental ray and ray trace shadows and reflections.

Master it   Add a Physical Sun and Sky network to the hound dog scene, and render with mental ray.

Solution   Open the hound_v09.ma scene, open the Render Settings window, and set the renderer to mental ray. In the Indirect Lighting tab, click the Add Physical Sun And Sky button. Render using the perspective camera. Be prepared for a long render!

Create dynamic curves.   A standard Maya curve can be made dynamic by using the Make Dynamic Curves action in the Hair menu. A copy of the curve is created that will respond to dynamic motion and forces. The curve can be used in skeletons for IK Spline tools, as a source for Paint Effects strokes, as a modeling tool, or for any other effect that requires curves.

Master it   Create a flag using dynamic curves.

Solution   Create two parallel curves and make both dynamic. Set the Point Lock attribute on both curves to Base. Loft a NURBS surface between the dynamic curves. Edit the dynamic properties of the curves, and apply fields to the curves to create a flapping motion for the flag.

Add hair to characters.   Hair is created using Paint Effects strokes that are controlled by follicles. The follicles are dynamic curves that respond to forces and movement. Follicles can be applied to polygon or NURBS surfaces as a grid or by painting on the surface. The Visor contains a number of hair presets that can be imported into a scene.

Master it   Add hair to the old man character from Chapter 9.

Solution   Open the UVMap_v06.ma scene from the chapter11\scenes folder on the DVD. Create a scalp surface for the old man by duplicating selected faces on the head. Paint follicles on the head to suggest hair growing from the sides and back of the head. Use Thinning and other hair properties to create the look of long and wispy hair.

Style hair.   Hair can be styled by painting attribute values on follicles, by using dynamic fields, or by directly editing the CVs of start or rest curves.

Master it   Create an avant-garde hairdo for the nancy character using fields.

Solution   Open the nancyHair_v06.ma scene. Apply a turbulence field to the hairSystem1 node. Set Magnitude to a high value (**10** to **20**) and set Attenuation to **0**. Play the animation. When the hair achieves an interesting state, select the follicles and set the state as the hair's rest position (and start position). Delete the field, and increase the hair's start curve Attract attribute.

Use hair constraints.   Hair constraints can be used to control the motion of hair or to connect the hair to props, such as hair ties and scrunchies.

Master it   Use a constraint to create a ponytail for a character.

Solution   Create hair for a character. Select a number of the start curves and apply a hair-to-hair constraint. Play the simulation, and adjust the properties of the constraint to create a ponytail at the back of the head. The effect of the motion of the constraint is visible in the hair strokes.

Render hair.   Hair can be rendered using mental ray or Maya. You can render as Paint Effects strokes or convert the strokes to geometry. Either method works in both Maya

Software and mental ray (in spite of the fact that Paint Effects cannot normally render in mental ray).

Master it Apply the Hair preset examples found in the Visor to a character, and render with mental ray.

Solution Open the Visor and import one of the hair examples into a scene with a character. Transplant the hair from the imported surface to your character, or just parent the imported hair surface to your character's rig. Import the `hairLights.ma` file from the Visor, and render using the Fine Trace Quality preset in the mental ray settings.

Create clothing for characters. Clothing is created by converting polygon geometry to an nCloth object. The object can be attached to a character using constraints.

Master it Create sweatpants and a sweatshirt with a hood for the simple man character.

Solution Open the `simpleMan_v01.ma` scene from the `chapter15\scenes` directory. Delete the existing shirt and pants objects. Model sweatpants and a hooded sweatshirt using polygon modeling techniques. Convert the pants and shirt to nCloth objects, and make the man's geometry a passive collider. Use a transform constraint to connect the vertices at the top of the sweatpants to the rootCtrl locator in the man's rig. Apply an nCloth preset, such as Heavy Knit, to the nCloth objects.

Paint nCloth properties. Properties such as Bounce, Stretch, and Wrinkle can be painted onto nCloth objects using either texture or vertex painting techniques. When painting properties, the Min and Max Value ranges in the Artisan interface may need to be altered to allow for values beyond the range of 0 to 1. Vertex maps have the advantage that the values are not stored in an external texture file.

Master it Add starch to the simple man's shirt by painting a Rigidity value on the shirt geometry.

Solution Open the `simpleMan_v06.ma` scene from the `chapter15\scenes` directory. Select the surface and paint a vertex map. Choose Rigidity as the property you want to paint. Set Max Value in the Artisan Tool options to **30**. Set the Max Color slider in the Artisan Display options to 30. Set the Paint value to somewhere between **20** and **30**, and paint on the surface where you want the shirt to be stiff. Adjust the values as needed.

Chapter 16: Maya Fluids

Use fluid containers. Fluid containers are used to create self-contained fluid effects. Fluid simulations use a special type of particle that is generated in the small subunits (called voxels) of a fluid container. Fluid containers can be 2D or 3D. 2D containers take less time to calculate and can be used in many cases to generate realistic fluid effects.

Master it Create a logo animation that dissolves like ink in water.

Solution Create a 2D fluid container, and use the Paint Fluids tool to paint density values in the container. Paint a logo or import a black-and-white image file of the logo. Set the Buoyancy of the fluid to **0**. Use dynamic fields to push the logo to create the dissolving motion. Try using turbulence, drag, and vortex fields on the logo.

Create a reaction.   A reaction can be simulated in a 3D container by combining temperature with fuel. Surfaces can be used as emitters within a fluid container.

Master it   Create a chain reaction of explosions using the Paint Fluids tool.

Solution   Create a 3D fluid container. Use the Paint Fluids tool to paint small blobs of fuel separated by short distances. The painted fuel blobs should be arranged so that they create a chain reaction when lit. Add an emitter that emits temperature, and place it below the first fuel blob in the container. Set the Ignition Temperature, Reaction Speed, and Heat Released attributes in the Fuel section of the container so the fuel burns and emits heat when a certain temperature is reached. Set Shading to Temperature so that you can see the reaction.

Render fluid containers.   Fluid containers can be rendered using Maya Software or mental ray. The fluids can react to lighting, cast shadows, and self-shadow.

Master it   Render the `TurbulentFlame.ma` example in the Visor so that it emits light onto nearby surfaces.

Solution   Create a scene that has simple modeled surfaces such as a floor and some logs. Import the `TurbulentFlame.ma` scene from the `Fire` folder of the Visor (under the Fluid Examples tab). Set the renderer to mental ray. In the Indirect Lighting section, turn on Final Gathering. Increase Final Gathering Scale to **4**. Turn off Default Light in the Common Attributes tab of the Render Settings window. Play the animation, and render a test frame when the fire is burning.

Use fluids with nParticles.   Fluid simulations can interact with nParticles to create a large array of interesting effects.

Master it   nCloth objects use nParticles and springs to simulate the behavior of cloth. If fluids can affect nParticles, it stands to reason that they can also affect nCloth objects. Test this by creating a simulation where a fluid emitter pushes around an nCloth object.

Solution   Create a 3D fluid container and an emitter that emits density and temperature. The fluid should rise in the container, and the Swirl attribute in Velocity should be set to **10** so that there is a turbulent motion. Create a polygon sphere and place it inside the fluid container above the emitter. Convert the sphere to an nCloth object. Use the Silk preset for the nCloth object, and set Gravity in the Nucleus tab to **0.1**. Play the animation, and experiment with the settings in the fluid container and on the nCloth object until the fluid pushes the nCloth object around.

Create a pond.   A pond uses a 2D fluid container and the Spring Mesh solver to create a pond surface. You can float objects in the pond and use wake emitters to create ripples. The pond can be converted to a polygon mesh to allow for more advanced shading techniques.

Master it   Open the `swamp.ma` scene in the `chapter16\scenes` directory, and create a pond. Add ripples to the surface.

Solution   Open the `swamp_v01.ma` scene from the `chapter16\scenes` directory. The scene has a small ditch and a few Paint Effects trees that have been converted to polygons. Create a pond surface. Add some wake emitters around the edges of the pond to create ripples. These can be hidden behind geometry in the scene. Convert the pond into polygons, and create a surface that looks like dark, brackish water.

Create an ocean.   Ocean effects are created and edited using the Ocean shader. Objects can float in the ocean using locators.

> **Master it**   Create an ocean effect that resembles stormy seas. Add the capsule geometry as a floating object.

> **Solution**   Import the WhiteCaps.ma scene from the Ocean Examples tab of the Visor. Import the capsule_v01.ma scene from the chapter16\scenes directory on the DVD. Use the Float Selected Objects command to make the capsule float on the surface of the water. Look at the settings in the ocean shader node to see how the stormy sea effect was created.

Chapter 17: MEL and Python

Use a MEL command.   MEL commands are used to perform many tasks within Maya. There are numerous ways to enter MEL commands in the Maya interface. These include the command shell, the command line, and the Script Editor.

> **Master it**   Create a polygon cube using the command shell. Create a NURBS cone using the command line. Create a polygonSphere using the Script Editor.

> **Solution**   Open the command shell and type **polyCube**. In the command line, type **cone**. In the work area of the Script Editor, type **polySphere**.

Use MEL scripting techniques.   Many basic MEL techniques can be used to reduce the number of repetitive tasks performed during a Maya session. Using commands, conditional statements, and loops, you can make simple scripts that make working in Maya faster and more efficient.

> **Master it**   Write a more efficient version of the mySpriteScript file that automatically selects all of the nParticle objects in a scene without the need for a conditional statement to test the type of the selected nodes.

> **Solution**   In the Script Editor choose History ➢ Echo All Commands. In a scene that contains nParticles, choose Edit ➢ Select All By Type ➢ nParticles. Observe the text in the history section of the Script Editor. The line that reads select -r `listTransforms "-type nParticle"`; can be used in the script to automatically select all of the nParticles in the scene, which means the conditional statement that tests the selection type is no longer needed. Edit the first few lines of mySpriteScript.mel to include the listTransforms command; then remove the conditional statement from the script. For an example of this alternate version, look at the mySpriteScript_v02.mel script in the chapter17\mel folder on the DVD.

Create a procedure.   Procedures are sections of code that can be called upon at any time within a script. Procedures can help make longer scripts more efficient by eliminating the need to repeat sections of code.

> **Master it**   Write a procedure that adds an expression to selected objects that use the noise function to randomly scale objects over time.

> **Solution**   Edit the shakeMeProc.mel file. Replace the text translateX=rand(-1,1); with **scaleX=noise(time);**. Repeat this for TranslateY and TranslateZ.

Use Python. Python can be used within the Script Editor to execute Python commands or to execute MEL commands within a Python script. The Maya commands must be imported at the start of Python script if you want to incorporate MEL into the Python code.

Master it Use Python to make a NURBS torus.

Solution Switch the Script Editor tab to Python mode. Import MEL commands by typing `maya.cmds`. Type `maya.cmds.torus`() to create the torus using default settings. Flags can be used to specify attributes of the torus. Look up Python commands in the Technical Documentation section of the Maya help files for more information.

Appendix B

About the Companion DVD

In this appendix:

- ◆ What you'll find on the DVD
- ◆ System requirements
- ◆ Using the DVD
- ◆ Troubleshooting

What You'll Find on the DVD

The following sections are arranged by category and provide a summary of the content you'll find on the DVD. If you need help with installing the items provided on the DVD, refer to the installation instructions in the "Using the DVD" section of this appendix.

Trial, demo, or *evaluation* versions of software are usually limited either by time or functionality (such as not letting you save a project after you create it).

Chapter Files

In the Chapter Files directory you will find all the files for completing the tutorials and understanding concepts in this book.

Many of the files can be found in Maya Project folders. Each folder contains all the scene and support files for that project. You can copy these project files to your hard drive and then work directly from them. Working with files directly from the DVD, however, is not encouraged. This is because of the fact that Maya scenes link to external files such as texture maps and dynamic caches. Copy the entire project for each chapter to your local drive, including the empty folders, to ensure that the example scenes function properly.

System Requirements

You will need to be running Maya 2009 to fully use all of the files on the DVD (the software is not included on the DVD). Make sure your computer meets the minimum system requirements shown in the following list. If your computer doesn't match up to these requirements, you may have problems using the files on the companion DVD. For the latest information, please refer to the ReadMe file located at the root of the DVD-ROM.

◆ A PC running Microsoft Windows XP (SP2 or higher) or Windows Vista

◆ A Macintosh running Apple OS X 10.5.2 or later

◆ An Internet connection

◆ A CD-ROM drive

For the latest information on system requirements for Maya, go to www.autodesk.com/maya. Although you can find specific hardware recommendations on these web pages, there is some general information that will help you determine if you're already set up to run Maya: You need a fast processor, a minimum 2GB of RAM, and a workstation graphics card for the best compatibility (rather than a consumer-grade gaming video card).

Using the DVD

To install the items from the DVD to your hard drive, follow these steps.

1. Insert the DVD into your computer's DVD-ROM drive. The license agreement appears.

AUTORUN

Windows users: The interface won't launch if you have AutoRun disabled. In that case, click Start ➤ Run (for Windows Vista, Start ➤ All Programs ➤ Accessories ➤ Run). In the dialog box that appears, type D:\Start.exe. (Replace *D* with the proper letter if your DVD drive uses a different letter. If you don't know the letter, see how your DVD drive is listed under My Computer.) Click OK.

---

2. Read through the license agreement, and then click the Accept button if you want to use the DVD.

The DVD interface appears. The interface allows you to access the content with just one or two clicks.

Troubleshooting

Wiley has attempted to provide programs that work on most computers with the minimum system requirements. Alas, your computer may differ, and some programs may not work properly for some reason.

The two likeliest problems are that you don't have enough memory (RAM) for the programs you want to use, or you have other programs running that are affecting the installation or running of a program. If you get an error message such as "Not enough memory" or "Setup cannot continue," try one or more of the following suggestions and then try using the software again:

Turn off any antivirus software running on your computer. Installation programs sometimes mimic virus activity and may make your computer incorrectly believe that it's being infected by a virus.

Close all running programs. The more programs you have running, the less memory is available to other programs. Installation programs typically update files and programs; so if you keep other programs running, installation may not work properly.

Have your local computer store add more RAM to your computer. This is, admittedly, a drastic and somewhat expensive step. However, adding more memory can really help the speed of your computer and allow more programs to run at the same time.

Customer Care

If you have trouble with the book's companion DVD-ROM, please call the Wiley Product Technical Support phone number at (800) 762-2974. Outside the United States, call +1(317) 572-3994. You can also contact Wiley Product Technical Support at `http://sybex.custhelp.com`. John Wiley & Sons will provide technical support only for installation and other general quality control items. For technical support on the applications themselves, consult the program's vendor or author.

To place additional orders or to request information about other Wiley products, please call (877) 762-2974.

Please check the book's website, `www.sybex.com/go/masteringmaya2009`, where we'll post additional content and updates that supplement this book should the need arise.

Index